FORMULA 1

ALL THE RACES

THE WORLD CHAMPIONSHIP STORY RACE-BY-RACE: 1950-2011

858 RACES • 192 CARS • 102 WINNERS • 62 SEASONS • 32 CHAMPIONS

ROGER SMITH

Haynes

Haynes Publishing

Dedication

This book is dedicated not to the F1 record-breakers but the F1 record-keepers. It is inspired by the works of authors such as Stephen Hirst (*Grand Prix Chronology*), David Hayhoe and David Holland (*Grand Prix Data Book*), Steve Small (*Grand Prix Who's Who*) and – especially – Mike Lang, who compiled a four-volume magnus opus (*Grand Prix!*). It is also inspired by *Autosport*'s F1 reporters, from founder Gregor Grant to Mark Hughes, who have sustained my perpetual joy in the Formula 1 world championship for over 50 of its 62 years.

First published in hardback in March 2012
This paperback edition published in August 2012

British Library Cataloguing in Publication Data
A catalogue record for this book is available from the British Library

ISBN 978 0 85733 309 4

Library of Congress catalog card no 2012940102

Published by Haynes Publishing,
Sparkford, Yeovil, Somerset BA22 7JJ, UK
Tel: 01963 442030 Fax: 01963 440001
Int. tel: +44 1963 442030 Int. fax: +44 1963 440001
E-mail: sales@haynes.co.uk
Website: www.haynes.co.uk

Haynes North America Inc.
861 Lawrence Drive, Newbury Park,
California 91320, USA

Printed and bound in the USA by Odcombe Press LP,
1299 Bridgestone Parkway, La Vergne, TN 37086

Author's acknowledgements

Special thanks to my long-suffering wife Rosemary, Mark Hughes and all at Haynes Publishing, Steve Small at ICON Publishing, Peter Higham and Kevin Wood at LAT Photographic and David Hayhoe. Alain Baudouin deserves special appreciation for providing superb illustrations of 192 winning cars – more details about Alain and his work may be found at www.abmotorart.com.

Photograph credits

All photographs from LAT Photographic except for the one on page 8, which is from Getty Images.

CONTENTS

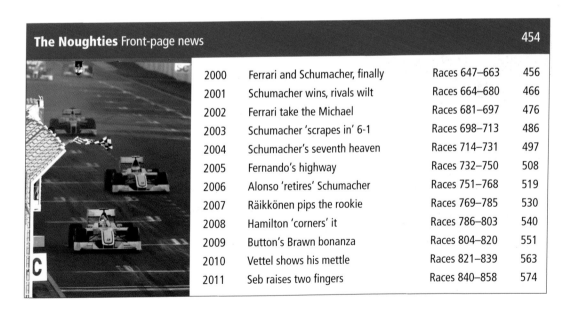

FOREWORD

by Martin Brundle

History always tells a fascinating story which is why it is so important that events are accurately recorded and easily researched. I know all too well from the commentary box that it is easy to get buried under too much information while following complex and fast-moving races.

One thing I find engaging about Sebastian Vettel, our new youngest back-to-back world champion, is his fascination with Formula 1 records. Drivers usually claim not to pay much attention to such matters, but we currently have a new German hero in Vettel aiming to knock his fellow countryman Michael Schumacher off the top of every league table of high achievement. Whenever he pushes unnecessarily hard in the closing laps of a Grand Prix to achieve yet another fastest lap, his intentions become ever clearer.

Many millions of people around the world extract great pleasure from the rich heritage of Grand Prix racing and, like Vettel, retain a healthy respect for the pioneers whilst focusing hard on the most important race of all. The next one.

To create records you need record-keepers. What I like about Roger Smith's *Formula 1: All the Races* is the clarity of thought and layout, and the ease of use. He has brought his marketing background to bear in identifying 'a gap in the market' with his very individual approach towards writing the history of the Formula 1 world championships.

For me he has struck a great balance between 'too much' versus 'too little'. The building blocks of his book are his unique 'race pods', which combine words and information to produce a three-minute 'heads-up' on every single one of the 858 championship races to date.

This book provides a comprehensive yet condensed record for posterity, even highlighting the author's take on the Top 100 races. But in his compact, direct style, he also tops and tails each season with a one-page 'executive summary' balanced by an insightful review of each season.

As I enter my 16th year of Formula 1 commentary I have engaged in an exciting challenge with the new and dedicated Sky Sports F1 HD channel. I can't wait to make lots more Formula 1 television, and you can be sure that this book will be near to hand for regular reference.

In 2012 I hope you enjoy with me the 63rd season of the FIA Formula 1 world championship to see if yet more records tumble… or not.

Martin Brundle, who donated his fee for writing this foreword to the Grand Prix Mechanics' Charitable Trust, interviews Sebastian Vettel at the 2011 Japanese Grand Prix.

INTRODUCTION

by Roger Smith

In meticulously writing and compiling *Formula 1: All the Races* I set twin goals. First, to fill a gap on my own Formula 1 bookshelf. Missing was a comprehensive yet compact history of the Formula 1 world championships that, through a combination of words and information, captured in microcosm the persona of each and every Grand Prix. From this 'race pods' were born.

My second goal was a book offering 'consumer choice'. Whether it's the latest fashion, a new car or just a cup of coffee, choice and flexibility counts these days. *Formula 1: All the Races* has been devised in just that way. You are invited to engage with different sections dependent upon time available, weight of significance, or the draw of your own curiosity. It has been conceived to present an informed storyline or an invaluable reference, to be read cover-to-cover or sliced-and-diced... favourite seasons, circuits, drivers, races attended, and so on. To help you navigate your way around the book, I hope you will find the following guidance useful.

The season overview
At the start of each season there is a one-page overview organised as bullet points beneath the heading 'The Tale of the Title'. Below this is a graph showing 'The Chase for the Championship', affording a swift appreciation of the nature of the championship battle.

But you want to know more...

The season race by race
My unique 'race pods', which form the building blocks of the book, have been carefully researched and written. Each pod features a surprising amount of detail about the race weekend, from qualifying to the race, from race results to their implications for the unfolding championship battle. The text in these pods records not only the key events of the individual race but also spotlights those incidental off-track happenings so singular to Formula 1. Nothing is missed – all significant events are recorded. Further, these race-by-race cameos are written to be enjoyed individually or sequentially, as a moment in time or as a continuing storyline.

An added bonus is my selection of 'Top 100 Races', those very special occasions that have entered Formula 1 folklore. In the same way that beauty is in the eye of the beholder, favourite races – identified in the book with a logo – are very much a personal choice, but I contend that at least 80 per cent of you will consider 80 per cent of my top 100 to be 'Grand Prix Gold'.

And if you want to go deeper still...

Season reviews, records and results
Immediately following the race pods is a section called 'Championship Facts and Folklore'. Here is an extensive season-by-season account of the evolution of Formula 1 in terms of races, countries and circuits, of teams and drivers and of rules and regulations. The technological, political and human aspects of Formula 1 are addressed both on and off track. New records are identified and even births and deaths are covered.

Finally there are the championship tables, for which the following is worth noting:

- The Drivers' and Constructors' tables list every driver and car/marque that had an influence on the given season by scoring championship points, taking pole position and/or setting fastest race lap. Any other participants are not listed.
- In the Drivers' Championship tables the column headed 'Car' shows all the cars the specific driver drove during that championship season, regardless of whether he scored points with the particular cars listed. In the same table, 'Triple Crown' refers to the number of races when the driver started from pole position, won the race and set fastest race lap.
- In the Constructors' Championship tables, the column headed 'Chassis' lists all the type numbers of the cars campaigned during the season for that particular team/marque, regardless of their points-scoring. A similar approach has been used for engine capacities and configurations recorded under the 'Engine' column.

Artwork
The illustrations by Alain Baudouin show 192 winning cars, from the 1950 Alfa Romeo 158 to the 2011 Red Bull-Renault RB7, providing an evocative and colourful record of the evolution of the Formula 1 car.

Appendices
At the back of the book there are three appendices listing the non-championship Formula 1 races, all the winners (drivers, constructors and engines) and all the champions.

So enjoy again all the races and championships you know and love... or those you would love to know.

EXPLANATORY NOTES AND ABBREVIATIONS

RACE PODS

Grid	Position on starting grid
NA	Not available
P1	Position 1 in qualifying and/or the race. Also P2, P3, etc.
Pole position	Figure in brackets is gap from pole to P2
r	Retired from race; not running at finish
SC	Safety Car
Stops	Pitstops from which car resumed race
str.	Streamliner
Time/gap	Duration of race and time gap from winner
Tyres	Tyre makes used: A = Avon, B = Bridgestone, C = Continental, D = Dunlop, E = Engelbert, F = Firestone, G = Goodyear, M = Michelin, P = Pirelli

CHAMPIONSHIP TABLES

1-2 finishes	Same team or marque finishing P1 and P2
Engines	F12 = 12 cylinders horizontally opposed or 'flat' (also F4 and F8); H16 = 16 cylinders formed by a pair of linked F8s; S4 = four cylinders in-line or 'straight' (also S6 and S8); s/c = forced induction by supercharging; t = forced induction by turbocharging; V8 = eight cylinders in 'vee' formation (also V6, V10, V12 and V16)
Nationalities	ARG = Argentina, AUS = Australia, AUT = Austria, BEL = Belgium, BRA = Brazil, CAN = Canada, CHL = Chile, CHN = China, COL = Colombia, GER = Germany, DNK = Denmark, ESP = Spain, FIN = Finland, FRA = France, GBR = United Kingdom, HKG = Hong Kong, HUN = Hungary, IND = India, IoM = Isle of Man, ITA = Italy, JPN = Japan, MEX = Mexico, NLD = Netherlands, NZL = New Zealand, POL = Poland, POR = Portugal, RSA = South Africa, RUS = Russia, SWE = Sweden, SUI = Switzerland, THI = Thailand/Siam, USA = United States, VEN = Venezuela, ZIM = Zimbabwe/Rhodesia

ORGANISATIONS

AAR	Anglo American Racers, Dan Gurney's F1 Eagle project
CSI	Commission Sportive Internationale
ECMA	European Car Manufacturers' Association
EU	European Union
FIA	Fédération Internationale de l'Automobile
FISA	Fédération Internationale du Sport Automobile
FOCA	Formula One Constructors Association
FOM	Formula One Management
FOTA	Formula One Teams Association
GPDA	Grand Prix Drivers' Association
GPWC	Grand Prix World Championship
GPMA	Grand Prix Manufacturers' Association
HANS	Head And Neck Support
NART	North American Racing Team
NASCAR	National Association for Stock Car Auto Racing
NSA	National Sporting Authority
RBR	Red Bull Racing

SEFAC	Societa Esercizio Fabbriche Automobili e Corse
STR	Scuderia Toro Rosso
TWG	Technical Working Group
USAC	United States Auto Club
WMSC	World Motor Sport Council
WRC	World Rally Championship

PEOPLE

ACBC	Anthony Colin Bruce Chapman
Commendatore	Italian 'knighthood' equivalent
DC	David Coulthard
Emo	Emerson Fittipaldi
GV	Gilles Villeneuve
H-HF	Heinz-Harald Frentzen
JB	Jenson Button
JMF	Juan Manuel Fangio
JPM	Juan Pablo Montoya
JV	Jacques Villeneuve
MS	Michael Schumacher
Regga	Clay Regazzoni
Seb	Sebastian Vettel
Tifosi	Italian F1 fans

TECHNICAL

a/c	Air-cooled
atmo	'Atmospheric', naturally aspirated engine
bhp	Brake horsepower
CAD/CAM	Computer Assisted Design/Computer Assisted Manufacture
CFD	Computational Fluid Dynamics
cvj	Constant-velocity joint
CVT	Continuously Variable Transmission
cwp	Crown wheel and pinion
de Dion	Type of suspension system
DFV	Ford Cosworth 'Double Four Valve'
Diff	Differential
DRS	Drag Reduction System
ECU	Electronic Control Unit
JAP	Motorcycle engines made by J A Prestwich Ltd
KERS	Kinetic Energy Recovery System
ohc	Overhead camshaft
Tacho	Tachometer or rev-counter
UJ	Universal joint

TRACKSIDE

Black-flagged	Directive to pit immediately for probable disqualification
BRG	British Racing Green
dnf	Did not finish race
dnq	Did not qualify to race
dns	Did not start race
dsq	Disqualified from race
F1	Formula 1 (also F2)
FP1	First free practice (also FP2 and FP3)
GP	Grand Prix
Grand Slam	A 'triple crown' plus leading every race lap
NC	Not classified in the race results
Q1	Qualifying session 1 (also Q2 and Q3)
red flag	The race has been stopped
T-car	Spare or Training car

RACE 79, French GP: It's Reims in 1959 and red front-engined Ferraris (Brooks 24, P Hill 26) battle for supremacy with green rear-engined Coopers (Brabham 8, Gregory 10), with Moss's BRM (2) in close attendance; by this time Stirling had replaced the retired Fangio as 'the man to beat'. This wonderful picture encapsulates the 'changing of the guard' that took place during the 1950s.

THE FIFTIES

From red to green

THE F1 EPICENTRE SHIFTED FROM ITALY TO BRITAIN, ENGINES SWITCHED FROM FRONT TO BACK, AND FANGIO WAS SUPREME

1950

Farina, first champion

THE TALE OF THE TITLE

- Pre-war 1.5-litre supercharged Alfa Romeos dominated the inaugural F1 world championship.
- Alfa Corse superiority was exemplified by their cars leading all but seven race-laps of the entire GP season.
- There were seven rounds including the Indy 500, Farina and Fangio winning three apiece.
- Nino Farina won the opening championship round at Silverstone, a race at which no Ferraris entered.
- The Italian went on to become the first world champion, at 43 still the all-time oldest.
- Ferrari made their debut at the second round, Monaco, their cars delayed by a chaotic first-lap mêleé.
- The Ferraris were frail and outclassed, even Rosier's Talbot-Lago beating Ascari to 'best of the rest'.
- The Scuderia quickly abandoned supercharging to develop normally aspirated V12s.
- And not forgetting: 'The Three Fs' – Fangio, Farina and Fagioli.

THE CHASE FOR THE CHAMPIONSHIP

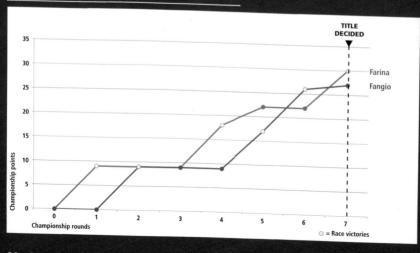

○ = Race victories

BRITISH GP Silverstone
13 May 1950
Race 1

Nino Far...
Alfa Romeo 158 14b...

Alfa Romeo entered four 158s which occupied the entire four-across front row, Farina on pole. Farina largely controlled the race, leading for 63 laps of the 70-lap distance, Fangio and Fagioli each briefly taking turns out front. Reg Parnell, a guest driver for his home Grand Prix, collided with a Silverstone hare while Fangio struck the straw bales at Stowe, both drivers surviving these encounters. But on lap 62 Fangio retired with engine trouble, leaving Farina to head an Alfa Corse 1-2-3 rout, all three completing the full distance. As an illustration of Italian superiority, the pair of French Talbot Lagos finished two laps in arrears and the British ERAs of Bob Gerard and Cuth Harrison crossed the line in a gaggle with the leaders, a further lap back.

POLE POSITION Farina, Alfa R...
151.063kph, 93.866mph
LAPS 70 x 4.649 km, 2.889 miles
DISTANCE 325.458 km, 202.230 miles
STARTERS/FINISHERS 21/11
WEATHER Sunny, warm, dry
LAP LEADERS Farina 1-9, 16-37, 39-70 (63); Fagioli 10-14, 38 (6); J M Fangio, Alfa Romeo 15 (1)
WINNER'S LAPS 1-9 P1, 10-15 P2, 16-37 P1, 38 P3, 39-70 P1
FASTEST LAP Farina, Alfa Romeo, 1m 50.6s (lap 2), 151.337kph, 94.036mph
CHAMPIONSHIP Farina 9, Fagioli 6, Parnell 4, Giraud-Cabantous 3, Rosier 2

Pos	Driver	Car	Time/gap	Grid	Stops	Tyres
1	N Farina	Alfa Romeo	2h 13m 23.6s	1	1	P
2	L Fagioli	Alfa Romeo	−2.6s	2	1	P
3	R Parnell	Alfa Romeo	−52.0s	4	1	P
4	Y Giraud-Cabantous	Talbot Lago	−2 laps	6	0	D
5	L Rosier	Talbot Lago	−2 laps	9	0	D
6	B Gerard	ERA	−3 laps	13	0	D

Alfa Romeo 158

MONACO GP Monte Carlo
21 May 1950
Race 2

Juan Manuel Fangio
Alfa Romeo 158 98.701kph, 61.330mph

In practice Fangio humbled the rest, annexing pole by an astonishing 2.6s from Farina. On the opening lap Farina, holding second spot, spun wildly at Tabac, the surface made wet by the sea dashing the harbour wall. Ten of the 19 starters were eliminated in the ensuing chaos while Fangio, unaffected by the accident, completed the 100 laps, taking over three hours at an average speed just a whisker below 100kph (61mph). Until his retirement with transmission failure on lap 63, the race was enlivened by Villoresi's duel with Ascari, both Ferrari-mounted, the Scuderia making its world championship debut. Ascari finally finished more than a lap behind, the supercharged Ferrari V12s requiring two fuel stops to Fangio's one.

POLE POSITION Fangio, Alfa Romeo, 1m 50.2s (0.2s), 103.884kph, 64.550mph
LAPS 100 x 3.180 km, 1.976 miles
DISTANCE 325.458 km, 202.230 miles
STARTERS/FINISHERS 19/7
WEATHER Sunny, cool, dry
LAP LEADERS Fangio 1-100 (100)
WINNER'S LAPS 1-100 P1
FASTEST LAP Fangio, Alfa Romeo, 1m 51.0s (lap NA), 103.135kph, 64.085mph
CHAMPIONSHIP Farina 9, Fangio 9, Fagioli 6, Ascari 6, Parnell 4

Pos	Driver	Car	Time/gap	Grid	Stops	Tyres
1	J M Fangio	Alfa Romeo	3h 13m 18.7s	1	1	P
2	A Ascari	Ferrari	−1 lap	7	2	P
3	L Chiron	Maserati	−2 laps	8	2	P
4	R Sommer	Ferrari	−3 laps	9	2	P
5	B Bira	Maserati	−5 laps	15	2	P
6	B Gerard	ERA	−6 laps	16	0	D

INDIANAPOLIS 500 Indianapolis
30 May 1950   Race 3

Johnnie Parsons
Kurtis Kraft-Offenhauser 199.562kph, 124.002mph

...on of the 500 by the FIA was purely an expedient to bring
...onal status to their new 'world' championship, which was otherwise
...n European circuits in its formative years. The Indy 500 was not run to
...mula 1 regulations and until the 1960s rarely attracted the interest of F1
...eams and drivers. As such the race had no bearing on the battle for the title,
the only GP drivers entered for the 1950 event being Nino Farina and Franco
Rol, neither turning up, Rol having broken his arm during the Monaco mêleé. A
rookie, Walt Faulkner, took pole for the first time, while Johnnie Parsons won
the race when a cloudburst ended it after 138 of the scheduled 200 laps. Unlike
GP racing, US oval racing was never run in the wet.

POLE POSITION W Faulkner, Kurtis Kraft, 4m 27.97s
(3.13s), 216.206kph, 134.344mph
LAPS 138 x 4.023 km, 2.500 miles (Stopped early due to
cloudburst)
DISTANCE 555.224 km, 345.000 miles
STARTERS/FINISHERS 33/22
WEATHER Warm and dry at the start, heavy rain later
LAP LEADERS Rose 1-9, 33, 105-109 (15); Parsons 10-32,
34-104, 118-138 (115); Holland 110-117 (8)
WINNER'S LAPS NA
FASTEST LAP Parsons, Kurtis Kraft, 1m 9.770s (lap NA),
207.600kph, 128.996mph
CHAMPIONSHIP Farina 9, Fangio 9, Parsons 9,
Fagioli 6, Ascari 6

Pos	Driver	Car	Time/gap	Grid	Stops	Tyres
1	J Parsons	Kurtis Kraft-Offy	2h 46m 55.970s	5	NA	F
2	B Holland	Deidt-Offenhauser	−1 lap	10	NA	F
3	M Rose	Deidt-Offenhauser	−1 lap	3	NA	F
4	C Green	Kurtis Kraft-Offy	−1 lap	12	NA	F
5	J Chitwood/T Bettenhausen	Kurtis Kraft-Offy	−2 laps	9	NA	F
6	L Wallard	Moore-Offy	−2 laps	23	NA	F

Round 4/7 — SWISS GP Bremgarten
4 June 1950   Race 4

Nino Farina
Alfa Romeo 158 149.279 kph, 92.757mph

Despite an uprated Ferrari, the three Alfas occupied the front row of the 3-2
grid. Villoresi's new de Dion Ferrari, also sporting a lengthened wheelbase,
claimed fourth spot but was still a full 10s off the pace. Fangio used his pole
position to lead initially but Farina was mainly in command, heading 33 of the
42 laps race distance. With nine to go Fangio retired with engine valve trouble,
leaving Farina to win from teammate Fagioli. The unreliable Ferraris retired
early on but might have been hard pressed to beat the non-stopping unblown
4.5-litre Talbot-Lago of Rosier, who came home third one lap down. Just
before half-distance Rosier's teammate, Eugène Martin, flew off the circuit and
sustained serious injuries.

POLE POSITION J M Fangio, Alfa Romeo, 2m 42.1s
(0.7s), 161.678kph, 100.462mph
LAPS 42 x 7.280 km, 4.524 miles
DISTANCE 305.760 km, 189.990 miles
STARTERS/FINISHERS 18/11
WEATHER Sunny, warm, dry
LAP LEADERS J M Fangio, Alfa Romeo 1-6, 21-22 (8);
Farina 7-20, 24-42 (33); Fagioli 23 (1)
WINNER'S LAPS 1-6 P2, 7-20 P1, 21 P2, 22 P3, 23 P2,
24-42 P1
FASTEST LAP Farina, Alfa Romeo, 2m 41.6s (lap 8),
162.178kph, 100.773mph
CHAMPIONSHIP Farina 18, Fagioli 12, Fangio 9,
Parsons 9, Ascari 6

Pos	Driver	Car	Time/gap	Grid	Stops	Tyres
1	N Farina	Alfa Romeo	2h 13m 23.6s	2	1	P
2	L Fagioli	Alfa Romeo	−1.4s	3	1	P
3	L Rosier	Talbot Lago	−1 lap	10	0	D
4	B Bira	Maserati	−2 laps	8	2	P
5	F Bonetto	Maserati Milano	−2 laps	12	2	P
6	E de Graffenried	Maserati	−2 laps	11	2	P

Round 5/7 — BELGIAN GP Spa-Francorchamps
18 June 1950   Race 5

Juan Manuel Fangio
Alfa Romeo 158 177.097kph, 110.043mph

The 'Three Fs', Farina, Fangio and Fagioli, took their customary positions on
the grid in that order. The mid-part of the race was enlivened by Raymond
Sommer, whose Talbot Lago led for three splendid laps during the thirsty
supercharged Alfas' first refuelling stop. But his engine could not sustain the
rigours beyond lap 20. This time Farina was the victim of poor Alfa reliability,
dropping to fourth with falling oil pressure. So Fangio led most of the race to
win from Fagioli, but once again it was Rosier who completed the podium for
Talbot Lago. The supercharged Ferraris were nowhere, but bearing in mind the
showing of the Talbot Lagos it was significant that an unsupercharged 3.3-litre
Ferrari appeared in practice.

POLE POSITION Farina, Alfa Romeo, 4m 37.0s (0.0s),
183.509kph, 114.027mph
LAPS 35 x 14.120 km, 8.774 miles
DISTANCE 494.200 km, 307.082 miles
STARTERS/FINISHERS 14/10
WEATHER Sunny, warm, dry
LAP LEADERS Fangio 1-6, 20-35 (22); Farina 7-11,
18-19 (7); Fagioli 12 (1); R Sommer, Talbot Lago 13-17 (5)
WINNER'S LAPS 1-6 P1, 7-10 P2, 11-12 P4, 13-17 P3,
18-19 P2, 20-35 P1
FASTEST LAP Farina, Alfa Romeo, 4m 34.1s (lap 18),
185.451kph, 115.234mph
CHAMPIONSHIP Farina 22, Fagioli 18, Fangio 17,
Rosier 10, J Parsons 9

Pos	Driver	Car	Time/gap	Grid	Stops	Tyres
1	J M Fangio	Alfa Romeo	2h 47m 26.0s	2	2	P
2	L Fagioli	Alfa Romeo	−2.6s	3	2	P
3	L Rosier	Talbot Lago	−2m 19.0s	6	0	D
4	N Farina	Alfa Romeo	−4m 5.0s	1	3	P
5	A Ascari	Ferrari	−1 laps	8	2	E
6	L Villoresi	Ferrari	−2 laps	4	2	E

Round 6/7	**FRENCH GP** Reims-Gueux		**Juan Manuel Fangio**
	2 July 1950	Race 6	Alfa Romeo 158 168.729kph, 104.843mph

The Alfas were completely at home on the fast Reims circuit, Fangio leading most of the way, Farina's challenge thwarted by fuel pump problems. Having led the opening phase, Farina tried his utmost to take something from the race, storming back to recover lost ground following at least two lengthy pit stops to cure his fuel starvation problem. As late as lap 50 he still held third place but his efforts ultimately proved in vain on lap 55. With the Talbot Lagos in cooling difficulties and no works Ferraris taking the start, Peter Whitehead brought his private entry home to finish third, albeit three laps behind the Alfas. Fangio now held a useful points lead in the title battle while a fourth second-place finish by Fagioli pushed Farina back to third.

POLE POSITION Fangio, Alfa Romeo, 2m 30.6s (1.9s), 186.837kph, 116.095mph
LAPS 64 x 7.816 km, 4.857 miles
DISTANCE 500.224 km, 310.825 miles
STARTERS/FINISHERS 18/8
WEATHER Sunny, hot, dry
LAP LEADERS N Farina, Alfa Romeo 1-16 (16); Fangio 17-64 (48)
WINNER'S LAPS 1-16 P2, 17-64 P1
FASTEST LAP Fangio, Alfa Romeo, 2m 35.6s (lap 52), 185.451kph, 115.234mph
CHAMPIONSHIP Fangio 26, Fagioli 24, Farina 22, Rosier 10, J Parsons 9

Pos	Driver	Car	Time/gap	Grid	Stops	Tyres
1	J M Fangio	Alfa Romeo	2h 57m 52.8s	1	2	P
2	L Fagioli	Alfa Romeo	−25.7s	3	2	P
3	P Whitehead	Ferrari	−3 laps	19	NA	D
4	R Manzon	Simca Gordini	−3 laps	13	NA	E
5	P Étançelin/E Chaboud	Talbot Lago	−5 laps	4	NA	D
6	C Pozzi/L Rosier	Talbot Lago	−8 laps	16	NA	D

Round 7/7	**ITALIAN GP** Monza		**Nino Farina**
	3 September 1950	Race 7	Alfa Romeo 159 176.543kph, 109.699mph

On pole, and leading the title battle into the deciding round, Fangio's dream of championship honours was shattered around quarter-distance when his gearbox seized. He took over Taruffi's car but that too failed. Meanwhile, after a classic early three-car duel teammate Farina, driving the new Tipo 159 with increased power and de Dion rear suspension, saw off the twin challenges of Fangio and Ascari in the long-awaited unblown 4.5-litre Ferrari 375, which exited the fray on lap 21. Farina swept to victory and to the inaugural world drivers' championship. But at last Ferrari had made a race of it, Ascari starting from the front row, leading two laps, and finishing second in his teammate's car. It augured well for the new season.

POLE POSITION J M Fangio, Alfa Romeo, 1m 58.6s (0.2s), 191.231kph, 118.825mph
LAPS 80 x 6.300 km, 3.915 miles
DISTANCE 500.224 km, 310.825 miles
STARTERS/FINISHERS 26/7
WEATHER Sunny, hot, dry, becoming overcast
LAP LEADERS Farina 1-13, 16-80 (78); Ascari 14-15 (2)
WINNER'S LAPS 1-13 P1, 14-15 P2, 16-80 P1
FASTEST LAP J M Fangio, Alfa Romeo, 2m 00.0s (lap 7), 189.000kph, 117.439mph
CHAMPIONSHIP Farina 30, Fangio 27, Fagioli 24, Rosier 13, Ascari 11

Pos	Driver	Car	Time/gap	Grid	Stops	Tyres
1	N Farina	Alfa Romeo	2h 51m 17.4s	3	2	P
2	D Serafini/A Ascari	Ferrari	−18.6s	6	2	P
3	L Fagioli	Alfa Romeo	−35.6s	5	2	P
4	L Rosier	Talbot Lago	−5 laps	13	NA	D
5	P Étançelin	Talbot Lago	−5 laps	16	NA	D
6	E de Graffenried	Maserati	−8 laps	17	NA	P

1950 CHAMPIONSHIP FACTS AND FOLKLORE

- The World Championship for Drivers was the creation of the recently formed *Fédération Internationale de l'Automobile*, the FIA.
- In that first year of the FIA World Championship as many as 22 races were organised for Formula 1 cars, many of which contained 'Grand Prix' in their title.
- But just six Grands Prix (or *Grandes Épreuves*) were selected to count towards the championship, plus the Indianapolis 500-mile race.
- The 'Indy 500', run annually in the United States since 1911 (except for the war years 1917–18 and 1942–45), was included to bestow the FIA championship with 'world' status.
- The inaugural championship race was held on 13 May 1950, the venue Silverstone, England.
- Ironically, Ferrari – the only marque to contest every year of the FIA world championships – missed that first round at Silverstone, making their debut at Monaco.

- The championship regulations called for cars with a maximum engine capacity of 4.5 litres normally aspirated or 1.5 litres supercharged.
- Supercharging produced prodigious power, but the downside was fuel consumption, tyre wear and even reliability, although F1 regulations initially imposed no fuel or weight restrictions.
- The minimum race distance was 300km (186.41 miles) or three hours, the first five finishers to be awarded championship points in the sequence 8, 6, 4, 3 and 2.
- Where drivers shared a car they shared the points, and an extra point was awarded to the driver posting the fastest race lap, fractions of that point being shared in the event of a joint fastest lap.
- Of the seven rounds in the championship, only the best four results would count.
- The list of teams and cars was headed by factory entries from Alfa Romeo SpA, Scuderia Ferrari and Officine Alfieri

Championship ranking	Championship points	Driver nationality	1950 Drivers Championship Driver	Car	Races contested	Race victories	Podiumse excl. victories	Races led	Flag to flag victories	Laps led	Poles	Fastest laps	Triple Crowns
1	30	ITA	Nino Farina	Alfa Romeo	6	3		5		197	2	3	1
2	27	ARG	Juan Manuel Fangio	Alfa Romeo	6	3		5	1	179	4	3	2
3	24	ITA	Luigi Fagioli	Alfa Romeo	6		5	3		8			
4	13	FRA	Louis Rosier	Talbot Lago	6		2						
5	11	ITA	Alberto Ascari	Ferrari	4		2	1		2			
6	9	USA	Johnnie Parsons	Kurtis Kraft-Offenhauser	1	1		1		115		1	
7	6	USA	Bill Holland	Deidt-Offenhauser	1		1	1		8			
8	5	THI	Prince Bira	Maserati	4								
9	4	GBR	Reg Parnell	Alfa Romeo (1) Maserati (1)	2		1						
10	4	FRA	Louis Chiron	Maserati	5		1						
11	4	USA	Mauri Rose	Deidt-Offenhauser	1		1	1		15			
12	4	GBR	Peter Whitehead	Ferrari	2		1						
13	3	ITA	Dorino Serafini	Ferrari	1		1						
14	3	FRA	Yves Giraud-Cabantous	Talbot Lago	4								
15	3	FRA	Raymond Sommer	Ferrari (2) Talbot Lago (3)	5				1	5			
16	3	USA	Cecil Green	Kurtis Kraft-Offenhauser	1								
17	3	FRA	Robert Manzon	Simca Gordini	3								
18	3	FRA	Philippe Etancelin	Talbot Lago	6								
19	2	ITA	Felice Bonetto	Maserati Milano	2								
20	1	USA	Tony Bettenhausen	Kurtis Kraft-Offenhauser	1								
20	1	USA	Joie Chitwood	Kurtis Kraft-Offenhauser	1								
22	1	FRA	Eugène Chaboud	Talbot Lago	2								
-	0	USA	Walt Faulkner	Kurtis Kraft-Offenhauser	1							1	

RACE 1, British GP: Alfa Romeo entered four 158s which occupied the entire four-across front row. From pole Farina (2) largely controlled the race, leading for 63 of the 70 laps.

RACE 1, British GP: Garlanded, Nino Farino receives congratulations after winning the first championship race. Within four months he was also hailed as the very first F1 World Champion.

Maserati representing Italy; Équipe Gordini and the Talbot Lagos from Automobiles Talbot-Darracq flying the flag for France, while outdated ERAs and underpowered private Altas embodied the British contingent.

■ Following World War Two, Grand Prix motor racing resumed in June 1947, inevitably most of the equipment being of pre-war origin, not least the Alfa Romeo 158. Originally designed by Gioacchino Colombo for 'voiturette' (Formula 2) racing just before the war, it was powered by a 1.5-litre straight-eight with two-stage supercharging, in 1950 form producing some 250bhp at 8,500rpm.

■ Still regarded as the car to beat, Alfa were able to attract a formidable driver line-up for this first championship season – Farina, Fangio and Fagioli, inevitably referred to as 'The Three Fs'.

■ Long before the Ferrari name became legend, the incomparable Enzo, 'the Commendatore', had run Alfa Romeo's motor racing department from 1929–39.

■ In 1945, free of the restrictions of his erstwhile employer, Ferrari began to build sports racing cars which carried his own name.

■ In 1948 Ferrari produced his first Grand Prix single-seater, the Tipo 125 with its 1.5-litre 60° V12 supercharged engine, and a development of this car was used to open their championship campaign.

■ However, Ferrari's new technical guru, Aurelio Lampredi, decided to explore the engine route adopted by the Talbot Lagos – a large-capacity normally aspirated motor, far more fuel-efficient than the supercharged alternative and bringing benefits in weight, tyre wear and fuel-stops.

■ Only Ferrari could reasonably be expected to compete with Alfa Romeo, the challenge from BRM never materialising.

■ The Monaco GP saw the first championship appearance for a rear-engined car, Harry Schell's T12 Cooper with 1.1-litre V2 JAP engine. It was not auspicious, starting last after not posting a time, then not completing the first lap, being caught up in the infamous first-lap pile-up at Tabac. After the race, winner Fangio, referring to the fracas, was quoted as saying 'I managed to pull up inches from the wreckage, and work my way towards the gap that remained.'

■ 1950 witnessed the birth of Gilles Villeneuve, Jody Scheckter, Flavio Briatore and Lord Alexander Hesketh.

Championship ranking	Championship points	Team/Marque nationality	1950 Constructors Results (Excl. Indy 500)		Engine maker nationality	Races contested	Race victories	1-2 finishes	Podiums excl. victories	Races led	Laps led	Poles	Fastest laps
			Chassis	Engine									
N/A	N/A	ITA	Alfa Romeo 158, 159	Alfa Romeo 1.5 S8 s/c	ITA	6	6	4	5	6	384	6	6
N/A	N/A	ITA	Ferrari 125, 166, 275, 375	Ferrari 1.5 V12 s/c, 3.3 V12, 4.5 V12	ITA	5			4	1	2		
N/A	N/A	FRA	Talbot Lago T26C, T26C-DA, T26C-GS	Talbot Lago 4.5 S6	FRA	6			2	1	5		
N/A	N/A	ITA	Maserati 4CL, 4CLT/48	Maserati 1.5 S4 s/c	ITA	6			1				
N/A	N/A	FRA	Simca Gordini T15	Gordini 1.5 S4 s/c	FRA	3							
N/A	N/A	ITA	Maserati Milano 4CLT/50	Maserati Milano 1.5 S4 s/c	ITA	3							

1951

Fangio repels Ferrari challenge

THE TALE OF THE TITLE

- Once more driving for Alfa Romeo, Fangio secured his first drivers' title
- The Argentinean won three, one shared, of Alfa's four race victories, defending champion Farina the other.
- This year, with their 4.5-litre V12, Ferrari took the fight to the thirsty fuel-stopping supercharged *Alfettas*.
- At Silverstone another Argentinean, Froilán González, took an historic maiden victory for SEFAC Ferrari.
- Enzo's emotional response to inflicting the first championship defeat on Alfa: "I have killed my mother."
- Ascari completed a Ferrari hat-trick, but at the season finale a disastrous tyre blunder ruined his challenge.
- It allowed Alfa Romeo to retire from F1 as undefeated champions, but only just.
- The V16 BRM made its long awaited championship debut, but it was a solitary and desultory appearance.
- G.A. (Tony) Vandervell entered privately a 4.5-litre Ferrari designated the 'Thin Wall Special'.
- And not forgetting: BRM use Girling disc brakes and Stirling Moss debuts.

THE CHASE FOR THE CHAMPIONSHIP

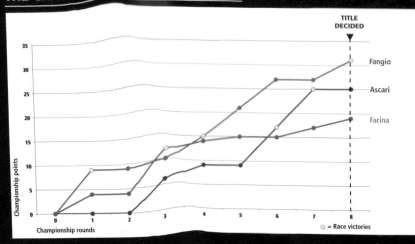

○ = Race victories

SWISS GP Bremgarten
27 May 1951
Race 8

Juan [...]
Alfa Romeo [...]

In a race run in heavy rain, Fangio won convincingly from pole with a superb display. Despite his fuel stop he finished almost a minute ahead of Taruffi's Ferrari 375. During the Argentinean's pit stop Farina led briefly, the fuel tanks of the reigning champion's Alfa 159 having been adapted to run the full distance in an effort to repulse the ever-increasing Ferrari challenge. But significantly Farina was still beaten by Taruffi's Ferrari, who hunted him down in the rain to snatch second place on the penultimate lap. Ascari finished sixth, handicapped by burns from a recent Formula 2 accident, while Stirling Moss made his debut in an HWM, coming home eighth.

POLE POSITION Fangi[...]
168.108kph, 104.457mph
LAPS 42 x 7.280 km, 4.524 mile[...]
DISTANCE 305.760 km, 189.990 m[...]
STARTERS/FINISHERS 21/14
WEATHER Overcast, heavy rain
LAP LEADERS Fangio 1-23, 29-42 (37); Farina [...]
WINNER'S LAPS 1-23 P1, 24-28 P2, 29-42 P1
FASTEST LAP Fangio, Alfa Romeo, 2m 51.1s (lap 33), 153.174kph, 95.178mph
CHAMPIONSHIP Fangio 9, Taruffi 6, Farina 4, Sanesi 3, de Graffenried 2

Pos	Driver	Car	Time/gap	Grid	Stops	Tyres
1	J M Fangio	Alfa Romeo	2h 7m 53.64s	1	1	P
2	P Taruffi	Ferrari	−55.24s	6	0	P
3	N Farina	Alfa Romeo	−1m 19.31s	2	0	P
4	C Sanesi	Alfa Romeo	−1 lap	4	1	P
5	E de Graffenried	Alfa Romeo	−2 laps	5	1	P
6	A Ascari	Ferrari	−2 laps	7	0	P

INDIANAPOLIS 500 Indianapolis
30 May 1951
Race 9

Lee Wallard
Kurtis Kraft-Offenhauser 203.171kph, 126.244mph

In year two of the championship 'Indy' was again the only race outside Europe, and once more had no bearing on the title outcome. Steeped in tradition, the Indy 500 was an all-American spectacular held on Memorial Day, the last Monday in May. The month of May was set aside for preparations including practice, 'carburation day' and finally qualification, held two weeks then one week prior to race day. 'Pole-day' decided grid positions 1–24 for the 33-car field, 'Bump-day' the remaining grid-slots, 'bumping' slower 'Pole-day' qualifiers off the grid but starting behind them even if faster. Lee Wallard, the 1951 winner, was the first to complete the full race-distance in less than four hours.

POLE POSITION D Nalon, Kurtis Kraft-Novi, 4m 23.74s (2.85s), 219.672kph, 136.498mph
LAPS 200 x 4.023 km, 2.500 miles
DISTANCE 804.672 km, 500.000 miles
STARTERS/FINISHERS 33/8
WEATHER Sunny, hot, dry
LAP LEADERS Wallard 1-2, 5-6, 16-26, 28-51, 81-200 (159); McGrath 3-4, 7-15 (11); C Green, Kurtis Kraft-Offy 27, 77-80 (5) J Davies, Silnes-Pawl-Offy 52-76 (25)
WINNER'S LAPS NA
FASTEST LAP Wallard, Kurtis Kraft-Offy, 1m 7.260s (lap 71), 215.345kph, 133.809mph
CHAMPIONSHIP Fangio 9, Wallard 9, Taruffi 6, Nazaruk 6, Farina 4

Pos	Driver	Car	Time/gap	Grid	Stops	Tyres
1	L Wallard	Kurtis Kraft-Offy	3h 57m 38.05s	2	NA	F
2	M Nazaruk	Kurtis Kraft-Offy	−1m 47.24s	7	NA	F
3	J McGrath/M Ayulu	Kurtis Kraft-Offy	−2m 51.39s	3	NA	F
4	A Linden	Silnes-Sherman-Offy	−4m 40.12s	31	NA	F
5	B Ball	Schroeder-Offy	−4m 52.23s	29	NA	F
6	H Banks	Moore-Offy	−5m 40.02s	17	NA	F

BELGIAN GP Spa-Francorchamps
17 June 1951
Race 10

Nino Farina
Alfa Romeo 159 183.985kph, 114.323mph

Although the Alfas had qualified first and second on the grid, the Ferraris got among the fuel-heavy *Alfettas* during the opening couple of laps, Villoresi leading. On lap 3 Farina got ahead and broke away, soon followed by Fangio, recovering from a poor start. Fangio was delayed badly during his lap 16 pit stop due to a stubborn broken wheel, leaving Farina to win comfortably despite making a second stop for fuel and tyres. The third Alfa of Sanesi retired, with a split radiator, as did Ferrari's third car, Taruffi's problem a rear axle. So Ascari and Villoresi completed the podium for Ferrari, albeit soundly beaten by defending champion Farina.

POLE POSITION J M Fangio, Alfa Romeo, 4m 25.0s (3.0s), 191.819kph, 119.191mph
LAPS 36 x 14.120 km, 8.774 miles
DISTANCE 508.320 km, 315.855 miles
STARTERS/FINISHERS 13/9
WEATHER Sunny, warm, dry
LAP LEADERS Villoresi 1-2 (2); Farina 3-14, 16-36 (33); Fangio 15 (1)
WINNER'S LAPS 1-2 P2, 3-14 P1, 15 P2, 16-36 P1
FASTEST LAP J M Fangio, Alfa Romeo, 4m 22.1s (lap 10), 193.941kph, 120.510mph
CHAMPIONSHIP Farina 12, Fangio 10, Wallard 9, Taruffi 6, Nazaruk 6

Pos	Driver	Car	Time/gap	Grid	Stops	Tyres
1	N Farina	Alfa Romeo	2h 45m 46.2s	2	2	P
2	A Ascari	Ferrari	−2m 51.0s	4	1	P
3	L Villoresi	Ferrari	−4m 21.9s	3	3	P
4	L Rosier	Talbot Lago	−2 laps	7	0	D
5	Y G.-Cabantous	Talbot Lago	−2 laps	8	0	D
6	A Pilette	Talbot Lago	−3 laps	12	0	E

FRENCH GP Reims-Gueux
1 July 1951   Race 11

...ging fortunes, Ascari initially led Fangio until gearbox
...d the Ferrari out on lap 10. But Fangio was in trouble too, a misfire
...n to pit then subsequently retire. For the next 35 laps Farina took
...d but meanwhile Fangio had commandeered Fagioli's car on lap 25,
...scari relieved González on lap 35. On lap 44 the flying Fangio pitted from
...ond place for tyres and fuel so that when Farina's leading Alfa threw a tread
on the very next lap it was Ascari who retook the lead. But this wasn't to be
Ferrari's victory breakthrough, a 40s pit stop for brake adjustment costing the
Ascari/González car the lead on lap 51, the Fangio/Fagioli Alfa triumphing by
almost a minute.

Pos	Driver	Car	Time/gap	Grid	Stops	Tyres
1	L Fagioli/J M Fangio	Alfa Romeo	3h 22m 11.0s	7	3	P
2	F González/A Ascari	Ferrari	−58.2s	6	2	P
3	L Villoresi	Ferrari	−3 laps	4	2	P
4	R Parnell	Ferrari	−4 laps	9	1	P
5	N Farina	Alfa Romeo	−4 laps	2	3	P
6	L Chiron	Talbot Lago	−6 laps	8	1	D

Luigi Fagioli/Juan Manuel Fangio
Alfa Romeo 159 178.600kph, 110.977mph

POLE POSITION Fangio, Alfa Romeo, 2m 25.7s (1.9s), 193.120kph, 119.999mph
LAPS 77 x 7.816 km, 4.857 miles
DISTANCE 601.832 km, 373.96119 miles
STARTERS/FINISHERS 23/11
WEATHER Sunny, hot, dry
LAP LEADERS Ascari 1-8, 45-50, (14); Fangio 9, 51-77 (28); N Farina 10-44 (35)
WINNER'S LAPS Fangio 1-8 P2, 9 P1, 10 P3, 11-13 P5, 14 P14, 15 P15, Fagioli/Fangio 16-20 P3, 21 P2, 22-24 P3, 25-33 P4, 34-36 P3, 37-43 P2, 44 P3, 45-50 P2, 51-77 P1
FASTEST LAP Fangio, Alfa Romeo, 2m 27.8s (lap 32), 190.376kph, 118.294mph
CHAMPIONSHIP Fangio 15, Farina 14, Wallard 9, Ascari 9, Taruffi 6

Round 5/8   BRITISH GP Silverstone
14 July 1951   Race 12

The distinction of being the first driver to win a world championship race for
Ferrari fell to Argentinean Froilán González, 'The Pampas Bull'. Highly deserved
it was too, claiming pole position with the first 100mph lap of Silverstone and
disputing the lead with Fangio until his Ferrari was able to pull away following
the Alfa's lap 49 pit stop. Twelve laps later González pitted without losing
his lead to win by 51s. At last the Alfa Romeo stranglehold had been broken.
Such was the pace of the race leaders that the third finisher was two laps
behind, neither Farina nor Ascari completing the course. This was the only
championship race ever contested by the BRM V16s, Parnell and Walker five
and six laps in arrears respectively.

Pos	Driver	Car	Time/gap	Grid	Stops	Tyres
1	F González	Ferrari	2h 42m 18.2s	1	1	P
2	J M Fangio	Alfa Romeo	−51.0s	2	1	P
3	L Villoresi	Ferrari	−2 laps	5	1	P
4	F Bonetto	Alfa Romeo	−3 laps	7	2	P
5	R Parnell	BRM	−5 laps	20	2	D
6	C Sanesi	Alfa Romeo	−6 laps	6	1	P

Froilán González
Ferrari 375 154.690kph, 96.120mph

POLE POSITION González, Ferrari, 1m 43.4s (1.0s), 161.874kph, 96.120mph
LAPS 90 x 4.649 km, 2.889 miles
DISTANCE 418.446 km, 260.010 miles
STARTERS/FINISHERS 20/13
WEATHER Sunny, warm, dry
LAP LEADERS Bonetto 1 (1); González 2-9, 39-47, 49-90 (59); Fangio 10-38, 48 (30)
WINNER'S LAPS 1 P2, 2-9 P1, 10-38 P2, 39-47 P1, 48 P2, 49-90 P1
FASTEST LAP N Farina, Alfa Romeo, 1m 44.0s (lap 38), 160.941kph, 100.004mph
CHAMPIONSHIP Fangio 21, Farina 15, Villoresi 12, González 11, Wallard 9

Round 6/8   GERMAN GP Nürburgring
29 July 1951   Race 13

Qualifying for the first post-war German Grand Prix suggested that Ferrari's
Silverstone form was no flash in the pan, the front row comprising Ferraris
1-2, Alfas 3-4. The race was an epic duel between Fangio and Ascari, the
Argentinean aware an extra fuel stop was likely. By lap 2 Fangio held a 7.1s
lead, but Ascari reeled it back and slipped by at Breidscheid on lap 5. Fangio,
having pitted on lap 7, regained the lead on lap 11 following Ascari's stop and
rebuilt his lead to almost 15s. But unless something went awry for Ascari it
was never enough to offset his second stop. Unexpectedly Ascari also made a
second stop, for tyres, but despite a jammed wheel still won comprehensively.

Pos	Driver	Car	Time/gap	Grid	Stops	Tyres
1	A Ascari	Ferrari	3h 23m 03.3s	1	2	P
2	J M Fangio	Alfa Romeo	−30.5s	3	2	P
3	F González	Ferrari	−4m 39.0s	2	1	P
4	L Villoresi	Ferrari	−5m 50.2s	5	1	P
5	P Taruffi	Ferrari	−7m 49.1s	6	2	P
6	R Fischer	Ferrari	−1 lap	8	1	P

Alberto Ascari
Ferrari 375 134.801kph, 83.761mph

POLE POSITION Ascari, Ferrari, 9m 55.8s (1.7s), 137.825kph, 85.640mph
LAPS 20 x 22.810 km, 14.173 miles
DISTANCE 456.200 km, 283.470 miles
STARTERS/FINISHERS 22/11
WEATHER Sunny, warm, dry
LAP LEADERS Fangio 1-4, 11-14 (8); Ascari 5-9, 15-20, (11); González 10 (1)
WINNER'S LAPS 1-4 P2, 5-9 P1, 10-14 P2, 15-20 P1
FASTEST LAP Fangio, Alfa Romeo, 9m 55.8s (lap 12), 137.825kph, 85.640mph
CHAMPIONSHIP Fangio 27, Ascari 17, González 15, Farina 15, Villoresi 15

Ferrari 375

Round 7/8	**ITALIAN GP** Monza **16 September 1951**	Race 14

Alberto Ascari

Ferrari 375 185.915kph, 115.522mph

Not wishing to be outshone by Ferrari on their mutual home territory, Alfa brought uprated 159Ms to Monza, qualifying 1-2. Fangio and Ascari initially disputed the lead until a thrown tyre tread delayed Fangio on lap 14 and a broken piston finally ended his race on lap 39 when holding third place behind the fleeing Ferrari pair. Farina had already retired his car early with engine failure, but now in Bonetto's car enlivened the second half of the race by chasing down the Ferraris not once but twice, finally finishing a gallant third spraying fuel behind him from a split tank. Ascari's victory completed a hat-trick for the Prancing Horse, and suddenly Fangio's championship lead had been cut to just two points.

POLE POSITION J M Fangio, Alfa Romeo, 1m 53.2s (0.7s), 200.353kph, 124.494mph
LAPS 80 x 6.300 km, 3.915 miles
DISTANCE 504.000 km, 313.171 miles
STARTERS/FINISHERS 20/9
WEATHER Sunny, hot, dry
LAP LEADERS Fangio 1-3, 8-13 (9); Ascari 4-7, 14-80 (71)
WINNER'S LAPS 1-3 P2, 4-7 P1, 8-13 P2, 14-80 P1
FASTEST LAP Farina, Alfa Romeo, 1m 56.5s (lap 64), 194.678kph, 120.967mph
CHAMPIONSHIP Fangio 27, Ascari 25, González 21, Farina 17, Villoresi 15

Pos	Driver	Car	Time/gap	Grid	Stops	Tyres
1	A Ascari	Ferrari	2h 42m 39.3s	3	2	P
2	F González	Ferrari	−35.6s	4	2	P
3	F Bonetto/N Farina	Alfa Romeo	−1 lap	7	3	P
4	L Villoresi	Ferrari	−1 lap	5	3	P
5	P Taruffi	Ferrari	−2 laps	6	2	P
6	A Simon	Simca Gordini	−6 laps	11	NA	E

Round 8/8	**SPANISH GP** Pedralbes **28 October 1951**	Race 15

Juan Manuel Fangio

Alfa Romeo 159 158.939kph, 98.760mph

With back-to-back late-season wins Ascari entered the final round as Fangio's only remaining rival for the title. But to secure the championship he still needed to finish strongly and ahead of his adversary. Pole position promised much but in the race Ascari's challenge fizzled out due to a disastrous blunder by his team: the size of wheels and tyres selected generated overheating and delamination. Taruffi's Ferrari was first to throw a tread on lap 6, Villoresi lap 7, Ascari lap 8, González lap 14. Fangio, meanwhile, sailed to a consummate victory and with it his first championship title. Ascari eventually came in a distant fourth, but second place for González ahead of outgoing champion Farina showed what might have been for Maranello.

POLE POSITION Ascari, Ferrari, 2m 10.59s (1.68s), 174.114kph, 108.190mph
LAPS 70 x 6.316 km, 3.925 miles
DISTANCE 442.120 km, 274.721 miles
STARTERS/FINISHERS 19/10
WEATHER Sunny, hot, dry
LAP LEADERS Ascari 1-3 (3); Fangio 4-70 (67)
WINNER'S LAPS 1-2 P3, 3 P2, 4-70 P1
FASTEST LAP Fangio, Alfa Romeo, 2m 16.93s (lap 3), 166.053kph, 103.180mph
CHAMPIONSHIP Fangio 31, Ascari 25, González 24, Farina 19, Villoresi 15

Pos	Driver	Car	Time/gap	Grid	Stops	Tyres
1	J M Fangio	Alfa Romeo	2h 46m 54.10s	2	2	P
2	F González	Ferrari	−54.28s	3	1	P
3	N Farina	Alfa Romeo	−1m 45.54s	4	2	P
4	A Ascari	Ferrari	−2 laps	1	3	P
5	F Bonetto	Alfa Romeo	−2 laps	8	2	P
6	E de Graffenried	Alfa Romeo	−4 laps	6	NA	P

Formula 1: All the Races – 1951   **23**

			Driver	Car	Races contested	Race victories	Podiumse excl. victories	Races led	Flag to flag victories	Laps led	Poles	Fastest laps	Triple Crowns
		ARG	Juan Manuel Fangio	Alfa Romeo	7	3	5	7		180	4	5	2
		ITA	Alberto Ascari	Ferrari	7	2	4	4		99	2		
	24	ARG	José Froilán González	Talbot Lago (1) Ferrari (5)	6	1	5	2		60	1		
4	19	ITA	Nino Farina	Alfa Romeo	7	1	4	3		73		2	
5	15	ITA	Luigi Villoresi	Ferrari	7		3	1		2			
6	10	ITA	Piero Taruffi	Ferrari	5		1						
7	9	USA	Lee Wallard	Kurtis Kraft-Offenhauser	1	1	1	1		159		1	
8	7	ITA	Felice Bonetto	Alfa Romeo	4		1	1		1			
9	6	USA	Mike Nazaruk	Kurtis Kraft-Offenhauser	1								
10	5	GBR	Reg Parnell	Thin Wall Ferrari (1) BRM (1)	2								
11	4	ITA	Luigi Fagioli	Alfa Romeo	1	1	1						
12	3	ITA	Consalvo Sanesi	Alfa Romeo	4								
12	3	USA	Andy Linden	Silnes-Sherman-Offenhauser	1								
12	3	FRA	Louis Rosier	Talbot Lago	7								
15	2	USA	Jack McGrath	Kurtis Kraft-Offenhauser	1				1	11			
15	2	USA	Manny Ayulo	Kurtis Kraft-Offenhauser	1								
17	2	SUI	Toulo de Graffenried	Alfa Romeo (3) Maserati (2)	5								
17	2	USA	Bobby Ball	Schroeder-Offenhauser	1								
17	2	FRA	Yves Giraud-Cabantous	Talbot Lago	6								
-	0	USA	Duke Nalon	Kurtis Kraft-Novi	1						1		
-	0	USA	Jimmy Davies	Pawl-Offenhauser	1				1	25			
-	0	USA	Cecil Green	Kurtis Kraft-Offenhauser	1				1	5			

1951 Drivers Championship

RACE 12, British GP: González (12) disputed the lead with Fangio (2) until, following the Alfa's lap 49 pit-stop, he was able to pull away to bring Ferrari a first championship race victory.

RACE 12, British GP: The V16 BRM certainly looked and sounded the part, but the 1951 British GP at Silverstone was its sole championship appearance; this is Reg Parnell's car.

1951 CHAMPIONSHIP FACTS AND FOLKLORE

- Including the Indy 500, the 1951 championship was run over eight rounds but without the Monaco GP, the Principality not returning until 1955.
- The first *Grandes Épreuves* were held at Pedralbes in Spain and the 14.173 miles of the mighty Nürburgring, snaking through the Eifel mountains.
- Technically 1951 was a fascinating encounter between two radically different schools of thought regarding engine design, Alfa Romeo's 1.5-litre supercharged straight-8 unit versus the unsupercharged 4.5-litre V12 Ferrari motor.
- To emphasise the key distinction, the normally aspirated Ferrari engine could achieve around 4.5mpg compared with the *Alfetta*'s 1.8mpg, or worse.
- The season was an Italian toe-to-toe, Alfa winning four races to Ferrari's three, no other team even reaching the podium.
- It was ironic that the *Alfettas* were the product of Alfa Romeo's Modena workshops back in 1937 under the stewardship of Scuderia Ferrari before Enzo's breakaway to form his own eponymous company and team.
- González's British Grand Prix victory was the watershed, and on learning the news Enzo Ferrari reacted with typical emotion and pomposity: 'When for the first time in the history of our direct rivalry González in a Ferrari showed his heels to the whole Alfa team, I wept with joy. But my tears of happiness were blended, too, with tears of sadness, for I thought that day: "I have killed my mother!"'
- The competetiveness of Ferrari in 1951 also enabled Alberto Ascari to showcase his talent and emerge as the driver

who would vie for supremacy with Fangio in these seminal championship seasons.
- But Alfa recognised that the writing was on the wall for its supercharged engine technology and, unable to raise the necessary funds for a new car, reluctantly withdrew at season's end, not returning until 1979.
- Alfa's decision put the fledgling FIA world drivers' championship into crisis, as other potential contenders such as Talbot Lago, Simca-Gordini and BRM were also proving unable to field competitive F1 machinery.
- BRM (British Racing Motors) was founded shortly after World War Two by Raymond Mays. Mays was determined to build an all-British Grand Prix challenger for the post-war era as a national prestige project, with financial and industrial backing from the British motor industry and its suppliers, channelled through a trust fund.
- An over-ambitious endeavour with cumbersome organisation, the project was doomed to failure, the car featuring an enormously powerful 1.5-litre V16 engine using two-stage Rolls Royce centrifugal superchargers. But its narrow power band, delivering some 430bhp through narrow tyres, made it very difficult to drive, let alone drive swiftly.
- Together with the demise of the Talbot Lago organisation and disintegration of the Simca-Gordini partnership, this left only Ferrari with competitive F1 cars.
- There was even talk of adopting Formula 2 rules for 1952, but one thing was certain – whether F1 or F2, Ferrari were in the box seat.

Championship ranking	Championship points	Team/Marque nationality	1951 Constructors Results (Excl. Indy 500)		Engine maker nationality	Races contested	Race victories	1-2 finishes	Podiums excl. victories	Races led	Laps led	Poles	Fastest laps
			Chassis	Engine									
N/A	N/A	ITA	Alfa Romeo 159	Alfa Romeo 1.5 S8 s/c	ITA	7	4		5	7	254	4	7
N/A	N/A	ITA	Ferrari 125, 212, 375, 375 TWSp	Ferrari 1.5 V12 s/c, 4.5 V12	ITA	7	3	1	9	6	161	3	
N/A	N/A	FRA	Talbot Lago T26C, T26C-DA, T26C-GS	Talbot Lago 4.5 S6	FRA	7							
N/A	N/A	GBR	BRM P15	BRM 1.5 V16 s/c	GBR	1							

1952

Ascari's Ferrari unbeatable

THE TALE OF THE TITLE

- With a dearth of competitive F1 cars, the 1952 championship was run to Formula 2 regulations.
- Ferrari fielded their Tipo 500 car, which had already enjoyed considerable F2 success in 1951.
- The Tipo 500 made a clean sweep of the season – seven races, seven wins, the Indy 500 excepted.
- Ascari dominated, victorious in all six GPs he started, Taruffi winning the opening round in his absence.
- Ascari's priority during May was leading Ferrari's one and only yet vain attempt at the Indy 500.
- In a one-sided championship, Fangio was unable to defend his title, sidelined with a broken neck.
- Maserati, Gordini, Cooper and Connaught were outclassed by the Ferrari 500, rarely showing much fight.
- Highlights included Mike Hawthorn's emergence in the Cooper-Bristol and the return by González at Monza.
- And not forgetting: HWM (Hersham & Walton Motors).

THE CHASE FOR THE CHAMPIONSHIP

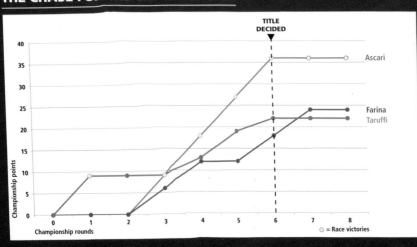

Ferrari 500

Round 1/8 **SWISS GP** Bremgarten 18 May 1952 Race 16	**Piero Taruffi** Ferrari 500 148.990kph, 92.578mph

In Ascari's absence at Indianapolis, Farina led the two-car works Ferrari entry and duly took pole position. From there he jumped straight into a steadily increasing lead, which he held until his retirement with magneto trouble at around quarter-distance. Teammate Taruffi then assumed the lead, reeling off the remaining 46 laps for an easy win. Farina took over Simon's car, overtaking Behra's Gordini for second place on lap 35, but he was out again with the same ailment by lap 51. A broken exhaust allowed Fischer's privately entered Ferrari 500 to get ahead of Behra's Gordini, the Frenchman making his championship debut along with Collins in an HWM. The HWMs were withdrawn when two of their number exited dramatically and simultaneously with de Dion failure.

POLE POSITION N Farina, Ferrari, 2m 47.5s (2.6s), 156.466kph, 97.223mph
LAPS 62 x 7.280 km, 4.524 miles
DISTANCE 451.360 km, 280.462 miles
STARTERS/FINISHERS 21/8
WEATHER Warm, dry
LAP LEADERS Farina 1-16 (16); Taruffi 17-62 (46)
WINNER'S LAPS 1-16 P2, 17-62 P1
FASTEST LAP Taruffi, Ferrari, 2m 49.1s (lap 46), 154.985kph, 96.303mph
CHAMPIONSHIP Taruffi 9, Fischer 6, Behra 4, Wharton 3, Brown 2

Pos	Driver	Car	Time/gap	Grid	Stops	Tyres
1	P Taruffi	Ferrari	3h 01m 46.1s	2	1	P
2	R Fischer	Ferrari	–2m 37.2s	5	0	P
3	J Behra	Gordini	–1 lap	7	3	E
4	K Wharton	Frazer Nash-Bristol	–2 laps	13	1	D
5	A Brown	Cooper-Bristol	–3 laps	15	0	D
6	E de Graffenried	Maserati Platé	–4 laps	8	1	P

Round 2/8 **INDIANAPOLIS 500** Indianapolis 30 May 1952 Race 17	**Troy Ruttman** Kuzma-Offenhauser 207.481kph, 128.922mph

The Indianapolis Motor Speedway, a 2.5-mile oval circuit, was built in 1909, getting its 'Brickyard' nickname the following year when it was repaved with 3.2 million bricks. Ascari's 1952 entry with Ferrari was the only attempt by a pukka F1 team/driver while the Indy 500 was officially part of the FIA world championship. The car was a beefed-up 1951 F1 car, designated the 375 Indy and entered by NART. Ascari was required to complete a 'rookie' test prior to qualifying 19th of the 33 starters. The Ferrari reached eighth place while it lasted, but on lap 40 of the 200 suffered a broken wire wheel hub. Troy Ruttman, 22, became the youngest-ever 500 winner when, with nine laps to go, long-term leader Bill Vukovich crashed with steering pin failure.

POLE POSITION F Agabashian, Kurtis Kraft-Cummins, 4m 20.85s (1.92s), 222.108kph, 138.011mph
LAPS 200 x 4.023 km, 2.500 miles
DISTANCE 804.672 km, 500.000 miles
STARTERS/FINISHERS 33/19
WEATHER Sunny, warm, dry
LAP LEADERS J McGrath, Kurtis Kraft-Offy 1-6 (6); Vukovich 7-11, 13-61, 83-134, 148-191 (150); Ruttman 12, 62-82, 135-147, 192-200 (44)
WINNER'S LAPS NA
FASTEST LAP B Vukovich, Kurtis Kraft-Offy, 1m 6.60s (lap 8), 217.479kph, 135.135mph
CHAMPIONSHIP Taruffi 9, Ruttman 8, Fischer 6, Rathmann 6, Behra 4

Pos	Driver	Car	Time/gap	Grid	Stops	Tyres
1	T Ruttman	Kuzma-Offy	3h 52m 41.88s	7	NA	F
2	J Rathmann	Kurtis Kraft-Offy	–4m 2.33s	10	NA	F
3	S Hanks	Kurtis Kraft-Offy	–6m 11.61s	5	NA	F
4	D Carter	Lesovsky-Offy	–6m 48.34s	6	NA	F
5	A Cross	Kurtis Kraft-Offy	–8m 40.15s	20	NA	F
6	J Bryan	Kurtis Kraft-Offy	–9m 24.32s	21	NA	F

BELGIAN GP Spa-Francorchamps
22 June 1952 — Race 18

Alberto Ascari
Ferrari 500 165.962kph, 103.124mph

...ks Ferraris locked out the front row, with Ascari – following his
...p to the USA – making his first championship appearance for the
...n over three hours of wet racing around the long Spa circuit, Ascari
...ina from pole to win by over two minutes. Behra's Gordini had given
...Ferraris a fright by leading early on until he spun on the second lap. Now
...ng third, he was passed by Taruffi on lap 14, the Italian making up ground
from a poor start. But just after making the pass Taruffi spun at Malmédy and
collected the closely following Behra, fortunately without consequence for
either driver. Mike Hawthorn, on his debut, finished a fine fourth in his Cooper-
Bristol in the difficult conditions.

POLE POSITION Ascari, Ferrari, 4m 37.0s (3.0s), 183.509kph, 114.027mph
LAPS 36 x 14.128 km, 8.774 miles
DISTANCE 508.320 km, 315.855 miles
STARTERS/FINISHERS 22/15
WEATHER Heavy rain
LAP LEADERS J Behra, Gordini 1 (1); Ascari 2-36 (35)
WINNER'S LAPS 1 P2, 2-36 P1
FASTEST LAP Ascari, Ferrari, 4m 55.0s (laps 2 & 7), 172.312kph, 107.070mph
CHAMPIONSHIP Taruffi 9, Ascari 9, Ruttman 8, Fischer 6, Rathmann 6

Pos	Driver	Car	Time/gap	Grid	Stops	Tyres
1	A Ascari	Ferrari	3h 3m 46.3s	1	0	P
2	N Farina	Ferrari	–1m 55.2s	2	0	P
3	R Manzon	Gordini	–4m 28.4s	4	0	E
4	M Hawthorn	Cooper-Bristol	–1 lap	6	2	D
5	P Frère	HWM-Alta	–2 laps	8	1	D
6	A Brown	Cooper-Bristol	–2 laps	9	0	D

Round 4/8
FRENCH GP Rouen-les-Essarts
6 July 1952 — Race 19

Alberto Ascari
Ferrari 500 128.958kph, 80.131mph

Apart from some spirited driving by Manzon and Behra in Gordinis during the
opening three or four laps, this race was a Ferrari benefit, the works cars led
by Ascari finishing 1-2-3 just as they had lined up on the grid. The rain-affected
race was stopped after three hours had elapsed and at the finish the top six
cars, except for Farina, were each separated by at least one lap. Hawthorn once
again made an impression with the Cooper-Bristol. Eighth on lap 20, he took
Macklin on lap 25, Collins lap 41, and Trintignant lap 44 to claim fifth behind
the Ferraris and Manzon, only for a misfire to develop which ended his race on
lap 51.

POLE POSITION Ascari, Ferrari, 2m 14.8s (1.4s), 136.202kph, 84.632mph
LAPS 76 x 5.100 km, 3.169 miles (Chequered flag shown at 3 hours)
DISTANCE 387.600 km, 240.843 miles
STARTERS/FINISHERS 20/12
WEATHER Overcast, rain later
LAP LEADERS Ascari 1-76 (77)
WINNER'S LAPS 1-76 P1
FASTEST LAP Ascari, Ferrari, 2m 17.3s (lap 28), 133.722kph, 83.091mph
CHAMPIONSHIP Ascari 18, Taruffi 13, Farina 12, Ruttman 8, Manzon 7

Pos	Driver	Car	Time/gap	Grid	Stops	Tyres
1	A Ascari	Ferrari	3h 00m 20.3s	1	0	P
2	N Farina	Ferrari	–44.4	2	0	P
3	P Taruffi	Ferrari	–1 lap	3	0	P
4	R Manzon	Gordini	–2 laps	5	0	E
5	M Trintignant	Simca Gordini	–4 laps	6	0	E
6	P Collins	HWM-Alta	–6 laps	8	0	D

Round 5/8
BRITISH GP Silverstone
19 July 1952 — Race 20

Alberto Ascari
Ferrari 500 146.323kph, 90.921mph

Another victory from pole by Ascari, this time followed home, a lap down, by
third driver Taruffi. Farina had been delayed by a misfire but managed to nurse
his car home sixth after a three-minute stop for a plug change. The race was
enlivened for the British crowd by a good showing from the new Connaughts,
making their first championship appearance. Drivers Poore, Thompson and
Downing had shown good pace in qualifying which they also brought to the
first half of the race, albeit often 5s a lap shy of the leading Ferrari. Their
Achilles heel was the need to make a fuel stop, which allowed Hawthorn to get
ahead to take a popular first podium for himself and Cooper.

POLE POSITION Farina, Ferrari, 1m 50.0s (0.0s), 154.163kph, 95.793mph
LAPS 85 x 4.711 km, 2.927 miles
DISTANCE 400.397 km, 248.795 miles
STARTERS/FINISHERS 31/22
WEATHER Overcast, but dry
LAP LEADERS Ascari 1-85 (85)
WINNER'S LAPS 1-85 P1
FASTEST LAP Ascari, Ferrari, 1m 52.0s (lap 9), 151.411kph, 94.082mph
CHAMPIONSHIP Ascari 27, Taruffi 19, Farina 12, Ruttman 8, Manzon 7

Pos	Driver	Car	Time/gap	Grid	Stops	Tyres
1	A Ascari	Ferrari	2h 44m 11.0s	2	0	P
2	P Taruffi	Ferrari	–1 lap	3	0	P
3	M Hawthorn	Cooper-Bristol	–2 laps	7	0	D
4	D Poore	Connaught-Lea Francis	–2 laps	8	1	D
5	E Thompson	Connaught-Lea Francis	–3 laps	9	1	D
6	N Farina	Ferrari	–3 laps	1	1	P

GERMAN GP Nürburgring
3 August 1952
Race 21

Alberto
Ferrari 500 132.288

Such was Ascari's supremacy that as early as 3 August his second successive victory at the Nürburgring also sealed his first championship – and this despite missing the opening round due to his Indy commitments. Another Ferrari procession was averted when Ascari pitted for oil on the penultimate lap. Farina's sister car took the lead but on his final tour Ascari overturned a 9s deficit to win by 14.1s. This time Ferraris finished 1-2-3-4, Behra's Gordini best of the rest. The 'rest' comprised a large entry of German F2 machinery, the British contingent largely absent. Attrition was heavy, less than half the 30 starters still circulating by lap 7, and just seven cars receiving the chequered flag.

POLE POSITION Ascari, Fer,
135.864kph, 84.422mph
LAPS 18 x 22.810 km, 14.173 miles
DISTANCE 410.580 km, 255.123 miles
STARTERS/FINISHERS 30/12
WEATHER Sunny, warm, dry
LAP LEADERS Ascari 1-18 (18)
WINNER'S LAPS 1-18 P1
FASTEST LAP Ascari, Ferrari, 10m 5.1s (lap 5),
135.706kph, 84.324mph
CHAMPIONSHIP Ascari 36, Taruffi 22, Farina 18,
Fischer 10, Ruttman 8

Pos	Driver	Car	Time/gap	Grid	Stops	Tyres
1	A Ascari	Ferrari	3h 2m 42.6s	1	2	P
2	N Farina	Ferrari	–14.1s	2	1	P
3	R Fischer	Ferrari	–7m 10.1s	6	0	P
4	P Taruffi	Ferrari	–1 lap	5	1	P
5	J Behra	Gordini	–1 lap	11	0	E
6	R Laurent	Ferrari	–2 laps	17	0	P

DUTCH GP Zandvoort
17 August 1952
Race 22

Alberto Ascari
Ferrari 500 130.521kph, 81.102mph

In qualifying for Holland's inaugural championship race, Hawthorn broke the usual Ferrari front-row stranglehold by pipping Villoresi in the third car. Then, for one glorious lap, he proceeded to hang on to the tail of the newly crowned world champion's car before Farina nipped past. Hawthorn may have finished two laps down to the unassailable works Ferraris but his fourth place, best of the rest, did not go unnoticed at Maranello. Next season he was at the wheel of a works Ferrari himself. Compatriot Moss started last, having recorded no time in qualifying, but lost a certain P7 finish when the con-rod broke on his ERA on lap 73.

POLE POSITION Ascari, Ferrari, 1m 46.5s (2.1s),
141.735kph, 88.070mph
LAPS 90 x 4.193 km, 2.605 miles
DISTANCE 377.370 km, 234.487 miles
STARTERS/FINISHERS 18/19
WEATHER Overcast, wet
LAP LEADERS Ascari 1-90 (90)
WINNER'S LAPS 1-90 P1
FASTEST LAP Ascari, Ferrari, 1m 49.8s (lap 89),
137.475kph, 85.423mph
CHAMPIONSHIP Ascari 36, Farina 24, Taruffi 22,
Fischer 10, Hawthorn 10

Pos	Driver	Car	Time/gap	Grid	Stops	Tyres
1	A Ascari	Ferrari	2h 53m 28.5s	1	0	P
2	N Farina	Ferrari	–40.1s	2	0	P
3	L Villoresi	Ferrari	–1m 34.4s	4	0	P
4	M Hawthorn	Cooper-Bristol	–2 laps	3	0	D
5	R Manzon	Gordini	–3 laps	8	1	E
6	M Trintignant	Gordini	–3 laps	5	0	E

ITALIAN GP Monza
7 September 1952
Race 23

Alberto Ascari
Ferrari 500 177.091kph, 110.039mph

At Monza González made a one-off appearance for Maserati, driving the comparatively new A6GCM model. He qualified fifth but shot into the lead and began drawing away from Ascari. This could be explained in part by the Maserati's smaller tanks and lighter fuel load, but it was still a fine drive. González made his expected fuel stop shortly before half-distance but was still able to vanquish all but Ascari's invincible Ferrari. It was hoped that Maserati's improved performance, and the return of Fangio, sidelined by injury all season, might give Ascari and his Ferrari 500 rather more of a test in 1953.

POLE POSITION Ascari, Ferrari, 2m 5.7s (0.9s),
180.430kph, 112.114mph
LAPS 80 x 6.300 km, 3.915 miles
DISTANCE 504.000 km, 313.171 miles
STARTERS/FINISHERS 24/15
WEATHER Sunny, warm, dry
LAP LEADERS González 1-36 (36); Ascari 37-80 (44)
WINNER'S LAPS 1-8 P2, 9 P3, 10 P2, 11 P3, 12-18 P2, 19
P3, 20 P2, 21 P3, 22-25 P2, 26-27 P3, 28-36 P2, 37-80 P1
FASTEST LAP Ascari, Ferrari/González, Maserati, 2m 6.1s
(lap 56/57 & 60), 179.857kph, 111.758mph
CHAMPIONSHIP Ascari 36, Farina 24, Taruffi 22,
Fischer 10, Hawthorn 10

Pos	Driver	Car	Time/gap	Grid	Stops	Tyres
1	A Ascari	Ferrari	2h 50m 45.6s	1	0	P
2	F González	Maserati	–1m 1.8s	5	1	P
3	L Villoresi	Ferrari	–2m 4.2s	2	1	P
4	N Farina	Ferrari	–2m 11.4s	3	0	P
5	F Bonetto	Maserati	–1 lap	13	2	P
6	A Simon	Ferrari	–1 lap	8	0	P

		nat.	Driver	Car	Races contested	Race victories	Podiumse excl. victories	Races led	Flag to flag victories	Laps led	Poles	Fastest laps	Triple Crowns
		ITA	Alberto Ascari	Ferrari	7	6		6	4	348	5	5	5
	4	ITA	Nino Farina	Ferrari	7		4	1		16	2		
22		ITA	Piero Taruffi	Ferrari	6	1	2	1		46		1	
10		SUI	Rudi Fischer	Ferrari	5		2						
4	10	GBR	Mike Hawthorn	Cooper-Bristol	5		1						
6	9	FRA	Robert Manzon	Gordini	7		1						
7	8	USA	Troy Ruttman	Kuzma-Offenhauser	1	1		1		44			
7	8	ITA	Luigi Villoresi	Ferrari	2		2						
9	6.5	ARG	José Froilán González	Maserati	1		1	1		36		1	
10	6	USA	Jim Rathmann	Kurtis Kraft-Offenhauser	1		1						
10	6	FRA	Jean Behra	Gordini	6		1	1		1			
12	4	USA	Sam Hanks	Kurtis Kraft-Offenhauser	1		1						
13	3	GBR	Ken Wharton	Frazer Nash-Bristol (3) Cooper-Bristol (1)	4								
13	3	USA	Duane Carter	Lesovsky-Offenhauser	1								
13	3	GBR	Dennis Poore	Connaught	2								
16	2	GBR	Alan Brown	Cooper-Bristol	4								
16	2	USA	Art Cross	Kurtis Kraft-Offenhauser	1								
16	2	BEL	Paul Frère	HWM (2) Simca Gordini (1)	3								
16	2	FRA	Maurice Trintignant	Gordini	5								
16	2	GBR	Eric Thompson	Connaught	1								
16	2	ITA	Felice Bonetto	Maserati	2								
22	1	USA	Bill Vukovich	Kurtis Kraft-Offenhauser	1			1		150		1	
-	0	USA	Fred Agabashian	Kurtis Kraft-Cummins	1						1		
-	0	USA	Jack McGrath	Kurtis Kraft-Offenhauser	1			1		6			

1952 Drivers Championship

1952 CHAMPIONSHIP FACTS AND FOLKLORE

■ With uncertainty over the ability of F1 teams such as Talbot Lago, Simca-Gordini and BRM to enter competitive machinery for 1952, Alfa Romeo's withdrawal from F1 towards the end of 1951 placed the nascent FIA drivers' world championship in jeopardy.

■ Having already announced a forthcoming new set of Formula 1 regulations, the FIA decided that for the two interim seasons the championship should continue but for 2-litre Formula 2 cars. This move also offered a proving ground for constructors' intent on participating in the new 2.5-litre Formula 1 set for 1954.

Championship ranking	Championship points	Team/Marque nationality	1952 Constructors Results (Excl. Indy 500) Chassis	Engine	Engine maker nationality	Races contested	Race victories	1-2 finishes	Podiums excl. victories	Races led	Laps led	Poles	Fastest laps
N/A	N/A	ITA	Ferrari 500, 125, 166, 212	Ferrari 2.0 S4, 2.0 V12	ITA	7	7	6	10	7	410	7	6
N/A	N/A	FRA	Gordini T16, T16S	Gordini 2.0 S6	FRA	7			2	1	1		
N/A	N/A	GBR	Cooper T20	Bristol 2.0 S6	GBR	6			1				
N/A	N/A	ITA	Maserati A6GCM	Maserati 2.0 S6	ITA	5			1	1	36		1
N/A	N/A	GBR	Connaught A	Lea Francis 2.0 S4	GBR	3							
N/A	N/A	GBR	Frazer Nash FN48, 421	Bristol 2.0 S6	GBR	4							
N/A	N/A	GBR	HWM (51), (52)	Alta 2.0 S4	GBR	6							
N/A	N/A	FRA	Simca Gordini T11, T15	Gordini 2.0 S4	FRA	5							

- The Formula 2 category had been conceived in 1948 for open-wheel monoposto cars with engines of 2 litres unblown or 500cc supercharged, no entrants taking the latter option.
- Ferrari, Maserati and Gordini could be relied upon to participate in the 1952 title fight but the adoption of F2 also undoubtedly provided a route for other constructors to aspire to world championship competition. From Britain it spawned the involvement of names such as HWM, Connaught, Fraser Nash and, most notably, Cooper; from Germany Veritas, AFM and EMW.
- Another significant development was that to avoid the cost and time of developing custom-built engines as used by the establishment represented by Ferrari, Maserati and Gordini, budding constructors instead tracked down extant units with racing potential. Cooper and Fraser-Nash turned to Bristol, Connaught to Lea Francis, and HWM to Alta. BMW was a popular choice with the German chassis builders.
- An increased incidence of British-based constructors inevitably led to the participation of more British drivers, together participating on a far more serious and professional footing than the true privateer acquiring and racing a Ferrari, Maserati or Talbot Lago.
- HWM (Hersham & Walton Motors) was typical of this breed of team, run by garage owners George Abecassis and John Heath. In 1951 Stirling Moss had made his debut in an HWM and in 1952 they gave 20-year-old Peter Collins his GP opportunity.
- Mike Hawthorn made his championship debut in 1951 at the wheel of a Cooper-Bristol, making a name for himself by bringing Cooper their first podium finish at Silverstone, their home GP.
- The Cooper Car Company was founded in 1946 by Charles Cooper and his son John who, taking advantage of the mushrooming post-war interest in motorsport, began building racing cars in their modest garage premises in Surbiton, Surrey. Together they built over 300 of their Formula 3 single-seaters powered by a 500cc JAP motorcycle engine.
- Connaught, another Surrey concern, was different again. Financed by Kenneth McAlpine, a member of the civil engineering family, the team had already built and raced a car in F2 with some success using a modified Lea Francis engine.
- But it was the car produced in Paris by Amédée Gordini, particularly in the hands of talented French driver Jean Behra, which occasionally, if only for a few laps, seemed to have the measure of the all-conquering Ferrari 500. During the winter Gordini had built a new 2-litre straight-six producing around 160bhp at 6,000rpm.
- This compared with the Ferrari 500's 170bhp at 7,000rpm four-cylinder engine, significantly mounted behind the front axle. Designed by Lampredi, the Tipo 500 first appeared in 1951 and was regarded as an entirely new concept by Ferrari, abandoning its sports car racing roots and V12 engines for lightness, weight distribution and agility.
- Of the former Alfa Romeo drivers, Farina joined Ascari at Ferrari, Fangio transferring to Maserati. But unfortunately Maserati's challenge was seriously blunted when the new world champion was unable to participate, injured in a non-title F2 race at Monza before the championship got under way.
- Starting in May and ending in September, 1952 was the shortest championship season on record, lasting just three months and 20 days.
- With Zandvoort added to the calendar, eight championship races were held including the Indy 500, with Rouen replacing Reims.
- In 1952 the Monaco GP was held for sports cars and during practice Luigi Fagioli was seriously injured when he lost control of his car exiting the tunnel and crashed broadside into a stone parapet. Aged 54, he died three weeks later.
- Future triple world champion Nelson Piquet was born in 1952.

RACE 22, Dutch GP: For one glorious lap, Hawthorn's Cooper-Bristol (32) hung on to the tail of newly crowned champion Ascari's Ferrari 500 (2) before Farina (16) nipped past.

1953

Ascari and Ferrari again

THE TALE OF THE TITLE

- Alberto Ascari, the first back-to-back champion, posted a still unbeaten record for consecutive race victories.
- In his first season for Ferrari, Mike Hawthorn became the first championship race winner from Britain.
- Hawthorn ended Ascari's nine-race winning streak at Reims, where he narrowly beat Fangio's Maserati.
- Now also Ferrari-mounted, Farina won his fifth and final championship race at the Nürburgring.
- Maserati were competitive but never had the beating of Ferrari, Fangio's challenge blunted by poor reliability.
- In five appearances prior to injury, González brought Maserati three thirds and a fourth.
- But Fangio won Maserati's first championship victory, Ascari spinning at the last corner of the Monza finale.
- The two Italian marques scored all but four points in the season, Trintignant twice finishing fifth for Gordini.
- And not forgetting: tragedy in Argentina.

THE CHASE FOR THE CHAMPIONSHIP

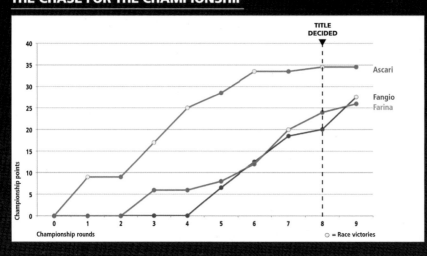

Round 1/9	**ARGENTINEAN GP** Buenos Aires No 2	**Alberto Ascari**
	18 January 1953 Race 24	Ferrari 500 125.736kph, 78.129mph

Fangio made his championship comeback at his home grand prix, getting among the Ferraris by qualifying second. With compatriot González also Maserati-mounted, a large but unruly crowd attended on race day. On lap 32, avoiding an errant spectator caused Farina to lose control, his Ferrari ploughing into the crown. Fifteen were killed, others seriously injured. The race was allowed to continue, lasting a further two hours. Ascari led from start to finish, easing away from Fangio and Farina by a second a lap. Shortly after the Farina hiatus Fangio retired when his prop-shaft UJ broke, Manzon's Gordini taking his place until losing a wheel. So when González made a late stop for fuel and tyres Villoresi finished runner-up.

POLE POSITION Ascari, Ferrari, 1m 55.4s (0.7s), 122.038kph, 75.831mph
LAPS 97 x 3.912 km, 2.431 miles (Race scheduled for three hours)
DISTANCE 379.464 km, 235.788 miles
STARTERS/FINISHERS 16/8
WEATHER Sunny, hot, dry
LAP LEADERS Ascari 1-97 (97)
WINNER'S LAPS 1-97 P1
FASTEST LAP Ascari, Ferrari, 1m 48.4s (laps 73), 129.919kph, 80.728mph
CHAMPIONSHIP Ascari 9, Villoresi 6, González 4, Hawthorn 3, Gálvez 2

Pos	Driver	Car	Time/gap	Grid	Stops	Tyres
1	A Ascari	Ferrari	3h 1m 4.6s	1	1	P
2	L Villoresi	Ferrari	–1 lap	3	1	P
3	F González	Maserati	–1 lap	5	2	P
4	M Hawthorn	Ferrari	–1 lap	6	2	P
5	O Gálvez	Maserati	–1 lap	9	0	P
6	J Behra	Gordini	–3 laps	11	0	E

Round 2/9	**INDIANAPOLIS 500** Indianapolis	**Bill Vukovich**
	30 May 1953 Race 25	Kurtis Kraft-Offenhauser 207.187kph, 128.740mph

After his near miss in 1952, Bill Vukovich made no mistake this year, achieving a dominant victory from pole. As the pace-car pulled off from the rolling start he assumed an immediate lead, recording the fastest lap on his 27th tour. The heat that day was intense, but while other drivers wilted Vukovich enhanced his burgeoning reputation to lead all but five laps and win by three. On lap 48 he stopped for fuel and tyres, rejoining the race 47s later in fifth place, retaking the lead on lap 54. The winner's car, like most on the Indy grid, was powered by the ubiquitous four-cylinder Offenhauser engine, or 'Offy'. Around lap 80, veteran Carl Scarborough handed over his car to Bob Scott. One hour later Scarborough died of heat exhaustion in the field hospital.

POLE POSITION Vukovich, Kurtis Kraft-Offy, 4m 20.13s (1.60s), 222.723kph, 138.393mph
LAPS 200 x 4.023 km, 2.500 miles
DISTANCE 804.672 km, 500.000 miles
STARTERS/FINISHERS 33/12
WEATHER Sunny, very hot, dry
LAP LEADERS Vukovich 1-48, 54-200 (195); Agabashian 49 (1); J Rathmann, Kurtis Kraft-Offy 50 (1); Hanks 51-53 (3)
WINNER'S LAPS NA
FASTEST LAP Vukovich, Kurtis Kraft-Offy, 1m 6.24s (lap 27), 218.661kph, 135.870mph
CHAMPIONSHIP Ascari 9, Vukovich 9, Villoresi 6, Cross 6, González 4

Pos	Driver	Car	Time/gap	Grid	Stops	Tyres
1	B Vukovich	Kurtis Kraft-Offy	3h 53m 1.69s	1	NA	F
2	A Cross	Kurtis Kraft-Offy	–3m 30.87s	12	NA	F
3	S Hanks/D Carter	Kurtis Kraft-Offy	–4m 11.50s	9	NA	F
4	F Agabashian/P Russo	Kurtis Kraft-Offy	–4m 39.24s	2	NA	F
5	J McGrath	Kurtis Kraft-Offy	–7m 49.64s	3	NA	F
6	J Daywalt	Kurtis Kraft-Offy	–8m 10.21s	21	NA	F

Round 3/9	**DUTCH GP** Zandvoort	**Alberto Ascari**
	7 June 1953 Race 26	Ferrari 500 130.430kph, 81.085mph

Now equipped with the latest A6GCM Maseratis, there was expectation that Fangio and González might present a greater threat to Ferrari. Fangio again made the front row but in the race both Maseratis suffered rear axle breakages well before half-distance. When González got back to the pits he took over Bonetto's third team car and made a storming recovery drive. He passed Trintignant for eighth, Schell for seventh and then Hawthorn's works Ferrari, although he was a lap ahead. De Graffenreid was next and with Fangio's retirement he was now fifth behind Hawthorn. Despite spinning at Tarzan on lap 48, González caught and passed Hawthorn a second time, and with Villoresi's retirement came home third behind Ascari and Farina to rapturous applause.

POLE POSITION Ascari, Ferrari, 1m 51.1s (1.6s), 135.867kph, 84.424mph
LAPS 90 x 4.193 km, 2.605 miles
DISTANCE 377.370 km, 234.487 miles
STARTERS/FINISHERS 19/9
WEATHER Sunny, warm, dry
LAP LEADERS Ascari 1-90 (90)
WINNER'S LAPS 1-90 P1
FASTEST LAP L Villoresi, Ferrari, 1m 52.8s (lap 59), 133.819kph, 83.151mph
CHAMPIONSHIP Ascari 17, Vukovich 9, Villoresi 7, Cross 6, Farina 6

Pos	Driver	Car	Time/gap	Grid	Stops	Tyres
1	A Ascari	Ferrari	2h 53m 35.8s	1	0	P
2	N Farina	Ferrari	–10.4s	3	0	P
3	F Bonetto/F González	Maserati	–1 lap	13	1	P
4	M Hawthorn	Ferrari	–1 lap	6	0	P
5	E de Graffenried	Maserati	–2 laps	7	0	P
6	M Trintignant	Gordini	–3 laps	12	0	E

<table>
<tr><td>Round 4/9</td><td colspan="2">BELGIAN GP Spa-Francorchamps</td><td colspan="2">Alberto Ascari</td></tr>
<tr><td></td><td>21 June 1953</td><td align="right">Race 27</td><td colspan="2">Ferrari 500 165.962kph, 103.124mph</td></tr>
</table>

Another Ferrari 1-2 masked a promising performance by the fast but fragile Maseratis. On the grid Ascari was the meat in a Maserati sandwich and had no answer to the flying cars from Modena for the first third of the race. Before his throttle broke on lap 12, leader González had built a gap of around a minute to Ascari. When on the following lap new leader Fangio also retired with engine trouble he took over Claes' car, resuming in eighth spot. Fangio charged back to third behind Ascari and Villoresi, but at the finish there was no sign of the Maserati. Fangio had suffered steering failure on the final lap, fortunately without personal mishap.

POLE POSITION J M Fangio, Maserati, 4m 30.0s (2.0s), 188.267kph, 116.983mph
LAPS 36 x 14.120 km, 8.774 miles
DISTANCE 508.320 km, 315.855 miles
STARTERS/FINISHERS 20/11
WEATHER Sunny, hot, dry
LAP LEADERS González 1-11 (11); Fangio 12-13 (2); Ascari 14-36 (23)
WINNER'S LAPS 1-11 P3, 12-13 P2, 14-36 P1
FASTEST LAP F González, Maserati, 4m 34.0s (laps 2, 3, 9 & 11), 185.518kph, 115.276mph
CHAMPIONSHIP Ascari 25, Villoresi 13, Vukovich 9, González 7, Cross 6

Pos	Driver	Car	Time/gap	Grid	Stops	Tyres
1	A Ascari	Ferrari	2h 48m 30.3s	2	0	P
2	L Villoresi	Ferrari	−2m 48.2s	5	0	P
3	O Marimón	Maserati	−1 lap	6	1	P
4	E de Graffenried	Maserati	−1 lap	9	0	P
5	M Trintignant	Gordini	−1 lap	8	1	E
6	M Hawthorn	Ferrari	−1 lap	7	2	P

<table>
<tr><td>Round 5/9</td><td colspan="2">FRENCH GP Reims</td><td colspan="2">Mike Hawthorn</td></tr>
<tr><td></td><td>5 July 1953</td><td align="right">Race 28</td><td colspan="2">Ferrari 500 182.881kph, 113.637mph</td></tr>
</table>

Qualifying pointed to a close race, the top six – three Ferraris, three Maseratis – covered by 1.3s. Widely regarded as one of the truly great races, González on low fuel led the first half until his pit stop. Thereafter Fangio and Hawthorn played out a spellbinding duel, repassing repeatedly (see Lap Leaders). Hawthorn finally won, saving Ferrari's blushes and becoming the first Englishman to win a World Championship race. There was little to choose between the two cars on top speed, but Ferrari had grunt out of corners, making the crucial difference from the Thillois hairpin to the finishing line. González was third, Ascari fourth, the first three covered by just 1.4s in an utterly thrilling race.

POLE POSITION Ascari, Ferrari, 2m 41.2s (1.4s), 186.409kph, 115.829mph
LAPS 60 x 8.347 km, 5.187 miles
DISTANCE 500.820 km, 311.195 miles
STARTERS/FINISHERS 25/15
WEATHER Sunny, hot, dry
LAP LEADERS González 1-29 (29); Fangio 30-31, 35-36, 39-41, 45-47, 49-53, 55-56 (17); Hawthorn 32-34, 37-38, 42-44, 48, 54, 57-60 (14)
WINNER'S LAPS 1-2 P5, 3 P4, 4 P3, 5 P4, 6 P3, 7 P4, 8 P3, 9-13 P2, 14-16 P3, 17-18 P4, 19 P3, 20 P2, 21 P3, 22 P2, 23 P4, 24 P3, 25 P4, 26 P6, 27 P5, 28-29 P4, 30-31 P2, 32-34 P1, 35-36 P2, 37-38 P1, 39-41 P2, 42-44 P1, 45-47 P2, 48 P1, 49-53 P2, 54 P1, 55-56 P2, 57-60 P1
FASTEST LAP Fangio, Maserati/Ascari, Ferrari, 2m 41.1s (laps 25/37), 186.525kph, 115.901mph
CHAMPIONSHIP Ascari 28.5, Hawthorn 14, Villoresi 13, González 11, Vukovich 9

TOP 100 RACE

Pos	Driver	Car	Time/gap	Grid	Stops	Tyres
1	M Hawthorn	Ferrari	2h 44m 18.6s	7	0	P
2	J M Fangio	Maserati	−1.0s	4	0	P
3	F González	Maserati	−1.4s	5	1	P
4	A Ascari	Ferrari	−4.6s	1	0	P
5	N Farina	Ferrari	−1m 7.6s	6	0	P
6	L Villoresi	Ferrari	−1m 15.9s	3	0	P

<table>
<tr><td>Round 6/9</td><td colspan="2">BRITISH GP Silverstone</td><td colspan="2">Alberto Ascari</td></tr>
<tr><td></td><td>18 July 1953</td><td align="right">Race 29</td><td colspan="2">Ferrari 500 149.629kph, 92.975mph</td></tr>
</table>

Following the excitement of Reims, the Silverstone front row – Ferrari, Maserati, Ferrari, Maserati – boded well for a resumption of the intense struggle between the two Italian marques. As it was, Ascari stamped his authority on the race from the start, beating Fangio by a full minute, the Argentine the only driver on the same lap as the victor. Ferrari beat Maserati for third place too, González losing out to Farina due to a black flag pit stop on lap 17 for dropping oil and a lap 56 stop to take on fuel and, of course, oil. On his home circuit, Reims hero Hawthorn finished fifth after an early spin. Heavy rain fell during the final half-hour.

POLE POSITION Ascari, Ferrari, 1m 48.0s (1.0s), 157.018kph, 97.567mph
LAPS 90 x 4.711 km, 2.927 miles
DISTANCE 423.949 km, 263.430 miles
STARTERS/FINISHERS 28/10
WEATHER Overcast, showers, heavy in final half-hour
LAP LEADERS Ascari 1-90 (90)
WINNER'S LAPS 1-90 P1
FASTEST LAP Ascari, Ferrari/F González, Maserati, 1m 50.0s (laps NA/NA), 154.163kph, 95.793mph
CHAMPIONSHIP Ascari 33.5, Hawthorn 16, González 13.5, Villoresi 13, Fangio 12.5

Pos	Driver	Car	Time/gap	Grid	Stops	Tyres
1	A Ascari	Ferrari	2h 50m 0.0s	1	0	P
2	J M Fangio	Maserati	−1m 0.0s	4	0	P
3	N Farina	Ferrari	−2 laps	5	0	P
4	F González	Maserati	−2 laps	2	2	P
5	M Hawthorn	Ferrari	−3 laps	3	1	P
6	F Bonetto	Maserati	−8 laps	16	1	P

GERMAN GP Nürburgring
2 August 1953
Race 30

Nino Farina
Ferrari 500 135.047kph, 83.914mph

Ascari, the only driver under ten minutes in qualifying and now leading the race by 40s, must have been contemplating a Nürburgring hat-trick, when, on lap 5 of 18, a wheel flew off approaching Tiergarten. Recovering brilliantly, Alberto limped the remainder of the lap on three wheels and a brake drum. Hawthorn and Fangio now duelled for the lead with Farina following. Perhaps energised by Ascari's ill fortune, the veteran Italian overtook them on lap 8 to draw away and win by over a minute. Bonetto was the only other driver to complete the full race-distance to finish fourth. Ascari's no-score and a third consecutive second place for Fangio kept the title battle mathematically open with two rounds remaining.

POLE POSITION A Ascari, Ferrari, 9m 59.8s (3.9s), 136.906kph, 85.069mph
LAPS 18 x 22.810 km, 14.173 miles
DISTANCE 410.580 km, 255.123 miles
STARTERS/FINISHERS 34/16
WEATHER Sunny, warm, dry
LAP LEADERS Ascari 1-4 (4); Hawthorn 5-7 (3); Farina 8-18 (11)
WINNER'S LAPS 1-5 P4, 6-7 P3, 8-18 P1
FASTEST LAP A Ascari, Ferrari, 9m 56.0s (lap 12), 137.779kph, 85.612mph
CHAMPIONSHIP Ascari 33.5, Farina 20, Fangio 18.5, Hawthorn 18, González 13.5

Pos	Driver	Car	Time/gap	Grid	Stops	Tyres
1	N Farina	Ferrari	3h 2m 25.0s	3	0	P
2	J M Fangio	Maserati	−1m 4.0s	2	0	P
3	M Hawthorn	Ferrari	−1m 43.6s	4	0	P
4	F Bonetto	Maserati	−8m 48.6s	7	0	P
5	E de Graffenried	Maserati	−1 lap	11	0	P
6	S Moss	Cooper-Alta	−1 lap	12	2	D

SWISS GP Bremgarten
23 August 1953
Race 31

Alberto Ascari
Ferrari 500 156.367kph, 97.162mph

A second Fangio pole restated the potential of Maserati and how close they were to a breakthrough victory. But in the race, an Ascari-led Ferrari 1-2-3 snuffed out any faint hope of a late season charge by Fangio for championship honours. The leadership battle between Ascari and Fangio lasted only until lap 8, when gearbox trouble slowed Fangio, pitting on lap 11 to take over Bonetto's car and go on to finish fourth. But Ascari too had his problems, losing a minute in the pits to have a carburettor jet cleaned after his engine went flat on lap 39, dropping him to third. The Italian then proceeded to storm past his teammates to win the title in style and become the first double champion.

POLE POSITION Fangio, Maserati, 2m 40.1s (2.6s), 163.698kph, 101.717mph
LAPS 65 x 7.280 km, 4.524 miles
DISTANCE 473.200 km, 294.033 miles
STARTERS/FINISHERS 20/9
WEATHER Sunny, warm, dry
LAP LEADERS Ascari 1-40, 54-65 (52); Farina 41-53 (13)
WINNER'S LAPS 1-40 P1, 41-46 P4, 47-51 P3, 52-53 P2, 54-65 P1
FASTEST LAP Ascari, Ferrari, 2m 41.3s (lap 50), 162.480kph, 100.960mph
CHAMPIONSHIP Ascari 34.5, Farina 24, Fangio 20, Hawthorn 19, González 13.5

Pos	Driver	Car	Time/gap	Grid	Stops	Tyres
1	A Ascari	Ferrari	3h 1m 34.40s	2	1	P
2	N Farina	Ferrari	−1m 12.93s	3	0	P
3	M Hawthorn	Ferrari	−1m 35.96s	7	0	P
4	F Bonetto/J M Fangio	Maserati	−1 lap	1	1	P
5	H Lang	Maserati	−3 laps	11	1	P
6	L Villoresi	Ferrari	−3 laps	6	3	P

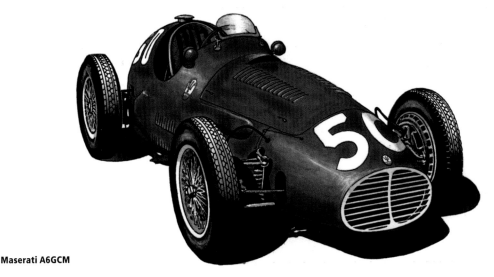

Maserati A6GCM

ITALIAN GP Monza
13 September 1953   Race 32

Juan Manuel Fangio
Maserati A6GCM 178.129kph, 110.684mph

For the sixth time that season Ascari and Fangio were side by side in the primary grid slots, Ascari claiming pole to win this particular personal duel 4-2. The race was a classic Monza slipstreamer with at times as many as six Italian cars disputing the lead and 24 lead changes recorded on the lap chart. But Ascari held the initiative, able to lead the gaggle over the line from lap 53 to 79. But on the 80th and final lap, at the final corner, Ascari and Fangio were side by side leading a five-car bunch when Ascari spun on oil. Fangio dodged by on the inside to seize a last-gasp home win and maiden championship victory for the ecstatic Maserati team. He was followed home by the three Ferraris, Ascari, who didn't complete the final lap, unplaced.

POLE POSITION A Ascari, Ferrari, 2m 2.7s (0.5s), 184.841kph, 114.855mph
LAPS 80 x 6.300 km, 3.915 miles
DISTANCE 504.000 km, 313.171 miles
STARTERS/FINISHERS 30/16
WEATHER Sunny, warm, dry
LAP LEADERS Ascari 1-6, 9, 14-22, 27-31, 34-36, 39-40, 42, 44-45, 47-49, 53-79 (59); Fangio 7-8, 11, 23, 25-26, 32-33, 37, 41, 50-52, 80 (14); Farina 10, 12-13, 24, 38, 43, 46 (7)
WINNER'S LAPS NA
FASTEST LAP Fangio, Maserati, 2m 4.5s (lap 39), 182.169kph, 113.194mph
CHAMPIONSHIP Ascari 34.5, Fangio 27.5, Farina 26, Hawthorn 19, Villoresi 17

Pos	Driver	Car	Time/gap	Grid	Stops	Tyres
1	J M Fangio	Maserati	2h 49m 45.9s	2	0	P
2	N Farina	Ferrari	−1.4s	3	0	P
3	L Villoresi	Ferrari	−1 lap	5	0	P
4	M Hawthorn	Ferrari	−1 lap	6	0	P
5	M Trintignant	Gordini	−1 lap	8	0	E
6	R Mières	Gordini	−3 laps	7	0	E

TOP **100** RACE

RACE 32, Italian GP: The race was a classic Monza slip-streamer with at times as many as six Italian cars disputing the lead. Fangio (50) won when Ascari (4) spun on the final lap. Here, Farina (6) and Marimón (54) give chase.

1953 CHAMPIONSHIP FACTS AND FOLKLORE

- With Fangio returning to the cockpit and the arrival of talented designer Gioacchino Colombo in the workshop, Officine Alfieri Maserati looked a far stronger proposition to take on Scuderia Ferrari in 1953.
- Maserati's new contender was an adaptation of their earlier A6GCM, but heavily revised by Colombo. Power from the redesigned six-cylinder engine was 190–195bhp at 8,000rpm.
- Despite this increased threat, for the second and final season of the world championship run to Formula 2 regulations Ferrari chose to again field their invincible Tipo 500 with improved power, 190bhp at 7,500rpm.
- Their judgement proved correct, the car victorious in all but the last race of the season, which was only lost due to driver error.
- Therefore, Indy 500 winners apart, in the two seasons run to F2 regulations Fangio's Maserati triumph at Monza was the only non-Ferrari victory from 15 GPs, of which Ascari won 11 from 14 starts.
- But unlike 1952, Ascari did not win every GP he entered. In addition to Fangio, he was beaten by teammates Hawthorn and Farina, each on one occasion.

- Nevertheless, excluding the Indy 500, by winning the first three races of the season between June 1952 and June 1953 Ascari won a record nine consecutive Grands Prix, a record which stands to this day.
- Including the Indy 500, the nine championship races in 1953 included a new venue, Buenos Aires, which opened the season. Extraordinarily, this race was Fangio's first competitive outing since breaking his neck the previous June in a non-championship race at Monza.
- As well as Fangio's homeland, Argentina was the first venture for the championship outside Europe, Indy 500 excepted. Wretchedly, the race produced a disaster of mammoth proportions.
- Speaking later of the tragic Argentinean GP where 15 spectators were killed, Mike Hawthorn said 'They began standing in the roadway holding shirts and pullovers, which they snatched away at the last moment like a toreador playing a bull.'
- 1952 witnessed the birth of a future world champion, Nigel Mansell.

Championship ranking	Championship points	Driver nationality	1953 Drivers Championship		Races contested	Race victories	Podiumse excl. victories	Races led	Flag to flag victories	Laps led	Poles	Fastest laps	Triple Crowns
			Driver	Car									
1	34.5	ITA	Alberto Ascari	Ferrari	8	5		7	3	415	6	5	2
2	27.5	ARG	Juan Manuel Fangio	Maserati	8	1	3	3		33	2	2	
3	26	ITA	Nino Farina	Ferrari	8	1	4	3		31			
4	19	GBR	Mike Hawthorn	Ferrari	8	1	2	2		17			
5	17	ITA	Luigi Villoresi	Ferrari	8		3					1	
6	13.5	ARG	José Froilán González	Maserati	5		3	2		40		2	
7	9	USA	Bill Vukovich	Kurtis Kraft-Offenhauser	1	1		1		195	1	1	1
8	7	SUI	Toulo de Graffenried	Maserati	7								
9	6.5	ITA	Felice Bonetto	Maserati	7		1						
10	6	USA	Art Cross	Kurtis Kraft-Offenhauser	1		1						
11	4	ARG	Onofre Marimón	Maserati	6		1						
12	4	FRA	Maurice Trintignant	Gordini	8								
13	2	USA	Duane Carter	Kurtis Kraft-Offenhauser	1		1						
13	2	USA	Sam Hanks	Kurtis Kraft-Offenhauser	1		1	1		3			
15	2	ARG	Oscar Galvez	Maserati	1								
15	2	USA	Jack McGrath	Kurtis Kraft-Offenhauser	1								
15	2	GER	Hermann Lang	Maserati	1								
18	1.5	USA	Fred Agabashian	Kurtis Kraft-Offenhauser	1				1		1		
18	1.5	USA	Paul Russo	Kurtis Kraft-Offenhauser	1								
-	0	USA	Jim Rathmann	Kurtis Kraft-Offenhauser	1				1		1		

Championship ranking	Championship points	Team/Marque nationality	1953 Constructors Results (Excl. Indy 500)		Engine maker nationality	Races contested	Race victories	1-2 finishes	Podiums excl. victories	Races led	Laps led	Poles	Fastest laps
			Chassis	Engine									
N/A	N/A	ITA	Ferrari 500, 553 Squalo, 166	Ferrari 2.0 S4, 2.0 V12	ITA	8	7	4	9	8	463	6	6
N/A	N/A	ITA	Maserati A6GCM	Maserati 2.0 S6	ITA	8	1		7	3	73	2	4
N/A	N/A	FRA	Gordini T16	Gordini 2.0 S6	FRA	8							

1954

Bullseye for Fangio's silver arrow

THE TALE OF THE TITLE

- New regulations revitalised the Formula 1 world championship.
- With six race victories from eight starts, Juan Manuel Fangio was undisputed champion, his second title.
- Fangio's 1954 crown was distinguished by being the only drivers' championship won with two teams.
- Before switching to Mercedes, he won twice with Maserati, without which González would have triumphed.
- On their debut at round four in France, Fangio led Mercedes-Benz to a crushing 1-2 triumph.
- But it was the only overwhelming victory by the German cars, subsequent success attributable to Fangio.
- Defending champion Ascari made no significant impression on the 1954 championship.
- Lancia, the team Ascari had signed to lead in 1954, did not appear until the very last round in October.
- Ferrari picked up the remaining two Grands Prix victories, González and Hawthorn winning a race apiece.
- Moss performed admirably in a Maserati 250F, but without tangible success.
- And not forgetting: the Mercedes *stromlinienwagens,* and tragedy at the Nürburgring.

THE CHASE FOR THE CHAMPIONSHIP

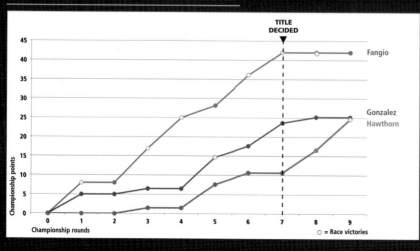

ARGENTINEAN GP Buenos Aires No 2

17 January 1954 — Race 33

Juan Manuel Fangio

Maserati 250F 112.865kph, 70.131mph

Over the opening 34 laps the Ferraris of Farina, González and Hawthorn each led and were lying 1-2-3 when a cloudburst enabled Fangio's Maserati to take the lead, Ferrari handling proving difficult in the wet. As the track dried González and Farina repassed Fangio until another downpour reversed the situation yet again. As conditions worsened, Fangio pitted on lap 61 to rejoin with hand-cut rain tyres. Ferrari then gave the 'SLOW' signal to their drivers, certain that the protest they had lodged against Fangio's pit stop – alleging more than the three permitted mechanics were used – would be upheld. This made it easy for Fangio to catch and pass both Ferraris and win, their objection not upheld even though Ferrari subsequently took the matter to the FIA.

POLE POSITION Farina, Ferrari, 1m 44.8s (0.1s), 134.382kph, 83.501mph
LAPS 87 x 3.912 km, 2.431 miles
DISTANCE 340.344 km, 211.480 miles
STARTERS/FINISHERS 16/9
WEATHER Overcast, dry at first, heavy showers during race
LAP LEADERS Farina 1-14, 63-64 (16); González 15-32, 47-58, 61-62 (32); M Hawthorn, Ferrari 33-34 (2); Fangio 35-46, 59-60, 65-87 (37)
WINNER'S LAPS NA
FASTEST LAP González, Ferrari, 1m 48.2s (lap NA), 130.159kph, 80.877mph
CHAMPIONSHIP Fangio 8, Farina 6, González 5, Trintignant 3, Bayol 2

Pos	Driver	Car	Time/gap	Grid	Stops	Tyres
1	J M Fangio	Maserati	3h 0m 55.8s	3	1	P
2	N Farina	Ferrari	–1m 19.0s	1	1	P
3	F González	Ferrari	–2m 1.0s	2	NA	P
4	M Trintignant	Ferrari	–1 lap	5	NA	P
5	É Bayol	Gordini	–2 laps	14	NA	E
6	H Schell	Maserati	–3 laps	10	NA	P

INDIANAPOLIS 500 Indianapolis

31 May 1954 — Race 34

Bill Vukovich

Kurtis Kraft-Offenhauser 210.566kph, 130.380mph

The addition of the Argentinean GP in 1954 meant that the Indy 500 was no longer the token 'non-European' event on the FIA world championship calendar, but this incongruous race was to remain an integral part for seven more F1 seasons. Jack McGrath took pole, the first driver to surpass the 140mph average for his four-lap qualifying run. In a race marked by a high incidence of pit stops, Bill Vukovich won again, this time from a row seven grid-slot. Not establishing a decisive lead until half-distance, he finally won by almost exactly one lap despite tyre worries in the closing stages. With back-to-back victories and the only driver ever to lead most race laps for three consecutive years, 'Vukie', the 'silent Serb', was attaining legendary status.

POLE POSITION McGrath, Kurtis Kraft-Offy, 4m 20.13s (2.27s), 226.970kph, 141.033mph
LAPS 200 x 4.023 km, 2.500 miles
DISTANCE 804.672 km, 500.000 miles
STARTERS/FINISHERS 33/19
WEATHER Sunny, very hot, dry
LAP LEADERS McGrath 1-44, 89-91 (47); J Daywalt, Kurtis Kraft-Offy 45-50, 55, 60 (8); A Cross, Kurtis Kraft-Offy 51-54, 56-59 (8); Vukovich 61, 92-129, 150-200 (90); S Hanks, Kurtis Kraft-Offy 62 (1); Bryan 63-88, 130-149 (46)
WINNER'S LAPS NA
FASTEST LAP McGrath, Kurtis Kraft-Offy, 1m 4.40s (lap 29), 226.173kph, 140.537mph
CHAMPIONSHIP Fangio 8, Vukovich 8, Farina 6, Bryan 6, González 5

Pos	Driver	Car	Time/gap	Grid	Stops	Tyres
1	B Vukovich	Kurtis Kraft-Offy	3h 49m 17.27s	19	NA	F
2	J Bryan	Kuzma-Offy	–1m 9.95s	3	NA	F
3	J McGrath	Kurtis Kraft-Offy	–1m 19.73s	1	NA	F
4	T Ruttman/D Carter	Kurtis Kraft-Offy	–2m 52.68s	11	NA	F
5	M Nazaruk	Kurtis Kraft-Offy	–3m 24.55s	14	NA	F
6	F Agabashian	Kurtis Kraft-Offy	–3m 47.55s	24	NA	F

BELGIAN GP Spa-Francorchamps

20 June 1954 — Race 35

Juan Manuel Fangio

Maserati 250F 185.173kph, 115.061mph

As in Argentina, Ascari was absent and Fangio still with Maserati. Despite Fangio's pole, Farina led initially before Fangio got by on lap 3. On lap 11, slowed by a broken visor strap, Fangio temporarily lost the lead to Farina but was able to regain it quite quickly. In any case Farina retired soon afterwards with ignition problems, and with the other Ferraris of González and Hawthorn also running into trouble Fangio continued unchallenged. It was left to Trintignant to uphold Ferrari honours with second place, Moss third in his privately entered Maserati 250F, a lap in arrears. A broken exhaust caused Hawthorn to be overcome by fumes, but González, having already retired, took over his car to finish fourth.

POLE POSITION Fangio, Maserati, 4m 22.1s (1.5s), 193.941kph, 120.510mph
LAPS 36 x 14.120 km, 8.774 miles
DISTANCE 508.320 km, 315.855 miles
STARTERS/FINISHERS 14/7
WEATHER Sunny, warm, dry
FASTEST LAP Fangio, Maserati, 4m 25.5s (lap 13), 191.458kph, 118.966mph
LAP LEADERS N Farina, Ferrari 1-2, 11-13 (5); Fangio 3-10, 14-36 (31)
WINNER'S LAPS 1 P3, 2 P2, 3-10 P1, 11-13 P2, 14-36 P1
CHAMPIONSHIP Fangio 17, Trintignant 9, Vukovich 8, González 6.5, Farina 6

Pos	Driver	Car	Time/gap	Grid	Stops	Tyres
1	J M Fangio	Maserati	2h 44m 42.4s	1	0	P
2	M Trintignant	Ferrari	–24.2s	6	0	P
3	S Moss	Maserati	–1 lap	9	0	P
4	M Hawthorn/F González	Ferrari	–1 lap	5	2	P
5	A Pilette	Gordini	–1 lap	8	0	E
6	B Bira	Maserati	–1 lap	13	1	P

Mercedes-Benz W196 *stromlinienwagen*

Round 4/9	**FRENCH** GP Reims		
	4 July 1954		**Race 36**

The reigning world champion made his first appearance of the year. He was driving for Maserati in place of Fangio, who had been called upon by Mercedes-Benz to lead their long-awaited championship debut. And what a debut it was for the W196 streamliners. From first and second on the grid, Fangio and Kling led every lap between them, the pair crossing the line a lap ahead in a formation finish 0.1s apart. With Ascari's Maserati out after just one lap with transmission trouble, Farina absent, and the other Ferraris of González and Hawthorn succumbing to engine gremlins by lap 13, it was all somewhat one-sided. The only blemish on the German team's performance was Herrmann's engine failure on lap 16.

Pos	Driver	Car	Time/gap	Grid	Stops	Tyres
1	J M Fangio	Mercedes-Benz	2h 42m 47.9s	1	0	C
2	K Kling	Mercedes-Benz	–0.1s	2	0	C
3	R Manzon	Ferrari	–1 lap	12	0	P
4	B Bira	Maserati	–1 lap	6	0	P
5	L Villoresi	Maserati	–3 laps	14	2	P
6	J Behra	Gordini	–5 laps	17	2	E

Juan Manuel Fangio
Mercedes-Benz W196 str. 186.644kph, 115.975mph

POLE POSITION Fangio, Mercedes-Benz, 2m 29.4s (1.0s), 200.048kph, 124.304mph
LAPS 61 x 8.302 km, 5.159 miles
DISTANCE 506.422 km, 314.676 miles
STARTERS/FINISHERS 21/6
WEATHER Overcast, dry then late rain
LAP LEADERS Kling 1-2, 29-33, 38, 54-57, 60 (13); Fangio 3-28, 34-37, 39-53, 58-59, 61 (48)
WINNER'S LAPS 1 P3, 2 P2, 3-28 P1, 29-33 P2, 34-37 P1, 38 P2, 39-53 P1, 54-57 P2, 58-59 P1,60 P2, 61 P1
FASTEST LAP H Herrmann, Mercedes-Benz, 2m 32.9s (lap 3), 195.469kph, 121.459mph
CHAMPIONSHIP Fangio 25, Trintignant 9, Vukovich 8, González 6.5, Farina 6

Round 5/9	**BRITISH GP** Silverstone		
	17 July 1954		**Race 37**

Silverstone proved a different story. González led from start to finish, winning by over a minute from Hawthorn in another Ferrari 625. Fangio was duly on pole in the W196, but in the race finished fourth, the aerodynamic bodywork proving unsuitable. The all-enveloping body obscured the front wheels and made cornering lines difficult to judge accurately, Fangio famously striking oil drums that marked out the track. Moss and Hawthorn had thrilled the crowd with some early dicing, but now firmly in second place, with a 26s lead over his compatriot, the rear axle on Moss' Maserati failed. Ascari's Maserati also suffered engine failure on lap 41. He was running seventh after starting last, having missed qualifying.

Pos	Driver	Car	Time/gap	Grid	Stops	Tyres
1	F González	Ferrari	2h 56m 14.0s	2	0	P
2	M Hawthorn	Ferrari	–1m 10.0s	3	0	P
3	O Marimón	Maserati	–1 lap	28	0	P
4	J M Fangio	Mercedes-Benz	–1 lap	1	0	C
5	M Trintignant	Ferrari	–3 laps	8	0	P
6	R Mières	Maserati	–3 laps	31	0	P

Froilán González
Ferrari 625 144.337kph, 89.687mph

POLE POSITION Fangio, Mercedes-Benz, 1m 45.0s (1.0s), 161.505kph, 100.354mph
LAPS 90 x 4.711 km, 2.927 miles
DISTANCE 423.949 km, 263.430 miles
STARTERS/FINISHERS 30/15
WEATHER Cold, dry then late heavy showers
LAP LEADERS González 1-90 (90)
WINNER'S LAPS 1-90 P1
FASTEST LAP A Ascari, Maserati/J Behra, Gordini/ Fangio/González/Hawthorn/Marimón/S Moss, Maserati, 1m 50.0s (laps NA/NA), 154.163kph, 95.793mph
CHAMPIONSHIP Fangio 28.14, González 14.64, Trintignant 11, Vukovich 8, Hawthorn 7.64

Round 6/9	**GERMAN GP** Nürburgring			
	1 August 1954		**Race 38**	

Juan Manuel Fangio

Mercedes-Benz W196 133.366kph, 82.870mph

For their home race, Mercedes fielded four cars, three with 'normal' bodywork. Fangio took pole, but before practice ended the news broke that his protégé Onofré Marimón had been killed, crashing his Maserati just before the Wehrseifen bridge. He was the first driver to lose his life at a championship grand prix meeting. The race went ahead the next day in front of an estimated 300,000 partisan crowd. They were not to be disappointed, Fangio taking victory for Mercedes. But this wasn't the hoped for dominant performance, Hans Herrmann retiring on lap 7 with a broken fuel pipe, veteran Herman Lang spinning out on lap 10, and Karl Kling managing fourth with a collapsed rear suspension.

POLE POSITION Fangio, Mercedes-Benz, 9m 50.1s (3.2s), 139.156kph, 86.468mph
LAPS 22 x 22.810 km, 14.173 miles
DISTANCE 501.820 km, 311.816 miles
STARTERS/FINISHERS 20/10
WEATHER Sunny, warm, dry
LAP LEADERS Fangio 1-14, 17-22 (20); Kling 15-16 (2)
WINNER'S LAPS 1-14 P1, 15-16 P2, 17-22 P1
FASTEST LAP Kling, Mercedes-Benz, 9m 55.1s (lap 16), 137.987kph, 85.741mph
CHAMPIONSHIP Fangio 36.14, González 17.64, Trintignant 15, Hawthorn 10.64, Kling 10

Pos	Driver	Car	Time/gap	Grid	Stops	Tyres
1	J M Fangio	Mercedes-Benz	3h 45m 45.8s	1	0	C
2	F González/M Hawthorn	Ferrari	–1m 36.5s	5	1	P
3	M Trintignant	Ferrari	–5m 8.6s	7	0	P
4	K Kling	Mercedes-Benz	–6m 6.5s	23	1	C
5	S Mantovani	Maserati	–8m 50.5s	15	0	P
6	P Taruffi	Ferrari	–1 lap	13	0	P

Round 7/9	**SWISS GP** Bremgarten			
	22 August 1954		**Race 39**	

Juan Manuel Fangio

Mercedes-Benz W196 159.650kph, 99.202mph

González had been particularly badly affected by the tragedy with had befallen his fellow countryman three weeks earlier but was back on form at Bremgarten to take pole from Fangio. And perhaps fittingly, first and second was how the two Argentinean drivers were to finish, Fangio a minute to the good having led from start to finish. With this his fifth victory of the season, Fangio regained the championship from Ascari, his points lead unassailable. In the early stages of the race Moss had overtaken González for second place and then Hawthorn had found his way past both of them in their vain pursuit of Fangio. But neither of the British drivers' cars lasted beyond lap 30.

POLE POSITION González, Ferrari, 2m 39.5s (0.2s), 164.313kph, 102.100mph
LAPS 66 x 7.280 km, 4.524 miles
DISTANCE 480.480 km, 298.556 miles
STARTERS/FINISHERS 16/8
WEATHER Overcast, wet track then drying
LAP LEADERS Fangio 1-66, (66)
WINNER'S LAPS 1-66 P1
FASTEST LAP Fangio, Mercedes-Benz, 2m 39.7s (lap 34), 164.108kph, 101.972mph
CHAMPIONSHIP Fangio 42, González 23.64, Trintignant 15, Hawthorn 10.64, Kling 10

Pos	Driver	Car	Time/gap	Grid	Stops	Tyres
1	J M Fangio	Mercedes-Benz	3h 0m 34.5s	2	0	C
2	F González	Ferrari	–57.8s	1	0	P
3	H Herrmann	Mercedes-Benz	–1 lap	7	0	C
4	R Mières	Maserati	–2 laps	12	0	P
5	S Mantovani	Maserati	–2 laps	9	0	P
6	K Wharton	Maserati	–2 laps	8	0	P

Round 8/9	**ITALIAN GP** Monza			
	5 September 1954		**Race 40**	

Juan Manuel Fangio

Mercedes-Benz W196 str. 180.216kph, 111.981mph

Fangio's Mercedes streamliner only just edged out Ascari for pole, the Italian champion back with Ferrari on a one-off basis. Moss completed the front row in his works-supported Maserati, these three making a race of it. Between laps 6 and 48 Ascari did most of the leading until, shortly after Moss had caught and passed him on lap 45, his engine dropped a valve. Moss now extended his lead until, on lap 68, a split oil pipe cruelly ended his challenge, having built up a 20s lead over Fangio. So Mercedes won again, but due solely to the presence of the redoubtable Fangio, there to pick up the pieces, teammates Herrmann coming in fourth three laps in arrears and Kling crashing out on lap 37.

POLE POSITION Fangio, Mercedes-Benz, 1m 59.0s (0.2s), 190.588kph, 118.426mph
LAPS 80 x 6.300 km, 3.915 miles
DISTANCE 504.000 km, 313.171 miles
STARTERS/FINISHERS 20/11
WEATHER Sunny, hot, dry
LAP LEADERS K Kling, Mercedes-Benz 1-3 (3); Fangio 4-5, 23, 68-80 (16); A Ascari, Ferrari 6-22, 24-44, 46-48 (41); S Moss, Maserati 45, 49-67 (20)
WINNER'S LAPS 1-3 P2, 4-5 P1, 6 P3, 7-22 P2, 23 P1, 24-37 P2, 38 P3, 39-40 P2, 41-42 P3, 43 P2, 44-48 P3, 49-67 P2, 68-80 P1
FASTEST LAP González, Ferrari, 2m 0.8s (lap 2), 187.748kph, 116.661mph
CHAMPIONSHIP Fangio 42, González 25.14, Trintignant 17, Hawthorn 16.64, Kling 10

Pos	Driver	Car	Time/gap	Grid	Stops	Tyres
1	J M Fangio	Mercedes-Benz	2h 47m 47.9s	1	0	C
2	M Hawthorn	Ferrari	–1 lap	7	0	P
3	U Maglioli/F González	Ferrari	–2 laps	13	2	P
4	H Herrmann	Mercedes-Benz	–3 laps	8	1	P
5	M Trintignant	Ferrari	–5 laps	11	2	P
6	F Wacker	Gordini	–5 laps	18	0	E

Ferrari 553 'Squalo'

Round 9/9	**SPANISH GP** Pedralbes 24 October 1954			Race 41

Mike Hawthorn
Ferrari 553 156.378kph, 97.169mph

Sensationally Ascari planted the brand new Lancia D50 on pole and built up a 10s lead in the first nine laps. His retirement with clutch trouble allowed Schell's Maserati and Trintignant's Ferrari to dice for the lead until Trintignant pitted with a broken gearbox oil-feed and Schell overdid it and spun on lap 24. This left Hawthorn's Ferrari in control 20s ahead of Fangio. Mercedes' performance was compromised by fuel injection being set for the very hot conditions forecast but not realised on race day. Worse still, in the late stages of the race Fangio slipped to third, the overheating Mercedes engine spraying its occupant with hot oil due to litter-clogged air intakes.

POLE POSITION A Ascari, Lancia, 2m 18.1s (1.0s), 164.646kph, 102.306mph
LAPS 80 x 6.316 km, 3.925 miles
DISTANCE 505.280 km, 313.966 miles
STARTERS/FINISHERS 21/9
WEATHER Sunny, warm, dry, windy
LAP LEADERS H Schell, Maserati 1-2, 10, 13, 15-17, 19, 21,23 (10); A Ascari, Lancia 3-9 (7); M Trintignant, Ferrari 11-12, 14, 18, 20 (5); Hawthorn 22, 24-80 (58)
WINNER'S LAPS 1-7 P3, 8 P2, 9 P3, 10 P2, 11-12 P3, 13 P4, 14-20 P3, 21 P2, 22 P1, 23 P2, 24-80 P1
FASTEST LAP A Ascari, Lancia, 2m 20.4s (lap 3), 161.949kph, 100.630mph
CHAMPIONSHIP Fangio 42, González 25.14, Hawthorn 24.64, Trintignant 17, Kling 12

Pos	Driver	Car	Time/gap	Grid	Stops	Tyres
1	M Hawthorn	Ferrari	3h 13m 52.1s	3	0	P
2	L Musso	Maserati	–1m 13.2s	7	0	P
3	J M Fangio	Mercedes-Benz	–1 lap	2	0	C
4	R Mières	Maserati	–1 lap	11	0	P
5	K Kling	Mercedes-Benz	–1 lap	12	0	C
6	C Godia	Maserati	–4 laps	13	1	P

1954 CHAMPIONSHIP FACTS AND FOLKLORE

■ The new-for-1954 regulations ushered in the first set of rules devised specifically for Formula 1 and the FIA world championship. These same regulations largely continued unchanged for the next seven seasons, heralding a new racing era.

■ The regulations were broadly straightforward, maximum engine capacity stipulated as 2.5 litres or 750cc supercharged, no other weight or fuel restrictions.

■ The minimum race-distance was raised from 300km (186.41 miles) to 500km (310.69 miles), or three hours, with nine races scheduled, still including the Indy 500. The points system was unchanged, the best five results counting towards the championship.

■ Most importantly, the promise of rules stability attracted new blood into F1 in the shape of car manufacturers Mercedes-Benz and Lancia, although neither team would be ready to commence their campaign until well after the start of the season.

■ The post-war return by Mercedes-Benz to the world's GP circuits was both emblematic and evocative, recollecting and connecting the 1930s 'golden era' of GP racing with the new FIA world championship.

■ The Mercedes-Benz contender, the W196, was designed and built to uncompromising standards hitherto unseen, the racing team managed in similar style by Alfred Neubauer, who had so successfully led the team before the war.

■ The mystique surrounding this team and its cars was generated not only from their track success but also through their stunning appearance. With shining paintwork and all-enveloping *stromlinienwagen* bodywork, the 'Silver Arrows' nickname was more than apt.

■ Technically advanced, the W196 dispensed with heavy ladder-frame chassis geometry in favour of stiff, load-bearing spaceframe construction. The 2.5-litre twin-ohc straight-eight produced 270bhp at 8,000rpm, featuring fuel injection and desmodromic valve gear.

- Mercedes recruited Fangio from Maserati to lead their assault, while double world champion Ascari switched from Ferrari to head Lancia's attack.
- But the Lancia D50 did not debut until the very final round in October, compromising Ascari's title defence, whereas Fangio crucially continued his partnership with Maserati until the Mercedes entry was ready.
- Therefore until the belated appearance of Mercedes in France, the first two rounds of the championship were a continuation of the all-Italian Ferrari versus Maserati affair from 1953, except Maserati won them both with their new 250F, an extensively revised A6GCM with 2.5-litre engine producing 240bhp at 6,800rpm.
- Ferrari essentially began the season with a Tipo 500 chassis with enlarged 2-litre engine designated the 625. In addition Ferrari produced a bespoke 2.5-litre four-cylinder engine for installation in the Tipo 553 'Squalo' (shark) cars that had made an appearance at Monza in 1953. With this car Hawthorn won the final round at Pedralbes, whereas the victory by González at Silverstone was with a 553 engine in a 625 chassis.
- The rest, notably Gordini, used their 1953 F2 machinery with stretched engines, and up against Mercedes, Maserati and Ferrari barely had a look-in. In three championship rounds Peter Collins campaigned the embryonic Vanwall, the 'Vanwall Special', the head of its four-cylinder engine based on a single-pot Norton motorcycle engine.
- With the 1954 championship already locked away by Fangio, at the final championship round in Spain defending double-champion Ascari was at last behind the wheel of the Lancia D50 and started from pole and led for seven spellbinding laps.
- It was a sensational debut for a car that at many levels would subsequently make a significant impression on the F1 championships. Designed by Vittorio Jani, the power unit was a 90° V8 giving 260bhp at 8,000rpm, the chassis distinguished by pannier fuel tanks out-rigged each side between the wheels to assist handling and aerodynamics.
- 1954 witnessed the first loss of a competitor's life at a championship event when Fangio's protégé, Onofré Marimón, was killed during practice at the Nürburgring.

RACE 36, French GP: Mercedes-Benz made their long-awaited championship debut at Reims, the W196 streamliners of Fangio (18) and Kling (20) leading every lap between them to finish 0.1s apart.

Championship ranking	Championship points	Driver nationality	1954 Drivers Championship — Driver	Car	Races contested	Race victories	Podiumse excl. victories	Races led	Flag to flag victories	Laps led	Poles	Fastest laps	Triple Crowns
1	42	ARG	Juan Manuel Fangio	Maserati (2) Mercedes-Benz (6)	8	6	1	6	1	218	5	3	1
2	25.14	ARG	José Froilán González	Ferrari	7	1	4	2	1	122	1	3	
3	24.64	GBR	Mike Hawthorn	Ferrari	8	1	3	2		60		1	
4	17	FRA	Maurice Trintignant	Ferrari	8		2	1		5			
5	12	GER	Karl Kling	Mercedes-Benz	6		1	3		18		1	
6	8	USA	Bill Vukovich	Kurtis Kraft-Offenhauser	1	1		1		90			
6	8	GER	Hans Herrmann	Mercedes-Benz	5		1					1	
8	6	ITA	Nino Farina	Ferrari	2		1	2		21	1		
8	6	USA	Jimmy Bryan	Kuzma-Offenhauser	1		1	1		46			
8	6	ITA	Luigi Musso	Maserati	2		1						
11	6	ARG	Roberto Mières	Maserati	8								
12	5	USA	Jack McGrath	Kurtis Kraft-Offenhauser	1		1	1		47	1	1	
13	4.14	GBR	Stirling Moss	Maserati	6		1	1		20		1	
13	4.14	ARG	Onofre Marimón	Maserati	4		1					1	
15	4	FRA	Robert Manzon	Ferrari	5		1						
16	4	ITA	Sergio Mantovani	Maserati	5								
17	3	THI	Prince Bira	Maserati	6								
18	2	ITA	Umberto Maglioli	Ferrari	3		1						
19	2	FRA	Elie Bayol	Gordini	1								
19	2	USA	Mike Nazaruk	Kurtis Kraft-Offenhauser	1								
19	2	BEL	André Pilette	Gordini	3								
19	2	ITA	Luigi Villoresi	Maserati (3) Lancia (1)	4								
23	1.5	USA	Duane Carter	Kurtis Kraft-Offenhauser	1								
23	1.5	USA	Troy Ruttman	Kurtis Kraft-Offenhauser	1								
25	1.14	ITA	Alberto Ascari	Maserati (2) Ferrari (1) Lancia (1)	4			2		48	1	2	
26	0.14	FRA	Jean Behra	Gordini	8							1	
-	0	USA	Harry Schell	Maserati	6			1		10			
-	0	USA	Jimmy Daywalt	Kurtis Kraft-Offenhauser	1			1		8			
-	0	USA	Art Cross	Kurtis Kraft-Offenhauser	1			1		8			
-	0	USA	Sam Hanks	Kurtis Kraft-Offenhauser	1			1		1			

Championship ranking	Championship points	Team/Marque nationality	1954 Constructors Results (Excl. Indy 500) — Chassis	Engine	Engine maker nationality	Races contested	Race victories	1-2 finishes	Podiums excl. victories	Races led	Laps led	Poles	Fastest laps
N/A	N/A	ITA	Ferrari 625, 553 Squalo, 500	Ferrari 2.5 S4	ITA	8	2	1	10	5	249	2	3
N/A	N/A	GER	Mercedes-Benz W196, W196 Streamliner	Mercedes-Benz 2.5 S8	GER	6	4	1	3	4	168	4	4
N/A	N/A	ITA	Maserati 250F, A6GCM	Maserati 2.5 S6	ITA	8	2		3	4	98	1	2
N/A	N/A	FRA	Gordini T16	Gordini 2.5 S6	FRA	8							1
N/A	N/A	ITA	Lancia D50	Lancia 2.5 V8	ITA	1			1	1	7	1	1

1955

Fangio triumphs in tragic year

THE TALE OF THE TITLE

- In a black year, Fangio and Mercedes successfully defended their title, the Argentinean's third.
- It was a truncated season, four Grands Prix cancelled in the aftermath of the Le Mans disaster on 11 June.
- 83 spectators were killed and over 100 injured at the La Sarthe circuit, the third motorsport tragedy in 17 days.
- On 26 May Ascari was killed testing at Monza, and on 30 May Bill Vukovich was killed at the Indy 500.
- With Ascari gone and Moss joining Fangio, Stuttgart domination was total, the Italian teams trounced.
- Mercedes won all but one of the six GPs, Fangio beaten only by Moss who won his first race at Aintree.
- At Monaco Ferrari won fortuitously, Ascari's Lancia, four days before his death, plunging into the harbour.
- Scuderia Lancia, devastated by the loss of their star, withdrew from F1, their cars taken over by Ferrari.
- Disenchanted by Vanwall, Hawthorn's Ferrari return was outshone by Castellotti, drafted in from Lancia.
- With podiums for Lancia and Ferrari, young Eugenio finished best of the rest to the matchless Mercedes pair.
- And not forgetting: Switzerland bans motorsport.

THE CHASE FOR THE CHAMPIONSHIP

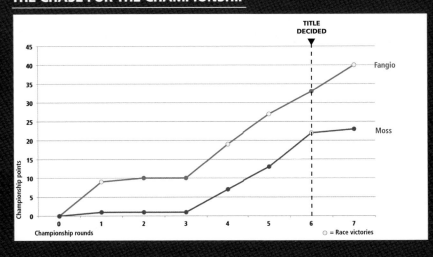

ARGENTINEAN GP Buenos Aires No 2
16 January 1955 — Race 42

Juan Manuel Fangio
Mercedes-Benz W196 124.738kph, 77.509mph

Four different marques shared the front row for the opening race: Ferrari, Lancia, Mercedes, Maserati. Due to the excessively hot weather the three-hour race became a question of endurance. After some initial jostling, Ascari established a lead until he spun out on oil, while Moss' Mercedes was out with fuel vaporisation. Then González gave up his lead to Fangio due to heat exhaustion, as did Schell some laps later. Fangio, after memorably calling in at the pits on lap 35 to douse himself with water, now took command, one of just two to finish without a relief driver. In all there were 16 driver substitutions, the second-placed González Ferrari passing to Farina, then Trintignant, back to González, and finally Farina once again.

POLE POSITION González, Ferrari, 1m 43.1s (0.5s), 136.597kph, 84.878mph
LAPS 96 x 3.921 km, 2.431 miles
DISTANCE 375.552 km, 233.357 miles
STARTERS/FINISHERS 21/7
WEATHER Very hot, humid, dry
LAP LEADERS Fangio 1-2, 27-35, 43-96 (65); A Ascari, Lancia 3-5, 12-21 (13); González 6-11, 22-26 (11); H Schell, Maserati 36-42 (7)
WINNER'S LAPS 1-2 P1, 3 P2, 4-21 P3, 22-26 P2, 27-35 P1, 36-38 P4, 39-41 P3, 42 P2, 43-96 P1
FASTEST LAP Fangio, Mercedes-Benz, 1m 48.3s (lap 45), 130.039kph, 80.802mph
CHAMPIONSHIP Fangio 9, Trintignant 3.33, Farina 3.33, González 2, R Mières 2

Pos	Driver	Car	Time/gap	Grid	Stops	Tyres
1	J M Fangio	Mercedes-Benz	3h 0m 38.6s	3	1	C
2	F González/N Farina/M Trintignant	Ferrari	−1m 29.6s	1	4	E
3	N Farina/U Maglioli/M Trintignant	Ferrari	−2 laps	5	3	E
4	H Herrmann/K Kling/S Moss	Mercedes-Benz	−2 laps	10	2	C
5	R Mières	Maserati	−5 laps	16	2	P
6	H Schell/J Behra	Maserati	−8 laps	7	3	P

Mercedes-Benz W196

MONACO GP Monte Carlo
22 May 1955 — Race 43

Maurice Trintignant
Ferrari 625 105.915kph, 65.813mph

This was the first championship race to be held at Monaco since 1950, which from now on would become a permanent fixture. Following some opening skirmishes, the Mercedes of Fangio and Moss soon had the race buttoned up. When Fangio retired at half-distance, Moss was there to take the lead and his maiden victory, until clouds of blue smoke signalled his demise on lap 81, the Mercedes trundling to a halt. Distracted by the crowd reaction to Moss' exit, Ascari shot out of the tunnel in his Lancia, misjudged the chicane and flew into the harbour in a cloud of steam, the driver shocked but lucky to survive the ducking. Despite a late challenge by Castellotti's Lancia, a surprised Trintignant completed the final 20 laps to record an unlikely Ferrari victory.

POLE POSITION J M Fangio, Mercedes-Benz, 1m 41.1s (0.0s), 111.988kph, 69.586mph
LAPS 100 x 3.145 km, 1.954 miles
DISTANCE 314.500 km, 195.421 miles
STARTERS/FINISHERS 20/9
WEATHER Sunny, hot, dry
LAP LEADERS Fangio 1-49 (49); S Moss, Mercedes-Benz 50-80 (31); Trintignant 81-100 (20)
WINNER'S LAPS 1-2 P10, 3-19 P9, 20-26 P7, 27-35 P6, 36-41 P5, 42-49 P4, 50-63 P3, 64 P4, 65-80 P3, 81-100 P1
FASTEST LAP J M Fangio, Mercedes-Benz, 1m 42.4s (lap 27), 110.566kph, 68.703mph
CHAMPIONSHIP Trintignant 11.33, Fangio 10, Farina 6.33, E Castellotti 6, González 2

Pos	Driver	Car	Time/gap	Grid	Stops	Tyres
1	M Trintignant	Ferrari	2h 58m 9.7s	9	0	E
2	E Castellotti	Lancia	−20.2s	4	1	P
3	J Behra/C Perdisa	Maserati	−1 lap	5	2	P
4	N Farina	Ferrari	−1 lap	14	1	E
5	L Villoresi	Lancia	−1 lap	7	1	P
6	L Chiron	Lancia	−5 laps	19	0	P

Ferrari 625

Round 3/7	**INDIANAPOLIS 500** Indianapolis
	30 May 1955 **Race 44**

Bob Sweikert
Kurtis Kraft-Offenhauser 206.333kph, 128.209mph

On 26 May, four days after Monaco, Alberto Ascari was killed at Monza. Four days after that a driver of equal stature on his own side of the Atlantic lost his life during the 39th running of the Indy 500. Seemingly well on his way to a hat-trick victory, holding a 17s lead, Bill Vukovich exited turn two behind slower traffic on the 57th lap to become an unwitting victim of a chain-reaction accident. Caught by a gust of wind, Rodger Ward's car swerved, caused Al Keller to lose control, who hit Johnny Boyd, pushing Boyd into the path of Vukovich. When their cars inevitably collided Vukovich's was launched, somersaulting airborne over the retaining wall to land upside down, bursting into flames. Bill Vukovich was the first driver to be killed during a championship race.

POLE POSITION J Hoyt, Stevens-Offy, 4m 17.06s (2.27s), 225.383kph, 140.045mph
LAPS 200 x 4.023 km, 2.500 miles
DISTANCE 804.672 km, 500.000 miles
STARTERS/FINISHERS 33/14
WEATHER Cold, windy, dry
LAP LEADERS J McGrath, Kurtis Kraft-Offy 1-3, 15, 25-26 (6); Vukovich 4-14, 16-24, 27-56 (50); J Bryan, Kuzma-Offy 57, 59-88 (31); Sweikert 58, 89-132, 160-200 (86); A Cross, Kurtis Kraft-Offy 133-156 (24); D Freeland, Phillips-Offy 157-159 (3)
WINNER'S LAPS NA
FASTEST LAP B Vukovich, Kurtis Kraft-Offy, 1m 3.67s (lap 29), 227.487kph, 141.354mph
CHAMPIONSHIP Trintignant 11.33, Fangio 10, Sweikert 8, Farina 6.33, E Castellotti 6

Pos	Driver	Car	Time/gap	Grid	Stops	Tyres
1	Bob Sweikert	Kurtis Kraft-Offy	3h 53m 59.530s	14	NA	F
2	T Bettenhausen/P Russo	Kurtis Kraft-Offy	–2m 43.56s	2	NA	F
3	J Davies	Kurtis Kraft-Offy	–3m 32.36s	10	NA	F
4	J Thomson	Kuzma-Offy	–3m 38.91s	33	NA	F
5	W Faulkner/B Homeier	Kurtis Kraft-Offy	–5m 17.17s	7	NA	F
6	A Linden	Kurtis Kraft-Offy	–5m 57.94s	8	NA	F

Round 4/7	**BELGIAN GP** Spa-Francorchamps
	5 June 1955 **Race 45**

Juan Manuel Fangio
Mercedes-Benz W196 191.238kph, 118.829mph

In the wake of the tragic death of lead driver Ascari, Lancia announced the immediate disbandment of the team. At the championship race held at Spa just ten days later, Lancia driver Castellotti, who had finished a strong second in Monte Carlo, persuaded the team to allow him to race as a private entrant and sensationally took pole position. The race itself turned into a high-speed procession, Fangio in the Mercedes-Benz leading all the way to win from teammate Moss. Driving the sole Lancia, Castellotti put on a fine display for the beleaguered team, second through Eau Rouge on lap 1 and maintaining a robust third place ahead of Farina's Ferrari. But at half-distance a split gearbox ended his race, Farina finishing a distant third. It was the fourth and final race for Lancia.

POLE POSITION E Castellotti, Lancia, 4m 18.1s (0.5s), 196.947kph, 122.377mph
LAPS 36 x 14.120 km, 8.774 miles
DISTANCE 508.320 km, 315.855 miles
STARTERS/FINISHERS 13/9
WEATHER Sunny, warm, dry
LAP LEADERS Fangio 1-36 (36)
WINNER'S LAPS 1-36 P1
FASTEST LAP Fangio, Mercedes-Benz, 4m 20.6s (lap 18), 195.058kph, 121.203mph
CHAMPIONSHIP Fangio 19, Trintignant 11.33, Farina 10.33, Sweikert 8, Moss 7

Pos	Driver	Car	Time/gap	Grid	Stops	Tyres
1	J M Fangio	Mercedes-Benz	2h 39m 29.0s	2	0	C
2	S Moss	Mercedes-Benz	–8.1s	3	0	C
3	N Farina	Ferrari	–1m 40.5s	4	0	E
4	P Frère	Ferrari	–3m 25.5s	8	0	E
5	R Mières/J Behra	Maserati	–1 lap	13	1	P
6	M Trintignant	Ferrari	–1 lap	10	1	E

Round 5/7	**DUTCH GP** Zandvoort	
	19 June 1955	**Race 46**

Juan Manuel Fangio
Mercedes-Benz W196 144.257kph, 89.637mph

Although the 1955 Le Mans disaster, when at least 80 spectators died, had only occurred the previous weekend, the Dutch organisers decided to proceed with their race, as did the three-car Mercedes Grand Prix team which locked out the front row. With Lancia now absent for the remainder of the season, Castellotti had been drafted into Ferrari, as had Hawthorn, returning to the Scuderia after expressing dissatisfaction with the Vanwall's performance. Fangio made his customary superb start and Moss once again took up station behind him after dealing with Musso's Maserati. Drizzle from lap 60 on made the job easier for Mercedes, Musso's spin adding 20s to his sizeable deficit. And that was how they finished, Moss shadowing Fangio who led all 100 laps.

POLE POSITION Fangio, Mercedes-Benz, 1m 40.0s (0.4s), 150.948kph, 93.795mph
LAPS 100 x 4.193 km, 2.605 miles
DISTANCE 419.300 km, 260.541 miles
STARTERS/FINISHERS 16/11
WEATHER Cold, drizzle from lap 60
LAP LEADERS Fangio 1-100 (100)
WINNER'S LAPS 1-100 P1
FASTEST LAP Mières, Maserati, 1m 40.9s (lap 3), 149.602kph, 92.958mph
CHAMPIONSHIP Fangio 27, Moss 13, Trintignant 11.33, Farina 10.33, Sweikert 8

Pos	Driver	Car	Time/gap	Grid	Stops	Tyres
1	J M Fangio	Mercedes-Benz	2h 54m 23.8s	1	0	C
2	S Moss	Mercedes-Benz	−0.3s	2	0	C
3	L Musso	Maserati	−57.1s	4	NA	P
4	R Mières	Maserati	−1 lap	7	NA	P
5	E Castellotti	Ferrari	−3 laps	9	NA	E
6	J Behra	Maserati	−3 laps	6	NA	P

Round 6/7	**BRITISH GP** Aintree	
	16 July 1955	**Race 47**

Stirling Moss
Mercedes-Benz 139.156kph, 86.468mph

For the British GP Aintree replaced Silverstone and Moss was in cracking form, out-qualifying his team leader for pole position. He then led for all but 10 laps, building a 12s advantage until ordered by team boss Neubauer to 'slow'. But Moss continued to lead, accepting the flag just 0.2s ahead of Fangio to head home a Mercedes 1-2-3-4. Did Fangio, crowned champion for the third time that same day, gift a first win on home turf to his young teammate? The jury remains out! Behra's front-row Maserati lay third until retirement on lap 10, Musso's similar car sparring with the lesser Mercedes team drivers to finish fifth. The best Ferrari could manage was to qualify tenth and finish sixth three laps down, Castellotti taking over Hawthorn's 625.

POLE POSITION Moss, Mercedes-Benz, 2m 0.4s (0.2s), 144.360kph, 189.701mph
LAPS 90 x 4.828 km, 3.000 miles
DISTANCE 434.523 km, 270.000 miles
STARTERS/FINISHERS 24/9
WEATHER Sunny, hot, dry
LAP LEADERS Fangio 1-2, 18-25 (10); Moss 3-17, 26-90 (80)
WINNER'S LAPS 1-2 P2, 3-17 P1, 18-25 P2, 26-90 P1
FASTEST LAP Moss, Mercedes-Benz, 2m 0.4s (lap 88), 144.360kph, 189.701mph
CHAMPIONSHIP Fangio 33, Moss 22, Trintignant 11.33, Farina 10.33, Sweikert 8

Pos	Driver	Car	Time/gap	Grid	Stops	Tyres
1	S Moss	Mercedes-Benz	3h 7m 21.2s	1	0	C
2	J M Fangio	Mercedes-Benz	−0.2s	2	0	C
3	K Kling	Mercedes-Benz	−1m 11.8s	4	0	C
4	P Taruffi	Mercedes-Benz	−1 lap	5	0	C
5	L Musso	Maserati	−1 lap	9	0	P
6	M Hawthorn/E Castellotti	Ferrari	−3 laps	12	1	E

Round 7/7	**ITALIAN GP** Monza	
	11 September 1955	**Race 48**

Juan Manuel Fangio
Mercedes-Benz W196 str. 206.792kph, 128.495mph

For the first time the new banked section was used at Autodromo di Monza. The Lancia team cars had been handed to Ferrari, and from a six-car entry by the Scuderia two Lancia-Ferraris would debut in the hands of Farina and Villoresi. But both were withdrawn on safety grounds due to a series of thrown tyre treads leading to a spectacular crash for Farina in practice, this his final F1 appearance. In their final race, having earlier announced their withdrawal, Mercedes reintroduced the streamliner bodywork for Fangio and Moss and by the end of the first lap had assumed a team order 1-2-3-4. But the rigours of the concrete banking caused over half the field to capitulate so by the finish it was Fangio and Taruffi in Mercedes from Castellotti's Ferrari 555 'Super Squalo'.

POLE POSITION Fangio, Mercedes-Benz, 2m 46.5s (0.3s), 216.216kph, 134.351mph
LAPS 50 x 10.000 km, 6.214 miles (New banked circuit)
DISTANCE 500.000 km, 310.686 miles
STARTERS/FINISHERS 20/9
WEATHER Sunny, warm, dry
LAP LEADERS Fangio 1-7, 9-50 (49); Moss 8 (1)
WINNER'S LAPS 1-7 P1, 8 P2, 9-50 P1
FASTEST LAP S Moss, Mercedes-Benz, 2m 46.9s (lap 21), 215.698kph, 134.029mph
CHAMPIONSHIP Fangio 40, Moss 23, Castellotti 12, Trintignant 11.33, Farina 10.33

Pos	Driver	Car	Time/gap	Grid	Stops	Tyres
1	J M Fangio	Mercedes-Benz	2h 25m 4.4s	1	0	C
2	P Taruffi	Mercedes-Benz	−0.7s	9	0	C
3	E Castellotti	Ferrari	−46.2s	4	0	E
4	J Behra	Maserati	−3m 57.5s	6	0	P
5	C Menditéguy	Maserati	−1 lap	16	1	P
6	U Maglioli	Ferrari	−1 lap	12	0	E

- 1955 was a tumultuous year for motorsport, with headlines and repercussions of equal moment.
- On 26 May double world champion Alberto Ascari lost his life in an accident while testing a Ferrari sports car at Monza. He was 36.
- The exact circumstances of the crash remain a mystery, although some felt it was because he had not fully recovered from the ordeal of his death-defying Monaco mishap just four short days earlier.
- Son of famous pre-war Grand Prix driver Antonio Ascari, Alberto's star burned brightly for a comparatively short time – 13 Grand Prix victories from just 17 starts between 1951 and 1953 – but long enough for many to regard him as the greatest driver of his age.
- On learning of Ascari's death, Fangio is reported to have said 'I have lost my greatest opponent.'
- Testament to their joint superiority is that, up until then, they had won between them over 70% of all the races since the inception of the F1 world championship in 1950 – Ascari 13, Fangio 14, Farina next with 5.
- To this day Ascari holds the record for the number of consecutive Grand Prix victories, nine.
- Just four days after the death of a F1 great, an equivalent figure in US open-wheel racing was killed during the Indy 500, Bill Vukovich. He had been well on his way to his third Indy victory in five starts, Vukovich extraordinarily leading nearly three out of every four laps he ever raced in the 500. Naturally his demise did not capture the headlines in Europe

as it did in the States, but there were banner headlines in all parts of the world for the third and worst motorsport calamity of all time.
- Barely two weeks after Ascari's death, the Le Mans disaster caused serious ramifications for the sport.
- On 11 June, a few hours into the race, a sequence of events – perhaps triggered by Mike Hawthorn's leading D-type Jaguar – caused the Mercedes driven by Pierre Levegh to collide with Lance Macklin's Austin-Healey on the pit straight at the La Sarthe circuit. The Mercedes was launched airborne, cartwheeling and disintegrating into the crowded grandstands where it annihilated at least 80 spectators and injured 120 more. Driver Levegh also lost his life.
- Four Grands Prix were subsequently cancelled (France, Germany, Switzerland, Spain), and motorsport underwent a temporary cessation in France. In Switzerland a total ban was invoked which remains in place to this day.
- The catastrophe, which had involved one of its cars, also led to the withdrawal of Mercedes-Benz from all motorsport at the end of only their second F1 championship season, albeit one of complete dominance. Whereas it might be said that Fangio brought Mercedes their first championship, the reverse was true in their second season together.
- Lancia, already under financial pressure, also abandoned racing with immediate effect following the loss of team leader Ascari.
- An intriguing consequence of this was the transfer to Ferrari of the Lancia D50 cars along with its designer Vittorio Jani,

RACE 47, British GP: On his home circuit, Moss (12) famously beat Fangio (10) to lead a Mercedes 1-2-3-4. Behra's front-row Maserati (2) lay third until retirement on lap ten.

although the Lancia Ferraris, as they became known, were not to make their first start until the following season.
- The 1955 championship was therefore decided over just six races plus the Indy 500, the best five results counting.
- Monaco returned to the abbreviated calendar and for the first time the British GP was held at Aintree, where Stirling Moss won his first championship race and Jack Brabham made his debut in a rear-engined Cooper-Bristol 'Bobtail' Special.
- Tony Brooks became the first British driver since Henry Seagrave's Sunbeam in 1923 to win a Grand Prix in a British car when he won the non-championship Syracuse GP in a Type B Connaught, thereafter dubbed the Connaught 'Syracuse'.
- Giuseppe Farina, the first Drivers' World Champion, retired from F1 at the end of the season.
- Alain Prost was born.

Championship ranking	Championship points	Driver nationality	1955 Drivers Championship		Races contested	Race victories	Podiumse excl. victories	Races led	Flag to flag victories	Laps led	Poles	Fastest laps	Triple Crowns
			Driver	Car									
1	40	ARG	Juan Manuel Fangio	Mercedes-Benz	6	4	1	6	2	309	3	3	
2	23	GBR	Stirling Moss	Mercedes-Benz	6	1	2	3		112	1	2	1
3	12	ITA	Eugenio Castellotti	Lancia (3) Ferrari (3)	6		2				1		
4	11.33	FRA	Maurice Trintignant	Ferrari	6	1	2	1		20			
5	10.33	ITA	Nino Farina	Ferrari	3		3						
6	9	ITA	Piero Taruffi	Ferrari (1) Mercedes-Benz (2)	3		1						
7	8	USA	Bob Sweikert	Kurtis Kraft-Offenhauser	1	1		1		86			
8	7	ARG	Roberto Mieres	Maserati	6							1	
9	6	FRA	Jean Behra	Maserati	6		1						
10	6	ITA	Luigi Musso	Maserati	6		1						
11	5	GER	Karl Kling	Mercedes-Benz	5		1						
12	4	USA	Jimmy Davies	Kurtis Kraft-Offenhauser	1		1						
13	3	USA	Paul Russo	Kurtis Kraft-Offenhauser	1		1						
13	3	USA	Tony Bettenhausen	Kurtis Kraft-Offenhauser	1		1						
15	3	USA	Johnny Thomson	Kuzma-Offenhauser	1								
15	3	BEL	Paul Frère	Ferrari	2								
17	2	ARG	José Froilán González	Ferrari	1		1	1		11	1		
18	2	ITA	Cesare Perdisa	Maserati	2		1						
19	2	ITA	Luigi Villoresi	Lancia	2								
19	2	ARG	Carlos Menditéguy	Maserati	2								
21	1.33	ITA	Umberto Maglioli	Ferrari	2		1						
22	1	GER	Hans Herrmann	Mercedes-Benz	1								
23	1	USA	Walt Faulkner	Kurtis Kraft-Offenhauser	1								
23	1	USA	Bill Homeier	Kurtis Kraft-Offenhauser	1								
25	1	USA	Bill Vukovich	Kurtis Kraft-Offenhauser	1			1		50		1	
-	0	USA	Jerry Hoyt	Stevens-Offenhauser	1						1		
-	0	USA	Jimmy Bryan	Kuzma-Offenhauser	1			1		31			
-	0	USA	Art Cross	Kurtis Kraft-Offenhauser	1			1		24			
-	0	USA	Jack McGrath	Kurtis Kraft-Offenhauser	1			1		6			
-	0	USA	Don Freeland	Phillips-Offenhauser	1			1		3			
-	0	ITA	Alberto Ascari	Lancia	2			1		13			
-	0	USA	Harry Schell	Maserati (1) Ferrari (1) Vanwall (2)	4			1		7			

Championship ranking	Championship points	Team/Marque nationality	1955 Constructors Results (Excl. Indy 500)		Engine maker nationality	Races contested	Race victories	1-2 finishes	Podiums excl. victories	Races led	Laps led	Poles	Fastest laps
			Chassis	Engine									
N/A	N/A	GER	Mercedes-Benz W196, W196 Streamliner	Mercedes-Benz 2.5 S8	GER	6	5	4	5	6	421	4	5
N/A	N/A	ITA	Ferrari 625, 555 Supersqualo, 500	Ferrari 2.5 S4	ITA	6	1		4	2	31	1	
N/A	N/A	ITA	Maserati 250F, A6GCM	Maserati 2.5 S6	ITA	6			2	1	7		1
N/A	N/A	ITA	Lancia D50	Lancia 2.5 V8	ITA	3			1	1	13	1	

1956

Collins hands Fangio his fourth

THE TALE OF THE TITLE

- Now with Ferrari, Fangio seized championship number four with three race wins, one shared with Musso.
- Fangio's title was assured when teammate Peter Collins nobly handed over his car during the final round.
- Collins, with two race victories of his own, selflessly sacrificed any personal chance of title honours.
- Mercedes' withdrawal brought a resurgence in Italian team ascendancy led by Fangio, Collins and Moss.
- Back with Maserati, Moss' two victories in the 250F brought championship runner-up spot for a second year.
- Moss was the only non-Lancia Ferrari winner, Maserati teammate Behra adding a string of podium finishes.
- Controversially reaping the benefit of Lancia technology, only the 250F challenged the Lancia Ferrari D50.
- Of the rest, two British marques began to show symptoms of promise, BRM and Vanwall.
- And not forgetting: Bugatti's fleeting return.

THE CHASE FOR THE CHAMPIONSHIP

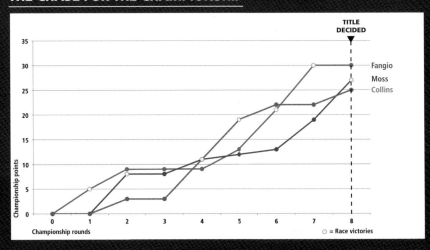

Round 1/8	**ARGENTINEAN GP** Buenos Aires No 2	**Luigi Musso/Juan Manuel Fangio**
	22 January 1956 Race 49	Lancia Ferrari D50 127.748kph, 79.379mph

The Lancia Ferraris sat 1-2-3 on the grid, Fangio in a commanding pole. Initially local driver Carlos Menditéguy, having a one-off drive for Maserati, enthralled the crowd by leading convincingly until almost half-distance. On his departure with a broken half-shaft, Moss took over the lead in his Maserati. Fangio, meanwhile, his Lancia Ferrari sidelined with fuel-pump trouble, had taken over Musso's similar car on lap 23 and once past Behra, and with the exodus of González, Castellotti and Menditéguy ahead of him, found himself behind Moss and closing. The leading Maserati had begun to trail smoke and misfire, such that to the joy of the locals Fangio inevitably took the lead on lap 67 to win from Behra's Maserati, Moss soldiering on until lap 82.

POLE POSITION Fangio, Lancia Ferrari, 1m 42.5s (2.2s), 137.397kph, 85.375mph
LAPS 98 x 3.912 km, 2.431 miles
DISTANCE 383.736 km, 238.219 miles
STARTERS/FINISHERS 13/6
WEATHER Overcast, warm, dry
LAP LEADERS F González, Maserati 1-3 (3); C Menditéguy, Maserati 4-42 (39); S Moss, Maserati 43-66 (24); Fangio 67-98 (32)
WINNER'S LAPS 1 P5, 2-6 P6, 7 P4, 8 P3, 9-10 P2, 11 P3, 12 P11, 13-15 P13, 16-17 P12, 17-22 P13, 27-40 P5, 41-42 P3, 43-66 P2, 67-98 P1
FASTEST LAP Fangio, Lancia Ferrari, 1m 45.3s (lap 42), 133.744kph, 83.104mph
CHAMPIONSHIP Behra 6, Fangio 5, Musso 4, Hawthorn 4, Gendebien 2

Pos	Driver	Car	Time/gap	Grid	Stops	Tyres
1	L Musso/J M Fangio	Lancia Ferrari	3h 0m 3.7s	3	1	E
2	J Behra	Maserati	−24.4s	4	0	P
3	M Hawthorn	Maserati	−2 laps	8	NA	P
4	C Landi/G Gerini	Maserati	−6 laps	11	NA	P
5	O Gendebien	Ferrari	−7 laps	10	NA	E
6	A Uria/O González	Maserati	−10 laps	13	NA	NA

Round 2/8	**MONACO GP** Monte Carlo	**Stirling Moss**
	13 May 1956 Race 50	Maserati 250F 104.515kph, 64.943mph

Fangio and Moss held the prime grid spots in that order, but it was Moss who led from start to finish. He drove superbly that day whereas Fangio seemed off his game, starting poorly, spinning at Ste Devote on lap two, striking numerous kerbs, and on lap 32 clouting the barriers. On lap 40 he handed his wheel-damaged car to Castellotti and 14 laps later took over Collins' second-placed car. Driving now with more characteristic skill, he took six laps to regain second place from Behra and on lap 70 was 47s behind Moss. Fangio chased down the gap to 6.1s by the end, posting fastest lap on his final tour, but Moss always had the situation under complete control.

POLE POSITION Fangio, Lancia Ferrari, 1m 44.0s (0.6s), 108.865kph, 67.646mph
LAPS 100 x 3.145 km, 1.954 miles
DISTANCE 314.500 km, 195.421 miles
STARTERS/FINISHERS 14/8
WEATHER Sunny, warm, dry
LAP LEADERS Moss 1-100 (100)
WINNER'S LAPS 1-100 P1
FASTEST LAP Fangio, Lancia Ferrari, 1m 44.4s (lap 100), 108.448kph, 67.387mph
CHAMPIONSHIP Behra 10, Fangio 9, Moss 8, Musso 4, Hawthorn 4

Pos	Driver	Car	Time/gap	Grid	Stops	Tyres
1	S Moss	Maserati	2h 58m 9.7s	2	0	P
2	P Collins/J M Fangio	Lancia Ferrari	−6.1s	9	1	E
3	J Behra	Maserati	−1 lap	4	0	P
4	J M Fangio/E Castellotti	Lancia Ferrari	−6 laps	1	1	E
5	N da Silva Ramos	Gordini	−7 laps	10	NA	E
6	É Bayol/A Pilette	Gordini	−10 laps	12	NA	E

Round 3/8	**INDIANAPOLIS 500** Indianapolis	**Pat Flaherty**
	30 May 1956 Race 51	Watson-Offenhauser 206.785kph, 128.490mph

Improvements to the Speedway included a new asphalt surface, a short stretch of the old bricks left visible along the main straight as a token reminder. The second qualifying weekend was almost a total washout, some quick cars unable to get their qualifying runs in before the track closed. This included 1950 world champion Nino Farina who had hoped to qualify a Bardahl-Ferrari. The race, now under the auspices of a new governing body, USAC, was won from pole by Pat Flaherty. Flaherty led for the last two-thirds of the race to win by 20s from Sam Hanks, who had raced well from 13th on the grid. There were numerous yellow-light periods triggered by accidents, Jimmy Daywalt sustaining serious head injuries in one when a tyre blew.

POLE POSITION Flaherty, Watson-Offy, 4m 7.26s (2.27s), 234.315kph, 145.596mph
LAPS 200 x 4.023 km, 2.500 miles
DISTANCE 804.672 km, 500.000 miles
STARTERS/FINISHERS 33/19
WEATHER Overcast, warm, dry
LAP LEADERS J Rathmann 1-3 (3); P O'Connor, Kurtis Kraft-Offy 4-10, 22-40, 42-44, 46-55 (39); P Russo, Kurtis Kraft-Offy 11-21 (11); Flaherty 41, 45, 76-200 (127); Parsons 56-71 (16); Freeland 72-75 (4)
WINNER'S LAPS NA
FASTEST LAP P Russo, Kurtis Kraft-Novi, 1m 2.32s (lap 19), 232.415kph, 144.416mph
CHAMPIONSHIP Behra 10, Fangio 9, Moss 8, Flaherty 8, Hanks 6

Pos	Driver	Car	Time/gap	Grid	Stops	Tyres
1	P Flaherty	Watson-Offy	3h 53m 28.84s	1	NA	F
2	S Hanks	Kurtis Kraft-Offy	−20.45s	13	NA	F
3	D Freeland	Phillips-Offy	−1m 30.23s	26	NA	F
4	J Parsons	Kuzma-Offy	−3m 25.69s	6	NA	F
5	D Rathmann	Kurtis Kraft-Offy	−4m 21.81s	4	NA	F
6	B Sweikert	Kuzma-Offy	−5m 35.05s	10	NA	F

Round 4/8	**BELGIAN GP** Spa-Francorchamps	**Peter Collins**

	3 June 1956	Race 52	Lancia Ferrari D50 190.614kph, 118.442mph

Making his third championship start for Ferrari, Collins justified their faith. Third on the grid beside Moss and Fangio, it was these three who dominated the race, initially in wet conditions. Moss led first until Fangio overtook on lap 5 and drew away, Moss' Maserati losing a wheel on lap 10. At half-distance the leading Lancia Ferraris were 30s apart, but when Fangio's transmission failed out on the circuit Collins had a comfortable lead to record his maiden victory 13 laps later. Moss had made his way back to the pits and resumed fifth in Perdisa's car, eventually finishing third ahead of Schell's Vanwall. During their dice while Moss was ahead, the Vanwall steamed past on the Masta straight, no doubt giving Stirling food for thought.

POLE POSITION J M Fangio, Lancia Ferrari, 4m 9.8s (4.9s), 203.491kph, 126.443mph
LAPS 36 x 14.120 km, 8.774 miles
DISTANCE 508.320 km, 315.855 miles
STARTERS/FINISHERS 15/8
WEATHER Overcast, rain at start, track drying from lap 10
LAP LEADERS Moss 1-4 (4); J M Fangio, Lancia Ferrari 5-23 (19); Collins 24-36 (13)
WINNER'S LAPS 1 P3, 2-6 P4, 7-10 P3, 11-23 P2, 24-36 P1
FASTEST LAP Moss, Maserati, 4m 14.7s (lap 30), 199.576kph, 124.011mph
CHAMPIONSHIP Collins 11, Moss 11, Behra 10, Fangio 9, Flaherty 8

Pos	Driver	Car	Time/gap	Grid	Stops	Tyres
1	P Collins	Lancia Ferrari	2h 40m 0.3s	3	0	E
2	P Frère	Lancia Ferrari	–1m 51.3s	8	0	E
3	C Perdisa/S Moss	Maserati	–3m 16.6s	9	1	P
4	H Schell	Vanwall	–1 lap	6	NA	P
5	L Villoresi	Maserati	–2 laps	11	NA	P
6	A Pilette	Lancia Ferrari	–3 laps	15	NA	E

Lancia Ferrari D50

Round 5/8	**FRENCH GP** Reims	**Peter Collins**

	1 July 1956	Race 53	Lancia Ferrari D50 196.809kph, 122.291mph

Three Lancia Ferraris headed qualifying, but unusually Vanwalls rather than Maseratis were next up. When Schell's Vanwall retired on lap 6 the Ferrari pit believed any challenge from the British team was spent, Hawthorn weary from the six-hours' race preceding the GP. But in an inspired drive by Schell, now in Hawthorn's car, the American driver caught the complacent Ferrari trio, overtaking Collins and Castellotti under braking for Thillois on lap 31, to then set off after leader Fangio. But Fangio responded and soon afterwards Schell fell back with fuel injection trouble, pitting on lap 38. But when Fangio was also delayed in the pits on lap 40 with a split fuel line, Collins led home Castellotti under team orders for back-to-back victories.

POLE POSITION Fangio, Lancia Ferrari, 2m 23.3s (1.3s), 208.564kph, 129.596mph
LAPS 61 x 8.302 km, 5.159 miles
DISTANCE 506.422 km, 314.676 miles
STARTERS/FINISHERS 19/11
WEATHER Overcast, warm, wet
LAP LEADERS Collins 1, 47-48, 50-61 (15); Castellotti 2-3, 39-46, 49 (11); Fangio 4-38 (35)
WINNER'S LAPS 1 P1, 2-30 P3, 31-34 P4, 35-38 P3, 39-46 P2, 47-48 P1, 49 P2, 50-61 P1
FASTEST LAP Fangio, Lancia Ferrari, 2m 25.8s (lap 61), 204.988kph, 127.373mph
CHAMPIONSHIP Collins 19, Behra 14, Fangio 13, Moss 12, Flaherty 8

Pos	Driver	Car	Time/gap	Grid	Stops	Tyres
1	P Collins	Lancia Ferrari	2h 34m 23.4s	3	0	E
2	E Castellotti	Lancia Ferrari	–0.3s	2	0	E
3	J Behra	Maserati	–1m 29.9s	7	0	P
4	J M Fangio	Lancia Ferrari	–1m 35.1s	1	1	E
5	C Perdisa/S Moss	Maserati	–2 laps	16	1	P
6	L Rosier	Maserati	–3 laps	13	NA	P

BRITISH GP Silverstone
14 July 1956   Race 54

Juan Manuel Fangio
Lancia Ferrari D50 158./80kph, 98.661mph

Fangio was the interloper in an all-British front row at Silverstone, Moss on pole, Hawthorn and Collins on the outside. Hawthorn, now BRM-mounted, gloriously led the first 15 laps before Moss went by and took command. But just as with Hawthorn, Moss was not to finish. First he pitted for oil on lap 60; stopped again, still first, on lap 69 to investigate a loss of power, and after replenishing oil again, retired from third place at Stowe on lap 94 with a broken rear axle. This gave Fangio a somewhat fortuitous victory that he appeared to have thrown away with a lap 8 spin at Becketts. Collins finished second in de Portago's car. Tony Brooks in the second BRM escaped serious injury when his car crashed and burned, the result of a stuck throttle in the fast Abbey Curve.

POLE POSITION S Moss, Maserati, 1m 41.0s (0.0s), 167.901kph, 104.329mph
LAPS 101 x 4.711 km, 2.927 miles
DISTANCE 475.766 km, 295.627 miles
STARTERS/FINISHERS 28/11
WEATHER Overcast, warm, dry
LAP LEADERS M Hawthorn, BRM 1-15 (15); S Moss, Maserati 16-68 (53); Fangio 69-101 (33)
WINNER'S LAPS 1-6 P3, 7-8 P2, 9-10 P6, 11-14 P5, 15-24 P4, 25-51 P3, 52-68 P2, 69-101 P1
FASTEST LAP S Moss, Maserati, 1m 43.2s (lap 71), 164.322kph, 102.105mph
CHAMPIONSHIP Collins 22, Fangio 21, Behra 18, Moss 13, Flaherty 8

Pos	Driver	Car	Time/gap	Grid	Stops	Tyres
1	J M Fangio	Lancia Ferrari	2h 59m 47.0s	2	0	E
2	A de Portago/P Collins	Lancia Ferrari	−1 lap	12	1	E
3	J Behra	Maserati	−2 laps	13	NA	P
4	J Fairman	Connaught-Alta	−3 laps	21	NA	P
5	H Gould	Maserati	−4 laps	14	NA	P
6	L Villoresi	Maserati	−5 laps	19	NA	P

GERMAN GP Nürburgring
5 August 1956   Race 55

Juan Manuel Fangio
Lancia Ferrari D50 137.656kph, 85.535mph

With no British teams entering, the Lancia Ferraris were the class of the field around the Nordschleife. Fangio dominated, leading every lap from pole and setting fastest lap. Moss at least kept Fangio honest, his Maserati completing the full distance less than a minute behind the winner in second place. Collins had a fraught race, overcome by fumes from a leaking fuel pipe to surrender a sound second place on lap 9. Recovered, he took over de Portago's car but spun out on lap 15 from third place, handing a crucial point to Behra. With one round remaining, the machinations of the championship points system had eliminated Moss, and with 30 points Fangio was the strong title favourite, but Collins and Behra were still in striking distance, just.

POLE POSITION Fangio, Lancia Ferrari, 9m 51.2s (0.3s), 138.897kph, 86.307mph
LAPS 22 x 22.810 km, 14.173 miles
DISTANCE 501.820 km, 311.816 miles
STARTERS/FINISHERS 19/5
WEATHER Sunny, warm, dry
LAP LEADERS Fangio 1-22 (22)
WINNER'S LAPS 1-22 P1
FASTEST LAP Fangio, Lancia Ferrari, 9m 41.6s (lap 14), 141.190kph, 87.731mph
CHAMPIONSHIP Fangio 30, Collins 22, Behra 22, Moss 19, Flaherty 8

Pos	Driver	Car	Time/gap	Grid	Stops	Tyres
1	J M Fangio	Lancia Ferrari	3h 38m 43.7s	1	0	E
2	S Moss	Maserati	−46.4s	4	0	P
3	J Behra	Maserati	−7m 38.3s	8	NA	P
4	C Godia	Maserati	−2 laps	16	NA	P
5	L Rosier	Maserati	−3 laps	14	NA	P
-	Only five classified finishers	-	-	-	-	-

ITALIAN GP Monza
2 September 1956   Race 56

Stirling Moss
Maserati 250F 208.785kph, 129.733mph

From the all Lancia Ferrari front row, Italians Musso and Castellotti put on a dazzling if foolhardy display for the *tifosi*. It only lasted four laps, the concrete Monza banking playing havoc with their tyres. Now Moss duelled for the lead with Schell's Vanwall until a rain shower helped him pull away. Five laps short of victory, a fuel leak caused Moss to run dry, but with a helping push into the pits from teammate Piotti's Maserati, he completed the distance the winner. Fangio had retired on lap 19 with a broken steering arm, Musso bluntly refusing to car-share here at Monza as he had in Buenos Aires. On lap 36, holding second place and extremely well placed to win both race and title, Collins handed his car over to Fangio, who finished just 5.7s behind Moss to secure his fourth title.

POLE POSITION Fangio, Lancia Ferrari, 2m 42.6s (0.8s), 221.402kph, 137.573mph
LAPS 50 x 10.000 km, 6.214 miles
DISTANCE 500.000 km, 310.686 miles
STARTERS/FINISHERS 24/11
WEATHER Warm with showers
LAP LEADERS E Castellotti, Lancia Ferrari 1-4 (4); Moss 5-10, 12-45, 48-50 (43); H Schell, Vanwall 11 (1); L Musso, Lancia Ferrari 46-47 (2)
WINNER'S LAPS 1-4 P6, 5-10 P1, 11 P2, 12-45 P1, 46-47 P2, 48-50 P1
FASTEST LAP Moss, Maserati, 2m 45.5s (lap 47), 217.523kph, 135.162mph
CHAMPIONSHIP Fangio 30, Moss 27, Collins 25, Behra 22, Flaherty 8

Pos	Driver	Car	Time/gap	Grid	Stops	Tyres
1	S Moss	Maserati	2h 23m 41.3s	6	1	P
2	P Collins /J M Fangio	Lancia Ferrari	−5.7s	7	1	E
3	R Flockhart	Connaught-Alta	−1 lap	23	NA	P/A
4	C Godia	Maserati	−1 lap	17	NA	P
5	J Fairman	Connaught-Alta	−3 laps	15	1	P/A
6	L Piotti	Maserati	−3 laps	14	NA	P

RACE 50, Monaco GP: Peter Collins handed his car over to team leader Fangio on two occasions during 1956, first here at Monaco and again at the Monza finale. Had he not done so, it is probable that he would have won the championship himself.

1956 CHAMPIONSHIP FACTS AND FOLKLORE

- The ban on motorsport in France following the Le Mans disaster had been lifted, so the French GP returned to a calendar of seven rounds including the Indy 500, the best five results counting towards the championship.
- In 1956 Ferrari could count themselves extremely fortunate to have inherited the cars of the insolvent Lancia team, along with designer Jani.
- Early on the Scuderia even fitted and raced the 555 'Super Squalo' with the excellent Lancia V8 engine, electing finally to campaign the D50 chassis in modified form, most notably the transfer of the fuel tanks from the distinctive panniers to the rear of the car to improve handling.
- Without Ferrari's controversial advantage other teams might have gained far greater success, especially Maserati. Moss and Behra enjoyed a strong season in the 250F, Moss leading more race laps than Fangio but on two occasions robbed of likely victory through mechanical unreliability.
- Fangio's fourth title was perhaps his least dominant display, he too suffering his share of car ailments. At the season's finale the Argentinean driver was in danger of losing his crown not to Moss but to his Lancia Ferrari teammate Peter Collins.
- At the showdown on the Monza banking, with just 14 laps remaining, Collins stood a very good chance of

becoming the first British world champion. Instead, in an astonishing act of sportsmanship by today's or any standards, he handed his car over to Fangio – 'Because he deserved it,' said Collins, perhaps implying that his own pair of race victories could have been regarded as gained at Fangio's expense.

- As well as epitomising the gallantry of the age, this remarkable act was acknowledgement that Fangio remained 'the man to beat', and that throughout the 1956 championship struggle no other driver, Collins included, had genuinely usurped that accepted status quo.
- The emergence of Collins as a force added to a groundswell of British success that was not confined merely to drivers.
- Under the patronage of industrialist Sir Alfred Owen, 1956 saw BRM return with the P25. By comparison with the excesses of the V16 concept, this was a fairly straightforward, light and compact car powered by a 2.5 four-cylinder engine producing around 100bhp per litre at 9,000rpm.
- The classic Vanwall silhouette inspired by aerodynamicist Frank Costin also graced the circuits for first time, showing flashes of its nascent potential. Costin's slippery bodywork enveloped a chassis designed by Colin Chapman, whose own Lotus cars would not appear in F1 for another two years.

- Chapman, no mean driver himself, entered the French GP in a Vanwall but after an accident in practice did not start.
- The British teams, leading in the use of disc brakes, seemed to be building some momentum in F1. The French, by contrast, were dissipating, Gordini gone at the end of the season along with Bugatti, which made a solitary post-war return appearance at the French GP. An adventurous design by Colombo, the straight-eight engine of the Type 251 Bugatti was mounted directly behind the driver.

Championship ranking	Championship points	Driver nationality	1956 Drivers Championship		Races contested	Race victories	Podiumse excl. victories	Races led	Flag to flag victories	Laps led	Poles	Fastest laps	Triple Crowns
			Driver	Car									
1	30	ARG	Juan Manuel Fangio	Lancia Ferrari	7	3	2	5	1	141	6	4	2
2	27	GBR	Stirling Moss	Maserati	7	2	2	5	1	224	1	3	
3	25	GBR	Peter Collins	Ferrari (1) Lancia Ferrari (6)	7	2	3	2		28			
4	22	FRA	Jean Behra	Maserati	7		5						
5	8	USA	Pat Flaherty	Watson-Offenhauser	1	1		1		127	1		
6	7.5	ITA	Eugenio Castellotti	Lancia Ferrari	7		1	2		15			
7	6	USA	Sam Hanks	Kurtis Kraft-Offenhauser	1		1	1					
7	6	BEL	Paul Frère	Lancia Ferrari	1		1	1					
9	6	ESP	Paco Godia	Maserati	5								
10	5	GBR	Jack Fairman	Connaught	2								
11	4	ITA	Luigi Musso	Lancia Ferrari	4	1		1		2			
12	4	GBR	Mike Hawthorn	Maserati (1) BRM (1) Vanwall (1)	3		1	1		15			
12	4	USA	Don Freeland	Phillips-Offenhauser	1		1	1		4			
12	4	GBR	Ron Flockhart	BRM (1) Connaught (1)	2		1						
15	3	ESP	Alfonso de Portago	Lancia Ferrari	4		1						
16	3	ITA	Cesare Perdisa	Maserati	4		1						
17	3	USA	Johnnie Parsons	Kuzma-Offenhauser	1			1		16			
17	3	USA	Harry Schell	Vanwall (5) Maserati (1)	6			1		1			
19	2	BEL	Olivier Gendebien	Ferrari-Lancia Ferrari (1) Lancia Ferrari (1)	2								
19	2	BRA	Nano da Silva Ramos	Gordini	4								
19	2	USA	Dick Rathmann	Kurtis Kraft-Offenhauser	1								
19	2	ITA	Luigi Villoresi	Maserati	5								
19	2	BRA	Horace Gould	Maserati	4								
19	2	FRA	Louis Rosier	Maserati	5								
25	1.5	ITA	Gerino Gerini	Maserati	2								
25	1.5	BRA	Chico Landi	Maserati	1								
27	1	USA	Paul Russo	Kurtis Kraft-Novi	1			1		11		1	
-	0	USA	Pat O'Connor	Kurtis Kraft-Offenhauser	1			1		39			
-	0	USA	Jim Rathmann	Kurtis Kraft-Offenhauser	1			1		3			
-	0	ARG	José Froilán González	Maserati (1) Vanwall (1)	2			1		3			
-	0	ARG	Carlos Menditéguy	Maserati	1			1		39			

Championship ranking	Championship points	Team/Marque nationality	1956 Constructors Results (Excl. Indy 500)		Engine maker nationality	Races contested	Race victories	1-2 finishes	Podiums excl. victories	Races led	Laps led	Poles	Fastest laps
			Chassis	Engine									
N/A	N/A	ITA	Lancia Ferrari D50, Ferrari 555 Super Squalo, 500	Lancia Ferrari 2.5 V8, Ferrari 2.5 S4	ITA	7	5	3	5	5	186	6	4
N/A	N/A	ITA	Maserati 250F, A6GCM	Maserati 2.5 S6	ITA	7	2		8	5	266	1	3
N/A	N/A	GBR	Connaught B	Alta 2.5 S4	GBR	3			1				
N/A	N/A	GBR	Vanwall VW56	Vanwall 2.5 S4	GBR	5				1	1		
N/A	N/A	FRA	Gordini T32, T16	Gordini 2.5 S8, 2.5 S6	FRA	5							
N/A	N/A	GBR	BRM P25	BRM 2.5 S4	GBR	1				1	15		

1957

Fangio saves best until last

THE TALE OF THE TITLE

■ Fangio clinched his fifth championship, rapidly securing the title by winning the first three rounds.
■ Unhappy at Ferrari, back with Maserati, his fourth and final victory was widely regarded as his finest.
■ At the daunting Nürburgring he famously thrashed the Lancia Ferraris of Hawthorn and Collins.
■ This superlative victory not only secured his fifth and final title but denied Ferrari any success in the season.
■ For a third successive year Moss finished runner-up to Fangio, taking three victories for Vanwall.
■ The last of these three, at Monza, signalled the nadir of 1950s supremacy by Italian teams.
■ Vanwall became the first British car to win a championship race when Moss won with Brooks at Aintree.
■ Jack Brabham debuted a works Cooper unusually featuring a rear-mounted engine from Coventry-Climax.
■ The most successful Ferrari driver was Musso, beating Hawthorn to third in the championship.
■ And not forgetting: Eugenio Castellotti lost his life.

THE CHASE FOR THE CHAMPIONSHIP

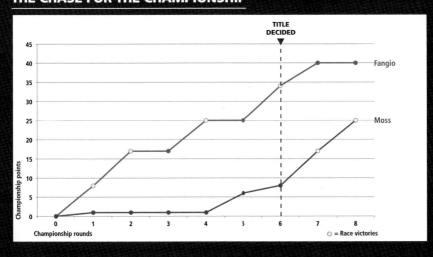

| Round 1/8 | **ARGENTINEAN GP** Buenos Aires No 2
 13 January 1957 | Race 57 | **Juan Manuel Fangio**
 Maserati 250F 129.729kph, 80.610mph |

With the British teams opting out of the trip to Buenos Aires, in an Italian benefit Maserati outshone Ferrari in qualifying and in the race, 250Fs finishing 1-2-3-4. Early on the Lancia Ferraris of Collins and Castellotti battled the Maseratis of Behra and Fangio, each leading briefly until clutch and other maladies saw their challenge wilt. With the Maserati of pole-sitter Moss losing nine laps at the start with a deranged throttle linkage, Fangio and Behra were soon in complete command. On lap 84 Behra led a lap for the final time, after which Fangio pulled away to eventually win by almost 20s from his teammate. It was the four-times champion's fourth consecutive home race victory and making his return to Maserati, trouncing Ferrari after their uneasy relationship.

POLE POSITION S Moss, Maserati, 1m 42.6s (1.1s), 137.263kph, 85.291mph
LAPS 100 x 3.912 km, 2.431 miles
DISTANCE 391.200 km, 243.080 miles
STARTERS/FINISHERS 14/10
WEATHER Sunny, hot, dry
LAP LEADERS Behra 1-2, 9-12, 81, 84 (8); E Castellotti, Lancia Ferrari 3-8 (6); P Collins, Lancia Ferrari 13-25 (13); Fangio 26-80,82-83, 85-100 (73)
WINNER'S LAPS 1-8 P3, 9-12 P4, 13-25 P3, 26-80 P1, 81 P2, 82-83 P1, 84 P2, 85-100 P1
FASTEST LAP S Moss, Maserati, 1m 44.7s (lap 75), 134.510kph, 83.518mph
CHAMPIONSHIP Fangio 8, Behra 6, Menditéguy 4, Schell 3, González 1

Pos	Driver	Car	Time/gap	Grid	Stops	Tyres
1	J M Fangio	Maserati	3h 0m 55.9s	2	1	P
2	J Behra	Maserati	–18.3s	3	1	P
3	C Menditéguy	Maserati	–1 lap	8	NA	P
4	H Schell	Maserati	–2 laps	9	NA	P
5	F González/A de Portago	Lancia Ferrari	–2 laps	10	1	E
6	C Perdisa/P Collins/W von Trips	Lancia Ferrari	–2 laps	11	2	E

| Round 2/8 | **MONACO GP** Monte Carlo
 19 May 1957 | Race 58 | **Juan Manuel Fangio**
 Maserati 250F 104.165kph, 64.725mph |

Fangio's Maserati on pole was followed by four British drivers – Collins, Moss and Brooks debuting for Vanwall, then Hawthorn's Lancia Ferrari. The race was effectively over after four laps due to an error by Moss. Exiting the tunnel in the lead chased by Collins, Moss misjudged the chicane and crashed. Collins, close behind, crashed in avoidance. Fangio picked his way through the mêlée, but a fast-arriving Brooks braked and was shunted by Hawthorn, his car ending up half on top of teammate Collins' Lancia Ferrari. Of the four British drivers involved only Brooks was able to continue, winding up a praiseworthy second behind Fangio. Significantly, with just six laps to go, Brabham's 2-litre Cooper-Climax lay third until a fuel pump bracket fractured.

POLE POSITION Fangio, Maserati, 1m 42.7s (0.6s), 110.243kph, 68.502mph
LAPS 105 x 3.145 km, 1.954 miles
DISTANCE 330.225 km, 205.192 miles
STARTERS/FINISHERS 16/6
WEATHER Sunny, warm, dry
LAP LEADERS S Moss, Vanwall 1-4 (4); Fangio 5-105 (101)
WINNER'S LAPS 1 P2, 2-4 P3, 5-105 P1
FASTEST LAP Fangio, Maserati, 1m 45.6s (lap NA), 107.216kph, 66.621mph
CHAMPIONSHIP Fangio 17, Behra 6, Brooks 6, Menditéguy 4, Gregory 4

Pos	Driver	Car	Time/gap	Grid	Stops	Tyres
1	J M Fangio	Maserati	3h 10m 12.8s	1	0	P
2	T Brooks	Vanwall	–25.2s	4	0	P
3	M Gregory	Maserati	–2 laps	10	0	P
4	S Lewis-Evans	Connaught-Alta	–3 laps	13	0	D
5	M Trintignant	Lancia Ferrari	–5 laps	6	1	E
6	J Brabham	Cooper-Climax	–5 laps	15	1	D

| Round 3/8 | **INDIANAPOLIS 500** Indianapolis
 30 May 1957 | Race 59 | **Sam Hanks**
 Epperly-Offenhauser 218.228kph, 135.601mph |

After his great showing to finish second in 1956, veteran Sam Hanks, who had been trying to win the '500' since 1940, finally made it at his 13th attempt. Amidst tears, he announced his retirement in victory lane, emulating inaugural '500' winner Ray Harroun, who made a similar pledge in 1911. Hanks won in a radical 'lay-down' roadster chassis designed and built by engineer George Salih, the regular 'Offy' engine tilted by 72° to create a car standing a mere 21in/530mm from the track. The sleek, low-profile Epperly-Offy performed flawlessly as Hanks beat Jim Rathmann, who had come through to challenge Hanks for the lead after a long climb through the field from the back row. Farina's attempts to qualify were again thwarted.

POLE POSITION P O'Connor, Kurtis Kraft-Offy, 4m 10.09s (0.22s), 231.664kph, 143.949mph
LAPS 200 x 4.023 km, 2.500 miles
DISTANCE 804.672 km, 500.000 miles
STARTERS/FINISHERS 33/17
WEATHER Cloudy, warm, dry
LAP LEADERS O'Connor 1-4, 7-9 (7); T Ruttman, Watson-Offy 5-6, 10-11 (4); Russo 12-35 (24); Hanks 36-48, 54-110, 135-200 (136); J Rathmann 111-134 (24)
WINNER'S LAPS NA
FASTEST LAP Rathmann, Epperly-Offy, 1m 2.75s (lap 127), 230.822kph, 143.426mph
CHAMPIONSHIP Fangio 17, Hanks 8, Rathmann 7, Behra 6, Brooks 6

Pos	Driver	Car	Time/gap	Grid	Stops	Tyres
1	S Hanks	Epperly-Offy	3h 41m 14.25s	13	NA	F
2	J Rathmann	Epperly-Offy	–21.46s	32	NA	F
3	J Bryan	Kuzma-Offy	–2m 13.97s	15	NA	F
4	P Russo	Kurtis Kraft-Novi	–2m 56.86s	10	NA	F
5	A Linden	Kurtis Kraft-Offy	–3m 14.27s	12	NA	F
6	J Boyd	Kurtis Kraft-Offy	–4m 35.27s	5	NA	F

| Round 4/8 | **FRENCH GP** Rouen-les-Essarts | | **Juan Manuel Fangio** |
| | 7 July 1957 | Race 60 | Maserati 250F 160.960kph, 100.016mph |

Fangio's third victory in as many Grands Prix saw a sublime drive on a revised and enhanced Rouen circuit. 'This is for me,' the Maestro remarked, nailing pole by more than a second. His task was made easier by the absence of Moss through sickness, and of Brooks following his Le Mans accident. Collins, Behra and Musso contested second place, the Italian eventually leading in the three Lancia Ferraris that followed in Fangio's wake. Behra pushed his lifeless Maserati across the line to collect the final championship points. Notable was the debut of American Herbert McKay-Fraser in a BRM. Starting P12, he was sixth on lap 1 and still seventh when he retired with engine trouble on lap 24. A week later he perished in a F2 race.

POLE POSITION Fangio, Maserati, 2m 21.5s (1.1s), 166.440kph, 103.421mph
LAPS 77 x 6.542 km, 4.065 miles
DISTANCE 503.734 km, 313.006 miles
STARTERS/FINISHERS 15/7
WEATHER Sunny, hot, dry
LAP LEADERS Musso 1-3 (3); Fangio 4-77 (74)
WINNER'S LAPS 1 P3, 2-3 P2, 4-77 P1
FASTEST LAP Musso, Lancia Ferrari, 2m 22.4s (lap 65), 165.388kph, 102.767mph
CHAMPIONSHIP Fangio 25, Hanks 8, Rathmann 7, Musso 7, Behra 6

Pos	Driver	Car	Time/gap	Grid	Stops	Tyres
1	J M Fangio	Maserati	3h 7m 46.4s	1	0	P
2	L Musso	Lancia Ferrari	–50.8s	3	0	E
3	P Collins	Lancia Ferrari	–2m 6.0s	5	0	E
4	M Hawthorn	Lancia Ferrari	–1 lap	7	0	E
5	J Behra	Maserati	–7 laps	2	1	P
6	H Schell	Maserati	–7 laps	4	1	P

| Round 5/8 | **BRITISH GP** Aintree | | **Tony Brooks/Stirling Moss** |
| | 20 July 1957 | Race 61 | Vanwall VW (57) 139.696kph, 86.803mph |

Fittingly at the British GP, Vanwall became the first British car to win a championship race, and with British drivers too. Moss led easily until engine trouble intervened, so on lap 26 he replaced the still injured Brooks, rejoining ninth. Battling through the field, catching race leader Behra, he was still some 50s in arrears at half-distance. Another 20 sizzling laps brought him into contention, then on lap 69 the clutch on the leading Maserati exploded, the debris punctured the tyre of Hawthorn's following Lancia Ferrari, and suddenly Vanwalls were leading 1-2. The Lewis-Evans Vanwall stopped soon afterwards but Moss sailed on to an historic victory, time even for a precautionary fuel stop. Fangio never featured, retiring his sick-sounding car mid-race.

POLE POSITION Moss, Vanwall, 2m 0.2s (0.0s), 144.600kph, 89.850mph
LAPS 90 x 4.828 km, 3.000 miles
DISTANCE 434.523 km, 270.000 miles
STARTERS/FINISHERS 18/8
WEATHER Overcast, warm, dry
LAP LEADERS Moss 1-22, 70-90 (43); J Behra, Maserati 23-69 (47)
WINNER'S LAPS 1-22 P1, 23 P7, 29 P8, 30-34 P7, 35-39 P6, 40-46 P5, 47-69 P4, 70-90 P1
FASTEST LAP Moss, Vanwall, 1m 59.2s (lap NA), 145.813kph, 90.604mph
CHAMPIONSHIP Fangio 25, Musso 13, Brooks 10, Hanks 8, Rathmann 7

Pos	Driver	Car	Time/gap	Grid	Stops	Tyres
1	T Brooks/S Moss	Vanwall	3h 6m 37.8s	3	2	P
2	L Musso	Lancia Ferrari	–25.6s	10	0	E
3	M Hawthorn	Lancia Ferrari	–42.8s	5	1	E
4	M Trintignant/P Collins	Lancia Ferrari	–2 laps	9	2	E
5	R Salvadori	Cooper-Climax	–5 laps	15	NA	E
6	B Gerard	Cooper-Bristol	–8 laps	18	NA	E

| Round 6/8 | **GERMAN GP** Nürburgring | | **Juan Manuel Fangio** |
| | 4 August 1957 | Race 62 | Maserati 250F 137.656kph, 85.535mph |

With the Vanwalls unsuited to the Nordschleife, Italian machinery occupied the four-across front row. Fuelled light, Fangio planned to build a lead over the non-stopping Lancia Ferraris, but spent the first two laps behind them. Once by he pulled away, but slow pit work on lap 12 turned his 30s lead into a 50s deficit to new leaders Collins and Hawthorn. As he reeled in the Lancia Ferrari pair, engaged in their own victory duel, Fangio exhibited what is regarded as the greatest drive of his illustrious career. On lap 19 he stole 11s from them, leaving the lap record in shreds. On lap 21, the penultimate, he took Collins at the North Curve and Hawthorn at Breidscheid to win by 3.6s and seal his fifth drivers' crown. Fangio's final victory was truly his greatest.

POLE POSITION Fangio, Maserati, 9m 25.6s (2.8s), 145.184kph, 90.213mph
LAPS 22 x 22.810 km, 14.173 miles
DISTANCE 501.820 km, 311.816 miles
STARTERS/FINISHERS 24/15 (Including F2 cars)
WEATHER Sunny, hot, dry
LAP LEADERS Hawthorn 1-2, 15-20 (8); Fangio 3-11, 21-22 (11); Collins 12-14 (3)
WINNER'S LAPS 1-2 P3, 3-11 P1, 12-20 P3, 21-22 P1
FASTEST LAP Fangio, Maserati, 9m 17.4s (lap 20), 147.320kph, 91.540mph
CHAMPIONSHIP Fangio 34, Musso 16, Hawthorn 13, Brooks 10, Moss 8

Pos	Driver	Car	Time/gap	Grid	Stops	Tyres
1	J M Fangio	Maserati	3h 30m 38.3s	1	1	P
2	M Hawthorn	Lancia Ferrari	–3.6s	2	0	E
3	P Collins	Lancia Ferrari	–35.6s	4	0	E
4	L Musso	Lancia Ferrari	–3m 37.6s	8	0	E
5	S Moss	Vanwall	–4m 37.5s	7	0	P
6	J Behra	Maserati	–4m 38.5s	3	1	P

Maserati 250F

Round 7/8	**PESCARA GP** Pescara						**Stirling Moss**
	18 August 1957					**Race 63**	Vanwall VW (57) 154.006kph, 95.695mph

For reasons of Italian politics, the Ferrari works team were absent, although a lone car was privately entered for Musso, who lined up on the front row to face 18 laps around the circa 16-mile Pescara road circuit. Alongside were Moss' Vanwall and Fangio's pole-sitting Maserati. For four laps Moss and Musso diced for the lead before Moss began to open some daylight, pulling out a 15s gap by half-distance. On lap 10 the Lancia Ferrari's oil tank split and Musso was out. Fangio, following, was caught out by this, spinning on the slick and buckling a wheel, but by coaxing his damaged car to the pits he retained second place. But by then Moss was almost three minutes ahead, having enough time in hand to stop for oil and a well-earned drink on lap 11.

POLE POSITION Fangio, Maserati, 9m 44.6s (10.1s), 157.517kph, 97.876mph
LAPS 18 x 25.579 km, 15.894 miles
DISTANCE 460.422 km, 286.093 miles
STARTERS/FINISHERS 16/7
WEATHER Sunny, very hot, dry
LAP LEADERS L Musso, Lancia Ferrari 1 (1); Moss 2-18 (17)
WINNER'S LAPS 1 P2, 2-18 P1
FASTEST LAP Moss, Vanwall, 9m 44.6s (lap 9), 157.517kph, 97.876mph
CHAMPIONSHIP Fangio 40, Moss 17, Musso 16, Hawthorn 13, Brooks 10

Pos	Driver	Car	Time/gap	Grid	Stops	Tyres
1	S Moss	Vanwall	2h 59m 22.7s	2	1	P
2	J M Fangio	Maserati	−3m 13.9s	1	1	P
3	H Schell	Maserati	−6m 46.8s	5	NA	P
4	M Gregory	Maserati	−8m 16.5s	7	1	P
5	S Lewis-Evans	Vanwall	−1 lap	8	2	P
6	G Scarlatti	Maserati	−1 lap	10	1	P

Round 8/8	**ITALIAN GP** Monza						**Stirling Moss**
	8 September 1957					**Race 64**	Vanwall VW (57) 193.564kph, 120.275mph

What a sight: the Monza front row comprised three green Vanwalls, each piloted by a British driver, Stuart Lewis-Evans on pole. After Fangio's Maserati 250F, Behra's V12 version was P5, the best Lancia Ferrari, that of Collins, P7. The first 20 laps were a close slipstreaming battle between the Vanwalls and the Maseratis of Fangio and Behra. Gradually cars dropped away until just Moss and Fangio remained, but the Vanwall was clearly faster and Moss pressed home the advantage. At two-thirds-distance, as much to the dismay of the World Champion as it no doubt was to the *tifosi*, Moss actually lapped the second-placed Maserati before making a precautionary late pit stop with ten laps to go. British Racing Green had spectacularly triumphed at the spiritual home of Italian motorsport.

POLE POSITION S Lewis-Evans, Vanwall, 1m 42.4s (0.3s), 202.148kph, 125.609mph
LAPS 87 x 5.750 km, 3.573 miles
DISTANCE 500.250 km, 310.841 miles
STARTERS/FINISHERS 18/11
WEATHER Sunny, hot, dry
LAP LEADERS Moss 1-3, 5, 11, 21-87 (72); J Behra, Maserati 4, 6 (2); Fangio 7-10 (4); Brooks, Vanwall 12-15 (4); Lewis-Evans, Vanwall 16-20 (5)
WINNER'S LAPS 1-3 P1, 4 P2, 5 P1, 6-8 P2, 9-10 P3, 11 P1, 12 P2, 13-14 P5, 16-18 P4, 19 P3, 20 P2, 21-87 P1
FASTEST LAP T Brooks, Vanwall, 1m 43.7s (lap 74), 199.614kph, 124.035mph
CHAMPIONSHIP Fangio 40, Moss 25, Musso 16, Hawthorn 13, Brooks 11

Pos	Driver	Car	Time/gap	Grid	Stops	Tyres
1	S Moss	Vanwall	2h 35m 3.9s	2	1	P
2	J M Fangio	Maserati	−41.2s	4	1	P
3	W von Trips	Lancia Ferrari	−2 laps	8	1	E
4	M Gregory	Maserati	−3 laps	11	NA	P
5	G Scarlatti/H Schell	Maserati	−3 laps	12	1	P
6	M Hawthorn	Lancia Ferrari	−4 laps	10	1	E

1957 CHAMPIONSHIP FACTS AND FOLKLORE

- 1957 was another curtailed championship series, although eight rounds were run, including the Indy 500, with the best five results counting as usual.
- Financial disputes had caused the cancellation of the Belgian, Dutch and Spanish races, the almost 16-mile Pescara road circuit – the longest track ever used in the history of the championship – providing a never-to-be-repeated substitute.

- Along with Monza, this race formed an end-of-season Italian double-header, the first time two rounds had been staged in one country. Ironically, both were won in style by Stirling Moss and Vanwall, the British car and driver by this time a threat to all-comers.
- Fittingly the British breakthrough had occurred at Aintree, when the nightmare memory of the BRM V16 debacle was

RACE 62, German GP: On the penultimate lap Fangio took Collins (7) at the North Curve and Hawthorn (8) at Breidscheid to win his final and greatest victory and to seal his fifth driver's crown.

finally eradicated with a dream result for industrialist and Vanwall team owner Tony Vandervell.

■ The impetus for British teams and drivers gathered pace in 1957, including events offstage which would have a significant bearing on the future of F1.

■ The revival of Formula 2 racing saw Cooper race a car with rear-mounted Coventry-Climax motor. Indeed, the latter was campaigned by Jack Brabham in six of the 1957 championship races and, especially in 2-litre form, raised a few eyebrows.

■ Also of future importance, Ferrari unveiled a 1.5-litre V6 engine to compete in F2.

■ But in F1, Ferrari's dismal 1957 started appallingly badly in March when talented young Italian Eugenio Castellotti

was killed testing a new Lancia Ferrari at Modena. Now designated the Tipo 801, the car was barely recognisable without its characteristic side panniers.

■ Despite the success and popularity of the 250F, which accounted for 13 of the 20 starters at Monza, 1957 proved to be the final year of participation for the Maserati factory due to financial difficulties.

■ In April they fielded a new V12 engine for the first time, which made its championship debut at Monza. Inevitably the project was shelved, only for the V12 to reappear nine years later in the back of the 1966 Cooper-Maseratis.

■ So Fangio's stunning Nürburgring triumph not only clinched his fifth and final championship, but proved to be his own final race victory, as well as that of *Officine Alfieri Maserati*.

Championship ranking	Championship points	Driver nationality	1957 Drivers Championship Driver	Car	Races contested	Race victories	Podiumse excl. victories	Races led	Flag to flag victories	Laps led	Poles	Fastest laps	Triple Crowns
1	40	ARG	Juan Manuel Fangio	Maserati	7	4	2	5		263	4	2	2
2	25	GBR	Stirling Moss	Maserati (1) Vanwall (5)	6	3		4		136	2	3	1
3	16	ITA	Luigi Musso	Lancia Ferrari	6		2	2		4		1	
4	13	GBR	Mike Hawthorn	Lancia Ferrari	6		2	1		8			
5	11	GBR	Tony Brooks	Vanwall	5	1	1	1		4		1	
6	10	USA	Masten Gregory	Maserati	4		1						
7	10	USA	Harry Schell	Maserati	7		1						
8	8	USA	Sam Hanks	Epperly-Offenhauser	1	1		1		136			
9	8	GBR	Peter Collins	Lancia Ferrari	6		2	2		16			
10	7	USA	Jim Rathmann	Epperly-Offenhauser	1		1	1		24		1	
11	6	FRA	Jean Behra	Maserati	6		1	3		57			
12	5	FRA	Maurice Trintignant	Lancia Ferrari	3								
12	5	GBR	Stuart Lewis-Evans	Connaught (1) Vanwall (5)	6			1		5	1		
14	4	ARG	Carlos Menditéguy	Maserati	4		1						
14	4	USA	Jimmy Bryan	Kuzma-Offenhauser	1		1						
14	4	GER	Wolfgang von Trips	Lancia Ferrari	3		1						
17	3	USA	Paul Russo	Kurtis Kraft-Offenhauser	1			1		24			
18	2	USA	Andy Linden	Kurtis Kraft-Offenhauser	1								
18	2	GBR	Roy Salvadori	Vanwall (1) Cooper-Climax (3)	4								
20	1	ESP	Alfonso de Portago	Lancia Ferrari	1								
20	1	ARG	José Froilán González	Lancia Ferrari	1								
20	1	ITA	Giorgio Scarlatti	Maserati	4								
-	0	USA	Pat O'Connor	Kurtis Kraft-Offenhauser	1			1		7	1		
-	0	USA	Johnny Thomson	Kuzma-Offenhauser	1			1		5			
-	0	USA	Troy Ruttman	Watson-Offenhauser	1			1		4			
-	0	ITA	Eugenio Castellotti	Lancia Ferrari	1			1		6			

Championship ranking	Championship points	Team/Marque nationality	1957 Constructors Results (Excl. Indy 500) Chassis	Engine	Engine maker nationality	Races contested	Race victories	1-2 finishes	Podiums excl. victories	Races led	Laps led	Poles	Fastest laps
N/A	N/A	ITA	Maserati 250F	Maserati 2.5 S6, 2.5 V12	ITA	7	4	1	6	6	320	5	3
N/A	N/A	ITA	Lancia Ferrari 801, Ferrari 500	Lancia Ferrari 2.5 V8, Ferrari 2.5 S4	ITA	7			7	4	34		1
N/A	N/A	GBR	Vanwall VW57	Vanwall 2.5 S4	GBR	6	3		1	4	145	2	3
N/A	N/A	GBR	Connaught B 'Syracuse'	Alta 2.5 S4	GBR	1							
N/A	N/A	GBR	Cooper T43	Coventry-Climax 1.5 S4, 2.0 S4	GBR	4							

1958

Mike pips magnanimous Moss

THE TALE OF THE TITLE

- 1958 was a 'Battle of Britain', fought out between Mike Hawthorn's Ferrari and Stirling Moss in the Vanwall.
- Moss won more races, four to one, but at the final round Hawthorn snatched the title by a single point.
- In Portugal, Moss' chivalrous gesture towards his opponent was decisive in the outcome of their rivalry.
- Vanwall deservedly landed the inaugural constructors' trophy, winning six rounds to Ferrari's two.
- Vanwall's Tony Brooks and Ferrari's Peter Collins each contributed superb victories for their teams.
- But the battle between Vanwall and Ferrari was hard fought, the cost heavy.
- Vanwall lost Stuart Lewis-Evans, Ferrari Luigi Musso and Peter Collins.
- The 1958 championship began with back-to-back wins for a diminutive Cooper, sparking a F1 revolution.
- Moss' Argentinean championship victory in the Walker Cooper-Climax was the first for a rear-engined car.
- Mid-season, five-times world champion Juan Manuel Fangio announced his retirement.
- But it was three events around the turn of the year that truly rocked the F1 world.
- The newly crowned F1 champions announced their exit, Hawthorn his retirement, Vanwall their withdrawal.
- Then, on 22 January 1959, Mike Hawthorn was killed in a road accident.
- And not forgetting: Avgas fuel.

THE CHASE FOR THE CHAMPIONSHIP

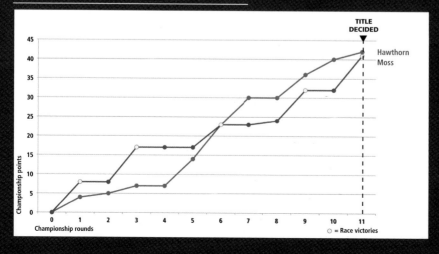

Round 1/11	**ARGENTINEAN GP** Buenos Aires No 2		**Stirling Moss**
	19 January 1958	**Race 65**	Cooper-Climax T43 134.547kph, 83.604mph

Stirling Moss began the new season by completing a championship victory hat-trick. Driving Rob Walker's private Cooper-Climax, he also recorded the second triumph for a British team/marque and the first championship race victory for a rear-engined car. Fangio had annexed his customary Buenos Aires pole, his quasi-works Maserati taking the lead from Hawthorn's Ferrari on lap 10. But a stop for tyres on lap 34 allowed Moss' Cooper to assume the lead, a lead he never lost because unexpectedly he did not stop, much to the chagrin of his rivals. It was a narrow victory, 3.6s from Musso's charging Ferrari, and a finely judged one, his tyres showing the canvas. Only ten cars participated, Vanwall and BRM still struggling to master the new fuel regulations.

POLE POSITION Fangio, Maserati, 1m 42.0s (0.6s), 138.071kph, 83.604mph
LAPS 80 x 3.912 km, 2.431 miles
DISTANCE 312.960 km, 194.464 miles
STARTERS/FINISHERS 10/9
WEATHER Sunny, warm, dry
LAP LEADERS Behra 1 (1); Hawthorn 2-9 (8); Fangio 10-34 (25); Moss 35-80 (46)
WINNER'S LAPS 1-2 P3, 3 P4, 4-9 P5, 10-17 P4, 18-20 P3, 21-34 P2, 35-80 P1
FASTEST LAP Fangio, Maserati, 1m 41.8s (lap 30), 138.382kph, 85.962mph
CHAMPIONSHIP Moss 8, Musso 6, Hawthorn 4, Fangio 4, Behra 2

Pos	Driver	Car	Time/gap	Grid	Stops	Tyres
1	S Moss	Cooper-Climax	2h 19m 33.7s	7	0	C
2	L Musso	Ferrari	−2.7s	5	1	E
3	M Hawthorn	Ferrari	−12.6s	2	1	E
4	J M Fangio	Maserati	−53.0s	1	1	P
5	J Behra	Maserati	−2 laps	4	2	P
6	H Schell	Maserati	−3 laps	8	NA	P

TOP **100** RACE

R.R.C. Walker Cooper-Climax T43

Round 2/11	**MONACO GP** Monte Carlo		**Maurice Trintignant**
	18 May 1958	**Race 66**	Cooper-Climax T45 109.414kph, 67.986mph

A second successive victory for Rob Walker's Cooper-Climax, this time Trintignant at the wheel. Brooks' Vanwall was on pole, but from the middle of the front row Behra's BRM led until quarter-distance. Brake problems put paid to him, leaving Hawthorn's Ferrari Dino leading from a challenging Moss, now Vanwall-mounted. Moss took the lead on lap 33 but it was short-lived as he retired with valve trouble six laps later. Hawthorn led again followed at 30s by Trintignant, who had started P5 but benefited from the attrition ahead of him. So when Hawthorn coasted to a halt with a broken fuel pump on lap 46, a rather surprised Trintignant won followed at a distance by the Ferraris of Musso and Collins.

POLE POSITION T Brooks, Vanwall, 1m 39.8s (1.0s), 113.447kph, 70.493mph
LAPS 100 x 3.145km, 1.954 miles
DISTANCE 314.500 km, 195.421 miles
STARTERS/FINISHERS 16/6
WEATHER Sunny, hot, dry
LAP LEADERS J Behra, BRM 1-27 (27); Hawthorn 28-32, 39-47 (14); S Moss, Vanwall 33-38 (6); Trintignant 48-100 (53)
WINNER'S LAPS 1-3 P5, 4-11 P6, 12-22 P5, 23-27 P4, 28-38 P3, 39-47 P2, 48-100 P1
FASTEST LAP M Hawthorn, Ferrari, 1m 40.6s (lap 36), 112.545kph, 69.932mph
CHAMPIONSHIP Musso 12, Moss 8, Trintignant 8, Hawthorn 5, Collins 4

Pos	Driver	Car	Time/gap	Grid	Stops	Tyres
1	M Trintignant	Cooper-Climax	2h 52m 27.9s	5	0	D
2	L Musso	Ferrari	−20.2s	10	0	E
3	P Collins	Ferrari	−38.8s	9	0	E
4	J Brabham	Cooper-Climax	−3 laps	3	1	D
5	H Schell	BRM	−9 laps	12	NA	D
6	W von Trips	Ferrari	−13 laps	11	NA	E

Round 3/11	**DUTCH GP** Zandvoort		**Stirling Moss**
	26 May 1958	**Race 67**	Vanwall VW (57) 151.166kph, 93.930mph

Vanwalls swept the front row, Lewis-Evans claiming a second pole ahead of Moss and Brooks. Behra's BRM and Brabham's Cooper were next, Hawthorn's best-placed Ferrari on the third row. Moss led from start to finish, winning at a canter. Hawthorn even had to bear the ignomity of being lapped by Moss on lap 49. With the Ferraris barely in the hunt and the other Vanwalls destined not to finish, it was the BRMs of Harry Schell and Jean Behra which took the remaining podium places, the team's best championship result to date, and the only other cars to be on the same lap as the flying winner. Hawthorn's Ferrari eventually finished fifth behind four British cars, and after three rounds already trailed Moss by the considerable margin of ten points.

POLE POSITION S Lewis-Evans, Vanwall, 1m 37.1s (0.9s), 155.456kph, 96.596mph
LAPS 75 x 4.193 km, 2.605 miles
DISTANCE 314.475 km, 195.406 miles
STARTERS/FINISHERS 17/11
WEATHER Overcast, dry, windy
LAP LEADERS Moss 1-75 (75)
WINNER'S LAPS 1-75 P1
FASTEST LAP Moss, Vanwall, 1m 37.6s (lap NA), 154.660kph, 96.101mph
CHAMPIONSHIP Moss 17, Musso 12, Trintignant 8, Schell 8, Hawthorn 7

Pos	Driver	Car	Time/gap	Grid	Stops	Tyres
1	S Moss	Vanwall	2h 4m 49.2s	2	0	D
2	H Schell	BRM	-47.9s	7	0	D
3	J Behra	BRM	-1m 42.3s	4	0	D
4	R Salvadori	Cooper-Climax	-1 lap	9	0	D
5	M Hawthorn	Ferrari	-1 lap	6	0	E
6	C Allison	Lotus-Climax	-2 laps	11	NA	D

Round 4/11	**INDIANAPOLIS 500** Indianapolis		**Jimmy Bryan**
	30 May 1958	**Race 68**	Epperly-Offenhauser 215.316kph, 133.791mph

Fangio took his rookie test but did not participate in qualifying. For a second year George Salih's Epperly-Offenhauser won, finishing 1, 2, 4 and 5, winner Jimmy Bryan successfully negotiating a first-lap pile-up to beat rookie George Amick in an accident strewn race, Pat O'Connor fatally injured. On lap 149 rookie A.J. Foyt spun out. Few would have recognised a future Indianapolis giant, AJ eventually becoming the first of just three drivers to win the '500' a record four times, 1961, 1964, 1967 and, remarkably, 1977, the others Al Unser Sr and Rick Mears. His first victory, 1961, was the first year that the Indy 500 was excluded from the championship. It also marked the second foray by a pukka F1 team, twice F1 champion Jack Brabham finishing ninth in a Cooper-Climax.

POLE POSITION Rathmann, Epperly-Offy, 4m 6.62s (0.08s), 234.922kph, 145.974mph
LAPS 200 x 4.023 km, 2.500 miles
DISTANCE 804.672 km, 500.000 miles
STARTERS/FINISHERS 33/13
WEATHER Sunny, warm, dry
LAP LEADERS Bryan 1-18, 26, 31, 47-48, 50-52, 66-104, 126-200 (139); Bettenhausen 19-20, 22-25, 35, 49, 53-65, 105-107 (24); E Sachs, Kuzma-Offy 21 (1); Amick 27-30, 32-34, 36-46 (18); Boyd 108-125 (18)
WINNER'S LAPS NA
FASTEST LAP Bettenhausen, Epperly-Offy, 1m 2.37s (lap 55), 232.229kph, 144.300mph
CHAMPIONSHIP Moss 17, Musso 12, Trintignant 8, Bryan 8, Schell 8

Pos	Driver	Car	Time/gap	Grid	Stops	Tyres
1	J Bryan	Epperly-Offy	3h 44m 13.80s	7	NA	F
2	G Amick	Epperly-Offy	-27.63s	25	NA	F
3	J Boyd	Kurtis Kraft-Offy	-1m 9.97s	8	NA	F
4	T Bettenhausen	Epperly-Offy	-1m 34.81s	9	NA	F
5	J Rathmann	Epperly-Offy	-1m 35.62s	20	NA	F
6	J Reece	Watson-Offy	-2m 16.95s	3	NA	F

Round 5/11	**BELGIAN GP** Spa-Francorchamps		**Tony Brooks**
	15 June 1958	**Race 69**	Vanwall VW (57) 209.093kph, 129.925mph

Ferrari returned to form at Spa with Hawthorn and Musso heading the Vanwalls after qualifying. Moss led but missed a gear out of Stavelot, buzzed his engine, and was out on lap 1. Brooks and Collins then duelled for the lead until the Ferrari went out with overheating after just five laps. But Ferrari were still in the hunt, Hawthorn and Musso chasing Brooks until the Italian crashed out with a tyre burst. Concerned it was Collins, Hawthorn slowed, and by the time he knew all was well Brooks was 40s up the road. Rounding La Source on the final lap Brooks' car appeared at a crawl, jammed in gear, Hawthorn's engine poured smoke and steam, and Lewis-Evans' tottered in on broken suspension, but that's the way the top three crossed the line.

POLE POSITION Hawthorn, Ferrari, 3m 57.1s (0.4s), 214.087kph, 133.027mph
LAPS 24 x 14.100 km, 8.761 miles
DISTANCE 338.400 km, 210.272 miles
STARTERS/FINISHERS 19/10
WEATHER Sunny, very hot, dry
LAP LEADERS Brooks 1, 3, 5-24 (22); Collins, Ferrari 2, 4 (2)
WINNER'S LAPS 1 P1, 2 P2, 3 P1, 4 P2, 5-24 P1
FASTEST LAP Hawthorn, Ferrari, 3m 58.3s (lap 24), 213.009kph, 132.358mph
CHAMPIONSHIP Moss 17, Hawthorn 14, Musso 12, Schell 10, Trintignant 8

Pos	Driver	Car	Time/gap	Grid	Stops	Tyres
1	T Brooks	Vanwall	1h 37m 6.3s	5	0	D
2	M Hawthorn	Ferrari	-20.7s	1	0	E
3	S Lewis-Evans	Vanwall	-3m 0.9s	11	0	D
4	C Allison	Lotus-Climax	-4m 15.5s	12	0	D
5	H Schell	BRM	-1 lap	7	0	D
6	O Gendebien	Ferrari	-1 lap	6	1	E

Vanwall VW (57)

Round 6/11	**FRENCH GP** Reims				
	6 July 1958				Race 70

Mike Hawthorn
Ferrari Dino 246 201.905kph, 125.458mph

Hawthorn was unstoppable at Reims, taking pole position, leading all the way and recording fastest lap. But Ferrari joy was to be muted as poor Luigi Musso suffered a fatal accident on lap 9. Running second to Hawthorn, he lost control of his Ferrari on the fast right-hand sweep after the pits, the Ferrari somersaulted over a ditch and the unfortunate driver was thrown out. The race continued and behind Hawthorn a hard-fought battle eventually saw Moss come through to second from von Trips in another Ferrari. Moss and Hawthorn were now locked together at the top of the points table. Making only his second appearance of the season, reigning World Champion Fangio finished fourth driving the Maserati 250F 'Piccolo' in what was to be his final Grand Prix.

POLE POSITION Hawthorn, Ferrari, 2m 21.7s (0.7s), 210.919kph, 131.059mph
LAPS 50 x 8.302 km, 5.159 miles
DISTANCE 415.100 km, 257.931 miles
STARTERS/FINISHERS 21/11
WEATHER Sunny, warm, dry
LAP LEADERS Hawthorn 1-50 (50)
WINNER'S LAPS 1-50 P1
FASTEST LAP Hawthorn, Ferrari, 2m 24.9s (lap 45), 206.261kph, 128.165mph
CHAMPIONSHIP Moss 23, Hawthorn 23, Musso 12, Schell 10, Trintignant 8

Pos	Driver	Car	Time/gap	Grid	Stops	Tyres
1	M Hawthorn	Ferrari	2h 3m 21.3s	1	0	E
2	S Moss	Vanwall	−24.6s	6	0	D
3	W von Trips	Ferrari	−59.7s	21	0	E
4	J M Fangio	Maserati	−2m 30.6s	8	1	P
5	P Collins	Ferrari	−5m 24.9s	4	0	E
6	J Brabham	Cooper-Climax	−1 lap	12	NA	D

Ferrari Dino 246

Round 7/11	**BRITISH GP** Silverstone							**Peter Collins**	
	19 July 1958					Race 71		Ferrari Dino 246 164.232kph, 102.049mph	

A second successive Ferrari victory, this time on Vanwall's home turf. Any disappointment for the crowd was assuaged by a British winner, Peter Collins. From row two, Collins snatched a lead at Becketts that he was never to relinquish. Moss' Vanwall, from pole, battled Hawthorn for second place but the Vanwall blew up in a big way on lap 26, Hawthorn's P2 now secure. Behind him, Salvadori's Cooper and the Lewis-Evans Vanwall scrapped over third until, on lap 44, Hawthorn screamed into the pits for more oil. He rejoined just ahead of Salvadori to assure a brilliant Ferrari 1-2 victory and, for the first time, Hawthorn led Moss in the championship. At the line, Salvadori narrowly beat Lewis-Evans by just 0.2s.

POLE POSITION S Moss, Vanwall, 1m 39.4s (0.4s), 170.603kph, 106.008mph
LAPS 75 x 4.711 km, 2.927 miles
DISTANCE 353.291 km, 219.525 miles
STARTERS/FINISHERS 20/9
WEATHER Sunny, warm, dry
LAP LEADERS Collins 1-75 (75)
WINNER'S LAPS 1-75 P1
FASTEST LAP Hawthorn, Ferrari, 1m 40.8s (lap 50), 168.234kph, 104.536mph
CHAMPIONSHIP Hawthorn 30, Moss 23, Collins 14, Musso 12, Schell 12

Pos	Driver	Car	Time/gap	Grid	Stops	Tyres
1	P Collins	Ferrari	2h 9m 4.2s	6	0	E
2	M Hawthorn	Ferrari	−24.2s	4	1	E
3	R Salvadori	Cooper-Climax	−50.6s	3	0	D
4	S Lewis-Evans	Vanwall	−50.8s	7	0	D
5	H Schell	BRM	−1m 14.8s	2	0	D
6	J Brabham	Cooper-Climax	−1m 23.2s	10	0	D

Round 8/11	**GERMAN GP** Nürburgring							**Tony Brooks**	
	3 August 1958					Race 72		Vanwall VW (57) 145.338kph, 90.309mph	

The Ferrari-Vanwall battle intensified. The contenders for race victory and championship honours filled the front row: Hawthorn, Brooks, Moss, Collins. First Moss led chased by Hawthorn and Collins, but on lap 4 he parked the Vanwall at Schwalbenschwar with magneto failure. With his team-leader out, Brooks rose to the challenge, reeling-in the 30s gap to the Ferrari drivers to overtake first Hawthorn then Collins to lead lap 11. Then tragedy. Collins, attempting to battle the rapid Vanwall, overdid it at Pflanzgarten and somersaulted with fatal consequences in full view of his teammate. Less than a lap later Hawthorn retired his Ferrari with a broken clutch. Brooks won from the Coopers of Salvadori and Trintignant.

POLE POSITION M Hawthorn, Ferrari, 9m 14.0s (1.0s), 148.224kph, 92.102mph
LAPS 15 x 22.810 km, 14.173 miles
DISTANCE 342.150 km, 212.602 miles
STARTERS/FINISHERS 25/11 (Including F2 cars)
WEATHER Overcast, warm, dry
LAP LEADERS Moss 1-3 (3); Hawthorn 4 (1); P Collins, Ferrari 5-10 (6); Brooks 11-15 (5)
WINNER'S LAPS 1-3 P4, 4-10 P3, 11-15 P1
FASTEST LAP S Moss, Vanwall, 9m 9.2s (lap 3), 149.519kph, 92.907mph
CHAMPIONSHIP Hawthorn 30, Moss 24, Brooks 16, Collins 14, Salvadori 13

Pos	Driver	Car	Time/gap	Grid	Stops	Tyres
1	T Brooks	Vanwall	2h 21m 15.0s	2	0	D
2	R Salvadori	Cooper-Climax	−3m 29.7s	6	0	D
3	M Trintignant	Cooper-Climax	−5m 11.2s	7	0	D
4	W von Trips	Ferrari	−6m 16.3s	5	1	E
5	C Allison	Lotus-Climax	−2 laps	24	1	D
-	Only five classified finishers	-	-	-	-	-

Round 9/11	**PORTUGUESE GP** Porto							**Stirling Moss**	
	24 August 1958					Race 73		Vanwall VW (57) 169.028kph, 105.029mph	

In qualifying, the title rivals were separated by five-hundredths of a second. From pole Moss led but up the main straight Hawthorn took the lead on lap 2 and held it for five more. But the Ferrari was in brake trouble, Moss going by to score his third victory. Stopping on lap 25 for attention to his brakes, Behra's BRM got ahead of Hawthorn but he battled back to P2, also setting fastest lap. Significantly for the eventual championship outcome, Moss misread his pit-signals and made no special effort to gain the extra point awarded for fastest lap. Further, Hawthorn spun on the final lap and by rejoining the track from the wrong direction was disqualified. In the post-race wrangle with the stewards, Moss intervened on Hawthorn's behalf, his P2, and six points, reinstated.

POLE POSITION Moss, Vanwall, 2m 34.21s (0.05s), 172.915kph, 107.444mph
LAPS 50 x 7.407 km, 4.602 miles
DISTANCE 370.350 km, 230.125 miles
STARTERS/FINISHERS 15/9
WEATHER Overcast, damp track then drying
LAP LEADERS Moss 1, 8-50 (44); Hawthorn 2-7 (6)
WINNER'S LAPS 1 P1, 2-7 P2, 8-50 P1
FASTEST LAP Hawthorn, Ferrari, 2m 32.37s (lap 36), 175.003kph, 108.742mph
CHAMPIONSHIP Hawthorn 36, Moss 32, Brooks 16, Collins 14, Salvadori 13

Pos	Driver	Car	Time/gap	Grid	Stops	Tyres
1	S Moss	Vanwall	2h 11m 27.80s	1	0	D
2	M Hawthorn	Ferrari	−5m 12.75s	2	1	E
3	S Lewis-Evans	Vanwall	−1 lap	3	0	D
4	J Behra	BRM	−1 lap	4	NA	D
5	W von Trips	Ferrari	−1 lap	6	NA	E
6	H Schell	BRM	−1 lap	7	NA	D

Round 10/11	**ITALIAN GP** Monza
	7 September 1958

Race 74

Tony Brooks
Vanwall VW (57) 195.078kph, 121.216mph

Following his brake troubles in Portugal, Hawthorn's Ferrari was sporting disc brakes for the first time, qualifying on the front row with three Vanwalls. After an incursion by Phil Hill's Ferrari in the opening laps, the Hawthorn/Moss battle quickly resumed at the head of the field until Moss retired with gearbox trouble on lap 17. The Ferraris took command, but once again Brooks played the perfect role for Vanwall. Delayed by an early pit visit, Brooks was now making relentless progress. When the Ferraris made tyre stops mid-race he was suddenly in contention, sweeping past Hawthorn with ten laps to go. His superb victory wrapped up the constructors' championship for Vanwall and kept open Moss' chances at the upcoming Casablanca finale.

POLE POSITION S Moss, Vanwall, 1m 40.5s (0.7s), 205.970kph, 127.984mph
LAPS 70 x 5.750 km, 3.573 miles
DISTANCE 402.500 km, 250.102 miles
STARTERS/FINISHERS 21//
WEATHER Sunny, hot, dry
LAP LEADERS P Hill 1-4, 35-37 (7); Hawthorn 5-6, 9, 15-34, 38-60 (46); Moss 7-8,10-14 (7); Brooks 61-70 (10)
WINNER'S LAPS 1-6 P5, 7-11 P4, 12-13 P5, 14 P9, 15-17 P8, 18-24 P7, 25-29 P6, 30 P5, 31-37 P4, 38-45 P3, 46-60 P2, 61-70 P1
FASTEST LAP P Hill, Ferrari, 1m 42.9s (lap 26), 201.166kph, 124.999mph
CHAMPIONSHIP Hawthorn 40, Moss 32, Brooks 24, Salvadori 15, Collins 14

Pos	Driver	Car	Time/gap	Grid	Stops	Tyres
1	T Brooks	Vanwall	2h 3m 47.8s	2	1	D
2	M Hawthorn	Ferrari	−24.2s	3	1	E
3	P Hill	Ferrari	−28.3s	7	2	E
4	M Gregory/C Shelby	Maserati	−1 lap	11	1	P
5	R Salvadori	Cooper-Climax	−8 laps	14	NA	D
6	G Hill	Lotus-Climax	−8 laps	12	NA	D

Round 11/11	**MOROCCAN GP** Âin-Diab, Casablanca
	19 October 1958

Race 75

Stirling Moss
Vanwall VW (57) 187.427kph, 116.462mph

Hawthorn and Moss lined up for the championship decider, the Ferrari on pole. Moss' only chance was to win the race and set fastest lap. This he did, leading all the way. But if Hawthorn finished second, the championship was his regardless. Moss looked home and dry when Hawthorn was relegated to fourth by Brooks on lap 19, but the Vanwall engine didn't last and Brooks retired on lap 30. Ferrari driver Phil Hill, running second, was asked to ease up and, with 13 laps remaining, waved his team leader through to championship glory. Two laps later Stuart Lewis-Evans' Vanwall, running fifth, blew its engine, ran off the circuit and caught fire. The unfortunate driver, overalls ablaze, leapt from the car but succumbed to serious burns the following week.

POLE POSITION Hawthorn, Ferrari, 2m 23.1s (0.1s), 191.648kph, 119.084mph
LAPS 53 x 7.618 km, 4.734 miles
DISTANCE 403.754 km, 250.881 miles
STARTERS/FINISHERS 25/16 (Including F2 cars)
WEATHER Sunny, warm, dry
LAP LEADERS Moss 1-53 (53)
WINNER'S LAPS 1-53 P1
FASTEST LAP Moss, Vanwall, 2m 22.5s (lap 21), 192.455kph, 119.586mph
CHAMPIONSHIP Hawthorn 42, Moss 41, Brooks 24, Salvadori 15, Collins 14

Pos	Driver	Car	Time/gap	Grid	Stops	Tyres
1	S Moss	Vanwall	2h 9m 15.1s	2	0	D
2	M Hawthorn	Ferrari	−1m 24.7s	1	0	E
3	P Hill	Ferrari	−1m 25.5s	5	0	E
4	J Bonnier	BRM	−1m 46.7s	8	0	D
5	H Schell	BRM	−2m 33.7s	10	NA	D
6	M Gregory	Maserati	−1 lap	13	NA	P

1958 CHAMPIONSHIP FACTS AND FOLKLORE

- Including the Indy 500, the calendar expanded to 11 rounds, with Portugal added and the championship extended to Africa by a one-off race in Casablanca, which would host the finale.
- Minimum race-distance reverted to 300km (186.41 miles) or two hours, 500km (310.69 miles) now the maximum duration.
- A world championship for constructors was introduced along similar lines to the drivers' contest, points awarded to the highest-placed team car/marque only.
- The best six results counted towards both championships, but drivers' points were no longer awarded for shared drives, this and the reduced minimum race-distance making pit-stops the exception rather then the rule.
- Alcohol-based fuel brews were banned, commercial 100–130 octane aviation fuel (Avgas) becoming the norm in response to lobbying by the oil companies to enhance their advertising opportunities.
- Having won three of the last four rounds the previous season, Vanwall entered 1958 odds-on favourite for the newly instigated constructors' championship, their number-one driver Stirling Moss favourite for the drivers' title, having been runner-up to Fangio the past three years.
- One unforeseen barrier to success was the difficulty Vanwall, and BRM for that matter, had encountered in adapting their engines to the new fuel regulations. This forced both teams to miss the first championship round, although Moss still won a landmark victory for Cooper.
- Moss became the first driver to win in a rear-engined car, driving R.R.C. Walker's blue privately entered 2-litre Cooper-Climax to victory in Argentina, Trintignant repeating the success at Monaco.
- Fangio, winner of the Argentinean GP the previous four years, had made the race his own. This time the reigning champion finished fourth in what turned out to be his penultimate Grand Prix, announcing his retirement later in the season.

- Fangio's decision to retire in 1958 was in recognition of an inescapable truth: a sea change had occurred in Grand Prix racing. He is reported to have said: 'Surrounded by rear-engined cars painted green, I realised it was the end of an era.'
- Probably the greatest driver of all time, he was undoubtedly the greatest exponent of taming the hefty, front-engined machines with their narrow, treaded tyres, so evocative of the 1950s.
- Stirling Moss stated: 'I have never driven against, nor subsequently identified, a driver who was better in a single-seater than the great Argentine, Juan Manuel Fangio…'
- Along with his five world titles, Fangio amassed a tally of 24 victories from 51 GP starts, an amazing strike-rate of 47%, unsurpassed to this day.
- In Fangio's absence, any significant challenge to Moss in 1958 was expected to materialise from Maranello, the Scuderia dumping the Lancia Ferrari derivatives and fielding new equipment, the Dino 246, for their primary drivers Hawthorn, Collins and Musso.

- The Ferrari 'Dino' was so named in memory of Enzo's 24-year-old son who sadly died of ill health in 1956. Derived from the F2 car, the 2.4-litre V6 engine produced 280bhp at 8,500rpm, the cylinder head, importantly, being originally designed for petrol rather than alcohol brews.
- A stirring championship battle ensued between two British drivers, Hawthorn and Moss, which was ultimately decided in favour of Hawthorn by a single point at the Casablanca showdown.
- With hindsight, the 'Battle of Britain' was effectively decided at Porto, due, from Moss's perspective, partly to a mistake and partly to his remarkable sporting magnanimity.
- What compelled the new world champion's post-season decision not to defend his title and retire aged 29 is open to conjecture. The tragedy which befell Collins, his 'Mon Ami, Mate', certainly sapped his motivation, but his kidney ailments may have been a factor too.
- On 22 January 1959, just months after his retirement announcement, Hawthorn died in a road accident on the Guildford bypass driving his potent British Racing Green 3.4 Mk 1 Jaguar, with Rob Walker in a Mercedes 300 SL ahead

RACE 66, Monaco GP: 1958 saw a 'Battle of Britain' between Mike Hawthorn's Ferrari (38) and Stirling Moss in the Vanwall (28), here fighting 'around the houses' at Monte Carlo.

of him. He lost control in rainy conditions and wrapped the car round a tree – some say a hawthorn. Whether it was driver error, mechanical failure or a blackout, Britain's 'Golden Boy' was dead.

■ In the same month, at the pinnacle of his success, Tony Vandervell announced his personal withdrawal from his Vanwall project, a decision partly stemming from the Lewis-Evans tragedy, but ostensibly due to ill-health. The marque stumbled on for a couple more years but made only two further championship appearances, one in 1959, the other 1960, both uncompetitive.

■ But as one door closes… Team Lotus made their debut in 1958 with a front-engined F2 derivative powered by the Coventry-Climax engine, the Lotus 16. Often called 'the mini-Vanwall' – the pens of Colin Chapman and Frank Costin prominent in both designs – the Lotus emphasised low frontal area.

■ Also debuting in 1958 was New Zealander Bruce McLaren in an F2 Cooper as well as two future world champions with a shared surname – Graham Hill with Team Lotus and, after a one-off Maserati drive, American Phil Hill with Ferrari.

■ At Spa, Signorina Maria de Filippis became the first woman to compete in a championship race, while at Monaco a certain Bernard Charles Ecclestone failed to qualify a Connaught.

■ Adrian Newey was born in 1958.

Championship ranking	Championship points	Driver nationality	1958 Drivers Championship		Races contested	Race victories	Podiumse victories	Podiumse excl. victories	Races led	Flag to flag victories	Laps led	Poles	Fastest laps	Triple Crowns
			Driver	Car										
1	42	GBR	Mike Hawthorn	Ferrari	10	1	6	6	1		125	4	5	1
2	41	GBR	Stirling Moss	Cooper-Climax (1) Vanwall (9)	10	4	1	7	1		234	3	3	
3	24	GBR	Tony Brooks	Vanwall	9	3		3	1		37	1		
4	15	GBR	Roy Salvadori	Cooper-Climax	9		2							
5	14	GBR	Peter Collins	Ferrari	7	1	1	3	1		83			
6	14	USA	Harry Schell	Maserati (1) BRM (9)	10		1							
7	12	FRA	Maurice Trintignant	Cooper-Climax (7) Maserati (1) BRM (1)	9	1	1	1			53			
8	12	ITA	Luigi Musso	Ferrari	5		2							
9	11	GBR	Stuart Lewis-Evans	Vanwall	8		2					1		
10	9	USA	Phil Hill	Maserati (1) Ferrari (3)	4		2	1			7		1	
11	9	GER	Wolfgang von Trips	Ferrari	6		1							
11	9	FRA	Jean Behra	Maserati (1) BRM (9)	10		1	2			28			
13	8	USA	Jimmy Bryan	Epperly-Offenhauser	1	1			1		139			
14	7	ARG	Juan Manuel Fangio	Maserati	2				1		25	1	1	
15	6	USA	George Amick	Epperly-Offenhauser	1		1		1		18			
16	4	USA	Johnny Boyd	Kurtis Kraft-Offenhauser	1		1		1		18			
17	4	USA	Tony Bettenhausen	Epperly-Offenhauser	1				1		24		1	
18	3	AUS	Jack Brabham	Cooper-Climax	9									
18	3	GBR	Cliff Allison	Lotus-Climax (8) Maserati (1)	9									
18	3	SWE	Jo Bonnier	Maserati (7) BRM (2)	9									
21	2	USA	Jim Rathmann	Epperly-Offenhauser	1									
-	0	USA	Dick Rathmann	Watson-Offenhauser	1								1	
-	0	USA	Eddie Sachs	Kuzma-Offenhauser	1			1			1			

Championship ranking	Championship points	Team/Marque nationality	1958 Constructors Championship (Excl. Indy 500)		Engine maker nationality	Races contested	Race victories	1-2 finishes	Podiums excl. victories	Races led	Laps led	Poles	Fastest laps
			Chassis	Engine									
1	48	GBR	Vanwall VW57	Vanwall 2.5 S4	GBR	9	6		3	7	225	5	3
2	40	ITA	Ferrari Dino 246	Ferrari 2.4 V6	ITA	10	2	1	12	8	215	4	6
3	31	GBR	Cooper T45, T43	Coventry-Climax 2.0 S4, 2.2 S4	GBR	10	2		3	2	99		
4	18	GBR	BRM P25	BRM 2.5 S4	GBR	9			2	1	27		
5	6	ITA	Maserati 250F	Maserati 2.5 S6	ITA	10			1		26	1	1
6	3	GBR	Lotus 12, 16	Coventry-Climax 2.0 S4, 2.2 S4	GBR	9							

1959

Cooper rewrite the rules

THE TALE OF THE TITLE

- In a sea-change season Jack Brabham won the title, rear-engined Coopers victorious in five of eight GPs.
- Cooper and Coventry-Climax were constructors' champions, three wins for the works team, two for Walker.
- Moss' potent challenge was punished by Coletti gearbox fallibility, depriving him of two certain victories.
- The front-engined Ferrari Dinos still had the legs of the Coopers on the French and German power circuits.
- Brooks' two victories for Ferrari matched Brabham and Moss, the title undecided until the Sebring finale.
- Another front-engined victor was Jo Bonnier at Zandvoort, BRM triumphing at long last.
- At Sebring, Bruce McLaren became the youngest-ever GP winner at the age of 22.
- 1959 saw Aston Martin make their GP debut and Porsche their first factory entry.
- And not forgetting: the Cooper streamliner.

THE CHASE FOR THE CHAMPIONSHIP

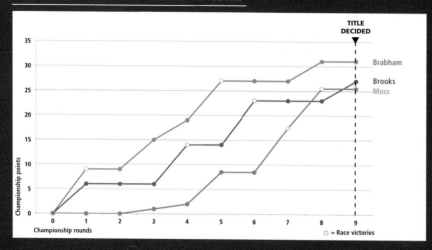

Cooper-Climax T51

| Round 1/9 | **MONACO GP** Monte Carlo | | | | | **Jack Brabham** |
| | 10 May 1959 | | | Race 76 | | Cooper-Climax T51 107.304kph, 66.676mph |

Moss in Rob Walker's Cooper, Behra's Ferrari, and Brabham in the works Cooper gave the front row of the new season a very different appearance. These three would lead the 100 laps 'round the houses', Behra initially by making a fine start to lead the opening 21 harried by Moss. First Moss then Brabham slipped by Behra, the Ferrari out soon afterwards with engine trouble. Moss pulled away relentlessly from Brabham, nearly 30s clear by lap 40, a full minute on lap 75. But six laps later certain victory was denied when his Colotti gearbox gave out. Brabham had it in the bag, a maiden victory for the driver as well as the Cooper works team, leading in Brooks in a Ferrari and the 1958 winner, Trintignant, in the second Walker Cooper.

POLE POSITION S Moss, Cooper-Climax, 1m 39.6s (0.4s), 113.675kph, 70.634mph
LAPS 100 x 3.145km, 1.954 miles
DISTANCE 314.500 km, 195.421 miles
STARTERS/FINISHERS 16/6
WEATHER Sunny, hot, dry
LAP LEADERS J Behra, Ferrari 1-21 (21); Moss 22-81 (60); Brabham 82-100 (19)
WINNER'S LAPS 1-22 P3, 23-81 P2, 82-100 P1
FASTEST LAP Brabham, Cooper-Climax, 1m 40.4s (lap 83), 112.769kph, 70.071mph
CHAMPIONSHIP Brabham 9, Brooks 6, Trintignant 4, P Hill 3, McLaren 2

Pos	Driver	Car	Time/gap	Grid	Stops	Tyres
1	J Brabham	Cooper-Climax	2h 55m 51.3s	3	0	D
2	T Brooks	Ferrari	−20.4s	4	0	D
3	M Trintignant	Cooper-Climax	−2 laps	6	1	D
4	P Hill	Ferrari	−3 laps	5	1	D
5	B McLaren	Cooper-Climax	−4 laps	13	1	D
6	R Salvadori	Cooper-Maserati	−17 laps	8	1	D

| Round 2/9 | **INDIANAPOLIS 500** Indianapolis | | | | | **Rodger Ward** |
| | 30 May 1959 | | | Race 77 | | Watson-Offenhauser 218.641kph, 135.857mph |

In practice, Jerry Unser died of burns and Bob Cortner was fatally injured when he hit the wall. In one of the most competitive races in history a record 16 cars finished the entire 500 miles. Rodger Ward, Jim Rathmann, Johnny Thomson and Pat Flaherty were evenly matched, their four cars engaged in a see-saw battle for the first three-quarters of the race. Eventually it was narrowed down to a two-way fight, Flaherty hitting the wall on lap 163 and spinning to a stop at the pit entrance, Thomson slowed by a broken torsion bar to finish third. As the laps were reeled off it became clear that Rodger Ward would hold off Rathmann for victory. He finally finished some 23s ahead of Rathmann, who ran out of fuel as he crossed the line.

POLE POSITION Thomson, Lesovsky-Offy, 4m 6.73s (0.82s), 234.815kph, 145.907mph
LAPS 200 x 4.023 km, 2.500 miles
DISTANCE 804.672 km, 500.000 miles
STARTERS/FINISHERS 33/16
WEATHER Cloudy, warm, dry
LAP LEADERS Thomson 1-4, 49-84 (40); Ward 5-12, 14-16, 46-48, 85-200 (130); Rathmann 13, 17-30, 32-33, 41-42 (19); P Flaherty, Watson-Offy, 31, 34-40, 43-45 (11)
WINNER'S LAPS NA
FASTEST LAP Thomson, Lesovsky-Offy, 1m 1.89s (lap 64), 234.030kph, 145.419mph
CHAMPIONSHIP Brabham 9, Ward 8, Brooks 6, Rathmann 6, Thomson 5

Pos	Driver	Car	Time/gap	Grid	Stops	Tyres
1	R Ward	Watson-Offy	3h 40m 49.20s	6	NA	F
2	J Rathmann	Watson-Offy	−23.28s	3	NA	F
3	J Thomson	Lesovsky-Offy	−50.64s	1	NA	F
4	T Bettenhausen	Epperly-Offy	−1m 47.09s	15	NA	F
5	P Goldsmith	Epperly-Offy	−2m 6.44s	16	NA	F
6	J Boyd	Epperly-Offy	−3m 16.98s	11	NA	F

BRM P25

Round 3/9	**DUTCH GP** Zandvoort						**Jo Bonnier**
	31 May 1959					Race 78	BRM P25 150.411kph, 93.461mph

Having tested extensively at Zandvoort the week prior, BRM took pole, Jo Bonnier leading most of the race to bring BRM championship glory at long last. Bonnier spent much of the race dicing with Coopers. Initially it was the works pair of Gregory and Brabham until both cars dropped back with similar gear selection difficulties, eventually finishing second and third. Keen to preserve his tyres, Moss had made a cautious start from P3, eighth on the first lap. Picking his way through the field, he passed Gregory on lap 27, Brabham lap 48, taking the lead from Bonnier on lap 60 as the pair lapped Behra. But just as at Monaco, the Colotti gearbox packed up and the unlucky Moss was out three laps later.

POLE POSITION Bonnier, BRM, 1m 36.0s (0.0s), 157.238kph, 97.703mph
LAPS 75 x 4.193 km, 2.605 miles
DISTANCE 314.475 km, 195.406 miles
STARTERS/FINISHERS 15/10
WEATHER Sunny, warm, dry
LAP LEADERS Bonnier 1, 12-29, 34-59, 63-75 (58); Gregory 2-11 (10); Brabham 30-33 (4); Moss 60-62 (3)
WINNER'S LAPS 1 P1, 2-11 P2, 12-29 P1, 30-33 P2, 34-59 P1, 60-62 P2, 63-75 P1
FASTEST LAP S Moss, Cooper-Climax, 1m 36.7s (lap 42), 156.099kph, 96.996mph
CHAMPIONSHIP Brabham 15, Ward 8, Bonnier 8, Brooks 6, Rathmann 6

Pos	Driver	Car	Time/gap	Grid	Stops	Tyres
1	J Bonnier	BRM	2h 5m 26.8s	1	0	D
2	J Brabham	Cooper-Climax	–14.2s	2	0	D
3	M Gregory	Cooper-Climax	–1m 23.0s	7	0	D
4	I Ireland	Lotus-Climax	–1 lap	9	0	D
5	J Behra	Ferrari	–1 lap	4	0	D
6	P Hill	Ferrari	–2 laps	12	0	D

Round 4/9	**FRENCH GP** Reims						**Tony Brooks**
	5 July 1959					Race 79	Ferrari Dino 246 205.086kph, 127.435mph

The fast Reims circuit suited the V6 Ferrari engine, Brooks using the power advantage to take pole and steadily ease away to lead every lap and a Ferrari 1-2 triumph. Teammate Phil Hill's race was more fraught, seeing off various challenges from Trintignant, Behra, Moss and Brabham in a high-speed slipstreamer made particularly challenging due to the hot sunshine melting the track surface at the Thillois hairpin. Its gradual disintegration caused numerous offs as well as driver abrasions from flying stones and tar. On lap 43 Moss, driving a BRP-entered BRM, spun at Thillois. Without a clutch since half-distance he was unable to restart unaided and disqualification was inevitable. With third place, Brabham now had 19 points, Moss still to score.

POLE POSITION T Brooks, Ferrari, 2m 19.4s (0.3s), 214.399kph, 133.211mph
LAPS 50 x 8.302 km, 5.159 miles
DISTANCE 415.100 km, 257.931 miles
STARTERS/FINISHERS 21/11
WEATHER Sunny, very hot, dry
LAP LEADERS Brooks 1-50 (50)
WINNER'S LAPS 1-50 P1
FASTEST LAP S Moss, BRM, 2m 22.8s (lap 40), 209.294kph, 130.049mph
CHAMPIONSHIP Brabham 19, Brooks 14, P Hill 9, Ward 8, Bonnier 8

Pos	Driver	Car	Time/gap	Grid	Stops	Tyres
1	T Brooks	Ferrari	2h 1m 26.5s	1	0	D
2	P Hill	Ferrari	–27.5s	3	0	D
3	J Brabham	Cooper-Climax	–1m 37.7s	2	0	D
4	O Gendebien	Ferrari	–1m 47.5s	11	0	D
5	B McLaren	Cooper-Climax	–1m 47.7s	10	0	D
6	R Flockhart	BRM	–2m 5.7s	13	0	D

Round 5/9	**BRITISH GP** Aintree						**Jack Brabham**
	18 July 1959					**Race 80**	Cooper-Climax T51 144.655kph, 89.884mph

A labour dispute absented Ferrari, while Salvadori caused a stir by planting the Aston Martin next to pole-man Brabham. The race initially appeared a Brabham walkover, the Australian running away as he pleased, 2.5s on the first lap, 10s by lap 5. Moss, again driving the pale green BRP BRM, had other ideas. Starting P7, he emerged from the early-laps squabble, and after a short dice with Schell's works car, was on his own. By lap 25 he had stabilised Brabham's advantage to 15s, down to 10s by lap 50. But it was an illusion, separate stops for tyres and fuel dropping him down to third. At least by pipping Bruce McLaren by 0.2s in an exciting climax Moss prevented a Cooper 1-2, McLaren almost getting alongside as they crossed the line.

POLE POSITION Brabham, Cooper-Climax, 1m 58.0s (0.0s), 147.296kph, 91.525mph
LAPS 75 x 4.828 km, 3.000 miles
DISTANCE 362.102 km, 225.000 miles
STARTERS/FINISHERS 24/13
WEATHER Sunny, warm, dry
LAP LEADERS Brabham 1-75 (75)
WINNER'S LAPS 1-75 P1
FASTEST LAP Moss, BRM/McLaren Cooper-Climax, 1m 57.0s (lap 69/75), 148.555kph, 92.308mph
CHAMPIONSHIP Brabham 27, Brooks 14, P Hill 9, Moss 8.5, McLaren 8.5

Pos	Driver	Car	Time/gap	Grid	Stops	Tyres
1	J Brabham	Cooper-Climax	2h 30m 11.6s	1	0	D
2	S Moss	BRM	–22.2s	7	2	D
3	B McLaren	Cooper-Climax	–22.4s	8	0	D
4	H Schell	BRM	–1 lap	3	1	D
5	M Trintignant	Cooper-Climax	–1 lap	4	0	D
6	R Salvadori	Aston Martin	–1 lap	2	0	A

Round 6/9	**GERMAN GP** AVUS						**Tony Brooks**
	2 August 1959					**Race 81**	Ferrari Dino 246 230.686kph, 143.342mph

The race was overshadowed by the death of Jean Behra in the supporting sports car event. Because of concern over tyre failures, particularly on the steeply banked North Curve, the race was held over two heats. As at Reims, the AVUS circuit suited Ferrari, Brooks leading from pole and generally having the measure of the rest in the closely fought slipstreaming battle. Moss' Walker Cooper was out after only two laps with transmission trouble, the works cars, notably Gregory, disputing the lead in heat 1. But Gregory's engine grenaded and Brabham's clutch packed up, so the three Ferraris headed the heat 2 grid, Brooks leading Gurney and Phil Hill to a resounding Ferrari 1-2-3, and suddenly challenging Brabham's championship points lead.

POLE POSITION Brooks, Ferrari, 2m 5.9s (0.9s), 237.331kph, 147.471mph
LAPS 60 x 8.300 km, 5.157 miles (2 x 30 lap heats, results aggregated)
DISTANCE 498.000 km, 309.443 miles
STARTERS/FINISHERS 15/7
WEATHER Overcast, warm, dry
LAP LEADERS Heat 1: Brooks 1-2, 4-13, 18, 20-21, 23-30 (23); M Gregory, Cooper-Climax 3, 15, 19, 22 (4); Gurney 14, 16-17 (3). Heat 2: P Hill 31, 36, 39, 45, 48-49 (6); Brooks 32-35, 37-38, 40, 42, 46-47, 52-60 (19); Gurney 41, 43-44, 50-51 (5)
WINNER'S LAPS Heat 1: 1-2 P1, 3 P2, 4-13 P1, 14-15 P2, 16 P3, 17 P2, 18 P1, 19 P2, 20-21 P1, 22 P2, 23-30 P1. Heat 2: 31 P3, 32-35 P1, 36 P2, 37-38 P1, 39 P2, 40 P1, 41 P2, 42 P1, 43 P2, 44 P3, 45 P2, 46-47 P1, 48 P3, 49-51 P2, 52-60 P1
FASTEST LAP S Brooks, Ferrari, 2m 4.5s (lap 18), 240.000kph, 149.129mph
CHAMPIONSHIP Brabham 27, Brooks 23, P Hill 13, Bonnier 10, Trintignant 9

Pos	Driver	Car	Time/gap	Grid	Stops	Tyres
1	T Brooks	Ferrari	2h 9m 31.6s	1	0	D
2	D Gurney	Ferrari	–2.9s	3	0	D
3	P Hill	Ferrari	–1m 4.8s	6	0	D
4	M Trintignant	Cooper-Climax	–1 lap	12	0	D
5	J Bonnier	BRM	–2 laps	7	1	D
6	I Burgess	Cooper-Maserati	–4 laps	15	0	D

Round 7/9	**PORTUGUESE GP** Monsanto Park						**Stirling Moss**
	23 August 1959					**Race 82**	Cooper-Climax T51 153.398kph, 95.317mph

Moss' Walker Cooper-Climax dominated practice. The works cars alongside beat him off the line but by the end of the first lap he had taken a lead he was never to lose, recording fastest lap and lapping the entire field. Championship points leader Brabham lay a safe second until lap 24, when, overtaking a backmarker, he misjudged his line into a corner, struck the straw bales and careered into a telegraph pole. Jack was flung from the car, fortunate to escape serious injury. What's more, Brooks, the other championship contender, also failed to score, the Ferraris in disappointing form throughout the meeting. Belatedly, Moss championship challenge sprang to life at last.

POLE POSITION Moss, Cooper-Climax, 2m 2.89s (2.0s), 159.632kph, 99.023mph
LAPS 62 x 5.440 km, 3.380 miles
DISTANCE 337.280 km, 209.576 miles
STARTERS/FINISHERS 16/10
WEATHER Sunny, hot, dry
LAP LEADERS Moss 1-62 (62)
WINNER'S LAPS 1-62 P1
FASTEST LAP Moss, Cooper-Climax, 2m 5.07s (lap 28), 156.584kph, 97.297mph
CHAMPIONSHIP Brabham 27, Brooks 23, Moss 17.5, P Hill 13, Trintignant 12

Pos	Driver	Car	Time/gap	Grid	Stops	Tyres
1	S Moss	Cooper-Climax	2h 11m 55.41s	1	0	D
2	M Gregory	Cooper-Climax	–1 lap	3	0	D
3	D Gurney	Ferrari	–1 lap	6	0	D
4	M Trintignant	Cooper-Climax	–2 laps	4	0	D
5	H Schell	BRM	–3 laps	9	0	D
6	R Salvadori	Aston Martin	–3 laps	12	0	A

Round 8/9	**ITALIAN GP** Monza						
	13 September 1959				Race 83		

Stirling Moss
Cooper-Climax T51 200.177kph, 124.384mph

The three championship contenders, Moss, Brooks and Brabham, occupied the front row. To the dismay of the *tifosi*, Brooks' Ferrari was out within yards of the start with clutch failure. Phil Hill kept Ferrari hopes alive by leading much of the first half of the race, Moss and Brabham content to conserve tyres. Around half-distance the Ferrari challenge for victory faded, Hill leading the four front-engined cars into their tyre stops. However, Hill managed to at least rejoin before Brabham went by, although even on fresh rubber he found Moss to be uncatchable. A second successive victory truly brought Moss into championship reckoning and clinched the constructors' title for Cooper. With P3, Brabham retained his slim but useful points lead.

POLE POSITION S Moss, Cooper-Climax, 1m 39.7s (0.1s), 207.623kph, 129.011mph
LAPS 72 x 5.750 km, 3.573 miles
DISTANCE 414.000 km, 257.248 miles
STARTERS/FINISHERS 21/15
WEATHER Sunny, warm, dry
LAP LEADERS Moss 1, 4, 15, 33-72 (43); P Hill 2-3, 5-14, 16-32 (29)
WINNER'S LAPS 1 P1, 2-3 P2, 4 P1, 5 P2, 6 P3, 7-14 P2, 15 P1, 16-32 P2, 33-72 P1
FASTEST LAP P Hill, Ferrari, 1m 40.4s (lap 32), 206.175kph, 128.111mph
CHAMPIONSHIP Brabham 31, Moss 25.5, Brooks 23, P Hill 20, Gurney 13

Pos	Driver	Car	Time/gap	Grid	Stops	Tyres
1	S Moss	Cooper-Climax	2h 4m 5.4s	1	0	D
2	P Hill	Ferrari	−46.7s	5	1	D
3	J Brabham	Cooper-Climax	−1m 12.5s	3	0	D
4	D Gurney	Ferrari	−1m 19.6s	4	1	D
5	C Allison	Ferrari	−1 lap	8	1	D
6	O Gendebien	Ferrari	−1 lap	6	1	D

Round 9/9	**UNITED STATES** GP Sebring						
	12 December 1959				Race 84		

Bruce McLaren
Cooper-Climax T51 159.047kph, 98.827mph

Because of the 'best five' scoring system, the three contenders each needed victory to be certain of the title. Chased by Brabham, Moss roared into a growing lead, but tension didn't last long. After a mere five laps Moss was out with yet another broken gearbox while Brooks was never in the hunt for victory. So Brabham became the new champion and looked to be about to lift his title in style with a third race victory. But on the final lap his Cooper ran dry, producing an exciting race finish. Teammate McLaren shot past Brabham to defy a fast-closing Trintignant by 0.6s and become the youngest-ever GP winner. The new champion didn't need to finish but elected to push his dead car a quarter-mile uphill to finish fourth in a virtual state of collapse.

POLE POSITION S Moss, Cooper-Climax, 3m 0.0s (3.0s), 167.372kph, 104.000mph
LAPS 42 x 8.369 km, 5.200 miles
DISTANCE 351.481 km, 218.400 miles
STARTERS/FINISHERS 18/7
WEATHER Sunny, warm, dry
LAP LEADERS Moss 1-5 (5); Brabham 6-41 (36); McLaren 42 (1)
WINNER'S LAPS 1-5 P3, 6-41 P2, 42 P1
FASTEST LAP Trintignant, Cooper-Climax, 3m 5.0s (lap 39), 162.848kph, 101.189mph
CHAMPIONSHIP Brabham 31, Brooks 27, Moss 25.5, P Hill 20, Trintignant 19

Pos	Driver	Car	Time/gap	Grid	Stops	Tyres
1	B McLaren	Cooper-Climax	2h 12m 35.7s	10	0	D
2	M Trintignant	Cooper-Climax	−0.6s	5	0	D
3	T Brooks	Ferrari	−3m 0.9s	4	0	D
4	J Brabham	Cooper-Climax	−4m 57.3s	2	0	D
5	I Ireland	Lotus-Climax	−3 laps	9	NA	D
6	W von Trips	Ferrari	−4 laps	6	NA	D

TOP **100** RACE

1959 CHAMPIONSHIP FACTS AND FOLKLORE

- Monsanto Park replaced Porto, the German GP transferred to the AVUS on a one-off basis, and America hosted a second championship round; the first official United States GP would be held at Sebring.
- US connections extended even further when Dan Gurney became the latest American driver to become a F1 regular, joining Schell, Phil Hill, Gregory and Shelby, while 1958 Indy 500 winner and USAC champion Rodger Ward was invited by the Sebring organisers to represent an all-American entry. Much to the surprise of the driver, the F1 brigade, especially around the corners, comprehensively blew off his Kurtis Kraft-Offy midget racer.
- Including the Indy 500 there were nine rounds, the best five results counting towards the championships.
- Without Vanwall, Maserati, Fangio and Hawthorn, the 1959 season saw a changing of the old guard, although some continuity would be provided by the presence of SEFAC Ferrari and Stirling Moss.
- F1 also took on a very different shape as the thinking behind

chassis design transformed forever.
- Moss campaigned a blue Rob Walker Cooper-Climax as well as making a couple of outings in a pale green BRM entered by the British Racing Partnership, a concern operated by Stirling's former manager Ken Gregory and his father Alfred Moss.
- Moss' temporary switch to BRP became necessary while Alf Francis attempted to rectify the Walker Cooper's Colotti gearbox gremlins, the Italian gearbox selected by patron Rob Walker in preference to the modified Citroën units used by the works team.
- For use by the Cooper and Lotus works teams and the Rob Walker cars, Coventry-Climax had developed a full-scale 2.5-litre FPF engine that at least partially narrowed the power deficit to the Ferraris.
- Although a comparative Grand Prix minnow, there were high expectations for the Cooper Car Company from Surbiton, with Jack Brabham, Bruce McLaren and Masten Gregory driving the green cars with their distinctive white trim.

- The seriousness of their 1959 campaign could be gauged by the development of all-enveloping streamlined bodywork, albeit only used in practice by Brabham at Reims, to help offset the Ferrari power advantage on high-speed tracks.
- Rear-engined Coopers of one hue or another were to win five of the eight championship rounds, the Indy 500 excepted, Brabham and Moss entering the final race at Sebring each capable of championship success. If Moss won and Brabham was second, the title would be decided by whichever one of them earned the extra point for fastest lap, it was that close.
- But there was a third contender, erstwhile Vanwall driver Tony Brooks replacing Hawthorn at Maranello.
- On the long straights of Reims and the AVUS Brooks used the power of his Ferrari to good effect to equal the two victories chalked up by both Brabham and Moss, so also went to Sebring with an outside chance of the title.

- Apart from an unrepresentative one-off victory in 1960, the resounding 1-2-3 in Germany was the last roll of the dice for the outmoded front-engined machines represented by Ferrari's Dino 246.
- The engine of the only other winning car was also forward of the driver, Jo Bonnier bringing belated joy to BRM eight years after their fanfare debut, the Bourne car at last combining some reliability with its undoubted speed.
- It was reliability, or the lack of it, which did for Moss' championship aspirations, eliminated at least twice on the verge of victory, the Colotti five-speed gearbox his Achilles heel.
- But that's motor racing, and with two wins plus three podiums Jack Brabham displayed a level of speed together with tenacity that marked him out as a new force in Formula 1.

Championship ranking	Championship points	Driver nationality	1959 Drivers Championship		Races contested	Race victories	Podiumse excl. victories	Races led	Flag to flag victories	Laps led	Poles	Fastest laps	Triple Crowns
			Driver	Car									
1	31	AUS	Jack Brabham	Cooper-Climax	8	2	3	4	1	134	1	1	
2	27	GBR	Tony Brooks	Ferrari (7) Vanwall (1)	8	2	2	2	1	92	2	1	1
3	25.5	GBR	Stirling Moss	Cooper-Climax (6) BRM (2)	8	2	1	5	1	173	4	4	1
4	20	USA	Phil Hill	Ferrari	7		3	2		35		1	
5	19	FRA	Maurice Trintignant	Cooper-Climax	8		2					1	
6	16.5	NZL	Bruce McLaren	Cooper-Climax	7	1	1	1		1		1	
7	13	USA	Dan Gurney	Ferrari	4		2	1		8			
8	10	SWE	Jo Bonnier	BRM	7	1		1		58	1		
9	10	USA	Masten Gregory	Cooper-Climax	6		2	2		14			
10	8	USA	Rodger Ward	Watson-Offenhauser (1) Kurtis Kraft-Offenhauser (1)	2	1		1		130			
11	6	USA	Jim Rathmann	Watson-Offenhauser	1		1	1		19			
12	5	USA	Johnny Thomson	Lesovsky-Offenhauser	1		1	1		40	1	1	
13	5	USA	Harry Schell	BRM (7) Cooper-Climax (1)	8								
13	5	GBR	Innes Ireland	Lotus-Climax	6								
15	3	USA	Tony Bettenhausen	Epperly-Offenhauser	1								
15	3	BEL	Olivier Gendebien	Ferrari	2								
17	2	USA	Paul Goldsmith	Epperly-Offenhauser	1								
17	2	FRA	Jean Behra	Ferrari	3			1		21			
17	2	GBR	Cliff Allison	Ferrari	5								
-	0	USA	Pat Flaherty	Watson-Offenhauser	1			1		11			

Championship ranking	Championship points	Team/Marque nationality	1959 Constructors Championship (Excl. Indy 500)		Engine maker nationality	Races contested	Race victories	1-2 finishes	Podiums excl. victories	Races led	Laps led	Poles	Fastest laps
			Chassis	Engine									
1	40	GBR	Cooper T51, T45	Coventry-Climax 2.5 S4, 2.2 S4	GBR	8	5	2	8	7	322	5	5
2	32	ITA	Ferrari Dino 246/256, Dino 156	2.4/2.5 V6, 1.5 V6	ITA	7	2	2	7	4	156	2	2
3	18	GBR	BRM P25	BRM 2.5 S4	GBR	7	1		1	1	58	1	2
4	5	GBR	Lotus 16	Coventry-Climax 2.5 S4, 1.5 S4	GBR	8							

◀ RACE 82, Portuguese GP: For Moss, 1959 was a second successive championship near miss. His potent challenge was punished by reliability, or the lack of it, depriving him of two certain victories. Here in Portugal the Colotti gearbox on his Walker Cooper-Climax held together for the first of his two late victories.

RACE 162, South African GP: On New Year's Day 1968, Jim Clark won at Kyalami, his 25th victory surpassing Fangio's benchmark. Round two held in May felt like a different era: no green-and-yellow Lotus livery; cars sprouting aerodynamic appendages; and no Jim Clark, his death casting a prolonged and gloomy shadow.

THE SIXTIES

Cigarettes and whisky

AEROFOILS AND SPONSORSHIP ARRIVED, AND BRITISH TEAMS AND DRIVERS, LED BY CLARK AND LOTUS, NEVER HAD IT SO GOOD

1960

Brabham back-to-back

THE TALE OF THE TITLE

- In the final season of the 2.5-litre Formula 1, Brabham and Cooper were conclusive back-to-back champions.
- Five successive wins pulverised the opposition, the T53 'lowline' Cooper-Climax quick and reliable.
- The works Coopers won six of eight rounds entered, the Surbiton marque populating up to half of some grids.
- The R.R.C. Walker team switched to Cheshunt, Moss bringing Lotus their first two championship victories.
- But at Spa an ill-fated GP curtailed his challenge, Moss and Taylor badly injured, Stacey and Bristow killed.
- Remarkably, Moss resumed F1 in eight weeks, his Riverside victory accentuating what might have been.
- The rear-engined Mk18 established Lotus, but team drivers Ireland, Surtees and Clark failed to win with it.
- Phil Hill's Ferrari won a hollow final victory for front-engined cars, the British teams boycotting Monza.
- Graham Hill's rear-engined BRM came oh-so-close to a Silverstone sensation.
- And not forgetting: the final championship Indy 500.

THE CHASE FOR THE CHAMPIONSHIP

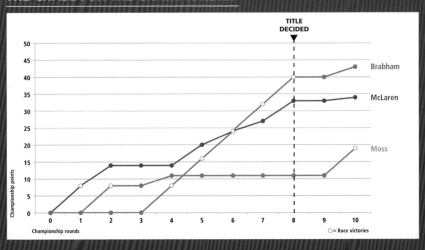

Round 1/10	**ARGENTINEAN GP** Buenos Aires No 2	**Bruce McLaren**
	7 February 1960 Race 85	Cooper-Climax T51 136.242kph, 84.657mph

The rear-engined Lotus 18 made its debut, Innes Ireland planting the new car alongside pole-sitter Moss in the Walker Cooper, the two front-engined BRMs of G. Hill and Bonnier completing the front row. The Lotus shot into the lead, and although short-lived – Ireland spinning down to sixth on lap 2 – the car's devastating performance and diminutive profile caused a sensation. For many laps Moss and Bonnier vied for the lead before Moss made his attack, pulling away until a suspension breakage put him out at half-distance. Bonnier regained the lead from Ireland's recovering Lotus until both hit problems, handing McLaren a second successive, albeit improbable, victory having started P12. Champion Brabham made an inauspicious start to his title defence.

POLE POSITION Moss, Cooper-Climax, 1m 36.9s (1.6s), 145.337kph, 90.309mph
LAPS 80 x 3.912 km, 2.431 miles
DISTANCE 312.960 km, 194.464 miles
STARTERS/FINISHERS 22/14
WEATHER Sunny, very hot, dry
LAP LEADERS I Ireland, Lotus-Climax 1 (1); J Bonnier, BRM 2-15, 21-36, 41-67 (57); Moss 16-20, 37-40 (9); McLaren 68-80 (13)
WINNER'S LAPS 1-4 P9, 5-25 P8, 26-32 P7, 33-37 P6, 38-40 P5, 41-42 P4, 43-62 P3, 63-67 P2, 68-80 P1
FASTEST LAP Moss, Cooper-Climax, 1m 38.9s (lap 37), 142.398kph, 88.482mph
CHAMPIONSHIP McLaren 8, Allison 6, Menditéguy 3, von Trips 2, Ireland 1

Pos	Driver	Car	Time/gap	Grid	Stops	Tyres
1	B McLaren	Cooper-Climax	2h 17m 49.5s	13	0	D
2	C Allison	Ferrari	–26.3s	7	0	D
3	M Trintignant/S Moss	Cooper-Climax	–36.9s	8	1	D
4	C Menditéguy	Cooper-Maserati	–53.3s	12	1	D
5	W von Trips	Ferrari	–1 lap	5	1	D
6	I Ireland	Lotus-Climax	–1 lap	2	1	D

R.R.C. Walker Lotus-Climax 18

Round 2/10	**MONACO GP** Monte Carlo	**Stirling Moss**
	29 May 1960 Race 86	Lotus-Climax 18 107.304kph, 66.676mph

Now driving an R.R.C. Walker Lotus 18, Moss took pole by a clear second from Brabham's new 'low-line' T53 Cooper. Race leadership changed five times between these two and Bonnier in the rear-engined BRM. Moss took the lead from Bonnier on lap 17 but lost it to Brabham when it began to rain around lap 30, only for the Australian to spin out in the treacherous conditions on lap 41, reinstating Moss. Then on lap 60 Moss pitted with a loose plug lead and his 20s advantage became a 10s deficit. On the now dry track, it took Stirling only seven laps to retake the lead from Bonnier, who cruelly failed to finish, only four cars left circulating. Moss' victory was the first for a Lotus while debutant Richie Ginther finished sixth in a rear-engined Ferrari.

POLE POSITION Moss, Lotus-Climax, 1m 36.3s (1.0s), 117.570kph, 73.055mph
LAPS 100 x 3.145km, 1.954 miles
DISTANCE 314.500 km, 195.421 miles
STARTERS/FINISHERS 16/9
WEATHER Dry start, rain then drying
LAP LEADERS Bonnier 1-16, 61-67 (23); Moss 17-33, 41-60, 68-100 (70); J Brabham, Cooper-Climax 34-40 (7)
WINNER'S LAPS 1-4 P3, 5-16 P2, 17-33 P1, 34-40 P2, 41-60 P1, 61-67 P2, 68-100 P1
FASTEST LAP McLaren, Cooper-Climax, 1m 36.2s (lap 11), 117.692kph, 73.131mph
CHAMPIONSHIP McLaren 14, Moss 8, Allison 6, P Hill 4, Menditéguy 3

Pos	Driver	Car	Time/gap	Grid	Stops	Tyres
1	S Moss	Lotus-Climax	2h 53m 45.5s	1	1	D
2	B McLaren	Cooper-Climax	–52.1s	11	0	D
3	P Hill	Ferrari	–1m 1.9s	10	0	D
4	T Brooks	Cooper-Climax	–1 lap	3	1	D
5	J Bonnier	BRM	–17 laps	5	0	D
6	R Ginther	Ferrari	–30 laps	9	0	D

INDIANAPOLIS 500 Indianapolis

30 May 1960   Race 87

Jim Rathmann
Watson-Offenhauser 223.324kph, 138.767mph

Finishing second in 1957 and 1959, Jim Rathmann's first and only victory marked the final inclusion of the Indy 500 in the F1 world championship. (The alliance with Indy would return 40 years on when F1 cars raced on a purpose-built track incorporating parts of the famous Indy 'oval'.) Just five years later Colin Chapman and Jim Clark finally proved with the Lotus-Ford 38 that F1 was indeed the technological pinnacle of motorsport, trouncing the local machinery after having given fair notice with a P2 in 1963 with the Lotus 29. But with the USA hosting their first F1 GP at Sebring in 1959 and the second at Riverside this year, the role of the Indianapolis 500-mile race – to bring world standing to the F1 championship – was over.

Pos	Driver	Car	Time/gap	Grid	Stops	Tyres
1	J Rathmann	Watson-Offy	3h 36m 11.36s	2	NA	F
2	R Ward	Watson-Offy	−12.75s	3	NA	F
3	P Goldsmith	Epperly-Offy	−3m 7.30s	26	NA	F
4	D Branson	Phillips-Offy	−3m 7.98s	8	NA	F
5	J Thomson	Lesovsky-Offy	−3m 11.35s	17	NA	F
6	E Johnson	Trevis-Offy	−4m 10.61s	7	NA	F

POLE POSITION E Sachs, Ewing-Offy, 4m 5.58s (0.37s), 235.917kph, 146.582mph
LAPS 200 x 4.023 km, 2.500 miles
DISTANCE 804.672 km, 500.000 miles
STARTERS/FINISHERS 33/16
WEATHER Cloudy, warm, dry
LAP LEADERS Ward 1, 4-18, 38-41, 123-127, 142-146, 148-151, 163-169, 171-177, 183-189,194-196 (58); Sachs, Ewing-Offy 2-3, 42-51, 57-61, 70-72, 75 (21); Ruttman, Watson-Offy 19-24, 52-56, (11); Rathmann 25-37, 62-69, 73-74, 76-85, 96-122, 128-141, 147, 152-162, 170, 178-182, 190-193, 197-200 (100); Thomson 86-95 (10)
WINNER'S LAPS NA
FASTEST LAP Rathmann, Watson-Offy, 1m 1.59s (lap 197), 235.170kph, 146.128mph
CHAMPIONSHIP McLaren 14, Moss 8, Rathmann 8, Allison 6, Ward 6

DUTCH GP Zandvoort

6 June 1960   Race 88

Jack Brabham
Cooper-Climax T53 154.931kph, 96.270mph

From his third consecutive pole, Moss chased Brabham for 17 laps until he was forced to make a pit stop for a punctured tyre caused by a piece of kerbing thrown up from the leading Cooper. From there Brabham's first victory of the season was never in doubt, attention turning to Moss' brilliant recovery drive, scything through the field and smashing the lap record repeatedly. Jim Clark debuted for Lotus, duelling impressively with Graham Hill until transmission trouble intervened. Hill achieved his first podium for BRM, finishing third behind Ireland and just managing to stay ahead of the flying Moss. A spectator died when Gurney's BRM left the track with brake failure. The youth had been standing in a prohibited area at Tarzan.

Pos	Driver	Car	Time/gap	Grid	Stops	Tyres
1	J Brabham	Cooper-Climax	2h 1m 47.2s	2	0	D
2	I Ireland	Lotus-Climax	−24.0s	3	0	D
3	G Hill	BRM	−56.6s	5	0	D
4	S Moss	Lotus-Climax	−57.7s	1	1	D
5	W von Trips	Ferrari	−1 lap	15	0	D
6	R Ginther	Ferrari	−1 lap	12	0	D

POLE POSITION Moss, Lotus-Climax, 1m 33.2s (0.2s), 161.961kph, 100.638mph
LAPS 75 x 4.193 km, 2.605 miles
DISTANCE 314.475 km, 195.406 miles
STARTERS/FINISHERS 17/8
WEATHER Sunny, warm, dry
LAP LEADERS Brabham 1-75 (75)
WINNER'S LAPS 1-75 P1
FASTEST LAP Moss, Lotus-Climax, 1m 33.8s (lap 75), 160.925kph, 99.994mph
CHAMPIONSHIP McLaren 14, Moss 11, Rathmann 8, Brabham 8, Ireland 7

BELGIAN GP Spa-Francorchamps

19 June 1960   Race 89

Jack Brabham
Cooper-Climax T53 215.052kph, 133.627mph

During practice Stirling Moss was seriously injured when his Lotus shed a wheel, as was Mike Taylor when the steering on his Lotus broke. On the super-fast circuit, Phil Hill exploited V6 power to put the front-engined Dino 246 Ferrari in amongst the British cars on the front row. For much of the race he put pressure on Brabham's leading Cooper but eventually finished fourth. Brabham led all the way from pole, Bruce McLaren making it a Cooper 1-2 when G. Hill lost second place, a BRM crankshaft letting go on the penultimate lap. But celebrations were muted. On lap 20 of the race Chris Bristow died instantly when he lost control of his Cooper. Four laps later Alan Stacey was killed when his Lotus crashed, the driver probably struck by a bird.

Pos	Driver	Car	Time/gap	Grid	Stops	Tyres
1	J Brabham	Cooper-Climax	2h 21m 37.3s	1	0	D
2	B McLaren	Cooper-Climax	−1m 3.3s	13	0	D
3	O Gendebien	Cooper-Climax	−1 lap	5	1	D
4	P Hill	Ferrari	−1 lap	4	1	D
5	J Clark	Lotus-Climax	−2 laps	3	1	D
6	L Bianchi	Cooper-Climax	−8 laps	9	1	D

POLE POSITION Brabham, Cooper-Climax, 3m 50.0s (2.5s), 220.696kph, 137.134mph
LAPS 36 x 14.100 km, 8.761 miles
DISTANCE 507.600 km, 315.408 miles
STARTERS/FINISHERS 17/6
WEATHER Sunny, warm, dry
LAP LEADERS Brabham 1-36 (36)
WINNER'S LAPS 1-36 P1
FASTEST LAP P Hill/Brabham/I Ireland, Lotus-Climax, 3m 51.9s (laps NA), 218.887kph, 136.010mph
CHAMPIONSHIP McLaren 20, Brabham 16, Moss 11, Rathmann 8, Ireland 7

| Round 6/10 | **FRENCH GP** Reims | | | | | | **Jack Brabham** |
| | **3 July 1960** | | | | Race 90 | | **Cooper-Climax T53** 212.119kph, 131.805mph |

Just as at the tragic Belgian race, Phil Hill kept the outmoded Ferrari machinery in the picture, taking another front-row spot and dicing with pole-sitter Brabham. For 29 laps Brabham struggled wheel-to-wheel with the Ferraris of Hill and von Trips, the three cars travelling at up to 190mph down the long Soissons straight. But Ferrari transmissions didn't last beyond lap 31, Brabham completing an unchallenged hat-trick victory. In a Cooper 1-2-3-4, Coventry-Climax engines were bolted in the back of the first eight finishers. Brabham now shared the championship lead with Cooper teammate McLaren, Moss still third some distance back but still out of action as the extensive injuries from his Spa accident healed.

POLE POSITION Brabham, Cooper-Climax, 2m 16.8s (1.4s), 218.474kph, 135.753mph
LAPS 50 x 8.302 km, 5.159 miles
DISTANCE 415.100 km, 257.931 miles
STARTERS/FINISHERS 20/12
WEATHER Overcast, warm, dry
LAP LEADERS Brabham 1-3, 5, 7, 9-10, 12, 14, 18-50 (42); P Hill, Ferrari 4, 6,8, 11, 13, 15-17 (8)
WINNER'S LAPS 1-3 P1, 4 P2, 5 P1, 6 P2, 7 P1, 8 P2, 9-10 P1, 11 P2, 12 P1, 13 P2, 14 P1, 15-17 P2, 18-50 P1
FASTEST LAP Brabham, Cooper-Climax, 2m 17.5s (lap 25), 217.361kph, 135.062mph
CHAMPIONSHIP Brabham 24, McLaren 24, Moss 11, Gendebien 10, Rathmann 8

Pos	Driver	Car	Time/gap	Grid	Stops	Tyres
1	J Brabham	Cooper-Climax	1h 57m 24.9s	1	0	D
2	O Gendebien	Cooper-Climax	−48.3s	11	0	D
3	B McLaren	Cooper-Climax	−51.9s	9	0	D
4	H Taylor	Cooper-Climax	−1 lap	13	0	D
5	J Clark	Lotus-Climax	−1 lap	12	0	D
6	R Flockhart	Lotus-Climax	−1 lap	8	0	D

Cooper-Climax T53

| Round 7/10 | **BRITISH GP** Silverstone | | | | | | **Jack Brabham** |
| | **16 July 1960** | | | | Race 91 | | **Cooper-Climax T53** 174.928kph, 108.695mph |

A race all about Graham Hill. As recuperating Stirling Moss dropped the flag, Hill stalled his BRM. From P2 on the grid alongside Brabham, he completed lap 1 in 22nd place. After ten laps he had reached seventh and from there dispensed with Bonnier, McLaren, Surtees, Clark, and Ireland, relieving Brabham of the lead on lap 55 and holding it for the next 17. But there was to be no fairy-tale victory. With just six laps remaining, hounded by Brabham, Hill spun-off at Copse while lapping the Ferraris, Brabham going on to receive the chequered flag. Making only his second championship start, John Surtees came home second for Team Lotus.

POLE POSITION Brabham, Cooper-Climax, 1m 34.6s (1.0s), 179.260kph, 111.387mph
LAPS 77 x 4.711 km, 2.927 miles
DISTANCE 362.712 km, 225.379 miles
STARTERS/FINISHERS 24/16
WEATHER Overcast, warm, dry
LAP LEADERS Brabham 1-54, 72-77 (60); G Hill 55-71 (17)
WINNER'S LAPS 1-54 P1, 55-71 P2, 72-77 P1
FASTEST LAP G Hill, BRM, 1m 34.4s (lap 56), 179.640kph, 111.623mph
CHAMPIONSHIP Brabham 32, McLaren 27, Moss 11, Ireland 11, Gendebien 10

Pos	Driver	Car	Time/gap	Grid	Stops	Tyres
1	J Brabham	Cooper-Climax	2h 4m 24.6s	1	0	D
2	J Surtees	Lotus-Climax	−49.6s	11	0	D
3	I Ireland	Lotus-Climax	−1m 29.6s	5	0	D
4	B McLaren	Cooper-Climax	−1 lap	3	0	D
5	T Brooks	Cooper-Climax	−1 lap	9	0	D
6	W von Trips	Ferrari	−2 laps	7	0	D

PORTUGUESE GP Porto

Race 92

Jack Brabham

Cooper-Climax T53 175.849kph, 109.268mph

Surtees' Lotus was on pole from Gurney's BRM, then Brabham. At the start the Australian led away but came out second best to Gurney at the hairpin, taking to the escape road and dropping to P8. Gurney led the first 10 laps from Surtees and Moss, making his comeback eight weeks after his Spa accident. As Gurney and Moss fell away with engine issues, Surtees looked well placed to win until lap 37, when his feet, petrol-soaked from a leaking tank, slipped on the pedals; in the resultant prang the Lotus radiator split on the high kerbing. So Brabham won easily from McLaren, a second 1-2 finish confirming Cooper's excellent reliability. Further, Brabham's fifth straight victory brought a second consecutive championship for both driver and constructor.

POLE POSITION J Surtees, Lotus-Climax, 2m 25.56s (0.07s), 183.190kph, 113.829mph
LAPS 55 x 7.407 km, 4.602 miles
DISTANCE 407.385 km, 253.137 miles
STARTERS/FINISHERS 15/7
WEATHER Sunny, hot, dry
LAP LEADERS D Gurney, BRM 1-10 (10); J Surtees, Lotus-Climax 11-35 (25); Brabham 36-55 (20)
WINNER'S LAPS 1 P1, 2-4 P8, 5-7 P6, 8-10 P5, 11-19 P4, 20-24 P3, 25 P2, 26-28 P3, 29-35 P2, 36-55 P1
FASTEST LAP J Surtees, Lotus-Climax, 2m 27.53s (lap 33), 180.744kph, 112.309mph
CHAMPIONSHIP Brabham 40, McLaren 33, Ireland 12, Moss 11, Gendebien 10

Pos	Driver	Car	Time/gap	Grid	Stops	Tyres
1	J Brabham	Cooper-Climax	2h 19m 0.03s	3	0	D
2	B McLaren	Cooper-Climax	−57.97s	6	0	D
3	J Clark	Lotus-Climax	−1m 53.23s	8	0	D
4	W von Trips	Ferrari	−1m 58.81s	9	0	D
5	T Brooks	Cooper-Climax	−6 laps	4	NA	D
6	I Ireland	Lotus-Climax	−7 laps	12	NA	D

ITALIAN GP Monza

Race 93

Phil Hill

Ferrari Dino 246 212.535kph, 132.063mph

This was something of a non-event. The Italian organisers insisted on using the Monza banking which led to a boycott by the British teams on the pretext that the banking was dangerous, that chassis and tyres were not designed for such loads. Without participation of works cars from Cooper, Lotus and BRM, it was a Ferrari walkover. Making two tyre-stops on his way, Phil Hill led a 1-2-3 to become the first American to win a championship GP as well as posting the final victory for a front-engined GP car. Wolfgang von Trips drove a 1.5-litre Ferrari F2 car with rear-mounted engine, finishing fifth behind another Ferrari-powered car, the Cooper of Cabianca which used a Castellotti-badged four-cylinder 'Squalo' engine.

POLE POSITION P Hill, Ferrari, 2m 41.4s (1.9s), 223.048kph, 138.596mph
LAPS 50 x 10.000 km, 6.214 miles
DISTANCE 500.000 km, 310.686 miles
STARTERS/FINISHERS 16/10
WEATHER Overcast, warm, dry
LAP LEADERS Ginther 1-16, 18-25 (24); P Hill 17, 26-50 (26)
WINNER'S LAPS 1-16 P2, 17 P1, 18-25 P2, 26-50 P1
FASTEST LAP P Hill, Ferrari, 2m 43.6s (lap 23), 220.049kph, 136.732mph
CHAMPIONSHIP Brabham 40, McLaren 33, P Hill 15, Ireland 12, Moss 11

Pos	Driver	Car	Time/gap	Grid	Stops	Tyres
1	P Hill	Ferrari	2h 21m 9.2s	1	2	D
2	R Ginther	Ferrari	−2m 27.6s	2	2	D
3	W Mairesse	Ferrari	−1 lap	3	2	D
4	G Cabianca	Cooper-Castellotti	−2 laps	4	1	D
5	W von Trips	Ferrari	−2 laps	6	1	D
6	H Herrmann	Porsche	−3 laps	10	1	D

UNITED STATES GP Riverside

Race 94

Stirling Moss

Lotus-Climax 18 159.318kph, 98.996mph

For the very final race of the 2.5-litre Formula no Ferraris showed, the *Commendatore* not considering the USA trip worthwhile for his obsolete machinery. An on-form Moss took pole position from Brabham and Gurney, going on to win the race from Ireland, the Walker Lotus easily outpacing the works car for a Lotus 1-2. Double world champion Jack Brabham led the first four laps but was delayed by two early pit stops to deal with a fuel leak fire. Once sorted he lapped very quickly to finally finish fourth behind teammate McLaren, these two completing their highly successful season first and second in the championship. Despite his abbreviated season, Moss edged Innes Ireland out of third spot in the points table.

POLE POSITION Moss, Lotus-Climax, 1m 54.4s (0.6s), 165.858kph, 103.059mph
LAPS 75 x 5.271 km, 3.275 miles
DISTANCE 395.295 km, 245.625 miles
STARTERS/FINISHERS 23/16
WEATHER Sunny, warm, dry
LAP LEADERS Brabham 1-4 (4); Moss 5-75 (71)
WINNER'S LAPS 1-4 P2, 5-75 P1
FASTEST LAP Brabham, Cooper-Climax, 1m 56.3s (lap 71), 163.148kph, 101.376mph
CHAMPIONSHIP Brabham 43, McLaren 34, Moss 19, Ireland 18, P Hill 16

Pos	Driver	Car	Time/gap	Grid	Stops	Tyres
1	S Moss	Lotus-Climax	2h 28m 52.2s	1	0	D
2	I Ireland	Lotus-Climax	−38.0s	7	0	D
3	B McLaren	Cooper-Climax	−52.0s	10	0	D
4	J Brabham	Cooper-Climax	−1 lap	2	2	D
5	J Bonnier	BRM	−1 lap	4	1	D
6	P Hill	Cooper-Climax	−1 lap	13	0	D

- The ten championship rounds included the Indy 500 for the very last time, with California's Riverside replacing Florida's Sebring for the US Grand Prix.
- For both the drivers' and constructors' championships a point would now be awarded for sixth place while the extra point for fastest lap was abolished. So points were 8, 6, 4, 3, 2, 1 to the top six finishers, the best five race results counting.
- 1960 was the seventh and final year of the 2.5-litre Formula 1 and spelled the swansong for GP cars with front-mounted engines. All race victories bar Indy and an unrepresentative Monza went to cars designed with the engine behind the driver.
- So impressed were Moss and Rob Walker by the new rear-engined Lotus 18, which made a sensational championship debut in Argentina, that the savvy pair switched from Surbiton to Cheshunt, and but for Moss' accident the Lotus marque might well have met with even greater early success.
- The season was marred by a catastrophic series of episodes at the Spa-Francorchamps circuit, where four totally unrelated incidents during practice and the race resulted in two fatalities and Moss lying seriously injured.
- With Moss *hors de combat* for three of the nine Grands Prix, world champion Jack Brabham became virtually invincible, his season defined by a remarkable sequence of five victories on the trot, the last of these bringing him and Cooper-Climax back-to-back titles.
- The Australian was again capably if unsensationally supported by New Zealander Bruce McLaren who, with a win and six podiums, proved the intrinsic unassailability of the 'lowline' T53 Cooper. Lower, slimmer and prettier, it was a logical development of its predecessor with updated rear suspension and gearbox.
- The Cooper Car Co had long been a 'volume' racing car manufacturers and now, with the availability of the 2.5-litre Coventry-Climax engine, there was a queue of F1 customers at Surbiton. One such was the Yeoman Credit Racing Team, a manifestation of the British Racing Partnership.
- BRP was the first F1 team to sell its identity in return for sponsorship by the Yeoman Credit hire purchase company for the 1960 season. The distinctive pale green year-old Coopers with red trim were driven by Tony Brooks, Olivier Gendebien and others, gaining a couple of podiums.
- During the season the team suffered much tragedy, Ivor Bueb killed in F2, the up-and-coming Chris Bristow at the tragic Spa event, and the previous month Harry Schell while practicing for the Silverstone International Trophy race.
- At the end of the year Yeoman Credit decided to transfer their sponsorship to Reg Parnell Racing and for 1961 and 1962 BRP was renamed UDT Laystall Racing under a new but similar sponsorship deal.
- Another team to adopt the Cooper chassis was Scuderia Castellotti, notable for installing Ferrari engines. Named after the talented Ferrari driver who died in testing at Modena in 1957, the Cooper used bored-out Ferrari Tipo 553 'Squalo' engines with 'Eugenio' on the cam covers.
- Another Italian team, Scuderia Centro Sud, shoehorned a four-cylinder Maserati into a T51 Cooper, one of these cars campaigned with verve by Masten Gregory.
- Whereas Cooper proved in 1960 that speed plus reliability was the essence of success in motorsport, Lotus offered the converse corollary. There was no question the rear-engined Lotus 18, especially in Moss' hands, often had the legs of the Cooper, especially through the corners, but

due to Chapman's obsession with weight-saving it was mechanically frail, and a Lotus reputation for swiftness with fragility was beginning to surface, Alan Stacey's fatal Spa accident no exception.
- BRM came away with little but encouragement as they developed their rear-engined P48, Graham Hill and Jo Bonnier each providing moments that would preserve the faith.
- Ferrari, their hollow Monza victory aside, were barely in the hunt for race victories, fielding a rear-engined chassis just twice but with little commitment.
- If it hadn't been blatantly obvious in 1959, 1960 proved beyond any doubt that the rear-mounted engine was the future, a fact evidenced in two starkly opposing ways:

RACE 92, Portuguese GP: Brabham's Cooper (2) won easily from teammate McLaren, his fifth straight victory bringing a second consecutive championship for both driver and constructor.

the success of Cooper and Lotus and the embarrassing uncompetitiveness of Aston Martin and Scarab, their designers still contending that the horse must pull the cart.
■ Lance Reventlow's Scarab project debuted in 1960, further verification of at least niche if not widespread enthusiasm for F1 Stateside. Son of Barbara Hutton, heiress to the Woolworth fortune, playboy Reventlow rapidly lost interest in automobile racing.
■ Two future champions also made their debut. Jim Clark and motorcycle world champion John Surtees, both signed for Colin Chapman's Team Lotus.
■ Also in 1960, Ayrton Senna and Damon Hill were born.

Championship ranking	Championship points	Driver nationality	1960 Drivers Championship		Races contested	Race victories	Podiumse excl. victories	Races led	Flag to flag victories	Laps led	Poles	Fastest laps	Triple Crowns
			Driver	Car									
1	43	AUS	Jack Brabham	Cooper-Climax	8	5		7	2	244	3	3	2
2	34	NZL	Bruce McLaren	Cooper-Climax	8	1	5	1		13		1	
3	19	GBR	Stirling Moss	Cooper-Climax (1) Lotus-Climax (4)	5	2	1	3		150	4	2	
4	18	GBR	Innes Ireland	Lotus-Climax	8		3	1		1		1	
5	16	USA	Phil Hill	Ferrari (8) Cooper-Climax (1)	9	1	1	2		34	1	2	1
6	10	BEL	Olivier Gendebien	Cooper-Climax	5		2						
6	10	GER	Wolfgang von Trips	Ferrari (8) Cooper-Maserati (8)	9								
8	8	USA	Jim Rathmann	Watson-Offenhauser	1	1		1		100		1	
8	8	USA	Richie Ginther	Ferrari	3		1	1		24			
8	8	GBR	Jim Clark	Lotus-Climax	6		1						
11	7	GBR	Tony Brooks	Cooper-Climax (6) Vanwall (1)	7								
12	6	GBR	Cliff Allison	Ferrari	1		1						
12	6	USA	Rodger Ward	Watson-Offenhauser	1		1	1		58			
12	6	GBR	John Surtees	Lotus-Climax	4		1	1		25	1	1	
15	4	USA	Paul Goldsmith	Epperly-Offenhauser	1		1						
15	4	GBR	Graham Hill	BRM	8		1	1		17		1	
15	4	BEL	Willy Mairesse	Ferrari	3		1						
18	4	SWE	Jo Bonnier	BRM	8			2		80			
19	3	ARG	Carlos Menditéguy	Cooper-Maserati	1								
19	3	USA	Don Branson	Phillips-Offenhauser	1								
19	3	GBR	Henry Taylor	Cooper-Climax	4								
19	3	ITA	Guilio Cabianca	Cooper-Ferrari	1								
23	2	USA	Johnny Thomson	Lesovsky-Offenhauser	1			1		10			
24	1	USA	Eddie Johnson	Trevis-Offenhauser	1								
24	1	BEL	Lucien Bianchi	Cooper-Climax	3								
24	1	GBR	Ron Flockhart	Lotus-Climax (1) Cooper-Climax (1)	2								
24	1	GER	Hans Herrmann	Porsche	1								
-	0	FRA	Maurice Trintignant	Cooper-Climax (1) Cooper-Maserati (4) Aston Martin (1)	6		1						
-	0	USA	Eddie Sachs	Ewing-Offenhauser	1			1		21	1		
-	0	USA	Troy Ruttman	Watson-Offenhauser	1			1		11			
-	0	USA	Dan Gurney	BRM	7			1		10			

Championship ranking	Championship points	Team/Marque nationality	1960 Constructors Championship (Excl. Indy 500)		Engine maker nationality	Races contested	Race victories	1-2 finishes	Podiums excl. victories	Races led	Laps led	Poles	Fastest laps
			Chassis	Engine									
1	48	GBR	Cooper T53, T51	Coventry-Climax 2.5 S4	GBR	9	6	3	8	8	266	4	5
2	34	GBR	Lotus 18, 16	Coventry-Climax 2.5 S4	GBR	8	2	1	5	4	167	4	3
3	26	ITA	Ferrari Dino 246/256, 246P, 156P	Ferrari 2.4/2.5 V6, 1.5 V6	ITA	9	1	1	4	2	58	1	2
4	8	GBR	BRM P48, P25	BRM 2.5 S4	GBR	8			1	4	107		1
5	3	GBR	Cooper T51	Maserati 2.5 S4	ITA	8							
5	3	GBR	Cooper T51, T45	Castellotti/Ferrari 2.5 S4	ITA	4							
7	1	GER	Porsche 718	Porsche 1.5 F4	GER	1							

1961

Phil Hill, first for USA

THE TALE OF THE TITLE

- New F1 regulations restored Ferrari supremacy, the 'shark-nose' 156 winning five of the eight rounds.
- With two race victories, Phil Hill became the first US world champion but in ill-fated circumstances.
- Ferrari teammate and closely matched rival Wolfgang von Trips plus 14 spectators were killed at Monza.
- Ferrari's third race winner, Giancarlo Baghetti, was the first and only driver to win on his championship debut.
- At Reims the Ferrari juggernaut faltered, rookie Baghetti fending off the works Porsche pair to win by 0.1s.
- The British teams were ill-prepared for the new F1, but Moss won brilliantly at Monaco and the Nürburgring.
- In the Walker Lotus, Moss sensationally defeated Ferrari twice, Team Lotus also taking their first victory.
- Champions Brabham and Cooper were nowhere, but late season the British V8s showed early promise.
- And not forgetting: non-stop Zandvoort; Ferrari 1-2-3-4 at Spa.

THE CHASE FOR THE CHAMPIONSHIP

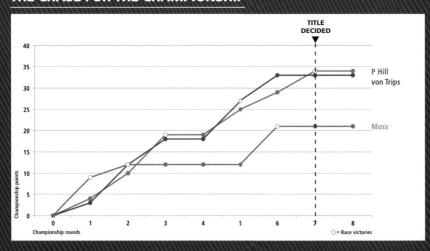

Round 1/8	**MONACO GP** Monte Carlo		**Stirling Moss**
	14 May 1961	**Race 95**	**Lotus-Climax 18** 113.788kph, 70.704mph

A famous against-the-odds victory by Stirling Moss, his nimble Walker Lotus-Climax giving away over 30bhp to the Ferraris. Moss took pole from Ginther's Ferrari and Clark's works Lotus. At the off Ginther led strongly, pulling out 7s in five laps until Moss began to reel him in. Once by on lap 14 Moss quickly built up a 10s lead. But then the superior Ferraris came back at him, the pursuit led by two Americans. In a tense and exciting two-hour chase, first Phil Hill then Richie Ginther tried to catch Moss but his cornering speed and race-craft, particularly in traffic, defied the might of Maranello. Soon after lap 70 the Ferrari pit signalled the faster Ginther to take up the attack from Hill, but at 100 laps he was still 3.6s short.

POLE POSITION Moss, Lotus-Climax, 1m 39.1s (0.2s), 114.248kph, 70.704mph
LAPS 100 x 3.145km, 1.954 miles
DISTANCE 314.500 km, 195.421 miles
STARTERS/FINISHERS 16/13
WEATHER Hazy, warm, dry
LAP LEADERS Ginther 1-13 (33); Moss 14-100 (100)
WINNER'S LAPS 1 P3, 2-13 P2, 14-100 P1
FASTEST LAP R Ginther, Ferrari/Moss, Lotus-Climax, 1m 36.3s (laps 84/85), 117.570kph, 73.055mph
CHAMPIONSHIP Moss 9, Ginther 6, P Hill 4, von Trips 3, Gurney 2

Pos	Driver	Car	Time/gap	Grid	Stops	Tyres
1	S Moss	Lotus-Climax	2h 45m 50.1s	1	0	D
2	R Ginther	Ferrari	−3.6s	2	0	D
3	P Hill	Ferrari	−41.3s	5	0	D
4r	W von Trips	Ferrari	−2 laps	6	0	D
5	D Gurney	Porsche	−2 laps	10	0	D
6	B McLaren	Cooper-Climax	−5 laps	7	1	D

Ferrari 156

Round 2/8	**DUTCH GP** Zandvoort		**Wolfgang von Trips**
	22 May 1961	**Race 96**	**Ferrari 156** 154.827kph, 96.205mph

Setting a pattern for the season, the Ferraris dominated qualifying with Phil Hill on pole, von Trips and Ginther alongside. Von Trips got the better of Hill at the start and broke away, maintaining his lead to the end to record the first of a string of Ferrari victories. At the finish Phil Hill was on his tail but holding station, the order pre-determined. For much of the race Hill had his hands full with a feisty Clark, who could overtake in the corners but lost out on the straights. Moss had similarly engaged Ginther and got ahead on the final lap, hanging on to fourth place by a hairsbreadth as Ferrari horsepower told down the finishing straight. This race is renowned as the only occasion when every starter finished, and made no pit visits to boot.

POLE POSITION P Hill, Ferrari, 1m 35.7s (0.0s), 157.730kph, 98.009mph
LAPS 75 x 4.193 km, 2.605 miles
DISTANCE 314.475 km, 195.406 miles
STARTERS/FINISHERS 15/15
WEATHER Sunny, warm, dry, windy
LAP LEADERS von Trips 1-75 (75)
WINNER'S LAPS 1-75 P1
FASTEST LAP Clark, Lotus-Climax, 1m 35.5s (lap 7), 158.051kph, 98.214mph
CHAMPIONSHIP von Trips 12, Moss 12, P Hill 10, Ginther 8, Clark 4

Pos	Driver	Car	Time/gap	Grid	Stops	Tyres
1	W von Trips	Ferrari	2h 1m 52.1s	2	0	D
2	P Hill	Ferrari	−0.9s	1	0	D
3	J Clark	Lotus-Climax	−13.1s	10	0	D
4	S Moss	Lotus-Climax	−22.2s	4	0	D
5	R Ginther	Ferrari	−22.3s	3	0	D
6	J Brabham	Cooper-Climax	−1m 20.1s	7	0	D

BELGIAN GP Spa-Francorchamps
18 June 1961   **Race 97**

Phil Hill
Ferrari 156 215.052kph, 133.627mph

Hill's turn to lead von Trips home in a Ferrari 1-2-3-4 landslide. Hill from pole led mostly, although von Trips and Belgian Gendebien in a fourth Ferrari – entered by Équipe National Belge and painted yellow for the occasion – also had their moments. Von Trips crossed the line right on Hill's tail in another Ferrari formation finish, the championship developing into a two-horse race between these two, separated by a single point after three rounds. Best of the rest in the totally outclassed field was John Surtees in a Yeoman Credit Cooper-Climax, beating Gurney's works Porsche into fifth. The works entries from Cooper, Lotus and BRM had a poor day, as did Moss, revisiting the place of his terrifying 1960 accident for the first time.

POLE POSITION P Hill, Ferrari, 3m 59.3s (0.8s), 212.119kph, 131.804mph
LAPS 30 x 14.100 km, 8.761 miles
DISTANCE 423.000 km, 262.840 miles
STARTERS/FINISHERS 21/13
WEATHER Overcast, warm, dry
LAP LEADERS P Hill 1, 3-5, 8, 11-13, 15, 17-18, 21-23, 25-30 (20); Gendebien 2, 6-7 (3); von Trips 9-10, 14, 16, 19-20, 24 (7)
WINNER'S LAPS 1 P1, 2 P2, 3-5 P1, 6-7 P2, 8 P1, 9-10 P2, 11-13 P1, 14 P2, 15 P1, 16 P2, 17-18 P1, 19-20 P2, 21-23 P1, 24 P2, 25-30 P1
FASTEST LAP Ginther, Ferrari, 3m 59.8s (lap 20), 211.676kph, 131.530mph
CHAMPIONSHIP P Hill 19, von Trips 18, Moss 12, Ginther 12, Clark 4

Pos	Driver	Car	Time/gap	Grid	Stops	Tyres
1	P Hill	Ferrari	2h 3m 3.8s	1	0	D
2	W von Trips	Ferrari	−0.7s	2	0	D
3	R Ginther	Ferrari	−19.5s	5	0	D
4	O Gendebien	Ferrari	−45.6s	3	0	D
5	J Surtees	Cooper-Climax	−1m 26.8s	4	0	D
6	D Gurney	Porsche	−1m 31.0s	10	0	D

FRENCH GP Reims
2 July 1961   **Race 98**

Giancarlo Baghetti
Ferrari 156 192.880kph, 119.850mph

At Reims the Ferrari juggernaut almost derailed. Utterly dominant as usual in qualifying, the race was a different matter. Von Trips' Ferrari was the first to yield, abandoned with a holed radiator, but pole-sitter Phil Hill was behind to regain his early lead. Then on lap 37 Hill spun it away at Thillois, losing much time, but Ginther was there to take over. With 12 laps to go Ginther stopped with zero oil pressure. But a fourth Ferrari was there to fill the void, a non-works entry driven by Baghetti, his first championship race. Under immense pressure from Bonnier and Gurney in Porches the excruciating final six laps went: 47 Baghetti, 48–49 Gurney, 50 Baghetti, 51 Gurney, and then on the final lap it was rookie Baghetti by one-tenth!

POLE POSITION P Hill, Ferrari, 2m 24.9s (1.5s), 206.261kph, 128.165mph
LAPS 52 x 8.302 km, 5.159 miles
DISTANCE 431.704 km, 268.248 miles
STARTERS/FINISHERS 26/15
WEATHER Sunny, very hot, dry
LAP LEADERS P Hill, Ferrari 1-12, 18-37 (32); W von Trips, Ferrari 13-17 (5); R Ginther, Ferrari 38-40 (3); Baghetti 41-43, 45, 47, 50, 52 (7); J Bonnier, Porsche 44 (1); Gurney 46, 48-49, 51 (4)
WINNER'S LAPS 1 P13, 2 P11, 3 P10, 4 P9, 5 P8, 6-7 P9, 8 P7, 9 P8, 10-13 P5, 14 P4, 15 P6, 16-18 P4, 19-22 P3, 23 P4, 24-32 P3, 33 P4, 34-38 P3, 39-40 P2, 41-43 P1, 44 P2, 45 P1, 46 P3, 47 P1, 48-49 P2, 50 P1, 51 P2, 52 P1
FASTEST LAP P Hill, Ferrari, 2m 27.1s (lap NA), 203.176kph, 126.248mph
CHAMPIONSHIP P Hill 19, von Trips 18, Moss 12, Ginther 12, Baghetti 9

Pos	Driver	Car	Time/gap	Grid	Stops	Tyres
1	G Baghetti	Ferrari	2h 14m 17.5s	12	0	D
2	D Gurney	Porsche	−0.1s	9	0	D
3	J Clark	Lotus-Climax	−1m 1.1s	5	0	D
4	I Ireland	Lotus-Climax	−1m 10.3s	10	0	D
5	B McLaren	Cooper-Climax	−1m 41.8s	8	0	D
6	G Hill	BRM	−1m 41.9s	6	0	D

BRITISH GP Aintree
15 July 1961   **Race 99**

Wolfgang von Trips
Ferrari 156 135.034kph, 83.907mph

The first half of the race was run in atrociously wet conditions during which von Trips demonstrated considerable skill to take the lead from Phil Hill on lap 7 and, unlike many others, keep it all together. This was particularly laudable as he was under sustained pressure from Moss in the Walker Lotus 18/21, the drenched track a great equaliser. But in the second half the weather eased, the Ferraris could apply their power advantage, and with Moss out with a broken brake pipe the Ferraris cruised to a 1-2-3 finish. His second victory gave von Trips a two-point margin over Hill. One month after Cliff Allison's career-ending accident at Spa, his UDT-Laystall teammate Henry Taylor suffered much the same fate at Aintree.

POLE POSITION P Hill, Ferrari, 1m 58.8s (0.0s), 146.304kph, 90.909mph
LAPS 75 x 4.828 km, 3.000 miles
DISTANCE 362.102 km, 225.000 miles
STARTERS/FINISHERS 30/17
WEATHER Overcast, cool, wet then drying
LAP LEADERS P Hill 1-6 (6); von Trips 7-75 (69)
WINNER'S LAPS 1-6 P2, 7-75 P1
FASTEST LAP T Brooks, BRM, 1m 57.8s (lap 72), 147.546kph, 91.681mph
CHAMPIONSHIP von Trips 27, P Hill 25, Ginther 16, Moss 12, Baghetti 9

Pos	Driver	Car	Time/gap	Grid	Stops	Tyres
1	W von Trips	Ferrari	2h 40m 53.6s	4	0	D
2	P Hill	Ferrari	−46.0s	1	0	D
3	R Ginther	Ferrari	−46.8s	2	0	D
4	J Brabham	Cooper-Climax	−1m 8.6s	9	0	D
5	J Bonnier	Porsche	−1m 16.2s	3	0	D
6	R Salvadori	Cooper-Climax	−1m 26.2s	13	0	D

Round 6/8	**GERMAN GP** Nürburgring						**Stirling Moss**
	6 August 1961					**Race 100**	Lotus-Climax 18/21 148.538kph, 92.297mph

Phil Hill's fifth pole with Brabham's Cooper alongside sporting the new Climax V8. The Australian led the first few miles before flying off in the wet/dry conditions to leave Moss leading Hill at the end of lap 1. As at Monaco, this was another mighty performance by Moss who had chosen 'wet' tyres, maintaining his lead brilliantly in the changeable conditions. The Ferraris had switched back to 'dries' on the grid, so as the track dried von Trips passed Hill and closed to 6.5s behind Moss at Adenau on lap 10 of 15. But further rain enabled Moss to finally win by 20s. As they raced for the line disputing second, von Trips, to the roar of the German crowd, slipstreamed by Hill to 'win' by 1.1s, edging his points lead to four.

POLE POSITION P Hill, Ferrari, 8m 55.2s (6.2s), 153.430kph, 95.337mph
LAPS 15 x 22.810 km, 14.173 miles
DISTANCE 342.150 km, 212.602 miles
STARTERS/FINISHERS 26/16
WEATHER Overcast, changeable, shower on final lap
LAP LEADERS Moss 1-15 (15)
WINNER'S LAPS 1-15 P1
FASTEST LAP P Hill, Ferrari, 8m 57.8s (lap 10), 152.689kph, 94.876mph
CHAMPIONSHIP von Trips 33, P Hill 29, Moss 21, Ginther 16, Clark 11

Pos	Driver	Car	Time/gap	Grid	Stops	Tyres
1	S Moss	Lotus-Climax	2h 18m 12.4s	3	0	D
2	W von Trips	Ferrari	−21.4s	5	0	D
3	P Hill	Ferrari	−22.5s	1	0	D
4	J Clark	Lotus-Climax	−1m 17.1s	8	0	D
5	J Surtees	Cooper-Climax	−1m 53.1s	10	0	D
6	B McLaren	Cooper-Climax	−2m 41.4s	9	0	D

TOP **100** RACE

Round 7/8	**ITALIAN GP** Monza						**Phil Hill**
	10 September 1961					**Race 101**	Ferrari 156 209.387kph, 130.107mph

After qualifying around the Monza banking – no British boycott this time – scarlet Ferraris resplendently occupied the first five grid-slots on the two-by-two grid. With only one round to follow Monza, the intra-Ferrari championship battle was tense. Von Trips had claimed pole but botched his start, Hill leading lap one from P4. Tragedy struck on lap 2. Under braking for Curva di Vedano, duelling over P4, von Trips got on the grass, then touched Clark. The Ferrari catapulted off the track, ejecting the driver and careering into the watching crowd. Von Trips and 14 spectators lost their lives. The remaining four Ferraris dominated but one by one fell out, leaving Phil Hill to win the race and, with the demise of his only rival, the championship too.

POLE POSITION W von Trips, Ferrari, 2m 46.3s (0.1s), 216.476kph, 134.512mph
LAPS 43 x 10.000 km, 6.214 miles
DISTANCE 430.000 km, 267.190 miles
STARTERS/FINISHERS 32/12
WEATHER Sunny, very hot, dry
LAP LEADERS P Hill 1-3, 5, 7, 10, 14-43 (36); R Ginther, Ferrari 4, 6, 8-9, 11-13 (7)
WINNER'S LAPS 1-3 P1, 4 P2, 5 P1, 6 P2, 7 P1, 8-9 P2, 10 P1, 11-13 P2, 14-43 P1
FASTEST LAP G Baghetti, Ferrari, 2m 48.4s (lap 2), 213.777kph, 132.835mph
CHAMPIONSHIP P Hill 34, von Trips 33, Moss 21, Ginther 16, Gurney 15

Pos	Driver	Car	Time/gap	Grid	Stops	Tyres
1	P Hill	Ferrari	2h 0m 13.0s	4	0	D
2	D Gurney	Porsche	−31.2s	12	0	D
3	B McLaren	Cooper-Climax	−2m 28.4s	14	0	D
4	J Lewis	Cooper-Climax	−2m 40.4s	16	0	D
5	T Brooks	BRM	−2m 40.5s	13	0	D
6	R Salvadori	Cooper-Climax	−1 lap	18	0	D

Lotus-Climax 21

Round 8/8	**UNITED STATES GP** Watkins Glen	**Innes Ireland**
	8 October 1961 **Race 102**	Lotus-Climax 21 166.032kph, 103.167mph

Citing their recent tragedy and with both championships settled, Ferrari as last year was absent. Brabham demonstrated the potential of the new Coventry-Climax V8 with pole by over a second. In the race he and Moss, using the old four-cylinder engine, exchanged the lead time and again until both forms of Climax engine expired shortly after half-distance. This left Innes Ireland fending off Graham Hill's BRM-Climax for 15 laps until Hill pitted with magneto trouble. Still Ireland couldn't relax, as first Salvadori's Yeoman Credit Cooper and then Gurney's Porsche challenged his lead. But finally, having survived a scary practice crash caused by broken steering and an early spin in the race, Ireland won the first of many for Team Lotus.

POLE POSITION J Brabham, Cooper-Climax, 1m 17.0s (1.1s), 173.057kph, 107.532mph
LAPS 100 x 3.701 km, 2.300 miles
DISTANCE 370.149 km, 230.000 miles
STARTERS/FINISHERS 19/11
WEATHER Sunny, warm, dry
LAP LEADERS S Moss, Lotus-Climax 1-5, 16, 24-25, 34-35, 39-58 (30); J Brabham, Cooper-Climax 6-15, 17-23, 26-33, 36-38 (28); Ireland 59-100 (42)
WINNER'S LAPS 1-2 P3, 3 P11, 4 P10, 5 P7, 6-7 P5, 8-33 P4, 34-44 P3, 45-58 P2, 59-100 P1
FASTEST LAP J Brabham, Cooper-Climax, 1m 18.2s (laps 28 & 30), 170.401kph, 105.882mph
CHAMPIONSHIP P Hill 34, von Trips 33, Moss 21, Gurney 21, Ginther 16

Pos	Driver	Car	Time/gap	Grid	Stops	Tyres
1	I Ireland	Lotus-Climax	2h 13m 45.8s	8	0	D
2	D Gurney	Porsche	−4.3s	7	0	D
3	T Brooks	BRM	−49.0s	6	0	D
4	B McLaren	Cooper-Climax	−58.0s	4	0	D
5	G Hill	BRM	−1 lap	2	1	D
6	J Bonnier	Porsche	−2 laps	10	1	D

1961 CHAMPIONSHIP FACTS AND FOLKLORE

■ With the Indianapolis 500-mile race no longer included there were eight championship rounds in 1961, the best five results counting.

■ Drivers' points were increased from 8 to 9 for a win, while the US GP found a new home at Watkins Glen.

■ The governing body introduced new Formula 1 regulations for 1961 intended to curb speeds in the interests of safety.

■ The key stipulation was a hefty cut in engine capacity to 1.3 litres minimum, 1.5 litres maximum, with supercharging outlawed and, for the first time, a dry weight limit of 450kg (992.08lb).

■ Compulsory were engine self-starter, a separate emergency braking system and rollover hoop.

■ Fuel tanks must be of the flexible aircraft safety type containing commercial 100-octane (maximum) 'pump' fuel, Avgas having been banned.

■ Also outlawed were enclosed 'streamliner' bodywork and oil replenishment during a race.

■ The change in formula brought a dramatic change in Ferrari fortunes. Essentially the FIA had readopted Formula 2 regulations for F1, and Ferrari had been successfully competing in the 1.5-litre Formula 2 since its restoration in 1957.

■ Their 1961 F1 car, the 'shark-nose' Tipo 156, naturally owed much to this F2 lineage, especially its powerful V6 engine, installed behind the driver in a multi-tubular chassis suspended front and rear by wishbones with helical spring/damper units.

■ The 1.5-litre 65° V6 engine was soon replaced by a 120° version pushing out 190bhp at 9,500rpm. It enjoyed a massive 30bhp advantage over the Coventry-Climax FPF four-cylinder in 1.5-litre form which the poorly prepared British teams, including BRM, relied upon.

RACE 96, Dutch GP: With his two victories Moss alone had the beating of the Ferrari 156 in 1961. Here he engages with Ginther's example, getting the better of the American on the final lap to take fourth place.

- The attitude of the British teams towards the unpopular new F1 had been ostrich-like and they were way behind in their preparations, having attempted to persuade the FIA to keep the existing 2.5-litre F1 going.
- Inevitably Ferrari became virtually unbeatable and the championship would be decided between their two leading drivers, American Phil Hill and Taffy von Trips from Germany.
- But there was one driver, Stirling Moss, who had their beating and his two peerless victories at Monaco and the Nürburgring in his outclassed Lotus were high points of the season.
- Another was the sensational Reims victory by Giancarlo Baghetti. Driving in his very first championship race he realised the fairy-tale feat of first-time rookie Grand Prix winner.
- But as well as these wonderful highs during the 1961 season there was a bottomless pit at Monza.
- The season-long battle between Ferrari teammates Hill and von Trips had been closely matched. On the winner's rostrum at Monza, Hill's emotions were simply torn to shreds. First elation that his Italian victory had put him right back in championship contention ... quickly turning to anguish on learning that his rival had perished in a second lap accident ... then the realisation that the coveted title was now his!
- Such a bittersweet circumstance in which to win the coveted crown was most unfortunate for the unassuming Hill, who will be best remembered as the first American world champion.

- Defending champion Jack Brabham scored a meagre four points but handled much of the race development for the new V8 Climax, which showed promise but lacked reliability early on.
- Besides Ferrari, the only other successful marque was Lotus. Along with Moss' pair of victories for Rob Walker's Lotus, Innes Ireland scored a maiden win for the works team in the USA, a race meeting Ferrari didn't enter.
- For 1961 Chapman came up with the Lotus 21, an interim car while the Coventry-Climax V8 was in development. It was a lower, sleeker, smoother car compared with the 18 that Moss used to win at Monaco.
- Moss' Nürburgring victory, the 100th championship race, was in a Lotus 18/21, a car developed specially for him, clashing fuel contracts preventing Rob Walker buying a 21.
- When Moss retired his Lotus 18/21 at Aintree, he amused the partisan crowd by taking over the Ferguson P99 entered for Jack Fairman. The Ferguson-Climax was not only the first 4WD F1 car, it was also the last front-engined car to win a F1 event, Moss driving it to victory at a damp Oulton Park Gold Cup meeting in September.
- In 1961 Moss was at the height of his powers, and when the Association of GP Drivers was formed, his peers elected 'Mr Motor Racing' its first chairman. But hindsight would later prove that Stirling Moss had already made his final world championship appearance.

Championship ranking	Championship points	Driver nationality	1961 Drivers Championship Driver	Car	Races contested	Race victories	Podiumse excl. victories	Races led	Flag to flag victories	Laps led	Poles	Fastest laps	Triple Crowns
1	34	USA	Phil Hill	Ferrari	7	2	4	4		94	5	2	
2	33	GER	Wolfgang von Trips	Ferrari	7	2	2	4	1	156	1		
3	21	GBR	Stirling Moss	Lotus-Climax (8) Ferguson-Climax (1)	8	2		3	1	132	1	1	
4	21	USA	Dan Gurney	Porsche	8		3	1		4			
5	16	USA	Richie Ginther	Ferrari	7		3	3		23		2	
6	12	GBR	Innes Ireland	Lotus-Climax	6	1		1		42			
7	11	GBR	Jim Clark	Lotus-Climax	8		2					1	
8	11	NZL	Bruce McLaren	Cooper-Climax	8		1						
9	9	ITA	Giancarlo Baghetti	Ferrari	3	1		1		7		1	
10	6	GBR	Tony Brooks	BRM-Climax	8		1					1	
11	4	AUS	Jack Brabham	Cooper-Climax	8			1		28	1	1	
12	4	GBR	John Surtees	Cooper-Climax	8								
13	3	BEL	Olivier Gendebien	Ferrari (1) Lotus-Climax (1)	2			1		3			
13	3	GBR	Jack Lewis	Cooper-Climax	5								
15	3	SWE	Jo Bonnier	Porsche	8		1			1			
15	3	GBR	Graham Hill	BRM-Climax	8								
17	2	GBR	Roy Salvadori	Cooper-Climax	6								

Championship ranking	Championship points	Team/Marque nationality	1961 Constructors Championship Chassis	Engine	Engine maker nationality	Races contested	Race victories	1-2 finishes	Podiums excl. victories	Races led	Laps led	Poles	Fastest laps
1	40	ITA	Ferrari 156	Ferrari 1.5 V6	ITA	7	5	3	9	6	283	6	5
2	32	GBR	Lotus 21, 18/21, 18	Coventry-Climax 1.5 S4	GBR	8	3		2		174	1	2
3	22	GER	Porsche 718, 787	Porsche 1.5 F4	GER	8			3		5		
4	14	GBR	Cooper T55, T53, T45, T58	Coventry-Climax 1.5 S4, 1.5 V8	GBR	8			1		28	1	1
5	7	GBR	BRM P48/57	Coventry-Climax 1.5 S4	GBR	8			1				1

1962

Graham Hill keeps Clark waiting

THE TALE OF THE TITLE

■ Following their 1961 mauling by Ferrari, British drivers and constructors bounced back.
■ A battle royal waged between Jim Clark and Graham Hill filled the void left by Stirling Moss.
■ A heavy accident at the pre-season Easter Goodwood meeting ended Moss' career.
■ Graham Hill took the title, his four wins including superlative triumphs at the Nürburgring and Monza.
■ BRM laid their 1950s ghosts forever with a deserved constructors' title for their excellent P57 V8.
■ But Chapman's monocoque chassis revolutionised F1 design, Clark's Lotus 25 fast but fragile.
■ Clark's moment of truth came at the Nürburgring, driver oversight leaving him stranded on the grid.
■ At Rouen Dan Gurney won in the Flat-8 Porsche, their only success as a constructor.
■ Reigning champions Ferrari were nowhere, their Tipo 156 V6 totally eclipsed by the svelte British V8s.
■ And not forgetting: the car that Jack built.

THE CHASE FOR THE CHAMPIONSHIP

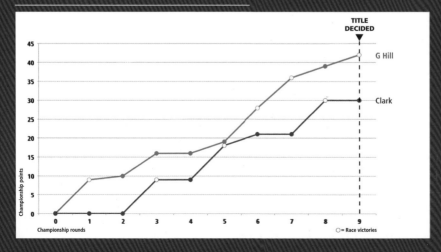

BRM P57

| Round 1/9 | **DUTCH GP** Zandvoort | | | | | **Graham Hill** |
| | 20 May 1962 | | | Race 103 | | BRM P57 153.596kph, 95.440mph |

The season began with two sensations: Colin Chapman launched his radical Lotus 25 for Clark, while Surtees stuck the new Lola-Climax on pole. These two and Graham Hill's BRM filled the front row. Chased by Hill, Clark shot into the lead for the first 11 laps until clutch trouble sidelined the brand new car. From there Hill had things much his own way, particularly following early retirements for both Gurney's Flat-8 Porsche and McLaren's Cooper, which set fastest lap. Trevor Taylor kept the Team Lotus flag flying with a superb second place after catching and passing the world champion's Ferrari. But the day belonged to Phil's namesake Graham, recording his maiden GP victory and bringing championship debut success to the BRM V8.

POLE POSITION J Surtees, Lola-Climax, 1m 32.5s (0.1s), 163.187kph, 101.400mph
LAPS 80 x 4.193 km, 2.605 miles
DISTANCE 335.440 km, 208.433 miles
STARTERS/FINISHERS 20/9
WEATHER Sunny, warm, dry
LAP LEADERS J Clark, Lotus-Climax 1-11 (11); G Hill 12-80 (69)
WINNER'S LAPS 1 P3, 2-11 P2, 12-80 P1
FASTEST LAP B McLaren, Cooper-Climax, 1m 34.4s (lap 5), 159.903kph, 99.359mph
CHAMPIONSHIP G Hill 9, Taylor 6, P Hill 4, Baghetti 3, Maggs 2

Pos	Driver	Car	Time/gap	Grid	Stops	Tyres
1	G Hill	BRM	2h 11m 2.1s	2	0	D
2	T Taylor	Lotus-Climax	−27.2s	10	0	D
3	P Hill	Ferrari	−1m 21.1s	9	0	D
4	G Baghetti	Ferrari	−1 lap	12	0	D
5	T Maggs	Cooper-Climax	−2 laps	15	0	D
6	C G de Beaufort	Porsche	−4 laps	14	NA	D

Cooper-Climax T60

MONACO GP Monte Carlo

3 June 1962   Race 104

Bruce McLaren

Cooper-Climax T60 113.337kph, 70.424mph

Qualifying had Clark on pole from Graham Hill and McLaren's Cooper-Climax. A first corner mêleé eliminated three cars, delayed Clark, but left McLaren leading from Hill. Hill took command on lap 7 but a recovering Clark had other ideas. Passing first Brabham and then McLaren on lap 27, the Lotus made up the 8s deficit to Hill and by lap 45 was on his gearbox. But that was as far as their duel went, clutch trouble again putting Clark out by lap 56. But Hill, now leading McLaren by 48s, was to endure even greater disappointment, suffering a smoky retirement just eight laps from the finish. So McLaren gave Cooper their first victory in approaching two years; the next would take even longer.

POLE POSITION J Clark, Lotus-Climax, 1m 35.4s (0.2s), 118.679kph, 73.744mph
LAPS 100 x 3.145km, 1.954 miles
DISTANCE 314.500 km, 195.421 miles
STARTERS/FINISHERS 16/8
WEATHER Overcast, dry
LAP LEADERS McLaren 1-6, 93-100 (14); G Hill 7-92 (86)
WINNER'S LAPS 1-6 P1, 7-27 P2, 28-29 P3, 30 P5, 31-55 P3, 56-92 P2, 93-100 P1
FASTEST LAP J Clark, Lotus-Climax, 1m 35.5s (lap 42), 118.555kph, 73.667mph
CHAMPIONSHIP G Hill 10, P Hill 10, McLaren 9, Taylor 6, Bandini 4

Pos	Driver	Car	Time/gap	Grid	Stops	Tyres
1	B McLaren	Cooper-Climax	2h 46m 29.7s	3	0	D
2	P Hill	Ferrari	−1.3s	9	0	D
3	L Bandini	Ferrari	−1m 24.1s	10	0	D
4	J Surtees	Lola-Climax	−1 lap	11	0	D
5	J Bonnier	Porsche	−7 laps	15	0	D
6r	G Hill	BRM	−8 laps	2	0	D

BELGIAN GP Spa-Francorchamps

17 June 1962   Race 105

Jim Clark

Lotus-Climax 25 212.266kph, 131.896mph

The first two rounds indicated that given reliability, Jim Clark's Lotus would be hard to beat. Spa proved the point. After a troubled practice, the Scotsman came from P12 on the grid to win by over 40s. It was his maiden GP victory as well as the first for a monocoque chassis. The race was highlighted by a spirited tussle, initially for the lead, between Clark's teammate Trevor Taylor and Willy Mairesse's Ferrari. It nearly ended in tragedy on lap 26 when they touched, Mairesse crashing in flames. Both cars were destroyed, the injured Mairesse lucky to survive. Pole-sitter G. Hill's spluttering BRM finished second and P. Hill's outclassed if reliable Ferrari completed a podium hat-trick.

POLE POSITION G Hill, BRM, 3m 57.0s (1.8s), 214.177kph, 133.084mph
LAPS 32 x 14.100 km, 8.761 miles
DISTANCE 451.200 km, 280.363 miles
STARTERS/FINISHERS 19/11
WEATHER Sunny, warm, dry
LAP LEADERS G Hill 1 (1); T Taylor, Lotus-Climax 2-3, 5, 7-8 (5); W Mairesse, Ferrari 4, 6 (2); Clark 9-32 (24)
WINNER'S LAPS 1 P4, 2 P5, 3 P4, 4-7 P5, 8 P2, 9-32 P1
FASTEST LAP Clark, Lotus-Climax, 3m 55.6s (lap 15), 215.450kph, 133.874mph
CHAMPIONSHIP G Hill 16, P Hill 14, McLaren 9, J Clark 9, Taylor 6

Pos	Driver	Car	Time/gap	Grid	Stops	Tyres
1	J Clark	Lotus-Climax	2h 7m 32.3s	12	0	D
2	G Hill	BRM	−44.1s	1	0	D
3	P Hill	Ferrari	−2m 6.5s	4	0	D
4	R Rodríguez	Ferrari	−2m 6.6s	7	0	D
5	J Surtees	Lola-Climax	−1 lap	11	NA	D
6	J Brabham	Lotus-Climax	−2 laps	15	NA	D

FRENCH GP Rouen-les-Essarts

8 July 1962   Race 106

Dan Gurney

Porsche 804 166.124kph, 103.225mph

This was one that got away for BRM's Graham Hill, who had the measure of everyone that day. Hill established a dominant lead over Surtees, Clark and the rest, leading 38 of 54 laps until hobbled by fuel injection trouble to finish ten laps down. He even survived a mid-race fracas when rammed by a backmarker, the ensuing spin giving Clark a short-lived lead. But it's the last lap that counts and, after finishing such a close second to Baghetti last year, Dan Gurney gave Porsche and himself their first victory. Trintignant limping home and Taylor finishing at high speed were luckily unscathed after a massive finish-line shunt, writing off both cars. Four races, four winners, Graham Hill from namesake Phil at the top of the points table.

POLE POSITION J Clark, Lotus-Climax, 2m 14.8s (0.2s), 174.712kph, 108.561mph
LAPS 54 x 6.542 km, 4.065 miles
DISTANCE 353.268 km, 219.511 miles
STARTERS/FINISHERS 17/9
WEATHER Sunny, warm, dry
LAP LEADERS G Hill 1-29, 33-41 (38); Clark 30-32 (3); Gurney 42-54 (13)
WINNER'S LAPS 1-9 P6, 10-13 P4, 14-32 P3, 33-41 P2, 42-54 P1
FASTEST LAP G Hill, BRM, 2m 16.9s (lap 32), 172.032kph, 106.896mph
CHAMPIONSHIP G Hill 16, P Hill 14, McLaren 12, J Clark 9, Gurney 9

Pos	Driver	Car	Time/gap	Grid	Stops	Tyres
1	D Gurney	Porsche	2h 7m 35.5s	6	0	D
2	T Maggs	Cooper-Climax	−1 lap	11	0	D
3	R Ginther	BRM	−2 laps	10	1	D
4	B McLaren	Cooper-Climax	−3 laps	3	1	D
5	J Surtees	Lola-Climax	−3 laps	5	1	D
6	C G de Beaufort	Porsche	−3 laps	17	0	D

Porsche 804

<table>
<tr><td colspan="2">**Round 5/9**</td><td>**BRITISH GP** Aintree</td><td></td><td>**Jim Clark**</td></tr>
<tr><td colspan="2"></td><td>21 July 1962</td><td>Race 107</td><td>Lotus-Climax 25 148.427kph, 92.247mph</td></tr>
</table>

The second successive but final British GP to be held at Aintree was utterly dominated by Jim Clark. From pole he led every lap, recorded fastest lap and won by almost a minute in the sun-soaked conditions. Although Surtees tried to make a race of it in the Lola, finishing second, Clark was simply in a class of his own, his second victory elevating him to just one point behind championship leader Graham Hill. Hill's BRM qualified poorly and was never in the hunt for victory, finishing fourth behind McLaren's Cooper. The Porsches and P. Hill's lone Ferrari were totally outperformed by the British machinery, Gurney best placed, starting sixth and finishing ninth.

POLE POSITION Clark, Lotus-Climax, 1m 53.6s (0.6s), 153.001kph, 95.070mph
LAPS 75 x 4.828 km, 3.000 miles
DISTANCE 362.100 km, 225.000 miles
STARTERS/FINISHERS 21/16
WEATHER Sunny, warm, dry
LAP LEADERS Clark 1-17 (75)
WINNER'S LAPS 1-75 P1
FASTEST LAP Clark, Lotus-Climax, 1m 55.0s (lap 36), 151.138kph, 93.913mph
CHAMPIONSHIP G Hill 19, J Clark 18, McLaren 16, P Hill 14, Surtees 13

Pos	Driver	Car	Time/gap	Grid	Stops	Tyres
1	J Clark	Lotus-Climax	2h 26m 20.8s	1	0	D
2	J Surtees	Lola-Climax	−49.2s	2	0	D
3	B McLaren	Cooper-Climax	−1m 44.8s	4	0	D
4	G Hill	BRM	−1m 56.8s	5	0	D
5	J Brabham	Lotus-Climax	−1 lap	9	0	D
6	T Maggs	Cooper-Climax	−1 lap	13	0	D

<table>
<tr><td colspan="2">**Round 6/9**</td><td>**GERMAN GP** Nürburgring</td><td></td><td>**Graham Hill**</td></tr>
<tr><td colspan="2"></td><td>5 August 1962</td><td>Race 108</td><td>BRM P57 129.312kph, 80.351mph</td></tr>
</table>

Gurney, Hill, Clark and Surtees made up the front row and were to fill the first four positions by the close. In wet and demanding conditions Hill won brilliantly from Surtees, Gurney and Clark, all four drivers putting on an impressive display of skill and courage around the notorious Nordschleife circuit. The first three battled throughout the almost two hours and 40 minutes' duration, crossing the line just 4.4s apart. Clark's fourth place came after a fine recovery drive from a grid delay caused by failure to switch on his petrol pump. He then clawed his way back from tenth place, even catching the leaders, until after a particularly frightening slide in the treacherous conditions on lap 11 he wisely settled for fourth. Jack debuted his Brabham-Climax.

POLE POSITION Gurney, Porsche, 8m 47.2s (3.0s), 155.759kph, 96.784mph
LAPS 15 x 22.810 km, 14.173 miles
DISTANCE 342.150 km, 212.602 miles
STARTERS/FINISHERS 26/16
WEATHER Rain throughout, often heavy
LAP LEADERS Gurney 1-2 (2); G Hill 3-15 (13)
WINNER'S LAPS 1-2 P2, 3-15 P1
FASTEST LAP G Hill, BRM, 10m 12.2s (lap 3), 134.133kph, 83.386mph
CHAMPIONSHIP G Hill 28, J Clark 21, Surtees 19, McLaren 18, P Hill 14

Pos	Driver	Car	Time/gap	Grid	Stops	Tyres
1	G Hill	BRM	2h 38m 45.3s	2	0	D
2	J Surtees	Lola-Climax	−2.4s	4	0	D
3	D Gurney	Porsche	−4.4s	1	0	D
4	J Clark	Lotus-Climax	−42.1s	3	0	D
5	B McLaren	Cooper-Climax	−1m 19.6s	5	0	D
6	R Rodríguez	Ferrari	−1m 23.8s	10	0	D

TOP **100** RACE

Round 7/9	**ITALIAN GP** Monza					**Graham Hill**		
	16 September 1962			Race 109		BRM P57 198.941kph, 123.616mph		

Monza being known as a power circuit, BRM cannily brought an uprated V8 and left with an overwhelming 1-2 victory. Such was winner Hill's pace, posting fastest laps on his third and fourth tours, it is hard to imagine a different result even if pole-sitter Clark had lasted more than three laps before pitting with gear selection difficulties. Hill's dominance was such that he won by almost half a minute from teammate Ginther and a minute over the pack led by McLaren's Cooper following a terrific tussle with the Porsches and Ferraris. Combining power with reliability, Hill and BRM had taken the championship by the throat and now led Clark by 15 points with just two rounds to go. In a soul-destroying season, this was Ferraris' final appearance.

POLE POSITION J Clark, Lotus-Climax, 1m 40.35s (0.03s), 206.278kph, 128.175mph
LAPS 86 x 5.750 km, 3.573 miles
DISTANCE 494.500 km, 307.268 miles
STARTERS/FINISHERS 21/14
WEATHER Overcast, late drizzle
LAP LEADERS G Hill 1-86
WINNER'S LAPS 1-86 P1
FASTEST LAP G Hill, BRM, 1m 42.30s (laps 3 & 4), 202.346kph, 125.732mph
CHAMPIONSHIP G Hill 36, McLaren 22, J Clark 21, Surtees 19, P Hill 14

Pos	Driver	Car	Time/gap	Grid	Stops	Tyres
1	G Hill	BRM	2h 29m 8.4s	2	0	D
2	R Ginther	BRM	−29.8s	3	0	D
3	B McLaren	Cooper-Climax	−57.8s	4	0	D
4	W Mairesse	Ferrari	−58.2s	10	0	D
5	G Baghetti	Ferrari	−1m 31.3s	18	0	D
6	J Bonnier	Porsche	−1 lap	9	0	D

Round 8/9	**UNITED STATES GP** Watkins Glen					**Jim Clark**		
	7 October 1962			Race 110		Lotus-Climax 25 174.576kph, 108.476mph		

In America Clark did what he had to – win. By so doing, despite rival Hill finishing second, Clark's championship hopes were kept alive as the combatants approached the final round of the season. Hill fought Clark all the way, overtaking in traffic to lead for seven laps. But just as in qualifying, Clark held the edge, going on to win by 9.2s despite racing half the distance without a clutch. McLaren was best of the rest, albeit a lap down. Brabham scored his first point in his own car with fourth, while Ferrari yet again decided not to travel to the States. But of greatest significance, a repeat performance by Clark in South Africa would bring him the title wherever Hill finished.

POLE POSITION Clark, Lotus-Climax, 1m 15.8s (0.8s), 175.796kph, 109.235mph
LAPS 100 x 3.701 km, 2.300 miles
DISTANCE 370.149 km, 230.000 miles
STARTERS/FINISHERS 18/13
WEATHER Overcast, dry
LAP LEADERS Clark 1-11, 19-100 (93); G Hill 12-18 (7)
WINNER'S LAPS 1-11 P1, 12-18 P2, 19-100 P1
FASTEST LAP Clark, Lotus-Climax, 1m 15.0s (lap 70), 177.672kph, 110.400mph
CHAMPIONSHIP G Hill 39, J Clark 30, McLaren 24, Surtees 19, Gurney 15

Pos	Driver	Car	Time/gap	Grid	Stops	Tyres
1	J Clark	Lotus-Climax	2h 7m 13.0s	1	0	D
2	G Hill	BRM	−9.2s	3	0	D
3	B McLaren	Cooper-Climax	−1 lap	6	0	D
4	J Brabham	Brabham-Climax	−1 lap	5	0	D
5	D Gurney	Porsche	−1 lap	4	0	D
6	M Gregory	Lotus-BRM	−1 lap	7	0	D

Round 9/9	**SOUTH AFRICAN GP** East London					**Graham Hill**		
	29 December 1962			Race 111		BRM P57 150.624kph, 93.594mph		

Yet again no Ferraris in South Africa, nor Porsches. Clark and Hill shared the front row, Brabham's Brabham a praiseworthy third. Clark set a furious pace from the start, Hill trying all he knew to hang on, the title protagonists way ahead of the rest. At three-quarter-distance with an unassailable lead, surely Clark had done it? Ominous puffs of smoke spelt otherwise. A bolt had dropped out of the engine crankcase, the resultant oil leak ending Clark's magnificent challenge on lap 62. With Clark's retirement Hill became champion but he proceeded to triumph in style with his fourth race victory of the season, which also underlined BRM's constructors' trophy.

POLE POSITION J Clark, Lotus-Climax, 1m 29.3s (1.1s), 158.044kph, 98.204mph
LAPS 82 x 3.920 km, 2.436 miles
DISTANCE 321.470 km, 199.752 miles
STARTERS/FINISHERS 17/11
WEATHER Sunny, warm, dry, windy
LAP LEADERS Clark 1-61 (61); G Hill 62-82 (21)
WINNER'S LAPS 1-61 P2, 62-82 P1
FASTEST LAP J Clark, Lotus-Climax, 1m 31.0s (lap 3), 155.091kph, 96.369mph
CHAMPIONSHIP G Hill 42, J Clark 30, McLaren 27, Surtees 19, Gurney 15

Pos	Driver	Car	Time/gap	Grid	Stops	Tyres
1	G Hill	BRM	2h 8m 3.3s	2	0	D
2	B McLaren	Cooper-Climax	−49.8s	8	0	D
3	T Maggs	Cooper-Climax	−50.3s	6	0	D
4	J Brabham	Brabham-Climax	−53.8s	3	0	D
5	I Ireland	Lotus-Climax	−1 lap	4	0	D
6	N Lederle	Lotus-Climax	−4 laps	10	0	D

1962 CHAMPIONSHIP FACTS AND FOLKLORE

- Nine races comprised the 1962 championship, the best five results counting and constructors' points brought into line with the drivers', nine points awarded for victory.
- Aintree staged its final Grand Prix while South Africa became a new race venue, hosting the championship finale.
- On 23 April Stirling Moss crashed heavily at the pre-season Easter Goodwood F1 race meeting, receiving severe head injuries, the circumstances of his accident never fully explained. He subsequently elected to retire from GP racing, feeling he no longer possessed that vital ingredient.
- Despite the absence of 'the man to beat', 1962 was a gripping championship battle between two very singular talents vying to fill the vacuum left by Moss.
- Neither Jim Clark nor Graham Hill had been a championship contender previously but as Clark's Lotus V8 and Hill's BRM V8 had each won two of the preliminary non-championship F1 encounters, their credentials for championship honours were building strongly.
- The British teams, left behind by Ferrari in 1961 after wasting time objecting to the implementation of the 1.5-litre F1

regulations, were now fully up to speed, with new multi-cylinder engines from Coventry-Climax and BRM.
- The svelte chassis and running gear of the new British V8s made last year's all-conquering Ferrari 156 look like a throwback to the 1950s, handsome as it may have been with its shark nose and wire wheels.
- Further adding to Ferrari woes, a serious disagreement led team manager Tavoni and other key technicians to walk out, hampering early season development.
- With Ferrari in the doldrums the championship quickly assumed the classic cocktail which makes Formula 1 so compelling, the fusion of driver brilliance with technical excellence, and in 1962 Lotus possessed the former and moved the goalposts for the latter. Yet still they lost.
- Successfully participating in the non-championship F1 warm-up races with the spaceframe Lotus 24, at the opening championship round they truly upset their customer teams by fielding the radical Lotus 25.
- From the ingenious pen of Colin Chapman, the innovative monocoque Lotus 25 took fundamentals of chassis design

RACE 108, German GP: In wet and demanding conditions Hill (11) won brilliantly from Surtees and Gurney (7), all three displaying immense skill and courage around the notorious Nordschleife circuit.

to new heights, especially lightness, rigidity and low frontal area assisted by a sharply reclined driver position.

- The monocoque chassis abandoned the multi-tubular spaceframe concept in favour of a pair of linked, stressed aluminium pontoons within which were housed the fuel tanks and between which sat the driver, this initial monocoque design nicknamed 'bathtub'.
- Records show that, on the brink of success in South Africa, Clark lost the title to Hill when loss of oil sidelined his monocoque Lotus, a bolt having dropped from the crankcase. In reality, however, Clark's moment of truth came at the Nürburgring, when he was left standing on the grid after failing to switch on his fuel pump.
- Hill went on to victory in Germany, and it was the nature of this win, plus the one that followed at Monza, which ensured he was the deserving recipient of the 1962 title.
- Lotus had yet to learn the F1 maxim, 'To finish first, first you have to finish'.
- Another precept for winning close-fought championships is to score big points when it's your rival's day of days. Across each of the races Clark won, Hill amassed 83% of the available points remaining, whereas Clark picked up a meagre 12% of the crumbs from Hill's table.

- The only other race victories were those somewhat fortuitously commandeered by Bruce McLaren's Cooper-Climax and the Porsche of Dan Gurney. These two, along with Surtees in the Lola and Brabham now driving his own car, played walk-on roles beside the two major players.
- Porsche withdrew from F1 at the end of the season to focus on sports car racing, but as one departed another arrived, Jack Brabham, turned constructor, debuting a car bearing his own name at the German GP.
- For 1962 Yeoman Credit had sold out to Bowmaker Finance to become the Bowmaker Racing Team, a quasi-works effort led by Reg Parnell and running the new Lola Mk4 designed by Eric Broadley with drivers John Surtees and Roy Salvadori. Despite success for Surtees in the pre-season Mallory Park International 2000 Guineas, and two championship P2s, the venture was generally a disappointment.
- In November, Mexican ace Ricardo Rodríguez was killed while practicing for a non-championship F1 race in his native country, a race staged as a preliminary to the first Mexican GP for 1963.

Championship ranking	Championship points	Driver nationality	1962 Drivers Championship		Races contested	Race victories	Podiums excl. victories	Races led	Flag to flag victories	Laps led	Poles	Fastest laps	Triple Crowns
			Driver	Car									
1	42	GBR	Graham Hill	BRM	9	4	2	8	1	321	1	3	
2	30	GBR	Jim Clark	Lotus-Climax	9	3		6	1	267	6	5	2
3	27	NZL	Bruce McLaren	Cooper-Climax	9	1	4	1		14		1	
4	19	GBR	John Surtees	Lola-Climax	9		2				1		
5	15	USA	Dan Gurney	Porsche	7	1	1	2		15	1		
6	14	USA	Phil Hill	Ferrari	6		3						
7	13	RSA	Tony Maggs	Cooper-Climax	9		2						
8	10	USA	Richie Ginther	BRM	9		2						
9	9	AUS	Jack Brabham	Lotus-Climax (5) Brabham-Climax (3)	8								
10	6	GBR	Trevor Taylor	Lotus-Climax	9		1	1		5			
11	5	ITA	Giancarlo Baghetti	Ferrari	4								
12	4	ITA	Lorenzo Bandini	Ferrari	3		1						
13	4	MEX	Ricardo Rodriguez	Ferrari	4								
14	3	BEL	Willy Mairesse	Ferrari	3			1		2			
15	3	SWE	Jo Bonnier	Porsche	7								
16	2	GBR	Innes Ireland	Lotus-Climax	8								
17	2	NLD	Carel Godin de Beaufort	Porsche	8								
18	1	USA	Masten Gregory	Lotus-Climax (2) Lotus-BRM (4)	6								
18	1	RSA	Neville Lederle	Lotus-Climax	1								

Championship ranking	Championship points	Team/Marque nationality	1962 Constructors Championship		Engine maker nationality	Races contested	Race victories	1-2 finishes	Podiums excl. victories	Races led	Laps led	Poles	Fastest laps
			Chassis	Engine									
1	42	GBR	BRM P57, P48/57	BRM 1.5 V8	GBR	9	4	1	4	8	321	1	3
2	36	GBR	Lotus 25, 24, 21, 18/21, 18	Coventry-Climax 1.5 V8, 1.5 S4	GBR	9	3		1	6	272	6	5
3	29	GBR	Cooper T60, T55, T53	Coventry-Climax 1.5 V8, 1.5 S4	GBR	9	1		6	1	14		1
4	19	GBR	Lola Mk4, Mk 4A	Coventry-Climax 1.5 V8	GBR	9			2			1	
5	18	GER	Porsche 804, 718, 787	Porsche 1.5 F8, 1.5 F4	GER	9	1		1	2	15	1	
6	18	ITA	Ferrari 156	Ferrari 1.5 V6	ITA	6			4	1	2		
7	6	AUS	Brabham BT3	Coventry-Climax 1.5 V8	GBR	3							
8	1	GBR	Lotus 24	BRM 1.5 V8	GBR	6							

1963

Jim Clark's highland fling

THE TALE OF THE TITLE

■ Clark and the monocoque Lotus 25 utterly dominated, winning seven races of the ten-race championship.
■ This set a new record for victories in a season and included five rampant flag-to-flag performances.
■ With a vast improvement in reliability, only minor gremlins prevented a Team Lotus clean-sweep.
■ The one-sided championship, settled by Monza, produced only two other winning drivers, also British.
■ In his first season with Ferrari, John Surtees returned the Scuderia to the winners' circle at the Nürburgring.
■ Graham Hill notched up two for BRM in the obsolete P57, their P61 'Lotus-eater' proving disappointing.
■ The Brabham team made a strong impression in their first full season, four podiums for Gurney and Jack.
■ Dutchman Carel Godin de Beaufort kept the Porsche flag flying with his orange Écurie Maarsbergen entry.
■ And not forgetting: ATS flop.

THE CHASE FOR THE CHAMPIONSHIP

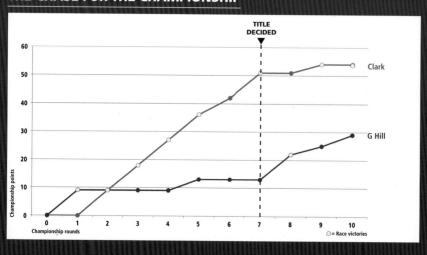

MONACO GP Monte Carlo
26 May 1963   Race 112

Graham Hill
BRM P57 116.605kph, 72.455mph

With Clark and Hill heading the grid, a resumption of their close rivalry seemed likely for 1963. Hill made the better start but after 17 laps Clark went ahead to eke out a 17s lead by lap 78. But, with shades of 1962, on the following lap he spun out with a jammed gearbox. So world champion Graham Hill's title defence got off to a flyer, leading a BRM 1-2 in a closely fought contest over the 100 laps. John Surtees, qualifying P3 on his championship debut for Ferrari, passed G. Hill for second on lap 57 but was repassed six laps later, falling back as he fumbled with oil smothered goggles. In his endeavours to wrench the final podium spot from last year's race winner Bruce McLaren in the Cooper-Climax, Surtees set a new lap record on the final lap.

POLE POSITION J Clark, Lotus-Climax, 1m 34.3s (0.2s), 120.064kph, 74.604mph
LAPS 100 x 3.145km, 1.954 miles
DISTANCE 314.500 km, 195.421 miles
STARTERS/FINISHERS 15/9
WEATHER Sunny, warm, dry
LAP LEADERS G Hill 1-17, 79-100 (39); J Clark, Lotus-Climax 18-78 (61)
WINNER'S LAPS 1-17 P1, 18-56 P2, 57-62 P3, 63-78 P2, 79-100 P1
FASTEST LAP J Surtees, Ferrari, 1m 34.5s (lap 100), 119.810kph, 74.446mph
CHAMPIONSHIP G Hill 9, Ginther 6, McLaren 4, Surtees 3, Maggs 2

Pos	Driver	Car	Time/gap	Grid	Stops	Tyres
1	G Hill	BRM	2h 41m 49.7s	2	0	D
2	R Ginther	BRM	−4.6s	4	0	D
3	B McLaren	Cooper-Climax	−12.8s	8	0	D
4	J Surtees	Ferrari	−14.1s	3	0	D
5	T Maggs	Cooper-Climax	−2 laps	10	NA	D
6	T Taylor	Lotus-Climax	−2 laps	9	NA	D

Lotus-Climax 25

BELGIAN GP Spa-Francorchamps
9 June 1963   Race 113

Jim Clark
Lotus-Climax 25 183.175kph, 113.819mph

After a troubled practice, Clark made a scintillating start from the third row to lead by Eau Rouge. In damp to wet conditions he pulled away at an astonishing rate from the rest of the field led by Hill from pole, the Lotus more then 30s to the good by half-distance. Hill's gearbox didn't last much longer and it was also around this time that a thunderstorm hit the circuit, the track awash, visibility minimal. Times increased from around four minutes per lap to more then six as the drivers tiptoed their way around. By this time Clark had lapped all but Bruce McLaren, who crossed the line to start his final lap just before Clark finished the race, Clark's extraordinary winning margin therefore very nearly five minutes.

POLE POSITION G Hill, BRM, 3m 54.1s (0.9s), 216.830kph, 134.732mph
LAPS 32 x 14.100 km, 8.761 miles
DISTANCE 451.200 km, 280.363 miles
STARTERS/FINISHERS 20/8
WEATHER Overcast, wet mid-race and very wet over closing laps
LAP LEADERS Clark 1-32 (32)
WINNER'S LAPS 1-32 P1
FASTEST LAP Clark, Lotus-Climax, 3m 58.1s (lap 16), 213.188kph, 132.469mph
CHAMPIONSHIP McLaren 10, G Hill 9, Clark 9, Ginther 9, Gurney 4

Pos	Driver	Car	Time/gap	Grid	Stops	Tyres
1	J Clark	Lotus-Climax	2h 27m 47.6s	8	0	D
2	B McLaren	Cooper-Climax	−4m 54.0s	5	0	D
3	D Gurney	Brabham-Climax	−1 lap	2	0	D
4	R Ginther	BRM	−1 lap	9	0	D
5	J Bonnier	Cooper-Climax	−2 laps	13	NA	D
6	C G de Beaufort	Porsche	−2 laps	18	NA	D

Round 3/10	**DUTCH GP** Zandvoort		**Jim Clark**
	23 June 1963	Race 114	Lotus-Climax 25 156.958kph, 97.529mph

In Holland Clark 'grand slammed' the opposition: won pole, led every lap, set fastest lap. He even lapped the entire field. Best of the rest came Dan Gurney, now driving for Jack Brabham's eponymous team. This was despite starting P14 due to engine problems during practice and a lap 30 pit stop during the race to fix a loose fuel pipe. At half-distance Gurney ran sixth behind Hill, Brabham, Surtees and Ireland. As Hill and Brabham both failed to make the finish due to late race mechanical retirements, Gurney's pursuit of Surtees, after overtaking Ireland, was for second place, which he took when Surtees spun the Ferrari at Tarzan on lap 63 and the Brabham-Climax flashed by.

POLE POSITION Clark, Lotus-Climax, 1m 31.6s (0.6s), 164.790kph, 102.396mph
LAPS 80 x 4.193 km, 2.605 miles
DISTANCE 335.440 km, 208.433 miles
STARTERS/FINISHERS 19/11
WEATHER Sunny, warm, dry
LAP LEADERS Clark 1-80 (80)
WINNER'S LAPS 1-80 P1
FASTEST LAP Clark, Lotus-Climax, 1m 33.7s (lap 56), 161.097kph, 100.101mph
CHAMPIONSHIP Clark 18, Ginther 11, McLaren 10, Gurney 10, G Hill 9

Pos	Driver	Car	Time/gap	Grid	Stops	Tyres
1	J Clark	Lotus-Climax	2h 8m 13.7s	1	0	D
2	D Gurney	Brabham-Climax	−1 lap	14	0	D
3	J Surtees	Ferrari	−1 lap	5	0	D
4	Ireland	BRP-BRM	−1 lap	7	0	D
5	R Ginther	BRM	−1 lap	6	0	D
6	L Scarfiotti	Ferrari	−2 laps	11	0	D

Round 4/10	**FRENCH GP** Reims		**Jim Clark**
	30 June 1963	Race 115	Lotus-Climax 25 201.676kph, 125.315mph

For the second successive race Clark was in 'grand slam' form, but this time failed to lap the field. He might well have done if his Coventry-Climax V8 motor had not lost its edge from lap 12. Despite having to nurse his engine Clark won easily from Maggs in the number two Cooper, who prevailed in a typical Reims slipstreaming gaggle during the early stages. Behind the vanishing Clark, this group included Hill, Brabham and Gurney who were next to finish, Hill giving the semi-monocoque BRM P61 its first outing and finishing third despite the addition of a one-minute penalty for a push-start on the grid. The Dunlops on Clark's winning Lotus had now completed their fourth GP.

POLE POSITION Clark, Lotus-Climax, 2m 20.2s (0.7s), 213.175kph, 132.461mph
LAPS 53 x 8.302 km, 5.159 miles
DISTANCE 440.006 km, 273.407 miles
STARTERS/FINISHERS 19/13
WEATHER Showers
LAP LEADERS Clark 1-53 (53)
WINNER'S LAPS 1-53 P1
FASTEST LAP Clark, Lotus-Climax, 2m 21.6s (lap 12), 211.068kph, 131.151mph
CHAMPIONSHIP Clark 27, Gurney 12, Ginther 11, McLaren 10, G Hill 9 (Hill awarded no points due to push start)

Pos	Driver	Car	Time/gap	Grid	Stops	Tyres
1	J Clark	Lotus-Climax	2h 10m 54.3s	1	0	D
2	T Maggs	Cooper-Climax	−1m 4.9s	8	0	D
3	G Hill	BRM	−2m 13.9s	2	0	D
4	J Brabham	Brabham-Climax	−2m 15.2s	5	0	D
5	D Gurney	Brabham-Climax	−2m 33.4s	3	1	D
6	J Siffert	Lotus-BRM	−1 lap	10	NA	D

Round 5/10	**BRITISH GP** Silverstone		**Jim Clark**
	20 July 1963	Race 116	Lotus-Climax 25 172.748kph, 107.341mph

From the front row the Brabhams completed the first lap 1-2, Jack leading, Clark uncharacteristically P5 despite his pole. Clark scuttled past Hill and McLaren on lap 2, Gurney lap 3, and on the next tour assumed his customary P1, pulling away to lead Gurney by 16s by half-distance. Brabham was already out with engine trouble and on lap 59 Gurney joined him. Attention now switched to the duel for second between Hill and Surtees, resolved in the Ferrari's favour when Hill's BRM coasted over the line, tanks dry. Another red car, Bandini's Centro-Sud BRM, might have taken fourth from Ginther's works entry but suffered a spectacular high-speed spin on lap 64 when the gearchange mounting broke.

POLE POSITION Clark, Lotus-Climax, 1m 34.4s (0.2s), 179.640kph, 111.623mph
LAPS 82 x 4.711 km, 2.927 miles
DISTANCE 386.265 km, 240.014 miles
STARTERS/FINISHERS 23/13
WEATHER Sunny, warm, dry
LAP LEADERS J Brabham, Brabham-Climax 1-3 (3); Clark 4-82 (79)
WINNER'S LAPS 1 P5, 2 P3, 3 P2, 4-82 P1
FASTEST LAP Surtees, Ferrari, 1m 36.0s (lap 3), 176.646kph, 109.763mph
CHAMPIONSHIP Clark 36, Ginther 14, G Hill 13, Surtees 13, Gurney 12

Pos	Driver	Car	Time/gap	Grid	Stops	Tyres
1	J Clark	Lotus-Climax	2h 14m 9.6s	1	0	D
2	J Surtees	Ferrari	−25.8s	5	0	D
3	G Hill	BRM	−37.6s	3	0	D
4	R Ginther	BRM	−1 lap	9	0	D
5	L Bandini	BRM	−1 lap	8	0	D
6	J Hall	Lotus-BRM	−2 laps	13	0	D

Ferrari 156

Round 6/10	**GERMAN GP** Nürburgring		**John Surtees**
	4 August 1963	Race 117	Ferrari 156 154.222kph, 95.829mph

John Surtees' first ever championship race victory also brought Ferrari their first GP success in almost two years. For much of the race he and Clark engaged in a fierce struggle for supremacy way ahead of the rest of the field. That Clark was hobbled by an increasingly worsening engine glitch – whereby, especially towards the end, his motor rarely ran on eight cylinders – detracted little from Surtees' fine accomplishment. Clark did well to finish, his final lap taking around a minute longer than usual as his engine maladies deepened. Richie Ginther's BRM came home a strong, consistent third, team leader Hill out early with gearbox trouble. There were a number of crashes during this race, McLaren ending up in hospital, Mairesse ending his career.

POLE POSITION Clark, Lotus-Climax, 8m 45.8s (0.9s), 156.173kph, 97.042mph
LAPS 15 x 22.810 km, 14.173 miles
DISTANCE 342.150 km, 212.602 miles
STARTERS/FINISHERS 22/10
WEATHER Sunny, warm, dry
LAP LEADERS Ginther 1 (1); Surtees 2-3, 5-15 (13); Clark 4 (1)
WINNER'S LAPS 1 P2, 2-3 P1, 4 P2, 5-15 P1
FASTEST LAP Surtees, Ferrari, 8m 47.0s (lap 9), 155.818kph, 96.821mph
CHAMPIONSHIP Clark 42, Surtees 22, Ginther 18, G Hill 13, Gurney 12

Pos	Driver	Car	Time/gap	Grid	Stops	Tyres
1	J Surtees	Ferrari	2h 13m 6.8s	2	0	D
2	J Clark	Lotus-Climax	–1m 17.5s	1	0	D
3	R Ginther	BRM	–2m 44.9s	6	0	D
4	G Mitter	Porsche	–8m 11.5s	15	0	D
5	J Hall	Lotus-BRM	–1 lap	16	0	D
6	J Bonnier	Cooper-Climax	–1 lap	12	1	D

Round 7/10	**ITALIAN GP** Monza		**Jim Clark**
	8 September 1963	Race 118	Lotus-Climax 25 205.575kph, 127.739mph

Surtees delighted the *tifosi* by putting the new semi-monocoque *Aero* V6 Ferrari on pole. Adding to Italian fervour, Lorenzo Bandini had been drafted in for Monza to drive the regular car, which he qualified P6. For the first 54 gripping laps of the race Hill, Surtees, Gurney and Clark disputed the lead until finally only Clark remained. The Surtees Ferrari was first to expire on lap 17, but the remaining three continued to chop and change the lead in typical Monza slipstreamer fashion until first Hill on lap 50 and then Gurney 13 laps later were forced to retire. A fifth victory for Clark from seven starts confirmed the Scotsman as undisputed champion, while Team Lotus, equally deservedly, picked up the constructors' cup.

POLE POSITION J Surtees, Ferrari, 1m 37.3s (0.03s), 212.744kph, 132.193mph
LAPS 86 x 5.750 km, 3.573 miles
DISTANCE 494.500 km, 307.268 miles
STARTERS/FINISHERS 20/16
WEATHER Sunny, warm, dry
LAP LEADERS G Hill, BRM 1-3, 23-26, 29-30, 32, 34-35, 39, 41 (13); J Surtees, Ferrari 4-16 (13); Clark 17-23, 28, 36, 40, 42-43, 45, 47-51, 53-54, 56-86 (50); D Gurney, Brabham-Climax 27, 31, 33, 37-38, 44, 46, 52, 55 (10)
WINNER'S LAPS 1-3 P3, 4-16 P2, 17-23 P1, 24-27 P3, 28 P1, 29 P2, 30 P3, 31 P2, 32-33 P3, 34-35 P2, 36 P1, 37-39 P3, 40 P1, 41 P2, 42-43 P1, 44 P2, 45 P1, 46 P2, 47-51 P1, 52 P2, 53-54 P1, 55 P2, 56-86 P1
FASTEST LAP Clark, Lotus-Climax, 1m 38.9s (lap 60), 209.302kph, 130.054mph
CHAMPIONSHIP Clark 51, Ginther 24, Surtees 22, McLaren 14, G Hill 13

Pos	Driver	Car	Time/gap	Grid	Stops	Tyres
1	J Clark	Lotus-Climax	2h 24m 19.6s	3	0	D
2	R Ginther	BRM	–1m 35.0s	4	0	D
3	B McLaren	Cooper-Climax	–1 lap	8	0	D
4r	I Ireland	BRP-BRM	–2 laps	10	0	D
5	J Brabham	Brabham-Climax	–2 laps	7	1	D
6	T Maggs	Cooper-Climax	–2 laps	13	0	D

Round 8/10	**UNITED STATES GP** Watkins Glen	**Graham Hill**
	6 October 1963 Race 119	BRM P57 175.290kph, 108.920mph

Hill on pole had his job made easier when Clark beside him failed to move up from the dummy grid due to a dud battery, only getting away after the rest had completed their first tour. Hill initially led Surtees, these two in close proximity until Hill's anti-roll bar came adrift shortly before half-distance. This allowed Surtees to pull away, but he was out of luck, a broken valve spring putting him out on lap 82. This left an understeering Hill to lead a BRM 1-2 from teammate Ginther. Although Clark finished a lap behind the triumphant Bourne cars, fast lapping and difficulties for both Brabhams enabled him to claim third place by the finish.

POLE POSITION G Hill, BRM 1m 13.4s (0.1s), 181.545kph, 112.807mph
LAPS 110 x 3.701 km, 2.300 miles
DISTANCE 407.164 km, 253.000 miles
STARTERS/FINISHERS 21/11
WEATHER Sunny, hot, dry
LAP LEADERS G Hill 1-6, 32, 35, 83-110 (36); J Surtees, Ferrari 7-31, 33-34, 36-82 (74)
WINNER'S LAPS 1-6 P1, 7-9 P2, 10-17 P3, 18-31 P2, 32 P1, 33-34 P2, 35 P1, 36-82 P2, 83-110 P1
FASTEST LAP Clark, Lotus-Climax, 1m 14.5s (laps 50, 59 & 61), 178.864kph, 111.141mph
CHAMPIONSHIP Clark 51, Ginther 28, G Hill 22, Surtees 22, McLaren 14

Pos	Driver	Car	Time/gap	Grid	Stops	Tyres
1	G Hill	BRM	2h 19m 22.1s	1	0	D
2	R Ginther	BRM	−34.3s	4	0	D
3	J Clark	Lotus-Climax	−1 lap	2	0	D
4	J Brabham	Brabham-Climax	−2 laps	5	0	D
5	L Bandini	Ferrari	−4 laps	9	NA	D
6	C G de Beaufort	Porsche	−11 laps	19	NA	D

Round 9/10	**MEXICAN GP** Mexico City	**Jim Clark**
	27 October 1963 Race 120	Lotus-Climax 25 150.152kph, 93.300mph

Clark's third 'grand slam' of the season simply trounced his opposition. At half-distance he was 48s clear of Gurney's Brabham-Climax, and by the finish his winning margin over Brabham's similar car had grown to more than 100s. In the non-Clark race the two Brabhams featured along with the BRMs and Surtees' Ferrari, although the latter failed to finish and Gurney's challenge was once again blunted by car ailments. At Watkins Glen Pedro Rodríguez had made his championship debut driving for Team Lotus, and made a second appearance here at his home circuit where just 12 months earlier brother Ricardo had lost his life.

POLE POSITION Clark, Lotus-Climax, 1m 58.8s (1.7s), 151.515ph, 94.147mph
LAPS 65 x 5.000 km, 3.107 miles
DISTANCE 325.000 km, 201.946 miles
STARTERS/FINISHERS 21/11
WEATHER Overcast, dry
LAP LEADERS Clark 1-65 (65)
WINNER'S LAPS 1-65 P1
FASTEST LAP Clark, Lotus-Climax, 1m 58.1s (lap NA), 152.413kph, 94.705mph
CHAMPIONSHIP Clark 54, Ginther 29, G Hill 25, Surtees 22, McLaren 14

Pos	Driver	Car	Time/gap	Grid	Stops	Tyres
1	J Clark	Lotus-Climax	2h 9m 52.1s	1	0	D
2	J Brabham	Brabham-Climax	−1m 41.1s	10	0	D
3	R Ginther	BRM	−1m 54.7s	5	0	D
4	G Hill	BRM	−1 lap	3	0	D
5	J Bonnier	Cooper-Climax	−3 laps	8	0	D
6	D Gurney	Brabham-Climax	−3 laps	4	0	D

Round 10/10	**SOUTH AFRICAN GP** East London	**Jim Clark**
	28 December 1963 Race 121	Lotus-Climax 25 153.075kph, 95.116mph

With this, his seventh victory of the season, Clark exceeded Ascari's record from 1952. Yet another start-to-finish victory from pole position put a final virtuoso stamp on his brilliant season. Behind the flying Scot, the Brabham team had now clearly surpassed BRM in their traditional role of 'best of the rest', Gurney comfortably beating Hill for second place. Indeed, the now former world champion, again driving the spaceframe BRM P57, suffered the ignominy of being lapped by Clark. Surtees' season also ended on a low note with more engine trouble, but Bandini – now the regular Ferrari number two – again scored points. So ended a season that had been long for everyone (May till December) save Clark and Lotus.

POLE POSITION Clark, Lotus-Climax, 1m 28.9s (0.1s), 158.755kph, 98.646mph
LAPS 85 x 3.920 km, 2.436 miles
DISTANCE 333.231 km, 207.060
STARTERS/FINISHERS 20/14
WEATHER Hot, dry, windy
LAP LEADERS Clark 1-85 (85)
WINNER'S LAPS 1-85 P1
FASTEST LAP Clark, Lotus-Climax, 1m 29.1s (lap 33), 158.398kph, 98.428mph
CHAMPIONSHIP Clark 54, G Hill 29, Ginther 29, Surtees 22, Gurney 19

Pos	Driver	Car	Time/gap	Grid	Stops	Tyres
1	J Clark	Lotus-Climax	2h 10m 36.9s	1	0	D
2	D Gurney	Brabham-Climax	−1m 6.8s	3	0	D
3	G Hill	BRM	−1 lap	6	0	D
4	B McLaren	Cooper-Climax	−1 lap	9	0	D
5	L Bandini	Ferrari	−1 lap	5	0	D
6	J Bonnier	Cooper-Climax	−2 laps	11	0	D

RACE 116, British GP: Clark's monocoque Lotus 25 utterly dominated 1963, winning seven of the ten championship races, five flag-to-flag. Here at Silverstone he at least let Brabham lead three laps.

1963 CHAMPIONSHIP FACTS AND FOLKLORE

- Ten races, the best six results counting, with Mexico City joining the championship calendar.
- A phenomenon first glimpsed in 1962, this was the season when Jim Clark unleashed the full latent potential of his brilliance behind the wheel of the monocoque Lotus 25.
- For 1963 Team Lotus had added one crucial missing ingredient – reliability.

- Conversely, their opposition lost some of theirs, preoccupied in their endeavours to play catch-up with Chapman's monocoque chassis revolution, and generally not making a particularly good fist of it either.
- Barring just three laps at Silverstone, six of Clark's seven victories were start-to-finish exhibitions with massive victory margins of well over a minute, although his extraordinary

4m 54s winning margin at Spa still did not exceed Moss' 1958 Porto equivalent of 5m 12.75s.
■ But such dominance hardly made for spellbinding racing or for a stirring championship battle.
■ Another factor that made the Clark-Lotus combo so potent was the Coventry-Climax V8 – the replacement of Weber carburettors by Lucas fuel injection for 1963 had eliminated the slight but telling power disadvantage it had endured against BRM and Ferrari engines. In this uprated form it produced 196bhp at 9,500rpm.
■ And finally, Clark's driving was not only devastatingly quick but also almost entirely error-free. It is a sobering thought that with 100% mechanical dependability, Clark may well have made a clean sweep of all ten championship rounds.
■ Two of these 'blemishes' enabled world champion Graham Hill to parade his undoubted prowess in what was increasingly an obsolete BRM.
■ This came about because both BRM and Ferrari's attempts to build new 'Lotus-eaters' by utilising a quasi-monocoque design were largely unsuccessful. This forced both teams to generally field lightly updated versions of last year's cars, Ferrari at last ditching spoke wheels for alloys.

■ Ironically, Brabham's designer Ron Tauranac flew in the face of the new chassis convention and continued to exploit multi-tubular spaceframe techniques with success, Gurney and Brabham turning in some highly competitive performances.
■ Ferrari too made progress, John Surtees beginning to lead the Scuderia back from the travails of 1962.
■ One such difficulty had been the exodus from Ferrari of certain key staff led by Carlo Chiti and Romolo Tavoni to form *Automobili Turismo e Sport* (ATS).
■ Securing the services of Phil Hill and Giancarlo Baghetti as drivers, during 1963 the ATS venture proved to be a calamitous embarrassment for all involved, the cars never qualifying better than 13th and finishing just twice from ten starts.
■ Finance companies Bowmaker and UDT had both exited the sport for 1963 so Reg Parnell ran the ex-Bowmaker Lolas, with 19-year-old New Zealander Chris Amon his lead driver.
■ With UDT gone the BRP name resurfaced and, disillusioned about reliance on Lotus customer cars, the team decided to become a constructor in its own right.
■ Another fleeting US-funded F1 venture was the Scirocco, built from the assets of the defunct Emeryson F1 project.

Championship ranking	Championship points	Driver nationality	1963 Drivers Championship		Races contested	Race victories	Podiumse excl. victories	Races led	Flag to flag victories	Laps led	Poles	Fastest laps	Triple Crowns
			Driver	Car									
1	54	GBR	Jim Clark	Lotus-Climax	10	7	2	9	5	506	7	6	3
2	29	GBR	Graham Hill	BRM	10	2	3	3		88	2		
3	29	USA	Richie Ginther	BRM	10		5	1		1			
4	22	GBR	John Surtees	Ferrari	10	1	2	3		100	1	3	
5	19	USA	Dan Gurney	Brabham-Climax	10		3	1		10		1	
6	17	NZL	Bruce McLaren	Cooper-Climax	10		3						
7	14	AUS	Jack Brabham	Lotus-Climax (1) Brabham-Climax (9)	10		1	1		3			
8	9	RSA	Tony Maggs	Cooper-Climax	10		1						
9	6	GBR	Innes Ireland	Lotus-BRM (2) BRP-BRM (5)	7								
10	6	ITA	Lorenzo Bandini	BRM (3) Ferrari (4)	7								
11	6	SWE	Jo Bonnier	Cooper-Climax	10								
12	3	GER	Gerhard Mitter	Porsche	2								
13	3	USA	Jim Hall	Lotus-BRM	9								
14	2	NDL	Carel Godin de Beaufort	Porsche	7								
15	1	GBR	Trevor Taylor	Lotus-Climax	9								
15	1	ITA	Ludovico Scarfiotti	Ferrari	1								
15	1	SUI	Jo Siffert	Lotus-BRM	9								

Championship ranking	Championship points	Team/Marque nationality	1963 Constructors Championship		Engine maker nationality	Races contested	Race victories	1-2 finishes	Podiums excl. victories	Races led	Laps led	Poles	Fastest laps
			Chassis	Engine									
1	54	GBR	Lotus 25, 24, 21	Coventry-Climax 1.5 V8, 1.5 S4	GBR	10	7		2	9	506	7	6
2	36	GBR	BRM P57, P61	BRM 1.5 V8	GBR	10	2	2	8	4	89	2	
3	28	AUS	Brabham BT7, BT3	Coventry-Climax 1.5 V8	GBR	10			4	2	13		1
4	26	ITA	Ferrari 156	Ferrari 1.5 V6	ITA	10	1		2	3	100	1	3
5	25	GBR	Cooper T66, T60, T55	Coventry-Climax 1.5 V8, 1.5 S4	GBR	10			4				
6	6	GBR	BRP Mk 1	BRM 1.5 V8	GBR	5							
7	5	GER	Porsche 718	Porsche 1.5 F4	GER	7							
8	4	GBR	Lotus 24	BRM 1.5 V8	GBR	9							

1964

Surtees does the improbable

THE TALE OF THE TITLE

- On the final lap of a three-way championship showdown, John Surtees and Ferrari snatched both titles.
- Ferrari number two Lorenzo Bandini infamously punted out rival Graham Hill, and later waved Surtees through.
- Surtees uniquely achieved the improbable feat of world championships on two wheels and on four.
- In a season of changing fortunes, Clark and Hill let their early advantage slip as Ferrari gained momentum.
- With his surprise Austrian victory, Bandini joined Surtees, Clark, Hill and Gurney on the podium top step.
- Four teams produced winning cars – Ferrari, Lotus and BRM with Brabham savouring their first success.
- In such an open season, three race victories was enough for Ferrari to clinch the constructors' title.
- Poor reliability remained a major results determinant, all teams proving susceptible.
- Better known for success in motorcycle racing, Honda brought Japan into the F1 world championships.
- And not forgetting: Carel Godin de Beaufort killed; 1961 champion Phil Hill retired.

THE CHASE FOR THE CHAMPIONSHIP

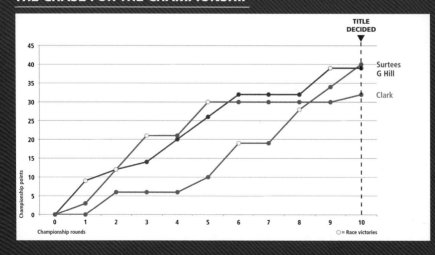

MONACO GP Monte Carlo
10 May 1964   Race 122

Graham Hill
BRM P261 116.969kph, 72.681mph

An uncharacteristic error by Clark on lap one, damaging an anti-roll bar at the chicane, caused him to lose his lead to Gurney on lap 37 when he pitted briefly to have the trailing debris removed. But the American's lead was short-lived, Hill driving superbly in the new monocoque BRM P261 to take the lead on lap 53 with fastest lap. Ten laps later Gurney's retirement allowed Clark to regain P2, but Hill would not be denied victory, pulling further away. Close to the end Clark's engine expired but he was still classified fourth, just six cars circulating at the chequered flag. Extraordinarily, Graham Hill's second successive victory round the houses was also a second successive BRM 1-2 at Monaco, Ginther finishing second, albeit a lap down from the winner.

POLE POSITION J Clark, Lotus-Climax, 1m 34.0s (0.1s), 120.447kph, 74.842mph
LAPS 100 x 3.145km, 1.954 miles
DISTANCE 314.500 km, 195.421 miles
STARTERS/FINISHERS 16/10
WEATHER Sunny, hot, dry
LAP LEADERS Clark 1-36 (36); D Gurney, Brabham-Climax 37-52 (16); G Hill 53-100 (48)
WINNER'S LAPS 1-10 P3, 11-12 P4, 13-36 P3, 37-52 P2, 53-100 P1
FASTEST LAP G Hill, BRM 1m 33.9s (lap 53), 120.575kph, 74.922mph
CHAMPIONSHIP G Hill 9, Ginther 6, Arundell 4, Clark 3, Bonnier 2

Pos	Driver	Car	Time/gap	Grid	Stops	Tyres
1	G Hill	BRM	2h 41m 19.5s	3	0	D
2	R Ginther	BRM	−1 lap	8	0	D
3	P Arundell	Lotus-Climax	−3 laps	6	1	D
4r	J Clark	Lotus-Climax	−4 laps	1	1	D
5	J Bonnier	Cooper-Climax	−4 laps	11	0	D
6	M Hailwood	Lotus-BRM	−4 laps	15	0	D

DUTCH GP Zandvoort
24 May 1964   Race 123

Jim Clark
Lotus-Climax 25 157.743kph, 98.017mph

After a repeat performance by BRM at Monaco, the second round was also reminiscent of last year in that Jim Clark led every lap and set fastest lap. But there were differences, Gurney ousting Clark from pole and Clark failing to lap the entire field. The only car not lapped was second-placed John Surtees in the V8-engined 'monocoque' Ferrari 158, albeit almost a minute behind the flying Scot in the Lotus 25. During the early stages Hill and Gurney had looked good for a podium finish but neither could complete the distance without problems intervening. Impressively, rookie Pete Arundell, as he had at Monaco, took another podium for Team Lotus.

POLE POSITION D Gurney, Brabham -Climax, 1m 31.2s (0.1s), 165.513kph, 102.845mph
LAPS 80 x 4.193 km, 2.605 miles
DISTANCE 335.440 km, 208.433 miles
STARTERS/FINISHERS 17/13
WEATHER Sunny, warm, dry
LAP LEADERS Clark 1-80 (80)
WINNER'S LAPS 1-80 P1
FASTEST LAP Clark, Lotus-Climax, 1m 32.8s (lap 6), 162.659kph, 101.072mph
CHAMPIONSHIP Clark 12, G Hill 12, Arundell 8, Ginther 6, Surtees 6

Pos	Driver	Car	Time/gap	Grid	Stops	Tyres
1	J Clark	Lotus-Climax	2h 7m 35.4s	2	0	D
2	J Surtees	Ferrari	−53.6s	4	0	D
3	P Arundell	Lotus-Climax	−1 lap	6	0	D
4	G Hill	BRM	−1 lap	3	1	D
5	C Amon	Lotus-BRM	−1 lap	13	0	D
6	B Anderson	Brabham-Climax	−2 laps	11	0	D

BELGIAN GP Spa-Francorchamps
14 June 1964   Race 124

Jim Clark
Lotus-Climax 25 213.712kph, 132.795mph

Despite a staggering pole time, an even quicker fastest lap and leading 28 of the 32 laps race-distance, Dan Gurney still couldn't bring the Brabham team their deserved maiden victory. Behind Gurney, Hill, McLaren and Clark – until delayed by a pit stop for water – closely contested second place. Then, two laps out, a bizarre sequence of events occurred. Leading by 40s Gurney pitted for fuel but found none to be available. This handed the lead to Hill, but during his final lap the Bendix fuel system failed on the BRM. Now McLaren's Cooper led, but his battery died at La Source. Coasting, 100 yards from the line, Bruce saw a flash of green and yellow as Clark snatched victory then promptly ran out of fuel.

POLE POSITION Gurney, Brabham-Climax, 3m 50.9s (1.8s), 219.835kph, 136.599mph
LAPS 32 x 14.100 km, 8.761 miles
DISTANCE 451.200 km, 280.363 miles
STARTERS/FINISHERS 18/10
WEATHER Overcast, dry
LAP LEADERS Gurney 1-2,4-29 (28); J Surtees, Ferrari 3 (1); G Hill 30-31 (2); Clark 32 (1)
WINNER'S LAPS 1-3 P3, 4-6 P2, 7-8 P3, 9-11 P4, 12 P2, 13-14 P3, 15 P2, 16, P3, 17-19 P2, 20-22 P3, 23 P4, 24-27 P3, 28-31 P4, 32 P1
FASTEST LAP Gurney, Brabham-Climax, 3m 49.2s (lap 27), 221.466kph, 137.613mph
CHAMPIONSHIP Clark 21, G Hill 14, Ginther 9, Arundell 8, Surtees 6

Pos	Driver	Car	Time/gap	Grid	Stops	Tyres
1	J Clark	Lotus-Climax	2h 6m 40.5s	6	1	D
2	B McLaren	Cooper-Climax	−3.4s	7	0	D
3	J Brabham	Brabham-Climax	−48.1s	3	0	D
4	R Ginther	BRM	−1m 58.6s	8	0	D
5r	G Hill	BRM	−1 lap	2	0	D
6r	D Gurney	Brabham-Climax	−1 lap	1	1	D

| Round 4/10 | **FRENCH GP** Rouen-les-Essarts | | **Dan Gurney** |
| | 28 June 1964 | Race 125 | Brabham-Climax BT7 175.042kph, 108.766mph |

Following heartbreak at Spa, Dan Gurney finally brought the Brabham team their very first championship victory. It was the venue of his own 1962 maiden win in a Porsche. In a role reversal of the extraordinary events in Belgium, Clark became the victim. Having led comfortably from pole, a holed piston on lap 31 of 57 ended his race. Gurney was there to assume an equally comfortable lead, which he maintained to the end. Following a lap 3 spin down to P13, Hill performed a strong recovery drive to thwart an historic Brabham 1-2. Fourth, for a while trading blows with Hill and Brabham, was Peter Arundell in his superb rookie season. Seven days later his F1 career was effectively ended in a serious F2 accident.

POLE POSITION J Clark, Lotus-Climax, 2m 9.6s (0.5s), 181.722kph, 112.917mph
LAPS 57 x 6.542 km, 4.065 miles
DISTANCE 372.894 km, 231.706 miles
STARTERS/FINISHERS 17/12
WEATHER Overcast, dry
LAP LEADERS Clark 1-30 (30); Gurney 31-57 (27)
WINNER'S LAPS 1-30 P2, 31-57 P1
FASTEST LAP Brabham, Brabham-Climax, 2m 11.4s (lap 44), 179.233kph, 111.370mph
CHAMPIONSHIP Clark 21, G Hill 20, Ginther 11, Arundell 11, Gurney 10

Pos	Driver	Car	Time/gap	Grid	Stops	Tyres
1	D Gurney	Brabham-Climax	2h 7m 49.1s	2	0	D
2	G Hill	BRM	–24.1s	6	0	D
3	J Brabham	Brabham-Climax	–24.9s	5	0	D
4	P Arundell	Lotus-Climax	–1m 10.6s	4	0	D
5	R Ginther	BRM	–2m 12.1s	9	0	D
6	B McLaren	Cooper-Climax	–1 lap	7	0	D

Brabham-Climax BT7

| Round 5/10 | **BRITISH GP** Brands Hatch | | **Jim Clark** |
| | 11 July 1964 | Race 126 | Lotus-Climax 25 151.505kph, 94.141mph |

Clark reserved his one and only 'grand slam' of the season for his home crowd. But this was no crushing victory – Graham Hill, in hot pursuit, was never more than 7.5s behind, and just 2.8s at the finish. It was a tense, determined struggle: first to blink would lose, but neither blinked. A third British driver completed the podium – John Surtees' Ferrari finished well behind the other two, but for only the second time in the five championship races to date he at least completed the course. Clark continued to lead the points table but the tenacious Hill was a mere four points behind. Surtees, 20 points in arrears, was seemingly out of the championship running.

POLE POSITION Clark, Lotus-Climax, 1m 38.1s (0.2s), 156.505kph, 97.248mph
LAPS 80 x 4.265 km, 2.650 miles
DISTANCE 341.181 km, 212.000 miles
STARTERS/FINISHERS 23/14
WEATHER Overcast, dry
LAP LEADERS Clark 1-80 (80)
WINNER'S LAPS 1-80 P1
FASTEST LAP Clark, Lotus-Climax, 1m 38.8s (lap 73), 155.396kph, 96.559mph
CHAMPIONSHIP Clark 30, G Hill 26, Ginther 11, Arundell 11, Brabham 11

Pos	Driver	Car	Time/gap	Grid	Stops	Tyres
1	J Clark	Lotus-Climax	2h 15m 7.0s	1	0	D
2	G Hill	BRM	–2.8s	2	0	D
3	J Surtees	Ferrari	–1m 20.6s	5	0	D
4	J Brabham	Brabham-Climax	–1 lap	4	2	D
5	L Bandini	Ferrari	–2 laps	8	0	D
6	P Hill	Cooper-Climax	–2 laps	15	0	D

Round 6/10	**GERMAN GP** Nürburgring					
	2 August 1964				Race 127	

Practice was marred when the amiable Dutchman and Porsche privateer Carel Godin de Beaufort crashed, later to die of his injuries. Surtees, looking particularly racy in practice, took pole position and in the race a forceful fist-shaking move on Clark at South Curve at the start of lap two gave him the lead. Until half-distance Clark initially and then Gurney battled closely with the V8 Ferrari but neither the Lotus nor the Brabham stayed healthy, enabling Surtees to repeat his victory of last year. Hill gave his championship chances a boost by coaxing his stuttering BRM into a third successive second place, Bandini in the V6 Ferrari finishing an excellent third. The race was also notable for the debut of the Honda V12.

Pos	Driver	Car	Time/gap	Grid	Stops	Tyres
1	J Surtees	Ferrari	2h 12m 4.8s	1	0	D
2	G Hill	BRM	−1m 15.6s	5	0	D
3	L Bandini	Ferrari	−4m 52.8s	4	0	D
4	J Siffert	Brabham-BRM	−5m 23.1s	10	0	D
5r	M Trintignant	BRM	−1 lap	14	0	D
6	T Maggs	BRM	−1 lap	16	0	D

John Surtees
Ferrari 158 155.429kph, 96.579mph

POLE POSITION Surtees, Ferrari, 8m 38.4s (0.4s), 158.403kph, 98.427mph
LAPS 15 x 22.810 km, 14.173 miles
DISTANCE 342.150 km, 212.602 miles
STARTERS/FINISHERS 22/14
WEATHER Overcast, cold, dry
LAP LEADERS J Clark, Lotus-Climax 1 (1); Surtees 2-3, 5-15 (13); D Gurney, Brabham-Climax 4 (1)
WINNER'S LAPS 1 P2, 2-3 P1, 4 P2, 5-15 P1
FASTEST LAP Surtees, Ferrari, 8m 39.0s (lap 11), 158.220kph, 98.313mph
CHAMPIONSHIP G Hill 32, Clark 30, Surtees 19, Ginther 11, Arundell 11

Ferrari 158

Round 7/10	**AUSTRIAN GP** Zeltweg					
	23 August 1964				Race 128	

Austria's very first championship race was held on the Zeltweg airfield circuit. Its uneven concrete surface caused havoc, all the fancied runners occupying the front row of the grid – Gurney, Clark, Surtees, Hill – being eliminated before half-distance. After just five laps Hill was out with a broken distributor, two laps later leader Surtees with a suspension rose-joint. Clark's half-shaft lasted until lap 40, his exit leaving Gurney with a huge lead over Bandini. But with over half the race still to run the Brabham's front suspension began to collapse. Bandini held off Ginther's BRM to record Ferrari's second successive victory, these two the only cars in the decimated field to complete the distance. Privateer Bob Anderson in third place was three laps adrift.

Pos	Driver	Car	Time/gap	Grid	Stops	Tyres
1	L Bandini	Ferrari	2h 6m 18.23s	7	0	D
2	R Ginther	BRM	−6.18s	5	0	D
3	B Anderson	Brabham-Climax	−3 laps	14	0	D
4	T Maggs	BRM	−3 laps	19	0	D
5	I Ireland	BRP-BRM	−3 laps	11	0	D
6	J Bonnier	Brabham-Climax	−4 laps	10	0	D

Lorenzo Bandini
Ferrari 156 159.615kph, 99.180mph

POLE POSITION G Hill, BRM, 1m 9.84s (0.32s), 164.948kph, 102.494mph
LAPS 105 x 3.200 km, 1.988 miles
DISTANCE 336.000 km, 208.781 miles
STARTERS/FINISHERS 20/9
WEATHER Cloudy, dry
LAP LEADERS Gurney 1, 8-46 (40); J Surtees, Ferrari 2-7 (6); Bandini 47-105 (59)
WINNER'S LAPS 1-7 P3, 8 P2, 9-40 P3, 41-46 P2, 47-105 P1
FASTEST LAP D Gurney, Brabham-Climax, 1m 10.56s (lap 32), 163.265kph, 101.448mph
CHAMPIONSHIP G Hill 32, Clark 30, Surtees 19, Ginther 17, Bandini 15

ITALIAN GP Monza
6 September 1964   **Race 129**

John Surtees
Ferrari 158 205.634kph, 127.775mph

At Monza Surtees brought Ferrari a hat-trick of race victories and the lead in the constructors' championship. It also launched the Englishman into contention for the drivers' title. Surtees and Gurney headed the grid and engaged in a thrilling lap-after-lap struggle, with 27 recorded lead changes over the first 56 laps. When Gurney dropped away with a flat battery misfire, Surtees powered round the final 22 laps to claim his nine points, now just four behind Hill and two from Clark, neither of whom finished. Indeed, Hill barely started, suffering a burned out clutch on the line; Clark a holed piston after 27 laps. McLaren's second gave Cooper a much needed fillip, Bandini bringing further joy for the *tifosi* with third in a photo-finish with Ginther.

POLE POSITION J Surtees, Ferrari, 1m 37.4s (0.8s), 212.526kph, 132.057mph
LAPS 78 x 5.750 km, 3.573 miles
DISTANCE 448.500 km, 278.685 miles
STARTERS/FINISHERS 20/14
WEATHER Overcast, dry
LAP LEADERS D Gurney, Brabham-Climax 1, 6-7, 10, 12-14, 16, 22, 25-26, 29, 32, 37-38, 45, 47-48, 50-52, 55 (22); Surtees 2-5, 8-9, 11, 15, 17-21, 23-24, 27-28, 30-31, 33-36, 39-44, 46, 49, 53-54, 56-78 (56)
WINNER'S LAPS 1 P2, 2-5 P1, 6 P3, 7 P2, 8-9 P1, 10 P2, 11 P1, 12-14 P2, 15 P1, 16 P2, 17-21 P1, 22 P2, 23-24 P1, 25-26 P2, 27-28 P1, 29 P2, 30-31 P1, 32 P2, 33-36 P1, 37-38 P2, 39-44 P1, 45 P2, 46 P1, 47-48 P2, 49 P1, 50-52 P2, 53-54 P1, 55 P2, 56-78 P1
FASTEST LAP J Surtees, Ferrari, 1m 38.8s (laps 63 & 67), 209.514kph, 130.186mph
CHAMPIONSHIP G Hill 32, Clark 30, Surtees 28, Ginther 20, Bandini 19

Pos	Driver	Car	Time/gap	Grid	Stops	Tyres
1	J Surtees	Ferrari	2h 10m 51.8s	1	0	D
2	B McLaren	Cooper-Climax	−1m 6.0s	5	0	D
3	L Bandini	Ferrari	−1 lap	7	0	D
4	R Ginther	BRM	−1 lap	9	0	D
5	I Ireland	BRP-BRM	−1 lap	13	0	D
6	M Spence	Lotus-Climax	−1 lap	8	0	D

BRM P261

UNITED STATES GP Watkins Glen
4 October 1964   **Race 130**

Graham Hill
BRM P261 178.799kph, 111.100mph

Clark won pole from Surtees, Gurney and Hill, these four contesting a closely fought race over almost 70 of the 110 laps race-distance. First Surtees led – his Ferrari in blue and white NART colours – then on lap 13 Clark forced his way through to leave the others disputing second a short distance behind. But Clark's luck was out, pitting on lap 44 with fuel injection trouble, an eventual dnf devastating for his championship aspirations. On lap 68 Surtees slid off on oil, fortunate to regain the circuit, and the very next lap Gurney was out with engine trouble. So Hill, always in contention, repeated his 1963 victory with Surtees second, and now looked favourite for his second world title. Bandini debuted a Flat-12 Ferrari.

POLE POSITION J Clark, Lotus-Climax 1m 12.65s (0.13s), 183.419kph, 113.971mph
LAPS 110 x 3.701 km, 2.300 miles
DISTANCE 407.164 km, 253.000 miles
STARTERS/FINISHERS 19/8
WEATHER Sunny, warm, dry
LAP LEADERS Surtees 1-12, 44 (13); Clark 13-43 (31); G Hill 45-110 (66)
WINNER'S LAPS 1-4 P3, 5 P2, 6-30 P3, 31-32 P2, 33-34 P3, 35-36 P2, 37 P3, 38-40 P2, 41 P3, 42-44 P2, 45-110 P1
FASTEST LAP J Clark, Lotus-Climax, 1m 12.70s (lap 81), 183.293kph, 113.893mph
CHAMPIONSHIP G Hill 39, Surtees 34, Clark 30, Ginther 23, Bandini 19

Pos	Driver	Car	Time/gap	Grid	Stops	Tyres
1	G Hill	BRM	2h 16m 38.0s	4	0	D
2	J Surtees	Ferrari	−30.5s	2	0	D
3	J Siffert	Brabham-BRM	−1 lap	12	0	D
4	R Ginther	BRM	−3 laps	13	0	D
5	W Hansgen	Lotus-Climax	−3 laps	17	0	D
6	T Taylor	BRP-BRM	−4 laps	15	0	D

| Round 10/10 | **MEXICAN GP** Mexico City
25 October 1964 | Race 131 | **Dan Gurney**
Brabham-Climax BT7 150.186kph, 93.321mph |

So the title would be decided between Hill, Surtees and Clark. From pole Clark eased out a lead over Gurney, in turn pulling away from the rest. By lap 11 Hill had moved into the crucial P3 which would deliver the title even if Clark was victorious. But Bandini in the Flat-12 Ferrari was constantly harrying him, and on lap 31 he got it wrong, controversially punting the BRM off. The title was now Clark's, Gurney's Brabham crucially occupying the P2 required by Surtees to snatch the title. But on the very last lap a split oil line put Clark out and for a few incredible moments it was Hill's title again – until Bandini waved Ferrari team-leader Surtees through into second place, and with it the championship by a single point.

POLE POSITION Clark, Lotus-Climax, 1m 57.24s (1.7s), 153.531ph, 95.400mph
LAPS 65 x 5.000 km, 3.107 miles
DISTANCE 325.000 km, 201.946 miles
STARTERS/FINISHERS 19/13
WEATHER Sunny, warm, dry
LAP LEADERS Clark 1-63 (63); Gurney 64-65 (2)
WINNER'S LAPS 1-63 P2, 64-65 P1
FASTEST LAP Clark, Lotus-Climax, 1m 58.37s (lap NA), 152.066kph, 94.489mph
CHAMPIONSHIP Surtees 40, G Hill 39, Clark 32, Bandini 23, Ginther 23

Pos	Driver	Car	Time/gap	Grid	Stops	Tyres
1	D Gurney	Brabham-Climax	2h 9m 5.32s	2	0	D
2	J Surtees	Ferrari	–1m 8.94s	4	0	D
3	L Bandini	Ferrari	–1m 9.63s	3	0	D
4	M Spence	Lotus-Climax	–1m 21.86s	5	0	D
5r	J Clark	Lotus-Climax	–1 lap	1	0	D
6	P Rodríguez	Ferrari	–1 lap	9	0	D

TOP **100** RACE

1964 CHAMPIONSHIP FACTS AND FOLKLORE

■ Ten races once again, the best six results counting towards the championships, with Brands Hatch and Zeltweg added to the list of GP circuits, the latter just this once.

■ In a season of changing fortunes that produced five different winners from four separate teams, John Surtees and Ferrari came out on top.

■ On the very last lap of the finale in Mexico, Lorenzo Bandini waved his team leader through to second place and the championship by a single point from Graham Hill, who

RACE 127, German GP: By repeating his victory of the previous year for Scuderia Ferrari at the Nürburgring, John Surtees suddenly began to look like a championship contender.

supposedly sent Bandini a book on driving lessons for Christmas because of the controversial part the Italian had played in Surtees' championship.

■ By winning, Surtees gained the special prominence of becoming the only winner of world championship titles on two wheels and on four, a remarkable accomplishment.

■ With their three victories Ferrari also secured the constructors' title, although at the final two rounds the Italian cars were not resplendent in traditional national *rosso*, but in the blue and white livery of the North American Racing Team (NART). This was *Commendatore* Enzo Ferrari's form of protest against the Automobile Club of Italy regarding the non-homologation of the Ferrari 250LM.

■ Lotus also scored three race victories, BRM and Brabham two apiece, the latter their first success.

■ At the halfway point of the season Clark with 30 points from three victories looked good for back-to-back titles, with Hill's 26-point haul showing BRM to be back in business after their 1963 drubbing.

■ Until then unreliability had restricted Surtees to just ten points, but in the second half of the season he added a further 30 in a purple patch of two wins and two seconds.

■ Hill added a more modest 13 points but by the championship showdown was still on course for the title regardless of the fortunes of others, whereas the outcome for Surtees and for Clark was dependent upon destiny.

■ This especially applied to Clark who, following his dominant Brands Hatch victory, added *nil points* from the following four race starts.

■ Although clearly their 1963 consistency had deserted them, calamitous reliability was not just the domain of Team Lotus, and if anything the finger could be pointed at Coventry-Climax rather than the Lotus 25 or its logical development the 33.

■ Despite the distinction of becoming a winning marque, reliability remained an Achilles heel at Brabham, otherwise Gurney might well have also joined in the title chase, the American leading more races and more laps than either Hill or Surtees.

■ BRM's full monocoque P261 chassis restored the Bourne team's competitiveness, their strong V8 engine now delivering over 200bhp at 11,000rpm. The team also experimented with a 4WD car during the year.

- Ferrari's revival was also technically led, albeit galvanised by Big John Surtees. His driving force, in all senses, plus the V8 engine in the monocoque Tipo 158, had coalesced to restore Ferrari to competitiveness. Maranello also introduced a 180° horizontally opposed Flat-12 engine towards the end of the season.
- Phil Hill joined Bruce McLaren at Cooper but the team continued to struggle, the ex-world champion having a particularly miserable season, his nadir two hefty crashes at Zeltweg. Phil retired from GP racing at the end of the season.
- The Cooper team were in all sorts of strife, son John seriously injured in a road accident in 1963 and father Charles sadly passing on in 1964 aged 70. Ken Tyrrell, who ran the Cooper Formula Junior team, was asked to deputise during these difficult times.

- In January Reg Parnell had died and son Tim took over the running of his team, Amon being joined – this time for a full season of GP racing – by another motorcycle world champion, Mike Hailwood, both using ex-works Lotus 25s.
- Another loss was Porsche privateer Carel Godin de Beaufort, fatally injured in practice at the Nürburgring. Porsche would return as an engine provider, but as a marque never raced in F1 again.
- Honda made their intriguing debut in Germany plus two other outings, American Ronnie Bucknam their development driver. The car was unusual in having its V12 engine transversely mounted behind the driver, the unit reputedly developing 225bhp at 12,500rpm.
- Austrian Jochen Rindt, a future world champion, made his debut at his inaugural home race.

Championship ranking	Championship points	Driver nationality	1964 Drivers Championship		Races contested	Race victories	Podiumse excl. victories	Races led	Flag to flag victories	Laps led	Poles	Fastest laps	Triple Crowns
			Driver	Car									
1	40	GBR	John Surtees	Ferrari	10	2	4	5		89	2	2	2
2	39	GBR	Graham Hill	BRM	10	2	3	3		116	1	1	
3	32	GBR	Jim Clark	Lotus-Climax	10	3		8	2	322	5	4	1
4	23	ITA	Lorenzo Bandini	Ferrari	10	1	3	1		59			
5	23	USA	Richie Ginther	BRM	10		2						
6	19	USA	Dan Gurney	Brabham-Climax	10	2		7		136	2	2	
7	13	NZL	Bruce McLaren	Cooper-Climax	10		2						
8	11	GBR	Peter Arundell	Lotus-Climax	4		2						
8	11	AUS	Jack Brabham	Brabham-Climax	10		2					1	
10	7	SUI	Jo Siffert	Lotus-BRM (1) Brabham-BRM (9)	10		1						
11	5	GBR	Bob Anderson	Brabham-Climax	7		1						
12	4	RSA	Tony Maggs	BRM	3								
12	4	GBR	Mike Spence	Lotus-Climax	6								
14	4	GBR	Innes Ireland	BRP-BRM	7								
15	3	SWE	Jo Bonnier	Cooper-Climax (1) Brabham-BRM (4) Brabham-Climax (4)	9								
16	2	NZL	Chris Amon	Lotus-BRM (7) Lotus-Climax (1)	8								
16	2	FRA	Maurice Trintignant	BRM	4								
16	2	USA	Walt Hansgen	Lotus-Climax	1								
19	1	GBR	Mike Hailwood	Lotus-BRM	9								
19	1	USA	Phil Hill	Cooper-Climax	9								
19	1	GBR	Trevor Taylor	BRP-BRM (6) Lotus-BRM (1)	7								
19	1	MEX	Pedro Rodriguez	Ferrari	1								

Championship ranking	Championship points	Team/Marque nationality	1964 Constructors Championship		Engine maker nationality	Races contested	Race victories	1-2 finishes	Podiums excl. victories	Races led	Laps led	Poles	Fastest laps
			Chassis	Engine									
1	45	ITA	Ferrari 158, 156, 1512	Ferrari 1.5 V8, 1.5 V6, 1.5 F12	ITA	10	3		7	5	148	2	2
2	42	GBR	BRM P261, P57	BRM 1.5 V8	GBR	10	2	1	5	3	116	1	1
3	37	GBR	Lotus 25, 33	Coventry-Climax 1.5 V8	GBR	10	3		2	9	322	5	4
4	30	AUS	Brabham BT7, BT11, BT3	Coventry-Climax 1.5 V8	GBR	10	2		3	7	136	2	3
5	16	GBR	Cooper T73, T66, T60	Coventry-Climax 1.5 V8	GBR	10			2				
6	7	AUS	Brabham BT11, BT3	BRM 1.5 V8	GBR	9			1				
7	5	GBR	BRP, Mk 1, Mk 2	BRM 1.5 V8	GBR	8							
8	3	GBR	Lotus 25, 24	BRM 1.5 V8	GBR	10							

1965

Clark's double scotch

THE TALE OF THE TITLE

- Clark's second title was as categorical as his first, his Lotus invincible during a five-race winning streak.
- During this astounding sequence, which lasted just seven weeks, he led every race lap bar five.
- He wrapped up the title even sooner than Ascari in 1952, and won the Indy 500 to boot.
- Team Lotus regained the constructors' title with six race victories to BRM's three
- Graham Hill scored a remarkable double hat-trick for BRM at Monte Carlo and Watkins Glen.
- In a sensational rookie season, Stewart landed his first GP victory to finish third in the title race.
- Champions Ferrari along with Brabham had a barren year, Surtees missing the final two races with injury.
- The sun rose on Honda with Richie Ginther's victory in the final race of the 1.5-litre Formula 1.
- It was also a first victory for Goodyear, fuelling the prospect of tyre wars in the upcoming season.
- Coventry-Climax withdrew at season's end while Ford announced their future participation in F1.
- And not forgetting: Cooper sell-up.

THE CHASE FOR THE CHAMPIONSHIP

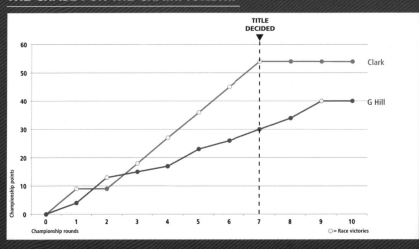

Lotus-Climax 33

Round 1/10	**SOUTH AFRICAN GP** East London					**Jim Clark**		
	1 January 1965				Race 132	Lotus-Climax 33 157.722kph, 98.004mph		

The day after Hogmanay the new season kicked off with Jim Clark in festive mood, at least by the end of the race. He completed a 'grand slam' performance by leading flag-to-flag from pole and setting fastest lap. Finishing in his wake were the other two title protagonists from last year. New world champion John Surtees and Graham Hill completed the distance closely together but well behind the flying Scot. Surprise of the race was Mike Spence in the number two Lotus 33, who demonstrated the intrinsic speed of the car by holding second place for 60 laps until spinning at Beacon Bend under pressure from Surtees. Jackie Stewart made an auspicious debut for BRM, scoring a championship point first time out.

POLE POSITION Clark, Lotus-Climax, 1m 27.2s (0.9s), 161.850kph, 100.569mph
LAPS 85 x 3.920 km, 2.436 miles
DISTANCE 333.231 km, 207.060
STARTERS/FINISHERS 20/15
WEATHER Overcast, dry, late light showers
LAP LEADERS Clark 1-85 (85)
WINNER'S LAPS 1-85 P1
FASTEST LAP Clark, Lotus-Climax, 1m 27.6s (lap 80), 161.111kph, 100.110mph
CHAMPIONSHIP Clark 9, Surtees 6, G Hill 4, Spence 3, McLaren 2

Pos	Driver	Car	Time/gap	Grid	Stops	Tyres
1	J Clark	Lotus-Climax	2h 6m 46.0s	1	0	D
2	J Surtees	Ferrari	–29.0s	2	0	D
3	G Hill	BRM	–31.8s	5	0	D
4	M Spence	Lotus-Climax	–54.4s	4	0	D
5	B McLaren	Cooper-Climax	–1 lap	8	0	D
6	J Stewart	BRM	–2 laps	11	0	D

Round 2/10	**MONACO GP** Monte Carlo					**Graham Hill**		
	30 May 1965				Race 133	BRM P261 119.688kph, 74.371mph		

Graham Hill scored a remarkable Monte Carlo hat-trick for BRM. The absence of Clark and Gurney at Indianapolis eased his task, but from pole position he was in irrepressible form. He led the opening laps but on lap 25 was forced to take to the chicane escape road to avoid a stricken car. Stewart now led but spun, then Brabham overtook new leader Bandini until his engine blew. It was now Hill's flying BRM versus the Ferrari pair, the Londoner passing Surtees on lap 53 and Bandini on lap 65. Surtees tried to get back on terms but ran out of fuel, elevating Bandini and Stewart to the podium. Paul Hawkins emulated Ascari's 1955 chicane mishap, his Lotus-Climax ending up in the harbour.

POLE POSITION G Hill, BRM, 1m 32.5s (0.1s), 122.400kph, 76.056mph
LAPS 100 x 3.145km, 1.954 miles
DISTANCE 314.500 km, 195.421 miles
STARTERS/FINISHERS 16/10
WEATHER Overcast, dry
LAP LEADERS G Hill 1-24, 65-100 (60); Stewart 25-29 (5); Bandini 30-33, 43-64 (26); J Brabham, Brabham-Climax 34-42 (9)
WINNER'S LAPS 1-24 P1, 25-33 P5, 34-42 P4, 43-52 P3, 53-64 P2, 65-100 P1
FASTEST LAP G Hill, BRM 1m 31.7s (lap 82), 123.468kph, 76.719mph
CHAMPIONSHIP G Hill 13, Clark 9, Surtees 9, Bandini 6, Stewart 5

Pos	Driver	Car	Time/gap	Grid	Stops	Tyres
1	G Hill	BRM	2h 37m 39.6s	1	0	D
2	L Bandini	Ferrari	–1m 4.0s	4	0	D
3	J Stewart	BRM	–1m 41.9s	3	0	D
4r	J Surtees	Ferrari	–1 lap	5	0	D
5	B McLaren	Cooper-Climax	–2 laps	7	0	D
6	J Siffert	Brabham-BRM	–2 laps	10	0	D

| Round 3/10 | **BELGIAN GP** Spa-Francorchamps | | **Jim Clark** |
| | 13 June 1965 | Race 134 | Lotus-Climax 33 188.550kph, 117.159mph |

The BRMs showed good practice form, flanking Clark's Lotus on the grid, Hill on pole. Race day was wet, track conditions sometimes indescribable. Clark and Stewart were in a race of their own, they alone able to fully master the conditions, the only drivers to complete the full race-distance. Stewart's performance was all the more remarkable as it was his first visit to Spa, although by the end Clark's winning margin was 44.8s over his fellow Scot. Clark's victory also marked his fourth consecutive triumph on the challenging Belgian circuit. The wet had turned Hill's BRM into a handful and he eventually fell back to fifth behind McLaren and Brabham, while Ginther took a first championship point for Honda.

POLE POSITION G Hill, BRM, 3m 45.4s (2.1s), 225.200kph, 139.933mph
LAPS 32 x 14.100 km, 8.761 miles
DISTANCE 451.200 km, 280.363 miles
STARTERS/FINISHERS 19/14
WEATHER Overcast, wet track at start, local rainstorms
LAP LEADERS Clark 1-32 (32)
WINNER'S LAPS 1-32 P1
FASTEST LAP Clark, Lotus-Climax, 4m 12.9s (lap 23), 200.712kph, 124.716mph
CHAMPIONSHIP Clark 18, G Hill 15, Stewart 11, Surtees 9, McLaren 8

Pos	Driver	Car	Time/gap	Grid	Stops	Tyres
1	J Clark	Lotus-Climax	2h 23m 34.8s	2	0	D
2	J Stewart	BRM	−44.8s	3	0	D
3	B McLaren	Cooper-Climax	−1 lap	9	0	D
4	J Brabham	Brabham-Climax	−1 lap	10	0	G
5	G Hill	BRM	−1 lap	1	0	D
6	R Ginther	Honda	−1 lap	4	0	G

| Round 4/10 | **FRENCH GP** Clermont-Ferrand | | **Jim Clark** |
| | 27 June 1965 | Race 135 | Lotus-Climax 25 143.583kph, 89.218mph |

Clark's second 'grand slam' of the season was around the Circuit du Charade, something of a mini-Nürburgring. On the tricky winding and undulating road course he broke the circuit record no less than 15 times over the 40 laps. Rookie Stewart repeated his role from two weeks earlier, not able to keep Clark in sight but by far the best of the rest to finish runner-up. A misfiring Surtees finished third, Denny Hulme in only his second outing for Brabham an excellent fourth, and an out-of-sorts Graham Hill fifth following a crash in practice caused by a stuck throttle. But as a race it was uninspiring, giving Clark a ten-point advantage in the championship over the two BRM drivers, only the Bourne team keeping Clark honest so far this season.

POLE POSITION Clark, Lotus-Climax, 3m 18.3s (0.5s), 146.233kph, 90.865mph
LAPS 40 x 8.055 km, 5.005 miles
DISTANCE 322.200 km, 200.206 miles
STARTERS/FINISHERS 17/9
WEATHER Sunny, warm, dry
LAP LEADERS Clark 1-40 (40)
WINNER'S LAPS 1-40 P1
FASTEST LAP Clark, Lotus-Climax, 3m 18.9s (lap 34), 145.792kph, 90.591mph
CHAMPIONSHIP Clark 27, G Hill 17, Stewart 17, Surtees 13, McLaren 8

Pos	Driver	Car	Time/gap	Grid	Stops	Tyres
1	J Clark	Lotus-Climax	2h 13m 38.4s	1	0	D
2	J Stewart	BRM	−26.3s	2	0	D
3	J Surtees	Ferrari	−2m 33.5s	4	0	D
4	D Hulme	Brabham-Climax	−2m 53.1s	6	0	G
5	G Hill	BRM	−1 lap	13	0	D
6	J Siffert	Brabham-BRM	−1 lap	14	0	D

| Round 5/10 | **BRITISH GP** Silverstone | | **Jim Clark** |
| | 10 July 1965 | Race 136 | Lotus-Climax 33 180.275kph, 112.017mph |

Clark's next triumph heralded his fourth successive British GP victory. Hill gave relentless pursuit but had mistakenly chosen rear 'wets', and steadily fell back. But with 20 laps left the latest 32-valve Climax engine installed behind Clark ran short of oil, sounding very sick indeed. Clark, with a 34s lead, began to switch it off while cornering to prevent oil-surge damage, sometimes losing 3s in a lap. The crowd began to urge Hill to reduce the deficit, but with his own brakes failing, and despite fastest lap on the final circuit, he was thwarted by 3.4s. 'Can't go beats can't stop' the headlines shrieked. With Surtees P3, the podium comprised the same British drivers for the third British GP in a row. While it lasted, the Honda was very quick.

POLE POSITION Clark, Lotus-Climax, 1m 30.8s (0.2s), 186.762kph, 116.048mph
LAPS 80 x 4.711 km, 2.927 miles
DISTANCE 376.844 km, 234.160 miles
STARTERS/FINISHERS 20/14
WEATHER Overcast, dry
LAP LEADERS Clark 1-80 (80)
WINNER'S LAPS 1-80 P1
FASTEST LAP G Hill, BRM, 1m 32.2s (lap 80), 183.926kph, 114.286mph
CHAMPIONSHIP Clark 36, G Hill 23, Stewart 19, Surtees 17, McLaren 8

Pos	Driver	Car	Time/gap	Grid	Stops	Tyres
1	J Clark	Lotus-Climax	2h 5m 25.4s	1	0	D
2	G Hill	BRM	−3.2s	2	0	D
3	J Surtees	Ferrari	−27.6s	5	0	D
4	M Spence	Lotus-Climax	−39.6s	6	0	D
5	J Stewart	BRM	−1m 14.6s	4	0	D
6	D Gurney	Brabham-Climax	−1 lap	7	0	G

TOP
100
RACE

Round 6/10	**DUTCH GP** Zandvoort		**Jim Clark**
	18 July 1965	**Race 137**	**Lotus-Climax 33** 162.329kph, 100.867mph

For the second successive race Ginther had the Honda on the front row and for the second successive race he beat the rest off the line. This time the ear-piercing Honda V12 led for a couple of laps before falling behind Hill and Clark. Once Clark got by Hill the race was effectively over, Hill *sans tacho* fading to finish fourth whereas teammate Stewart was upwardly mobile from P6 on the grid, taking second place from Gurney on lap 32 to finish only 8s behind Clark. Ginther scored another point for Honda, the Japanese team making palpable progress. There was an unseemly incident on the grid involving Colin Chapman and a Dutch policeman that reached Consular proportions, Chapman locked up overnight.

POLE POSITION G Hill, BRM, 1m 30.7s (0.3s), 166.426kph, 103.412mph
LAPS 80 x 4.193 km, 2.605 miles
DISTANCE 335.440 km, 208.433 miles
STARTERS/FINISHERS 17/13
WEATHER Overcast, dry
LAP LEADERS Ginther 1-2 (2); G Hill 3-5 (3); Clark 6-80 (75)
WINNER'S LAPS 1-4 P3, 5 P2, 6-80 P1
FASTEST LAP Clark, Lotus-Climax, 1m 30.6s (lap 5), 166.609kph, 103.526mph
CHAMPIONSHIP Clark 45, G Hill 26, Stewart 25, Surtees 17, McLaren 8

Pos	Driver	Car	Time/gap	Grid	Stops	Tyres
1	J Clark	Lotus-Climax	2h 3m 59.1s	2	0	D
2	J Stewart	BRM	−8.0s	6	0	D
3	D Gurney	Brabham-Climax	−13.0s	5	0	G
4	G Hill	BRM	−45.1s	1	0	D
5	D Hulme	Brabham-Climax	−1 lap	7	1	G
6	R Ginther	Honda	−1 lap	3	0	G

Round 7/10	**GERMAN GP** Nürburgring		**Jim Clark**
	1 August 1965	**Race 138**	**Lotus-Climax 33** 160.542kph, 99.756mph

Victory number six for Clark was another 'grand slam', his fifth win in a row and his sixth from six starts. This, his first Nordschleife triumph, also brought Clark his second world drivers' title, and by the date of 1 August beat Ascari's 1952 record by two days. Clark was fortunate to survive the opening lap when his car hit a bump and aviated, the Climax motor reaching an explosive 11,600rpm as the rear wheels lost traction. The BRM driver in runner-up spot was Hill, by nearly 16s, Stewart bending his suspension with an off on lap 2. Rindt notably finished fourth for Cooper-Climax. Despite the impressive showing by BRM, Team Lotus also wrapped up the constructors' cup with three championship rounds remaining.

POLE POSITION Clark, Lotus-Climax, 8m 22.7s (3.4s), 163.350kph, 101.501mph
LAPS 15 x 22.810 km, 14.173 miles
DISTANCE 342.150 km, 212.602 miles
STARTERS/FINISHERS 19/8
WEATHER Overcast, dry
LAP LEADERS Clark 1-15 (15)
WINNER'S LAPS 1-15 P1
FASTEST LAP Clark, Lotus-Climax, 8m 24.1s (lap 10), 162.896kph, 101.219mph
CHAMPIONSHIP Clark 54, G Hill 30, Stewart 25, Surtees 17, Gurney 9

Pos	Driver	Car	Time/gap	Grid	Stops	Tyres
1	J Clark	Lotus-Climax	2h 7m 52.4s	1	0	D
2	G Hill	BRM	−15.9s	3	0	D
3	D Gurney	Brabham-Climax	−21.4s	5	0	G
4	J Rindt	Cooper-Climax	−3m 29.6s	8	0	D
5	J Brabham	Brabham-Climax	−4m 41.2s	14	0	G
6	L Bandini	Ferrari	−5m 8.6s	7	0	D

Round 8/10	**ITALIAN GP** Monza		**Jackie Stewart**
	12 September 1965	**Race 139**	**BRM P261** 209.962kph, 130.464mph

The battle for championship runner-up spot between the BRM boys was far from over, and Monza produced another 1-2 for the team. In his rookie season Stewart beat team leader Hill to the line by 3.3s, to leave them separated by a single point with just two rounds remaining. The race was sensational with 43 lap-lead changes – an all-time record – between Stewart, Hill and Clark. Although these were the only three to lead over the timing line, Gurney, Surtees and Bandini participated in the spectacular slipstreamer. The clutch of the F12 Ferrari put Surtees out on lap 34 while Clark made a late exit with fuel pump failure on lap 63. The BRM twins were together with one to go but it went to Stewart when Hill slid on the loose stuff at South Curve.

POLE POSITION J Clark, Lotus-Climax, 1m 35.9s (0.2s), 215.850kph, 134.123mph
LAPS 76 x 5.750 km, 3.573 miles
DISTANCE 437.000 km, 271.539 miles
STARTERS/FINISHERS 23/14
WEATHER Sunny, warm, dry
LAP LEADERS Clark 1-2, 4, 7, 10, 18, 21, 27, 33-36, 38, 44, 46, 51, 53-54, 57 (19); G Hill 3, 5, 25-26, 28, 40-41, 43, 45, 50, 55-56, 64, 70-71, 73, 74 (17); Stewart 6, 8-9, 11-17, 19-20, 22-24, 29-32, 37, 39, 42, 47-49, 52, 58-63, 65-69, 72, 75-76 (40)
WINNER'S LAPS 1 P2, 2 P3, 3 P2, 4 P3, 5 P2, 6 P1, 7 P2, 8-9 P1, 10 P2, 11-17 P1, 18 P3, 19-20 P1, 21 P2, 22-24 P1, 25-28 P2, 29-32 P1, 33-36 P2, 37 P1, 38 P2, 39 P1, 40-41 P2, 42 P1, 43-44 P2, 45 P3, 46 P2, 47-49 P1, 50 P3, 51 P2, 52 P1, 53 P2, 54-55 P3, 56 P2, 57 P3, 58-63 P1, 64 P2, 65-69 P1, 70-71 P2, 72 P1, 73-74 P2, 75-76 P1
FASTEST LAP J Clark, Lotus-Climax, 1m 36.4s (lap 46), 214.730kph, 133.427mph
CHAMPIONSHIP Clark 54, G Hill 34, Stewart 33, Surtees 17, Gurney 13

TOP **100** RACE

Pos	Driver	Car	Time/gap	Grid	Stops	Tyres
1	J Stewart	BRM	2h 4m 52.8s	3	0	D
2	G Hill	BRM	−3.3s	4	0	D
3	D Gurney	Brabham-Climax	−16.5s	9	0	G
4	L Bandini	Ferrari	−1m 15.9	5	0	D
5	B McLaren	Cooper-Climax	−1 lap	11	0	D
6	D Attwood	Lotus-BRM	−1 lap	13	0	D

UNITED STATES GP Watkins Glen

3 October 1965   **Race 140**

Graham Hill

BRM P261 173.752kph, 107.965mph

Three weeks later Hill put rookie Stewart firmly back in his place with his hat-trick victory at Watkins Glen. In a race made tricky by showers, Hill, from pole, saw off Clark's early challenge and then kept the Brabhams at bay to win by 12.5s. Both Clark (engine trouble) and Stewart (throttle cable and suspension) were out inside a dozen laps. Behind the determined Brabhams of Gurney and Black Jack, which gave Hill little peace for much of the race, came the Ferraris of Bandini and Rodríguez, the Mexican subbing for Surtees, absent through injury. Driving a Lola T70, Big John was in hospital following a heavy accident during practice for the Canadian GP sports car race at Mosport Park.

POLE POSITION G Hill, BRM 1m 11.25s (0.10s), 187.023kph, 116.211mph
LAPS 110 x 3.701 km, 2.300 miles
DISTANCE 407.164 km, 253.000 miles
STARTERS/FINISHERS 18/13
WEATHER Overcast, cold, showers, windy
LAP LEADERS G Hill 1, 5-110 (107); J Clark, Lotus-Climax 2-4 (3)
WINNER'S LAPS 1 P1, 2-4 P2, 5-110 P1
FASTEST LAP G Hill, BRM, 1m 11.90s (lap 105), 185.332kph, 115.160mph
CHAMPIONSHIP Clark 54, G Hill 40, Stewart 33, Gurney 19, Surtees 17

Pos	Driver	Car	Time/gap	Grid	Stops	Tyres
1	G Hill	BRM	2h 20m 36.1s	1	0	D
2	D Gurney	Brabham-Climax	–12.5s	8	0	G
3	J Brabham	Brabham-Climax	–57.5s	7	0	G
4	L Bandini	Ferrari	–1 lap	5	0	D
5	P Rodríguez	Ferrari	–1 lap	15	0	D
4	J Rindt	Cooper-Climax	–2 laps	13	0	D

Honda RA272

MEXICAN GP Mexico City

24 October 1965   **Race 141**

Richie Ginther

Honda RA272 151.710kph, 94.268mph

In the rarefied atmosphere of Mexico City, a Honda technician predicted: 'If fuel injection work, we win!' It did, Ginther, Honda and Goodyear each notching up their first championship victories and bringing to a close the 1.5-litre Formula 1 on a high note of future expectation. Clark from pole made a good start but on the main straight ten cars swept by the sick-sounding Lotus, out after just eight laps. So Ginther led lap 1 and the remaining 64, but it wasn't a runaway victory, Gurney, also on Goodyears, pursuing his compatriot all the way. When Dan took P2 from Spence on lap 20 he was 7s adrift, but still three back by the chequered flag. Neither BRM finished but even so Hill completed the season runner-up to the superlative Clark.

POLE POSITION J Clark, Lotus-Climax, 1m 56.17s (0.07s), 154.945ph, 96.279mph
LAPS 65 x 5.000 km, 3.107 miles
DISTANCE 325.000 km, 201.946 miles
STARTERS/FINISHERS 17/8
WEATHER Sunny, warm, dry
LAP LEADERS Ginther 1-65 (65)
WINNER'S LAPS 1-65 P1
FASTEST LAP Gurney, Brabham-Climax, 1m 55.84s (lap 57), 155.387kph, 96.553mph
CHAMPIONSHIP Clark 54, G Hill 40, Stewart 33, Gurney 25, Surtees 17

Pos	Driver	Car	Time/gap	Grid	Stops	Tyres
1	R Ginther	Honda	2h 8m 32.10s	3	0	G
2	D Gurney	Brabham-Climax	–2.89s	2	0	G
3	M Spence	Lotus-Climax	–1m 0.15s	6	0	D
4	J Siffert	Brabham-BRM	–1m 54.42s	11	0	D
5	R Bucknum	Honda	–1 lap	10	0	G
6	D Attwood	Lotus-BRM	–1 lap	16	0	D

1965 CHAMPIONSHIP FACTS AND FOLKLORE

- A ten-race championship, the best six results counting, with Clermont-Ferrand staging the French GP for the first time and the South African GP held at East London for the final time.
- Jim Clark's second world championship was as uncompromising as his first. The title was his by the Nürburgring, by which time he had won the first six races in which he participated.
- Adding a surreal quality to the legend, Clark only missed the second championship round at Monaco because he was busy in the USA at the Indy 500, which he, Lotus and Ford also won.

- Having stitched up his second championship, the Lotus-Climax unreliability curse returned with a vengeance, Clark adding not a single point to his tally over the final three rounds.
- The engine department was again the troublesome area, the new 32-valve version of the Coventry-Climax V8 highly capricious.
- On the other hand, the BRMs of Graham Hill and newcomer Jackie Stewart suffered only four dnfs between them. Such reliability along with tremendous speed brought the BRM drivers highly praiseworthy second and third positions in the championship standings.

RACE 140, United States GP: New York State, a chilly October day. Although a second title is already his, Jim Clark looks pensive ahead of the race, rightly fearing further engine woes.

- Graham Hill did extremely well to come out on top, Stewart displaying a prodigious talent to win his first Grand Prix in only his eighth championship race.
- Hill was victorious twice, and if any proof were ever needed to support the maxim 'horses for courses', this would be it. He scored hat-trick victories at both Monaco and Watkins Glen.
- But even in this respect Clark seemed to have the upper hand, his Belgian GP win being his fourth on the trot at the challenging Spa-Francorchamps, a circuit he personally hated, considering it highly dangerous.
- But, as exemplified in qualifying by Hill's four poles to Clark's six, over the season Hill and his V8 BRM P261 remained Clark's main adversary, as had been the case since their championship rivalry commenced in 1962.
- But what of reigning world champions Surtees and Ferrari in 1965? Not much, is the answer, despite an estimated 220bhp at 12,000rpm from the Flat-12 engine used for much of the season.
- The outgoing world champion was in any case unable to complete the season through a serious back injury sustained in a sports car accident in Canada.
- Surtees' replacement, Pedro Rodríguez, acquitted himself well, but a handful of podium finishes was all Ferrari had to show for their season.

- This also applied to Jack Brabham's team, Denny Hulme – destined to become world champion with the team – having a successful debut season in place of Dan Gurney. But this year's Brabham-Climax BT11 rarely had the legs of BRM, let alone Clark's Lotus 33.
- Having the legs of everyone in the final race of the 1.5-litre Formula 1 was Honda, their Rising Sun livery symbolic of the Japanese manufacturers' unremitting progress and commitment.
- The most important pointer towards the development path of Formula 1 in general and the new 3-litre F1 in particular was that Honda gave Goodyear their first victory over incumbent Dunlop. With the presence of Firestone also, and with tyres becoming noticeably wider during 1965, the prospect of 'tyre wars' in 1966 was now a certainty.
- On the engine front things were less clear for the new 3-litre formula. Coventry-Climax, having already abandoned development of the Flat-16 engine for the 1.5-litre formula, left a seemingly unfillable void by deciding not to participate in the new formula for financial reasons.
- Fortunately, on 6 October 1965 Ford announced plans involving Cosworth Engineering and Lotus which would bring them into F1 racing, but not before 1967.
- Following the death of his father, John Cooper sold the Cooper Formula 1 team to the Chipstead Motor Group in April 1965.

1965 Drivers Championship

Championship ranking	Championship points	Driver nationality	Driver	Car	Races contested	Race victories	Podiumse excl. victories	Races led	Flag to flag victories	Laps led	Poles	Fastest laps	Triple Crowns
1	54	GBR	Jim Clark	Lotus-Climax	9	6		8	5	349	6	6	3
2	40	GBR	Graham Hill	BRM	10	2	4	4		187	4	3	1
3	33	GBR	Jackie Stewart	BRM	10	1	4	2		45			
4	25	USA	Dan Gurney	Brabham-Climax	9		5					1	
5	17	GBR	John Surtees	Ferrari	8		3						
6	13	ITA	Lorenzo Bandini	Ferrari	10		1	1		26			
7	11	USA	Richie Ginther	Honda	8	1		2	1	67			
8	10	GBR	Mike Spence	Lotus-Climax	9		1						
9	10	NZL	Bruce McLaren	Cooper-Climax	10		1						
10	9	AUS	Jack Brabham	Brabham-Climax	6		1	1		9			
11	5	NZL	Denny Hulme	Brabham-Climax	6								
12	5	SUI	Jo Siffert	Brabham-BRM	10								
13	4	AUT	Jochen Rindt	Cooper-Climax	9								
14	2	MEX	Pedro Rodriguez	Ferrari	2								
14	2	USA	Ronnie Bucknum	Honda	6								
16	2	GBR	Richard Attwood	Lotus-BRM	8								

1965 Constructors Championship

Championship ranking	Championship points	Team/Marque nationality	Chassis	Engine	Engine maker nationality	Races contested	Race victories	1-2 finishes	Podiums excl. victories	Races led	Laps led	Poles	Fastest laps
1	54	GBR	Lotus 33, 25	Coventry-Climax 1.5 V8	GBR	10	6		1	8	349	6	6
2	45	GBR	BRM P261	BRM 1.5 V8	GBR	10	3	1	8	4	232	4	3
3	27	AUS	Brabham BT11	Coventry-Climax 1.5 V8	GBR	10			6	1	9		1
4	26	ITA	Ferrari 1512, 158	Ferrari 1.5 F12, 1.5 V8	ITA	10			4	1	26		
5	14	GBR	Cooper T77	Coventry-Climax 1.5 V8	GBR	10			1				
6	11	JPN	Honda RA272	Honda 1.5 V12	JPN	8	1			2	67		
7	5	AUS	Brabham BT11	BRM 1.5 V8	GBR	10							
8	2	GBR	Lotus 25	BRM 1.5 V8	GBR	10							

1966

Uniquely Brabham's Brabham

THE TALE OF THE TITLE

- ■ A new 3-litre Formula 1 heralded the 'return to power'.
- ■ Six years since his last title, Australian Jack Brabham won his third championship at the age of 40.
- ■ Brabham became the only driver to win the championship in a car bearing his own name.
- ■ With four race victories, two more than Ferrari, Brabham-Repco also took the constructors' title.
- ■ Limited engine options left many teams poorly prepared and mechanical reliability was low.
- ■ Brabham's uncomplicated Repco V8 solution produced four decisive straight victories mid-season.
- ■ Pre-season favourites Ferrari self-destructed through internal politics, John Surtees switching to Cooper.
- ■ Surtees brought Cooper, using Maserati V12 engines, their first race victory in four seasons.
- ■ Stewart won for BRM at Monaco and Clark for Lotus using the recalcitrant H16 BRM engine.
- ■ New driver/constructor team McLaren made its championship debut, as did Dan Gurney's AAR Eagle.
- ■ And not forgetting: first victory for Firestone; John Frankenheimer's movie *Grand Prix*.

THE CHASE FOR THE CHAMPIONSHIP

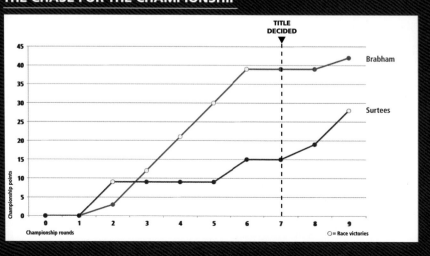

| Round 1/9 | **MONACO GP** Monte Carlo | | **Jackie Stewart** |
| | 22 May 1966 | Race 142 | BRM P261 123.192kph, 76.548mph |

With his second victory in only his 11th GP start, Jackie Stewart made it four-in-a-row for BRM at Monaco. In this opening race of the new Formula only around half the field were pukka 3-litre cars, and reliability was poor. There were only four classified finishers (three BRMs and Bandini's Ferrari), all up-rated 1965 cars. Clark took pole in a 2-litre Lotus-Climax from Surtees in the 3-litre Ferrari V12, the latter making his championship return after injury. The 2-litre BRMs of Stewart and Hill filled row two. With Clark left behind at the start, stuck in gear, the Ferrari led but was out early, leaving Stewart to dominate the remaining 86 laps. Bandini brought the 2.4-litre V6 Ferrari into second place from the clutch-slipping BRM of Hill.

POLE POSITION J Clark, Lotus-Climax, 1m 29.9s (0.2s), 125.940kph, 78.255mph
LAPS 100 x 3.145km, 1.954 miles
DISTANCE 314.500 km, 195.421 miles
STARTERS/FINISHERS 16/4
WEATHER Cloudy, warm, dry
LAP LEADERS J Surtees 1-14 (14); Stewart 15-100 (86)
WINNER'S LAPS 1-44 P2, 15-100 P1
FASTEST LAP L Bandini, Ferrari 1m 29.8s (lap 80), 126.080kph, 78.343mph
CHAMPIONSHIP Stewart 9, Bandini 6, G Hill 4, Bondurant 3

Pos	Driver	Car	Time/gap	Grid	Stops	Tyres
1	J Stewart	BRM	2h 33m 10.5s	3	0	D
2	L Bandini	Ferrari	−40.2s	5	0	F
3	G Hill	BRM	1 lap	4	0	D
4	B Bondurant	BRM	−5 laps	16	1	G
-	Only four classified finishers	-	-	-	-	-
-	-	-	-	-	-	-

Ferrari 312

Round 2/9	**BELGIAN GP** Spa-Francorchamps	**John Surtees**

BELGIAN GP Spa-Francorchamps
12 June 1966   **Race 143**

John Surtees
Ferrari 312 183.360kph, 113.935mph

The already small field was decimated when a rain squall caught out many drivers. Eight cars, including Clark's with a broken Climax motor, failed to complete the first lap. Stewart lost his BRM approaching the Masta Straight and, soaked in fuel, was trapped in the wreckage for 20-plus minutes while BRM teammates Hill and Bondurant bravely worked to extricate him. For most of the race, on a steaming track, Jochen Rindt led superbly in the Cooper-Maserati. But towards the end, as the track dried out, various technical niggles caused the handling to deteriorate, enabling Surtees' pole-sitting Ferrari to retake the lead and pull away, despite occasionally losing drive with an intermittent fuel-pump problem. Not one for the spectators.

POLE POSITION J Surtees, Ferrari, 3m 38.0s (3.2s), 232.844kph, 144.683mph
LAPS 28 x 14.100 km, 8.761 miles
DISTANCE 394.800 km, 245.317 miles
STARTERS/FINISHERS 15/5
WEATHER Overcast, rain squalls, drying later
LAP LEADERS Surtees 1, 3, 24-28 (7); Bandini 2 (1); Rindt 4-23 (20)
WINNER'S LAPS 1 P1, 2 P2, 3 P1, 4-23 P2, 24-28 P1
FASTEST LAP J Surtees, Ferrari, 4m 18.7s (lap 18), 196.212kph, 121.920mph
CHAMPIONSHIP Bandini 10, Stewart 9, Surtees 9, Rindt 6, G Hill 4

Pos	Driver	Car	Time/gap	Grid	Stops	Tyres
1	J Surtees	Ferrari	2h 9m 11.3s	1	0	D
2	J Rindt	Cooper-Maserati	−42.1s	2	0	D
3	L Bandini	Ferrari	−1 lap	5	0	F
4	J Brabham	Brabham-Repco	−2 laps	4	0	G
5	R Ginther	Cooper-Maserati	−3 laps	8	0	D
-	Only five classified finishers	-		-	-	-

Round 3/9	**FRENCH GP** Reims	**Jack Brabham**

FRENCH GP Reims
3 July 1966   **Race 144**

Jack Brabham
Brabham-Repco BT19 220.322kph, 136.902mph

A famous victory for Jack Brabham, the first driver to win in a car bearing his own name. It was also his first for almost six years. After qualifying, John Surtees was on the front row flanked by the Ferraris of Bandini on pole and Mike Parkes, but Surtees was driving a Cooper-Maserati. New Ferrari team leader Bandini was out of luck when, with only 11 laps to run, a broken throttle cable denied him certain victory in the 3-litre car. Brabham, at the time trailing the Italian by some 25s, swept through to win from Parkes and teammate Denny Hulme. The driver/constructor flag was truly waved that day when Dan Gurney also scored the first points for his own car, the AAR Eagle. Clark did not start due to an eye injury, hit by a bird during practice.

POLE POSITION L Bandini, Ferrari, 2m 7.8s (0.5s), 233.859kph, 145.313mph
LAPS 48 x 8.302 km, 5.159 miles
DISTANCE 398.496 km, 247.614 miles
STARTERS/FINISHERS 17/8
WEATHER Sunny, very hot, dry
LAP LEADERS Bandini 1-31 (31); Brabham 32-48 (17)
WINNER'S LAPS 1-31 P2, 32-48 P1
FASTEST LAP L Bandini, Ferrari, 2m 11.3s (lap 30), 227.625kph, 141.440mph
CHAMPIONSHIP Brabham 12, Bandini 10, Stewart 9, Surtees 9, Rindt 9

Pos	Driver	Car	Time/gap	Grid	Stops	Tyres
1	J Brabham	Brabham-Repco	1h 48m 31.3s	4	0	G
2	M Parkes	Ferrari	−9.5s	3	0	F
3	D Hulme	Brabham-Repco	−2 laps	9	0	G
4	J Rindt	Cooper-Maserati	−2 laps	5	1	D
5	D Gurney	Eagle-Climax	−3 laps	14	0	G
6	J Taylor	Brabham-BRM	−3 laps	15	0	G

Brabham-Repco BT19

<table>
<tr><td>

Round 4/9

</td><td>

BRITISH GP Brands Hatch
16 July 1966 Race 145

</td><td>

Jack Brabham
Brabham-Repco BT19 153.658kph, 95.479mph

</td></tr>
</table>

With Ferrari absent supposedly due to a general strike in Italy, Brabham-Repcos took 1-2 on the grid, Gurney's Eagle-Climax alongside, Hill and Clark in 2-litre cars on row two. This second Brabham victory was a far more convincing display than Reims. He led every lap from pole and recorded fastest lap, a classic 'grand slam', leading in a Brabham 1-2. Initially wet track conditions had allowed the Coopers of Surtees and Rindt, on rain tyres, to pursue Brabham, but by the finish, as the track dried out, teammate Hulme had come through to P2 after a slow start. Hill and Clark never looked like winners but finished third and fourth after strong races. Another driver/constructor scored his first point, Bruce finishing sixth for McLaren.

POLE POSITION Brabham, Brabham-Repco, 1m 34.5s (0.3s), 162.467kph, 100.952mph
LAPS 80 x 4.265 km, 2.650 miles
DISTANCE 341.181 km, 212.000 miles
STARTERS/FINISHERS 20/11
WEATHER Overcast, damp early laps, drying later
LAP LEADERS Brabham 1-80 (80)
WINNER'S LAPS 1-80 P1
FASTEST LAP Brabham, Brabham-Repco, 1m 37.0s (lap 60), 158.280kph, 98.351mph
CHAMPIONSHIP Brabham 21, Rindt 11, Bandini 10, Hulme 10, Stewart 9

Pos	Driver	Car	Time/gap	Grid	Stops	Tyres
1	J Brabham	Brabham-Repco	2h 13m 13.4s	1	0	G
2	D Hulme	Brabham-Repco	−9.6s	2	0	G
3	G Hill	BRM	−1 lap	4	0	D
4	J Clark	Lotus-Climax	−1 lap	5	0	F
5	J Rindt	Cooper-Maserati	−1 lap	7	0	D
6	B McLaren	McLaren-Serenissima	−2 laps	13	0	F

<table>
<tr><td>

Round 5/9

</td><td>

DUTCH GP Zandvoort
24 July 1966 Race 146

</td><td>

Jack Brabham
Brabham-Repco BT19 161.107kph, 100.107mph

</td></tr>
</table>

The Ferraris and Cooper-Maseratis disappointed in qualifying, best placed being the Parkes Ferrari in P5. They were hardly to feature in an exciting race in which Jim Clark reminded everyone why he was the reigning double champion. His 2-litre Lotus-Climax shared the front row with the pair of 3-litre Brabham-Repcos, and from the start relentlessly pursued Brabham for the first 26 laps. Getting ahead in traffic, Clark then proceeded to pull out a 10s lead until, with only 15 laps remaining, he was forced to stop to top up water. In truth, Brabham had already begun his bid, reducing Clark's advantage to a mere 2–3s, but when Clark pitted the final outcome was still very much in doubt. So Brabham won from Hill, Clark still managing third.

POLE POSITION Brabham, Brabham-Repco, 1m 28.1s (0.3s), 171.337kph, 106.464mph
LAPS 90 x 4.193 km, 2.605 miles
DISTANCE 377.370 km, 234.487 miles
STARTERS/FINISHERS 17/9
WEATHER Sunny, warm, dry
LAP LEADERS Brabham 1-26, 76-90 (41); Clark 27-75 (49)
WINNER'S LAPS 1-26 P1, 27-75 P2, 76-90 P1
FASTEST LAP D Hulme, Brabham-Repco, 1m 30.6s (lap 2), 166.609kph, 103.526mph
CHAMPIONSHIP Brabham 30, G Hill 14, Stewart 12, Bandini 11, Rindt 11

Pos	Driver	Car	Time/gap	Grid	Stops	Tyres
1	J Brabham	Brabham-Repco	2h 20m 32.5s	1	0	G
2	G Hill	BRM	−1 lap	7	0	G
3	J Clark	Lotus-Climax	−2 laps	3	2	F
4	J Stewart	BRM	−2 laps	8	0	G
5	M Spence	Lotus-BRM	−3 laps	12	0	F
6	L Bandini	Ferrari	−3 laps	9	0	F

<table>
<tr><td>

Round 6/9

</td><td>

GERMAN GP Nürburgring
7 August 1966 Race 147

</td><td>

Jack Brabham
Brabham-Repco BT19 139.606kph, 86.747mph

</td></tr>
</table>

F2 cars boosted the modest F1 field for the long Nordschleife circuit. On the opening lap John Taylor's F1 Brabham ran into the back of Jacky Ickx's F2 Matra and crashed in flames at Flugplatz, the unfortunate driver later succumbing to severe burns. Although Brabham led every lap across the line for his fourth consecutive victory, John Surtees in the Cooper-Maserati fought him closely, leading most of lap 1, the two cars rarely separated by more than a second or two, both contending with a wet or damp track throughout. Only over the final two laps did Surtees fall back, stuck in fourth gear. The second Cooper-Maserati of Jochen Rindt finished third. On lap 12 Clark flew off the road at Flugplatz in his pursuit of the 2-litre BRMs of Hill and Stewart.

POLE POSITION J Clark, Lotus-Climax, 8m 16.5s (3.4s), 165.390kph, 102.768mph
LAPS 15 x 22.810 km, 14.173 miles
DISTANCE 342.150 km, 212.602 miles
STARTERS/FINISHERS 19/8 (Excluding F2 cars)
WEATHER Overcast, wet
LAP LEADERS Brabham 1-15 (15)
WINNER'S LAPS 1-15 P1
FASTEST LAP Surtees, Cooper-Maserati, 8m 49.0s (lap 4), 155.229kph, 96.455mph
CHAMPIONSHIP Brabham 39, G Hill 17, Surtees 15, Rindt 15, Stewart 14

Pos	Driver	Car	Time/gap	Grid	Stops	Tyres
1	J Brabham	Brabham-Repco	2h 27m 3.0s	5	0	G
2	J Surtees	Cooper-Maserati	−44.4s	2	0	D
3	J Rindt	Cooper-Maserati	−2m 32.6s	9	0	D
4	G Hill	BRM	−6m 41.4s	10	0	D
5	J Stewart	BRM	−8m 28.9s	3	0	D
6	L Bandini	Ferrari	−10m 56.4s	6	0	F

ITALIAN GP Monza
4 September 1966   **Race 148**

Ludovico Scarfiotti
Ferrari 312 218.748kph, 135.924mph

A resurgent Ferrari, their cars sporting new 36-valve versions of the V12, had Parkes, Scarfiotti and Bandini 1, 2 and 5 on the grid. Clark slotted his Lotus-BRM H16 on the outside of the front row. Each of the Ferraris led, as did Brabham, Surtees and Hulme, up to seven cars engaged in a slipstreaming battle for the lead. But gradually, as others, including Bandini, wilted, Scarfiotti edged away, leading 55 of the 68 laps to eventually finish 15s ahead of Parkes in a famous Ferrari 1-2. Scarfiotti was the first Italian to win at Monza in a Ferrari since Ascari in 1952. It was also the first GP victory for Firestone tyres. Brabham failed to finish, but Surtees' retirement assured the 40-year-old Australian his third world title.

POLE POSITION Parkes, Ferrari, 1m 31.3s (0.3s), 226.725kph, 140.880mph
LAPS 68 x 5.750 km, 3.573 miles
DISTANCE 391.000 km, 242.956 miles
STARTERS/FINISHERS 20/9
WEATHER Sunny, warm, dry
LAP LEADERS L Bandini, Ferrari 1 (1); Parkes 2, 8-10, 12, 27 (6); J Surtees, Cooper-Maserati 3 (1); J Brabham, Brabham-Repco 4-7 (4); Hulme 11 (1); Scarfiotti 13-26, 28-68 (55)
WINNER'S LAPS 1 P7, 2-3 P6, 4 P7, 5-6 P6, 7 P7, 8 P5, 9-10 P4, 11 P3, 12 P2, 13-26 P1, 27 P2, 28-68 P1
FASTEST LAP Scarfiotti, Ferrari, 1m 32.4s (lap 49), 224.026kph, 139.203mph
CHAMPIONSHIP Brabham 39, Rindt 18, G Hill 17, Surtees 15, Stewart 14

Pos	Driver	Car	Time/gap	Grid	Stops	Tyres
1	L Scarfiotti	Ferrari	1h 47m 14.8s	2	0	F
2	M Parkes	Ferrari	–5.8s	1	0	F
3	D Hulme	Brabham-Repco	–6.1s	10	0	G
4	J Rindt	Cooper-Maserati	–1 lap	8	0	F
5	M Spence	Lotus-BRM	–1 lap	14	0	F
6	B Anderson	Brabham-Climax	–2 laps	15	0	F

Lotus-BRM 43

UNITED STATES GP Watkins Glen
2 October 1966   **Race 149**

Jim Clark
Lotus-BRM 43 184.977kph, 114.939mph

After qualifying, Clark had his Lotus-BRM alongside the new world champion's pole-sitting Brabham-Repco. Initially Bandini and Brabham disputed the lead, Surtees and Clark also well placed. On lap 35 the head gasket blew on Bandini's singleton NART-entered Ferrari, so Brabham took over the lead 14s clear of Clark. Some 20 laps later Brabham's Repco broke a tappet, Clark assuming the lead but with over 50 laps to go. No one, least of all Clark, expected the chronically unreliable BRM H16 engine to complete the distance, the similarly powered works BRMs of Hill and Stewart already out. Cooper-Maseratis finished 2-3-4 but if Surtees had not collided with a backmarker on lap 15 the result might well have been very different.

POLE POSITION J Brabham, Brabham-Repco 1m 8.42s (0.11s), 194.758kph, 121.017mph
LAPS 108 x 3.701 km, 2.300 miles
DISTANCE 399.761 km, 248.400 miles
STARTERS/FINISHERS 19/6
WEATHER Cool, dry
LAP LEADERS L Bandini, Ferrari 1-9, 20-34 (24); J Brabham, Brabham-Repco 10-19, 35-55 (31); Clark 56-108 (53)
WINNER'S LAPS 1-3 P2, 4-8 P3, 9-16 P4, 17-34 P3, 35-55, P2, 56-108 P1
FASTEST LAP Surtees, Cooper-Maserati, 1m 9.67s (lap 31), 191.264kph, 118.846mph
CHAMPIONSHIP Brabham 39, Rindt 22, Surtees 19, G Hill 17, Clark 16

Pos	Driver	Car	Time/gap	Grid	Stops	Tyres
1	J Clark	Lotus-BRM	2h 9m 40.1s	2	0	F
2	J Rindt	Cooper-Maserati	–1 lap	9	0	F
3	J Surtees	Cooper-Maserati	–1 lap	4	1	F
4	J Siffert	Cooper-Maserati	–3 laps	13	0	D
5	B McLaren	McLaren-Ford	–3 laps	11	0	F
6	P Arundell	Lotus-Climax	–7 laps	19	NA	F

MEXICAN GP Mexico City

Round 9/9
23 October 1966 — Race 150

John Surtees
Cooper-Maserati T81 154.042kph, 95.717mph

Making only its third appearance of the season, and from P3 on the grid, Richie Ginther commemorated last season's first Honda victory by leading the opening lap before Brabham took over, the Japanese V12 dropping back to finish a close fourth to Hulme, albeit both cars one lap behind. Surtees soon demonstrated the speed his Cooper-Maserati had already shown in qualifying to claim pole position, usurping Brabham's lead on lap 6 and going on to win by 7.88s. It was the first Cooper victory since 1962 and completed an end of season hat-trick for Firestone tyres. Jack Brabham and teammate Denny Hulme finished 2-3, consolidating the constructors' title they had secured at Watkins Glen and rounding off a superb season for the Brabham team.

POLE POSITION Surtees, Cooper-Maserati, 1m 53.18s (0.32s), 159.039ph, 98.822mph
LAPS 65 x 5.000 km, 3.107 miles
DISTANCE 325.000 km, 201.946 miles
STARTERS/FINISHERS 18/8
WEATHER Sunny, hot, dry
LAP LEADERS Ginther 1 (1); Brabham 2-5 (4); Surtees 6-65 (60)
WINNER'S LAPS 1-2 P5, 3-4 P3, 5 P2, 6-65 P1
FASTEST LAP Ginther, Honda, 1m 53.75s (lap 58), 158.242kph, 98.327mph
CHAMPIONSHIP Brabham 42, Surtees 28, Rindt 22, Hulme 18, G Hill 17

Pos	Driver	Car	Time/gap	Grid	Stops	Tyres
1	J Surtees	Cooper-Maserati	2h 6m 35.34s	1	0	F
2	J Brabham	Brabham-Repco	−7.88s	4	0	G
3	D Hulme	Brabham-Repco	−1 lap	6	0	G
4	R Ginther	Honda	−1 lap	3	0	G
5	D Gurney	Eagle-Climax	−1 lap	9	0	G
6	J Bonnier	Cooper-Maserati	−2 laps	12	0	F

1966 CHAMPIONSHIP FACTS AND FOLKLORE

■ The new Formula 1 regulations doubled maximum engine capacity to 3 litres with the option of 1.5 litres if supercharged. Minimum overall dry weight was raised from 450 to 500kg (1102.31lb).

■ The best five results would count from the nine championship rounds, the minimum race-distance still 300km (186.41 miles) but the maximum reduced from 500 to 400km (248.55 miles).

■ Just as in 1961, the British teams were in disarray at the commencement of a new formula. This time it was consequential upon the shock decision by Coventry-Climax not to support the 3-litre regulations, withdrawing from Grand Prix racing ostensibly for financial reasons.

■ BRM's solution to the 3-litre formula was effectively to 'flatten' two 1.5-litre V8s and mate them in tandem in an 'H' configuration. Simple in theory, complex in practice, the heavy BRM H16 rekindled the ghastly spectre of the disastrous V16 of 1950–51.

■ For much of the season BRM were compelled to turn to a 2-litre version of their excellent V8. Stewart used a 2-litre version of this engine to good effect around the streets of Monte Carlo to win the opening championship round, but at the following race on the perilous Spa circuit he was lucky to escape from his wreck with comparatively minor injuries.

■ It was from this traumatic experience that Stewart's campaign for F1 safety took root. His rescuers, Hill and Bondurant, had to borrow a spanner from a local farm to remove the steering wheel boss, Stewart binding a spanner to his steering wheel in future races.

■ Awaiting his Ford-Cosworth engine for next season, Lotus had also arranged to employ the BRM H16 power unit, but until it was raceworthy Clark used an enlarged V8 Climax. Extraordinarily, it transpired to be the H16 that gave Clark an improbable victory, the only 1966 success for the reigning world champions.

■ The recent new owners of Cooper, the Chipstead Group, was headed by Jonathan Sieff, his considerable wealth derived from the Marks & Spencer retail empire. Chipstead were the UK Maserati concessionaires so the F1 team ended up with a development of the 60° Italian V12 Grand Prix engine which had first appeared in 1957. In early carburettor

form the engine produced 330bhp, fuel injection adding an extra 30bhp at 9,500rpm. Importantly, in testing the engine proved remarkably reliable.

■ Jochen Rindt benefitted from regular points finishes with the T81 and by season's end the Cooper-Maserati was competitive enough to give Surtees the unusual distinction of winning for two teams in the same season.

■ The 1964 world champion began his fourth season with Ferrari looking like odds-on favourite for his second title. Unlike most teams, the Prancing Horse engine supply was not a constraint, de-stroking a 60° twin-ohc 3.3-litre V12 from the P2 'Le Mans' sports cars to meet their F1 requirements giving them an engine which developed 360bhp at 10,000rpm.

■ At the second race at Spa Surtees won for Maranello, but by round three he was racing with Cooper, having fallen out with Ferrari team manager Dragoni during the Le Mans weekend in June. Ferrari won only once more, but it was a memorable 1-2 triumph at Autodromo di Monza, with an Italian driver at the wheel.

■ Monza was also where Honda made their first appearance of the season along with the V12 Weslake engine for Dan Gurney's Eagle. Dan's car had made its debut earlier in the season, as had Bruce's new M2B McLaren, his first F1 car.

■ It was extraordinary that in Bruce McLaren Motor Racing, the Cooper Cars Co connection had spawned yet another driver/constructor in the image of the Brabham Racing Organisation, while Brabham driver Dan Gurney had in turn aspired to become a F1 constructor in his own right.

■ Gurney's Anglo American Racers project represented a serious US-inspired entry into F1, despite strong UK influence through chassis designer Len Terry and an engine commissioned from Weslake Engineering to a design by Aubrey Woods, joint-designer of the successful 1.5-litre BRM V8 motor. For the handsome Eagle T1G chassis their efforts produced a 60° 3.0-litre V12 that was smooth and powerful, producing 370bhp at 9,500rpm.

■ As expected, Honda's 90 V12 was powerful enough (385bhp at 10,000rpm), but when the car weighed in for its debut at Monza it was, at 743kg, nearly half as much again as the 500kg minimum weight limit, something of a handicap.

RACE 146, Dutch GP: After a stirring battle, Jack Brabham in the 3-litre Brabham-Repco (16) finally overcame the 2-litre Lotus-Climax of Jim Clark (6) to record a hat-trick of victories. Hulme (18) and G. Hill are also pictured.

■ Although he also used a V8 Serenissima sports car engine, Bruce McLaren's initial choice of a sleeved down, destroked 4.2-litre V8 Ford Indianapolis engine made low chassis weight vital to offset the bulky power plant. This led McLaren and his designer Robin Herd to innovate with Mallite – an aerospace industry material consisting of a sandwich of balsa wood between aluminium sheets – in the construction of the first McLaren F1 chassis, the M2B.

■ So that was the somewhat motley opposition arrayed against Jack Brabham. In sharp contrast to BRM, Brabham had elected for a conservative route to engine sourcing. The single-ohc 3-litre V8 Repco initially produced only 285bhp, hardly the much vaunted 'return to power' the 3-litre

formula represented, but it was reliable and in Tauranac's spaceframe BT19 certainly quick enough.

■ Australian engineering company Repco were already developing for the Tasman series a 2.5-litre 90° V8 based on an Oldsmobile block to replace the Climax FPF engine. A 3-litre version was a comparatively simple development.

■ On the tyres front, Goodyear won four races with Brabham, Firestone three through Ferrari (at Monza), Lotus and Cooper, while for Dunlop it was the first two, Ferrari at Spa and the BRM victory which started off this eccentric season.

■ But it was Jack Brabham who, just as in his second championship year of 1960, pulverised the opposition mid-season with a string of wins, his fourth in a row in Germany

effectively sealing the title. It is his third race, at Zandvoort, which will be best remembered. Playing to the gallery, wearing a long beard along with his crash helmet, Brabham hobbled with a stick towards his pole-sitting car, responding to the 'old man' moniker the media had bestowed on him after he turned 40.
- In 1966 this singular 'old man' achieved his third world championship, and remains the only driver to have won the title in a car bearing his own name.

- Sadly, Formula 1's very first drivers' world champion, Giuseppe 'Nino' Farina, was killed in a road accident aged 59. He was travelling in a Lotus-Cortina to the French GP, the very last one to be held on the classic Reims circuit.
- Another sad loss was John Taylor, victim of the tragic first lap accident at the Nürburgring.
- During the year Hollywood came to F1, John Frankenheimer's film *Grand Prix* being set around the 1966 season.

Championship ranking	Championship points	Driver nationality	1966 Drivers Championship		Races contested	Race victories	Podiumse excl. victories	Races led	Flag to flag victories	Laps led	Poles	Fastest laps	Triple Crowns
			Driver	Car									
1	42	AUS	Jack Brabham	Brabham-Repco	9	4	1	7	2	192	3	1	1
2	28	GBR	John Surtees	Ferrari (2) Cooper-Maserati (7)	9	2	2	4		82	2	3	1
3	22	AUT	Jochen Rindt	Cooper-Maserati	9		3	1		20			
4	18	NZL	Denny Hulme	Brabham-Climax (2) Brabham-Repco (7)	9		4	1		1		1	
5	17	GBR	Graham Hill	BRM	9		3						
6	16	GBR	Jim Clark	Lotus-Climax (5) Lotus-BRM (3)	8	1	1	2		102	2		
7	14	GBR	Jackie Stewart	BRM	8	1		1		86			
8	12	GBR	Mike Parkes	Ferrari	4		2	1		6	1		
9	12	ITA	Lorenzo Bandini	Ferrari	7		2	4		57	1	2	
10	9	ITA	Ludovico Scarfiotti	Ferrari	2	1		1		55		1	
11	5	USA	Richie Ginther	Cooper-Maserati (2) Honda (3)	5			1		1		1	
12	4	GBR	Mike Spence	Lotus-BRM	8								
12	4	USA	Dan Gurney	Eagle-Climax (6) Eagle-Weslake (2)	8								
14	3	USA	Bob Bondurant	BRM (5) Eagle-Climax (1) Eagle-Weslake (1)	7								
14	3	SUI	Jo Siffert	Brabham-BRM (1) Cooper-Maserati (7)	8								
16	3	NZL	Bruce McLaren	McLaren-Ford (3) McLaren-Serenissima (1)	4								
17	1	GBR	John Taylor	Brabham- BRM	4								
17	1	GBR	Bob Anderson	Brabham-Climax	6								
17	1	GBR	Peter Arundell	Lotus-BRM (6) Lotus-Climax (1)	7								
17	1	SWE	Jo Bonnier	Cooper-Maserati (7) Brabham-Climax (2)	9								

Championship ranking	Championship points	Team/Marque nationality	1966 Constructors Championship		Engine maker nationality	Races contested	Race victories	1-2 finishes	Podiums excl. victories	Races led	Laps led	Poles	Fastest laps
			Chassis	Engine									
1	42	AUS	Brabham BT19, BT20	Repco 3.0 V8	AUS	9	4	1	5	7	193	3	2
2	31	ITA	Ferrari 312, Dino 246	Ferrari 3.0 V12, 2.4 V6	ITA	7	2	1	4	5	139	3	4
3	30	GBR	Cooper T81	Maserati 3.0 V12	ITA	9	1		5	3	81	1	2
4	22	GBR	BRM P261, P83	BRM 2.0 V8, 3.0 H16	GBR	9	1		3	1	86		
5	13	GBR	Lotus 43, 25	BRM 3.0 H16, 2.0 V8	GBR	9	1		1	1	53	1	
6	8	GBR	Lotus 33	Coventry-Climax 2.0 V8	GBR	9			1	1	49	1	
7	4	USA	Eagle T1G	Coventry-Climax 2.7 S4	GBR	7							
8	3	JPN	Honda RA273	Honda 3.0 V12	JPN	3			1	1	1		1
9	2	NZL	McLaren M2B	Ford 3.0 V8	USA	3							
10	1	AUS	Brabham BT11	BRM 2.0 V8	GBR	5							
10	1	NZL	McLaren M2B	Serenissima 3.0 V8	ITA	1							
10	1	AUS	Brabham BT11	Coventry-Climax 2.7 S4	GBR	7							

1967

Hulme brings it home

THE TALE OF THE TITLE

- Victories at Monaco and the Nürburgring underpinned Denny Hulme's steady march to the championship.
- With two wins for Jack also, the Brabham team won both championships for the second year running.
- In its latest guise, the Brabham-Repco was again a blend of agility, speed and bulletproof reliability.
- The new Lotus 49 with Ford-Cosworth DFV engine took a stunning debut victory at Zandvoort.
- Jim Clark won four races with the Lotus-Ford plus a miracle drive at Monza, but reliability was fickle.
- At Monza Surtees finally won in the 'Hondola', a collaborative effort with Lola to bring success to Honda.
- Dan Gurney's Eagle soared high at Spa, but victory was a false dawn, the car finishing only one other race.
- In an outdated Cooper-Climax, John Love performed a near miracle by so nearly winning at Kyalami.
- That race, the opening championship round in January, went to Pedro Rodríguez in the Cooper-Maserati.
- Jackie Stewart spent a dismal third and final season with BRM, struggling to tame the intractable H16.
- Ferrari, rarely finding race-winning pace, also had to grapple with Bandini's fatal accident at Monaco.
- And not forgetting: Matra arrive; cars sprout wings.

THE CHASE FOR THE CHAMPIONSHIP

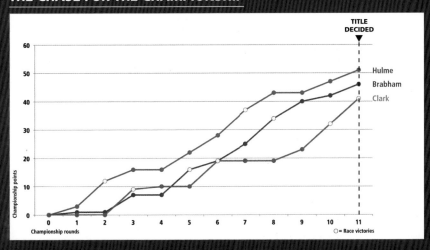

Cooper-Maserati T81

Round 1/11	**SOUTH AFRICAN GP** Kyalami		**Pedro Rodríguez**
	2 January 1967	**Race 151**	Cooper-Maserati T81 156.260kph, 97.095mph

Pedro Rodríguez, now at Cooper, qualified fourth behind Brabham, Hulme and Clark and immediately ahead of local driver John Love in an elderly four-cylinder 2.7-litre Cooper-Climax, the ex-Bruce McLaren Tasman car. Hulme shot into a growing lead, victory certain until, with 20 laps to go, he rushed into the pits to replenish brake fluid. With other fancied runners such as Brabham, Rindt, Gurney and the Surtees Honda already out or in trouble, Love found himself in the lead of his home GP, the ageing Cooper 24s ahead of Rodríguez in the works car. But there was to be no fairy-tale ending. To complete the distance Love needed to make a splash and dash, Rodríguez leading in a Cooper 1-2, their second victory in as many races.

POLE POSITION J Brabham, Brabham-Repco, 1m 28.3s (0.6s), 166.920kph, 103.719mph
LAPS 80 x 4.094 km, 2.544 miles
DISTANCE 327.534 km, 203.520 miles
STARTERS/FINISHERS 18/6
WEATHER Sunny, hot, dry
LAP LEADERS Hulme 1-60 (60); Love 61-73 (13); Rodríguez 74-80 (7)
WINNER'S LAPS 1-2 P4, 3-4 P5, 6-17 P4, 18 P3, 19-25 P5, 26-38 P7, 39-40 P6, 41-44 P5, 45-53 P4, 54-60 P3, 61-73 P2, 74-80 P1
FASTEST LAP D Hulme, Brabham-Repco, 1m 29.9s (lap 3), 163.949kph, 101.873mph
CHAMPIONSHIP Rodríguez 9, Love 6, Surtees 4, Hulme 3, Anderson 2

Pos	Driver	Car	Time/gap	Grid	Stops	Tyres
1	P Rodríguez	Cooper-Maserati	2h 5m 45.9s	4	0	F
2	J Love	Cooper-Climax	−26.4s	5	1	F
3	J Surtees	Honda	−1 lap	6	0	F
4	D Hulme	Brabham-Repco	−2 laps	2	3	G
5	B Anderson	Brabham-Climax	−2 laps	10	0	F
6	J Brabham	Brabham-Repco	−4 laps	1	1	G

Round 2/11	**MONACO GP** Monte Carlo		**Denny Hulme**
	7 May 1967	**Race 152**	Brabham-Repco BT20 122.079kph, 75.857mph

On lap 82 Bandini's Ferrari, holding second place, crashed at the chicane, turned over and burst into flames. Poor Lorenzo, trapped beneath the car, died from dreadful burns. Inevitably this cast a dark shadow over Denny Hulme's first championship victory. From P2 on the grid Bandini had led the first lap, then it was Hulme, then last year's winner Stewart took over from lap 6 and began to break away from those behind. But once the cwp broke on Stewart's 2.1-litre BRM V8 Hulme led to the finish, chased by Bandini until that fateful lap. Graham Hill maintained his remarkable Monaco finishing record with second in the 2.1 Lotus-BRM. Ferrari's new signing, Chris Amon, came third.

POLE POSITION J Brabham, Brabham-Repco, 1m 27.6s (0.7s), 129.247kph, 80.310mph
LAPS 100 x 3.145km, 1.954 miles
DISTANCE 314.500 km, 195.421 miles
STARTERS/FINISHERS 16/6
WEATHER Sunny, warm, dry
LAP LEADERS L Bandini, Ferrari 1 (1); Hulme 2-5, 15-100 (90); J Stewart, BRM 6-14 (9)
WINNER'S LAPS 1 P2, 2-5 P1, 6-14 P2, 15-100 P1
FASTEST LAP J Clark, Lotus-Climax 1m 29.5s (lap 38), 126.503kph, 78.605mph
CHAMPIONSHIP Hulme 12, Rodríguez 11, Love 6, G Hill 6, Surtees 4

Pos	Driver	Car	Time/gap	Grid	Stops	Tyres
1	D Hulme	Brabham-Repco	2h 34m 34.3s	4	0	G
2	G Hill	Lotus-BRM	−1 lap	8	0	F
3	C Amon	Ferrari	−2 laps	14	1	F
4	B McLaren	McLaren-BRM	−3 laps	10	1	G
5	P Rodríguez	Cooper-Maserati	−4 laps	16	0	F
6	M Spence	BRM	−4 laps	12	0	G

Round 3/11	**DUTCH GP** Zandvoort					**Jim Clark**		

DUTCH GP Zandvoort
4 June 1967 · Race 153

Jim Clark
Lotus-Ford 49 168.029kph, 104.408mph

The debut of the Lotus 49 was a sensation. Fitted with the 3-litre V8 Ford-Cosworth DFV, Graham Hill, back with Lotus, put the brand new car on pole from Gurney's Eagle-Weslake V12 and Brabham. Hill led the opening ten laps until a camshaft broke in the new engine, but Brabham's ensuing lead didn't last long. Starting P8 after a troubled practice, Clark was scything through the field in the new car, separating Brabham from the lead on lap 16 and then pulling away, the car never missing a beat. Such a resounding victory for a brand new car and engine was an astonishing achievement. Brabham and Hulme's Brabham-Repcos finished 2-3 then three Ferraris, these and other teams having much to contemplate.

POLE POSITION G Hill, Lotus-Ford, 1m 24.60s (0.5s), 178.426kph, 110.868mph
LAPS 90 x 4.193 km, 2.605 miles
DISTANCE 377.370 km, 234.487 miles
STARTERS/FINISHERS 17/10
WEATHER Overcast, dry
LAP LEADERS G Hill 1-10 (10); Brabham 11-15 (5); Clark 16-90 (75)
WINNER'S LAPS 1-3 P6, 4-6 P5, 7-10 P4, 11-14 P3, 15 P2, 16-90 P1
FASTEST LAP Clark, Lotus-Ford, 1m 28.08s (lap 67), 171.376kph, 106.488mph
CHAMPIONSHIP Hulme 16, Rodríguez 11, Clark 9, Brabham 7, Amon 7

Pos	Driver	Car	Time/gap	Grid	Stops	Tyres
1	J Clark	Lotus-Ford	2h 14m 45.1s	8	0	F
2	J Brabham	Brabham-Repco	−23.6s	3	0	G
3	D Hulme	Brabham-Repco	−25.7s	7	0	G
4	C Amon	Ferrari	−27.3s	9	0	F
5	M Parkes	Ferrari	−1 lap	10	0	F
6	L Scarfiotti	Ferrari	−1 lap	15	0	F

Eagle-Weslake T1G

BELGIAN GP Spa-Francorchamps
18 June 1967 · Race 154

Dan Gurney
Eagle-Weslake T1G 234.946kph, 145.988mph

Round 4/11

Just as it had in practice, Clark's Lotus 49 dominated the race, but shortly before half-distance made a couple of pit-stops with spark-plug trouble. Stewart now led, for once enjoying a fine drive in the H16 BRM, but Dan Gurney was closing in the V12 Eagle-Weslake. But just as Clark made his stop for attention so too did the Eagle, Gurney complaining of fluctuating fuel pressure. He quickly rejoined, still in second place, and again began to reel in the BRM, in part because Stewart was driving one-handed, the other holding his car in gear. With eight laps left the Eagle took the lead, and despite some alarms over fuel pressure held on to the finish. Although neither Brabham featured or finished, Hulme retained the championship lead.

POLE POSITION Clark, Lotus-Ford, 3m 28.1s (3.1s), 243.921kph, 151.566mph
LAPS 28 x 14.100 km, 8.761 miles
DISTANCE 394.800 km, 245.317 miles
STARTERS/FINISHERS 18/10
WEATHER Sunny, warm, dry
LAP LEADERS Clark 1-12 (12); Stewart 13-20 (8); Gurney 21-28 (8)
WINNER'S LAPS 1 P5, 2-12 P3, 13-20 P2, 21-28 P1
FASTEST LAP Gurney, Eagle-Weslake, 3m 31.9s (lap 19), 239.547kph, 148.848mph
CHAMPIONSHIP Hulme 16, Rodríguez 11, Amon 11, Clark 10, Gurney 9

Pos	Driver	Car	Time/gap	Grid	Stops	Tyres
1	D Gurney	Eagle-Weslake	2h 40m 49.4s	2	1	G
2	J Stewart	BRM	−1m 3.0s	6	0	G
3	C Amon	Ferrari	−1m 40.0s	5	0	F
4	J Rindt	Cooper-Maserati	−2m 13.9s	4	0	F
5	M Spence	BRM	−1 lap	11	0	G
6	J Clark	Lotus-Ford	−1 lap	1	2	F

Round 5/11	**FRENCH GP** Bugatti au Mans		
	2 July 1967		Race 155

FRENCH GP Bugatti au Mans

Round 5/11 — 2 July 1967 — Race 155

Jack Brabham
Brabham-Repco BT24 159.166kph, 98.901mph

The top six grid slots comprised a pair of cars from each of the leading teams of the moment, Lotus-Ford, Brabham-Repco and Eagle-Weslake, Hill's Lotus 49 on pole. McLaren was driving Gurney's second car, neither McLaren nor Honda cars present due to engine shortages and Ferrari down to a single car following Parkes' Spa injury. Hill and Clark dominated the race until both succumbed to transmission failure, handing the lead to Brabham closely chased by Gurney. But by half-distance Gurney too was out and the second half of the race was a breeze for the Brabhams, fielding for the first time a pair of their latest cars, the diminutive F2-based BT24. They finished the race 1-2, the positions they now occupied in the championship points table.

POLE POSITION G Hill, Lotus-Ford, 1m 36.2s (0.1s), 165.480kph, 102.825mph
LAPS 80 x 4.422 km, 2.748 miles
DISTANCE 353.760 km, 219.816 miles
STARTERS/FINISHERS 15/6
WEATHER Sunny, warm, dry
LAP LEADERS G Hill 1, 11-13 (4); Brabham 2-4, 24-80 (60); J Clark, Lotus-Ford 5-10, 14-23 (16)
WINNER'S LAPS 1 P3, 2-4 P1, 5-6 P2, 7-13 P3, 14-23 P2, 24-80 P1
FASTEST LAP G Hill, Lotus-Ford, 1m 36.7s (lap 7), 164.625kph, 102.293mph
CHAMPIONSHIP Hulme 22, Brabham 16, Rodríguez 12, Amon 11, Clark 10

Pos	Driver	Car	Time/gap	Grid	Stops	Tyres
1	J Brabham	Brabham-Repco	2h 13m 21.3s	2	0	G
2	D Hulme	Brabham-Repco	–49.5s	6	0	G
3	J Stewart	BRM	–1 lap	10	0	G
4	J Siffert	Cooper-Maserati	–3 laps	11	0	F
5r	C Irwin	BRM	–4 laps	9	0	G
6	P Rodríguez	Cooper-Maserati	–4 laps	13	1	F

Lotus-Ford 49

BRITISH GP Silverstone

Round 6/11 — 15 July 1967 — Race 156

Jim Clark
Lotus-Ford 49 189.327kph, 117.642mph

Clark took pole, Hill alongside despite his Lotus sustaining heavy damage when its rear suspension collapsed during practice. Clark led away from the start whereas Hill was pushed down to P3 by Brabham, but once Hill found his stride in the rebuilt Lotus he retook Brabham on lap 8 and set off after Clark. Eighteen laps later he took the lead and kept it for the next 28 laps, Clark never far behind. But on lap 55 Hill pitted, a rear wheel askew. A bolt had dropped out of the hastily rebuilt suspension. Clark, untroubled, won his fifth British GP, but Hulme's second place increased his championship advantage, now up to nine points. Chris Amon's Ferrari completed the podium followed by Brabham, these four alone finishing the distance.

POLE POSITION Clark, Lotus-Ford, 1m 25.3s (0.7s), 198.804kph, 123.531mph
LAPS 80 x 4.711 km, 2.927 miles
DISTANCE 376.844 km, 234.160 miles
STARTERS/FINISHERS 20/10
WEATHER Sunny, warm, dry
LAP LEADERS Clark 1-25, 55-80 (51); G Hill, Lotus-Ford 26-54 (29)
WINNER'S LAPS 1-25 P1, 26-54 P2, 55-80 P1
FASTEST LAP Hulme, Brabham-Repco, 1m 27.0s (lap 3), 194.919kph, 121.117mph
CHAMPIONSHIP Hulme 28, Clark 19, Brabham 19, Amon 15, Rodríguez 14

Pos	Driver	Car	Time/gap	Grid	Stops	Tyres
1	J Clark	Lotus-Ford	1h 59m 25.6s	1	0	F
2	D Hulme	Brabham-Repco	–12.8s	4	0	G
3	C Amon	Ferrari	–16.6s	6	0	F
4	J Brabham	Brabham-Repco	–21.8s	3	0	G
5	P Rodríguez	Cooper-Maserati	–1 lap	9	0	F
6	J Surtees	Honda	–2 laps	7	0	F

Round 7/11	**GERMAN GP** Nürburgring		
	6 August 1967	Race 157	

Denny Hulme
Brabham-Repco BT24 163.200kph, 101.408mph

Denny Hulme's German GP victory significantly tightened his grip on the 1967 title, his championship lead extending to 12 points. Clark, once more on pole, led the opening three laps but was out soon afterwards, neither Team Lotus car reaching the finish with sundry suspension difficulties. Gurney now took command, easily pulling away, a clear-cut victory in sight more than a minute ahead of Hulme. If Clark's retirement was disappointing, Gurney's was devastating. With two laps remaining the Eagle's driveshaft let go. So Denis Hulme led another Brabham 1-2, with Chris Amon's Ferrari third for the fourth time in six races. Jackie Oliver finished fifth on the road to win the concurrent F2 race in a works Lotus-Ford.

POLE POSITION J Clark, Lotus-Ford, 8m 4.1s (9.4s), 169.812kph, 105.516mph
LAPS 15 x 22.835km, 14.189 miles
DISTANCE 342.525 km, 212.835 miles
STARTERS/FINISHERS 17/8 (Excluding F2 cars)
WEATHER Sunny, warm, dry
LAP LEADERS Clark 1-3 (3); Gurney 4-12 (9); Hulme 13-15 (3)
WINNER'S LAPS 1-12 P2, 13-15 P1
FASTEST LAP D Gurney, Eagle-Weslake, 8m 15.1s (lap 3), 166.039kph, 103.172mph
CHAMPIONSHIP Hulme 37, Brabham 25, Clark 19, Amon 19, Rodríguez 14

Pos	Driver	Car	Time/gap	Grid	Stops	Tyres
1	D Hulme	Brabham-Repco	2h 5m 55.7s	2	0	G
2	J Brabham	Brabham-Repco	–38.5s	7	0	G
3	C Amon	Ferrari	–39.0s	8	0	F
4	J Surtees	Honda	–2m 25.7s	6	0	F
5	J Bonnier	Cooper-Maserati	–8m 42.1s	16	0	F
6	G Ligier	Brabham-Repco	–1 lap	17	0	F

Brabham-Repco BT24

Round 8/11	**CANADIAN GP** Mosport Park		
	27 August 1967	Race 158	

Jack Brabham
Brabham-Repco BT24 133.007kph, 82.647mph

Another Brabham-Repco 1-2 hammer-blow, this time the boss leading the way, the team's superb points-scoring form clinching the constructors' championship. From the outside of the front row, Hulme got ahead of pole-sitter Clark on lap 4 and led for over 50 laps. In treacherous early conditions Hulme established a useful lead but had to surrender it to Clark on lap 58, the drying track benefitting his Lotus. Renewed rainfall caused Clark's retirement on lap 68 with wet electrics, and Hulme to pit to replace muddy goggles with a visor. Brabham took the lead during all of this, having made a last-minute grid decision to fit rain tyres. Bruce McLaren made a promising impression in the McLaren M5A fitted with the new V12 BRM engine.

POLE POSITION J Clark, Lotus-Ford, 1m 22.4s (0.3s), 172.895kph, 107.432mph
LAPS 90 x 3.957 km, 2.459 miles
DISTANCE 356.164 km, 221.310 miles
STARTERS/FINISHERS 17/11
WEATHER Wet
LAP LEADERS Clark 1-3, 58-67 (13); Hulme 4-57 (54); Brabham 68-90 (23)
WINNER'S LAPS 1 P5, 2-6 P4, 7-12 P3, 13-21 P4, 22-33 P5, 34-45 P4, 46-67 P2, 68-90 P1
FASTEST LAP J Clark, Lotus-Ford, 1m 23.1s (lap 54), 171.439kph, 106.527mph
CHAMPIONSHIP Hulme 43, Brabham 34, Amon 20, Clark 19, Rodríguez 14

Pos	Driver	Car	Time/gap	Grid	Stops	Tyres
1	J Brabham	Brabham-Repco	2h 40m 40.0s	7	0	G
2	D Hulme	Brabham-Repco	–1m 1.9s	3	2	G
3	D Gurney	Eagle-Weslake	–1 lap	5	0	G
4	G Hill	Lotus-Ford	–2 laps	6	0	F
5	M Spence	BRM	–3 laps	10	0	G
6	C Amon	Ferrari	–3 laps	4	0	F

Honda RA300

Round 9/11	**ITALIAN GP** Monza						**John Surtees**
	10 September 1967					**Race 159**	Honda RA300 226.120kph, 140.505mph

Leading a four-car slipstreaming gaggle of Lotuses and Brabhams, a deflating tyre forced Clark to pit on lap 13, losing a lap in the process. On lap 61 he retook the lead from Brabham, having made up 100s in 46 laps, one of the most incredible comeback drives in the annals of F1. Regrettably, fuel pump failure on the very last lap ruined one fairy tale yet wrote quite another. Surtees overtook a very sideways Brabham on the exit to Parabolica to win by 0.2s, the new 'Hondola' only ahead for those final few hundred metres. In truth, if Graham Hill's engine had not broken ten laps from the end when 75s ahead of Brabham, Clark could not have retaken the lead, but it takes nothing from his feat or the myth surrounding it.

POLE POSITION Clark, Lotus-Ford, 1m 28.5s (0.3s), 233.898kph, 145.338mph
LAPS 68 x 5.750 km, 3.573 miles
DISTANCE 391.000 km, 242.956 miles
STARTERS/FINISHERS 18/7
WEATHER Sunny, warm, dry
LAP LEADERS D Gurney, Eagle-Weslake 1-2 (2); Clark 3-9, 11-12, 61-67 (16); D Hulme, Brabham-Repco 10, 13-15, 17, 24-27 (9); Brabham 16, 59-60 (3); G Hill, Lotus-Ford 18-23, 28-58 (37); Surtees 68 (1)
WINNER'S LAPS 1 P10, 2-4 P9, 5-6 P8, 7 P7, 8 P6, 9 P5, 10 P6, 11-12 P5, 13-30 P4, 31-36 P3, 37 P4, 38-41 P3, 42 P4, 43-64 P3, 65-67 P2, 68 P1
FASTEST LAP Clark, Lotus-Ford, 1m 28.5s (lap 26), 233.898kph, 145.338mph
CHAMPIONSHIP Hulme 43, Brabham 40, Clark 23, Amon 20, Surtees 17

Pos	Driver	Car	Time/gap	Grid	Stops	Tyres
1	J Surtees	Honda	1h 43m 45.0s	9	0	F
2	J Brabham	Brabham-Repco	−0.2s	2	0	G
3	J Clark	Lotus-Ford	−23.1s	1	1	F
4	J Rindt	Cooper-Maserati	−56.6s	11	0	F
5	M Spence	BRM	−1 lap	12	0	G
6	J Ickx	Cooper-Maserati	−2 laps	15	0	F

Round 10/11	**UNITED STATES GP** Watkins Glen						**Jim Clark**
	1 October 1967					**Race 160**	Lotus-Ford 49 184.977kph, 114.939mph

Monza had put paid to Clark's title aspirations so a Clark-led 1-2 for Team Lotus in the USA was simply too late. Hill from Clark on the grid, Clark from Hill at the finish looked straightforward enough, but it wasn't. For 40 laps Hill led until gear selection problems slowed him. Clark then looked set for an easy victory until with two to go, a rear wheel adopted a drunken angle. But he nursed his stricken car to the finish to just take it from Hill. Although the Brabhams were way off the pace, another team kept Lotus honest and but for their own late misfortunes most likely would have won the race. This was Ferrari, Amon always close enough to the Lotus pair that, but for engine failure 13 laps from the end, the outcome might have been different.

POLE POSITION G Hill, Lotus-Ford 1m 5.48s (0.59s), 203.503kph, 126.451mph
LAPS 108 x 3.701 km, 2.300 miles
DISTANCE 399.761 km, 248.400 miles
STARTERS/FINISHERS 18/7
WEATHER Sunny, cool, dry
LAP LEADERS G Hill 1-40 (40); Clark 41-108 (68)
WINNER'S LAPS 1 P2, 2-7 P3, 8-40 P2, 41-108 P1
FASTEST LAP G Hill, Lotus-Ford, 1m 6.00s (lap 81), 201.900kph, 125.455mph
CHAMPIONSHIP Hulme 47, Brabham 42, Clark 32, Amon 20, Surtees 17

Pos	Driver	Car	Time/gap	Grid	Stops	Tyres
1	J Clark	Lotus-Ford	2h 3m 13.2s	2	0	F
2	G Hill	Lotus-Ford	−6.3s	1	0	F
3	D Hulme	Brabham-Repco	−1 lap	6	0	G
4	J Siffert	Cooper-Maserati	−2 laps	12	0	F
5	J Brabham	Brabham-Repco	−4 laps	5	1	G
6	J Bonnier	Cooper-Maserati	−7 laps	15	NA	F

MEXICAN GP Mexico City
22 October 1967   Race 161

Jim Clark
Lotus-Ford 49 163.210kph, 101.414mph

Only Jack Brabham could deny Hulme the 1967 title, and to do so he had to win in Mexico whereas Hulme could seal it with fourth place or better. In the race Brabham never looked likely to beat Clark for the required victory, and Hulme never looked likely to finish below fourth, especially following the early retirement of Hill from P2 and the late retirement of Amon also from second place, running out of fuel three laps from the flag. A degree of championship tension held up until the end, as late retirements by Clark and Hulme might have gifted Brabham a fourth title, but as the final laps to the championship counted down a surprise outcome became steadily less likely, Hulme's sixth podium finish, plus two wins, being the model of consistency.

POLE POSITION Clark, Lotus-Ford, 1m 47.56s (0.48s), 167.348ph, 103.986mph
LAPS 65 x 5.000 km, 3.107 miles
DISTANCE 325.000 km, 201.946 miles
STARTERS/FINISHERS 18/12
WEATHER Sunny, warm, dry
LAP LEADERS G Hill 1-2 (2); Clark 3-65 (63)
WINNER'S LAPS 1 P3, 2 P2, 3-65 P1
FASTEST LAP Clark, Lotus-Ford, 1m 48.13s (lap 52), 166.466kph, 103.437mph
CHAMPIONSHIP Hulme 51, Brabham 46, Clark 41, Surtees 20, Amon 20

Pos	Driver	Car	Time/gap	Grid	Stops	Tyres
1	J Clark	Lotus-Ford	1h 59m 28.7s	1	0	F
2	J Brabham	Brabham-Repco	−7.88s	4	0	G
3	D Hulme	Brabham-Repco	−1 lap	6	0	G
4	J Surtees	Honda	−1 lap	3	0	F
5	M Spence	BRM	−1 lap	9	0	G
6	P Rodríguez	Cooper-Maserati	−2 laps	12	0	F

1967 CHAMPIONSHIP FACTS AND FOLKLORE

■ For only the second time there were 11 races, but rather than just the best six scores counting as in 1958 it was decided to raise this to nine but split the season into two parts. The best five results from the first six races, plus the best four from the remaining five would decide the championships.

■ Mosport Park brought Canada on to the GP map and Kyalami became the new home for the South African race. The French GP was held just the once at the Bugatti au Mans track, a circuit that utilised part of the famous 24 Hours Sarthe circuit.

■ New Zealander Denny Hulme made an early claim to the 1967 title with a well-judged Monaco victory at the start of the European season.

■ His second win was also on a drivers' circuit, two hours and five minutes around the Nürburgring, making him one of just 15 revered Nordschleife grand prix winners; a true badge of honour.

■ But Jim Clark remained very much the man to beat in 1967, bagging four race victories, twice as many as the new world champion.

■ Over the season Clark led four more races and 100 more laps then Hulme, stats which tell the real tale of the title – reliability.

■ As usual Clark and his Lotus were win or bust, whereas Hulme was the model of consistency and dependability coupled with no mean turn of speed.

■ If anything, Clark's pre-eminence was endorsed by the arrival of a new teammate, albeit an old adversary, Graham Hill returning to Lotus after seven seasons with BRM.

■ Similarly equipped with the Lotus 49, Clark out-qualified Hill 6-3 and Hill also failed to win a race, although in that particular respect improved reliability might well have led to a three-all draw.

■ With hindsight, the arrival of the Lotus 49 and the Cosworth DFV V8 was a Formula 1 landmark, a watershed, and in many ways that was how it seemed at the time.

■ In discussion with Colin Chapman of Lotus about the void left in F1 by the withdrawal of Coventry-Climax, Keith Duckworth of Cosworth Engineering claimed he could produce a competitive 3-litre F1 engine given a development budget of £100,000. Chapman approached Walter Hayes at Ford to sponsor the project, Ford's Blue Oval to grace the cam-covers.

■ Hayes later claimed it was the best £100,000 Ford ever spent,

as once the initially exclusive arrangement with Chapman and Lotus ended, the Ford-Cosworth DFV (short for 'double four valve') spawned the F1 'kit-car' era and would still be promoting Ford's prowess in F1 some 15 years later.

■ Naturally Lotus and Cosworth worked closely on the Lotus-Ford project, and it showed. As a package it was so right, the design so beautifully conceived and integrated, the engine forming a stressed chassis member to which the rear suspension was bolted. It made the offerings from Cooper, BRM, Honda, Ferrari and even the elegant Eagle look and seem cumbersome, even archaic.

■ The Ford-Cosworth DFV engine was a jewel, a neat, compact, all-aluminium 90° twin-ohc V8. Incorporating four valves per cylinder and Lucas fuel injection, initial output was 400bhp at 9,000rpm.

■ Only Brabham measured up with their diminutive and nimble F2-based BT24, powered by a further development of the Repco V8.

■ Brabham-Repco were worthy winners of the constructors' cup with four victories plus ten podiums, failing to score points just once, at Spa.

■ The singleton victories by Cooper-Maserati, Eagle-Weslake and Honda added spice to the season but were each somewhat fortuitous.

■ The Eagle-Weslake clearly showed the greatest potential, but whether engine or chassis, its mechanical reliability was lamentable.

■ The 'Hondola' victory was the product of Surtees' move to Honda and his collaboration with Eric Broadly of Lola to produce a better, lighter Honda chassis. Monza was only Honda's second victory in four years of trying. Their third victory, as a fully-fledged constructor, would come 39 years later, courtesy of Jenson Button in 2006.

■ What of BRM and Ferrari in 1967? By providing a new V12 engine to Bruce McLaren for his new M5A chassis BRM signalled their future intent to dump the ill-conceived H16 project, which over two seasons had brought no tangible success to the Bourne concern.

■ Ferrari, following the Bandini tragedy, often entered just one car for new team-leader Chris Amon, who delivered with four podiums for the Scuderia. The adoption of the 48-valve

RACE 152, Monaco GP: Bandini's dreadful accident inevitably cast a dark shadow over Denny Hulme's first championship victory. Here he leads Stewart's BRM.

V12 from Monza, delivering 410bhp at 10,600rpm, brought Amon much closer to a potential victory in the final rounds.
■ But in view of what was to happen the following April at a F2 race in Germany, the defining moment of 1967 must be Clark at Monza. When he took the lead for the second time it was hard to believe quite what was happening. Clark appeared to have done the impossible, as only he knew how.
■ In 1967 Tony Vandervell of Vanwall fame died aged 68 and regular F1 privateer Bob Anderson was killed testing at Silverstone.

■ Looking ahead, there was an important new entrant in 1967 – Matra Sports, a successful French F2 team and chassis manufacturer. They entered ballasted F2 cars in three Grands Prix for Jean-Pierre Beltoise and Johnny Servoz-Gavin.
■ But it was Belgian driver Jacky Ickx who really made the F1 establishment sit up. In the combined F1/F2 race at the German GP he clocked the third fastest qualifying time around the Nordschleife in his 1,600cc F2 Matra-Ford MS7 entered by Ken Tyrrell. A sign of things to come.

Championship ranking	Championship points	Driver nationality	1967 Drivers Championship		Races contested	Race victories	Podiumse excl. victories	Races led	Flag to flag victories	Laps led	Poles	Fastest laps	Triple Crowns
			Driver	Car									
1	51	NZL	Denny Hulme	Brabham-Repco	11	2	6	5		216		2	
2	46	AUS	Jack Brabham	Brabham-Repco	11	2	4	4		91	2		
3	41	GBR	Jim Clark	Lotus-BRM (1) Lotus-Climax (1) Lotus-Ford (9)	11	4	1	9		317	6	5	1
4	20	GBR	John Surtees	Honda	9	1	1	1		1			
5	20	NZL	Chris Amon	Ferrari	10		4						
6	15	MEX	Pedro Rodriguez	Cooper-Maserati	8	1		1		7			
7	15	GBR	Graham Hill	Lotus-BRM (2) Lotus-Ford (9)	11		2	6		122	3	2	
8	13	USA	Dan Gurney	Eagle-Climax (1) Eagle-Weslake (10)	11	1	1	3		19		2	
9	10	GBR	Jackie Stewart	BRM	11		2	2		17			
10	9	GBR	Mike Spence	BRM	11								
11	6	ZIM	John Love	Cooper-Climax	1		1	1		13			
12	6	AUT	Jochen Rindt	Cooper-Maserati	10								
12	6	SUI	Jo Siffert	Cooper-Maserati	10								
14	3	NZL	Bruce McLaren	McLaren-BRM (6) Eagle-Weslake (3)	9								
15	3	SWE	Jo Bonnier	Cooper-Maserati	8								
16	2	GBR	Bob Anderson	Brabham-Climax	5								
16	2	GBR	Mike Parkes	Ferrari	2								
16	2	GBR	Chris Irwin	Lotus-BRM (1) BRM (8)	9								
19	1	ITA	Ludovico Scarfiotti	Ferrari (2) Eagle-Weslake (1)	3								
19	1	FRA	Guy Ligier	Cooper-Maserati (2) Brabham-Repco (5)	7								
19	1	BEL	Jacky Ickx	Matra-Ford Cosworth (1) Cooper-Maserati (2)	3								
-	0	ITA	Lorenzo Bandini	Ferrari	1			1		1			

Championship ranking	Championship points	Team/Marque nationality	1967 Constructors Championship		Engine maker nationality	Races contested	Race victories	1-2 finishes	Podiums excl. victories	Races led	Laps led	Poles	Fastest laps
			Chassis	Engine									
1	63	AUS	Brabham BT24, BT20, BT19	Repco 3.0 V8	AUS	11	4	3	10	7	307	2	2
2	44	GBR	Lotus 49	Ford Cosworth 3.0 V8	GBR	9	4	1	3	9	439	9	7
3	28	GBR	Cooper T81, T81B, T86	Maserati 3.0 V12	ITA	11	1			1	7		
4	20	JPN	Honda RA273, RA 300	Honda 3.0 V12	JPN	9	1		1	1	1		
5	20	ITA	Ferrari 312	Ferrari 3.0 V12	ITA	10			4	1	1		
6	17	GBR	BRM P83, P115, P261	BRM 3.0 H16, 2.1 V8	GBR	11			2	2	17		
7	13	USA	Eagle T1G	Weslake 3.0 V12	GBR	10	1		1	3	19		2
8	6	GBR	Cooper T79	Coventry-Climax 2.7 S4	GBR	1			1	1	13		
8	6	GBR	Lotus 33, 43	BRM 2.1 V8, 3.0 H16	GBR	4							
10	3	NZL	McLaren M4B, M5A	BRM 2.1 V8, 3.0 V12	GBR	6							
11	2	AUS	Brabham BT11	Coventry-Climax 2.7 S4	GBR	5							

1968

Graham Hill steps up

THE TALE OF THE TITLE

- On 7 April 1968 Jim Clark was killed in a F2 race at Hockenheim.
- Graham Hill turned Lotus tragedy into triumph with his second drivers' championship.
- At the Mexico finale he defeated Stewart and Hulme, his three wins including a fourth Monaco victory.
- Five race wins, including one for Siffert in Rob Walker's car, brought Lotus-Ford the constructors' title.
- McLaren and the Tyrrell Matra team joined Lotus in using the Ford-Cosworth DFV engine.
- The DFV powered the winner of all 12 championship rounds save one – Ickx's Ferrari in France.
- Dire problems for the latest Repco V8 totally sidelined reigning double constructors' champions Brabham.
- Seven drivers from five teams won races, Mario Andretti taking pole position on his F1 debut with Lotus.
- Bruce was first to win for McLaren, other first-time victors being the Tyrrell Matras and drivers Ickx and Siffert.
- On New Year's Day, Jim Clark's 25th and last victory at Kyalami surpassed Fangio's benchmark.
- And not forgetting: high-mounted aerofoils; Gold Leaf Team Lotus.

THE CHASE FOR THE CHAMPIONSHIP

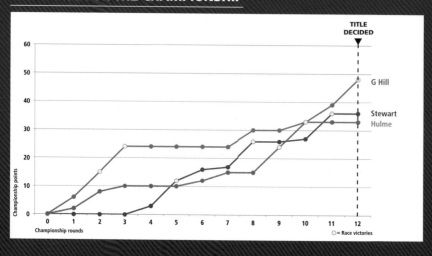

SOUTH AFRICAN GP Kyalami
1 January 1968 Race 162

Jim Clark
Lotus-Ford 49 172.878kph, 107.422mph

New Year's Day and a new season. Jim Clark won as he pleased from pole, which, including the final two races of last year, made it three in a row. With teammate Hill making it a 1-2 on the grid and in the race, prospects for 1968 appeared to be a return to the halcyon Lotus days of 1963 and 1965. However, the race contained performances that suggested otherwise, notably a strong showing for 20 laps by Stewart in the Tyrrell-run Matra-Ford DFV, and Rindt making a promising debut for Brabham-Repco in the BT24. Adding to the prospect of increased competition, from the start of the European season the DFV would also be bolted in the back of the McLaren. This was Clark's 25th championship victory, beating Fangio's 1957 benchmark.

POLE POSITION Clark, Lotus-Climax, 1m 21.6s (1.0s), 166.920kph, 103.719mph
LAPS 80 x 4.104 km, 2.550 miles
DISTANCE 328.306 km, 204.000 miles
STARTERS/FINISHERS 23/9
WEATHER Sunny, very hot, dry
LAP LEADERS Stewart, Matra-Ford 1 (1); Clark 2-80 (79)
WINNER'S LAPS 1 P2, 2-80 P1
FASTEST LAP Clark, Lotus-Climax, 1m 23.7s (lap 73), 163.949kph, 101.873mph
CHAMPIONSHIP Clark 9, G Hill 6, Rindt 4, Amon, 3, Hulme 2

Pos	Driver	Car	Time/gap	Grid	Stops	Tyres
1	J Clark	Lotus-Ford	1h 53m 56.6s	1	0	F
2	G Hill	Lotus-Ford	−25.3s	2	0	F
3	J Rindt	Brabham-Repco	−30.4s	4	0	G
4	C Amon	Ferrari	−2 laps	8	1	F
5	D Hulme	McLaren-BRM	−2 laps	9	0	G
6	J-P Beltoise	Matra-Ford	−3 laps	18	0	D

SPANISH GP Jarama
12 May 1968 Race 163

Graham Hill
Lotus-Ford 49 135.823kph, 84.396mph

Round two felt like a different era: no Jim Clark; no green-and-yellow Lotus livery, and no Stewart either, legacy of a wrist damaged in a F2 accident. And a Ferrari on pole, Chris Amon. From P2 on the grid, Rodríguez in the V12 BRM led until he was passed by the smoking Matra-DFV of Beltoise on lap 12. When Beltoise pitted to investigate the oil smoke Amon was able to steadily draw away from Hill, now leading the chase. But on lap 58, with a big lead, Amon 'luck' put him out with fuel-pump failure. Hill sailed by to give the beleaguered Gold Leaf Team Lotus a much needed fillip, which in the circumstances few would begrudge. Bruce McLaren and Denny Hulme debuted the new McLaren M7A with Ford DFV, the reigning champion finishing second.

POLE POSITION C Amon, Ferrari, 1m 27.9s (0.2s), 139.413kph, 86.627mph
LAPS 90 x 3.404 km, 2.115 miles
DISTANCE 306.360 km, 190.363 miles
STARTERS/FINISHERS 13/5
WEATHER Sunny, hot, dry
LAP LEADERS P Rodríguez, BRM 1-11 (11); Beltoise 12-15 (4); Amon 16-57 (42); G Hill 58-90 (33)
WINNER'S LAPS 1-4 P7, 5 P6, 6-11, P5, 12-16 P4, 17-27 P3, 28-57 P2, 58-90 P1
FASTEST LAP Beltoise, Matra-Ford, 1m 28.3s (lap 47), 138.781kph, 86.235mph
CHAMPIONSHIP G Hill 15, Clark 9, Hulme 8, Rindt 4, Redman 4

Pos	Driver	Car	Time/gap	Grid	Stops	Tyres
1	G Hill	Lotus-Ford	2h 15m 20.1s	6	0	F
2	D Hulme	McLaren-Ford	−15.9s	3	0	G
3	B Redman	Cooper-BRM	−1 lap	13	0	F
4	L Scarfiotti	Cooper-BRM	−1 lap	12	0	F
5	J-P Beltoise	Matra-Ford	−9 laps	5	2	D
-	Only five classified finishers	-	-	-	-	-

Lotus-Ford 49B

Round 3/12	**MONACO GP** Monte Carlo		**Graham Hill**	
	26 May 1968	Race 164	Lotus-Ford 49B 125.238kph, 77.819mph	

The fifth successive victory for Team Lotus was Graham Hill's fourth at Monaco. Johnny Servoz-Gavin, deputising for Stewart, led three frenetic opening laps before breaking the Tyrrell Matra driveshaft when he clipped a barrier. This enabled Hill to lead the rest of the way from his pole position and give himself a blistering start in the title race. In fact he was not to win again until October. Monaco's car-busting reputation was preserved, just five cars still running at the end. Challenges from Siffert in the Walker Lotus-DFV and Surtees in the Honda were over well before quarter-distance, but race interest was just about kept up, at least in the closing stages, by Attwood's BRM, setting a new lap record on the final tour to finish just 2.2s from Hill.

POLE POSITION G Hill, Lotus-Climax, 1m 28.2s (0.6s), 128.367kph, 79.764mph
LAPS 80 x 3.145km, 1.954 miles
DISTANCE 251.600 km, 156.337 miles
STARTERS/FINISHERS 16/5
WEATHER Sunny, warm, dry
LAP LEADERS J Servoz-Gavin, Matra-Ford 1-3 (3); G Hill 4-80 (77)
WINNER'S LAPS 1-3 P2, 4-80 P1
FASTEST LAP D Attwood, BRM 1m 28.1s (lap 80), 128.513kph, 79.854mph
CHAMPIONSHIP G Hill 24, Hulme 10, Clark 9, Attwood 6, Scarfiotti 6

Pos	Driver	Car	Time/gap	Grid	Stops	Tyres
1	G Hill	Lotus-Ford	2h 0m 32.3s	1	0	F
2	D Attwood	BRM	–2.2s	6	0	G
3	L Bianchi	Cooper-BRM	–4 laps	14	0	F
4	L Scarfiotti	Cooper-BRM	–4 laps	15	0	F
5	D Hulme	McLaren-Ford	–7 laps	10	1	G
-	Only five classified finishers	-		-	-	-

Round 4/12	**BELGIAN GP** Spa-Francorchamps		**Bruce McLaren**	
	9 June 1968	Race 165	McLaren-Ford M7A 236.797kph, 147.139mph	

Missing Monaco, Ferrari returned with a bang, Amon on pole. Alongside him Stewart was also back, his wrist still in plaster. Amon battled with Surtees until a stone pierced the Ferrari oil radiator on lap 8. Two laps later Surtees lost an 18s lead when the rear wishbone pulled out from the chassis, leaving Hulme and Stewart now scrapping for victory. Once Hulme retired on lap 19 with a broken half-shaft Stewart was on his own, over half-a-minute ahead of the duelling McLaren and Rodríguez. But Stewart's DFV had consumed more fuel than expected, running dry on the penultimate lap. When the Rodríguez BRM also began to suffer fuel starvation Bruce McLaren became, somewhat fortuitously, the second driver to win in a car bearing his name.

POLE POSITION C Amon, Ferrari, 3m 28.6s (3.7s), 243.337kph, 151.202mph
LAPS 28 x 14.100 km, 8.761 miles
DISTANCE 394.800 km, 245.317 miles
STARTERS/FINISHERS 18/8
WEATHER Overcast, dry
LAP LEADERS Amon 1 (1); Surtees 2-10 (9); D Hulme, McLaren-Ford 11, 15 (2); Stewart 12-14, 16-27 (15); McLaren 28 (1)
WINNER'S LAPS 1 P11, 2-7 P9, 8 P8, 9-10 P5, 11-13 P3, 14-16 P4, 17 P3, 18 P2, 19-21 P3, 22-27 P2, 28 P1
FASTEST LAP J Surtees, Honda 3m 30.5s (lap 5), 241.140kph, 149.838mph
CHAMPIONSHIP G Hill 24, Hulme 10, Clark 9, McLaren 9, Attwood 6

Pos	Driver	Car	Time/gap	Grid	Stops	Tyres
1	B McLaren	McLaren-Ford	1h 40m 2.1s	6	0	G
2	P Rodríguez	BRM	–12.1s	8	0	G
3	J Ickx	Ferrari	–39.6s	3	0	F
4	J Stewart	Matra-Ford	–1 lap	2	1	D
5r	J Oliver	Lotus-Ford	–2 laps	15	1	F
6	L Bianchi	Cooper-BRM	–2 laps	12	0	F

Round 5/12	**DUTCH GP** Zandvoort		**Jackie Stewart**	
	23 June 1968	Race 166	Matra-Ford MS10 136.245kph, 84.659mph	

Amon's Ferrari took pole again. In rainy race conditions, Hill was first to show until Stewart came by on lap 4, grooved Dunlop wets clearly the tyres to have. This was demonstrated most vividly by Beltoise in the V12 Matra. Starting P16, he quickly made up places to catch and pass Hill for second and close on Stewart. On lap 21 the Frenchman spun at Tarzan and this and the ensuing pit stop dropped him to seventh. He then did the whole thing again, passing car after car and making up around 50s on Hill, who he re-passed for second place on lap 51. Stewart apart, driving with a wrist support, few drivers did not gyrate on the treacherous track, including points-leader Graham Hill who in the end failed to score.

POLE POSITION Amon, Ferrari, 1m 23.54s (0.16s), 180.689kph, 112.275mph
LAPS 90 x 4.193 km, 2.605 miles
DISTANCE 377.370 km, 234.487 miles
STARTERS/FINISHERS 19/9
WEATHER Heavy showers
LAP LEADERS G Hill, Lotus-Ford 1-3 (3); Stewart 4-90 (87)
WINNER'S LAPS 1-3 P2, 4-90 P1
FASTEST LAP Beltoise, Matra, 1m 45.91s (lap 6), 142.525kph, 88.561mph
CHAMPIONSHIP G Hill 24, Stewart 12, Rodríguez 10, Hulme 10, Clark 9

Pos	Driver	Car	Time/gap	Grid	Stops	Tyres
1	J Stewart	Matra-Ford	2h 46m 11.26s	5	0	D
2	J-P Beltoise	Matra	–1m 33.93s	16	1	D
3	P Rodríguez	BRM	–1 lap	11	0	G
4	J Ickx	Ferrari	–2 laps	6	0	F
5	S Moser	Brabham-Repco	–3 laps	17	0	G
6	C Amon	Ferrari	–5 laps	1	1	F

| Round 6/12 | **FRENCH GP** Rouen-les-Essarts | **Jacky Ickx** |
| | 7 July 1968   Race 167 | Ferrari 312 161.662kph, 100.452mph |

After maiden victories for McLaren and for Matra, the next two races produced first-time wins for drivers. Another wet race saw Jacky Ickx bring Ferrari their first for two years. For 20 laps Ickx battled intensely with Rodríguez and Surtees. Ickx, unlike most of the field, had opted for full-wets, but even he had a brief spin, dropping behind his two pursuers on lap 19. Maybe this indiscretion was a wake-up call, as the following lap he was back in the lead and from there pulled away steadily. Conditions were far too tricky for debutant Jo Schlesser in the new air-cooled V8 Honda, who stood no chance when he crashed heavily on lap 3 and overturned in flames. Stewart finished third, Hill out of the points yet again.

POLE POSITION J Rindt, Brabham-Repco, 1m 56.1s (1.2s), 202.853kph, 126.047mph
LAPS 60 x 6.542 km, 4.065 miles
DISTANCE 392.520 km, 243.901 miles
STARTERS/FINISHERS 17/11
WEATHER Wet
LAP LEADERS Ickx 1-18, 20-60 (59); Rodríguez 19 (1)
WINNER'S LAPS 1-18 P1, 19 P3, 20-60 P1
FASTEST LAP P Rodríguez, BRM, 2m 11.5s (lap 19), 179.097kph, 111.285mph
CHAMPIONSHIP G Hill 24, Ickx 16, Stewart 16, Hulme 12, Rodríguez 10

Pos	Driver	Car	Time/gap	Grid	Stops	Tyres
1	J Ickx	Ferrari	2h 25m 40.9s	3	0	F
2	J Surtees	Honda	–1 m 58.6s	7	1	F
3	J Stewart	Matra-Ford	–1 lap	2	1	D
4	V Elford	Cooper-BRM	–2 laps	17	0	F
5	D Hulme	McLaren-Ford	–2 laps	4	1	G
6	P Courage	BRM	–3 laps	14	1	D

Ferrari 312

| Round 7/12 | **BRITISH GP** Brands Hatch | **Jo Siffert** |
| | 4 August 1968   Race 168 | Lotus-Ford 49B 168.709kph, 104.831mph |

Jo Siffert's maiden victory was the first for Rob Walker since 1961. Hill was in authoritative mood at his home circuit with a scintillating pole and a clear early lead. For the first 20 laps the sight of three Lotuses in echelon, their massive rear wings on high struts shaking and wobbling, was awe-inspiring. But on lap 26 the spell was broken, yet another car breakage for Hill promoting Lotus number two Jackie Oliver. More than 20s behind Oliver, Siffert driving the Walker/Durlacher Lotus 49B was engaged in an intense duel with Amon's Ferrari, the red car getting ahead on lap 37, Siffert retaking on lap 43. The very next lap it became the lead, Oliver out. Over the final 37 laps Amon tried everything to displace the Swiss driver but without success.

POLE POSITION G Hill, Lotus-Ford, 1m 28.9s (0.5s), 107.312kph, 123.531mph
LAPS 80 x 4.265 km, 2.650 miles
DISTANCE 341.181 km, 212.000 miles
STARTERS/FINISHERS 20/8
WEATHER Sunny, hot, dry
LAP LEADERS J Oliver, Lotus-Ford 1-3, 27-43 (20); G Hill 4-26 (23); Siffert 44-80 (37)
WINNER'S LAPS 1-26 P3, 27-36 P2, 37-42 P3, 43 P2, 44-80 P1
FASTEST LAP Siffert, Lotus-Ford, 1m 29.7s (lap 42), 171.161kph, 106.355mph
CHAMPIONSHIP G Hill 24, Ickx 20, Stewart 17, Hulme 15, Rodríguez 10

Pos	Driver	Car	Time/gap	Grid	Stops	Tyres
1	J Siffert	Lotus-Ford	2h 1m 20.3s	4	0	F
2	C Amon	Ferrari	–4.4s	3	0	F
3	J Ickx	Ferrari	–1 lap	12	0	F
4	D Hulme	McLaren-Ford	–1 lap	11	0	G
5	J Surtees	Honda	–2 laps	9	0	F
6	J Stewart	Matra-Ford	–2 laps	7	0	D

Walker/Durlacher Lotus-Ford 49B

Round 8/12 | GERMAN GP Nürburgring
4 August 1968   Race 169

Jackie Stewart
Matra-Ford MS10 137.943kph, 85.714mph

Stewart's tame British GP showing, inhibited by his painful wrist injury, made his Nürburgring drive even more extraordinary, winning by over four minutes from Graham Hill. Maybe the atrocious weather made it easier on the injury, but even equipped with Dunlop 'super-wets', 2 hours 19 minutes around the Nordschleife wearing a wrist support did seem Herculean. Starting from only the third row, Stewart took the lead halfway around the first lap and pulled steadily away in the rain and mist. Hill, behind him, was preoccupied for much of the race with Amon until a differential problem spun the Ferrari out. The Ferrari pair had been 1-2 on the grid, Ickx's remarkable pole almost breaking the nine-minute barrier. Stewart now lay just four points behind Hill.

POLE POSITION Ickx, Ferrari, 9m 4.0s (10.9s), 151.114kph, 93.898mph
LAPS 14 x 22.835km, 14.189 miles
DISTANCE 319.690 km, 198.646 miles
STARTERS/FINISHERS 20/14
WEATHER Murky, very wet
LAP LEADERS Stewart 1-14 (14)
WINNER'S LAPS 1-14 P1
FASTEST LAP Stewart, Matra-Ford, 9m 36.0s (lap 8), 142.719kph, 88.681mph
CHAMPIONSHIP G Hill 30, Stewart 26, Ickx 23, Hulme 15, Rodríguez 11

Pos	Driver	Car	Time/gap	Grid	Stops	Tyres
1	J Stewart	Matra-Ford	2h 19m 3.2s	6	0	D
2	G Hill	Lotus-Ford	–4m 3.2s	4	0	F
3	J Rindt	Brabham-Repco	–4m 9.4s	3	0	G
4	J Ickx	Ferrari	–5m 55.2s	1	2	F
5	J Brabham	Brabham-Repco	–6m 21.1s	15	0	G
6	P Rodríguez	BRM	–6m 25.0s	14	0	G

TOP 100 RACE

Round 9/12 | ITALIAN GP Monza
8 September 1968   Race 170

Denny Hulme
McLaren-Ford M7A 226.120kph, 140.505mph

Last year's winner Surtees was on pole but reigning world champion Denny Hulme won the race for McLaren and for Goodyear, Akron bringing new improved rubber to good effect. The race soon developed into a typical Monza slipstreamer, as many as seven cars dicing in the leading group with five different leaders crossing the timing line. Surtees went out early, caught up in Amon's spin on oil at Lesmo on lap 5, and gradually the leading group was whittled down until Hulme managed to break free in the final ten laps. When Ickx pitted on lap 61, Servoz-Gavin, in only his second race, suddenly realised P2 was possible, unlapped himself and pipped Ickx on the line. Neither Hill nor Stewart added to their championship points totals.

POLE POSITION J Surtees, Honda, 1m 28.5s (0.04s), 240.502kph, 149.441mph
LAPS 68 x 5.750 km, 3.573 miles
DISTANCE 391.000 km, 242.956 miles
STARTERS/FINISHERS 20/6
WEATHER Sunny, hot, dry
LAP LEADERS B McLaren, McLaren-Ford 1-6, 8-12, 14 (12); J Surtees, Honda 7 (1); J Stewart, Matra-Ford 13, 17-18, 27, 30, 33, 40 (7); J Siffert, Lotus-Ford 15-16 (2); Hulme 19-26, 28-29, 31-32, 34-39, 41-68 (46)
WINNER'S LAPS 1 P8, 2-8 P7, 9-10 P5, 11-15 P4, 16-18 P3, 19-26 P1, 27 P2, 28-29 P1, 30 P2, 31-32 P1, 33 P2, 34-39 P1, 40 P2, 41-68 P1
FASTEST LAP J Oliver, Lotus-Ford, 1m 26.5s (lap 7), 239.306kph, 148.698mph
CHAMPIONSHIP G Hill 30, Ickx 27, Stewart 26, Hulme 24, Rodríguez 11

Pos	Driver	Car	Time/gap	Grid	Stops	Tyres
1	D Hulme	McLaren-Ford	1h 40m 14.8s	7	0	G
2	J Servoz-Gavin	Matra-Ford	–1m 28.4s	13	0	D
3	J Ickx	Ferrari	–1m 28.6s	4	1	F
4	P Courage	BRM	–1 lap	17	0	D
5	J-P Beltoise	Matra	–2 laps	18	0	D
6	J Bonnier	McLaren-BRM	–4 laps	19	0	G

CANADIAN GP St Jovite
22 September 1968   Race 171

Denny Hulme
McLaren-Ford M7A 156.466kph, 97.223mph

Rindt took pole, demonstrating the potential of the latest twin-ohc Repco engine. Hulme's second win in as many races, leading a McLaren 1-2, was one of resilience over speed. There were only two race leaders, Amon's Ferrari leading every lap until 72 of the 90, when transmission failure intervened. For the first 29 laps his old Brands Hatch adversary Jo Siffert had given him a hard time, but abandoned the race with an oil leak. Further back, although not challenging for the lead, were pole-sitter Rindt, Dan Gurney in a McLaren and Graham Hill, but all but Hill retired. Hulme and Hill now jointly led the championship points table, six ahead of Stewart and Ickx, although the latter was out of the running having sustained a broken leg in an accident during practice.

POLE POSITION J Rindt, Brabham-Repco, 1m 33.8s (0.0s), 163.680kph, 101.706mph
LAPS 90 x 4.265 km, 2.650 miles
DISTANCE 383.829 km, 238.500 miles
STARTERS/FINISHERS 20/6
WEATHER Sunny, warm, dry
LAP LEADERS C Amon, Ferrari 1-72 (72); Hulme 73-90 (18)
WINNER'S LAPS 1-26 P6, 27-29 P5, 30-38 P4, 39-44 P3, 45-72 P2, 73-90 P1
FASTEST LAP J Siffert, Lotus-Ford, 1m 35.1s (lap 22), 161.442kph, 100.315mph
CHAMPIONSHIP G Hill 33, Hulme 33, Stewart 27, Ickx 27, McLaren 15

Pos	Driver	Car	Time/gap	Grid	Stops	Tyres
1	D Hulme	McLaren-Ford	2h 27m 11.2s	6	0	G
2	B McLaren	McLaren-Ford	−1 lap	8	0	G
3	P Rodríguez	BRM	−2 laps	12	1	G
4	G Hill	Lotus-Ford	−4 laps	5	1	F
5	V Elford	Cooper-BRM	−4 laps	16	0	F
6	J Stewart	Matra-Ford	−7 laps	11	1	D

Matra-Ford MS10

UNITED STATES GP Watkins Glen
6 October 1968   Race 172

Jackie Stewart
Matra-Ford MS10 200.989kph, 124.889mph

Although mechanical ailments spoilt Mario Andretti's first championship race, pitting on lap 14 with a collapsed front wing when running second, his F1 debut at his home race in a works Lotus was a sensation, taking pole from Stewart and Hill. To keep his championship chances alive Stewart needed to win. Andretti beat Stewart off the line but at the end of the main straight the Scot out-braked the American to take a lead he would keep for the duration. But main rival Hill, hampered by a loose steering wheel, still finished second to retain his points lead into the final round. Despite his eventful race, spinning twice and finally damaging his car extensively, defending champion Hulme was also still in contention for another title.

POLE POSITION M Andretti, Lotus-Ford 1m 4.20s (0.07s), 207.560kph, 128.972mph
LAPS 108 x 3.701 km, 2.300 miles
DISTANCE 399.761 km, 248.400 miles
STARTERS/FINISHERS 19/6
WEATHER Overcast, dry
LAP LEADERS Stewart 1-108 (108)
WINNER'S LAPS 1-108 P1
FASTEST LAP Stewart, Matra-Ford, 1m 5.22s (lap 52), 204.314kph, 126.955mph
CHAMPIONSHIP G Hill 39, Stewart 36, Hulme 33, Ickx 27, McLaren 16

Pos	Driver	Car	Time/gap	Grid	Stops	Tyres
1	J Stewart	Matra-Ford	1h 59m 20.29s	2	0	F
2	G Hill	Lotus-Ford	−6.3s	3	0	F
3	J Surtees	Honda	−1 lap	9	0	G
4	D Gurney	McLaren-Ford	−1 lap	7	0	F
5	J Siffert	Lotus-Ford	−3 laps	12	1	G
6	B McLaren	McLaren-Ford	−5 laps	10	1	F

| Round 12/12 | **MEXICAN GP** Mexico City | | | | | | **Graham Hill** |
| | 3 November 1968 | | | | Race 173 | | Lotus-Ford 49B 167.049kph, 103.799mph |

<table>
<tr><td>

Put simply, to be certain of championship honours all three contenders had to win the showdown. None of them qualified especially well, but when pole-sitter Siffert botched his start Hill seized the initiative, leading lap 1 from P3. Stewart was third from P7, Hulme fifth from P4. On lap 5 they were 1-2-3, Stewart ahead of Hill. Hill retook the lead on lap 9, Hulme out with a broken damper the following lap. Despite the brief intervention of the rapid Siffert, by half-distance the two protagonists were still only separated by a second. Soon afterwards the gap widened as a misfire and other difficulties set in, Stewart eventually finishing seventh a lap behind. Hill was champion, his skill and fortitude having hauled Team Lotus back from the depths.

</td><td>

POLE POSITION Siffert, Lotus-Ford, 1m 45.22s (0.40s), 171.070ph, 106.298mph
LAPS 65 x 5.000 km, 3.107 miles
DISTANCE 325.000 km, 201.946 miles
STARTERS/FINISHERS 21/10
WEATHER Sunny, warm, dry
LAP LEADERS G Hill 1-4, 9-21, 25-65 (58); J Stewart, Matra-Ford 5-8 (4); Siffert 22-24 (3)
WINNER'S LAPS 1-4 P1, 5-8 P2, 9-21 P1, 22-24 P2, 25-65 P1
FASTEST LAP Siffert, Lotus-Ford, 1m 44.23s (lap 52), 172.695kph, 107.308mph
CHAMPIONSHIP G Hill 48, Stewart 36, Hulme 33, Ickx 27, McLaren 22

</td></tr>
</table>

Pos	Driver	Car	Time/gap	Grid	Stops	Tyres
1	G Hill	Lotus-Ford	1h 56m 43.95s	3	0	F
2	B McLaren	McLaren-Ford	−1m 19.32s	9	0	G
3	J Oliver	Lotus-Ford	−1m 40.65s	14	0	F
4	P Rodríguez	BRM	−1m 41.09s	12	0	G
5	J Bonnier	Honda	−1 lap	18	0	F
6	J Siffert	Lotus-Ford	−1 lap	1	1	F

RACE 173, Mexican GP: Graham Hill (10) on his way to winning the race and with it his second title, having hauled Gold Leaf Team Lotus back from the depths following Clark's sad demise. Siffert (16) and Stewart (15) pursue.

Championship ranking	Championship points	Driver nationality	Driver	Car	Races contested	Race victories	Podiumse excl. victories	Races led	Flag to flag victories	Laps led	Poles	Fastest laps	Triple Crowns
1	48	GBR	Graham Hill	Lotus-Ford	12	3	3	5		194	2		
2	36	GBR	Jackie Stewart	Matra-Ford	10	3	1	7	2	236		2	
3	33	NZL	Denny Hulme	McLaren-BRM (1) McLaren-Ford (11)	12	2	1	3		66			
4	27	BEL	Jacky Ickx	Ferrari	9	1	3	1		59	1		
5	22	NZL	Bruce McLaren	McLaren-Ford	11	1	2	2		13			
6	18	MEX	Pedro Rodriguez	BRM	12		3	2		12		1	
7	12	SUI	Jo Siffert	Cooper-Maserati (1) Lotus-Ford (11)	12	1		3		42	1	3	
8	12	GBR	John Surtees	Honda	12		2	2		10	1	1	
9	11	FRA	Jean-Pierre Beltoise	Matra-Ford (2) Matra (10)	12		1	1		4		2	
10	10	NZL	Chris Amon	Ferrari	11		1	3		115	3		
11	9	GBR	Jim Clark	Lotus-Ford	1	1		1		79	1	1	1
12	8	AUT	Jochen Rindt	Brabham-Repco	12		2				2		
13	6	GBR	Richard Attwood	BRM	6		1					1	
13	6	FRA	Johnny Servoz-Gavin	Matra-Ford (4) Cooper-BRM (1)	5		1	1		3			
15	6	GBR	Jackie Oliver	Lotus-Ford	8		1	1		20		1	
16	6	ITA	Ludovico Scarfiotti	Cooper-Maserati (1) Cooper-BRM (2)	3								
17	5	BEL	Lucien Bianchi	Cooper-BRM	7		1						
18	5	GBR	Vic Elford	Cooper-BRM	7								
19	4	GBR	Brian Redman	Cooper-Maserati (1) Cooper-BRM (2)	3		1						
20	4	GBR	Piers Courage	BRM	11								
21	3	USA	Dan Gurney	Eagle-Weslake (5) Brabham-Repco (1) McLaren-Ford (3)	9								
22	3	SWE	Jo Bonnier	Cooper-Maserati (1) McLaren-BRM (6) Honda (1)	8								
23	2	SUI	Silvio Moser	Brabham-Repco	2								
23	2	AUS	Jack Brabham	Brabham-Repco	11								
-	0	USA	Mario Andretti	Lotus-Ford	1						1		

1968 CHAMPIONSHIP FACTS AND FOLKLORE

■ 1968 was the longest season on record, lasting ten months and two days, and for the first time a 12-race season divided into two parts, the best five results from each half counting towards the championships.

■ St Jovite in Canada joined the GP calendar, and after an interval of 14 years Spain returned at Járama.

■ Jim Clark's fatal accident on 7 April 1968 at a Hockenheim F2 race has never been fully explained, although a tyre deflation was suspected, the Lotus leaving the tree-lined track to devastating effect.

■ If the news caused shockwaves throughout the motor racing world, it was utter devastation for Colin Chapman. Team Lotus was bereft. After the frustrations of the previous season, the team was ready to enjoy the spoils of the Lotus 49 in the hands of the great Scotsman, to replicate the glory days of 1963 and 1965.

■ Fortuitously in 1967 Chapman had rehired Graham Hill to partner Clark and it was he who stepped up as team leader in their hour of need by securing the championship in the final race of the season in Mexico.

■ A win in Spain followed by a record fourth Monaco triumph put Hill and his beleaguered team on an early path towards championship honours, but then a spate of dnfs, largely reliability induced, allowed challenges from first Stewart's Tyrrell Matra, and then Hulme's McLaren, to gather momentum.

■ For 1968 the Tyrrell and McLaren teams also had use of the Ford-Cosworth DFV engine to power, respectively, Stewart's Matra MS10 and the M7A chassis for world champion Denny Hulme.

■ Hulme had departed Brabham to join fellow Kiwi Bruce McLaren. One unusual feature of the McLaren was the provision for pannier tanks to be mounted each side between the wheels, similar in concept to the 1954 Lancia D50.

■ Matra, a French aerospace and defence armament company, entered F1 through their subsidiary Matra Sports with a two-pronged attack. Their works team would use a new 60° Matra V12 while their chassis would also be supplied to entrant Ken Tyrrell, mirroring their existing arrangement in F2.

■ Stewart and Tyrrell, who had enjoyed a highly successful

RACE 162, South African GP: Little did F1 appreciate that Jim Clark's 25th victory – surpassing Fangio's record – was the final time his sublime skills would grace the world championship.

driver/entrant relationship in Formula Junior running the Cooper-BMC works team, would renew that partnership in an assault on the F1 world championships, the duo convinced that the Ford-Cosworth DFV was fundamental to success.

■ But Stewart's championship campaign was disrupted due to a F2 accident, a broken wrist causing him to miss two races and suffer discomfiture for much of the season.

■ However, three Stewart victories and two by Hulme propelled three title protagonists towards a championship showdown in Mexico, ultimately resolved in Hill's favour.

■ As aerodynamic wings became de rigueur, Lotus exploited the high-mounted concept to the full and, sporting ground-breaking Golf Leaf livery, were worthy winners of the constructors' cup with five race victories.

■ These included Jo Siffert's British Grand Prix success, the first for Rob Walker in seven years but the last ever for a F1 private entrant.

■ Following a change in the regulations concerning sponsorship in F1, the striking Gold Leaf livery worn by the Team Lotus cars heralded the commencement of overt recognition of team support and funding, and the start of a massive influx of tobacco money into the sport, which would endure for over three decades.

■ McLaren's three race wins included a landmark victory for Bruce at Spa, where, two years after Jack Brabham, he became the second-ever driver to win in a self-named car, and the third to win in a car of his own construction following Gurney's Eagle triumph at the same circuit 12 months earlier.

■ All bar one of the dozen championship rounds therefore went to the remarkable Ford-Cosworth DFV engine, the exception resulting from a Ferrari victory, the first in two years. This was delivered by the talented Belgian driver Jacky Ickx, who even brought himself into championship contention until breaking his leg in a practice accident in Canada. Four poles, three down to Amon, also indicated a gradual re-emergence of Ferrari as a force.

■ Ferrari's French win was the first for a car fitted with a rear 'wing' aerodynamic device, the Scuderia also experimenting with adjustable aerofoils, both automatic and driver-actuated.

■ 1968 was a complete disaster for Brabham, the unreliability of the latest Repco engine a lamentable experience for Jochen Rindt, who had replaced Denny Hulme.

■ The new version of the Repco V8 had gear-driven double overhead camshafts and four valves per cylinder producing 400bhp at 9,500rpm, but it suffered from insurmountable valve gear problems.

■ Gurney's AAR Eagle project was losing impetus as the American's focus increasingly turned to USAC racing. This was the final season for Eagle works entries.

■ As well as Lotus, three other teams suffered driver losses during the season, BRM, Cooper and Honda.

■ BRM's Mike Spence was killed in a freak accident while practising for the Indy 500. Cooper, switching from V12 Maserati to V12 BRM engines, lost lead driver Ludo Scarfiotti at a German Hillclimb.

■ Honda's misfortune happened to poor Jo Schlesser on the opening lap of the treacherously wet French GP. He was driving a prototype air-cooled V8 Honda, much against the better judgement of John Surtees, who considered that the radical car required far more development.

■ The Schlesser tragedy knocked the stuffing out of Honda, and of these three blighted teams only BRM would continue the following season.

■ In 1968 Mika Häkkinen was born.

Championship ranking	Championship points	Team/Marque nationality	1968 Constructors Championship		Engine maker nationality	Races contested	Race victories	1-2 finishes	Podiums excl. victories	Races led	Laps led	Poles	Fastest laps
			Chassis	Engine									
1	62	GBR	Lotus 49, 49B	Ford Cosworth 3.0 V8	GBR	12	5	1	4	7	335	5	5
2	49	NZL	McLaren M7A	Ford Cosworth 3.0 V8	GBR	11	3	1	3	3	79		
3	45	FRA	Matra MS9, MS10, MS7	Ford Cosworth 3.0 V8, 1.6 S4	GBR	12	3		2	9	243		3
4	32	ITA	Ferrari 312	Ferrari 3.0 V12	ITA	11	1		3	4	174	4	
5	28	GBR	BRM P126, P133, P115	BRM 3.0 V12, 3.0 H16	GBR	12			4	2	12		2
6	14	JPN	Honda RA 300, RA301, RA302	Honda 3.0 V12, 3.0 V8 a/c	JPN	12			2	2	10	1	1
7	14	GBR	Cooper T86B	BRM 3.0 V12	GBR	11			3				
8	10	AUS	Brabham BT26, BT24, BT20	Repco 3.0 V8	AUS	12			2			2	
9	8	FRA	Matra MS11	Matra 3.0 V12	FRA	10			1				1
10	3	NZL	McLaren M5A	BRM 3.0 V12	GBR	7							

1969

Stewart's entente cordiale

THE TALE OF THE TITLE

- France's Matra chassis shot Stewart to his and their first title, the combo winning six of the first eight races.
- Ken Tyrrell fused the French chassis, Ford DFV engine and Dunlop tyres into a potent package for Stewart.
- The Anglo-French enterprise benefitted from the lack of any consistent championship-winning opposition.
- Ditching Repco for the DFV, Brabham bounced back, new signing Jacky Ickx championship runner-up.
- Jochen Rindt's first season at Lotus was a disappointment, his first victory not until the penultimate round.
- Tall strut-mounted wings were banned after failure led to horrifying accidents for the Lotus pair in Spain.
- Graham Hill won his fifth Monaco GP in seven years, only to later suffer serious injury at Watkins Glen.
- The Ford DFV powered all 11 race winners, Matra six, Brabham and Lotus two, Hulme's McLaren one.
- Non-DFV teams BRM and Ferrari scored seven championship points apiece over the whole season.
- And not forgetting: Frank Williams, F1 entrant; 4WD cars flop.

THE CHASE FOR THE CHAMPIONSHIP

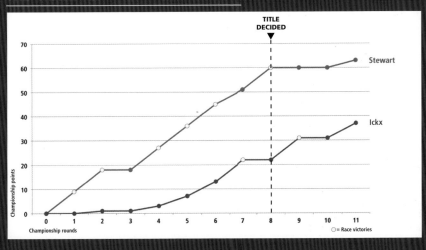

| Round 1/11 | **SOUTH AFRICAN GP** Kyalami | | **Jackie Stewart** |
| | 1 March 1969 | Race 174 | Matra-Ford MS10 178.021kph, 110.617mph |

The first race of the new season saw the three title rivals from last year finish 1-2-3. Brabham was on pole, having switched from Repco V8 to Cosworth DFV, but at the start Stewart blasted the Tyrrell-Matra MS10 into the lead from the second row, chased by the pole-sitter. But Brabham's race only lasted until lap 6, when his high-mounted rear aerofoil collapsed, the same fate befalling Ickx making his Brabham debut. The three entries from Gold Leaf Team Lotus, Hill, Rindt and Andretti, provided Stewart with some early competition but only Hill's car survived, completing the distance well behind Stewart's comfortable flag-to-flag victory. Front and rear-mounted high wing aerofoils were evident on many cars, some driver-adjustable.

POLE POSITION J Brabham, Brabham-Ford, 1m 20.0s (0.2s), 184.672kph, 114.750mph
LAPS 80 x 4.104 km, 2.550 miles
DISTANCE 328.306 km, 204.000 miles
STARTERS/FINISHERS 18/8
WEATHER Sunny, hot, dry
LAP LEADERS Stewart 1-80 (80)
WINNER'S LAPS 1-80 P1
FASTEST LAP Stewart, Matra-Ford, 1m 21.6s (lap 50), 181.051kph, 112.500mph
CHAMPIONSHIP Stewart 9, G Hill 6, Hulme 4, Siffert 3, McLaren 2

Pos	Driver	Car	Time/gap	Grid	Stops	Tyres
1	J Stewart	Matra-Ford	1h 50m 39.1s	4	0	D
2	G Hill	Lotus-Ford	−18.8s	7	0	F
3	D Hulme	McLaren-Ford	−31.8s	3	0	G
4	J Siffert	Lotus-Ford	−49.2s	12	0	F
5	B McLaren	McLaren-Ford	−1 lap	8	0	G
6	J-P Beltoise	Matra-Ford	−2 laps	11	0	D

| Round 2/11 | **SPANISH GP** Montjuïc | | **Jackie Stewart** |
| | 4 May 1969 | Race 175 | Matra-Ford MS80 149.536kph, 92.917mph |

The undulations of this road circuit exposed the folly of mounting massive aerofoil wings on tall spindly struts. First Hill, in third place, crashed heavily on lap 8 when the rear wing structure collapsed, two rows of Armco preventing the Lotus scything down trees, lamp-posts and the dense crowd. Then on lap 20, in the lead from Amon's Ferrari by 7s, teammate Rindt's wing similarly failed. The Austrian was even luckier to escape with minor injuries, smashing first into the barrier, then Hill's wreck. The Armco barriers, derided as lending the track a 'slot-car racing' appearance, had averted utter catastrophe. Amon then seemed a certain winner until, with a 40s lead, engine trouble on lap 56 gifted Stewart the race.

POLE POSITION J Rindt, Lotus-Ford, 1m 25.7s (0.5s), 159.249kph, 98.952mph
LAPS 90 x 3.791 km, 2.356 miles
DISTANCE 341.190 km, 212.006 miles
STARTERS/FINISHERS 14/6
WEATHER Sunny, warm, dry
LAP LEADERS Rindt 1-19 (19); C Amon, Ferrari 20-56 (37); Stewart 57-90 (34)
WINNER'S LAPS 1-6 P6, 7-8 P5, 9-19, P4, 20-30 P3, 31-56 P2, 57-90 P1
FASTEST LAP J Rindt, Lotus-Ford, 1m 28.3s (lap 15), 154.559kph, 96.039mph
CHAMPIONSHIP Stewart 18, McLaren 8, Hulme 7, G Hill 6, Beltoise 5

Pos	Driver	Car	Time/gap	Grid	Stops	Tyres
1	J Stewart	Matra-Ford	2h 16m 53.99s	4	0	D
2	B McLaren	McLaren-Ford	−2 laps	13	0	G
3	J-P Beltoise	Matra-Ford	−3 laps	12	2	D
4	D Hulme	McLaren-Ford	−3 laps	8	1	G
5	J Surtees	BRM	−6 laps	9	2	D
6r	J Ickx	Brabham-Ford	−7 laps	7	1	G

| Round 3/11 | **MONACO GP** Monte Carlo | | **Graham Hill** |
| | 18 May 1969 | Race 176 | Lotus-Ford 49B 129.037kph, 80.180mph |

At Monaco high wings were banned. Teams protested that being designed around wings, cars would become more dangerous without them. The CSI remained adamant, the race proceeding without wings and the still recovering Rindt. After his fortuitous Spanish victory, Stewart now had the new Tyrrell Matra MS80 motoring, leading from pole to build up a massive early lead from Amon and Hill. On lap 17 car failure put Amon out, and then around quarter-distance, Stewart, leading by 20s, also ground to a halt. Hill swept by for his fifth Monaco triumph, a record lasting 24 years. It was a good day for privateers, Piers Courage bringing the Frank Williams-entered Brabham home second, Siffert in the Walker Lotus third.

POLE POSITION J Stewart, Matra-Ford, 1m 24.6s (0.4s), 133.830kph, 83.158mph
LAPS 80 x 3.145km, 1.954 miles
DISTANCE 251.600 km, 156.337 miles
STARTERS/FINISHERS 16/7
WEATHER Overcast, warm, dry
LAP LEADERS Stewart 1-22 (22); G Hill 23-80 (58)
WINNER'S LAPS 1 P4, 2-16 P3, 17-22 P2, 23-80 P1
FASTEST LAP J Stewart, Matra-Ford 1m 25.1s (lap 16), 133.043kph, 82.669mph
CHAMPIONSHIP Stewart 18, G Hill 15, McLaren 10, Hulme 8, Siffert 7

Pos	Driver	Car	Time/gap	Grid	Stops	Tyres
1	G Hill	Lotus-Ford	1h 56m 59.4s	4	0	F
2	P Courage	Brabham-Ford	−17.3s	9	0	D
3	J Siffert	Lotus-Ford	−34.6s	5	0	F
4	D Attwood	Lotus-Ford	−52.9s	10	0	F
5	B McLaren	McLaren-Ford	−1 lap	11	0	G
6	D Hulme	McLaren-Ford	−2 laps	12	0	G

Matra Ford MS80

Round 4/11	**DUTCH GP** Zandvoort						Jackie Stewart
	21 June 1969					Race 177	Matra-Ford MS80 178.705kph, 111.042mph

Cancellation of Spa on safety grounds gave teams the opportunity to respond to the revised wing regulations. Rear wings integrated into the bodywork became commonplace and in coming races front and rear aerodynamic appendages steadily evolved to assume a recognisable norm. Rindt proclaimed his return with an impressive pole from Stewart and Hill, then over the opening 17 laps built up a 10s lead. When driveshaft failure concluded Rindt's race Stewart was left to win easily from Siffert's well-driven Walker Lotus. The race was enlivened by a terrific mid-race scrap for P3 between Hulme, Amon, Ickx and Brabham. With Hill out of the points with a badly handling Lotus, Stewart assumed a significant championship lead.

POLE POSITION J Rindt, Lotus-Ford, 1m 20.85s (0.29s), 186.701kph, 116.011mph
LAPS 90 x 4.193 km, 2.605 miles
DISTANCE 377.370 km, 234.487 miles
STARTERS/FINISHERS 15/10
WEATHER Sunny, warm, dry
LAP LEADERS G Hill, Lotus-Ford 1-2 (2); Rindt 3-16 (14); Stewart 17-90 (74)
WINNER'S LAPS 1-4 P3, 5-16 P2, 17-90 P1
FASTEST LAP Stewart, Matra-Ford, 1m 22.94s (lap 5), 181.997kph, 113.087mph
CHAMPIONSHIP Stewart 27, G Hill 15, Siffert 13, Hulme 11, McLaren 10

Pos	Driver	Car	Time/gap	Grid	Stops	Tyres
1	J Stewart	Matra-Ford	2h 6m 42.08s	2	0	D
2	J Siffert	Lotus-Ford	–24.52s	10	0	F
3	C Amon	Ferrari	–30.51s	4	0	F
4	D Hulme	McLaren-Ford	–37.16s	7	0	G
5	J Ickx	Brabham-Ford	–37.67s	5	0	G
6	J Brabham	Brabham-Ford	–1m 33.93s	8	0	G

Round 5/11	**FRENCH GP** Clermont-Ferrand						Jackie Stewart
	6 July 1969					Race 178	Matra-Ford MS80 157.251kph, 97.712mph

Jackie Stewart was in irrepressible form around this picturesque and undulating five-mile mini-Nürburgring. A massive pole, start-to-finish leader, fastest lap, and winner by over a minute, Stewart's performance was reminiscent of another Scottish victor when the circuit was last used in 1965. Frenchman Beltoise made it a *jour de gloire*, bringing the second French-built chassis home second for a Tyrrell Matra 1-2 in France. Having tracked Ickx for lap after lap, Beltoise literally pipped the Brabham at the post to the delight of the French crowd. Early on Hulme had looked good for second spot while both Lotus drivers were distinctly off the pace, Rindt retiring suffering from sickness and double vision around the sinuous Circuit du Charade.

POLE POSITION Stewart, Matra-Ford, 3m 0.6s (1.8s), 160.565kph, 99.770mph
LAPS 38 x 8.055 km, 5.005 miles
DISTANCE 306.090 km, 190.196 miles
STARTERS/FINISHERS 13/9
WEATHER Sunny, warm, dry
LAP LEADERS Stewart 1-38 (38)
WINNER'S LAPS 1-38 P1
FASTEST LAP Stewart, Matra-Ford, 3m 2.7s (lap 27), 158.719kph, 98.624mph
CHAMPIONSHIP Stewart 36, G Hill 16, Siffert 13, McLaren 13, Beltoise 11

Pos	Driver	Car	Time/gap	Grid	Stops	Tyres
1	J Stewart	Matra-Ford	1h 56m 47.4s	1	0	D
2	J-P Beltoise	Matra-Ford	–57.1s	5	0	D
3	J Ickx	Brabham-Ford	–57.3s	4	0	G
4	B McLaren	McLaren-Ford	–1 lap	7	0	G
5	V Elford	McLaren-Ford	–1 lap	10	0	G
6	G Hill	Lotus-Ford	–1 lap	8	0	F

McLaren-Ford M7C

Round 6/11	**BRITISH GP** Silverstone					**Jackie Stewart**		
	19 July 1969				Race 179	Matra-Ford MS80 204.795kph, 127.254mph		

Despite a hefty practice prang due to loose kerbing at Woodcote, Stewart lined up beside Rindt on pole. At last their long overdue duel looked set, and this time a titanic struggle ensued, lap after lap. Rindt did most of the leading, Stewart never more than a few car-lengths behind, the pair lapping the entire field. But on lap 63 of 84 the spell was broken, Rindt pitting to fix a rear-wing endplate which threatened to puncture his rear tyre. Later, a further stop for fuel dropped him to fourth. At the start Ickx had fallen from P4 to P10. Over the following 28 laps he sliced through the field, eventually taking McLaren for third place – second with Rindt's tribulations – only to almost lose out to McLaren again when he ran out of fuel on his final lap.

POLE POSITION Rindt, Lotus-Ford, 1m 20.8s (0.4s), 209.876kph, 130.411mph
LAPS 84 x 4.711 km, 2.927 miles
DISTANCE 395.686 km, 245.868 miles
STARTERS/FINISHERS 17/10
WEATHER Overcast, dry
LAP LEADERS Rindt 1-5, 16-61 (51); Stewart 6-15, 62-84 (33)
WINNER'S LAPS 1-5 P2, 6-15 P1, 16-61 P2, 62-84 P1
FASTEST LAP Stewart, Matra-Ford, 1m 21.3s (laps 57 & 60), 208.585kph, 129.609mph
CHAMPIONSHIP Stewart 45, McLaren 17, G Hill 16, Siffert 13, Ickx 13

Pos	Driver	Car	Time/gap	Grid	Stops	Tyres
1	J Stewart	Matra-Ford	1h 55m 55.6s	2	0	D
2	J Ickx	Brabham-Ford	–1 lap	4	0	G
3	B McLaren	McLaren-Ford	–1 lap	7	0	G
4	J Rindt	Lotus-Ford	–1 lap	1	2	F
5	P Courage	Brabham-Ford	–1 lap	10	0	D
6	V Elford	McLaren-Ford	–2 laps	11	0	G

TOP **100** RACE

Round 7/11	**GERMAN GP** Nürburgring					**Jacky Ickx**		
	3 August 1969				Race 180	Brabham-Ford BT26A 174.498kph, 108.428mph		

At the Nürburgring, Stewart and Rindt had to cede pole to Ickx. Making poor use of his advantage, Ickx was P9 as they rounded the South Curve and completed the first lap P4, Stewart leading. He then proceeded to overtake Rindt on lap 2, Siffert on lap 3 and Stewart for the lead on lap 7, simultaneously posting fastest race lap. Their struggle continued until eventually Stewart began to fall away with gear selection difficulties, but on that day Ickx in the Brabham were supreme. Only four F1 cars were running at the end, Siffert still classified despite crashing out of third place at high speed with front suspension failure two laps from the end. Sadly, Gerhard Mitter lost his life while practising for the concurrent F2 race.

POLE POSITION Ickx, Brabham-Ford, 7m 42.1s (0.3s), 177.897kph, 110.540mph
LAPS 14 x 22.835km, 14.189 miles
DISTANCE 319.690 km, 198.646 miles
STARTERS/FINISHERS 14/6 (Excluding F2 cars)
WEATHER Sunny, warm, dry
LAP LEADERS Stewart 1-6 (6); Ickx 7-14 (8)
WINNER'S LAPS 1 P4, 2 P3, 3-6 P2, 7-14 P1
FASTEST LAP Ickx, Brabham-Ford, 7m 43.8s (lap 7), 177.245kph, 110.135mph
CHAMPIONSHIP Stewart 51, Ickx 22, McLaren 21, G Hill 19, Siffert 15

Pos	Driver	Car	Time/gap	Grid	Stops	Tyres
1	J Ickx	Brabham-Ford	1h 49m 55.4s	1	0	G
2	J Stewart	Matra-Ford	–57.7s	2	0	D
3	B McLaren	McLaren-Ford	–3m 21.6s	8	0	G
4	G Hill	Lotus-Ford	–3m 58.8s	9	0	F
5	J Siffert	Lotus-Ford	–2 laps	4	0	F
6	J-P Beltoise	Matra-Ford	–2 laps	10	0	D

ITALIAN GP Monza

7 September 1969 Race 181

The race quickly developed into a classic Monza slipstreamer, as many as eight cars tied together, vying for the lead lap after lap, ducking and diving to gain any small advantage. Gradually the leading bunch thinned out as some retired – Hill on lap 63, driveshaft; Siffert lap 65, piston – while others fell back, notably the Frank Williams Brabham, the tiny team nevertheless elated to have led their first GP. By the flag the first four cars crossed the line separated by less than 0.2s – Stewart, Rindt, Beltoise, McLaren. Stewart's sixth win from eight races gave him an unassailable points lead. He was the new world champion and with victory at Monza he had won the title in style.

Pos	Driver	Car	Time/gap	Grid	Stops	Tyres
1	J Stewart	Matra-Ford	1h 39m 11.26s	3	0	D
2	J Rindt	Lotus-Ford	–0.08s	1	0	F
3	J-P Beltoise	Matra-Ford	–0.17s	6	0	D
4	B McLaren	McLaren-Ford	–0.19s	5	0	G
5	P Courage	Brabham-Ford	–33.44s	4	0	D
6	P Rodríguez	Ferrari	–2 laps	12	0	F

Jackie Stewart

Matra-Ford MS80 236.521kph, 146.968mph

POLE POSITION Rindt, Lotus-Ford, 1m 25.48s (0.21s), 242.162kph, 150.472mph
LAPS 68 x 5.750 km, 3.573 miles
DISTANCE 391.000 km, 242.956 miles
STARTERS/FINISHERS 15/10
WEATHER Sunny, warm, dry
LAP LEADERS Stewart 1-6, 9-17, 19-24, 28-30, 33, 35-36, 38-68 (58); Rindt 7, 25-27, 31, 34, 37 (7); D Hulme, McLaren-Ford 8 (1); Courage 18, 32 (2)
WINNER'S LAPS 1-6 P1, 7-8 P2, 9-17 P1, 18 P2, 19-24 P1, 25-26 P3, 27 P2, 28-30 P1, 31-32 P2, 33 P1, 34 P2, 35-36 P1, 37 P2, 38-68 P1
FASTEST LAP Beltoise, Matra-Ford, 1m 25.20s (lap 64), 242.958kph, 150.967mph
CHAMPIONSHIP Stewart 60, McLaren 24, Ickx 22, G Hill 19, Beltoise 16

TOP **100** RACE

CANADIAN GP Mosport Park

20 September 1969 Race 182

Almost as remarkable as Stewart's six-from-eight victories was that the new world champion would not win another race this year. His first disappointment came here in Canada and was somewhat controversial. Stewart had qualified P4 but quickly disposed of Beltoise, pole-man Ickx and Rindt to take the lead on the sixth lap. Two laps later Ickx overtook Rindt for second and was soon engaged in a close tussle for the lead with Stewart. On the 33rd lap, as the pair lapped a backmarker, Ickx made to pass at a dubious spot, wheels touched and Stewart was eliminated. Ickx lost a dozen seconds but regained the track still in the lead. Brabham eventually got the better of Rindt to make it a Brabham 1-2.

Pos	Driver	Car	Time/gap	Grid	Stops	Tyres
1	J Ickx	Brabham-Ford	1h 59m 25.7s	1	0	G
2	J Brabham	Brabham-Ford	–46.2s	6	0	G
3	J Rindt	Lotus-Ford	–52.0s	3	0	F
4	J-P Beltoise	Matra-Ford	–1 lap	2	0	D
5	B McLaren	McLaren-Ford	–3 laps	9	0	G
6	J Servoz-Gavin	Matra-Ford	–6 laps	15	0	D

Jacky Ickx

Brabham-Ford BT26A 178.934kph, 111.185mph

POLE POSITION Ickx, Brabham-Ford, 1m 17.4s (0.5s), 184.064kph, 114.372mph
LAPS 90 x 3.957 km, 2.459 miles
DISTANCE 356.164 km, 221.310 miles
STARTERS/FINISHERS 20/7
WEATHER Sunny, warm, dry
LAP LEADERS Rindt 1-5 (5); J Stewart, Matra-Ford 6-32 (27); Ickx 33-90 (58)
WINNER'S LAPS 1-4 P2, 5-7 P3, 8-32 P2, 33-90 P1
FASTEST LAP Ickx, Brabham-Ford/Brabham, Brabham-Ford, 1m 18.1s (laps 30/62), 182.414kph, 113.347mph
CHAMPIONSHIP Stewart 60, Ickx 31, McLaren 26, G Hill 19, Beltoise 19

Brabham-Ford BT26A

Round 10/11	**UNITED STATES GP** Watkins Glen	**Jochen Rindt**

UNITED STATES GP Watkins Glen
5 October 1969   Race 183

Jochen Rindt
Lotus-Ford 49B 203.359kph, 126.361mph

A wet Friday practice exploded the 4WD myth, their performance nothing special. Jochen Rindt's Lotus claimed his sixth pole, and having already led five Grands Prix and 96 laps during the season the car at last held together for a full race distance. Result: his first victory. Stewart did not give Rindt an easy ride, stealing the lead for nine laps until his engine expired on lap 36. Stewart's departure gave Rindt a substantial lead over three Brabhams, which battled together for over an hour, Piers Courage in the Frank Williams car ultimately finishing second. Graham Hill suffered serious leg injuries. Having spun on oil, he dismounted to push-start his car, but, unable to refasten his seat-belts, he was flung from the car in a second spin when a tyre deflated.

POLE POSITION Rindt, Lotus-Ford, 1m 3.62s (0.03s), 207.560kph, 128.972mph
LAPS 108 x 3.701 km, 2.300 miles
DISTANCE 399.761 km, 248.400 miles
STARTERS/FINISHERS 17/6
WEATHER Sunny, hot, dry
LAP LEADERS Rindt 1-11, 21-108 (99); Stewart 12-20 (9)
WINNER'S LAPS 1-11 P1, 12-20 P2, 21-108 P1
FASTEST LAP Rindt, Lotus-Ford, 1m 4.34s (lap 69), 204.314kph, 126.955mph
CHAMPIONSHIP Stewart 60, Ickx 31, McLaren 26, J Rindt 22, G Hill 19

Pos	Driver	Car	Time/gap	Grid	Stops	Tyres
1	J Rindt	Lotus-Ford	1h 57m 56.84s	1	0	F
2	P Courage	Brabham-Ford	–46.99s	9	0	D
3	J Surtees	BRM	–2 laps	11	1	D
4	J Brabham	Brabham-Ford	–2 laps	10	1	G
5	P Rodríguez	Ferrari	–7 laps	12	1	D
6	S Moser	Brabham-Ford	–10 laps	17	1	G

Round 11/11	**MEXICAN GP** Mexico City	**Denny Hulme**

MEXICAN GP Mexico City
19 October 1969   Race 184

Denny Hulme
McLaren-Ford M7A 170.833kph, 106.151mph

Denny Hulme's unproductive season ended on a high with victory. He beat the Brabham pair which had sewn-up the front row of the grid. Qualifying and the race were determined by the new G20 compound from Goodyear. At the off, Stewart shot into the lead before Ickx got past on lap 6. But from fifth place on lap 1 Hulme overtook Rindt, pole-sitter Brabham, Stewart and finally Ickx on lap 10. Hulme never fully shook off the Belgian ace, who ended up less than 3s behind. Ickx also, most creditably, finished runner-up to Stewart in the drivers' championship. A three-car Lotus entry completed their erratic season 44 laps prematurely, whereas world champions Stewart and Tyrrell Matra finished fourth behind the Goodyear trio.

POLE POSITION Brabham, Brabham-Ford, 1m 42.90s (0.70s), 174.927ph, 108.695mph
LAPS 65 x 5.000 km, 3.107 miles
DISTANCE 325.000 km, 201.946 miles
STARTERS/FINISHERS 16/11
WEATHER Sunny, warm, dry
LAP LEADERS Stewart 1-5 (5); Ickx 6-9 (4); Hulme 10-65 (56)
WINNER'S LAPS 1 P5, 2-5 P4, 6 P3, 7-9 P2, 10-65 P1
FASTEST LAP Ickx, Brabham-Ford, 1m 43.05s (lap 64), 174.672kph, 108.536mph
CHAMPIONSHIP Stewart 63, Ickx 37, McLaren 26, J Rindt 22, Beltoise 21

Pos	Driver	Car	Time/gap	Grid	Stops	Tyres
1	D Hulme	McLaren-Ford	1h 54m 8.80s	4	0	G
2	J Ickx	Brabham-Ford	–2.56s	2	0	G
3	J Brabham	Brabham-Ford	–38.48s	1	0	G
4	J Stewart	Matra-Ford	–47.04s	3	0	D
5	J-P Beltoise	Matra-Ford	–1m 38.52s	8	0	D
6	J Oliver	BRM	–2 laps	12	0	D

1969 CHAMPIONSHIP FACTS AND FOLKLORE

- For 1969 the minimum dry weight for F1 cars was raised from 500 to 530kg (1168.45lb) to allow for the addition of mandatory fire extinguisher systems and strengthened rollover hoops.
- Following near disaster at Montjuïc, high-mounted and movable aerofoils were banned from Monaco. Subsequent limits were also placed on car height and rear wing overhang, and the width of coachwork ahead of the front wheels.
- In an 11-race two-part championship – the best five results from the first six races, the best four from the remaining five – the first GP was to be staged at Barcelona's Montjuïc Park.
- Even with an interim F2-based car, the combination of Ken Tyrrell, Jackie Stewart, the Ford-Cosworth engine and the French Matra chassis had shown great promise in 1968.
- For 1969 Matra shelved their own Équipe along with development of their V12 engine to focus all their energies on Ken Tyrrell's team, for whom they introduced a brand new chassis design, the MS80.
- The results were stunning. Stewart led at every round of the 11-race championship, winning six from the first eight.

- In reality, his French GP triumph apart, Stewart's superiority was not as great as the facts suggest. His success hinged as much on the fact that the opponent expected to be his strongest rival, Jochen Rindt having joined Gold Leaf Team Lotus, simply did not produce the goods.
- This shortfall was far more car than it was driver. The Lotus 49B continued to prove mechanically fragile whereas much of the in-season development was diverted towards the experimental R63 4WD car, which, just as those from Matra, McLaren and Cosworth – yes, Cosworth – failed to impress.
- Further, Rindt missed Monaco, the victim of a heavy accident in Spain from which he was fortunate to emerge in one piece. Spain saw both Rindt and Hill's cars wiped out when their high-wing aerofoils collapsed, and looking back with 21st-century hindsight, the whole affair verged on scandalous.
- Thankfully, during Monaco practice, the governing body acted abruptly and decisively to instantly ban the ungainly and dangerous devices before something truly catastrophic happened.
- Catastrophe still pursued reigning champion Graham Hill,

ironically to the site of so many former glories, Watkins Glen. Having already had reason to unfasten his seatbelts, a deflating tyre caused him to lose control; the car rolled, and the hapless driver was flung out, his legs mutilated.

■ So whereas Watkins Glen was the scene of Jochen Rindt's first victory, it was where Graham Hill's winning ways finally ended, although he would compete in Grand Prix for a further six seasons.

■ The other Lotus win in 1969 was Graham's final victory, and, famously, his fifth around the Principality, a landmark victory which stood until Ayton Senna went one better in 1993.

■ With Rindt's move to Lotus, Jacky Ickx had taken over his seat at Brabham and it was he who put up the strongest all-round challenge to Stewart's Matra. Two victories and a handful of podiums showed the Brabham team to be back in the running having dumped their Repco motor for the DFV.

■ They became the fourth team to adopt the ubiquitous engine, all four DFV teams enjoying at least one victory when Denny Hulme won the final round for McLaren to complete a Ford-Cosworth clean sweep of the season.

■ Non-DFV teams, Ferrari and BRM, barely had a look in despite entering drivers of the calibre of Amon at Maranello, Surtees at Bourne, both of whom were gone by the end of the season, as was Tony Rudd, a BRM stalwart of 20-years standing. No question, Cosworth was king.

■ Early in 1969 Fiat took a 50% stake in Ferrari, which secured

RACE 179, British GP: Stewart (3) lined up beside Rindt (2) on pole. At last their long overdue duel looked set and this time a titanic struggle ensued, lap after lap.

its future and increased available investment funds, but any benefits would take time to show.

■ Frank Williams became a GP entrant in 1969, entering with notable success a Brabham-Ford BT26A for friend and heir to the brewing dynasty Piers Courage.

■ Regrettably, Gerhard Mitter died at the Nürburgring practising for the concurrent F2 race.

■ Michael Schumacher was born.

Championship ranking	Championship points	Driver nationality	1969 Drivers Championship		Races contested	Race victories	Podiumse excl. victories	Races led	Flag to flag victories	Laps led	Poles	Fastest laps	Triple Crowns
			Driver	Car									
1	63	GBR	Jackie Stewart	Matra-Ford	11	6	1	11	2	386	2	5	1
2	37	BEL	Jacky Ickx	Brabham-Ford	11	2	3	3		70	2	3	2
3	26	NZL	Bruce McLaren	McLaren-Ford	9		3						
4	22	AUT	Jochen Rindt	Lotus-Ford	10	1	2	6		195	5	2	1
5	21	FRA	Jean-Pierre Beltoise	Matra-Ford	11		3					1	
6	20	NZL	Denny Hulme	McLaren-Ford	11	1	1	2		57			
7	19	GBR	Graham Hill	Lotus-Ford	10	1	1	2		60			
8	16	GBR	Piers Courage	Brabham-Ford	10		2	1		2			
9	15	SUI	Jo Siffert	Lotus-Ford	11		2						
10	14	AUS	Jack Brabham	Brabham-Ford	8		2				2	1	
11	6	GBR	John Surtees	BRM	9		1						
12	4	NZL	Chris Amon	Ferrari	6		1	1		37			
13	3	GBR	Richard Attwood	Lotus-Ford	1								
14	3	GBR	Vic Elford	Cooper-Maserati (1) McLaren-Ford (4)	5								
14	3	MEX	Pedro Rodriguez	BRM (3) Ferrari (5)	8								
16	1	FRA	Johnny Servoz-Gavin	Matra-Ford	4								
16	1	SUI	Silvio Moser	Brabham-Ford	7								
16	1	GBR	Jackie Oliver	BRM	10								

Championship ranking	Championship points	Team/Marque nationality	1969 Constructors Championship		Engine maker nationality	Races contested	Race victories	1-2 finishes	Podiums excl. victories	Races led	Laps led	Poles	Fastest laps
			Chassis	Engine									
1	66	FRA	Matra MS80, MS84, MS10	Ford Cosworth 3.0 V8	GBR	11	6	1	4	11	386	2	6
2	49	AUS	Brabham BT26A, BT24	Ford Cosworth 3.0 V8	GBR	11	2	1	7	4	72	4	4
3	47	GBR	Lotus 49B, 63	Ford Cosworth 3.0 V8	GBR	11	2		5	7	255	5	2
4	38	NZL	McLaren M7C, M7A, M9A	Ford Cosworth 3.0 V8	GBR	11	1		4	2	57		
5	7	ITA	Ferrari 312	Ferrari 3.0 V12	ITA	10			1	1	37		
5	7	GBR	BRM P139, P138	BRM 3.0 V12	GBR	10			1				

RACE 265, Brazilian GP: The opening moments of what was to become one of the greatest championship battles in F1 history. At the start of the opening round, Lauda's Ferrari (1) has already snatched the advantage from poleman Hunt's McLaren (11).

THE SEVENTIES

Television stardom

BORN AGAIN FERRARI v THE FORD 'KIT CAR', EPITOMISED BY LAUDA v HUNT, THE EPIC TITLE STRUGGLE WHICH MADE F1 A TV SPORT

1970

Rindt gives his all

THE TALE OF THE TITLE

- Runaway championship leader Jochen Rindt was killed qualifying the revolutionary Lotus 72 at Monza.
- With his championship points score remaining unbeaten, Rindt was awarded his world title posthumously.
- Before disaster at Monza, Jochen won four consecutive races and wove a piece of magic winning Monaco.
- The Lotus 72 redefined F1 chassis design and brought Team Lotus another constructors' championship.
- Ickx in a resurgent Ferrari mounted a vain late title charge, impartial fans generally relieved it fell short.
- Rindt's title was assured when rookie Fittipaldi took a surprise win in only his fourth race for Lotus.
- Three times world champion Jack Brabham retired from F1, still a race winner in his final season.
- A new F1 constructor, March Engineering, flooded the grid by supplying four teams with cars.
- One was champion Tyrrell, Stewart bringing the new marque victory on its second appearance.
- Ken Tyrrell astounded F1 by turning constructor, the Tyrrell-Ford's debut 'the best kept secret in F1'.
- Tyrrell, March, Surtees and de Tomaso joined the three existing DFV teams in the 'kit-car' revolution.
- But Ferrari and BRM 12-cylinder engines defeated the Ford DFV in five of the 13 championship rounds.
- In a harrowing season, Bruce McLaren and Piers Courage also died at the wheel.
- And not forgetting: Dunlop withdraw from Formula 1.

THE CHASE FOR THE CHAMPIONSHIP

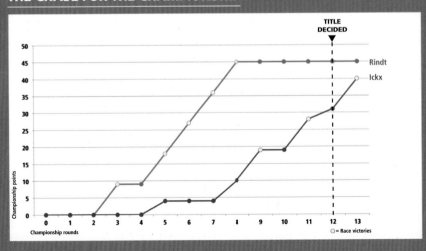

Brabham-Ford BT33

| Round 1/13 | SOUTH AFRICAN GP Kyalami | Jack Brabham |
| | 7 March 1970   Race 185 | Brabham-Ford BT33 179.768kph, 111.703mph |

No less than five of the new March 701 cars had been entered for the race and remarkably two of them headed the grid, Stewart's blue Tyrrell version on pole. Jack Brabham's monocoque BT33 completed the front row but over-exuberance by Rindt at the start knocked him back to P6. But within 20 laps Brabham had passed McLaren, Oliver, Beltoise, Ickx and finally Stewart for the lead. Hulme, significantly also on Goodyears, like Brabham, broke away from the bunch to claim second, Stewart's Dunlop-shod March finishing third. At the end the loudest round of applause was reserved for the still hobbling Graham Hill, making his return five months after his big accident and taking a plucky sixth place in the BBO/Rob Walker Lotus 49C.

POLE POSITION Stewart, March-Ford, 1m 19.3s (0.2s), 186.302kph, 115.763mph
LAPS 80 x 4.104 km, 2.550 miles
DISTANCE 328.306 km, 204.000 miles
STARTERS/FINISHERS 23/13
WEATHER Sunny, very hot, dry
LAP LEADERS Stewart 1-19 (19); Brabham 20-80 (61)
WINNER'S LAPS 1-3 P6, 4 P4, 5 P3, 6-19 P2, 20-80 P1
FASTEST LAP J Surtees, McLaren-Ford/Brabham, Brabham-Ford, 1m 20.8s (laps 6/71), 182.844kph, 113.614mph
CHAMPIONSHIP Brabham 9, Hulme 6, Stewart 4, Beltoise 3, Miles 2

Pos	Driver	Car	Time/gap	Grid	Stops	Tyres
1	J Brabham	Brabham-Ford	1h 49m 34.6s	3	0	G
2	D Hulme	McLaren-Ford	−8.1s	6	0	G
3	J Stewart	March-Ford	−17.1s	1	0	D
4	J-P Beltoise	Matra	−1m 13.1s	8	0	G
5	J Miles	Lotus-Ford	−1 lap	14	0	F
6	G Hill	Lotus-Ford	−1 lap	19	0	F

| Round 2/13 | SPANISH GP Jarama | Jackie Stewart |
| | 19 April 1970   Race 186 | March-Ford 701 140.350kph, 87.209mph |

Brabham's first monocoque, the BT33, again showed its paces with pole. This time Brabham could not catch the fast-starting Stewart, who led all the way to give March victory in only the marque's second race. Brabham pressed Stewart closely for two-thirds of the race distance but suffered engine failure on lap 62 when it appeared he might soon be about to pass. His retirement enabled McLaren to finish P2, albeit a lap behind. On lap 1 a breakage caused Oliver to lose control of his BRM, T-boning Ickx's Ferrari and rupturing its fully fuelled tanks. Ickx was fortunate to escape the resultant conflagration with minor burns. Despite the chaos – the blazing Ferrari rolling back across the track and water and foam causing cars to spin – the race continued.

POLE POSITION J Brabham, Brabham-Ford, 1m 23.9s (0.2s), 146.060kph, 90.757mph
LAPS 90 x 3.404 km, 2.115 miles
DISTANCE 306.360 km, 190.363 miles
STARTERS/FINISHERS 16/5
WEATHER Sunny, very hot, dry
LAP LEADERS Stewart 1-90 (90)
WINNER'S LAPS 1-90 P1
FASTEST LAP J Brabham, Brabham-Ford, 1m 24.3s (lap 19), 145.367kph, 90.327mph
CHAMPIONSHIP Stewart 13, Brabham 9, Hulme 6, McLaren 6, Andretti 4

Pos	Driver	Car	Time/gap	Grid	Stops	Tyres
1	J Stewart	March-Ford	2h 10m 58.2s	3	0	D
2	B McLaren	McLaren-Ford	−1 lap	11	0	G
3	M Andretti	March-Ford	−1 lap	16	0	F
4	G Hill	Lotus-Ford	−1 lap	15	0	F
5	J Servoz-Gavin	March-Ford	−2 laps	14	0	D
-	Only five classified finishers	-		-	-	-

March-Ford 701

Round 3/13	**MONACO GP** Monte Carlo					
	10 May 1970			Race 187		

Jochen Rindt
Lotus-Ford 49C 131.716kph, 81.845mph

For 27 laps Stewart ran away with it from pole, but once he pitted with ignition trouble it was Brabham leading Amon. Rindt meanwhile had moved up through the field from his P8 grid spot, overtaking Hulme for third on lap 41, which became second 20 laps later when Amon dropped out. For ten laps Brabham held the gap to Rindt at a comfortable 10s, but with only four to go lost a big chunk of time to a backmarker. Suddenly scenting an improbable victory, Rindt literally danced his Lotus 49C around the classic street circuit, his final lap 0.8s faster than pole – and 2.7s quicker than his own grid time! Little wonder he pressured the Australian into a braking error at the final corner, sweeping past to a famous victory.

POLE POSITION J Stewart, March-Ford, 1m 24.0s (0.6s), 134.786kph, 83.752mph
LAPS 80 x 3.145km, 1.954 miles
DISTANCE 251.600 km, 156.337 miles
STARTERS/FINISHERS 16/8
WEATHER Sunny, warm, dry
LAP LEADERS Stewart 1-27 (27); Brabham 28-79 (52); Rindt 80 (1)
WINNER'S LAPS 1-2 P7, 3-11 P8, 12-21 P7, 22-27 P6, 28-35 P5, 36-40 P4, 41-60 P3, 61-79 P2, 80 P1
FASTEST LAP Rindt, Lotus-Ford, 1m 23.2s (lap 80), 136.082kph, 84.557mph
CHAMPIONSHIP Brabham 15, Stewart 13, Rindt 9, Hulme 9, McLaren 6

Pos	Driver	Car	Time/gap	Grid	Stops	Tyres
1	J Rindt	Lotus-Ford	1h 54m 36.6s	8	0	F
2	J Brabham	Brabham-Ford	−23.1s	4	0	G
3	H Pescarolo	Matra	−51.4s	7	0	G
4	D Hulme	McLaren-Ford	−1m 28.3s	3	0	G
5	G Hill	Lotus-Ford	−1 lap	12	0	F
6	P Rodríguez	BRM	−2 laps	16	0	D

TOP **100** RACE

BRM P153

| Round 4/13 | **BELGIAN GP** Spa-Francorchamps | | | | | | **Pedro Rodríguez** |
| | **7 June 1970** | | | | **Race 188** | | BRM P153 241.308kph, 149.942mph |

The McLaren team was absent in deference to the death of their founder five days earlier. World Champion Jackie Stewart was in sparkling qualifying form with pole, and in the race he and Amon, both in Marches, disputed the lead initially. Pedro Rodríguez, driving the Yardley BRM P153, took Rindt's Lotus 49C for third on lap 3, then Stewart and Amon on successive laps to lead by lap 5. Amon's works March shadowed the Mexican all the way but could never fully get to grips with the swift V12, just 1.1s behind at the line. The Spa circuit, always good to unleash V12 power, had two Matras and a Ferrari joining the BRM in the top six, Rodríguez bringing victory to the Bourne team for the first time since 1966. Stewart retired with engine trouble on lap 14.

POLE POSITION J Stewart, March-Ford, 3m 28.0s (2.1s), 244.038kph, 151.638mph
LAPS 28 x 14.100 km, 8.761 miles
DISTANCE 394.800 km, 245.317 miles
STARTERS/FINISHERS 17/8
WEATHER Sunny, warm, dry
LAP LEADERS Amon 1, 3-4 (3); Stewart 2 (1); Rodríguez 5-28 (24)
WINNER'S LAPS 1-2 P4, 3 P3, 4 P2, 5-28 P 1
FASTEST LAP Amon, March-Ford 3m 27.4s (lap 28), 244.744kph, 152.077mph
CHAMPIONSHIP Brabham 15, Stewart 13, Rodríguez 10, Rindt 9, Hulme 9

Pos	Driver	Car	Time/gap	Grid	Stops	Tyres
1	P Rodríguez	BRM	1h 38m 9.9s	6	0	D
2	C Amon	March-Ford	−1.1s	3	0	F
3	J-P Beltoise	Matra	−1m 43.7s	11	0	G
4	I Giunti	Ferrari	−2m 38.5s	8	1	F
5	R Stommelen	Brabham-Ford	−3m 31.8s	7	0	G
6r	H Pescarolo	Matra	−1 lap	17	1	G

| Round 5/13 | **DUTCH GP** Zandvoort | | | | | | **Jochen Rindt** |
| | **21 June 1970** | | | | **Race 189** | | Lotus-Ford 72C 181.772kph, 112.948mph |

Team Lotus, working hard to bring their revolutionary Lotus 72 up to speed, fielded the 'C' spec for Rindt. Now it began to fly, annexing pole from Stewart's March and Ickx in the Flat-12 Ferrari. Ickx made a superb start, chased by Rindt, Stewart back to P4. As the leaders approached Tarzan for the third time Rindt out-braked the Ferrari and then eased away to give the radical 72C its first victory. Stewart gave Ickx a hard time over P2, but just as it appeared that Ickx had won that particular contest a puncture brought him into the pits on lap 51. Rindt's victory was inevitably overshadowed by the fiery and fatal accident that befell his friend Piers Courage on lap 22, behind the wheel of the Frank Williams de Tomaso.

POLE POSITION Rindt, Lotus-Ford, 1m 18.50s (0.23s), 192.290kph, 119.484mph
LAPS 80 x 4.193 km, 2.605 miles
DISTANCE 335.440 km, 208.433 miles
STARTERS/FINISHERS 20/11
WEATHER Overcast, dry
LAP LEADERS Ickx 1-2 (2); Rindt 3-80 (78)
WINNER'S LAPS 1-2 P2, 3-80 P1
FASTEST LAP Ickx, Ferrari, 1m 19.23s (lap 22), 190.519kph, 118.383mph
CHAMPIONSHIP Stewart 19, Rindt 18, Brabham 15, Rodríguez 10, Hulme 9

Pos	Driver	Car	Time/gap	Grid	Stops	Tyres
1	J Rindt	Lotus-Ford	1h 50m 43.41s	1	0	F
2	J Stewart	March-Ford	−30.00s	2	0	D
3	J Ickx	Ferrari	−1 lap	3	1	F
4	C Regazzoni	Ferrari	−1 lap	6	0	F
5	J-P Beltoise	Matra	−1 lap	10	0	G
6	J Surtees	McLaren-Ford	−1 lap	14	0	F

| Round 6/13 | **FRENCH GP** Clermont-Ferrand | | | | | | **Jochen Rindt** |
| | **5 July 1970** | | | | **Race 190** | | Lotus-Ford 72C 158.391kph, 98.419mph |

In France, Ickx's Ferrari claimed the first non-DFV pole in almost two years. Further, another 12-cylinder, the Matra of J-P Beltoise, was alongside. From the start these two simply left the rest standing, closely contesting the lead until on lap 15 the Ferrari engine burnt a valve. Frenchman, French car, French GP, the crowd went crazy for Beltoise, now leading. But no Gallic fairy tale here, a softening tyre destroying his 17s lead and, 13 laps from *la gloire*, first Rindt and then Amon slipped through. Beltoise had little option but to pit, now completely out of the running. A second successive victory, albeit less convincing than the first, suddenly put Rindt in command of the title race.

POLE POSITION J Ickx, Ferrari, 2m 58.22s (0.48s), 162.709kph,101.103mph
LAPS 38 x 8.055 km, 5.005 miles
DISTANCE 306.090 km, 190.196 miles
STARTERS/FINISHERS 20/14
WEATHER Sunny, warm, dry
LAP LEADERS Ickx 1-14 (14); J-P Beltoise, Matra 15-25 (11); Rindt 26-38 (13)
WINNER'S LAPS 1-4 P5, 5-6 P4, 7-15 P3, 16-25 P2, 26-38 P1
FASTEST LAP Brabham, Brabham-Ford, 3m 00.75s (lap 29), 160.432kph, 99.688mph
CHAMPIONSHIP Rindt 27, Stewart 19, Brabham 19, Amon 12, Hulme 12

Pos	Driver	Car	Time/gap	Grid	Stops	Tyres
1	J Rindt	Lotus-Ford	1h 55m 57.00s	6	0	F
2	C Amon	March-Ford	−7.61s	3	0	F
3	J Brabham	Brabham-Ford	−44.83s	5	0	G
4	D Hulme	McLaren-Ford	−45.66s	7	0	G
5	H Pescarolo	Matra	−1m 19.42s	8	0	G
6	D Gurney	McLaren-Ford	−1m 19.65s	17	0	G

BRITISH GP Brands Hatch
18 July 1970

Race 191

Jochen Rindt
Lotus-Ford **72C** 174.915kph, 108.687mph

Rindt's third consecutive victory was also fortuitous. He and Brabham shared the front row with identical times and in the race seemed closely matched, the pair pulling well clear of the rest once Ickx's Ferrari dropped out having easily led the opening six laps. Brabham tailed Rindt relentlessly for 62 laps, then with 12 to go it appeared Black Jack had been sandbagging. He shot past Rindt and established a lead of over 10s in no time. But on his final tour he ran out of fuel, to trundle in second behind the astonished Rindt. It wasn't over. The Lotus rear wing failed post-race scrutineering, Brabham declared the winner. But more then three hours after the race, following a lengthy meeting with Chapman and Rindt, the scrutineers reversed their decision.

POLE POSITION Rindt, Lotus-Ford, 1m 24.8s (0.0s), 181.051kph, 112.500mph
LAPS 80 x 4.265 km, 2.650 miles
DISTANCE 341.181 km, 212.000 miles
STARTERS/FINISHERS 22/9
WEATHER Sunny, warm, dry
LAP LEADERS J Ickx, Ferrari 1-6 (6); Rindt 7-68, 80 (63); Brabham 69-79 (11)
WINNER'S LAPS 1-6 P3, 7-68 P1, 69-79 P2, 80 P1
FASTEST LAP Brabham, Brabham-Ford, 1m 25.9s (lap 70), 178.733kph, 111.059mph
CHAMPIONSHIP Rindt 36, Brabham 25, Stewart 19, Hulme 16, Amon 14

Pos	Driver	Car	Time/gap	Grid	Stops	Tyres
1	J Rindt	Lotus-Ford	1h 57m 2.0s	1	0	F
2	J Brabham	Brabham-Ford	−32.9s	2	0	G
3	D Hulme	McLaren-Ford	−54.4s	5	0	G
4	C Regazzoni	Ferrari	−54.8s	6	0	F
5	C Amon	March-Ford	−1 lap	17	0	F
6	G Hill	Lotus-Ford	−1 lap	22	0	F

Lotus-Ford 72C

GERMAN GP Hockenheim
2 August 1970

Race 192

Jochen Rindt
Lotus-Ford **72C** 199.667kph, 124.067mph

For his fourth consecutive victory Rindt had to work hard to hang on to Ickx in the ever-improving Ferrari 312B. These two filled the front row, the Ferrari on pole. From the off a five-car slipstreaming battle ensued between Rindt, the two Ferraris, and the works March pair of Amon and Siffert. As the flat-out pace took its toll of engines, just two remained, never more than 2s between them: lap 45–46 Ickx, 47 Rindt, 48 Ickx, 49 Rindt and finally 50 Rindt, to win by 0.7s. In this high-speed thrash, chassis/aero had overcome horsepower/grunt, but only just, a fascinating encounter. Hard luck story of the race was John Surtees, making his way up from P15 to a secure third until the motor in his own Surtees TS7 blew four laps short.

POLE POSITION Ickx, Ferrari, 1m 59.5s (0.2s), 204.522kph, 127.084mph
LAPS 50 x 6.789 km, 4.218 miles
DISTANCE 339.450 km, 210.924 miles
STARTERS/FINISHERS 21/9
WEATHER Sunny, hot, dry
LAP LEADERS Ickx 1-6, 10-17, 26-31, 36-43, 45-46, 48 (31); Rindt 7-9, 18-21, 24-25, 32-35, 44, 47, 49-50 (17); C Regazzoni, Ferrari 22-23 (2)
WINNER'S LAPS 1-6 P2, 7-9 P1, 10-11 P2, 12 P3, 13-17 P2, 18-21 P1, 22-23 P2, 24-25 P1, 26-28 P2, 29 P3, 30-31 P2, 32-35 P1, 36-43 P2, 44 P1, 45-46 P2, 47 P1, 48 P2, 49-50 P1
FASTEST LAP Ickx, Ferrari, 2m 00.5s (lap 49), 202.825kph, 126.030mph
CHAMPIONSHIP Rindt 45, Brabham 25, Hulme 20, Stewart 19, Amon 14

Pos	Driver	Car	Time/gap	Grid	Stops	Tyres
1	J Rindt	Lotus-Ford	1h 42m 0.3s	2	0	F
2	J Ickx	Ferrari	−0.7s	1	0	F
3	D Hulme	McLaren-Ford	−1m 21.8s	16	0	G
4	E Fittipaldi	Lotus-Ford	−1m 55.1s	13	0	F
5	R Stommelen	Brabham-Ford	−1 lap	11	0	G
6	H Pescarolo	Matra	−1 lap	5	1	G

TOP **100** RACE

AUSTRIAN GP Österreichring
16 August 1970   **Race 193**

Jacky Ickx
Ferrari 312B 208.035kph, 129.267mph

The characteristics of the new Österreichring suited the 12-cylinder cars, although Rindt still managed pole at his home GP. For the fifth race running Ickx took an early lead and this time was there at the finish, the Scuderia's first victory in two years. Teammate Regazzoni underlined the Ferrari renaissance 0.61s behind, the two scarlet cars circulating in tandem lap after lap. For half the race another 12-cylinder, Beltoise's Matra, joined the Ferraris, then fell away, losing a secure P3 near the end by running out of fuel. Only one V8 finished in the top seven, Rindt going out with engine trouble. Ickx now featured on the championship leader-board, but despite failing to score Rindt's advantage over Ickx was a seemingly unassailable 26 points.

POLE POSITION J Rindt, Lotus-Ford, 1m 39.23s (0.47s), 214.447kph, 133.251mph
LAPS 60 x 5.911 km, 3.673 miles
DISTANCE 354.660 km, 220.376 miles
STARTERS/FINISHERS 24/15
WEATHER Sunny, warm, dry
LAP LEADERS Regazzoni 1 (1); Ickx 2-60 (59)
WINNER'S LAPS 1 P2, 2-60 P1
FASTEST LAP Ickx, Ferrari/Regazzoni, Ferrari, 1m 40.40s (lap 45), 211.948kph, 131.699mph
CHAMPIONSHIP Rindt 45, Brabham 25, Hulme 20, Stewart 19, Ickx 19

Pos	Driver	Car	Time/gap	Grid	Stops	Tyres
1	J Ickx	Ferrari	1h 42m 17.32s	3	0	F
2	C Regazzoni	Ferrari	−0.61s	2	0	F
3	R Stommelen	Brabham-Ford	−1m 27.88s	17	0	G
4	P Rodríguez	BRM	−1 lap	22	0	D
5	J Oliver	BRM	−1 lap	14	0	D
6	J-P Beltoise	Matra	−1 lap	7	0	G

ITALIAN GP Monza
6 September 1970   **Race 194**

Clay Regazzoni
Ferrari 312B 236.696kph, 147.076mph

During final practice, championship leader Jochen Rindt's Lotus 72C inexplicably veered sharply under braking for the Parabolica, forcefully striking the guardrail with fatal consequences for the driver. The remaining Lotus cars were withdrawn. The race the following day was a Monza slipstreamer, six lap leaders – Ickx, Rodríguez, Stewart, Regazzoni, Oliver, Hulme – chopping and changing until Regazzoni's surviving Ferrari finally broke away from the bunch to score a fine victory in his rookie season. The Ferraris of Ickx and Giunti, and the BRMs of Rodríguez and Oliver, all participated in the leading mêlée but failed to finish, reigning champion Stewart, a close friend of Rindt, scoring his best result in a while with second.

POLE POSITION J Ickx, Ferrari, 1m 24.14s (0.22s), 246.019kph, 152.869mph
LAPS 68 x 5.750 km, 3.573 miles
DISTANCE 391.000 km, 242.956 miles
STARTERS/FINISHERS 20/8
WEATHER Sunny, hot, dry
LAP LEADERS Ickx 1-3, 19-20 (5); P Rodríguez, BRM 4, 7-8 (3); Stewart 5-6, 9, 11, 14-17, 26-27, 31, 35, 37, 42-43, 51, 53 (17); Regazzoni 10, 12, 32-34, 36, 38-41, 44-50, 52, 54-68 (33); J Oliver, BRM 13, 18, 21-25, 28, 30 (9); Hulme 29 (1)
WINNER'S LAPS 1 P4, 2 P3, 3-5 P4, 6-7 P3, 8-9 P4, 10 P1, 11 P4, 12 P1, 13 P3, 14-15 P4, 16 P3, 17-18 P4, 19-20 P3, 21-22 P2, 23 P3, 24 P2, 25 P3, 26-30 P4, 31 P3, 32-34 P1, 35 P2, 36 P1, 37 P2, 38-41 P1, 42-43 P2, 44-50 P1, 51 P2, 52 P1, 53 P2, 54-68 P1
FASTEST LAP Regazzoni, Ferrari, 1m 25.20s (lap 65), 242.958kph, 150.967mph
CHAMPIONSHIP Rindt 45, Brabham 25, Stewart 25, Hulme 23, Regazzoni 21

Pos	Driver	Car	Time/gap	Grid	Stops	Tyres
1	C Regazzoni	Ferrari	1h 39m 6.88s	3	0	F
2	J Stewart	March-Ford	−5.73s	4	0	D
3	J-P Beltoise	Matra	−5.80s	14	0	G
4	D Hulme	McLaren-Ford	−6.15s	9	0	G
5	R Stommelen	Brabham-Ford	−6.41s	17	0	G
6	F Cevert	March-Ford	−1m 3.46s	11	0	D

CANADIAN GP St Jovite
20 September 1970   **Race 195**

Jacky Ickx
Ferrari 312B 162.977kph, 101.269mph

Jackie Stewart staggered the F1 fraternity with pole position on the GP race debut of Ken Tyrrell's first F1 contender. He then proceeded to rapidly build a 16s lead until a stub-axle broke at one-third-distance on the badly rippled track surface. Ickx then proceeded to bring Ferrari their third race win in a row. Regazzoni made a poor start, but once he had disposed of the Marches of Cevert and Amon and the Rodríguez BRM he was up to P3 and, once Stewart went out, completed a second Ferrari 1-2 in three races, although Stewart's Tyrrell had given them a fright. Ickx was now the only driver in a position to beat Rindt's points total, but to do so he had to win the two remaining races.

POLE POSITION J Stewart, Tyrrell-Ford, 1m 31.5s (0.1s), 167.794kph, 104.262mph
LAPS 90 x 4.265 km, 2.650 miles
DISTANCE 383.829 km, 238.500 miles
STARTERS/FINISHERS 20/10
WEATHER Sunny, warm, dry
LAP LEADERS Stewart 1-31 (31); Ickx 32-90 (59)
WINNER'S LAPS 1-31 P2, 32-90 P1
FASTEST LAP Regazzoni, Ferrari, 1m 32.2s (lap 75), 166.520kph, 103.471mph
CHAMPIONSHIP Rindt 45, Ickx 28, Regazzoni 27, Brabham 25, Stewart 25

Pos	Driver	Car	Time/gap	Grid	Stops	Tyres
1	J Ickx	Ferrari	2h 21m 18.4s	2	0	F
2	C Regazzoni	Ferrari	−14.8s	3	0	F
3	C Amon	March-Ford	−57.9s	6	0	F
4	P Rodríguez	BRM	−1 lap	7	0	D
5	J Surtees	Surtees-Ford	−1 lap	5	1	F
6	P Gethin	McLaren-Ford	−2 laps	11	0	G

UNITED STATES GP Watkins Glen
4 October 1970   Race 196

Emerson Fittipaldi
Lotus-Ford 72C 204.053kph, 126.792mph

Despite taking pole, Ickx's championship challenge evaporated before half-distance when he pitted with a fuel leak, any chance of the victory he vitally needed gone. It had in any case looked slim, Stewart's Tyrrell again rushing off into the distance. But when Stewart retired with an oil leak on lap 82 Ickx was not there to assume the lead. The new leader was Rodríguez, his BRM well ahead until, on lap 101 of 108, he pitted for fuel and Emerson Fittipaldi, making only his fourth GP start, won for beleaguered Team Lotus. Teammate Reine Wisell in his very first GP came third behind Rodríguez, Lotus now assured of the constructors' championship along with Jochen Rindt's posthumous drivers' title, which was now a certainty.

POLE POSITION Ickx, Ferrari, 1m 03.07s (0.03s), 211.269kph, 131.283mph
LAPS 108 x 3.701 km, 2.300 miles
DISTANCE 399.761 km, 248.400 miles
STARTERS/FINISHERS 24/14
WEATHER Cloudy, cold, dry
LAP LEADERS J Stewart, Tyrrell-Ford 1-82 (82); Rodríguez 83-100 (18); Fittipaldi 101-108 (8)
WINNER'S LAPS 1-4 P8, 5-14 P7, 15-37 P6, 38-47 P5, 48-56 P4, 57-82 P3, 83-100 P2, 101-108 P1
FASTEST LAP Ickx, Ferrari, 1m 02.74s (lap 105), 212.390kph, 131.973mph
CHAMPIONSHIP Rindt 45, Ickx 31, Regazzoni 27, Brabham 25, Stewart 25

Pos	Driver	Car	Time/gap	Grid	Stops	Tyres
1	E Fittipaldi	Lotus-Ford	1h 57m 32.79s	3	0	F
2	P Rodríguez	BRM	−36.39s	4	1	D
3	R Wisell	Lotus-Ford	−45.17s	9	0	F
4	J Ickx	Ferrari	−1 lap	1	1	F
5	C Amon	March-Ford	−1 lap	5	1	F
6	D Bell	Surtees-Ford	−1 lap	13	0	F

Ferrari 312B

MEXICAN GP Mexico City
25 October 1970   Race 197

Jacky Ickx
Ferrari 312B 171.848kph, 106.781mph

The start was delayed when a massive crowd climbed the fences, walls of spectators lining the track, some running across during the race. Ferrari completed the season in the ascendant with their third 1-2 finish. As Ickx crossed the line a track invasion created extreme danger, especially as Hulme and Amon were still racing for third place, finishing a second apart. The only challenge to Ferrari domination came from Stewart's Tyrrell, pushing the leading Ferrari for 13 laps until pitting with a loose steering column, later retiring after hitting a stray dog. Running third behind the Ferraris with just 13 laps to go, Jack Brabham – having announced his intention to retire during practice – failed to finish his farewell race when his engine blew.

POLE POSITION Regazzoni, Ferrari, 1m 41.86s (0.02s), 176.713ph, 109.804mph
LAPS 65 x 5.000 km, 3.107 miles
DISTANCE 325.000 km, 201.946 miles
STARTERS/FINISHERS 18/9
WEATHER Sunny, warm, dry
LAP LEADERS Regazzoni 1 (1); Ickx 2-65 (64)
WINNER'S LAPS 1 P2, 2-65 P1
FASTEST LAP Ickx, Ferrari, 1m 43.11s (lap 46), 174.571kph, 108.473mph
CHAMPIONSHIP Rindt 45, Ickx 40, Regazzoni 33, Hulme 27, Brabham 25

Pos	Driver	Car	Time/gap	Grid	Stops	Tyres
1	J Ickx	Ferrari	1h 53m 28.36s	3	0	F
2	C Regazzoni	Ferrari	−24.64s	1	0	F
3	D Hulme	McLaren-Ford	−45.97s	14	0	G
4	C Amon	March-Ford	−47.05s	5	0	F
5	J-P Beltoise	Matra	−50.11s	6	0	G
6	P Rodríguez	BRM	−1m 24.76s	7	0	D

1970 CHAMPIONSHIP FACTS AND FOLKLORE

- For the first time the championship season reached 13 rounds, including the first GPs at Hockenheim and the Österreichring. The points-earning races were split seven-six, the score from one round dropped in each part.
- The romantic view of the 1970 championship was that in only his fourth GP start, 23-year-old Emerson Fittipaldi won at Watkins Glen to guarantee that erstwhile team leader, the late Jochen Rindt, could not be beaten to the championship by the charging Ickx, who had been taking chunks out of the Austrian's frozen points advantage.
- In reality Fittipaldi's victory did clinch the constructors' cup for Lotus, but Ickx's challenge for the drivers' title was spent about an hour earlier when his Ferrari visited the pits with a fuel leak.
- However, putting a fanciful spin on the grim events of 1970 might well be excused. Not only did Rindt die at the wheel but so too Piers Courage and Bruce McLaren.
- For Colin Chapman, just as in 1968, the triumph of landing both championships was bittersweet. The team had worked hard to perfect the groundbreaking Lotus 72, and on the brink of fully merited championship glory had come Rindt's fatal practice accident at Monza.
- By shifting the radiators to each side the Lotus 72 reinvented the aerodynamic silhouette of the F1 car, also paying close attention to airflow and unsprung weight with inboard disc brakes and torsion-bar suspension.
- After a period in the doldrums, the black stallion was prancing again, Ferrari winning four of the last five races of the season including three 1-2 finishes. At the heart of this success was a new Flat-12 'Boxer' engine capable of 460bhp at 11,600rpm, with Marelli transistorised ignition.
- The earlier part of the year appeared very much as though Jack Brabham would once again confound all-comers as he put together a series of potentially championship winning performances in his first monocoque F1 car, but providence was against him.
- After his British Grand Prix disappointment, not another point was to come his way and the 44-year-old triple champion announced his retirement at the end of the season, handing over team ownership to designer/partner Ron Tauranac.

- But what of reigning champion, Jackie Stewart? He too started more strongly than he finished, at least in terms of hard results, but 1970 was a year of transition for the Tyrrell Racing Organisation which would pay off handsomely in the future.
- The highly successful partnership with Matra Elf had drawn to a close through insistence that L'Équipe must be an all-French affair technically, thus the Ford-Cosworth should be supplanted by their own V12. Matra's links to Chrysler through Simca ruled out use of the Ford engine.
- Tyrrell and Stewart were resolute that the DFV was essential to future success and were forced to find another chassis supplier.
- March Engineering provided that answer, an entirely new and highly ambitious organisation founded, inter alia, by Max Mosley and Robin Herd, which in a blaze of publicity fielded no less than five new 701s at their Kyalami debut. Two of these were blue Tyrrell-entered cars, Stewart giving the new marque their maiden race victory at the following Jarama round.
- March's second victory would be five years yonder, not that Ken Tyrrell could possibly know that. But what he had concluded from the Matra/March experience was that if he was to hang on to Stewart, and if they were to win more championships together, they had to be masters of their own destiny.
- In one of the best-kept secrets in Formula 1, the Tyrrell 001 with its Ford-Cosworth DFV was launched to a startled world on 22 August at the Oulton Park Gold Cup.
- Teething troubles prevented hard results, but Tyrrell 001 competed in the final three GPs of the season, started from the front row in each, once from pole, and led two of the races quite easily.
- McLaren, still reeling from Bruce's fatal Goodwood accident on 2 June testing a Can-Am sports car, were unable to rediscover the key to winning races in 1970 with the new M14A chassis.
- Dan Gurney made his final championship appearance, driving three races for McLaren following the death of Bruce.

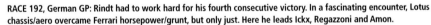

RACE 192, German GP: Rindt had to work hard for his fourth consecutive victory. In a fascinating encounter, Lotus chassis/aero overcame Ferrari horsepower/grunt, but only just. Here he leads Ickx, Regazzoni and Amon.

- Alfa Romeo made a tentative return to GP racing as an engine supplier, a modified V8 sports car engine with factory support fitted to a works McLaren M7D for Andrea de Adamich.
- Following the internal strife of last year, BRM had turned things around and produced a car with real potential. The P153 brought the Yardley-sponsored team victory at Spa, the final GP ever to be held at the perilously alluring original long circuit.
- After his frustrations with Honda and then BRM, John Surtees chose to go the driver/constructor 'kit car' route, debuting his own chassis with DFV engine and Hewland gearbox at the British GP, ironically soon after BRM had demonstrated that they were becoming a genuine force again.
- Following their successful 1969 season together, Frank Williams entered a De Tomaso-DFV for Piers Courage, only for tragedy to strike at the Dutch GP when Piers crashed and was killed. Despite the addition of further compulsory regulations in the area of fuel tank safety, fire continued to constitute a massive risk for drivers in the event of an accident.
- Having officially entered GP racing in 1958 in association with the momentum of British teams Vanwall and Cooper, Dunlop withdrew at the end of 1970, unable to compete financially with US rivals Goodyear and Firestone.
- Ronnie Peterson made his debut in 1970 driving a privately entered March.

Championship ranking	Championship points	Driver nationality	1970 Drivers Championship Driver	Car	Races contested	Race victories	Podiumse excl. victories	Races led	Flag to flag victories	Laps led	Poles	Fastest laps	Triple Crowns
1	45	AUT	Jochen Rindt	Lotus-Ford	9	5		5		172	3	1	
2	40	BEL	Jacky Ickx	Ferrari	13	3	2	8		240	4	5	
3	33	SUI	Clay Regazzoni	Ferrari	8	1	3	4		37	1	3	
4	27	NZL	Denny Hulme	McLaren-Ford	11		4	1		1			
5	25	AUS	Jack Brabham	Brabham-Ford	13	1	3	3		124	1	4	
5	25	GBR	Jackie Stewart	March-Ford (10) Tyrrell-Ford (3)	13	1	3	7	1	267	4		
7	23	MEX	Pedro Rodriguez	BRM	13	1	1	3		45			
8	23	NZL	Chris Amon	March-Ford	13		3	1		3		1	
9	16	FRA	Jean-Pierre Beltoise	Matra	13		2	1		11			
10	12	BRA	Emerson Fittipaldi	Lotus-Ford	5	1		1		8			
11	10	GER	Rolf Stommelen	Brabham-Ford	10		1						
12	8	FRA	Henri Pescarolo	Matra	13		1						
13	7	GBR	Graham Hill	Lotus-Ford	11								
14	6	NZL	Bruce McLaren	McLaren-Ford	3		1						
15	4	USA	Mario Andretti	March-Ford	5		1						
15	4	SWE	Reine Wisell	Lotus-Ford	2		1						
17	3	ITA	Ignazio Giunti	Ferrari	4								
18	3	GBR	John Surtees	McLaren-Ford (4) Surtees-Ford (7)	11							1	
19	2	GBR	John Miles	Lotus-Ford	7								
19	2	FRA	Johnny Servoz-Gavin	March-Ford	2								
19	2	GBR	Jackie Oliver	BRM	13				1	9			
22	1	USA	Dan Gurney	McLaren-Ford	3								
22	1	FRA	François Cevert	March-Ford	9								
22	1	GBR	Peter Gethin	McLaren-Ford	7								
22	1	GBR	Derek Bell	Brabham-Ford (1) Surtees-Ford (1)	2								

Championship ranking	Championship points	Team/Marque nationality	1970 Constructors Championship Chassis	Engine	Engine maker nationality	Races contested	Race victories	1-2 finishes	Podiums excl. victories	Races led	Laps led	Poles	Fastest laps
1	59	GBR	Lotus 72, 72B, 72C, 49C	Ford Cosworth 3.0 V8	GBR	12	6		1	6	180	3	1
2	52	ITA	Ferrari 312B	Ferrari 3.0 F12	ITA	13	4	3	5	8	277	5	8
3	48	GBR	March 701	Ford Cosworth 3.0 V8	GBR	13	1		7	5	157	3	1
4	35	AUS	Brabham BT33, BT26A	Ford Cosworth 3.0 V8	GBR	13	1		4	3	124	1	4
5	35	NZL	McLaren M14A, M7C	Ford Cosworth 3.0 V8	GBR	12			5	1	1		1
6	23	GBR	BRM P153	BRM 3.0 V12	GBR	13	1		1	3	54		
7	23	FRA	Matra MS120	Matra 3.0 V12	FRA	13			3	1	11		
8	3	GBR	Surtees TS7	Ford Cosworth 3.0 V8	GBR	7							
-	0	GBR	Tyrrell 001	Ford Cosworth 3.0 V8	GBR	3				2	113	1	

1971

Stewarts's stylish supremacy

THE TALE OF THE TITLE

- Elf Team Tyrrell trounced the rest with seven superb victories in an 11-round championship.
- Jackie Stewart won six races, three flag-to-flag victories sweeping him to a second world title.
- Tyrrell-Ford easily won the constructors' cup, Cevert adding a seventh victory and a pair of 1-2 finishes.
- Ronnie Peterson was championship runner-up in a March 711, his maiden victory eluding him by 0.01s.
- Peter Gethin in a BRM famously beat Peterson at Monza in the closest race finish of all time.
- Although Ferrari and BRM each won on two occasions, the 12-cylinder cars were a disappointment.
- Making occasional appearances at the wheel of a Ferrari, Mario Andretti recorded his maiden GP victory.
- BRM drivers Pedro Rodríguez and Jo Siffert both died at the wheel, neither in championship events.
- Slicks arrived, tyres playing an increasingly vital factor as Goodyear and Firestone went head to head.
- And not forgetting: engine airboxes and 'sports car' noses.

THE CHASE FOR THE CHAMPIONSHIP

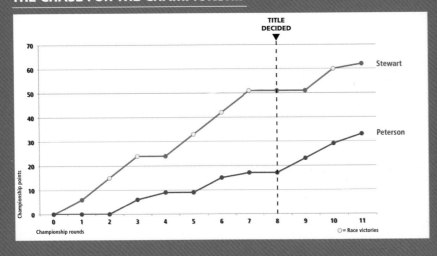

Round 1/11	**SOUTH AFRICAN GP** Kyalami		**Mario Andretti**
	6 March 1971	**Race 198**	Ferrari 312B 180.804kph, 112.346mph

Once Hulme, driving the new Goodyear-shod M19A McLaren, had dispensed with Ickx and Fittipaldi, he took another dozen laps to catch and pass Regazzoni's leading Ferrari, then held sway for 59 laps. Meanwhile Andretti's Firestone-shod Ferrari, coming through from as low as P7, began to put pressure on the leader in the closing stages. But Hulme's lead looked safe enough until suspension failure allowed Mario by with just four laps to go, his maiden GP victory achieved in his first race for Ferrari. Pole-sitter Stewart made a poor start but came in second, the race demonstrating that tyre development was fast becoming the prime performance differential, cars losing or gaining position due to variations in temperature or wear cycles.

POLE POSITION Stewart, Tyrrell-Ford, 1m 17.8s (0.6s), 189.902kph, 118.000mph
LAPS 79 x 4.104 km, 2.550 miles
DISTANCE 324.216 km, 201.458 miles
STARTERS/FINISHERS 25/13
WEATHER Sunny, hot, dry
LAP LEADERS Regazzoni 1-16 (16); Hulme 17-75 (59); Andretti 76-79 (4)
WINNER'S LAPS 1 P6, 2-4 P7, 5-7 P6, 8-10 P5, 11-21 P6, 22 P5, 23-37 P4, 38-43 P3, 44-75 P2, 76-79 P1
FASTEST LAP Andretti, Ferrari, 1m 20.3s (lap 73), 183.990kph, 114.326mph
CHAMPIONSHIP Andretti 9, Stewart 6, Regazzoni 4, Wisell 3, Amon 2

Pos	Driver	Car	Time/gap	Grid	Stops	Tyres
1	M Andretti	Ferrari	1h 37m 35.5s	4	0	F
2	J Stewart	Tyrrell-Ford	−20.9s	1	0	G
3	C Regazzoni	Ferrari	−31.4s	3	0	F
4	R Wisell	Lotus-Ford	−1m 9.4s	14	0	F
5	C Amon	Matra	−1 lap	2	0	G
6	D Hulme	McLaren-Ford	−1 lap	7	0	G

Round 2/11	**SPANISH GP** Montjuïc		**Jackie Stewart**
	18 April 1971	**Race 199**	Tyrrell-Ford 003 156.428kph, 97.200mph

Led by Ickx, the front of the grid was peppered with 12-cylinder cars from Ferrari, Matra and BRM. Qualifying, therefore, had given little hint that Jackie Stewart would bring marque Tyrrell their maiden win from only their fifth GP start. But Stewart, the only DFV-powered car in the top seven during the early laps, managed to overtake Ickx for the lead on lap 6 and gradually pull away to a 10s advantage. Towards the end of the race Ickx turned-up the wick, setting a succession of fastest laps and eventually getting below his own pole time on lap 69. But he finished 3.4s behind, the 12-cylinder Matra of Amon and BRM V12 of Rodríguez also giving best to the jubilant Scot.

POLE POSITION Ickx, Ferrari, 1m 25.9s (0.1s), 158.878kph, 98.722mph
LAPS 75 x 3.791 km, 2.356 miles
DISTANCE 284.325 km, 176.671 miles
STARTERS/FINISHERS 22/11
WEATHER Sunny, hot, dry
LAP LEADERS Ickx 1-5 95); Stewart 6-75 (70)
WINNER'S LAPS 1-5 P2, 6-75 P1
FASTEST LAP Ickx, Ferrari, 1m 25.1s (lap 69), 160.371kph, 99.650mph
CHAMPIONSHIP Stewart 15, Andretti 9, Ickx 6, Amon 6, Regazzoni 4

Pos	Driver	Car	Time/gap	Grid	Stops	Tyres
1	J Stewart	Tyrrell-Ford	1h 49m 3.4s	4	0	G
2	J Ickx	Ferrari	−3.4s	1	0	F
3	C Amon	Matra	−58.1s	3	0	G
4	P Rodríguez	BRM	−1m 17.9s	5	0	F
5	D Hulme	McLaren-Ford	−1m 27.0s	9	0	G
6	J-P Beltoise	Matra	−1 lap	6	0	G

Round 3/11	**MONACO GP** Monte Carlo		**Jackie Stewart**
	23 May 1971	**Race 200**	Tyrrell-Ford 003 134.360kph, 83.487mph

As Roman Polanski's film of the event depicts, Jackie Stewart and his Tyrrell were simply unbeatable at Monaco. Pole by 1.2s, start-to-finish leader, and a fastest race lap 1s under pole, his performance made all the more extraordinary by the effective loss of his rear brakes due to maladjustment prior to the start. Another driver to excel that day was Ronnie Peterson in the works March 711. From eighth on the grid he finished a fine second on merit. Fifth after a brilliant first lap, Ronnie took Ickx for third on lap 30 and the following lap second place from Siffert's BRM. This was the first of some strong finishes that would bring the talented Swede Peterson championship runner-up spot.

POLE POSITION Stewart, Tyrrell-Ford, 1m 23.2s (1.2s), 136.082kph, 84.557mph
LAPS 80 x 3.145km, 1.954 miles
DISTANCE 251.600 km, 156.337 miles
STARTERS/FINISHERS 18/10
WEATHER Overcast, dry
LAP LEADERS Stewart 1-80 (80)
WINNER'S LAPS 1-80 P1
FASTEST LAP Stewart, Tyrrell-Ford, 1m 22.2s (lap 57), 137.737kph, 85.586mph
CHAMPIONSHIP Stewart 24, Ickx 10, Andretti 9, Peterson 6, Amon 6

Pos	Driver	Car	Time/gap	Grid	Stops	Tyres
1	J Stewart	Tyrrell-Ford	1h 52m 21.3s	1	0	G
2	R Peterson	March-Ford	−25.6s	8	0	F
3	J Ickx	Ferrari	−53.3s	2	0	F
4	D Hulme	McLaren-Ford	−1m 6.7s	6	0	G
5	E Fittipaldi	Lotus-Ford	−1 lap	17	0	F
6	R Stommelen	Surtees-Ford	−1 lap	16	0	F

<table>
<tr><td>**Round 4/11**</td><td colspan="2">**DUTCH GP** Zandvoort
20 June 1971   **Race 201**</td><td>**Jacky Ickx**
Ferrari 312B2 151.379kph, 94.062mph</td></tr>
</table>

Ickx, Rodríguez and Stewart on the front row, but in very wet race conditions Stewart was soon in trouble, as were most of the Goodyear runners, Firestone wets making a clean sweep of all the championship points on offer. Ickx in the Ferrari and Rodríguez in the BRM proceeded to put on a masterly display of wet-weather driving, leaving the rest of the field way behind in the process. First Ickx led, then Rodríguez until from lap 32 Ickx began to edge away, 15s up by lap 60. But as the rain intensified in the final ten laps the BRM again closed right up on the Ferrari, eventually crossing the line 8s behind. Dave Walker debuted the 4WD Lotus 56B turbine car. Starting P22, he was P10 after five laps, crashing out on the next.

POLE POSITION Ickx, Ferrari, 1m 17.42s (0.04s), 194.973kph, 121.151mph
LAPS 70 x 4.193 km, 2.605 miles
DISTANCE 293.510 km, 182.379 miles
STARTERS/FINISHERS 24/12
WEATHER Overcast, rain
LAP LEADERS Ickx 1-8, 30, 32-70 (48); Rodríguez 9-29, 31 (22)
WINNER'S LAPS 1-8 P1, 9-29 P2, 30 P1, 31 P2, 32-70 P1
FASTEST LAP Ickx, Ferrari, 1m 34.95s (lap 49), 158.976kph, 98.783mph
CHAMPIONSHIP Stewart 24, Ickx 19, Andretti 9, Peterson 9, Rodríguez 9

Pos	Driver	Car	Time/gap	Grid	Stops	Tyres
1	J Ickx	Ferrari	1h 56m 20.09s	1	0	F
2	P Rodríguez	BRM	−7.99s	2	0	F
3	C Regazzoni	Ferrari	−1 lap	4	0	F
4	R Peterson	March-Ford	−2 laps	13	0	F
5	J Surtees	Surtees-Ford	−2 laps	7	0	F
6	J Siffert	BRM	−2 laps	8	0	F

<table>
<tr><td>**Round 5/11**</td><td colspan="2">**FRENCH GP** Paul Ricard
4 July 1971   **Race 202**</td><td>**Jackie Stewart**
Tyrrell-Ford 003 179.700kph, 111.660mph</td></tr>
</table>

The French GP was held at the new Circuit Paul Ricard with its unusually long Mistral straight. For this race Tyrrell introduced a new streamlined full-width 'sports car' nose cowling. Along with enhanced engine power assisted by a new 'airbox', the Tyrrell was by far the fastest projectile down the Mistral. It enabled Stewart to grand-slam the opposition, leading every lap from pole and setting fastest lap. Adding further joy, teammate Cevert brought the second car home for a Tyrrell 1-2, made possible when, on lap 20, Regazzoni spun out of P2 on oil and Rodríguez vacated the same position seven laps later with ignition trouble. Fittipaldi finished third, closing on Cevert, having brought the Gold Leaf Team Lotus 72D up from P17 on the grid.

POLE POSITION Stewart, Tyrrell-Ford, 1m 50.71s (0.82s), 188.926kph,117.393mph
LAPS 55 x 5.810 km, 3.610 miles
DISTANCE 319.550 km, 198.559 miles
STARTERS/FINISHERS 23/13
WEATHER Sunny, hot, dry
LAP LEADERS Stewart 1-55 (55)
WINNER'S LAPS 1-55 P1
FASTEST LAP Stewart, Tyrrell-Ford, 1m 54.09s (lap 2), 183.329kph, 113.915mph
CHAMPIONSHIP Stewart 33, Ickx 19, Andretti 9, Peterson 9, Rodríguez 9

Pos	Driver	Car	Time/gap	Grid	Stops	Tyres
1	J Stewart	Tyrrell-Ford	1h 46m 41.68s	1	0	G
2	F Cevert	Tyrrell-Ford	−28.12s	7	0	G
3	E Fittipaldi	Lotus-Ford	−34.07s	17	0	F
4	J Siffert	BRM	−37.17s	6	0	F
5	C Amon	Matra	−41.08s	9	0	G
6	R Wisell	Lotus-Ford	−1m 16.02s	15	0	F

<table>
<tr><td>**Round 6/11**</td><td colspan="2">**BRITISH GP** Silverstone
17 July 1971   **Race 203**</td><td>**Jackie Stewart**
Tyrrell-Ford 003 209.987kph, 130.480mph</td></tr>
</table>

It took Stewart just three laps to dispense with the fast-starting Ferraris of pole-man Regazzoni and Jacky Ickx. Once ahead he sailed away into an undisputed lead. On lap 5 Siffert chopped inside compatriot Regazzoni at Copse for second place and for a dozen laps looked as though he might make a race of it. But tyre vibrations caused the rear wing to slip and the BRM lost its competitive edge. Neither Ferrari finished and by the end it was Peterson in second place, albeit more than 30s behind the rampant Tyrrell. At the halfway stage of the championship Stewart had scored more than twice the points of Ickx and his Flat-12 Ferrari, who for many had been the pre-season favourite.

POLE POSITION C Regazzoni, Ferrari, 1m 18.1s (0.0s), 134.919kph, 112.500mph
LAPS 68 x 4.711 km, 2.927 miles
DISTANCE 320.317 km, 199.036 miles
STARTERS/FINISHERS 24/12
WEATHER Sunny, warm, dry
LAP LEADERS Regazzoni 1-3 (3); Stewart 4-68 (65)
WINNER'S LAPS 1 P3, 2-3 P2, 4-68 P1
FASTEST LAP Stewart, Tyrrell-Ford, 1m 19.9s (lap 45), 212.240kph, 131.880mph
CHAMPIONSHIP Stewart 42, Ickx 19, Peterson 15, Fittipaldi 10, Andretti 9

Pos	Driver	Car	Time/gap	Grid	Stops	Tyres
1	J Stewart	Tyrrell-Ford	1h 31m 31.5s	2	0	G
2	R Peterson	March-Ford	−36.1s	5	0	F
3	E Fittipaldi	Lotus-Ford	−50.5s	4	0	F
4	H Pescarolo	March-Ford	−1 lap	17	0	G
5	R Stommelen	Surtees-Ford	−1 lap	12	0	F
6	J Surtees	Surtees-Ford	−1 lap	18	0	F

Round 7/11	**GERMAN GP** Nürburgring		**Jackie Stewart**
	1 August 1971	Race 204	Tyrrell-Ford 003 184.191kph, 114.451mph

Stewart's fifth race victory of the season was his hat-trick and the second Tyrrell 1-2 finish in three events. It was another scintillating display to which no other team could summon an effective response. Not only was the speed of the Tyrrells so crushing but so was the reliability. Cevert came through to finish second, having been down in P8 on lap 1. His battle with Regazzoni and Siffert kept alive the first half of the race as Stewart made serene progress up front. Uncharacteristically Ickx spun out on lap 2 but Regazzoni and Andretti made recompense, finishing 3-4 for Ferrari.

POLE POSITION Stewart, Tyrrell-Ford, 7m 19.0s (0.2s), 187.257kph, 116.356mph
LAPS 12 x 22.835 km, 14.189 miles
DISTANCE 274.020 km, 170.268 miles
STARTERS/FINISHERS 22/12
WEATHER Sunny, warm, dry
LAP LEADERS Stewart 1-12 (12)
WINNER'S LAPS 1-12 P1
FASTEST LAP Cevert, Tyrrell-Ford, 7m 20.1s (lap 10), 186.789kph, 116.066mph
CHAMPIONSHIP Stewart 51, Ickx 19, Peterson 17, Andretti 12, Cevert 12

Pos	Driver	Car	Time/gap	Grid	Stops	Tyres
1	J Stewart	Tyrrell-Ford	1h 29m 15.7s	1	0	G
2	F Cevert	Tyrrell-Ford	−30.1s	5	0	G
3	C Regazzoni	Ferrari	−37.1s	4	0	F
4	M Andretti	Ferrari	−2m 5.0s	11	0	F
5	R Peterson	March-Ford	−2m 29.1s	7	1	F
6	T Schenken	Brabham-Ford	−2m 58.6s	9	0	G

BRM P160

Round 8/11	**AUSTRIAN GP** Österreichring		**Jo Siffert**
	15 August 1971	Race 205	BRM P160 211.858kph, 131.642mph

Last year the Österreichring had proved a happy hunting ground for 12-cylinder engines. This time, rather than the expected Ferrari on pole it was the Swiss driver Jo Siffert's V12 Yardley BRM. Yet more surprising, the Tyrrell twins qualified 2-3. Despite losing a large chunk of his lead towards the end with a deflating tyre, Siffert's was a glorious flag-to-flag victory, the BRM P160 uncatchable. The two Tyrrells gave stern chase, but for the only time this year both retired, Stewart shedding a wheel, Cevert a broken DFV. With his only possible championship challenger, Ickx, also out of the race, Stewart – bizarrely after such a dominant season – won his second world title making his way back to the pits on foot, mobbed by screaming autograph hunters.

POLE POSITION Siffert, BRM, 1m 37.44s (0.21s), 218.387kph, 135.699mph
LAPS 54 x 5.911 km, 3.673 miles
DISTANCE 319.194 km, 198.338 miles
STARTERS/FINISHERS 21/12
WEATHER Sunny, warm, dry
LAP LEADERS Siffert 1-54 (54)
WINNER'S LAPS 1-54 P1
FASTEST LAP Siffert, BRM, 1m 38.47s (lap 22), 216.102kph, 134.280mph
CHAMPIONSHIP Stewart 51, Ickx 19, Peterson 17, Fittipaldi 16, Siffert 13

Pos	Driver	Car	Time/gap	Grid	Stops	Tyres
1	J Siffert	BRM	1h 30m 23.91s	1	0	F
2	E Fittipaldi	Lotus-Ford	−4.12s	5	0	F
3	T Schenken	Brabham-Ford	−19.77s	7	0	G
4	R Wisell	Lotus-Ford	−31.87s	10	0	F
5	G Hill	Brabham-Ford	−48.43s	8	0	G
6	H Pescarolo	March-Ford	−1m 24.51s	13	0	G

ITALIAN GP Monza
5 September 1971   **Race 206**

Peter Gethin
BRM P160 242.616kph, 150.755mph

BRM's second consecutive victory was the final Monza 'slipstreamer', five cars hurtling over the line covered by 0.61s. This race was and remains the closest finish in GP history, Peter Gethin's winning margin over Ronnie Peterson officially 0.01s or about 70cm, a couple of feet. Peterson led by far the most laps, 23, Gethin just three, the BRM driver making a tyre-smoking pass between the Swede and Cevert under braking at Parabolica to snatch victory. The race, the fastest at that time and the first run at over 150mph, also tops the list for the most race leaders, eight. Both Ferraris went out early and for the only time this year Stewart broke an engine. Pole-sitter Amon's V12 Matra dropped out of the lead when his visor came off.

POLE POSITION Amon, Matra, 1m 24.40s (0.42s), 251.214kph, 156.097mph
LAPS 55 x 5.750 km, 3.573 miles
DISTANCE 316.250 km, 196.509 miles
STARTERS/FINISHERS 23/10
WEATHER Sunny, hot, dry
LAP LEADERS C Regazzoni, Ferrari 1-3, 9 (4); Peterson 4-7, 10-14, 17-22, 24, 26, 33, 47-50, 54 (23); J Stewart, Tyrrell-Ford 8 (1); Cevert 15-16, 23, 31-32, 34, 36 (7); Hailwood 25, 27, 35, 42, 51 (5); Siffert, BRM 28-30 (3); Amon 37-41, 43-46 (9); Gethin 52-53, 55 (3)
WINNER'S LAPS 1 P9, 2 P8, 3 P10, 4-11 P8, 12 P9, 13 P10, 14 P9, 15 P10, 16-17 P8, 18 P7, 19 P8, 20-31 P7, 32-47 P6, 48-49 P5, 50-51 P3, 52-53 P1, 54 P4, 55 P1
FASTEST LAP H Pescarolo, March-Ford, 1m 23.80s (lap 9), 247.017kph, 153.489mph
CHAMPIONSHIP Stewart 51, Peterson 23, Ickx 19, Cevert 16, Fittipaldi 16

Pos	Driver	Car	Time/gap	Grid	Stops	Tyres
1	P Gethin	BRM	1h 18m 12.60s	11	0	F
2	R Peterson	March-Ford	−0.01s	6	0	F
3	F Cevert	Tyrrell-Ford	−0.09s	5	0	G
4	M Hailwood	Surtees-Ford	−0.18s	17	0	F
5	H Ganley	BRM	−0.61s	4	0	F
6	C Amon	Matra	−32.36s	1	0	G

CANADIAN GP Mosport Park
19 September 1971   **Race 207**

Jackie Stewart
Tyrrell-Ford 003 131.895kph, 81.956mph

Twelve months on from the Tyrrell's sensational debut, Canada saw the resumption of normal service with another Stewart victory. Race conditions were wet and misty, and on this occasion the opposition, in the shape of Ronnie Peterson, took the fight to Stewart, at least for half the race. Stewart led from pole for 17 laps, the Swede the next 13, although they exchanged the lead more times than the lap-chart indicates. Regrettably the tense duel was brought to a premature conclusion when, lapping a backmarker on lap 32, the March's nose nudged a rear wheel and the car slewed across the track, its front wing askew. The incident cost Peterson 13s, although he was still able to come home second. Mark Donohue made a fine debut, finishing third.

POLE POSITION Stewart, Tyrrell-Ford, 1m 15.3s (0.2s), 189.197kph, 117.562mph
LAPS 64 x 3.957 km, 2.459 miles (Scheduled for 80 laps but stopped due to rain)
DISTANCE 253.272 km, 157.376 miles
STARTERS/FINISHERS 24/16
WEATHER Murky, rain
LAP LEADERS Stewart 1-17, 31-64 (51); Peterson 18-30 (13)
WINNER'S LAPS 1-17 P1, 18-30 P2, 31-64 P1
FASTEST LAP Hulme, McLaren-Ford, 1m 43.5s (lap 57), 137.648kph, 85.530mph
CHAMPIONSHIP Stewart 60, Peterson 29, Ickx 19, Cevert 17, Fittipaldi 16

Pos	Driver	Car	Time/gap	Grid	Stops	Tyres
1	J Stewart	Tyrrell-Ford	1h 55m 12.9s	1	0	G
2	R Peterson	March-Ford	−38.3s	6	0	F
3	M Donohue	McLaren-Ford	−1m 35.8s	8	1	G
4	D Hulme	McLaren-Ford	−1 lap	10	0	G
5	R Wisell	Lotus-Ford	−1 lap	7	0	F
6	F Cevert	Tyrrell-Ford	−2 laps	3	0	G

Tyrrell-Ford 002

Round 11/11	**UNITED STATES GP** Watkins Glen	**François Cevert**
	3 October 1971 **Race 208**	Tyrrell-Ford 002 185.228kph, 115.096mph

Tyrrell's seventh victory of the season confirmed the burgeoning talent of their number two driver, who twice already had backed up his team-leader with 1-2 finishes and now brought the team victory when Stewart's car faded with poor handling. From his sixth pole of the year, Stewart led from the start, Cevert initially holding P3 behind Hulme. On lap 7 Cevert took Hulme, such that seven laps later the understeering Stewart could wave him through as the Scot steadily slipped back through the field to finish fifth. Until the closing stages Cevert had to resist increasing pressure from Ickx, closing to within 2s, although the Ferrari was not to finish. His maiden victory gave Cevert third place in the championship behind Stewart and Peterson.

POLE POSITION Stewart, Tyrrell-Ford, 1m 42.642s (0.017s), 190.615kph, 118.443mph
LAPS 59 x 5.435 km, 3.377 miles
DISTANCE 320.651 km, 199.243 miles
STARTERS/FINISHERS 29/17
WEATHER Sunny, warm, dry
LAP LEADERS Stewart 1-13 (13); Cevert 14-59 (46)
WINNER'S LAPS 1-6 P3, 7-13 P2, 14-59 P1
FASTEST LAP J Ickx, Ferrari, 1m 43.474s (lap 43), 189.082kph, 117.490mph
CHAMPIONSHIP Stewart 62, Peterson 33, Cevert 26, Ickx 19, Siffert 19

Pos	Driver	Car	Time/gap	Grid	Stops	Tyres
1	F Cevert	Tyrrell-Ford	1h 43m 51.991s	5	0	G
2	J Siffert	BRM	−40.062s	6	0	F
3	R Peterson	March-Ford	−44.070s	11	0	F
4	H Ganley	BRM	−56.749s	12	0	F
5	J Stewart	Tyrrell-Ford	−1m 0.003s	1	0	G
6	C Regazzoni	Ferrari	−1m 16.426s	4	1	F

1971 CHAMPIONSHIP FACTS AND FOLKLORE

■ With maximum race-distance reduced to 200 miles (321.87km), the 11-round championship was again in two parts, the best five results from the first six races counting plus the best four from the remaining five.

■ Paul Ricard hosted the French GP for the first time, while sponsorship spread to race promotion with the 'Woolmark' British GP. Monaco marked the 200th championship race.

■ Greater emphasis on safety continued, additional Armco barriers and catch-fencing used at the circuits and red rear

RACE 199, Spanish GP: Qualifying at Montjuïc had given little hint that Jackie Stewart would bring Tyrrell their maiden win from only their fifth GP start.

lights made compulsory on cars to be used in poor visibility, notably during wet-weather racing.

■ Three appearances at the end of the previous season gave fair warning that the new Tyrrell was a quick car, but no one quite expected such superiority. This was most apparent at Paul Ricard when the Tyrrell twins, sporting new thinking in front-end aero treatment, simply trounced the opposition.

■ In fact, Jackie Stewart posted the first Tyrrell-Ford victory in the new marque's second race of the season, but once the breakthrough occurred six more quickly followed, including a pair of 1-2 finishes and one by Stewart's teammate François Cevert.

■ These three results pointed to the fact that the car was capable of winning races without Stewart at the wheel, though his dynamic 'on it' driving style was invariably the ingredient which made the package so successful across the season, and in the face of some powerful opposition.

■ Powerful in more than one sense, as many pre-season pundits expected that the 12-cylinder brigade, enjoying up to 10% more engine power, would see off the V8 DFV. But Cosworth responded with an important extra 10bhp and the ram effect of a new development, the engine 'airbox', also assisted.

■ Further, by out-sourcing part of their engine rebuild programme, Cosworth also found improved reliability. But as well as power wars, tyre wars were playing an ever-increasing role in GP racing.

■ For their new treadless 'slicks', Goodyear and Firestone began bringing new compounds or constructions to almost every race.

■ Vibration became a common tyre trouble, one that Goodyear overcame quicker than Firestone, again to the advantage of Tyrrell.

■ Nevertheless, Firestone-shod Ferrari and BRM notched up two race victories apiece, confirming their potential, whereas none of the other DFV teams won, reaffirming Tyrrell superiority.

■ Lotus, failing to win a race for the first time since 1959, was hampered on two fronts. An early season car accident to their new star driver Emerson Fittipaldi affected his season appreciably. Secondly, Chapman's pursuit of the 'unfair advantage' turned this time towards the Pratt & Whitney gas-turbine powered Lotus 56B, an unsuccessful experiment shelved at the end of the season.

■ McLaren lost much development time trying to make rising-rate suspension function on their new M19A, and March employed Frank Costin's principles of the 'slippery' aerodynamic profile with their second F1 design, the eccentric 711 with its 'tea-tray' front wing.

■ Ronnie Peterson made good use of this peculiar looking car such that he finished runner-up to Stewart in the championship, but he couldn't wring a victory from it, despite getting closer to winning a race than anyone before or since.

■ 0.01s was the margin Peterson lost to Gethin's BRM at Monza, a famous victory on numerous counts: the closest-ever race victory; the greatest number of race leaders, eight, and the first race average to exceed 150mph, a record which stood for 32 years.

■ Despite their two race victories, the BRM team suffered two devastating blows during 1971, losing both of their wonderful drivers, Pedro Rodríguez and Jo Siffert, who were paired together in the muscular P160 V12.

■ On 11 July Pedro was killed in a sports car race at the Norisring. Then on 24 October, three weeks after the end of the Grand Prix season, an additional non-championship F1 race took place at Brands Hatch, the scene of Jo Siffert's 1968 GP victory. During the race 'Seppi' crashed at Hawthorn's bend and died when his BRM burst into flames.

■ Cancellation of the Mexican GP and the acclaimed success for Stewart and Tyrrell had given race promoter John Webb the idea of staging this additional event. It was billed 'The Rothmans World Championships Victory Race'.

■ In 1971 Jo Bonnier retired from F1 but died at Le Mans the following June; Niki Lauda made his debut in a March, and Jacques Villeneuve was born.

Championship ranking	Championship points	Driver nationality	1971 Drivers Championship		Races contested	Race victories	Podiumse excl. victories	Races led	Flag to flag victories	Laps led	Poles	Fastest laps	Triple Crowns
			Driver	Car									
1	62	GBR	Jackie Stewart	Tyrrell-Ford	11	6	1	8	3	347	6	3	2
2	33	SWE	Ronnie Peterson	March-Ford (10) March-Alfa Romeo (1)	11		5	2		36			
3	26	FRA	François Cevert	Tyrrell-Ford	11	1	3	2		53		1	
4	19	BEL	Jacky Ickx	Ferrari	11	1	2	2		53	2	3	1
5	19	SUI	Jo Siffert	BRM	11	1	1	2	1	57	1	1	1
6	16	BRA	Emerson Fittipaldi	Lotus-Ford (9) Lotus Pratt & Whitney (1)	10		3						
7	13	SUI	Clay Regazzoni	Ferrari	11		3	3		23	1		
8	12	USA	Mario Andretti	Ferrari	5	1		1		4		1	
9	9	GBR	Peter Gethin	BRM	11	1		1		3			
10	9	MEX	Pedro Rodriguez	BRM	5		1	1		22			
11	9	NZL	Chris Amon	Matra	10		1	1		9	1		
12	9	SWE	Reine Wisell	Lotus-Ford (9) Lotus Pratt & Whitney (1)	10								
12	9	NZL	Denny Hulme	McLaren-Ford	10			1		59		1	
14	5	AUS	Tim Schenken	Brabham-Ford	10		1						
15	5	NZL	Howden Ganley	BRM	9								
16	4	USA	Mark Donohue	McLaren-Ford	1		1						
17	4	FRA	Henri Pescarolo	March-Ford	10							1	
18	3	GBR	Mike Hailwood	Surtees-Ford	2		1			5			
19	3	GER	Rolf Stommelen	Surtees-Ford	9								
19	3	GBR	John Surtees	Surtees-Ford	11								
21	2	GBR	Graham Hill	Brabham-Ford	11								
22	1	FRA	Jean-Pierre Beltoise	Matra	7								

Championship ranking	Championship points	Team/Marque nationality	1971 Constructors Championship		Engine maker nationality	Races contested	Race victories	1-2 finishes	Podiums excl. victories	Races led	Laps led	Poles	Fastest laps
			Chassis	Engine									
1	73	GBR	Tyrrell 001, 002, 003	Ford Cosworth 3.0 V8	GBR	11	7	2	4	8	400	6	4
2	36	GBR	BRM P160, P153	BRM 3.0 V12	GBR	11	2		2	3	82	1	1
3	33	ITA	Ferrari 312B2, 312B	Ferrari 3.0 F12	ITA	11	2		5	5	80	3	4
4	33	GBR	March 711, 701	Ford Cosworth 3.0 V8	GBR	11			5	2	36		1
5	21	GBR	Lotus 72D, 72C	Ford Cosworth 3.0 V8	GBR	10			3				
6	10	NZL	McLaren M19A, M14A	Ford Cosworth 3.0 V8	GBR	11			1	1	59		1
7	9	FRA	Matra MS120B	Matra 3.0 V12	FRA	10			1	1	9	1	
8	8	GBR	Surtees TS9, TS7	Ford Cosworth 3.0 V8	GBR	11				1	5		
9	5	AUS	Brabham BT 34, BT33	Ford Cosworth 3.0 V8	GBR	11			1				

1972

Fittipaldi's mardi gras

THE TALE OF THE TITLE

- Lotus, led by Emerson Fittipaldi and resplendent in JPS black and gold, made a spectacular return to form.
- He became the youngest-ever champion, five victories toppling Stewart and Tyrrell from both titles.
- Stewart won four times, twice in a new Tyrrell but only after the titles had already changed hands.
- The Ford DFV still ruled, just two non-Cosworth victories in the 12-race season.
- One was the unexpected yet brilliant win by Jean-Pierre Beltoise for BRM at a rain-drenched Monaco.
- The other a singleton victory by Jacky Ickx in the promising but ultimately disappointing Ferrari 312B2.
- A season of regular points and podiums for Yardley McLaren saw Hulme return to the winner's circle.
- Goodyear and Firestone introduced sticky qualifying tyres, the latter edging it 5–7 for poles, and for wins.
- And not forgetting: Bernie Ecclestone buys Brabham.

THE CHASE FOR THE CHAMPIONSHIP

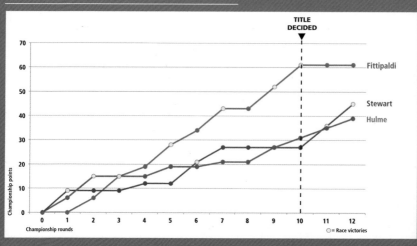

Round 1/12	**ARGENTINEAN GP** Buenos Aires No 9	**Jackie Stewart**
	23 January 1972 Race 209	Tyrrell-Ford 003 161.607kph, 100.418mph

After a 12-year absence F1 returned to Latin America, inspiring local hero Carlos Reutemann to annex pole on his GP debut. His car was the lobster-claw Brabham BT34, the team now owned by Bernie Ecclestone. In the race, to the delight of the partisan crowd, Reutemann pressed Stewart's leading Tyrrell closely for seven glorious laps until Fittipaldi's Lotus got ahead and the Brabham gradually fell away. The team had gambled on super-sticky Goodyears and the gamble had failed in the very hot conditions. On lap 35 Hulme's Yardley-McLaren overtook Fittipaldi for second, where he finished, leading in the Ferrari pair. The new world champion had started the season superbly, Fittipaldi losing P3 on lap 60 with suspension failure.

POLE POSITION C Reutemann, Brabham-Ford, 1m 12.46s (0.6s), 166.188kph, 103.265mph
LAPS 95 x 3.345 km, 2.078 miles
DISTANCE 317.775 km, 197.456 miles
STARTERS/FINISHERS 21/11
WEATHER Sunny, very hot, dry
LAP LEADERS Stewart 1-95 (95)
WINNER'S LAPS 1-95 P1
FASTEST LAP Stewart, Tyrrell-Ford, 1m 13.66s (lap 25), 163.481kph, 101.582mph
CHAMPIONSHIP Stewart 9, Hulme 6, Ickx 4, Regazzoni 3, Schenken 2

Pos	Driver	Car	Time/gap	Grid	Stops	Tyres
1	J Stewart	Tyrrell-Ford	1h 57m 58.82s	2	0	G
2	D Hulme	McLaren-Ford	−25.96s	4	0	G
3	J Ickx	Ferrari	−59.39s	8	0	F
4	C Regazzoni	Ferrari	−1m 6.72s	6	0	F
5	T Schenken	Surtees-Ford	−1m 9.11s	11	0	F
6	R Peterson	March-Ford	−1 lap	10	0	G

McLaren-Ford M19A

Round 2/12	**SOUTH AFRICAN GP** Kyalami	**Denny Hulme**
	4 March 1972 Race 210	McLaren-Ford M19A 183.834kph, 114.229mph

The early stages followed the established pattern, Stewart taking the lead from pole then building it. Behind him, Hulme, Fittipaldi and Hailwood's Surtees engaged in a close battle and began to reel in the leader. Hailwood was even challenging Stewart's lead when his suspension broke on lap 29. Fittipaldi was next to try to unseat the champion, but on lap 44 a seized gearbox put Stewart out. However, Fittipaldi's lead was short-lived. As his tanks lightened increasing oversteer made him easy pray to Hulme, bringing McLaren their first victory since 1969, indeed their first in the post-Bruce McLaren period. Behind Fittipaldi, Peter Revson also added a podium for McLaren.

POLE POSITION J Stewart, Tyrrell-Ford, 1m 17.0s (0.3s), 191.875kph, 119.226mph
LAPS 79 x 4.104 km, 2.550 miles
DISTANCE 324.216 km, 201.458 miles
STARTERS/FINISHERS 26/17
WEATHER Sunny, hot, dry
LAP LEADERS Hulme 1, 57-79 (24); Stewart 2-44 (43); Fittipaldi 45-56 (12)
WINNER'S LAPS 1 P1, 2-16 P2, 17 P3, 18-28 P4, 29-44 P3, 45-56 P2, 57-79 P1
FASTEST LAP M Hailwood, Surtees-Ford, 1m 18.9s (lap 20), 187.255kph, 116.355mph
CHAMPIONSHIP Hulme 15, Stewart 9, Fittipaldi 6, Ickx 4, Revson 4

Pos	Driver	Car	Time/gap	Grid	Stops	Tyres
1	D Hulme	McLaren-Ford	1h 45m 49.1s	5	0	G
2	E Fittipaldi	Lotus-Ford	−14.1s	3	0	F
3	P Revson	McLaren-Ford	−25.8s	12	0	G
4	M Andretti	Ferrari	−38.5s	6	0	F
5	R Peterson	March-Ford	−49.0s	9	0	G
6	G Hill	Brabham-Ford	−1 lap	14	0	G

Round 3/12	**SPANISH GP** Jarama				
	1 May 1972				Race 211

SPANISH GP Jarama

Emerson Fittipaldi

Lotus-Ford 72D 148.614kph, 92.344mph

Ickx was on pole but it was Hulme, alongside, who was first to lead until Stewart hit the front on lap 5. But by lap 9 Fittipaldi had carved his way through to the lead and stayed there to the end, finishing almost 20s ahead of Ickx and Regazzoni in the Ferraris. The way Fittipaldi had steadily picked off Regazzoni, Hulme, Ickx and finally Stewart during those early laps was impressive and ominous for his rivals, the young Brazilian having also looked very strong in the early-season non-championship races. Firestone equipment on the first four finishers suggested a tyre advantage, but only time would tell if this would be a lasting one. On lap 70 Stewart retired from third with extensive damage following an inexplicable spin.

FASTEST LAP Ickx, Ferrari, 1m 21.01s (lap 52), 151.270kph, 93.995mph
LAPS 90 x 3.404 km, 2.115 miles
DISTANCE 306.360 km, 190.363 miles
STARTERS/FINISHERS 25/11
WEATHER Cold, showers, windy
LAP LEADERS Hulme 1-4 (4); J Stewart, Tyrrell-Ford 5-8 (4); Fittipaldi 9-90 (82)
WINNER'S LAPS 1-2 P5, 3-5 P4, 6-8 P2, 9-90 P1
POLE POSITION Ickx, Ferrari, 1m 18.43s (0.75s), 156.246kph, 97.087mph
CHAMPIONSHIP Hulme 15, Fittipaldi 15, Ickx 10, Stewart 9, Regazzoni 7

Pos	Driver	Car	Time/gap	Grid	Stops	Tyres
1	E Fittipaldi	Lotus-Ford	2h 3m 41.23s	3	0	F
2	J Ickx	Ferrari	−18.92s	1	0	F
3	C Regazzoni	Ferrari	−1 lap	8	0	F
4	A de Adamich	Surtees-Ford	−1 lap	13	0	F
5	P Revson	McLaren-Ford	−1 lap	11	0	G
6	C Pace	March-Ford	−1 lap	16	0	G

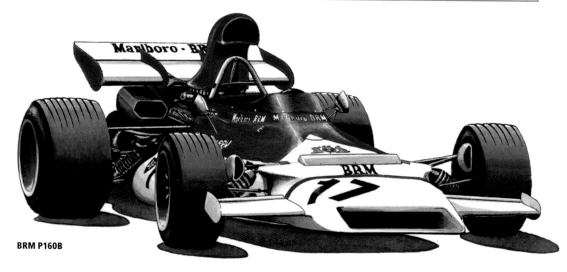

BRM P160B

Round 4/12	**MONACO GP** Monte Carlo				
	14 May 1972				Race 212

MONACO GP Monte Carlo

Jean-Pierre Beltoise

BRM P160B 102.756kph, 63.849mph

From row two in the teeming rain, Jean-Pierre Beltoise aimed his BRM down the inside at Ste Devote to lead up the hill in a ball of spray. The advantage of a clear track ahead enabled him to pull away from the rest, but it was more than that – he was driving brilliantly. By half-distance even the sceptics had stopped waiting for the Frenchman's inevitable collision with the barriers. After 2½ hours in unrelenting weather, he finished more than 30s ahead of the Ickx Ferrari, the only two cars to complete the course. Beltoise's one and only GP victory was a virtuoso performance, the exceptional conditions he coped with illustrated by this being the slowest championship race on record. Near the end Stewart lost P3 to Fittipaldi with water in the electrics.

POLE POSITION Fittipaldi, Lotus-Ford, 1m 21.4s (0.2s), 139.091kph, 86.427mph
LAPS 80 x 3.145km, 1.954 miles
DISTANCE 251.600 km, 156.337 miles
STARTERS/FINISHERS 25/17
WEATHER Overcast, rain
LAP LEADERS Beltoise 1-80 (80)
WINNER'S LAPS 1-80 P1
FASTEST LAP Beltoise, BRM, 1m 40.0s (lap 9), 113.220kph, 70.352mph
CHAMPIONSHIP Fittipaldi 19, Ickx 16, Hulme 15, Stewart 12, Regazzoni 7

Pos	Driver	Car	Time/gap	Grid	Stops	Tyres
1	J-P Beltoise	BRM	2h 26m 54.7s	4	0	F
2	J Ickx	Ferrari	−38.2s	2	0	F
3	E Fittipaldi	Lotus-Ford	−1 lap	1	0	F
4	J Stewart	Tyrrell-Ford	−2 laps	8	0	G
5	B Redman	McLaren-Ford	−3 laps	10	0	G
6	C Amon	Matra	−3 laps	6	4	G

Round 5/12	**BELGIAN GP** Nivelles-Baulers		**Emerson Fittipaldi**
	4 June 1972	Race 213	Lotus-Ford 72D 182.423kph, 113.353mph

Fittipaldi was now getting into his stride with a second successive pole. His task was eased by the absence of the world champion, Stewart suffering from a stomach ulcer. Fittipaldi harried Regazzoni's fast-starting Ferrari before squeezing by on lap 9 and steadily disappearing into the distance, the superior road-holding and braking of the black and gold Lotus shown to good effect on the new Nivelles circuit. A terrific battle raged for second place between the Ferraris, Cevert, Hulme and Amon, eventually settled in the Frenchman's favour, albeit nearly 30s behind the JPS Lotus. Hulme took third, but neither Ferrari finished – Regazzoni colliding with a spinning Tecno – and Amon's Matra ran short of fuel when third.

POLE POSITION Fittipaldi, Lotus-Ford, 1m 11.43s (0.15s), 187.686kph, 116.623mph
LAPS 85 x 3.724 km, 2.314 miles
DISTANCE 316.540 km, 196.689 miles
STARTERS/FINISHERS 25/14
WEATHER Sunny, warm, dry
LAP LEADERS C Regazzoni, Ferrari 1-8 (8); Fittipaldi 9-85 (77)
WINNER'S LAPS 1-8 P2, 9-85 P1
FASTEST LAP Amon, Matra, 1m 12.12s (lap 66), 185.890kph, 115.507mph
CHAMPIONSHIP Fittipaldi 28, Hulme 19, Ickx 16, Stewart 12, Beltoise 9

Pos	Driver	Car	Time/gap	Grid	Stops	Tyres
1	E Fittipaldi	Lotus-Ford	1h 44m 6.7s	1	0	F
2	F Cevert	Tyrrell-Ford	−26.6s	5	0	G
3	D Hulme	McLaren-Ford	−58.1s	3	0	G
4	M Hailwood	Surtees-Ford	−1m 12.0s	8	0	F
5	C Pace	March-Ford	−1 lap	11	0	G
6	C Amon	Matra	−1 lap	13	1	G

Round 6/12	**FRENCH GP** Clermont-Ferrand		**Jackie Stewart**
	2 July 1972	Race 214	Tyrrell-Ford 003 163.454kph, 101.566mph

The Dutch GP cancelled, Stewart returned refreshed from a six-week layoff to a familiar track, the 51 corners of *le Circuit de Charade*. Amon's V12 Matra – the French constructor recently victorious at *Le 24 heures du Mans* – looked to be the main obstacle to the victory Stewart needed to get back into championship contention. From pole Amon narrowly led Hulme and Stewart until a mid-race puncture handed the Tyrrell victory. Amon stormed back from midfield, but just failed to catch Fittipaldi in second place. Eight cars were delayed by punctures, including Hulme. Stewart had said that the way to win was to keep it on the tarmac and avoid the stones. On lap 9 Helmut Marko lost an eye when a stone thrown up by another car pierced his visor.

POLE POSITION Amon, Matra, 2m 53.4s (0.8s), 167.232kph,103.913mph
LAPS 38 x 8.055 km, 5.005 miles
DISTANCE 306.090 km, 190.196 miles
STARTERS/FINISHERS 24/19
WEATHER Sunny, hot, dry
LAP LEADERS Amon 1-19 (19); Stewart 20-38 (19)
WINNER'S LAPS 1-16 P3, 17-19 P2, 20-38 P1
FASTEST LAP Amon, Matra, 2m 53.9s (lap 32), 166.751kph, 103.614mph
CHAMPIONSHIP Fittipaldi 34, Stewart 21, Hulme 19, Ickx 16, Beltoise 9

Pos	Driver	Car	Time/gap	Grid	Stops	Tyres
1	J Stewart	Tyrrell-Ford	1h 52m 21.5s	3	0	G
2	E Fittipaldi	Lotus-Ford	−27.7s	8	0	F
3	C Amon	Matra	−31.9s	1	1	G
4	F Cevert	Tyrrell-Ford	−49.3s	7	0	G
5	R Peterson	March-Ford	−56.8s	9	0	G
6	M Hailwood	Surtees-Ford	−1m 36.1s	10	0	F

Round 7/12	**BRITISH GP** Brands Hatch		**Emerson Fittipaldi**
	15 July 1972	Race 215	Lotus-Ford 72D 180.340kph, 112.058mph

Brands Hatch kicked off the second half of the season, champion and challenger each with two race victories. Having ceded to Stewart in France, young Fittipaldi knew that in the Briton's back yard he must reassert his advantage. From the front row, Ickx and Emerson immediately began a battle for the lead, joined at quarter-distance by Stewart, making up time from P5 on lap 1. On lap 25 Stewart and Fittipaldi switched positions out of Druids, reversed at the same spot 11 laps later. On lap 49 the Lotus went through in the lead, Ickx pitting with lack of lubricant, an oil cooler leak. Never separated by more than a few seconds, the titanic battle between the two title protagonists ensued, finishing 4.1s apart at the end. Was this the tipping point?

POLE POSITION J Ickx, Ferrari, 1m 22.2s (0.4s), 186.778kph, 116.058mph
LAPS 76 x 4.265 km, 2.650 miles
DISTANCE 324.122 km, 201.400 miles
STARTERS/FINISHERS 26/13
WEATHER Sunny, warm, dry
LAP LEADERS Ickx 1-48 (48); Fittipaldi 49-76 (28)
WINNER'S LAPS 1-24 P2, 25-35 P3, 36-48 P2, 49-76 P1
FASTEST LAP Stewart, Tyrrell-Ford, 1m 24.0s (laps 58 & 60), 182.775kph, 113.571mph
CHAMPIONSHIP Fittipaldi 43, Stewart 27, Hulme 21, Ickx 16, Revson 10

Pos	Driver	Car	Time/gap	Grid	Stops	Tyres
1	E Fittipaldi	Lotus-Ford	1h 47m 50.2s	2	0	F
2	J Stewart	Tyrrell-Ford	−4.1s	4	0	G
3	P Revson	McLaren-Ford	−1m 12.5s	3	0	G
4	C Amon	Matra	−1 lap	17	0	G
5	D Hulme	McLaren-Ford	−1 lap	11	0	G
6	A Merzario	Ferrari	−1 lap	9	1	F

| Round 8/12 | **GERMAN GP** Nürburgring | | | | | **Jacky Ickx** |
| | 30 July 1972 | | | Race 216 | | Ferrari 312B2 187.676kph, 116.616mph |

After disappointment at Brands Hatch, three years after his first Nürburgring victory for Brabham Ickx repeated it in grand style. He was untouchable, leading throughout from pole and recording the fastest lap. Peterson and Fittipaldi gave ever-distant chase during much of the race until Ronnie spun back behind Regazzoni on lap 9, and Fittipaldi lost a certain P2 finish when his gearbox seized two laps later. So Regazzoni made it a Ferrari 1-2 but somewhat controversially. In a wheel-to-wheel battle for second, the Swiss driver slid wide on the final lap and as Stewart attempted to pass the two cars touched, eliminating the Tyrrell. With Fittipaldi already out, the loss of points was crucial to Stewart's championship chances.

POLE POSITION Ickx, Ferrari, 7m 07.0s (1.7s), 192.520kph, 119.626mph
LAPS 14 x 22.835 km, 14.189 miles
DISTANCE 319.960 km, 198.646 miles
STARTERS/FINISHERS 27/15
WEATHER Sunny, warm, dry
LAP LEADERS Ickx 1-14 (14)
WINNER'S LAPS 1-14 P1
FASTEST LAP Ickx, Ferrari, 7m 13.6s (lap 10), 189.589kph, 117.805mph
CHAMPIONSHIP Fittipaldi 43, Stewart 27, Ickx 25, Hulme 21, Regazzoni 13

Pos	Driver	Car	Time/gap	Grid	Stops	Tyres
1	J Ickx	Ferrari	1h 42m 12.3s	1	0	F
2	C Regazzoni	Ferrari	−48.3s	7	0	F
3	R Peterson	March-Ford	−1m 6.7s	4	0	G
4	H Ganley	BRM	−2m 20.2s	18	0	F
5	B Redman	McLaren-Ford	−2m 35.7s	19	0	G
6	G Hill	Brabham-Ford	−2m 59.6s	15	0	G

| Round 9/12 | **AUSTRIAN GP** Österreichring | | | | | **Emerson Fittipaldi** |
| | 13 August 1972 | | | Race 217 | | Lotus-Ford 72D 214.518kph, 133.295mph |

In Austria Fittipaldi turned the screw. The Brazilian's pole didn't pay off, as Stewart – debuting the new Tyrrell 005 – shot into the lead from row two and began to pull away. But just before half-distance Fittipaldi dived ahead as chronic handling set in causing the Tyrrell to fall back steadily, Stewart finishing seventh, more than a minute behind. Back at the front, a terrific tussle was developing as Hulme began to perceptibly make up ground on the leader, the McLaren faster on the straights, the Lotus in the corners. The final ten laps were very tense, Hulme getting alongside at one point, but at the finish just 1.18s separated them. Although arithmetically the championship was still undecided, victory had given Fittipaldi a virtually unassailable lead.

POLE POSITION Fittipaldi, Lotus-Ford, 1m 35.97s (0.07s), 221.732kph, 137.778mph
LAPS 54 x 5.911 km, 3.673 miles
DISTANCE 319.194 km, 198.338 miles
STARTERS/FINISHERS 25/14
WEATHER Sunny, very hot, dry
LAP LEADERS J Stewart, Tyrrell-Ford 1-23 (23); Fittipaldi 24-54 (31)
WINNER'S LAPS 1-4 P3, 5-23 P2, 24-54 P1
FASTEST LAP Hulme, McLaren-Ford, 1m 38.32s (lap 47), 216.432kph, 134.485mph
CHAMPIONSHIP Fittipaldi 52, Stewart 27, Hulme 27, Ickx 25, Revson 14

Pos	Driver	Car	Time/gap	Grid	Stops	Tyres
1	E Fittipaldi	Lotus-Ford	1h 29m 16.66s	1	0	F
2	D Hulme	McLaren-Ford	−1.18s	7	0	G
3	P Revson	McLaren-Ford	−36.53s	4	0	G
4	M Hailwood	Surtees-Ford	−44.76s	12	0	F
5	C Amon	Matra	−45.64s	6	0	G
6	H Ganley	BRM	−1m 1.19s	10	0	F

| Round 10/12 | **ITALIAN GP** Monza | | | | | **Emerson Fittipaldi** |
| | 10 September 1972 | | | Race 218 | | Lotus-Ford 72D 211.813kph, 131.614mph |

The introduction of two chicanes had totally altered Monza and its slipstreaming character. As the flag fell, Stewart lost his clutch and his championship. The rest rushed down to the first chicane led by the two Ferraris. Ickx, having annexed pole, also led the race in the main, although Fittipaldi was never far behind once he had made up ground from his P6 grid slot after earlier troubles. But there was to be no grandstand finish, the Ferraris dropping out, first Regazzoni through an accident not of his making on lap 17, then Ickx with an electrical fault ten laps from the end. This enabled Hailwood to take second place for the ecstatic Surtees team. So Fittipaldi's Lotus won the race, his fifth of the season, and with it wrapped up both championships.

POLE POSITION J Ickx, Ferrari, 1m 35.65s (0.04s), 217.355kph, 135.058mph
LAPS 55 x 5.775 km, 3.588 miles
DISTANCE 317.625 km, 197.363 miles
STARTERS/FINISHERS 25/13
WEATHER Overcast, dry
LAP LEADERS Ickx 1-13, 17-45 (42); C Regazzoni, Ferrari 14-16 (3); Fittipaldi 46-55 (10)
WINNER'S LAPS 1-16 P3, 17-45 P2, 46-55 P1
FASTEST LAP J Ickx, Ferrari, 1m 36.30s (lap 44), 215.888kph, 134.146mph
CHAMPIONSHIP Fittipaldi 61, Hulme 31, Stewart 27, Ickx 25, Revson 17

Pos	Driver	Car	Time/gap	Grid	Stops	Tyres
1	E Fittipaldi	Lotus-Ford	1h 29m 58.6s	6	0	F
2	M Hailwood	Surtees-Ford	−14.5s	9	0	F
3	D Hulme	McLaren-Ford	−23.8s	5	0	G
4	P Revson	McLaren-Ford	−35.7s	8	0	G
5	G Hill	Brabham-Ford	−1m 5.6s	13	0	G
6	P Gethin	BRM	−1m 21.9s	12	0	F

Round 11/12	**CANADIAN GP** Mosport Park		**Jackie Stewart**
	24 September 1972	Race 219	Tyrrell-Ford 005 183.918kph, 114.282mph

The new world champion and the deposed champion only managed row two in Canada. Ahead sat two McLarens and Peterson's March, Revson on pole. At the off, delayed by fog, the McLaren's bogged down, Peterson shooting into the lead. Stewart gave him just three laps before taking over, and that was that, driving away from the field in a manner reminiscent of last year to give the new Tyrrell its first victory. When Peterson tripped up lapping Hill's Brabham the two McLarens went through to finish a remote 2-3, Revson's best finish to date. Fittipaldi, when fighting with Revson for third, had to pit to replace a broken nose wing, finishing well down the field.

POLE POSITION Revson, McLaren-Ford, 1m 13.6s (0.3s), 193.587kph, 120.277mph
LAPS 80 x 3.957 km, 2.459 miles
DISTANCE 316.590 km, 196.720 miles
STARTERS/FINISHERS 24/13
WEATHER Misty, dry
LAP LEADERS R Peterson, March-Ford 1-3 (3); Stewart 4-80 (77)
WINNER'S LAPS 1-3 P2, 4-80 P1
FASTEST LAP Stewart, Tyrrell-Ford, 1m 15.7s (lap 25), 188.198kph, 116.941mph
CHAMPIONSHIP Fittipaldi 61, Stewart 36, Hulme 35, Ickx 25, Revson 23

Pos	Driver	Car	Time/gap	Grid	Stops	Tyres
1	J Stewart	Tyrrell-Ford	1h 43m 16.9s	5	0	G
2	P Revson	McLaren-Ford	−48.2s	1	0	G
3	D Hulme	McLaren-Ford	−54.6s	2	0	G
4	C Reutemann	Brabham-Ford	−1m 0.7s	9	0	G
5	C Regazzoni	Ferrari	−1m 7.0s	7	0	F
6	C Amon	Matra	1 lap	10	0	G

Round 12/12	**UNITED STATES GP** Watkins Glen		**Jackie Stewart**
	8 October 1972	Race 220	Tyrrell-Ford 005 189.070kph, 117.483mph

Any loitering queries over Stewart's health were dispelled at Watkins Glen with an awe-inspiring grand-slam performance. Last year's winner, Cevert, made it a Tyrrell 1-2 and, ever the showman, after crossing the line Stewart slowed to enable himself, Cevert and the lapped third Tyrrell entry of Depailler to come home in team formation. By contrast, Fittipaldi ended his championship year with an early retirement, only one of the three black and gold cars finishing, and then out of the points. Hulme finished third, the McLarens continuing to look strong, highlighted by debutant Jody Scheckter in a third car, who overtook Fittipaldi early on for third but was caught out by a light shower when running fourth on lap 40.

POLE POSITION Stewart, Tyrrell-Ford, 1m 40.481s (0.046s), 194.715kph, 120.990mph
LAPS 59 x 5.435 km, 3.377 miles
DISTANCE 320.651 km, 199.243 miles
STARTERS/FINISHERS 31/18
WEATHER Cold, dry, some rain later
LAP LEADERS Stewart 1-59 (59)
WINNER'S LAPS 1-59 P1
FASTEST LAP Stewart, Tyrrell-Ford, 1m 41.644s (lap 33), 192.487kph, 119.606mph
CHAMPIONSHIP Fittipaldi 61, Stewart 45, Hulme 39, Ickx 27, Revson 23

Pos	Driver	Car	Time/gap	Grid	Stops	Tyres
1	J Stewart	Tyrrell-Ford	1h 41m 45.354s	1	0	G
2	F Cevert	Tyrrell-Ford	−32.268s	4	0	G
3	D Hulme	McLaren-Ford	−37.528s	3	0	G
4	R Peterson	March-Ford	−1m 22.516s	26	0	G
5	J Ickx	Ferrari	−1m 23.119s	12	0	F
6	M Andretti	Ferrari	−1 lap	10	0	F

1972 CHAMPIONSHIP FACTS AND FOLKLORE

- Regulation changes included a restriction to a maximum of 12 cylinders for engines and, on the safety front, minimum dry weight raised to 550kg (1,212.54lb) to accommodate heavier-gauge aluminium in monocoque construction, foam-filled fuel tanks and a mandatory six-point driver harness.
- In a 12-race calendar, the first GP took place at Nivelles, the last at Clermont-Ferrand, the championship season again split into the usual two parts, the best five results counting from each group of six.
- Having failed last season to win a GP for the first time since 1959, Lotus – now wearing the striking black and gold insignia of John Player Special – came back to the fore with Emerson Fittipaldi.
- Regalvanised around an enhanced sponsorship deal with Imperial Tobacco, and having shown well in the early-season non-championship races, together they won five races to triumph in both championships.

- In so doing, at the age of 25, Emerson assumed Jim Clark's mantle of the youngest-ever World Champion, a distinction he held for over 30 years.
- Lotus didn't achieve this monumental change in fortunes through some earth-shattering technical innovation but with the Lotus 72, now in its third year. In 'D' spec it was a very different machine from the original 1970 car, but apart from the new paint job it was little changed from last year.
- Neither could the upswing in fortunes be accounted for by a switch in tyre supplier, Lotus sticking with Firestone. Perhaps the inexplicable could be accorded to the men in the cockpits. Certainly Fittipaldi had now fully recovered from appreciable injuries endured in a road accident in June 1971, whereas 12 months further on it was his chief rival, reigning world champion Jackie Stewart, who was suffering from his own health issues, which caused him to miss the Belgian GP.

- That largely unpredictable factor, reliability, also played its part, Stewart leading more GPs and more laps than Fittipaldi during the year, yet winning one race less.
- If there was a watershed, it was the Brazilian's ultimate victory resulting from the protagonists' gladiatorial struggle around Brands Hatch. From then on Stewart was playing catch-up, and unless Emerson faltered…
- But he didn't, far from it. It was Stewart and Tyrrell that faded, and by the time they rallied it was too late.
- McLaren too were sporting a new colour scheme, having wooed Yardley from BRM, but BRM had attracted yet another new sponsor into F1, and one that would stick around for a very long time.
- The Marlboro-BRM set-up was an overly ambitious multi-car, multi-national team intended to field six entries, although it never managed more than five.
- Tribulations with the new P180s as well as the career-ending eye injury to Dr Helmut Marko at stone-strewn Clermont-Ferrand were major setbacks for the over-extended team, but there was one unexpected diamond.
- It was to prove to be the BRM marque's last hurrah, but Beltoise's victory in the pouring rain at Monaco was something to behold, a faultless drive of remarkable precision in extremely demanding conditions.
- This was one of just two non-DFV race victories, the other also a victory of brilliance by Jackie Ickx for Ferrari at the Nürburgring.

- Besides the two races they won, 12-cylinder cars only led four of the remaining ten, including a classy French GP showing by Amon for Matra, the disillusioned French team unexpectedly deciding to withdrew at season's end.
- The 12-cylinder exponents were simply outclassed by Lotus, Tyrrell and the resurgent McLaren team.
- Kyalami winner Denny Hulme wound up third in the drivers' championship, the team similarly positioned in the constructors' cup, new signing Peter Revson contributing some useful points to those of Hulme.
- March had a disastrous season, Robin Herd exploring 'low polar moment of inertia' with the errant 721X while Brabham were regrouping under new management, Ron Tauranac having sold-up to Bernie Ecclestone.
- To illustrate the difficulty of attaining success in F1, Team Surtees – John now retired as a driver to focus on team management – scored a respectable 18 points in their third season, with five points-scoring finishes. Little did they know that 1972 would be by far their most successful year – and Mike Hailwood's second place at Monza their best-ever finish – in what would be six further years of endeavour to follow.
- Undeterred by such prospects, Frank Williams became a constructor with his Politoys-Ford.
- In the final championship round future world champion Jody Scheckter made an impressive debut for McLaren.
- Emerson and Wilson Fittipaldi became the first brothers to race together in the championship.

RACE 217, Austrian GP: Fittipaldi confers with Colin Chapman prior to his fourth of five race victories which made him 1972 world champion, the youngest ever.

RACE 212, Monaco GP: The surprise victory of the 1972 season was achieved by Jean-Pierre Beltoise on a streaming wet Monte Carlo circuit. In a virtuoso performance he led every lap over a period of almost two-and-a-half hours.

Championship ranking	Championship points	Driver nationality	1972 Drivers Championship		Races contested	Race victories	Podiumse excl. victories	Races led	Flag to flag victories	Laps led	Poles	Fastest laps	Triple Crowns
			Driver	Car									
1	61	BRA	Emerson Fittipaldi	Lotus-Ford	12	5	3	6		240	3		
2	45	GBR	Jackie Stewart	Tyrrell-Ford	11	4	1	7	2	320	2	4	1
3	39	NZL	Denny Hulme	McLaren-Ford	12	1	6	2		28		1	
4	27	BEL	Jacky Ickx	Ferrari	12	1	3	3	1	104	4	3	1
5	23	USA	Peter Revson	McLaren-Ford	9		4				1		
6	15	FRA	François Cevert	Tyrrell-Ford	12		2						
7	15	SUI	Clay Regazzoni	Ferrari	10		2	2		11			
8	13	GBR	Mike Hailwood	Surtees-Ford	10		1					1	
9	12	SWE	Ronnie Peterson	March-Ford	12		1	1		3			
10	12	NZL	Chris Amon	Matra	11		1	1		19	1	2	
11	9	FRA	Jean-Pierre Beltoise	BRM	11	1		1	1	80		1	
12	4	NZL	Howden Ganley	BRM	10								
12	4	USA	Mario Andretti	Ferrari	5								
14	4	GBR	Brian Redman	McLaren-Ford (3) BRM (1)	4								
15	4	GBR	Graham Hill	Brabham-Ford	12								
16	3	ITA	Andrea de Adamich	Surtees-Ford	12								
16	3	ARG	Carlos Reutemann	Brabham-Ford	10						1		
18	3	BRA	Carlos Pace	March-Ford	11								
19	2	AUS	Tim Schenken	Surtees-Ford	12								
20	1	ITA	Arturo Merzario	Ferrari	2								
20	1	GBR	Peter Gethin	BRM	10								

Championship ranking	Championship points	Team/Marque nationality	1972 Constructors Championship		Engine maker nationality	Races contested	Race victories	1-2 finishes	Podiums excl. victories	Races led	Laps led	Poles	Fastest laps
			Chassis	Engine									
1	61	GBR	Lotus 72D	Ford Cosworth 3.0 V8	GBR	12	5		3	6	240	3	
2	51	GBR	Tyrrell 002, 003, 004, 005, 006	Ford Cosworth 3.0 V8	GBR	12	4	1	3	7	320	2	4
3	47	NZL	McLaren M19A	Ford Cosworth DFV 3.0 V8	GBR	12	1		10	2	28	1	1
4	33	ITA	Ferrari 312B2	Ferrari 3.0 F12	ITA	12	1	1	5	4	115	4	3
5	18	GBR	Surtees TS9B, TS14	Ford Cosworth 3.0 V8	GBR	12			1				1
6	15	GBR	March 721, 721X, 721G, 711	Ford Cosworth 3.0 V8	GBR	12			1	1	3		
7	14	GBR	BRM P160B, P160C, P180	BRM 3.0 V12	GBR	12	1			1	80		1
8	12	FRA	Matra MS120D, MS120C	Matra 3.0 V12	FRA	11			1	1	19	1	2
9	7	GBR	Brabham BT37, BT34, BT33	Ford Cosworth 3.0 V8	GBR	12						1	

1973

Tragedy mars Stewart's third

THE TALE OF THE TITLE

- A blighted year saw disaster befall Roger Williamson and Stewart's Tyrrell teammate François Cevert.
- In a continuation of his struggle for supremacy with Fittipaldi, five race wins gave Stewart a third title.
- The Cevert tragedy during practice for the final round brought forward Stewart's planned retirement.
- Lotus kept their constructors' title, Peterson at last catching the race-winning bug with four of their seven.
- The M23 reinstated McLaren as the third force, winning three races, Peter Revson a pair of them.
- At Silverstone, occasional McLaren driver Jody Scheckter triggered possibly the worst F1 pile-up yet seen.
- The Ford DFV made another clean sweep, BRM limited by Firestone, Ferrari in virtual disarray.
- Mike Hailwood and David Purley won George Medals, each independently displaying immense bravery.
- And not forgetting: Bernie Ecclestone forms FOCA.

THE CHASE FOR THE CHAMPIONSHIP

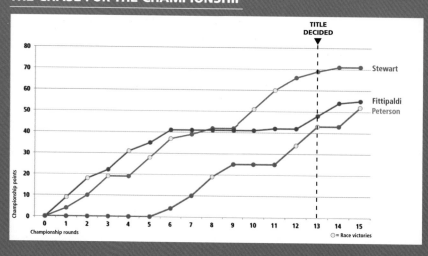

ARGENTINEAN GP Buenos Aires No 9
28 January 1973   **Race 221**

Emerson Fittipaldi
Lotus-Ford 72D 165.663kph, 102.938mph

Clay Regazzoni impressed BRM, his new team, with pole and then by leading the opening 28 laps, going away from the field. As his Firestones went off Cevert took over, having made a lighting start from row three. By lap 34 the Tyrrell twins were being followed by the JPS Lotus pair, the uniformity eventually broken when Peterson dropped out and Stewart fell back with a softening tyre. Fittipaldi was now tracking the tiring Cevert, and made his move with 11 laps remaining to win by 4.69s. The new champion had begun his defence in the best possible fashion, roared over the line by the jubilant Argentinean crowd, conveniently forgetting their rivalry with Brazil in their preference for a Latino victory.

POLE POSITION C Regazzoni, BRM, 1m 10.54s (0.30s), 170.712kph, 106.075mph
LAPS 96 x 3.345 km, 2.078 miles
DISTANCE 321.120 km, 199.535 miles
STARTERS/FINISHERS 19/10
WEATHER Sunny, hot, dry
LAP LEADERS Regazzoni 1-28 (28); Cevert 29-85 (57); Fittipaldi 86-96 (11)
WINNER'S LAPS 1-29 P3, 30-32 P4, 33-75 P3, 76-85 P2, 86-96 P1
FASTEST LAP E Fittipaldi, Lotus-Ford, 1m 11.22s (lap 79), 169.082kph, 105.063mph
CHAMPIONSHIP Fittipaldi 9, Cevert 6, Stewart 4, Ickx 3, Hulme 2

Pos	Driver	Car	Time/gap	Grid	Stops	Tyres
1	E Fittipaldi	Lotus-Ford	1h 56m 18.22s	2	0	G
2	F Cevert	Tyrrell-Ford	–4.69s	6	0	G
3	J Stewart	Tyrrell-Ford	–33.19s	4	0	G
4	J Ickx	Ferrari	–42.57s	3	0	G
5	D Hulme	McLaren-Ford	–1 lap	8	0	G
6	W Fittipaldi	Brabham-Ford	–1 lap	12	0	G

BRAZILIAN GP Interlagos
11 February 1973   **Race 222**

Emerson Fittipaldi
Lotus-Ford 72D 183.822kph, 114.222mph

At the next round things got even better for Fittipaldi, winning at Interlagos, the very first championship race to be held in his homeland. Tiresomely, although the Lotus pair dominated qualifying teammate Peterson had stolen pole. But Emerson would not be denied this one, making no mistake at the start to lead from flag-to-flag and win by almost 15s. The partisan crowd were further elated by fellow Brazilian Carlos Pace's early *banzai* laps in a Surtees, and Emerson's elder brother Wilson finishing sixth in a Brabham. Stewart again finished on the podium with second, minimising the impact of the champion's early season purple patch. Peterson failed to score, a broken wheel on lap 6.

POLE POSITION R Peterson, Lotus-Ford, 2m 30.5s (0.2s), 190.405kph, 118.312mph
LAPS 40 x 7.960 km, 4.946 miles
DISTANCE 318.400 km, 197.845 miles
STARTERS/FINISHERS 20/12
WEATHER Sunny, very hot, dry
LAP LEADERS Fittipaldi 1-40 (95)
WINNER'S LAPS 1-40 P1
FASTEST LAP Fittipaldi, Lotus-Ford/Hulme, McLaren-Ford 2m 35.0s (laps 14/20), 184.877kph, 114.878mph
CHAMPIONSHIP Fittipaldi 18, Stewart 10, Cevert 6, Hulme 6, Ickx 5

Pos	Driver	Car	Time/gap	Grid	Stops	Tyres
1	E Fittipaldi	Lotus-Ford	1h 43m 55.6s	2	0	G
2	J Stewart	Tyrrell-Ford	–13.5s	8	0	G
3	D Hulme	McLaren-Ford	–1m 46.4s	5	0	G
4	A Merzario	Ferrari	–1 lap	17	0	G
5	J Ickx	Ferrari	–1 lap	3	1	G
6	C Regazzoni	BRM	–1 lap	4	1	F

SOUTH AFRICAN GP Kyalami
3 March 1973   **Race 223**

Jackie Stewart
Tyrrell-Ford 006 188.526kph, 117.145mph

The new McLaren M23 made an auspicious debut, giving Hulme his very first pole position after 72 race starts. Following a practice accident Stewart chose to use his teammate's car, even though this left him 16th on the grid. By lap 7 he had taken the lead. In part this was explained by a hiatus on lap 3 when, in a four-car contretemps, Mike Hailwood, his own race-suit burning, bravely rescued unconscious Regazzoni from his blazing BRM. Approaching the accident scene, Stewart was later reprimanded by the stewards for overtaking Revson under yellow, who finished second. Despite this controversy, in race trim Stewart essentially had the legs of the rest. Fittipaldi finished third, Peterson failed to score, throttle linkage.

POLE POSITION Hulme, McLaren-Ford, 1m 16.28s (0.13s), 193.686kph, 120.351mph
LAPS 79 x 4.104 km, 2.550 miles
DISTANCE 324.216 km, 201.458 miles
STARTERS/FINISHERS 25/11
WEATHER Heavy cloud, dry
LAP LEADERS Hulme 1-4 (4); J Scheckter, McLaren-Ford 5-6 (2); Stewart 7-79 (73)
WINNER'S LAPS 1-2 P10, 3-4 P7, 5 P4, 6 P3, 7-79 P1
FASTEST LAP Fittipaldi, Lotus-Ford, 1m 17.10s (lap 76), 191.626kph, 119.071mph
CHAMPIONSHIP Fittipaldi 22, Stewart 19, Hulme 8, Cevert 6, Revson 6

Pos	Driver	Car	Time/gap	Grid	Stops	Tyres
1	J Stewart	Tyrrell-Ford	1h 43m 11.07s	16	0	G
2	P Revson	McLaren-Ford	–24.55s	6	0	G
3	E Fittipaldi	Lotus-Ford	–25.06s	2	0	G
4	A Merzario	Ferrari	–1 lap	15	0	G
5	D Hulme	McLaren-Ford	–2 laps	1	2	G
6	G Follmer	Shadow-Ford	–2 laps	21	0	G

Round 4/15	**SPANISH GP** Montjuïc						**Emerson Fittipaldi**

Round 4/15 — **SPANISH GP** Montjuïc
29 April 1973 — Race 224 — **Emerson Fittipaldi** Lotus-Ford 72E 157.504kph, 97.868mph

Fittipaldi struck back immediately, his third victory from four starts giving him a significant championship lead over Stewart. But for 56 laps it was Fittipaldi's teammate Peterson who led from a mighty pole, but again failed to score, gearbox this time. Stewart had also retired from a comfortable second on lap 47 with brake problems. But Fittipaldi, now leading, was in trouble himself, a rear tyre deflating, and was caught by Reutemann. But on lap 66 Reutemann too was out with driveshaft failure, and with no other immediate threat Fittipaldi skilfully nursed his car home. This victory was the 50th for Team Lotus, and remarkably exceeded the 47 race victories achieved by Ferrari, despite the Scuderia entering the championship eight years sooner.

POLE POSITION R Peterson, Lotus-Ford, 1m 21.8s (0.7s), 166.851kph, 103.670mph
LAPS 75 x 3.791 km, 2.356 miles
DISTANCE 284.325 km, 176.671 miles
STARTERS/FINISHERS 22/12
WEATHER Sunny, warm, dry
LAP LEADERS Peterson 1-56 (56); Fittipaldi 57-75 (19)
WINNER'S LAPS 1 P7, 2 P6, 3-19 P5, 20-26 P4, 27-46 P3, 47-56 P2, 57-75 P1
FASTEST LAP R Peterson, Lotus-Ford, 1m 23.8s (lap 13), 162.859kph, 101.196mph
CHAMPIONSHIP Fittipaldi 31, Stewart 19, Cevert 12, Revson 9, Hulme 9

Pos	Driver	Car	Time/gap	Grid	Stops	Tyres
1	E Fittipaldi	Lotus-Ford	1h 48m 18.7s	7	0	G
2	F Cevert	Tyrrell-Ford	−42.7s	3	1	G
3	G Follmer	Shadow-Ford	−1m 13.1s	14	0	G
4	P Revson	McLaren-Ford	−1 lap	5	0	G
5	J-P Beltoise	BRM	−1 lap	10	0	F
6	D Hulme	McLaren-Ford	−1 lap	2	2	G

Round 5/15 — **BELGIAN GP** Zolder
20 May 1973 — Race 225 — **Jackie Stewart** Tyrrell-Ford 006 173.384kph, 107.736mph

Freshly laid tarmac caused strife in practice and the race. Peterson, once again on pole, spun off on the loose surface when third. Ahead, Fittipaldi led Stewart until on lap 25 the Scot forced by and pulled away. But it was his teammate Cevert who had been the sensation, overtaking Peterson on the second lap to draw away swiftly until he spun away his lead on lap 20 with brake fade. Rejoining eighth, he still beat Fittipaldi into second place by the finish to make it the first Tyrrell 1-2 of the season. But Emerson still finished third to retain a seven-point lead in the championship table as a result of his 3-2 advantage in race victories. Niki Lauda, who last year had spent a desperate and pointless first season with March, won his first points, P5 for BRM.

POLE POSITION R Peterson, Lotus-Ford, 1m 22.46s (0.15s), 184.235kph, 114.478mph
LAPS 70 x 4.220 km, 2.622 miles
DISTANCE 295.400 km, 183.553 miles
STARTERS/FINISHERS 23/11
WEATHER Sunny, warm, dry
LAP LEADERS Peterson 1 (1); Cevert 2-19 (18); Fittipaldi 20-24 (5); Stewart 25-70 (46)
WINNER'S LAPS 1-3 P8, 4 P9, 5 P8, 6 P7, 7-8 P6, 9-13 P5, 14-18 P4, 19 P3, 20-24 P2, 25-70 P1
FASTEST LAP Cevert, Tyrrell-Ford, 1m 25.42s (lap 28), 177.851kph, 110.511mph
CHAMPIONSHIP Fittipaldi 35, Stewart 28, Cevert 18, Revson 9, Hulme 9

Pos	Driver	Car	Time/gap	Grid	Stops	Tyres
1	J Stewart	Tyrrell-Ford	1h 42m 13.43s	6	0	G
2	F Cevert	Tyrrell-Ford	−31.84s	4	0	G
3	E Fittipaldi	Lotus-Ford	−2m 2.79s	9	0	G
4	A de Adamich	Brabham-Ford	−1 lap	18	0	G
5	N Lauda	BRM	−1 lap	14	1	F
6	C Amon	Tecno	−3 laps	15	0	F

Round 6/15 — **MONACO GP** Monte Carlo
3 June 1973 — Race 226 — **Jackie Stewart** Tyrrell-Ford 006 130.298kph, 80.963mph

From row two Cevert shot into the lead, but glory lasted just one lap when he punctured a tyre on a kerb. Now Peterson led until pole-sitter Stewart took command on lap 8. By half-distance Stewart led Fittipaldi by 12s, but towards the end the world champion brought it down to just 1.3s, recording fastest lap on his final tour. But in reality Stewart had the whole thing under control, his 25th race victory equalling Clark's all-time record. With three wins apiece, only four points now separated the two rivals. The two early leaders, Cevert and Peterson, finished 3-4 a lap behind, the McLaren pair completing the top six, two laps short, these three teams nevertheless asserting their superiority over the rest.

POLE POSITION Stewart, Tyrrell-Ford, 1m 27.5s (0.2s), 134.866kph, 83.802mph
LAPS 78 x 3.278 km, 2.037 miles
DISTANCE 255.684 km, 158.875 miles
STARTERS/FINISHERS 25/11
WEATHER Sunny, warm, dry
LAP LEADERS Cevert 1 (1); Peterson 2-7 (6); Stewart 8-78 (71)
WINNER'S LAPS 1 P4, 2-5 P3, 6-7 P2, 8-78 P1
FASTEST LAP Fittipaldi, Lotus-Ford, 1m 28.1s (lap 78), 133.948kph, 83.231mph
CHAMPIONSHIP Fittipaldi 41, Stewart 37, Cevert 21, Revson 11, Hulme 10

Pos	Driver	Car	Time/gap	Grid	Stops	Tyres
1	J Stewart	Tyrrell-Ford	1h 57m 44.3s	1	0	G
2	E Fittipaldi	Lotus-Ford	−1.3s	5	0	G
3	R Peterson	Lotus-Ford	−1 lap	2	0	G
4	F Cevert	Tyrrell-Ford	−1 lap	4	1	G
5	P Revson	McLaren-Ford	−2 laps	15	0	G
6	D Hulme	McLaren-Ford	−2 laps	3	0	G

| Round 7/15 | **SWEDISH GP** Anderstorp | | | | | | **Denny Hulme** |
| | **17 June 1973** | | | **Race 227** | | | McLaren-Ford M23 165.169kph, 102.631mph |

Despite good form, Peterson had only four points from six races. Surely his very first home GP would change that? And from pole position he led every lap … except the last two. Peterson headed an exciting five-car train of two Lotuses, two Tyrrells and Hulme in fifth. Shortly after quarter-distance, running about 4s behind the leaders, a cloud of sand was thrown up by a backmarker, jamming Hulme's throttle slides. He managed to sort it out without stopping but had lost 15s. The Bear put his head down, and as those ahead struck trouble he caught and passed Cevert on lap 61, Stewart lap 70 and Fittipaldi for second on lap 76 to challenge Peterson for the lead, which became victory when the Swede slowed with a deflating rear tyre.

POLE POSITION Peterson, Lotus-Ford, 1m 23.810s (0.089s), 172.590kph, 107.243mph
LAPS 80 x 4.018 km, 2.497 miles
DISTANCE 321.440 km, 199.734 miles
STARTERS/FINISHERS 20/14
WEATHER Sunny, warm, dry
LAP LEADERS Peterson 1-78 (78); Hulme 79-80 (2)
WINNER'S LAPS 1-2 P6, 3-59 P5, 60-69 P4, 70-75 P3, 76-78 P2, 79-80 P1
FASTEST LAP Hulme, McLaren-Ford, 1m 26.146s (lap 7), 167.910kph, 104.335mph
CHAMPIONSHIP Fittipaldi 41, Stewart 39, Cevert 25, Hulme 19, Revson 11

Pos	Driver	Car	Time/gap	Grid	Stops	Tyres
1	D Hulme	McLaren-Ford	1h 56m 46.049s	6	0	G
2	R Peterson	Lotus-Ford	−4.039s	1	0	G
3	F Cevert	Tyrrell-Ford	−14.667s	2	0	G
4	C Reutemann	Brabham-Ford	−18.068s	5	0	G
5	J Stewart	Tyrrell-Ford	−25.992s	3	0	G
6	J Ickx	Ferrari	−1 lap	8	0	G

Lotus-Ford 72E

| Round 8/15 | **FRENCH GP** Paul Ricard | | | | | | **Ronnie Peterson** |
| | **1 July 1973** | | | **Race 228** | | | Lotus-Ford 72E 185.268kph, 115.118mph |

Subbing for Revson, Jody Scheckter's third-ever GP start was made from P2 on the grid between reigning champion Fittipaldi and double-champion Stewart on pole. The 23-year-old South African then proceeded not only to lead the first lap but the next 40, his M23 McLaren very quick down the Mistral straight. Led by the Lotus pair, a four-car train followed until Hulme and Stewart dropped back with chunking tyres. Unfortunately, it all ended badly on the 42nd lap when Fittipaldi attempted to pass Scheckter when they were lapping a backmarker – the Lotus rammed the McLaren, eliminating both cars with suspension damage. At his 40th attempt Peterson was a GP winner at last.

POLE POSITION Stewart, Tyrrell-Ford, 1m 48.37s (0.81s), 193.005kph,119.928mph
LAPS 54 x 5.810 km, 3.610 miles
DISTANCE 313.740 km, 194.949 miles
STARTERS/FINISHERS 25/16
WEATHER Sunny, very hot, dry
LAP LEADERS J Scheckter, McLaren-Ford 1-41 (41); Peterson 42-54 (13)
WINNER'S LAPS 1-20 P2, 21-41 P3, 42-54 P1
FASTEST LAP D Hulme, McLaren-Ford, 1m 50.99s (lap 52), 188.449kph, 117.097mph
CHAMPIONSHIP Stewart 42, Fittipaldi 41, Cevert 31, Peterson 19, Hulme 19

Pos	Driver	Car	Time/gap	Grid	Stops	Tyres
1	R Peterson	Lotus-Ford	1h 41m 36.52	5	0	G
2	F Cevert	Tyrrell-Ford	−40.92s	4	0	G
3	C Reutemann	Brabham-Ford	−46.48s	8	0	G
4	J Stewart	Tyrrell-Ford	−46.93s	1	1	G
5	J Ickx	Ferrari	−48.90s	12	0	G
6	J Hunt	March-Ford	−1m 22.54s	14	0	F

McLaren-Ford M23

BRITISH GP Silverstone

14 July 1973   Race 229

Peter Revson

McLaren-Ford M23 212.034kph, 131.752mph

Scheckter's short GP career created yet more sensation. From his third-row grid spot he was up to fourth at the end of lap 1 when he lost control at Woodcote, spun, then cannoned off the pit wall to end up in the midst of the oncoming pack. There was carnage, nine cars failing to make the restart, but mercifully only one minor driver injury. In the restarted race, as he was making to pass Peterson for the lead on lap 6 a gearbox glitch pitched Stewart into his celebrated cornfield excursion at Stowe. For half the race the McLaren pair stalked the Lotus twins until Fittipaldi went out and then a light shower helped Revson overtake Peterson on lap 39. The American held on to take his first GP victory by 2.8s, Hunt finishing a close fourth.

POLE POSITION R Peterson, Lotus-Ford, 1m 16.3s (0.2s), 222.254kph, 138.102mph
LAPS 67 x 4.711 km, 2.927 miles (Restarted over original distance following accident)
DISTANCE 315.607 km, 196.109 miles
STARTERS/FINISHERS 28/13
WEATHER Overcast, mainly dry
LAP LEADERS Peterson 1-38 (38); Revson 39-67 (29)
WINNER'S LAPS 1-6 P6, 7 P4, 8-36 P3, 37-38 P2, 39-67 P1
FASTEST LAP Hunt, March-Ford, 1m 18.6s (lap 63), 215.750kph, 134.061mph
CHAMPIONSHIP Stewart 42, Fittipaldi 41, Cevert 33, Peterson 25, Hulme 23

Pos	Driver	Car	Time/gap	Grid	Stops	Tyres
1	P Revson	McLaren-Ford	1h 29m 18.5s	3	0	G
2	R Peterson	Lotus-Ford	−2.8s	1	0	G
3	D Hulme	McLaren-Ford	−3.0s	2	0	G
4	J Hunt	March-Ford	−3.4s	11	0	F
5	F Cevert	Tyrrell-Ford	−36.6s	7	0	G
6	C Reutemann	Brabham-Ford	−44.7s	8	0	G

Tyrrell-Ford 006

DUTCH GP Zandvoort

29 July 1973   Race 230

Jackie Stewart

Tyrrell-Ford 006 184.022kph, 114.346mph

Peterson on pole, the Tyrrells completing the front row, these three running 1-2-3 in a processional race. At one time Peterson was 14s ahead, but mechanical maladies with only nine laps remaining enabled Stewart to win from teammate Cevert. It was Stewart's fourth of the season and 26th all-time victory, exceeding Clark's career record. Fittipaldi gave up after two laps in discomfort, having hurt his ankles in a massive practice accident caused by a wheel breakage. Suddenly Stewart had a ten-point margin over the Brazilian. When Roger Williamson's March 731 left the track on lap 8, overturned and caught fire, David Purley's heroic rescue bid could not save him. The fire took several laps to control, the race continuing.

POLE POSITION R Peterson, Lotus-Ford, 1m 19.47s (0.50s), 191.438kph, 118.954mph
LAPS 72 x 4.226 km, 2.626 miles
DISTANCE 304.272 km, 189.066 miles
STARTERS/FINISHERS 23/11
WEATHER Overcast, dry
LAP LEADERS Peterson 1-63 (63); Stewart 64-72 (9)
WINNER'S LAPS 1-63 P2, 64-72 P1
FASTEST LAP R Peterson, Lotus-Ford, 1m 20.31s (lap 42), 189.436kph, 117.710mph
CHAMPIONSHIP Stewart 51, Fittipaldi 41, Cevert 39, Peterson 25, Revson 23

Pos	Driver	Car	Time/gap	Grid	Stops	Tyres
1	J Stewart	Tyrrell-Ford	1h 39m 12.45s	2	0	G
2	F Cevert	Tyrrell-Ford	−15.83s	3	0	G
3	J Hunt	March-Ford	−1m 3.01s	7	0	F
4	P Revson	McLaren-Ford	−1m 9.13s	6	0	G
5	J-P Beltoise	BRM	−1m 13.37s	9	0	F
6	G van Lennep	Iso Marlboro-Ford	−2 laps	20	0	F

GERMAN GP Nürburgring

5 August 1973   Race 231

Jackie Stewart

Tyrrell-Ford 006 187.961kph, 116.793mph

Stewart's third victory around the swoops and plunges of the fearsome Eifel circuit equalled Fangio's great feat. Right from the off the Tyrrells pulled away, spending much of the race in team formation to finish just 1.6s apart for a second successive 1-2. The absent Ferrari team released Nürburgring aficionado Ickx to McLaren. The Belgian qualified fourth, eclipsing the two regular drivers, and raced to third place behind the Tyrrell twins, albeit 40s in arrears. Peterson went out from third place on the very first lap with ignition trouble while Fittipaldi scored a point, less troubled by his ankles than expected. But in the championship battle, Stewart now held a significant lead and Fittipaldi had lost runner-up spot to Cevert.

POLE POSITION Stewart, Tyrrell-Ford, 7m 07.8s (0.5s), 192.160kph, 119.403mph
LAPS 14 x 22.835 km, 14.189 miles
DISTANCE 319.960 km, 198.646 miles
STARTERS/FINISHERS 22/16
WEATHER Sunny, warm, dry
LAP LEADERS Stewart 1-14 (14)
WINNER'S LAPS 1-14 P1
FASTEST LAP Pace, Surtees-Ford, 7m 11.4s (lap 13), 190.556kph, 118.406mph
CHAMPIONSHIP Stewart 60, Cevert 45, Fittipaldi 42, Peterson 25, Revson 23

Pos	Driver	Car	Time/gap	Grid	Stops	Tyres
1	J Stewart	Tyrrell-Ford	1h 42m 3.0s	1	0	G
2	F Cevert	Tyrrell-Ford	−1.6s	3	0	G
3	J Ickx	McLaren-Ford	−41.2s	4	0	G
4	C Pace	Surtees-Ford	−53.8s	11	0	F
5	W Fittipaldi	Brabham-Ford	−1m 19.9s	13	0	G
6	E Fittipaldi	Lotus-Ford	−1m 24.3s	14	0	G

AUSTRIAN GP Österreichring

19 August 1973   Race 232

Ronnie Peterson

Lotus-Ford 72E 215.640kph, 133.993mph

A pair of Lotuses followed by a pair of McLarens led the grid, Fittipaldi on pole, the Tyrrells strangely out of it. One McLaren went out at the start with clutch trouble but the other, Hulme's, chased Peterson for 11 laps until having to pit to reconnect a plug lead. With the McLaren threat gone, Peterson dutifully waved Fittipaldi through on lap 16 to keep his championship chances alive. But on lap 49, five from the end, Peterson came through alone, Fittipaldi stranded out on the circuit with a broken fuel line. From his fourth-row grid placing Stewart made his way through to finish second, and now needed just four points from three races to regain the title. Pace finished an excellent third for Team Surtees, at one point pressurising Stewart.

POLE POSITION E Fittipaldi, Lotus-Ford, 1m 34.98s (0.39s), 224.043kph, 139.214mph
LAPS 54 x 5.911 km, 3.673 miles
DISTANCE 319.194 km, 198.338 miles
STARTERS/FINISHERS 23/10
WEATHER Sunny, very hot, dry
LAP LEADERS Peterson 1-16, 49-54 (22); E Fittipaldi, Lotus-Ford 17-48 (32)
WINNER'S LAPS 1-16 P1, 17-48 P2, 49-54 P1
FASTEST LAP Pace, Surtees-Ford, 1m 37.29s (lap 46), 218.723kph, 135.908mph
CHAMPIONSHIP Stewart 66, Cevert 45, Fittipaldi 42, Peterson 34, Revson 23

Pos	Driver	Car	Time/gap	Grid	Stops	Tyres
1	R Peterson	Lotus-Ford	1h 28m 48.78s	2	0	G
2	J Stewart	Tyrrell-Ford	−9.01s	7	0	G
3	C Pace	Surtees-Ford	−46.64s	8	0	F
4	C Reutemann	Brabham-Ford	−47.91s	5	0	G
5	J-P Beltoise	BRM	−1m 21.60s	13	0	F
6	C Regazzoni	BRM	−1m 38.40s	14	0	F

Round 13/15	**ITALIAN GP** Monza	**Ronnie Peterson**
	9 September 1973 Race 233	Lotus-Ford 72E 213.450kph, 132.631mph

Stewart regained the title from Fittipaldi at Monza despite the Lotus pair dominating the race, rarely more than a few car lengths apart. A puncture on lap 8 dropped Stewart down from fourth to twentieth, from where he made a thrilling climb back through the field, passing car after car, to regain his fourth position and the points he needed to clinch the title in style. Stewart's three points meant that for Peterson, who had led all the way from pole, there was nothing to be gained by letting Fittipaldi through to retain an infinitesimal mathematical chance of the title, and therefore he took the flag just 0.8s ahead for the first Team Lotus 1-2 in six years.

POLE POSITION Peterson, Lotus-Ford, 1m 34.80s (0.49s), 219.304kph, 136.269mph
LAPS 55 x 5.775 km, 3.588 miles
DISTANCE 317.625 km, 197.363 miles
STARTERS/FINISHERS 24/15
WEATHER Sunny, hot, dry
LAP LEADERS Peterson 1-55 (55)
WINNER'S LAPS 1-55 P1
FASTEST LAP Stewart, Tyrrell-Ford, 1m 35.30s (lap 51), 218.153kph, 135.554mph
CHAMPIONSHIP Stewart 69, Fittipaldi 48, Cevert 47, Peterson 43, Revson 27

Pos	Driver	Car	Time/gap	Grid	Stops	Tyres
1	R Peterson	Lotus-Ford	1h 29m 17.0s	1	0	G
2	E Fittipaldi	Lotus-Ford	−0.8s	4	0	G
3	P Revson	McLaren-Ford	−28.8s	2	0	G
4	J Stewart	Tyrrell-Ford	−33.2s	6	1	G
5	F Cevert	Tyrrell-Ford	−46.2s	11	0	G
6	C Reutemann	Brabham-Ford	−59.8s	10	0	G

Round 14/15	**CANADIAN GP** Mosport Park	**Peter Revson**
	23 September 1973 Race 234	McLaren-Ford M23 159.534kph, 99.130mph

Revson's second victory was a bewildering race with seven leaders. Uncertainty arose from a combination of wet weather, pit stops to change from wets and the intervention of the very first Safety Car, which picked up the wrong 'leader'. On a wet surface, Peterson led from pole until Lauda's BRM on Firestone wets shot by, only to lose a big lead to Fittipaldi by pitting for inters. On lap 33 Scheckter and Cevert collided, triggering the SC, which assisted some drivers to gain a lap whereby it was subsequently discovered that an incredibly close and exciting finish between Fittipaldi, Oliver and Beltoise was not for victory … but for P2. Revson had passed Oliver when the Shadow slowed with throttle trouble, confirmed as winner after three hours of confusion.

POLE POSITION R Peterson, Lotus-Ford, 1m 13.697s (1.040s), 193.313kph, 120.119mph
LAPS 80 x 3.957 km, 2.459 miles
DISTANCE 316.590 km, 196.720 miles
STARTERS/FINISHERS 26/18
WEATHER Wet start, drying later
LAP LEADERS R Peterson, Lotus-Ford 1-2 (2); N Lauda, BRM 3-19 (17); Fittipaldi 20-32 (13); Stewart 33 (1); Beltoise 34-39 (6); Oliver 40-46 (7); Revson 47-80 (34); SC 34-42 (9)
WINNER'S LAPS 1-2 P7, 3-4 P8, 5 P9, 6 P10, 7 P11, 8-9 P13, 10-16 P14, 17-18 P12, 19 P10, 20-23 P9, 24 P13, 25-28 P12, 29-30 P10, 31-32 P9, 33-34 P4, 35-39 P3, 40-46 P2, 47-80 P1
FASTEST LAP Fittipaldi, Lotus-Ford, 1m 15.496s (lap NA), 188.706kph, 117.257mph
CHAMPIONSHIP Stewart 71, Fittipaldi 54, Cevert 47, Peterson 43, Revson 36

Pos	Driver	Car	Time/gap	Grid	Stops	Tyres
1	P Revson	McLaren-Ford	1h 59m 4.083s	2	1	G
2	E Fittipaldi	Lotus-Ford	−32.734s	5	1	G
3	J Oliver	Shadow-Ford	−34.505s	14	1	G
4	J-P Beltoise	BRM	−36.514s	16	1	F
5	J Stewart	Tyrrell-Ford	1 lap	9	2	G
6	H Ganley	Iso Marlboro-Ford	1 lap	22	1	F

Round 15/15	**UNITED STATES GP** Watkins Glen	**Ronnie Peterson**
	7 October 1973 Race 235	Lotus-Ford 72E 189.991kph, 118.055mph

When teammate Françoise Cevert was killed in practice, Jackie Stewart, as a mark of respect, retired from Formula 1 immediately rather than take his final and 100th GP start. From his ninth pole of the season, Peterson led all the way and, after Team Tyrrell's withdrawal, Lotus retained their constructors' crown. However, the race was better than the bald facts portray. Hunt's Hesketh March, qualifying P4, took Reutemann for second on lap 4 and thereafter chased Peterson mercilessly – at one point getting alongside – and scarcely ever more than a second behind and less than one second at the finish after 101 minutes of flat-out racing. Hunt's performance also demonstrated that Firestone had at last regained parity with Goodyear.

POLE POSITION Peterson, Lotus-Ford, 1m 39.657s (0.356s), 196.325kph, 121.990mph
LAPS 59 x 5.435 km, 3.377 miles
DISTANCE 320.651 km, 199.243 miles
STARTERS/FINISHERS 25/16
WEATHER Cold, dry
LAP LEADERS Peterson 1-59 (59)
WINNER'S LAPS 1-59 P1
FASTEST LAP Hunt, March-Ford, 1m 41.652s (lap 58), 192.472kph, 119.590mph
CHAMPIONSHIP Stewart 71, Fittipaldi 55, Peterson 52, Cevert 47, Revson 38

Pos	Driver	Car	Time/gap	Grid	Stops	Tyres
1	R Peterson	Lotus-Ford	1h 41m 15.779s	1	0	G
2	J Hunt	March-Ford	−0.668s	4	0	F
3	C Reutemann	Brabham-Ford	−22.930s	2	0	G
4	D Hulme	McLaren-Ford	−50.226s	8	0	G
5	P Revson	McLaren-Ford	−1m 20.367s	7	0	G
6	E Fittipaldi	Lotus-Ford	−1m 47.945s	3	1	G

■ Fire risk continued to preoccupy the minds of the rule makers. To accommodate compulsory fuel tank protection cladding along the flanks of each chassis known as 'deformable structures', minimum dry weight for F1 cars was increased to 575kg (1,267.66lb). Introduced from the Spanish GP, deformable structures were rigid foam-filled fibreglass side-pods containing no fuel, fuel lines or electric power.

■ F1 fuel tankage was also restricted to a maximum of 250 litres (55 gallons), and a piped air delivery system to drivers' helmets introduced.

■ The Safety Car (née Pace Car) concept was also initiated and first deployed at the Canadian GP, and from the German GP two-by-two grids were adopted.

■ Led by Brabham team-owner Bernie Ecclestone, the Formula 1 Constructors' Association (FOCA) was formed and immediately became entangled in a pre-season clash with the circuit owners … over money.

■ From the Belgian GP teams would retain the same car numbers throughout the season, the reigning world champion being No1.

■ 1973 was the first 15-round championship, the success of Fittipaldi and of Peterson the factor in the addition of Brazil and Sweden to the GP calendar.

■ Races would now be 200 miles (321.87km) or two hours, whichever was shorter, the championship season divided as usual, the best seven results from the first eight races, and the best six from the last seven counting for points.

■ In a season interspersed with tragedy, the ferocious battle between Tyrrell and JPS Lotus and their lead drivers Jackie Stewart and Emerson Fittipaldi continued unabated for a second year.

■ In the drivers' championship the pendulum swung back towards Stewart, claiming the title for the third and final time with five race victories to Fittipaldi's three.

■ This drew to a conclusion the comparatively short yet illustrious nine-year F1 career of John Young Stewart which, along with his three drivers' titles, additionally established a new benchmark for race victories, Stewart's final GP victory at the Nürburgring leaving his tally at 27, surpassing Jim Clark's 25 and the 24 of Juan Manuel Fangio.

■ Stewart's decision to retire also concluded one of the great Formula 1 team owner/driver relationships but, wretchedly, in the most shocking of circumstances. Charismatic Frenchman Françoise Cevert had been groomed by Tyrrell and Stewart to lead the team into 1974 following Stewart's planned departure, so his tragic loss when practising for the final race of the season was agonising in so many ways.

■ Stewart naturally chose not to participate in his final race, which was to have been his 100th championship start, and instead had to walk away from F1 on such a low note.

■ For Tyrrell, the withdrawal of his cars effectively handed the constructors' championship to rivals JPS Lotus.

■ Fittipaldi's Spanish win had been the 50th championship victory for Lotus and significantly one more than Ferrari, despite Team Lotus giving the Scuderia an eight-year start.

■ In its forth season, the Lotus 72, now in 'E' configuration, continued to be a potent weapon in the hands of Fittipaldi and also, after a slow start, new Chapman signing Ronnie Peterson.

■ As the season wore on, 'Superswede' steadily outshone the reigning world champion as the stats illustrate so well, Peterson first: qualifying 11:4; poles 9:1; races led 11:6; laps led 393:120, and finally race wins 4:3.

■ After a blazing start winning three of the first four rounds,

Emerson didn't win again, whereas, with spooky palindromic symmetry, Ronnie won three of the last four rounds.

■ Most telling was Peterson's Monza victory, when by not waving his teammate through he snuffed out any lingering chance Fittipaldi had of retaining his title, minuscule as it was.

■ Peterson was now Chapman's leading man and it was no surprise when Fittipaldi joined McLaren for the following season.

■ Since their founder's death the McLaren team had been led by trusted lieutenants Teddy Mayer and Tyler Alexander, both Americans. With their latest M23 chassis McLaren continued onwards and upwards in 1973, and three race victories made them decidedly a third force alongside JPS Lotus and Tyrrell.

■ Revson twice and Hulme delivered the victories, while occasional third driver Scheckter supplied the havoc – positive havoc within the F1 establishment by virtue of some stunning performances, and negative havoc at Silverstone with his infamous first-lap faux pas.

■ For a second season the Ford-Cosworth DFV made a clean sweep of the 15 championship rounds – Lotus seven,

RACE 231, German GP: Stewart's third Nürburgring victory equalled Fangio's great feat, the Tyrrell pair pulling away to finish just 1.6s apart for a second successive 1-2.

Tyrrell five, McLaren three – leaving just crumbs for Ferrari and BRM, neither team even reaching the top step of the podium.
- As the disillusioned Ickx drifted away from the Scuderia, a singleton entry for Arturo Merzario in the latter part of the season evidenced the depths to which the Ferrari decline had plumbed.
- Coincidentally, and highly significantly as it was to prove, Niki Lauda was building a reputation with some dynamic drives for BRM which were enough to catch the eye of the *Commendatore*.
- A notable newcomer was Shadow, another US-inspired F1 entry led by Don Nichols and sponsored by UOP, Universal

Oil Products. In Spain, Graham Hill became a F1 driver/entrant with a white and red Shadow DN1 for his newly formed 'Embassy Racing with Graham Hill'.
- And finally, exemplifying the agony and the ecstasy of Grand Prix racing, two British drivers made their debut in 1973, each driving a March.
- Roger Williamson was to lose his life in only his second GP, at Zandvoort.
- In his second GP, James Hunt scored a championship point driving the Hesketh March and went on to finish with a glorious second place in the final race of the season. This was the very same race at which François Cevert died and Jackie Stewart retired as three-time world champion.

Championship ranking	Championship points	Driver nationality	1973 Drivers Championship		Races contested	Race victories	Podiumse excl. victories	Race led	Flag to flag victories	Laps led	Poles	Fastest laps	Triple Crowns
			Driver	Car									
1	71	GBR	Jackie Stewart	Tyrrell-Ford	14	5	3	6	1	214	3	1	
2	55	BRA	Emerson Fittipaldi	Lotus-Ford	15	3	5	6	1	120	1	5	
3	52	SWE	Ronnie Peterson	Lotus-Ford	15	4	3	11	2	393	9	2	
4	47	FRA	François Cevert	Tyrrell-Ford	14		7	3		76		1	
5	38	USA	Peter Revson	McLaren-Ford	14	2	2	2		63			
6	26	NZL	Denny Hulme	McLaren-Ford	15	1	2	2		6	1	3	
7	16	ARG	Carlos Reutemann	Brabham-Ford	15		2						
8	14	GBR	James Hunt	March-Ford	7		2					2	
9	12	BEL	Jacky Ickx	Ferrari (10) McLaren-Ford (1) Iso Marlboro-Ford (1)	12		1						
10	9	FRA	Jean-Pierre Beltoise	BRM	15			1		6			
11	7	BRA	Carlos Pace	Surtees-Ford	15		1					2	
12	6	ITA	Arturo Merzario	Ferrari	9								
13	5	USA	George Follmer	Shadow-Ford	12		1						
14	4	GBR	Jackie Oliver	Shadow-Ford	13		1	1		7			
15	3	ITA	Andrea de Adamich	Surtees-Ford (1) Brabham-Ford (5)	6								
16	3	BRA	Wilson Fittipaldi	Brabham-Ford	15								
17	2	AUT	Niki Lauda	BRM	14			1		17			
18	2	SUI	Clay Regazzoni	BRM	14			1		28	1		
19	1	NZL	Chris Amon	Tecno (4) Tyrrell-Ford (1)	5								
19	1	NDL	Gijs van Lennep	Iso Marlboro-Ford	3								
19	1	NZL	Howden Ganley	Iso Marlboro-Ford	14								
-	0	RSA	Jody Scheckter	McLaren-Ford	5			2		43			

Championship ranking	Championship points	Team/Marque nationality	1973 Constructors Championship		Engine maker nationality	Races contested	Race victories	1-2 finishes	Podiums excl. victories	Races led	Laps led	Poles	Fastest laps
			Chassis	Engine									
1	92	GBR	Lotus 72D, 72E	Ford Cosworth 3.0 V8	GBR	15	7	1	8	13	513	10	7
2	82	GBR	Tyrrell 005, 006	Ford Cosworth 3.0 V8	GBR	14	5	3	10	7	290	3	2
3	58	NZL	McLaren M23, M19C	Ford Cosworth 3.0 V8	GBR	15	3		5	5	112	1	3
4	22	GBR	Brabham BT42, BT37	Ford Cosworth 3.0 V8	GBR	15			2				
5	14	GBR	March 731, 721G	Ford Cosworth 3.0 V8	GBR	15			2				2
6	12	ITA	Ferrari 312B3, 312B2	Ferrari 3.0 F12	ITA	13							
7	12	GBR	BRM P160E, P160D	BRM 3.0 V12	GBR	15				2	51	1	
8	9	USA	Shadow-Ford DN1	Ford Cosworth 3.0 V8	GBR	13			2	1	7		
9	7	GBR	Surtees TS14A	Ford Cosworth 3.0 V8	GBR	15			1				2
10	2	GBR	Iso-Marlboro IR, FX3B	Ford Cosworth 3.0 V8	GBR	14							
11	1	ITA	Tecno PA123	Tecno 3.0 F12	ITA	4							

1974

Emerson's second, McLaren's first

THE TALE OF THE TITLE

- A close-fought championship produced seven race-winners from five teams.
- Consistent and reliable, Emerson Fittipaldi won his second championship, this time with McLaren.
- With four race wins McLaren took their first constructors' title, achieved having led a mere 79 racing laps.
- Luca di Montezemolo inspired a Ferrari renaissance which was only to prove that speed isn't everything.
- Ferrari's Niki Lauda emerged as the man to beat, nine poles deserving far more than two race victories.
- The resurgence of Brabham under Bernie Ecclestone also proved that speed is only part of winning.
- With three victories Reutemann came good for Brabham, Scheckter's pair keeping Tyrell in the frame.
- The new Lotus 76 failed but Ronnie Peterson won three times with the ageing 72, now in its fifth season.
- Kit cars multiplied, 34 cars from 17 teams entering for 25 available grid slots at the British GP.
- The F1 death toll rose, Peter Revson and Helmuth Koinigg the latest casualties.
- And not forgetting: tyre problems proliferate; 1967 champion Denny Hulme retires.

THE CHASE FOR THE CHAMPIONSHIP

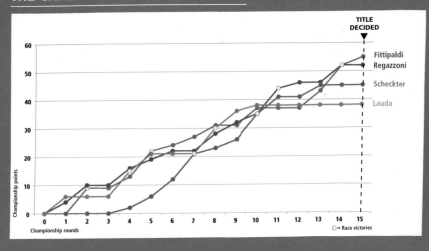

ARGENTINEAN GP Buenos Aires No 15

13 January 1974 — **Race 236**

Denny Hulme
McLaren-Ford M23 187.841kph, 116.719mph

On the opening lap, it was Peterson from pole leading Reutemann. But the Lotus was not on full-song, and to a deafening roar 'Lole' took the lead on lap 3 and pulled away remorselessly thereafter. It was a wondrous site, the first time a Brabham had led a race since 1970. At two-thirds-distance a loose airbox scoop affected performance and Reutemann's half-minute lead over Hulme began to shrink. But it wasn't until six to go that true disaster struck, a loose ignition wire putting the Brabham on to seven cylinders, and less than two laps from winning his home GP Carlos, placed P7, was powerless to prevent Hulme going by followed by the promising new Ferrari pairing, Lauda and Regazzoni.

POLE POSITION R Peterson, Lotus-Ford, 1m 50.78s (0.30s), 193.941kph, 120.509mph
LAPS 53 x 5.968 km, 3.708 miles
DISTANCE 316.304 km, 196.542 miles
STARTERS/FINISHERS 25/13
WEATHER Sunny, hot, dry
LAP LEADERS Peterson 1-2 (2); C Reutemann, Brabham-Ford 3-51 (49); Hulme 52-53 (2)
WINNER'S LAPS 1-3 P6, 4-6 P4, 7-9 P3, 10-51 P2, 52-53 P1
FASTEST LAP Regazzoni, Ferrari, 1m 52.10s (lap 38), 191.657kph, 119.090mph
CHAMPIONSHIP Hulme 9, Lauda 6, Regazzoni 4, Hailwood 3, Beltoise 2

Pos	Driver	Car	Time/gap	Grid	Stops	Tyres
1	D Hulme	McLaren-Ford	1h 41m 2.01s	10	0	G
2	N Lauda	Ferrari	−9.27s	8	0	G
3	C Regazzoni	Ferrari	−20.41s	2	0	G
4	M Hailwood	McLaren-Ford	−31.79s	9	0	G
5	J-P Beltoise	BRM	−51.84s	14	0	F
6	P Depailler	Tyrrell-Ford	−1m 52.48s	15	0	G

Round 2/15 — BRAZILIAN GP Interlagos

27 January 1974 — **Race 237**

Emerson Fittipaldi
McLaren-Ford M23 180.615kph, 112.229mph

McLaren won again, new signing Emerson Fittipaldi doing what Reutemann so nearly achieved two weeks earlier. It was Fittipaldi's second successive home victory and this time he did it from pole and saw off ex-teammate Peterson in the process. The early race was a series of nose-to-tail dices, the leading one between Reutemann, Peterson and Fittipaldi, not lasting long before the Brabham's front tyres went off. From there it was a Ronnie versus Emo needle match, the JPS leading until the McLaren got ahead on lap 16 when lapping a backmarker. Four laps later the JPS was delayed by a deflating tyre and finally a sudden downpour caused the race to be stopped early. Regazzoni's second place reaffirmed the Ferrari revival.

POLE POSITION Fittipaldi, McLaren-Ford, 2m 32.97s (0.24s), 187.331kph, 116.402mph
LAPS 32 x 7.960 km, 4.946 miles (Scheduled for 40 laps but stopped due to rain)
DISTANCE 254.720 km, 158.276 miles
STARTERS/FINISHERS 25/17
WEATHER Cloudy, hot, showers, heavy later
LAP LEADERS C Reutemann, Brabham-Ford 1-3 (3); R Peterson, Lotus-Ford 4-15 (12); Fittipaldi 16-32 (17)
WINNER'S LAPS 1-3 P3, 4-15 P2, 16-32 P1
FASTEST LAP Regazzoni, Ferrari, 2m 36.05s (lap 26), 183.633kph, 114.105mph
CHAMPIONSHIP Regazzoni 10, Hulme 9, Fittipaldi 9, Lauda 6, Hailwood 5

Pos	Driver	Car	Time/gap	Grid	Stops	Tyres
1	E Fittipaldi	McLaren-Ford	1h 24m 37.06s	1	0	G
2	C Regazzoni	Ferrari	−13.57s	8	0	G
3	J Ickx	Lotus-Ford	−1 lap	5	0	G
4	C Pace	Surtees-Ford	−1 lap	12	0	F
5	M Hailwood	McLaren-Ford	−1 lap	7	0	G
6	R Peterson	Lotus-Ford	−1 lap	4	2	G

Round 3/15 — SOUTH AFRICAN GP Kyalami

30 March 1974 — **Race 238**

Carlos Reutemann
Brabham-Ford BT44 187.049kph, 116.227mph

An unusual grid, the first 14 within 1s, Pace's Surtees P2 and Merzario's Iso Marlboro P3. But from his maiden pole Lauda led until Reutemann came by on lap 9. This time Carlos delivered the first Brabham victory since Jack's own Kyalami triumph in 1970, and the first under Bernie Ecclestone. Lauda clung on to the leader but Ferrari reliability did not match their speed, he and Regazzoni both losing certain podium finishes late on with engine-related issues. The drive of the race came from Beltoise in the new BRM P201 on Firestones, finishing second from his P11 grid slot, Hailwood's Yardley McLaren completing the podium. Sadly, Peter Revson, now leading the Shadow team, had been killed in pre-race testing at the circuit.

POLE POSITION N Lauda, Ferrari, 1m 16.58s (0.05s), 192.928kph, 119.880mph
LAPS 78 x 4.104 km, 2.550 miles
DISTANCE 320.112 km, 198.908 miles
STARTERS/FINISHERS 27/19
WEATHER Sunny, warm, dry
LAP LEADERS Lauda 1-8 (8); Reutemann 9-78 (70)
WINNER'S LAPS 1-8 P2, 9-78 P1
FASTEST LAP Reutemann, Brabham-Ford, 1m 18.16s (lap 58), 189.028kph, 117.456mph
CHAMPIONSHIP Regazzoni 10, Hulme 9, Fittipaldi 9, Reutemann 9, Hailwood 9

Pos	Driver	Car	Time/gap	Grid	Stops	Tyres
1	C Reutemann	Brabham-Ford	1h 42m 40.96s	4	0	G
2	J-P Beltoise	BRM	−33.94s	11	0	F
3	M Hailwood	McLaren-Ford	−42.16s	12	0	G
4	P Depailler	Tyrrell-Ford	−44.19s	15	0	G
5	H-J Stuck	March-Ford	−46.23s	7	0	G
6	A Merzario	Iso Marlboro-Ford	−56.04s	3	0	F

Ferrari 312 B3

Round 4/15	**SPANISH GP** Jarama				
	28 April 1974			**Race 239**	

Niki Lauda

Ferrari 312B3 142.383kph, 88.473mph

Niki Lauda on pole again but, in wet conditions, Peterson got ahead off the line to lead the two Ferraris and teammate Ickx. The two red and two black cars maintained station, pulling away from the rest until, as the track dried, tyre-stops became necessary around lap 20. Whereas the Ferrari stops were proficient, those by Lotus were shambolic, but in any case the two new Lotus 76 cars were out with mechanical defects well before lap 30. It was Lauda's maiden GP victory and the first for Ferrari in two seasons, Regazzoni completing the triumph with a 1-2 finish. The rain produced a slow race speed, ending at the two-hour cut-off point with six laps to go, by which time Lauda had lapped all but his teammate, Fittipaldi a lapped third.

POLE POSITION Lauda, Ferrari, 1m 18.44s (0.03s), 156.226kph, 97.075mph
LAPS 84 x 3.404 km, 2.115 miles (Scheduled for 90 laps but stopped after two hours)
DISTANCE 285.936 km, 177.672 miles
STARTERS/FINISHERS 25/14
WEATHER Overcast, wet start, drying later
LAP LEADERS R Peterson, Lotus-Ford 1-20 (20); Lauda 21-22, 25-84 (62); J Ickx, Lotus-Ford 23-24 (2)
WINNER'S LAPS 1-20 P2, 21-22 P1, 23-24 P2, 25-84 P1
FASTEST LAP Lauda, Ferrari, 1m 20.83s (lap 47), 151.607kph, 94.204mph
CHAMPIONSHIP Regazzoni 16, Lauda 15, Fittipaldi 13, Hulme 10, Reutemann 9

Pos	Driver	Car	Time/gap	Grid	Stops	Tyres
1	N Lauda	Ferrari	2h 0m 29.56s	1	1	G
2	C Regazzoni	Ferrari	−35.61s	3	1	G
3	E Fittipaldi	McLaren-Ford	−1 lap	4	1	G
4	H-J Stuck	March-Ford	−2 laps	13	1	G
5	J Scheckter	Tyrrell-Ford	−2 laps	9	1	G
6	D Hulme	McLaren-Ford	−2 laps	8	1	G

Round 5/15	**BELGIAN GP** Nivelles-Baulers				
	12 May 1974			**Race 240**	

Emerson Fittipaldi

McLaren-Ford M23 182.019kph, 113.101mph

A third Ferrari pole, this time Regazzoni, but as a result of a timing error, Scheckter the hard-done-by fastest qualifier. Initially six cars formed a leading train – Regazzoni, Fittipaldi, Lauda, Scheckter, Peterson, Hunt – things only changing when the leaders encountered heavy traffic around half-distance. Once clear of the disruptive backmarkers two separate duels formed: Fittipaldi from Lauda; Regazzoni from Scheckter. Emerson was able to hold Niki at a 3s interval until he wound down on his final lap to finish a mere 0.35s to the good. Scheckter pipped Regazzoni at the finish as the Ferrari ran dry. First to record a second win of the season, Fittipaldi took the championship lead, but both Ferrari drivers were within three points.

POLE POSITION Regazzoni, Ferrari, 1m 09.82s (1.04s), 192.014kph, 119.312mph
LAPS 85 x 3.724 km, 2.314 miles
DISTANCE 316.540 km, 196.689 miles
STARTERS/FINISHERS 31/18
WEATHER Sunny, warm, dry
LAP LEADERS Regazzoni 1-38 (38); Fittipaldi 39-85 (47)
WINNER'S LAPS 1-38 P2, 39-85 P1
FASTEST LAP Hulme, McLaren-Ford, 1m 11.31s (lap 37), 188.002kph, 116.819mph
CHAMPIONSHIP Fittipaldi 22, Lauda 21, Regazzoni 19, Hulme 11, Beltoise 10

Pos	Driver	Car	Time/gap	Grid	Stops	Tyres
1	E Fittipaldi	McLaren-Ford	1h 44m 20.57s	4	0	G
2	N Lauda	Ferrari	−0.35s	3	0	G
3	J Scheckter	Tyrrell-Ford	−45.61s	2	0	G
4	C Regazzoni	Ferrari	−52.02s	1	0	G
5	J-P Beltoise	BRM	−1m 8.05s	7	0	F
6	D Hulme	McLaren-Ford	−1m 10.54s	12	0	G

MONACO GP Monte Carlo

26 May 1974   Race 241

Ronnie Peterson
Lotus-Ford 72E 129.941kph, 80.742mph

After qualifying a superb 1-2 at Monte Carlo, Regazzoni's Ferrari got the better of Lauda's pole-sitting car only to spin away his lead at Rascasse on lap 20 and finish up fourth. Lauda led the next 12 laps until ignition failure put paid to his bid. Peterson, who had been pressing Lauda, now took over but up until then his had not been an easy ride. Qualifying the 'old' Lotus 72 third, Ronnie spent the first two laps behind Jarier's faster-starting Shadow, but once past was now able to attack the Ferrari pair. But on lap 6 he spun at Rascasse, rejoining P6. Hailwood ahead of him crashed out, so once he had disposed of first Scheckter and then Jarier for a second time he was perfectly placed for victory once Lauda retired.

POLE POSITION N Lauda, Ferrari, 1m 26.3s (0.2s), 136.742kph, 84.967mph
LAPS 78 x 3.278 km, 2.037 miles
DISTANCE 255.684 km, 158.875 miles
STARTERS/FINISHERS 25/9
WEATHER Sunny, warm, dry
LAP LEADERS Regazzoni 1-20 (20); Lauda 21-32 (12); Peterson 33-78 (46)
WINNER'S LAPS 1-2 P4, 3-5 P3, 6-11 P6, 12-18 P5, 19-20 P4, 21-24 P3, 25-32 P2, 33-78 P1
FASTEST LAP Peterson, Lotus-Ford, 1m 27.9s (lap 57), 134.253kph, 83.421mph
CHAMPIONSHIP Fittipaldi 24, Regazzoni 22, Lauda 21, Scheckter 12, Hulme 11

Pos	Driver	Car	Time/gap	Grid	Stops	Tyres
1	R Peterson	Lotus-Ford	1h 58m 3.7s	3	0	G
2	J Scheckter	Tyrrell-Ford	−28.8s	5	0	G
3	J-P Jarier	Shadow-Ford	−48.9s	6	0	G
4	C Regazzoni	Ferrari	−1m 3.1s	2	0	G
5	E Fittipaldi	McLaren-Ford	−1 lap	13	0	G
6	J Watson	Brabham-Ford	−1 lap	23	0	F

Tyrrell-Ford 007

SWEDISH GP Anderstorp

9 June 1974   Race 242

Jody Scheckter
Tyrrell-Ford 007 162.723kph, 101.111mph

Once again the Ferraris paired-off on the grid, only this time on row two, the front row occupied by two blue Tyrrells. Making their fourth race appearance, the 007 Tyrrells found themselves well suited to this particular circuit and their drivers took full advantage with a 1-2 team-formation finish, just 0.38s apart. Depailler fluffed his start from pole, initially lying third to Scheckter and Peterson, the latter from the third row highly intent upon victory in his home race. But eight laps in local hero Ronnie was out with a broken driveshaft. Hunt's Hesketh kept the leaders honest, chasing down the Tyrrell twins to finish just 3s back. Scheckter's maiden victory was the sixth different winner in the first seven races.

POLE POSITION Depailler, Tyrrell-Ford, 1m 24.758s (0.318s), 170.660kph, 106.043mph
LAPS 80 x 4.018 km, 2.497 miles
DISTANCE 321.440 km, 199.734 miles
STARTERS/FINISHERS 26/11
WEATHER Sunny, warm, dry
LAP LEADERS Scheckter 1-80 (80)
WINNER'S LAPS 1-80 P1
FASTEST LAP Depailler, Tyrrell-Ford, 1m 27.262s (lap 72), 165.763kph, 103.000mph
CHAMPIONSHIP Fittipaldi 27, Regazzoni 22, Lauda 21, Scheckter 21, Hulme 11

Pos	Driver	Car	Time/gap	Grid	Stops	Tyres
1	J Scheckter	Tyrrell-Ford	1h 58m 39.391s	2	0	G
2	P Depailler	Tyrrell-Ford	−0.380s	1	0	G
3	J Hunt	Hesketh-Ford	−3.325s	6	0	F
4	E Fittipaldi	McLaren-Ford	−53.507s	9	0	G
5	J-P Jarier	Shadow-Ford	−1m 16.403s	8	0	G
6	G Hill	Lola-Ford	−1 lap	15	0	F

DUTCH GP Zandvoort

23 June 1974   Race 243

Niki Lauda

Ferrari 312B3 184.621kph, 114.718mph

Following practice the Ferraris were again paired-up, again fastest. Lauda's pole was a full second quicker than his nearest Ford-powered rival, Fittipaldi's McLaren. This time Lauda got away well at the start, and 103 minutes later he was still there, 8s ahead of his teammate. If anything the Ferraris had shown even greater superiority than the Tyrrells in Sweden. Fittipaldi won the Ford-Cosworth race, overtaking Scheckter, Hailwood and Depailler to take third place. Lauda now joined Fittipaldi with two race victories, these two and Regazzoni tightly bunched at the head of the points table, this race completing the first segment of the two-part season.

POLE POSITION Lauda, Ferrari, 1m 18.31s (0.50s), 194.274kph, 120.716mph
LAPS 75 x 4.226 km, 2.626 miles
DISTANCE 316.950 km, 196.944 miles
STARTERS/FINISHERS 25/12
WEATHER Sunny, warm, dry
LAP LEADERS Lauda 1-75 (75)
WINNER'S LAPS 1-75 P1
FASTEST LAP R Peterson, Lotus-Ford, 1m 21.44s (lap 63), 186.807kph, 116.077mph
CHAMPIONSHIP Fittipaldi 31, Lauda 30, Regazzoni 28, Scheckter 23, Hailwood 12

Pos	Driver	Car	Time/gap	Grid	Stops	Tyres
1	N Lauda	Ferrari	1h 43m 0.35s	1	0	G
2	C Regazzoni	Ferrari	−8.25s	2	0	G
3	E Fittipaldi	McLaren-Ford	−30.27s	3	0	G
4	M Hailwood	McLaren-Ford	−31.29s	4	0	G
5	J Scheckter	Tyrrell-Ford	−34.28s	5	0	G
6	P Depailler	Tyrrell-Ford	−51.52s	8	0	G

FRENCH GP Dijon-Prenois

7 July 1974   Race 244

Ronnie Peterson

Lotus-Ford 72E 192.722kph, 119.752mph

A laggardly start by Pryce's Shadow from row two caused a start-line fracas. This allowed the front three – Lauda, Peterson and Regazzoni – to break away from the rest of the grid. Peterson's ageing Lotus 72E was losing out to the Flat-12 Ferraris down the straight but working far better around the twists of this short, simplistic track. It took Peterson a while to find a way past, but once he had superbly out-braked Lauda on lap 16 he could pull away despite his straight-line speed deficit. For a car in its fourth season up against the latest from Maranello, it was a tour de force by Peterson, although Lauda later complained of worsening front-tyre vibrations handicapping his vision. Scheckter added interest in his attempts to relieve Regazzoni of third.

POLE POSITION Lauda, Ferrari, 0m 58.79s (0.29s), 201.402kph, 125.145mph
LAPS 80 x 3.289 km, 2.044 miles
DISTANCE 263.120 km, 163.495 miles
STARTERS/FINISHERS 22/16
WEATHER Sunny, warm, dry
LAP LEADERS Lauda 1-16 (16); Peterson 17-80 (64)
WINNER'S LAPS 1-16 P2, 17-80 P1
FASTEST LAP Scheckter, Tyrrell-Ford, 1m 00.00s (lap 10), 197.340kph, 122.621mph
CHAMPIONSHIP Lauda 36, Regazzoni 32, Fittipaldi 31, Scheckter 26, Peterson 19

Pos	Driver	Car	Time/gap	Grid	Stops	Tyres
1	R Peterson	Lotus-Ford	1h 21m 55.02	2	0	G
2	N Lauda	Ferrari	−20.36s	1	0	G
3	C Regazzoni	Ferrari	−27.84s	4	0	G
4	J Scheckter	Tyrrell-Ford	−28.11s	7	0	G
5	J Ickx	Lotus-Ford	−37.54s	13	0	G
6	D Hulme	McLaren-Ford	−38.14s	11	0	G

BRITISH GP Brands Hatch

20 July 1974   Race 245

Jody Scheckter

Tyrrell-Ford 007 186.258kph, 115.735mph

Last year Scheckter made British GP headlines for the wrong reasons. This time he brought himself into championship contention. Lauda appeared the certain winner, leading from pole, Scheckter's Tyrrell in relentless pursuit. As these two reeled off the laps it became clear Lauda was controlling his 8s advantage, Scheckter helpless to challenge. With 20 laps left, the sharp-eyed observed an alteration in the profile of Lauda's right rear Goodyear, and as handling deteriorated with the slowly escaping air Scheckter went past with six to go. Lauda stayed out but when forced in on lap 74 officials prevented him rejoining because the crowded pit lane exit was blocked. Classified ninth, Lauda was reinstated to fifth on appeal.

POLE POSITION Lauda, Ferrari, 1m 19.7s (0.0s), 192.637kph, 119.699mph
LAPS 75 x 4.265 km, 2.650 miles
DISTANCE 319.857 km, 198.750 miles
STARTERS/FINISHERS 25/14
WEATHER Sunny, warm, dry
LAP LEADERS Lauda 1-69 (69); Scheckter 70-75 (6)
WINNER'S LAPS 1-69 P2, 70-75 P1
FASTEST LAP Lauda, Ferrari, 1m 21.1s (lap 25), 189.311kph, 117.633mph
CHAMPIONSHIP Lauda 38, Fittipaldi 37, Scheckter 35, Regazzoni 35, Peterson 19

Pos	Driver	Car	Time/gap	Grid	Stops	Tyres
1	J Scheckter	Tyrrell-Ford	1h 43m 2.2s	3	0	G
2	E Fittipaldi	McLaren-Ford	−15.3s	8	0	G
3	J Ickx	Lotus-Ford	−1m 1.5s	12	0	G
4	C Regazzoni	Ferrari	−1m 7.2s	7	1	G
5	N Lauda	Ferrari	−1 lap	1	1	G
6	C Reutemann	Brabham-Ford	−1 lap	4	0	G

Round 11/15	**GERMAN GP** Nürburgring		**Clay Regazzoni**
	4 August 1974	Race 246	Ferrari 312B3 188.824kph, 117.330mph

Regazzoni renewed his championship challenge at the perilous Nürburgring. The Ferraris, quick in practice, hogged the front row, and then two of Regga's chief rivals were quickly eliminated. Lauda, from pole, tried to win the race at the North Curve on lap 1 and was nurfed-off when he attempted to out-brake Scheckter. Fittipaldi, fastest of the Ford-engined qualifiers, couldn't find a gear on the grid, the McLaren retiring with collision damage. Meanwhile, Regazzoni successfully negotiated the rain showers and came home 50s ahead of Scheckter. Mike Hailwood suffered career-ending leg injuries when his Yardley-McLaren, dicing with the JPS pair for fourth on lap 12, landed awkwardly at Pflanzgarten, crashing heavily.

POLE POSITION N Lauda, Ferrari, 7m 00.8s (0.3s), 195.356kph, 121.389mph
LAPS 14 x 22.835 km, 14.189 miles
DISTANCE 319.960 km, 198.646 miles
STARTERS/FINISHERS 26/15
WEATHER Overcast, showers
LAP LEADERS Regazzoni 1-14 (14)
WINNER'S LAPS 1-14 P1
FASTEST LAP Scheckter, Tyrrell-Ford, 7m 11.1s (lap 11), 190.689kph, 118.489mph
CHAMPIONSHIP Regazzoni 44, Scheckter 41, Lauda 38, Fittipaldi 37, Peterson 22

Pos	Driver	Car	Time/gap	Grid	Stops	Tyres
1	C Regazzoni	Ferrari	1h 41m 35.0s	2	0	G
2	J Scheckter	Tyrrell-Ford	−50.7s	4	0	G
3	C Reutemann	Brabham-Ford	−1m 23.3s	6	0	G
4	R Peterson	Lotus-Ford	−1m 24.2s	8	0	G
5	J Ickx	Lotus-Ford	−1m 25.0s	9	0	G
6	T Pryce	Shadow-Ford	−2m 18.1s	11	0	G

Round 12/15	**AUSTRIAN GP** Österreichring		**Carlos Reutemann**
	18 August 1974	Race 247	Brabham-Ford BT44 215.804kph, 134.095mph

The Brabhams were flying in practice, another case of horses for courses, but Lauda managed to snatch his eighth pole. At flag-fall Reutemann made amends, leading all the way from P2 but having to work hard for his second victory. It was a very fast, hot and close race, initially seven cars streaming round line astern behind the leading Brabham. The strongest and longest challenge came from Regazzoni, Peterson and Pace, the second Brabham driver at one time positioned to make it a triumphant 1-2. But when engine or other problems put paid to these three, as it had Scheckter, Lauda and Fittipaldi earlier on, Reutemann could complete the final laps with ease to finish well ahead of Hulme. Of the title contenders, only Regazzoni scored.

POLE POSITION N Lauda, Ferrari, 1m 35.40s (0.16s), 223.057kph, 138.601mph
LAPS 54 x 5.911 km, 3.673 miles
DISTANCE 319.194 km, 198.338 miles
STARTERS/FINISHERS 25/12
WEATHER Sunny, very hot, dry
LAP LEADERS Reutemann 1-54 (54)
WINNER'S LAPS 1-54 P1
FASTEST LAP Regazzoni, Ferrari, 1m 37.22s (lap 46), 218.881kph, 136.006mph
CHAMPIONSHIP Regazzoni 46, Scheckter 41, Lauda 38, Fittipaldi 37, Reutemann 23

Pos	Driver	Car	Time/gap	Grid	Stops	Tyres
1	C Reutemann	Brabham-Ford	1h 28m 44.72s	2	0	G
2	D Hulme	McLaren-Ford	−42.92s	10	0	G
3	J Hunt	Hesketh-Ford	−1m 1.54s	7	0	F
4	J Watson	Brabham-Ford	−1m 9.39s	11	0	F
5	C Regazzoni	Ferrari	−1m 13.08s	8	1	G
6	V Brambilla	March-Ford	−1m 13.82s	20	0	G

Round 13/15	**ITALIAN GP** Monza		**Ronnie Peterson**
	8 September 1974	Race 248	Lotus-Ford 72E 213.450kph, 132.631mph

Lauda's ninth pole headed three Brabhams, a works car on loan to John Watson. To the delight of the *tifosi*, the Ferraris were soon running 1-2, the triple-Brabham challenge having evaporated. It wasn't especially exciting, but there were many worse things than watching red cars demolish the opposition at Monza. But was that smoke on the overrun from Lauda's exhausts? The elation when Regazzoni came out of Parabolica on lap 30 was only matched by the dismay when the second Ferrari also began to smoke. With 12 laps to go it was suddenly a repeat of last year, Peterson versus Fittipaldi, only this time JPS Lotus versus Marlboro-Texaco McLaren. The result was the same, and extraordinarily by an identical winning margin, 0.8s.

POLE POSITION N Lauda, Ferrari, 1m 33.16s (0.11s), 223.358kph, 138.788mph
LAPS 52 x 5.780 km, 3.592 miles
DISTANCE 300.560 km, 186.759 miles
STARTERS/FINISHERS 25/11
WEATHER Sunny, very hot, dry
LAP LEADERS Lauda 1-29 (29); C Regazzoni, Ferrari 30-40 (11); Peterson 41-52 (12)
WINNER'S LAPS 1 P6, 2-6 P5, 7-11 P4, 12-32 P3, 33-40 P2, 41-52 P1
FASTEST LAP Pace, Brabham-Ford, 1m 34.20s (lap 46), 220.892kph, 137.256mph
CHAMPIONSHIP Regazzoni 46, Scheckter 45, Fittipaldi 43, Lauda 38, Peterson 31

Pos	Driver	Car	Time/gap	Grid	Stops	Tyres
1	R Peterson	Lotus-Ford	1h 22m 56.6s	7	0	G
2	E Fittipaldi	McLaren-Ford	−0.8s	6	0	G
3	J Scheckter	Tyrrell-Ford	−24.7s	12	0	G
4	A Merzario	Iso Marlboro-Ford	−1m 27.7s	15	0	F
5	C Pace	Brabham-Ford	−1 lap	3	1	G
6	D Hulme	McLaren-Ford	−1 lap	19	0	G

Round 14/15	**CANADIAN GP** Mosport Park		**Emerson Fittipaldi**
	22 September 1974	**Race 249**	McLaren-Ford M23 189.130kph, 117.520mph

Fittipaldi showed himself to be up for the title fight by thwarting Lauda's tenth pole of the season. But Lauda, driving a must-win race, forged ahead at the start and easily controlled a 5s gap to the Brazilian. On lap 68, with everything nicely under control, Lauda took his usual line at normal speed for the blind turn three right-hand sweep and promptly skated off track on debris dumped by another competitor's off, ending his championship challenge thump against the barriers. Scheckter also crashed out on lap 49 from third place when his brakes failed, but he at least still retained an outside chance of the title. By finishing second, Regazzoni went to the final round showdown equal on points with race winner Fittipaldi.

POLE POSITION Fittipaldi, Lotus-Ford, 1m 13.188s (0.042s), 194.657kph, 120.954mph
LAPS 80 x 3.957 km, 2.459 miles
DISTANCE 316.590 km, 196.720 miles
STARTERS/FINISHERS 26/16
WEATHER Cold, dry
LAP LEADERS Lauda 1-67 (67); Fittipaldi 68-80 (13)
WINNER'S LAPS 1-67 P2, 68-80 P1
FASTEST LAP N Lauda, Ferrari, 1m 13.659s (lap 60), 193.412kph, 120.181mph
CHAMPIONSHIP Fittipaldi 52, Regazzoni 52, Scheckter 45, Lauda 38, Peterson 35

Pos	Driver	Car	Time/gap	Grid	Stops	Tyres
1	E Fittipaldi	McLaren-Ford	1h 40m 26.136s	1	0	G
2	C Regazzoni	Ferrari	−13.034s	6	0	G
3	R Peterson	Lotus-Ford	−14.494s	10	0	G
4	J Hunt	Hesketh-Ford	−15.669s	8	0	F
5	P Depailler	Tyrrell-Ford	−55.322s	7	0	G
6	D Hulme	McLaren-Ford	−1 lap	14	0	G

Round 15/15	**UNITED STATES GP** Watkins Glen		**Carlos Reutemann**
	6 October 1974	**Race 250**	Brabham-Ford BT44 191.705kph, 119.120mph

Scheckter had to win, Fittipaldi and Regazzoni score points and beat one another. Disappointingly the three contenders qualified sixth, eighth and ninth respectively. It was a downbeat conclusion to the title battle, Fittipaldi always holding tactical track position over Regazzoni and Scheckter, neither of whom finished in the points. Ferrari's dismal showing at this race also gave McLaren the constructors' title to cap their maiden championship season. The race itself was a Brabham 1-2 runaway, although Hunt in third had challenged winner Reutemann before gremlins slowed his Hesketh. Mirroring the season-ending Cevert tragedy 12 months ago, Austrian Helmuth Koinigg was killed when his Surtees TS16 inexplicably crashed on lap 9.

POLE POSITION Reutemann, Brabham-Ford, 1m 38.978s (0.017s), 197.671kph, 122.827mph
LAPS 59 x 5.435 km, 3.377 miles
DISTANCE 320.651 km, 199.243 miles
STARTERS/FINISHERS 27/12
WEATHER Sunny, warm, dry
LAP LEADERS Reutemann 1-59 (59)
WINNER'S LAPS 1-59 P1
FASTEST LAP Pace, Brabham-Ford, 1m 40.608s (lap 54), 194.469kph, 120.837mph
CHAMPIONSHIP Fittipaldi 55, Regazzoni 52, Scheckter 45, Lauda 38, Peterson 35

Pos	Driver	Car	Time/gap	Grid	Stops	Tyres
1	C Reutemann	Brabham-Ford	1h 40m 21.439s	1	0	G
2	C Pace	Brabham-Ford	−10.735s	4	0	G
3	J Hunt	Hesketh-Ford	−1m 10.384s	2	0	F
4	E Fittipaldi	McLaren-Ford	−1m 17.753s	8	0	G
5	J Watson	Brabham-Ford	−1m 25.804s	7	0	F
6	P Depailler	Tyrrell-Ford	−1m 27.506s	13	0	G

1974 CHAMPIONSHIP FACTS AND FOLKLORE

■ 1974 witnessed the 'oil crisis', when OPEC countries placed an embargo on supply, yet remarkably no GPs were cancelled.

■ With 15 championship rounds, the best seven results counted from the first eight, for the second part of the season six from seven. Dijon-Prenois became the sixth venue to stage the French GP within nine years.

■ A tightly fought and highly competitive championship produced seven different race winners, five drivers still in contention with two rounds to go, and three who went into the final showdown.

■ It was almost as if Stewart's retirement had left a void, a vacuum, and the rest were wrangling over who should fill it and be anointed the 'man to beat'.

■ The driver who made the most persuasive case did not actually win the championship. For a second time the champion was Emerson Fittipaldi, who put together a very measured, assured season-long performance befitting his new double world champion status.

■ But the driver and team that really turned heads in 1974 were Niki Lauda and Ferrari. Designer Mauro Forghieri had extensively modified his 312B3 especially in the area of weight distribution, the cockpit moved forward to allow the fuel load to be carried more centrally.

■ With its distinctive full-width front wing and tall, narrow airbox, the 312B3 looked every bit a winner, improvements to the Flat-12 also adding low-speed grunt.

■ Ferrari's return to winning form under the charismatic leadership of Luca di Montezemolo was one of two factors that defined the season. The other was the profusion of new teams spawned by the 'kit car' phenomenon.

■ 'Kit car' was the term used to describe a chassis designed around the Ford-Cosworth DFV engine/Hewland gearbox combination that offered all-comers a potentially high-performance, comparatively low cost entry into GP racing.

■ 1974 saw seven new constructors – Hesketh, Trojan, Token, Lola, Amon, Parnelli, Penske – added to the existing 11, the most notable Hesketh and, representing the USA, Penske and Parnelli. The Embassy-Hill team switched from Shadow to Lola chassis.

- Just two of the 18 teams were non-DFV powered, these being BRM and Ferrari, just three different F1 power units the fewest raced in one season before or since.
- Up against this horde of Ford-powered cars, Ferrari's revival was doubly impressive, although Lauda's championship run was blighted by poor reliability, failing to finish nine of the fifteen rounds and scoring not one point in the final five races, having led the championship before that juncture.
- In truth, two of his dnfs could be attributed to the driver, and it should be remembered that prior to 1974 he had only competed in two full GP seasons.
- For this reason a back-to-back comparison of his results with champion Fittipaldi is illuminating, Lauda first: qualifying

13:2; poles 9:2; races led 8:3; laps led 338:77, but finally race wins 2:3.
- Two other drivers emerged as winners during the season. With six podiums including two victories, Jody Scheckter quickly demonstrated why Ken Tyrrell had shown faith in him despite his impetuous induction with McLaren. Stewart and Cevert were big boots to fill and Scheckter in particular did a fine job to keep Tyrrell on the winning trail, still in the world championship frame at the finale.
- The other was Carlos Reutemann, who made very good use of the pretty and effective Gordon Murray-designed BT44 to return the Brabham name to the winners' circle under the new Bernie Ecclestone regime.

RACE 237, Brazilian GP: Having switched to McLaren, Fittipaldi won second time out for his new team, also his second successive home race victory. It was the perfect platform for a championship season.

- Brabham, with three victories, were one of five successful teams as far as race-winning was concerned, the others being Tyrrell two, Lotus three, Ferrari three and McLaren four.
- Denny Hulme's season-opening victory pleased new sponsors Texaco-Marlboro and assisted McLaren to win the constructors' cup for the first time in their ninth year of GP racing.
- It was a positive way for the 1967 world champion to end his career, 'The bear' electing to retire at the end of the year.
- But what of former champions Lotus? Fraught is the only word to describe their struggle to make the new Lotus 76 work, let alone win, the car featuring an electric clutch operated by a gear-lever button and a split two-footed brake pedal. All their winning was done with the ageing Lotus 72E, still competitive in its fifth season, at least in the hands of Ronnie Peterson. Changes were largely confined to the new rear-wing overhang restriction, to be one metre from the rear-axle centre-line, and the larger rear tyres.
- Lotus, as with many of the teams, had to bear their share of tyre-related maladies largely associated with the introduction by Goodyear of larger 28ln diameter rears. These were not only prone to punctures but also to loss of pressure and, in the interests of overall progress, more than one fine drive was jeopardised in this manner.
- Thankfully tyres did not directly impact yet another sorry season for safety. Despite numerous initiatives for improvement of cars and circuits, Peter Revson at Kyalami and Helmuth Koinigg at Watkins Glen lost their lives and Mike Hailwood received career-ending injuries at the Nürburgring.
- At the conclusion of its 25th year, and after exactly 250 championship races, Formula 1 remained a highly dangerous activity.

Championship ranking	Championship points	Driver nationality	1974 Drivers Championship		Races contested	Race victories	Podiumse excl. victories	Races led	Flag to flag victories	Laps led	Poles	Fastest laps	Triple Crowns
			Driver	Car									
1	55	BRA	Emerson Fittipaldi	McLaren-Ford	15	3	4	3		77	2		
2	52	SUI	Clay Regazzoni	Ferrari	15	1	6	4	1	83	1	3	
3	45	RSA	Jody Scheckter	Tyrrell-Ford	15	2	4	2	1	86		2	
4	38	AUT	Niki Lauda	Ferrari	15	2	3	8	1	338	9	3	1
5	35	SWE	Ronnie Peterson	Lotus-Ford	15	3	1	6		156	1	2	
6	32	ARG	Carlos Reutemann	Brabham-Ford	15	3	1	5	2	235	1	1	
7	20	NZL	Denny Hulme	McLaren-Ford	15	1	1	1		2		1	
8	15	GBR	James Hunt	March-Ford (2) Hesketh-Ford (13)	15		3						
9	14	FRA	Patrick Depailler	Tyrrell-Ford	15		1				1	1	
10	12	BEL	Jacky Ickx	Lotus-Ford	15		2	1		2			
11	12	GBR	Mike Hailwood	McLaren-Ford	11		1						
12	11	BRA	Carlos Pace	Surtees-Ford (7) Brabham-Ford (6)	13		1					2	
13	10	FRA	Jean-Pierre Beltoise	BRM	14		1						
14	6	FRA	Jean-Pierre Jarier	Shadow-Ford	14		1						
15	6	GBR	John Watson	Brabham-Ford	15								
16	5	GER	Hans-Joachim Stuck	March-Ford	12								
17	4	ITA	Arturo Merzario	Iso Marlboro-Ford	14								
18	1	GBR	Graham Hill	Lola-Ford	15								
18	1	GBR	Tom Pryce	Token-Ford (1) Shadow-Ford (8)	9								
18	1	ITA	Vittorio Brambilla	March-Ford	11								

Championship ranking	Championship points	Team/Marque nationality	1974 Constructors Championship		Engine maker nationality	Races contested	Race victories	1-2 finishes	Podiums excl. victories	Races led	Laps led	Poles	Fastest laps
			Chassis	Engine									
1	73	NZL	McLaren M23	Ford Cosworth 3.0 V8	GBR	15	4		6	4	79	2	1
2	65	ITA	Ferrari 312B3	Ferrari 3.0 F12	ITA	15	3	2	9	10	421	10	6
3	52	GBR	Tyrrell 007, 005, 006	Ford Cosworth 3.0 V8	GBR	15	2	1	5	2	86	1	3
4	42	GBR	Lotus 76, 72E	Ford Cosworth 3.0 V8	GBR	15	3		3	6	158	1	2
5	35	GBR	Brabham BT44, BT42	Ford Cosworth 3.0 V8	GBR	15	3	1	2	5	235	1	3
6	15	GBR	Hesketh 308	Ford Cosworth 3.0 V8	GBR	13			3				
7	10	GBR	BRM P201, P160E	BRM 3.0 V12	GBR	15			1				
8	7	USA	Shadow-Ford DN3, DN1	Ford Cosworth 3.0 V8	GBR	14			1				
9	6	GBR	March 741, 731	Ford Cosworth 3.0 V8	GBR	15							
10	4	GBR	Iso-Marlboro FW	Ford Cosworth 3.0 V8	GBR	15							
11	3	GBR	Surtees TS16	Ford Cosworth 3.0 V8	GBR	14							
12	1	GBR	Lola T370	Ford Cosworth 3.0 V8	GBR	15							

1975

Lauda stakes his claim

THE TALE OF THE TITLE

■ Lauda's championship endorsed the Ferrari renaissance, Maranello taking both titles, their first in 11 years.
■ Six race wins for Forghieri's 312T eclipsed the DFV teams, the rest spread over seven drivers, five teams.
■ After a slow start, no one got close to challenging Lauda's championship run, holder Fittipaldi runner-up.
■ Lord Alexander Hesketh's tiny outfit won a sole GP victory when Hunt squarely beat Lauda at Zandvoort.
■ Three races were red-flagged, half-points awarded in two of these abbreviated races.
■ Each produced surprise winners, Jochen Mass in Spain, Vittorio Brambilla in Austria, both tragic events.
■ Five bystanders died in Spain, and in Austria Mark Donohue and a circuit marshal died in the race-day warm-up.
■ In Spain Lella Lombardi became the first, and so far only, female to win a (half) championship point.
■ Graham Hill retired from driving then lost his life in a plane crash that also took the life of Tony Brise.
■ And not forgetting: catch-fencing; Firestone withdraw.

THE CHASE FOR THE CHAMPIONSHIP

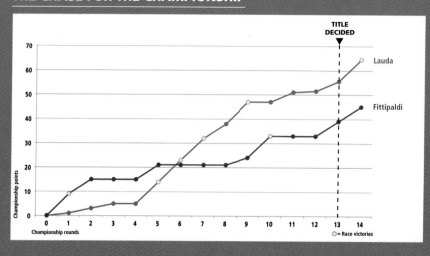

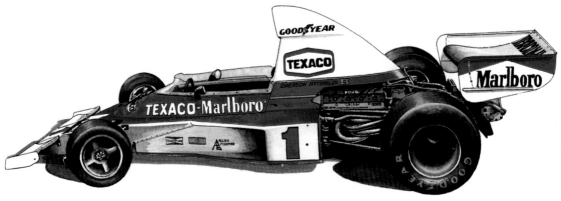

McLaren-Ford M23

ARGENTINEAN GP Buenos Aires No 15
12 January 1975   **Race 251**

Emerson Fittipaldi
McLaren-Ford M23 190.855kph, 118.592mph

A fresh season and a fresh combination on pole: Jarier in the Shadow. But when he was unable to take his place on the grid, the cwp breaking on the warm-up lap, 'Lole', somewhat prematurely from row two, gave the partisan crowd just what they wanted. He was chased by teammate Pace, who took the lead on lap 15 only to spin off before completing it. Reutemann was next to make a slip, such that from lap 26 it became a two-man race, Hunt's Hesketh leading the reigning world champion. Then on lap 35 Hunt, having just set fastest lap, became the third race leader to pirouette, Fittipaldi pressurising the Hesketh driver into a brief spin. James recovered quickly but Emo held him off by 5s to the flag. Lauda finished sixth.

POLE POSITION J-P Jarier, Shadow-Ford, 1m 49.21s (0.43s), 196.729kph, 122.242mph
LAPS 53 x 5.968 km, 3.708 miles
DISTANCE 316.304 km, 196.542 miles
STARTERS/FINISHERS 22/14
WEATHER Sunny, hot, dry
LAP LEADERS Reutemann 1-25 (25); Hunt 26-34 (9); Fittipaldi 35-53 (19)
WINNER'S LAPS 1-14 P5, 15-22 P4, 23-26 P3, 27-34 P2, 35-53 P1
FASTEST LAP Hunt, Hesketh-Ford, 1m 50.91s (lap 34), 193.714kph, 120.368mph
CHAMPIONSHIP Fittipaldi 9, Hunt 6, Reutemann 4, Regazzoni 3, Depailler 2

Pos	Driver	Car	Time/gap	Grid	Stops	Tyres
1	E Fittipaldi	McLaren-Ford	1h 39m 26.29s	5	0	G
2	J Hunt	Hesketh-Ford	–5.91s	6	0	G
3	C Reutemann	Brabham-Ford	–17.06s	3	0	G
4	C Regazzoni	Ferrari	–35.79s	7	0	G
5	P Depailler	Tyrrell-Ford	–54.25s	8	0	G
6	N Lauda	Ferrari	–1m 19.65s	4	0	G

BRAZILIAN GP Interlagos
26 January 1975   **Race 252**

Carlos Pace
Brabham-Ford BT44B 182.488kph, 113.393mph

Jarier's Shadow, on pole yet again by an even wider margin, dispensed with the fast-starting Reutemann on lap 5, then proceeded to disappear up the road posting fastest lap on his tenth tour. But a 25s lead soon dissolved with a faulty fuel-metering unit, the unfortunate Frenchman facing heartbreak once more when he went out with only eight laps remaining. The crowd didn't care. Local boy Carlos Pace had moved quickly through from row three to P3 at the start, eased past his Martini Brabham teammate for second on lap 14, and recorded his maiden win chased home by fellow 'Paulista' Emerson Fittipaldi, now firmly leading the championship following the opening LatAm double-header. Lauda came fifth.

POLE POSITION J-P Jarier, Shadow-Ford, 2m 29.88s (0.80s), 191.193kph, 118.802mph
LAPS 40 x 7.960 km, 4.946 miles
DISTANCE 318.400 km, 197.845 miles
STARTERS/FINISHERS 23/15
WEATHER Sunny, very hot, dry
LAP LEADERS C Reutemann, Brabham-Ford 1-4 (4); Jarier 5-32 (28); Pace 33-40 (8)
WINNER'S LAPS 1-13 P3, 14-32 P2, 33-40 P1
FASTEST LAP J-P Jarier, Shadow-Ford, 2m 34.16s (lap 10), 185.885kph, 115.503mph
CHAMPIONSHIP Fittipaldi 15, Pace 9, Hunt 7, Regazzoni 6, Reutemann 4

Pos	Driver	Car	Time/gap	Grid	Stops	Tyres
1	C Pace	Brabham-Ford	1h 44m 41.17s	6	0	G
2	E Fittipaldi	McLaren-Ford	–5.79s	2	0	G
3	J Mass	McLaren-Ford	–26.66s	10	0	G
4	C Regazzoni	Ferrari	–43.28s	5	0	F
5	N Lauda	Ferrari	–1m 1.88s	4	0	G
6	J Hunt	Hesketh-Ford	–1m 5.12s	7	0	G

Brabham-Ford BT44B

Round 3/14	**SOUTH AFRICAN GP** Kyalami		**Jody Scheckter**
	1 March 1975	Race 253	Tyrrell-Ford 007 185.964kph, 115.553mph

The local lad won this GP as well. Jody didn't look much like a winner on race-day morning when his engine blew in the spare chassis after a driver-induced practice prang in the race car. But from third on the grid behind a Martini-Brabham front row, Scheckter forced his way past pole-sitter Carlos Pace at Crowthorne on lap 3 to bring Tyrrell their only win of the season. First one Carlos, then the Argentinean one proceeded to shadow Scheckter throughout the race, making it a hard-fought victory if a highly popular one, which demonstrated an impressive race-winning determination in Scheckter. At the finish Tyrrell and Brabham also occupied third and fourth. Lauda came fifth.

POLE POSITION Pace, Brabham-Ford, 1m 16.41s (0.07s), 193.357kph, 120.146mph
LAPS 78 x 4.104 km, 2.550 miles
DISTANCE 320.112 km, 198.908 miles
STARTERS/FINISHERS 27/17
WEATHER Overcast, warm, dry
LAP LEADERS Pace 1-2 (2); Scheckter 3-78 (76)
WINNER'S LAPS 1-2 P2, 3-78 P1
FASTEST LAP Pace, Brabham-Ford, 1m 17.20s (lap 11), 191.378kph, 118.917mph
CHAMPIONSHIP Fittipaldi 15, Pace 12, Reutemann 10, Scheckter 9, Hunt 7

Pos	Driver	Car	Time/gap	Grid	Stops	Tyres
1	J Scheckter	Tyrrell-Ford	1h 43m 16.90s	3	0	G
2	C Reutemann	Brabham-Ford	−3.74s	2	0	G
3	P Depailler	Tyrrell-Ford	−16.92s	5	0	G
4	C Pace	Brabham-Ford	−17.31s	1	0	G
5	N Lauda	Ferrari	−28.64s	4	0	G
6	J Mass	McLaren-Ford	−1m 3.34s	16	0	G

Round 4/14	**SPANISH GP** Montjuïc		**Jochen Mass**
	27 April 1975	Race 254	McLaren-Ford M23 153.779kph, 95.554mph

The drivers initially boycotted practice, installation of the Armco barriers clearly defective. But pressure was brought to bear, a grid formed and the race proceeded. On the 25th of the 75 laps the rear wing detached from Stommelen's leading Embassy-Hill. In the inevitable crash his car leapt the guardrail and five bystanders were killed. The race was stopped, Mass in the McLaren declared winner at 29 laps, hence half-points were awarded. From the very first corner – at which the front-row Ferrari pair had collided – accidents had blighted the race, eliminating 11 cars by the time the red flag was shown. On his journey from P10 on lap 1, winner Mass' only pass was his repass of Ickx on lap 29, allegedly under yellow but subsequently vindicated.

POLE POSITION N Lauda, Ferrari, 1m 23.4s (0.1s), 163.640kph, 101.681mph
LAPS 29 x 3.791 km, 2.356 miles (Scheduled for 75 laps but stopped after fatal accident)
DISTANCE 109.939 km, 68.313 miles (Minimum distance incomplete; half points awarded)
STARTERS/FINISHERS 25/8
WEATHER Sunny, warm, dry
LAP LEADERS J Hunt, Hesketh-Ford 1-6 (6); Andretti 7-16 (10); R Stommelen, Hill-Ford 17-21, 23-25 (8); C Pace, Brabham-Ford 22 (1); Mass 26-27, 29 (3); Ickx 28 (1)
WINNER'S LAPS 1 P10, 2 P11, 3 P10, 4-6 P9, 7-10 P6, 11-16 P5, 17-23 P4, 24-25 P3, 26-27 P1, 28 P2, 29 P1
FASTEST LAP M Andretti, Parnelli-Ford, 1m 25.1s (lap 14), 160.371kph, 99.650mph
CHAMPIONSHIP Fittipaldi 15, Pace 12, Reutemann 12, Mass 9.5, Scheckter 9

Pos	Driver	Car	Time/gap	Grid	Stops	Tyres
1	J Mass	McLaren-Ford	42m 53.7s	11	0	G
2	J Ickx	Lotus-Ford	−1.1s	16	0	G
3	C Reutemann	Brabham-Ford	−1 lap	15	0	G
4	J-P Jarier	Shadow-Ford	−1 lap	10	1	G
5	V Brambilla	March-Ford	−1 lap	5	1	G
6	L Lombardi	March-Ford	−2 laps	24	0	G

Round 5/14	**MONACO GP** Monte Carlo						**Niki Lauda**
	11 May 1975					Race 255	Ferrari 312T 121.552kph, 75.529mph

Despite the wet track Lauda got away well from pole, only losing his lead to the chasing Peterson when making the switch to dries on lap 24. As they all rushed in, a slick McLaren tyre-stop moved Fittipaldi up to second but put Peterson out of contention, a wheel-nut rolling beneath the Lotus 72E. At 60 laps, determined to give the Scuderia its first Monaco victory since 1955, Lauda had a 16s cushion. But as the race entered the closing laps Lauda's lead over Fittipaldi shrank alarmingly as he nursed falling oil pressure. Aware that the two-hour mark would be reached before the full race distance, the canny Austrian handled it perfectly, at the chequer, which was three laps short, still 2.78s ahead for his first win in 11 months.

POLE POSITION Lauda, Ferrari, 1m 26.40s (0.69s), 136.583kph, 84.869mph
LAPS 75 x 3.278 km, 2.037 miles (Scheduled for 78 laps but stopped after two hours)
DISTANCE 245.850 km, 152.764 miles
STARTERS/FINISHERS 18/9
WEATHER Rain at start, drying later
LAP LEADERS Lauda 1-23, 25-75 (74); Peterson 24 (1)
WINNER'S LAPS 1-23 P1, 24 P2, 25-75 P1
FASTEST LAP Depailler, Tyrrell-Ford, 1m 28.67s (lap 68), 133.087kph, 82.696mph
CHAMPIONSHIP Fittipaldi 21, Pace 16, Lauda 14, Reutemann 12, Mass 10.5

Pos	Driver	Car	Time/gap	Grid	Stops	Tyres
1	N Lauda	Ferrari	2h 1m 21.31s	1	1	G
2	E Fittipaldi	McLaren-Ford	−2.78s	9	1	G
3	C Pace	Brabham-Ford	−17.81s	8	1	G
4	R Peterson	Lotus-Ford	−38.45s	4	1	G
5	P Depailler	Tyrrell-Ford	−40.86s	12	1	G
6	J Mass	McLaren-Ford	−42.07s	15	1	G

Round 6/14	**BELGIAN GP** Zolder						**Niki Lauda**
	25 May 1975					Race 256	Ferrari 312T 172.285kph, 107.053mph

After five different race winners this year, Niki Lauda was the first to strike with successive victories, indeed the first back-to-back winner since 1973. This abrupt turn in fortunes catapulted him from also-ran to championship leader. Carlos Pace had led the opening three laps, giving way to the on-form Vittorio Brambilla, who had qualified the Beta March on the second row and pushed Lauda down to third on lap 3. But on a circuit notoriously hard on brakes the March challenge could not be sustained. Just as at Monaco, as the race wound down an off-tune Ferrari engine – this time a broken exhaust – gave hope to pursuing Scheckter, but his own developing problems enabled Lauda to finish well ahead.

POLE POSITION Lauda, Ferrari, 1m 25.43s (0.04s), 192.014kph, 119.312mph
LAPS 70 x 4.262 km, 2.648 miles
DISTANCE 298.340 km, 185.380 miles
STARTERS/FINISHERS 24/12
WEATHER Overcast, dry
LAP LEADERS C Pace, Brabham-Ford 1-3 (3); V Brambilla, March-Ford 4-5 (2); Lauda 6-70 (65)
WINNER'S LAPS 1-2 P2, 3-4 P3, 5 P2, 6-70 P1
FASTEST LAP Regazzoni, Ferrari, 1m 26.76s (lap 11), 188.002kph, 116.819mph
CHAMPIONSHIP Lauda 23, Fittipaldi 21, Pace 16, Reutemann 16, Scheckter 15

Pos	Driver	Car	Time/gap	Grid	Stops	Tyres
1	N Lauda	Ferrari	1h 43m 53.98s	4	0	G
2	J Scheckter	Tyrrell-Ford	−19.22s	3	0	G
3	C Reutemann	Brabham-Ford	−41.82s	2	0	G
4	P Depailler	Tyrrell-Ford	−1m 0.08s	1	0	G
5	C Regazzoni	Ferrari	−1m 3.86s	7	1	G
6	T Pryce	Shadow-Ford	−1m 28.45s	12	0	G

Round 7/14	**SWEDISH GP** Anderstorp						**Niki Lauda**
	8 June 1975					Race 257	Ferrari 312T 161.656kph, 100.448mph

Was Brambilla's orange Beta Tools March emerging as a front-runner, or was it the maverick characteristics of the Anderstorp circuit? The Italian took a surprise pole by 0.4s from last year's grid-topper, Depailler's Tyrrell, and led the opening 15 laps before tyre-wear forced a stop. New leader Reutemann was chased for many laps by Jarier until the Shadow's engine blew. So with less than half the race to run Reutemann had a 9s lead from Lauda, steadily making his way up from P6 on lap 1 as others fell by the wayside. But as the two entered the closing stages and the Brabham's handling deteriorated, Carlos was steadily losing his precious lead to the looming Lauda, and with 11 left Niki went ahead for his hat-trick.

POLE POSITION V Brambilla, March-Ford, 1m 24.630s (0.380s), 170.918kph, 106.204mph
LAPS 80 x 4.018 km, 2.497 miles
DISTANCE 321.440 km, 199.734 miles
STARTERS/FINISHERS 26/17
WEATHER Sunny, warm, dry
LAP LEADERS Brambilla 1-15 (15); Reutemann 16-69 (54); Lauda 70-80 (11)
WINNER'S LAPS 1-13 P6, 14-17 P5, 18-38 P4, 39-41 P3, 42-69 P2, 70-80 P1
FASTEST LAP Lauda, Ferrari, 1m 28.267s (lap 61), 163.876kph, 101.828mph
CHAMPIONSHIP Lauda 32, Reutemann 22, Fittipaldi 21, Pace 16, Scheckter 15

Pos	Driver	Car	Time/gap	Grid	Stops	Tyres
1	N Lauda	Ferrari	1h 59m 18.319s	5	0	G
2	C Reutemann	Brabham-Ford	−6.288s	4	0	G
3	C Regazzoni	Ferrari	−29.095s	12	0	G
4	M Andretti	Parnelli-Ford	−44.380s	15	0	G
5	M Donohue	Penske-Ford	−1m 30.763s	16	0	G
6	T Brise	Hill-Ford	−1 lap	17	0	G

Hesketh-Ford 308

Round 8/14	**DUTCH GP** Zandvoort					
	22 June 1975					Race 258

With Lauda on pole and a winning roll, was there no one to defy the might of Maranello? Enter James Hunt. This was a classic victory by the Englishman and the tiny Hesketh team as well as the first skirmish in the fabled Hunt versus Lauda saga. Hunt qualified best of the rest behind the Ferrari pair but the key moment was the canny tyre change from wets to dries. Running fourth, Hunt was the first of the leaders on the still slick track to pit, a full six laps sooner than leader Lauda and dropping to P19 in the process. But as Lauda rejoined Hunt had gone by, and worse still Jarier pushed him back to third for 28 laps. Once released, still with over 30 laps to go, Lauda did close the 10s gap to Hunt, but pass he could not.

James Hunt

Hesketh-Ford 308 177.801kph, 110.480mph

POLE POSITION Lauda, Ferrari, 1m 20.29s (0.28s), 189.483kph, 117.739mph
LAPS 75 x 4.226 km, 2.626 miles
DISTANCE 316.950 km, 196.944 miles
STARTERS/FINISHERS 24/16
WEATHER Rain, then dry
LAP LEADERS Lauda 1-12 (12); Regazzoni 13-14 (2); Hunt 15-75 (61)
WINNER'S LAPS 1-7 P4, 8 P19, 9-10 P17, 11 P15, 12 P9, 13 P3, 14 P2, 15-75 P1
FASTEST LAP Lauda, Ferrari, 1m 21.54s (lap 55), 186.578kph, 115.934mph
CHAMPIONSHIP Lauda 38, Reutemann 25, Fittipaldi 21, Pace 18, Hunt 16

Pos	Driver	Car	Time/gap	Grid	Stops	Tyres
1	J Hunt	Hesketh-Ford	1h 46m 57.40s	3	1	G
2	N Lauda	Ferrari	–1.06s	1	1	G
3	C Regazzoni	Ferrari	–55.06s	2	1	G
4	C Reutemann	Brabham-Ford	–1 lap	5	1	G
5	C Pace	Brabham-Ford	–1 lap	9	1	G
6	T Pryce	Shadow-Ford	–1 lap	12	1	G

TOP **100** RACE

Round 9/14	**FRENCH GP** Paul Ricard					
	6 July 1975					Race 259

The next race was role reversal, Lauda beating Hunt by just over a second. What's more, Jochen Mass was much the same distance behind Master James to produce a thrilling finish. It had looked like a Lauda benefit to begin with as the Ferrari from pole quickly established an increasing lead over Scheckter. The Tyrrell was holding others back and once past on lap 8 Hunt pulled away. But it wasn't until Jochen got by Jody and started gaining little by little on James that the Hesketh began to also catch the now understeering Ferrari. Maybe Niki always had it covered, but over those final thrilling laps the cars were so evenly matched that the slightest error would radically alter the outcome, demanding of the highest driving skills.

Niki Lauda

Ferrari 312T 187.655kph, 116.603mph

POLE POSITION Lauda, Ferrari, 1m 47.82s (0.40s), 193.990kph, 120.540mph
LAPS 54 x 5.810 km, 3.610 miles
DISTANCE 313.740 km, 194.949 miles
STARTERS/FINISHERS 25/18
WEATHER Sunny, hot, dry
LAP LEADERS Lauda 1-54 (54)
WINNER'S LAPS 1-54 P1
FASTEST LAP Mass, McLaren-Ford, 1m 50.60s (lap 38), 189.114kph, 117.510mph
CHAMPIONSHIP Lauda 47, Reutemann 25, Fittipaldi 24, Hunt 22, Pace 18

Pos	Driver	Car	Time/gap	Grid	Stops	Tyres
1	N Lauda	Ferrari	1h 40m 18.84	1	0	G
2	J Hunt	Hesketh-Ford	–1.59s	3	0	G
3	J Mass	McLaren-Ford	–2.31s	7	0	G
4	E Fittipaldi	McLaren-Ford	–39.77s	10	0	G
5	M Andretti	Parnelli-Ford	–1m 2.08s	15	0	G
6	P Depailler	Tyrrell-Ford	–1m 7.40s	13	0	G

TOP **100** RACE

BRITISH GP Silverstone
19 July 1975 — Race 260

Emerson Fittipaldi
McLaren-Ford M23 193.151kph, 120.019mph

Tom Pryce's Shadow was on pole, but it was the world champion who returned to the winner's circle in a bizarre event. Showers shaped the race, sweeping through on separate occasions, sometimes localised to different parts of the Silverstone circuit. Some drivers switched to wets, others not, producing seven different race leaders. Around half-distance Brise, making a big impression in the Embassy Hill, moved into P6, and to the further excitement of the damp crowd Hunt took the lead, holding it for eight laps until first Fittipaldi and then Pace got by. But the skies were darkening again, and when 12 cars – eight a multiple pile-up at Club corner – failed to negotiate lap 56, the race was stopped, leader Fittipaldi one of very few not to go off.

POLE POSITION T Pryce, Shadow-Ford, 1m 19.36s (0.14s), 214.049kph, 133.004mph
LAPS 56 x 4.719 km, 2.932 miles (Scheduled for 67 laps but stopped due to rain)
DISTANCE 264.241 km, 164.192 miles
STARTERS/FINISHERS 26/19
WEATHER Showers, heavy later
LAP LEADERS Pace 1-12, 22-26 (17); Regazzoni 13-18 (6); Pryce 19-20 (2); Scheckter 21, 27-32 (7); J-P Jarier, Shadow-Ford 33-34 (2); Hunt 35-42 (8); Fittipaldi 43-56 (14)
WINNER'S LAPS 1 P8, 2-8 P7, 9-18 P6, 19-20 P5, 21 P4, 22-26 P2, 27-28 P5, 29-32 P4, 33-34 P3, 35-42 P2, 43-56 P1
FASTEST LAP C Regazzoni, Ferrari, 1m 20.90s (lap 16), 209.975kph, 130.472mph
CHAMPIONSHIP Lauda 47, Fittipaldi 33, Hunt 25, Reutemann 25, Pace 24

TOP **100** RACE

Pos	Driver	Car	Time/gap	Grid	Stops	Tyres
1	E Fittipaldi	McLaren-Ford	1h 22m 5.0s	7	1	G
2r	C Pace	Brabham-Ford	–1 lap	2	0	G
3r	J Scheckter	Tyrrell-Ford	–1 lap	6	2	G
4r	J Hunt	Hesketh-Ford	–1 lap	9	0	G
5r	M Donohue	March-Ford	–1 lap	15	0	G
6	V Brambilla	March-Ford	–1 lap	5	1	G

GERMAN GP Nürburgring
3 August 1975 — Race 261

Carlos Reutemann
Brabham-Ford BT44B 188.824kph, 117.330mph

Lauda's pole was the first, and only, sub-seven-minute F1 lap of the Nordschleife. Punctures caused by stones blighted both practice and the race, losing Lauda a commanding lead over his teammate at two-thirds-distance, rejoining after a tyre change to finish third. But Regazzoni's engine had blown, so it was Carlos Reutemann leading at the end of the tenth lap. Reutemann had made a great start from a lowly P10 to complete the first lap fourth, so when the Ferraris faltered – along with the Depailler Tyrrell which hounded Lauda for more than half the race – the race was his. Just nine of the 24 starters finished, only the first two going through trouble-free, Laffite's distant second bringing Frank Williams his first podium as a constructor.

POLE POSITION Lauda, Ferrari, 6m 58.6s (1.4s), 196.383kph, 122.027mph
LAPS 14 x 22.835 km, 14.189 miles
DISTANCE 319.960 km, 198.646 miles
STARTERS/FINISHERS 24/10
WEATHER Sunny, warm, dry
LAP LEADERS Lauda 1-9 (9); Reutemann 10-14 (5)
WINNER'S LAPS 1-2 P4, 3-4 P5, 5-8 P4, 9 P3, 10-14 P1
FASTEST LAP C Regazzoni, Ferrari, 7m 06.4s (lap 7), 192.791kph, 119.795mph
CHAMPIONSHIP Lauda 51, Reutemann 34, Fittipaldi 33, Hunt 25, Pace 24

Pos	Driver	Car	Time/gap	Grid	Stops	Tyres
1	C Reutemann	Brabham-Ford	1h 41m 14.1s	10	0	G
2	J Laffite	Williams-Ford	–1m 37.7s	15	0	G
3	N Lauda	Ferrari	–2m 23.3s	1	1	G
4	T Pryce	Shadow-Ford	–3m 31.4s	16	0	G
5	A Jones	Hill-Ford	–3m 50.3s	21	0	G
6	G van Lennep	Ensign-Ford	–5m 5.5s	24	0	G

AUSTRIAN GP Österreichring
17 August 1975 — Race 262

Vittorio Brambilla
March-Ford 751 177.499kph, 110.293mph

A tragicomedy. In race-day warm-up Mark Donohue and a track marshal lost their lives when the Penske March left the circuit due to tyre failure. The comedy came at the finish. Extreme weather stopped the race prematurely – the third red flag this season and the second awarded half-points. After a brilliant wet-weather drive, astonished winner Vittorio Brambilla crashed after receiving the chequer, completing his jubilant *tour d'honour* in a very battered March 751. Lauda, starting his home GP from pole – car wrongly set up anticipating a drying circuit – resisted Hunt until lap 15. But within four laps Brambilla was leading, and once the Hesketh lost a cylinder, he pulled out 27s over 11 laps for victory from a P8 start.

POLE POSITION Lauda, Ferrari, 1m 34.85s (0.12s), 224.350kph, 139.405mph
LAPS 29 x 5.911 km, 3.673 miles (Scheduled for 54 laps but stopped due to rain)
DISTANCE 171.419 km, 106.515 miles (Minimum distance incomplete; half points awarded)
STARTERS/FINISHERS 26/17
WEATHER Very wet thoughout
LAP LEADERS Lauda 1-14 (14); Hunt 15-18 (4); Brambilla 19-29 (11)
WINNER'S LAPS 1 P6, 2-4 P5, 5 P4, 6-14 P3, 15-18 P2, 19-29 P1
FASTEST LAP Brambilla, March-Ford, 1m 53.90s (lap 11), 186.827kph, 116.089mph
CHAMPIONSHIP Lauda 51.5, Reutemann 34, Fittipaldi 33, Hunt 28, Pace 24

Pos	Driver	Car	Time/gap	Grid	Stops	Tyres
1	V Brambilla	March-Ford	57m 56.69s	8	0	G
2	J Hunt	Hesketh-Ford	–27.03s	2	0	G
3	T Pryce	Shadow-Ford	–34.85s	15	0	F
4	J Mass	McLaren-Ford	–1m 12.66s	9	0	F
5	R Peterson	Lotus-Ford	–1m 23.33s	13	1	G
6	N Lauda	Ferrari	–1m 30.28s	1	0	G

March-Ford 751

Round 13/14	**ITALIAN GP** Monza		
	7 September 1975		**Race 263**

Clay Regazzoni
Ferrari 312T 218.034kph, 135.480mph

This was a Ferrari festival: an all-red front row, then Regazzoni leading all the way to give Ferrari their first Monza victory since his last in 1970. By finishing third Lauda wrapped up both drivers' and constructors' titles, the Scuderia's first championships in 11 long years. For the *tifosi* it couldn't get much better. A first chicane fracas on lap 2 assisted the Ferraris in their escape and eliminated a handful of runners, the gap 6.5s after two laps. Reutemann, Fittipaldi and Hunt gave vain pursuit. But on lap 14 Emo moved ahead of Carlos and, as Lauda fell back into his clutches with a rear damper problem, with seven to go the reigning champion overtook the champion-elect to stave off the inevitable exchange of titles for a further 6.6s.

POLE POSITION Lauda, Ferrari, 1m 32.24s (0.51s), 225.585kph, 140.172mph
LAPS 52 x 5.780 km, 3.592 miles
DISTANCE 300.560 km, 186.759 miles
STARTERS/FINISHERS 26/14
WEATHER Overcast, dry
LAP LEADERS Regazzoni 1-52 (52)
WINNER'S LAPS 1-52 P1
FASTEST LAP Regazzoni, Ferrari, 1m 33.10s (lap 47), 223.502kph, 138.877mph
CHAMPIONSHIP Lauda 55.5, Fittipaldi 39, Reutemann 37, Hunt 30, Regazzoni 25

Pos	Driver	Car	Time/gap	Grid	Stops	Tyres
1	C Regazzoni	Ferrari	1h 22m 42.6s	2	0	G
2	E Fittipaldi	McLaren-Ford	−16.6s	3	0	G
3	N Lauda	Ferrari	−23.2s	1	0	G
4	C Reutemann	Brabham-Ford	−55.1s	7	0	G
5	J Hunt	Hesketh-Ford	−57.1s	8	0	G
6	T Pryce	Shadow-Ford	−1m 15.9s	14	0	G

Round 14/14	**UNITED STATES GP** Watkins Glen		
	5 October 1975		**Race 264**

Niki Lauda
Ferrari 312T 186.842kph, 116.098mph

As if to strut his newfound status, the new world champion rounded out his brilliant season with a ninth pole followed by his fifth win. Also somehow symbolic was outgoing champion Emerson Fittipaldi's spirited drive to second place, a contest which would have been even more stirring if Lauda's teammate, Regazzoni, hadn't let Niki by on lap 20 and then held up the McLaren until he was black-flagged. Over five laps Regazzoni's blocking persisted, a mesmerising race between two champions completely demolished, the gap expanding from 1.2s to 12.2s. Montezemolo was livid. Mass-Hunt-Peterson-Scheckter finished like that, 3-4-5-6, but Lauda was undisputed champion and now wore Stewart's mantle as the man to beat.

POLE POSITION Lauda, Ferrari, 1m 42.003s (0.357s), 191.809kph, 119.185mph
LAPS 59 x 5.435 km, 3.377 miles
DISTANCE 320.651 km, 199.243 miles
STARTERS/FINISHERS 22/10
WEATHER Cool, dry
LAP LEADERS Lauda 1-59 (59)
WINNER'S LAPS 1-59 P1
FASTEST LAP Fittipaldi, McLaren-Ford, 1m 43.374s (lap 43), 189.265kph, 117.604mph
CHAMPIONSHIP Lauda 64.5, Fittipaldi 45, Reutemann 37, Hunt 33, Regazzoni 25

Pos	Driver	Car	Time/gap	Grid	Stops	Tyres
1	N Lauda	Ferrari	1h 42m 58.175s	1	0	G
2	E Fittipaldi	McLaren-Ford	−4.943s	2	0	G
3	J Mass	McLaren-Ford	−47.637s	9	0	G
4	J Hunt	Hesketh-Ford	−49.475s	15	0	G
5	R Peterson	Lotus-Ford	−49.986s	14	0	G
6	J Scheckter	Tyrrell-Ford	−50.321s	10	0	G

RACE 258, Dutch GP: In what turned out to be a rehearsal for their titanic championship duel the following year, James Hunt (24) beat Niki Lauda (12) fair and square at Zandvoort, but by a mere 1.060s.

1975 CHAMPIONSHIP FACTS AND FOLKLORE

■ The 14-race season was split into two as usual, the best seven results from the first eight races, the best five from the remaining six counting towards the championships.

■ After a comparatively slow start to the season, Niki Lauda's Monaco triumph began a sequence of successes that rocketed him from points deficit to points leader, an advantage he was never to lose. It was an onslaught to which his main rival, reigning champion Emerson Fittipaldi, simply had no answer.

■ 1975 witnessed Lauda fulfil the latent promise he had revealed last year. His was an aptitude which exploited the full potential of Mauro Forghieri's latest manifestation of the Flat-12 series, the 312T with its *trasversale* gearbox, honing the design through extensive testing around Fiorano, Ferrari's private test track built in 1972.

■ Speed with reliability is a potent blend in any car, but Lauda proved more than once that he could adapt his skills to a given situation and deliver results that might otherwise evade others.

■ As many as nine drivers won Grands Prix this year but Lauda's five victories stood head and shoulders above his peers, none of whom, besides Fittipaldi's pair of wins, recorded more than a singleton victory.

■ Emerson's title defence started and finished positively but there was a lengthy mid-season lacklustre patch when the pace just wasn't there.

■ If anything James Hunt and the diminutive Hesketh Racing team provided the sternest opposition to the Maranello juggernaut, but just as the other Cosworth teams, it was not a sustained assault.

■ So Ferrari took the constructors' cup with six wins to McLaren's three, Brabham with two and one each for Tyrrell, Hesketh and March.

■ Lotus didn't even make the podium and Shadow was unable to translate three pole positions into tangible results.

■ The European season began in Spain in a manner that was as unfortunate as it was sobering. A motorsport accident causing multiple fatalities is burdensome enough, but it

RACE 261, German GP: After posting the first, and only, sub-seven-minute F1 lap of the Nordschleife, poleman Lauda lost a commanding lead at two-thirds distance due to a puncture.

was made doubly onerous due to the drivers' protest that preceded it.

■ The drivers acted through their collective organisation the GPDA to protest about the inadequacy of the barriers at a track which, by its nature, demanded the highest attention to security.

■ Despite improvements, the Fittipaldi brothers remained dissatisfied. Reigning world champion Emerson boycotted the race while brother Wilson made one slow protest lap before retiring his car. Lamentably, events were to vindicate their misgivings.

■ But at least the horror of Montjuïc made the race promoters sit up. For example, the double Armco barriers surrounding the Monte Carlo circuit were reinforced generally and heightened in places, and at Silverstone a chicane was introduced at Woodcote corner, at the time regarded as one of the great 'driver' corners in F1.

■ But another measure added at the Woodcote chicane, as well as to many other parts of the circuit, was catch-fencing, designed to reduce the velocity of an off-course car before it connected with anything solid.

■ But catch-fencing was a flawed concept. During the Silverstone race Jarier graphically demonstrated some of its inadequacies. A wooden post struck his head an injurious blow and a spectator in the adjoining grandstand was hurt by flying debris.

■ At the Österreichring a month later, catch-fencing also behaved unpredictably in regard to the two further fatalities which occurred during the season. This time the posts and fencing actually assisted Mark Donohue's Penske March 751 to vault the Armco guard-rail and collect two marshals.

■ This accident, probably caused by front tyre failure, was of course a terrible setback for the Penske team, turning to the March while they worked on getting their PC1 car raceworthy. Donohue appeared initially to have survived the accident, speaking lucidly, only to lose consciousness and die later from head injuries.

■ The races in Spain (accident) and Austria (rain) were both stopped before 60% of the race distance had been completed and so became the first where only half-points were awarded.

■ One recipient of these truncated awards was Lella Lombardi. With her sixth-place finish in Spain, she remains the only woman to win a championship point, albeit a half-point.

■ At Monaco, of all places, Graham Hill failed to qualify his own car, the Hill GH1, and effectively retired from driving to focus on managing his Embassy Racing Team. He announced his decision at Silverstone in July.

■ In late November the motor racing world was stunned by his death in a light aircraft crash returning from F1 testing at Paul Ricard. The nucleus of Hill's burgeoning team died with

him, including the young highly talented driver Tony Brise along with four others.
- Firestone withdrew early in the season, leaving Goodyear the sole tyre supplier. Goodyear introduced 'control tyres' but tyre reliability remained dubious.
- Innovation saw carbon-fibre rear wings appear at Embassy Hill and Hesketh, and at Silverstone a revised starting procedure with lights was first used.
- The primary safety measure for cars was a mandatory fire extinguisher system to be installed in the engine

compartment, but safety – a key issue towards the successful future of F1 – continued to be approached in a somewhat random manner.
- The best example of this was that whereas the Safety Car had made its first appearance in 1973, there was no sign of this particular safety measure during a season when it could have been appropriately deployed for all three of the foreshortened races.
- Alan Jones, destined to be the 1980 world champion, made his GP debut in 1975.

Championship ranking	Championship points	Driver nationality	1975 Drivers Championship		Races contested	Race victories	Podiumse excl. victories	Races led	Lights to flag victories	Laps led	Poles	Fastest laps	Triple Crowns
			Driver	Car									
1	64.5	AUT	Niki Lauda	Ferrari	14	5	3	8		298	9	2	
2	45	BRA	Emerson Fittipaldi	McLaren-Ford	13	2	4	2		33		1	
3	37	ARG	Carlos Reutemann	Brabham-Ford	14	1	5	4		88			
4	33	GBR	James Hunt	Hesketh-Ford	14	1	3	5		88		1	
5	25	SUI	Clay Regazzoni	Ferrari	14	1	2	3		60		4	
6	24	BRA	Carlos Pace	Brabham-Ford	14	1	2	5		31	1	1	
7	20	RSA	Jody Scheckter	Tyrrell-Ford	14	1	2	2		83			
8	20	GER	Jochen Mass	McLaren-Ford	14	1	3	1		3		1	
9	12	FRA	Patrick Depailler	Tyrrell-Ford	14		1					1	
10	8	GBR	Tom Pryce	Shadow-Ford	14		1	1		2	1		
11	6.5	ITA	Vittorio Brambilla	March-Ford	14	1		3		28	1	1	
12	6	FRA	Jacques Laffite	Williams-Ford	10		1						
13	6	SWE	Ronnie Peterson	Lotus-Ford	14		1			1			
14	5	USA	Mario Andretti	Parnelli-Ford	12			1		10		1	
15	4	USA	Mark Donohue	Penske-Ford (9) March-Ford (2)	11								
16	3	BEL	Jacky Ickx	Lotus-Ford	9		1	1		1			
17	2	AUS	Alan Jones	Hesketh-Ford (4) Hill-Ford (4)	8								
18	1.5	FRA	Jean-Pierre Jarier	Shadow-Ford (11) Shadow-Matra (2)	13			2		30	2	1	
19	1	GBR	Tony Brise	Williams-Ford (1) Hill-Ford (9)	10								
19	1	NDL	Gijs van Lennep	Ensign-Ford	3								
21	0.5	ITA	Lella Lombardi	March-Ford	10								
-	0	GER	Rolf Stommelen	Lola-Ford (3) Hill-Ford (3)	6								

Championship ranking	Championship points	Team/Marque nationality	1975 Constructors Championship		Engine maker nationality	Races contested	Race victories	1-2 finishes	Podiums excl. victories	Races led	Laps led	Poles	Fastest laps
			Chassis	Engine									
1	72.5	ITA	Ferrari 312T, 312B3	Ferrari 3.0 F12	ITA	14	6		5	10	358	9	6
2	54	GBR	Brabham BT44B	Ford Cosworth 3.0 V8	GBR	14	2		7	8	129	1	1
3	53	NZL	McLaren M23	Ford Cosworth 3.0 V8	GBR	14	3		7	3	36		2
4	33	GBR	Hesketh 308, 308C	Ford Cosworth 3.0 V8	GBR	14	1		3	5	88		1
5	25	GBR	Tyrrell 007	Ford Cosworth 3.0 V8	GBR	14	1		3	2	83		1
6	9.5	USA	Shadow-Ford DN5, DN3B	Ford Cosworth 3.0 V8	GBR	14			1	2	32	3	1
7	9	GBR	Lotus 72E, 72F	Ford Cosworth 3.0 V8	GBR	14			1	2	2		
8	7.5	GBR	March 751, 741	Ford Cosworth 3.0 V8	GBR	14	1			2	28	1	1
9	6	GBR	Williams FW04, FW	Ford Cosworth 3.0 V8	GBR	12			1				
10	5	USA	Parnelli VPJ4	Ford Cosworth 3.0 V8	GBR	12				1	10		1
11	3	GBR	Hill GH1	Ford Cosworth 3.0 V8	GBR	10				1	8		
12	2	USA	Penske PC1	Ford Cosworth 3.0 V8	GBR	10							
13	1	GBR	Ensign N175, N174	Ford Cosworth 3.0 V8	GBR	7							

1976

Hunt prevails in epic duel

THE TALE OF THE TITLE

- 'The greatest story ever told', the 1976 championship contained every facet that makes F1 so compelling.
- A spellbinding Fuji finale gave Hunt the title by one point after an heroic season-long battle with Lauda.
- Fittipaldi's move to Copersucar and Hesketh's withdrawal put Hunt in the number one seat at McLaren.
- A titanic championship battle was anticipated, Hunt versus Lauda, McLaren versus Ferrari.
- But Lauda romped to a huge early lead in the championship, Hunt's challenge dogged by controversy.
- Disaster at the Nürburgring altered everything, Lauda miraculously surviving to courageously return.
- Meanwhile, during Lauda's three-race absence Hunt's fraught points chase set up the Fuji showdown.
- McLaren and Ferrari won six races apiece, but it was Maranello's constructors' championship again.
- The startling six-wheeler spearheaded Tyrrell's strong season, a Scheckter victory plus 11 podiums.
- Twelve months after tragedy struck, John Watson gave Team Penske a poignant first victory in Austria.
- Andretti returned Lotus to winning ways and Peterson took his third Italian GP, this time for March.
- And not forgetting: no more 'Green Hell'.

THE CHASE FOR THE CHAMPIONSHIP

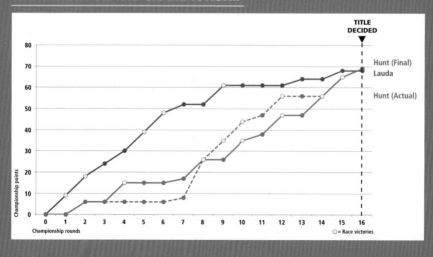

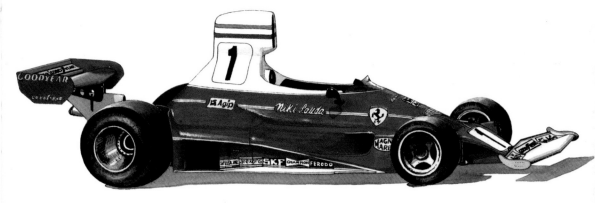

Ferrari 312T

Round 1/16	**BRAZILIAN GP** Interlagos		Niki Lauda
	25 January 1976	Race 265	Ferrari 312T 181.460kph, 112.754mph

Hunt on pole, Lauda alongside, the eagerly anticipated Ferrari versus McLaren duel looked all set. But it was Regazzoni from row two who led the opening eight laps until delayed by a puncture. Now Lauda took over with Hunt tussling with Jarier's Shadow close behind. This dice continued until Hunt fell back with metering unit problems on lap 27 and finally spun out from fifth with a stuck throttle eight laps from the end. Jarier meanwhile, posting fastest lap on lap 31, had reduced the gap to Lauda from 6s to 2s, only to spin out on oil dropped the previous lap in the Hunt incident. So Lauda took a comfortable victory, claiming afterwards that Jarier had posed no threat. Depailler's Tyrrell and Pryce's Shadow completed the podium.

POLE POSITION J Hunt, McLaren-Ford, 2m 32.50s (0.02s), 187.908kph, 116.761mph
LAPS 40 x 7.960 km, 4.946 miles
DISTANCE 318.400 km, 197.845 miles
STARTERS/FINISHERS 22/14
WEATHER Sunny, very hot, dry
LAP LEADERS C Regazzoni, Ferrari 1-8 (8); Lauda 9-40 (32)
WINNER'S LAPS 1-8 P2, 9-40 P1
FASTEST LAP J-P Jarier, Shadow-Ford, 2m 35.07s (lap 31), 184.794kph, 114.826mph
CHAMPIONSHIP Lauda 9, Depailler 6, Pryce 4, Stuck 3, Scheckter 2

Pos	Driver	Car	Time/gap	Grid	Stops	Tyres
1	N Lauda	Ferrari	1h 45m 16.78s	2	0	G
2	P Depailler	Tyrrell-Ford	–21.47s	9	0	G
3	T Pryce	Shadow-Ford	–23.84s	12	0	G
4	H-J Stuck	March-Ford	–1m 28.17s	14	0	G
5	J Scheckter	Tyrrell-Ford	–1m 56.46s	13	0	G
6	J Mass	McLaren-Ford	–1m 58.27s	6	1	G

Round 2/16	**SOUTH AFRICAN GP** Kyalami		Niki Lauda
	6 March 1976	Race 266	Ferrari 312T 187.737kph, 116.654mph

Once again Hunt and Lauda occupied the front row but Hunt wasted his pole position, crucially slipping to fourth on the first lap from a poor start. Lauda took an immediate lead which, by the time Hunt passed Brambilla's March for second place on lap 6, was 6s. At its maximum it became 10s, but, as tyre and track conditions altered, the gap began to slowly shrink. In the closing laps it also became apparent that the rear tyre on the Ferrari was deflating. With three to go Hunt was 3.6s behind, the last lap 2.7s and at the line 1.3s. But for his bad start James might have made it. Yet despite this second defeat, with teammate Jochen Mass finishing third McLaren at least looked competitive and Hunt had now opened his account.

POLE POSITION Hunt, McLaren-Ford, 1m 16.41s (0.07s), 193.357kph, 120.146mph
LAPS 78 x 4.104 km, 2.550 miles
DISTANCE 320.112 km, 198.908 miles
STARTERS/FINISHERS 25/17
WEATHER Sunny, hot, dry
LAP LEADERS Lauda 1-78 (78)
WINNER'S LAPS 1-78 P1
FASTEST LAP Lauda, Ferrari, 1m 17.20s (lap 11), 191.378kph, 118.917mph
CHAMPIONSHIP Lauda 18, Depailler 6, Hunt 6, Mass 5, Scheckter 5

Pos	Driver	Car	Time/gap	Grid	Stops	Tyres
1	N Lauda	Ferrari	1h 42m 18.4s	2	0	G
2	J Hunt	McLaren-Ford	–1.3s	1	0	G
3	J Mass	McLaren-Ford	–45.9s	4	0	G
4	J Scheckter	Tyrrell-Ford	–1m 8.4s	12	0	G
5	J Watson	Penske-Ford	–1 lap	3	0	G
6	M Andretti	Parnelli-Ford	–1 lap	13	0	G

Round 3/16	UNITED STATES GP WEST Long Beach	Clay Regazzoni
	28 March 1976 · Race 267	Ferrari 312T 137.715kph, 85.572mph

A resounding Regazzoni-led 1-2 finish heralded a Ferrari hat-trick of victories in the opening three races. At the very first GP to be held on the Long Beach street circuit, Regazzoni took pole, led every one of the 80 laps, his 61st the fastest lap. Lauda from P4 after a troubled practice found himself promoted to second on lap 5 but with 'transmission vibration' was glad just to finish, and never challenged for victory. Lauda's elevation to P2 came from controversy, Hunt clashing with Depailler's Tyrrell on lap 3 in an attempt to wrest second place from the Frenchman. Hunt was furious, the unscathed Tyrrell finishing third, but the fracas was not caused blatantly, just part of the rough and tumble of street racing.

POLE POSITION Regazzoni, Ferrari, 1m 23.099s (0.193s), 140.834kph, 87.510mph
LAPS 80 x 3.251 km, 2.020 miles
DISTANCE 260.070 km, 161.600 miles
STARTERS/FINISHERS 20/10
WEATHER Sunny, hot, dry
LAP LEADERS Regazzoni 1-80 (80)
WINNER'S LAPS 1-80 P1
FASTEST LAP Regazzoni, Ferrari, 1m 23.076s (lap 61), 140.873kph, 87.534mph
CHAMPIONSHIP Lauda 24, Depailler 10, Regazzoni 9, Mass 7, Hunt 6

Pos	Driver	Car	Time/gap	Grid	Stops	Tyres
1	C Regazzoni	Ferrari	1h 53m 18.471s	1	0	G
2	N Lauda	Ferrari	−42.414s	4	0	G
3	P Depailler	Tyrrell-Ford	−49.972s	2	0	G
4	J Laffite	Ligier-Matra	−1m 12.828s	12	0	G
5	J Mass	McLaren-Ford	−1m 22.292s	14	0	G
6	E Fittipaldi	Copersucar-Ford	−1 lap	16	1	G

McLaren-Ford M23

Round 4/16	SPANISH GP Jarama	James Hunt
	2 May 1976 · Race 268	McLaren-Ford M23 149.677kph, 93.005mph

Another poor pole getaway by Hunt gave Lauda the lead, the following McLaren pair sandwiching a strange blue, six-wheeled car. Depailler had qualified the Tyrrell P34 third on debut and was going well until running out of brakes on lap 25. Hounded by the two McLarens, and driving with a broken rib from a tractor accident, Lauda was tiring. On lap 32 Hunt went by, Mass three later. Trailing Lauda in points, Hunt's first McLaren win was very welcome until post-race scrutineering ignited the contention that characterised the rest of the season. His McLaren was disqualified for failing the newly introduced width regulations, handing victory and yet another nine points to Lauda. (Some two months later Hunt's victory was reinstated on appeal.)

POLE POSITION Hunt, McLaren-Ford, 1m 18.52s (0.32s), 156.067kph, 96.976mph
LAPS 75 x 3.404 km, 2.115 miles
DISTANCE 255.300 km, 158.636 miles
STARTERS/FINISHERS 24/13
WEATHER Sunny, hot, dry
LAP LEADERS Lauda 1-31 (31); Hunt 32-75 (44)
WINNER'S LAPS 1-31 P2, 32-75 P1 (Hunt disqualified but reinstated later after appeal)
FASTEST LAP J Mass, McLaren-Ford, 1m 20.93s (lap 52), 151.420kph, 94.088mph
CHAMPIONSHIP Lauda 30, Hunt 15, Depailler 10, Regazzoni 9, Mass 7 (Points reflect final results)

Pos	Driver	Car	Time/gap	Grid	Stops	Tyres
1	J Hunt	McLaren-Ford	1h 42m 20.43s	1	0	G
2	N Lauda	Ferrari	−30.97s	2	0	G
3	G Nilsson	Lotus-Ford	−48.02s	7	0	G
4	C Reutemann	Brabham-Alfa	−1 lap	12	0	G
5	C Amon	Ensign-Ford	−1 lap	10	0	G
6	C Pace	Brabham-Alfa	−1 lap	11	0	G

Round 5/16	**BELGIAN GP** Zolder	**Niki Lauda**
	16 May 1976 Race 269	Ferrari 312T2 173.981kph, 108.107mph

With McLaren on the back foot, Ferrari capitalised with another convincing 1-2, Lauda from Regga in qualifying and the race. More disconcerting for the DFV brigade, Jacques Laffite rubbed in 12-cylinder superiority with a first podium for the new Ligier-Matra. Hunt's poorly handling M23, barely in contention for a top-three place, convinced McLaren critics that post-Spain mods had removed the unfair advantage. He retired at half-distance with transmission woes, still with only six points to his name, 36 behind Lauda's rampant Ferrari. The six-wheelers kept the Ford flag flying, but Scheckter in fourth was close to being lapped by Lauda. Amon, running fifth on lap 52, had a narrow squeak when his Ensign lost a wheel.

POLE POSITION Lauda, Ferrari, 1m 26.55s (0.05s), 177.276kph, 110.154mph
LAPS 70 x 4.262 km, 2.648 miles
DISTANCE 298.340 km, 185.380 miles
STARTERS/FINISHERS 26/12
WEATHER Sunny, warm, dry
LAP LEADERS Lauda 1-70 (70)
WINNER'S LAPS 1-70 P1
FASTEST LAP Lauda, Ferrari, 1m 25.98s (lap NA), 178.451kph, 110.884mph
CHAMPIONSHIP Lauda 39, Hunt 15, Regazzoni 15, Depailler 10, Mass 8

Pos	Driver	Car	Time/gap	Grid	Stops	Tyres
1	N Lauda	Ferrari	1h 42m 53.23s	1	0	G
2	C Regazzoni	Ferrari	−3.46s	2	0	G
3	J Laffite	Ligier-Matra	−35.38s	6	0	G
4	J Scheckter	Tyrrell-Ford	−1m 31.08s	7	0	G
5	A Jones	Surtees-Ford	−1 lap	16	0	G
6	J Mass	McLaren-Ford	−1 lap	18	0	G

Round 6/16	**MONACO GP** Monte Carlo	**Niki Lauda**
	30 May 1976 Race 270	Ferrari 312T2 129.321kph, 80.356mph

Ferrari locked out the front row a second time. From pole Lauda then proceeded to lead every lap in dominant style. For the first 26 he was chased by a March 761, Peterson showing a welcome return to form before coming unstuck at Tabac. Two laps sooner and Regazzoni would have made it a Ferrari 1-2, but he too had a moment which had led the two six-wheelers by. They finished second and third, Regazzoni's late attack ending when he clipped the barriers with five laps remaining. Hunt qualified poorly, didn't feature in the race and went out with engine trouble. After six championship rounds Lauda was just three points short of a maximum, Hunt still on six.

POLE POSITION Lauda, Ferrari, 1m 29.65s (0.26s), 132.997kph, 82.641mph
LAPS 78 x 3.312 km, 2.058 miles
DISTANCE 258.336 km, 160.523 miles
STARTERS/FINISHERS 20/14
WEATHER Cloudy with sunny intervals, warm, dry
LAP LEADERS Lauda 1-78 (78)
WINNER'S LAPS 1-78 P1
FASTEST LAP C Regazzoni, Ferrari, 1m 30.28s (lap 60), 132.069kph, 82.064mph
CHAMPIONSHIP Lauda 48, Hunt 15, Regazzoni 15, Depailler 14, Scheckter 14

Pos	Driver	Car	Time/gap	Grid	Stops	Tyres
1	N Lauda	Ferrari	1h 59m 51.47s	1	0	G
2	J Scheckter	Tyrrell-Ford	−11.13s	5	0	G
3	P Depailler	Tyrrell-Ford	−1m 4.84s	4	0	G
4	H-J Stuck	March-Ford	−1 lap	6	0	G
5	J Mass	McLaren-Ford	−1 lap	11	0	G
6	E Fittipaldi	Copersucar-Ford	−1 lap	7	0	G

Round 7/16	**SWEDISH GP** Anderstorp	**Jody Scheckter**
	13 June 1976 Race 271	Tyrrell-Ford P34 162.381kph, 100.899mph

Anderstorp produced its usual, unusual grid, six-wheelers one and three sandwiching Andretti's Lotus 77, Amon's Ensign four, Ferraris six and twelve. For 30-odd laps until the engine went off Andretti held sway, but when it finally expired on lap 46 the Tyrrell six-wheelers were there to stun the Grand Prix world with a 1-2 victory. It was a result strangely reminiscent of 1974, when once again the Tyrrells, this time without their newfangled wheel configuration, ideally suited the Anderstorp track. At half-distance, running a strong fourth, Amon had another nasty fright when front suspension failure pitched him into the barrier. Lauda started fifth and finished third; Hunt started seventh and finished fifth, his points deficit to Lauda now 47.

POLE POSITION Scheckter, Tyrrell-Ford, 1m 25.659s (0.349s), 168.865kph, 104.928mph
LAPS 72 x 4.018 km, 2.497 miles
DISTANCE 289.296 km, 179.760 miles
STARTERS/FINISHERS 26/15
WEATHER Overcast, dry
LAP LEADERS (On the road) Andretti 1-45 (45); Scheckter 46-72 (27)
WINNER'S LAPS 1-45 P2, 46-72 P1
FASTEST LAP M Andretti, Lotus-Ford, 1m 28.002s (lap 11), 164.369kph, 102.134mph
CHAMPIONSHIP Lauda 52, Scheckter 23, Depailler 20, Hunt 17, Regazzoni 16

Pos	Driver	Car	Time/gap	Grid	Stops	Tyres
1	J Scheckter	Tyrrell-Ford	1h 46m 53.729s	1	0	G
2	P Depailler	Tyrrell-Ford	−19.766s	4	0	G
3	N Lauda	Ferrari	−33.866s	5	0	G
4	J Laffite	Ligier-Matra	−55.819s	7	0	G
5	J Hunt	McLaren-Ford	−59.483s	8	0	G
6	C Regazzoni	Ferrari	−1m 0.366s	11	0	G

Tyrrell-Ford P34

Round 8/16	**FRENCH GP** Paul Ricard	**James Hunt**
	4 July 1976 Race 272	McLaren-Ford M23 186.423kph, 115.838mph

For the forth time in eight races Hunt and Lauda shared the front row. And for the forth time Hunt failed to capitalise, Lauda grabbing an initial lead, Hunt meat in a Ferrari sandwich. But not for long. First Lauda 8s ahead and then Regazzoni 1s behind were both out by lap 17 with falling oil pressure. Depailler finished second in the six-wheeler and Peterson's March held third until the metering unit failed three laps from the finish. So Watson narrowly beat Pace's Brabham-Alfa into third until the Ulsterman's Penske was disqualified over rear-wing height, later reinstated. Also reinstated in Paris the following day was Hunt's Spanish win, the gap to Lauda suddenly slashed to 26 championship points.

POLE POSITION Hunt, McLaren-Ford, 1m 47.89s (0.28s), 193.864kph, 120.642mph
LAPS 54 x 5.810 km, 3.610 miles
DISTANCE 313.740 km, 194.949 miles
STARTERS/FINISHERS 27/19
WEATHER Sunny, hot, dry
LAP LEADERS Lauda 1-8 (8); Hunt 9-54 (46)
WINNER'S LAPS 1-8 P2, 9-54 P1
FASTEST LAP N Lauda, Ferrari, 1m 51.00s (lap 4), 188.432kph, 117.086mph
CHAMPIONSHIP Lauda 52, Hunt 26, Depailler 26, Scheckter 24, Regazzoni 16

Pos	Driver	Car	Time/gap	Grid	Stops	Tyres
1	J Hunt	McLaren-Ford	1h 40m 58.60s	1	0	G
2	P Depailler	Tyrrell-Ford	–12.70s	3	0	G
3	J Watson	Penske-Ford	–23.55s	8	0	G
4	C Pace	Brabham-Alfa	–24.82s	5	0	G
5	M Andretti	Lotus-Ford	–43.92s	7	0	G
6	J Scheckter	Tyrrell-Ford	–55.07s	9	0	G

Round 9/16	**BRITISH GP** Brands Hatch	**Niki Lauda**
	18 July 1976 Race 273	Ferrari 312T2 183.874kph, 114.254mph

A Hunt-Lauda front row, but the red cars led into Paddock and touched. Bedlam, red flag. When it was announced that Hunt would not be allowed to restart, spectator people-power – jeering, clapping, stamping – reversed the stewards' decision. For 44 laps of the re-run race Lauda led Hunt, pulling a 6s gap which then shrank back to nothing. Hunt took the lead at Druids, the crowd ecstatic, to win by almost one minute. Hunt had taken the restart in his spare car, the race-car damaged in the Ferrari-induced first corner chaos. Ferrari had also argued, and been granted, that Regazzoni use his spare. Nevertheless, after the race the Scuderia lodged a protest on those same grounds against the winner, the result therefore provisional pending McLaren's appeal.

POLE POSITION Lauda, Ferrari, 1m 19.35s (0.06s), 214.049kph, 133.004mph
LAPS 76 x 4.207 km, 2.614 miles (Race restarted for scheduled 76 laps following accident)
DISTANCE 319.719 km, 198.664 miles
STARTERS/FINISHERS 26/9
WEATHER Sunny, warm, dry
LAP LEADERS (On the road) Lauda 1-44 (44); J Hunt, McLaren-Ford 45-76 (32)
WINNER'S LAPS 1-44 P1, 45-76 P2 (Hunt disqualified from first place)
FASTEST LAP Lauda, Ferrari, 1m 19.91s (lap 41), 209.975kph, 130.472mph
CHAMPIONSHIP Lauda 61, Scheckter 30, Hunt 26, Depailler 26, Regazzoni 16 (Points reflect final results)

Pos	Driver	Car	Time/gap	Grid	Stops	Tyres
1	N Lauda	Ferrari	1h 44m 19.66s	1	0	G
2	J Scheckter	Tyrrell-Ford	–16.18s	8	0	G
3	J Watson	Penske-Ford	–1 lap	11	1	G
4	T Pryce	Shadow-Ford	–1 lap	20	0	G
5	A Jones	Surtees-Ford	–1 lap	19	0	G
6	E Fittipaldi	Copersucar-Ford	–2 laps	21	0	G

TOP **100** RACE

Round 10/16	**GERMAN GP** Nürburgring			James Hunt
	1 August 1976		**Race 274**	McLaren-Ford M23 188.586kph, 117.182mph

For the sixth time Hunt and Lauda occupied the front row but this time it was Niki who fluffed his start, dropping to seventh. During the first wet-dry lap of the 14-mile Nordschleife circuit Lauda's Ferrari, on slicks, went off at Bergwerk, crashing in flames. His survival in doubt, the last rites were administered in hospital, but after three days on the brink a miraculous recovery began. In now dry conditions, Hunt led the restarted race from pole, winning as he pleased once Regazzoni spun on the opening lap. A Tyrrell six-wheeler was runner-up yet again, and Mass in the second McLaren, who had 'won' the first two-lap race, came in third. Hunt's third successive victory reduced the points gap to 14.

POLE POSITION Hunt, McLaren-Ford, 7m 06.5s (0.9s), 192.746kph, 119.767mph
LAPS 14 x 22.835 km, 14.189 miles (Race restarted for scheduled 14 laps following accident)
DISTANCE 319.960 km, 198.646 miles
STARTERS/FINISHERS 26/15
WEATHER Wet start, drying later
LAP LEADERS Hunt 1-14 (14)
WINNER'S LAPS 1-14 P1
FASTEST LAP Scheckter, Tyrrell-Ford, 7m 10.8s (lap 13), 190.822kph, 118.571mph
CHAMPIONSHIP Lauda 61, Scheckter 36, Hunt 35, Depailler 26, Regazzoni 16

Pos	Driver	Car	Time/gap	Grid	Stops	Tyres
1	J Hunt	McLaren-Ford	1h 41m 42.7s	1	0	G
2	J Scheckter	Tyrrell-Ford	–27.7s	8	0	G
3	J Mass	McLaren-Ford	–52.4s	9	0	G
4	C Pace	Brabham-Alfa	–54.2s	7	0	G
5	G Nilsson	Lotus-Ford	–1m 57.3s	16	0	G
6	R Stommelen	Brabham-Alfa	–2m 30.3s	15	0	G

Penske-Ford PC4

Round 11/16	**AUSTRIAN GP** Österreichring			John Watson
	15 August 1976		**Race 275**	Penske-Ford PC4 212.451kph, 132.011mph

Hunt on pole from Watson's Penske, no Ferraris present. The opening laps were tricky, the grid wearing slicks on a damp track that got wetter. But the unexpected shower was brief, pit stops for wets unnecessary, and an exciting race ensued. Watson and Peterson shared the lead initially but Scheckter made rapid progress from a P10 start and led lap 10, only to crash soon afterwards when a wishbone broke. By half-distance Watson led by 7s and at the finish by 10s, Laffite-Nilsson-Hunt finishing 2-3-4 like that. For Hunt, with Lauda on the mend, two miserly points seemed an opportunity missed. Watson's maiden victory for Penske was poignant, the anniversary of Mark Donohue's fatal accident at the same circuit two days away.

POLE POSITION Hunt, McLaren-Ford, 1m 35.02s (0.12s), 223.911kph, 139.132mph
LAPS 54 x 5.910 km, 3.672 miles
DISTANCE 319.140 km, 198.304 miles
STARTERS/FINISHERS 25/12
WEATHER Warm, wet track then drying
LAP LEADERS Watson 1-2, 12-54 (45); Peterson 3-9, 11 (8); J Scheckter, Tyrrell-Ford 10 (1)
WINNER'S LAPS 1-2 P1, 3-6 P2, 7-10 P3, 11 P2, 12-54 P1
FASTEST LAP Hunt, McLaren-Ford, 1m 35.91s (lap NA), 221.833kph, 137.841mph
CHAMPIONSHIP Lauda 61, Hunt 38, Scheckter 36, Depailler 26, Watson 19

Pos	Driver	Car	Time/gap	Grid	Stops	Tyres
1	J Watson	Penske-Ford	1h 30m 7.86s	2	0	G
2	J Laffite	Ligier-Matra	–10.79s	5	0	G
3	G Nilsson	Lotus-Ford	–11.98s	4	0	G
4	J Hunt	McLaren-Ford	–12.44s	1	0	G
5	M Andretti	Lotus-Ford	–21.49s	9	0	G
6	R Peterson	March-Ford	–34.34s	3	0	G

Round 12/16	**DUTCH GP** Zandvoort			**James Hunt**

DUTCH GP Zandvoort
29 August 1976   Race 276

James Hunt
McLaren-Ford M23 177.801kph, 110.480mph

At the scene of his Hesketh victory a year ago, Hunt triumphed again. From the front row he completed lap 1 third behind pole-sitter Peterson and Watson. As Watson attempted to pass Peterson on lap 8, Hunt slipped by and four laps later passed the understeering March for the lead. Hunt and Watson, in the quicker car, then slugged it out for 35 laps until the Penske gearbox quit. Hunt, handling deteriorating, next came under pressure from Regazzoni in the singleton Ferrari. But much to the *Commendatore*'s displeasure, Regazzoni fell short by less than a second. Lauda's championship lead was now two points, but news of the reigning world champion was that he had left hospital and, incredibly, was well on the way to recovery.

POLE POSITION R Peterson, March-Ford, 1m 21.31s (0.08s), 187.106kph, 116.262mph
LAPS 75 x 4.226 km, 2.626 miles
DISTANCE 316.950 km, 196.944 miles
STARTERS/FINISHERS 26/12
WEATHER Sunny, warm, dry
LAP LEADERS Peterson 1-11 (11); Hunt 12-75 (64)
WINNER'S LAPS 1-7 P3, 8-11 P2, 12-75 P1
FASTEST LAP Regazzoni, Ferrari, 1m 22.59s (lap 49), 184.206kph, 114.461mph
CHAMPIONSHIP Lauda 61, Hunt 47, Scheckter 38, Depailler 26, Regazzoni 22

Pos	Driver	Car	Time/gap	Grid	Stops	Tyres
1	J Hunt	McLaren-Ford	1h 44m 52.09s	2	0	G
2	C Regazzoni	Ferrari	−0.92s	5	0	G
3	M Andretti	Lotus-Ford	−2.09s	6	0	G
4	T Pryce	Shadow-Ford	−6.94s	3	0	G
5	J Scheckter	Tyrrell-Ford	−22.46s	8	0	G
6	V Brambilla	March-Ford	−45.03s	7	0	G

March-Ford 761

Round 13/16	**ITALIAN GP** Monza			**Ronnie Peterson**

ITALIAN GP Monza
12 September 1976   Race 277

Ronnie Peterson
March-Ford 761 199.750kph, 124.119mph

Ronnie Peterson won the Italian GP for the third time, this time for March. He led from lap 11 to the end, Regazzoni's Ferrari and pole-man Laffite's Ligier-Matra close behind. Both Tyrrells led but faded towards the end. With his facial burns still swathed in bandages, Lauda made a miraculous return to the wheel just six weeks after his death-defying accident. He qualified fifth, fastest of the three Ferraris entered, Carlos Reutemann having been drafted in from Brabham as his replacement. Meanwhile, the Italian officials dispatched Hunt to the back of the grid for an alleged fuel octane irregularity. Attempting to come back through the field, Hunt crashed out. Lauda finished a courageous fourth, extending his points lead to five.

POLE POSITION Laffite, Ligier-Matra, 1m 41.35s (0.03s), 206.019kph, 128.014mph
LAPS 52 x 5.800 km, 3.604 miles
DISTANCE 301.600 km, 187.406 miles
STARTERS/FINISHERS 26/10
WEATHER Warm, some light rain
LAP LEADERS Scheckter 1-10 (10); Peterson 11-52 (42)
WINNER'S LAPS 1-2 P4, 3 P3, 4-10 P2, 11-52 P1
FASTEST LAP Peterson, March-Ford, 1m 41.30s (lap 50), 206.120kph, 128.077mph
CHAMPIONSHIP Lauda 64, Hunt 47, Scheckter 40, Regazzoni 28, Depailler 27

Pos	Driver	Car	Time/gap	Grid	Stops	Tyres
1	R Peterson	March-Ford	1h 30m 35.6s	8	0	G
2	C Regazzoni	Ferrari	−2.3s	9	0	G
3	J Laffite	Ligier-Matra	−3.0s	1	0	G
4	N Lauda	Ferrari	−19.4s	5	0	G
5	J Scheckter	Tyrrell-Ford	−19.5s	2	0	G
6	P Depailler	Tyrrell-Ford	−35.7s	4	0	G

Round 14/16	**CANADIAN GP** Mosport Park	**James Hunt**
	3 October 1976 Race 278	McLaren-Ford M23 189.650kph, 117.843mph

In Paris McLaren's British GP appeal had been quashed, so Lauda entered the back-to-back North American rounds with his lead not five points but seventeen. Hunt rose to the challenge, beginning with another pole position. Off the line, second-fastest qualifier Peterson's March led Hunt for eight laps before increasing handling trouble set in. Hunt and Depailler then staged a stirring pursuit dice for lap after lap until the Tyrrell fell back in the closing laps, the Frenchman affected by fumes. Andretti's ever-improving Lotus came third while Regazzoni was widely censured for pushing Pace into the pit wall to prevent him overtaking for sixth place. Hampered by suspension maladies, Lauda failed to score, his points advantage over Hunt now eight.

POLE POSITION Hunt, McLaren-Ford, 1m 12.389s (0.394s), 196.806kph, 122.289mph
LAPS 80 x 3.957 km, 2.459 miles
DISTANCE 316.590 km, 196.720 miles
STARTERS/FINISHERS 24/20
WEATHER Sunny, warm, dry
LAP LEADERS R Peterson, March-Ford 1-8 (8); Hunt 9-80 (72)
WINNER'S LAPS 1-8 P2, 9-80 P1
FASTEST LAP Depailler, Tyrrell-Ford, 1m 13.817s (lap 60), 192.998kph, 119.924mph
CHAMPIONSHIP Lauda 64, Hunt 56, Scheckter 43, Depailler 33, Regazzoni 29

Pos	Driver	Car	Time/gap	Grid	Stops	Tyres
1	J Hunt	McLaren-Ford	1h 40m 9.626s	1	0	G
2	P Depailler	Tyrrell-Ford	−6.331s	4	0	G
3	M Andretti	Lotus-Ford	−10.366s	5	0	G
4	J Scheckter	Tyrrell-Ford	−19.745s	7	0	G
5	J Mass	McLaren-Ford	−41.811s	11	0	G
6	C Regazzoni	Ferrari	−46.256s	12	0	G

Round 15/16	**UNITED STATES GP EAST** Watkins Glen	**James Hunt**
	10 October 1976 Race 279	McLaren-Ford M23 187.371kph, 116.427mph

At the Glen Hunt completed a North American clean sweep, and just as in Canada his chief opposition came from a six-wheeler. For half the race Lauda ran third, a few seconds behind Scheckter and Hunt, but as oversteer set in the Ferrari almost fell into the grips of the second McLaren. At the front, James, having failed to convert his pole, tracked Jody, cannily saving his tyres on full tanks. As the McLaren handling became neutral, Hunt closed in and took the lead on lap 37. Scheckter briefly got back ahead in traffic, forcing Hunt to repeat the exercise, but once by he pulled out 8s in the final 14 laps. But Lauda's gritty third-place meant the defending champion went to the Fuji finale still holding a slender three-point lead.

POLE POSITION Hunt, McLaren-Ford, 1m 43.622s (0.248s), 188.812kph, 117.323mph
LAPS 59 x 5.435 km, 3.377 miles
DISTANCE 320.651 km, 199.243 miles
STARTERS/FINISHERS 26/14
WEATHER Cold, dry
LAP LEADERS Scheckter 1-36, 41-45 (41); Hunt 37-40, 46-59 (18)
WINNER'S LAPS 1-36 P2, 37-40 P1, 41-45 P2, 46-59 P1
FASTEST LAP Hunt, McLaren-Ford, 1m 42.851s (lap 53), 190.228kph, 118.202mph
CHAMPIONSHIP Lauda 68, Hunt 65, Scheckter 49, Depailler 33, Regazzoni 29

Pos	Driver	Car	Time/gap	Grid	Stops	Tyres
1	J Hunt	McLaren-Ford	1h 42m 40.741s	1	0	G
2	J Scheckter	Tyrrell-Ford	−8.030s	2	0	G
3	N Lauda	Ferrari	−1m 2.324s	5	0	G
4	J Mass	McLaren-Ford	−1m 2.458s	17	0	G
5	H-J Stuck	March-Ford	−1m 7.978s	6	0	G
6	J Watson	Penske-Ford	−1m 8.190s	8	0	G

Lotus-Ford 77

Round 16/16	**JAPANESE GP** Fuji		**Mario Andretti**
	24 October 1976	Race 280	Lotus-Ford 77 183.615kph, 114.093mph

If Hunt won the race the title was his regardless. If he didn't, Lauda needed to finish close enough to the McLaren to retain it. These scenarios were valid for a mere two laps, Lauda, along with three others, withdrawing their cars, deciding the atrociously wet and misty weather to be unsuitable for racing. Meanwhile Hunt had taken the lead, holding it for 61 laps of the 73-lap race. But as the track dried he was forced to pit for new tyres, dropping him to fifth with five laps to go, the championship now Lauda's. But on the penultimate lap Hunt charged back on fresh rubber and overtook non-stopping cars struggling on worn tyres, regaining the crucial P4, then P3 and with it the championship by one point. Pole-man Andretti won the race for Lotus.

POLE POSITION Andretti, Lotus-Ford, 1m 12.77s (0.03s), 215.644kph, 133.995mph
LAPS 73 x 4.359 km, 2.709 miles
DISTANCE 318.207 km, 197.725 miles
STARTERS/FINISHERS 25/11
WEATHER Overcast, rain, misty
LAP LEADERS Hunt 1-61 (61); Depailler 62-63 (2); Andretti 64-73 (10)
WINNER'S LAPS 1 P3, 2 P2, 3-5 P3, 6-15 P2, 16-20 P3, 21 P4, 22-32 P5, 33-35 P6, 36-38 P5, 39-46 P4, 47-61 P3, 62-63 P2, 64-73 P1
FASTEST LAP J Laffite, Ligier-Matra, 1m 19.97s (lap NA), 196.229kph, 121.931mph
CHAMPIONSHIP Hunt 69, Lauda 68, Scheckter 49, Depailler 39, Regazzoni 31

Pos	Driver	Car	Time/gap	Grid	Stops	Tyres
1	M Andretti	Lotus-Ford	1h 43m 58.86s	1	0	G
2	P Depailler	Tyrrell-Ford	−1 lap	13	1	G
3	J Hunt	McLaren-Ford	−1 lap	2	1	G
4	A Jones	Surtees-Ford	−1 lap	20	0	G
5	C Regazzoni	Ferrari	−1 lap	7	0	G
6	G Nilsson	Lotus-Ford	−1 lap	16	0	G

TOP 100 RACE

1976 CHAMPIONSHIP FACTS AND FOLKLORE

- Regulation changes addressed new limits on front and rear wing overhang, maximum chassis and wheel width, rear wheel/tyre diameter and engine airbox height, with driver's foot-well reinforcement and dash-panel rollover protection now mandatory.
- Sixteen races for the first time in a two-part season, the best seven from each half counting for the championship, the calendar including the first Japanese GP and a second US GP run at Long Beach. Following the Lauda accident, the Nürburgring Nordschleife circuit, nicknamed 'The Green Hell', was never again used for Grand Prix racing.
- The championship battle between James Hunt and Niki Lauda tops F1 folklore. The events that unfolded were laced with nerve, skill, courage and controversy, but ultimately, after Lauda had led the points table all season, Hunt snatched the championship at the Fuji finale by a single point. It was that close, that tense.
- Lauda's near-fatal accident halfway through the opening lap at the Nürburgring was the pivotal moment that abruptly curtailed his romp to a second consecutive championship.
- Could Hunt close a 26-point deficit in the races that remained? Or would Lauda rise from his deathbed to defend his title?
- Lauda's accident was exceptionally violent, his Ferrari cannoning off an embankment to come to rest engulfed in flames in the middle of the track. The wreck was subsequently and unavoidably struck by two following cars.
- These drivers made valiant attempts to free Lauda but it was the diminutive Arturo Merzario who dived into the flames to release the jammed safety harness, so enabling the stricken driver to be pulled clear.
- Burns to Lauda's face were intensified because catch-fencing had wrenched off his helmet, but hospital tests were needed to identify serious internal injuries to his lungs and blood system caused by the inhalation of toxic fumes from the inferno.
- His life lay in the balance for three days, following which a remarkable recovery began. Miraculously, Lauda returned to the cockpit a mere six weeks after his brush with death, a demonstration of courage and determination beyond measure.

RACE 280, Japanese GP: A late tyre stop for long-term race leader Hunt, here leading teammate Mass, set up a spellbinding ending, James taking the title by one point after an heroic season-long battle with Lauda.

- What was it that made the 1976 championship so utterly compelling? Was it Hunt versus Lauda, McLaren versus Maranello, Ford versus Ferrari? Probably all of these and more.
- It seemed to have every facet which transforms a good script into great theatre: the unexpected, disqualifications, reinstatements, intrigue, dirty tricks, last rites, courage, bravery, all culminating in a showdown at the Fuji finale.
- And it was there, if any further evidence were needed of Lauda's strength of character, that he took a decision requiring real guts, withdrawing his car on the grounds that the appalling weather conditions were unsuitable for racing. Yes, Niki Lauda was undoubtedly his own man.
- The 100 minutes of racing at Fuji was in itself a microcosm of all the emotional turmoil that had gone before as, within the space of the last dozen laps, the world championship was ripped from the grasp of one deserving player to be placed in the hands of the other equally deserving character, and back again, finally to be resolved by that single point!
- The 1976 championship has been parodied 'The greatest story ever told' because its intensity was not just confined to the Fuji finale. Tension steadily mounted throughout its entire nine-month duration, had even begun during the preceding close season. Why James Hunt found himself driving for McLaren in 1976 owed itself to two totally unrelated departures.
- First, Lord Alexander Hesketh effectively wound up his underfunded team, releasing Hunt from his obligations, although the remnants of the team continued without his Lordship's patronage. Second, Emerson Fittipaldi left McLaren in the lurch with a late decision to join his brother at Copersucar-Fittipaldi.
- Miraculously, Hunt, the only driver in 1975 to truly take the fight to Lauda and Ferrari, suddenly found himself no longer driving for a minnow but for a top team, a team that could deliver regular race wins, even championships.
- Ferrari's burgeoning success against the multifarious talents of the Ford-powered teams called for a white knight to take on the Prancing Horse. Hunt became this formidable warrior, the McLaren M23 his charger.
- Even in its 1974 championship-winning year the McLaren M23 had never been dominant, but invariably it proved competitive, having won nine Grands Prix since inception.
- First introduced in 1973, preparation of the M23 chassis for what would be its fourth season of competition focussed in the main on weight-saving measures. These included the use of Kevlar and Nomex in the fabrication of the monocoque and a compressed air starter system.
- McLaren also developed their own six-speed gearbox using Hewland internals, intended as much for the M23's replacement which was already in the pipeline.
- The new M26 made its debut at the Dutch Grand Prix, but in the end – as McLaren and Ford desperately attempted to wrest the titles back from Ferrari – the team decided to stick with the trusty M23 for the remainder of such an intense season.

- The two main protagonists left very little for the other teams although the race victories incidental to the main theme added further texture to this extraordinary season: Scheckter's six-wheeler in Sweden; Watson and Penske in Austria; Peterson's March at Monza, and the one of greatest future significance, Mario Andretti bringing Lotus back in from the cold at Fuji.
- A significant new arrival was the French Ligier équipe using the V12 Matra power plant, distinguished by a ludicrously oversized airbox which was thankfully cut down to size by new regulations effective from the Spanish GP. The JS prefix to the type number of his cars was Guy Ligier's tribute to his great friend Jo Schlesser, killed at Rouen in 1968.

- The Martini Brabhams also switched to 12 cylinders, now using Alfa Romeo's Flat-12 engine but without notable success.
- Both US teams withdrew in 1976, Parnelli after just two showings, Penske at the end of the season but with that precious single victory to their name.
- But the epic 1976 season was all about the championship battle. Its singular edginess derived from the collision of two worlds each superbly championing the cause of a converse Grand Prix culture. Colnbrook the kit car, the *garagistas*; Maranello the antithesis, all pedigree, each epitomised by McLaren versus Ferrari.

Championship ranking	Championship points	Driver nationality	1976 Drivers Championship		Races contested	Race victories	Podiumse excl. victories	Races led	Lights to flag victories	Laps led	Poles	Fastest laps	Triple Crowns
			Driver	Car									
1	69	GBR	James Hunt	McLaren-Ford	16	6	2	8	1	351	8	2	1
2	68	AUT	Niki Lauda	Ferrari	14	5	4	7	3	341	3	4	2
3	49	RSA	Jody Scheckter	Tyrrell-Ford	16	1	4	4		79	1	1	
4	39	FRA	Patrick Depailler	Tyrrell-Ford	16		7	1		2		1	
5	31	SUI	Clay Regazzoni	Ferrari	15	1	3	2	1	88	1	3	1
6	22	USA	Mario Andretti	Parnelli-Ford (2) Lotus-Ford (13)	15	1	2	2		55	1	1	
7	20	GBR	John Watson	Penske-Ford	16	1	2	1		45			
8	20	FRA	Jacques Laffite	Ligier-Matra	16		3				1	1	
9	19	GER	Jochen Mass	McLaren-Ford	16		2					1	
10	11	SWE	Gunnar Nilsson	Lotus-Ford	15		2						
11	10	SWE	Ronnie Peterson	Lotus-Ford (1) March-Ford (15)	16	1		4		69	1	1	
12	10	GBR	Tom Pryce	Shadow-Ford	16		1						
13	8	GER	Hans-Joachim Stuck	March-Ford	16								
14	7	BRA	Carlos Pace	Brabham-Alfa	16								
15	7	AUS	Alan Jones	Surtees-Ford	14								
16	3	ARG	Carlos Reutemann	Brabham-Alfa (12) Ferrari (1)	13								
17	3	BRA	Emerson Fittipaldi	Fittipaldi-Ford	15								
18	2	NZL	Chris Amon	Ensign-Ford	8								
19	1	GER	Rolf Stommelen	Brabham-Alfa (2) Hesketh-Ford (1)	3								
19	1	ITA	Vittorio Brambilla	March-Ford	16								
-	-	FRA	Jean-Pierre Jarier	Shadow-Ford	16							1	

Championship ranking	Championship points	Team/Marque nationality	1976 Constructors Championship		Engine maker nationality	Races contested	Race victories	1-2 finishes	Podiums excl. victories	Races led	Laps led	Poles	Fastest laps
			Chassis	Engine									
1	83	ITA	Ferrari 312T2	Ferrari 3.0 F12	ITA	15	6	2	7	9	429	4	7
2	74	NZL	McLaren M23	Ford Cosworth 3.0 V8	GBR	16	6		4	8	351	8	3
3	71	GBR	Tyrrell 007 & P34	Ford Cosworth 3.0 V8	GBR	16	1	1	11	5	81	1	2
4	29	GBR	Lotus 77	Ford Cosworth 3.0 V8	GBR	16	1		4	2	55	1	1
5	20	USA	Penske PC3 & PC4	Ford Cosworth 3.0 V8	GBR	16	1		2	1	45		
6	20	FRA	Ligier JS5	Matra 3.0 V12	FRA	16			3			1	1
7	19	GBR	March 761	Ford Cosworth 3.0 V8	GBR	16	1			4	69	1	1
8	10	USA	Shadow DN5B, DN8	Ford Cosworth 3.0 V8	GBR	16			1				1
9	9	GBR	Brabham BT45	Alfa Romeo 3.0 F12	ITA	16							
10	7	GBR	Surtees TS19	Ford Cosworth 3.0 V8	GBR	15							
11	3	BRA	Fittipaldi FD04	Ford Cosworth 3.0 V8	GBR	15							
12	2	GBR	Ensign N175, N174	Ford Cosworth 3.0 V8	GBR	14							
13	1	USA	Parnelli VPJ4	Ford Cosworth 3.0 V8	GBR	2							

1977

Niki storms back

THE TALE OF THE TITLE

- ◼ Niki Lauda conclusively regained the drivers' championship, then walked out on Ferrari polemics.
- ◼ His three race victories, with Reutemann adding a fourth, led Ferrari to their third consecutive constructors' title.
- ◼ The Lotus 78 pioneered 'ground effect', Andretti's four victories signalling a resurgence in Lotus fortunes.
- ◼ But the Cosworth 'development' engine's poor reliability caused another Lotus 'win or bust' campaign.
- ◼ Jody Scheckter driving for the new Wolf team mounted a genuine title challenge with three race victories.
- ◼ The McLaren M26, also with three wins, came good far too late for James Hunt to defend his hard-won title.
- ◼ Victories were spread across eight drivers, Gunnar Nilsson, Jacques Laffite and Alan Jones new winners.
- ◼ Jones gave Shadow a one and only win, Laffite the first championship success for a French car, Ligier-Matra.
- ◼ At Silverstone the F1 French connection escalated, Renault debuting an innovative turbocharged car.
- ◼ A freak accident killed Tom Pryce, and two spectators died when Gilles Villeneuve's Ferrari cartwheeled.
- ◼ And not forgetting: Renault bring Michelin to F1; Tyrrell's six-wheeler abandoned.

THE CHASE FOR THE CHAMPIONSHIP

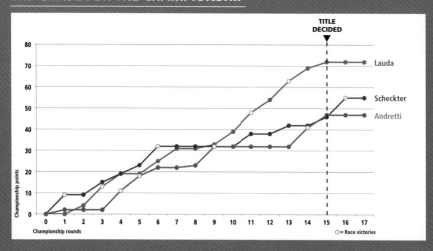

Wolf-Ford WR1

ARGENTINEAN GP Buenos Aires No 15

9 January 1977   Race 281

Jody Scheckter
Wolf-Ford WR1 189.429kph, 117.706mph

Jody Scheckter, driving for his brand new team in their brand new car, the Wolf-Ford, won first time out. From a P11 grid spot he made steady progress, leading the closing six laps as others wilted. The new champion was on pole, Watson alongside in the now competitive Brabham-Alfa, these two looking likely winners for much of the race. But mechanical failure put paid to both, Hunt's suspension on lap 31, gearbox mountings for Watson ten laps later. Meanwhile Pace in the other Brabham-Alfa, having slipped to P9 behind Scheckter at the start, was coming through even stronger, taking teammate Watson for the lead on lap 35. But affected by the heat, the slowing Pace finished second, only just pipping Reutemann's Ferrari.

POLE POSITION J Hunt, McLaren-Ford, 1m 48.68s (0.28s), 197.689kph, 122.838mph
LAPS 53 x 5.968 km, 3.708 miles
DISTANCE 316.304 km, 196.542 miles
STARTERS/FINISHERS 20/7
WEATHER Sunny, very hot, dry
LAP LEADERS J Watson, Brabham-Alfa 1-10, 32-34 (13); Hunt 11-31 (21); Pace 35-47 (13); Scheckter 48-53 (6)
WINNER'S LAPS 1-2 P8, 3-5 P7, 6 P8, 7-9 P9, 10-11 P8, 12-19 P7, 20-28 P6, 29-31 P5, 32-37 P4, 38-41 P3, 42-47 P2, 48-53 P1
FASTEST LAP J Hunt, McLaren-Ford, 1m 51.06s (lap 21), 193.452kph, 120.206mph
CHAMPIONSHIP Scheckter 9, Pace 6, Reutemann 4, Fittipaldi 3, Andretti 2

Pos	Driver	Car	Time/gap	Grid	Stops	Tyres
1	J Scheckter	Wolf-Ford	1h 40m 11.19s	11	0	G
2	C Pace	Brabham-Alfa	−43.24s	6	0	G
3	C Reutemann	Ferrari	−46.02s	7	1	G
4	E Fittipaldi	Copersucar-Ford	−55.48s	16	1	G
5r	M Andretti	Lotus-Ford	−2 laps	8	0	G
6	C Regazzoni	Ensign-Ford	−2 laps	12	1	G

BRAZILIAN GP Interlagos

23 January 1977   Race 282

Carlos Reutemann
Ferrari 312T 181.720kph, 112.916mph

Carlos Pace sent the crowd wild by rocketing into the lead from the third row only to be one of the first of the 'turn three' casualties, the surface breaking up under sticky rubber and hot sun. So pole-man Hunt went ahead on lap 7, but by lap 23 he had to give best to Reutemann's front-row Ferrari, the McLaren driver in handling difficulties immediately pitting for fresh rubber. Hunt charged back to second place but there was no catching Reutemann, a winner in only his third outing for Ferrari and taking an early lead in the points table. Behind these two, Lauda's Ferrari came from a lowly seventh row to finish third and open his championship account. Only seven cars finished, the same number eliminated by the 'turn three' marbles.

POLE POSITION Hunt, McLaren-Ford, 2m 30.11s (0.07s), 190.900kph, 118.620mph
LAPS 40 x 7.960 km, 4.946 miles
DISTANCE 318.400 km, 197.845 miles
STARTERS/FINISHERS 22/7
WEATHER Sunny, very hot, dry
LAP LEADERS C Pace, Brabham-Alfa 1-6 (6); Hunt 7-22 (16); Reutemann 23-40 (18)
WINNER'S LAPS 1-2 P2, 3-6 P3, 7-22 P2, 23-40 P1
FASTEST LAP Hunt, McLaren-Ford, 2m 34.55s (lap 33), 185.416kph, 115.212mph
CHAMPIONSHIP Reutemann 13, Scheckter 9, Pace 6, Hunt 6, Fittipaldi 6

Pos	Driver	Car	Time/gap	Grid	Stops	Tyres
1	C Reutemann	Ferrari	1h 45m 7.72s	2	0	G
2	J Hunt	McLaren -Ford	−10.71s	1	1	G
3	N Lauda	Ferrari	−1m 47.51s	13	0	G
4	E Fittipaldi	Copersucar-Ford	−1 lap	16	1	G
5	G Nilsson	Lotus-Ford	−1 lap	10	1	G
6	R Zorzi	Shadow-Ford	−1 lap	18	0	G

| Round 3/17 | **SOUTH AFRICAN GP** Kyalami | | | **Niki Lauda** | | |
| | **5 March 1977** | | **Race 283** | Ferrari 312T2 187.737kph, 116.654mph | | |

Lauda's first victory since his Nürburgring ordeal was impressive, nursing his lead in an ailing car, its water system damaged by debris. The debris resulted from a bizarre fatal collision on lap 23 between Tom Pryce's Shadow and an over-zealous marshal, crossing the track to lend assistance elsewhere. The unfortunate driver was struck by the fire extinguisher the marshal was carrying, killing Pryce instantly, the car careering down the straight to crash at Crowthorne. From his third successive pole Hunt led for only six laps before tyre problems caused first Lauda, then Scheckter on lap 18, and finally Depailler to come by in a very hairy move on lap 67. By the finish of this joyless race these four were separated by only 10s.

POLE POSITION Hunt, McLaren-Ford, 1m 15.96s (0.05s), 194.502kph, 120.858mph
LAPS 78 x 4.104 km, 2.550 miles
DISTANCE 320.112 km, 198.908 miles
STARTERS/FINISHERS 23/15
WEATHER Overcast, dry
LAP LEADERS Hunt 1-6 (6); Lauda 7-78 (72)
WINNER'S LAPS 1-6 P2, 7-78 P1
FASTEST LAP Watson, Brabham-Alfa, 1m 17.63s (lap 7), 190.318kph, 118.258mph
CHAMPIONSHIP Scheckter 15, Reutemann 13, Lauda 13, Hunt 9, Pace 6

Pos	Driver	Car	Time/gap	Grid	Stops	Tyres
1	N Lauda	Ferrari	1h 42m 21.6s	3	0	G
2	J Scheckter	Wolf-Ford	−5.2s	5	0	G
3	P Depailler	Tyrrell-Ford	−5.7s	4	0	G
4	J Hunt	McLaren-Ford	−9.5s	1	0	G
5	J Mass	McLaren-Ford	−19.9s	13	0	G
6	J Watson	Brabham-Alfa	−20.2s	11	0	G

Ferrari 312T2

| Round 4/17 | **UNITED STATES GP WEST** Long Beach | | | **Mario Andretti** | | |
| | **3 April 1977** | | **Race 284** | Lotus-Ford 78 139.834kph, 86.889mph | | |

Lauda and Andretti filled the front row but Scheckter from immediately behind beat them both to the first corner. A first lap shenanigans enabled these three to break clear and a tense and thrilling battle ensued. On a track with limited overtaking opportunities the lap chart read 20, 5, 11, Scheckter, Andretti, Lauda for lap after lap until, with only four of the 80 remaining, a deflating front tyre cost Scheckter the race, Andretti and Lauda crossing the line just 0.773s apart. It was tough for Scheckter but sweet for Andretti in front of his home crowd, but the upshot was that Lauda and Scheckter now jointly led the championship from Reutemann, these three looking like candidates, the strength of Mario's claim still unclear.

POLE POSITION Lauda, Ferrari, 1m 21.650s (0.238s), 143.333kph, 89.063mph
LAPS 80 x 3.251 km, 2.020 miles
DISTANCE 260.070 km, 161.600 miles
STARTERS/FINISHERS 22/11
WEATHER Sunny, warm, dry
LAP LEADERS Scheckter 1-76 (76); Andretti 77-80 (4)
WINNER'S LAPS 1-76 P2, 77-80 P1
FASTEST LAP Lauda, Ferrari, 1m 22.753s (lap 62), 141.423kph, 87.876mph
CHAMPIONSHIP Scheckter 19, Lauda 19, Reutemann 13, Andretti 11, Hunt 9

Pos	Driver	Car	Time/gap	Grid	Stops	Tyres
1	M Andretti	Lotus-Ford	1h 51m 35.470s	2	0	G
2	N Lauda	Ferrari	−0.773s	1	0	G
3	J Scheckter	Wolf-Ford	−4.857s	3	0	G
4	P Depailler	Tyrrell-Ford	−1m 14.487s	12	0	G
5	E Fittipaldi	Copersucar-Ford	−1m 20.908s	7	0	G
6	J-P Jarier	Penske-Ford	−1 lap	9	0	G

Round 5/17	**SPANISH GP** Jarama					
	8 May 1977				**Race 285**	

Mario Andretti
Lotus-Ford 78 149.677kph, 93.005mph

A second and far more convincing Andretti victory followed immediately, lifting the American into contention on the championship points table. What's more, Niki Lauda was unable to take part because of a rib injury, a hangover from his tractor accident ten months earlier. The JPS Lotus 78 enjoyed a significant performance advantage, fastest in all three qualifying sessions and topped by a scintillating pole. Leading every lap, the race was a foregone conclusion, especially when Laffite's chasing Ligier-Matra V12 pitted for attention on lap 12. So Andretti won handsomely from two other championship contenders, Reutemann and Scheckter. Hunt made a miserable debut in the M26 McLaren, retiring within a handful of laps.

POLE POSITION Andretti, Lotus-Ford, 1m 18.70s (0.72s), 155.710kph, 96.754mph
LAPS 75 x 3.404 km, 2.115 miles
DISTANCE 255.300 km, 158.636 miles
STARTERS/FINISHERS 24/14
WEATHER Sunny, warm, dry
LAP LEADERS Andretti 1-75 (75)
WINNER'S LAPS 1-75 P1
FASTEST LAP J Laffite, Ligier-Matra, 1m 20.81s (lap 5), 151.645kph, 94.228mph
CHAMPIONSHIP Scheckter 23, Andretti 20, Lauda 19, Reutemann 19, Hunt 9

Pos	Driver	Car	Time/gap	Grid	Stops	Tyres
1	M Andretti	Lotus-Ford	1h 42m 52.22s	1	0	G
2	C Reutemann	Ferrari	−15.85s	4	0	G
3	J Scheckter	Wolf-Ford	−24.51s	5	0	G
4	J Mass	McLaren-Ford	−24.87s	9	0	G
5	G Nilsson	Lotus-Ford	−1m 5.83s	12	0	G
6	H-J Stuck	Brabham-Alfa	−1 lap	13	0	G

Round 6/17	**MONACO GP** Monte Carlo					
	22 May 1977				**Race 286**	

Jody Scheckter
Wolf-Ford WR1 128.120kph, 79.610mph

Just as at Long Beach, Scheckter reaffirmed his street circuit mastery with a second victory for Wolf. Excellent slow-corner traction put Watson's Flat-12 Braham-Alfa on pole, but Scheckter beat him from the front row and was never headed. For half the race Watson hassled the Wolf but gear difficulties set in, spinning the Brabham out on lap 48. Scheckter apart, the 12-cylinder cars went well around the houses, the Ferrari pair completing the podium. Lauda drove a tremendous race. Out-qualified by Reutemann, he passed his Ferrari teammate on lap 26 and as the fuel-starved Wolf spluttered around its final lap, finished within a second of a Monaco hat-trick. This marked the 100th victory for the Ford Cosworth DFV engine.

POLE POSITION J Watson, Brabham-Alfa, 1m 29.86s (0.41s), 132.686kph, 82.448mph
LAPS 76 x 3.312 km, 2.058 miles
DISTANCE 251.712 km, 156.407 miles
STARTERS/FINISHERS 20/12
WEATHER Sunny, warm, dry
LAP LEADERS Scheckter 1-76 (76)
WINNER'S LAPS 1-76 P1
FASTEST LAP Scheckter, Wolf-Ford, 1m 31.07s (lap 35), 130.923kph, 81.352mph
CHAMPIONSHIP Scheckter 32, Lauda 25, Reutemann 23, Andretti 22, Hunt 9

Pos	Driver	Car	Time/gap	Grid	Stops	Tyres
1	J Scheckter	Wolf-Ford	1h 57m 52.77s	2	0	G
2	N Lauda	Ferrari	−0.89s	6	0	G
3	C Reutemann	Ferrari	−32.80s	3	0	G
4	J Mass	McLaren-Ford	−34.60s	9	0	G
5	M Andretti	Lotus-Ford	−35.55s	10	0	G
6	A Jones	Shadow-Ford	−36.61s	11	0	G

Round 7/17	**BELGIAN GP** Zolder					
	5 June 1977				**Race 287**	

Gunnar Nilsson
Lotus-Ford 78 155.527kph, 96.640mph

The first wet race of the year produced a maiden victory, Gunnar Nilsson giving the JPS Lotus 78 its third win. Team-leader Andretti seized pole by a massive 1.5s, but in atrocious conditions collided with Watson on lap 1. This gave Scheckter an initial lead, but as the track dried a chaotic period of tyre stops followed, more complex than any lap chart conveys. David Purley leading briefly in the LEC. When things settled down Lauda held a commanding lead, although he lost time with a spin when lapping Purley. But once the rain returned Nilsson reeled in the Ferrari to lead the final 20 laps and win by nearly 15s. Third and fourth brought first points for Peterson in the Tyrrell six-wheeler, and Brambilla for Team Surtees.

POLE POSITION M Andretti, Lotus-Ford, 1m 24.64s (1.54s), 181.276kph, 112.640mph
LAPS 70 x 4.262 km, 2.648 miles
DISTANCE 298.340 km, 185.380 miles
STARTERS/FINISHERS 26/14
WEATHER Overcast, cold, rain
LAP LEADERS J Scheckter, Wolf-Ford 1-16 (16); J Mass, McLaren-Ford 17-18 (2); Lauda 23-49 (27); Brambilla 19-22 (4); Nilsson 50-70 (21)
WINNER'S LAPS 1-17 P2, 18 P13, 19-20 P12, 21-22 P9, 23-25 P8, 26 P7, 27-29 P6, 30 P5, 31-32 P6, 33-34 P5, 35 P4, 36-39 P3, 40-49 P2, 50-70 P1
FASTEST LAP Nilsson, Lotus-Ford, 1m 27.54s (lap 53), 175.271kph, 108.908mph
CHAMPIONSHIP Scheckter 32, Lauda 31, Reutemann 23, Andretti 22, Nilsson 13

Pos	Driver	Car	Time/gap	Grid	Stops	Tyres
1	G Nilsson	Lotus-Ford	1h 55m 5.71s	3	1	G
2	N Lauda	Ferrari	−14.19s	11	1	G
3	R Peterson	Tyrrell-Ford	−19.95s	8	1	G
4	V Brambilla	Surtees-Ford	−24.98s	12	1	G
5	A Jones	Shadow-Ford	−1m 15.47s	17	1	G
6	H-J Stuck	Brabham-Alfa	−1 lap	18	1	G

Lotus-Ford 78

Round 8/17	SWEDISH GP Anderstorp		Jacques Laffite
	19 June 1977	Race 288	Ligier-Matra JS7 162.335kph, 100.871mph

Jacques Laffite's win was the first-ever all-French championship victory – car, engine, driver. Although he only led the final three laps, the Ligier was in second place on merit, having bested a tight group of seven cars – the others Watson, Scheckter, Hunt, Depailler, Reutemann, Mass – vying behind race-leader Andretti. Initially seventh, Laffite moved up from fifth to second over four laps, and once there even began reducing Andretti's 15s advantage. Again on pole, Andretti had led convincingly from lap 2 until an over-rich mixture caused a last-minute splash and dash, pushing him back to sixth. Champion Hunt gave the McLaren M26 its best outing to date, spoilt by a late tyre-stop, Mass ironically finishing a good second in the old faithful M23.

POLE POSITION Andretti, Lotus-Ford, 1m 25.404s (0.141s), 169.369kph, 105.241mph
LAPS 72 x 4.018 km, 2.497 miles
DISTANCE 289.296 km, 179.760 miles
STARTERS/FINISHERS 24/19
WEATHER Sunny, warm, dry
LAP LEADERS Watson 1 (1); Andretti 2-69 (68); Laffite 70-72 (3)
WINNER'S LAPS 1-5 P11, 6 P10, 7-10 P9, 11-22 P8, 23-29 P7, 30-37 P5, 38 P4, 39-40 P3, 41-69 P2, 70-72 P1
FASTEST LAP Andretti, Lotus-Ford, 1m 27.607s (lap ?), 165.110kph, 102.595mph
CHAMPIONSHIP Scheckter 32, Lauda 31, Reutemann 27, Andretti 23, Mass 14

Pos	Driver	Car	Time/gap	Grid	Stops	Tyres
1	J Laffite	Ligier-Matra	1h 46m 55.520s	8	0	G
2	J Mass	McLaren-Ford	–8.449s	9	0	G
3	C Reutemann	Ferrari	–14.369s	12	0	G
4	P Depailler	Tyrrell-Ford	–16.308s	6	0	G
5	J Watson	Brabham-Alfa	–18.735s	2	0	G
6	M Andretti	Lotus-Ford	–25.277s	1	1	G

Ligier-Matra JS7

FRENCH GP Dijon-Prenois

3 July 1977   Race 289

Mario Andretti

Lotus-Ford 78 183.006kph, 113.715mph

The top three on the grid, Andretti, Hunt and Watson, embarked on a battle royal around the quaint little Dijon track. Hunt led initially, keeping Watson at bay for four laps, and then Andretti, down to third after a poor start, for a further 13. But then the handling bugbear intervened and Hunt eventually finished a distant third – but at least the M26 had put its first points on the board. By then Watson was 5s ahead and, driving beautifully, keeping Andretti at arm's length. On the final lap, half a minute from a glorious victory, the Alfa Flat-12 coughed, short of fuel, and Andretti was by in a flash, a mirror image of his own plight a fortnight ago. At the halfway stage of the championship just five points separated the top five drivers.

POLE POSITION Andretti, Lotus-Ford, 1m 12.21s (0.52s), 189.447kph, 117.717mph
LAPS 80 x 3.800 km, 2.361 miles
DISTANCE 304.000 km, 188.897 miles
STARTERS/FINISHERS 22/13
WEATHER Sunny, hot, dry
LAP LEADERS Hunt 1-4 (4); Watson 5-79 (75); Andretti 80 (1)
WINNER'S LAPS 1-16 P3, 17-79 P2, 80 P1
FASTEST LAP Andretti, Lotus-Ford, 1m 13.75s (lap 76), 185.492kph, 115.259mph
CHAMPIONSHIP Lauda 33, Andretti 32, Scheckter 32, Reutemann 28, Nilsson 16

Pos	Driver	Car	Time/gap	Grid	Stops	Tyres
1	M Andretti	Lotus-Ford	1h 39m 40.13	1	0	G
2	J Watson	Brabham-Alfa	−1.55s	4	0	G
3	J Hunt	McLaren-Ford	−33.87s	2	0	G
4	G Nilsson	Lotus-Ford	−1m 11.08s	3	0	G
5	N Lauda	Ferrari	−1m 14.15s	9	0	G
6	C Reutemann	Ferrari	−1 lap	6	0	G

TOP **100** RACE

BRITISH GP Silverstone

16 July 1977   Race 290

James Hunt

McLaren M26 209.789kph, 130.357mph

At last McLaren had got their M26 motoring and, to the delight of the British crowd, Hunt took pole from Watson. A troublesome clutch caused Hunt a shocking start, dropping to fourth. Reasserting his qualifying form, he passed Scheckter on lap 7, Lauda on lap 23 and zeroed in on Watson. For 25 laps these two kept the crowd spellbound, content that either way a home victory was a certainty. But for the second time in a fortnight Watson was denied victory, pitting from the lead with fuel injection trouble on lap 50. It had been a long, lean period for the world champion but was Hunt's return to form simply too late to mount a realistic title defence? With Lauda finishing second, his most competitive showing in three starts, it looked like it.

POLE POSITION Hunt, McLaren-Ford, 1m 18.49s (0.28s), 216.422kph, 134.478mph
LAPS 68 x 4.719 km, 2.932 miles
DISTANCE 320.865 km, 199.376 miles
STARTERS/FINISHERS 26/15
WEATHER Sunny, warm, dry
LAP LEADERS J Watson, Brabham-Alfa 1-49 (49); Hunt 50-68 (19)
WINNER'S LAPS 1-6 P4, 7-22 P3, 23-49 P2, 50-68 P1
FASTEST LAP Hunt, McLaren-Ford, 1m 19.60s (lap 48), 213.404kph, 132.603mph
CHAMPIONSHIP Lauda 39, Andretti 32, Scheckter 32, Reutemann 28, Hunt 22

Pos	Driver	Car	Time/gap	Grid	Stops	Tyres
1	J Hunt	McLaren-Ford	1h 31m 46.06s	1	0	G
2	N Lauda	Ferrari	−18.31s	3	0	G
3	G Nilsson	Lotus-Ford	−19.57s	5	0	G
4	J Mass	McLaren-Ford	−47.76s	11	0	G
5	H-J Stuck	Brabham-Alfa	−1m 11.73s	7	0	G
6	J Laffite	Ligier-Matra	−1 lap	15	0	G

McLaren-Ford M26

<table>
<tr><td>Round 11/17</td><td>GERMAN GP Hockenheim
31 July 1977   Race 291</td><td>Niki Lauda
Ferrari 312T2 208.528kph, 129.573mph</td></tr>
</table>

Twelve months less one day after his near-death experience, Niki Lauda won the German Grand Prix at its new venue, Hockenheim. The fitting nature of this victory was not lost on anyone who had observed Lauda's miraculous restoration to F1 winner and championship contender. At the start, Scheckter, from pole, led Watson and Lauda, the Brabham-Alfa lasting a mere eight laps. By lap 13 Lauda had caught and passed Scheckter, the Wolf slowed by fuel pressure problems. A P2 finish after a four-race points famine rekindled Scheckter's championship aspirations, but victory put Lauda solidly on course for his second title, especially with a rather ordinary fourth from his Ferrari teammate and *nil points* for Andretti and Hunt.

POLE POSITION Scheckter, Wolf-Ford, 1m 53.07s (0.27s), 216.153kph, 134.311mph
LAPS 47 x 6.789 km, 4.218 miles
DISTANCE 319.083 km, 198.269 miles
STARTERS/FINISHERS 25/10
WEATHER Sunny, warm, dry
LAP LEADERS Scheckter 1-12 (12); Lauda 13-47 (35)
WINNER'S LAPS 1-7 P3, 8-12 P2, 13-47 P1
FASTEST LAP Lauda, Ferrari, 1m 55.99s (lap 28), 210.711kph, 130.930mph
CHAMPIONSHIP Lauda 48, Scheckter 38, Andretti 32, Reutemann 31, Hunt 22

Pos	Driver	Car	Time/gap	Grid	Stops	Tyres
1	N Lauda	Ferrari	1h 31m 48.62s	3	0	G
2	J Scheckter	Wolf-Ford	−14.33s	1	0	G
3	H-J Stuck	Brabham-Alfa	−20.90s	5	0	G
4	C Reutemann	Ferrari	−1m 0.27s	8	0	G
5	V Brambilla	Surtees-Ford	−1m 27.37s	10	0	G
6	P Tambay	Ensign-Ford	−1m 29.81s	11	0	G

Shadow-Ford DN8

<table>
<tr><td>Round 12/17</td><td>AUSTRIAN GP Österreichring
14 August 1977   Race 292</td><td>Alan Jones
Shadow-Ford DN8 197.914kph, 122.978mph</td></tr>
</table>

Lauda's resurgence brought pole for his home GP, Hunt alongside. With the track drenched from recent rain, most teams opted to start the race on wets. Andretti led until yet another engine failure on lap 12 presented Hunt with the lead. Meanwhile, the Shadow of Alan Jones was working well in the conditions and from 14th on the grid came through to P2 on merit. So when leader Hunt's engine let go Jones was there to complete the final 11 laps and claim his and Shadow's maiden victory. It was difficult to comprehend that Lauda had finished second to an apparent also-ran, but in the bigger picture of the championship Lauda would have been quietly content with a 16-point lead over nearest rival Scheckter.

POLE POSITION Lauda, Ferrari, 1m 39.32s (0.13s), 215.377kph, 133.829mph
LAPS 54 x 5.942 km, 3.692 miles
DISTANCE 320.868 km, 199.378 miles
STARTERS/FINISHERS 26/17
WEATHER Damp track, drying
LAP LEADERS M Andretti, Lotus-Ford 1-11 (11); J Hunt, McLaren-Ford 12-43 (32); Jones 44-54 (11)
WINNER'S LAPS 1 P13, 2-4 P12, 5 P11, 6-7 P10, 8 P9, 9 P8, 10 P6, 11 P5, 12-14 P4, 15 P3, 16-43 P2, 44-54 P1
FASTEST LAP J Watson, Brabham-Alfa, 1m 40.96s (lap 52), 211.878kph, 131.655mph
CHAMPIONSHIP Lauda 54, Scheckter 38, Reutemann 34, Andretti 32, Hunt 22

Pos	Driver	Car	Time/gap	Grid	Stops	Tyres
1	A Jones	Shadow-Ford	1h 37m 16.49s	14	0	G
2	N Lauda	Ferrari	−20.13s	1	0	G
3	H-J Stuck	Brabham-Alfa	−34.50s	4	0	G
4	C Reutemann	Ferrari	−34.75s	5	0	G
5	R Peterson	Tyrrell-Ford	−1m 2.09s	15	0	G
6	J Mass	McLaren-Ford	−1 lap	9	1	G

Round 13/17	**DUTCH GP** Zandvoort	**Niki Lauda**
	28 August 1977 Race 293	Ferrari 312T2 186.871kph, 116.116mph

Another Lotus 'wing-car' circuit, Andretti a dominant pole. Hunt made a scintillating start from row two which led to an incident that ended championship hopes for both drivers, each blaming the other. Andretti attempted a pass round the outside at Tarzan, they touched, the McLaren leapt in the air, Hunt out. The Lotus had spun but nine laps later Andretti dropped out from P3 with another engine failure. Laffite had assumed the lead from Hunt, chased by Lauda, the Ferrari out-braking the Ligier at Tarzan on lap 20. Laffite, rarely more than a few seconds in arrears, finished second and, having started P15, Scheckter's third place kept his championship hopes alive. But this third victory gave Lauda an almost unassailable championship lead.

POLE POSITION M Andretti, Lotus-Ford, 1m 18.65s (0.62s), 193.434kph, 120.194mph
LAPS 75 x 4.226 km, 2.626 miles
DISTANCE 316.950 km, 196.944 miles
STARTERS/FINISHERS 26/13
WEATHER Sunny, warm, dry
LAP LEADERS J Hunt, McLaren-Ford 1-5 (5); Laffite 6-19 (14); Lauda 20-75 (56)
WINNER'S LAPS 1-5 P4, 6-19 P2, 20-75 P1
FASTEST LAP Lauda, Ferrari, 1m 19.99s (lap 72), 190.194kph, 118.181mph
CHAMPIONSHIP Lauda 63, Scheckter 42, Reutemann 35, Andretti 32, Hunt 22

Pos	Driver	Car	Time/gap	Grid	Stops	Tyres
1	N Lauda	Ferrari	1h 41m 45.93s	4	0	G
2	J Laffite	Ligier-Matra	−1.89s	2	0	G
3	J Scheckter	Wolf-Ford	−1 lap	15	0	G
4	E Fittipaldi	Copersucar-Ford	−1 lap	17	0	G
5r	P Tambay	Ensign-Ford	−2 laps	12	0	G
6	C Reutemann	Ferrari	−2 laps	6	1	G

Round 14/17	**ITALIAN GP** Monza	**Mario Andretti**
	11 September 1977 Race 294	Lotus-Ford 78 206.015kph, 128.012mph

Italian-born Andretti was delighted to win at Monza, his fourth victory of the season. He overtook pole-sitter Hunt for second on lap 2 and Scheckter for the lead on lap 10, both with comparative ease, and then drove into the distance. This time his Ford-DFV, a standard unit replacing the recalcitrant Cosworth development engine, didn't miss a beat. Hunt had a miserable race, spinning away P3 at the first chicane on lap 12, while Scheckter only completed 23 laps before his engine let go when running an easy second. This allowed champion-elect Lauda, never a threat to Andretti, to gather another six points, bringing Ferrari their third successive constructors' cup. From his P16 start Jones finished a fine third for Shadow.

POLE POSITION J Hunt, McLaren-Ford, 1m 38.08s (0.07s), 212.887kph, 132.282mph
LAPS 52 x 5.800 km, 3.604 miles
DISTANCE 301.600 km, 187.406 miles
STARTERS/FINISHERS 24/9
WEATHER Sunny, warm, dry
LAP LEADERS J Scheckter, Wolf-Ford 1-9 (9); Andretti 10-52 (43)
WINNER'S LAPS 1 P3, 2-9 P2, 10-52 P1
FASTEST LAP Andretti, Lotus-Ford, 1m 39.10s (lap 31), 210.696kph, 130.921mph
CHAMPIONSHIP Lauda 69, Scheckter 42, Andretti 41, Reutemann 35, Hunt 22

Pos	Driver	Car	Time/gap	Grid	Stops	Tyres
1	M Andretti	Lotus-Ford	1h 27m 50.30s	4	0	G
2	N Lauda	Ferrari	−16.96s	5	0	G
3	A Jones	Shadow-Ford	−23.63s	16	0	G
4	J Mass	McLaren-Ford	−28.48s	9	0	G
5	C Regazzoni	Ensign-Ford	−30.11s	7	0	G
6	R Peterson	Tyrrell-Ford	−1m 19.22s	12	0	G

Round 15/17	**UNITED STATES GP EAST** Watkins Glen	**James Hunt**
	2 October 1977 Race 295	McLaren-Ford M26 162.509kph, 100.978mph

Mischievously, Lauda chose Monza to make the shock announcement that he would join Brabham next year. Brabham-Alfa's two and three on the Watkins Glen grid hinted at one reason why. A cold and wet race saw Hans Stuck's Brabham beat pole-man Hunt off the front row and lead 14 laps until he spun, his clutchless car jumping out of gear. This enabled Hunt, his McLaren set up for a wet race, to repeat his win of last year, despite nearly getting caught by Andretti as his wet tyres wore out on a drying track. It was a close call, Hunt unaware of the threat, Andretti making up 13s in the final ten laps. Scheckter was third while Lauda, making his final appearance for Ferrari, came fourth to regain the title from race-winner Hunt.

POLE POSITION Hunt, McLaren-Ford, 1m 40.863s (0.275s), 193.977kph, 120.532mph
LAPS 59 x 5.435 km, 3.377 miles
DISTANCE 320.651 km, 199.243 miles
STARTERS/FINISHERS 26/19
WEATHER Cold, rain
LAP LEADERS H-J Stuck, Brabham-Alfa 1-14 (14); Hunt 15-59 (45)
WINNER'S LAPS 1-14 P2, 15-59 P1
FASTEST LAP R Peterson, Tyrrell-Ford, 1m 51.854s (lap 56), 174.917kph, 108.688mph
CHAMPIONSHIP Lauda 72, Andretti 47, Scheckter 46, Reutemann 36, Hunt 31

Pos	Driver	Car	Time/gap	Grid	Stops	Tyres
1	J Hunt	McLaren-Ford	1h 58m 23.267s	1	0	G
2	M Andretti	Lotus-Ford	−2.026s	4	0	G
3	J Scheckter	Wolf-Ford	−1m 18.879s	9	0	G
4	N Lauda	Ferrari	−1m 40.615s	7	0	G
5	C Regazzoni	Ensign-Ford	−1m 48.138s	19	0	G
6	C Reutemann	Ferrari	−1 lap	6	0	G

| Round 16/17 | **CANADIAN GP** Mosport Park | | | | **Jody Scheckter** |
| | **9 October 1977** | | | **Race 296** | Wolf-Ford WR1 189.954kph, 118.032mph |

From the front row, Andretti and Hunt performed a high-speed duel that left the rest gasping. Hunt could hang on but not challenge the JPS Lotus for the lead. That was until lap 60, when they came up to lap McLaren teammate Mass. This hiatus caused Andretti to lose his lead but extraordinarily for one lap only, the McLaren pair contriving to collide as the lapped Mass waved the new leader through, putting Hunt out. Andretti resumed in front, but unbelievably – with just two laps to go – his development DFV blew yet again. So Scheckter, unlapping himself as Andretti began to slow, unexpectedly inherited the lead from almost a lap behind to give Wolf a third victory. Depailler gave the six-wheeler a rare podium, Mass finished third.

POLE POSITION M Andretti, Lotus-Ford, 1m 11.385s (0.394s), 199.574kph, 124.009mph
LAPS 80 x 3.957 km, 2.459 miles
DISTANCE 316.590 km, 196.720 miles
STARTERS/FINISHERS 25/12
WEATHER Overcast, dry
LAP LEADERS Andretti 1-60, 62-77 (76); J Hunt, McLaren-Ford 61 (1); Scheckter 78-80 (3)
WINNER'S LAPS 1 P9, 2-6 P8, 7-9 P7, 10-14 P6, 15-17 P5, 18-60 P4, 61 P3, 62-77 P2, 78-80 P1
FASTEST LAP M Andretti, Lotus-Ford, 1m 13.299s (lap 56), 194.362kph, 120.771mph
CHAMPIONSHIP Lauda 72, Scheckter 55, Andretti 47, Reutemann 36, Hunt 31

Pos	Driver	Car	Time/gap	Grid	Stops	Tyres
1	J Scheckter	Wolf-Ford	1h 40m 00.0s	9	0	G
2	P Depailler	Tyrrell-Ford	−6.77s	6	0	G
3	J Mass	McLaren-Ford	−15.76s	5	0	G
4	A Jones	Shadow-Ford	−46.69s	7	0	G
5	P Tambay	Ensign-Ford	−1m 3.26s	16	0	G
6r	V Brambilla	Surtees-Ford	−2 laps	15	0	G

| Round 17/17 | **JAPANESE GP** Fuji | | | | **James Hunt** |
| | **23 October 1977** | | | **Race 297** | McLaren-Ford M26 207.840kph, 129.146mph |

Hunt shot into a lead he would never lose while pole-man Andretti messed up, dropping to P8. Playing catch-up, Andretti tangled with Laffite and was out on lap 2, confirming Scheckter as championship runner-up. Five cars occupied P2 at some stage, Laffite's the worst hard-luck story by running out of fuel 500 yards from the line, Reutemann the beneficiary. On lap 6, under braking at the end of the main straight, Villeneuve's Ferrari ran into Peterson's Tyrrell. The Ferrari cartwheeled into a prohibited area full of spectators. The drivers were unharmed but two bystanders were killed and seven seriously injured. The accident, the absence of world champion Lauda, and winner Hunt shunning the podium ceremony, ended the season on a sour note.

POLE POSITION M Andretti, Lotus-Ford, 1m 12.23s (0.16s), 217.256kph, 134.997mph
LAPS 73 x 4.359 km, 2.709 miles
DISTANCE 318.207 km, 197.725 miles
STARTERS/FINISHERS 23/12
WEATHER Sunny, warm, dry
LAP LEADERS Hunt 1-73 (73)
WINNER'S LAPS 1-73 P1
FASTEST LAP J Scheckter, Wolf-Ford, 1m 14.30s (lap 72), 211.203kph, 131.236mph
CHAMPIONSHIP Lauda 72, Scheckter 55, Andretti 47, Reutemann 42, Hunt 40

Pos	Driver	Car	Time/gap	Grid	Stops	Tyres
1	J Hunt	McLaren-Ford	1h 31m 51.68s	2	0	G
2	C Reutemann	Ferrari	−1m 2.45s	7	0	G
3	P Depailler	Tyrrell-Ford	−1m 6.39s	15	0	G
4	A Jones	Shadow-Ford	−1m 6.61s	12	0	G
5r	J Laffite	Ligier-Matra	−1 lap	5	0	G
6	R Patrese	Shadow-Ford	−1 lap	13	0	G

1977 CHAMPIONSHIP FACTS AND FOLKLORE

■ Regulation changes were modest. For cars the maximum airbox height was increased, although the 'low-line' appearance was retained. For the races a minimum distance of 250km (155.34 miles) was introduced, while 200 miles (321.87km) or two hours was now regarded as the maximum.

■ A 17-race season was a new high, split into two parts nine/eight, every race bar one in each part counting towards the championships.

■ In the frenetic climax to the 1976 Hunt/Lauda title battle, a win by Mario Andretti's Lotus at the rain-soaked Fuji showdown went almost unnoticed. In reality it signalled a resurgence in Lotus fortunes, at its forefront for 1977 an innovative chassis design based on the principles of 'ground effect'.

■ Ground effect applied the lift principles of an aircraft wing in reverse, using an inverted aerofoil section to suck the car to the ground, so increasing tyre load, improving cornering grip and raising tyre operating temperatures to their optimum. A very powerful concept.

■ The inverted aerofoil section was located beneath the water radiators in long side-pods each side of the chassis into which the car's slipstream was channelled, airflow spillage reduced by plastic skirts which closed the gap between side-pod and track. The more rapid the airstream exposed to the inverted aerofoil, the greater the downforce created.

■ Four victories with the Lotus 78 'wing car' should have been enough to present Andretti with his first drivers' title, but the Lotus Achilles heel, reliability, restricted the other points finishes needed to build a championship-winning season.

■ As so often before, there was a win-or-bust tendency at Lotus, although in fairness engine failure was the prime cause of the dnfs, and this could be laid squarely at the feet of Cosworth and their development engine.

■ Extraction of greater power was essential for DFV users to remain competitive with the 12-cylinder teams, but the downside was the effect this could have on durability, and this was a problem not confined to Lotus during 1977.

- Despite this, Ford-Cosworth teams won 12 of the 17 championship rounds and Scheckter's Monaco win marked the DFV's 100th victory, an extraordinary accomplishment.
- Engine aside, the Lotus 78 chassis was at times unbeatable, and for some of the seven pole positions Andretti posted the performance superiority verged on demoralising for their opposition.
- Mystery surrounded the use by Lotus of a locked differential, the car sometimes appearing to corner 'on rails'. But ground effect wasn't all good news, as increased drag could reduce straight-line velocity considerably.
- But net-net, Lotus had found a new 'unfair advantage', and it required someone special to put together a championship-winning season against the formidable Andretti/Lotus combination.
- The prime candidates were reigning champion Hunt and ex-champion Lauda, but a third contender emerged early on in the shape of Jody Scheckter.
- The South African had abandoned Ken Tyrrell's trudge down his six-wheeled cul-de-sac to join a new team headed by Walter Wolf .
- Wolf had financed the Williams F1 operation in 1976, but dissatisfied had bought-out Frank to establish his own operation. For this reason the Wolf team's unprecedented golden race-winning rookie season remains a moot point.
- The Wolf WR1, a conventional Harvey Postlethwaite design, proved an effective mount for Jody, who astonishingly if fortuitously won first time out.
- Two more victories plus six podiums was destroyed by a gaping, pointless black hole mid-season which killed off Scheckter's championship hopes in much the same way it did for Andretti.
- Lauda, on the other hand, was always there-and-thereabouts throughout the season. Three wins and a string of podiums gave him his second drivers' title, and Ferrari, displaying a FIAT logo for the first time, their third consecutive constructors' championship.
- His new teammate Carlos Reutemann looked extremely dangerous when he won the second championship round in Brazil, but after that Lauda invariably had his measure and the Argentinean was only in the frame for championship honours during the first half of the season.
- At Monza rumour became fact when Lauda announced his departure from Maranello to end a four-year association that had realised two drivers' and three constructors' titles from 15 race victories. Lauda's relationship with Enzo Ferrari had never truly survived the repercussions from his 1976 Fuji decision, and the grooming of a youthful third driver, Gilles Villeneuve, was the last straw.
- Once the 1977 championships were done and dusted, Lauda announced his future plans with Brabham and sat out the final two races of the season.
- His replacement Villeneuve ended the season with a tumultuous crash in Japan which sadly killed a marshal and a photographer.
- Once again the GP victories in 1977 were scattered, eight drivers from six teams finding success, but three victories by the 1976 world champion should not be overlooked.
- Six poles and ten races led, three more than anyone else, suggested that Hunt had done his part in defending the title Lauda had loaned him for 12 months. But despite the three race victories, Hunt and his team found the transition from the McLaren M23 to the M26 to be a trial.
- For Shadow it was a bittersweet season, scarred by the loss of their driver Tom Pryce who, together with Roger Williamson

RACE 291, German GP: Twelve months less one day after his near-death experience, Niki Lauda won the German Grand Prix at its new venue, Hockenheim. He shares the podium with Stuck (left) and Scheckter.

and Tony Brise, was the third talented British driver to die in little over 12 months, truly a lost generation.

■ Alan Jones brought Shadow the unexpected, victory from 14th on the grid, exceeding Bruce McLaren's 1960 landmark win from P13, while Riccardo Patrese made his debut for the team at the start of his record breaking 17-year, 256-race career.

■ After years of decline, the one-time distinguished and sometime despised BRM name finally disappeared, last heard of as Rotary Watches-Stanley BRM.

■ Renault's arrival, debuting their novel 1.5-litre turbocharged car at Silverstone, also brought Michelin tyres into GP racing. In preparation for a resumption of 'tyre wars', Goodyear began to offer a choice of compounds. Lauda's Hockenheim victory was Goodyear's 100th Grand Prix win.

■ One team that won nothing but showed bags of potential was Brabham-Alfa, and this was despite their number-one driver Carlos Pace perishing in a light-aircraft accident in his native Brazil in March.

■ The Alfa-Romeo Flat-12 engine was a development of their successful sports car unit and initially could produce over 500bhp at 12,000rpm. In an endeavour to extract more power and improve reliability for 1977, Alfa produced new cylinder heads and other refinements along with a six-speed gearbox.

■ Four podium finishes for the Brabham-Alfa BT45B doesn't sound like much to get excited about, but seven front-row starts including pole at Monaco had caught the eye of the new double world champion in selecting his berth for the 1978 championship campaign.

Championship ranking	Championship points	Driver nationality	1977 Drivers Championship		Races contested	Race victories	Podiumse excl. victories	Races led	Lights to flag victories	Laps led	Poles	Fastest laps	Triple Crowns
			Driver	Car									
1	72	AUT	Niki Lauda	Ferrari	14	3	7	4		190	2	3	
2	55	RSA	Jody Scheckter	Wolf-Ford	17	3	6	7	1	198	1	2	
3	47	USA	Mario Andretti	Lotus-Ford	17	4	1	7	1	278	7	4	1
4	42	ARG	Carlos Reutemann	Ferrari	17	1	5	1		18			
5	40	GBR	James Hunt	McLaren-Ford	17	3	2	10	1	222	6	3	1
6	25	GER	Jochen Mass	McLaren-Ford	17		2	1		2			
7	22	AUS	Alan Jones	Shadow-Ford	14	1	1	1		11			
8	20	SWE	Gunnar Nilsson	Lotus-Ford	16	1	1	1		21		1	
9	20	FRA	Patrick Depailler	Tyrrell-Ford	17		3						
10	18	FRA	Jacques Laffite	Ligier-Matra	17	1	1	2		17		1	
11	12	GER	Hans-Joachim Stuck	March-Ford (1) Brabham-Alfa (14)	15		2	1		14			
12	11	BRA	Emerson Fittipaldi	Fittipaldi-Ford	14								
13	9	GBR	John Watson	Brabham-Alfa	17		1	4		138	1	2	
14	7	SWE	Ronnie Peterson	Tyrrell-Ford	17		1					1	
15	6	BRA	Carlos Pace	Brabham-Alfa	3		1	2		19			
16	6	ITA	Vittorio Brambilla	Surtees-Ford	17			1		4			
17	5	SUI	Clay Regazzoni	Ensign-Ford	15								
17	5	FRA	Patrick Tambay	Ensign-Ford	7								
19	1	ITA	Renzo Zorzi	Shadow-Ford	5								
19	1	FRA	Jean-Pierre Jarier	Penske-Ford (10) Shadow-Ford (1) Ligier-Matra (1)	12								
19	1	ITA	Riccardo Patrese	Shadow-Ford	9								

Championship ranking	Championship points	Team/Marque nationality	1977 Constructors Championship		Engine maker nationality	Races contested	Race victories	1-2 finishes	Podiums excl. victories	Races led	Laps led	Poles	Fastest laps
			Chassis	Engine									
1	95	ITA	Ferrari 312T2	Ferrari 3.0 F12	ITA	17	4		12	5	208	2	3
2	62	GBR	Lotus 78	Ford Cosworth 3.0 V8	GBR	17	5		2	7	299	7	5
3	60	NZL	McLaren M26, M23	Ford Cosworth 3.0 V8	GBR	17	3		4	11	224	6	3
4	55	CAN	Wolf WR1, WR2, WR3	Ford Cosworth 3.0 V8	GBR	17	3		6	7	198	1	2
5	27	GBR	Brabham BT45, BT45B	Alfa Romeo 3.0 F12	ITA	17			4	6	171	1	2
6	27	GBR	Tyrrell P34	Ford Cosworth 3.0 V8	GBR	17			4				1
7	23	USA	Shadow DN8, DN5B	Ford Cosworth 3.0 V8	GBR	17	1		1	1	11		
8	18	FRA	Ligier JS7	Matra 3.0 V12	FRA	17	1		1	2	17		1
9	11	BRA	Fittipaldi FD04, F5	Ford Cosworth 3.0 V8	GBR	14							
10	10	GBR	Ensign N177	Ford Cosworth 3.0 V8	GBR	17							
11	6	GBR	Surtees TS19	Ford Cosworth 3.0 V8	GBR	17			1	4			
12	1	USA	Penske PC4	Ford Cosworth 3.0 V8	GBR	12							

1978

Andretti breaks new ground

THE TALE OF THE TITLE

- With six race victories, Mario Andretti became the second drivers' champion from the USA.
- Chapman's latest, the Lotus 79, significantly advanced the principles of ground effect pioneered last year.
- Eight wins by Andretti and Peterson gave Lotus a seventh title, yet almost understated the 79's superiority.
- Echoing 1968 and 1970, Ronnie Peterson's death at Monza was shattering for the triumphant Team Lotus.
- Swedish motorsport also mourned Gunnar Nilsson, who lost his fight with cancer soon afterwards.
- Gordon Murray's interpretation of ground effect was the Brabham 'fan car', banned after a winning debut.
- Gilles Villeneuve's first win was one of five for Ferrari, finding erratic success with Michelin radials.
- McLaren and Wolf were nowhere, but, back on four wheels, Depailler won Monaco for Tyrrell.
- Frank Williams and Patrick Head formed Williams GP Engineering, their FW06 showing promise.
- Arrows, a breakaway racing team from Shadow, made their debut amid controversy over copyright.
- And not forgetting: Balestre elected FISA President.

THE CHASE FOR THE CHAMPIONSHIP

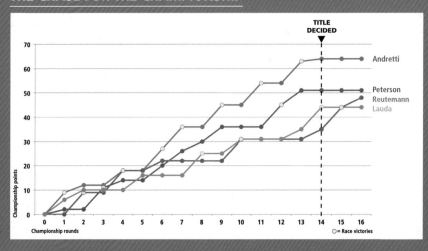

ARGENTINEAN GP Buenos Aires No 15
15 January 1978   Race 298

Mario Andretti
Lotus-Ford 78 191.813kph, 119.817mph

Andretti kicked-off the new season in fine style with a lights-to-flag victory from pole position. Reutemann's front row Ferrari initially gave chase but soon fell back, the team making the wrong tyre choice as they adjusted to their new supplier, Michelin. The Brabham-Alfas both showed well, Niki Lauda taking second when teammate Watson relinquished P2 with a late engine blow-up. The surprise was Depailler's Tyrrell, back to four wheels, which came through to finish third, close behind Lauda, from a P10 start. Hunt finished a 'poorly balanced' fourth, and last year's winner, Scheckter's Wolf, was never in the picture. With the new car yet to come, it was ominous that Andretti had won so easily using the 'old' Lotus 78.

POLE POSITION Andretti, Lotus-Ford, 1m 47.75s (0.09s), 199.395kph, 123.898mph
LAPS 52 x 5.968 km, 3.708 miles
DISTANCE 310.336 km, 192.834 miles
STARTERS/FINISHERS 24/18
WEATHER Sunny, hot, dry
LAP LEADERS Andretti 1-52 (52)
WINNER'S LAPS 1-52 P1
FASTEST LAP G Villeneuve, Ferrari, 1m 49.76s (lap 3), 195.743kph, 121.629mph
CHAMPIONSHIP Andretti 9, Lauda 6, Depailler 4, Hunt 3, Peterson 2

Pos	Driver	Car	Time/gap	Grid	Stops	Tyres
1	M Andretti	Lotus-Ford	1h 37m 4.47s	1	0	G
2	N Lauda	Brabham-Alfa	−13.21s	5	0	G
3	P Depailler	Tyrrell-Ford	−13.64s	10	0	G
4	J Hunt	McLaren -Ford	−16.05s	6	0	G
5	R Peterson	Lotus-Ford	−1m 14.85s	3	0	G
6	P Tambay	McLaren -Ford	−1m 19.90s	9	0	G

BRAZILIAN GP Rio de Janeiro
29 January 1978   Race 299

Carlos Reutemann
Ferrari 312T2 172.887kph, 107.427mph

Carlos Reutemann never did win his home GP but was now twice winner in Brazil. The crowd would have preferred a dnf, because finishing second was Brazilian hero Emerson Fittipaldi, bringing his eponymous car its best-ever finish, before or since. By lap 12 Fittipaldi had got the better of a three-way battle with Hunt and pole-man Peterson for P3, which became second when Andretti's Lotus jammed in fourth gear within ten laps of the finish. Reutemann's dominant display, rocketing away from the start and at times pulling out 2s a lap, was a comprehensive maiden victory for Michelin, justification for Ferrari's tyre strategy, and confirmation that ground effect was not yet supreme. Davina Galica made her third and final attempt to qualify for a GP.

POLE POSITION R Peterson, Lotus-Ford, 1m 40.45s (0.08s), 180.305kph, 112.036mph
LAPS 63 x 5.031 km, 3.126 miles
DISTANCE 316.953 km, 196.945 miles
STARTERS/FINISHERS 22/11
WEATHER Sunny, very hot, dry
LAP LEADERS Reutemann 1-63 (63)
WINNER'S LAPS 1-63 P1
FASTEST LAP Reutemann, Ferrari, 1m 43.07s (lap 35), 175.721kph, 109.188mph
CHAMPIONSHIP Andretti 12, Lauda 10, Reutemann 9, Fittipaldi 6, Depailler 4

Pos	Driver	Car	Time/gap	Grid	Stops	Tyres
1	C Reutemann	Ferrari	1h 49m 59.86s	4	0	M
2	E Fittipaldi	Copersucar-Ford	−49.13s	7	0	G
3	N Lauda	Brabham-Alfa	−57.02s	10	0	G
4	M Andretti	Lotus-Ford	−1m 33.2s	3	0	G
5	C Regazzoni	Shadow-Ford	−1 lap	15	1	G
6	D Pironi	Tyrrell-Ford	−1 lap	19	0	G

SOUTH AFRICAN GP Kyalami
4 March 1978   Race 300

Ronnie Peterson
Lotus-Ford 78 187.817kph, 116.704mph

An action-packed race with five leaders and two memorable happenings. The first was that on its second appearance, Riccardo Patrese looked odds-on to win on merit in the controversial new Arrows until its engine expired. Then Depailler led in the new Tyrrell 008 – and now the second happening – only to run short of fuel and lose out to Peterson by 0.466s on their final wheel-banging lap. Initial race leaders were Andretti and Scheckter until they both had to back off to conserve tyres, and then for 37 extraordinary laps the race was Patrese's to lose. His wretched luck left Depailler ahead of Andretti, Watson and Peterson. Watson spun on oil, Andretti pitted for fuel, leaving Patrick and Ronnie to engage in an unforgettable final lap race for the flag.

POLE POSITION N Lauda, Brabham-Alfa, 1m 14.65s (0.25s), 197.916kph, 122.979mph
LAPS 78 x 4.104 km, 2.550 miles
DISTANCE 320.112 km, 198.908 miles
STARTERS/FINISHERS 26/12
WEATHER Sunny, hot, dry
LAP LEADERS Andretti 1-20 (20); J Scheckter, Wolf-Ford 21-26 (6); R Patrese, Arrows-Ford 27-63 (37); Depailler 64-77 (14); Peterson 78 (1)
WINNER'S LAPS 1 P10, 2 P9, 3-4 P10, 5 P9, 6-14 P10, 15-22 P11, 23-29 P10, 30-33 P9, 34 P8, 35-51 P7, 52 P6, 53-54 P5, 55-63 P4, 64-74 P3, 75-77 P2, 78 P1
FASTEST LAP M Andretti, Lotus-Ford, 1m 17.09s (lap 2), 191.651kph, 119.087mph
CHAMPIONSHIP Andretti 12, Peterson 11, Lauda 10, Depailler 10, Reutemann 9

Pos	Driver	Car	Time/gap	Grid	Stops	Tyres
1	R Peterson	Lotus-Ford	1h 42m 15.767s	11	0	G
2	P Depailler	Tyrrell-Ford	−0.466s	12	0	G
3	J Watson	Brabham-Alfa	−4.442s	10	0	G
4	A Jones	Williams-Ford	−38.986s	18	0	G
5	J Laffite	Ligier-Matra	−1m 9.218s	14	0	G
6	D Pironi	Tyrrell-Ford	−1 lap	13	0	G

TOP 100 RACE

Ferrari 312T3

Round 4/16	UNITED STATES GP WEST Long Beach	Carlos Reutemann
	2 April 1978 Race 301	Ferrari 312T3 140.172kph, 87.099mph

From 1-2 on the grid, the Michelin-shod Ferraris led all the way, Villeneuve for the first half until he made a misjudgement overtaking backmarkers and spun out. Reutemann took the lead chased closely by a Williams. Jones' climb through the field in the FW06 from P8 on the grid had been sensational. For a brief period, until first the front wings collapsed and then the fuel pump faltered, the Williams was a genuine threat to the leader. Both Brabhams featured but were out before one-third-distance. Reutemann's was a debut victory for the new 312T3 Ferrari, designed specifically around the Michelin radials. Andretti finished second and now Ferrari and Lotus had each won two of the opening rounds, Carlos and Mario tied at the top of the points table.

POLE POSITION Reutemann, Ferrari, 1m 20.636s (0.200s), 145.141kph, 90.187mph
LAPS 80.5 x 3.251 km, 2.020 miles
DISTANCE 261.706 km, 162.616 miles
STARTERS/FINISHERS 22/12
WEATHER Sunny, warm, dry
LAP LEADERS G Villeneuve, Ferrari 1-38 (38.5); Reutemann 39-80 (42)
WINNER'S LAPS 1-9 P4, 10-27 P3, 28-38 P2, 39-80 P1
FASTEST LAP A Jones, Williams-Ford, 1m 22.215s (lap 27), 142.354kph, 88.454mph
CHAMPIONSHIP Reutemann 18, Andretti 18, Peterson 14, Depailler 14, Lauda 10

Pos	Driver	Car	Time/gap	Grid	Stops	Tyres
1	C Reutemann	Ferrari	1h 52m 1.301s	1	0	M
2	M Andretti	Lotus-Ford	−11.061s	4	0	G
3	P Depailler	Tyrrell-Ford	−28.951s	12	0	G
4	R Peterson	Lotus-Ford	−45.603s	6	0	G
5	J Laffite	Ligier-Matra	−1m 22.884s	14	0	G
6	R Patrese	Arrows-Ford	−1 lap	9	1	G

Round 5/16	MONACO GP Monte Carlo	Patrick Depailler
	7 May 1978 Race 302	Tyrrell-Ford 008 129.325kph, 80.359mph

So close at Kyalami, Depailler finally won his maiden GP in his sixth season with Tyrrell. Reutemann from pole lost out in the first lap squabble so Watson led from Depailler, who had started from the third row. Brake trouble cost Watson the lead at half-distance, but all along the Tyrrell had been snapping at his tyre-treads. Depailler's lead was briefly menaced by Lauda, but on lap 45 Niki pitted with a puncture. Now took place a classic recovery drive through the field by the world champion, shattering the lap record with a time almost 2s faster, and with three laps to go Lauda regained his second place from Scheckter. But Depailler was the glorious victor and, with Reutemann and Andretti failing to score, also headed the points table.

POLE POSITION C Reutemann, Ferrari, 1m 28.34s (0.49s), 134.969kph, 83.866mph
LAPS 75 x 3.312 km, 2.058 miles
DISTANCE 248.400 km, 154.349 miles
STARTERS/FINISHERS 20/11
WEATHER Sunny, warm, dry
LAP LEADERS Watson 1-37 (37); Depailler 38-75 (38)
WINNER'S LAPS 1-37 P2, 38-75 P1
FASTEST LAP Lauda, Brabham-Alfa, 1m 28.65s (lap 72), 134.497kph, 83.573mph
CHAMPIONSHIP Depailler 23, Reutemann 18, Andretti 18, Lauda 16, Peterson 14

Pos	Driver	Car	Time/gap	Grid	Stops	Tyres
1	P Depailler	Tyrrell-Ford	1h 55m 14.66s	5	0	G
2	N Lauda	Brabham-Alfa	−22.45s	3	1	G
3	J Scheckter	Wolf-Ford	−32.29s	9	0	G
4	J Watson	Brabham-Alfa	−33.53s	2	0	G
5	D Pironi	Tyrrell-Ford	−1m 8.06s	13	0	G
6	R Patrese	Arrows-Ford	−1m 8.77s	14	0	G

Tyrrell-Ford 008

| Round 6/16 | **BELGIAN GP** Zolder | | | | | | **Mario Andretti** |
| | 21 May 1978 | | | | | Race 303 | **Lotus-Ford 79** 179.242kph, 111.376mph |

Andretti made his first start in the new Lotus 79, the latest expression of the 'wing car'. He trounced the opposition, leading all the way from a demoralising pole. To rub it in, on ACBC's birthday, Peterson came second in the 'old' Lotus 78. Ronnie's ride was not so easy, a puncture on lap 56 requiring a charge from fourth to second in the closing laps. An incident-ridden start left Lauda, Hunt and ultimately Scheckter on the sidelines but Villeneuve chasing Andretti. Gilles' splendid yet vain attempt to hang on to the Lotus ended on lap 39 when smoke plumed from his left front tyre, Villeneuve crawling round on the rim for almost a whole lap to change the punctured tyre. He still finished fourth, the Ferraris 3-4 behind the Lotus 1-2.

POLE POSITION Andretti, Lotus-Ford, 1m 20.90s (0.79s), 189.656kph, 117.847mph
LAPS 70 x 4.262 km, 2.648 miles
DISTANCE 298.340 km, 185.380 miles
STARTERS/FINISHERS 24/13
WEATHER Overcast, dry
LAP LEADERS Andretti 1-70 (70)
WINNER'S LAPS 1-70 P1
FASTEST LAP Peterson, Lotus-Ford, 1m 23.13s (lap 66), 184.569kph, 114.686mph
CHAMPIONSHIP Andretti 27, Depailler 23, Reutemann 22, Peterson 20, Lauda 16

Pos	Driver	Car	Time/gap	Grid	Stops	Tyres
1	M Andretti	Lotus-Ford	1h 39m 52.02s	1	0	G
2	R Peterson	Lotus-Ford	−9.90s	7	1	G
3	C Reutemann	Ferrari	−24.34s	2	0	M
4	G Villeneuve	Ferrari	−47.04s	4	1	M
5r	J Laffite	Ligier-Matra	−1 lap	14	0	G
6	D Pironi	Tyrrell-Ford	−1 lap	23	0	G

Lotus-Ford 79

Round 7/16	**SPANISH GP** Jarama		**Mario Andretti**	
	4 June 1978	Race 304	Lotus-Ford 79 150.495kph, 93.513mph	

Andretti's pole was a second quicker than Reutemann's Ferrari, the first non-Lotus. It was therefore no surprise when he repeated his Jarama victory of last year in the Lotus 79. Peterson, having his first outing in the new car, made it a back-to-back 1-2 team finish, and that's exactly how the two Lotus twins also stood in the championship. Hunt took advantage of the Swede's muffed start, catapulting through to lead the opening laps, but on sticky tyres a pit stop was almost inevitable, and it came on lap 60 when lying fourth, finishing sixth. The fact that Peterson could complete lap 1 P8 and yet displace Hunt for second on lap 53 vividly illustrated Lotus supremacy. Lauda retired while Reutemann had a lucky escape when his throttle stuck open.

POLE POSITION Andretti, Lotus-Ford, 1m 18.70s (0.72s), 155.710kph, 96.754mph
LAPS 75 x 3.404 km, 2.115 miles
DISTANCE 255.300 km, 158.636 miles
STARTERS/FINISHERS 24/15
WEATHER Sunny, warm, dry
LAP LEADERS Hunt 1-5 (5); Andretti 6-75 (70)
WINNER'S LAPS 1-5 P2, 6-75 P1
FASTEST LAP Andretti, Lotus-Ford, 1m 20.81s (lap 5), 151.645kph, 94.228mph
CHAMPIONSHIP Andretti 36, Peterson 26, Depailler 23, Reutemann 22, Lauda 16

Pos	Driver	Car	Time/gap	Grid	Stops	Tyres
1	M Andretti	Lotus-Ford	1h 41m 47.06s	1	0	G
2	R Peterson	Lotus-Ford	−19.56s	2	0	G
3	J Laffite	Ligier-Matra	−37.24s	10	0	G
4	J Scheckter	Wolf-Ford	−1m 0.06s	9	0	G
5	J Watson	Brabham-Alfa	−1m 5.93s	7	0	G
6	J Hunt	McLaren-Ford	−1 lap	4	1	G

Round 8/16	**SWEDISH GP** Anderstorp		**Niki Lauda**	
	17 June 1978	Race 305	Brabham-Alfa Romeo BT46B 167.609kph, 104.147mph	

Brabham's 'fan car' won the battle, yet lost the war. After this single victory it was banned, the fan deemed a movable aero device that also vented dangerous debris. In their only head-to-head, Brabham's alternative 'ground effect' beat the Lotus solution: unacceptable 'fan-suck' outperforming acceptable 'venturi-suck'. Andretti's venturi won pole from Watson's fan, and in the race led the first 38 laps from Lauda's fan. But on the 39th tour Andretti made that tiny slip Lauda needed and once by, the Brabham pulled easily ahead on the oily track surface. Watson's fan Brabham went out on lap 19, and after an early puncture Peterson's venturi Lotus just failed to chase down Patrese for second after Andretti blew up on lap 47.

POLE POSITION M Andretti, Lotus-Ford, 1m 22.058s (0.679s), 176.846kph, 109.887mph
LAPS 70 x 4.031 km, 2.505 miles
DISTANCE 282.170 km, 175.332 miles
STARTERS/FINISHERS 24/15
WEATHER Sunny, warm, dry
LAP LEADERS Andretti 1-38 (38); Lauda 39-70 (32)
WINNER'S LAPS 1-38 P2, 39-70 P1
FASTEST LAP Lauda, Brabham-Alfa, 1m 24.836s (lap 33), 171.055kph, 106.288mph
CHAMPIONSHIP Andretti 36, Peterson 30, Lauda 25, Depailler 23, Reutemann 22

Pos	Driver	Car	Time/gap	Grid	Stops	Tyres
1	N Lauda	Brabham-Alfa	1h 41m 0.606s	3	0	G
2	R Patrese	Arrows-Ford	−34.019s	5	0	G
3	R Peterson	Lotus-Ford	−34.105s	4	1	G
4	P Tambay	McLaren-Ford	−1 lap	15	0	G
5	C Regazzoni	Shadow-Ford	−1 lap	16	0	G
6	E Fittipaldi	Copersucar-Ford	−1 lap	13	0	G

Round 9/16	**FRENCH GP** Paul Ricard		**Mario Andretti**	
	2 July 1978	Race 306	Lotus-Ford 79 190.404kph, 118.312mph	

A third Lotus 1-2 in four races annihilated the opposition. With the Brabham 'fan car' debarred, the championship was psychologically if not mathematically over. But even *sans* fan the Brabham-Alfa continued to be effective in qualifying, if brittle in the races. Lauda qualified P3 but was victim to engine trouble after only ten laps. Watson took pole, led half a lap, but could only finish fourth behind the car that gave the Lotus pair the hardest time, Hunt's McLaren. As Peterson made his way though from a poor row three starting position, James more than hung on to Ronnie's coat tails to finish a valiant third behind the black and gold cars. Michelin had a bad French GP, Ferrari qualifying 8-9 and finishing 12-18.

POLE POSITION Watson, Brabham-Alfa, 1m 44.41s (0.05s), 200.326kph, 124.477mph
LAPS 54 x 5.810 km, 3.610 miles
DISTANCE 313.740 km, 194.949 miles
STARTERS/FINISHERS 26/18
WEATHER Sunny, hot, dry
LAP LEADERS Andretti 1-54 (54)
WINNER'S LAPS 1-54 P1
FASTEST LAP C Reutemann, Ferrari, 1m 48.56s (lap 48), 192.668kph, 119.718mph
CHAMPIONSHIP Andretti 45, Peterson 36, Lauda 25, Depailler 23, Reutemann 22

Pos	Driver	Car	Time/gap	Grid	Stops	Tyres
1	M Andretti	Lotus-Ford	1h 38m 51.92	2	0	G
2	R Peterson	Lotus-Ford	−2.93s	5	0	G
3	J Hunt	McLaren-Ford	−19.80s	4	0	G
4	J Watson	Brabham-Alfa	−36.88s	1	0	G
5	A Jones	Williams-Ford	−41.81s	14	0	G
6	J Scheckter	Wolf-Ford	−54.53s	7	0	G

BRITISH GP Brands Hatch

16 July 1978   Race 307

Carlos Reutemann

Ferrari 312T3 187.690kph, 116.625mph

This was the race when fans had to decide where their support lay, with Ferrari or with Lauda. High attrition included the front-row Lotus twins, pole-man Peterson with fuel pump, Andretti on lap 23 with another engine failure when leading. Once second leader Scheckter was out with gearbox problems just before half-distance – along with Peterson, Jones and Patrese who had challenged for the lead – it became a struggle between ex-Ferrari number one Lauda leading and fast-closing replacement Reutemann. Michelins and a piece of backmarker opportunism at Clearways on lap 60 gave Reutemann victory, but a 1.23s gap at the finish and fastest lap on 72 of 76 laps suggested Lauda did not submit readily to this particular defeat.

POLE POSITION R Peterson, Lotus-Ford, 1m 16.80s (0.26s), 197.195kph, 122.531mph
LAPS 76 x 4.207 km, 2.614 miles
DISTANCE 319.719 km, 198.664 miles
STARTERS/FINISHERS 26/10
WEATHER Sunny, warm, dry
LAP LEADERS M Andretti, Lotus-Ford 1-23 (23); J Scheckter Wolf-Ford 24-33 (10); Lauda 34-59 (26); Reutemann 60-76 (17)
WINNER'S LAPS 1-6 P7, 7-23 P6, 24-26 P5, 27-35 P4, 36-39 P3, 40-59 P2, 60-76 P1
FASTEST LAP Lauda, Brabham-Alfa, 1m 18.60s (lap 72), 192.679kph, 119.725mph
CHAMPIONSHIP Andretti 45, Peterson 36, Reutemann 31, Lauda 31, Depailler 26

Pos	Driver	Car	Time/gap	Grid	Stops	Tyres
1	C Reutemann	Ferrari	1h 42m 12.39s	8	0	M
2	N Lauda	Brabham-Alfa	−1.23s	4	0	G
3	J Watson	Brabham-Alfa	−37.25s	9	0	G
4	P Depailler	Tyrrell-Ford	−1m 13.27s	10	1	G
5	H-J Stuck	Shadow-Ford	−1 lap	18	0	G
6	P Tambay	McLaren-Ford	−1 lap	20	0	G

GERMAN GP Hockenheim

30 July 1978   Race 308

Mario Andretti

Lotus-Ford 79 208.263kph, 129.409mph

Eight laps short of their fourth 1-2 finish of the year, Peterson's gearbox failure left Andretti to share the podium with Scheckter and Laffite. Scheckter's Wolf WR5 was a quasi-ground-effect machine, his storming drive from last place but one to second providing further evidence of the effectiveness of the science. His Wolf was delayed on the warm-up lap by fuel vaporisation, a problem that afflicted many cars in the relentless heat. One such was Alan Jones in the Williams, who retired from a strong third place on lap 29. On the podium Andretti was in buoyant spirits, now with an 18-point championship lead, none of his rivals scoring. Scheckter shared his mood, having just announced that for 1979 he would leave Wolf and join Ferrari.

POLE POSITION Andretti, Lotus-Ford, 1m 51.90s (0.09s), 218.413kph, 135.715mph
LAPS 45 x 6.789 km, 4.218 miles
DISTANCE 305.505 km, 189.832 miles
STARTERS/FINISHERS 24/11
WEATHER Sunny, very hot, dry
LAP LEADERS Peterson 1-4 (4); Andretti 5-45 (41)
WINNER'S LAPS 1-4 P2, 5-45 P1
FASTEST LAP R Peterson, Lotus-Ford, 1m 55.62s (lap 26), 211.386kph, 131.349mph
CHAMPIONSHIP Andretti 54, Peterson 36, Reutemann 31, Lauda 31, Depailler 26

Pos	Driver	Car	Time/gap	Grid	Stops	Tyres
1	M Andretti	Lotus-Ford	1h 28m 0.90s	1	0	G
2	J Scheckter	Wolf-Ford	−15.35s	4	0	G
3	J Laffite	Ligier-Matra	−28.01s	7	0	G
4	E Fittipaldi	Copersucar-Ford	−36.88s	10	0	G
5	D Pironi	Tyrrell-Ford	−57.26s	16	0	G
6	H Rebaque	Lotus-Ford	−1m 37.86s	18	0	G

AUSTRIAN GP Österreichring

13 August 1978   Race 309

Ronnie Peterson

Lotus-Ford 79 189.939kph, 118.022mph

On a damp track the entire field fitted slicks, gambling further rain would hold off. They were wrong, the race stopped after seven laps due to a series of spins and accidents which included pole-sitter and race leader Peterson, but on his eighth tour and without harm. Andretti was already out, trying to pass Reutemann on lap 1. Wet tyres now fitted, the race was restarted over 47 laps to be decided on aggregate. Apart from the Michelin-shod Ferraris taking the lead during the switch back to slicks, Peterson drove away from the rest just as he had in the first part. There were only nine finishers, the retirements list littered with big names who had succumbed to the treacherous conditions, including Scheckter, Jones, Hunt, Reutemann and Lauda.

POLE POSITION Peterson, Lotus-Ford, 1m 37.71s (0.05s), 218.925kph, 136.034mph
LAPS 54 x 5.942 km, 3.692 miles (54 lap race interrupted due to accident. Result aggregate of 7 + 47 laps)
DISTANCE 320.868 km, 199.378 miles
STARTERS/FINISHERS 26/9
WEATHER Very wet
LAP LEADERS (On the road) Peterson 1-18, 29-54 (44); C Reutemann 19-22 (4); Villeneuve 23-28 (6)
WINNER'S LAPS 1-18 P1, 19 P6, 20 P4, 21-23 P3, 24-28 P2, 29-54 P1
FASTEST LAP Peterson, Lotus-Ford, 1m 43.12s (lap NA), 207.440kph, 128.897mph
CHAMPIONSHIP Andretti 54, Peterson 45, Depailler 32, Reutemann 31, Lauda 31

Pos	Driver	Car	Time/gap	Grid	Stops	Tyres
1	R Peterson	Lotus-Ford	1h 41m 21.57s	1	1	G
2	P Depailler	Tyrrell-Ford	−47.44s	13	1	G
3	G Villeneuve	Ferrari	−1m 39.76s	11	2	M
4	E Fittipaldi	Copersucar-Ford	−1 lap	6	2	G
5	J Laffite	Ligier-Matra	−1 lap	5	1	G
6	V Brambilla	Surtees-Ford	−1 lap	21	1	G

DUTCH GP Zandvoort
27 August 1978   Race 310

Mario Andretti
Lotus-Ford 79 186.871kph, 116.116mph

With the constructors' title wrapped up in Austria, JPS Lotus stole the front row for the fourth race running. There was an alarming moment as the leaders began lap 2. They encountered Patrese's immovable wreck in the middle of the track, legacy of a blameless yet violent collision with Pironi's Tyrrell that had been tapped from behind. For three laps the field threaded their way past the stricken car before its removal. For the eighth JPS Lotus win of the season both cars managed to finish, 0.32s separating another staged 1-2. The Brabham-Alfas finished 3-4, demonstrating that when they held together they could be best of the rest. Lauda had chased hard, setting fastest lap on lap 57 when he got to within a second of the black and gold cars.

POLE POSITION Andretti, Lotus-Ford, 1m 16.36s (0.61s), 199.235kph, 123.799mph
LAPS 75 x 4.226 km, 2.626 miles
DISTANCE 316.950 km, 196.944 miles
STARTERS/FINISHERS 26/12
WEATHER Dry, windy
LAP LEADERS Andretti 1-75 (75)
WINNER'S LAPS 1-75 P1
FASTEST LAP Lauda, Brabham-Alfa, 1m 19.57s (lap 57), 191.198kph, 118.805mph
CHAMPIONSHIP Andretti 63, Peterson 51, Lauda 35, Depailler 32, Reutemann 31

Pos	Driver	Car	Time/gap	Grid	Stops	Tyres
1	M Andretti	Lotus-Ford	1h 41m 4.23s	1	0	G
2	R Peterson	Lotus-Ford	−0.32s	2	0	G
3	N Lauda	Brabham-Alfa	−12.21s	3	0	G
4	J Watson	Brabham-Alfa	−20.92s	8	0	G
5	E Fittipaldi	Copersucar-Ford	−21.50s	10	0	G
6	G Villeneuve	Ferrari	−45.95s	5	0	M

Brabham-Alfa Romeo BT46

ITALIAN GP Monza
10 September 1978   Race 311

Niki Lauda
Brabham-Alfa Romeo BT46 207.527kph, 128.951mph

Peterson alone could prevent an Andretti championship but patently he intended to behave honourably. But the point became irrelevant when once again tragedy stalked Lotus in their hour of triumph. A shambolic start triggered a controversial and horrific 11-car accident, Hunt and Regazzoni releasing Peterson from his burning wreck with severe leg injuries. If anything Brambilla's head injuries appeared more life-threatening, but it was Peterson who died the following morning when complications set in. Andretti 'won' the restarted and shortened race, Villeneuve leading all but the final six laps. But they each received a 60s penalty for jumping the start, handing Lauda victory and Brabham a 1-2 finish. Andretti's championship was joyless.

POLE POSITION Andretti, Lotus-Ford, 1m 37.52s (0.346s), 214.110kph, 133.042mph
LAPS 40 x 5.800 km, 3.604 miles (Race shortened from 52 laps following accident.)
DISTANCE 232.000 km, 144.158 miles
STARTERS/FINISHERS 24/14
WEATHER Sunny, warm, dry
LAP LEADERS (On the road) G Villeneuve, Ferrari 1-34 (34); Andretti 35-40 (6)
WINNER'S LAPS 1-5 P4, 6-40 P3 (Andretti and G Villeneuve, Ferrari finished first and second but were both penalised one minute for jumped start)
FASTEST LAP Andretti, Lotus-Ford, 1m 38.23s (lap 33), 212.562kph, 132.080mph
CHAMPIONSHIP Andretti 64, Peterson 51, Lauda 44, Reutemann 35, Depailler 32

Pos	Driver	Car	Time/gap	Grid	Stops	Tyres
1	N Lauda	Brabham-Alfa	1h 7m 4.54s	4	0	G
2	J Watson	Brabham-Alfa	−1.48s	7	0	G
3	C Reutemann	Ferrari	−20.47s	11	0	M
4	J Laffite	Ligier-Matra	−37.53s	8	0	G
5	P Tambay	McLaren-Ford	−40.39s	19	0	G
6	M Andretti	Lotus-Ford	−46.33s	1	0	G

Round 15/16	**UNITED STATES GP EAST** Watkins Glen	**Carlos Reutemann**
	1 October 1978 **Race 312**	Ferrari 312T3 190.838kph, 118.581mph

Despite taking pole by a second, a late car switch ruined any chance Andretti had to win his home GP. Reutemann was able to pass the oversteering Lotus on lap 4 and after 27 laps Mario was out with a blown engine. Five laps earlier the same fate befell Villeneuve when Ferrari looked good for a 1-2 finish. So from lap 23 Jones in the Williams FW06 held a fine second place, although he came under pressure from Jarier in the number two Lotus towards the finish. Like Andretti, Jarier was using a car he had not driven in anger before the flag fell, and after an early tyre stop he carved his way through the field from P21 on lap 12 to P3 on lap 53, only to run out of fuel with four laps to go. Jabouille scored Renault's first points with fourth.

POLE POSITION M Andretti, Lotus-Ford, 1m 38.114s (1.065s), 199.412kph, 123.909mph
LAPS 59 x 5.435 km, 3.377 miles
DISTANCE 320.651 km, 199.243 miles
STARTERS/FINISHERS 26/16
WEATHER Overcast, dry
LAP LEADERS Andretti 1-2 (2); Reutemann 3-59 (57)
WINNER'S LAPS 1-2 P2, 3-59 P1
FASTEST LAP J-P Jarier, Lotus-Ford, 1m 39.557s (lap 55), 196.522kph, 122.113mph
CHAMPIONSHIP Andretti 64, Peterson 51, Reutemann 44, Lauda 44, Depailler 32

Pos	Driver	Car	Time/gap	Grid	Stops	Tyres
1	C Reutemann	Ferrari	1h 40m 48.800s	2	0	M
2	A Jones	Williams-Ford	−19.738s	3	0	G
3	J Scheckter	Wolf-Ford	−45.701s	11	0	G
4	J-P Jabouille	Renault	−1m 25.007s	9	0	M
5	E Fittipaldi	Copersucar-Ford	−1m 28.089s	13	0	G
6	P Tambay	McLaren-Ford	−1m 50.210s	18	0	G

Round 16/16	**CANADIAN GP** Montréal	**Gilles Villeneuve**
	8 October 1978 **Race 313**	Ferrari 312T3 160.414kph, 99.677mph

A Quebecois winning his and Canada's very first GP at the new Île Notre-Dame circuit sounds like fiction, but that's exactly what Gilles Villeneuve did. Adding to the local euphoria, second place went to Canadian oil-billionaire Walter Wolf's car driven for the final time by Jody Scheckter. But the story of the race was Jean-Pierre Jarier. The Frenchman had replaced poor Ronnie and demonstrated his undoubted talent with pole and 49 dominant laps in the Lotus 79. A holed oil radiator handed the lead to Villeneuve, who had overtaken Jones for third on lap 19 and Scheckter for second six laps later. Reutemann finished third in the other Ferrari while new champion Andretti collided with Watson and didn't even complete lap 6.

POLE POSITION J-P Jarier, Lotus-Ford, 1m 38.015s (0.011s), 165.281kph, 102.701mph
LAPS 70 x 4.500 km, 2.796 miles
DISTANCE 315.000 km, 195.732 miles
STARTERS/FINISHERS 22/12
WEATHER Cold, dry
LAP LEADERS Jarier 1-49 (49); Villeneuve 50-70 (21)
WINNER'S LAPS 1-18 P4, 19-24 P3, 25-49 P2, 50-70 P1
FASTEST LAP A Jones, Williams-Ford, 1m 38.072s (lap 70), 165.185kph, 102.641mph
CHAMPIONSHIP Andretti 64, Peterson 51, Reutemann 48, Lauda 44, Depailler 34

Pos	Driver	Car	Time/gap	Grid	Stops	Tyres
1	G Villeneuve	Ferrari	1h 57m 49.196s	3	0	M
2	J Scheckter	Wolf-Ford	−13.372s	2	0	G
3	C Reutemann	Ferrari	−19.408s	11	0	M
4	R Patrese	Arrows-Ford	−24.667s	12	0	G
5	P Depailler	Tyrrell-Ford	−28.558s	13	1	G
6	D Daly	Ensign-Ford	−54.476s	15	0	G

1978 CHAMPIONSHIP FACTS AND FOLKLORE

■ Under the auspices of the FIA, the CSI was replaced by *La Fédération Internationale du Sport Automobile* (FISA), with Jean-Marie Balestre elected President with responsibility for the governance of Formula 1.

■ Wankel, diesel, two-stroke and gas turbine engines were now prohibited, also cars with more than four wheels.

■ In a 16-race season the first GPs were held at Rio de Janeiro and the Île Notre Dame circuit in Montréal. South Africa was the 300th race in the F1 world championship series.

■ It was the usual two-part season, equally divided, the best seven results from each part counting towards the championships.

■ Having demonstrated its immense potential the preceding year, in 1978 Lotus duly reaped the rewards of ground effect, Andretti and new teammate Peterson, returning to Cheshunt after two years, sweeping to eight victories including four 1-2 finishes.

■ This gave Lotus the constructors' title for the seventh and, as it transpired, final time.

■ Mario Andretti, with six wins, duly became drivers' world champion, the second American to win the title, but again the last to do so.

■ But just as in 1968 and 1970, so too in 1978 tragedy once more overshadowed Lotus triumph, this time Sweden's Ronnie Peterson another Monza victim in controversial circumstances.

■ Andretti's practice form at Monza had been irresistible whereas problems forced Peterson to start in the old 78 from fifth. A chaotic starting procedure combined with, possibly, some reckless driving led to a massive start-line accident.

■ Three drivers were injured while James Hunt and Clay Regazzoni displayed immense gallantry in extricating Peterson from his burning wreck.

■ Peterson's shattered legs were serious injuries but did not appear to be life-threatening. Unexpectedly and shockingly he died the next morning through complications.

■ Arrows driver Patrese was blackballed for one race following Peterson's fatal accident, the obvious inference unstated and fervently denied.

RACE 310, Dutch GP: Andretti leads Peterson for the eighth JPS Lotus win of the season, 0.32s separating another staged 1-2. It would be Ronnie's final finish.

■ Spookily remarkable coincidences of Andretti's championship were parallels with that of the first American world champion, Phil Hill in 1961. In both cases they clinched their titles at the Italian Grand Prix at Monza; in both cases on Sunday 10 September; in both cases they entered that race with only their teammate still in contention for the title, and in both cases the teammate was killed in the race, sealing the title.

■ The month following Peterson's death another Swede, Gunnar Nilsson, a Grand Prix winner for Lotus the previous year, succumbed to his battle with cancer.

■ Earlier in the season, Sweden had been the scene of Niki Lauda's attempt to halt the Andretti/Lotus rollercoaster and revitalise his own attempt to retain his championship crown. Gordon Murray's ingenious concept, the Brabham 'fan car', pushed the F1 envelope and appeared to have the beating of Lotus, but after winning its debut at Anderstorp this particular solution to ground effect was outlawed by the authorities.

■ Unfortunately for the reigning world champion, the reason he had chosen Brabham-Alfa in 1977 – its nascent potential – continued into 1978, that is to say, the BT46 flattered to deceive as poor reliability again undermined its undoubted performance.

■ Even without Lauda, Ferrari continued to be a significant force by finding a competitive edge through their new tyre

supplier, Michelin. Once the differing characteristics of radials were matched to the bespoke 312T3 chassis, the Ferrari became either highly competitive or seriously off the pace, but the highs steadily became more frequent and were enough to bring a further clutch of five wins to the Scuderia.

■ Multiple race winners from last season McLaren and Wolf found no joy this year, and consequentially each lost or fired their number-one driver, Scheckter going to Ferrari, Hunt replacing Jody at Wolf.

■ Back on four wheels, Tyrrell did return to the winners circle at Monte Carlo. Monaco winner Depailler was one of two new race victors, the other Gilles Villeneuve at the inaugural GP held at the Île Notre Dame circuit in Montréal, later renamed after this illustrious French-Canadian hero.

■ Future world champions Nelson Piquet and Keke Rosberg made their debuts. Frank Williams and Patrick Head joined up to form Williams GP Engineering, the start of something big, whereas Team Surtees withdrew at season's end, never a winner.

■ There was a row between Shadow and new breakaway constructor Arrows over copyright, Don Nichols claiming that the Arrows FA1 was a straight copy of the Shadow DN9. The high courts agreed, after all the DN9 had been penned by Tony Southgate and Dave Wass before they departed from Shadow with Alan Rees and Jack Oliver to form Arrows, the name derived from an amalgam of their initials.

Lotus experimented with a Getrag clutchless gearchange, Parmalat-Brabham with carbon-fibre disc brakes, and Tyrrell with data logging, an early telemetry. But the dominating performance differentiators in 1978 were ground effect and tyres.

- The Lotus 79, 'Black Beauty' as it was nicknamed, frequently humbled the opposition by taking the principle of ground effect to new heights, increasing the low-pressure venturi effect beneath the car by paying even greater attention to unhindered under-car airflow to the side-pods containing the inverted aerofoil section.

- Tyres, on the other hand, added an indeterminate ingredient.

Firstly, compound choice had become hugely important because performance varied widely over a race distance – ie they could go 'off'. In response to the new challenge from Michelin, Goodyear provided increased choice of compounds to selected drivers.

- Secondly, wet-weather covers were an area of acute competiveness within the Goodyear/Michelin tyre wars, but thirdly, punctures or pressure-loss remained a bugbear.

- But for next year, most teams recognised that the comprehension of ground effect and its physical transference into their 1979 designs was where future success truly lay.

Championship ranking	Championship points	Driver nationality	1978 Drivers Championship		Races contested	Race victories	Podiumse excl. victories	Races led	Lights to flag victories	Laps led	Poles	Fastest laps	Triple Crowns
			Driver	Car									
1	64	USA	Mario Andretti	Lotus-Ford	16	6	1	11	4	451	8	3	1
2	51	SWE	Ronnie Peterson	Lotus-Ford	14	2	5	3		49	3	3	1
3	48	ARG	Carlos Reutemann	Ferrari	16	4	3	5	1	183	2	2	
4	44	AUT	Niki Lauda	Brabham-Alfa	16	2	5	2		58	1	4	
5	34	FRA	Patrick Depailler	Tyrrell-Ford	16	1	4	2		52			
6	25	GBR	John Watson	Brabham-Alfa	16		3	1		37	1		
7	24	RSA	Jody Scheckter	Wolf-Ford	16		4	2		16			
8	19	FRA	Jacques Laffite	Ligier-Matra	16		2						
9	17	CAN	Gilles Villeneuve	Ferrari	16	1	1	4		99.5		1	
10	17	BRA	Emerson Fittipaldi	Fittipaldi-Ford	16		1						
11	11	AUS	Alan Jones	Williams-Ford	16		1					2	
12	11	ITA	Riccardo Patrese	Arrows-Ford	14		1	1		37			
13	8	GBR	James Hunt	McLaren-Ford	16		1	1		5			
14	8	FRA	Patrick Tambay	McLaren-Ford	15								
15	7	FRA	Didier Pironi	Tyrrell-Ford	16								
16	4	SUI	Clay Regazzoni	Shadow-Ford	11								
17	3	FRA	Jean-Pierre Jabouille	Renault	14								
18	2	GER	Hans-Joachim Stuck	Shadow-Ford	14								
19	1	MEX	Hector Rebaque	Lotus-Ford	9								
19	1	ITA	Vittorio Brambilla	Surtees-Ford	12								
19	1	IRL	Derek Daly	Ensign-Ford	6								
-	0	FRA	Jean-Pierre Jarier	ATS-Ford (3) Lotus-Ford (2)	5				1	49	1	1	

Championship ranking	Championship points	Team/Marque nationality	1978 Constructors Championship		Engine maker nationality	Races contested	Race victories	1-2 finishes	Podiums excl. victories	Races led	Laps led	Poles	Fastest laps
			Chassis	Engine									
1	86	GBR	Lotus 79, 78	Ford Cosworth 3.0 V8	GBR	16	8	4	6	14	549	12	7
2	58	ITA	Ferrari 312T3, 312T2	Ferrari 3.0 F12	ITA	16	5		4	9	282.5	2	3
3	53	GBR	Brabham BT46, BT45C	Alfa Romeo 3.0 F12	ITA	16	2	1	8	3	95	2	4
4	38	GBR	Tyrrell 008	Ford Cosworth 3.0 V8	GBR	16	1		4	2	52		
5	24	CAN	Wolf WR1, WR3, WR4, WR5, WR6	Ford Cosworth 3.0 V8	GBR	16			4	2	16		
6	19	FRA	Ligier JS7, JS7/9, JS9	Matra 3.0 V12	FRA	16			2				
7	17	BRA	Fittipaldi F5A	Ford Cosworth 3.0 V8	GBR	16			1				
8	15	NZL	McLaren M26	Ford Cosworth 3.0 V8	GBR	16			1	1	5		
9	11	GBR	Williams FW06	Ford Cosworth 3.0 V8	GBR	16			1				2
10	11	GBR	Arrows FA1, A1	Ford Cosworth 3.0 V8	GBR	15			1	1	37		
11	6	USA	Shadow DN9, DN8	Ford Cosworth 3.0 V8	GBR	15							
12	3	FRA	Renault RS01	Renault 1.5 V6t	FRA	14							
13	1	GBR	Surtees TS20, TS19	Ford Cosworth 3.0 V8	GBR	16							
13	1	GBR	Ensign N177	Ford Cosworth 3.0 V8	GBR	12							

1979

Scheckter wins team game

THE TALE OF THE TITLE

- The Ferrari T4 with Michelin tyres put the Scuderia back on top of their British and French opposition.
- Jody Scheckter built a fine championship season, Gilles Villeneuve sportingly playing second fiddle.
- Three race wins apiece brought Ferrari their fourth constructors' cup in five seasons.
- Switching from Matra to Ford power, Ligier started strongly with three victories from the first five races.
- Williams finished even stronger, five from the last seven, Regazzoni winning their breakthrough race.
- Despite four Williams victories for Alan Jones, a bizarre revised points system obstructed his title hopes.
- In a fine season for French cars and drivers, Renault scored an historic first victory for a turbo-powered car.
- Behind winner Jabouille, Gilles Villeneuve and René Arnoux battled memorably over two points at Dijon.
- The Lotus 80 was too advanced to tame, Andretti making one of the feeblest title defences in F1 history.
- Former champions and 1976 rivals Hunt and Lauda both walked away from Formula 1 before season's end.
- And not forgetting: Ferrari's 75th GP victory; Alfa Romeo return.

THE CHASE FOR THE CHAMPIONSHIP

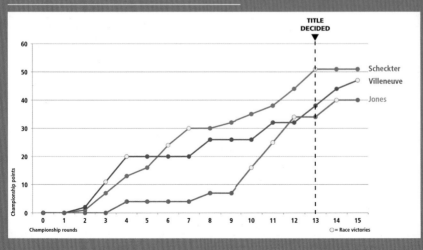

ARGENTINEAN GP Buenos Aires No 15
21 January 1979 — Race 314

Jacques Laffite
Ligier-Ford JS11 197.580kph, 122.770mph

Équipe Gitanes Ligier, having switched from Matra V12 to DFV V8, had also made the best fist of mastering ground effect over the winter, Laffite and Depailler 1-2 on the grid. The season began with a first-lap accident involving eight cars and eliminating five, including the new number one at Ferrari, Jody Scheckter. At the restart Depailler led the first ten laps until Laffite overtook his misfiring teammate to accomplish a first-time-out win for the new car. Reutemann kept the race alive for the locals as the troubled Depailler, little by little over 30 laps, fell into his grasp. So behind Laffite the podium was completed by Reutemann, replacing Peterson at Lotus, and Watson, driving Peterson's favoured 1979 mount, the McLaren M28.

POLE POSITION Laffite, Ligier-Ford, 1m 44.20s (1.04s), 206.188kph, 128.119mph
LAPS 53 x 5.968 km, 3.708 miles (Race restarted for scheduled 53 laps following accident)
DISTANCE 316.304 km, 196.542 miles
STARTERS/FINISHERS 24/11
WEATHER Sunny, very hot, dry
LAP LEADERS Depailler 1-10 (10); Laffite 11-53 (43)
WINNER'S LAPS 1 P4, 2-4 P3, 5-10 P2, 11-53 P1
FASTEST LAP Laffite, Ligier-Ford, 1m 46.91s (lap 42), 200.962kph, 124.872mph
CHAMPIONSHIP Laffite 9, Reutemann 6, Watson 4, Depailler 3, Andretti 2

Pos	Driver	Car	Time/gap	Grid	Stops	Tyres
1	J Laffite	Ligier-Ford	1h 36m 3.21s	1	0	G
2	C Reutemann	Lotus-Ford	−14.94s	3	0	G
3	J Watson	McLaren -Ford	−1m 28.81s	6	0	G
4	P Depailler	Ligier-Ford	−1m 41.72s	2	1	G
5	M Andretti	Lotus-Ford	−1 lap	7	0	G
6	E Fittipaldi	Copersucar-Ford	−1 lap	11	0	G

BRAZILIAN GP Interlagos
4 February 1979 — Race 315

Jacques Laffite
Ligier-Ford JS11 188.673kph, 117.236mph

Vive La France! Another Ligier victory, this time a 1-2. Ligier dominance was such that Laffite grand-slammed the opposition, leading from pole to flag and recording fastest lap. On the grid the Ligier pair was followed by the Lotus pair and the Ferrari pair, establishing some sort of early-season pecking order. Again Reutemann's Martini Lotus 79 was best of the rest, the world champion having exited on lap 2 when a fuel leak led to a small fire. The Ferraris finished where they started, a lap behind the flying Ligiers, having both needed to make tyre stops. The real race was for fourth place involving Fittipaldi, Scheckter and Pironi, the French Tyrrell driver coming out on top when local hero Emerson had to stop to fix a loose rear wheel.

POLE POSITION Laffite, Ligier-Ford, 2m 23.07s (0.92s), 198.130kph, 123.112mph
LAPS 40 x 7.874 km, 4.893 miles
DISTANCE 314.960 km, 195.707 miles
STARTERS/FINISHERS 23/15
WEATHER Sunny, very hot, dry
LAP LEADERS Laffite 1-40 (40)
WINNER'S LAPS 1-40 P1
FASTEST LAP Laffite, Ligier-Ford, 2m 28.76s (lap 23), 190.551kph, 118.403mph
CHAMPIONSHIP Laffite 18, Reutemann 10, Depailler 9, Watson 4, Pironi 3

Pos	Driver	Car	Time/gap	Grid	Stops	Tyres
1	J Laffite	Ligier-Ford	1h 40m 9.64s	1	0	G
2	P Depailler	Ligier-Ford	−5.28s	2	0	G
3	C Reutemann	Lotus-Ford	−44.14s	3	0	G
4	D Pironi	Tyrrell-Ford	−1m 25.88s	8	0	G
5	G Villeneuve	Ferrari	−1 lap	5	1	M
6	J Scheckter	Ferrari	−1 lap	6	1	M

SOUTH AFRICAN GP Kyalami
3 March 1979 — Race 316

Gilles Villeneuve
Ferrari 312T4 188.611kph, 117.197mph

Kyalami's altitude assisted Renault to their first pole. The new ground-effect 312T4 Ferraris were next, the Ligiers on row three. A cloudburst stopped the race after two laps, restarted over the distance remaining. The Ferraris led, Scheckter just one of four drivers who had decided to start with slicks on the wet track. When chasing teammate Villeneuve pitted for slicks on lap 15 Scheckter had a 30s lead and with the rain holding off looked good for victory. But he had overworked his tyres and left his pit stop too late, rejoining 36s behind Villeneuve on lap 53. To the delight of his home crowd Scheckter used his fresh rubber to fight back and finish just 3s short. A delighted Jarier, Tyrrell, beat Andretti's Lotus for third.

POLE POSITION J-P Jabouille, Renault, 1m 11.800s (0.240s), 205.772kph, 127.861mph
LAPS 78 x 4.104 km, 2.550 miles (78 lap race interrupted due to accident. Result aggregate of 2 + 76 laps)
DISTANCE 320.112 km, 198.908 miles
STARTERS/FINISHERS 24/13
WEATHER Overcast, intermittent heavy rain
LAP LEADERS (On the road) Jabouille 1 (1); Villeneuve 2-14, 53-78 (39); Scheckter 15-52 (38)
WINNER'S LAPS 1 P3, 2-14 P1, 15-52 P2, 53-78 P1
FASTEST LAP Villeneuve, Ferrari, 1m 14.412s (lap 23), 198.549kph, 123.372mph
CHAMPIONSHIP Laffite 18, Reutemann 12, Villeneuve 11, Depailler 9, Watson 4

Pos	Driver	Car	Time/gap	Grid	Stops	Tyres
1	G Villeneuve	Ferrari	1h 41m 49.96s	3	1	M
2	J Scheckter	Ferrari	−3.42s	2	1	M
3	J-P Jarier	Tyrrell-Ford	−22.11s	9	1	G
4	M Andretti	Lotus-Ford	−27.88s	8	1	G
5	C Reutemann	Lotus-Ford	−1m 6.97s	11	1	G
6	N Lauda	Brabham-Alfa	−1 lap	4	1	G

Round 4/15	**UNITED STATES GP WEST** Long Beach	**Gilles Villeneuve**
	8 April 1979 Race 317	Ferrari 312T4 141.313kph, 87.808mph

With the advantage of his first pole, and by making a more suitable tyre choice, Villeneuve was never headed. Technical difficulties meant Reutemann didn't occupy his front row place. This gave row two the opportunity to attack Villeneuve for the lead on lap 1 at the hairpin, the upshot Depailler second and Scheckter back to third with an askew front wing. Jody took 27 laps to dislodge Depailler and Jarier, who had also got ahead in their three-way tussle, to reach second place and get after Villeneuve, but by then Gilles was gone and continued to pull away to lead another Ferrari 1-2, the Scuderia's 75th GP victory. A minute back, the Williams FW06 of a determined Alan Jones ultimately won a fierce midfield battle for third.

POLE POSITION Villeneuve, Ferrari, 1m 18.825s (0.061s), 148.476kph, 92.259mph
LAPS 80.5 x 3.251 km, 2.020 miles
DISTANCE 261.706 km, 162.616 miles
STARTERS/FINISHERS 24/9
WEATHER Sunny, warm, dry
LAP LEADERS Villeneuve 1-80.5 (80.5)
WINNER'S LAPS 1-80.5 P1
FASTEST LAP Villeneuve, Ferrari, 1m 21.200s (lap NA), 144.133kph, 89.560mph
CHAMPIONSHIP Villeneuve 20, Laffite 18, Scheckter 13, Reutemann 12, Depailler 11

Pos	Driver	Car	Time/gap	Grid	Stops	Tyres
1	G Villeneuve	Ferrari	1h 50m 25.40s	1	0	M
2	J Scheckter	Ferrari	–29.38s	3	0	M
3	A Jones	Williams-Ford	–59.69s	10	0	G
4	M Andretti	Lotus-Ford	–1m 4.33s	6	0	G
5	P Depailler	Ligier-Ford	–1m 23.52s	4	0	G
6	J-P Jarier	Tyrrell-Ford	–1 lap	7	0	G

Round 5/15	**SPANISH GP** Jarama	**Patrick Depailler**
	29 April 1979 Race 318	Ligier-Ford JS11 154.419kph, 95.952mph

Ligier regained the initiative at the start of the European season, once again locking out the front row. Also side by side, but six rows behind the flying Ligiers, the new ground-effect Williams FW07s made an inauspicious debut. A more impressive first entrance was made by the new Lotus 80, Andretti qualifying P4, P8 for Reutemann's 79. In the race, once pole-sitting Laffite missed a gearchange, out on lap 15 with a buzzed Cosworth, Depailler cruised home the lights-to-flag winner. The Lotuses finished an encouraging 2-3, old beating new, but both heading Scheckter's Ferrari. Championship leader Villeneuve spun away his race chances not once but twice. When Jones' new Williams was running it was impressively quick.

POLE POSITION J Laffite, Ligier-Ford, 1m 14.50s (0.29s), 164.489kph, 102.208mph
LAPS 75 x 3.404 km, 2.115 miles
DISTANCE 255.300 km, 158.636 miles
STARTERS/FINISHERS 24/14
WEATHER Sunny, cool, dry
LAP LEADERS Depailler 1-75 (75)
WINNER'S LAPS 1-75 P1
FASTEST LAP G Villeneuve, Ferrari, 1m 16.44s (lap 72), 160.314kph, 99.614mph
CHAMPIONSHIP Villeneuve 20, Depailler 20, Laffite 18, Reutemann 18, Scheckter 16

Pos	Driver	Car	Time/gap	Grid	Stops	Tyres
1	P Depailler	Ligier-Ford	1h 39m 11.84s	2	0	G
2	C Reutemann	Lotus-Ford	–20.94s	8	0	G
3	M Andretti	Lotus-Ford	–27.31s	4	0	G
4	J Scheckter	Ferrari	–28.68s	5	0	M
5	J-P Jarier	Tyrrell-Ford	–30.39s	12	0	G
6	D Pironi	Tyrrell-Ford	–48.43s	10	0	G

Round 6/15	**BELGIAN GP** Zolder	**Jody Scheckter**
	13 May 1979 Race 319	Ferrari 312T4 179.018kph, 111.237mph

Laffite's fourth pole, Depailler likewise alongside. Initially the Ligiers shared leadership, but in a fascinating race with five lead changes, on lap 24 a Williams led a GP for the very first time. Jones had the measure of everyone that day, pulling out a 12s lead until electrics forced him out on lap 40. Soon afterwards leader Depailler missed his apex and crashed, returning the lead to Laffite. Scheckter had never looked a winner on sheer pace, largely running P4, but Laffite's poor grip could not hold the Ferrari, which moved past on lap 54 to win his first for the *Commendatore*. Villeneuve, unlucky to tangle early on, pitted, stormed back to third but ran dry in sight of the flag. After 27 years Alfa Romeo returned to the F1 racetrack.

POLE POSITION Laffite, Ligier-Ford, 1m 21.13s (0.07s), 189.119kph, 117.513mph
LAPS 70 x 4.262 km, 2.648 miles
DISTANCE 298.340 km, 185.380 miles
STARTERS/FINISHERS 24/11
WEATHER Sunny, hot, dry
LAP LEADERS P Depailler, Ligier-Ford 1-18, 40-46 (25); Laffite 19-23, 47-53 (12); A Jones Williams-Ford 24-39 (16); Scheckter 54-70 (17)
WINNER'S LAPS 1 P7, 2-3 P6, 4-5 P5, 6-39 P4, 40-46 P3, 47-53 P2, 54-70 P1
FASTEST LAP G Villeneuve, Ferrari, 1m 23.09s (lap 63), 184.658kph, 114.741mph
CHAMPIONSHIP Laffite 24, Scheckter 24, Villeneuve 20, Depailler 20, Reutemann 19

Pos	Driver	Car	Time/gap	Grid	Stops	Tyres
1	J Scheckter	Ferrari	1h 39m 59.53s	7	0	M
2	J Laffite	Ligier-Ford	–15.36s	1	0	G
3	D Pironi	Tyrrell-Ford	–46.49s	12	0	G
4	C Reutemann	Lotus-Ford	–1m 4.31s	10	0	G
5	R Patrese	Arrows-Ford	–1m 5.85s	16	0	G
6	J Watson	McLaren -Ford	–1 lap	19	0	G

Ferrari 312T4

Round 7/15	**MONACO GP** Monte Carlo		
	27 May 1979		**Race 320**

Jody Scheckter

Ferrari 312T4 130.902kph, 81.338mph

The Michelin-shod Ferraris were the class in qualifying and quickly established a 1-2 lead in the race. Behind the escaping Ferraris, Lauda kept the Ligiers in check followed by Pironi and Jones. Laffite's pit stop released a fired-up Pironi who made contact first with Depailler on lap 19 and then Lauda on lap 22. With all three sidelined the track ahead opened up for Jones, soon in a three-car train with the Ferraris. But on lap 43 a brush with the barriers put Jones out, and Villeneuve's transmission broke on lap 54. But the race wasn't over. Regazzoni in the other Williams, having starting fifth-last, was up to second with Villeneuve gone, and in the final 15 laps closed by as many seconds to within 0.44s of Scheckter in a thrilling chase to the flag.

POLE POSITION Scheckter, Ferrari, 1m 26.45s (0.07s), 137.920kph, 85.700mph
LAPS 76 x 3.312 km, 2.058 miles
DISTANCE 251.712 km, 156.407 miles
STARTERS/FINISHERS 20/6
WEATHER Sunny, warm, dry
LAP LEADERS Scheckter 1-77 (76)
WINNER'S LAPS 1-76 P1
FASTEST LAP Depailler, Ligier-Ford, 1m 28.82s (lap 69), 134.240kph, 83.413mph
CHAMPIONSHIP Scheckter 30, Laffite 24, Villeneuve 20, Depailler 20, Reutemann 20

Pos	Driver	Car	Time/gap	Grid	Stops	Tyres
1	J Scheckter	Ferrari	1h 55m 22.48s	1	0	M
2	C Regazzoni	Williams-Ford	−0.44s	16	0	G
3	C Reutemann	Lotus-Ford	−8.57s	11	0	G
4	J Watson	McLaren -Ford	−41.31s	14	0	G
5r	P Depailler	Ligier-Ford	−1 lap	3	1	G
6	J Mass	Arrows-Ford	−7 laps	8	1	G

Round 8/15	**FRENCH GP** Dijon-Prenois		
	1 July 1979		**Race 321**

Jean-Pierre Jabouille

Renault RS10 191.315kph, 118.877mph

An all-Renault front row but Arnoux almost stalled, dropping to ninth, and Jabouille was outgunned by Villeneuve from row two. On lap 47 Jabouille finally powered by the Ferrari, now on worn tyres, which was falling into the grasp of the recovering Arnoux. On lap 77, urged on by the patriotic crowd, he took Villeneuve for second, but Gilles was having none of it. Over those final three crazy, awe-inspiring, wheel-banging laps Arnoux and Villeneuve fought uncompromisingly over second place, passing and repassing, the epitome of motor-*racing*. Two years after Renault's debut, Jabouille's first turbo victory was an historic F1 landmark and a triumph more Gallic than even the Ligier wins: driver, car, engine, tyres, fuel, and at Dijon.

POLE POSITION Jabouille, Renault, 1m 07.19s (0.26s), 203.602kph, 126.512mph
LAPS 80 x 3.800 km, 2.361 miles
DISTANCE 304.000 km, 188.897 miles
STARTERS/FINISHERS 24/18
WEATHER Overcast, dry
LAP LEADERS Villeneuve 1-46 (46); Jabouille 47-80 (34)
WINNER'S LAPS 1-46 P2, 47-80 P1
FASTEST LAP Arnoux, Renault, 1m 09.16s (lap 71), 197.802kph, 122.909mph
CHAMPIONSHIP Scheckter 30, Villeneuve 26, Laffite 24, Depailler 20, Reutemann 20

Pos	Driver	Car	Time/gap	Grid	Stops	Tyres
1	J-P Jabouille	Renault	1h 35m 20.42	1	0	M
2	G Villeneuve	Ferrari	−14.59s	3	0	M
3	R Arnoux	Renault	−14.83s	2	0	M
4	A Jones	Williams-Ford	−36.61s	7	0	G
5	J-P Jarier	Tyrrell-Ford	−1m 4.51s	10	0	G
6	C Regazzoni	Williams-Ford	−1m 5.51s	9	0	G

TOP **100** RACE

Renault RS10

Round 9/15	**BRITISH GP** Silverstone						**Clay Regazzoni**
	14 July 1979					**Race 322**	Williams-Ford FW07 223.375kph, 138.799mph

A great weekend for the French was followed by a pretty good one for the British. At Silverstone, fittingly, Frank Williams' first victory in his 11th season as a GP entrant was also the precursor for the start of something big. Ever since its second outing a FW07 victory had looked on the cards. From the first pole for team and driver, only Jabouille could keep Jones in sight, and when his Renault expired on lap 17 the second Williams took over P2. Twenty-two laps later it became P1 when a water-pump seal ended the race for Jones. So the number two Williams won from the number two Renault, no one else even on the same lap. When finally it happened for Williams it all looked so easy, but ten prior seasons suggested otherwise.

POLE POSITION A Jones, Williams-Ford, 1m 11.88s (0.60s), 236.324kph, 146.845mph
LAPS 68 x 4.719 km, 2.932 miles
DISTANCE 320.865 km, 199.376 miles
STARTERS/FINISHERS 24/14
WEATHER Sunny, warm, dry
LAP LEADERS Jones 1-38 (38); Regazzoni 39-68 (30)
WINNER'S LAPS 1-16 P3, 17-38 P2, 39-68 P1
FASTEST LAP Regazzoni, Williams-Ford, 1m 14.40s (lap 39), 228.319kph, 141.871mph
CHAMPIONSHIP Scheckter 33, Villeneuve 26, Laffite 24, Depailler 20, Reutemann 20

Pos	Driver	Car	Time/gap	Grid	Stops	Tyres
1	C Regazzoni	Williams-Ford	1h 26m 11.17s	4	0	G
2	R Arnoux	Renault	−24.28s	5	0	M
3	J-P Jarier	Tyrrell-Ford	−1 lap	16	0	G
4	J Watson	McLaren-Ford	−1 lap	7	0	G
5	J Scheckter	Ferrari	−1 lap	11	0	M
6	J Ickx	Ligier-Ford	−1 lap	17	0	G

Williams-Ford FW07

Round 10/15	**GERMAN GP** Hockenheim			
	29 July 1979		Race 323	

Alan Jones
Williams-Ford FW07 216.124kph, 134.293mph

Alan Jones had only to wait two weeks to make good his Silverstone disappointment. Jabouille was on pole, Hockenheim suiting turbo power. Jones, alongside, made a lightning start knowing that if the Renault got ahead it would be hard to pass. So Jones led, Jabouille menacing for seven laps until, just as he mounted an attack for the lead, the Frenchman made an error under braking and spun out. Now Laffite was second, but not for long. The second Williams was marching up the order, taking Scheckter on lap 8 and depriving Laffite of P2 five laps later, now some 15s behind his team leader. But Jones' first Williams victory kept his pit anxious, a softening rear tyre and fuel vaporisation prolonging tension.

POLE POSITION J-P Jabouille, Renault, 1m 48.48s (0.27s), 225.299kph, 139.994mph
LAPS 45 x 6.789 km, 4.218 miles
DISTANCE 305.505 km, 189.832 miles
STARTERS/FINISHERS 24/12
WEATHER Sunny, very hot, dry
LAP LEADERS Jones 1-45 (45)
WINNER'S LAPS 1-45 P1
FASTEST LAP G Villeneuve, Ferrari, 1m 51.89s (lap 40), 218.432kph, 135.728mph
CHAMPIONSHIP Scheckter 35, Laffite 28, Villeneuve 26, Regazzoni 22, Depailler 20

Pos	Driver	Car	Time/gap	Grid	Stops	Tyres
1	A Jones	Williams-Ford	1h 24m 48.83s	2	0	G
2	C Regazzoni	Williams-Ford	−2.91s	6	0	G
3	J Laffite	Ligier-Ford	−18.39s	3	0	G
4	J Scheckter	Ferrari	−31.20s	5	0	M
5	J Watson	McLaren-Ford	−1m 37.80s	12	0	G
6	J Mass	Arrows-Ford	−1 lap	18	0	G

Round 11/15	**AUSTRIAN GP** Österreichring			
	12 August 1979		Race 324	

Alan Jones
Williams-Ford FW07 219.689kph, 136.508mph

Three cars fought for pole, the two Renaults with Jones' Williams, Arnoux claiming his first. But at the start Villeneuve shot into the lead from row three. It took Jones three laps to get past the Ferrari and sail away to another victory, a Williams hat-trick. The Renaults battled with Villeneuve but neither finished, so Villeneuve led in Laffite and Scheckter. In the early season these three had been the leading lights but now could not hold on to the Renaults, let alone Jones' Williams. However, they still led the championship, separated by just six points. What's more, because of the peculiar 'best four results' from each part of the two-part season, due to their modest results in the first seven races the Williams drivers could not realistically win the title.

POLE POSITION Arnoux, Renault, 1m 34.07s (0.21s), 227.397kph, 141.298mph
LAPS 54 x 5.942 km, 3.692 miles
DISTANCE 320.868 km, 199.378 miles
STARTERS/FINISHERS 24/10
WEATHER Sunny, warm, dry
LAP LEADERS Villeneuve 1-3 (3); Jones 4-54 (51)
WINNER'S LAPS 1-3 P2, 4-54 P1
FASTEST LAP Arnoux, Renault, 1m 35.77s (lap 40), 223.360kph, 138.790mph
CHAMPIONSHIP Scheckter 38, Villeneuve 32, Laffite 32, Jones 25, Regazzoni 24

Pos	Driver	Car	Time/gap	Grid	Stops	Tyres
1	A Jones	Williams-Ford	1h 27m 38.01s	2	0	G
2	G Villeneuve	Ferrari	−36.05s	5	0	M
3	J Laffite	Ligier-Ford	−46.77s	8	0	G
4	J Scheckter	Ferrari	−47.21s	9	0	M
5	C Regazzoni	Williams-Ford	−48.92s	6	0	G
6	R Arnoux	Renault	−1 lap	1	1	M

Round 12/15	**DUTCH GP** Zandvoort			
	26 August 1979		Race 325	

Alan Jones
Williams-Ford FW07 187.675kph, 116.616mph

Pole-sitter Arnoux and Regazzoni went out in a four abreast incident on lap 1. The two survivors, Villeneuve and Jabouille, set off after leader Jones. As these three began lap 11 Villeneuve found his way around the outside at Tarzan, the Williams' gearbox temperamental. Separated by no more than 4s, Villeneuve led Jones until a deflating rear tyre finally disintegrated, pitching him off approaching Tarzan. Gilles memorably if futilely returned to the pits on three wheels, wrecking his car in the process. This effectively finished Villeneuve's title chances as Scheckter, having overcooked his clutch at the start, made a great comeback drive from P19 on lap 1 to finish second and stretch his lead over Villeneuve to 12 points.

POLE POSITION R Arnoux, Renault, 1m 15.461s (0.185s), 201.609kph, 125.274mph
LAPS 75 x 4.226 km, 2.626 miles
DISTANCE 316.950 km, 196.944 miles
STARTERS/FINISHERS 24/7
WEATHER Overcast, dry
LAP LEADERS Jones 1-10, 47-75 (39); Villeneuve 11-46 (36)
WINNER'S LAPS 1-10 P1, 11-46 P2, 47-75 P1
FASTEST LAP G Villeneuve, Ferrari, 1m 19.438s (lap 39), 191.515kph, 119.002mph
CHAMPIONSHIP Scheckter 44, Laffite 36, Jones 34, Villeneuve 32, Regazzoni 24

Pos	Driver	Car	Time/gap	Grid	Stops	Tyres
1	A Jones	Williams-Ford	1h 41m 19.775s	2	0	G
2	J Scheckter	Ferrari	−21.783s	5	0	M
3	J Laffite	Ligier-Ford	−1m 3.253s	7	0	G
4	N Piquet	Brabham-Alfa	−1 lap	11	0	G
5	J Ickx	Ligier-Ford	−1 lap	20	0	G
6	J Mass	Arrows-Ford	−2 laps	18	0	G

Round 13/15	**ITALIAN GP** Monza					
	9 September 1979				**Race 326**	

And suddenly it was all over. Scheckter's Monza victory clinched the drivers' championship, and with the dutiful Villeneuve second by 0.46s Ferrari simultaneously won the constructors' cup. Qualifying hadn't looked that promising, the Renaults 1-2, the Ferraris 3-5, but the French challenge capitulated rapidly, the British challenge from Williams little better. Arnoux dropped out with electrics when leading lap 13 while pole-man Jabouille never featured higher than fourth. Jones' battery went flat, pitting on lap 5 from where he made a wonderful comeback drive, but even Regazzoni's late charge for Williams spluttered out on the penultimate lap with fuel starvation. For the *tifosi*, race and championship results couldn't get any better.

Jody Scheckter
Ferrari 312T4 212.186kph, 131.846mph

POLE POSITION J-P Jabouille, Renault, 1m 34.580s (0.124s), 220.765kph, 137.177mph
LAPS 50 x 5.800 km, 3.604 miles
DISTANCE 290.000 km, 180.198 miles
STARTERS/FINISHERS 24/14
WEATHER Sunny, warm, dry
LAP LEADERS Scheckter 1, 13-50 (39); R Arnoux, Renault 2-12 (11)
WINNER'S LAPS 1 P1, 2-12 P2, 13-50 P1
FASTEST LAP Regazzoni, Williams-Ford, 1m 35.600s (lap 46), 218.410kph, 135.714mph
CHAMPIONSHIP Scheckter 51, Villeneuve 38, Laffite 36, Jones 34, Regazzoni 27

Pos	Driver	Car	Time/gap	Grid	Stops	Tyres
1	J Scheckter	Ferrari	1h 22m 0.22s	3	0	M
2	G Villeneuve	Ferrari	−0.46s	5	0	M
3	C Regazzoni	Williams-Ford	−4.78s	6	0	G
4	N Lauda	Brabham-Alfa	−54.40s	9	0	G
5	M Andretti	Lotus-Ford	−59.70s	10	0	G
6	J-P Jarier	Tyrrell-Ford	−1m 1.55s	16	0	G

Round 14/15	**CANADIAN GP** Montréal					
	30 September 1979				**Race 327**	

No wonder the circuit was renamed after him in 1982. Last year's winner Gilles Villeneuve put on an unforgettable display for his home crowd. He gave his all to finish just 1s behind winner Alan Jones. It was a titanic contest between two spirited and relentless drivers at their absolute peak. Villeneuve kept pole-man Jones at bay for 50 laps, Jones likewise for the final 22 after a ballsy pass. Gilles had offered Alan that minuscule opportunity, a fractionally slower exit from one of the tight corners. It was enough. On the Friday double world champion Lauda walked away to retirement, leaving Piquet to make a brilliant race debut for the new Ford DFV-engined Brabham BT49. He lost P3 close to the end with gearbox maladies.

Alan Jones
Williams-Ford FW07 169.926kph, 105.587mph

POLE POSITION Jones, Williams-Ford, 1m 29.892s (0.662s), 176.612kph, 109.742mph
LAPS 72 x 4.410 km, 2.740 miles
DISTANCE 317.520 km, 197.298 miles
STARTERS/FINISHERS 24/10
WEATHER Sunny, warm, dry
LAP LEADERS Villeneuve 1-50 (50); Jones 51-72 (22)
WINNER'S LAPS 1-50 P2, 51-72 P1
FASTEST LAP Jones, Williams-Ford, 1m 31.272s (lap 65), 173.942kph, 108.082mph
CHAMPIONSHIP Scheckter 51, Villeneuve 44, Jones 40, Laffite 36, Regazzoni 29

Pos	Driver	Car	Time/gap	Grid	Stops	Tyres
1	A Jones	Williams-Ford	1h 52m 6.892s	1	0	G
2	G Villeneuve	Ferrari	−1.080s	2	0	M
3	C Regazzoni	Williams-Ford	−1m 13.656s	3	0	G
4	J Scheckter	Ferrari	−1 lap	9	1	M
5	D Pironi	Tyrrell-Ford	−1 lap	6	0	G
6	J Watson	McLaren-Ford	−2 laps	17	1	G

Round 15/15	**UNITED STATES GP EAST** Watkins Glen					
	7 October 1979				**Race 328**	

In dry qualifying Jones posted a stunning pole, over a second better than next man, Piquet's Brabham-Ford. But the race was wet. Villeneuve plus Michelin wets held sway until the track began to dry, letting Jones ahead for laps 32–36. On lap 34 Villeneuve switched to slicks, Jones disastrously two laps later, losing 10s to the Ferrari with a sticking rear. Under pressure the Williams crew released Jones before fully tightening the recalcitrant wheel, which parted company with the car during his rejoining lap. So with his third race victory of the season Villeneuve cemented runner-up position in the championship and equalled teammate and champion Scheckter with three race wins. But neither matched Alan Jones' four victories for Williams.

Gilles Villeneuve
Ferrari 312T4 171.325kph, 106.456mph

POLE POSITION A Jones, Williams-Ford, 1m 35.615s (1.299s), 204.624kph, 127.147mph
LAPS 59 x 5.435 km, 3.377 miles
DISTANCE 320.651 km, 199.243 miles
STARTERS/FINISHERS 24/7
WEATHER Overcast, cold, wet
LAP LEADERS Villeneuve 1-31, 37-59 (54); Jones 32-36 (5)
WINNER'S LAPS 1-31 P1, 32-36 P2, 37-59 P1
FASTEST LAP N Piquet, Brabham-Ford, 1m 40.054s (lap 51), 195.546kph, 121.506mph
CHAMPIONSHIP Scheckter 51, Villeneuve 47, Jones 40, Laffite 36, Regazzoni 29

Pos	Driver	Car	Time/gap	Grid	Stops	Tyres
1	G Villeneuve	Ferrari	1h 52m 17.734s	3	1	M
2	R Arnoux	Renault	−48.787s	7	1	M
3	D Pironi	Tyrrell-Ford	−53.199s	10	1	G
4	E de Angelis	Shadow-Ford	−1m 30.512s	20	1	G
5	H-J Stuck	ATS-Ford	−1m 41.259s	14	1	G
6	J Watson	McLaren-Ford	−1 lap	13	1	G

- Car regulation changes were confined to dimensional restrictions, including maximum overall length.
- The championship points system received a makeover. Positive was that constructors could now claim points for all their entries, not just the highest placed car in a race, and that points in all races would count.
- Conversely and bizarrely, only eight of the fifteen championship rounds would count towards the drivers' title, the best four results from each of the first seven and the final eight races.
- Sponsorship difficulties saw the cancellation of Anderstorp, and, after the tragic losses of Peterson and Nilsson, Sweden would never reappear on the GP calendar.
- Tyre barriers were introduced at Long Beach, and in qualifying two 90-minute sessions became the established norm.
- Inevitably, ground effect was the name of the game in 1979 and sliding skirts became de rigueur.
- With their flat-12 engine configuration, Ferrari was possibly least best-placed to exploit venturi tunnels, but as a package, with its powerful engine and Michelin tyres, the Ferrari 312T4 was highly effective and more reliable than most.
- Add to this a strong driver line-up – Jody Scheckter having joined Gilles Villeneuve – and six race victories, three for each driver including three 1-2s, was more than enough to land the constructors' championship for the Scuderia and the drivers' title for Scheckter.

- Scheckter had caught Enzo Ferrari's eye as a potential team-leader not only as a proven race-winner, but because he could build a championship season. He had demonstrated this at both Tyrrell and at Wolf, and it was exactly the performance he gave in 1979.
- He failed to finish in just two races – the first an accident, the last a puncture – scoring points in the rest bar one seventh, these including his three wins plus three podiums.
- Villeneuve delivered four podiums with his three wins, but also suffered five dnfs, the killer blow being the legendary tyre-burst sequence when leading at Zandvoort.
- The other iconic Villeneuve imagery of the season was his never to be forgotten wheel-to-wheel battle with Arnoux's Renault at Dijon for second place.
- The final championship-deciding moment was his acceptance of team orders not to challenge Scheckter for the Monza victory. GV was an uncompromising racing driver, yes, but one with strong principles, and in any case, other championship chances would come his way, wouldn't they?
- Another contributor towards Ferrari success was that while the Scuderia failed to score in just one championship round, their strongest challengers zero-scored in eleven Renault, nine Williams and five Ligier.
- No one team or driver put together a sustained challenge, Ligier unable to maintain their early advantage, the Williams charge beginning too late.
- Initially Ligier had looked the car to beat, winning three

RACE 323, German GP: A man of principle, Gilles Villeneuve – as required of him – frequently played follow-my-leader to his team leader during the 1979 season. Here he follows in Jody Scheckter's tyre tracks at Hockenheim.

from the first five races, but the loss of Patrick Depailler mid-season, suffering serious leg injuries in a hang-gliding accident, didn't help their cause, replacement Ickx not the force he once was.

■ The real star of the season was the Williams FW07, bringing Frank his overdue breakthrough, which landed five victories from the final seven races.

■ Also breaking through was Renault with a single but significant win, fittingly at the French Grand Prix. Two years on from their debut, a switch from Garrett to KKK twin-turbos had begun to tame the undoubted power and improve reliability, but there was still some way to go, particularly getting the turbo off the start-line.

■ Jabouille was one of seven winning drivers in 1979, the pairs of drivers from Ferrari, Williams and Ligier completing the list, Jones the most successful individually with his four late-season victories.

■ After 27 years Alfa Romeo were back, making an appearance in five of the fifteen rounds, their car fitted with their new V12 engine, which Brabham had also switched to.

■ The unreliability of the V12 and the now non-exclusive engine supply contributed to Brabham's decision to end their arrangement with Alfa and revert to Cosworth power for the final two championship rounds.

■ So what of the dominant 1978 champions Andretti and Lotus? Wretchedly, unable to make the new Lotus 80

RACE 321, French GP: Behind Renault's historic first turbo victory, Gilles Villeneuve's Ferrari and Rene Arnoux's Renault battled memorably over second place at Dijon.

function they plunged from heroes to zeroes, Andretti suffering one of the most unsuccessful title defences in F1 annals, accumulating just 14 points, third place his best finish.

■ The American was not the only despairing ex-world champion. Shortly after yet another early retirement at Monaco, James Hunt turned his back on his new team and on GP racing, citing self-preservation.

■ Extraordinarily, another ex-world champion prematurely exited the sport, Niki Lauda making the same decision in Canada, giving up on Brabham with two races remaining, his rationale 'I am tired of driving round and round in circles'! He rescinded this opinion with a successful comeback for McLaren in 1982.

■ Although their stated reasons differed, Hunt and Lauda were both thoroughly disillusioned, each experiencing an utterly abysmal season which jointly garnered three race finishes and four points from 20 starts.

■ If new world champion Jody Scheckter had been able to project himself forward just 12 months, he would first have shuddered, then nodded with resigned sympathy and understanding.

■ Kimi Räikkönen was born in 1979, and dubbed by the Queen of England for distinguished services to British motorsport, Sir Jack Brabham became the first Formula 1 knight.

Championship ranking	Championship points	Driver nationality	1979 Drivers Championship		Races contested	Race victories	Podiumse excl. victories	Races led	Lights to flag victories	Laps led	Poles	Fastest laps	Triple Crowns
			Driver	Car									
1	51	RSA	Jody Scheckter	Ferrari	15	3	3	4	1	170	1		
2	47	CAN	Gilles Villeneuve	Ferrari	15	3	4	7	1	308.5	1	6	1
3	40	AUS	Alan Jones	Williams-Ford	15	4	1	7	1	216	3	1	1
4	36	FRA	Jacques Laffite	Ligier-Ford	15	2	4	3	1	95	4	2	2
5	29	SUI	Clay Regazzoni	Williams-Ford	15	1	4	1		30		2	
6	20	FRA	Patrick Depailler	Ligier-Ford	7	1	1	3	1	110		1	
7	20	ARG	Carlos Reutemann	Lotus-Ford	15		4						
8	17	FRA	René Arnoux	Renault	14		3	1		11	2	2	
9	15	GBR	John Watson	McLaren-Ford	15		1						
10	14	FRA	Didier Pironi	Tyrrell-Ford	15		2						
11	14	FRA	Jean-Pierre Jarier	Tyrrell-Ford	12		2						
12	14	USA	Mario Andretti	Lotus-Ford	15		1						
13	9	FRA	Jean-Pierre Jabouille	Renault	14	1		2		35	4		
14	4	AUT	Niki Lauda	Brabham-Alfa	13								
15	3	BRA	Nelson Piquet	Brabham-Alfa (13) Brabham-Ford (2)	15							1	
15	3	ITA	Elio de Angelis	Shadow-Ford	14								
17	3	BEL	Jacky Ickx	Ligier-Ford	8								
18	3	GER	Jochen Mass	Arrows-Ford	13								
19	2	ITA	Riccardo Patrese	Arrows-Ford	14								
19	2	GER	Hans-Joachim Stuck	ATS-Ford	12								
21	1	BRA	Emerson Fittipaldi	Fittipaldi-Ford	15								

Championship ranking	Championship points	Team/Marque nationality	1979 Constructors Championship		Engine maker nationality	Races contested	Race victories	1-2 finishes	Podiums excl. victories	Races led	Laps led	Poles	Fastest laps
			Chassis	Engine									
1	113	ITA	Ferrari 312T4, 312T3	Ferrari 3.0 F12	ITA	15	6	3	7	11	478.5	2	6
2	75	GBR	Williams FW07, FW06	Ford Cosworth 3.0 V8	GBR	15	5	1	5	8	246	3	3
3	61	FRA	Ligier JS11	Ford Cosworth 3.0 V8	GBR	15	3	1	5	6	205	4	3
4	39	GBR	Lotus 79, 80	Ford Cosworth 3.0 V8	GBR	15			5				
5	28	GBR	Tyrrell 009	Ford Cosworth 3.0 V8	GBR	15			4				
6	26	FRA	Renault RS10, RS01	Renault 1.5 V6t	FRA	14	1		3	3	46	6	2
7	15	NZL	McLaren M28, M29	Ford Cosworth 3.0 V8	GBR	15			1				
8	7	GBR	Brabham BT48, BT46	Alfa Romeo 3.0 V12, 3.0 F12	ITA	13							
9	5	GBR	Arrows A2, A1B	Ford Cosworth 3.0 V8	GBR	15							
10	3	USA	Shadow DN9	Ford Cosworth 3.0 V8	GBR	14							
11	2	GER	ATS D2, D3	Ford Cosworth 3.0 V8	GBR	12							
12	1	BRA	Fittipaldi F5A, F6A	Ford Cosworth 3.0 V8	GBR	15							
-	0	GBR	Brabham BT49	Ford Cosworth 3.0 V8	GBR	2							1

RACE 349, Spanish GP: The 1980s were defined by the turbo era and *le professeur*, Alain Prost, was the undoubted master of this F1 genre. But behind the wheel of a turbo, the driver who made the blood race was Gilles Villeneuve, here winning the second of his two remarkable 1981 victories.

THE EIGHTIES

Bernie's travelling circus

INTERSPERSED WITH FISA/FOCA WARS, GROUND EFFECT AND TURBOS, ECCLESTONE'S F1 BUSINESS MODEL GREW RELENTLESSLY

1980

Then along came Jones

THE TALE OF THE TITLE

- With five race victories Alan Jones won the world drivers' title for Williams.
- In his 12th season as an F1 entrant, Frank's cars dominated the constructors' championship.
- Piquet and Brabham, occasionally unbeatable, mounted a serious challenge for the drivers' title.
- The FISA/FOCA wars caused the Spanish GP, won by Jones, to be struck from the championship calendar.
- French teams Ligier and Renault competed strongly, bringing race success to four French drivers.
- From an abundance of French drivers one was sadly lost, Patrick Depailler killed testing for Alfa Romeo.
- Despite this tragic setback, the Italian outfit revealed occasional glimpses of winning form.
- Renault, with three race victories, again demonstrated the brittle potential of turbo-power.
- Ferrari were nowhere, focussing their energies on a new turbo car for next year.
- Scheckter's lame title defence decided his retirement at the end of a miserable season.
- Twice champion Fittipaldi also retired from F1 after a fruitless five-year struggle with the family team.
- And not forgetting: Goodyear withdraw; Ron Dennis moves in at McLaren.

THE CHASE FOR THE CHAMPIONSHIP

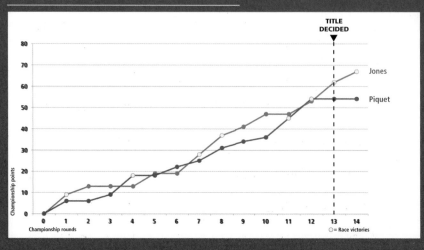

Round 1/14	**ARGENTINEAN GP** Buenos Aires No 15		**Alan Jones**	
	13 January 1980	Race 329	Williams-Ford FW07 183.531kph, 114.041mph	

Alan Jones began the new season with his fifth win from the last seven races. Despite his pole advantage it was an arduous victory in blistering weather, disintegration of the track causing difficulties for everyone. On lap 17 race leader Jones became another victim of the treacherous 'marbles' building up on several corners. As a consequence of his spin rubbish became trapped in his radiator, causing overheating and a pit stop. Rejoining fourth, Jones fought back to retake the lead on lap 30 from last year's winner Laffite, the Ligier soon out with engine trouble. Jones was then pressured by Villeneuve until the Ferrari ploughed off the track on lap 36 with suspension failure. Despite two more brief offs, Jones won from Piquet's Brabham.

POLE POSITION Jones, Williams-Ford, 1m 44.17s (0.27s), 206.247kph, 128.156mph
LAPS 53 x 5.968 km, 3.708 miles
DISTANCE 316.304 km, 196.542 miles
STARTERS/FINISHERS 24/7
WEATHER Sunny, very hot, dry
LAP LEADERS Jones 1-17, 30-53 (41); Laffite 18-29 (12)
WINNER'S LAPS 1-17 P1, 18-24 P4, 25 P3, 26-29 P2, 30-53 P1
FASTEST LAP Jones, Williams-Ford, 1m 50.45s (lap 5), 194.521kph, 120.869mph
CHAMPIONSHIP Jones 9, Piquet 6, Rosberg 4, Daly 3, Giacomelli 2

Pos	Driver	Car	Time/gap	Grid	Stops	Tyres
1	A Jones	Williams-Ford	1h 43m 24.38s	1	1	G
2	N Piquet	Brabham-Ford	−24.59s	4	0	G
3	K Rosberg	Fittipaldi-Ford	−1m 18.64s	13	0	G
4	D Daly	Tyrrell-Ford	−1m 23.48s	22	0	G
5	B Giacomelli	Alfa Romeo	−1 lap	20	0	G
6	A Prost	McLaren-Ford	−1 lap	12	0	G

Renault RE20

Round 2/14	**BRAZILIAN GP** Interlagos		**René Arnoux**	
	27 January 1980	Race 330	Renault RE20 188.934kph, 117.398mph	

Jabouille lost his advantage of pole to a lightning start by Villeneuve from immediately behind, but by lap 2 had assumed the lead chased by last year's winner Laffite. The Ligier challenge only lasted until lap 14, out with electrical problems. By the halfway stage Arnoux, from P6 on the grid, had seen off the de Angelis Lotus and now found himself second to Jabouille. But at an advanced stage of the race a glorious Renault 1-2 was spoilt by turbo failure for the race leader, Arnoux's maiden victory coming 16 laps later. De Angelis might so nearly have claimed a last-minute victory himself when the winner failed to complete the slowing-down lap, out of fuel. Jones joined them on the podium, thus retaining his championship lead.

POLE POSITION Arnoux, Renault, 2m 23.07s (0.92s), 198.130kph, 123.112mph
LAPS 40 x 7.874 km, 4.893 miles
DISTANCE 314.960 km, 195.707 miles
STARTERS/FINISHERS 24/16
WEATHER Sunny, very hot, dry
LAP LEADERS G Villeneuve, Ferrari 1 (1); Jabouille 2-24 (23); Arnoux 25-40 (16)
WINNER'S LAPS 1 P5, 2-3 P4, 4-13 P3, 14-24 P2, 25-40 P1
FASTEST LAP J-P Jabouille, Renault, 2m 28.76s (lap 23), 190.551kph, 118.403mph
CHAMPIONSHIP Jones 13, Arnoux 9, Piquet 6, de Angelis 6, Rosberg 4

Pos	Driver	Car	Time/gap	Grid	Stops	Tyres
1	R Arnoux	Renault	1h 40m 1.33s	6	0	M
2	E de Angelis	Lotus-Ford	−21.86s	7	0	G
3	A Jones	Williams-Ford	−1m 6.11s	10	0	G
4	D Pironi	Ligier-Ford	−1m 40.13s	2	1	G
5	A Prost	McLaren-Ford	−2m 25.41s	13	0	G
6	R Patrese	Arrows-Ford	−1 lap	14	0	G

Round 3/14	SOUTH AFRICAN GP Kyalami		René Arnoux

SOUTH AFRICAN GP Kyalami
1 March 1980 — Race 331

René Arnoux
Renault RE20 198.262kph, 123.194mph

In the rarefied Kyalami atmosphere Renault tied up the front row, both cars getting on for 2s quicker than the Ford-engined cars. Pole-man Jabouille led for 61 laps until he rolled to a halt on the main straight with front tyre failure caused by track debris. So Arnoux completed the final 17 laps, his second victory at the expense of his team-leader holding similarities with his first, but also a key difference in that this time he closely stalked Jabouille throughout. Behind the dominant Renaults Laffite got the better of the Williams pair, a French 1-2-3 completed by Pironi in the second Ligier. He chiselled away at the gap to Piquet ahead to take P3 with nine laps remaining, the Brabham suffering from slowly worsening understeer.

POLE POSITION J-P Jabouille, Renault, 1m 10.00s (0.21s), 211.063kph, 131.148mph
LAPS 78 x 4.104 km, 2.550 miles
DISTANCE 320.112 km, 198.908 miles
STARTERS/FINISHERS 24/13
WEATHER Sunny, warm, dry
LAP LEADERS J-P Jabouille, Renault 1-61 (61); Arnoux 62-78 (17)
WINNER'S LAPS 1-61 P2, 62-78 P1
FASTEST LAP Arnoux, Renault, 1m 13.15s (lap 51), 201.974kph, 125.501mph
CHAMPIONSHIP Arnoux 18, Jones 13, Piquet 9, Pironi 7, de Angelis 6

Pos	Driver	Car	Time/gap	Grid	Stops	Tyres
1	R Arnoux	Renault	1h 36m 52.54s	2	0	M
2	J Laffite	Ligier-Ford	−34.07s	4	0	G
3	D Pironi	Ligier-Ford	−52.49s	5	0	G
4	N Piquet	Brabham-Ford	−1m 1.02s	3	0	G
5	C Reutemann	Williams-Ford	−1 lap	6	0	G
6	J Mass	Arrows-Ford	−1 lap	19	0	G

UNITED STATES GP WEST Long Beach
30 March 1980 — Race 332

Nelson Piquet
Brabham-Ford BT49 142.348kph, 88.451mph

Nelson Piquet's maiden GP victory was a tour de force: a commanding pole, leading all the way, fastest lap and an almost 50s winning margin. It was an accident-strewn race, the field decimated in a first-lap crash caused by Giacomelli's spinning Alfa. The culprit survived but on lap 40 was involved in a further misdemeanour when being lapped by Jones, the Australian at the time running a strong if distant second behind Piquet. So Patrese took over second, and remarkably Fittipaldi finished third, having started from last place. But by far the worst incident in this race was brake failure at the end of the main straight for the sole Ensign, the unfortunate Clay Regazzoni's legs paralysed from spinal damage sustained in the resultant crash.

POLE POSITION Piquet, Brabham-Ford, 1m 17.694s (0.995s), 150.637kph, 93.602mph
LAPS 80.5 x 3.251 km, 2.020 miles
DISTANCE 261.706 km, 162.616 miles
STARTERS/FINISHERS 24/10
WEATHER Sunny, warm, dry
LAP LEADERS Piquet 1-80.5 (80.5)
WINNER'S LAPS 1-80.5 P1
FASTEST LAP Piquet, Brabham-Ford, 1m 19.830s (lap 38), 146.607kph, 91.097mph
CHAMPIONSHIP Arnoux 18, Piquet 18, Jones 13, Pironi 8, Patrese 7

Pos	Driver	Car	Time/gap	Grid	Stops	Tyres
1	N Piquet	Brabham-Ford	1h 50m 18.550s	1	0	G
2	R Patrese	Arrows-Ford	−49.212s	8	0	G
3	E Fittipaldi	Fittipaldi-Ford	−1m 18.563s	24	0	G
4	J Watson	McLaren-Ford	−1 lap	21	0	G
5	J Scheckter	Ferrari	−1 lap	16	1	M
6	D Pironi	Ligier-Ford	−1 lap	9	1	G

BELGIAN GP Zolder
4 May 1980 — Race 333

Didier Pironi
Ligier-Ford JS11/15 186.402kph, 115.825mph

Only the fifth round of the season and the third new race winner, Didier Pironi's maiden victory almost as dominant as Piquet's. Taking the lead from pole-sitter Jones at the first corner the Frenchman was never headed. It was an inspired drive, Jones unable to stay with the Ligier and finishing nearly 50s in arrears. For half the race Jones resisted the attentions of Laffite, but unlike the winning Ligier brake trouble required a visit to the pits on lap 40. This allowed Reutemann into third, the Williams pair the only unlapped cars. Piquet spun out of an isolated fifth spot on lap 32 having over-adjusted his brake balance, while Arnoux snatched fourth on the final lap following an unforced spin that dropped him to tenth on lap 17.

POLE POSITION Jones, Williams-Ford, 1m 19.12s (0.23s), 189.119kph, 117.513mph
LAPS 72 x 4.262 km, 2.648 miles
DISTANCE 306.864 km, 190.676 miles
STARTERS/FINISHERS 24/12
WEATHER Dry, windy
LAP LEADERS Pironi 1-72 (72)
WINNER'S LAPS 1-72 P1
FASTEST LAP J Laffite, Ligier-Ford, 1m 20.88s (lap 57), 184.658kph, 114.741mph
CHAMPIONSHIP Arnoux 21, Jones 19, Piquet 18, Pironi 17, Patrese 7

Pos	Driver	Car	Time/gap	Grid	Stops	Tyres
1	D Pironi	Ligier-Ford	1h 38m 46.51s	2	0	G
2	A Jones	Williams-Ford	−47.37s	1	0	G
3	C Reutemann	Williams-Ford	−1m 24.12s	4	0	G
4	R Arnoux	Renault	−1 lap	6	0	M
5	J-P Jarier	Tyrrell-Ford	−1 lap	9	0	G
6	G Villeneuve	Ferrari	−1 lap	12	0	M

Ligier-Ford JS11/15

Round 6/14	**MONACO GP** Monte Carlo						**Carlos Reutemann**
	16 May 1980					**Race 334**	Williams-Ford FW07B 130.677kph, 81.199mph

Within moments of the start, Derek Daly's Tyrrell famously went flying at Ste Dévote, landing on its sister car and eliminating four cars on the spot. By three-quarter-distance Pironi looked on course for a double. Taking full advantage of his very first pole position, he controlled the race just ahead of the chasing Williams pair. At one-third-distance Jones went out with transmission trouble while shortly after half-distance rain began to fall. Most chose to cautiously continue on slicks but the combination of gearbox gremlins and a wet track was the leader's undoing, the Ligier striking the barriers hard at Casino Square. For Reutemann the rest was easy, winning by over a minute from Laffite then Piquet, the Argentinean's first victory for Williams.

POLE POSITION D Pironi, Ligier-Ford, 1m 24.813s (0.069s), 140.582kph, 87.354mph
LAPS 76 x 3.312 km, 2.058 miles
DISTANCE 251.712 km, 156.407 miles
STARTERS/FINISHERS 20/9
WEATHER Cloudy, showers
LAP LEADERS Pironi 1-54 (54); Reutemann 55-76 (22)
WINNER'S LAPS 1-24 P3, 25-54 P2, 55-76 P1
FASTEST LAP Reutemann, Williams-Ford, 1m 27.418s (lap 40), 136.393kph, 84.751mph
CHAMPIONSHIP Piquet 22, Arnoux 21, Jones 19, Pironi 17, Reutemann 15

Pos	Driver	Car	Time/gap	Grid	Stops	Tyres
1	C Reutemann	Williams-Ford	1h 55m 34.365s	2	0	G
2	J Laffite	Ligier-Ford	–1m 13.629s	5	0	G
3	N Piquet	Brabham-Ford	–1m 17.726s	4	0	G
4	J Mass	Arrows-Ford	–1 lap	15	0	G
5	G Villeneuve	Ferrari	–1 lap	6	1	M
6	E Fittipaldi	Fittipaldi-Ford	–2 laps	18	0	G

Round 7/14	**FRENCH GP** Paul Ricard						**Alan Jones**
	29 June 1980					**Race 335**	Williams-Ford FW07B 203.016kph, 126.148mph

After qualifying, the top seven grid-slots were populated by French cars and/or drivers, Arnoux's Renault, quick along the Mistral straight, vying for pole with the Ligiers. The Williams pair, P5 and P6, didn't look a particular threat to French *gloire en France*. Laffite led two-thirds of the race from pole, but once Jones extricated himself from a stirring early skirmish with Pironi and Arnoux he proceeded to reel-in the Ligier, its tyres beginning to go away in the blistering heat of Le Castellet. To the dismay of the French crowd Jones went by on lap 35 to win at a canter. It was a timely return to the top-step for Jones, making up for his disallowed win in the Spanish GP and regaining the championship lead from Piquet.

POLE POSITION Laffite, Ligier-Ford, 1m 38.88s (0.61s), 211.529kph, 131.438mph
LAPS 54 x 5.810 km, 3.610 miles
DISTANCE 313.740 km, 194.949 miles
STARTERS/FINISHERS 24/14
WEATHER Sunny, very hot, dry, windy
LAP LEADERS Laffite 1-34 (34); Jones 35-54 (20)
WINNER'S LAPS 1-3 P4, 4-7 P3, 8-34 P2, 35-54 P1
FASTEST LAP Jones, Williams-Ford, 1m 41.45s (lap 48), 206.171kph, 128.108mph
CHAMPIONSHIP Jones 28, Piquet 25, Arnoux 23, Pironi 23, Reutemann 16

Pos	Driver	Car	Time/gap	Grid	Stops	Tyres
1	A Jones	Williams-Ford	1h 32m 43.42s	4	0	G
2	D Pironi	Ligier-Ford	–4.52s	3	0	G
3	J Laffite	Ligier-Ford	–30.26s	1	0	G
4	N Piquet	Brabham-Ford	–1m 14.88s	8	0	G
5	R Arnoux	Renault	–1m 16.15s	2	0	M
6	C Reutemann	Williams-Ford	–1m 16.74s	5	0	G

| Round 8/14 | **BRITISH GP** Brands Hatch | | | | | | **Alan Jones** |
| | 13 July 1980 | | | Race 336 | | | Williams-Ford FW07B 202.310kph, 125.710mph |

Beaten in their own backyard two weeks prior, the Ligier pair were out for revenge at Brands Hatch, 1-2 on the grid. For the first 30 laps first one then the other blue car led easily, but wheel-rim and tyre problems intervened. Pironi managed to reach the pits for a wheel-change on lap 19 whilst Laffite's exit from the lead 11 laps later was more spectacular, spinning into the barriers at Hawthorns. Jones led the second half of a rather uneventful race enlivened by Pironi's superb yet ultimately unproductive comeback drive and Reutemann's equally fruitless late attempt to separate Piquet from second. So one year on from their inaugural race victory the Williams team celebrated number nine. Desiré Wilson failed to qualify her Williams FW07.

POLE POSITION D Pironi, Ligier-Ford, 1m 11.004s (0.391s), 213.292kph, 132.533mph
LAPS 76 x 4.207 km, 2.614 miles
DISTANCE 319.719 km, 198.664 miles
STARTERS/FINISHERS 24/13
WEATHER Overcast, dry
LAP LEADERS Pironi 1-18 (18); J Laffite, Ligier-Ford 19-30 (12); Jones 31-76 (46)
WINNER'S LAPS 1-18 P3, 19-30 P2, 31-76 P1
FASTEST LAP D Pironi, Ligier-Ford, 1m 12.368s (lap 54), 209.272kph, 130.035mph
CHAMPIONSHIP Jones 37, Piquet 31, Arnoux 23, Pironi 23, Reutemann 20

Pos	Driver	Car	Time/gap	Grid	Stops	Tyres
1	A Jones	Williams-Ford	1h 34m 49.228s	3	0	G
2	N Piquet	Brabham-Ford	−11.007s	5	0	G
3	C Reutemann	Williams-Ford	−13.285s	4	0	G
4	D Daly	Tyrrell-Ford	−1 lap	10	0	G
5	J-P Jarier	Tyrrell-Ford	−1 lap	11	0	G
6	A Prost	McLaren-Ford	−1 lap	7	0	G

| Round 9/14 | **GERMAN GP** Hockenheim | | | | | | **Jacques Laffite** |
| | 10 August 1980 | | | Race 337 | | | Ligier-Ford JS11/15 220.859kph, 137.235mph |

Gloomy weather captured the mood, Patrick Depailler killed in his Alfa during pre-race testing. Pole-man Jones knew he was in trouble when Jabouille blasted past before they even reached the first chicane. But shortly after half-distance, within a lap of one another, both Renaults retired from first and third with broken valve springs, a persistent problem during practice. This elevated Jones and Laffite, who had started P6, to first and second, and when Jones pitted with a puncture Laffite completed the remaining five laps to claim an unexpected win. Reutemann was second and Jones, after his tyre stop, just held off Piquet's clutchless Brabham for third, these two breaking away from the rest at the top of the championship points table.

POLE POSITION Jones, Williams-Ford, 1m 45.85s (0.27s), 230.897kph, 143.472mph
LAPS 45 x 6.789 km, 4.218 miles
DISTANCE 305.505 km, 189.832 miles
STARTERS/FINISHERS 24/16
WEATHER Overcast, dry
LAP LEADERS J-P Jabouille, Renault 1-26 (26); Jones 27-40 (14); Laffite 41-45 (5)
WINNER'S LAPS 1-2 P5, 3-26 P4, 27-40 P2, 41-45 P1
FASTEST LAP Jones, Williams-Ford, 1m 48.49s (lap 43), 225.278kph, 139.981mph
CHAMPIONSHIP Jones 41, Piquet 34, Reutemann 26, Laffite 25, Arnoux 23

Pos	Driver	Car	Time/gap	Grid	Stops	Tyres
1	J Laffite	Ligier-Ford	1h 22m 59.73s	5	0	G
2	C Reutemann	Williams-Ford	−3.19s	4	0	G
3	A Jones	Williams-Ford	−43.53s	1	1	G
4	N Piquet	Brabham-Ford	−44.48s	6	0	G
5	B Giacomelli	Alfa Romeo	−1m 16.49s	19	0	G
6	G Villeneuve	Ferrari	−1m 28.72s	16	1	M

| Round 10/14 | **AUSTRIAN GP** Österreichring | | | | | | **Jean-Pierre Jabouille** |
| | 17 August 1980 | | | Race 338 | | | Renault RE20 223.181kph, 138.678mph |

Arnoux's pole, bettering his teammate by more than a second, demonstrated turbo superiority on this ultra-fast circuit. Disposing quickly of a fast-starting Jones, the Renaults waltzed into the lead. But leader Arnoux, having selected a different tyre choice, pitted after 20 laps leaving Jabouille in control 11s up on Jones. However, Jabouille's Michelins were also deteriorating and in the closing stages an exciting chase to the line developed, Jones short by just 0.82s, both drivers registering their fastest lap on that final frantic tour. Reutemann maintained the astonishing Williams finishing record with third. After Brazil and Argentina Jabouille deserved a little *bon chance*, but both Renault drivers were now out of championship contention.

POLE POSITION R Arnoux, Renault, 1m 30.27s (1.21s), 236.969kph, 147.246mph
LAPS 54 x 5.942 km, 3.692 miles
DISTANCE 320.868 km, 199.378 miles
STARTERS/FINISHERS 24/16
WEATHER Sunny, warm, dry
LAP LEADERS Jones 1-2 (2); Arnoux 3-20 (18); Jabouille 21-54 (34)
WINNER'S LAPS 1-3 P3, 4-20 P2, 21-54 P1
FASTEST LAP R Arnoux, Renault, 1m 32.53s (lap 50), 231.181kph, 143.649mph
CHAMPIONSHIP Jones 47, Piquet 36, Reutemann 30, Laffite 28, Arnoux 23

Pos	Driver	Car	Time/gap	Grid	Stops	Tyres
1	J-P Jabouille	Renault	1h 26m 15.73s	2	0	M
2	A Jones	Williams-Ford	−0.82s	3	0	G
3	C Reutemann	Williams-Ford	−19.36s	4	0	G
4	J Laffite	Ligier-Ford	−42.02s	5	0	G
5	N Piquet	Brabham-Ford	−1m 2.81s	7	0	G
6	E de Angelis	Lotus-Ford	−1m 14.97s	9	0	G

Brabham-Ford BT49

DUTCH GP Zandvoort

31 August 1980   Race 339

Nelson Piquet

Brabham-Ford BT49 187.675kph, 116.616mph

Back at sea level, the Renaults were still good for the front row, next the Williams pair, Piquet fifth. Jones negated his wonderful start and ruined his race by 'kerbing' his sliding-skirt when leading the opening lap. Arnoux led lap 2 before Laffite scrambled past, only lasting until Piquet became the fourth race leader on lap 13. From P6 on lap 1 the Brazilian had made his way past Villeneuve and Arnoux and once in clean air pulled away to a well-earned win. Behind, a frantic fight over third was resolved in Giacomelli's favour, but on lap 38 the Alfa V12 driver spun away a fantastic drive in a muffed pass of Laffite for P2. Thinking his position now safe, just three laps from the end Laffite got mugged by the fast-closing Arnoux.

POLE POSITION Arnoux, Renault, 1m 17.44s (0.30s), 197.665kph, 122.824mph
LAPS 72 x 4.252 km, 2.642 miles
DISTANCE 306.144 km, 190.229 miles
STARTERS/FINISHERS 24/11
WEATHER Sunny, warm, dry
LAP LEADERS A Jones, Williams-Ford 1 (1); Arnoux 2 (1); Laffite 3-12 (10); Piquet 13-72 (60)
WINNER'S LAPS 1 P6, 2-5 P5, 6-7 P4, 8-10 P3, 11-12 P2, 13-72 P1
FASTEST LAP Arnoux, Renault, 1m 19.35s (lap 67), 192.907kph, 119.867mph
CHAMPIONSHIP Jones 47, Piquet 45, Reutemann 33, Laffite 32, Arnoux 29

Pos	Driver	Car	Time/gap	Grid	Stops	Tyres
1	N Piquet	Brabham-Ford	1h 38m 13.83s	5	0	G
2	R Arnoux	Renault	−12.93s	1	0	M
3	J Laffite	Ligier-Ford	−13.43s	6	0	G
4	C Reutemann	Williams-Ford	−15.29s	3	0	G
5	J-P Jarier	Tyrrell-Ford	−1m 0.02s	17	0	G
6	A Prost	McLaren-Ford	−1m 22.62s	18	0	G

ITALIAN GP Imola

14 September 1980   Race 340

Nelson Piquet

Brabham-Ford BT49 183.439kph, 113.984mph

During practice Ferrari debuted a turbo-powered car, and for the third race turbos bestrode the front row. But in the race Renault could not replicate qualifying form and neither car completed the race distance. Piquet, starting fifth, only took three laps to overcome the Renaults – the BT49 was just too good that day, cruising home well ahead of Jones. Clutch and gearbox difficulties saw Reutemann drop from first to last on lap 1 and yet finish third after a fine recovery drive. Alfa Romeo were delighted to out-qualify Ferrari at Imola but it nearly ended badly on lap 5. A tyre burst eliminated Villeneuve and Giacomelli simultaneously, Gilles lucky to escape injury. So Piquet topped the points table, one ahead of Jones with two rounds to go.

POLE POSITION R Arnoux, Renault, 1m 33.988s (0.351s), 191.514kph, 119.001mph
LAPS 60 x 5.000 km, 3.107 miles
DISTANCE 300.000 km, 186.411 miles
STARTERS/FINISHERS 24/13
WEATHER Sunny, warm, dry
LAP LEADERS Arnoux 1-2 (2); J-P Jabouille, Renault 3 (1); Piquet 4-60 (57)
WINNER'S LAPS 1-2 P3, 3 P2, 4-60 P1
FASTEST LAP Jones, Williams-Ford, 1m 36.089s (lap 47), 187.326kph, 116.399mph
CHAMPIONSHIP Piquet 54, Jones 53, Reutemann 37, Laffite 32, Arnoux 29

Pos	Driver	Car	Time/gap	Grid	Stops	Tyres
1	N Piquet	Brabham-Ford	1h 38m 7.52s	5	0	G
2	A Jones	Williams-Ford	−28.93s	6	0	G
3	C Reutemann	Williams-Ford	−1m 13.67s	3	0	G
4	E de Angelis	Lotus-Ford	−1 lap	18	0	G
5	K Rosberg	Fittipaldi-Ford	−1 lap	11	0	G
6	D Pironi	Ligier-Ford	−1 lap	13	0	G

Round 13/14	**CANADIAN GP** Montréal		**Alan Jones**
	28 September 1980	Race 341	Williams-Ford FW07B 173.494kph, 107.804mph

The two title contenders qualified 1-2, Piquet a scorching pole. At the first corner they collided, spun and set off a chain reaction, the youngest ever F1 starter, Mike Thackwell, eliminated in the mêleé. At the restart Jones led Pironi from Piquet in his spare chassis, but such was its superiority that the Brabham took the lead on lap 3 and quickly established a 10s gap. But on lap 24 engine failure handed the race to Jones. For the final 27 laps Pironi led on the road but, docked a minute for a jumped start, he was eventually classified third. So the jubilant Williams pair finished 1-2, a drivers' championship for Jones now added to the constructors' title secured at Imola. By contrast, outgoing champion Jody Scheckter had failed to qualify.

POLE POSITION N Piquet, Brabham-Ford, 1m 27.328s (0.836s), 181.797kph, 112.964mph
LAPS 70 x 4.410 km, 2.740 miles (Race restarted for scheduled 70 laps following accident)
DISTANCE 308.700 km, 191.817 miles
STARTERS/FINISHERS 24/12
WEATHER Cold, dry
LAP LEADERS (On the road) Jones 1-2, 24-43 (22); Piquet 3-23 (21); D Pironi 44-70 (27)
WINNER'S LAPS 1-2 P1, 3-23 P2, 24-43 P1, 44-70 P2 (Pironi finished first but was penalised one minute for jumped start)
FASTEST LAP Pironi, Ligier-Ford, 1m 28.769s (lap 62), 178.846kph, 111.130mph
CHAMPIONSHIP Jones 62, Piquet 54, Reutemann 40, Laffite 32, Arnoux 29

Pos	Driver	Car	Time/gap	Grid	Stops	Tyres
1	A Jones	Williams-Ford	1h 46m 45.53s	2	0	G
2	C Reutemann	Williams-Ford	−15.54s	5	0	G
3	D Pironi	Ligier-Ford	−19.07s	3	0	G
4	J Watson	McLaren-Ford	−30.98s	7	0	G
5	G Villeneuve	Ferrari	−55.23s	22	0	M
6	H Rebaque	Brabham-Ford	−1 lap	10	0	G

Round 14/14	**UNITED STATES GP EAST** Watkins Glen	**Alan Jones**
	5 October 1980 Race 342	Williams-Ford FW07B 203.371kph, 126.369mph

Giacomelli put the Alfa Romeo on pole by a wide margin and then proceeded to lead the race handsomely. On lap 32, 13s ahead and still pulling away, a fairy-tale victory ended with electrical failure. Jones took over the lead, which was remarkable considering a mistake had seen him leave the road at the first corner and complete the first lap P12. It was a tigering drive by the new world champion during which he overtook the likes of Villeneuve, Andretti, Laffite, Pironi and finally teammate Reutemann for second on lap 30. Five laps earlier his main championship adversary, Piquet, ended his season dismally, spinning away second place. So Jones led in a second successive Williams 1-2 and ended the season just as it had begun, with victory.

POLE POSITION B Giacomelli, Alfa Romeo, 1m 33.291s (0.789s), 209.721kph, 130.315mph
LAPS 59 x 5.435 km, 3.377 miles
DISTANCE 320.651 km, 199.243 miles
STARTERS/FINISHERS 24/11
WEATHER Cold, dry
LAP LEADERS Giacomelli 1-31 (31); Jones 32-59 (28)
WINNER'S LAPS 1 P12, 2 P11, 3 P9, 4-9 P8, 10 P7, 11-22 P6, 23-24 P5, 25-27 P4, 28-29 P3, 30-31 P2, 32-59 P1
FASTEST LAP Jones, Williams-Ford, 1m 34.068s (lap 44), 207.989kph, 129.238mph
CHAMPIONSHIP Jones 67, Piquet 54, Reutemann 42, Laffite 34, Pironi 32

Pos	Driver	Car	Time/gap	Grid	Stops	Tyres
1	A Jones	Williams-Ford	1h 34m 36.05s	5	0	G
2	C Reutemann	Williams-Ford	−4.21s	3	0	G
3	D Pironi	Ligier-Ford	−12.57s	7	0	G
4	E de Angelis	Lotus-Ford	−29.69s	4	0	G
5	J Laffite	Ligier-Ford	−1 lap	12	0	G
6	M Andretti	Lotus-Ford	−1 lap	11	0	G

1980 CHAMPIONSHIP FACTS AND FOLKLORE

■ Following the exclusion of Jarama, 1980 was a two-part, 14-race season, ten rounds counting towards the drivers' championship, the best five results from each of the first and last seven rounds. Constructors' points remained as 1979.

■ The final GP was held at Watkins Glen and, for the first and only time, Imola replaced Monza as the venue for the Italian GP. Subsequently Imola would host the San Marino GP.

■ Staggered one-by-one starting grids were introduced and qualifying tyres were banned from the Belgian GP.

■ The Spanish round lost its championship status, arising from the increasing disharmony between FISA and FOCA.

■ The conflict arose though the non-payment of certain drivers' fines, these penalties imposed by FISA for non-attendance at the Zolder and Monte Carlo driver briefings. This action by the drivers was orchestrated by FOCA as a direct provocation to FISA authority. This escalated to the running of the Spanish GP outside FISA jurisdiction and the

boycotting of the race by the FISA-aligned manufacturer teams, Ferrari, Renault and Alfa Romeo.

■ As part of a wider negotiation, the fines were eventually paid and the Spanish GP annulled. An uneasy truce prevailed for the remainder of the season, but it was the end of the beginning, not the beginning of the end.

■ Alan Jones and Williams had looked every part potential champions in the second half of 1979, and in 1980 they duly delivered. But it was by no means the anticipated walkover, due mainly to a strong championship challenge from Nelson Piquet and a Brabham team rejuvenated since ditching the Alfa engine for the trusty Ford-Cosworth and successfully experimenting with the Weismann gearbox and carbon brake discs.

■ Jones won five races to Piquet's three, although it might have appeared even more conclusive if Jones had been allowed to also keep his Spanish victory.

- As it was, two convincing late-season victories had put Piquet right back on course for championship honours, but Piquet's championship hopes exploded with his engine while leading the following and penultimate round in Canada.
- In any case, Jones and Williams answered the challenge in the most emphatic manner possible, a pair of 1-2 team finishes to round out the season in North America, leaving Piquet and Brabham only with 'what ifs'.
- Whereas Piquet carried the Brabham team virtually alone, scoring all bar one of the team's constructors' points, Jones' teammate Carlos Reutemann not only won Monaco, he also contributed a bag full of points to those amassed by Williams, more than double those of Brabham.
- Indeed, Brabham were beaten into second place in the constructors' championship by Équipe Ligier, their two drivers winning a race apiece. Indeed it was a highly successful year for French teams and drivers, apart, that is, from the tragedy which befell Patrick Depailler at Hockenheim.
- Thankfully his was the only fatality, but there were career-ending injuries to Regazzoni, much the same for Jabouille, as well as a number of near misses, not least Villeneuve's colossal accident at Imola.
- Renault once again demonstrated the potential for turbocharged power with three race wins, a point not lost on Ferrari who debuted a similarly powered car in practice at Imola.
- So from the seven winning drivers during 1980, four were French and in addition a new star was born. Compatriot Alain Prost accomplished a highly praiseworthy rookie season in the uncompetitive McLaren.
- But perhaps better times lay ahead for McLaren, as during the year it was merged with Ron Dennis' Project 4 team.
- Shadow didn't complete the season and morphed into

RACE 336, British GP: One year on from their inaugural race victory, Frank Williams and Patrick Head tend the FW07B of Alan Jones. Later the team celebrated win number nine.

Theodore Racing the following year, while with the arrival of Osella, Italian teams numbered three. Alfa made some progress but Ferrari was simply nowhere.

■ Whereas Michelin tyres had been an asset for Ferrari last year, now they were a liability, but the inferior results could not be totally placed at the feet of the jovial Bibendum as, although Renault too had found problems with the French rubber, they had also enjoyed their fair share of success.

■ Another factor was that during 1980 Ferrari were preoccupied with development of the successor to the F1 Flat-12 '312' family, having taken the strategic decision to follow Renault along the turbocharged engine route.

■ Some felt that after his triumphant 1979 Scheckter had lost his mojo in 1980, and there was some evidence of this, but teammate Villeneuve most certainly had not, yet his meagre pickings from the season were only six championship points from two fifths and two sixth places.

■ But Scheckter scored just two points, was ranked 19th in the championship and failed to qualify for the Canadian GP. It was the worst defence by a reigning world champion before or since and it was hardly a shock when in August the South African announced his decision to retire at the end of the season.

■ So too did another former world champion, Emerson Fittipaldi, although he was set to race on successfully in the USA.

■ The new world champion, Australian Alan Jones, followed his illustrious compatriot Jack Brabham into the record books, and helped bring to Frank Williams the ultimate success he had striven for since a car was first entered under his name back in 1969.

■ As well as Alain Prost, future world champion Nigel Mansell lined up on the GP grid for the first time in 1980, and future champion Jenson Button was born.

Championship ranking	Championship points	Driver nationality	1980 Drivers Championship		Races contested	Race victories	Podiumse excl. victories	Races led	Lights to flag victories	Laps led	Poles	Fastest laps	Triple Crowns
			Driver	Car									
1	67	AUS	Alan Jones	Williams-Ford	14	5	5	8		174	3	5	1
2	54	BRA	Nelson Piquet	Brabham-Ford	14	3	3	4	1	218.5	2	1	1
3	42	ARG	Carlos Reutemann	Williams-Ford	14	1	7	1		22		1	
4	34	FRA	Jacques Laffite	Ligier-Ford	14	1	4	5		73	1	1	
5	32	FRA	Didier Pironi	Ligier-Ford	14	1	4	4	1	171	2	2	
6	29	FRA	René Arnoux	Renault	14	2	1	5		54	3	4	
7	13	ITA	Elio de Angelis	Lotus-Ford	14		1						
8	9	FRA	Jean-Pierre Jabouille	Renault	13	1		5		145	2		
9	7	ITA	Riccardo Patrese	Arrows-Ford	14		1						
10	6	FIN	Keke Rosberg	Fittipaldi-Ford	11		1						
11	6	IRL	Derek Daly	Tyrrell-Ford	14								
11	6	GBR	John Watson	McLaren-Ford	13								
13	6	FRA	Jean-Pierre Jarier	Tyrrell-Ford	14								
14	6	CAN	Gilles Villeneuve	Ferrari	14			1		1			
15	5	BRA	Emerson Fittipaldi	Fittipaldi-Ford	14		1						
16	5	FRA	Alain Prost	McLaren-Ford	11								
17	4	GER	Jochen Mass	Arrows-Ford	11								
18	4	ITA	Bruno Giacomelli	Alfa Romeo	14			1		31	1		
19	2	RSA	Jody Scheckter	Ferrari	13								
20	1	MEX	Hector Rebaque	Brabham-Ford	7								
20	1	USA	Mario Andretti	Lotus-Ford	14								

Championship ranking	Championship points	Team/Marque nationality	1980 Constructors Championship		Engine maker nationality	Races contested	Race victories	1-2 finishes	Podiums excl. victories	Races led	Laps led	Poles	Fastest laps
			Chassis	Engine									
1	120	GBR	Williams FW07B, FW07	Ford Cosworth 3.0 V8	GBR	14	6	2	12	9	196	3	6
2	66	FRA	Ligier JS11/15	Ford Cosworth 3.0 V8	GBR	14	2		8	8	244	3	3
3	55	GBR	Brabham BT49	Ford Cosworth 3.0 V8	GBR	14	3		3	4	218.5	2	1
4	38	FRA	Renault RE20	Renault 1.5 V6t	FRA	14	3		1	6	199	5	4
5	14	GBR	Lotus 81, 81B	Ford Cosworth 3.0 V8	GBR	14			1				
6	12	GBR	Tyrrell 010, 009	Ford Cosworth 3.0 V8	GBR	14							
7	11	GBR	Arrows A3	Ford Cosworth 3.0 V8	GBR	14			1				
8	11	BRA	Fittipaldi F7, F8	Ford Cosworth 3.0 V8	GBR	14			2				
9	11	NZL	McLaren M29B, M29C, M30	Ford Cosworth 3.0 V8	GBR	14							
10	8	ITA	Ferrari 312T5	Ferrari 3.0 F12	ITA	14				1	1		
11	4	ITA	Alfa Romeo 179	Alfa Romeo 3.0 V12	ITA	14				1	31	1	

1981

Piquet raises his game

THE TALE OF THE TITLE

- In a bizarre season, the title was decided by a single point at a finale held in a Las Vegas car park.
- At Caesar's Palace, Piquet prised the title from the grasp of long-term championship leader Reutemann.
- Laffite and Ligier, reunited with Matra, also maintained a championship challenge into that final round.
- Williams kept their constructors' title with four wins, Reutemann defying team orders for one of his pair.
- The FISA/FOCA war rumbled on, Kyalami another casualty, but culminated in the Concorde Agreement.
- Rock-hard 'trick' suspension, a flagrant rules breach, reduced F1 to farce, even endangering drivers' lives.
- FISA banned the 'twin-chassis' Lotus 88 yet approved the Brabham-inspired hydro-pneumatic suspension.
- Disillusioned with the development path for F1 cars, Jones opted to retire, but signed-off in winning style.
- Race victories were distributed across seven drivers from six teams, Alain Prost breaking his duck.
- Prost's three wins for Renault matched champion Piquet's haul, but there were too many dnfs for a title challenge.
- Turbo power restored Ferrari to the winners' enclosure with two classic Gilles Villeneuve victories.
- After four wilderness years McLaren also won, their carbon-fibre MP4 pioneering a chassis revolution in F1.
- And not forgetting: harrowing Belgian GP.

THE CHASE FOR THE CHAMPIONSHIP

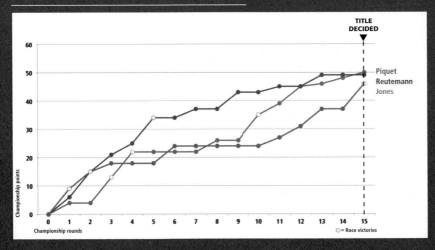

| Round 1/15 | **UNITED STATES GP WEST** Long Beach | **Alan Jones** |
| | 15 March 1981   Race 343 | Williams-Ford FW07C 140.974kph, 87.597mph |

The season-opening South African GP was a victim of the FISA/FOCA wars, so the championship season proper kicked off in America. The surprise package was Patrese's Arrows, which easily led from pole for 24 laps until sidelined with fuel-feed problems. This left Kyalami non-championship race winner Reutemann looking good for a back-to-back. But a lapse of concentration let Jones through on lap 32 and that's how it stayed for a third successive Williams 1-2. World champion Jones finished 35s ahead of last year's winner, Piquet's Brabham in P3, Andretti's Alfa a fine fourth. The Villeneuve and Pironi turbo Ferraris made a competitive first showing but the twin-chassis Lotus 88 was controversially banned by the race stewards.

POLE POSITION R Patrese, Arrows-Ford, 1m 19.399s (0.009s), 147.402kph, 91.592mph
LAPS 80.5 x 3.251 km, 2.020 miles
DISTANCE 261.706 km, 162.616 miles
STARTERS/FINISHERS 24/8
WEATHER Sunny, hot, dry
LAP LEADERS Patrese 1-24 (24.5); Reutemann 25-31 (7); Jones 32-80 (49)
WINNER'S LAPS 1-25 P3, 26-31 P2, 32-80 P1
FASTEST LAP Jones, Williams-Ford, 1m 20.901s (lap 31), 144.666kph, 89.891mph
CHAMPIONSHIP Jones 9, Reutemann 6, Piquet 4, Andretti 3, Cheever 2

Pos	Driver	Car	Time/gap	Grid	Stops	Tyres
1	A Jones	Williams-Ford	1h 50m 41.33s	2	0	M
2	C Reutemann	Williams-Ford	–9.19s	3	0	M
3	N Piquet	Brabham-Ford	–34.92s	4	0	M
4	M Andretti	Alfa Romeo	–49.31s	6	0	M
5	E Cheever	Tyrrell-Ford	–1m 6.70s	8	0	M
6	P Tambay	Theodore-Ford	–1 lap	17	0	M

Williams-Ford FW07C

| Round 2/15 | **BRAZILIAN GP** Rio de Janeiro | **Carlos Reutemann** |
| | 29 March 1981   Race 344 | Williams-Ford FW07C 155.450kph, 96.592mph |

The fourth successive Williams 1-2 was flawed. It finished 2-1. Contrary to explicit JONES-REUT pit signals, Reutemann refused to give way. The Aussie world champion and team leader was not amused. It was a wet race that got wetter, reaching the two-hour mark one lap ahead of the completion of the full race distance. The podium established itself quickly, Reutemann leading all the way from a closely following Jones, Patrese's Arrows third at some distance. Piquet's hydro-pneumatic suspended Brabham was on pole but the Brazilian ruled himself out of his home GP by gambling on dry tyres and improving conditions. A start-line shunt eliminated three and delayed three more while the Lotus 88 was again barred from racing.

POLE POSITION N Piquet, Brabham-Ford, 1m 35.079s (0.311s), 190.490kph, 118.365mph
LAPS 62 x 5.031 km, 3.126 miles (Scheduled for 63 laps but stopped after two hours)
DISTANCE 311.922 km, 193.819 miles
STARTERS/FINISHERS 24/13
WEATHER Overcast, cool, rain
LAP LEADERS Reutemann 1-62 (62)
WINNER'S LAPS 1-62 P1
FASTEST LAP Surer, Ensign-Ford, 1m 54.302s (lap 36), 158.454kph, 98.459mph
CHAMPIONSHIP Jones 15, Reutemann 15, Piquet 4, Patrese 4, Andretti 3

Pos	Driver	Car	Time/gap	Grid	Stops	Tyres
1	C Reutemann	Williams-Ford	2h 0m 23.66s	2	0	M
2	A Jones	Williams-Ford	–4.44s	3	0	M
3	R Patrese	Arrows-Ford	–1m 3.08s	4	0	M
4	M Surer	Ensign-Ford	–1m 17.03s	18	0	M
5	E de Angelis	Lotus-Ford	–1m 26.42s	10	0	M
6	J Laffite	Ligier-Matra	–1m 26.83s	16	0	M

Round 3/15	**ARGENTINEAN GP** Buenos Aires No 15	**Nelson Piquet**
	12 April 1981 Race 345	Brabham-Ford BT49C 200.731kph, 124.728mph

Following protests, the hydro-pneumatic Brabham was allowed to run, the Lotus 88 was not. Inevitably the Brabham was simply in a different class. This was evidenced by Piquet's pole, a second clear of Jones; Piquet pulling away from Reutemann in second place by up to 2s a lap, and perhaps most of all by Rebaque overtaking Arnoux, Patrese, Prost and finally Reutemann to make it a runaway Brabham 1-2. But Rebaque didn't make the finish, so after Piquet and Reutemann, Prost's Renault finished third followed by the down-on-power Jones. After three races the championship already looked to be between Piquet and the Williams pair, the surprising absentee Prost's Renault, the combination expected to feature prominently.

POLE POSITION Piquet, Brabham-Ford, 1m 42.665s (0.316s), 209.271kph, 130.035mph
LAPS 53 x 5.968 km, 3.708 miles
DISTANCE 316.304 km, 196.542 miles
STARTERS/FINISHERS 24/13
WEATHER Sunny, hot, dry
LAP LEADERS Piquet 1-53 (53)
WINNER'S LAPS 1-53 P1
FASTEST LAP Piquet, Brabham-Ford, 1m 45.287s (lap 6), 204.059kph, 126.797mph
CHAMPIONSHIP Reutemann 21, Jones 18, Piquet 13, Patrese 4, Prost 4

Pos	Driver	Car	Time/gap	Grid	Stops	Tyres
1	N Piquet	Brabham-Ford	1h 34m 32.74s	1	0	M
2	C Reutemann	Williams-Ford	−26.61s	4	0	M
3	A Prost	Renault	−49.98s	2	0	M
4	A Jones	Williams-Ford	−1m 7.88s	3	0	M
5	R Arnoux	Renault	−1m 31.85s	5	0	M
6	E de Angelis	Lotus-Ford	−1 lap	10	0	M

Round 4/15	**SAN MARINO GP** Imola	**Nelson Piquet**
	3 May 1981 Race 346	Brabham-Ford BT49C 162.873kph, 101.205mph

Practice saw an attempt by officialdom to assert itself over flexible skirts, ride-height and 'trick' suspension, but nothing altered. The key message from the first San Marino GP was simple – Ferrari were back. Villeneuve's turbocharged Ferrari took pole and led a wet race from teammate Pironi. A lap 15 pit stop for dry tyres was followed by a renewed shower requiring a second stop two laps later. So Pironi, staying on wets, led for 32 laps, half the race. But as his tyres wore Pironi lost the lead to Piquet, the Brabham coming on strong as the race developed, and gradually fell away to finish fifth behind Patrese, Reutemann and Rebaque. For the first time this season Jones failed to score whereas his teammate did not.

POLE POSITION G Villeneuve, Ferrari, 1m 34.523s (0.706s), 191.953kph, 119.274mph
LAPS 60 x 5.040 km, 3.132 miles
DISTANCE 302.400 km, 187.903 miles
STARTERS/FINISHERS 24/13
WEATHER Overcast, cool, rain
LAP LEADERS Villeneuve 1-14 (14); Pironi 15-46 (32); Piquet 47-60 (14)
WINNER'S LAPS 1-2 P9, 3-5 P8, 6 P7, 7-14 P5, 15-21 P3, 22-46 P2, 47-60 P1
FASTEST LAP G Villeneuve, Ferrari, 1m 48.064s (lap 46), 167.901kph, 104.329mph
CHAMPIONSHIP Reutemann 25, Piquet 22, Jones 18, Patrese 10, Prost 4

Pos	Driver	Car	Time/gap	Grid	Stops	Tyres
1	N Piquet	Brabham-Ford	1h 51m 23.97s	5	0	M
2	R Patrese	Arrows-Ford	−4.58s	9	0	M
3	C Reutemann	Williams-Ford	−6.34s	2	0	M
4	H Rebaque	Brabham-Ford	−22.89s	13	0	M
5	D Pironi	Ferrari	−25.87s	6	0	M
6	A de Cesaris	McLaren-Ford	−1m 6.61s	14	0	M

Round 5/15	**BELGIAN GP** Zolder	**Carlos Reutemann**
	17 May 1981 Race 347	Williams-Ford FW07C 180.445kph, 112.123mph

During practice an Osella mechanic was killed in the narrow pit lane. Then a grid protest led to a confused start. Mechanic Dave Luckett returned to the stationary grid to fire-up Patrese's stalled car in P4, during which the grid was released. Somehow all dodged by except Stohr's Arrows, which shunted the rear of the stranded sister car, Luckett pinned between the two. Miraculously he sustained only light injuries. At the restart Pironi led, but Jones was on the move from a P6 grid-slot, taking the lead on lap 13. In the process he and Piquet touched, the Brabham eliminated, only for Jones to spin out himself with a gearbox glitch a few laps later. Mercifully rain cut short this dour race, Reutemann's victory his 15th consecutive points-paying finish.

POLE POSITION Reutemann, Williams-Ford, 1m 22.28s (0.85s), 186.475kph, 115.870mph
LAPS 54 x 4.262 km, 2.648 miles (Race restarted for scheduled 70 laps following accident. Stopped early due to rain)
DISTANCE 230.148 km, 143.007 miles
STARTERS/FINISHERS 24/13
WEATHER Cloudy, warm, dry, rain later
LAP LEADERS D Pironi, Ferrari 1-12 (12); A Jones, Williams-Ford 13-19 (7); Reutemann 20-54 (35)
WINNER'S LAPS 1-9 P2, 10 P4, 11-12 P3, 13-19 P2, 20-54 P1
FASTEST LAP Reutemann, Williams-Ford, 1m 23.30s (lap 37), 184.192kph, 114.452mph
CHAMPIONSHIP Reutemann 34, Piquet 22, Jones 18, Patrese 10, Laffite 7

Pos	Driver	Car	Time/gap	Grid	Stops	Tyres
1	C Reutemann	Williams-Ford	1h 16m 31.61s	1	0	M
2	J Laffite	Ligier-Matra	−36.6s	9	0	M
3	N Mansell	Lotus-Ford	−43.69s	10	0	M
4	G Villeneuve	Ferrari	−47.64s	7	0	M
5	E de Angelis	Lotus-Ford	−49.20s	14	0	M
6	E Cheever	Tyrrell-Ford	−52.51s	8	0	M

Ferrari 126CK

Round 6/15	**MONACO GP** Monte Carlo						**Gilles Villeneuve**
	31 May 1981					**Race 348**	Ferrari 126CK 132.029kph, 82.039mph

Bizarrely, the race was delayed by a flood in the tunnel due to a fire at Lowes Hotel. Piquet, leading from pole, had the measure of the chasing Villeneuve. But Jones was again coming through from a modest grid-slot and took Gilles for second through Casino Square. At lap 20 Piquet's lead was 9s; by lap 40 they were together, Jones gaining through traffic. On lap 54 the leader, still under pressure, tripped over a backmarker and clattered the barriers at Tabac. Jones now led Villeneuve by over 30s, time enough to pit for a splash to cure fuel vaporisation. The Williams re-emerged 6s ahead but still spluttering, Villeneuve sweeping by on lap 73 for a popular victory, the first for the Ferrari turbo and his first since 1979.

POLE POSITION N Piquet, Brabham-Ford, 1m 25.710s (0.078s), 139.111kph, 86.440mph
LAPS 76 x 3.312 km, 2.058 miles
DISTANCE 251.712 km, 156.407 miles
STARTERS/FINISHERS 20/7
WEATHER Sunny, hot, dry
LAP LEADERS Piquet 1-53 (53); Jones 54-72 (19); Villeneuve 73-76 (4)
WINNER'S LAPS 1-19 P2, 20-24 P3, 25-29 P4, 30-53 P3, 54-72 P2, 73-76 P1
FASTEST LAP Jones, Williams-Ford, 1m 27.470s (lap 48), 136.312kph, 84.700mph
CHAMPIONSHIP Reutemann 34, Jones 24, Piquet 22, Villeneuve 12, Laffite 11

Pos	Driver	Car	Time/gap	Grid	Stops	Tyres
1	G Villeneuve	Ferrari	1h 54m 23.38s	2	0	M
2	A Jones	Williams-Ford	−39.91s	7	1	M
3	J Laffite	Ligier-Matra	−1m 29.24s	8	0	M
4	D Pironi	Ferrari	−1 lap	17	0	M
5	E Cheever	Tyrrell-Ford	−2 laps	15	0	M
6	M Surer	Ensign-Ford	−2 laps	19	1	M

Round 7/15	**SPANISH GP** Jarama						**Gilles Villeneuve**
	21 June 1981					**Race 349**	Ferrari 126CK 149.156kph, 92.681mph

Laffite in the Ligier-Matra took pole but completed the first lap P11. As he finally finished second, his botched start cost him dear. So Jones led from Reutemann then Villeneuve, a blistering turbo-charged start from row four. On lap 2 Villeneuve overtook Reutemann, the unwieldy Ferrari, acting as a mobile chicane, helping Jones to disappear into the distance. But on lap 14, with a 10s lead, Jones unaccountably flew off the road. Famously, lap after lap for the next 67, Villeneuve defied the efforts of the potentially quicker following cars, uncatchable on the straights, unconquerable in the corners. By the finish he was leading a thrilling convoy of five cars covered by little more than a second. The stuff of legends.

POLE POSITION Laffite, Ligier-Matra, 1m 13.754s (0.270s), 161.662kph, 100.452mph
LAPS 80 x 3.312 km, 2.058 miles
DISTANCE 264.960 km, 164.639 miles
STARTERS/FINISHERS 24/16
WEATHER Sunny, very hot, dry
LAP LEADERS Jones 1-13 (13); Villeneuve 14-80 (67)
WINNER'S LAPS 1 P3, 2-13 P2, 14-80 P1
FASTEST LAP A Jones, Williams-Ford, 1m 17.818s (lap 5), 153.219kph, 95.206mph
CHAMPIONSHIP Reutemann 37, Jones 24, Piquet 22, Villeneuve 21, Laffite 17

Pos	Driver	Car	Time/gap	Grid	Stops	Tyres
1	G Villeneuve	Ferrari	1h 46m 35.01s	7	0	M
2	J Laffite	Ligier-Matra	−0.22s	1	0	M
3	J Watson	McLaren-Ford	−0.58s	4	0	M
4	C Reutemann	Williams-Ford	−1.01s	3	0	M
5	E de Angelis	Lotus-Ford	−1.24s	10	0	M
6	N Mansell	Lotus-Ford	−28.58s	11	0	M

Renault RE30

<table>
<tr><td>Round 8/15</td><td colspan="2">FRENCH GP Dijon-Prenois</td><td></td></tr>
<tr><td></td><td colspan="2">5 July 1981</td><td align="right">Race 350</td></tr>
</table>

Alain Prost

Renault RE30 190.392kph, 118.304mph

Prost's first GP victory was an unsatisfactory affair, but the winner wouldn't have cared, especially at his home track. Halted by a sudden deluge after 58 laps – two before three-quarter-distance when the results would have stood – the race was run in two parts, the result decided on aggregate. With tyre wars resumed, Goodyear back since their withdrawal, the first part was led convincingly by Goodyear-shod Piquet, who 'won' from Prost and Watson. The grid for the remaining 22 laps was determined by the finishing order in the first. But during the interval, with under 30 minutes of the race remaining and the damp track drying, the Michelin runners switched to soft slicks, giving Prost his maiden win after 19 race starts.

POLE POSITION Arnoux, Renault, 1m 05.95s (0.41s), 207.430kph, 128.891mph
LAPS 80 x 3.800 km, 2.361 miles (80 lap race interrupted due to rain. Result aggregate of 58 + 22 laps)
DISTANCE 304.000 km, 188.897 miles
STARTERS/FINISHERS 23/17
WEATHER Cloudy, cool, dry, rain later, drying at restart
LAP LEADERS (On the road) Piquet 1-58 (58); Prost 59-80 (22)
WINNER'S LAPS 1-2 P3, 2-58 P2, 59-80 P1
FASTEST LAP Prost, Renault, 1m 09.14s (lap 64), 197.859kph, 122.944mph
CHAMPIONSHIP Reutemann 37, Piquet 26, Jones 24, Villeneuve 21, Laffite 17

Pos	Driver	Car	Time/gap	Grid	Stops	Tyres
1	A Prost	Renault	1h 35m 48.13s	3	0	M
2	J Watson	McLaren-Ford	−2.29s	2	0	M
3	N Piquet	Brabham-Ford	−24.262	4	0	G
4	R Arnoux	Renault	−42.30s	1	0	M
5	D Pironi	Ferrari	−1 lap	14	0	M
6	E de Angelis	Lotus-Ford	−1 lap	8	0	M

<table>
<tr><td>Round 9/15</td><td colspan="2">BRITISH GP Silverstone</td><td></td></tr>
<tr><td></td><td colspan="2">18 July 1981</td><td align="right">Race 351</td></tr>
</table>

John Watson

McLaren-Ford MP4 221.507kph, 137.638mph

The Renaults were very quick at Silverstone, qualifying 1-2 and easily leading the race. On lap 17 leader Prost's engine expired so Arnoux took up the Renault assault, way ahead of Watson. On lap 3 Watson had fallen to P10, the innocent victim of a Villeneuve spin at the Woodcote chicane, but within ten laps he emerged on merit at the head of the Renault-chasing pack. Assisting his progress to P2 was Piquet's heavy prang at Beckett's on lap 12 due to tyre failure when lying third. With 15 laps to go the leader's engine began to falter, to the delight of the partisan crowd, and in an exciting pursuit Arnoux's 30s lead evaporated steadily. With eight laps to go Watson snatched the lead and a highly popular victory.

POLE POSITION R Arnoux, Renault, 1m 11.000s (0.046s), 239.253kph, 148.665mph
LAPS 68 x 4.719 km, 2.932 miles
DISTANCE 320.865 km, 199.376 miles
STARTERS/FINISHERS 24/11
WEATHER Cloudy, warm, dry
LAP LEADERS A Prost, Renault 1-16 (16); Arnoux 17-60 (44); Watson 61-68 (8)
WINNER'S LAPS 1-3 P7, 4 P8, 5 P9, 6-11 P7, 12 P5, 13 P4, 14-17 P3, 18-60 P2, 61-68 P1
FASTEST LAP R Arnoux, Renault, 1m 15.067s (lap 50), 226.290kph, 140.610mph
CHAMPIONSHIP Reutemann 43, Piquet 26, Jones 24, Villeneuve 21, Laffite 21

Pos	Driver	Car	Time/gap	Grid	Stops	Tyres
1	J Watson	McLaren-Ford	1h 26m 54.801s	5	0	M
2	C Reutemann	Williams-Ford	−40.652s	9	0	G
3	J Laffite	Ligier-Matra	−1 lap	14	0	M
4	E Cheever	Tyrrell-Ford	−1 lap	23	0	M
5	H Rebaque	Brabham-Ford	−1 lap	13	2	G
6	S Borgudd	ATS-Ford	−1 lap	21	0	A

TOP 100 RACE

McLaren-Ford MP4

GERMAN GP Hockenheim
2 August 1981   Race 352

Nelson Piquet
Brabham-Ford BT49C 213.325kph, 132.554mph

Hockenheim also suited Renault, Prost taking his maiden pole. In a power versus handling contest, the Williams pair lined up behind the French cars. Chased by Jones, Prost led until on lap 21 he encountered a delayed teammate. Arnoux offered hindrance not help, enabling Jones an opportunistic pass and then to quickly disappear, 10s ahead by lap 30. Until, that is, the dreaded Williams misfire returned, Jones' head jerking out of slow corners as the engine caught and died spasmodically. But it was not Prost who took the lead just seven laps from the flag but a resurgent Piquet, having overtaken the Renault two laps earlier. With Reutemann failing to finish, the Argentinean's championship points lead was suddenly in jeopardy.

POLE POSITION Prost, Renault, 1m 47.50s (0.46s), 227.353kph, 141.270mph
LAPS 45 x 6.789 km, 4.218 miles
DISTANCE 305.505 km, 189.832 miles
STARTERS/FINISHERS 24/15
WEATHER Sunny, hot, dry
LAP LEADERS Prost 1-20 (20); Jones 21-38 (18); Piquet 39-45 (7)
WINNER'S LAPS 1 P6, 2 P5, 3-8 P4, 9-14 P3, 15-26 P4, 27-36 P3, 37-38 P2, 39-45 P1
FASTEST LAP A Jones, Williams-Ford, 1m 52.42s (lap 4), 217.403kph, 135.088mph
CHAMPIONSHIP Reutemann 43, Piquet 35, Laffite 25, Jones 24, Villeneuve 21

Pos	Driver	Car	Time/gap	Grid	Stops	Tyres
1	N Piquet	Brabham-Ford	1h 25m 55.60s	6	0	G
2	A Prost	Renault	–11.52s	1	0	M
3	J Laffite	Ligier-Matra	–1m 4.60s	7	0	M
4	H Rebaque	Brabham-Ford	–1m 39.69s	16	0	G
5	E Cheever	Tyrrell-Ford	–1m 50.52s	18	0	A
6	J Watson	McLaren-Ford	–1 lap	9	0	M

Ligier-Matra JS17

Round 11/15	**AUSTRIAN GP** Österreichring	**Jacques Laffite**
	16 August 1981 Race 353	Ligier-Matra JS17 215.683kph, 134.019mph

Another all-Renault front row, pole bringing an Austrian hat-trick to Arnoux. After the early laps scramble which briefly featured the Ferrari pair, the Renaults simply disappeared up the road. And soon it became a French festival, Laffite's Ligier-Matra taking up third place from Piquet and the Williams pair. Handling superbly, the Ligier began to reel-in the now understeering Renaults, his task made easier when leader Prost crashed harmlessly at half-distance with suspension failure. Eventually, on lap 39, Laffite caught and passed Arnoux for a conclusive victory which, following a string of podiums, brought Jacques into championship contention. In addition Piquet's third had further shrunk Reutemann's 17-point Silverstone lead to just six.

POLE POSITION Arnoux, Renault, 1m 32.018s (0.303s), 232.468kph, 144.449mph
LAPS 53 x 5.942 km, 3.692 miles
DISTANCE 314.926 km, 195.686 miles
STARTERS/FINISHERS 24/11
WEATHER Sunny, hot, dry
LAP LEADERS G Villeneuve, Ferrari 1 (1); A Prost, Renault 2-26 (25); Arnoux 27-38 (12); Laffite 39-53 (15)
WINNER'S LAPS 1 P5, 2-5 P4, 6-7 P5, 8 P4, 9-26 P3, 27-38 P2, 39-53 P1
FASTEST LAP Laffite, Ligier-Matra, 1m 37.620s (lap 47), 219.127kph, 136.159mph
CHAMPIONSHIP Reutemann 45, Piquet 39, Laffite 34, Jones 27, Villeneuve 21

Pos	Driver	Car	Time/gap	Grid	Stops	Tyres
1	J Laffite	Ligier-Matra	1h 27m 36.47s	4	0	M
2	R Arnoux	Renault	−5.17s	1	0	M
3	N Piquet	Brabham-Ford	−7.34s	7	0	G
4	A Jones	Williams-Ford	−12.04s	6	0	G
5	C Reutemann	Williams-Ford	−31.85s	5	0	G
6	J Watson	McLaren-Ford	−1m 31.14s	12	0	M

Round 12/15	**DUTCH GP** Zandvoort	**Alain Prost**
	30 August 1981 Race 354	Renault RE30 183.002kph, 113.712mph

The fourth successive Renault front row. A fascinating duel developed between Prost and Jones, the Renault 'on rails', its horsepower advantage enabling a massive rear wing, the Williams much looser, adopting the 'skinny' aero option. After unsuccessful attempts to pass around the outside at Tarzan, on lap 23 a backmarker presented an opportunity and Jones dived ahead at 'Bos uit'. Backmarker-Jones-Prost slipstreamed down the straight as one, first Jones then Prost flicking out to pass, Prost retaking the lead at Tarzan. Soon afterwards tyre wear caused Jones to fall back into the clutches of Piquet, and with Reutemann eliminated in a clash with Laffite, second place put the Brazilian and the Argentinean level on points with just three races left.

POLE POSITION Prost, Renault, 1m 18.176s (0.079s), 195.804kph, 121.667mph
LAPS 72 x 4.252 km, 2.642 miles
DISTANCE 306.144 km, 190.229 miles
STARTERS/FINISHERS 24/10
WEATHER Sunny, warm, dry
LAP LEADERS Prost 1-22, 24-72 (71); Jones 23 (1)
WINNER'S LAPS 1-22 P1, 23 P2, 24-72 P1
FASTEST LAP Jones, Williams-Ford, 1m 21.830s (lap 15), 187.061kph, 116.234mph
CHAMPIONSHIP Piquet 45, Reutemann 45, Laffite 34, Jones 31, Prost 28

Pos	Driver	Car	Time/gap	Grid	Stops	Tyres
1	A Prost	Renault	1h 40m 22.43s	1	0	M
2	N Piquet	Brabham-Ford	−8.24s	3	0	G
3	A Jones	Williams-Ford	−35.50s	4	0	G
4	H Rebaque	Brabham-Ford	−1 lap	15	0	G
5	E de Angelis	Lotus-Ford	−1 lap	9	0	G
6	E Salazar	Ensign-Ford	−2 laps	24	0	A

Round 13/15	**ITALIAN GP** Monza	**Alain Prost**
	13 September 1981 Race 355	Renault RE30 209.045kph, 129.895mph

Prost made the business of winning look easy, leading at the first corner from P3 and never headed thereafter. Behind there was quite a battle on a track made slippery by localised showers. After an initial surge by Pironi, Arnoux held P2 until he slipped off on lap 13. Now it was Jones followed by teammate Reutemann, but the latter's Williams on a dry set-up performed poorly in the damp, although he rallied as the track improved. By then, however, prime championship rival Piquet was firmly ahead. But when Piquet's engine let go on the final lap Reutemann snatched a vital third place. Watson was fortunate to be unhurt in a violent smash at Lesmo 2, the McLaren chassis/fuel tank separating from the engine/gearbox in a ball of flame.

POLE POSITION R Arnoux, Renault, 1m 33.467s (0.673s), 223.394kph, 138.811mph
LAPS 52 x 5.800 km, 3.604 miles
DISTANCE 301.600 km, 187.406 miles
STARTERS/FINISHERS 24/10
WEATHER Overcast, warm, occasional showers
LAP LEADERS Prost 1-52 (52)
WINNER'S LAPS 1-52 P1
FASTEST LAP Reutemann, Williams-Ford, 1m 37.528s (lap 48), 214.092kph, 133.031mph
CHAMPIONSHIP Reutemann 49, Piquet 46, Prost 37, Jones 37, Laffite 34

Pos	Driver	Car	Time/gap	Grid	Stops	Tyres
1	A Prost	Renault	1h 26m 33.897s	3	0	M
2	A Jones	Williams-Ford	−22.175s	5	0	G
3	C Reutemann	Williams-Ford	−50.587s	2	0	G
4	E de Angelis	Lotus-Ford	−1m 32.902s	11	0	G
5	D Pironi	Ferrari	−1m 34.522s	8	0	M
6r	N Piquet	Brabham-Ford	−1 lap	6	0	G

CANADIAN GP Montréal

27 September 1981   **Race 356**

Jacques Laffite
Ligier-Matra JS17 137.290kph, 85.308mph

Title protagonists Piquet and Reutemann headed the grid, but by the conclusion of a very wet race a third contender had brought himself into play. Laffite's torquey Ligier-Matra proved best-suited to take advantage of Michelin wets, the Goodyear offering totally outshone by the French rubber which furnished the first four finishers. Starting tenth, Laffite's masterly drive took him into the lead on lap 13, the race halted at the two-hour mark seven laps short. Watson and Villeneuve completed the podium, their intense mid-race battle keeping the crowd warm, while by salvaging a crucial point Piquet went to the championship finale just one point down on Reutemann. Despite no points in Canada, Williams retained their constructors' title.

POLE POSITION Piquet, Brabham-Ford, 1m 29.211s (0.148s), 177.960kph, 110.579mph
LAPS 63 x 4.410 km, 2.740 miles (Scheduled for 70 laps but stopped after two hours)
DISTANCE 277.830 km, 172.636 miles
STARTERS/FINISHERS 24/12
WEATHER Overcast, rain
LAP LEADERS A Jones, Williams-Ford 1-6 (6); A Prost, Renault 7-12 (6); Laffite 13-63 (51)
WINNER'S LAPS 1 P6, 2-4 P5, 5-6 P4, 7-12 P2, 13-63 P1
FASTEST LAP Watson, McLaren-Ford, 1m 49.475s (lap 43), 145.019kph, 90.111mph
CHAMPIONSHIP Reutemann 49, Piquet 48, Laffite 43, Prost 37, Jones 37

Pos	Driver	Car	Time/gap	Grid	Stops	Tyres
1	J Laffite	Ligier-Matra	2h 1m 25.20s	10	0	M
2	J Watson	McLaren-Ford	−6.23s	9	0	M
3	G Villeneuve	Ferrari	−1m 50.27s	11	0	M
4	B Giacomelli	Alfa Romeo	−1 lap	15	0	M
5	N Piquet	Brabham-Ford	−1 lap	1	0	G
6	E de Angelis	Lotus-Ford	−1 lap	7	0	G

CAESARS PALACE GP Las Vegas

17 October 1981   **Race 357**

Alan Jones
Williams-Ford FW07C 157.703kph, 97.992mph

And finally to a hotel car park, not the only bizarre aspect of the 1981 title showdown. Reutemann started from pole but even allowing for gearbox difficulties drove a lacklustre race to finish a lap down and out of the points. Piquet, head lolling from physical and heat exhaustion around this anticlockwise circuit, finished a distant fifth, needing to be lifted from his car. But outgoing champion Jones, having already announced his retirement, showed them both how to do it, sprinting to an uncontested victory. Michelins were not the tyre for Vegas, almost all so-equipped needing to stop for fresh rubber. This put paid to Laffite's challenge when lying P2, although Prost stormed back to second after his stop. But Piquet was champion, by a single point.

POLE POSITION C Reutemann, Williams-Ford, 1m 17.821s (0.174s), 168.849kph, 104.918mph
LAPS 75 x 3.650 km, 2.268 miles
DISTANCE 273.749 km, 170.100 miles
STARTERS/FINISHERS 24/12
WEATHER Sunny, warm, dry
LAP LEADERS Jones 1-75 (75)
WINNER'S LAPS 1-75 P1
FASTEST LAP D Pironi, Ferrari, 1m 20.156s (lap 49), 163.930kph, 101.861mph
CHAMPIONSHIP Piquet 50, Reutemann 49, Jones 46, Laffite 44, Prost 43

Pos	Driver	Car	Time/gap	Grid	Stops	Tyres
1	A Jones	Williams-Ford	1h 44m 9.077s	2	0	G
2	A Prost	Renault	−20.048s	5	1	M
3	B Giacomelli	Alfa Romeo	−20.428s	8	0	M
4	N Mansell	Lotus-Ford	−47.473s	9	0	G
5	N Piquet	Brabham-Ford	−1m 16.438s	4	0	G
6	J Laffite	Ligier-Matra	−1m 18.175s	12	1	M

1981 CHAMPIONSHIP FACTS AND FOLKLORE

■ Lamentably, the 1981 season cannot be reviewed adequately without reference to the political turmoil that engulfed Formula 1 over the winter of 1980–81.

■ In summary, FISA president Jean Marie Balestre, on behalf of the FIA, set out to wrest back the initiative for governance of Formula 1 from FOCA, the constructors' body.

■ Headed by Bernie Ecclestone, FOCA had steadily assumed increasing control of commercial and operational aspects of the sport, formerly the sole domain of the FIA. This included central negotiation with race promoters and TV companies, guaranteeing 'the show', and sensibly addressing other organisational and procedural issues.

■ The battleground Balestre chose to reassert FISA's authority was the banning of sliding skirts from 1 January 1981 and insistence upon a 6cm ride-height. By imposing this change on safety grounds – to reduce excessive cornering speeds – Balestre avoided the two-year-notice rule normally required for major regulation amendments.

■ Superior chassis dynamics, specifically the use of ground effect to enhance cornering performance, was the means by which the Ford-Cosworth powered teams – which were generally aligned with FOCA – could successfully compete with the FISA-aligned teams – notably Ferrari and Renault – which were investing heavily in the development of high-power turbo engines that enjoyed a straight-line speed advantage.

■ Despite breakaway threats by FOCA, the sliding skirts ban and 6cm minimum ride-height constraints were implemented and this fierce dispute ultimately culminated in the Concorde Agreement, under the terms of which the 1981 season was run.

■ There were various new or revised regulations, notably:
   ◆ Minimum dry weight raised from 575kg (1,267.66lb) to 585kg (1,289.70lb).
   ◆ Minimum race distance 250km (155.34 miles), and maximum 320km (198.84 miles) or two hours.
   ◆ A minimum of 18 starters for each race and a maximum of 30 cars for qualifying.

- ◆ A limit of eight tyres per car per timed practice session.
- ◆ The drivers' championship no longer split into two parts, the best 11 results from all 15 races to count.
- ■ But the FISA/FOCA wars directly impacted the 1981 season in at least two other ways: first, championship status for the opening round in February, the South African GP, was revoked, the round excluded from the calendar having been boycotted by the FISA-aligned 'Grandee' teams – Ferrari, Renault, Alfa Romeo, Osella and Toleman – due to the use of sliding skirts by the FOCA teams. Carlos Reutemann won this disallowed South African GP from Nelson Piquet.
- ■ Second, Bernie Ecclestone's Brabham team designer, Gordon Murray, came up with an ingenious way to circumnavigate the restrictions placed on sliding skirts and ride-height: hydro-pneumatic suspension.
- ■ Instead of banning the Brabham BT49C, as they did the twin-chassis Lotus 88, the governing body prevaricated and condemned the season to ridicule.
- ■ The performance advantage of this blatant abuse of the spirit of the agreed rules was such that all teams were forced to follow suit and introduce similar 'trick' suspension systems. The 'trick' was to pneumatically raise the ride-height above 6cm when the car was accessible to scrutineers in the pit-lane area, but once on the circuit at speed to lower the chassis to skim along the track surface and, with fixed, rigid skirts replacing sliding skirts, retain much of the benefits of ground effect.
- ■ This arrangement required rock-hard suspension with minimal travel and proved highly unpopular with the drivers due to discomfort – every undulation of the track surface was transmitted to the driver – and due to safety – in certain circumstances a bump could chuck the car off-line and provoke an accident, such as Watson's near miss at Monza.
- ■ Certainly the unrewarding nature of driving a giant roller-skate was a significant factor in disenchanted reigning world champion Alan Jones calling time on his career at season's end.
- ■ Another disruptive factor in the season was the temporary withdrawal of Goodyear for the first half of the season. This required all but Michelin-shod Renault, Ferrari and Ligier, plus Toleman on Pirellis, to adapt to either a 'standard' Michelin or to switch to Avons.
- ■ Back on track, pre-season favourites Williams were again

RACE 357, Caesars Palace GP: The 1981 championship opened and closed Stateside, the decisive championship finale bizarrely held in a Las Vegas hotel car park. Here, lap one, turn one, race winner Jones leads Villeneuve, Prost, Reutemann, Giacomelli and Piquet, the eventual champion.

constructors' champions with four victories, two apiece for Jones and Reutemann.

■ With wins distributed across seven drivers and six teams, resolution of the championship went down to the final race, although Reutemann had led the points table, at times handsomely, throughout most of the season. But he capitulated at the finale with a strangely low-energy drive which allowed Nelson Piquet, finishing only fifth, to snatch the championship by a single point, having won three races during the year.

■ At his 19th attempt Alain Prost broke his duck with three wins for Renault, and with Laffite's Ligier-Matra also picking up two victories France were again well represented in the winners' circle.

■ Gilles Villeneuve won twice for Ferrari, now also turbo powered, and John Watson took a popular victory at Silverstone, the first for McLaren since James Hunt in 1977; the first for a chassis of carbon-fibre construction, and the first under the leadership of Ron Dennis.

■ A new team, Toleman, entered with Pirelli tyres, a turbocharged Hart engine and a chassis designed by Rory Byrne. Toleman, already known for offshore powerboat racing, were European F2 champions in 1980.

■ After hosting the 1980 Italian GP Imola became a regular fixture from 1981 as the venue for the San Marino GP, while the track for the first Caesar's Palace GP partly utilised a Las Vegas hotel car park.

■ 1981 was a bizarre year for F1, and was also the year in which Fernando Alonso was born.

Championship ranking	Championship points	Driver nationality	1981 Drivers Championship		Races contested	Race victories	Podiumse excl. victories	Races led	Lights to flag victories	Laps led	Poles	Fastest laps	Triple Crowns
			Driver	Car									
1	50	BRA	Nelson Piquet	Brabham-Ford	15	3	4	5	1	185	4	1	1
2	49	ARG	Carlos Reutemann	Williams-Ford	15	2	5	3	1	104	2	2	1
3	46	AUS	Alan Jones	Williams-Ford	15	2	4	8	1	188		5	
4	44	FRA	Jacques Laffite	Ligier-Matra	15	2	5	2		66	1	1	
5	43	FRA	Alain Prost	Renault	15	3	3	7	1	212	2	1	
6	27	GBR	John Watson	McLaren-Ford	15	1	3	1		8		1	
7	25	CAN	Gilles Villeneuve	Ferrari	15	2	1	4		86	1	1	
8	14	ITA	Elio de Angelis	Lotus-Ford	14								
9	11	FRA	René Arnoux	Renault	14		1	2		56	4	1	
10	11	MEX	Hector Rebaque	Brabham-Ford	14								
11	10	ITA	Riccardo Patrese	Arrows-Ford	15		2	1		24.5	1		
12	10	USA	Eddie Cheever	Tyrrell-Ford	14								
13	9	FRA	Didier Pironi	Ferrari	15			2		44		1	
14	8	GBR	Nigel Mansell	Lotus-Ford	13		1						
15	7	ITA	Bruno Giacomelli	Alfa Romeo	15		1						
16	4	SUI	Marc Surer	Ensign-Ford (6) Theodore-Ford (7)	13							1	
17	3	USA	Mario Andretti	Alfa Romeo	15								
18	1	FRA	Patrick Tambay	Theodore-Ford (6) Ligier-Matra (8)	14								
18	1	ITA	Andrea de Cesaris	McLaren-Ford	14								
18	1	SWE	Slim Borgudd	ATS-Ford	7								
18	1	CHL	Eliseo Salazar	March-Ford (1) Ensign-Ford (8)	9								

Championship ranking	Championship points	Team/Marque nationality	1981 Constructors Championship		Engine maker nationality	Races contested	Race victories	1-2 finishes	Podiums excl. victories	Races led	Laps led	Poles	Fastest laps
			Chassis	Engine									
1	95	GBR	Williams FW07C, FW07D	Ford Cosworth 3.0 V8	GBR	15	4	2	9	9	292	2	7
2	61	GBR	Brabham BT49C	Ford Cosworth 3.0 V8	GBR	15	3		4	5	185	4	1
3	54	FRA	Renault RE30, RE20B	Renault 1.5 V6t	FRA	15	3		4	7	268	6	2
4	44	FRA	Ligier JS17	Matra 3.0 V12	FRA	15	2		5	2	66	1	1
5	34	ITA	Ferrari 126CK	Ferrari 1.5 V6t	ITA	15	2		1	5	130	1	2
6	28	GBR	McLaren MP4, M29F	Ford Cosworth 3.0 V8	GBR	15	1		3	1	8		1
7	22	GBR	Lotus 87, 81	Ford Cosworth 3.0 V8	GBR	14			1				
8	10	GBR	Arrows A3	Ford Cosworth 3.0 V8	GBR	15			2	1	24.5	1	
9	10	ITA	Alfa Romeo 179B, 179C, 179D	Alfa Romeo 3.0 V12	ITA	15			1				
10	10	GBR	Tyrrell 010, 011	Ford Cosworth 3.0 V8	GBR	15							
11	5	GBR	Ensign N180B	Ford Cosworth 3.0 V8	GBR	14							1
12	1	HKG	Theodore TY01	Ford Cosworth 3.0 V8	GBR	13							
12	1	GER	ATS D4, HGS1	Ford Cosworth 3.0 V8	GBR	9							

1982

It's Rosberg at the Finnish

THE TALE OF THE TITLE

- In a troubled season of tragedy and controversy Keke Rosberg seized the title with a single race victory.
- No individual won more than twice, victories spread across a record 11 drivers from seven teams.
- It was honours even in the technological struggle, turbo and atmo (non-turbo) winning eight apiece.
- Ferrari became the first turbo constructors' champions, an atmo Williams the world champion's mount.
- Reliability remained the curse of the turbo engine, shattering a season of great promise for Renault.
- Renault drivers Prost and Arnoux led far more races and laps than any other but only won four times.
- Ferrari's bid for the drivers' title was tragically derailed by Villeneuve's death and Pironi's accident.
- Brabham's switch to turbo power with BMW proved exasperating, but the potential was undeniable.
- Niki Lauda returned with McLaren, he and Watson delivering four victories with the MP4.
- John Watson was a title contender to the end, his remarkable Detroit victory from the lowest grid-slot ever.
- The Austrian GP victory by the Lotus of Elio de Angelis was the closest finish of all time, bar one.
- Contentious were the drivers' superlicence strike, and at Imola the FOCA boycott and Pironi's duplicity.
- Calamitous were the deaths of Gilles Villeneuve and Riccardo Paletti and the passing of Colin Chapman.
- And not forgetting: mid-race refuelling returns; 'water-cooled' brakes.

THE CHASE FOR THE CHAMPIONSHIP

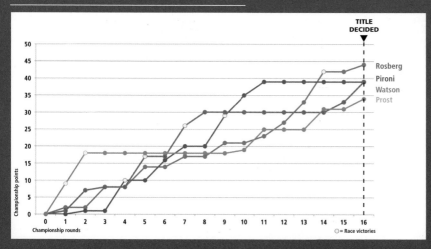

Renault RE30B

| Round 1/16 | **SOUTH AFRICAN GP** Kyalami | | | | | **Alain Prost** |
| | 23 January 1982 | | | | Race 358 | Renault RE30B 205.779kph, 127.865mph |

During Thursday practice Niki Lauda, returning with McLaren, was the ringleader in a drivers' strike over superlicences. Rosberg, replacing Jones at Williams, qualified P7, the fastest non-turbo now that Brabham-BMW had joined the turbo brigade. The Renaults took command from the off, pole-man Arnoux leading until a backmarker helped Prost ahead on lap 14. On lap 41, holding an 11s lead, a puncture dropped Prost to eighth, a lap behind Arnoux. A superb comeback drive on fresh rubber saw Prost retake the lead from his slowing teammate on lap 68 of 77. Arnoux's tyre problems – vibration caused by rubber pick-up – became so acute he lost second to Reutemann. Lauda finished fourth, the Ferraris and Brabhams failing.

POLE POSITION Arnoux, Renault, 1m 06.351s (0.274s), 222.670kph, 138.361mph
LAPS 77 x 4.104 km, 2.550 miles
DISTANCE 316.008 km, 196.358 miles
STARTERS/FINISHERS 26/18
WEATHER Sunny, hot, dry
LAP LEADERS Arnoux 1-13, 41-67 (40); Prost 14-40, 68-77 (37)
WINNER'S LAPS 1-13 P2, 14-40 P1, 41-43 P8, 44-50 P7, 51-53 P6, 54 P5, 55-60 P4, 61 P3, 62-67 P2, 68-77 P1
FASTEST LAP Prost, Renault, 1m 08.278s (lap 49), 216.386kph, 134.456mph
CHAMPIONSHIP Prost 9, Reutemann 6, Arnoux 4, Lauda 3, Rosberg 2

Pos	Driver	Car	Time/gap	Grid	Stops	Tyres
1	A Prost	Renault	1h 32m 8.401s	5	1	M
2	C Reutemann	Williams-Ford	−14.946s	8	0	G
3	R Arnoux	Renault	−27.900s	1	0	M
4	N Lauda	McLaren-Ford	−32.133s	13	0	M
5	K Rosberg	Williams-Ford	−46.139s	7	0	G
6	J Watson	McLaren-Ford	−50.993s	9	0	M

TOP **100** RACE

| Round 2/16 | **BRAZILIAN GP** Rio de Janeiro | | | | | **Alain Prost** |
| | 21 March 1982 | | | | Race 359 | Renault RE30B 181.892kph, 113.022mph |

From the front row Villeneuve's Ferrari led, Piquet and Rosberg soon chasing after getting the better of the Renaults. Around half-distance, resolutely defending a forceful overtaking manoeuvre by Piquet, Gilles spun out. Now it was Piquet versus Rosberg, the 2–3s gap only widening over the final dozen laps, Keke's tyres shot. Heat, humidity, G-forces, the constant battering from solid suspension, the winner of his home GP and reigning champion collapsed on the podium. Subsequently Piquet and Rosberg were disqualified for contravening weight regulations, their cars using ballast thinly disguised as 'water-cooled brakes'. So Prost, who despite a misfire had finished third with one of his stealthy, calculated drives, was proclaimed winner.

POLE POSITION Prost, Renault, 1m 28.808s (0.365s), 203.941kph, 126.723mph
LAPS 63 x 5.031 km, 3.126 miles
DISTANCE 316.953 km, 196.945 miles
STARTERS/FINISHERS 26/10
WEATHER Sunny, hot, dry
LAP LEADERS (On the road) G Villeneuve, Ferrari 1-29 (29); N Piquet, Brabham-Ford 30-63 (34)
WINNER'S LAPS 1-5 P3, 6-10 P5, 11-18 P6, 19 P7, 20 P8, 21-29 P5, 30-32 P4, 33-63 P3 (Piquet and K Rosberg, Williams-Ford finished first and second but both were disqualified for under-weight cars)
FASTEST LAP Prost, Renault, 1m 37.016s (lap 36), 186.687kph, 116.002mph
CHAMPIONSHIP Prost 18, Watson 7, Reutemann 6, Arnoux 4, Mansell 4

Pos	Driver	Car	Time/gap	Grid	Stops	Tyres
1	A Prost	Renault	1h 44m 33.134s	1	0	M
2	J Watson	McLaren-Ford	−2.990s	12	0	M
3	N Mansell	Lotus-Ford	−36.859s	14	0	G
4	M Alboreto	Tyrrell-Ford	−50.761s	13	0	G
5	M Winkelhock	ATS-Ford	−1 lap	15	0	A
6	D Pironi	Ferrari	−1 lap	8	0	G

| Round 3/16 | **UNITED STATES GP WEST** Long Beach | | Niki Lauda |

UNITED STATES GP WEST Long Beach
Round 3/16
4 April 1982   Race 360

Niki Lauda
McLaren-Ford MP4B 131.128kph, 81.479mph

In his comeback season, Niki Lauda won round three. He was just too good for the young Italian de Cesaris who, exploiting the slow-corner torque of his V12 Alfa Romeo, had snatched an impressive last-minute pole from Lauda and led the opening laps. The inevitable lead-change happened on lap 15, Lauda smoothly past and cunningly working the traffic to inch away. On lap 34 de Cesaris became one of many to fall foul of the Long Beach walls as the track broke up in places, championship leader Prost one of them. Ferrari protested Lauda and second-placed Rosberg for 'water-cooled brakes', but ironically it was their driver Villeneuve who was disqualified from third for the use of an unusual and illegal 'double' rear wing.

POLE POSITION A de Cesaris, Alfa Romeo, 1m 27.316s (0.120s), 141.331kph, 87.819mph
LAPS 75.5 x 3.428 km, 2.130 miles
DISTANCE 258.807 km, 160.815 miles
STARTERS/FINISHERS 26/10
WEATHER Sunny, hot, dry
LAP LEADERS de Cesaris 1-14 (14.5); Lauda 15-75 (61)
WINNER'S LAPS 1-5 P3, 6-14 P2, 15-75 P1
FASTEST LAP Lauda, McLaren-Ford, 1m 30.831s (lap 12), 135.862kph, 84.421mph
CHAMPIONSHIP Prost 18, Lauda 12, Rosberg 8, Watson 8, Reutemann 6

Pos	Driver	Car	Time/gap	Grid	Stops	Tyres
1	N Lauda	McLaren-Ford	1h 58m 25.318s	2	0	M
2	K Rosberg	Williams-Ford	–14.660s	8	0	G
3	R Patrese	Brabham-Ford	–1m 19.143s	18	0	G
4	M Alboreto	Tyrrell-Ford	–1m 20.947s	12	0	G
5	E de Angelis	Lotus-Ford	–1 lap	16	0	G
6	J Watson	McLaren-Ford	–1 lap	11	0	M

SAN MARINO GP Imola
Round 4/16
25 April 1982   Race 361

Didier Pironi
Ferrari 126C2 187.733kph, 116.652mph

In the face of the FIA ban on 'water-cooled brakes' and the disqualification of Piquet and Rosberg from the Brazilian GP, the FOCA teams boycotted Imola, just 14 cars competing. In essence the race was between Renault and Ferrari, the front row yellow, the second row red. Pole-man Arnoux led from the Ferraris, Prost out early. For lap after lap an enthralling struggle for the lead developed between the three remaining cars, the Ferraris cutting and thrusting just behind Arnoux, who was briefly deprived of his lead by Villeneuve mid-race. On lap 44 the Renault engine broke the spell, only the Ferrari pair remaining. Pironi committed a piece of F1 infamy by ignoring pit signals and overtaking on the final lap, Villeneuve incensed by the duplicity.

POLE POSITION R Arnoux, Renault, 1m 29.765s (0.484s), 202.128kph, 125.596mph
LAPS 60 x 5.040 km, 3.132 miles
DISTANCE 302.400 km, 187.903 miles
STARTERS/FINISHERS 13/5
WEATHER Sunny, hot, dry
LAP LEADERS Arnoux 1-26, 31-43 (39); Villeneuve 27-30, 44-45, 49-52, 59 (11); Pironi 46-48, 53-58, 60 (10)
WINNER'S LAPS 1-21 P3, 22-25 P2, 26-35 P3, 36-40 P2, 41-44 P3, 45 P2, 46-48 P1, 49-52 P2, 53-58 P1, 59 P2, 60 P1
FASTEST LAP Pironi, Ferrari, 1m 35.036s (lap 44), 190.917kph, 118.630mph
CHAMPIONSHIP Prost 18, Lauda 12, Pironi 10, Alboreto 10, Rosberg 8

Pos	Driver	Car	Time/gap	Grid	Stops	Tyres
1	D Pironi	Ferrari	1h 36m 38.887s	4	0	G
2	G Villeneuve	Ferrari	–0.366s	3	0	G
3	M Alboreto	Tyrrell-Ford	–1m 7.684s	5	0	G
4	J-P Jarier	Osella-Ford	–1 lap	9	0	P
5	E Salazar	ATS-Ford	–3 laps	14	1	A
-	No other classified finishers	-	-	-	-	-

TOP **100** RACE

BELGIAN GP Zolder
Round 5/16
9 May 1982   Race 362

John Watson
McLaren-Ford MP4B 187.047kph, 116.226mph

Gilles Villeneuve died following an appalling accident in final qualifying. The Ferraris were withdrawn. Renaults filled the front row but inside five laps any threat had vanished. Rosberg qualified the new Williams FW08 third and now made a splendid bid for victory, leading the next 64 laps. Behind the flying Finn, de Cesaris impressed again with the Alfa V12 while it was healthy, holding second on lap 34, after which the McLarens took up the challenge. Both were beginning to motor on their Michelins, especially Watson on a harder compound. John overtook Lauda on lap 47, reeled in Rosberg's 20s lead – his Goodyears shot – going by on the penultimate lap as Rosberg ran wide. Underweight Lauda was disqualified from third.

POLE POSITION A Prost, Renault, 1m 15.701s (0.029s), 202.682kph, 125.941mph
LAPS 70 x 4.262 km, 2.648 miles
DISTANCE 298.340 km, 185.380 miles
STARTERS/FINISHERS 26/9
WEATHER Sunny, warm, dry
LAP LEADERS R Arnoux, Renault 1-4 (4); Rosberg 5-68 (64); Watson 69-70 (2)
WINNER'S LAPS 1-4 P9, 5 P8, 6-7 P7, 8 P6, 9-30 P5, 31-34 P4, 35-46 P3, 47-68 P2, 69-70 P1
FASTEST LAP Watson, McLaren-Ford, 1m 20.214s (lap 67), 191.278kph, 118.855mph
CHAMPIONSHIP Prost 18, Watson 17, Rosberg 14, Lauda 12, Pironi 10

Pos	Driver	Car	Time/gap	Grid	Stops	Tyres
1	J Watson	McLaren-Ford	1h 35m 41.995s	10	0	M
2	K Rosberg	Williams-Ford	–7.268s	3	0	G
3	E Cheever	Ligier-Matra	–1 lap	14	0	M
4	E de Angelis	Lotus-Ford	–2 laps	11	1	G
5	N Piquet	Brabham-BMW	–3 laps	8	1	G
6	C Serra	Fittipaldi-Ford	–3 laps	23	0	P

Round 6/16	**MONACO GP** Monte Carlo	**Riccardo Patrese**
	23 May 1982 Race 363	Brabham-Ford BT49D 132.262kph, 82.184mph

When pole-man Arnoux spun away his lead on lap 15 Prost looked the certain winner until two-and-a-half laps from glory. Heading towards Tabac, the track surface greasy from drizzle, he lost control as he negotiated a backmarker and struck the barriers hard. For Patrese, running within a few seconds of Prost for most of the race, a maiden victory seemed assured. But approaching the hairpin he too spun away the lead, allowing Pironi and de Cesaris by. But fate granted Patrese another chance. First he was push-started, his car deemed to be in a dangerous position; then de Cesaris ran out of fuel, and finally Pironi's battery failed, Patrese the only driver to complete the full distance. Prost's late crash had triggered five minutes of F1 magic.

POLE POSITION R Arnoux, Renault, 1m 23.281s (0.510s), 143.168kph, 88.961mph
LAPS 76 x 3.312 km, 2.058 miles
DISTANCE 251.712 km, 156.407 miles
STARTERS/FINISHERS 20/10
WEATHER Warm and dry, rain in closing laps
LAP LEADERS Arnoux 1-14 (14); A Prost, Renault 15-73 (59); Patrese 74, 76 (2); Pironi 75 (1)
WINNER'S LAPS 1-4 P4, 5-15 P3, 16-73 P2, 74 P1, 75 P3, 76 P1
FASTEST LAP Patrese, Brabham-Ford, 1m 26.354s (lap 69), 138.074kph, 85.795mph
CHAMPIONSHIP Prost 18, Watson 17, Pironi 16, Rosberg 14, Patrese 13

Pos	Driver	Car	Time/gap	Grid	Stops	Tyres
1	R Patrese	Brabham-Ford	1h 54m 11.259s	2	0	G
2r	D Pironi	Ferrari	−1 lap	5	0	G
3r	A de Cesaris	Alfa Romeo	−1 lap	7	0	M
4	N Mansell	Lotus-Ford	−1 lap	11	1	G
5	E de Angelis	Lotus-Ford	−1 lap	15	0	G
6r	D Daly	Williams-Ford	−2 laps	8	0	G

Round 7/16	**UNITED STATES GP** Detroit	**John Watson**
	6 June 1982 Race 364	McLaren-Ford MP4B 125.754kph, 78.140mph

The first Motown GP was impulsively red-flagged after six laps. At the restart – the result aggregated – Prost continued to lead from Rosberg and Pironi, Keke moving ahead on lap 23 as the Renault began to misfire. Watson had qualified P17 and for the restart lined up P13 on harder Michelins. On his way to a quite remarkable victory, Watson clinically overtook car after car. In a single lap, to move from P5 to P2, he passed Lauda, Cheever and Pironi. In the next four laps Watson slashed the 12s gap to Rosberg, taking the lead on lap 37. It might well have been a McLaren 1-2, but, trying to emulate his teammate's progress, Lauda crashed out. Watson now led the title race, defending champion Piquet failing to qualify the Brabham-BMW.

POLE POSITION A Prost, Renault, 1m 48.537s (0.335s), 133.075kph, 82.689mph
LAPS 62 x 4.012 km, 2.493 miles (70 lap race interrupted due to accident. Stopped after two hours, result aggregate of 6 + 56 laps)
DISTANCE 248.750 km, 154.566 miles
STARTERS/FINISHERS 25/11
WEATHER Cloudy with sunny intervals, warm, dry
LAP LEADERS (On the road) Prost 1-22 (22); Rosberg 23-36 (14); Watson 37-62 (26)
WINNER'S LAPS 1 P15, 2 P14, 3 P15, 4-6 P14, 7-15 P13, 16 P11, 17-18 P10, 19-23 P9, 24 P8, 25-28 P7, 29 P6, 30-32 P5, 33-36 P2, 37-62 P1
FASTEST LAP A Prost, Renault, 1m 50.438s (lap 45), 130.784kph, 81.266mph
CHAMPIONSHIP Watson 26, Pironi 20, Prost 18, Rosberg 17, Patrese 13

Pos	Driver	Car	Time/gap	Grid	Stops	Tyres
1	J Watson	McLaren-Ford	1h 58m 41.043s	17	0	M
2	E Cheever	Ligier-Matra	−15.726s	9	0	M
3	D Pironi	Ferrari	−28.077s	4	0	G
4	K Rosberg	Williams-Ford	−1m 11.976s	3	0	G
5	D Daly	Williams-Ford	−1m 23.757s	12	0	G
6	J Laffite	Ligier-Matra	−1 lap	13	0	M

Round 8/16	**CANADIAN GP** Montréal	**Nelson Piquet**
	13 June 1982 Race 365	Brabham-BMW BT50 173.655kph, 107.904mph

When Pironi stalled on pole, Paletti's Osella slammed into the stationery Ferrari at speed and briefly caught fire. The young Italian died of his injuries. The race was restarted, but perhaps understandably Pironi, driving a singleton Ferrari entry, was not the force he had been in qualifying and victory lay between the Renaults and Piquet. Nelson relieved René of the lead on lap 9 and by mid-race he was cruising, Prost out with engine trouble, Arnoux spinning and stalling. From non-qualifier in Detroit, the world champion's only (legal) victory of 1982 confirmed the potential of the Brabham-BMW, its maiden victory. Patrese's Brabham-Ford delivered the team a 1-2, and third gave Watson a ten-point championship lead at the halfway stage.

POLE POSITION D Pironi, Ferrari, 1m 27.509s (0.386s), 181.421kph, 112.730mph
LAPS 70 x 4.410 km, 2.740 miles (Race restarted for scheduled 70 laps following accident)
DISTANCE 308.700 km, 191.817 miles
STARTERS/FINISHERS 26/11
WEATHER Overcast, cold, dry
LAP LEADERS Pironi 1 (1); R Arnoux, Renault 2-8 (7); Piquet 9-70 (62)
WINNER'S LAPS 1 P4, 2 P3, 3-8 P2, 9-70 P1
FASTEST LAP D Pironi, Ferrari, 1m 28.323s (lap 66), 179.749kph, 111.691mph
CHAMPIONSHIP Watson 30, Pironi 20, Patrese 19, Prost 18, Rosberg 17

Pos	Driver	Car	Time/gap	Grid	Stops	Tyres
1	N Piquet	Brabham-BMW	1h 46m 39.577s	4	0	G
2	R Patrese	Brabham-Ford	−13.799s	8	0	G
3	J Watson	McLaren-Ford	−1m 1.836s	6	0	M
4	E de Angelis	Lotus-Ford	−1 lap	10	0	G
5	M Surer	Arrows-Ford	−1 lap	16	0	P
6r	A de Cesaris	Alfa Romeo	−2 laps	9	0	M

Brabham-BMW BT50

<table>
<tr><td>**Round 9/16**</td><td>**DUTCH GP** Zandvoort</td><td>**Didier Pironi**</td></tr>
<tr><td></td><td>**3 July 1982**   **Race 366**</td><td>**Ferrari 126C2** 187.331kph, 116.402mph</td></tr>
</table>

1-2 on the grid, another troubled race saw both Renaults out before half-distance. Prost suffered the seemingly inevitable engine trouble while Arnoux survived a massive accident when the left-front wheel parted company under braking for Tarzan. But neither would have beaten Pironi's Ferrari that day, revised pull-rod suspension adding improved handling to its undoubted power. Calmly out-braking Prost at Tarzan for the lead on lap 5, Pironi was able to pull away to a resounding victory, his second of the season. This elevated the Frenchman into championship contention, points-leader Watson finishing a dismal ninth. Piquet's Brabham-BMW came in second, while Rosberg's fighting third overshadowed the rest of the non-turbo runners.

POLE POSITION R Arnoux, Renault, 1m 14.233s (0.427s), 206.205kph, 128.130mph
LAPS 72 x 4.252 km, 2.642 miles
DISTANCE 306.144 km, 190.229 miles
STARTERS/FINISHERS 26/15
WEATHER Cloudy with sunny intervals, warm, dry
LAP LEADERS Prost 1-4 (4); Pironi 5-72 (68)
WINNER'S LAPS 1 P3, 2-4 P2, 5-72 P1
FASTEST LAP D Warwick, Toleman-Hart, 1m 19.780s (lap 13), 191.868kph, 119.221mph
CHAMPIONSHIP Watson 30, Pironi 29, Rosberg 21, Patrese 19, Prost 18

Pos	Driver	Car	Time/gap	Grid	Stops	Tyres
1	D Pironi	Ferrari	1h 38m 3.254s	4	1	G
2	N Piquet	Brabham-BMW	−21.649s	3	1	G
3	K Rosberg	Williams-Ford	−22.365s	7	1	G
4	N Lauda	McLaren-Ford	−1m 23.720s	5	1	M
5	D Daly	Williams-Ford	−1 lap	12	1	G
6	M Baldi	Arrows-Ford	−1 lap	16	1	P

<table>
<tr><td>**Round 10/16**</td><td>**BRITISH GP** Brands Hatch</td><td>**Niki Lauda**</td></tr>
<tr><td></td><td>**18 July 1982**   **Race 367**</td><td>**McLaren-Ford MP4B** 200.737kph, 124.732mph</td></tr>
</table>

Last moment problems forced maiden pole-winner Rosberg to start from the back. Surrogate pole-man Patrese stalled, start-line chaos ensued, three cars instantly *hors de combat* including Arnoux. A couple of laps later another incident eliminated three more, Watson included. Planning to stop for fuel, Piquet's 'light-fuelled' Brabham charged into the lead, but on lap 9, with a 10s lead, the fuel-injection belt broke on the BMW. Lauda then took over and, driving in his neat, calm, efficient style, won comfortably from the two Ferraris. Derek Warwick inspired the British crowd with his performance in the Toleman-Hart. From his P16 grid-slot he rocketed through the field, taking second from Pironi on lap 26 and holding it easily until the CV joint broke.

POLE POSITION K Rosberg, Williams-Ford, 1m 09.540s (0.087s), 217.782kph, 135.324mph
LAPS 76 x 4.207 km, 2.614 miles
DISTANCE 319.719 km, 198.664 miles
STARTERS/FINISHERS 26/10
WEATHER Sunny, hot, dry
LAP LEADERS N Piquet, Brabham-BMW 1-9 (9); Lauda 10-76 (67)
WINNER'S LAPS 1-9 P2, 10-76 P1
FASTEST LAP B Henton, Tyrrell-Ford, 1m 13.028s (lap 63), 207.380kph, 128.860mph
CHAMPIONSHIP Pironi 35, Watson 30, Lauda 24, Rosberg 21, Prost 19

Pos	Driver	Car	Time/gap	Grid	Stops	Tyres
1	N Lauda	McLaren-Ford	1h 35m 33.812s	5	0	M
2	D Pironi	Ferrari	−25.726s	4	0	G
3	P Tambay	Ferrari	−38.436s	13	0	G
4	E de Angelis	Lotus-Ford	−41.242s	7	0	G
5	D Daly	Williams-Ford	−41.430s	10	1	G
6	A Prost	Renault	−41.636s	8	0	M

FRENCH GP Paul Ricard

25 July 1982   Race 368

René Arnoux
Renault RE30B 201.215kph, 125.029mph

Renault restored some credibility to their disastrous season with a 1-2 finish at home, their first in five years of competition. Initially they were forced to play second fiddle to the Brabham pair operating their low fuel/soft tyres strategy, but prior to their stops both BMWs expired spectacularly, Patrese *'boom'* on lap 8, Piquet *'boom'* lap 23. A damaged skirt meant title contender Prost was slower that day, but in defiance of team orders Arnoux still went on to win. So French cars 1-2, French drivers 1-2-3-4 and with third place Pironi began to look on course for the title. In a potentially catastrophic accident on lap 11 about 12 spectators were lightly injured in a massive cartwheeling crash involving Mass' March and Baldi's Arrows.

POLE POSITION Arnoux, Renault, 1m 34.406s (0.282s), 221.554kph, 137.667mph
LAPS 54 x 5.810 km, 3.610 miles
DISTANCE 313.740 km, 194.949 miles
STARTERS/FINISHERS 26/16
WEATHER Sunny, hot, dry
LAP LEADERS Arnoux 1-2, 24-54 (33); Patrese 3-7 (5); N Piquet, Brabham-BMW 8-23 (16)
WINNER'S LAPS 1-2 P1, 3-4 P2, 5-7 P3, 8-23 P2, 24-54 P1
FASTEST LAP R Patrese, Brabham-BMW, 1m 40.075s (lap 4), 209.003kph, 129.869mph
CHAMPIONSHIP Pironi 39, Watson 30, Prost 25, Lauda 24, Rosberg 23

Pos	Driver	Car	Time/gap	Grid	Stops	Tyres
1	R Arnoux	Renault	1h 33m 33.217s	1	0	M
2	A Prost	Renault	−17.308s	2	0	M
3	D Pironi	Ferrari	−42.128s	3	0	G
4	P Tambay	Ferrari	−1m 16.241s	5	0	G
5	K Rosberg	Williams-Ford	−1m 30.994s	10	0	G
6	M Alboreto	Tyrrell-Ford	−1m 32.339s	15	0	G

Ferrari 126C2

GERMAN GP Hockenheim

8 August 1982   Race 369

Patrick Tambay
Ferrari 126C2 209.929kph, 130.444mph

Shattered legs in a horrifying wet practice smash put paid to Pironi's championship and his career. Tambay's lone Ferrari started behind both Renaults and Piquet, the lightweight Brabham scampering off into a massive lead. Prior to his fuel stop, Piquet tripped over backmarker Salazar, eliminating them both. Infamously, in front of worldwide TV, the world champion proceeded to punch and kick the bewildered Chilean. But there to pick up the pieces was Tambay, having disposed of both Renaults within ten laps of the start. Nine laps from the end Watson lost a certain P3 with suspension failure, Lauda not even starting, injured in a practice off. But with Pironi out the McLaren pair plus Rosberg and Prost now looked championship favourites.

POLE POSITION D Pironi, Ferrari, 1m 47.947s (0.943s), 226.678kph, 140.851mph
LAPS 45 x 6.797 km, 4.223 miles
DISTANCE 305.865 km, 190.056 miles
STARTERS/FINISHERS 25/11
WEATHER Cloudy with sunny intervals, hot, dry
LAP LEADERS Arnoux 1 (1); Piquet 2-18 (17); Tambay 19-45 (27)
WINNER'S LAPS 1-3 P4, 4-9 P3, 10-18 P2, 19-45 P1
FASTEST LAP N Piquet, Brabham-BMW, 1m 54.035s (lap 7), 214.576kph, 133.331mph
CHAMPIONSHIP Pironi 39, Watson 30, Rosberg 27, Prost 25, Lauda 24

Pos	Driver	Car	Time/gap	Grid	Stops	Tyres
1	P Tambay	Ferrari	1h 27m 25.178s	5	0	G
2	R Arnoux	Renault	−16.379s	3	0	M
3	K Rosberg	Williams-Ford	−1 lap	9	0	G
4	M Alboreto	Tyrrell-Ford	−1 lap	7	0	G
5	B Giacomelli	Alfa Romeo	−1 lap	11	0	M
6	M Surer	Arrows-Ford	−1 lap	26	0	P

Lotus-Ford 91

Round 13/16	AUSTRIAN GP Österreichring
	15 August 1982

Race 370

Elio de Angelis
Lotus-Ford 91 222.204kph, 138.071mph

The Brabham-BMW pair dominated qualifying and, employing their unique one-stop race strategy, rushed off into the distance. But this time at least the pit stops were enacted before the BMWs broke, fuel and tyres on Patrese's leading car replenished in 14s. Now Prost, the last turbo runner in with a chance, held a commanding lead from de Angelis, his Lotus leading the non-turbo brigade, normally the province of Rosberg's Williams. With just five laps remaining the Renault fuel injection packed up, leaving de Angelis 3s ahead of Rosberg. For lap after thrilling lap the two cars closed, Rosberg failing by just 0.050s at the line, the second-closest GP finish of all time. After four seasons, Lotus was a winner again.

POLE POSITION N Piquet, Brabham-BMW, 1m 27.612s (0.359s), 244.158kph, 151.713mph
LAPS 53 x 5.942 km, 3.692 miles
DISTANCE 314.926 km, 195.686 miles
STARTERS/FINISHERS 26/8
WEATHER Sunny, hot, dry
LAP LEADERS Piquet 1 (1); R Patrese, Brabham-BMW 2-27 (26); A Prost, Renault 28-48 (21); de Angelis 49-53 (5)
WINNER'S LAPS 1 P6, 2-14 P5, 15-17 P4, 18-27 P3, 28-48 P2, 49-53 P1
FASTEST LAP N Piquet, Brabham-BMW, 1m 33.699s (lap 5), 228.297kph, 141.857mph
CHAMPIONSHIP Pironi 39, Rosberg 33, Watson 30, Lauda 26, Prost 25

Pos	Driver	Car	Time/gap	Grid	Stops	Tyres
1	E de Angelis	Lotus-Ford	1h 25m 2.212s	7	0	G
2	K Rosberg	Williams-Ford	−0.050s	6	0	G
3	J Laffite	Ligier-Matra	−1 lap	14	0	M
4	P Tambay	Ferrari	−1 lap	4	1	G
5	N Lauda	McLaren-Ford	−1 lap	10	0	M
6	M Baldi	Arrows-Ford	−1 lap	23	0	P

Round 14/16	SWISS GP Dijon-Prenois
	29 August 1982

Race 371

Keke Rosberg
Williams-Ford FW08 196.796kph, 122.283mph

Rosberg didn't have to wait long for his maiden victory. The circumstances were not dissimilar in character to his near-miss in Austria, closing down the leader in a final charge for the line. Prost had led from lap 2 but in the closing stages, hobbled by skirt-damage, he was in danger from his teammate. But equally, both Renaults were under pressure from the meteoric Rosberg. With a handful of laps remaining Arnoux's fuel injection packed up, giving Rosberg a clear run at Prost, who he passed on the penultimate lap despite the (French) organisers attempting to bring things to an early conclusion. With Pironi in hospital and Watson not scoring for the seventh successive race, Rosberg's maiden victory suddenly made him title favourite.

POLE POSITION Prost, Renault, 1m 01.380s (0.360s), 222.874kph, 138.487mph
LAPS 80 x 3.800 km, 2.361 miles
DISTANCE 304.000 km, 188.897 miles
STARTERS/FINISHERS 25/16
WEATHER Sunny, hot, dry
LAP LEADERS R Arnoux, Renault 1 (1); Prost 2-78 (77); Rosberg 79-80 (2)
WINNER'S LAPS 1-4 P6, 5 P5, 6-39 P4, 40-72 P3, 73-78 P2, 79-80 P1
FASTEST LAP Prost, Renault, 1m 07.477s (lap 2), 202.736kph, 125.974mph
CHAMPIONSHIP Rosberg 42, Pironi 39, Prost 31, Watson 30, Lauda 30

Pos	Driver	Car	Time/gap	Grid	Stops	Tyres
1	K Rosberg	Williams-Ford	1h 32m 41.087s	8	0	G
2	A Prost	Renault	−4.442s	1	0	M
3	N Lauda	McLaren-Ford	−1m 0.343s	4	0	M
4	N Piquet	Brabham-BMW	−1 lap	6	1	G
5	R Patrese	Brabham-BMW	−1 lap	3	0	G
6	E de Angelis	Lotus-Ford	−1 lap	15	0	G

Williams-Ford FW08

Round 15/16	**ITALIAN GP** Monza		
	12 September 1982		Race 372

Mario Andretti, recalled to the Scuderia for Monza, did the business for the *tifosi* with a wonderful pole. Unusually the Renault's qualified 'third' behind the Ferraris and the Brabhams, but it was Arnoux from P6 who led lap 1. That he was never headed and finished in front of the Ferrari pair may have influenced the fact that at Monza 12 months on René Arnoux was a Ferrari driver. This wasn't a great race but, as so often, an unexciting race result can add intrigue to the interrelated championship battle. In this case, with Rosberg finishing out of the points in eighth, Watson's fourth gave the Ulsterman the faintest hope possible of beating the Finn to the title. Rosberg required just one point, whereas Watson needed to win.

René Arnoux

Renault RE30B 219.535kph, 136.413mph

POLE POSITION M Andretti, Ferrari, 1m 28.473s (0.035s), 236.004kph, 146.646mph
LAPS 52 x 5.800 km, 3.604 miles
DISTANCE 301.600 km, 187.406 miles
STARTERS/FINISHERS 26/12
WEATHER Sunny, hot, dry
LAP LEADERS Arnoux 1-52 (52)
WINNER'S LAPS 1-52 P1
FASTEST LAP Arnoux, Renault, 1m 33.619 lap 25), 223.032kph, 138.585mph
CHAMPIONSHIP Rosberg 42, Pironi 39, Watson 33, Prost 31, Lauda 30

Pos	Driver	Car	Time/gap	Grid	Stops	Tyres
1	R Arnoux	Renault	1h 22m 25.734s	6	0	M
2	P Tambay	Ferrari	−14.064s	3	0	G
3	M Andretti	Ferrari	−48.452s	1	0	G
4	J Watson	McLaren-Ford	−1m 27.845s	12	0	M
5	M Alboreto	Tyrrell-Ford	−1 lap	11	0	G
6	E Cheever	Ligier-Matra	−1 lap	14	0	M

Tyrrell-Ford 011

CAESARS PALACE GP Las Vegas

25 September 1982   **Race 373**

Michele Alboreto

Tyrrell-Ford 011 161.111kph, 100.110mph

In many ways the final round was a microcosm of the season: Prost losing the lead to the winner in the closing stages and the Brabhams expiring before half-distance. Alboreto won, his maiden victory the first Tyrrell triumph in over four years. Qualifying third, Michele paced himself, his car and his tyres to perfection, taking the lead on lap 54. Watson made a brilliant effort to win. Qualifying difficulties had him P11 on lap 1, chasing Alboreto by lap 20, but tyre vibrations ruled out victory. In any case, all Keke Rosberg needed to land the world championship was a points finish, which is exactly what he did with a circumspect fifth. Although neither car finished, the constructors' title went to Ferrari, the first turbo champions.

POLE POSITION Prost, Renault, 1m 16.356s (0.430s), 172.088kph, 106.931mph
LAPS 75 x 3.650 km, 2.268 miles
DISTANCE 273.749 km, 170.100 miles
STARTERS/FINISHERS 24/13
WEATHER Cloudy with sunny intervals, hot, dry
LAP LEADERS Prost 1,15-51 (38); R Arnoux, Renault 2-14 (13); Alboreto 52-75 (24)
WINNER'S LAPS 1-19 P3, 20-51 P2, 52-75 P1
FASTEST LAP Alboreto, Tyrrell-Ford, 1m 19.639s (lap 59), 164.994kph, 102.523mph
CHAMPIONSHIP Rosberg 44, Pironi 39, Watson 39, Prost 34, Lauda 30

Pos	Driver	Car	Time/gap	Grid	Stops	Tyres
1	M Alboreto	Tyrrell-Ford	1h 41m 56.888s	3	0	G
2	J Watson	McLaren-Ford	−27.292s	9	0	M
3	E Cheever	Ligier-Matra	−56.450s	4	0	M
4	A Prost	Renault	−1m 8.648s	1	0	M
5	K Rosberg	Williams-Ford	−1m 11.375s	6	0	G
6	D Daly	Williams-Ford	−1 lap	14	0	G

1982 CHAMPIONSHIP FACTS AND FOLKLORE

- The minimum dry weight for F1 cars was reduced from 585kg (1,289.70lb) to 580kg (1,278.68lb), along with a driver 'survival cell' cockpit protection featuring a compulsory pedal box.
- Ground clearance checks were abolished, eliminating the need for hydro-pneumatic suspension, while fixed, rigid skirts and rubbing strips were now officially permitted.
- The maximum number of race entries was raised from 30 to 34, but the 30-car maximum for qualifying was retained. The maximum number of starters was raised from 24 to 26 except 20 at Monaco.
- For the drivers' title the best 11 results counted from 16 championship rounds, the Argentine GP a casualty of the drivers' superlicence dispute, the race not regaining the F1 calendar for 14 years.
- One factor in this long absence was that at the end of March, Argentinean Carlos Reutemann dropped a bombshell on Williams, announcing his retirement from F1. The Falklands invasion began one week later.
- 1982 was an emotional rollercoaster, sporadic peaks interspersed by numerous troughs. Almost every one of the 16-race series was eventful, but as a whole the prevailing mood of the season was one of anguish rooted in concern over safety and disquiet over political strife.
- The FISA/FOCA wars had generated an absurd breed of car that made unacceptable demands of the driver through massive cornering G-forces combined with 'solid' suspension. On a bumpy track, drivers continued to take a fearful pounding due to the stiff suspensions required to make fixed skirts operate efficiently.
- Additionally, a different form of war – tyre wars – had sustained the folly of super-sticky qualifiers.
- Tambay's spinal problems and Piquet's podium collapse were both symptoms of rock-hard suspension, while the ludicrously short life-cycle of qualifying tyres was instrumental in the tragedy which befell Gilles Villeneuve.
- Super-sticky qualifying tyres, ostensibly banned in 1980, had found their way back into use. Restricted to two sets per car per session, they were proving potentially dangerous because they barely lasted one flying lap, forcing drivers to take unacceptable risks to avoid being baulked by traffic.
- 'Water-cooled brakes' made a brief appearance before being outlawed. In reality they were a thinly disguised attempt to circumnavigate the weight rules in order to keep non-turbo-powered cars competitive.
- Even though the wellbeing of participants was at stake, even their lives, rationality had been abandoned in the face of power politics.
- As well as the loss of their adored Gilles Villeneuve at Zolder, Canada also had to endure a fatal accident at their own Grand Prix the following month, the Montréal track having just been renamed in memoriam Circuit Gilles Villeneuve. Mercifully, Riccardo Paletti was the last driver to die at a Grand Prix race meeting for 12 years, and as a direct result of this and similar episodes 'aborted-start' procedures were introduced.
- But the most disconcerting safety aspect was cars becoming airborne through wheel-to-wheel contact, evident in both the Villeneuve and Pironi accidents and, because it involved spectators, Mass' potentially even more catastrophic crash.
- So safety issues exerted one level of bleakness upon the season while ill-tempered political wrangling and questionable ethics added another: The drivers' strike; the stark blatancy of 'water-cooled brakes'; the San Marino FOCA boycott and, at the same race, the Villeneuve/Pironi affair, all added a sourness which was impossible to ignore.
- To top it all, the championship itself failed to capture the imagination. This is no refection on the eventual champion Keke Rosberg, who was as deserving as the next man, but probably had more to do with the void left by Villeneuve, whose time had come, many hoped and believed.
- Then, just as Pironi emerged as title favourite, he too vanished from the fray.
- The other strong pre-season candidate for champion was Alain Prost, and it is staggering that from 16 championship rounds he and Renault teammate Arnoux only won two races apiece, despite enjoying positions of potential superiority which far surpassed any other team or driver. These included ten poles, leading all but three races, and running P1 in nearly half of all the laps raced during the season. The trouble was, more often than not the Renaults led the laps at the beginning of the race, not when it counted.

- No wonder there was growing frisson in the French camp especially, after six years of pioneering effort, having to watch Ferrari become the first constructor to win the championship with a turbo car.
- The Harvey Postlethwaite designed 126C2 was a significant step forward for Ferrari but rarely showed a clean pair of Goodyears to the rest. It was ironic that Tambay's Hockenheim victory, the day following the Pironi disaster and driving Villeneuve's No27, was the race which decisively put Ferrari on course for the constructors' title.
- Mario Andretti's two late-season appearances for the beleaguered Ferrari team drew a line beneath his fine GP career.
- The third team to embrace turbo technology, once they ditched the 'water-cooled brakes' farce, was Brabham. Piquet demonstrated his belief in and commitment to the project, accepting the peaks and troughs associated with race-proving the BMW turbo, particularly exemplified by his failure to qualify in Detroit followed by victory in Montréal one week later.
- This particular success was accomplished without the benefit of the mid-race fuel stop, a smart tactic introduced by Brabham during the latter part of the season but frustratingly never rewarded. Brabham's reintroduction of refuelling pit stops also saw ovens used to pre-heat fresh soft tyres to optimum working temperature.
- In most cases failure for the Brabham team was down to their engine supplier, the BMW capable of spectacular detonation. But on one notorious occasion, at Hockenheim, the particular circumstances for Piquet's exit led to an undignified trackside brawl, hardly the behaviour expected of the reigning world champion.

- A former world champion, Niki Lauda, returned from a two-year sabbatical. At his first race back he led the drivers' 'strike' over superlicences, and at his third race back he won.
- He and teammate Watson won two races apiece for the resurgent McLaren team, but their switch to Michelin radials produced a somewhat inconsistent performance that occasionally could produce exceptional results, typified by Watson's Detroit victory.
- The first event staged around the streets of Motown saw John Watson establish a remarkable record, P17 being the lowest-ever grid slot for a winner.
- Indeed, Watson was a championship contender throughout the season, even mathematically at the final race, but a long lean spell from mid-season destroyed his prospects.
- The other Ford DFV successes were singleton wins by Lotus and Tyrrell – each the first in four years – and for reigning double champions Williams, who also experimented with a six-wheeler with four rear driven wheels.
- It was this unprecedented spread of victories between 11 drivers across seven teams which enabled Keke Rosberg to win his championship with just a single victory.
- But this most disagreeable of seasons still had a sting in the tail. In December, Colin Chapman, the founder of Lotus and great visionary in GP racing car design, died prematurely at the age of only 54.
- The 0.050s victory by Elio de Angelis in Austria was not only the second-closest finish of all time, it was also the 150th DFV victory, and, from his 301 races at the helm, it was poignantly Colin Chapman's final F1 triumph. Perhaps appropriately it was the 72nd Lotus championship victory, a memento of probably Chapman's greatest creation, the Lotus 72.

RACE 370, Austrian GP: For lap after thrilling lap Rosberg (6) closed on de Angelis (11), failing by just 0.050 seconds at the line, the second-closest GP finish of all time.

Championship ranking	Championship points	Driver nationality	1982 Drivers Championship		Races contested	Race victories	Podiumse excl. victories	Races led	Lights to flag victories	Laps led	Poles	Fastest laps	Triple Crowns
			Driver	Car									
1	44	FIN	Keke Rosberg	Williams-Ford	15	1	5	3		80	1		
2	39	FRA	Didier Pironi	Ferrari	10	2	4	4		80	2	2	
3	39	GBR	John Watson	McLaren-Ford	15	2	3	2		28		1	
4	34	FRA	Alain Prost	Renault	16	2	2	7		258	5	4	1
5	30	AUT	Niki Lauda	McLaren-Ford	14	2	1	2		128		1	
6	28	FRA	René Arnoux	Renault	16	2	2	10	1	204	5	1	
7	25	FRA	Patrick Tambay	Ferrari	6	1	2	1		27			
8	25	ITA	Michele Alboreto	Tyrrell-Ford	16	1	1	1		24		1	
9	23	ITA	Elio de Angelis	Lotus-Ford	15	1		1		5			
10	21	ITA	Riccardo Patrese	Brabham-Ford (5) Brabham-BMW (10)	15	1	2	3		33		2	
11	20	BRA	Nelson Piquet	Brabham-Ford (2) Brabham-BMW (12)	14	1	1	6		139	1	2	
12	15	USA	Eddie Cheever	Ligier-Matra	14		3						
13	8	IRL	Derek Daly	Theodore-Ford (3) Williams-Ford (12)	15								
14	7	GBR	Nigel Mansell	Lotus-Ford	13		1						
15	6	ARG	Carlos Reutemann	Williams-Ford	2		1						
15	6	CAN	Gilles Villeneuve	Ferrari	4		1	2		40			
17	5	ITA	Andrea de Cesaris	Alfa Romeo	16		1	1		14.5	1		
17	5	FRA	Jacques Laffite	Ligier-Matra	15		1						
19	4	USA	Mario Andretti	Williams-Ford (1) Ferrari (2)	3		1				1		
20	3	FRA	Jean-Pierre Jarier	Osella-Ford	13								
21	3	SUI	Marc Surer	Arrows-Ford	12								
22	2	GER	Manfred Winkelhock	ATS-Ford	13								
22	2	CHL	Elio Salazar	ATS-Ford	13								
22	2	ITA	Bruno Giacomelli	Alfa Romeo	16								
25	2	ITA	Mauro Baldi	Arrows-Ford	11								
26	1	BRA	Chico Serra	Fittipaldi-Ford	9								
-	0	GBR	Derek Warwick	Toleman-Hart	10							1	
-	0	GBR	Brian Henton	Arrows-Ford (1) Tyrrell-Ford (13)	14							1	

Championship ranking	Championship points	Team/Marque nationality	1982 Constructors Championship		Engine maker nationality	Races contested	Race victories	1-2 finishes	Podiums excl. victories	Races led	Laps led	Poles	Fastest laps
			Chassis	Engine									
1	74	ITA	Ferrari 126C2	Ferrari 1.5 V6t	ITA	14	3	1	8	4	147	3	2
2	69	GBR	McLaren MP4B, MP4	Ford Cosworth 3.0 V8	GBR	15	4		4	4	156		2
3	62	FRA	Renault RE30B	Renault 1.5 V6t	FRA	16	4	1	4	13	462	10	5
4	58	GBR	Williams FW08, FW07D, FW07C	Ford Cosworth 3.0 V8	GBR	15	1		6	3	80	1	
5	30	GBR	Lotus 91, 87B	Ford Cosworth 3.0 V8	GBR	15	1		1	1	5		
6	25	GBR	Tyrrell 011	Ford Cosworth 3.0 V8	GBR	16	1		1	1	24		2
7	22	GBR	Brabham BT50	BMW 1.5 4t	GER	12	1	0.5	1	5	136	1	3
8	20	FRA	Ligier JS19, JS17B, JS17	Matra 3.0 V12	FRA	15			4				
9	19	GBR	Brabham BT49D, BT49C	Ford Cosworth 3.0 V8	GBR	5	1	0.5	2	2	36		1
10	7	ITA	Alfa Romeo 182, 179D	Alfa Romeo 3.0 V12	ITA	16			1	1	14.5	1	
11	5	GBR	Arrows A4, A5, A3	Ford Cosworth 3.0 V8	GBR	14							
12	4	GER	ATS D5	Ford Cosworth 3.0 V8	GBR	15							
13	3	ITA	Osella FA1C, FA1D	Ford Cosworth 3.0 V8	GBR	13							
14	1	BRA	Fittipaldi F8D, F9	Ford Cosworth 3.0 V8	GBR	9							
-	0	GBR	Toleman TG181C, TG183	Hart 1.5 4t	GBR	11							1

1983

Piquet power blows Prost away

THE TALE OF THE TITLE

- In a late-season charge Nelson Piquet blitzed hot favourite Prost, snatching the title in the finale shoot-out.
- An end of season Brabham-BMW hat-trick brought Piquet the accolade 'first turbo drivers' champion'.
- Prost's 14-point lead melted over the final four rounds, his Zandvoort mistake starting the rot.
- Yet again, turbo pioneers Renault went away empty-handed and, amid recriminations, fired both drivers.
- Turbos dominated the season, Brabham-BMW, Ferrari and Renault each winning four races.
- Ferrari won the constructors' cup, displaying superior consistency over their more frail turbo rivals.
- FISA finally outlawed ground effect, 'flat-bottomed' Ford-Cosworth atmo cars completely outclassed.
- Street circuits gave the DFV its last hurrah, one win each for McLaren, Williams and Tyrrell.
- For McLaren, Watson's amazing Long Beach victory began from P22, unprecedented before or since.
- In late season McLaren debuted their TAG Porsche engine, and Honda returned after 14 years away.
- This time their F1 incursion was not as constructor but an engine supplier, partnering with Williams for 1984.
- And not forgetting: no more 'solid' suspension; accidents sharply reduced.

THE CHASE FOR THE CHAMPIONSHIP

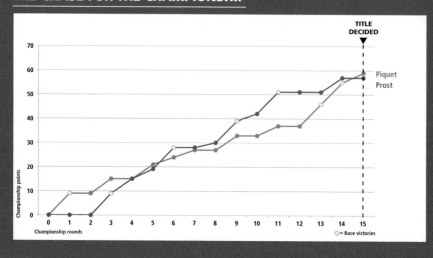

BRAZILIAN GP Rio de Janeiro
13 March 1983   Race 374

Nelson Piquet
Brabham-BMW BT52 175.335kph, 108.948mph

With ground effect banned, new champion Rosberg unexpectedly out-qualified the turbos to give the 'flat-bottomed' Williams pole. Adopting fuel-stop strategy, Rosberg scampered off pursued by the also light-running Brabhams. In seven laps Piquet displaced Rosberg and, despite gearbox scares in practice, the Brabham-BMW ran like clockwork, the stop for fuel/tyres also faultless. By contrast, a flash-fire disrupted Rosberg's pit stop and he fell to eighth. On fresh tyres, Keke tigered back to second but was disqualified for a push-start during the frenetic stop. McLaren were strong, Watson in a threatening P2 at half-distance when his engine seized while Lauda finished third. Tyre vibrations ruined front-row qualifier Prost's race.

POLE POSITION Rosberg, Williams-Ford, 1m 34.526s (0.146s), 191.604kph, 119.057mph
LAPS 63 x 5.031 km, 3.126 miles
DISTANCE 316.953 km, 196.945 miles
STARTERS/FINISHERS 26/14
WEATHER Cloudy with sunny intervals, hot, dry
LAP LEADERS Rosberg 1-6 (6); Piquet 7-63 (57)
WINNER'S LAPS 1 P3, 2-6 P2, 7-63 P1
FASTEST LAP Piquet, Brabham-BMW, 1m 39.829s (lap 4), 181.426kph, 112.733mph
CHAMPIONSHIP Piquet 9, Lauda 4, Laffite 3, Tambay 2, Surer 1

Pos	Driver	Car	Time/gap	Grid	Stops	Tyres
1	N Piquet	Brabham-BMW	1h 48m 27.731s	4	1	M
dsq	K Rosberg	Williams-Ford	push start	1	1	G
3	N Lauda	McLaren-Ford	–51.883s	9	0	M
4	J Laffite	Williams-Ford	–1m 13.951s	18	0	G
5	P Tambay	Ferrari	–1m 18.117s	3	0	G
6	M Surer	Arrows-Ford	–1m 18.207s	20	0	G

McLaren-Ford MP4/1C

UNITED STATES GP WEST Long Beach
27 March 1983   Race 375

John Watson
McLaren-Ford MP4/1C 129.753kph, 80.625mph

Two Ferraris then two Williamses filled the sharp end of the grid. Near the back, the McLarens started P22 and P23. Around two hours later Watson led in a McLaren 1-2. To prove this extraordinary result was about drivers and Michelins rather than reliability and attrition, a Ferrari finished third, a Williams fourth. True, around lap 25 the McLarens were assisted by the elimination of three of a front-running quartet. In a failed overtaking attempt, Rosberg punted out leader Tambay while at the very next corner Jarier paid Rosberg a similar compliment, both out. The survivor, Laffite's Williams, led until the remarkable Watson overtook him on lap 45 of 75. Watson made numerous passes that day, most crucially teammate Lauda on lap 33.

POLE POSITION P Tambay, Ferrari, 1m 26.117s (0.818s), 136.907kph, 85.070mph
LAPS 75 x 3.275 km, 2.035 miles
DISTANCE 245.626 km, 152.625 miles
STARTERS/FINISHERS 26/12
WEATHER Sunny, hot, dry
LAP LEADERS Tambay 1-25 (25); Laffite 26-44 (19); Watson 45-75 (31)
WINNER'S LAPS 1-3 P20, 4-5 P21, 6 P20, 7-10 P19, 11 P18, 12, P17, 13-14 P16, 15 P15, 16-23 P13, 24 P12, 25 P10, 26 P7, 27 P5, 28-32 P4, 33-43 P3, 44 P2, 45-75 P1
FASTEST LAP Lauda, McLaren-Ford, 1m 28.330s (lap 42), 133.477kph, 82.939mph
CHAMPIONSHIP Lauda 10, Piquet 9, Watson 9, Laffite 6, Arnoux 4

Pos	Driver	Car	Time/gap	Grid	Stops	Tyres
1	J Watson	McLaren-Ford	1h 53m 34.889s	22	0	M
2	N Lauda	McLaren-Ford	–27.993s	23	0	M
3	R Arnoux	Ferrari	–1m 13.638s	2	2	G
4	J Laffite	Williams-Ford	–1 lap	4	0	G
5	M Surer	Arrows-Ford	–1 lap	16	0	G
6	J Cecotto	Theodore-Ford	–1 lap	17	0	G

Renault RE40

Round 3/15	**FRENCH GP** Paul Ricard						**Alain Prost**
	17 April 1983					**Race 376**	Renault RE40 199.767kph, 124.129mph

Pre-season championship favourite Prost began his title claim with a home-race hat-trick for Renault, the Régie's fourth from the last five. Posting an incredible pole in the RE40 and employing fuel-stop strategy for the first time, Prost posted fastest lap and led all but three mid-race laps, this the result of a fumbled pit stop. Even with this hiccup, Prost beat Piquet by a convincing 30s, the ill-handling but powerful Brabham only 10s clear of Cheever's number two Renault. The long Mistral straight meant the DFV-engined cars were totally outclassed, Lauda's McLaren the highest atmo qualifier at P12. Rosberg, starting P16, drove his heart out to finish fifth, but lapped. Prost won, but with P2 Piquet retook the championship lead.

POLE POSITION Prost, Renault, 1m 36.672s (2.308s), 216.360kph, 134.440mph
LAPS 54 x 5.810 km, 3.610 miles
DISTANCE 313.740 km, 194.949 miles
STARTERS/FINISHERS 26/13
WEATHER Cloudy, cool, dry
LAP LEADERS Prost 1-29, 33-54 (51); Piquet 30-32 (3)
WINNER'S LAPS 1-29 P1, 30-32 P2, 33-54 P1
FASTEST LAP Prost, Renault, 1m 42.695s (lap 34), 203.671kph, 126.555mph
CHAMPIONSHIP Piquet 15, Lauda 10, Watson 9, Prost 9, Laffite 7

Pos	Driver	Car	Time/gap	Grid	Stops	Tyres
1	A Prost	Renault	1h 34m 13.913s	1	1	M
2	N Piquet	Brabham-BMW	−29.720s	6	1	M
3	E Cheever	Renault	−40.232s	2	1	M
4	P Tambay	Ferrari	−1m 6.880s	11	1	G
5	K Rosberg	Williams-Ford	−1 lap	16	1	G
6	J Laffite	Williams-Ford	−1 lap	19	1	G

Round 4/15	**SAN MARINO GP** Imola						**Patrick Tambay**
	1 May 1983					**Race 377**	Ferrari 126C2B 185.381kph, 115.190mph

Tambay gave the *tifosi* exactly what they wanted: victory for Ferrari No27 twelve months after Gilles' last race. Six laps from the finish the perfect result seemed unlikely as the clearly quicker Brabham-BMW of Patrese closed in. Riccardo had taken the lead from pole-man Arnoux on lap 6 but lost it to Tambay at the pit stops, the delay due to his Brabham overshooting its markings. Having now made up the lost time he went by Tambay just before Tosa, only to lose his composure yet again by going off 30s later. The *tifosi* cheered as the Italian driver hit the tyre wall and their sacred Ferrari went by, driven by a Frenchman. Arnoux spun away second to Prost, and with Piquet stalling on the line Prost and Piquet shared the points table lead.

POLE POSITION Arnoux, Ferrari, 1m 31.238s (0.726s), 198.865kph, 123.569mph
LAPS 60 x 5.040 km, 3.132 miles
DISTANCE 302.400 km, 187.903 miles
STARTERS/FINISHERS 26/12
WEATHER Cloudy with sunny intervals, warm, dry
LAP LEADERS Arnoux 1-5 (5); Patrese 6-33 (28); Tambay 34-60 (27)
WINNER'S LAPS 1-2 P2, 3-19 P3, 20-33 P2, 34-60 P1
FASTEST LAP R Patrese, Brabham-BMW, 1m 34.437s (lap 47), 192.128kph, 119.383mph
CHAMPIONSHIP Piquet 15, Prost 15, Tambay 14, Watson 11, Lauda 10

Pos	Driver	Car	Time/gap	Grid	Stops	Tyres
1	P Tambay	Ferrari	1h 37m 52.460s	3	1	G
2	A Prost	Renault	−48.781s	4	1	M
3	R Arnoux	Ferrari	−1 lap	1	2	G
4	K Rosberg	Williams-Ford	−1 lap	11	1	G
5	J Watson	McLaren-Ford	−1 lap	24	0	M
6	M Surer	Arrows-Ford	−1 lap	12	1	G

Williams-Ford FW08C

| Round 5/15 | **MONACO GP** Monte Carlo | | | | | | **Keke Rosberg** |
| | 15 May 1983 | | | Race 378 | | | Williams-Ford FW08C 129.487kph, 80.459mph |

Fifth race, fifth winner – shades of the 1982 championship lottery. The world champion's second-ever GP win was typical Rosberg. Aided by a brave-hearted decision by Williams to run dry tyres on a damp track, Keke took the race by the scruff of the neck with energy and conviction to lead every lap bar the first. Starting fifth on the grid, he rocketed away on slicks, in the wet, to slot in at Ste Devote behind pole-man Prost on Michelin wets. One lap later, at that very same point, he out-braked Prost and that was that. For over 50 laps a Williams 1-2 looked likely but gearbox problems sidelined Laffite. The other bad news for Williams was that Piquet and Prost had finished second and third behind Rosberg, and further that his Rio disqualification had been upheld.

POLE POSITION Prost, Renault, 1m 24.840s (0.342s), 140.537kph, 87.326mph
LAPS 76 x 3.312 km, 2.058 miles
DISTANCE 251.712 km, 156.407 miles
STARTERS/FINISHERS 20/7
WEATHER Cloudy, damp track then drying
LAP LEADERS Prost 1 (1); Rosberg 2-76 (75)
WINNER'S LAPS 1 P2, 2-76 P1
FASTEST LAP Piquet, Brabham-BMW, 1m 27.283s (lap 69), 136.604kph, 84.882mph
CHAMPIONSHIP Piquet 21, Prost 19, Tambay 17, Rosberg 14, Watson 11

Pos	Driver	Car	Time/gap	Grid	Stops	Tyres
1	K Rosberg	Williams-Ford	1h 56m 38.121s	5	0	G
2	N Piquet	Brabham-BMW	−18.475s	6	1	M
3	A Prost	Renault	−31.366s	1	1	M
4	P Tambay	Ferrari	−1m 4.297s	4	1	G
5	D Sullivan	Tyrrell-Ford	−2 laps	20	0	G
6	M Baldi	Alfa Romeo	−2 laps	13	1	M

| Round 6/15 | **BELGIAN GP** Spa-Francorchamps | | | | | | **Alain Prost** |
| | 22 May 1983 | | | Race 379 | | | Renault RE40 191.729kph, 119.135mph |

After 13 years the F1 circus returned to a splendid new Spa-Francorchamps. A power circuit, the turbos ruled, and following an aborted start it was de Cesaris in the Alfa Romeo V8 turbo who rocketed from row two to lead from Prost on pole. Seven seconds to the good by his stop on lap 19, the dream didn't last, the Alfa pit crew mucking up and then engine failure finishing it on lap 25. So with no serious challenger without de Cesaris, Prost was the first to record a second victory in the year. Piquet held P2 until gearbox maladies dropped him to fourth, Tambay and Cheever completing the podium. The championship was boiling up nicely into a three-way contest between turbo teams Renault, Brabham-BMW and Ferrari.

POLE POSITION A Prost, Renault, 2m 04.615s (0.029s), 200.750kph, 124.740mph
LAPS 40 x 6.949 km, 4.318 miles
DISTANCE 278.620 km, 173.126 miles
STARTERS/FINISHERS 26/14
WEATHER Cloudy with sunny intervals, warm, dry
LAP LEADERS de Cesaris 1-18 (18); Prost 19-22, 24-40 (21); N Piquet 23 (1)
WINNER'S LAPS 1-18 P2, 19-22 P1, 23 P2, 24-40 P1
FASTEST LAP A de Cesaris, Alfa Romeo, 2m 07.493s (lap 17), 196.218kph, 121.924mph
CHAMPIONSHIP Prost 28, Piquet 24, Tambay 23, Rosberg 16, Watson 11

Pos	Driver	Car	Time/gap	Grid	Stops	Tyres
1	A Prost	Renault	1h 27m 11.502s	1	1	M
2	P Tambay	Ferrari	−23.182s	2	1	G
3	E Cheever	Renault	−39.869s	8	1	M
4	N Piquet	Brabham-BMW	−42.295s	4	1	M
5	K Rosberg	Williams-Ford	−50.480s	9	1	G
6	J Laffite	Williams-Ford	−1m 33.107s	11	1	G

Tyrrell-Ford 011

Round 7/15	**UNITED STATES GP** Detroit					
	5 June 1983				**Race 380**	

Fuel strategy pioneers Brabham craftily ran Piquet non-stop, 'heavy' Nelson getting the drop on Arnoux's 'light' pole-sitting Ferrari to lead the opening laps. Once ahead Arnoux galloped away, just managing to make his stop without losing the lead. But two laps later he was out with electrics. Tyrrell had also chosen the non-stop strategy and from mid-distance the little green car, sporting a development Ford Cosworth DFY engine, became a genuine threat to leader Piquet. But with just nine laps to go the matter was resolved when the Brabham pitted with a puncture. So Alboreto's non-stopping Tyrrell beat Rosberg's one-stopping Williams, the 155th and final victory for the DFV-series engine, which filled five of the top six places.

Michele Alboreto
Tyrrell-Ford 011 130.612kph, 81.158mph

POLE POSITION R Arnoux, Ferrari, 1m 44.734s (0.199s), 138.294kph, 85.932mph
LAPS 60 x 4.023 km, 2.500 miles
DISTANCE 241.402 km, 150.000 miles
STARTERS/FINISHERS 26/12
WEATHER Sunny, hot, dry
LAP LEADERS Piquet 1-9, 32-50 (28); Arnoux 10-31 (22); Alboreto 51-60 (10)
WINNER'S LAPS 1-5 P5, 6-7 P4, 8-13 P5, 14-28 P4, 29-31 P3, 32-50 P2, 51 -60 P1
FASTEST LAP Watson, McLaren-Ford, 1m 47.668s (lap 55), 134.526kph, 83.590mph
CHAMPIONSHIP Prost 28, Piquet 27, Tambay 23, Rosberg 22, Watson 15

Pos	Driver	Car	Time/gap	Grid	Stops	Tyres
1	M Alboreto	Tyrrell-Ford	1h 50m 53.669s	6	0	G
2	K Rosberg	Williams-Ford	–7.702s	12	1	G
3	J Watson	McLaren-Ford	–9.283s	21	0	M
4	N Piquet	Brabham-BMW	–1m 12.185s	2	1	M
5	J Laffite	Williams-Ford	–1m 32.603s	20	1	G
6	N Mansell	Lotus-Ford	–1 lap	14	0	P

Round 8/15	**CANADIAN GP** Montréal					
	12 June 1983				**Race 381**	

The following week Arnoux's Ferrari turbo didn't falter and he won from pole. It was a resounding victory, his first for the Scuderia. It was also Goodyear's 150th Grand Prix win. Patrese in the Brabham-BMW pursued Arnoux at a distance for much of the race until gearbox trouble intervened, team-leader Piquet out early with a broken throttle when third. But for a misfire Tambay might have made it a Ferrari 1-2, passed by Cheever's Renault mid-race when the vapour-lock problem was most acute. Prost's Renault was also in trouble, 800 revs short plus a late puncture, but at least netting two points. Against the odds Rosberg's Williams finished fourth and, but for his Rio disqualification, Keke would have been leading the championship at the halfway stage.

René Arnoux
Ferrari 126C2B 170.661kph, 106.044mph

POLE POSITION Arnoux, Ferrari, 1m 28.729s (0.101s), 178.927kph, 111.180mph
LAPS 70 x 4.410 km, 2.740 miles
DISTANCE 308.700 km, 191.817 miles
STARTERS/FINISHERS 26/10
WEATHER Sunny, very hot, dry
LAP LEADERS Arnoux 1-34, 39-70 (66); R Patrese, Brabham-BMW 35-37 (3); Tambay 38 (1)
WINNER'S LAPS 1-34 P1, 35-37 P3, 38 P2, 39-70 P1
FASTEST LAP Tambay, Ferrari, 1m 30.851s (lap 42), 174.748kph, 108.583mph
CHAMPIONSHIP Prost 30, Piquet 27, Tambay 27, Rosberg 25, Arnoux 17

Pos	Driver	Car	Time/gap	Grid	Stops	Tyres
1	R Arnoux	Ferrari	1h 48m 31.838s	1	1	G
2	E Cheever	Renault	–42.029s	6	1	M
3	P Tambay	Ferrari	–52.610s	4	1	G
4	K Rosberg	Williams-Ford	–1m 17.048s	9	1	G
5	A Prost	Renault	–1 lap	2	2	M
6	J Watson	McLaren-Ford	–1 lap	20	0	M

Ferrari 126C2B

<table>
<tr><td>**Round 9/15**</td><td>**BRITISH GP** Silverstone</td><td></td><td>**Alain Prost**</td></tr>
<tr><td></td><td>**16 July 1983**</td><td>**Race 382**</td><td>Renault RE40 224.050kph, 139.218mph</td></tr>
</table>

Ferrari locked out the front row with their new C3, Arnoux's pole lap the first at Silverstone under 70s and over 150mph. The first non-turbo qualifier, Rosberg, was over 4s slower in P13. But on race day Michelin radials were the tyres to have, and after leading the opening 19 laps the scarlet cars were overwhelmed first by Prost and then Piquet, which is how they finished. Tambay salvaged third for Ferrari, while Mansell caused much excitement by finishing fourth in the new Lotus-Renault 94T, having stormed up from P18. Another notable debutant was the Honda V6 turbo installed behind driver Johansson in the new Spirit 201. A third victory gave Prost a useful points advantage, but not decisive, his main rivals finishing 2-3.

POLE POSITION Arnoux, Ferrari, 1m 09.462s (0.642s), 244.550kph, 151.956mph
LAPS 67 x 4.719 km, 2.932 miles
DISTANCE 316.146 km, 196.444 miles
STARTERS/FINISHERS 26/17
WEATHER Sunny, hot, dry
LAP LEADERS Tambay 1-19 (19); Prost 20-36, 42-67 (43); Piquet 37-41 (5)
WINNER'S LAPS 1-13 P3, 14-19 P2, 20-36 P1, 37-41 P2, 42-67 P1
FASTEST LAP Prost, Renault, 1m 14.212s (lap 32), 228.898kph, 142.230mph
CHAMPIONSHIP Prost 39, Piquet 33, Tambay 31, Rosberg 25, Arnoux 19

Pos	Driver	Car	Time/gap	Grid	Stops	Tyres
1	A Prost	Renault	1h 24m 39.780s	3	1	M
2	N Piquet	Brabham-BMW	−19.161s	6	1	M
3	P Tambay	Ferrari	−26.246s	2	1	G
4	N Mansell	Lotus-Renault	−38.952s	18	1	P
5	R Arnoux	Ferrari	−58.874s	1	1	G
6	N Lauda	McLaren-Ford	−1 lap	15	1	M

<table>
<tr><td>**Round 10/15**</td><td>**GERMAN GP** Hockenheim</td><td></td><td>**René Arnoux**</td></tr>
<tr><td></td><td>**7 August 1983**</td><td>**Race 383**</td><td>Ferrari 126C3 210.525kph, 130.814mph</td></tr>
</table>

From their front row slots the race was initially a Ferrari runaway, Arnoux leading. But Tambay's engine lasted just ten laps, leaving Piquet to take up the chase, albeit some 15s in arrears when Arnoux made his stop. Piquet took the lead for seven laps until his own stop, the gap unchanged on resumption. Then quite quickly he whittled down Arnoux's lead to just 5s with six laps to go. But a cracked fuel filter and a sheet of flame signalled the end for Piquet's BMW turbo, Arnoux winning by over a minute. De Cesaris had qualified his Alfa turbo P3, and although never in contention for victory finished second, the team's best result since 1951. Despite loss of fifth gear Prost nudged his championship total forward another three points.

POLE POSITION P Tambay, Ferrari, 1m 47.947s (0.107s), 223.815kph, 139.072mph
LAPS 45 x 6.797 km, 4.223 miles
DISTANCE 305.865 km, 190.056 miles
STARTERS/FINISHERS 26/13
WEATHER Cloudy with sunny intervals, warm, dry
LAP LEADERS Tambay 1 (1); Arnoux 2-23, 31-45 (37); N Piquet, Brabham-BMW 24-30 (7)
WINNER'S LAPS 1 P2, 2-23 P1, 24 P3, 25-30 P2, 31-45 P1
FASTEST LAP Arnoux, Ferrari, 1m 54.035s (lap 12), 214.759kph, 133.445mph
CHAMPIONSHIP Prost 42, Piquet 33, Tambay 31, Arnoux 28, Rosberg 25

Pos	Driver	Car	Time/gap	Grid	Stops	Tyres
1	R Arnoux	Ferrari	1h 27m 10.319s	2	1	G
2	A de Cesaris	Alfa Romeo	−1m 10.652s	3	1	M
3	R Patrese	Brabham-BMW	−1m 44.093s	8	1	M
4	A Prost	Renault	−2m 0.750s	5	1	M
5	J Watson	McLaren-Ford	−1 lap	23	1	M
6	J Laffite	Williams-Ford	−1 lap	15	1	G

Round 11/15	**AUSTRIAN GP** Österreichring						**Alain Prost**	
	14 August 1983				**Race 384**		Renault RE40 223.495kph, 138.873mph	

For the third race running Ferrari wrapped up the front row. Tambay led 21 laps until a crass piece of baulking by backmarker Jarier gave Arnoux the lead, Piquet also getting by. Shortly afterwards slick pit-work by Brabham got Piquet ahead, but only six laps after his stop, with 15 still remaining, Arnoux and Prost went by as the BMW lost boost pressure. The two French former teammates fought hard until, as the Ferrari's defective gearbox hesitated once too often, Prost got past to lead the final six laps for his fourth victory of the season and a 14-point championship lead. As Prost crossed the line the Renault pit erupted with joy. At last it looked as though Renault, and Prost, were on course for the titles few would deny they deserved.

POLE POSITION P Tambay, Ferrari, 1m 29.871s (0.064s), 238.021kph, 147.899mph
LAPS 53 x 5.942 km, 3.692 miles
DISTANCE 314.926 km, 195.686 miles
STARTERS/FINISHERS 26/13
WEATHER Sunny, hot, dry
LAP LEADERS Tambay 1-21 (21); Arnoux 22-27, 38-47 (16); Piquet 28-37 (10); Prost 48-53 (6)
WINNER'S LAPS 1-21 P4, 22 P5, 23-26 P7, 27-28 P6, 29-30 P5, 31-37 P3, 38-47 P2, 48-53 P1
FASTEST LAP Prost, Renault, 1m 33.961s (lap 20), 227.660kph, 141.462mph
CHAMPIONSHIP Prost 51, Piquet 37, Arnoux 34, Tambay 31, Rosberg 25

Pos	Driver	Car	Time/gap	Grid	Stops	Tyres
1	A Prost	Renault	1h 24m 32.745s	5	1	M
2	R Arnoux	Ferrari	–6.835s	2	1	G
3	N Piquet	Brabham-BMW	–27.659s	4	1	M
4	E Cheever	Renault	–28.395s	8	1	M
5	N Mansell	Lotus-Renault	–1 lap	3	1	P
6	N Lauda	McLaren-Ford	–2 laps	14	1	M

Round 12/15	**DUTCH GP** Zandvoort						**René Arnoux**	
	28 August 1983				**Race 385**		Ferrari 126C3 186.107kph, 115.642mph	

From his first pole this year, Piquet established an early lead over Prost until tyre wear reduced the gap. Around half-distance, despite imminent pit stops for both, Prost attempted an uncharacteristically clumsy passing manoeuvre at Tarzan which eliminated both cars, the hapless Piquet immediately, the damaged Renault smiting the barriers two miles further on. This presented Ferrari with a fortuitous 1-2 victory led by Arnoux. At the start it hadn't looked likely, Arnoux a lowly P9 and Tambay cooking his clutch to fall from P2 to P21. As a bemused Forghieri said afterwards, 'Everyone get out the way for us.' McLaren debuted their TAG Porsche turbo promisingly but Watson stole the plaudits with a stunning drive to third in the atmo car.

POLE POSITION N Piquet, Brabham-BMW, 1m 15.630s (0.740s), 202.396kph, 125.763mph
LAPS 72 x 4.252 km, 2.642 miles
DISTANCE 306.144 km, 190.229 miles
STARTERS/FINISHERS 26/14
WEATHER Overcast, cool, dry
LAP LEADERS Piquet 1-41 (41); Arnoux 42-72 (31)
WINNER'S LAPS 1 P7, 2-4 P6, 5-14 P5, 15-21 P4, 22-41 P3, 42-72 P1
FASTEST LAP R Arnoux, Renault, 1m 19.863s (lap 33), 191.668kph, 119.097mph
CHAMPIONSHIP Prost 51, Arnoux 43, Piquet 37, Tambay 37, Rosberg 25

Pos	Driver	Car	Time/gap	Grid	Stops	Tyres
1	R Arnoux	Ferrari	1h 38m 41.950s	10	1	G
2	P Tambay	Ferrari	–20.839s	2	1	G
3	J Watson	McLaren-Ford	–43.741s	15	1	M
4	D Warwick	Toleman-Hart	–1m 16.839s	7	1	P
5	M Baldi	Alfa Romeo	–1m 24.292s	12	1	M
6	M Alboreto	Tyrrell-Ford	–1 lap	18	1	G

Round 13/15	**ITALIAN GP** Monza						**Nelson Piquet**	
	11 September 1983				**Race 386**		Brabham-BMW BT52B 217.549kph, 135.179mph	

Patrese took pole but his BMW lasted just two laps, after which team-leader Piquet was never threatened, able to turn down his boost and stroke home, an utterly dominant victory in Ferrari's backyard. For the *tifosi* Arnoux chased vainly to finish second, Tambay's down-on-power Ferrari fourth. Sandwiched between them came Cheever, significantly the only Renault to finish. These were crucial results for Ferrari, seizing the lead from Renault in their quest to retain the constructors' cup, while in the drivers', Arnoux now lay just one shy of points-leader Prost with only two rounds remaining. As for Prost's race, soon after the start he flat-spotted his tyres avoiding an accident, but more fundamentally the Renault turbo did not last beyond half-distance.

POLE POSITION R Patrese, Brabham-BMW, 1m 29.122s (0.528s), 234.286kph, 145.578mph
LAPS 52 x 5.800 km, 3.604 miles
DISTANCE 301.600 km, 187.406 miles
STARTERS/FINISHERS 26/13
WEATHER Sunny, warm, dry
LAP LEADERS Patrese 1-2 (2); Piquet 3-52 (50)
WINNER'S LAPS 1-2 P2, 3-52 P1
FASTEST LAP Piquet, Brabham-BMW, 1m 34.431s (lap 20), 221.114kph, 137.394mph
CHAMPIONSHIP Prost 51, Arnoux 49, Piquet 46, Tambay 40, Rosberg 25

Pos	Driver	Car	Time/gap	Grid	Stops	Tyres
1	N Piquet	Brabham-BMW	1h 23m 10.880s	4	1	M
2	R Arnoux	Ferrari	–10.212s	3	1	G
3	E Cheever	Renault	–18.612s	7	1	M
4	P Tambay	Ferrari	–29.023s	2	1	G
5	E de Angelis	Lotus-Renault	–53.680s	8	1	P
6	D Warwick	Toleman-Hart	–1m 13.348s	12	1	P

Brabham-BMW BT52B

Round 14/15	**EUROPEAN GP** Brands Hatch					**Nelson Piquet**
	25 September 1983			Race 387		Brabham-BMW BT52B 198.246kph, 123.184mph

Patrese's Brabham-BMW led the opening laps until an overtaking attempt by surprise pole-sitter de Angelis in the Lotus-Renault had both cars spinning at South Bank. Piquet swept by to a second successive victory, only this time, from lap 15 onwards, Prost was an ever-present threat 10s back, the time it had taken him to make up ground from his poor P8 grid-slot. So Prost and Piquet went to the Kyalami finale separated by just two points, while the chances for the Ferrari drivers faded. Tambay was running third late in the race when his brakes failed, while Arnoux spun away fifth on lap 19 and with it all but a very slim chance of championship glory. Mansell qualified P3 in the Lotus-Renault, and after a slow start finished there.

POLE POSITION E de Angelis, Lotus-Renault, 1m 12.092s (0.366s), 210.073kph, 130.533mph
LAPS 76 x 4.207 km, 2.614 miles
DISTANCE 319.719 km, 198.664 miles
STARTERS/FINISHERS 26/15
WEATHER Sunny, hot, dry
LAP LEADERS R Patrese, Brabham-BMW 1-10 (10); Piquet 11-76 (66)
WINNER'S LAPS 1 P4, 2-10 P3, 11-76 P1
FASTEST LAP Mansell, Lotus-Renault, 1m 14.342s (lap 70), 203.715kph, 126.583mph
CHAMPIONSHIP Prost 57, Piquet 55, Arnoux 49, Tambay 40, Rosberg 25

Pos	Driver	Car	Time/gap	Grid	Stops	Tyres
1	N Piquet	Brabham-BMW	1h 36m 45.865s	4	1	M
2	A Prost	Renault	−6.571s	8	1	M
3	N Mansell	Lotus-Renault	−30.315s	3	1	P
4	A de Cesaris	Alfa Romeo	−34.396s	14	1	M
5	D Warwick	Toleman-Hart	−44.915s	11	1	P
6	B Giacomelli	Toleman-Hart	−52.190s	12	1	P

Round 15/15	**SOUTH AFRICAN GP** Kyalami					**Riccardo Patrese**
	15 October 1983			Race 388		Brabham-BMW BT52B 202.941kph, 126.102mph

The Brabham team showed immense self-belief to win both race and drivers' title. A Piquet hat-trick would settle it regardless of Prost, so he set a blistering winning pace on an exceptionally light fuel-load in the added hope that the Renault turbo might not stand the pace. Just before half-distance – Prost holding a 'losing' P3 behind the Brabhams – that was exactly what happened. As Piquet no longer needed to win, just score enough points, he turned down the wick and stroked home to third place and the championship. Ferrari won the constructors' title and portents for next season were the promising debut of the Williams-Honda by Rosberg and the performance of Lauda's McLaren-TAG, getting to within 4s of Patrese towards the end before electrics intervened.

POLE POSITION P Tambay, Ferrari, 1m 06.554s (0.238s), 221.991kph, 137.939mph
LAPS 77 x 4.104 km, 2.550 miles
DISTANCE 316.008 km, 196.358 miles
STARTERS/FINISHERS 26/12
WEATHER Sunny, hot, dry
LAP LEADERS Piquet 1-59 (59); Patrese 60-77 (18)
WINNER'S LAPS 1-59 P2, 60-77 P1
FASTEST LAP Piquet, Brabham-BMW, 1m 09.948s (lap 6), 211.220kph, 131.246mph
CHAMPIONSHIP Piquet 59, Prost 57, Arnoux 49, Tambay 40, Rosberg 27

Pos	Driver	Car	Time/gap	Grid	Stops	Tyres
1	R Patrese	Brabham-BMW	1h 33m 25.708s	3	1	M
2	A de Cesaris	Alfa Romeo	−9.319s	9	1	M
3	N Piquet	Brabham-BMW	−21.969s	2	1	M
4	D Warwick	Toleman-Hart	−1 lap	13	1	P
5	K Rosberg	Williams-Honda	−1 lap	6	1	G
6	E Cheever	Renault	−1 lap	14	1	M

- For 1983 the best 11 results from 15 championship rounds counted for the drivers' title.
- For the first time a GP was held at a splendid new circuit at Spa-Francorchamps, while the European GP, held at Brands Hatch, was the first occasion this designation had been used as its own GP entity.
- Four-wheel drive and cars with more than four wheels were banned; minimum dry weight reduced to 540kg (1,190.5lb); the dimensions for the pedal box were increased, and rear wing width and overhang was reduced, with the height raised to improve rearward vision.
- But the most radical as well as the most telling regulation change for 1983 was an obligatory flat bottom between front and rear wheels, this and the banning of side-skirts effectively eliminating ground effect and so reducing cornering speeds, at least in the short term.
- The 1983 championship would therefore be fought between turbo teams, the atmo cars largely making up the numbers, with the smart money on Ferrari, Brabham-BMW and particularly Renault, these three teams fielding second-generation turbo designs.
- The 90° V6 EF1 Renault engine now featured water injection for combustion chamber cooling, with power reaching

RACE 385, Dutch GP: Prost attempted an uncharacteristically clumsy pass on Piquet's Brabham-BMW at Tarzan, eliminating both cars, the damaged Renault hitting the barriers.

650bhp at 11,500rpm. This compared with the four-cylinder BMW's 640bhp at 11,000rpm and the 620bhp at 11,500rpm of the 120° V6 Ferrari engine.
- And so it transpired that pre-season favourites and long-term championship leaders Prost and Renault appeared well on course to scoop the honours, their fourth victory giving Prost a 14-point lead with but four races to go.
- But it all went terribly wrong, Prost's mistake at Zandvoort bursting the Renault bubble. Alain only added a further six points in those final four races to Piquet's additional 22.
- This dire conclusion to their campaign should hardly be heaped on Prost alone, although at Zandvoort Renault did lose their precious lead in the constructors' championship to Ferrari who scored maximum points, Renault zero.
- Anyway Prost, so often the victim of his equipment, felt he had been made the fall-guy for collective failure and after three seasons left the Régie for pastures new with nine race victories to his name.
- Ferrari won the constructors' championship on merit, the 126C3 keeping Arnoux in with a chance of the title until the end, a chance he somewhat squandered. Once Arnoux broke through for the Scuderia in Canada, he won three from five starts, although Tambay delivered the stronger first half to the season.
- After winning with No27 at Imola, Patrick Tambay phoned Gilles Villeneuve's wife to utter one word, 'Vengé.'
- On the tyre-wars front Michelin beat Goodyear 9–6, and on balance, at least in race trim, the Goodyear-shod Ferraris were sometimes at a disadvantage compared with Renault and Brabham on their Michelin radials. Ferrari's unexpected 1-2 in Canada, however, was Goodyear's 150th Grand Prix win.
- Where Ferrari did enjoy some advantage was in the reliability stakes. Turbos in general continued to be fickle machines, not least Gordon Murray's striking-looking dart-shaped Brabham-BMW BT52. Capable of blistering pace, it led more races and more laps than either Ferrari or Renault yet finished behind these two in the constructors' championship, Patrese's contribution minimal.
- But it did provide a potent mount for Nelson Piquet, the combo coming on good and strong in a sensational closing sequence to the season to snatch the title at the 11th hour and the kudos of first turbo-powered drivers' champion, an accolade probably of greater significance to turbo pioneers Renault than to anyone else.
- Alfa Romeo switched to turbo power with a V8 engine and finished two races in second place, but that was as close as they would ever get to revisiting their 1950s successes.
- Towards the end of their second full season of competition Toleman began to score regular points finishes by finding some reliability to match their occasional yet conspicuous displays of speed.
- Lotus joined the turbo brigade with Renault power and began to show some potential, also experimenting with active suspension, computer-controlled hydraulic jacks replacing conventional suspension.
- It was the improving longevity and performance by Lotus-Renault and Toleman-Hart that produced a modest milestone at Monza when for the first time ever the top six finishers were all turbo-powered.
- As for the non-turbo teams, windows of opportunity for the normally aspirated V8 cars were limited, their virtues chiefly nimbleness, reliability and the adoption of an alternate non-stop approach in the face of the widely used one-stop fuel

and tyres strategy. But on the street circuits of Long Beach, Monaco and Detroit they delivered.

- At the final GP to be held at Long Beach, John Watson exceeded his extraordinary feat of the previous season by winning from 22nd on the grid, a 'from back to front' record still standing to this day.
- Including his storming Monaco victory, defending world champion Keke Rosberg produced a spirited early sequence of strong finishes, and remarkably stayed in contention for the championship for the first half of the season.
- The 155th and final triumph for the most successful grand prix engine of all time, the Ford Cosworth DFV, albeit in DFY form, was Alboreto's Detroit victory, which also marked the last win for Ken Tyrrell.
- But although it was slim pickings for Williams and for McLaren in 1983, plans were afoot to change all that and join the turbo club.
- These two teams trod very different paths to source their motors, but at the end of the season both unveiled their turbo contenders, each fitted with an engine which severally would redefine turbo technology over the next five years of F1.

Championship ranking	Championship points	Driver nationality	1983 Drivers Championship Driver	Car	Races contested	Race victories	Podiumse excl. victories	Races led	Lights to flag victories	Laps led	Poles	Fastest laps	Triple Crowns
1	59	BRA	Nelson Piquet	Brabham-BMW	15	3	5	11		327	1	4	
2	57	FRA	Alain Prost	Renault	15	4	3	4		121	3	3	1
3	49	FRA	René Arnoux	Ferrari	15	3	4	6		177	4	2	
4	40	FRA	Patrick Tambay	Ferrari	15	1	4	6		94	4	1	
5	27	FIN	Keke Rosberg	Williams-Ford (14) Williams-Honda (1)	15	1	1	2		82	1		
6	22	GBR	John Watson	McLaren-Ford (11) McLaren-TAG (3)	14	1	2	1		31		1	
7	22	USA	Eddie Cheever	Renault	15		4						
8	15	ITA	Andrea de Cesaris	Alfa Romeo	14		2	1		18.1		1	
9	13	ITA	Riccardo Patrese	Brabham-BMW	15	1	1	5		61	1	1	
10	12	AUT	Niki Lauda	McLaren-Ford (10) McLaren-TAG (4)	14		2					1	
11	11	FRA	Jacques Laffite	Williams-Ford (12) Williams-Honda (1)	13			1		19			
12	10	ITA	Michele Alboreto	Tyrrell-Ford	15	1		1		10			
13	10	GBR	Nigel Mansell	Lotus-Ford (8) Lotus-Renault (7)	15		1					1	
14	9	GBR	Derek Warwick	Toleman-Hart	15								
15	4	SUI	Marc Surer	Arrows-Ford	15								
16	3	ITA	Mauro Baldi	Alfa Romeo	15								
17	2	USA	Danny Sullivan	Tyrrell-Ford	15								
17	2	ITA	Elio de Angelis	Lotus-Ford (1) Lotus-Renault (14)	15						1		
19	1	VEN	Johnny Cecotto	Theodore-Ford	9								
19	1	ITA	Bruno Giacomelli	Toleman-Hart	14								

Championship ranking	Championship points	Team/Marque nationality	1983 Constructors Championship Chassis	Engine	Engine maker nationality	Races contested	Race victories	1-2 finishes	Podiums excl. victories	Races led	Laps led	Poles	Fastest laps
1	89	ITA	Ferrari 126C3, 126C2B	Ferrari 1.5 V6t	ITA	15	4	1	8	8	271	8	3
2	79	FRA	Renault RE40, RE30C	Renault 1.5 V6t	FRA	15	4		7	4	121	3	3
3	72	GBR	Brabham BT52, BT52B	BMW 1.5 4t	GER	15	4		6	13	388	2	5
4	36	GBR	Williams FW08C	Ford Cosworth 3.0 V8	GBR	14	1		1	3	101	1	
5	34	GBR	McLaren MP4-1C	Ford Cosworth 3.0 V8	GBR	11	1	1	4	1	31		2
6	18	ITA	Alfa Romeo 183T	Alfa Romeo 1.5 V8t	ITA	15			2	1	18.1		1
7	12	GBR	Tyrrell 011, 012	Ford Cosworth 3.0 V8	GBR	15	1			1	10		
8	11	GBR	Lotus 93T, 94T	Renault 1.5 V6t	FRA	14			1			1	1
9	10	GBR	Toleman TG183B	Hart 1.5 4t	GBR	15							
10	4	GBR	Arrows A6	Ford Cosworth 3.0 V8	GBR	15							
11	2	GBR	Williams FW09	Honda 1.5 V6t	JAP	1							
12	1	HKG	Theodore N183	Ford Cosworth 3.0 V8	GBR	13							
12	1	GBR	Lotus 92	Ford Cosworth 3.0 V8	GBR	8							

1984

Lauda makes his (half) point

THE TALE OF THE TITLE

- A second championship slipped through Prost's fingers, this time by half a point.
- McLaren teammate Niki Lauda nabbed his third world title by the narrowest possible margin.
- New regulations placed emphasis on fuel efficiency but endangered the expression F1 *racing*.
- 'Not running at finish; out of fuel' became a regular entry on the results sheets.
- McLaren's TAG Porsche turbo dominated, winning a record 12 of the 16 rounds.
- With seven race victories Prost equalled Clark's 1963 record, and beat Lauda's tally 7-5.
- Defending champion Piquet's challenge was blunted by dire BMW reliability.
- But Piquet and Brabham-BMW presented the only genuine challenge to McLaren supremacy.
- Ferrari and Renault never fully mastered fuel efficiency, their drivers' only choice 'to race or to finish'.
- Even so, Team Lotus with Renault power took third in the championship, a serious proposition once again.
- Rosberg gave Williams-Honda a first victory despite the inability to conquer 'light-switch' power delivery.
- Ballast dubiously featured again, this time not 'water-cooled brakes' but 'engine water-injection'.
- Following appeal, atmo Tyrrells were expunged from the championship for cheating.
- Rookie Ayrton Senna made his mark at Monaco, challenging Prost for victory in the rain.
- And not forgetting: 'barn-door' rear wings; 'Coke-bottle' rear ends; potent fuel brews.

THE CHASE FOR THE CHAMPIONSHIP

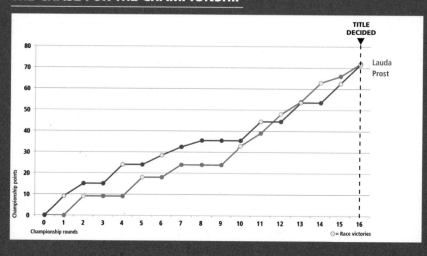

BRAZILIAN GP Rio de Janeiro
25 March 1984 Race 389

Alain Prost
McLaren-TAG Porsche MP4/2 179.512kph, 111.544mph

Ferrari recruit Alboreto led the opening 11 laps until a brake problem caused a spin. Now it was Lauda's McLaren-TAG from Warwick's Renault with Prost making up ground after a slow start. On lap 29 Warwick pitted for fresh, softer Michelins and really began to motor, such that on lap 38 – as Lauda pitted with electrics and Prost's concurrent pit stop was consequentially delayed – the Renault went ahead. With ten laps to go holding a 35s lead, Warwick looked the certain winner until his front suspension let go, ironically the probable consequence of an earlier overtaking nudge from Lauda around lap 10. Behind Prost, Rosberg's Williams-Honda and the Lotus-Renault of pole-man de Angelis struggled in, two of only eight survivors.

POLE POSITION de Angelis, Lotus-Renault, 1m 28.392s (0.506s), 204.901kph, 127.320mph
LAPS 61 x 5.031 km, 3.126 miles
DISTANCE 306.891 km, 190.693 miles
STARTERS/FINISHERS 26/8
WEATHER Sunny, very hot, dry
LAP LEADERS M Alboreto, Ferrari 1-11 (11); N Lauda, McLaren-TAG 12-37 (26); Prost 38, 51-61 (12); D Warwick, Renault 39-50 (12)
WINNER'S LAPS 1 P10, 2 P9, 3-4 P8, 5-8 P7, 9-12 P6, 13-15 P4, 16-23 P3, 24-37 P2, 38 P1, 39-50 P2, 51-61 P1
FASTEST LAP Prost, McLaren-TAG, 1m 36.499s (lap 42), 187.687kph, 116.623mph
CHAMPIONSHIP Prost 9, Rosberg 6, de Angelis 4, Cheever 3, Tambay 2

Pos	Driver	Car	Time/gap	Grid	Stops	Tyres
1	A Prost	McLaren-TAG	1h 42m 34.492s	4	1	M
2	K Rosberg	Williams- Honda	–40.514s	9	1	G
3	E de Angelis	Lotus-Renault	–59.128s	1	1	G
4	E Cheever	Alfa Romeo	–1 lap	12	1	G
5r	P Tambay	Renault	–2 laps	8	1	M
6	T Boutsen	Arrows-Ford	–2 laps	20	0	G

McLaren-TAG Porsche MP4/2

SOUTH AFRICAN GP Kyalami
7 April 1984 Race 390

Niki Lauda
McLaren-TAG Porsche MP4/2 206.599kph, 128.375mph

Defending champion Piquet almost stalled on pole, allowing Rosberg's front row Williams-Honda to lead lap 1. Second time round Nelson scorched ahead until on lap 21, under pressure from Lauda, tyre-blistering forced a pit stop. But the Brabham challenge was over, the BMW turbo only lasting another eight laps. McLaren's all-round superiority was demonstrated by Prost. Despite starting from the pit lane in the spare, he finished second to Lauda, the only other car to complete the full race distance. So close to victory in Rio, Warwick came in third despite a second tyre-stop for a puncture, while Renault teammate Tambay once again ran out of fuel near the end when well-placed. Rookie Senna scored his first point for Toleman-Hart.

POLE POSITION N Piquet, Brabham-BMW, 1m 04.871s (0.187s), 227.750kph, 141.518mph
LAPS 75 x 4.104 km, 2.550 miles
DISTANCE 307.800 km, 191.258 miles
STARTERS/FINISHERS 26/12
WEATHER Cloudy with sunny intervals, hot, dry
LAP LEADERS K Rosberg, Williams-Honda 1 (1); Piquet 2-20 (19); Lauda 21-75 (55)
WINNER'S LAPS 1-3 P4, 4-9 P3, 10-20 P2, 21-75 P1
FASTEST LAP P Tambay, Renault, 1m 08.877s (lap 64), 214.504kph, 133.287mph
CHAMPIONSHIP Prost 15, Lauda 9, Rosberg 6, de Angelis 4, Warwick 4

Pos	Driver	Car	Time/gap	Grid	Stops	Tyres
1	N Lauda	McLaren-TAG	1h 29m 23.430s	3	1	M
2	A Prost	McLaren-TAG	–1m 5.950s	9	1	M
3	D Warwick	Renault	–1 lap	2	2	M
4	R Patrese	Alfa Romeo	–2 laps	13	1	G
5	A de Cesaris	Ligier-Renault	–2 laps	6	1	M
6	A Senna	Toleman-Hart	–3 laps	14	0	P

Ferrari 126C4

Round 3/16	**BELGIAN GP** Zolder						**Michele Alboreto**		
	29 April 1984					**Race 391**	Ferrari 126C4 185.431kph, 115.221mph		

Alboreto used his first pole and a Goodyear tyre advantage to put on a polished display, leading every lap to win by over 40s. Poignantly, being Zolder, he won in No27, the first Italian Ferrari winner since 1966. Teammate Arnoux, alongside on the front row, had a less auspicious drive but still finished on the podium behind the excellent Warwick, the leading Michelin runner. In the closing laps Piquet's BMW blew when fourth, but the drive of the day came from Rosberg. Bogging down at the start, he was P20 on lap 1 only to run out of fuel on the penultimate lap when third after a meteoric display. By half-distance both McLarens had succumbed, piston failure and electrics, neither featuring on the leader-board having started P8 and P14.

POLE POSITION M Alboreto, Ferrari, 1m 14.846s (0.552s), 204.997kph, 127.379mph
LAPS 70 x 4.262 km, 2.648 miles
DISTANCE 298.340 km, 185.380 miles
STARTERS/FINISHERS 26/10
WEATHER Sunny, warm, dry
LAP LEADERS Alboreto 1-70 (70)
WINNER'S LAPS 1-70 P1
FASTEST LAP R Arnoux, Ferrari, 1m 19.294s (lap 64), 193.498kph, 120.234mph
CHAMPIONSHIP Prost 15, Warwick 10, Lauda 9, Alboreto 9, Rosberg 9

Pos	Driver	Car	Time/gap	Grid	Stops	Tyres
1	M Alboreto	Ferrari	1h 36m 32.048s	1	1	G
2	D Warwick	Renault	–42.386s	4	1	M
3	R Arnoux	Ferrari	–1m 9.803s	2	1	G
4r	K Rosberg	Williams-Honda	–1 lap	3	1	G
5	E de Angelis	Lotus-Renault	–1 lap	5	0	G
6	A Senna	Toleman-Hart	–2 laps	21	1	P

Round 4/16	**SAN MARINO GP** Imola						**Alain Prost**		
	6 May 1984					**Race 392**	McLaren-TAG Porsche MP4/2 187.255kph, 116.355mph		

Piquet and Prost on the front row, Prost taking the lead at turn one. He just drove away from the Brabham at over a second per lap, never relinquishing his lead despite a harmless spin on lap 23 and a tyre stop seven laps later. Behind Prost a race of attrition developed with only six cars still running at the finish, three others classified but stationary, out of fuel. Mechanical carnage included Lauda's engine on lap 15, Alboreto's exhaust on lap 24 and Piquet losing P2 on lap 49 when, you guessed it, thick black smoke signalled another turbo failure. Excessive Renault fuel consumption had Warwick finishing fourth, in the points again after a frustrating economy run, but suddenly Prost held an 11-point championship lead after only four rounds.

POLE POSITION N Piquet, Brabham-BMW, 1m 28.517s (0.111s), 204.978kph, 127.367mph
LAPS 60 x 5.040 km, 3.132 miles
DISTANCE 302.400 km, 187.903 miles
STARTERS/FINISHERS 26/9
WEATHER Cloudy with sunny intervals, warm, dry
LAP LEADERS Prost 1-60 (60)
WINNER'S LAPS 1-60 P1
FASTEST LAP N Piquet, Brabham-BMW, 1m 33.275s (lap 48), 194.522kph, 120.870mph
CHAMPIONSHIP Prost 24, Warwick 13, Arnoux 10, de Angelis 10, Lauda 9

Pos	Driver	Car	Time/gap	Grid	Stops	Tyres
1	A Prost	McLaren-TAG	1h 36m 53.679s	2	1	M
2	R Arnoux	Ferrari	–13.416s	6	1	G
3r	E de Angelis	Lotus-Renault	–1 lap	11	1	G
4	D Warwick	Renault	–1 lap	4	0	M
5	T Boutsen	Arrows-Ford	–1 lap	21	0	G
6r	A de Cesaris	Ligier-Renault	–2 laps	20	0	M

Round 5/16	**FRENCH GP** Dijon-Prenois				
	20 May 1984			Race 393	

FRENCH GP Dijon-Prenois

Round 5/16 — 20 May 1984 — Race 393

Niki Lauda
McLaren-TAG Porsche MP4/2 202.024kph, 125.532mph

Tambay gave Renault their first pole of the year, leading the early stages chased by the Renault-engined Lotus pair to the joy of the partisan crowd. Difficulties had caused the McLarens to qualify poorly, but in race trim their speed looked ominous, Prost homing in on the leading Renault. On the verge of displacing Tambay, a loose front wheel ended Prost's challenge although by then Lauda was there to take it up. With a groan from the crowd, Niki took the lead on lap 41, only to lose it again when his crew made a sluggish tyre change on lap 54. Even though Tambay's fuel consumption was behaving, it only took Lauda seven laps to dash the home victory dream once again. With two wins apiece, the championship was becoming a McLaren benefit.

POLE POSITION Tambay, Renault, 1m 02.200s (0.136s), 224.971kph, 139.791mph
LAPS 79 x 3.887 km, 2.415 miles
DISTANCE 307.073 km, 190.806 miles
STARTERS/FINISHERS 26/13
WEATHER Cloudy with sunny intervals, warm, dry
LAP LEADERS Tambay 1-38, 40, 54-61 (47); Lauda 39, 41-53, 62-79 (32)
WINNER'S LAPS 1 P10, 2 P9, 3 P8, 4-11 P7, 12-14 P6, 15-16 P5, 17-20 P4, 21-27 P3, 28-38 P2, 39 P1, 40 P2, 41-53 P1, 54-61 P2, 62-79 P1
FASTEST LAP A Prost, McLaren-TAG, 1m 05.257s (lap 59), 214.432kph, 133.242mph
CHAMPIONSHIP Prost 24, Lauda 18, Warwick 13, Arnoux 13, de Angelis 12

Pos	Driver	Car	Time/gap	Grid	Stops	Tyres
1	N Lauda	McLaren-TAG	1h 31m 11.951s	9	1	M
2	P Tambay	Renault	–7.154s	1	1	M
3	N Mansell	Lotus-Renault	–23.969s	6	1	G
4	R Arnoux	Ferrari	–43.706s	11	1	G
5	E de Angelis	Lotus-Renault	–1m 6.125s	2	1	G
6	K Rosberg	Williams-Honda	–1 lap	4	1	G

MONACO GP Monte Carlo

Round 6/16 — 3 June 1984 — Race 394

Alain Prost
McLaren-TAG Porsche MP4/2 100.776kph, 62.618mph

In streaming wet conditions, Prost led from pole chased by Mansell from P2. On lap 11 the Lotus got by, and for five glorious laps Nigel led his first GP only to loose it on the slick road markings going up the hill. Other casualties were the Renault pair, both out within a few hundred metres of the start, and Lauda who spun away third at Casino Square. But increasingly all eyes turned to the charge through the field by rookies Senna and Bellof, the Toleman displacing Lauda from second on lap 19 and now reeling in the leader. Prost meanwhile was gesticulating for the rain-hit race to be stopped, and controversially, well before half-distance, race director Jacky Ickx obliged, leaving many unanswered questions and Prost with a half-points victory.

POLE POSITION Prost, McLaren-TAG, 1m 22.661s (0.091s), 144.242kph, 89.628mph
LAPS 31 x 3.312 km, 2.058 miles (Race scheduled for 77 laps but stopped due to rain)
DISTANCE 102.672 km, 63.797 miles (Minimum distance incomplete; half points awarded)
STARTERS/FINISHERS 20/8
WEATHER Overcast, cold, very wet
LAP LEADERS Prost 1-10, 16-31 (26); N Mansell, Lotus-Renault 11-15 (5)
WINNER'S LAPS 1-10 P1, 11-15 P2, 16-31 P1
FASTEST LAP Senna, Toleman-Hart, 1m 54.334s (lap 24), 104.284kph, 64.799mph
CHAMPIONSHIP Prost 28.5, Lauda 18, Arnoux 15, Warwick 13, de Angelis 13

Pos	Driver	Car	Time/gap	Grid	Stops	Tyres
1	A Prost	McLaren-TAG	1h 1m 7.740s	1	0	M
2	A Senna	Toleman-Hart	–7.446s	13	0	P
3	R Arnoux	Ferrari	–29.077s	20	0	G
4	K Rosberg	Williams-Honda	–35.246s	3	0	G
5	E de Angelis	Lotus-Renault	–35.246s	10	0	G
6	M Alboreto	Ferrari	–1 lap	11	0	G

CANADIAN GP Montréal

Round 7/16 — 17 June 1984 — Race 395

Nelson Piquet
Brabham-BMW BT53 174.086kph, 108.172mph

The three-race North American tour began with the reigning world champion on pole for a third time but still with no points to his name. This time the BMW turbo held together, Piquet leading all the way once he blasted past Prost on the return leg of the opening lap. It was a beautifully controlled victory, leading Lauda home by a mere 2–3s to provide the first tangible evidence that the BMW possessed competitive, race-long fuel-efficiency. Although his car benefitted from the altered weight distribution, Piquet's only difficulty was burned feet caused by the new nose-mounted oil cooler. In a tense rather than exciting race, Lauda replaced Prost on lap 44 as Piquet's principal challenger, Alain's TAG-turbo short of 1,000 revs later on.

POLE POSITION Piquet, Brabham-BMW, 1m 25.442s (0.101s), 185.810kph, 115.457mph
LAPS 70 x 4.410 km, 2.740 miles
DISTANCE 308.700 km, 191.817 miles
STARTERS/FINISHERS 26/11
WEATHER Sunny, hot, dry
LAP LEADERS Piquet 1-70 (70)
WINNER'S LAPS 1-70 P1
FASTEST LAP Piquet, Brabham-BMW, 1m 28.763s (lap 55), 178.858kph, 111.137mph
CHAMPIONSHIP Prost 32.5, Lauda 24, Arnoux 17, de Angelis 16, Warwick 13

Pos	Driver	Car	Time/gap	Grid	Stops	Tyres
1	N Piquet	Brabham-BMW	1h 46m 23.748s	1	0	M
2	N Lauda	McLaren-TAG	–2.612s	8	0	M
3	A Prost	McLaren-TAG	–1m 28.032s	2	0	M
4	E de Angelis	Lotus-Renault	–1 lap	3	0	G
5	R Arnoux	Ferrari	–2 laps	5	1	G
6	N Mansell	Lotus-Renault	–2 laps	7	0	G

Brabham-BMW BT53

Round 8/16	UNITED STATES GP Detroit		Nelson Piquet
	24 June 1984	Race 396	Brabham-BMW BT53 131.449kph, 81.679mph

Following a restart, even in the spare Brabham Piquet completed a second lights-to-flag win, 18 points in eight days giving McLaren food for thought if not yet sleepless nights. Only six cars finished the race, the field decimated by numerous accidents and mechanical failures. Various cars sniped at Piquet's lead, Mansell early on, Alboreto later, but even the McLarens made little impact, Lauda never higher than P6, Prost making two stops for tyres. At least the closing laps were enlivened by Brundle's pursuit of the leader, falling short by less than a second, but in reality it was an illusion. Piquet had the situation fully under control, and at post-race scrutineering the Tyrrell team were called to answer charges relating to fuel and weight irregularities.

POLE POSITION Piquet, Brabham-BMW, 1m 40.980s (0.660s), 143.435kph, 89.127mph
LAPS 63 x 4.023 km, 2.500 miles (Race restarted for scheduled 63 laps following accident)
DISTANCE 253.472 km, 157.500 miles
STARTERS/FINISHERS 26/5
WEATHER Sunny, hot, dry
LAP LEADERS Piquet 1-63 (63)
WINNER'S LAPS 1-63 P1
FASTEST LAP D Warwick, Renault, 1m 46.221s (lap 32), 136.358kph, 84.729mph
CHAMPIONSHIP Prost 35.5, Lauda 24, de Angelis 22, Piquet 18, Arnoux 17

Pos	Driver	Car	Time/gap	Grid	Stops	Tyres
1	N Piquet	Brabham-BMW	1h 55m 41.842s	1	0	M
2	E de Angelis	Lotus-Renault	−32.638s	5	1	G
3	T Fabi	Brabham-BMW	−1m 26.528s	23	0	M
4	A Prost	McLaren-TAG	−1m 55.258s	2	0	M
5	J Laffite	Williams-Honda	−1 lap	19	1	G
-	No other classified finishers after Brundle's Tyrrell was later disqualified from P2					−

Williams-Honda FW09

UNITED STATES GP Dallas
8 July 1984   Race 397

Keke Rosberg
Williams-Honda FW09 129.203kph, 80.283mph

At the one and only GP to be held in Dallas, only seven cars made the finish, the deteriorating track surface causing numerous indiscretions against the concrete walls. From his maiden pole Mansell led the first half, but always under pressure from first Warwick, then teammate de Angelis, and finally Rosberg, who took the lead on lap 36 when Mansell made a stop for fresh rubber, having skimmed the wall. Soon the clumsy point-and-squirt Williams-Honda was pursued by the McLaren pair. Prost took the lead on lap 49 but on lap 56 touched the wall, and four laps later Lauda was also out through the same misdemeanour. So Keke won to give Williams-Honda their first success, and equally brilliantly Arnoux came second, having started dead last.

Pos	Driver	Car	Time/gap	Grid	Stops	Tyres
1	K Rosberg	Williams-Honda	2h 1m 22.617s	8	0	G
2	R Arnoux	Ferrari	−22.464s	4	0	G
3	E de Angelis	Lotus-Renault	−1 lap	2	0	G
4	J Laffite	Williams-Honda	−2 laps	24	0	G
5	P Ghinzani	Osella-Alfa	−2 laps	18	1	P
6r	N Mansell	Lotus-Renault	−3 laps	1	1	G

POLE POSITION Mansell, Lotus-Renault, 1m 37.041s (0.594s), 144.720kph, 89.925mph
LAPS 67 x 3.901 km, 2.424 miles (Scheduled for 78 laps but stopped after two hours)
DISTANCE 261.370 km, 162.408 miles
STARTERS/FINISHERS 25/8
WEATHER Sunny, very hot, dry
LAP LEADERS Mansell 1-35 (35); Rosberg 36-48, 57-67 (24); A Prost, McLaren-TAG 49-56 (8)
WINNER'S LAPS 1 P6, 2-10 P5, 11-13 P4, 14-18 P3, 19-32 P2, 33-34 P3, 35 P2, 36-48 P1, 49-56 P2, 57-67 P1
FASTEST LAP N Lauda, McLaren-TAG, 1m 45.353s (lap 22), 133.302kph, 82.830mph
CHAMPIONSHIP Prost 35.5, de Angelis 26, Lauda 24, Arnoux 23, Rosberg 20.5

BRITISH GP Brands Hatch
22 July 1984   Race 398

Niki Lauda
McLaren-TAG Porsche MP4/2 200.290kph, 124.455mph

A lap 11 accident at Clearways caused the race to become a two-part affair decided on aggregate. Despite this disruption it quickly developed into a struggle between world champion Piquet on pole and the two McLarens. First Piquet led, but following the restart Prost took command until on lap 37, with an 11-second lead, he retired with a broken gearbox. Lauda assumed the lead, having got past Piquet under braking for Druids on lap 29. From there it was Lauda the rest of the way, Piquet's late efforts foiled by sagging boost pressure to finally finish seventh. Warwick brought the British crowd some cheer with second, his first points finish in six races, while Senna gained more points for Toleman-Hart with a popular third.

Pos	Driver	Car	Time/gap	Grid	Stops	Tyres
1	N Lauda	McLaren-TAG	1h 29m 28.532s	3	0	M
2	D Warwick	Renault	−42.123s	6	0	M
3	A Senna	Toleman-Hart	−1m 3.328s	7	0	G
4	E de Angelis	Lotus-Renault	−1 lap	4	0	G
5	M Alboreto	Ferrari	−1 lap	9	0	G
6	R Arnoux	Ferrari	−1 lap	13	0	G

POLE POSITION N Piquet, Brabham-BMW, 1m 10.869s (0.207s), 213.698kph, 132.786mph
LAPS 71 x 4.207 km, 2.614 miles (75 lap race interrupted due to accident. Result aggregate of 11 + 60 laps)
DISTANCE 298.685 km, 185.594 miles
STARTERS/FINISHERS 27/12
WEATHER Sunny, hot, dry
LAP LEADERS (On the road) Piquet 1-11 (11); A Prost, McLaren-TAG 12-37 (26); Lauda 38-71 (34)
WINNER'S LAPS 1 P4, 2-28 P3, 29-37 P2, 38-71 P1
FASTEST LAP Lauda, McLaren-TAG, 1m 13.191s (lap 57), 206.918kph, 128.573mph
CHAMPIONSHIP Prost 35.5, Lauda 33, de Angelis 29, Arnoux 24, Rosberg 20.5

GERMAN GP Hockenheim
5 August 1984   Race 399

Alain Prost
McLaren-TAG Porsche MP4/2 211.804kph, 131.609mph

The first half of the race belonged first to de Angelis, leading the opening seven laps until his Renault motor blew, and then Piquet, who retired on lap 23 when the Brabham gearbox broke. After that it became a rather dull procession led by pole-sitter Prost followed not that closely by teammate Lauda. McLaren, Porsche – especially at Hockenheim – and Michelin were delighted with the 1-2 result. As were the drivers, extending their points lead significantly at the head of the championship table. For all these good people it was a great day. For the rest, including the thousands of trackside spectators and the millions watching on TV, it wasn't. Even a British 3-4 didn't alleviate the tedium.

Pos	Driver	Car	Time/gap	Grid	Stops	Tyres
1	A Prost	McLaren-TAG	1h 24m 43.210s	1	0	M
2	N Lauda	McLaren-TAG	−3.149s	7	0	M
3	D Warwick	Renault	−36.423s	3	0	M
4	N Mansell	Lotus-Renault	−51.663s	16	0	G
5	P Tambay	Renault	−1m 11.949s	4	0	M
6	R Arnoux	Ferrari	−1 lap	10	1	G

POLE POSITION Prost, McLaren-TAG, 1m 47.012s (0.053s), 228.658kph, 142.082mph
LAPS 44 x 6.797 km, 4.223 miles
DISTANCE 299.068 km, 185.832 miles
STARTERS/FINISHERS 26/9
WEATHER Cloudy with sunny intervals, warm, dry
LAP LEADERS E de Angelis, Lotus-Renault 1-7 (7); N Piquet, Brabham-BMW 8-21 (14); Prost 22-44 (23)
WINNER'S LAPS 1-21 P2, 22-44 P1
FASTEST LAP Prost, McLaren-TAG, 1m 53.538s (lap 31), 215.516kph, 133.915mph
CHAMPIONSHIP Prost 44.5, Lauda 39, de Angelis 29, Arnoux 25, Warwick 23

Round 12/16	**AUSTRIAN GP** Österreichring **19 August 1984** **Race 400**	**Niki Lauda** McLaren-TAG Porsche MP4/2 223.884kph, 139.115mph

Piquet versus the McLarens again, this time the Brazilian holding them at bay by a second or three for most of the race, Prost leading the attack, Lauda hovering behind. On lap 29 the leading trio hit oil dropped by de Angelis, causing Prost, holding the gear lever in fourth, to spin into the catch-fencing. Now Lauda moved in, Piquet resolutely defending just as he had against Prost, the exciting duel even closer now that the Brabham's rear Michelins were badly worn. In ten starts Lauda had never won his own GP but with 12 laps to go, to the delight of the crowd, he took the lead. Three laps later, exiting the Boschkurve, he almost ground to a halt with severe gearbox problems, but somehow coaxed it home to beat Piquet, unsuspecting of Lauda's plight.

POLE POSITION Piquet, Brabham-BMW, 1m 26.173s (0.030s), 248.236kph, 154.246mph
LAPS 51 x 5.942 km, 3.692 miles (Aborted start; restarted from original distance)
DISTANCE 303.042 km, 188.302 miles
STARTERS/FINISHERS 25/12
WEATHER Sunny, warm, dry
LAP LEADERS Piquet 1-39 (39); Lauda 40-51 (12)
WINNER'S LAPS 1 P6, 2 P5, 3-8 P4, 9-28 P3, 29-39 P2, 40-51 P1
FASTEST LAP Lauda, McLaren-TAG, 1m 32.882s (lap 23), 230.305kph, 143.105mph
CHAMPIONSHIP Lauda 48, Prost 44.5, de Angelis 29, Arnoux 25, Piquet 24

Pos	Driver	Car	Time/gap	Grid	Stops	Tyres
1	N Lauda	McLaren-TAG	1h 21m 12.851s	4	0	M
2	N Piquet	Brabham-BMW	–23.525s	1	0	M
3	M Alboreto	Ferrari	–48.998s	12	0	G
4	T Fabi	Brabham-BMW	–56.312s	7	0	M
5	T Boutsen	Arrows-BMW	–1 lap	17	0	G
6	M Surer	Arrows-BMW	–1 lap	19	0	G

Round 13/16	**DUTCH GP** Zandvoort **26 August 1984** **Race 401**	**Alain Prost** McLaren-TAG Porsche MP4/2 186.051kph, 115.607mph

Once leader Piquet went out after a mere ten laps with a broken oil union, Prost restored his championship momentum with a clear-cut victory from pole. But as so often previously, Lauda, from an inferior grid position, came through strongly in the race to finish just 10s behind. He therefore maintained the points lead he had opened up with his Austrian victory, but by half of one point. With their third 1-2 finish of the year McLaren deservedly became constructors' champions at the circuit where exactly one year ago Lauda had debuted the McLaren-TAG Porsche. The Lotus-Renaults finished 3-4, Mansell's a strong drive to third from P12. Rosberg held third for much of the race, his ill-handling Williams running dry three laps from the finish.

POLE POSITION Prost, McLaren-TAG, 1m 13.567s (0.305s), 208.072kph, 129.290mph
LAPS 71 x 4.252 km, 2.642 miles
DISTANCE 301.892 km, 187.587 miles
STARTERS/FINISHERS 27/13
WEATHER Sunny, warm, dry
LAP LEADERS N Piquet, Brabham-BMW 1-10 (10); Prost 11-71 (61)
WINNER'S LAPS 1-10 P2, 11-71 P1
FASTEST LAP R Arnoux, Ferrari, 1m 19.465s (lap 64), 192.628kph, 119.694mph
CHAMPIONSHIP Lauda 54, Prost 53.5, de Angelis 32, Arnoux 25, Piquet 24

Pos	Driver	Car	Time/gap	Grid	Stops	Tyres
1	A Prost	McLaren-TAG	1h 37m 21.468s	1	0	M
2	N Lauda	McLaren-TAG	–10.283s	6	0	M
3	N Mansell	Lotus-Renault	–1m 19.544s	12	0	G
4	E de Angelis	Lotus-Renault	–1 lap	3	0	G
5	T Fabi	Brabham-BMW	–1 lap	10	1	M
6	P Tambay	Renault	–1 lap	5	1	M

Round 14/16	**ITALIAN GP** Monza **9 September 1984** **Race 402**	**Niki Lauda** McLaren-TAG Porsche MP4/2 220.515kph, 137.022mph

Same old story: Piquet on pole; leads opening laps; turbo blows. But just a minute, it's not a McLaren now leading, it's Tambay's Renault, 7s up on lap 16. What's more, Prost's TAG let go on lap 4 and on lap 17 Lauda was overtaken by the feisty Teo Fabi in the number two Brabham-BMW. It didn't take long for the Fabi/Lauda twosome to become a threesome as they reeled-in Tambay, the trio circulating together for many laps until Fabi retired with engine trouble on lap 43, Tambay a broken throttle linkage the following lap. In a race of high attrition, reliability not pace brought Alboreto second. It was also a good day for Austrian drivers, three starting, all finishing in the points: Lauda P1, Gartner P5, Berger P6.

POLE POSITION N Piquet, Brabham-BMW, 1m 26.584s (0.087s), 241.153kph, 149.846mph
LAPS 51 x 5.800 km, 3.604 miles
DISTANCE 295.800 km, 183.802 miles
STARTERS/FINISHERS 25/10
WEATHER Cloudy with sunny intervals, hot, dry
FASTEST LAP Lauda, McLaren-TAG, 1m 31.912s (lap 42), 227.174kph, 141.159mph
WINNER'S LAPS 1-2 P6, 3 P5, 4-7 P4, 8-15 P3, 16 P2, 17-39 P3, 40-42 P2, 43-51 P1
LAP LEADERS Piquet 1-15 (15); P Tambay, Renault 16-42 (27); Lauda 43-51 (9)
CHAMPIONSHIP Lauda 63, Prost 53.5, de Angelis 32, Arnoux 25, Piquet 24

Pos	Driver	Car	Time/gap	Grid	Stops	Tyres
1	N Lauda	McLaren-TAG	1h 20m 29.065s	4	0	M
2	M Alboreto	Ferrari	–24.249s	11	0	G
3	R Patrese	Alfa Romeo	–1 lap	9	0	G
4	S Johansson	Toleman-Hart	–2 laps	17	1	M
5	J Gartner	Osella-Alfa	–2 laps	24	0	P
6	G Berger	ATS-BMW	–2 laps	20	0	P

Round 15/16	**EUROPEAN GP** Nürburgring						**Alain Prost**
	7 October 1984				Race 403		McLaren-TAG Porsche MP4/2 191.751kph, 119.149mph

At the first corner of the first GP held at the new Nürburgring an accident eliminated five cars on the spot. But this did not prevent Prost dominating the race with a lights-to-flag win, a victory he needed badly to keep his championship alive. Only beaten by Piquet in qualifying, even a heavy shunt in race-day warm-up didn't put him off his stride for a consummate sixth victory. His adversary had a miserable time, qualifying 15th and spinning when lapping a backmarker to finish fourth. It could so easily have been second, Alboreto and Piquet both running out of fuel as they approached the flag. With one race left Lauda's points advantage was 4.5, but the following week Tyrrell lost their Detroit appeal, were excluded from the championship, the gap now 3.5.

POLE POSITION Piquet, Brabham-BMW, 1m 18.071s (0.304s), 207.316kph, 128.820mph
LAPS 67 x 4.542 km, 2.822 miles
DISTANCE 304.314 km, 189.092 miles
STARTERS/FINISHERS 26/11
WEATHER Overcast, cold, dry
LAP LEADERS Prost 1-67 (67)
WINNER'S LAPS 1-67 P1
FASTEST LAP Piquet, Brabham-BMW/Alboreto, Ferrari, 1m 23.146s (lap 62/62), 196.656kph, 122.197mph
CHAMPIONSHIP Lauda 66, Prost 62.5, de Angelis 32, Piquet 28, Alboreto 27.5

Pos	Driver	Car	Time/gap	Grid	Stops	Tyres
1	A Prost	McLaren-TAG	1h 35m 13.284s	2	0	M
2	M Alboreto	Ferrari	−23.911s	5	0	G
3	N Piquet	Brabham-BMW	−24.922s	1	0	M
4	N Lauda	McLaren-TAG	−43.086s	15	0	M
5	R Arnoux	Ferrari	−1m 1.430s	6	0	G
6	R Patrese	Alfa Romeo	−1 lap	9	0	G

Round 16/16	**PORTUGUESE GP** Estoril						**Alain Prost**
	21 October 1984				Race 404		McLaren-TAG Porsche MP4/2 180.541kph, 112.183mph

Put simply, even if Prost won, second would bring Lauda the championship. Once Prost dispensed with the fast-starting Rosberg, he did everything required of him by winning. Now it was up to Lauda who had only qualified P13. Relentlessly he made his way through until on lap 33 he reached third. There progress stalled, Mansell, driving his Lotus swansong, way ahead. *La France* prepared to crown their first champion until, 18 laps from *le gloire*, Mansell retired brakeless from the crucial P2, handing Lauda a third championship. Despite his 7-5 race win superiority, another title had slipped by Prost, this time by the narrowest margin of half a point. And by qualifying and finishing P3, Senna had put down a marker for 1985.

POLE POSITION Piquet, Brabham-BMW, 1m 21.703s (0.071s), 191.670kph, 119.098mph
LAPS 70 x 4.350 km, 2.703 miles
DISTANCE 304.500 km, 189.208 miles
STARTERS/FINISHERS 27/17
WEATHER Sunny, hot, dry
LAP LEADERS K Rosberg, Williams-Honda 1-8 (8); Prost 9-70 (62)
WINNER'S LAPS 1 P3, 2-8 P2, 9-70 P1
FASTEST LAP Lauda, McLaren-TAG, 1m 22.996s (lap 51), 188.684kph, 117.243mph
CHAMPIONSHIP Lauda 72, Prost 71.5, de Angelis 34, Alboreto 30.5, Piquet 29

Pos	Driver	Car	Time/gap	Grid	Stops	Tyres
1	A Prost	McLaren-TAG	1h 41m 11.753s	2	0	M
2	N Lauda	McLaren-TAG	−13.425s	11	0	M
3	A Senna	Toleman-Hart	−20.042s	3	0	M
4	M Alboreto	Ferrari	−20.317s	8	0	G
5	E de Angelis	Lotus-Renault	−1m 32.169s	5	0	G
6	N Piquet	Brabham-BMW	−1 lap	1	1	M

1984 CHAMPIONSHIP FACTS AND FOLKLORE

- The best 11 results from 16 championship rounds counted towards the 1984 drivers' title.
- The title European GP enabled a new circuit at the Nürburgring to join the calendar alongside the German GP at Hockenheim; a GP was held at Dallas for the one and only time, while the championship finale at Estoril was the first GP in Portugal since 1960.
- The Austrian GP was the 400th world championship event. Coincidentally, when the Tyrrells failed to qualify it became the first all-turbo grid, another nail in the coffin of the venerable Ford-Cosworth DFV engine.
- The warm-up lap became part of the race distance, the minimum 300km (186.41 miles), the maximum 320km (198.84 miles) or two hours. But the regulation changes that made a massive impact on the 1984 season were that fuel tanks were reduced to 220 litres (48.39 gallons) and mid-race refuelling was banned in an endeavour to restrict escalating turbo horsepower.
- To maximise power from this prescribed fuel measure, fuel

suppliers increasingly concocted bespoke brews developed for specific circuits, let alone specific engines, while teams soon introduced fuel coolers to increase density and so exceed the 220-litre limit.
- Another ploy was water ballast under the pretext of water injection tanks designed to cool engine combustion. For many it was no more than a device to run cars underweight for half the race, the empty water reservoirs replenished at the tyre stop, so ballasting the chassis back up to the required weight limit.
- Team Tyrrell, the only team committed to atmo engines throughout the season, were purported to have pushed the ballast envelope to an unacceptable degree by also inserting lead shot during water-tank replenishment. There was also the discovery of minute traces of hydrocarbons in the water-injection fluid.
- Whichever, although the team was allowed to race for a further five races under appeal, Tyrrell was ultimately disqualified from the championship with exclusion from the

final three rounds and all previous points erased.

- Even in the absence of Colin Chapman, Lotus still searched for the unfair advantage, leading the development in 'qualifying specials', engines with larger turbochargers and other enhancements to deliver increased power for just a few short laps, but which might be good for pole and track position advantage.
- On the other side of reason, the improved safety record from last year was largely sustained, although during the race warm-up in South Africa Ghinzani miraculously escaped with minor burns from a somersaulting inferno.
- Also fortunate was rookie Martin Brundle, escaping virtually unscathed in a massive crash during practice at Monaco. He was less lucky at Dallas a month later, out for the rest of the season with foot and leg injuries. Johnny Cecotto's career was terminated by similar damage received at Brands Hatch.
- Brabham-BMW's hat-trick to end 1983 may well have pointed to more of the same this year, but the aforementioned fuel regulation changes completely altered the F1 landscape.
- From this, Ron Dennis' McLaren emerged as a force in F1 which would last a generation and longer.
- Designer John Barnard called the shots and Ron made sure he got 'it', and that the team delivered on 'it'.
- 'It', ultimately, was a bespoke engine to create a total racing package, chassis and engine designed as a coherent whole rather than compromised by engine dimensions, configuration, or simply the whims of the supplier.
- Dennis' partner Mansour Ojjeh, the man behind TAG, *Techniques d'Avant Garde*, bankrolled the project and Porsche were commissioned to manufacture the engine under the direction of Hans Mezger, the McLaren/Porsche relationship first established in August 1981.

- The key design criteria were that Barnard and Mezger both recognised from the beginning that fuel efficiency would inevitably become the turbo performance limiter, and that once the balance between output and fuel consumption was deemed critical, an 80° V6 was optimal together with the Bosche Motronic management system developed through Porsche's successful endurance racing activities.
- Secondly, a 'short' V6 crankshaft and absolute control over the positioning of its ancillaries enabled Barnard to package the engine for aero advantage, leading to the waisted 'coke-bottle' rear end and the embryonic diffuser.
- The upshot was excellent downforce, superb aerodynamics, competitive power, exceptional fuel economy, reduced throttle lag and awesome reliability, and the results were simply phenomenal: world drivers' champion Lauda; McLaren-TAG Porsche constructors' champions; McLaren raising the bar for wins in a season to 12 from Lotus' eight wins in 1978, and finally Prost equalling Clark's 1963 seven wins in a season – formidable.
- To the great credit of Ron Dennis, John Barnard and for that matter Hans Mezger, the rest fell woefully short in 1984, believing that the F1 turbo era was a power race.
- This was possibly best demonstrated by Piquet's nine poles in a season, equalling Peterson in 1973 and Lauda in 1974–75, although over the balance of the season Brabham-BMW made a better fist of challenging McLaren than any other team.
- Even so, the reigning world champion began his title defence with six retirements. Poor reliability, a universal characteristic of turbo technology so far, became even worse this year as engines either blew up or ran short of fuel as engineers struggled to balance performance with durability.
- The three mid-season North America races was the only

RACE 401, Dutch GP: From row three Lauda came through strongly in the race to finish ten seconds behind winner Prost and so maintain his championship lead by half-a-point. Behind the shades, FISA President Jean-Marie Balestre appears unimpressed.

period that the McLaren team lost its winning momentum, Piquet's Brabham-BMW winning two on the trot followed by Rosberg's Williams-Honda.

■ This was the first Honda success since 1967, but it had far more to do with driver Rosberg than either Williams or Honda, Keke wrestling a brute of a car. Williams and Renault innovated with driver-to-pits radio communications in 1984, and Keke's feedback during that race must have been something.

■ Rosberg's Dallas victory was one of only two for Goodyear who finally if inevitably this season were forced to adopt radial tyre construction as pioneered by rivals Michelin, although the French company withdrew at the end of the season.

■ Ayrton Senna graduated to GP racing, joining Toleman. He made his mark quickly, challenging Prost for victory at a rain-shortened Monaco race, and later showed his ruthless ambition by reneging on his three-year Toleman contract to sign a new two-year deal with Lotus for 1985.

■ The final thought goes to Alain Prost, losing yet another championship opportunity at the final hurdle, and this time by half a point. Since his debut five years ago he had won more Grands Prix than any other, including twice world champion Nelson Piquet. Now that Prost's tally had reached 16, equalling that of Stirling Moss, an inevitable parallel could be drawn: two prolific race winners denied their deserved world crown.

■ But at least for Prost, there was always next year.

Championship ranking	Championship points	Driver nationality	1984 Drivers Championship		Races contested	Race victories	Podiumse excl. victories	Races led	Lights to flag victories	Laps led	Poles	Fastest laps	Triple Crowns
			Driver	Car									
1	72	AUT	Niki Lauda	McLaren-TAG	16	5	4	6		168		5	
2	71.5	FRA	Alain Prost	McLaren-TAG	16	7	2	9	2	345	3	3	1
3	34	ITA	Elio de Angelis	Lotus-Renault	16		4	1		7	1		
4	30.5	ITA	Michele Alboreto	Ferrari	16	1	3	2	1	81	1	1	
5	29	BRA	Nelson Piquet	Brabham-BMW	16	2	2	8	2	241	9	3	1
6	27	FRA	René Arnoux	Ferrari	16		4					2	
7	23	GBR	Derek Warwick	Renault	16		4	1		12		1	
8	20.5	FIN	Keke Rosberg	Williams-Honda	16	1	1	3		33			
9	13	BRA	Ayrton Senna	Toleman-Hart	14		3					1	
10	13	GBR	Nigel Mansell	Lotus-Renault	16		2	2		40	1		
11	11	FRA	Patrick Tambay	Renault	15		1	2		74	1	1	
12	9	ITA	Teo Fabi	Brabham-BMW	12		1						
13	8	ITA	Riccardo Patrese	Alfa Romeo	16		1						
14	5	FRA	Jacques Laffite	Williams-Honda	16								
15	5	BEL	Thierry Boutsen	Arrows-Ford (3) Arrows-BMW (12)	15								
16	3	USA	Eddie Cheever	Alfa Romeo	15								
16	3	SWE	Stefan Johansson	Tyrrell-Ford (3) Toleman-Hart (3)	6								
18	3	ITA	Andrea de Cesaris	Ligier-Renault	16								
19	2	ITA	Piercarlo Ghinzani	Osella-Alfa Romeo	14								
20	1	SUI	Marc Surer	Arrows-Ford (6) Arrows-BMW (9)	15								

Championship ranking	Championship points	Team/Marque nationality	1984 Constructors Championship		Engine maker nationality	Races contested	Race victories	1-2 finishes	Podiums excl. victories	Races led	Laps led	Poles	Fastest laps
			Chassis	Engine									
1	143.5	GBR	McLaren MP4-2	TAG Porsche 1.5 V6t	GER	16	12	4	6	13	513	3	8
2	57.5	ITA	Ferrari 126C4	Ferrari 1.5 V6t	ITA	16	1		7	2	81	1	3
3	47	GBR	Lotus 95T	Renault 1.5 V6t	FRA	16			6	3	47	2	
4	38	GBR	Brabham BT53	BMW 1.5 S4t	GER	16	2		3	8	241	9	3
5	34	FRA	Renault RE50	Renault 1.5 V6t	FRA	16			5	3	86	1	2
6	25.5	GBR	Williams FW09, FW09B	Honda 1.5 V6t	JAP	16	1		1	3	33		
7	16	GBR	Toleman TG183B, TG184	Hart 1.5 S4t	GBR	16			3				1
8	11	ITA	Alfa Romeo 184T	Alfa Romeo 1.5 V8t	ITA	16			1				
9	3	GBR	Arrows A6	Ford Cosworth 3.0 V8	GBR	8							
9	3	FRA	Ligier JS23, JS23B	Renault 1.5 V6t	FRA	16							
9	3	GBR	Arrows A7	BMW 1.5 S4t	GER	13							
12	2	ITA	Osella FA1F	Alfa Romeo 1.5 V8t	ITA	15							
12	2	ITA	Osella FA1F	Alfa Romeo 1.5 V8t	ITA	15							

1985

Prost's promise fulfilled

THE TALE OF THE TITLE

- At last Alain Prost won that elusive title to become the first, and still the only, drivers' champion from France.
- His five race wins numbered three more than the next best, teammate and champion Lauda victor just once.
- Alboreto's Ferrari was a genuine contender until Monza, but what started with a flourish ended in a whimper.
- McLaren-TAG retained the constructors' cup with six victories, but formidable new competitors emerged.
- Williams-Honda began to realise their colossal winning potential with an end of season hat-trick.
- Senna put Lotus-Renault back on the map with seven poles, although race victories were harder to come by.
- Senna was one of two new race-winners to emerge, Ayrton at his 16th attempt, Nigel Mansell at his 72nd.
- Piquet, Brabham-BMW and Pirelli had a miserable season together, enjoying just one day in the sun at Ricard.
- At season-end Piquet switched from Brabham to Williams, Rosberg joining Prost at McLaren.
- Farewells were also conveyed to Niki Lauda, the Zandvoort circuit, and teams Renault and Alfa Romeo.
- And not forgetting: digital fuel readouts; 1,000+ bhp qualifying engines.

THE CHASE FOR THE CHAMPIONSHIP

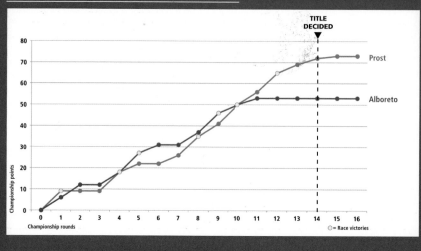

McLaren-TAG Porsche MP4/2B

Round 1/16	**BRAZILIAN GP** Rio de Janeiro		**Alain Prost**
	7 April 1985	Race 405	McLaren-TAG Porsche MP4/2B 181.529kph, 112.797mph

As last year, Prost began the season with victory. In qualifying the McLarens were not that competitive, making their way from P6 and P9 to reach the front, but by lap 14 were lying 2-3 behind leader and pole-man Alboreto. Rosberg had been first to lead but the Honda didn't last ten laps. On lap 18 Alboreto finally lost the struggle to remain ahead of Prost, having next to contend with the other McLaren, but a 1-2 was thwarted by an electronics glitch for world champion Lauda. Alboreto kept his second place and Ferrari teammate Arnoux made a fine comeback drive to fourth. The new Lotus pairing vied for team supremacy, De Angelis finishing third, Senna out with electronics. Fellow Brazilian Piquet spun his Brabham out on lap 2.

POLE POSITION Alboreto, Ferrari, 1m 27.768s (0.096s), 206.358kph, 128.225mph
LAPS 61 x 5.031 km, 3.126 miles
DISTANCE 306.891 km, 190.693 miles
STARTERS/FINISHERS 25/13
WEATHER Sunny, hot, dry
LAP LEADERS K Rosberg, Williams-Honda 1-9 (9); Alboreto 10-17 (8); Prost 18-61 (44)
WINNER'S LAPS 1-9 P3, 10-17 P2, 18-61 P1
FASTEST LAP Prost, McLaren-TAG, 1m 36.702s (lap 34), 187.293kph, 116.378mph
CHAMPIONSHIP Prost 9, Alboreto 6, de Angelis 4, Arnoux 3, Tambay 2

Pos	Driver	Car	Time/gap	Grid	Stops	Tyres
1	A Prost	McLaren-TAG	1h 41m 26.115s	6	1	G
2	M Alboreto	Ferrari	-3.259s	1	1	G
3	E de Angelis	Lotus-Renault	-1 lap	3	1	G
4	R Arnoux	Ferrari	-2 laps	7	1	G
5	P Tambay	Renault	-2 laps	11	1	G
6	J Laffite	Ligier-Renault	-2 laps	15	0	P

Round 2/16	**PORTUGUESE GP** Estoril		**Ayrton Senna**
	21 April 1985	Race 406	Lotus-Renault 97T 145.160kph, 90.198mph

From only his 16th GP start, Senna made his presence known with a stunning pole in the dry and a stupendous win in the wet. Never headed over the two-hour duration, it was a mesmeric error-free performance when many others, including Prost and Rosberg, were bested by the atrocious conditions. For over half the race teammate de Angelis held P2, albeit an ever-widening gap, finishing up fourth with a deflating tyre. Alboreto took another well-driven second and an early championship lead, but finished a minute behind Senna, the remainder lapped. Near half-distance an incident emphasised the magnitude of Senna's feat. Chasing de Angelis, Prost's McLaren fishtailed, spun, then crashed, but this was on the straight.

POLE POSITION Senna, Lotus-Renault, 1m 21.007s (0.413s), 193.317kph, 120.121mph
LAPS 67 x 4.350 km, 2.703 miles (Scheduled for 69 laps but stopped after two hours)
DISTANCE 291.450 km, 181.099 miles
STARTERS/FINISHERS 26/9
WEATHER Overcast, cold, rain
LAP LEADERS Senna 1-67 (67)
WINNER'S LAPS 1-67 P1
FASTEST LAP Senna, Lotus-Renault, 1m 44.121s (lap 15), 150.402kph, 93.455mph
CHAMPIONSHIP Alboreto 12, Prost 9, Senna 9, de Angelis 7, Tambay 6

Pos	Driver	Car	Time/gap	Grid	Stops	Tyres
1	A Senna	Lotus-Renault	2h 0m 28.006s	1	0	G
2	M Alboreto	Ferrari	-1m 2.978s	5	0	G
3	P Tambay	Renault	-1 lap	12	0	G
4	E de Angelis	Lotus-Renault	-1 lap	4	0	G
5	N Mansell	Williams-Honda	-2 laps	9	0	G
6	S Bellof	Tyrrell-Ford	-2 laps	21	0	G

SAN MARINO GP Imola
5 May 1985 **Race 407**

Elio de Angelis
Lotus-Renault 97T 191.799kph, 119.178mph

Senna from pole led a fascinating duel, the opening laps disputed with de Angelis, Alboreto and Prost. De Angelis slowed with failing brakes, Alboreto went out with electrics, but for much of the race Prost kept pressure on Senna. But on lap 54 he was overtaken by Arnoux's Ferrari replacement Stefan Johansson, who had started a lowly P15. With four laps to go with a 10s lead Senna ran out of fuel, and suddenly Johansson found himself leading. But the Swedish fairy-tale lasted half a lap, he too running dry. Prost won and promptly ran out of fuel, but was disqualified for an underweight car, the tanks bone-dry. So de Angelis inherited victory without once leading a lap, no doubt blessing the new fuel-efficient EF15 Renault powering his Lotus.

POLE POSITION A Senna, Lotus-Renault, 1m 27.327s (0.027s), 204.978kph, 127.367mph
LAPS 60 x 5.040 km, 3.132 miles
DISTANCE 302.400 km, 187.903 miles
STARTERS/FINISHERS 25/10
WEATHER Cloudy with sunny intervals, warm, dry
LAP LEADERS (On the road) Senna 1-56 (56); Johansson 57 (1); A Prost, McLaren-TAG 58-60 (3)
WINNER'S LAPS 1-10 P2, 11 P3, 12-16 P4, 17-23 P5, 24-34 P4, 35-49 P3, 50-57 P4, 58-60 P2 (Prost finished first but was disqualified for an under-weight car)
FASTEST LAP M Alboreto, Ferrari, 1m 30.961s (lap 29), 194.522kph, 120.870mph
CHAMPIONSHIP de Angelis 16, Alboreto 12, Tambay 10, Prost 9, Senna 9

Pos	Driver	Car	Time/gap	Grid	Stops	Tyres
1	E de Angelis	Lotus-Renault	1h 34m 35.955s	3	0	G
2	T Boutsen	Arrows-BMW	−1 lap	5	0	G
3	P Tambay	Renault	−1 lap	11	0	G
4	N Lauda	McLaren-TAG	−1 lap	8	0	G
5	N Mansell	Williams-Honda	−2 laps	7	0	G
6	S Johansson	Ferrari	−3 laps	15	0	G

MONACO GP Monte Carlo
19 May 1985 **Race 408**

Alain Prost
McLaren-TAG Porsche MP4/2B 138.435kph, 86.019mph

Senna led from pole, but the Renault EF15 motor in his Lotus only lasted 20 minutes. Alboreto took over appearing to have the measure of Prost, whose TAG turbo boost pressure was fluctuating. But after only four laps in the lead Michele slid wide on oil and, worse still, picked up debris. This hazard had arisen from a dangerous clash between Patrese, the culprit, and Piquet during a tail-end battle, both cars pointlessly destroyed. It only took Alboreto seven laps to reclaim his lost lead from Prost but a slow puncture had developed, dropping him to fourth. From there he fought back to second, unable to catch winner Prost but importantly relegating championship points leader de Angelis to third.

POLE POSITION A Senna, Lotus-Renault, 1m 20.450s (0.086s), 148.206kph, 92.091mph
LAPS 78 x 3.312 km, 2.058 miles
DISTANCE 258.336 km, 160.523 miles
STARTERS/FINISHERS 25/11
WEATHER Overcast, cool, dry, light rain later
LAP LEADERS Senna 1-13 (13); Alboreto 14-17, 24-31 (12); Prost 18-23, 32-78 (53)
WINNER'S LAPS 1 P4, 2-13 P3, 14-17 P2, 18-23 P1, 24-31 P2, 32-78 P1
FASTEST LAP Alboreto, Ferrari, 1m 22.637s (lap 60), 144.284kph, 89.659mph
CHAMPIONSHIP de Angelis 20, Prost 18, Alboreto 18, Tambay 10, Senna 9

Pos	Driver	Car	Time/gap	Grid	Stops	Tyres
1	A Prost	McLaren-TAG	1h 51m 58.034s	5	0	G
2	M Alboreto	Ferrari	−7.541s	3	1	G
3	E de Angelis	Lotus-Renault	−1m 27.171s	9	0	G
4	A de Cesaris	Ligier-Renault	−1 lap	8	0	P
5	D Warwick	Renault	−1 lap	10	0	G
6	J Laffite	Ligier-Renault	−1 lap	16	0	P

CANADIAN GP Montréal
16 June 1985 **Race 409**

Michele Alboreto
Ferrari 156/85 174.686kph, 108.545mph

Two black Lotuses on the front row, two scarlet Ferraris next. All four finished, the Ferraris 1-2, the Lotus duo P5 and P16. De Angelis set the pace from pole, Senna's chase only lasting six laps, time lost in the pits with a broken turbo clip. When Senna rejoined he and Rosberg, separated by five laps, enlivened a 'fuel-consumption race' with a no-holds-barred duel. Rosberg's verdict: 'Senna's really good. I was impressed – but, Jesus, he takes some risks…' After 15 laps, dictated by fuel consumption, de Angelis gave up his lead to Alboreto and faded to fifth. Now Prost, having conserved fuel for 50 laps, mounted his attack on the leading Ferrari pair in the final 20. But he left it too late, 5s covering the top three at the finish.

POLE POSITION de Angelis, Lotus-Renault, 1m 24.567s (0.249s), 187.733kph, 116.652mph
LAPS 70 x 4.410 km, 2.740 miles
DISTANCE 308.700 km, 191.817 miles
STARTERS/FINISHERS 25/17
WEATHER Cloudy, cool, dry
LAP LEADERS de Angelis 1-15 (15); Alboreto 16-70 (55)
WINNER'S LAPS 1-5 P3, 6-15 P2, 16-70 P1
FASTEST LAP A Senna, Lotus-Renault, 1m 27.445s (lap 45), 181.554kph, 112.812mph
CHAMPIONSHIP Alboreto 27, Prost 22, de Angelis 22, Tambay 10, Senna 9

Pos	Driver	Car	Time/gap	Grid	Stops	Tyres
1	M Alboreto	Ferrari	1h 46m 1.813s	3	0	G
2	S Johansson	Ferrari	−1.957s	4	0	G
3	A Prost	McLaren-TAG	−4.341s	5	0	G
4	K Rosberg	Williams-Honda	−27.821s	8	2	G
5	E de Angelis	Lotus-Renault	−43.349s	1	0	G
6	N Mansell	Williams-Honda	−1m 17.878s	16	0	G

Ferrari 156/85

Round 6/16	**UNITED STATES GP** Detroit	
	23 June 1985	Race 410

Senna mistakenly chose unsuitable race rubber, pitting from the lead on lap 8. Rosberg was on it from the outset, from the third row blasting by Alboreto, Prost and Mansell on lap 1 and dominating from the moment he took over the lead from Senna. It was Keke at his virtuoso best, winning by almost a minute and even just having time to pit to extract litter from a sidepod without losing his lead to Johansson, the Ferraris finishing 2-3. Recently equipped with the latest E-Type Honda engine, the Williams FW10 was getting there. Brundle and Bellof gave Tyrrell something to smile about, running 4-5 mid-race in the DFY-engined cars, Bellof winning three priceless points. The choice of carbon over steel brakes accounted for both McLarens.

Keke Rosberg
Williams-Honda FW10 131.487kph, 81.702mph

POLE POSITION A Senna, Lotus-Renault, 1m 42.051s (1.198s), 141.930kph, 88.191mph
LAPS 63 x 4.023 km, 2.500 miles
DISTANCE 253.472 km, 157.500 miles
STARTERS/FINISHERS 25/12
WEATHER Sunny, hot, dry
LAP LEADERS Senna 1-7 (7); Rosberg 8-63 (56)
WINNER'S LAPS 1-7 P2, 8-63 P1
FASTEST LAP A Senna, Lotus-Renault, 1m 45.612s (lap 51), 137.144kph, 85.218mph
CHAMPIONSHIP Alboreto 31, de Angelis 24, Prost 22, Johansson 13, Rosberg 12

Pos	Driver	Car	Time/gap	Grid	Stops	Tyres
1	K Rosberg	Williams-Honda	1h 55m 39.851s	5	1	G
2	S Johansson	Ferrari	−57.549s	9	0	G
3	M Alboreto	Ferrari	−1m 3.170s	3	0	G
4	S Bellof	Tyrrell-Ford	−1m 6.225s	19	0	G
5	E de Angelis	Lotus-Renault	−1m 26.966s	8	1	G
6	N Piquet	Brabham-BMW	−1 lap	10	1	P

Round 7/16	**FRENCH GP** Paul Ricard	
	7 July 1985	Race 411

High race-day temperatures saw an abrupt change in Piquet's nightmare season. P5 in qualifying hadn't looked that promising, but the Pirelli-shod Brabham-BMW was third on lap 1, second on lap 7, and P1 on lap 11. Rosberg led the first ten laps from pole but the tyre choice was wrong and he spent the afternoon fending off the McLarens. When Lauda's gearbox gave up on lap 30 Prost moved up to third and on lap 39 got by the Williams for second. But on the final lap Rosberg, now on fresh tyres, managed to pinch back the runner-up spot from a slowing Prost. Johansson came from 15th to fourth, but Alboreto was a non-finisher. Mansell survived a 180mph tyre-burst approaching Signes in practice, and posted a dns.

Nelson Piquet
Brabham-BMW BT54 201.325kph, 125.097mph

POLE POSITION Rosberg, Williams-Honda, 1m 32.462s (0.373s), 226.212kph, 140.562mph
LAPS 53 x 5.810 km, 3.610 miles
DISTANCE 307.930 km, 191.339 miles
STARTERS/FINISHERS 25/15
WEATHER Sunny, hot, dry
LAP LEADERS Rosberg 1-10 (10); Piquet 11-53 (43)
WINNER'S LAPS 1-6 P3, 7-10 P2, 11-53 P1
FASTEST LAP Rosberg, Williams-Honda, 1m 39.914s (lap 46), 209.340kph, 130.078mph
CHAMPIONSHIP Alboreto 31, Prost 26, de Angelis 26, Rosberg 18, Johansson 16

Pos	Driver	Car	Time/gap	Grid	Stops	Tyres
1	N Piquet	Brabham-BMW	1h 31m 46.266s	5	0	P
2	K Rosberg	Williams-Honda	−6.660s	1	1	G
3	A Prost	McLaren-TAG	−9.285s	4	0	G
4	S Johansson	Ferrari	−53.491s	15	0	G
5	E de Angelis	Lotus-Renault	−53.690s	7	0	G
6	P Tambay	Renault	−1m 15.167s	9	0	G

Brabham-BMW BT54

Round 8/16	**BRITISH GP** Silverstone			**Alain Prost**
	21 July 1985		Race 412	McLaren-TAG Porsche MP4/2B 235.405kph, 146.274mph

Rosberg's stunning 65.591s pole was the first 160mph lap around Silverstone. Senna made a flyer from the second row to lead lap 1 and most of the race, but he never got fully clear of first Rosberg, until his exhaust broke on lap 21, then Prost as *le professeur* homed in from a carefully judged start. For 30 laps it was cat and mouse until the Renault turbo faltered and Prost was by. The engine re-caught, Senna briefly regained the lead, but with six to go parked, out of fuel. Was it driver or car? Anyway, Prost won from the uncompetitive and lapped Alboreto, who still led Prost by two points in the championship. Erroneously the flag was shown one lap early, Piquet denied third much to his chagrin, Laffite running dry on lap 66.

POLE POSITION K Rosberg, Williams-Honda, 1m 05.591s (0.658s), 258.983kph, 160.925mph
LAPS 65 x 4.719 km, 2.932 miles (Scheduled for 66 laps but stopped one lap early in error)
DISTANCE 306.709 km, 190.580 miles
STARTERS/FINISHERS 26/11
WEATHER Cloudy with sunny intervals, warm, dry
LAP LEADERS A Senna, Lotus-Renault 1-57, 59 (58); Prost 58, 60-65 (7)
WINNER'S LAPS 1 P4, 2-6 P5, 7-8 P4, 9-15 P3, 16-57 P2, 58 P1, 59 P2, 60-65 P1
FASTEST LAP Prost, McLaren-TAG, 1m 09.886s (lap 43), 243.067kph, 151.035mph
CHAMPIONSHIP Alboreto 37, Prost 35, de Angelis 26, Rosberg 18, Johansson 16

Pos	Driver	Car	Time/gap	Grid	Stops	Tyres
1	A Prost	McLaren-TAG	1h 18m 10.436s	3	0	G
2	M Alboreto	Ferrari	−1 lap	6	0	G
3	J Laffite	Ligier-Renault	−1 lap	16	0	P
4	N Piquet	Brabham-BMW	−1 lap	2	0	P
5	D Warwick	Renault	−1 lap	12	0	G
6	M Surer	Brabham-BMW	−2 laps	15	0	P

Round 9/16	**GERMAN GP** Nürburgring			**Michele Alboreto**
	4 August 1985		Race 413	Ferrari 156/85 191.147kph, 118.774mph

Rosberg led the first 15 laps, Senna the next 11, but just as the Lotus began to make a break the CV joint did the same. His lead restored, a duelling threesome, Alboreto, de Angelis and Prost, began reeling Rosberg in and on lap 45 they both went by, having been reduced to a twosome when the other Lotus expired. The Ferrari, which had started P8, continued to maintain the upper hand such that as Prost tried to hang on he indulged in a late spin. Alboreto went on to win but was fortunate to survive two car clashes during the journey. One was clumsily banging wheels as he took the lead from Rosberg. The other, at the start, ruined the day for his teammate, Johansson having qualified beside pole-man Teo Fabi, his and Toleman-Hart's first ever.

POLE POSITION T Fabi, Toleman-Hart, 1m 17.429s (1.187s), 211.177kph, 131.219mph
LAPS 67 x 4.542 km, 2.822 miles
DISTANCE 304.314 km, 189.092 miles
STARTERS/FINISHERS 27/12
WEATHER Overcast, cool, dry
LAP LEADERS K Rosberg, Williams-Honda 1-15, 27-44 (33); A Senna, Lotus-Renault 16-26 (11); Alboreto 45-67 (23)
WINNER'S LAPS 1-26 P3, 27-44 P2, 45-67 P1
FASTEST LAP Lauda, McLaren-TAG, 1m 22.806s (lap 53), 197.464kph, 122.698mph
CHAMPIONSHIP Alboreto 46, Prost 41, de Angelis 26, Rosberg 18, Johansson 16

Pos	Driver	Car	Time/gap	Grid	Stops	Tyres
1	M Alboreto	Ferrari	1h 35m 31.337s	8	0	G
2	A Prost	McLaren-TAG	−11.661s	3	0	G
3	J Laffite	Ligier-Renault	−51.154s	13	0	P
4	T Boutsen	Arrows-BMW	−55.279s	15	1	G
5	N Lauda	McLaren-TAG	−1m 13.972s	12	1	G
6	N Mansell	Williams-Honda	−1m 16.820s	10	0	G

Round 10/16	**AUSTRIAN GP** Österreichring					
	18 August 1985				**Race 414**	

AUSTRIAN GP Österreichring — Alain Prost

Alain Prost
McLaren-TAG Porsche MP4/2B 231.132kph, 143.619mph

After a restart, on the fast sweeps of Zeltweg the McLarens ran away with it. At half-distance Lauda, who had recently announced his intention to retire, took the lead when Prost pitted for tyres. Over the next 13 laps, on fresh rubber, Prost reeled Lauda in by 15s. But suddenly, with 13 laps to go but still 15s to the good, Lauda suffered turbo failure. It would have been close, very close. The rest were nowhere. The Williams-Hondas showed speed but no reliability; the performance of the Lotus-Renaults was strangely muted yet unusually reliable, and the Ferraris were just uncompetitive. So Senna led in the Ferraris and his teammate, while de Cesaris was a very lucky Italian, escaping a spectacular barrel-rolling crash.

POLE POSITION Prost, McLaren-TAG, 1m 25.490s (0.562s), 250.219kph, 155.479mph
LAPS 52 x 5.942 km, 3.692 miles (Race restarted for scheduled 52 laps following accident)
DISTANCE 308.984 km, 191.994 miles
STARTERS/FINISHERS 26/10
WEATHER Cloudy with sunny intervals, warm, dry
LAP LEADERS Prost 1-25, 40-52 (38); N Lauda, McLaren-TAG 26-39 (14)
WINNER'S LAPS 1-25 P1, 26-39 P2, 40-52 P1
FASTEST LAP Prost, McLaren-TAG, 1m 29.241s (lap 39), 239.701kph, 148.944mph
CHAMPIONSHIP Prost 50, Alboreto 50, de Angelis 28, Johansson 19, Rosberg 18

Pos	Driver	Car	Time/gap	Grid	Stops	Tyres
1	A Prost	McLaren-TAG	1h 20m 12.583s	1	1	G
2	A Senna	Lotus-Renault	–30.002s	14	0	G
3	M Alboreto	Ferrari	–34.356s	9	0	G
4	S Johansson	Ferrari	–39.073s	12	0	G
5	E de Angelis	Lotus-Renault	–1m 22.092s	7	1	G
6	M Surer	Brabham-BMW	–1 lap	11	0	P

Round 11/16	**DUTCH GP** Zandvoort					
	25 August 1985				**Race 415**	

Niki Lauda
McLaren-TAG Porsche MP4/2B 193.089kph, 119.980mph

After Austria, no one begrudged the reigning champion this tactical victory, not even teammate Prost beaten by a mere 0.232s, two to three car lengths. Both McLarens one-stopped, Lauda early and swift, Prost later but sluggish, rejoining 17s in arrears and needing 30 laps to catch up. But catching is one thing, passing quite another, both drivers at ten-tenths over the final five, Lauda hanging on to win once again at a former happy hunting ground. Earlier, Piquet had stalled on pole; Rosberg led for 19 laps until the Honda failed, while Senna, perhaps significantly in a still close championship battle, denied the charging Alboreto a point, holding on for third. With five rounds to go, three points separated the championship rivals.

POLE POSITION N Piquet, Brabham-BMW, 1m 11.074s (0.573s), 215.370kph, 133.825mph
LAPS 70 x 4.252 km, 2.642 miles
DISTANCE 297.640 km, 184.945 miles
STARTERS/FINISHERS 26/10
WEATHER Cool, dry
LAP LEADERS K Rosberg, Williams-Honda 1-19 (19); Prost 20-33 (14); Lauda 34-70 (37)
WINNER'S LAPS 1-4 P5, 5-13 P4, 14-20 P3, 21-22 P8, 23-24 P7, 25-26 P6, 27 P5, 28-31 P3, 32-33 P2, 34-70 P1
FASTEST LAP Prost, McLaren-TAG, 1m 16.538s (lap 57), 199.995kph, 124.271mph
CHAMPIONSHIP Prost 56, Alboreto 53, de Angelis 30, Senna 19, Johansson 19

Pos	Driver	Car	Time/gap	Grid	Stops	Tyres
1	N Lauda	McLaren-TAG	1h 32m 29.263s	10	1	G
2	A Prost	McLaren-TAG	–0.232s	3	1	G
3	A Senna	Lotus-Renault	–48.491s	4	1	G
4	M Alboreto	Ferrari	–48.837s	16	1	G
5	E de Angelis	Lotus-Renault	–1 lap	11	1	G
6	N Mansell	Williams-Honda	–1 lap	7	2	G

Round 12/16	**ITALIAN GP** Monza					
	8 September 1985				**Race 416**	

Alain Prost
McLaren-TAG Porsche MP4/2B 227.565kph, 141.402mph

The *tifosi* departed Monza early. Alboreto had started a paltry P7, retired a feeble P5 and was now 12 points shy of Prost with four races left. His title dream had effectively died with his Ferrari turbo on lap 45. Adding insult to injury, on that very same lap Prost assumed the race lead from Rosberg and Ferrari conceded their constructors' points lead to McLaren. The Williams-Honda had looked good for victory from the opening lap. Prost would not stop, opting for harder tyres, but could not live with Rosberg who led easily before and after his own tyre stop until that critical 45th lap when the Honda V6 broke. Piquet's early tyre change tactic paid off with second place, the underpowered Senna third after another scintillating pole.

POLE POSITION Senna, Lotus-Renault, 1m 25.084s (0.146s), 245.405kph, 152.487mph
LAPS 51 x 5.800 km, 3.604 miles
DISTANCE 295.800 km, 183.802 miles
STARTERS/FINISHERS 26/13
WEATHER Cloudy with sunny intervals, hot, dry
LAP LEADERS K Rosberg, Williams-Honda 1-27, 40-44 (32); Prost 28-39, 45-51 (19)
WINNER'S LAPS 1-2 P4, 3 P3, 4-27 P2, 28-39 P1, 40-44 P2, 45-51 P1
FASTEST LAP N Mansell, Williams-Honda, 1m 28.283s (lap 38), 236.512kph, 146.962mph
CHAMPIONSHIP Prost 65, Alboreto 53, de Angelis 31, Senna 23, Johansson 21

Pos	Driver	Car	Time/gap	Grid	Stops	Tyres
1	A Prost	McLaren-TAG	1h 17m 59.451s	5	0	G
2	N Piquet	Brabham-BMW	–51.635s	4	1	P
3	A Senna	Lotus-Renault	–1m 0.390s	1	0	G
4	M Surer	Brabham-BMW	–1m 0.609s	9	0	P
5r	S Johansson	Ferrari	–1 lap	10	1	G
6	E de Angelis	Lotus-Renault	–1 lap	6	0	G

BELGIAN GP Spa Francorchamps

15 September 1985   **Race 417**

Ayrton Senna

Lotus-Renault 97T 189.811kph, 117.943mph

Problems with newly laid asphalt postponed Spa from June to less clement September. The rain had stopped by the start of the race but everyone fitted wets. Prost was on pole, but once he heard that championship rival Alboreto was out on lap 3 with clutch trouble he decided to drive for points in the tricky conditions, third place stretching his championship lead. Despite a worsening misfire, Senna's second GP victory was another consummate display on the wet then drying track. He didn't put a wheel wrong, pitting on lap 8 for pre-heated slicks and rejoining without losing his lead. Although presenting no threat to the lights-to-flag winner, the Williams-Honda pair raced strongly to finish second and fourth, Mansell's podium his best GP drive yet.

POLE POSITION Prost, McLaren-TAG, 1m 55.306s (0.097s), 216.676kph, 134.636mph
LAPS 43 x 6.940 km, 4.312 miles
DISTANCE 298.420 km, 185.430 miles
STARTERS/FINISHERS 24/13
WEATHER Overcast, cool, wet, drying later
LAP LEADERS Senna 1-8, 10-43 (42); E de Angelis, Lotus-Renault 9 (1)
WINNER'S LAPS 1-8 P1, 9 P2, 10-43 P1
FASTEST LAP Prost, McLaren-TAG, 2m 01.730s (lap 38), 205.241kph, 127.531mph
CHAMPIONSHIP Prost 69, Alboreto 53, Senna 32, de Angelis 31, Rosberg 21

Pos	Driver	Car	Time/gap	Grid	Stops	Tyres
1	A Senna	Lotus-Renault	1h 34m 19.893s	2	1	G
2	N Mansell	Williams-Honda	−28.422s	7	1	G
3	A Prost	McLaren-TAG	−55.109s	1	1	G
4	K Rosberg	Williams-Honda	−1m 15.290s	10	2	G
5	N Piquet	Brabham-BMW	−1 lap	3	1	G
6	D Warwick	Renault	−1 lap	14	1	P

Williams-Honda FW10

EUROPEAN GP Brands Hatch

6 October 1985   **Race 418**

Nigel Mansell

Williams-Honda FW10 203.625kph, 126.527mph

The podium was the scene of much elation as new race winner Mansell and new world champion Prost sprayed the bubbly. The race's defining moment came on lap 7. For six laps it had been shaping up beautifully: Senna, Rosberg, Piquet, Mansell, but on the seventh Rosberg tried to pass Senna at Surtees, spun and collected Piquet. Nelson was out, but Rosberg made it back to the pits, rear tyre flapping. On lap 9 the now lapped Rosberg helped Mansell do the overtaking piece properly, and the race was over. Senna, once again from pole, finished second and Rosberg tigered back to third. The championship's defining moment came on lap 13 when No27 made a fiery exit at the Ferrari pit. P4 was all Prost needed to clinch it.

POLE POSITION Senna, Lotus-Renault, 1m 07.169s (0.313s), 225.470kph, 140.100mph
LAPS 75 x 4.207 km, 2.614 miles
DISTANCE 315.512 km, 196.050 miles
STARTERS/FINISHERS 26/12
WEATHER Cloudy with sunny intervals, warm, dry
LAP LEADERS Senna 1-8 (8); Mansell 9-75 (67)
WINNER'S LAPS 1-6 P4, 7-8 P2, 9-75 P1
FASTEST LAP J Laffite, Ligier-Renault, 1m 11.526s (lap 55), 211.735kph, 131.566mph
CHAMPIONSHIP Prost 72, Alboreto 53, Senna 38, de Angelis 33, Rosberg 25

Pos	Driver	Car	Time/gap	Grid	Stops	Tyres
1	N Mansell	Williams-Honda	1h 32m 58.109s	3	0	G
2	A Senna	Lotus-Renault	−21.396s	1	0	G
3	K Rosberg	Williams-Honda	−58.533s	4	0	G
4	A Prost	McLaren-TAG	−1m 6.121s	6	1	G
5	E de Angelis	Lotus-Renault	−1 lap	9	0	G
6	T Boutsen	Arrows-BMW	−2 laps	12	0	G

Round 15/16	**SOUTH AFRICAN GP** Kyalami		**Nigel Mansell**

SOUTH AFRICAN GP Kyalami
19 October 1985 — Race 419

Nigel Mansell
Williams-Honda FW10 208.959kph, 129.841mph

His first victory took 72 starts, his second just the one. From pole, Mansell led every lap bar one. On lap 8 Mansell waved his hard-charging teammate through, only for Rosberg to spin next time around on oil just laid at Crowthorne. But Keke kept the engine running and despite two tyre stops, tigered back to pass a now misfiring Prost for second on lap 71. Mansell sailed on his way but under unrelenting threat from not one but two McLarens, a challenge he resisted with pace and guile. Outgoing champion Lauda lost a strong P2 with turbo troubles on lap 37 while new champion Prost consolidated his championship with third. Neither Lotus-Renault finished and for the fourth time this season Piquet was out within ten laps: car three, driver one.

POLE POSITION Mansell, Williams-Honda, 1m 02.366s (0.124s), 236.898kph, 147.202mph
LAPS 75 x 4.104 km, 2.550 miles
DISTANCE 307.800 km, 191.258 miles
STARTERS/FINISHERS 20/7
WEATHER Sunny, hot, dry
LAP LEADERS Mansell 1-7, 9-75 (74); Rosberg 8 (1)
WINNER'S LAPS 1-7 P1, 8 P2, 9-75 P1
FASTEST LAP Rosberg, Williams-Honda, 1m 08.149s (lap 74), 216.796kph, 134.711mph
CHAMPIONSHIP Prost 73, Alboreto 53, Senna 38, de Angelis 33, Mansell 31

Pos	Driver	Car	Time/gap	Grid	Stops	Tyres
1	N Mansell	Williams-Honda	1h 28m 22.866s	1	1	G
2	K Rosberg	Williams-Honda	−7.572s	3	2	G
3	A Prost	McLaren-TAG	−1 lap	9	1	G
4	S Johansson	Ferrari	−1 lap	16	1	G
5	G Berger	Arrows-BMW	−1 lap	11	1	G
6	T Boutsen	Arrows-BMW	−1 lap	10	2	G

Round 16/16	**AUSTRALIAN GP** Adelaide		**Keke Rosberg**

AUSTRALIAN GP Adelaide
3 November 1985 — Race 420

Keke Rosberg
Williams-Honda FW10 154.032kph, 95.711mph

Australia's first GP was a cracker. Rosberg, his final appearance for Williams, won handsomely from two squabbling Ligiers. Remarkably and excitingly, he achieved this with three tyre stops, during which time both the one-stopping Senna and the non-stopping Lauda were each given a brief sniff of victory. Lauda crashed out brakeless when leading his farewell GP, at that moment, after 57 laps of racing, the top three still covered by only 10s despite their very different race strategies. Five laps after Lauda's exit Senna was out too, and with dnf for Prost, Piquet, de Angelis, Alboreto and Mansell lower order grid teams earned some points. Despite their blank score-card, McLaren secured the constructors' title by eight points from Ferrari.

POLE POSITION A Senna, Lotus-Renault, 1m 19.843s (0.694s), 170.344kph, 105.847mph
LAPS 82 x 3.778 km, 2.348 miles
DISTANCE 309.796 km, 192.498 miles
STARTERS/FINISHERS 25/8
WEATHER Sunny, hot, dry
LAP LEADERS Rosberg 1-41, 44-52, 62-82 (71); Senna 42-43, 53-55, 58-61 (9); N Lauda, McLaren-TAG 56-57 (2)
WINNER'S LAPS 1-41 P1, 42-43 P2, 44-52 P1, 53-57 P3, 58-61 P2, 62-82 P1
FASTEST LAP Rosberg, Williams-Honda, 1m 23.758s (lap 57), 162.382kph, 100.900mph
CHAMPIONSHIP Prost 73, Alboreto 53, Rosberg 40, Senna 38, de Angelis 33

Pos	Driver	Car	Time/gap	Grid	Stops	Tyres
1	K Rosberg	Williams-Honda	2h 0m 40.473s	3	3	G
2	J Laffite	Ligier-Renault	−46.130s	20	1	P
3	P Streiff	Ligier-Renault	−1m 28.536s	18	1	P
4	I Capelli	Tyrrell-Renault	−1 lap	22	0	G
5	S Johansson	Ferrari	−1 lap	15	2	G
6	G Berger	Arrows-BMW	−1 lap	7	3	G

1985 CHAMPIONSHIP FACTS AND FOLKLORE

- Banned for 1985 was the practice of fuel freezing, along with winglet extensions to rear wing endplates. Conversely, qualifying engines and tyres were not.
- The foremost car safety feature was a mandatory crush-box in the nose, and another F1 season passed without disturbing safety incidents, if not without F1 tragedy. Mid-season, within a month of each other, the two German F1 drivers Manfred Winkelhock and Stefan Bellof both lost their lives in sports car racing.
- Once again the best 11 results counted for the drivers' title taken from a 16-round championship which included the last GP at Zandvoort and the first in Australia, rounding out the season in Adelaide.
- Alain Prost's first championship was overdue, and when it finally came it was thoroughly convincing and well deserved. On his way to becoming France's first F1 world champion he added another five race victories to his impressive tally, three more than any other driver this year.
- Having twice before missed out on that elusive title in

the final championship round, he was determined that there should be no mistake this time, prepared at Spa and Brands to drive for points if need be. After all, it had been a long wait, 87 races, second only to Jody Scheckter's title apprenticeship.
- Thankfully, the constructors' title in 1985 was a harder ask for McLaren, but a second championship came their way for much the same reasons, fuel efficiency, race pace and reliability. Their focus was on Sunday results not Saturday headlines. They chose to shun qualifying engines and boost switches, the latter because there wasn't much more to offer.
- Niki Lauda won just once in 1985, his motivation in question. However, while Prost retired just thrice, this equalled Niki's record of race finishes, and at the end of the season he retired for the second and final time.
- Lauda's four-season comeback with McLaren had yielded a third world title and eight further race wins, leaving his career tally at 25, beating Fangio, equalling Clark and exceeded only by Stewart's 27.

Championship ranking	Championship points	Driver nationality	Driver	Car	Races contested	Race victories	Podiumse excl. victories	Races led	Lights to flag victories	Laps led	Poles	Fastest laps	Triple Crowns
				1985 Drivers Championship									
1	73	FRA	Alain Prost	McLaren-TAG	16	5	6	7		178	2	5	1
2	53	ITA	Michele Alboreto	Ferrari	16	2	6	4		98	1	2	
3	40	FIN	Keke Rosberg	Williams-Honda	16	2	3	8		231	2	3	
4	38	BRA	Ayrton Senna	Lotus-Renault	16	2	4	9	1	271	7	3	1
5	33	ITA	Elio de Angelis	Lotus-Renault	16	1	2	2		16	1		
6	31	GBR	Nigel Mansell	Williams-Honda	15	2	1	2		141	1	1	
7	26	SWE	Stefan Johansson	Tyrrell-Ford (1) Ferrari (15)	16		2	1		1			
8	21	BRA	Nelson Piquet	Brabham-BMW	16	1	1	1		43	1		
9	16	FRA	Jacques Laffite	Ligier-Renault	15		3					1	
10	14	AUT	Niki Lauda	McLaren-TAG	14	1		3		53		1	
11	11	BEL	Thierry Boutsen	Arrows-BMW	16		1						
12	11	FRA	Patrick Tambay	Renault	15		2						
13	5	SUI	Marc Surer	Brabham-BMW	12								
14	5	GBR	Derek Warwick	Renault	15								
15	4	FRA	Philippe Streiff	Ligier-Renault (4) Tyrrell-Renault (1)	5		1						
16	4	GER	Stefan Bellof	Tyrrell-Ford (6) Tyrrell-Renault (3)	9								
17	3	FRA	René Arnoux	Ferrari	1								
17	3	ITA	Andrea de Cesaris	Ligier-Renault	11								
17	3	ITA	Ivan Capelli	Tyrrell-Renault	2								
20	3	AUT	Gerhard Berger	Arrows-BMW	16								
-	0	ITA	Teo Fabi	Toleman-Hart	13						1		

RACE 405, Brazilian GP: On lap 18 Alboreto finally lost the struggle to remain ahead of Prost, and just as the previous year, the Frenchman began the season with victory.

RACE 406, Portuguese GP: In only his second race for Lotus, his 16th GP start, Senna won his first of 41 championship race victories. In demanding conditions it was a virtuoso performance by the 25-year-old.

- How the Prancing Horse ended the season so lamely is still difficult to fathom. Alboreto was in championship contention right up until Monza. For an answer, most point to the revised suspension introduced as early as Paul Ricard.
- Whatever, Ferrari's diabolical run from Monza on – during which five races Alboreto scored *nil points* to Prost's net 17 – was the first and last time, at the wheel of a Ferrari or otherwise, that an Italian fought for F1 championship honours since Ascari 30 years before.
- McLaren and Ferrari aside, this still left a further five drivers from three teams as 1985 winners.
- It had taken time, but at last Williams and Honda were getting there. Williams' 1985 offering was the carbon composite FW10 while Honda contributed a second generation turbo, significantly both chassis and engine far stiffer than their predecessors.
- Mansell's debut win at the European Grand Prix was the first of a hat-trick for Williams-Honda in the final three races of the season. It portended things to come, Williams-Honda dominating the next two seasons while Mansell went on to win a further 30 races even though his first victory had taken 72 starts, the longest wait yet recorded.
- Adelaide proved to be Keke Rosberg's final GP victory. His other success that year was Detroit in June, just four days before son Nico was born.

- 1985 also witnessed the first triumph for another prolific future winner, Ayrton Senna. Over the decade spanning 1984 to 1993, Senna would join three other drivers – Prost, Mansell and Piquet – to dominate race winning, one of these four victorious in all but 32 of the 160 Grands Prix run.
- Piquet's 1985 French GP victory was the first for Pirelli since the 1950s.
- French teams Renault and Ligier-Renault staged a political withdrawal from the South African GP on anti-apartheid grounds, Kyalami subsequently dropped from the calendar for seven years, returning in 1992.
- After nine years in vain pursuit of a championship, the end of the season also saw turbo pioneers Renault wind up their works team but continue as engine supplier to Lotus, Ligier and Tyrrell.
- Similarly, Alfa Romeo's comeback seven years earlier had produced very little, 50 championship points to be precise, and they too withdrew at season's end, supplying their turbo V8 to Osella for one further season.
- At the start of the 1985 season Toleman had been left high and dry without a tyre contract, missing the opening three rounds. Sponsor Benetton assisted the Oxfordshire team with the purchase of the Pirelli contract from Spirit, and on the 1986 grid the Toleman moniker had been supplanted by Benetton.

Championship ranking	Championship points	Team/Marque nationality	1985 Constructors Championship		Engine maker nationality	Races contested	Race victories	1-2 finishes	Podiums excl. victories	Races led	Laps led	Poles	Fastest laps
			Chassis	Engine									
1	90	GBR	McLaren MP4-2B	TAG Porsche 1.5 V6t	GER	16	6	1	6	8	231	2	6
2	82	ITA	Ferrari 156/85	Ferrari 1.5 V6t	ITA	16	2	1	8	4	99	1	2
3	71	GBR	Williams FW10	Honda 1.5 V6t	JAP	16	4	1	4	9	372	3	4
4	71	GBR	Lotus 97T	Renault 1.5 V6t	FRA	16	3		6	11	287	8	3
5	26	GBR	Brabham BT54	BMW 1.5 S4t	GER	16	1		1	1	43	1	
6	23	FRA	Ligier JS25	Renault 1.5 V6t	FRA	16			4				1
7	16	FRA	Renault RE60, RE60B	Renault 1.5 V6t	FRA	16			2				
8	14	GBR	Arrows A8	BMW 1.5 S4t	GER	16			1				
9	4	GBR	Tyrrell 012	Ford Cosworth 3.0 V8	GBR	9							
10	3	GBR	Tyrrell 014	Renault 1.5 V6t	FRA	10							
-	0	GBR	Toleman TG 185	Hart 1.5 S4t	GBR	13						1	

1986

Prost elated, Mansell deflated

THE TALE OF THE TITLE

- A spectacular rear tyre burst denied Nigel Mansell the championship at the final round in Australia.
- Alain Prost won the Adelaide finale to become the first back-to-back champion in 26 years.
- Williams-Honda superiority produced nine race victories and the constructors' championship.
- But warring Williams drivers Mansell and Piquet divided the Williams spoils between them, letting Prost in.
- Fuel and tyre management defined turbo era 'racing', Prost, *le professeur*, proving master of the genre.
- For much of the season Ayrton Senna was a genuine fourth championship contender in the Lotus-Renault.
- Mansell with five victories was the most successful of the five race winners over the 16 championship rounds.
- Benetton joined Williams, McLaren and Lotus in the winners' circle, Gerhard Berger triumphant in Mexico.
- For the first time since going turbo in 1981, Ferrari failed to win while Brabham-BMW were also-rans.
- Frank Williams endured a shocking pre-season car crash and Elio de Angelis was killed testing at Paul Ricard.
- And not forgetting: two-way radios and tyre blankets.

THE CHASE FOR THE CHAMPIONSHIP

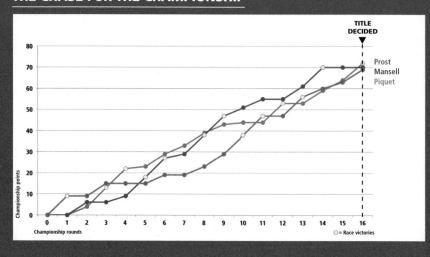

Round 1/16	**BRAZILIAN GP** Rio de Janeiro					**Nelson Piquet**
	23 March 1986			**Race 421**		Williams-Honda FW11 184.980kph, 114.941mph

On his first appearance for Williams-Honda, Piquet sent hospitalised team owner Frank the best possible 'get well' message. The result also thrilled the partisan crowd, Senna making it a Brazilian 1-2 having won pole yet again. After two fervent laps Piquet disposed of his countryman's Lotus-Renault, and 16 later, at the first of his two stops, his lead was out to 12s, and by the flag more than 30s. Piquet's greater threat was world champion Prost. On a one-stop strategy, Prost's only chance from a P9 grid slot, he took the lead at one-third-distance, but two laps after his pit stop the TAG engine failed. Piquet's other danger-man, teammate Mansell, lasted barely a lap, eliminated in an overtaking contretemps with Senna. The Ligier-Renaults finished 3-4.

POLE POSITION Senna, Lotus-Renault, 1m 25.501s (0.765s), 211.829kph, 131.625mph
LAPS 61 x 5.031 km, 3.126 miles
DISTANCE 306.891 km, 190.693 miles
STARTERS/FINISHERS 25/10
WEATHER Cloudy with sunny intervals, hot, dry
LAP LEADERS Senna 1-2, 19, 41 (4); Piquet 3-18, 27-40, 42-61 (50); A Prost, McLaren-TAG 20-26 (7)
WINNER'S LAPS 1-2 P2, 3-18 P1, 19-21 P3, 22-26 P2, 27-40 P1, 41 P2, 42-61 P1
FASTEST LAP Piquet, Williams-Honda, 1m 33.546s (lap 46), 193.612kph, 120.305mph
CHAMPIONSHIP Piquet 9, Senna 6, Laffite 4, Arnoux 3, Brundle 2

Pos	Driver	Car	Time/gap	Grid	Stops	Tyres
1	N Piquet	Williams-Honda	1h 39m 32.583s	2	2	G
2	A Senna	Lotus-Renault	−34.827s	1	2	G
3	J Laffite	Ligier-Renault	−59.579s	5	1	P
4	R Arnoux	Ligier-Renault	−1m 28.428s	4	1	P
5	M Brundle	Tyrrell-Renault	−1 lap	17	2	G
6	G Berger	Benetton-BMW	−2 laps	16	2	P

Lotus-Renault 98T

Round 2/16	**SPANISH GP** Jerez					**Ayrton Senna**
	13 April 1986			**Race 422**		Lotus-Renault 98T 167.486kph, 104.071mph

Senna on pole from the Williams pair then the two McLarens, these five breaking clear from the start. The race was all about fuel and tyre management. Senna led the first half from Piquet until his retirement on lap 39. The following lap Mansell, never far adrift, took the lead and held it until he began to run out of rubber, pitting on lap 63. On fresh tyres the Williams driver rejoined with nine laps to go and 20s to make up. It was a thrilling chase, both drivers ten-tenths lap after lap, Mansell carving great slices through the gap. In the drag race from the final corner to the line he fell short by 14/100ths. The race was decided with five to go, Mansell losing crucial time overtaking Prost. The McLarens finished 3-4, slowed by pessimistic fuel readouts.

POLE POSITION Senna, Lotus-Renault, 1m 21.605s (0.826s), 186.077kph, 115.623mph
LAPS 72 x 4.218 km, 2.621 miles
DISTANCE 303.696 km, 188.708 miles
STARTERS/FINISHERS 24/8
WEATHER Sunny, warm, dry
LAP LEADERS Senna 1-39, 63-72 (49); Mansell 40-62 (23)
WINNER'S LAPS 1-39 P1, 40-62 P2, 63-72 P1
FASTEST LAP Mansell, Williams-Honda, 1m 27.176s (lap 65), 174.186kph, 108.234mph
CHAMPIONSHIP Senna 15, Piquet 9, Mansell 6, Laffite 4, Prost 4

Pos	Driver	Car	Time/gap	Grid	Stops	Tyres
1	A Senna	Lotus-Renault	1h 48m 47.735s	1	0	G
2	N Mansell	Williams-Honda	−0.014s	3	1	G
3	A Prost	McLaren-TAG	−21.552s	4	0	G
4	K Rosberg	McLaren-TAG	−1 lap	5	1	G
5	T Fabi	Benetton-BMW	−1 lap	9	1	P
6	G Berger	Benetton-BMW	−1 lap	7	1	P

TOP **100** RACE

McLaren-TAG Porsche MP4/2C

Round 3/16	**SAN MARINO GP** Imola					**Alain Prost**
	27 April 1986			Race 423		McLaren-TAG Porsche MP4/2C 196.208kph, 121.918mph

Imola, always heavy on fuel consumption, was an economy run: 190 miles from 195 litres in the shortest time. The result was Prost perfect, *le professeur* crossing the line, engine dead, tanks dry, flik-flakking the car to suck the final dregs. Piquet's approach was different. Sprint into the lead, cruise after the fuel stop behind the McLarens when the fuel readout looked threatening, then sprint again at the end. But he misjudged it, finishing second with fuel to spare. But he was righter than Rosberg, who ran dry with two laps left when defending second place from Piquet's late attack. Senna, who had annexed his third pole in as many races this season, didn't feature, out after 11 laps with a wheel bearing, Mansell even sooner with engine trouble.

POLE POSITION A Senna, Lotus-Renault, 1m 25.050s (0.027s), 213.333kph, 132.559mph
LAPS 60 x 5.040 km, 3.132 miles
DISTANCE 302.400 km, 187.903 miles
STARTERS/FINISHERS 26/10
WEATHER Cloudy with sunny intervals, warm, dry
LAP LEADERS Piquet 1-28 (28); Rosberg 29-32 (4); Prost 33-60 (28)
WINNER'S LAPS 1-3 P3, 4 P2, 5-11 P3, 12 P2, 13-28 P3, 29-32 P2, 33-60 P1
FASTEST LAP Piquet, Williams-Honda, 1m 28.667s (lap 57), 204.631kph, 127.152mph
CHAMPIONSHIP Senna 15, Piquet 15, Prost 13, Mansell 6, Berger 6

Pos	Driver	Car	Time/gap	Grid	Stops	Tyres
1	A Prost	McLaren-TAG	1h 32m 28.408s	4	1	G
2	N Piquet	Williams-Honda	–7.645s	2	1	G
3	G Berger	Benetton-BMW	–1 lap	9	1	P
4	S Johansson	Ferrari	–1 lap	7	1	G
5r	K Rosberg	McLaren-TAG	–2 laps	6	1	G
6r	R Patrese	Brabham-BMW	–2 laps	16	0	P

Round 4/16	**MONACO GP** Monte Carlo					**Alain Prost**
	11 May 1986			Race 424		McLaren-TAG Porsche MP4/2C 134.634kph, 83.658mph

No one could challenge Prost. From pole he lost the lead briefly to Senna during his tyre stop, otherwise his totally faultless drive provoked very little race excitement. By the end Senna's outclassed Lotus-Renault was actually a distant third behind a McLaren 1-2, Rosberg demonstrating McLaren superiority around the houses by coming through from a modest P9 qualification. 'Light-switch' Honda power delivery had the Williams drivers helmets jerking back and forth, but Mansell came in next, Piquet seventh. Towards the end, near catastrophe: At Mirabeau Tambay's Lola barrel-rolled, launched off Brundle's Tyrrell, both drivers, indeed F1 itself, very lucky. Prost's Monaco hat-trick relegated Senna from his early championship lead.

POLE POSITION Prost, McLaren-TAG, 1m 22.627s (0.420s), 144.999kph, 90.098mph
LAPS 78 x 3.328 km, 2.068 miles
DISTANCE 259.584 km, 161.298 miles
STARTERS/FINISHERS 20/12
WEATHER Sunny, warm, dry
LAP LEADERS Prost 1-34, 42-78 (71); Senna 35-41 (7)
WINNER'S LAPS 1-34 P1, 35-41 P2, 42-78 P1
FASTEST LAP Prost, McLaren-TAG, 1m 26.607s (lap 51), 138.335kph, 85.958mph
CHAMPIONSHIP Prost 22, Senna 19, Piquet 15, Rosberg 11, Mansell 9

Pos	Driver	Car	Time/gap	Grid	Stops	Tyres
1	A Prost	McLaren-TAG	1h 55m 41.060s	1	1	G
2	K Rosberg	McLaren-TAG	–25.022s	9	1	G
3	A Senna	Lotus-Renault	–53.646s	3	2	G
4	N Mansell	Williams-Honda	–1m 11.402s	2	1	G
5	R Arnoux	Ligier-Renault	–1 lap	12	0	P
6	J Laffite	Ligier-Renault	–1 lap	7	0	P

Round 5/16	**BELGIAN GP** Spa Francorchamps	**Nigel Mansell**
	25 May 1986 Race 425	Williams-Honda FW11 203.548kph, 126.479mph

Berger's Benetton-BMW sat alongside Piquet on pole, the Austrian instrumental in a first corner mêleé at La Source that effectively eliminated the McLarens, although subsequently Prost drove a lonely blinder back to P6. Unaffected, the remainder of the 'big four' rushed off led by Piquet, drawing away. Behind, Mansell quickly took Senna then spun back to fourth at the Bus Stop. When Piquet's engine failed on lap 16 Senna led but lost out to Mansell during the tyre stops, Nigel subsequently doing the better job balancing fuel with pace. Mansell dedicated his victory to former teammate Elio de Angelis, killed ten days earlier testing at Ricard. After just one prior points finish Ferrari's came in 3-4, while P2 restored Senna's championship points lead.

POLE POSITION N Piquet, Williams-Honda, 1m 54.331s (0.137s), 218.523kph, 135.784mph
LAPS 43 x 6.940 km, 4.312 miles
DISTANCE 298.420 km, 185.430 miles
STARTERS/FINISHERS 25/13
WEATHER Sunny, hot, dry
LAP LEADERS Piquet 1-16 (16); Senna 17-21 (5); Johansson 22-23 (2); Mansell 24-43 (20)
WINNER'S LAPS 1-2 P3, 3-4 P2, 5-14 P4, 15-16 P3, 17-20 P2, 21 P3, 22-23 P2, 24-43 P1
FASTEST LAP Prost, McLaren-TAG, 1m 59.282s (lap 31), 209.453kph, 130.148mph
CHAMPIONSHIP Senna 25, Prost 23, Mansell 18, Piquet 15, Rosberg 11

Pos	Driver	Car	Time/gap	Grid	Stops	Tyres
1	N Mansell	Williams-Honda	1h 27m 57.925s	5	1	G
2	A Senna	Lotus-Renault	−19.827s	4	1	G
3	S Johansson	Ferrari	−26.592s	11	1	G
4	M Alboreto	Ferrari	−29.634s	9	1	G
5	J Laffite	Ligier-Renault	−1m 10.690s	17	1	P
6	A Prost	McLaren-TAG	−2m 17.772s	3	1	G

Williams-Honda FW11

Round 6/16	**CANADIAN GP** Montréal	**Nigel Mansell**
	15 June 1986 Race 426	Williams-Honda FW11 178.225kph, 110.744mph

With a second successive victory Mansell brought himself into genuine championship contention, now matching Senna's points haul and just two shy of Prost, who had resumed the lead in the title race. It was a commanding victory, pipping Senna for pole, then controlling the race from the front, although around quarter-distance Rosberg relieved Mansell of his lead for five laps before dropping back to conserve fuel. Mansell was followed home by the remainder of the 'gang of four': Prost runner-up, simply unable to run with the Williams that day; a lacklustre Piquet third; and following Rosberg, an off-the-pace Senna, ignominiously lapped by the leader ten from the finish.

POLE POSITION Mansell, Williams-Honda, 1m 24.118s (0.070s), 188.735kph, 117.274mph
LAPS 69 x 4.410 km, 2.740 miles
DISTANCE 304.290 km, 189.077 miles
STARTERS/FINISHERS 24/13
WEATHER Sunny, warm, dry
LAP LEADERS Mansell 1-16, 22-30, 32-69 (63); Rosberg 17-21 (5); Prost 31 (1)
WINNER'S LAPS 1-16 P1, 17-21 P2, 22-30 P1, 31 P2, 32-69 P1
FASTEST LAP Piquet, Williams-Honda, 1m 25.443s (lap 63), 185.808kph, 115.456mph
CHAMPIONSHIP Prost 29, Mansell 27, Senna 27, Piquet 19, Rosberg 14

Pos	Driver	Car	Time/gap	Grid	Stops	Tyres
1	N Mansell	Williams-Honda	1h 42m 26.415s	1	1	G
2	A Prost	McLaren-TAG	−20.659s	4	1	G
3	N Piquet	Williams-Honda	−36.262s	3	2	G
4	K Rosberg	McLaren-TAG	−1m 35.673s	6	1	G
5	A Senna	Lotus-Renault	−1 lap	2	1	G
6	R Arnoux	Ligier-Renault	−1 lap	5	0	P

Round 7/16	**UNITED STATES GP** Detroit						**Ayrton Senna**	
	22 June 1986					Race 427	Lotus-Renault 98T 136.748kph, 84.971mph	

In a race with five separate leaders, pole-sitter Senna saw off every challenge for a fine victory. The first came from Mansell but faded with his brakes, the Williams-Honda taking the lead from Senna on lap 2 but only for six laps. On lap 14 a puncture caused Senna to lose the lead a second time, Ayrton scything back from eighth to brilliantly regain the lead at the two-thirds mark, holding it to the end. During Senna's recovery drive the race was led by the Ligier duo, Arnoux and Laffite, then finally Piquet until his lap 39 stop let Senna back ahead. In his subsequent chase of Senna, Piquet clipped the barrier and crashed heavily, Arnoux's challenge also ending when he collided with the wreckage. So Laffite finished P2, pipping the troubled Prost.

POLE POSITION Senna, Lotus-Renault, 1m 38.301s (0.538s), 147.344kph, 91.556mph
LAPS 63 x 4.023 km, 2.500 miles
DISTANCE 253.472 km, 157.500 miles
STARTERS/FINISHERS 25/10
WEATHER Sunny, hot, dry, windy
LAP LEADERS Senna 1, 8-13, 39-63 (32); Mansell 2-7 (6); R Arnoux, Ligier-Renault 14-17 (4); Laffite 18-30 (13); Piquet 31-38 (8)
WINNER'S LAPS 1 P1, 2-7 P2, 8-13 P1, 14-16 P8, 17-18, P7, 19-26 P6, 27-29 P4, 30 P3, 31-38 P2, 39-63 P1
FASTEST LAP N Piquet, Williams-Honda, 1m 41.233s (lap 41), 143.077kph, 88.908mph
CHAMPIONSHIP Senna 36, Prost 33, Mansell 29, Piquet 19, Rosberg 14

Pos	Driver	Car	Time/gap	Grid	Stops	Tyres
1	A Senna	Lotus-Renault	1h 51m 12.847s	1	2	G
2	J Laffite	Ligier-Renault	−31.017s	6	1	P
3	A Prost	McLaren-TAG	−31.824s	7	1	G
4	M Alboreto	Ferrari	−1m 30.936s	11	1	G
5	N Mansell	Williams-Honda	−1 lap	2	1	G
6	R Patrese	Brabham-BMW	−1 lap	8	0	P

Round 8/16	**FRENCH GP** Paul Ricard						**Nigel Mansell**	
	6 July 1986					Race 428	Williams-Honda FW11 188.062kph, 116.856mph	

At the first corner Mansell chopped past pole-man Senna for the lead and then drove a fast, composed, two-stop race to beat the one-stopping Prost by 17s. During the first half Prost's alternate pit stop strategy appeared menacing, but concerns over fuel consumption constrained his victory challenge and he settled for second, which nevertheless jumped him back into the points lead. Senna had a costly afternoon for his championship hopes. On lap 4 Mansell saw the oil dropped at Signes, Senna didn't, plunging off the track, hard into the barrier. Arnoux cheered the French crowd, holding P2 for several laps, and despite slow pit stops the Ligiers again finished in the points, P5 and P6, albeit a lap behind the Williams and McLaren cars ahead.

POLE POSITION A Senna, Lotus-Renault, 1m 06.526s (0.229s), 206.337kph, 128.212mph
LAPS 80 x 3.813 km, 2.369 miles
DISTANCE 305.040 km, 189.543 miles
STARTERS/FINISHERS 26/11
WEATHER Cloudy with sunny intervals, warm, dry
LAP LEADERS Mansell 1-25, 37-53, 59-80 (64); Prost 26-36, 54-58 (16)
WINNER'S LAPS 1-25 P1, 26-30 P3, 31-36 P2, 37-53 P1, 54-58 P2, 59-80 P1
FASTEST LAP Rosberg, McLaren-TAG, 1m 09.993s (lap 57), 196.117kph, 121.861mph
CHAMPIONSHIP Prost 39, Mansell 38, Senna 36, Piquet 23, Rosberg 17

Pos	Driver	Car	Time/gap	Grid	Stops	Tyres
1	N Mansell	Williams-Honda	1h 37m 19.272s	2	2	G
2	A Prost	McLaren-TAG	−17.128s	5	1	G
3	N Piquet	Williams-Honda	−37.545s	3	2	G
4	K Rosberg	McLaren-TAG	−48.703s	7	1	G
5	R Arnoux	Ligier-Renault	−1 lap	4	2	P
6	J Laffite	Ligier-Renault	−1 lap	11	2	P

Round 9/16	**BRITISH GP** Brands Hatch						**Nigel Mansell**	
	13 July 1986					Race 429	Williams-Honda FW11 208.853kph, 129.775mph	

As Mansell left the grid his driveshaft broke. Seconds later a multiple accident at Paddock Hill Bend produced a red flag, four cars eliminated and Jacques Laffite with career-ending leg injuries. For Mansell, now strapped into Piquet's spare, the restarted race was a reprieve. Quickly it developed into an unyielding man-on-man duel between the Williams-Honda pair, never more than 2s apart for 70 laps, Prost finishing a lapped third. Out of South Bank on lap 23 Piquet missed a gear, Mansell through to the audible approval of the crowd. There was other British interest too, Warwick out on his final lap, the Brabham tank dry, his fifth place taken by Brundle's Tyrrell. But all that paled alongside the 'Mansell mania' that gripped Silverstone.

POLE POSITION Piquet, Williams-Honda, 1m 06.961s (0.438s), 226.170kph, 140.536mph
LAPS 75 x 4.207 km, 2.614 miles (Race restarted for scheduled 75 laps following accident)
DISTANCE 315.512 km, 196.050 miles
STARTERS/FINISHERS 26/9
WEATHER Sunny, warm, dry
LAP LEADERS Piquet 1-22 (22); Mansell 23-75 (53)
WINNER'S LAPS 1-2 P3, 3-22 P2, 23-75 P1
FASTEST LAP Mansell, Williams-Honda, 1m 09.593s (lap 69), 217.616kph, 135.220mph
CHAMPIONSHIP Mansell 47, Prost 43, Senna 36, Piquet 29, Rosberg 17

Pos	Driver	Car	Time/gap	Grid	Stops	Tyres
1	N Mansell	Williams-Honda	1h 30m 38.471s	2	1	G
2	N Piquet	Williams-Honda	−5.574s	1	1	G
3	A Prost	McLaren-TAG	−1 lap	6	2	G
4	R Arnoux	Ligier-Renault	−2 laps	8	2	P
5	M Brundle	Tyrrell-Renault	−3 laps	11	1	G
6	P Streiff	Tyrrell-Renault	−3 laps	16	1	G

GERMAN GP Hockenheim
27 July 1986   Race 430

Nelson Piquet
Williams-Honda FW11 218.463kph, 135.747mph

Over a race distance the fuel efficiency of the Honda was approaching invincibility, victorious in eight of the last 12 races. Piquet made it nine from 13, even able to luxuriate in a two-stop strategy and still outclass the one-stopping rest. On Friday Rosberg announced his retirement then stuck it on pole, also competing robustly if vainly by leading just as many race laps as Piquet, but not the one that mattered. Indeed, neither he nor Prost completed the final lap, their probable 2-3 finish dwindling to 5-6, tanks dry. Senna, who also finished out of fuel, inherited second, while Mansell, despite a race handicapped by handling difficulties due to a partially broken rear diffuser, was glad of podium points which extended his championship lead to seven.

POLE POSITION Rosberg, McLaren-TAG, 1m 42.013s (0.153s), 239.864kph, 149.044mph
LAPS 44 x 6.797 km, 4.223 miles
DISTANCE 299.068 km, 185.832 miles
STARTERS/FINISHERS 26/12
WEATHER Sunny, warm, dry
LAP LEADERS Senna 1 (1); Rosberg 2-5, 15-19, 27-38 (21); Piquet 6-14, 21-26, 39-44 (21); Prost 20 (1)
WINNER'S LAPS 1-2 P4, 3-5 P2, 6-14 P1, 15 P2, 16-19 P4, 20 P2, 21-26 P1, 27 P2, 28-30 P3, 31-38 P1, 39-44 P1
FASTEST LAP G Berger, Benetton-BMW, 1m 46.604s (lap 35), 229.534kph, 142.626mph
CHAMPIONSHIP Mansell 51, Prost 44, Senna 42, Piquet 38, Rosberg 19

Pos	Driver	Car	Time/gap	Grid	Stops	Tyres
1	N Piquet	Williams-Honda	1h 22m 8.263s	5	2	G
2	A Senna	Lotus-Renault	−15.437s	3	1	G
3	N Mansell	Williams-Honda	−44.580s	6	2	G
4	R Arnoux	Ligier-Renault	−1m 15.176s	8	1	P
5r	K Rosberg	McLaren-TAG	−1 lap	1	1	G
6r	A Prost	McLaren-TAG	−1 lap	2	1	G

HUNGARIAN GP Hungaroring
10 August 1986   Race 431

Nelson Piquet
Williams-Honda FW11 151.804kph, 94.327mph

At the first Soviet bloc GP, a repeat Piquet victory put him squarely on the championship map, although compatriot Senna made him work hard for it. From the front row the two Brazilians engaged in a dramatic two-hour battle. Until lap 50 the Lotus was looking good, but then Nelson came on strong, making up 9s in five laps. On lap 57 the race settled as Piquet made a lurid pass of the robustly defensive Senna at turn one. Mansell maintained his title momentum with another podium, albeit lapped. Relationships between the Williams drivers were beginning to unravel, Piquet, with his T-car advantage, not sharing the diff benefit he had discovered during practice. Prost damaged his championship prospects by posting a dnf.

POLE POSITION Senna, Lotus-Renault, 1m 29.450s (0.335s), 161.547kph, 100.381mph
LAPS 76 x 4.014 km, 2.494 miles (Scheduled for 77 laps but stopped after two hours)
DISTANCE 305.064 km, 189.558 miles
STARTERS/FINISHERS 26/10
WEATHER Sunny, hot, dry
LAP LEADERS Senna 1-11, 36-56 (32); Piquet 12-35, 57-76 (44)
WINNER'S LAPS 1-2 P3, 3-11 P2, 12-35 P1, 36-56 P2, 57-76 P1
FASTEST LAP Piquet, Williams-Honda, 1m 31.001s (lap 73), 158.794kph, 98.670mph
CHAMPIONSHIP Mansell 55, Senna 48, Piquet 47, Prost 44, Rosberg 19

Pos	Driver	Car	Time/gap	Grid	Stops	Tyres
1	N Piquet	Williams-Honda	2h 0m 34.508s	2	1	G
2	A Senna	Lotus-Renault	−17.673s	1	1	G
3	N Mansell	Williams-Honda	−1 lap	4	2	G
4	S Johansson	Ferrari	−1 lap	7	2	G
5	J Dumfries	Lotus-Renault	−2 laps	8	1	G
6	M Brundle	Tyrrell-Renault	−2 laps	16	1	G

AUSTRIAN GP Österreichring
17 August 1986   Race 432

Alain Prost
McLaren-TAG Porsche MP4/2C 227.821kph, 141.561mph

A week later Prost bounced back with his third victory of the season, and, as the only championship contender to score, boosted his chances appreciably. Benetton stood the formbook on its head by qualifying 1-2 and then leading going away. Fabi was first to falter when the BMW broke on lap 17, teammate Berger gloriously leading half of his home GP until delayed with a flat battery. Behind the Benettons Prost disputed P3 with Mansell but was home clear when a Williams half-shaft failed on lap 32. Prost was the only car to complete the full race-distance, but it wasn't quite that easy, both McLarens in serious electronics trouble in the final laps. Prost nursed his home, Rosberg didn't, handing Ferrari their best result so far, a lapped second.

POLE POSITION T Fabi, Benetton-BMW, 1m 25.549s (0.194s), 256.032kph, 159.091mph
LAPS 52 x 5.942 km, 3.692 miles
DISTANCE 308.984 km, 191.994 miles
STARTERS/FINISHERS 25/11
WEATHER Sunny, hot, dry
LAP LEADERS Berger 1-25 (25); N Mansell, Williams-Honda 26-28 (3); Prost 29-52 (24)
WINNER'S LAPS 1-16 P3, 17-20 P2, 21 P3, 22-23 P4, 24-25 P3, 26-28 P2, 29-52 P1
FASTEST LAP G Berger, Benetton-BMW, 1m 29.444s (lap 49), 239.157kph, 148.606mph
CHAMPIONSHIP Mansell 55, Prost 53, Senna 48, Piquet 47, Rosberg 19

Pos	Driver	Car	Time/gap	Grid	Stops	Tyres
1	A Prost	McLaren-TAG	1h 21m 22.531s	5	1	G
2	M Alboreto	Ferrari	−1 lap	9	1	G
3	S Johansson	Ferrari	−2 laps	14	2	G
4	A Jones	Lola-Ford	−2 laps	16	0	G
5	P Tambay	Lola-Ford	−2 laps	13	2	G
6	C Danner	Arrows-BMW	−3 laps	22	2	G

| **Round 13/16** | **ITALIAN GP** Monza | | **Nelson Piquet** |

ITALIAN GP Monza
7 September 1986   **Race 433**

Nelson Piquet
Williams-Honda FW11 228.373kph, 141.905mph

With Ferrari in the doldrums, surrogate Italian team Benetton again showed strongly at Monza, Fabi on pole, Berger leading the opening six laps, still there vying for third until the BMW went sick over the final ten. Up ahead the Williams pair fought for victory, Mansell leading in the main but maybe pushing his Goodyears too hard, Piquet's late charge proving irresistible. Not yet level on points, the Williams drivers were now equal on race wins, four apiece. And the rest were scratching: nothing for Prost, engine on lap 27; Rosberg a distant fourth behind Johansson's Ferrari, a mere sop for the disenchanted *tifosi*, and nothing for Senna, transmission failure on the start line almost but not quite bringing his championship challenge to a close.

POLE POSITION T Fabi, Benetton-BMW, 1m 24.078s (0.436s), 248.341kph, 154.312mph
LAPS 51 x 5.800 km, 3.604 miles
DISTANCE 295.800 km, 183.802 miles
STARTERS/FINISHERS 27/10
WEATHER Cloudy with sunny intervals, warm, dry
LAP LEADERS Berger 1-6, 25-26 (8); Mansell 7-24, 27-37 (29); Piquet 38-51 (14)
WINNER'S LAPS 1-7 P3, 8-21 P2, 22 P5, 23 P6, 24-26 P4, 27-28 P3, 29-37 P2, 38-51 P1
FASTEST LAP T Fabi, Benetton-BMW, 1m 28.099 (lap 35), 237.006kph, 147.269mph
CHAMPIONSHIP Mansell 61, Piquet 56, Prost 53, Senna 48, Rosberg 22

Pos	Driver	Car	Time/gap	Grid	Stops	Tyres
1	N Piquet	Williams-Honda	1h 17m 42.889s	6	1	G
2	N Mansell	Williams-Honda	–9.828s	3	1	G
3	S Johansson	Ferrari	–22.915s	1	1	G
4	K Rosberg	McLaren-TAG	–53.809s	8	1	G
5	G Berger	Benetton-BMW	–1 lap	4	1	P
6	A Jones	Lola-Ford	–2 laps	18	2	G

PORTUGUESE GP Estoril
21 September 1986   **Race 434**

Nigel Mansell
Williams-Honda FW11 187.644kph, 116.597mph

In the face of Piquet's recent form, three wins from the last four races, Mansell brilliantly reasserted his title claim with a crushing lights-to-flag victory, opening up a significant ten-point championship advantage. Mansell, now equipped with his own T-car, started from the front row, smoked past poleman Senna, and was never seen again. The Brazilian rivals fought over second but it was Prost who ultimately claimed that position. Piquet's late spin caused by locking rear brakes dropped him to third, and dry tanks sent Senna down to fourth and conclusively out of the title run-in. The early-season 'big four' was now three: Prost versus Williams-Honda, their ninth win of 1986 bringing the Oxfordshire team the constructors' championship.

POLE POSITION Senna, Lotus-Renault, 1m 16.673s (0.816s), 204.244kph, 126.911mph
LAPS 70 x 4.350 km, 2.703 miles
DISTANCE 304.500 km, 189.208 miles
STARTERS/FINISHERS 27/13
WEATHER Cloudy with sunny intervals, hot, dry
LAP LEADERS Mansell 1-70 (70)
WINNER'S LAPS 1-70 (70)
FASTEST LAP Mansell, Williams-Honda, 1m 20.943s (lap 53), 193.469kph, 120.216mph
CHAMPIONSHIP Mansell 70, Piquet 60, Prost 59, Senna 51, Rosberg 22

Pos	Driver	Car	Time/gap	Grid	Stops	Tyres
1	N Mansell	Williams-Honda	1h 37m 21.900s	2	1	G
2	A Prost	McLaren-TAG	–18.772s	3	1	G
3	N Piquet	Williams-Honda	–49.274s	6	1	G
4r	A Senna	Lotus-Renault	–1 lap	1	1	G
5	M Alboreto	Ferrari	–1 lap	13	1	G
6	S Johansson	Ferrari	–1 lap	8	1	G

Benetton-BMW B186

Round 15/16	**MEXICAN GP** Mexico City		**Gerhard Berger**
	12 October 1986	Race 435	Benetton-BMW B186 193.306kph, 120.115mph

If Mansell finished ahead of Piquet and Prost the title was his, but instead of sealing it Mansell failed to engage gear on the start-line, completing the first lap P18, finishing fifth. For almost half the race rival Piquet looked the winner, but tyre blistering and repeated stops by the leading Goodyear-shod runners changed everything. Piquet used four sets, which left him fourth behind Senna, who managed the race on three. Berger's Benetton meanwhile, never more than a few seconds behind the leaders, went the distance for a conclusive maiden victory, his Pirellis working better and better. Wily Prost coaxed home a sick McLaren for second, but realistically, to retain his championship in the final round the Williams duo would need to fail.

POLE POSITION Senna, Lotus-Renault, 1m 16.990s (0.289s), 206.723kph, 128.452mph
LAPS 68 x 4.421 km, 2.747 miles
DISTANCE 300.628 km, 186.802 miles
STARTERS/FINISHERS 25/16
WEATHER Cloudy with sunny intervals, hot, dry, humid
LAP LEADERS Piquet 1-31 (31); Senna 32-35 (4); Berger 36-68 (33)
WINNER'S LAPS 1-6 P3, 7-29 P4, 30-31 P3, 32-35 P2, 36-68 P1
FASTEST LAP Piquet, Williams-Honda, 1m 19.360s (lap 64), 200.549kph, 124.616mph
CHAMPIONSHIP Mansell 70, Prost 64, Piquet 63, Senna 55, Rosberg 22

Pos	Driver	Car	Time/gap	Grid	Stops	Tyres
1	G Berger	Benetton-BMW	1h 33m 18.700s	4	0	P
2	A Prost	McLaren-TAG	−25.438s	6	1	G
3	A Senna	Lotus-Renault	−52.513s	1	2	G
4	N Piquet	Williams-Honda	−1 lap	2	3	G
5	N Mansell	Williams-Honda	−1 lap	3	2	G
6	P Alliot	Ligier-Renault	−1 lap	10	1	P

Round 16/16	**AUSTRALIAN GP** Adelaide		**Alain Prost**
	26 October 1986	Race 436	McLaren-TAG Porsche MP4/2C 162.609kph, 101.041mph

On lap 63, easy leader Rosberg, on the threshold of a swansong victory, heard his engine blow. Actually a rear Goodyear had unaccountably delaminated, stripped tread flailing bodywork being the death-rattle Keke misheard. The next lap, holding P3 and so perfectly poised for the title, Mansell spectacularly suffered the same fate at 180mph, wrestling his swerving, bucking steed to a standstill for 14s. Piquet, now leading Prost and the race, would become champion – until, that is, Goodyear advised a precautionary tyre stop. Prost, on fresher tyres due to a lap 32 puncture, but troubled by a negative cockpit readout, conserved fuel by giving up most of his 20s cushion, going on to win the race and become the first back-to-back title holder in 26 years.

POLE POSITION N Mansell, Williams-Honda, 1m 18.403s (0.311s), 173.519kph, 107.820mph
LAPS 82 x 3.779 km, 2.348 miles
DISTANCE 309.878 km, 192.549 miles
STARTERS/FINISHERS 26/10
WEATHER Cloudy with sunny intervals, warm, dry
LAP LEADERS Piquet 1-6,63-64 (8); K Rosberg, McLaren-TAG 7-62 (56); Prost 65-82 (18)
WINNER'S LAPS 1-6 P5, 7-10 P4, 11-22 P3, 23-31 P2, 32-62 P4, 63-64 P2, 65-82 P1
FASTEST LAP Piquet, Williams-Honda, 1m 20.787s (lap 82), 168.398kph, 104.638mph
CHAMPIONSHIP Prost 72, Mansell 70, Piquet 69, Senna 55, Johansson 23

Pos	Driver	Car	Time/gap	Grid	Stops	Tyres
1	A Prost	McLaren-TAG	1h 54m 20.388s	4	1	G
2	N Piquet	Williams-Honda	−4.205s	2	1	G
3	S Johansson	Ferrari	−1 lap	12	1	G
4	M Brundle	Tyrrell-Renault	−1 lap	16	0	G
5r	P Streiff	Tyrrell-Renault	−2 laps	10	0	G
6	J Dumfries	Lotus-Renault	−2 laps	14	1	G

1986 CHAMPIONSHIP FACTS AND FOLKLORE

- For this one and only season, turbo engines exclusively were permitted to contest the championship.
- Fuel stops remained prohibited while tank capacity was further restricted from 220 to 195 litres (42.89 gallons), with a further stipulation that tanks be housed within the main structure of the car.
- The best 11 results would count for the drivers' title, the 16-race championship calendar seeing the last GP at Brands Hatch and the first in a Communist bloc country at the Hungaroring.
- Although Prost won the drivers' championship in 1986, Williams supplanted McLaren as top team, presaged by their winning streak to close out 1985.
- An excellent team, chassis, tyres and driver pairing was a formidable package, but the magic ingredient was the unmatched power-to-consumption ratio and sound reliability of the Honda V6 turbo, Williams-Honda comfortably taking the constructors' cup with nine wins from the 16 rounds.
- The fatal flaw turned out to be the driver pairing chemistry.

- Against expectations nominal number two Mansell proved far too strong for double world champion Piquet, drafted in from Brabham to replace McLaren-bound Rosberg.
- Mansell won five times to Piquet's four, which would not have been at issue if Piquet hadn't so manifestly played second fiddle to Mansell on most of his winning occasions, notably their 1-2 finish at Brands Hatch.
- In March 1986, prior to the start of the season, an accident while driving a hire car between Paul Ricard Circuit and Nice Airport resulted in quadriplegia for Frank Williams.
- Whether Frank's absence for much of the season was significant in the enmity that developed between the two sides of the Williams pit is open to conjecture, but regardless of the 'no team orders' mantra, firm leadership was called for.
- Not only did Williams lose a championship, they lost the confidence of their engine supplier, Soichiro Honda unimpressed to be denied his first drivers' title.
- In fairness, Williams-Honda was on the very brink of

RACE 434, Portuguese GP: That pre-race photo-call by the 'big four' title contenders – Senna, Prost, Mansell, Piquet. Afterwards, Senna's bid now over, it became Prost versus Williams-Honda.

championship glory, Nigel Mansell's spectacular tyre burst at the finale in Australia the defining moment of the 1986 season, but on such inexactitudes championships are won and lost.

■ So against the odds Prost went on to win his fourth race of the season and with it his second successive title. Having shadowed the warring Williams 'teammates' all year, he was there to seize the spoils as they faltered at the last, the first back-to-back champion since Jack Brabham in 1960, his feat also replicating Ascari and Fangio.

■ The McLaren-TAG MP4/2C was a logical development of its highly successful predecessors but rarely a match for Williams-Honda, only winning overwhelmingly at Monaco where fuel consumption was not a consideration. Most notable improvements were a six-speed box and a more sophisticated Bosch Motronic engine management system, although the latter was the root of certain unreliability issues.

■ Rosberg joined Prost, Keke's more physical driving style contrasting sharply with Alain's silky smoothness and, at odds with designer John Barnard's thinking, Rosberg was never able to hustle a McLaren as he could a Williams.

■ At Hockenheim Rosberg announced his retirement, five race victories from 114 starts and the 1982 championship to his name. The two enduring memories of his wretched final season say it all: his McLaren decked in gaudy yellow livery in deference to Marlboro Lights in Portugal; dominating his

final race at Adelaide while the car lasted with that pleasing darty Rosberg 'body language'.

■ A factor in Rosberg's better showing in Adelaide was that Barnard had severed his sometime prickly relationship with Ron Dennis, departing McLaren before the end of the season bound for Maranello.

■ For 1987 Dennis drafted in highly successful Brabham designer Gordon Murray. In his final Brabham season Murray had pursued an innovative low-line design path which would later pay off in his immensely successful 1988 McLaren design, the MP4/4.

■ But in 1986 the skateboard Brabham with its 'lay-down' BMW engine scored just two points, the team's plight magnified through the terrible blow suffered by the death of Elio de Angelis in a testing accident at Paul Ricard in May, the last driver to die at the wheel of a Formula 1 car until the Imola tragedies of 1994.

■ Sadly, the following month a former F1 driver died, 1984 Osella driver Jo Gartner killed instantly at Le Mans, his Porsche crashing in the middle of the night on the Mulsanne straight.

■ Senna's second Lotus season again produced just two race victories although it could be judged a step forward from the first. Unlike last year, in 1986 the combo mounted a genuine title challenge that only faded in the final few rounds when that additional race victory so desperately needed just wasn't there.

- Senna's pole position strike rate remained formidable, eight from 16, Jerez marking the 100th pole for Lotus while his subsequent narrow 0.014s victory over Mansell stood only behind Gethin's 1971 Monza winning margin of 0.010s.
- Renault squeezed out yet more bhp in 1986, finding another 1,000rpm by introducing pneumatic valves, but fuel efficiency was the limiting factor, not power.
- Having already blocked Warwick as his 1986 teammate, Senna next informed Peter Warr that it was either him or Renault for 1987, and sure enough, Senna was Honda-powered for next year and at the end of this season Renault withdrew not only as engine supplier to Lotus, but to Ligier and Tyrrell also.
- Toleman's sponsor Benetton had bought out the team for 1986, switching from Hart to BMW power plants and achieving early success. Their first win was the BMW turbo's last and also a rare Pirelli victory, the tyre company withdrawing from F1 at the end of the year.
- Benetton's Mexico success was designer Rory Byrne's first win, first of many, while for his final qualifying run in Austria, Berger's BMW was purported to be pumping out close to 1,400 bhp.
- Next year Benetton would switch to the Ford Cosworth V6 turbo developed for Team Haas (USA) Ltd and their big-bucks sponsor Beatrice Foods. Alan Jones had been lured back to full-time GP racing in 1986 but retired for good, the team disbanding at the end of a dismal season that marked the final foray into F1 by a USA-led team.
- Dismal was also the word to describe Ferrari's year, the Scuderia failing to win a race for the first time since 1980, the prospect never looking remotely likely.
- Ligier had a better season than of late but one inevitably disrupted by the career-ending leg injuries suffered by Jacques Laffite at Brands Hatch.
- If Jacques had fared better and been able to take the grid for the restarted race, the popular Frenchman, winner of six GPs, would have exceeded Graham Hill's record of 176 GP starts.

Championship ranking	Championship points	Driver nationality	1986 Drivers Championship		Races contested	Race victories	Podiumse excl. victories	Races led	Lights to flag victories	Laps led	Poles	Fastest laps	Triple Crowns
			Driver	Car									
1	72	FRA	Alain Prost	McLaren-TAG	16	4	7	8		242	1	2	1
2	70	GBR	Nigel Mansell	Williams-Honda	16	5	4	9	1	331	2	4	
3	69	BRA	Nelson Piquet	Williams-Honda	16	4	6	10		166	2	7	
4	55	BRA	Ayrton Senna	Lotus-Renault	16	2	6	8		134	8		
5	23	SWE	Stefan Johansson	Ferrari	16		4	1		2			
6	22	FIN	Keke Rosberg	McLaren-TAG	16		1	4		86	1		
7	17	AUT	Gerhard Berger	Benetton-BMW	16	1	1	3		66		2	
8	14	FRA	Jacques Laffite	Ligier-Renault	9		2	1		13			
9	14	ITA	Michele Alboreto	Ferrari	16		1						
10	14	FRA	René Arnoux	Ligier-Renault	16			1		4			
11	8	GBR	Martin Brundle	Tyrrell-Renault	16								
12	4	AUS	Alan Jones	Lola-Hart (2) Lola-Ford (14)	16								
13	3	FRA	Philippe Streiff	Tyrrell-Renault	16								
13	3	GBR	Johnny Dumfries	Lotus-Renault	15								
15	2	ITA	Teo Fabi	Benetton-BMW	16							2	1
15	2	FRA	Patrick Tambay	Lola-Hart (3) Lola-Ford (11)	14								
17	2	ITA	Riccardo Patrese	Brabham-BMW	16								
18	1	GER	Christian Danner	Osella-Alfa Romeo (5) Arrows-BMW (10)	15								
18	1	FRA	Philippe Alliot	Ligier-Renault	7								

Championship ranking	Championship points	Team/Marque nationality	1986 Constructors Championship		Engine maker nationality	Races contested	Race victories	1-2 finishes	Podiums excl. victories	Races led	Laps led	Poles	Fastest laps
			Chassis	Engine									
1	141	GBR	Williams FW11	Honda 1.5 V6t	JAP	16	9	2	10	15	497	4	11
2	96	GBR	McLaren MP4-2C	TAG Porsche 1.5 V6t	GER	16	4	1	8	8	328	2	2
3	58	GBR	Lotus 98T	Renault 1.5 V6t	FRA	16	2		6	8	134	8	
4	37	ITA	Ferrari F1-86	Ferrari 1.5 V6t	ITA	16			5	1	2		
5	29	FRA	Ligier JS27	Renault 1.5 V6t	FRA	16			2	1	17		
6	19	GBR	Benetton B186	BMW 1.5 S4t	GER	16	1		1	3	66	2	3
7	11	GBR	Tyrrell 014, 015	Renault 1.5 V6t	FRA	16							
8	6	USA	Lola THL2	Ford Cosworth 1.5 V6t	GBR	14							
9	2	GBR	Brabham BT55, BT54	BMW 1.5 S4t	GER	16							
10	1	GBR	Arrows A8, A9	BMW 1.5 S4t	GER	16							

1987

Piquet reaps more Mansell misery

THE TALE OF THE TITLE

- Nelson Piquet won his third drivers' title as Mansell crashed out injured at the penultimate round in Japan.
- With eight poles and six race victories Mansell had been the dominant driver throughout the season.
- But while Mansell accrued race wins, Piquet amassed points, including two fortuitous wins of his three.
- Dominant team Williams won both championships but lost their Honda engine supply to McLaren.
- Honda-powered cars won 11 of the 16 rounds, Senna twice victorious for Camel Team Lotus Honda.
- Lotus and Williams each won races with cars equipped with active suspension.
- Prost and Senna, to be paired at McLaren in 1988, both contested the title for much of the season.
- With three more McLaren-TAG victories, Prost surpassed Jackie Stewart's record with 28 race victories.
- Ferrari re-emerged as winners, Gerhard Berger triumphing in the final two races of the season.
- The Jim Clark Trophy went to Jonathan Palmer, seven atmo class wins producing seven points for Tyrrell.
- And not forgetting: Mansell's Stowe pass on Piquet; sparking skid-blocks and turbo flame-outs.

THE CHASE FOR THE CHAMPIONSHIP

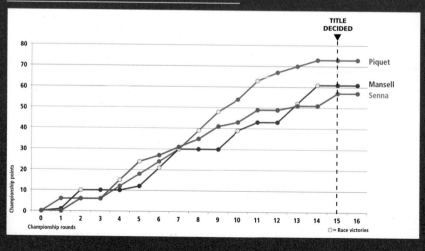

McLaren-TAG Porsche MP4/3

Round 1/16	**BRAZILIAN GP** Rio de Janeiro						**Alain Prost**		
	12 April 1987				**Race 437**		McLaren-TAG Porsche MP4/3 184.592kph, 114.700mph		

The 'big four' were straight back on it: Mansell pole, Piquet and Senna race leaders, but Prost the winner. Victory was typical of the double champion, fuel, tyres, and mind managed perfectly to produce the fastest time over the given distance. The Williams duo were untouchable in qualifying but experienced overheating in the race. Mansell endured a poor start and a puncture to finish sixth, while Piquet shot into an early lead but changed tyres on laps 4, 20 and 38, the first stop necessary to extract radiator-intake debris. Senna also stopped three times, the Honda in his active suspension Lotus failing on lap 51 when fourth. Prost started P5, led by lap 13, losing it briefly during the first of his two stops to beat Piquet by 40s. A tour de force.

POLE POSITION Mansell, Williams-Honda, 1m 26.128s (0.439s), 210.287kph, 130.666mph
LAPS 61 x 5.031 km, 3.126 miles
DISTANCE 306.891 km, 190.693 miles
STARTERS/FINISHERS 22/12
WEATHER Sunny, hot, dry
LAP LEADERS Piquet 1-7, 17-20 (11); A Senna, Lotus-Honda 8-12 (5); Prost 13-16, 21-61 (45)
WINNER'S LAPS 1-2 P6, 3-7 P5, 8-10 P3, 11-12 P2, 13-16 P1, 17 P5, 18-19 P4, 20 P3, 21-61 P1
FASTEST LAP Piquet, Williams-Honda, 1m 33.861s (lap 42), 192.962kph, 119.901mph
CHAMPIONSHIP Prost 9, Piquet 6, Johansson 4, Berger 3, Boutsen 2

Pos	Driver	Car	Time/gap	Grid	Stops	Tyres
1	A Prost	McLaren-TAG	1h 39m 45.141s	5	2	G
2	N Piquet	Williams-Honda	−40.547s	2	3	G
3	S Johansson	McLaren-TAG	−56.758s	10	2	G
4	G Berger	Ferrari	−1m 39.235s	7	2	G
5	T Boutsen	Benetton-Ford	−1 lap	6	2	G
6	N Mansell	Williams-Honda	−1 lap	1	2	G

Round 2/16	**SAN MARINO GP** Imola						**Nigel Mansell**		
	3 May 1987				**Race 438**		Williams-Honda FW11B 195.201kph, 121.292mph		

Piquet's Tamburello accident during qualifying was massive, a tyre the probable cause. Fortunate to survive, he sat out the race. Goodyear withdrew that particular tyre type the next morning. Senna claimed the first pole for active suspension and led lap 1, but once by Mansell's victory was never in doubt, despite the loss of wheel balance weights. This was especially so when Prost retired on lap 15 with a duff alternator when his McLaren was closely stalking the Williams. Senna's Lotus never presented a serious threat, finishing second, while Patrese's Brabham-BMW looked racy for a time, holding P2 as late as lap 49. Alboreto too duelled with Senna for second until the Ferrari fell away over the final ten laps with dwindling turbo boost to finish third.

POLE POSITION Senna, Lotus-Honda, 1m 25.826s (0.120s), 211.404kph, 131.361mph
LAPS 59 x 5.040 km, 3.132 miles
DISTANCE 297.360 km, 184.771 miles
STARTERS/FINISHERS 25/13
WEATHER Cloudy, warm, dry
LAP LEADERS Senna 1, 25-26 (3); Mansell 2-21, 27-59 (53); Alboreto 22-24 (3)
WINNER'S LAPS 1 P2, 2-21 P1, 22 P4, 23 P5, 24 P4, 25-26 P2, 27-59 P1
FASTEST LAP T Fabi, Benetton-Ford, 1m 29.246s (lap 51), 203.303kph, 126.327mph
CHAMPIONSHIP Mansell 10, Prost 9, Johansson 7, Piquet 6, Senna 6

Pos	Driver	Car	Time/gap	Grid	Stops	Tyres
1	N Mansell	Williams-Honda	1h 31m 24.076s	2	1	G
2	A Senna	Lotus-Honda	−27.545s	1	1	G
3	M Alboreto	Ferrari	−39.144s	6	1	G
4	S Johansson	McLaren-TAG	−1m 0.588s	8	2	G
5	M Brundle	Zakspeed	−2 laps	14	0	G
6	S Nakajima	Lotus-Honda	−2 laps	12	1	G

Round 3/16	**BELGIAN GP** Spa Francorchamps		**Alain Prost**	
	17 May 1987	**Race 439**	McLaren-TAG Porsche MP4/3 205.680kph, 127.804mph	

Ardennes weather made qualifying a lottery, Prost sixth, his three primary rivals 1-2-3. With pole-man Mansell leading by 2s, the race was red-flagged on lap 2 when both Tyrrells crashed exiting Eau Rouge, Palmer caught up in Streiff's massive accident, both drivers unscathed. At the restart leader Senna and Mansell effectively eliminated each other in a controversial first lap coming-together in an apparent passing manoeuvre approaching Blanchimont. Piquet now led Alboreto and Prost until the Ferrari gearbox broke on lap 9 and the Honda turbo on lap 11. From there it was a cakewalk for Prost, the threatened rain holding off. By making it a 1-2, Johansson rammed home the twin McLaren advantages of race pace plus reliability.

POLE POSITION N Mansell, Williams-Honda, 1m 52.026s (1.390s), 223.020kph, 138.578mph
LAPS 43 x 6.940 km, 4.312 miles (Race restarted for scheduled 43 laps following accident)
DISTANCE 298.420 km, 185.430 miles
STARTERS/FINISHERS 26/10
WEATHER Overcast, cool, dry
LAP LEADERS N Piquet, Williams-Honda 1-9 (9); Prost 10-43 (34)
WINNER'S LAPS 1-9 P3, 10-43 P1
FASTEST LAP Prost, McLaren-TAG, 1m 57.153s (lap 26), 213.260kph, 132.513mph
CHAMPIONSHIP Prost 18, Johansson 13, Mansell 10, Piquet 6, Senna 6

Pos	Driver	Car	Time/gap	Grid	Stops	Tyres
1	A Prost	McLaren-TAG	1h 27m 3.217s	6	1	G
2	S Johansson	McLaren-TAG	−24.764s	10	1	G
3r	A de Cesaris	Brabham-BMW	−1 lap	13	0	G
4	E Cheever	Arrows-Megatron	−1 lap	11	1	G
5	S Nakajima	Lotus-Honda	−1 lap	15	1	G
6	R Arnoux	Ligier-Megatron	−2 laps	16	1	G

Lotus-Honda 99T

Round 4/16	**MONACO GP** Monte Carlo		**Ayrton Senna**	
	31 May 1987	**Race 440**	Lotus-Honda 99T 132.102kph, 82.085mph	

Mansell, in sparkling form around the houses, streaked ahead from his commanding pole to pull out 11s over the chasing Senna, but on lap 29 a fractured exhaust weld robbed him of probable victory. Senna, more than a match for everyone bar Mansell, reeled off the remaining 49 lonely laps, elated to win at Monaco and post the first victory for active suspension. Piquet, never a Monaco aficionado and still stiff from his Imola shunt, was second. Prost's five-cylinder motor quit with three to go when third, giving Alboreto's Ferrari a welcome podium after a major practice accident. Fourth was Berger's Ferrari, the top six completed by 3.5-litre atmo cars, Palmer's Tyrrell beating Capelli's March in their tussle for the Jim Clark Trophy.

POLE POSITION N Mansell, Williams-Honda, 1m 23.039s (0.672s), 144.279kph, 89.651mph
LAPS 78 x 3.328 km, 2.068 miles
DISTANCE 259.584 km, 161.298 miles
STARTERS/FINISHERS 24/13
WEATHER Sunny, warm, dry
LAP LEADERS Mansell 1-29 (29); Senna 30-78 (49)
WINNER'S LAPS 1-29 P2, 30-78 P1
FASTEST LAP Senna, Lotus-Honda, 1m 27.685s (lap 72), 136.635kph, 84.901mph
CHAMPIONSHIP Prost 18, Senna 15, Johansson 13, Piquet 12, Mansell 10

Pos	Driver	Car	Time/gap	Grid	Stops	Tyres
1	A Senna	Lotus-Honda	1h 57m 54.085s	2	1	G
2	N Piquet	Williams-Honda	−33.212s	3	1	G
3	M Alboreto	Ferrari	−1m 12.839s	5	1	G
4	G Berger	Ferrari	−1 lap	8	1	G
5	J Palmer	Tyrrell-Ford	−2 laps	15	0	G
6	I Capelli	March-Ford	−2 laps	19	0	G

<table>
<tr><td>Round 5/16</td><td colspan="2">UNITED STATES GP Detroit
21 June 1987   Race 441</td></tr>
</table>

Round 5/16 — UNITED STATES GP Detroit
21 June 1987 — Race 441

Ayrton Senna
Lotus-Honda 99T 137.915kph, 85.697mph

Senna's second successive win was a repeat of his Motown victory last year, active suspension helping him run the distance on one set of tyres. Just as at Monaco, dominant pole-winner Mansell again looked the likely race victor until his mid-race tyre stop. Soon afterwards he began to fall away, suffering increasing exhaustion due to agonising leg cramp, finally finishing fifth with poor tyre grip too. Following a puncture on lap 3 which dropped him to P21, Piquet made a superb recovery drive, depriving Prost of second on lap 43 and Mansell waving him through for second ten laps later. Despite a 'long' brake pedal and gearbox issues, Prost held on for third to keep him within two points of new championship leader Senna.

POLE POSITION Mansell, Williams-Honda, 1m 39.264s (1.343s), 145.915kph, 90.667mph
LAPS 63 x 4.023 km, 2.500 miles
DISTANCE 253.472 km, 157.500 miles
STARTERS/FINISHERS 26/12
WEATHER Cloudy, warm, dry, humid
LAP LEADERS Mansell 1-33 (33); Senna 34-63 (30)
WINNER'S LAPS 1-33 P2, 34-63 P1
FASTEST LAP Senna, Lotus-Honda, 1m 40.464s (lap 39), 144.172kph, 89.584mph
CHAMPIONSHIP Senna 24, Prost 22, Piquet 18, Johansson 13, Mansell 12

Pos	Driver	Car	Time/gap	Grid	Stops	Tyres
1	A Senna	Lotus-Honda	1h 50m 16.358s	2	0	G
2	N Piquet	Williams-Honda	−33.819s	3	1	G
3	A Prost	McLaren-TAG	−45.327s	5	1	G
4	G Berger	Ferrari	−1m 2.601s	12	1	G
5	N Mansell	Williams-Honda	−1 lap	1	1	G
6r	E Cheever	Arrows-Megatron	−3 laps	6	1	G

Round 6/16 — FRENCH GP Paul Ricard
5 July 1987 — Race 442

Nigel Mansell
Williams-Honda FW11B 188.560kph, 117.166mph

The 'big four' filled the front two rows at the start and the first four places by the finish, Piquet the only mover, starting P4, finishing P2, a position he claimed initially on the first lap. On lap 19 Prost retook Piquet and began to give pole-sitter and race-leader Mansell a hard time. The race was clearly between these three, Senna finishing a lapped fourth, unable to replicate the challenge he presented on the street circuits. Piquet stopped first, taking the lead when Prost and Mansell made theirs. But while Prost dropped back with engine gremlins, Mansell took around ten laps to close the 5s gap and on lap 46 he was by as Piquet ran wide. Nelson played his fresh tyres ace far too late, allowing 16 laps to regain 25s and make the pass. He fell well short.

POLE POSITION Mansell, Williams-Honda, 1m 06.454s (0.423s), 206.561kph, 128.351mph
LAPS 80 x 3.813 km, 2.369 miles
DISTANCE 305.040 km, 189.543 miles
STARTERS/FINISHERS 26/9
WEATHER Cloudy with sunny intervals, hot, dry
LAP LEADERS Mansell 1-35, 46-80 (70); Piquet 36-45 (10)
WINNER'S LAPS 1-35 P1, 36-37 P3, 38-45 P2, 46-80 P1
FASTEST LAP Piquet, Williams-Honda, 1m 09.548s (lap 68), 197.372kph, 122.641mph
CHAMPIONSHIP Senna 27, Prost 26, Piquet 24, Mansell 21, Johansson 13

Pos	Driver	Car	Time/gap	Grid	Stops	Tyres
1	N Mansell	Williams-Honda	1h 37m 3.839s	1	1	G
2	N Piquet	Williams-Honda	−7.711s	4	2	G
3	A Prost	McLaren-TAG	−55.255s	2	1	G
4	A Senna	Lotus-Honda	−1 lap	3	1	G
5r	T Fabi	Benetton-Ford	−3 laps	7	1	G
6	J Streiff	Tyrrell-Ford	−4 laps	25	0	G

Round 7/16 — BRITISH GP Silverstone
12 July 1987 — Race 443

Nigel Mansell
Williams-Honda FW11B 235.298kph, 146.208mph

Later, on his victory lap, showman Mansell stopped at Stowe to kiss the tarmac where he had executed one of the great passing moves of all time. With 2½ laps remaining, Mansell sold Piquet the perfect dummy then sliced past the sister car on the inside at Stowe, Nelson having led from pole for the previous 62½. The chase had begun with 30 to go when Mansell exited 28s in arrears from a tyre stop forced upon him by extreme vibrations, the loss of a front wheel balance weight. Surely his task was impossible, but driving at ten-tenths and urged on by the frenzied, partisan crowd, Mansell lowered the lap record nine times, taking great chunks out of Nelson's lead. Hondas finished 1-2-3-4, but Senna's Lotus was a lap behind, Nakajima's two.

POLE POSITION Piquet, Williams-Honda, 1m 07.110s (0.070s), 256.315kph, 159.267mph
LAPS 65 x 4.778 km, 2.969 miles
DISTANCE 310.579 km, 192.985 miles
STARTERS/FINISHERS 25/9
WEATHER Cloudy with sunny intervals, warm, dry
LAP LEADERS Piquet 1-62 (62); Mansell 63-65 (3)
WINNER'S LAPS 1-62 P2, 63-65 P1
FASTEST LAP Mansell, Williams-Honda, 1m 09.832s (lap 58), 246.324kph, 153.059mph
CHAMPIONSHIP Senna 31, Mansell 30, Piquet 30, Prost 26, Johansson 13

Pos	Driver	Car	Time/gap	Grid	Stops	Tyres
1	N Mansell	Williams-Honda	1h 19m 11.780s	2	1	G
2	N Piquet	Williams-Honda	−1.918s	1	0	G
3	A Senna	Lotus-Honda	−1 lap	3	0	G
4	S Nakajima	Lotus-Honda	−2 laps	12	0	G
5	D Warwick	Arrows-Megatron	−2 laps	13	0	G
6	T Fabi	Benetton-Ford	−2 laps	6	0	G

TOP **100** RACE

Williams-Honda FW11B

Round 8/16	**GERMAN GP** Hockenheim		**Nelson Piquet**
	26 July 1987	Race 444	Williams-Honda FW11B 218.463kph, 135.747mph

Just five points blanketed the 'big four', one of their number yet to win, but Hockenheim saw a seismic shift in fortunes, Piquet inheriting his first victory at Mansell and Prost's expense. Following fleeting intervention by Senna, who finished a lapped third, Mansell from pole soon led Prost. On lap 8 at the first chicane Alain took the lead and began to inch away, holding a 5s gap after the stops. Disappointingly Mansell's Honda seized, his eagerly anticipated fresh-tyres chase lasting just three laps. But Prost's was the real hard-luck story, losing a one-time 30s plus lead to Piquet when he parked at the Östkurve with alternator failure, the Brazilian leading the final five. Johansson struggled in P2 on three wheels, his front tyre shredded.

POLE POSITION N Mansell, Williams-Honda, 1m 42.616s (0.257s), 238.454kph, 148.168mph
LAPS 44 x 6.797 km, 4.223 miles
DISTANCE 299.068 km, 185.832 miles
STARTERS/FINISHERS 26/7
WEATHER Cloudy with sunny intervals, warm, dry
LAP LEADERS Senna 1 (1); Mansell 2-7, 19-22 (10); A Prost, McLaren-TAG 8-18, 23-39 (28); Piquet 40-44 (5)
WINNER'S LAPS 1-2 P4, 3-20 P3, 21 P5, 22 P4, 23-25 P3, 26-39 P2, 40-44 P1
FASTEST LAP N Mansell, Williams-Honda, 1m 45.716s (lap 24), 231.462kph, 143.824mph
CHAMPIONSHIP Piquet 39, Senna 35, Mansell 30, Prost 26, Johansson 19

Pos	Driver	Car	Time/gap	Grid	Stops	Tyres
1	N Piquet	Williams-Honda	1h 21m 25.091s	4	1	G
2	S Johansson	McLaren-TAG	–1m 39.591s	8	1	G
3	A Senna	Lotus-Honda	–1 lap	2	3	G
4	J Streiff	Tyrrell-Ford	–1 lap	22	0	G
5	J Palmer	Tyrrell-Ford	–1 lap	23	0	G
6	P Alliot	Lola-Ford	–2 laps	21	0	G

Round 9/16	**HUNGARIAN GP** Hungaroring		**Nelson Piquet**
	9 August 1987	Race 445	Williams-Honda FW11B 153.239kph, 95.218mph

Two weeks later it happened again, this time Piquet leading the final six laps, the ill luck befalling Mansell, memorably losing victory and a wheel-nut just 15 miles short. Consummately he had led every inch of the way from pole until the nut worked free, flying off the right rear. Berger's front row was the best Ferrari grid slot in two years, both Ferraris getting between the Williams pair at the start. By the time Piquet eventually moved up to P2 on lap 29, Mansell was untouchable, his lead 14s. Senna, serious tyre vibrations, and Prost, persistent misfire, completed the podium but the championship landscape had radically altered. Two fortuitous wins had rocketed Piquet ahead of Senna by seven points and Prost and Mansell by a massive 18.

POLE POSITION N Mansell, Williams-Honda, 1m 28.047s (0.502s), 164.121kph, 101.980mph
LAPS 76 x 4.014 km, 2.494 miles
DISTANCE 305.064 km, 189.558 miles
STARTERS/FINISHERS 26/14
WEATHER Sunny, hot, dry
LAP LEADERS Mansell 1-70 (70); Piquet 71-76 (6)
WINNER'S LAPS 1-12 P4, 13-28 P3, 29-70 P2, 71-76 P1
FASTEST LAP Piquet, Williams-Honda, 1m 30.149s (lap 63), 160.295kph, 99.602mph
CHAMPIONSHIP Piquet 48, Senna 41, Mansell 30, Prost 30, Johansson 19

Pos	Driver	Car	Time/gap	Grid	Stops	Tyres
1	N Piquet	Williams-Honda	1h 59m 26.793s	3	0	G
2	A Senna	Lotus-Honda	–37.727s	6	0	G
3	A Prost	McLaren-TAG	–1m 27.456s	4	0	G
4	T Boutsen	Benetton-Ford	–1 lap	7	0	G
5	R Patrese	Brabham-BMW	–1 lap	10	0	G
6	D Warwick	Arrows-Megatron	–2 laps	9	0	G

AUSTRIAN GP Österreichring
16 August 1987
Race 446

Nigel Mansell
Williams-Honda FW11B 235.421kph, 146.284mph

Three starts spelt the end for the menacing Österreichring with its precariously narrow pits straight and errant deer. Mansell's clutch difficulties triggered the second red flag, so at the third start, eschewing the spare FW11B, he made a careful getaway. From P3, just seconds back, he stalked Piquet, who had led from pole, closing in once Boutsen pitted to decisively overtake the flustered Brazilian on lap 21, driving away to a dominant victory. But coming home second, albeit a minute behind, the humbled Piquet conceded only three points. Senna, Prost and Alboreto all started from the pit lane, entertainingly charging through, the former pair taking points, but ultimately the Benetton-Ford turbos finished 3-4, disappointed not to be closer to Piquet.

POLE POSITION Piquet, Williams-Honda, 1m 23.357s (0.102s), 256.622kph, 159.547mph
LAPS 52 x 5.942 km, 3.692 miles (Race twice restarted for scheduled 52 laps following accidents)
DISTANCE 308.984 km, 191.994 miles
STARTERS/FINISHERS 26/14
WEATHER Cloudy, hot, dry
LAP LEADERS Piquet 1-20 (20); Mansell 21-52 (32)
WINNER'S LAPS 1-3 P4, 4-14 P3, 15-20 P2, 21-52 P1
FASTEST LAP Mansell, Williams-Honda, 1m 28.318s (lap 31), 242.207kph, 150.500mph
CHAMPIONSHIP Piquet 54, Senna 43, Mansell 39, Prost 31, Johansson 19

Pos	Driver	Car	Time/gap	Grid	Stops	Tyres
1	N Mansell	Williams-Honda	1h 18m 44.898s	2	0	G
2	N Piquet	Williams-Honda	−55.704s	1	1	G
3	T Fabi	Benetton-Ford	−1 lap	5	2	G
4	T Boutsen	Benetton-Ford	−1 lap	4	2	G
5	A Senna	Lotus-Honda	−2 laps	7	2	G
6	A Prost	McLaren-TAG	−2 laps	9	1	G

ITALIAN GP Monza
6 September 1987
Race 447

Nelson Piquet
Williams-Honda FW11B 232.636kph, 144.553mph

Piquet's grip on the title tightened with his third victory from four races, beating compatriot Senna. Both Brazilians drove Honda-powered cars with active suspension, the newly so-equipped Williams appearing far the quicker. P6 on lap 1, Senna boldly decided his only chance was to run one set of tyres, taking the lead on lap 24 when Piquet made his stop. On fresh rubber Piquet chased Senna, a very tight finish forecast until, eight laps short, Senna slid wide on worn tyres at Parabolica lapping a backmarker. Mansell's conventional Williams had only been a tenth shy of pole-man Piquet, but finished the race a distant third due to high engine temperatures and power loss. Prost's troubled McLaren finished four laps down out of the points.

POLE POSITION Piquet, Williams-Honda, 1m 23.460s (0.099s), 250.180kph, 155.454mph
LAPS 50 x 5.800 km, 3.604 miles
DISTANCE 290.000 km, 180.198 miles
STARTERS/FINISHERS 26/16
WEATHER Sunny, hot, dry
LAP LEADERS Piquet 1-23, 43-50 (31); Senna 24-42 (19)
WINNER'S LAPS 1-23 P1, 24-42 P2, 43-50 P1
FASTEST LAP Senna, Lotus-Honda, 1m 26.796 (lap 49), 240.564kph, 149.480mph
CHAMPIONSHIP Piquet 63, Senna 49, Mansell 43, Prost 31, Johansson 20

Pos	Driver	Car	Time/gap	Grid	Stops	Tyres
1	N Piquet	Williams-Honda	1h 14m 47.707s	1	1	G
2	A Senna	Lotus-Honda	−1.806s	4	0	G
3	N Mansell	Williams-Honda	−49.036s	2	1	G
4	G Berger	Ferrari	−57.979s	3	1	G
5	T Boutsen	Benetton-Ford	−1m 21.319s	6	1	G
6	S Johansson	McLaren-TAG	−1m 28.787s	11	1	G

PORTUGUESE GP Estoril
20 September 1987
Race 448

Alain Prost
McLaren-TAG Porsche MP4/3 188.224kph, 116.957mph

Tyres shot, under pressure from Prost, Berger spun it away three laps from what could have been a glorious red revival. It was only a half-spin, but Prost pounced and it was all over, a galling outcome for the Austrian Ferrari driver who led almost all the way from his maiden pole. But a triumphal result for Prost, his 28th race victory eclipsing Stewart's long-standing record. As low as P6 early on, Prost drove brilliantly to make up over 20s on Berger, pressurising the Ferrari driver remorselessly over the final 15 laps, Alain's car also at the edge of adhesion. And with Mansell, electrics, and Senna, seventh, coming away empty-handed, the destination of the championship seemed clear with another distant podium for Piquet in the active Williams.

POLE POSITION Berger, Ferrari, 1m 17.620s (0.331s), 201.752kph, 125.363mph
LAPS 70 x 4.350 km, 2.703 miles (Race restarted for scheduled 70 laps following accident)
DISTANCE 304.500 km, 189.208 miles
STARTERS/FINISHERS 26/14
WEATHER Cloudy with sunny intervals, warm, dry
LAP LEADERS N Mansell, Williams-Honda 1 (1); Berger 2-33, 36-67 (64); M Alboreto, Ferrari 34-35 (2); Prost 68-70 (3)
WINNER'S LAPS 1-2 P5, 3-11 P6, 12-13 P5, 14-29 P4, 30-31 P3, 32-36 P4, 37-38 P3, 39-67 P2, 68-70 P1
FASTEST LAP Berger, Ferrari, 1m 19.282s (lap 66), 197.523kph, 122.735mph
CHAMPIONSHIP Piquet 67, Senna 49, Mansell 43, Prost 40, Johansson 22

Pos	Driver	Car	Time/gap	Grid	Stops	Tyres
1	A Prost	McLaren-TAG	1h 37m 3.906s	3	1	G
2	G Berger	Ferrari	−20.493s	1	1	G
3	N Piquet	Williams-Honda	−1m 3.295s	4	1	G
4r	T Fabi	Benetton-Ford	−1 lap	10	0	G
5	S Johansson	McLaren-TAG	−1 lap	8	1	G
6	E Cheever	Arrows-Megatron	−2 laps	11	0	G

Round 13/16	**SPANISH GP** Jerez				
	27 September 1987		Race 449		

Choosing his conventionally-sprung Williams, Mansell drove an aggressive first lap, passed Piquet's pole-sitting active car, after which it was plain sailing, even retaining the lead during his tyre stop. Behind these two a bizarre race unfolded, Senna's 'non-stopping-minimal-wing' strategy producing a Lotus-Honda slow in the corners, fast down the straights. Behind Senna's 'mobile chicane' a crocodile of five cars formed, Senna keeping them all at bay for 62 laps. On lap 46 Piquet joined Senna's queue when he bungled his pit stop, the championship points leader also spinning twice in an error-strewn performance. Eventually the cork came out of the bottle, the McLarens bursting past Senna's tyre-weary Lotus to finish 2-3, Piquet fourth, Senna fifth.

Nigel Mansell
Williams-Honda FW11B 166.848kph, 103.675mph

POLE POSITION Piquet, Williams-Honda, 1m 22.461s (0.620s), 184.145kph, 114.423mph
LAPS 72 x 4.218 km, 2.621 miles
DISTANCE 303.696 km, 188.708 miles
STARTERS/FINISHERS 26/16
WEATHER Cloudy with sunny intervals, warm, dry
LAP LEADERS Mansell 1-72 (72)
WINNER'S LAPS 1-72 P1
FASTEST LAP G Berger, Ferrari, 1m 26.986s (lap 49), 174.566kph, 108.470mph
CHAMPIONSHIP Piquet 70, Mansell 52, Senna 51, Prost 46, Johansson 26

Pos	Driver	Car	Time/gap	Grid	Stops	Tyres
1	N Mansell	Williams-Honda	1h 49m 12.692s	2	1	G
2	A Prost	McLaren-TAG	−22.225s	7	1	G
3	S Johansson	McLaren-TAG	−30.818s	11	1	G
4	N Piquet	Williams-Honda	−31.450s	1	2	G
5	A Senna	Lotus-Honda	−1m 13.507s	5	0	G
6	P Alliot	Lola-Ford	−1 lap	17	0	G

Round 14/16	**MEXICAN GP** Mexico City				
	18 October 1987		Race 450		

The bumpy track surface caused numerous accidents in qualifying but a closely competitive grid, the Williams-Hondas 1-3, Berger's Ferrari and Boutsen's Benetton 2-4. These two initially outpaced pole-man Mansell but neither lasted, first the Benetton sidelined with electrics on lap 15, five later the Ferrari turbo breaking. Mansell restored normality until lap 30 when the race was stopped somewhat needlessly when a horrifying accident for Warwick's Arrows appeared fully under control. In the 33-lap part two, all Mansell had to do was stalk Piquet to win easily. After a first lap collision that eliminated Prost, Piquet was fortunate not to be disqualified for a push-start, while late on Senna spun his clutchless Lotus from third.

Nigel Mansell
Williams-Honda FW11B 193.411kph, 120.180mph

POLE POSITION Mansell, Williams-Honda, 1m 18.383s (0.043s), 203.049kph, 126.169mph
LAPS 63 x 4.421 km, 2.747 miles (68 lap race interrupted due to accident. Result aggregate of 30 + 33 laps)
DISTANCE 278.523 km, 173.066 miles
STARTERS/FINISHERS 26/9
WEATHER Sunny, hot, dry
LAP LEADERS (On the road) G Berger, Ferrari 1, 15-20 (7); T Boutsen, Benetton-Ford 2-14 (13); Mansell 21-30 (10); Piquet 31-63 (33)
WINNER'S LAPS 1-15 P3, 16-20 P2, 21-63 P1
FASTEST LAP Piquet, Williams-Honda, 1m 19.132s (lap 57), 201.127kph, 124.975mph
CHAMPIONSHIP Piquet 73, Mansell 61, Senna 51, Prost 46, Johansson 26

Pos	Driver	Car	Time/gap	Grid	Stops	Tyres
1	N Mansell	Williams-Honda	1h 26m 24.207s	1	0	G
2	N Piquet	Williams-Honda	−26.176s	3	0	G
3	R Patrese	Brabham-BMW	−1m 26.879s	8	0	G
4	E Cheever	Arrows-Megatron	−1m 41.352s	12	0	G
5	T Fabi	Benetton-Ford	−2 laps	6	2	G
6	P Alliot	Lola-Ford	−3 laps	24	0	G

Round 15/16	**JAPANESE GP** Suzuka				
	1 November 1987		Race 451		

The constructors' championship theirs at Jerez, from now on the drivers' title was also an all-Williams affair, Mansell back in the frame due to the idiosyncrasies of the points system. But with startling suddenness it was over. During Friday practice Mansell ran wide at the chicane, a hefty accident ensued, Nigel ruled out for the rest of the season with a back injury. Piquet was champion and at Honda's own circuit, a subtlety not lost on Enzo Ferrari, whose car trounced the Honda-powered cars on Sunday. From pole Berger comfortably led all bar one lap for Ferrari's first victory in 2½ years. It might have been different if departing champion Prost hadn't punctured on lap 2 when second, but the new champion was never a threat, the Honda failing when P4.

Gerhard Berger
Ferrari F1-87 192.847kph, 119.829mph

POLE POSITION Berger, Ferrari, 1m 40.042s (0.610s), 210.835kph, 131.007mph
LAPS 51 x 5.859 km, 3.641 miles
DISTANCE 298.809 km, 185.671 miles
STARTERS/FINISHERS 26/15
WEATHER Cloudy, cool, dry
LAP LEADERS Berger 1-24, 26-51 (50); Senna 25 (1)
WINNER'S LAPS 1-24 P1, 25 P3, 26-51 P1
FASTEST LAP A Prost, McLaren-TAG, 1m 43.844s (lap 35), 203.116kph, 126.211mph
CHAMPIONSHIP Piquet 73, Mansell 61, Senna 57, Prost 46, Johansson 30

Pos	Driver	Car	Time/gap	Grid	Stops	Tyres
1	G Berger	Ferrari	1h 32m 58.072s	1	1	G
2	A Senna	Lotus-Honda	−17.384s	7	1	G
3	S Johansson	McLaren-TAG	−17.694s	9	1	G
4	M Alboreto	Ferrari	−1m 20.441s	4	1	G
5	T Boutsen	Benetton-Ford	−1m 25.576s	3	1	G
6	S Nakajima	Lotus-Honda	−1m 36.479s	11	1	G

AUSTRALIAN GP Adelaide

15 November 1987   Race 452

Gerhard Berger

Ferrari F1-87 164.631kph, 102.297mph

Two weeks later Berger repeated the exercise even more convincingly, leading every lap in a Ferrari 1-2 after Senna's second-place Lotus failed post-race scrutineering. Berger took a comfortable pole from Prost, Piquet and Senna, the two Ps both succumbing to braking deficiencies around two-thirds race-distance. Using what subsequently turned out to be illegal brake ducts, Senna mounted a spirited attack in the second half but Berger always had him covered. It was a race of attrition, just eight cars finishing, the 'big four', so central to the championship battle, curiously making minimal impact on the final two races of the season. Maybe it was due to the enforced absence of the dominant figure, not the new world champion but his indisposed teammate.

POLE POSITION Berger, Ferrari, 1m 17.267s (0.700s), 176.070kph, 109.405mph
LAPS 82 x 3.779 km, 2.348 miles
DISTANCE 309.878 km, 192.549 miles
STARTERS/FINISHERS 26/9
WEATHER Sunny, hot, dry
LAP LEADERS Berger 1-82 (82)
WINNER'S LAPS 1-82 P1
FASTEST LAP Berger, Ferrari, 1m 20.416s (lap 72), 169.175kph, 105.121mph
CHAMPIONSHIP Piquet 73, Mansell 61, Senna 57, Prost 46, Berger 36

Pos	Driver	Car	Time/gap	Grid	Stops	Tyres
1	G Berger	Ferrari	1h 52m 56.144s	1	0	G
2	M Alboreto	Ferrari	–7.884s	6	0	G
3	T Boutsen	Benetton-Ford	–1 lap	5	0	G
4	J Palmer	Tyrrell-Ford	–2 laps	19	1	G
5	Y Dalmas	Lola-Ford	–3 laps	21	0	G
6	R Moreno	AGS-Ford	–3 laps	25	0	G

1987 CHAMPIONSHIP FACTS AND FOLKLORE

- In October 1986 a declaration by FISA outlined a three-year transition to a new Formula 1, effectively a shift from turbocharged engines exclusively in 1986 to solely atmospheric engines from 1989. 1987 was the first year of transition open to both forms of engine as follows:
- Cars with 1.5-litre turbo engines: unchanged 540kg (1,190,7lb) weight and 195 litres (42.9 gallons) fuel capacity; a FISA pop-off valve to limit boost pressure to 4.0 bar; the banning of multi-stage turbochargers, intercoolers using liquids, water injection and oval pistons.
- Cars with 3.5-litre atmospheric engines: same 195 litres fuel tankage but lower weight of 500kg (1,102.31lb); engines of up to 12 cylinders but again oval pistons banned.
- The introduction of turbo pop-off valves and Pirelli's withdrawal at the end of 1986 effectively eradicated the use of special qualifying engines and tyres. Goodyear brought one tyre type for all participants to each meeting.
- In parallel with the F1 world championships, normally aspirated cars would contest their own championships in 1987, the Jim Clark Trophy for drivers and the Colin Chapman Cup for constructors.
- The drivers' title was again the best 11 results from 16 championship rounds, which included the return, after a ten-year absence, of the Japanese GP, its new venue Suzuka, a circuit owned by Honda.
- The last GP was held at the Österreichring after Stefan Johansson had a terrifying 140mph encounter with a deer during practice, deer killed, car wrecked, driver lucky. Then in the race, the ludicrously narrow pit straight was a factor in two red flags, three starts.
- Leading up to the first round in Rio the superlicence row resurfaced. FISA introduced a sliding scale based on points won the previous season. The logic was that more successful drivers were better paid and should pay (be taxed) more. The leading drivers refuted the principle but paid up in the end.
- 1987 was another nine wins for Williams-Honda and another lost championship for Nigel Mansell. His crash and resultant injury in first qualifying at the penultimate round in Japan sidelined him for the rest of the season.
- Williams teammate Piquet was the beneficiary of Mansell's

rare but critical error in a season in which he dominated the track and his teammate.
- Silverstone saw Mansell on fresh rubber come from a long way back to take Piquet in the closing moments at Stowe in one of the great overtaking manoeuvres of all time.
- Piquet's Tamburello accident at round two may have blunted his subsequent form but it wouldn't explain similarly losing out to Mansell in their first season alongside one another last year.
- Over their two seasons together their stats read, Piquet first: qualifying 12:17; poles 6:10; laps led 353:714, and race wins 7:11.
- Piquet looked for and found an advantage in active ride suspension, developing it, adapting to it, and benefitting from it earlier than Mansell, this technical advance in itself contributing to their continuing poor relationship, one driver certain that Williams were showing favouritism, the other that Honda were biased.
- But very much in their tradition of technical innovation, Team Lotus were first to race and win with computer controlled active suspension, although the more revolutionary Lotus version proved more challenging to master than the simpler 'hydro-pneumatic' system from Williams.
- From the outset Senna committed to the new technology, gaining two early successes on the unevenness of street circuits, his Monaco victory turning out to be the 79th and final GP success for Lotus, at the time a total only eclipsed by Ferrari's 91. Their tally for championships was equally impressive, six drivers' and seven constructors' titles won by Lotus.
- 1987 also brought a new look for Lotus, now sporting Camel yellow along with Honda power, but these changes and the struggle with active suspension did not bring the championship-winning form Senna expected from his third year with the team. After six wins from 16 pole positions over the three years, Senna left Lotus to join Prost at McLaren, his seat to be taken by the new world champion.
- In May distinguished design engineer Gioacchino Colombo died at the age of 84. He was leader of the Scuderia Ferrari design team which produced the original Alfa Romeo 158 in 1937–38; the man who laid the foundations of Ferrari's legendary post-war V12 road and race engines, and responsible for the original Maserati 250F design of 1954.

RACE 443, British GP: Mansell, in 'Red 5', lining up Piquet to execute one of the great passing moves of all time, selling the perfect dummy then slicing past the sister car at Stowe.

- Colombo, therefore, did not witness the latest fruits of his successors, Ferrari enjoying a pair of convincing race victories to round out the season, their first success in two years.
- John Barnard had joined Ferrari from McLaren, but although he can take a share of the credit for this revival, the mid-season return to the front-line of Harvey Postlethwaite had far more to do with making Gustav Brunner's original design go fast in the hands of Gerhard Berger.
- Tyrrell enjoyed some modest success by winning the Colin Chapman Cup for 3.5-litre atmo cars, competing against such as Larrousse Lola, AGS and Leyton House March. Jonathan Palmer won the Jim Clark Trophy from his Tyrrell teammate Philippe Streiff.
- Tyrrell's yet closer alliance with title sponsor Data General saw the DG prefix added to the type number, the computer company assisting the team to move forward in the areas of telemetry and CAD-CAM.
- Alain Prost won three times in the final iteration of the now outclassed McLaren-TAG Porsche, and in so doing took his race win tally to 28, surpassing the 24-year record held by Jackie Stewart.
- Having chalked up 25 wins over just four seasons, McLaren discarded the TAG Porsche engine at the end of the year and switched to Honda, who in turn had separated from Williams with one year of their contract still to run.
- For their competitors, Prost and Senna in Honda-powered McLarens presented a daunting prospect for 1988.

Championship ranking	Championship points	Driver nationality	1987 Drivers Championship		Races contested	Race victories	Podiums excl. victories	Races led	Lights to flag victories	Laps led	Poles	Fastest laps	Triple Crowns
			Driver	Car									
1	73	BRA	Nelson Piquet	Williams-Honda	15	3	8	9		187	4	4	
2	61	GBR	Nigel Mansell	Williams-Honda	14	6	1	11	1	383	8	3	
3	57	BRA	Ayrton Senna	Lotus-Honda	16	2	6	7		108	1	3	
4	46	FRA	Alain Prost	McLaren-TAG	16	3	4	4		110		2	
5	36	AUT	Gerhard Berger	Ferrari	16	2	1	4	1	203	3	3	
6	30	SWE	Stefan Johansson	McLaren-TAG	16		5						
7	17	ITA	Michele Alboreto	Ferrari	16		3	2		5			
8	16	BEL	Thierry Boutsen	Benetton-Ford	16		1	1		13			
9	12	ITA	Teo Fabi	Benetton-Ford	16		1					1	
10	8	USA	Eddie Cheever	Arrows-Megatron	16								
11	7	GBR	Jonathan Palmer	Tyrrell-Ford	16								
12	7	JAP	Satoru Nakajima	Lotus-Honda	16								
13	6	ITA	Riccardo Patrese	Brabham-BMW (15) Williams-Honda (1)	16		1						
14	4	ITA	Andrea de Cesaris	Brabham-BMW	16		1						
15	4	FRA	Philippe Streiff	Tyrrell-Ford	16								
16	3	GBR	Derek Warwick	Arrows-Megatron	16								
17	3	FRA	Philippe Alliot	Lola-Ford	15								
18	2	GBR	Martin Brundle	Zakspeed	16								
19	1	FRA	René Arnoux	Ligier-Megatron	14								
19	1	ITA	Ivan Capelli	March-Ford	15								
19	1	BRA	Roberto Moreno	AGS-Ford	2								

Championship ranking	Championship points	Team/Marque nationality	1987 Constructors Championship		Engine maker nationality	Races contested	Race victories	1-2 finishes	Podiums excl. victories	Races led	Laps led	Poles	Fastest laps
			Chassis	Engine									
1	137	GBR	Williams FW11B	Honda 1.5 V6t	JAP	16	9	4	9	14	570	12	7
2	76	GBR	McLaren MP4-3	TAG Porsche 1.5 V6t	GER	16	3	1	9	4	110		2
3	64	GBR	Lotus 99T	Honda 1.5 V6t	JAP	16	2		6	7	108	1	3
4	53	ITA	Ferrari F1-87	Ferrari 1.5 V6t	ITA	16	2		4	5	208	3	3
5	28	GBR	Benetton B187	Ford Cosworth 1.5 V6t	GBR	16			2	1	13		1
6	11	GBR	Tyrrell DG016	Ford Cosworth 3.5 V8	GBR	16							
7	11	GBR	Arrows A10	Megatron 1.5 S4t	GER	16							
8	10	GBR	Brabham BT56	BMW 1.5 S4t	GER	16			2				
9	3	GBR	Lola LC87	Ford Cosworth 3.5 V8	GBR	15							
10	2	GER	Zakspeed 871, 861B, 861	Zakspeed 1.5 S4t	GER	16							
11	1	FRA	Ligier JS29B, JS29C	Megatron 1.5 S4t	GER	15							
11	1	GBR	March 871	Ford Cosworth 3.5 V8	GBR	15							
11	1	FRA	AGS JH22	Ford Cosworth 3.5 V8	GBR	13							

1988

Prost yields to ruthless Senna

THE TALE OF THE TITLE

- Senna joined Prost at McLaren and, in the most intense intra-team rivalry of all time, drew first blood.
- Following a season-long battle, on a damp Suzuka track surface Senna's uncanny skills secured his first title.
- From a remarkable 13 poles he was victorious in eight races, each a new record in a season.
- But ultimately his race-win tally was only one more than Prost, who also grossed appreciably more points.
- It truly was a battle of titans, the king versus the man who would be king.
- 1-2 in ten races, McLaren-Honda failed to win just one of the 16 rounds to dominate the constructors' contest.
- Senna's Monza slip-up gifted Ferrari an emotional 1-2 victory just weeks after the death of Enzo Ferrari.
- Completely outclassed, Berger and the Ferrari turbo were distant runners-up to McLaren and their drivers.
- Adrian Newey began to make his mark on F1 with success for the Leyton House March Team.
- But of the non-turbo teams, Benetton was by far the most successful with seven podiums.
- And not forgetting: the turbo era ends.

THE CHASE FOR THE CHAMPIONSHIP

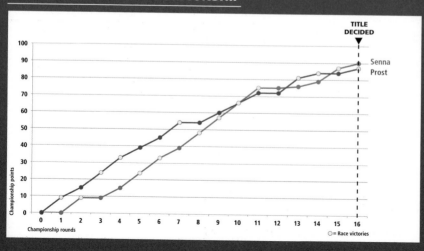

<table>
<tr><td>**Round 1/16**</td><td>**BRAZILIAN GP** Rio de Janeiro
3 April 1988   **Race 453**</td><td>**Alain Prost**
McLaren-Honda MP4/4 188.438kph, 117.090mph</td></tr>
</table>

Making his first McLaren appearance Senna took pole, but sat alongside was not Prost but Mansell in the Williams-Judd, 1.5s quicker than the next normally aspirated car in P7. A gear-linkage problem for Senna caused an aborted start and a pit-lane getaway in the T-car, opening the way for Prost to be first to exhibit McLaren-Honda superiority with a perfect lights-to-flag display, his fifth Rio victory in seven years. Senna stormed through to P2 by lap 20 but was black-flagged for switching cars: 1-0 Prost. Mansell went out with overheating when P3 on lap 18, Berger and Piquet completing the podium having made two tyre stops to Prost's one. Despite boost cuts and fuel and weight penalties for turbos, the best atmo finished seventh.

POLE POSITION A Senna, McLaren-Honda, 1m 28.096s (0.536s), 205.589kph, 127.747mph
LAPS 60 x 5.031 km, 3.126 miles (Scheduled for 61 laps but reduced after aborted start)
DISTANCE 301.860 km, 187.567 miles
STARTERS/FINISHERS 25/9
WEATHER Cloudy, hot, dry
LAP LEADERS Prost 1-60 (60)
WINNER'S LAPS 1-60 P1
FASTEST LAP Berger, Ferrari, 1m 32.943s (lap 45), 194.868kph, 121.085mph
CHAMPIONSHIP Prost 9, Berger 6, Piquet 4, Warwick 3, Alboreto 2

Pos	Driver	Car	Time/gap	Grid	Stops	Tyres
1	A Prost	McLaren-Honda	1h 36m 6.857s	3	1	G
2	G Berger	Ferrari	−9.873s	4	2	G
3	N Piquet	Lotus-Honda	−1m 8.521s	5	2	G
4	D Warwick	Arrows-Megatron	−1m 13.348s	11	1	G
5	M Alboreto	Ferrari	−1m 14.556s	6	1	G
6	S Nakajima	Lotus-Honda	−1 lap	10	2	G

McLaren-Honda MP4/4

<table>
<tr><td>**Round 2/16**</td><td>**SAN MARINO GP** Imola
1 May 1988   **Race 454**</td><td>**Ayrton Senna**
McLaren-Honda MP4/4 195.754kph, 121.636mph</td></tr>
</table>

Senna qualified 0.771s faster than Prost and an unheard of 3.352s up on Piquet in P3 driving his former mount, the Lotus-Honda. From pole Senna led throughout. Prost, just managing to save an engine-stall on the grid, fell to seventh on lap 1, recovering to second by lap 8. The 10s gap ebbed and flowed, neither planning to stop. Prost gained on pace but lost out in traffic. 1-1. The race for third was more entertaining, Piquet holding off the faster atmo cars, viz the Benettons and Mansell. This was more like it, Imola regarded as the race when the 150-litre fuel limit for turbos was expected to make them most vulnerable to the atmos. But nobody told McLaren, the fastest race-lap for both cars quicker than Piquet's qualifying lap.

POLE POSITION Senna, McLaren-Honda, 1m 27.148s (0.771s), 208.198kph, 129.368mph
LAPS 60 x 5.040 km, 3.132 miles
DISTANCE 302.400 km, 187.903 miles
STARTERS/FINISHERS 26/18
WEATHER Cloudy, warm, dry
LAP LEADERS Senna 1-60 (60)
WINNER'S LAPS 1-60 P1
FASTEST LAP Prost, McLaren-Honda, 1m 29.685s (lap 53), 202.308kph, 125.708mph
CHAMPIONSHIP Prost 15, Senna 9, Berger 8, Piquet 8, Warwick 3

Pos	Driver	Car	Time/gap	Grid	Stops	Tyres
1	A Senna	McLaren-Honda	1h 32m 41.264s	1	0	G
2	A Prost	McLaren-Honda	−2.334s	2	0	G
3	N Piquet	Lotus-Honda	−1 lap	3	0	G
4	T Boutsen	Benetton-Ford	−1 lap	8	0	G
5	G Berger	Ferrari	−1 lap	5	0	G
6	A Nannini	Benetton-Ford	−1 lap	4	0	G

Round 3/16	**MONACO GP** Monte Carlo	**Alain Prost**
	15 May 1988 Race 455	McLaren-Honda MP4/4 132.797kph, 82.516mph

Senna on pole by 1.427s from Prost. And for 66 of 78 laps Senna was in a different league. Indeed, when the Ferrari snicked by in the first hundred yards Prost was trapped behind Berger for 54 laps, almost a minute in arrears when he at last broke free. Until, that is, Senna binned it at Portiers, probably a lapse of concentration. Prost 2-1 for 1988 and 4-1 for Monte Carlo. No wonder Ayrton went AWOL for 24 hours. The Ferraris finished 2-3, Alboreto spinning Mansell out of the race in an attempted pass for P4 around the swimming pool esses on lap 33. But when the dust settled no one could ignore that Prost had 24 championship points, Senna 9, and that making up a 15-point deficit on the double world champion was not the work of a moment.

POLE POSITION A Senna, McLaren-Honda, 1m 23.998s (1.427s), 142.632kph, 88.627mph
LAPS 78 x 3.328 km, 2.068 miles
DISTANCE 259.584 km, 161.298 miles
STARTERS/FINISHERS 25/10
WEATHER Cloudy, warm, dry
LAP LEADERS Senna 1-66 (66); Prost 67-78 (12)
WINNER'S LAPS 1-66 P2, 67-78 P1
FASTEST LAP A Senna, McLaren-Honda, 1m 26.321s (lap 59), 138.794kph, 86.242mph
CHAMPIONSHIP Prost 24, Berger 14, Senna 9, Piquet 8, Alboreto 6

Pos	Driver	Car	Time/gap	Grid	Stops	Tyres
1	A Prost	McLaren-Honda	1h 57m 17.077s	2	0	G
2	G Berger	Ferrari	−20.453s	3	0	G
3	M Alboreto	Ferrari	−41.229s	4	0	G
4	D Warwick	Arrows-Megatron	−1 lap	7	0	G
5	J Palmer	Tyrrell-Ford	−1 lap	10	0	G
6	R Patrese	Williams-Judd	−1 lap	8	1	G

Round 4/16	**MEXICAN GP** Mexico City	**Alain Prost**
	29 May 1988 Race 456	McLaren-Honda MP4/4 196.898kph, 122.346mph

In qualifying, Alliot survived a monumental cartwheeling accident of immense violence. Senna's fourth pole, Prost alongside, the start quite probably deciding the race. Senna's was good, Prost's better, but Piquet's the best from P4, his brief intervention assisting Prost to lead lap 1 by 2s from Senna, and very gradually pull away. Ninety minutes later that's how it finished. Prost 3-1. Neither driver was entirely happy with their car, Prost dealing with an overheating engine and marginal tyre wear; Senna tyre issues and unexpectedly high fuel consumption. But both drivers were mistake-free and closely matched. As was the final result, the McLaren, Ferrari, Arrows and Benetton teams all finishing two-by-two, all but Berger lapped.

POLE POSITION Senna, McLaren-Honda, 1m 17.468s (0.629s), 205.447kph, 127.659mph
LAPS 67 x 4.421 km, 2.747 miles
DISTANCE 296.207 km, 184.054 miles
STARTERS/FINISHERS 26/16
WEATHER Cloudy with sunny intervals, hot, dry
LAP LEADERS Prost 1-67 (67)
WINNER'S LAPS 1-67 P1
FASTEST LAP Prost, McLaren-Honda, 1m 18.608s (lap 52), 202.468kph, 125.808mph
CHAMPIONSHIP Prost 33, Berger 18, Senna 15, Alboreto 9, Piquet 8

Pos	Driver	Car	Time/gap	Grid	Stops	Tyres
1	A Prost	McLaren-Honda	1h 30m 15.737s	2	0	G
2	A Senna	McLaren-Honda	−7.104s	1	0	G
3	G Berger	Ferrari	−57.314s	3	0	G
4	M Alboreto	Ferrari	−1 lap	5	0	G
5	D Warwick	Arrows-Megatron	−1 lap	9	0	G
6	E Cheever	Arrows-Megatron	−1 lap	7	0	G

Round 5/16	**CANADIAN GP** Montréal	**Ayrton Senna**
	12 June 1988 Race 457	McLaren-Honda MP4/4 182.152kph, 113.184mph

Warwick endured a colossal qualifying accident, the next day gallantly racing to seventh. Senna's fifth pole, Prost alongside, the rest not even close. Prost got away the better but this time Senna pressed from the off, the pair exchanging fastest laps over the first ten. On lap 19, busy with backmarkers, Senna closed right up. Approaching the chicane he flicked right, went by on the inside, Prost making no attempt to block. 20 laps later the gap was still only 2s, after which it began to open up as overheating and fuel consumption hindered Prost. 3-2. In the other race, the usually reliable Ferraris both failed mechanically, leaving the way clear for the racy atmo Benetton-Fords to star, Boutsen on the podium and the same lap as the McLarens.

POLE POSITION Senna, McLaren-Honda, 1m 21.681s (0.182s), 193.484kph, 120.226mph
LAPS 69 x 4.390 km, 2.728 miles
DISTANCE 302.910 km, 188.220 miles
STARTERS/FINISHERS 26/14
WEATHER Hot, dry, sunny
LAP LEADERS Prost 1-18 (18); Senna 19-69 (51)
WINNER'S LAPS 1-18 P2, 19-69 P1
FASTEST LAP Senna, McLaren-Honda, 1m 24.973s (Lap 53), 185.988kph, 115.568mph
CHAMPIONSHIP Prost 39, Senna 24, Berger 18, Piquet 11, Alboreto 9

Pos	Driver	Car	Time/gap	Grid	Stops	Tyres
1	A Senna	McLaren-Honda	1h 39m 46.618s	1	0	G
2	A Prost	McLaren-Honda	−5.934s	2	0	G
3	T Boutsen	Benetton-Ford	−51.409s	7	0	G
4	N Piquet	Lotus-Honda	−1 lap	6	0	G
5	I Capelli	March-Judd	−1 lap	14	0	G
6	J Palmer	Tyrrell-Ford	−2 laps	19	0	G

<table>
<tr><td>**Round 6/16**</td><td>**UNITED STATES GP** Detroit
19 June 1988　　　　　　　　　**Race 458**</td><td>**Ayrton Senna**
McLaren-Honda MP4/4 132.322kph, 82.221mph</td></tr>
</table>

Senna's sixth pole was not only a prelude to his Detroit hat-trick, it also restored equilibrium to his 1988 race-win tally versus Prost, 3-3. But not his points – by again finishing second Prost still held a 12-point advantage. Qualifying placed two Ferraris between the McLarens, reflecting in part Prost's dislike of the circuit. But in the race he only needed six laps to reach P2, but by then Senna was long gone. As too were the Ferraris by the finish, bringing Boutsen's Benetton another podium. A deteriorating track surface caused many spins and offs, only eight running by the end of an almost two-hour marathon. De Cesaris' Rial came fourth; Palmer came from dead last to a fighting fifth, and after four years Minardi scored their first championship point.

POLE POSITION Senna, McLaren-Honda, 1m 40.606s (0.858), 143.969kph, 89.458mph
LAPS 63 x 4.023 km, 2.500 miles
DISTANCE 253.472 km, 157.500 miles
STARTERS/FINISHERS 26/9
WEATHER Cloudy with sunny intervals, hot, dry
LAP LEADERS Senna 1-63 (63)
WINNER'S LAPS 1-63 P1
FASTEST LAP Prost, McLaren-Honda, 1m 44.836s (lap 4), 138.160kph, 85.848mph
CHAMPIONSHIP Prost 45, Senna 33, Berger 18, Boutsen 11, Piquet 11

Pos	Driver	Car	Time/gap	Grid	Stops	Tyres
1	A Senna	McLaren-Honda	1h 54m 56.035s	1	1	G
2	A Prost	McLaren-Honda	−38.713s	4	1	G
3	T Boutsen	Benetton-Ford	−1 lap	5	0	G
4	A de Cesaris	Rial-Ford	−1 lap	12	0	G
5	J Palmer	Tyrrell-Ford	−1 lap	17	1	G
6	P Martini	Minardi-Ford	−1 lap	16	0	G

<table>
<tr><td>**Round 7/16**</td><td>**FRENCH GP** Paul Ricard
3 July 1988　　　　　　　　　**Race 459**</td><td>**Alain Prost**
McLaren-Honda MP4/4 187.482kph, 116.496mph</td></tr>
</table>

On pole for the first time in two years, Prost made it pay. But after leading the opening 36 laps he lost out on the tyre stops. However, this was France and Prost was on Senna's tail and feeling confident. On lap 61 of 80 Senna's rhythm was disturbed just a fraction by a backmarker, and cornering slightly wide, Prost nailed him down the inside. Mildly handicapped by a gearbox problem, Senna was unable to re-engage with the flying Frenchman. 4-3 to Prost on race wins and his points lead over Senna back to 15. The Ferraris were 3-4, their fourth 'best of the rest' finish, Alboreto beating Berger for the first time. Next came Piquet's Lotus-Honda then the highest finishing atmo sixth, Nannini's Benetton noticeably short of grunt down the Mistral straight.

POLE POSITION Prost, McLaren-Honda, 1m 07.589s (0.479), 203.092kph, 126.196mph
LAPS 80 x 3.813 km, 2.369 miles
DISTANCE 305.040 km, 189.543 miles
STARTERS/FINISHERS 26/15
WEATHER Cloudy with sunny intervals, hot, dry
LAP LEADERS Prost 1-36, 61-80 (56); Senna 37-60 (24)
WINNER'S LAPS 1-36 P1, 37-60 P2, 61-80 P1
FASTEST LAP Prost, McLaren-Honda, 1m 11.737s (lap 45), 191.349kph, 118.899mph
CHAMPIONSHIP Prost 54, Senna 39, Berger 21, Piquet 13, Alboreto 13

Pos	Driver	Car	Time/gap	Grid	Stops	Tyres
1	A Prost	McLaren-Honda	1h 30m 15.737s	2	1	G
2	A Senna	McLaren-Honda	−7.104s	1	1	G
3	M Alboreto	Ferrari	−57.314s	3	1	G
4	G Berger	Ferrari	−1 lap	5	1	G
5	N Piquet	Lotus-Honda	−1 lap	9	1	G
6	A Nannini	Benetton-Ford	−1 lap	7	1	G

<table>
<tr><td>**Round 8/16**</td><td>**BRITISH GP** Silverstone
10 July 1988　　　　　　　　　**Race 460**</td><td>**Ayrton Senna**
McLaren-Honda MP4/4 199.788kph, 124.142mph</td></tr>
</table>

Silverstone, halfway and perhaps a watershed. Not only a sublime Senna victory in difficult, wet conditions, but more significantly the first Prost dnf, surrendering to poor handling and the weather on lap 24. Eight rounds, 4-4, and now just six points separating them. Silverstone was notable in other ways too: the first non-McLaren pole, the grid comprising two Ferraris from two McLarens from two March-Judds; the first race laps led by other than a McLaren, Berger throwing fuel considerations to the wind for the first 13 laps, losing P6 as the starved engine gasped on his final lap, and lastly, Mansell finishing his first race of the season in a 'passive' Williams-Judd, and doing so in style with a crowd-rousing charge to P2 in the dank conditions.

POLE POSITION G Berger, Ferrari, 1m 07.110s (0.070s), 245.267kph, 152.402mph
LAPS 65 x 4.778 km, 2.969 miles
DISTANCE 310.579 km, 192.985 miles
STARTERS/FINISHERS 26/19
WEATHER Overcast, cool, intermittent rain
LAP LEADERS Berger 1-13 (13); Senna 14-65 (52)
WINNER'S LAPS 1-13 P2, 14-65 P1
FASTEST LAP Mansell, Williams-Judd, 1m 23.308s (lap 48), 206.479kph, 128.300mph
CHAMPIONSHIP Prost 54, Senna 48, Berger 21, Piquet 15, Alboreto 13

Pos	Driver	Car	Time/gap	Grid	Stops	Tyres
1	A Senna	McLaren-Honda	1h 33m 16.367s	3	0	G
2	N Mansell	Williams-Judd	−23.344s	11	0	G
3	A Nannini	Benetton-Ford	−51.214s	8	0	G
4	M Gugelmin	March-Judd	−1m 11.368s	5	0	G
5	N Piquet	Lotus-Honda	−1m 20.835s	7	0	G
6	D Warwick	Arrows-Megatron	−1 lap	9	0	G

Round 9/16	**GERMAN GP** Hockenheim		**Ayrton Senna**
	24 July 1988	Race 461	McLaren-Honda MP4/4 193.148kph, 120.017mph

At Hockenheim normal order was restored, McLarens ahead of Ferraris in qualifying, Senna's seventh pole. And 44 laps later, that's how they finished, Senna immaculate in the wet as he had been two weeks before. 4-5 to Senna. Prost's afternoon was less clear-cut. Too few revs and a hesitant getaway required him to dispense with Nannini and Berger before he got behind Senna, by then 12s ahead. Mid-race Prost successfully reduced the gap for a while, but delays due to a tangle in traffic and a later spin on fading rain tyres resolved the matter. As Silverstone, Ferrari race pace was fuel-governed, but here they didn't run short, finishing 3-4. And next, for a change, was a new winner of the atmo class, Ivan Capelli's March-Judd.

POLE POSITION Senna, McLaren-Honda, 1m 44.596s (0.277s), 233.940kph, 145.364mph
LAPS 44 x 6.797 km, 4.223 miles
DISTANCE 299.068 km, 185.832 miles
STARTERS/FINISHERS 26/19
WEATHER Overcast, cool, intermittent drizzle
LAP LEADERS Senna 1-44 (44)
WINNER'S LAPS 1-44 P1
FASTEST LAP A Nannini, Benetton-Ford, 2m 03.032s (lap 40), 198.885kph, 123.581mph
CHAMPIONSHIP Prost 60, Senna 57, Berger 25, Alboreto 16, Piquet 15

Pos	Driver	Car	Time/gap	Grid	Stops	Tyres
1	A Senna	McLaren-Honda	1h 32m 54.118s	1	0	G
2	A Prost	McLaren-Honda	–13.609s	2	0	G
3	G Berger	Ferrari	–52.095s	3	0	G
4	M Alboreto	Ferrari	–1m 40.912s	4	0	G
5	I Capelli	March-Judd	–1m 49.606s	7	0	G
6	T Boutsen	Benetton-Ford	–1 lap	9	0	G

Round 10/16	**HUNGARIAN GP** Hungaroring		**Ayrton Senna**
	7 August 1988	Race 462	McLaren-Honda MP4/4 155.401kph, 96.562mph

An atmo circuit, but Senna still edged his eighth pole from Mansell's Williams-Judd, first of a string of atmo cars before reaching Prost's McLaren at P7. Remarkably, at a notorious circuit for overtaking, Prost worked his way from P9 on lap 1 to pass Boutsen, running a close second, on lap 47. Starting lap 49, Prost saw a glimmer of a chance to depose Senna of his lead. A momentary hesitation in traffic and Prost was down the inside at turn one, but his entry speed forced a wide exit line and Senna nipped back inside the frustrated Frenchman. 4-6 for races, but more importantly, even-steven on points. Boutsen took a fine third for Benetton, and early on Mansell chased Senna relentlessly until a high-speed spin, finally retiring from exhaustion.

POLE POSITION Senna, McLaren-Honda, 1m 27.635s (0.108s), 164.893kph, 102.460mph
LAPS 76 x 4.014 km, 2.494 miles
DISTANCE 305.064 km, 189.558 miles
STARTERS/FINISHERS 26/13
WEATHER Sunny, hot, dry
LAP LEADERS Senna 1-76 (76)
WINNER'S LAPS 1-76 P1
FASTEST LAP Prost, McLaren-Honda, 1m 30.639s (lap 51), 159.429kph, 99.064mph
CHAMPIONSHIP Prost 66, Senna 66, Berger 28, Alboreto 16, Boutsen 16

Pos	Driver	Car	Time/gap	Grid	Stops	Tyres
1	A Senna	McLaren-Honda	1h 57m 47.081s	1	0	G
2	A Prost	McLaren-Honda	–0.529s	7	0	G
3	T Boutsen	Benetton-Ford	–31.410s	3	0	G
4	G Berger	Ferrari	–1m 28.670s	9	0	G
5	M Gugelmin	March-Judd	–1 lap	8	0	G
6	R Patrese	Williams-Judd	–1 lap	6	0	G

Round 11/16	**BELGIAN GP** Spa Francorchamps		**Ayrton Senna**
	28 August 1988	Race 463	McLaren-Honda MP4/4 203.447kph, 126.416mph

From his ninth pole Senna won his fourth successive race, having led every lap of the last three. So the wins score stood 4-7 and for the very first time Senna headed the points table. Struggling with set-up, Prost was soundly beaten into second despite making the better getaway from the front row to lead the first half-lap. But Senna exited Eau Rouge much faster and took Prost up the hill to Les Combes. It was a demoralising opening lap by Senna, and afterwards Prost conceded the championship, aware that the scoring system would play out against him. McLaren's eighth 1-2 sealed the constructors' championship and Senna's seventh win equalled the record held by Clark, and Prost. Disqualification over fuel irregularities denied Benetton a 2-3 result.

POLE POSITION Senna, McLaren-Honda, 1m 53.718s (0.410s), 219.701kph, 136.516mph
LAPS 43 x 6.940 km, 4.312 miles
DISTANCE 298.420 km, 185.430 miles
STARTERS/FINISHERS 26/13
WEATHER Cloudy, warm, dry
LAP LEADERS Senna 1-43 (43)
WINNER'S LAPS 1-43 P1
FASTEST LAP G Berger, Ferrari, 2m 00.772s (lap 10), 206.869kph, 128.543mph
CHAMPIONSHIP Senna 75, Prost 72, Berger 28, Boutsen 20, Alboreto 16

Pos	Driver	Car	Time/gap	Grid	Stops	Tyres
1	A Senna	McLaren-Honda	1h 28m 0.549s	1	0	G
2	A Prost	McLaren-Honda	–30.470s	2	0	G
3	I Capelli	March-Judd	–1m 15.768s	6	0	G
4	N Piquet	Lotus-Honda	–1m 23.628s	7	0	G
5	D Warwick	Arrows-Megatron	–1m 25.355s	14	0	G
6	E Cheever	Arrows-Megatron	–1 lap	9	0	G

Ferrari F1-87/88C

Round 12/16	**ITALIAN GP** Monza					**Gerhard Berger**	
	11 September 1988			Race 464		Ferrari F1-87/88C 228.528kph, 142.000mph	

The one that got away. McLaren posted their first and only mechanical retirement, Prost, close behind Senna, out at two-thirds distance with engine trouble. Senna, fuel marginal, eased up, the chasing Ferraris closing in from 25s to just five. With two laps left, the charging Ferraris bearing down, Senna saw a backmarker ahead, the Williams-Judd of Jean-Louis Schlesser, subbing for the ill Nigel Mansell in his one and only GP appearance. At the first chicane things went awry and they collided, a mixture of Schlesser's desperation to steer clear and Senna's impetuosity. With both McLarens out Ferrari were gifted an unexpected and emotional 1-2 *doppietta* at Monza, just four weeks following the death of the *Commendatore*, Enzo Ferrari.

POLE POSITION A Senna, McLaren-Honda, 1m 25.974s (0.303s), 242.864kph, 150.909mph
LAPS 51 x 5.800 km, 3.604 miles
DISTANCE 295.800 km, 183.802 miles
STARTERS/FINISHERS 26/13
WEATHER Cloudy with sunny intervals, hot, dry
LAP LEADERS Senna 1-49 (49); Berger 50-51 (2)
WINNER'S LAPS 1-34 P3, 35-49 P2, 50-51 P1
FASTEST LAP Alboreto, Ferrari, 1m 29.070 (lap 44), 234.422kph, 145.663mph
CHAMPIONSHIP Senna 75, Prost 72, Berger 37, Alboreto 22, Boutsen 21

Pos	Driver	Car	Time/gap	Grid	Stops	Tyres
1	G Berger	Ferrari	1h 17m 39.744s	3	0	G
2	M Alboreto	Ferrari	−0.502s	4	0	G
3	E Cheever	Arrows-Megatron	−35.532s	5	0	G
4	D Warwick	Arrows-Megatron	−36.114s	6	0	G
5	I Capelli	March-Judd	−52.522s	11	0	G
6	T Boutsen	Benetton-Ford	−59.878s	8	0	G

Round 13/16	**PORTUGUESE GP** Estoril					**Alain Prost**	
	25 September 1988			Race 465		McLaren-Honda MP4/4 187.034kph, 116.218mph	

Prost, from his second pole, led all except lap 1, but had to battle hard for victory. Not with Senna but Capelli's March-Judd. 5-7. After one abort and one restart Senna led away, but as Prost confidently breezed past commencing lap 2 Senna deliberately and dangerously squeezed him towards the pit wall. Prost was not amused, yet for now at least the Prost/Senna relationship survived the incident. Capelli's Newey-designed car had qualified P3, demonstrating superior aero traits, and was now tormenting Senna. Getting by on lap 21, Capelli quickly closed on the leader, but Prost was able to respond and pull away. Senna meanwhile battled an engine problem and Mansell until he spun off, Senna finishing P6. So the championship wasn't over.

POLE POSITION Prost, McLaren-Honda, 1m 17.411s (0.458s), 202.297kph, 125.701mph
LAPS 70 x 4.350 km, 2.703 miles
DISTANCE 304.500 km, 189.208 miles
STARTERS/FINISHERS 26/12
WEATHER Sunny, hot, dry
LAP LEADERS Senna 1 (1); Prost 2-70 (69)
WINNER'S LAPS 1 P2, 2-70 P1
FASTEST LAP G Berger, Ferrari, 1m 21.961s (lap 31), 191.066kph, 118.723mph
CHAMPIONSHIP Prost 81, Senna 76, Berger 37, Boutsen 25, Alboreto 24

Pos	Driver	Car	Time/gap	Grid	Stops	Tyres
1	A Prost	McLaren-Honda	1h 37m 40.958s	1	0	G
2	I Capelli	March-Judd	−9.553s	3	0	G
3	T Boutsen	Benetton-Ford	−44.619s	13	0	G
4	D Warwick	Arrows-Megatron	−1m 7.419s	10	0	G
5	M Alboreto	Ferrari	−1m 11.884s	7	0	G
6	A Senna	McLaren-Honda	−1m 18.269s	2	1	G

| Round 14/16 | **SPANISH GP** Jerez | | | | Alain Prost | |
| | 2 October 1988 | | | Race 466 | McLaren-Honda MP4/4 167.586kph, 104.133mph | |

From his 11th pole, Senna was beaten away by Prost and by Mansell. By the end of a storming opening lap Prost was 2s up and never looked back. This was despite Mansell's close attention for half the race until Nigel lost time at his tyre stop with a stubborn left rear. 6-7. As Prost's radio wasn't working he decided not to risk a stop, but with the pressure now off he made it and all went smoothly. Senna, hampered by his fuel readout and again off the pace, finished fourth, beaten to the podium by Nannini's Benetton. With two wins in one week the Frenchman had restored a points lead of five with two rounds remaining. But due to the vagaries of the scoring system, one more race victory would guarantee the Brazilian championship glory.

POLE POSITION Senna, McLaren- Honda, 1m 24.067s (0.067s), 180.627kph, 112.237mph
LAPS 72 x 4.218 km, 2.621 miles
DISTANCE 303.696 km, 188.708 miles
STARTERS/FINISHERS 26/14
WEATHER Sunny, hot, dry
LAP LEADERS Prost 1-72 (72)
WINNER'S LAPS 1-72 P1
FASTEST LAP Prost, McLaren- Honda, 1m 27.845s (lap 60), 172.859kph, 107.410mph
CHAMPIONSHIP Prost 84, Senna 79, Berger 38, Boutsen 25, Alboreto 24

Pos	Driver	Car	Time/gap	Grid	Stops	Tyres
1	A Prost	McLaren- Honda	1h 48m 43.851s	2	1	G
2	N Mansell	Williams-Judd	−26.232s	3	1	G
3	A Nannini	Benetton-Ford	−35.446s	5	1	G
4	A Senna	McLaren- Honda	−46.710s	1	1	G
5	R Patrese	Williams-Judd	−47.430s	7	0	G
6	G Berger	Ferrari	−51.813s	8	1	G

| Round 15/16 | **JAPANESE GP** Suzuka | | | | Ayrton Senna | |
| | 30 October 1988 | | | Race 467 | McLaren-Honda MP4/4 191.880kph, 119.229mph | |

Senna stalled his 12th pole, finding just enough momentum for a bump-start. He rounded the first corner P14, the first lap in P8. With Prost leading, championship destiny would now surely await Adelaide. But it drizzled, periodically, slicks on a damp surface meat and drink to Senna. Displaying uncanny skills, he sliced through the field and by lap 28 of 51 dispossessed Prost of the lead, and his title ambitions. 6-8, game, set, match and championship to Senna. Earlier, Prost had initially seen off Berger's brief, fuel-limited Ferrari challenge but then had to resist far greater pressure from Capelli's March. When Prost was slowed by Suzuki's spinning Lola on lap 16, Capelli broke the timing beam P1, the first lap led by an atmo in four years.

POLE POSITION Senna, McLaren- Honda, 1m 41.853s (0.324s), 207.087kph, 128.678mph
LAPS 51 x 5.859 km, 3.641 miles
DISTANCE 298.809 km, 185.671 miles
STARTERS/FINISHERS 26/17
WEATHER Overcast, cool, occasional light rain
LAP LEADERS Prost 1-15, 17-27 (26); I Capelli, March-Judd 16 (1); Senna 28-51 (24)
WINNER'S LAPS 1 P8, 2 P6, 3 P5, 4-10 P4, 11-19 P3, 20-27 P2, 28-51 P1
FASTEST LAP Senna, McLaren- Honda, 1m 46.326s (lap 33), 198.375kph, 123.264mph
CHAMPIONSHIP Senna 87, Prost 84, Berger 41, Boutsen 29, Alboreto 24

Pos	Driver	Car	Time/gap	Grid	Stops	Tyres
1	A Senna	McLaren-Honda	1h 33m 26.173s	1	0	G
2	A Prost	McLaren-Honda	−13.363s	2	0	G
3	T Boutsen	Benetton-Ford	−36.109s	10	0	G
4	G Berger	Ferrari	−1m 26.714s	3	0	G
5	A Nannini	Benetton-Ford	−1m 30.603s	12	0	G
6	R Patrese	Williams-Judd	−1m 37.615s	11	0	G

| Round 16/16 | **AUSTRALIAN GP** Adelaide | | | | Alain Prost | |
| | 13 November 1988 | | | Race 468 | McLaren-Honda MP4/4 164.225kph, 102.085mph | |

Fittingly, the final turbo race went to Prost and McLaren, the dominant driver and team of the six-year era. New champion Senna duly annexed his record 13th pole, but Prost led him comfortably all the way – as he did the race, apart from while Berger cast fuel-caution to the winds for 12 laps, only to collide lapping a backmarker on lap 26. Outgoing champion Piquet – remember him? – finished third to make it a Honda 1-2-3, also a fitting result for the dominant engine of the era. So the final 1988 race tally was 7-8 to Senna. But since Hungary when they were tied on points, Prost had won more victories (3-2), won more points (39-28) and had wound up with a gross championship score greater than Senna's (105-94). Curious business, Formula 1.

POLE POSITION Senna, McLaren- Honda, 1m 17.748s (0.132s), 175.027kph, 108.757mph
LAPS 82 x 3.780 km, 2.349 miles
DISTANCE 309.960 km, 192.600 miles
STARTERS/FINISHERS 26/13
WEATHER Cloudy with sunny intervals, hot, dry
LAP LEADERS Prost 1-13, 26-82 (70); G Berger, Ferrari 14-25 (12)
WINNER'S LAPS 1-13 P1, 14-25 P2, 26-82 P1
FASTEST LAP Prost, McLaren- Honda, 1m 21.216s (lap 59), 167.553kph, 104.113mph
CHAMPIONSHIP Senna 90, Prost 87, Berger 41, Boutsen 31, Alboreto 24

Pos	Driver	Car	Time/gap	Grid	Stops	Tyres
1	A Prost	McLaren-Honda	1h 53m 14.676s	2	0	G
2	A Senna	McLaren-Honda	−36.787s	1	0	G
3	N Piquet	Lotus-Honda	−47.546s	5	0	G
4	R Patrese	Williams-Judd	−1m 20.088s	6	0	G
5	T Boutsen	Benetton-Ford	−1 lap	10	0	G
6	I Capelli	March-Judd	−1 lap	9	1	G

RACE 465, Portuguese GP: Ayrton led off the grid, but as Prost breezed past commencing lap two, Senna deliberately and dangerously squeezed him towards the pit-wall.

1988 CHAMPIONSHIP FACTS AND FOLKLORE

- 1988 was the second transition year from turbos to atmos. The two forms of engine would compete directly against one another with no separate competition for normally aspirated entries, the regulations supposedly having been written to favour the atmos.
- The performance of turbo-engined cars was further limited through yet another reduction in fuel tankage to 150 litres (33 gallons) and even more restriction of turbo boost with a pop-off valve of only 2.5 bar.
- This represented a significant reduction in bhp and resulted in the increased possibility of tyres lasting a whole race without the need for a pit stop. Turbo cars also continued to carry a 40kg dry weight penalty.
- 3.5-litre atmospheric-engined cars had no fuel tank restriction, but on a safety note the pedal box had to be behind the front axle, beginning to address the menace of foot and leg injuries associated with the forward driver position latterly adopted by designers.
- Brabham withdrew for this season resuming in 1989, but even so, no less than 18 teams entered, six opting for the turbo option. With up to 31 cars competing for 26 grid slots the early-morning ritual of pre-qualifying resumed.
- For the 16-round series the minimum race-distance was set at 300km (186.41 miles) excluding the warm-up lap, with a maximum of 320km (198.84 miles) or two hours.
- As usual the best 11 results would count for the drivers' title, which, in his close championship battle with Senna, played out severely against Prost.
- The season was all about Senna, Prost and the McLaren-Honda. Everyone else had walk-on parts as the McLaren team and drivers totally dominated, seeming to break every record going.
- 15 of the 16 championship rounds went to the pair, Senna taking the championship with eight race victories, a new record exceeding the seven held by Clark (1963) and Prost (1984 and 1988).
- Senna's 13 poles in the year also established a new benchmark with the six consecutive poles that began the season equalling the record set by Moss (1959–60) and Lauda (1974).
- Prost won seven races, finished second seven times and scored 105 points gross, also a record, and 11 more than Senna.
- Among the leading teams for the final year of the turbo era, McLaren alone built a brand new car, the MP4/4, and their new engine partner also uniquely did the same, and it showed.
- Of the 1,031 laps raced in 1988, just 28 were not led by a McLaren-Honda, Berger's Ferrari leading 27 laps, Capelli's March-Judd just the one.
- McLaren won the constructors' championship with a record 199 points and on no less than ten occasions finished 1-2.
- The single race win which got away from McLaren gifted Ferrari an unexpected and emotional win at Monza, just four weeks after the death of the great Enzo Ferrari, the epitome of a motor racing mogul.
- Enzo Ferrari (1898–1988) died at the age of 90. A racing driver in the 1920s, team principal for Alfa Romeo's factory team in the 1930s, his fame emanated from the road and racing cars bearing his name, a business he established at Maranello in the 1940s, and partially sold to FIAT in 1969.
- The scarlet Ferraris with their Prancing Horse emblem are the only team to have participated in every year of the F1 world championships. At the time of Ing Ferrari's death his legendary marque had won 91 GPs, bringing nine drivers' and eight constructors' titles over 37 championship seasons.
- In 1988, having won the last two races of the previous season, Ferrari raced a development of their existing chassis and turbo engine. They were a distant second place in the constructors' championship but beat all other teams, proving that, the remarkable McLaren-Honda apart, even in heavily restricted form a 1.5 turbo still outperformed a 3.5 atmo.

- Berger, with his single victory and four other podium results, finished third in the drivers championship behind Senna and Prost.
- Despite running the same new Honda engine, Lotus with reigning champion Piquet at the wheel achieved very little, finishing equal fourth with Arrows who ran a Megatron turbo (née BMW).
- Of the atmo teams, March-Judd and their designer Adrian Newey deservedly received rave reviews when Capelli put genuine pressure on winner Prost at Estoril and finished a strong second, but undoubtedly the most successful atmo team was Benetton-Ford.
- Ford elected to drop their V6 turbo and instead provide Benetton with the latest incarnation of the venerable DFV, the 3.5-litre DFL. In the back of Rory Byrne's B188 chassis the package worked well, the team finishing third in the championship and Boutsen on five occasions beaten only by the McLarens.
- What of Williams, dominant champions for the last two years? With Honda now aligned with McLaren, Williams turned to John Judd's V8 and they and Mansell had a 'character-building' year.
- Overheating and problems with the reactive suspension had

Mansell only finish twice. On both occasions it was a fine P2 and at Silverstone only following the FW12 being stripped of its trick suspension.
- Mansell also missed two races through chickenpox. His replacement at Monza, Jean-Louis Schlesser, will forever be remembered for the infamous Monza incident when Senna tripped over backmarker Schlesser in the closing moments. McLaren a 1988 clean sweep of race victories when Senna Jean-Louis was the nephew of the late Jo Schlesser, killed at the French GP in 1968.
- So 1988 was the swansong for turbo-powered F1 cars. First introduced to F1 by Renault in 1977, it was not until 1983 that turbo cars became predominant and the six-year turbo era truly began.
- Over that six-year period, 95 world championship GPs were run. The most successful driver was Prost with 30 victories (32%); the most successful team McLaren, 41 wins (43%), each of these more than double the next, Senna and Williams respectively. The stats for engines were closer, Honda 34 wins (36%) versus TAG Porsche 25 victories (26%).
- It had been an extraordinary period for Formula 1. With their fuel limitations and variable boost pressure, turbos required a special form of race craft, but was it racing?

Championship ranking	Championship points	Driver nationality	1988 Drivers Championship		Races contested	Race victories	Podiumse excl. victories	Races led	Lights to flag victories	Laps led	Poles	Fastest laps	Triple Crowns
			Driver	Car									
1	90	BRA	Ayrton Senna	McLaren-Honda	16	8	3	12	5	553	13	3	2
2	87	FRA	Alain Prost	McLaren-Honda	16	7	7	9	3	450	2	7	1
3	41	AUT	Gerhard Berger	Ferrari	16	1	4	3		27	1	3	
4	27	BEL	Thierry Boutsen	Benetton-Ford	16		5						
5	24	ITA	Michele Alboreto	Ferrari	16		3					1	
6	22	BRA	Nelson Piquet	Lotus-Honda	16		3						
7	17	ITA	Ivan Capelli	March-Judd	15		2	1		1			
8	17	GBR	Derek Warwick	Arrows-Megatron	16								
9	12	GBR	Nigel Mansell	Williams-Judd	14		2					1	
10	12	ITA	Alessandro Nannini	Benetton-Ford	16		2					1	
11	8	ITA	Riccardo Patrese	Williams-Judd	16								
12	6	USA	Eddie Cheever	Arrows-Megatron	16		1						
13	5	BRA	Mauricio Gugelmin	March-Judd	16								
14	5	GBR	Jonathan Palmer	Tyrrell-Ford	14								
15	3	ITA	Andrea de Cesaris	Rial-Ford	16								
16	1	JAP	Satoru Nakajima	Lotus-Honda	14								
16	1	ITA	Pierluigi Martini	Minardi-Ford	9								

Championship ranking	Championship points	Team/Marque nationality	1988 Constructors Championship		Engine maker nationality	Races contested	Race victories	1-2 finishes	Podiums excl. victories	Races led	Laps led	Poles	Fastest laps
			Chassis	Engine									
1	199	GBR	McLaren MP4-4	Honda 1.5 V6t	JPN	16	15	10	10	16	1003	15	10
2	65	ITA	Ferrari F1-87/88C	Ferrari 1.5 V6t	ITA	16	1	1	7	3	27	1	4
3	39	GBR	Benetton B188	Ford Cosworth 3.5 V8	GBR	16			7				1
4	23	GBR	Lotus 100T	Honda 1.5 V6t	JAP	16			3				
5	23	GBR	Arrows A10B, A10	Megatron 1.5 S4t	GER	16			1				
6	22	GBR	March 881	Judd 3.5 V8	GBR	16			2	1	1		
7	20	GBR	Williams FW12	Judd 3.5 V8	GBR	16			2				1
8	5	GBR	Tyrrell 017	Ford Cosworth 3.5 V8	GBR	15							
9	3	GER	Rial ARC-01	Ford Cosworth 3.5 V8	GBR	16							
10	1	ITA	Minardi M188	Ford Cosworth 3.5 V8	GBR	14							

1989

Prost's Suzuka chicanery

THE TALE OF THE TITLE

- Round two of Prost versus Senna culminated in their notorious yet decisive Suzuka chicane collision.
- Consistent Alain Prost with 11 podiums including four race victories regained the title from hit-or-miss Senna.
- Senna won more races, six, but his nine dnfs could reasonably be ascribed five car, four driver.
- Bad blood characterised the second and final season of their McLaren internecine rivalry.
- After six seasons that brought seven titles to McLaren, Prost took 'number one' to Maranello for 1990.
- The McLaren-Honda switch from turbo to atmo was seamless, bringing another landslide constructors' cup.
- The McLaren-Honda V10 won ten races, but the V12 Ferrari and Williams-Renault V10 also won on merit.
- Mansell won on debut for Ferrari, his superb pass of Senna in Hungary illustrating Ferrari chassis superiority.
- Ferrari's John Barnard-designed 640 chassis with paddle-shift gearbox pointed the way ahead.
- Gerhard Berger survived a fiery accident at Imola but later won for Ferrari at Estoril.
- Although both victories were in the wet, Thierry Boutsen won twice for a new F1 alliance, Williams-Renault.
- And not forgetting: real-time telemetry; Senna's winter of discontent.

THE CHASE FOR THE CHAMPIONSHIP

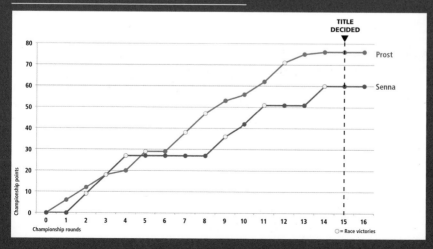

Ferrari 640

Round 1/16	**BRAZILIAN GP** Rio de Janeiro		**Nigel Mansell**
	26 March 1989	Race 469	Ferrari 640 186.034kph, 115.596mph

Dawn of the new 3.5-litre atmo F1 found the top six grid-slots populated by McLaren-Honda V10, Williams-Renault V10 and Ferrari V12. Pole-man Senna went out in a macho first-corner collision with Berger, so initially Patrese's Williams led teammate Boutsen for the few laps his Renault lasted, then Mansell and Prost from row three. Following tribulations with the paddle-shift gearbox in practice, Mansell's Ferrari was now running faultlessly, on lap 16 taking the lead from Patrese which he would only lose during his tyre stops. So Mansell won first time out for Ferrari from a clutchless Prost, powerless due to this to make his second tyre stop. Patrese's Renault also failed, so Gugelmin's March took P3 from Herbert, P4 on debut.

POLE POSITION A Senna, McLaren-Honda, 1m 25.302s (0.870s), 212.323kph, 131.932mph
LAPS 61 x 5.031 km, 3.126 miles
DISTANCE 306.891 km, 190.693 miles
STARTERS/FINISHERS 26/14
WEATHER Sunny, very hot, dry
LAP LEADERS R Patrese 1-15, 21-22 (17); Mansell 16-20, 28-44, 47-61 (37); Prost 23-27, 45-46 (7)
WINNER'S LAPS 1 P6, 2-3 P3, 4-15 P2, 16-20 P1, 21-23 P3, 24-27 P2, 28-44 P1, 45-46 P2, 47-61 P1
FASTEST LAP R Patrese, Williams-Renault, 1m 32.507s (lap 47), 195.786kph, 121.656mph
CHAMPIONSHIP Mansell 9, Prost 6, Gugelmin 4, Herbert 3, Warwick 2

Pos	Driver	Car	Time/gap	Grid	Stops	Tyres
1	N Mansell	Ferrari	1h 38m 58.744s	6	2	G
2	A Prost	McLaren-Honda	–7.809s	5	1	G
3	M Gugelmin	March-Judd	–9.370s	12	1	G
4	J Herbert	Benetton-Ford	–10.493s	10	2	G
5	D Warwick	Arrows-Ford	–17.866s	8	2	G
6	A Nannini	Benetton-Ford	–18.241s	11	3	G

McLaren-Honda MP4/5

SAN MARINO GP Imola

23 April 1989   **Race 470**

Ayrton Senna

McLaren-Honda MP4/5 201.939kph, 125.479mph

At Tamburello on lap 4, Gerhard Berger escaped with his life as his Ferrari left the track when the front wing broke, striking the barrier at undiminished speed, bursting into flames. The race was restarted, the results aggregated. Despite the switch from V6 turbo to V10 atmo, the superiority of the McLaren-Hondas was as last year, their race laps quicker than the rest's qualifying pace. The entire field was lapped for a 1-2 walkover, neither driver stopping, the new champion leading a disgruntled Prost home, Alain spinning briefly and complaining of a broken agreement. Mansell and Patrese fought over third for 20 laps, both cars succumbing to their Achilles heels, Williams-Renault the engine, Ferrari the gearbox. Nannini finished P3 for Benetton.

POLE POSITION Senna, McLaren-Honda, 1m 26.010s (0.225s), 210.952kph, 131.080mph
LAPS 58 x 5.040 km, 3.132 miles (61 lap race interrupted due to accident. Result aggregate of 3 + 55 laps)
DISTANCE 292.320 km, 181.639 miles
STARTERS/FINISHERS 25/12
WEATHER Cloudy with sunny intervals, warm, dry
LAP LEADERS Senna 1-58 (58)
WINNER'S LAPS 1-58 P1
FASTEST LAP Prost, McLaren-Honda, 1m 26.795s (lap 45), 209.044kph, 129.894mph
CHAMPIONSHIP Prost 12, Mansell 9, Senna 9, Nannini 5, Gugelmin 4

Pos	Driver	Car	Time/gap	Grid	Stops	Tyres
1	A Senna	McLaren-Honda	1h 26m 51.245s	1	0	G
2	A Prost	McLaren-Honda	−40.225s	2	0	G
3	A Nannini	Benetton-Ford	−1 lap	7	0	G
4	T Boutsen	Williams-Renault	−1 lap	6	0	G
5	D Warwick	Arrows-Ford	−1 lap	12	0	G
6	J Palmer	Tyrrell-Ford	−1 lap	25	0	G

MONACO GP Monte Carlo

7 May 1989   **Race 471**

Ayrton Senna

McLaren-Honda MP4/5 135.401kph, 84.134mph

As last year, Senna's pole was over a second up on Prost alongside. But unlike last year his race was faultless, leading throughout. Prost harried for the first 14 laps until they met traffic, the gap widening when Alain was cynically baulked by backmarker Arnoux, and later coming to a standstill for 30s when Piquet and de Cesaris gridlocked the Loews hairpin. Prost then settled for P2 but might have kept the hammer down if he had realised that Senna was in gearbox difficulties, a fact skilfully concealed through tactical driving. Brabham-Judd pre-qualifiers Brundle and Modena qualified P5 and P9 on their Pirellis. When Mansell's gearbox broke Brundle looked on for the podium until he stopped with a misfire on lap 49, but Modena kept going for P3.

POLE POSITION Senna, McLaren-Honda, 1m 22.308s (1.148s), 145.561kph, 90.447mph
LAPS 77 x 3.328 km, 2.068 miles
DISTANCE 256.256 km, 159.230 miles
STARTERS/FINISHERS 26/15
WEATHER Cloudy with sunny intervals, warm, dry
LAP LEADERS Senna 1-77 (77)
WINNER'S LAPS 1-77 P1
FASTEST LAP Prost, McLaren-Honda, 1m 25.501s (lap 59), 140.125kph, 87.069mph
CHAMPIONSHIP Prost 18, Senna 18, Mansell 9, Nannini 5, Gugelmin 4

Pos	Driver	Car	Time/gap	Grid	Stops	Tyres
1	A Senna	McLaren-Honda	1h 53m 33.251s	1	0	G
2	A Prost	McLaren-Honda	−52.528s	2	0	G
3	S Modena	Brabham-Judd	−1 lap	8	0	P
4	A Caffi	Dallara-Ford	−2 laps	9	0	P
5	M Alboreto	Tyrrell-Ford	−2 laps	12	0	P
6	M Brundle	Brabham-Judd	−2 laps	4	1	P

MEXICAN GP Mexico City

28 May 1989   **Race 472**

Ayrton Senna

McLaren-Honda MP4/5 191.941kph, 119.267mph

Senna and Prost 1-2 on the grid as usual, Mansell P3, but at P6 the second Ferrari, Berger making a welcome and feisty return. At the second start he ran third until Mansell took over, but the revolutionary Ferrari gearbox/transmission was fragile, Berger out on lap 16 and Mansell retiring from a strong second at two-thirds-distance. The race between the McLarens was decided by tyre compounds, the non-stopping Senna selecting harder Bs on the left, Prost mistakenly Cs all-round, stopping a second time when the pit fitted the wrong type. Patrese gave the improving Williams-Renault its first podium, but with four poles from four, and three from four victories, Senna was looking invincible, and with Prost P5 opened up a useful points lead.

POLE POSITION Senna, McLaren-Honda, 1m 17.876s (0.897s), 204.371kph, 126.990mph
LAPS 69 x 4.421 km, 2.747 miles (Race restarted for scheduled 69 laps following accident)
DISTANCE 305.049 km, 189.549 miles
STARTERS/FINISHERS 26/15
WEATHER Sunny, hot, dry
LAP LEADERS Senna 1-69 (69)
WINNER'S LAPS 1-69 P1
FASTEST LAP N Mansell, Ferrari, 1m 20.420s (lap 41), 197.906kph, 122.973mph
CHAMPIONSHIP Senna 27, Prost 20, Mansell 9, Nannini 8, Patrese 6

Pos	Driver	Car	Time/gap	Grid	Stops	Tyres
1	A Senna	McLaren-Honda	1h 35m 21.431s	1	0	G
2	R Patrese	Williams-Renault	−15.560s	5	0	G
3	M Alboreto	Tyrrell-Ford	−31.254s	7	0	G
4	A Nannini	Benetton-Ford	−45.495s	13	0	G
5	A Prost	McLaren-Honda	−56.113s	2	2	G
6	G Tarquini	AGS-Ford	−1 lap	17	0	G

	UNITED STATES GP Phoenix							Alain Prost
Round 5/16	**4 June 1989**					**Race 473**		**McLaren-Honda MP4/5** 140.608kph, 87.370mph

Senna's 34th pole broke Clark's old record. Well on his way to his fourth consecutive lights-to-flag victory, a misfire developed around lap 30 which led to Senna's first technical retirement since his Lotus days 21 races ago. Prost was the inevitable beneficiary, a victory sorely needed if the title fight was not to become a total forgone conclusion. In practice Prost wrote off his first McLaren chassis in 5½ years, the two-hour inaugural Arizona street race notable for accidents and mechanical carnage, just six cars still running at the finish. Mansell lay third before his alternator failed, Berger out exactly the same way, while Patrese again finished second for Williams-Renault from Cheever's Arrows, the pair finishing 3.5s apart after a lively race-long scrap.

POLE POSITION A Senna, McLaren-Honda, 1m 30.108s (1.409s), 151.740kph, 94.287mph
LAPS 75 x 3.798 km, 2.360 miles (Scheduled for 81 laps but stopped after two hours)
DISTANCE 284.854 km, 177.000 miles
STARTERS/FINISHERS 26/9
WEATHER Sunny, hot, dry
LAP LEADERS Senna 1-33 (33); Prost 34-75 (42)
WINNER'S LAPS 1-33 P2, 34-75 P1
FASTEST LAP A Senna, McLaren-Honda, 1m 33.969s (lap 38), 145.505kph, 90.413mph
CHAMPIONSHIP Prost 29, Senna 27, Patrese 12, Mansell 9, Nannini 8

Pos	Driver	Car	Time/gap	Grid	Stops	Tyres
1	A Prost	McLaren-Honda	2h 1m 33.133s	2	0	G
2	R Patrese	Williams-Renault	–39.696s	14	0	G
3	E Cheever	Arrows-Ford	–43.210s	17	0	G
4	C Danner	Rial-Ford	–1 lap	26	0	G
5	J Herbert	Benetton-Ford	–1 lap	25	0	G
6	T Boutsen	Williams-Renault	–1 lap	16	1	G

Williams-Renault FW12C

	CANADIAN GP Montréal							Thierry Boutsen
Round 6/16	**18 June 1989**					**Race 474**		**Williams-Renault FW12C** 149.707kph, 93.024mph

The season badly needed an atypical result and a wet race contributed towards a Williams-Renault 1-2, the de Cesaris Dallara third. But it was close, Senna's Honda failing just four laps short to give an incredulous Boutsen his maiden victory. On lap 4 leader Senna pitted for slicks but was forced back to wets on lap 21, the rain having intensified. By lap 39 he retook the lead from Warwick's Arrows, which had only recently assumed P1 from long-term leader Patrese, who had pitted for fresh wets. Meanwhile Boutsen, now on wets having also wrongly stopped for slicks, was coming through strongly, and, with Patrese struggling with a loose under-tray, took his teammate and victory. And pole-sitter Prost? Suspension failure, out on lap 2.

POLE POSITION A Prost, McLaren-Honda, 1m 20.973s (0.076s), 195.176kph, 121.277mph
LAPS 69 x 4.390 km, 2.728 miles
DISTANCE 302.910 km, 188.220 miles
STARTERS/FINISHERS 26/8
WEATHER Cool, cloudy, intermittent rain, heavy at times
LAP LEADERS Prost 1 (1); A Senna, McLaren-Honda 2-3, 39-66 (30); Patrese 4-34 (31); D Warwick, Arrows-Ford 35-38 (4); Boutsen 67-69 (3)
WINNER'S LAPS 1 P5, 2-3 P3, 4 P2, 5-6 P3, 7-10 P2, 11 P11, 12-14 P10, 15 P9, 16 P8, 17-18 P7, 19-20 P12, 21 P11, 22-23 P10, 24-26 P8, 27 P7, 28 P6, 29-33 P5, 34-40 P4, 41-62 P3, 63-66 P2, 67-69 P1
FASTEST LAP J Palmer, Tyrrell-Ford, 1m 31.925s (Lap 11), 171.923kph, 106.828mph
CHAMPIONSHIP Prost 29, Senna 27, Patrese 18, Boutsen 13, Mansell 9

Pos	Driver	Car	Time/gap	Grid	Stops	Tyres
1	T Boutsen	Williams-Renault	2h 1m 24.073s	6	2	G
2	R Patrese	Williams-Renault	–30.007s	3	1	G
3	A de Cesaris	Dallara-Ford	–1m 36.649s	9	1	P
4	N Piquet	Lotus-Judd	–1m 41.484s	19	1	G
5	R Arnoux	Ligier-Ford	–1 lap	22	0	G
6	A Caffi	Dallara-Ford	–2 laps	8	2	P

| Round 7/16 | **FRENCH GP** Paul Ricard | | | | | | **Alain Prost** |
| | 9 July 1989 | | | Race 475 | | | McLaren-Honda MP4/5 185.830kph, 115.469mph |

Having announced his split with McLaren, Prost repeated his home GP success of last year, winning from pole. He led throughout following a restarted race when Gugelmin indulged in some inverted low-level flying at the first corner, mercifully without harm. For the third race in succession Senna was out with car ailments, barely leaving the grid, differential failure at the second start. Prost's lead was never threatened, Berger initially, then Nannini and finally Boutsen all holding P2 but none of them lasting much beyond half-distance. Thankfully Mansell enlivened proceedings. Starting from the pit lane in Berger's discarded car, his own damaged by the flying Gugelmin, he drove a stormer to P2, Alesi also notable, P4 on debut for Tyrrell-Ford.

POLE POSITION Prost, McLaren-Honda, 1m 07.203s (0.025), 204.259kph, 126.920mph
LAPS 80 x 3.813 km, 2.369 miles (Race restarted for scheduled 80 laps following accident)
DISTANCE 305.040 km, 189.543 miles
STARTERS/FINISHERS 26/13
WEATHER Sunny, very hot, dry
LAP LEADERS Prost 1-80 (80)
WINNER'S LAPS 1-80 P1
FASTEST LAP M Gugelmin, March-Judd, 1m 12.090s (lap 29), 190.412kph, 118.317mph
CHAMPIONSHIP Prost 38, Senna 27, Patrese 22, Mansell 15, Boutsen 13

Pos	Driver	Car	Time/gap	Grid	Stops	Tyres
1	A Prost	McLaren-Honda	1h 38m 29.411s	1	1	G
2	N Mansell	Ferrari	–44.017s	3	1	G
3	R Patrese	Williams-Renault	–1m 6.921s	8	1	G
4	J Alesi	Tyrrell-Ford	–1m 13.232s	16	1	G
5	S Johansson	Onyx-Ford	–1 lap	13	1	G
6	O Grouillard	Ligier-Ford	–1 lap	17	0	G

| Round 8/16 | **BRITISH GP** Silverstone | | | | | | **Alain Prost** |
| | 16 July 1989 | | | Race 476 | | | McLaren-Honda MP4/5 231.253kph, 143.694mph |

Mansell in a Ferrari gave extra energy to the Silverstone *tifosi*. Qualifying produced a McLaren front row, Ferrari 3-4. Senna led, his race ending on lap 12, spinning at Becketts when the new transverse gearbox played up. With Prost's McLaren, now leading, emitting puffs of smoke, a famous victory looked plausible. But Prost's car never faltered and Honda power seemed to have the better of Ferrari poise, Prost eking out his lead to 10s. Then down Hangar Straight on lap 43 a slow puncture finally deflated, Mansell's delay leaving Prost to win comfortably despite a McLaren pit-stop hitch. Nannini and Piquet also completed the distance, the Minardi pair 5-6. But with Senna's fourth dnf in a row Prost's points lead was now vast.

POLE POSITION A Senna, McLaren-Honda, 1m 09.099s (0.167s), 249.021kph, 154.735mph
LAPS 64 x 4.780 km, 2.970 miles
DISTANCE 305.904 km, 190.080 miles
STARTERS/FINISHERS 26/12
WEATHER Sunny, warm, dry
LAP LEADERS Senna 1-11 (11); Prost 12-64 (53)
WINNER'S LAPS 1-11 P2, 12-64 P1
FASTEST LAP Mansell, Ferrari, 1m 12.017s (lap 57), 238.931kph, 148.465mph
CHAMPIONSHIP Prost 47, Senna 27, Patrese 22, Mansell 21, Boutsen 13

Pos	Driver	Car	Time/gap	Grid	Stops	Tyres
1	A Prost	McLaren-Honda	1h 19m 22.131s	2	1	G
2	N Mansell	Ferrari	–19.369s	3	1	G
3	A Nannini	Benetton-Ford	–48.019s	9	1	G
4	N Piquet	Lotus-Judd	–1m 6.735s	10	0	G
5	P Martini	Minardi-Ford	–1 lap	11	1	P
6	L Sala	Minardi-Ford	–1 lap	15	0	P

| Round 9/16 | **GERMAN GP** Hockenheim | | | | | | **Ayrton Senna** |
| | 30 July 1989 | | | Race 477 | | | McLaren-Honda MP4/5 224.566kph, 139.539mph |

This time Prost was the McLaren transverse gearbox victim, Senna the beneficiary. But Prost got his car home P2, losing only three points to his rival. The Hockenheim grid mirrored the current pecking order, McLaren, Ferrari, Williams paired off on the first three rows. The red and white pair led, tied together, pulling away from the red pair as Honda acceleration and power exploited the long, chicane-punctuated straights. Prost pitted for tyres on lap 17, Senna lap 19, both stops less than perfect, the outcome Prost with a small but growing lead. As the race drew to its close Senna cut the gap to 1s but turbulence prevented further progress. But with just three to go Prost lost top gear and Senna went by. Mansell completed the podium.

POLE POSITION Senna, McLaren-Honda, 1m 42.300s (1.006s), 239.191kph, 148.626mph
LAPS 45 x 6.797 km, 4.223 miles
DISTANCE 305.865 km, 190.056 miles
STARTERS/FINISHERS 26/12
WEATHER Cloudy, warm, dry
LAP LEADERS Senna 1-19, 43-45 (22); Prost 20-42 (23)
WINNER'S LAPS 1-19 P1, 20-42 P2, 43-45 P1
FASTEST LAP Senna, McLaren-Honda, 1m 45.884s (lap 43), 231.094kph, 143.595mph
CHAMPIONSHIP Prost 53, Senna 36, Patrese 25, Mansell 25, Boutsen 13

Pos	Driver	Car	Time/gap	Grid	Stops	Tyres
1	A Senna	McLaren-Honda	1h 21m 43.302s	1	1	G
2	A Prost	McLaren-Honda	–18.151s	2	1	G
3	N Mansell	Ferrari	–1m 23.254s	3	1	G
4	R Patrese	Williams-Renault	–1 lap	5	1	G
5	N Piquet	Lotus-Judd	–1 lap	8	1	G
6	D Warwick	Arrows-Ford	–1 lap	17	0	G

HUNGARIAN GP Hungaroring

13 August 1989   **Race 478**

Nigel Mansell

Ferrari 640 167.197kph, 103.891mph

The first non-McLaren pole in 13 months for Patrese's Williams-Renault. And in the race he kept Senna at bay for 52 laps until a holed radiator ended it. Mansell, having carved his way up from a P12 grid-slot, now hounded Senna. On qualifying tyres his Ferrari had been hopeless so he had spent the final practice session on race rubber and set-up. Now the strategy was paying dividends, the Ferrari handling beautifully if not the measure of the McLaren on the straights. On his way to the front Mansell had made up four places on lap 1, then overtaken Boutsen, Caffi, who had qualified the Dallara P3, Prost and the fading Patrese. The endgame was sheer poetry: a backmarker; Senna hesitated; Mansell swooped; game over on lap 58.

POLE POSITION R Patrese, Williams-Renault, 1m 19.726s (0.313s), 179.174kph, 111.333mph
LAPS 77 x 3.968 km, 2.466 miles
DISTANCE 305.536 km, 189.851 miles
STARTERS/FINISHERS 26/13
WEATHER Sunny, hot, dry
LAP LEADERS Patrese 1-52 (52); Senna 53-57 (5); Mansell 58-77 (20)
WINNER'S LAPS 1-11 P8, 12-19 P7, 20-21 P6, 22-29 P5, 30-40 P4, 41-52 P3, 53-57 P2, 58-77 P1
FASTEST LAP Mansell, Ferrari, 1m 22.637s (lap 66), 172.862kph, 107.411mph
CHAMPIONSHIP Prost 56, Senna 42, Mansell 34, Patrese 25, Boutsen 17

Pos	Driver	Car	Time/gap	Grid	Stops	Tyres
1	N Mansell	Ferrari	1h 49m 38.650s	12	0	G
2	A Senna	McLaren-Honda	−25.967s	2	0	G
3	T Boutsen	Williams-Renault	−38.354s	4	1	G
4	A Prost	McLaren-Honda	−44.177s	5	1	G
5	E Cheever	Arrows-Ford	−45.106s	16	0	G
6	N Piquet	Lotus-Judd	−1m 12.039s	17	1	G

BELGIAN GP Spa Francorchamps

27 August 1989   **Race 479**

Ayrton Senna

McLaren-Honda MP4/5 181.576kph, 112.826mph

Less a race, more a display of brio. Ardennes weather means it is easy to picture Spa in the pouring rain, Eau Rouge streaming wet. But on this occasion add the three most prolific GP winners of their time strutting their stuff to finish within 2s of each other – Senna, Prost, Mansell. Not necessarily exciting, simply riveting, awe-inspiring, the three driving at speeds only 10, maybe 12mph shy of a dry race-average. Berger, initially heading his teammate, lost control, as did Patrese, leaving Boutsen, Nannini and Warwick the unlapped heroes. But on the podium stood Senna, his fourth lights-to-flag victory of the year; Prost resisting extraordinary pressure to the end, and Mansell spectacularly exerting that pressure as only he knows how.

POLE POSITION Senna, McLaren-Honda, 1m 50.867s (0.596s), 225.351kph, 140.027mph
LAPS 44 x 6.940 km, 4.312 miles
DISTANCE 305.360 km, 189.742 miles
STARTERS/FINISHERS 26/16
WEATHER Overcast, cool, rain
LAP LEADERS Senna 1-44 (44)
WINNER'S LAPS 1-44 P1
FASTEST LAP Prost, McLaren-Honda, 2m 11.571s (lap 44), 189.890kph, 117.992mph
CHAMPIONSHIP Prost 62, Senna 51, Mansell 38, Patrese 25, Boutsen 20

Pos	Driver	Car	Time/gap	Grid	Stops	Tyres
1	A Senna	McLaren-Honda	1h 40m 54.196s	1	0	G
2	A Prost	McLaren-Honda	−1.304s	2	0	G
3	N Mansell	Ferrari	−1.824s	6	0	G
4	T Boutsen	Williams-Renault	−54.418s	4	0	G
5	A Nannini	Benetton-Ford	−1m 8.805s	7	0	G
6	D Warwick	Arrows-Ford	−1m 18.316s	10	0	G

ITALIAN GP Monza

10 September 1989   **Race 480**

Alain Prost

McLaren-Honda MP4/5 232.119kph, 144.232mph

Nine laps from victory, with a 22s lead, Senna's engine blew. Having just signed for Ferrari Prost's subsequent victory was popular and restored his 20-point championship advantage. But he was disgruntled, irked by a gap in qualifying of almost 2s to Senna, at Monza! It smacked of unequal equipment from Honda, from McLaren, or maybe both? Had their drivers' feud permeated team impartiality? Was Ferrari-bound Prost now a pariah in Senna's camp? Tossing his winner's trophy from the podium to the *tifosi* couldn't have helped team ambience. In a dull race, it had taken Prost 41 laps to correct the consequences of his performance deficit, finally overtaking the second of the two Ferraris that had qualified ahead of him.

POLE POSITION A Senna, McLaren-Honda, 1m 23.720s (1.014s), 249.403kph, 154.972mph
LAPS 53 x 5.800 km, 3.604 miles
DISTANCE 307.400 km, 191.010 miles
STARTERS/FINISHERS 26/11
WEATHER Cloudy with sunny intervals, hot, dry
LAP LEADERS Senna 1-44 (44); Prost 45-53 (9)
WINNER'S LAPS 1-20 P4, 21-40 P3, 41-44 P2, 45-53 P1
FASTEST LAP Prost, McLaren-Honda, 1m 28.107 (lap 43), 236.985kph, 147.255mph
CHAMPIONSHIP Prost 71, Senna 51, Mansell 38, Patrese 28, Boutsen 24

Pos	Driver	Car	Time/gap	Grid	Stops	Tyres
1	A Prost	McLaren-Honda	1h 19m 27.550s	4	0	G
2	G Berger	Ferrari	−7.326s	2	0	G
3	T Boutsen	Williams-Renault	−14.975s	6	0	G
4	R Patrese	Williams-Renault	−38.722s	5	0	G
5	J Alesi	Tyrrell-Ford	−1 lap	10	0	G
6	M Brundle	Brabham-Judd	−1 lap	12	0	P

Round 13/16	**PORTUGUESE GP** Estoril	**Gerhard Berger**
	24 September 1989 Race 481	Ferrari 640 191.418kph, 118.942mph

Having secured the constructors' title at Monza, McLaren dominance lapsed. For the first time in 29 GPs a McLaren did not lead. And for the first time ever a Minardi did, albeit a solitary lap during the tyre stops. Initially the Ferraris had the measure of the McLarens, Berger leading 23 laps, losing it to Mansell for 16, then regaining it when Mansell made his stop. But Mansell overshot his overcrowded pit, and by reversing in the pit lane was disqualified. But he raced on, resuming an earlier tussle with Senna until, controversially, they collided well after the Ferrari should have been withdrawn. So Berger won easily; Prost finishing P2 to extend his points lead, while Mansell received a one race ban for ignoring the black flag, claiming he didn't see it.

POLE POSITION A Senna, McLaren-Honda, 1m 15.468s (0.591s), 207.505kph, 128.938mph
LAPS 71 x 4.350 km, 2.703 miles
DISTANCE 308.850 km, 191.910 miles
STARTERS/FINISHERS 26/14
WEATHER Sunny, hot, dry
LAP LEADERS Berger 1-23, 41-71 (54); N Mansell, Ferrari 24-39 (16); Martini 40 (1)
WINNER'S LAPS 1-23 P1, 24-33 P2, 34 P5, 36-38 P4, 39 P3, 40 P2, 41-71 P1
FASTEST LAP Berger, Ferrari, 1m 18.986s (lap 49), 198.263kph, 123.195mph
CHAMPIONSHIP Prost 75, Senna 51, Mansell 38, Patrese 28, Boutsen 24

Pos	Driver	Car	Time/gap	Grid	Stops	Tyres
1	G Berger	Ferrari	1h 36m 48.546s	2	1	G
2	A Prost	McLaren-Honda	−32.637s	4	1	G
3	S Johansson	Onyx-Ford	−55.325s	12	0	G
4	A Nannini	Benetton-Ford	−1m 22.369s	13	0	G
5	P Martini	Minardi-Ford	−1 lap	5	1	P
6	J Palmer	Tyrrell-Ford	−1 lap	18	0	G

Round 14/16	**SPANISH GP** Jerez	**Ayrton Senna**
	1 October 1989 Race 482	McLaren-Honda MP4/5 171.374kph, 106.487mph

With Prost 24 points ahead, Senna's championship mission was now plain: he had to win the three remaining races. In Spain he accomplished the task perfectly, winning his 20th victory from his 40th pole, leading all the way and recording the fastest lap. He finished almost 30s clear of Berger and nearly a minute up on Prost, these three 1-2-3 from lights to flag and lapping the rest of the field. Mansell, the man who might have turned it into a race, sat it out at home serving his one race ban. Nigel's emotive press conference at the circuit on Thursday created as many column inches as the race, which was a somewhat routine affair. Mansell was piqued to be both fined and banned. 'To be made a scapegoat for ruining the championship is ridiculous.'

POLE POSITION Senna, McLaren-Honda, 1m 20.291s (0.274s), 189.122kph, 117.515mph
LAPS 73 x 4.218 km, 2.621 miles
DISTANCE 307.914 km, 191.329 miles
STARTERS/FINISHERS 26/10
WEATHER Sunny, hot, dry
LAP LEADERS Senna 1-73 (73)
WINNER'S LAPS 1-73 P1
FASTEST LAP Senna, McLaren-Honda, 1m 25.779s (lap 55), 177.022kph, 109.997mph
CHAMPIONSHIP Prost 76, Senna 60, Mansell 38, Patrese 30, Boutsen 24

Pos	Driver	Car	Time/gap	Grid	Stops	Tyres
1	A Senna	McLaren-Honda	1h 47m 48.264s	1	1	G
2	G Berger	Ferrari	−27.051s	2	1	G
3	A Prost	McLaren-Honda	−53.788s	3	1	G
4	J Alesi	Tyrrell-Ford	−1 lap	9	1	G
5	R Patrese	Williams-Renault	−1 lap	6	2	G
6	P Alliot	Lola-Lamborghini	−1 lap	5	1	G

Round 15/16	**JAPANESE GP** Suzuka	**Alessandro Nannini**
	22 October 1989 Race 483	Benetton-Ford B189 195.907kph, 121.731mph

By a massive 1.7s Senna won pole, but crucially Prost won the first corner. To keep Senna at bay, Prost had painstakingly set up his car for straight-line speed, and after the tyre stops he was still ahead. Senna would now have to pass on track or concede his title. With six to go, Senna attempted a do-or-die lunge at the chicane from a long way back, but Prost closed the door, unwilling to 'co-operate'. The resultant collision eliminated Prost whereas Senna resumed, pitted for a new nose, raced the remaining laps passing new leader Nannini in the process to win. But on the podium no Senna, disqualified for regaining the circuit improperly, Nannini declared the winner. So the result of race and championship now had to await McLaren's appeal.

POLE POSITION A Senna, McLaren-Honda, 1m 38.041s (1.730s), 215.139kph, 133.681mph
LAPS 53 x 5.859 km, 3.641 miles
DISTANCE 310.527 km, 192.953 miles
STARTERS/FINISHERS 26/10
WEATHER Cloudy with sunny intervals, warm, dry
LAP LEADERS (On the road) A Prost, McLaren-Honda 1-20, 24-46 (43); A Senna 21-23, 47-48, 51-53 (8); Nannini 49-50 (2)
WINNER'S LAPS 1-20 P4, 21 P6, 22-23 P5, 24-33 P4, 34-46 P3, 47-48 P2, 49-50 P1, 51-53 P2 (Senna finished first but was disqualified for rejoining the circuit illegally)
FASTEST LAP Prost, McLaren-Honda, 1m 43.506s (lap 43), 203.779kph, 126.623mph
CHAMPIONSHIP Prost 76, Senna 60, Mansell 38, Patrese 36, Boutsen 28

Pos	Driver	Car	Time/gap	Grid	Stops	Tyres
1	A Nannini	Benetton-Ford	1h 35m 6.277s	6	1	G
2	R Patrese	Williams-Renault	−11.904s	5	1	G
3	T Boutsen	Williams-Renault	−13.446s	7	1	G
4	N Piquet	Lotus-Judd	−1m 44.225s	11	0	G
5	M Brundle	Brabham-Judd	−1 lap	13	1	P
6	D Warwick	Arrows-Ford	−1 lap	25	1	G

Benetton-Ford B189

Round 16/16	AUSTRALIAN GP Adelaide		Thierry Boutsen
	5 November 1989	Race 484	Williams-Renault FW13 131.981kph, 82.009mph

With McLaren's Suzuka appeal pending, Senna still had a title chance if his disqualification was overturned. But he must win the final round, nothing less. With atrocious race-day weather, Senna alone was ready to race in the diabolical conditions. Eventually it started but was red-flagged on lap 2, Prost withdrawing after the first lap. At the restart Senna sailed into the distance. On lap 10 he was 30s ahead; on lap 11 he spun like a top, three times, and on lap 14 he rammed the tail of Brundle's Brabham, concealed in a ball of spray. At that moment Prost, sitting it out, became undisputed champion. Boutsen inherited Senna's lead and after two hours, having brilliantly completed 70 of the scheduled 81 laps, he led home eight dishevelled survivors.

POLE POSITION A Senna, McLaren- Honda, 1m 16.665s (0.738s), 177.500kph, 110.293mph
LAPS 70 x 3.780 km, 2.349 miles (81 lap race interrupted due to rain. Stopped after two hours)
DISTANCE 264.600 km, 164.415 miles
STARTERS/FINISHERS 26/8
WEATHER Overcast, cool, rain
LAP LEADERS Senna 1-13 (13); Boutsen 14-70 (57)
WINNER'S LAPS 1-2 P3, 3-13 P2, 14-70 P1
FASTEST LAP Nakajima, Lotus-Judd 1m 38.480s (lap 64), 138.180kph, 85.861mph
CHAMPIONSHIP Prost 76, Senna 60, Patrese 40, Mansell 38, Boutsen 37

Pos	Driver	Car	Time/gap	Grid	Stops	Tyres
1	T Boutsen	Williams-Renault	2h 0m 17.421s	5	0	G
2	A Nannini	Benetton-Ford	–28.658s	4	0	G
3	R Patrese	Williams-Renault	–37.683s	6	0	G
4	S Nakajima	Lotus-Judd	–42.331s	23	0	G
5	E Pirro	Benetton-Ford	–2 laps	13	0	G
6	P Martini	Minardi-Ford	–3 laps	3	0	P

Williams-Renault FW13

- In the third year of the three-year transition of Formula 1, turbo engines were banned and only 3.5-litre atmospheric engines as defined for 1988 were permitted.
- With 20 teams fielding close to 40 cars, pre-qualifying became a regular feature at GP race meetings.
- Once again it was a 16-round series with the accepted practice of the best 11 results counting towards the drivers' title. Races would be 305km (189.52 miles) or two hours, whichever was shorter.
- A street circuit in Phoenix, Arizona, became the seventh venue to stage a championship GP in the USA.
- Senna and Prost again stole most of the headlines, but Mansell at Ferrari and the emergence of Williams-Renault added further spice to the season.
- Honda gave McLaren exclusivity for their 3.5-litre V10, which was powerful and reliable following thousands of testing miles. It was installed in the new Neil Oatley-drawn MP4/5 chassis which retained many of the design cues of earlier chassis.

- This car brought Prost his third title in his sixth consecutive season with McLaren. He finished in all but three races, and setting aside the unusual circumstances at Suzuka and Adelaide, it might well have been just one dnf.
- In this same car Senna lost his title despite generally holding the upper hand over Prost in both qualifying and the race, winning more races but also leading many more races and laps from his 13 poles. At Phoenix, his 34th, Senna exceeded Clark's poles record dating back to 1968.
- But the heart was ripped out of Senna's championship campaign by four successive dnfs in the second quarter of the season, all car-related. But damningly, there were four other occasions when collisions with others terminated his races.
- Regardless of whether it was a case of Senna losing his title rather than Prost winning it, their fragile relationship disintegrated after the Imola 'broken agreement', culminating in Prost's departure to Ferrari and their Suzuka collision which effectively settled the title in Prost's favour.

RACE 478, Hungarian GP: Mansell's Ferrari, not the measure of Senna's McLaren on the straights, was handling beautifully. The endgame was sheer poetry: a backmarker, Senna hesitated, Mansell swooped, game over.

Championship ranking	Championship points	Driver nationality	Driver	Car	Races contested	Race victories	Podiumse excl. victories	Races led	Lights to flag victories	Laps led	Poles	Fastest laps	Triple Crowns
				1989 Drivers Championship									
1	76	FRA	Alain Prost	McLaren-Honda	16	4	7	8	1	258	2	5	
2	60	BRA	Ayrton Senna	McLaren-Honda	16	6	1	13	5	487	13	3	2
3	40	ITA	Riccardo Patrese	Williams-Renault	16		6	3		100	1	1	
4	38	GBR	Nigel Mansell	Ferrari	15	2	4	3		73		3	
5	37	BEL	Thierry Boutsen	Williams-Renault	16	2	3	2		60			
6	32	ITA	Alessandro Nannini	Benetton-Ford	16	1	3	1		2			
7	21	AUT	Gerhard Berger	Ferrari	15	1	2	1		54		1	
8	12	BRA	Nelson Piquet	Lotus-Judd	15								
9	8	FRA	Jean Alesi	Tyrrell-Ford	8								
10	7	GBR	Derek Warwick	Arrows-Ford	15			1		4			
11	6	ITA	Michele Alboreto	Tyrrell-Ford (5) Lola-Lamborghini (5)	10		1						
11	6	USA	Eddie Cheever	Arrows-Ford	14		1						
11	6	SWE	Stefan Johansson	Onyx-Ford	8		1						
14	5	GBR	Johnny Herbert	Benetton-Ford (5) Tyrrell-Ford (1)	6								
15	5	ITA	Pierluigi Martini	Minardi-Ford	15			1		1			
16	4	BRA	Mauricio Gugelmin	March-Judd	15		1					1	
16	4	ITA	Stefano Modena	Brabham-Judd	15		1						
16	4	ITA	Andrea de Cesaris	Dallara-Ford	15		1						
19	4	ITA	Alex Caffi	Dallara-Ford	14								
20	4	GBR	Martin Brundle	Brabham-Judd	14								
21	3	GER	Christian Danner	Rial-Ford	4								
21	3	JAP	Satoru Nakajima	Lotus-Judd	13							1	
23	2	FRA	René Arnoux	Ligier-Ford	9								
23	2	ITA	Emanuele Pirro	Benetton-Ford	10								
25	2	GBR	Jonathan Palmer	Tyrrell-Ford	15							1	
26	1	ITA	Gabriele Tarquini	AGS-Ford	6								
26	1	FRA	Olivier Grouillard	Ligier-Ford	12								
26	1	ESP	Luis Perez Sala	Minardi-Ford	12								
26	1	FRA	Philippe Alliot	Lola-Lamborghini	15								

■ There was of course a conspiracy theory, the French connection between FISA President Jean Marie Balestre and Alain Prost. But while Senna might have successfully argued that the push-start he received from the marshals, normally an offence for immediate disqualification, was justifiable – his car in a dangerous position – his second offence was not. In the heat of the moment Senna blundered by rejoining the track from the escape road, a misdemeanour FISA would have found difficult to erase following the inevitable protest by Benetton.

■ But the premise that Balestre actually persecuted Senna gained momentum when FISA fined Senna $100,000 plus a six-month suspended ban for dangerous driving, linking his Suzuka collision with others in this and earlier seasons. At Adelaide the mortified Senna spoke animatedly to the press for 90 minutes.

■ When Senna refused to pay his fine the now personal feud with Balestre escalated, the FISA President threatening to withhold his superlicence for 1990. The matter was only finally resolved a few weeks before the new season began.

■ So after two seasons the most antagonistic driver paring in F1 history ended, Prost and Senna, both quite exceptional drivers, each winning a championship. They started 32 races in similar equipment, both finishing in 20.

■ In this astonishingly vehement heavyweight championship contest, the equivalent of Ali versus Frazier, who came out on top? Undoubtedly Prost would have won on points,

186:154, but it was Senna who delivered the knockout punch. In their 20 races in which both cars finished, Prost won 6, Senna 14.

■ John Barnard's three-year tenure at Ferrari ended with his move to Benetton for 1990, but from his purpose-built technology centre in Guildford he had penned the 640 chassis with its advanced aerodynamics and semi-automatic paddle-shift gearbox, a concept quicker, less distracting, less error-prone and physically easier on the driver than the conventional manual shift.

■ Barnard might have claimed that if the Magneti-Marelli side of the new electro-magnetic gearbox had worked, and the 65° Ferrari V12 had generated greater power, far more success than just three race victories might have been achieved.

■ Mansell slotted into Scuderia Ferrari as though born to it, revelling in the kudos proffered by Maranello and the adulation by the *tifosi. Il Leone*, they soon called him, his debut victory in Rio, defeat of Senna in Hungary, and their early-race combat in Portugal producing some of the great moments of the season.

■ As so, for different reasons, was Berger's fiery Tamburello accident, the horror of which together with the relief that his injuries were comparatively minor remains a deep-seated memory for all. Intriguingly, his rapid return to racing was assisted by the paddle-shift gearbox, requiring only fingertip operation by his burn-damaged hands.

RACE 483, Japanese GP: With six laps to go, Senna (1) attempted a do-or-die lunge at the chicane, but Prost (2) closed the door, this act the precursor to the escape of an ugly genie from the F1 bottle.

- Disaster also befell AGS driver Philippe Streiff, his racing career curtailed when he suffered paralysis following a massive testing accident at Rio 11 days before the opening race of the season.
- After only two seasons away from the fray, coming to terms with the disappointment of their ten-year turbo venture which begat no championships from 20 race victories, Renault returned with a 3.5-litre V10 featuring pneumatic valve-gear for exclusive use by Honda exiles Williams.
- In what was to become a highly successful partnership, Boutsen won twice in their first season together, while in the championship teammate Patrese finished best of the rest to Prost and Senna. The Italian veteran also exceeded Graham Hill's 1975 record for championship GPs, matched by Jacques Laffite in 1986, making his 177th start at Rio.
- The fourth winning team of 1989 was Benetton, Nannini's Suzuka victory admittedly only awarded following Senna's disqualification. But after the McLaren chicane fracas, that the Benetton was there to pick up the pieces was evidence of a highly competitive package. It was Ford's first win in six years.
- For 1989 and 1990 Benetton had exclusive call on Ford's

successor to the DFV, the Cosworth HB engine. Its arrival was delayed until mid-season, after which it showed well. But by then the unfortunate Johnny Herbert had been dropped, his obvious talent compromised by legs still in recovery from the devastating F3000 Brands Hatch accident the previous summer.
- But Benetton continued to give every hint that it was a team of the future, the 1990 package encompassing Barnard, Piquet, and under Luciano Benetton, an F1 newcomer as team director, Flavio Briatore.
- Of the 48 podium finishes available in 1989, the four race-winning teams accounted for a greedy 42. This left just six P3 crumbs for Gugelmin's March-Judd; Modena's Brabham-Judd on the team's return to competition; Alboreto's Tyrrell-Cosworth DFR; Cheever's Arrows-Cosworth DFR; de Cesaris' Dallara-Cosworth DFR and, remarkably, Johansson's Onyx-Cosworth DFR, coming home P3 as late as the 13th round at Estoril.
- And lest we forget, Pirelli, making their return, led a GP courtesy of Minardi (later to be known as Toro Rosso). It was just the one lap by Pierluigi Martini during tyre stops in Portugal, but that plus podiums for Brabham and Dallara BMS gave at least some hope.

Championship ranking	Championship points	Team/Marque nationality	1989 Constructors Championship		Engine maker nationality	Races contested	Race victories	1-2 finishes	Podiums excl. victories	Races led	Laps led	Poles	Fastest laps
			Chassis	Engine									
1	141	GBR	McLaren MP4-5	Honda 3.5 V10	JPN	16	10	4	8	15	745	15	8
2	77	GBR	Williams FW12C, FW13	Renault 3.5 V10	FRA	16	2		9	4	160	1	1
3	59	ITA	Ferrari 640	Ferrari 3.5 V12	ITA	16	3		6	4	127		4
4	39	GBR	Benetton B188, B189	Ford Cosworth 3.5 V8	GBR	16	1		3	1	2		
5	16	GBR	Tyrrell 018, 017B	Ford Cosworth 3.5 V8	GBR	16			1				1
6	15	GBR	Lotus 101	Judd 3.5 V8	GBR	15							1
7	13	GBR	Arrows A11	Ford Cosworth 3.5 V8	GBR	16			1	1	4		
8	8	ITA	Dallara BMS189	Ford Cosworth 3.5 V8	GBR	16			1				
9	8	GBR	Brabham BT58	Judd 3.5 V8	GBR	16			1				
10	6	GBR	Onyx ORE-1	Ford Cosworth 3.5 V8	GBR	12			1				
11	6	ITA	Minardi M189, M188B	Ford Cosworth 3.5 V8	GBR	16				1	1		
12	4	GBR	March CG891, 881	Judd 3.5 V8	GBR	16			1				1
13	3	GER	Rial ARC-02	Ford Cosworth 3.5 V8	GBR	4							
14	3	FRA	Ligier JS33	Ford Cosworth 3.5 V8	GBR	14							
15	1	FRA	AGS JH24, JS23B	Ford Cosworth 3.5 V8	GBR	6							
15	1	GBR	Lola LC89	Lamborghini 3.5 V12	ITA	16							

RACE 522, Monaco GP: Ayrton Senna, like the Colossus, bestrode the 1990s in life and in death. Always at his astonishing best in adversity, here in 1992 he rounds the Loews hairpin when he famously denied Nigel Mansell his sixth successive victory.

THE NINETIES

Going global

WHILE THE INGENUITY OF FRANK AND RON DOMINATED THE TRACK, VISIONARY BERNIE BEGAN TO EXPAND F1 TO SIX CONTINENTS

1990

Senna wreaks ruthless revenge

THE TALE OF THE TITLE

- With 11 victories between them, for a third successive season Senna and Prost bestrode the championship.
- Now driving for competing teams, Senna's six victories regained the title from Prost, who scored five.
- But echoing Suzuka last year, contact decided it, Senna deliberately ramming Prost at the first corner.
- Further staining the sport's tarnished image, FISA failed to take action over Senna's reprehensible act.
- McLaren-Honda V10 and Ferrari V12 were closely matched, each winning six race victories.
- But Honda horses had the edge over Ferrari handling, McLaren securing a constructors' hat-trick.
- Williams-Renault V10 and Benetton-Ford V8 also won two each, Capelli the nearly man for Leyton House.
- Jean Alesi and Harvey Postlethwaite brought Tyrrell back into the reckoning with a pair of P2 finishes.
- At Silverstone Mansell announced his F1 retirement and ten weeks later his F1 return with Williams.
- And not forgetting: raised noses and traction control.

THE CHASE FOR THE CHAMPIONSHIP

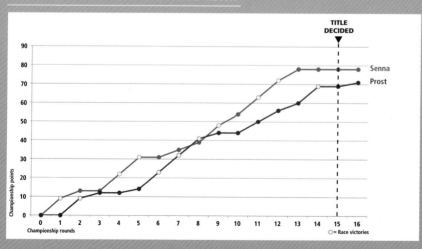

McLaren-Honda MP4/5B

UNITED STATES GP Phoenix

11 March 1990 **Race 485**

Berger's McLaren on pole from a Minardi, a Dallara and a Tyrrell, Senna P5. The grid was partly Pirelli qualifiers, partly Saturday rain, but a Tyrrell leading the first 34 laps was all Jean Alesi. Rocketing from row two he led the first corner and pulled away. Berger spun out on lap 9, so now only Senna could catch the flying Tyrrell, hopping and skipping like a kart over the bumpy street circuit. Once Senna assumed Berger's P2 he began to whittle away the 8s deficit. When it came on lap 34, the confrontation was brief but explosive. Senna overtook at the 90° right-hander but Alesi boldly repassed at the next and kept ahead. Next time round Senna made it stick and drew away, but the heroic Alesi brought Tyrrell and Pirelli a fine podium.

Ayrton Senna

McLaren-Honda MP4/5B 145.784kph, 90.586mph

POLE POSITION G Berger, McLaren-Honda, 1m 28.664s (0.067s), 154.211kph, 95.822mph
LAPS 72 x 3.798 km, 2.360 miles
DISTANCE 273.460 km, 169.920 miles
STARTERS/FINISHERS 25/14
WEATHER Cloudy, cool, dry
LAP LEADERS Alesi 1-34 (34); Senna 35-72 (38)
WINNER'S LAPS 1-3 P4, 4-8 P3, 9-34 P2, 35-72 P1
FASTEST LAP Berger, McLaren-Honda, 1m 31.050s (lap 34), 150.170kph, 93.311mph
CHAMPIONSHIP Senna 9, Alesi 6, Boutsen 4, Piquet 3, Modena 2

Pos	Driver	Car	Time/gap	Grid	Stops	Tyres
1	A Senna	McLaren-Honda	1h 52m 32.829s	5	0	G
2	J Alesi	Tyrrell-Ford	−8.685s	4	0	P
3	T Boutsen	Williams-Renault	−54.080s	9	0	G
4	N Piquet	Benetton-Ford	−1m 8.358s	6	1	G
5	S Modena	Brabham-Judd	−1m 9.503s	10	0	P
6	S Nakajima	Tyrrell-Ford	−1 lap	11	0	P

TOP **100** RACE

BRAZILIAN GP Interlagos

25 March 1990 **Race 486**

For the first time in ten years F1 returned to São Paulo and, according to the script, Senna comfortably led his home-town GP from pole. But on lap 41, for the second race running, he ran into Tyrrell trouble, but this time of a different kind. Nakajima made room to be lapped, lost it on the marbles, and trying to recover inadvertently knocked the McLaren front wing askew, a replacement needed. And there was his nemesis, Prost, now with Ferrari, having moved steadily up from P6 on the grid, to assume his lead and go on to win. Prost's first for Ferrari was his sixth in Brazil. Senna finished a disappointed third behind teammate Berger, Mansell fourth. The Williams challenge, from a promising 3-4 on the grid, faded around half-distance.

Alain Prost

Ferrari 641 189.252kph, 117.596mph

POLE POSITION Senna, McLaren-Honda, 1m 17.277s (0.611s), 201.483kph, 125.196mph
LAPS 71 x 4.325 km, 2.687 miles
DISTANCE 307.075 km, 190.808 miles
STARTERS/FINISHERS 26/14
WEATHER Cloudy with sunny intervals, hot, dry
LAP LEADERS Senna 1-32, 35-40 (38); Berger 33-34 (2); Prost 41-71 (31)
WINNER'S LAPS 1-16 P4, 17-29 P3, 30 P2, 31 P3, 32 P4, 33-34 P3, 35-40 P2, 41-71 P1
FASTEST LAP Berger, McLaren-Honda, 1m 19.899s (lap 55), 194.871kph, 121.087mph
CHAMPIONSHIP Senna 13, Prost 9, Alesi 6, Berger 6, Boutsen 6

Pos	Driver	Car	Time/gap	Grid	Stops	Tyres
1	A Prost	Ferrari	1h 37m 21.258s	6	1	G
2	G Berger	McLaren-Honda	−13.564s	2	1	G
3	A Senna	McLaren-Honda	−37.722s	1	1	G
4	N Mansell	Ferrari	−47.266s	3	1	G
5	T Boutsen	Williams-Renault	−1 lap	5	1	G
6	N Piquet	Benetton-Ford	−1 lap	13	2	G

Ferrari 641

SAN MARINO GP Imola

13 May 1990   Race 487

In qualifying Martini escaped a massive accident at Acque Minerale. The grid again comprised paired McLarens, Williamses and Ferraris, and once early leaders Senna, wheel rim lap 3, and Boutsen, engine lap 17, retired, Berger led. Mid-race, Mansell closed in fast. Tucked in tight behind Berger through Tamburello, Mansell flicked left to take the inside line into Tosa. There were two versions of what happened, but the Ferrari went on the grass and at 190mph spun twice, Mansell remarkably gathering it up to resume the chase. Three laps later his Ferrari engine expired. Berger, however, still wasn't home free, unable to defend against Patrese's late charge, the Italian elated to lay his 1983 Imola ghost and take his first victory in seven years.

Pos	Driver	Car	Time/gap	Grid	Stops	Tyres
1	R Patrese	Williams-Renault	1h 30m 55.478s	3	0	G
2	G Berger	McLaren-Honda	–5.117s	2	0	G
3	A Nannini	Benetton-Ford	–6.240s	9	0	G
4	A Prost	Ferrari	–6.843s	6	1	G
5	N Piquet	Benetton-Ford	–53.112s	8	0	G
6	J Alesi	Tyrrell-Ford	–1 lap	7	1	P

Riccardo Patrese

Williams-Renault FW13B 202.876kph, 126.061mph

POLE POSITION A Senna, McLaren-Honda, 1m 23.220s (0.561s), 218.025kph, 135.474mph
LAPS 61 x 5.040 km, 3.132 miles
DISTANCE 307.440 km, 191.034 miles
STARTERS/FINISHERS 26/13
WEATHER Cloudy with sunny intervals, hot, dry
LAP LEADERS Senna 1-3 (3); T Boutsen, Williams-Renault 4-17 (14); Berger 18-50 (33); Patrese 51-61 (11)
WINNER'S LAPS 1-3 P4, 4-17 P3, 18-21 P2, 22-38 P3, 39-50 P2, 51-61 P1
FASTEST LAP Nannini, Benetton-Ford, 1m 27.156s (lap 60), 208.178kph, 129.356mph
CHAMPIONSHIP Senna 13, Prost 12, Berger 12, Patrese 9, Alesi 7

MONACO GP Monte Carlo

27 May 1990   Race 488

Senna, Prost and Alesi headed the grid and on lap 1 the Tyrrell was by the Ferrari at Mirabeau. Over-ambitiously Berger attempted to follow but nurfed Prost off. Red flag. At the restart Prost, driving cautiously in the T-car, didn't fall for Alesi opportunism a second time and so the race became a cakewalk for Senna. No one got near him apart from when he slowed towards the end to save a suspect engine. Any challenge from the Ferraris vanished with their gearbox electronics and Boutsen's Williams-Renault was a lapped fourth. After Prost's departure it fell to Alesi to take on the McLarens. He managed to defeat one but never seriously troubled the other. However, P2 was an impressive debut for the radical new 'raised-nose' Tyrrell 019.

Pos	Driver	Car	Time/gap	Grid	Stops	Tyres
1	A Senna	McLaren-Honda	1h 52m 46.982s	1	0	G
2	J Alesi	Tyrrell-Ford	–1.087s	3	0	P
3	G Berger	McLaren-Honda	–2.073s	5	0	G
4	T Boutsen	Williams-Renault	–1 lap	6	0	G
5	A Caffi	Arrows-Ford	–2 laps	22	0	G
6	E Bernard	Lola-Lamborghini	–2 laps	24	0	G

Ayrton Senna

McLaren-Honda MP4/5B 138.097kph, 85.810mph

POLE POSITION Senna, McLaren-Honda, 1m 21.314s (0.462s), 147.340kph, 91.553mph
LAPS 78 x 3.328 km, 2.068 miles (Race restarted for scheduled 78 laps following accident)
DISTANCE 259.584 km, 161.298 miles
STARTERS/FINISHERS 26/7
WEATHER Cloudy with sunny intervals, warm, dry
LAP LEADERS Senna 1-78 (78)
WINNER'S LAPS 1-78 P1
FASTEST LAP Senna, McLaren-Honda, 1m 24.468s (lap 59), 141.838kph, 88.134mph
CHAMPIONSHIP Senna 22, Berger 16, Alesi 13, Prost 12, Patrese 9

CANADIAN GP Montréal
10 June 1990   **Race 489**

Ayrton Senna
McLaren-Honda MP4/5B 179.114kph, 111.296mph

A McLaren 1-2 finish but not a 1-2 result. Berger 'won' but was penalised a minute for a jump-start. To negate the penalty he took a gamble on lap 10, first of the leaders to switch from wets to slicks, and so doing got ahead of Senna to lead on the road. He then drove hard, making up 45s, Senna naturally fully aware of the circumstances. Berger finally finished fourth between the Ferrari pair, the three separated by just 1.5s. Mansell won his first podium of the season but had to give best to his old sparring partner Piquet in the Benetton, P2 his best result since his 1987 halcyon days with Williams. Senna's 30th pole from 37 McLaren starts brought his third victory of the year from five races, rewarded by a sizeable points lead.

POLE POSITION A Senna, McLaren-Honda, 1m 20.399s (0.066s), 196.570kph, 122.143mph
LAPS 70 x 4.390 km, 2.728 miles
DISTANCE 307.300 km, 190.947 miles
STARTERS/FINISHERS 26/8
WEATHER Overcast, warm, damp then drying
LAP LEADERS (On the road) Senna 1-11 (11); A Nannini 12-14 (3); G Berger 15-70 (56)
WINNER'S LAPS 1-11 P1, 12 P5, 13 P2, 14 P3, 15-70 P2 (Berger finished first but was penalised one minute for jumping the start)
FASTEST LAP Berger, McLaren-Honda, 1m 22.077s (Lap 70), 192.551kph, 119.646mph
CHAMPIONSHIP Senna 31, Berger 19, Prost 14, Alesi 13, Piquet 12

Pos	Driver	Car	Time/gap	Grid	Stops	Tyres
1	A Senna	McLaren-Honda	1h 42m 56.400s	1	1	G
2	N Piquet	Benetton-Ford	−10.497s	5	1	G
3	N Mansell	Ferrari	−13.385s	7	1	G
4	G Berger	McLaren-Honda	−14.854s	2	1	G
5	A Prost	Ferrari	−15.820s	3	1	G
6	D Warwick	Lotus-Lamborghini	−2 laps	11	1	G

MEXICAN GP Mexico City
24 June 1990   **Race 490**

Alain Prost
Ferrari 641/2 197.664kph, 122.823mph

Prost's P13 grid-slot was his worst since his 1980 rookie season, but ten on-track passes brought him into play. Also significant, both McLarens made mistakes, Berger burning out his tyres within 12 laps, and leader Senna believing a slow puncture to be tyre wear, his right-rear collapsing nine laps from home. So a fortuitous victory? Maybe. But what brilliance to even get into a position to win. Lap 55: Prost overtook teammate Mansell. Lap 60: Senna, Prost and Mansell crossed the line separated by 0.4s. Lap 61: Prost led. Lap 63: Senna's tyre finally let go. Lap 64: Mansell half-spun, passed by the recovering Berger. Lap 68, the penultimate: Mansell retakes Berger around the outside of the banked final Curva Peralta for a Ferrari 1-2.

POLE POSITION Berger, McLaren-Honda, 1m 17.227s (0.271s), 206.089kph, 128.057mph
LAPS 69 x 4.421 km, 2.747 miles
DISTANCE 305.049 km, 189.549 miles
STARTERS/FINISHERS 26/20
WEATHER Cloudy, warm, dry
LAP LEADERS Senna 1-60 (60), Prost 61-69 (9)
WINNER'S LAPS 1 P13, 2 P12, 3 P11, 4-6 P10, 7-8 P9, 9-11 P8, 12 P7, 13-25 P6, 26-30 P5, 31-41 P4, 42-54 P3, 55-60 P2, 61-69 P1
FASTEST LAP Prost, Ferrari, 1m 17.958s (lap 58), 204.156kph, 126.857mph
CHAMPIONSHIP Senna 31, Prost 23, Berger 23, Alesi 13, Mansell 13

Pos	Driver	Car	Time/gap	Grid	Stops	Tyres
1	A Prost	Ferrari	1h 32m 35.783s	13	0	G
2	N Mansell	Ferrari	−25.351s	4	0	G
3	G Berger	McLaren-Honda	−25.530s	1	1	G
4	A Nannini	Benetton-Ford	−41.099s	14	0	G
5	T Boutsen	Williams-Renault	−46.669s	5	0	G
6	N Piquet	Benetton-Ford	−46.943s	8	1	G

FRENCH GP Paul Ricard
8 July 1990   **Race 491**

Alain Prost
Ferrari 641/2 195.761kph, 121.640mph

Mansell's first-ever Ferrari pole but it was teammate Prost who won again for Ferrari's 100th GP victory. Initially the McLarens led from Mansell, Prost down in P6. Trapped behind Patrese, Alain decided to make an early tyre stop, then banged in some very fast lappery, this and swift Ferrari pit-work the foundation of his victory. The three early leaders all had comparatively poor stops, the McLarens rejoining P8 and P9, Mansell P6 having lost 11s to Prost in the process. Leading the race now were the pair of Leyton House-Judds, neither of which had even qualified in Mexico. By relinquishing his tyre stop Capelli led 45 laps, Prost harrying but unable to pass, a shock result looking on. But with three to go he did it, the Judd engine faltering.

POLE POSITION N Mansell, Ferrari, 1m 04.402s (0.110), 213.142kph, 132.441mph
LAPS 80 x 3.813 km, 2.369 miles
DISTANCE 305.040 km, 189.543 miles
STARTERS/FINISHERS 26/18
WEATHER Sunny, hot, dry
LAP LEADERS Berger 1-27 (27); Senna 28-29 (2); Mansell 30-31 (2); Patrese 32 (1); Capelli 33-77 (45); Prost 78-80 (3)
WINNER'S LAPS 1-26 P6, 27 P7, 28 P8, 29-30 P6, 31 P5, 32-33 P4, 34-53 P3, 54-77 P2, 78-80 P1
FASTEST LAP N Mansell, Ferrari, 1m 08.012s (lap 64), 201.829kph, 125.411mph
CHAMPIONSHIP Senna 35, Prost 32, Berger 25, Piquet 16, Alesi 13

Pos	Driver	Car	Time/gap	Grid	Stops	Tyres
1	A Prost	Ferrari	1h 33m 29.606s	4	1	G
2	I Capelli	Leyton House-Judd	−8.626s	7	0	G
3	A Senna	McLaren-Honda	−11.606s	3	1	G
4	N Piquet	Benetton-Ford	−41.207s	9	1	G
5	G Berger	McLaren-Honda	−42.219s	2	1	G
6	R Patrese	Williams-Renault	−1m 9.351s	6	1	G

Round 8/16 · BRITISH GP Silverstone

15 July 1990 — Race 492

Alain Prost
Ferrari 641/2 233.762kph, 145.253mph

Mansell's second Ferrari pole also ended in disappointment, contributing in part to his post-race shock announcement that he would retire at season's end. Despite gearbox trouble he still led most of his home GP only to finally retire on lap 55 and watch his teammate take the glory. Senna led the first 11 laps but then faded to finish an ill-handling third. Now Mansell led, quickly pulling 4s on Berger, Prost up to third. Suddenly on lap 22 it was Berger leading Mansell, the Ferrari gearbox having a mind of its own. On lap 28 all was well again, Mansell back ahead, Prost soon following. But another dose of gearbox gremlins gave Prost the lead on lap 41 for his first hat-trick in 43 race victories, and to lead the points table for the first time.

POLE POSITION N Mansell, Ferrari, 1m 07.428s (0.643s), 255.192kph, 158.569mph
LAPS 64 x 4.780 km, 2.970 miles
DISTANCE 305.904 km, 190.080 miles
STARTERS/FINISHERS 25/14
WEATHER Cloudy with sunny intervals, hot, dry
LAP LEADERS Senna 1-11 (11); Mansell 12-21, 28-42 (25); G Berger, McLaren-Honda 22-27 (6); Prost 43-64 (22)
WINNER'S LAPS 1-13 P5, 14-15 P4, 16-30 P3, 31-42 P2, 43-64 P1
FASTEST LAP N Mansell, Ferrari, 1m 11.291s (lap 51), 241.364kph, 149.997mph
CHAMPIONSHIP Prost 41, Senna 39, Berger 25, Piquet 18, Boutsen 17

Pos	Driver	Car	Time/gap	Grid	Stops	Tyres
1	A Prost	Ferrari	1h 18m 30.999s	5	0	G
2	T Boutsen	Williams-Renault	−39.092s	4	0	G
3	A Senna	McLaren-Honda	−43.088s	2	1	G
4	E Bernard	Lola-Lamborghini	−1m 15.302s	8	0	G
5	N Piquet	Benetton-Ford	−1m 24.003s	11	0	G
6	A Suzuki	Lola-Lamborghini	−1 lap	9	1	G

Round 9/16 · GERMAN GP Hockenheim

29 July 1990 — Race 493

Ayrton Senna
McLaren-Honda MP4/5B 227.334kph, 141.259mph

The usual suspects lined up in their predictable pairs, McLarens, Ferraris, Williamses, but with tyre wear marginal Benetton, using the latest series IV Ford V8, went tactical. Senna led, but Nannini's Benetton, starting from P9 on hard tyres, was handling beautifully. On lap 18, 16s behind, Sandro just managed to snatch the lead when Senna made his stop. As the laps ticked by it became clear Nannini was not going to, and surprisingly, despite fresh rubber, the McLaren seemed unable to reclaim the lead. Finally, on lap 34, Senna passed him at the first chicane, Nannini baulked by a backmarker. Also troubled with tyres, exhaust and the oil light, Sandro still finished a fine P2. Senna and Prost, four points apart, had each won four races.

POLE POSITION Senna, McLaren-Honda, 1m 40.198s (0.236s), 244.388kph, 151.856mph
LAPS 45 x 6.802 km, 4.227 miles
DISTANCE 306.090 km, 190.196 miles
STARTERS/FINISHERS 26/11
WEATHER Sunny, hot, dry
LAP LEADERS Senna 1-17, 34-45 (29); Nannini 18-33 (16)
WINNER'S LAPS 1-17 P1, 18-33 P2, 34-45 P1
FASTEST LAP Boutsen, Williams-Renault, 1m 45.602s (lap 31), 231.882kph, 144.085mph
CHAMPIONSHIP Senna 48, Prost 44, Berger 29, Boutsen 18, Piquet 18

Pos	Driver	Car	Time/gap	Grid	Stops	Tyres
1	A Senna	McLaren-Honda	1h 20m 47.164s	1	1	G
2	A Nannini	Benetton-Ford	−6.520s	9	0	G
3	G Berger	McLaren-Honda	−8.553s	2	1	G
4	A Prost	Ferrari	−45.270s	3	1	G
5	R Patrese	Williams-Renault	−48.028s	5	1	G
6	T Boutsen	Williams-Renault	−1m 23.254s	6	1	G

Round 10/16 · HUNGARIAN GP Hungaroring

12 August 1990 — Race 494

Thierry Boutsen
Williams-Renault FW13B 167.402kph, 104.019mph

From his maiden pole Boutsen controlled the race from the front, withstanding nearly two hours of pressure from Berger, Nannini, and finally Senna. It was a gruelling, closely fought race, Boutsen, Berger, Patrese and Mansell within a few seconds of each other for the first 47 laps. Tyre pit stops broke this pattern and enabled Nannini and Senna to get involved. On lap 63, with Boutsen, Nannini, Senna, Mansell and Berger covered by just 2s, Senna survived his own injudicious passing attempt, punting Nannini's car high into the air. With six to go, at the self-same ess-bend the other McLaren driver committed precisely the same felony on Mansell, both cars out. But worn tyres and all, Boutsen held off Senna by a whisker, a virtuoso performance.

POLE POSITION Boutsen, Williams-Renault, 1m 17.919s (0.036s), 183.329kph, 113.915mph
LAPS 77 x 3.968 km, 2.466 miles
DISTANCE 305.536 km, 189.851 miles
STARTERS/FINISHERS 26/13
WEATHER Sunny, hot, dry
LAP LEADERS Boutsen 1-77 (77)
WINNER'S LAPS 1-77 P1
FASTEST LAP Patrese, Williams-Renault, 1m 22.058s (lap 63), 174.082kph, 108.169mph
CHAMPIONSHIP Senna 54, Prost 44, Berger 29, Boutsen 27, Piquet 22

Pos	Driver	Car	Time/gap	Grid	Stops	Tyres
1	T Boutsen	Williams-Renault	1h 49m 30.597s	1	0	G
2	A Senna	McLaren-Honda	−0.288s	4	1	G
3	N Piquet	Benetton-Ford	−27.893s	9	0	G
4	R Patrese	Williams-Renault	−31.833s	2	1	G
5	D Warwick	Lotus-Lamborghini	−1m 14.244s	11	0	G
6	E Bernard	Lola-Lamborghini	−1m 24.308s	12	0	G

TOP
100
RACE

Williams-Renault FW13B

BELGIAN GP Spa Francorchamps
26 August 1990   Race 495

Ayrton Senna
McLaren-Honda MP4/5B 211.729kph, 131.562mph

First lap accidents at La Source and Eau Rouge caused two red flags. From the third start Senna took the lead from pole and was never headed. His only real challenger was Prost, the Ferrari quicker in the corners, slower down the straights. But Berger had done a sound job for his team-leader, keeping Prost at bay for the first 13 laps such that he presented no immediate threat at the pit stop. In fact they pitted simultaneously on lap 22, but Prost's took 4s longer, rejoining third behind non-stop Nannini who only just failed to pip Senna for P1 as the McLaren exited the pits. Berger eventually fought past Nannini for third and by the finish Prost's gap to Senna was only 3s, but crucially it added three more to Senna's growing points lead.

POLE POSITION Senna, McLaren-Honda, 1m 50.365s (0.583s), 226.376kph, 140.664mph
LAPS 44 x 6.940 km, 4.312 miles (Race twice restarted for scheduled 44 laps following accidents)
DISTANCE 305.360 km, 189.742 miles
STARTERS/FINISHERS 26/17
WEATHER Overcast, warm, dry
LAP LEADERS Senna 1-44 (44)
WINNER'S LAPS 1-44 P1
FASTEST LAP Prost, Ferrari, 1m 55.087s (lap 38), 217.088kph, 134.892mph
CHAMPIONSHIP Senna 63, Prost 50, Berger 33, Boutsen 27, Piquet 24

Pos	Driver	Car	Time/gap	Grid	Stops	Tyres
1	A Senna	McLaren-Honda	1h 26m 31.997s	1	1	G
2	A Prost	Ferrari	–3.550s	3	1	G
3	G Berger	McLaren-Honda	–28.462s	2	1	G
4	A Nannini	Benetton-Ford	–49.337s	6	0	G
5	N Piquet	Benetton-Ford	–1m 29.650s	8	1	G
6	M Gugelmin	Leyton House-Judd	–1m 48.851s	14	0	G

ITALIAN GP Monza
9 September 1990   Race 496

Ayrton Senna
McLaren-Honda MP4/5B 236.569kph, 146.997mph

McLarens and Ferraris headed the grid, Senna on pole, Prost alongside. And that was how it ended, Senna's sixth win this year and his first Monza victory. There were two starts caused by a red flag when Warwick shockingly flipped his Lotus exiting Parabolica, doggedly restarting in the spare. On both occasions the McLarens scampered away on acceleration pursued by Alesi, who got the better of Prost each time. But after four laps Alesi spun it all away. Once Prost took Berger on lap 21 a race developed as the Ferrari traded fastest laps with the McLaren. Senna always held sway, but it was a worthy duel that perhaps engendered a sense of mutual respect. At the press conference, to spontaneous applause, the arch-rivals shook hands.

POLE POSITION Senna, McLaren-Honda, 1m 22.533s (0.402s), 252.990kph, 157.201mph
LAPS 53 x 5.800 km, 3.604 miles (Race restarted for scheduled 53 laps following accident)
DISTANCE 307.400 km, 191.010 miles
STARTERS/FINISHERS 26/13
WEATHER Cloudy with sunny intervals, warm, dry
LAP LEADERS Senna 1-53 (53)
WINNER'S LAPS 1-53 P1
FASTEST LAP Senna, McLaren-Honda, 1m 26.254s (lap 46), 242.076kph, 150.419mph
CHAMPIONSHIP Senna 72, Prost 56, Berger 37, Boutsen 27, Piquet 24

Pos	Driver	Car	Time/gap	Grid	Stops	Tyres
1	A Senna	McLaren-Honda	1h 17m 57.878s	1	0	G
2	A Prost	Ferrari	–6.054s	2	0	G
3	G Berger	McLaren-Honda	–7.404s	3	0	G
4	N Mansell	Ferrari	–56.219s	4	0	G
5	R Patrese	Williams-Renault	–1m 25.274s	7	0	G
6	S Nakajima	Tyrrell-Ford	–1 lap	14	0	P

PORTUGUESE GP Estoril
23 September 1990
Race 497

Nigel Mansell
Ferrari 641/2 193.725kph, 120.375mph

Mansell ended his 13-month win drought with his third Ferrari victory from his third Ferrari pole. Prost, alongside, determined to win to keep championship hopes alive, had been working hard on starts at the Fiorano test facility. But it was all to no avail, Mansell somehow contriving to half-spin at the start, almost collecting his teammate, and allowing the McLaren pair from row two to lead until the stops. Worse still for Prost, he became trapped behind Nannini for the first 12 laps, effectively putting paid to any chance of victory. Once on new tyres Mansell attacked Senna, taking the lead on lap 50. Prost relieved Berger of third, but before he could engage in his crucial scrap with Senna an accident halted the race ten laps prematurely.

Pos	Driver	Car	Time/gap	Grid	Stops	Tyres
1	N Mansell	Ferrari	1h 22m 11.014s	1	1	G
2	A Senna	McLaren-Honda	−2.808s	3	1	G
3	A Prost	Ferrari	−4.189s	2	1	G
4	G Berger	McLaren-Honda	−5.896s	4	1	G
5	N Piquet	Benetton-Ford	−57.418s	6	1	G
6	A Nannini	Benetton-Ford	−58.249s	9	1	G

POLE POSITION Mansell, Ferrari, 1m 13.557s (0.591s), 207.505kph, 128.938mph
LAPS 61 x 4.350 km, 2.703 miles (Scheduled for 71 laps but stopped following accident)
DISTANCE 265.350 km, 164.881 miles
STARTERS/FINISHERS 25/15
WEATHER Cloudy with sunny intervals, hot, dry
LAP LEADERS Senna 1-28, 32-49 (46); Berger 29-31 (3); Mansell 50-61 (12)
WINNER'S LAPS 1-26 P3, 27-28 P4, 29-30 P5, 31 P3, 32-49 P2, 50-61 P1
FASTEST LAP R Patrese, Williams-Renault, 1m 18.306s (lap 56), 199.985kph, 124.265mph
CHAMPIONSHIP Senna 78, Prost 60, Berger 40, Boutsen 27, Piquet 26

SPANISH GP Jerez
30 September 1990
Race 498

Alain Prost
Ferrari 641/2 171.025kph, 106.270mph

Martin Donnelly experienced a qualifying accident of such ferocity that his survival was truly miraculous. Senna led from his 50th pole closely chased by Prost, giving every indication that at Jerez Honda horsepower could not live with Ferrari handling. And so the tyre stops proved, Senna losing out to the rampant Ferrari, which pulled away to a dominant win. Senna settled for second knowing it would bring the title, but on lap 52 returned to the pits believing he had a tyre issue, only to discover the problem was terminal, a holed radiator. So Prost led in a Ferrari 1-2, his fifth win of the season, and with Senna failing to score and Berger foolishly colliding with Boutsen, a glimmer of hope returned to the title aspirations of both Prost and Ferrari.

Pos	Driver	Car	Time/gap	Grid	Stops	Tyres
1	A Prost	Ferrari	1h 48m 1.461s	2	2	G
2	N Mansell	Ferrari	−22.064s	3	1	G
3	A Nannini	Benetton-Ford	−34.878s	9	1	G
4	T Boutsen	Williams-Renault	−43.296s	7	1	G
5	R Patrese	Williams-Renault	−57.530s	6	1	G
6	A Suzuki	Lola-Lamborghini	−1m 3.728s	15	1	G

POLE POSITION A Senna, McLaren-Honda, 1m 18.387s (0.437s), 193.716kph, 120.369mph
LAPS 73 x 4.218 km, 2.621 miles
DISTANCE 307.914 km, 191.329 miles
STARTERS/FINISHERS 25/10
WEATHER Cloudy with sunny intervals, hot, dry
LAP LEADERS Senna 1-26 (26); N Piquet, Benetton-Ford 27-28 (2); Prost 29-73 (45)
WINNER'S LAPS 1-24 P2, 25 P3, 26 P4, 27-28 P2, 29-73 P1
FASTEST LAP Patrese, Williams-Renault, 1m 24.513s (lap 53), 179.674kph, 111.674mph
CHAMPIONSHIP Senna 78, Prost 69, Berger 40, Mansell 31, Boutsen 30

JAPANESE GP Suzuka
21 October 1990
Race 499

Nelson Piquet
Benetton-Ford B190 196.923kph, 122.362mph

For the third championship running, Senna versus Prost went unresolved to Suzuka, the place where twice before it had been settled by fair means or foul. In a reverse of last year, the 'must win' pressure was all on Prost, failure to finish and the title was Senna's. Warm-up suggested that in race trim the Ferrari would outpace the McLaren, but Senna held pole, his request that it be moved to the clean side of the track denied. So Prost, with better traction, led into the first corner where Senna cynically drove into him, eliminating them both, and so regaining the title from his adversary. Berger led lap 1 but spun off, then Mansell until transmission failure on lap 26, leaving Piquet to head a jubilant Benetton 1-2, but overall, sport was the loser.

Pos	Driver	Car	Time/gap	Grid	Stops	Tyres
1	N Piquet	Benetton-Ford	1h 34m 36.824s	6	0	G
2	R Moreno	Benetton-Ford	−7.223s	8	0	G
3	A Suzuki	Lola-Lamborghini	−22.469s	9	1	G
4	R Patrese	Williams-Renault	−36.258s	7	1	G
5	T Boutsen	Williams-Renault	−46.884s	5	1	G
6	S Nakajima	Tyrrell-Ford	−1m 12.350s	13	1	P

POLE POSITION A Senna, McLaren-Honda, 1m 39.996s (0.232s), 217.456kph, 135.121mph
LAPS 53 x 5.859 km, 3.641 miles
DISTANCE 310.527 km, 192.953 miles
STARTERS/FINISHERS 25/10
WEATHER Cloudy with sunny intervals, hot, dry
LAP LEADERS G Berger, McLaren-Honda 1 (1); N Mansell, Ferrari 2-26 (25); Piquet 27-53 (27)
WINNER'S LAPS 1 P3, 2-26 P2, 27-53 P1
FASTEST LAP Patrese, Williams-Renault, 1m 44.233s (lap 40), 202.358kph, 125.740mph
CHAMPIONSHIP Senna 78, Prost 69, Berger 40, Piquet 35, Boutsen 32

Benetton-Ford B190

| Round 16/16 | AUSTRALIAN GP Adelaide | | Nelson Piquet |
| | 4 November 1990 | Race 500 | Benetton-Ford B190 167.399kph, 104.017mph |

When Senna missed a gear spinning away certain victory on lap 61, few grieved for a world champion who had totally lost the plot in Japan. Sentiments were similar when Mansell swept by teammate Prost – the other not-so-innocent party in the tedious Senna grudge-match – in order to chase down leader Piquet over the closing laps. Mansell didn't quite make it, although the two old intra-team rivals certainly went for it. Their race conduct served to remind that Mansell/Piquet maintained on-track principles that Senna/Prost sullied. When a brake-problem spin and pit stop had dropped Mansell from P2 at half-distance, his tigering comeback drive was raw excitement. It was gratifying that this was only arrivederci Ferrari, not his last F1 race after all.

POLE POSITION A Senna, McLaren-Honda, 1m 15.671s (0.573s), 179.831kph, 111.742mph
LAPS 81 x 3.780 km, 2.349 miles
DISTANCE 306.180 km, 190.251 miles
STARTERS/FINISHERS 26/13
WEATHER Sunny, very hot, dry
LAP LEADERS Senna 1-61 (61); Piquet 62-81 (20)
WINNER'S LAPS 1-2 P5, 3-8 P4, 9-45 P3, 46-61 P2, 62-81 P1
FASTEST LAP Mansell, Ferrari, 1m 18.203s (lap 75), 174.009kph, 108.124mph
CHAMPIONSHIP Senna 78, Prost 71, Piquet 43, Berger 43, Mansell 37

Pos	Driver	Car	Time/gap	Grid	Stops	Tyres
1	N Piquet	Benetton-Ford	1h 49m 44.570s	7	0	G
2	N Mansell	Ferrari	−3.129s	3	1	G
3	A Prost	Ferrari	−37.259s	4	0	G
4	G Berger	McLaren-Honda	−46.862s	2	0	G
5	T Boutsen	Williams-Renault	−1m 51.160s	9	0	G
6	R Patrese	Williams-Renault	−1 lap	6	1	G

1990 CHAMPIONSHIP FACTS AND FOLKLORE

■ 1990 was Prost versus Senna round three, a 16-race championship with the now customary best 11 results to decide the drivers' title.

■ Senna entered the year still in dispute with FISA over his disqualification in Japan, which he considered unjust, while Prost had decided to leave the increasing rancour at McLaren, latterly infecting his relationship with Ron Dennis, and seek refuge at Ferrari.

■ Although no longer driving identical equipment, another close championship battle ensued, Prost briefly snatching the lead mid-season with a hat-trick of wins.

■ Undoubtedly Ferrari made up ground on McLaren this year, the 641 a logical development of last year's deft-handling Barnard design plus enhanced aero and a significant power increase. By the end of the season Ferrari possibly matched Honda in top-end power, 680bhp at 12,750rpm, over 700bhp in qualifying.

■ Where Ferrari continued to fall short was low down grunt, McLaren acceleration from the start-line and out of slow

corners still outstanding, and leading Ferrari to explore alternate means to improve race starts.

■ Despite losing out to McLaren for the constructors' title, Ferrari enjoyed their winningest season since 1979, Prost adding five to bring his personal total to 44, Mansell's single victory his 16th.

■ McLaren fielded an update on last year's car, but deprived of its significant power advantage, which permitted a hefty rear-wing angle to disguise any handling deficiencies, the MP4/5B could not dominate like its predecessor, as Ferrari, Williams and even Benetton proved on occasion.

■ Honda fed the MP4/5B chassis with an array of circuit-bespoke V10 motors, but that a V12 Honda was on the stocks for 1991 indicated the line of thinking to regain ascendancy.

■ By the time of Suzuka, Ferrari had conclusively beaten McLaren in the two preceding rounds, a factor no doubt heavily influencing Senna's shameful behaviour when Prost beat him off the line.

- Senna would no doubt have it that the root cause of this was that pole position had been 'unfairly' sited on the dirty side of the track. In reality, for Japan Ferrari introduced what would later become known as 'traction control', a driver-controlled device with three settings, sensors cutting the engine when rear-wheel rotation speed exceeded the fronts, minimising wheelspin and optimising traction.
- In advance of Suzuka expectancy was at fever pitch, the championship peaking to a wonderful climax. That it was all over in seconds was disappointing, the manner of its happening disgraceful.
- With another six race victories to his name, Senna's tally reached 26, surpassing Piquet as the most successful Brazilian and Fangio as the most prolific winner from Latin America.
- Alongside Senna and Prost, teammates Berger and Mansell had a tough time. Berger's season was error prone, which only in part could be explained by the difficulties he experienced fitting his frame into the car.

- By most comparative performance indicators Mansell and Prost related closely apart for the important one, race wins. Mansell the showman, revelling in the limelight, begrudged the growing shadow Prost cast at Ferrari and, additionally perturbed by a spate of car unreliability, announced at Silverstone that he would retire at the end of the season.
- Adding insult to Mansell's injury, Prost had won in Britain having already delivered Ferrari their 100th GP victory in France. All seemed well for the French champion, but even in this his honeymoon season, the cracks which would later become fissures were already beginning to show in his relationship with the Italian team.
- Unexpectedly perhaps, Benetton beat Williams to third place in the constructors' championship. Both teams scored points regularly throughout the year but Benetton clinched it with their two late-season victories.
- More than once Nannini had demonstrated the potential of the Benetton-Ford package, which had clearly benefitted

RACE 499, Japanese GP: Prost led into the first corner where Senna cynically drove into him, eliminating them both, so regaining the title from his adversary.

from Barnard influence, but his helicopter accident in October finished not only his season but his F1 career, his right arm severed, although surgeons managed to reattach it.

- It was sadly ironic that the first race Nannini missed was the place of his one and only GP triumph of a year ago, Japan, where Sandro's replacement Roberto Moreno made it an all Brazilian affair, finishing second to teammate Piquet
- In Australia, the 500th championship race, Nelson more convincingly made it two in a row, the Benetton-Ford package further strengthened by the latest HB 75° V8, which by now could output 650bhp at 13,000rpm.
- After the high promise of their first season together, Williams-Renault didn't make the progress expected in year two, Boutsen and Patrese winning one apiece.
- Much more was forecast for next year, Adrian Newey joining the team mid-season and Mansell 'unretiring' himself to drive next year alongside veteran Patrese, who at Silverstone celebrated 200 GP starts.
- March became Leyton House in 1990 but lost Adrian Newey to Williams, Capelli again so nearly bringing the team success in France.
- Jean Alesi's star burned brightly this season, his leading stint

in Phoenix the first time for a Tyrrell since Alboreto won in Detroit in 1983. Alesi was much in demand for a 1991 seat and somehow contrived to be simultaneously signed-up with Tyrrell, Williams and Ferrari. He chose the mystique of Maranello, often regarded as the worst driver-decision ever in view of what life at Williams would hold in coming seasons.

- Harvey Postlethwaite, another crucial ingredient in the comparative revival for Team Tyrrell, introduced a radical new design at Imola. The Tyrrell 019 was the first F1 car with a raised nose, this concept bringing far-reaching airflow benefits and revolutionising the shape of the F1 car.
- Drivers continued to walk away from some horrendous accidents largely unharmed, the notable exception Martin Donnelly. During qualifying in Spain he was critically injured when a mechanical failure sent his Lotus-Lamborghini spearing head-on into the crash barrier. The Lotus disintegrated, the unfortunate Ulsterman thrown from the car to be deposited on the track like a rag-doll. His survival was miraculous but his F1 career was over, his recovery long and painful.
- In 1990 David Brabham, youngest of Sir Jack's three sons, emulated dad and so became the first son of a world champion to start a GP. Fittingly he was driving a Brabham.

Championship ranking	Championship points	Driver nationality	1990 Drivers Championship		Races contested	Race victories	Podiums excl. victories	Races led	Lights to flag victories	Laps led	Poles	Fastest laps	Triple Crowns
			Driver	Car									
1	78	BRA	Ayrton Senna	McLaren-Honda	16	6	5	14	3	500	10	2	2
2	71	FRA	Alain Prost	Ferrari	16	5	4	5		110		2	
3	43	BRA	Nelson Piquet	Benetton-Ford	16	2	2	3		49			
4	43	AUT	Gerhard Berger	McLaren-Honda	16		7	7		128	2	3	
5	37	GBR	Nigel Mansell	Ferrari	16	1	4	4		64	3	3	
6	34	BEL	Thierry Boutsen	Williams-Renault	16	1	2	2	1	91	1	1	
7	23	ITA	Riccardo Patrese	Williams-Renault	16	1		2		12		4	
8	21	ITA	Alessandro Nannini	Benetton-Ford	14		3	2		19		1	
9	13	FRA	Jean Alesi	Tyrrell-Ford	15		2	1		34			
10	6	ITA	Ivan Capelli	Leyton House-Judd	14		1	1		45			
10	6	BRA	Roberto Moreno	EuroBrun-Judd (2) Benetton-Ford (2)	4		1						
12	6	JPN	Aguri Suzuki	Lola-Lamborghini	16		1						
13	5	FRA	Éric Bernard	Lola-Lamborghini	16								
14	3	GBR	Derek Warwick	Lotus-Lamborghini	16								
15	3	JPN	Satoru Nakajima	Tyrrell-Ford	15								
16	2	ITA	Stefano Modena	Brabham-Judd	16								
16	2	ITA	Alex Caffi	Arrows-Ford	11								
18	1	BRA	Mauricio Gugelmin	Leyton House-Judd	11								

Championship ranking	Championship points	Team/Marque nationality	1990 Constructors Championship		Engine maker nationality	Races contested	Race victories	1-2 finishes	Podiums excl. victories	Races led	Laps led	Poles	Fastest laps
			Chassis	Engine									
1	121	GBR	McLaren MP4-5B	Honda 3.5 V10	JPN	16	6		12	9	628	12	5
2	110	ITA	Ferrari 641, 641/2	Ferrari 3.5 V12	ITA	16	6	2	8	5	174	3	5
3	71	GBR	Benetton B190, B189B	Ford Cosworth 3.5 V8	GBR	16	2	1	6	5	68		1
4	57	GBR	Williams FW13B	Renault 3.5 V10	FRA	16	2		2	2	103	1	5
5	16	GBR	Tyrrell 019, 018	Ford Cosworth 3.5 V8	GBR	16			2	1	34		
6	11	GBR	Lola 90, LC89B	Lamborghini 3.5 V12	ITA	16			1				
7	7	JPN	Leyton House CG901	Judd 3.5 V8	GBR	14			1	1	45		
8	3	GBR	Lotus 102	Lamborghini 3.5 V12	GBR	16							
9	2	GBR	Brabham BT59, BT58	Judd 3.5 V8	GBR	16							
9	2	GBR	Arrows A11B, A11	Ford Cosworth 3.5 V8	GBR	14							

1991

Senna's triple crown

THE TALE OF THE TITLE

- Senna's third title in four years, McLaren-Honda's fourth, but both driver and team faced stiff opposition.
- This came not from Prost and Ferrari, enduring a fruitless season, but from Nigel Mansell and Williams-Renault.
- Their ultimately unsuccessful campaign was strewn with lost opportunities, the Estoril fiasco the killer blow.
- Senna instead started with four straight wins and maintained a season-long points-scoring momentum.
- These teams dominated the season, McLaren-Honda V12 with eight wins, Williams-Renault V10 seven.
- Patrese won two for Williams while Gerhard Berger was gracelessly gifted an empty victory by Senna.
- Another squandered Williams victory in Canada brought Piquet and Benetton-Ford a lucky win.
- For the first time in ten years Prost failed to win a race, fired by Ferrari for likening his car to a truck.
- Mosley's defeat of Balestre enabled Senna to vent his spleen about the former FISA president.
- Another grubby episode was the Schumacher affair, the German rookie snatched from Jordan by Benetton.
- And not forgetting: Mansell and Senna 'sitting it out' at Cataluña.

THE CHASE FOR THE CHAMPIONSHIP

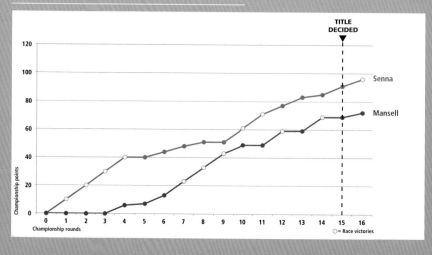

McLaren-Honda MP4/6

UNITED STATES GP Phoenix

10 March 1991   Race 501

Ayrton Senna

McLaren-Honda MP4/6 149.698kph, 93.018mph

Sporting the new Honda V12 in the latest McLaren, reigning champion Senna served ominous notice for the new season with pole a second quicker than Prost's Ferrari alongside. And so it proved in the race, not only quicker but more reliable too, teammate Berger, the Williams-Renault pair Mansell and Patrese, and Alesi's Ferrari all falling by the wayside. Prost lay second for much of the race, seeing off challenges from Mansell, Alesi and Patrese until all three succumbed to gearbox gremlins. Prost then had to fight back from P7 after a fumbled pit-stop cost 15s. And after two hours that was the gap Senna finished ahead of Prost. His lead had been up to 45s, but towards the end he struggled with his own gearbox issues.

POLE POSITION Senna, McLaren-Honda, 1m 21.434s (1.121s), 164.488kph, 102.208mph
LAPS 81 x 3.721 km, 2.312 miles (Scheduled for 82 laps but stopped after two hours)
DISTANCE 301.385 km, 187.272 miles
STARTERS/FINISHERS 26/12
WEATHER Cloudy, warm, dry
LAP LEADERS Senna 1-81 (81)
WINNER'S LAPS 1-81 P1
FASTEST LAP J Alesi, Ferrari, 1m 26.758s (lap 49), 154.394kph, 95.936mph
CHAMPIONSHIP Senna 10, Prost 6, Piquet 4, Modena 3, Nakajima 2

Pos	Driver	Car	Time/gap	Grid	Stops	Tyres
1	A Senna	McLaren-Honda	2h 0m 47.828s	1	1	G
2	A Prost	Ferrari	−16.322s	2	1	G
3	N Piquet	Benetton-Ford	−17.376s	5	0	P
4	S Modena	Tyrrell-Honda	−25.409s	11	0	P
5	S Nakajima	Tyrrell-Honda	−1 lap	16	0	P
6	A Suzuki	Lola-Ford	−2 laps	21	1	G

BRAZILIAN GP Interlagos

24 March 1991   Race 502

Ayrton Senna

McLaren-Honda MP4/6 187.110kph, 116.265mph

The results show Senna led throughout from pole, but the Williams-Renault pair made him work in a frenetic race. Mansell, chasing, forced Senna to set a tremendous early pace until a slow Williams tyre stop on lap 25 alleviated the pressure. Over the next 15 laps Mansell pulled back five of the lost seconds, back hounding Senna again. Then Mansell had to fight back a third time after an unscheduled stop for a puncture. Suddenly the gap was closing fast, Senna in gearbox trouble confined to sixth gear. But with 12 laps to go and 19s to find, Mansell went out with gearbox failure, the Patrese Williams now threatening Senna. Then it rained. Racked with painful cramp, Senna somehow coaxed his crippled car to a joyous first home GP victory.

POLE POSITION Senna, McLaren-Honda, 1m 16.392s (0.383s), 203.817kph, 126.646mph
LAPS 71 x 4.325 km, 2.687 miles
DISTANCE 307.075 km, 190.808 miles
STARTERS/FINISHERS 25/13
WEATHER Overcast, warm, wet in closing laps
LAP LEADERS Senna 1-71 (71)
WINNER'S LAPS 1-71 P1
FASTEST LAP N Mansell, Williams-Renault, 1m 20.436s (lap 35), 193.570kph, 120.279mph
CHAMPIONSHIP Senna 20, Prost 9, Patrese 6, Piquet 6, Berger 4

Pos	Driver	Car	Time/gap	Grid	Stops	Tyres
1	A Senna	McLaren-Honda	1h 38m 28.128s	1	1	G
2	R Patrese	Williams-Renault	−2.991s	2	1	G
3	G Berger	McLaren-Honda	−5.416s	4	1	G
4	A Prost	Ferrari	−19.369s	6	2	G
5	N Piquet	Benetton-Ford	−21.960s	7	1	P
6	J Alesi	Ferrari	−23.641s	5	2	G

Round 3/16	**SAN MARINO GP** Imola		**Ayrton Senna**
	28 April 1991	**Race 503**	McLaren-Honda MP4/6 193.671kph, 120.342mph

A heavy shower just before the start caused the elimination of both Ferraris by lap 3. Prost didn't even complete the parade lap, aquaplaning off backwards at Rivazza, while Alesi ended up in a sand trap after a failed overtake for fourth. Patrese gave the *tifosi* something to cheer by leading Senna for nine laps until pitting with an engine malady. Berger made it a 1-2, both McLarens lapping the field. Moreno looked good for P3 in the new Benetton before gearbox trouble with ten to go, so JJ Lehto made his first visit to the rostrum for Dallara-Judd, and fourth, two laps down, a Minardi-Ferrari. It was that sort of race. The bloke who might have produced a different outcome, Mansell, was rammed on lap 1 when he couldn't find gears.

POLE POSITION Senna, McLaren-Honda, 1m 21.877s (0.080s), 221.601kph, 137.696mph
LAPS 61 x 5.040 km, 3.132 miles
DISTANCE 307.440 km, 191.034 miles
STARTERS/FINISHERS 25/13
WEATHER Overcast, warm, wet then drying
LAP LEADERS R Patrese, Williams-Renault 1-9 (9); Senna 10-61 (52)
WINNER'S LAPS 1-9 P2, 10-61 P1
FASTEST LAP Berger, McLaren-Honda, 1m 26.531s (lap 55), 209.682kph, 130.290mph
CHAMPIONSHIP Senna 30, Berger 10, Prost 9, Patrese 6, Piquet 6

Pos	Driver	Car	Time/gap	Grid	Stops	Tyres
1	A Senna	McLaren-Honda	1h 35m 14.750s	1	1	G
2	G Berger	McLaren-Honda	–1.675s	5	1	G
3	J J Lehto	Dallara-Judd	–1 lap	16	1	P
4	P Martini	Minardi-Ferrari	–2 laps	9	1	G
5	M Häkkinen	Lotus-Judd	–3 laps	25	1	G
6	J Bailey	Lotus-Judd	–3 laps	26	2	G

Round 4/16	**MONACO GP** Monte Carlo		**Ayrton Senna**
	12 May 1991	**Race 504**	McLaren-Honda MP4/6 137.785kph, 85.615mph

An all-Honda front row had Modena's Tyrrell-Honda V10 next to the inevitable Senna. These two led away, Modena holding the gap to 5s for the first 25 laps until it opened up in traffic. On lap 43, the gap now 20s, the Tyrrell's Honda engine detonated without warning, the unfortunate Patrese, closing on Modena, spinning out on the oil. Senna's lead suddenly doubled over next man Prost. He and Mansell had been in combat until the Renault engine started cutting in and out. From half-distance, power restored, Mansell closed in, daringly taking the Ferrari at the chicane, Prost dropping to fifth with a loose front upright. Mansell's first finish was Senna's fourth Monaco victory. It was also a record-breaking four wins from the first four races.

POLE POSITION Senna, McLaren-Honda, 1m 20.344s (0.465s), 149.119kph, 92.648mph
LAPS 78 x 3.328 km, 2.068 miles
DISTANCE 259.584 km, 161.298 miles
STARTERS/FINISHERS 26/12
WEATHER Cloudy with sunny intervals, warm, dry
LAP LEADERS Senna 1-78 (78)
WINNER'S LAPS 1-78 P1
FASTEST LAP Prost, Ferrari, 1m 24.368s (lap 77), 142.006kph, 88.239mph
CHAMPIONSHIP Senna 40, Prost 11, Berger 10, Patrese 6, Mansell 6

Pos	Driver	Car	Time/gap	Grid	Stops	Tyres
1	A Senna	McLaren-Honda	1h 53m 2.334s	1	0	G
2	N Mansell	Williams-Renault	–18.348s	5	0	G
3	J Alesi	Ferrari	–47.455s	9	0	G
4	R Moreno	Benetton-Ford	–1 lap	8	0	P
5	A Prost	Ferrari	–1 lap	7	1	G
6	E Pirro	Dallara-Judd	–1 lap	12	0	P

Round 5/16	**CANADIAN GP** Montréal		**Nelson Piquet**
	2 June 1991	**Race 505**	Benetton-Ford B191 185.520kph, 115.277mph

Piquet gained his 23rd and final GP win with a rare last-lap victory. It came at the expense of arch-opponent Mansell, who had majestically led the previous 68. The Williams-Renaults were the class in Canada, locking out the front row then leading with ease. When a puncture delayed pole-man Patrese, suffering whiplash from a nasty off in practice, Mansell's lead was 60s over Piquet. Showboating near the end, Mansell hammered in the fastest lap then slowed it down on the final one, acknowledging the crowd, his first victory of the season. It never happened. The semi-auto gearbox engaged neutral, the engine stalled, Mansell coasting to a standstill in sight of the finish. On a day McLaren were crushed and neither car finished, this was a cruel ending.

POLE POSITION Patrese, Williams-Renault, 1m 19.837s (0.388s), 199.757kph, 124.123mph
LAPS 69 x 4.430 km, 2.753 miles
DISTANCE 305.670 km, 189.935 miles
STARTERS/FINISHERS 26/10
WEATHER Sunny, hot, dry
LAP LEADERS Mansell 1-68 (68); Piquet 69 (1)
WINNER'S LAPS 1 P8, 2-10 P6, 11-25 P5, 26 P3, 27-28 P4, 29-40 P3, 41-68 P2, 69 P1
FASTEST LAP Mansell, Williams-Renault, 1m 22.385s (Lap 65), 193.579kph, 120.284mph
CHAMPIONSHIP Senna 40, Piquet 16, Prost 11, Berger 10, Patrese 10

Pos	Driver	Car	Time/gap	Grid	Stops	Tyres
1	N Piquet	Benetton-Ford	1h 38m 51.490s	8	1	P
2	S Modena	Tyrrell-Honda	–31.832s	9	1	P
3	R Patrese	Williams-Renault	–42.217s	1	1	G
4	A de Cesaris	Jordan-Ford	–1m 20.210s	11	1	G
5	B Gachot	Jordan-Ford	–1m 22.351s	14	1	G
6r	N Mansell	Williams-Renault	–1 lap	2	0	G

Benetton-Ford B191

<table>
<tr><td>**Round 6/16**</td><td colspan="2">**MEXICAN GP** Mexico City</td><td colspan="2">**Riccardo Patrese**</td></tr>
<tr><td></td><td>**16 June 1991**</td><td>**Race 506**</td><td colspan="2">Williams-Renault FW14 197.757kph, 122.880mph</td></tr>
</table>

In practice Senna lost control at Peraltada, spinning then rolling. Williams-Renault again qualified 1-2, and again it was Patrese, Mansell. And that was how they finished. After two aborted starts, Patrese made it difficult for himself by rounding the first corner fourth, but then he drove past Alesi, Senna and Mansell for a resounding victory, his fourth from his fifth pole. Mansell, down on power with an overheating Renault, didn't allow his number two to get away with it entirely. In an exciting three-lap dispute he made Patrese fight to take the lead on lap 15, and then, when a fuel mixture adjustment restored engine power, drove a string of fastest laps to haul back 20s in as many laps, finishing within two. Senna came a distant third.

POLE POSITION Patrese, Williams-Renault, 1m 16.696s (0.282s), 207.515kph, 128.944mph
LAPS 67 x 4.421 km, 2.747 miles
DISTANCE 296.207 km, 184.054 miles
STARTERS/FINISHERS 26/12
WEATHER Cloudy with sunny intervals, warm, dry
LAP LEADERS Mansell 1-14 (14), Patrese 15-67 (53)
WINNER'S LAPS 1-3 P4, 4-10 P3, 11-14 P2, 15-67 P1
FASTEST LAP Mansell, Williams-Renault, 1m 16.788s (lap 61), 207.267kph, 128.790mph
CHAMPIONSHIP Senna 44, Patrese 20, Piquet 16, Mansell 13, Prost 11

Pos	Driver	Car	Time/gap	Grid	Stops	Tyres
1	R Patrese	Williams-Renault	1h 29m 52.205s	1	0	G
2	N Mansell	Williams-Renault	–1.336s	2	0	G
3	A Senna	McLaren-Honda	–57.357s	3	0	G
4r	A de Cesaris	Jordan-Ford	–1 lap	11	0	G
5	R Moreno	Benetton-Ford	–1 lap	9	1	P
6	E Bernard	Lola-Ford	–1 lap	18	0	G

Williams-Renault FW14

FRENCH GP Magny-Cours
7 July 1991   Race 507

Nigel Mansell
Williams-Renault FW14 188.271kph, 116.986mph

Prost came back to the front in France with a revamped Ferrari. Patrese pipped him for pole but got left at the start, finishing a lapped fifth. The race developed into a duel between five-time French GP winner Prost and the chasing Mansell. On lap 21 Mansell made one of those opportunistic moves of his, down the inside in traffic at the Adelaide hairpin. But the Williams team blundered tactically, delaying his tyre stop too long after Prost's, and then making a slow wheel change. His lead lost, Mansell had it all to do again. After closing quickly, he tailed Prost for some 15 laps until the opportunity came, this time around the outside at Adelaide on lap 54 for an overdue first win of the season. Senna retained his big championship lead with another P3.

POLE POSITION Patrese, Williams-Renault, 1m 14.559s (0.230), 206.221kph, 128.140mph
LAPS 72 x 4.271 km, 2.654 miles
DISTANCE 307.512 km, 191.079 miles
STARTERS/FINISHERS 26/12
WEATHER Overcast, warm, dry
LAP LEADERS Prost 1-21, 32-54 (44); Mansell 22-31, 55-72 (28)
WINNER'S LAPS 1-21 P2, 22-31 P1, 32-54 P2, 55-72 P1
FASTEST LAP Mansell, Williams-Renault, 1m 19.168s (lap 49), 194.215kph, 120.680mph
CHAMPIONSHIP Senna 48, Mansell 23, Patrese 22, Prost 17, Piquet 16

Pos	Driver	Car	Time/gap	Grid	Stops	Tyres
1	N Mansell	Williams-Renault	1h 38m 0.056s	4	1	G
2	A Prost	Ferrari	−5.003s	2	1	G
3	A Senna	McLaren-Honda	−34.934s	3	1	G
4	J Alesi	Ferrari	−35.920s	6	1	G
5	R Patrese	Williams-Renault	−1 lap	1	1	G
6	A de Cesaris	Jordan-Ford	−1 lap	13	1	G

BRITISH GP Silverstone
14 July 1991   Race 508

Nigel Mansell
Williams-Renault FW14 211.189kph, 131.227mph

One year on from announcing his F1 retirement, Mansell was unstoppable at Silverstone, giving the crowd what he couldn't deliver 12 months ago in a Ferrari. He was fastest in every session including race warm-up and would have led all the way had not Senna beaten him off the line. The Williams powered past at Stowe to draw steadily away with a succession of fastest laps. When he pitted for tyres on lap 36 his lead over Senna was 25s. Patrese's Williams was out, colliding with Berger at the first corner, so Senna, choosing not to change tyres, had the measure of the rest until a faulty fuel readout caused him to run dry on the final lap, memorably hitching a ride home astride Mansell's victorious car. Berger and Prost completed the podium.

POLE POSITION Mansell, Williams-Renault, 1m 20.939s (0.679s), 232.421kph, 144.420mph
LAPS 59 x 5.226 km, 3.247 miles
DISTANCE 308.307 km, 191.573 miles
STARTERS/FINISHERS 26/14
WEATHER Sunny, warm, dry
LAP LEADERS Mansell 1-59 (59)
WINNER'S LAPS 1-59 P1
FASTEST LAP Mansell, Williams-Renault, 1m 26.379s (lap 43), 217.784kph, 135.325mph
CHAMPIONSHIP Senna 51, Mansell 33, Patrese 22, Prost 21, Piquet 18

Pos	Driver	Car	Time/gap	Grid	Stops	Tyres
1	N Mansell	Williams-Renault	1h 17m 35.479s	1	1	G
2	G Berger	McLaren-Honda	−42.293s	4	1	G
3	A Prost	Ferrari	−1m 0.150s	5	1	G
4r	A Senna	McLaren-Honda	−1 lap	2	0	G
5	N Piquet	Benetton-Ford	−1 lap	8	1	P
6	B Gachot	Jordan-Ford	−1 lap	17	0	G

GERMAN GP Hockenheim
28 July 1991   Race 509

Nigel Mansell
Williams-Renault FW14 231.028kph, 143.554mph

Mansell maintained momentum with his hat-trick win, only briefly losing the lead during his tyre stop to the non-stopping Alesi. For five laps he kept his lead to a couple of seconds, then once his tyres had gone through their cycle, pulverised the opposition, pulling away by a second a lap. Behind, a stirring battle ensued between Berger, Senna, Prost and Patrese but ended in tears when Senna ran Prost off the track when the Ferrari attempted a pass at the first chicane. Afterwards there were angry words. Alesi, his best showing to date for Ferrari, was eventually passed by Patrese for a Williams 1-2. At the finish Senna was apoplectic, losing P4 by running out of fuel yet again, Mansell grossing another ten points to close in for the championship battle.

POLE POSITION Mansell, Williams-Renault, 1m 37.087s (0.187s), 252.219kph, 156.722mph
LAPS 45 x 6.802 km, 4.227 miles
DISTANCE 306.090 km, 190.196 miles
STARTERS/FINISHERS 26/13
WEATHER Cloudy with sunny intervals, hot, dry
LAP LEADERS Mansell 1-18, 21-45 (43); Alesi 19-20 (2)
WINNER'S LAPS 1-18 P1, 19 P3, 20 P2, 21-45 P1
FASTEST LAP Patrese, Williams-Renault, 1m 43.569s (lap 35), 236.434kph, 146.913mph
CHAMPIONSHIP Senna 51, Mansell 43, Patrese 28, Prost 21, Berger 19

Pos	Driver	Car	Time/gap	Grid	Stops	Tyres
1	N Mansell	Williams-Renault	1h 19m 29.661s	1	1	G
2	R Patrese	Williams-Renault	−13.779s	4	1	G
3	J Alesi	Ferrari	−17.618s	6	0	G
4	G Berger	McLaren-Honda	−32.651s	3	1	G
5	A de Cesaris	Jordan-Ford	−1m 17.537s	7	1	G
6	B Gachot	Jordan-Ford	−1m 40.605s	11	1	G

HUNGARIAN GP Hungaroring

11 August 1991   **Race 510**

Ayrton Senna

McLaren-Honda MP4/6 167.857kph, 104.301mph

Senna halted the Mansell juggernaut assisted by an entirely new Honda V12. His incredible pole-lap made the Williams-Renault duo look ordinary, and in the race he led imperiously. In a typical Hungaroring high-speed train, the Williams pair snapped at his rear tyres for much of the race, first Patrese, later Mansell, but by three-quarters-distance, their brakes cooked, Senna put in some quick laps to draw away and this time did not run out of fuel on the final lap. For their conduct during the Hockenheim race, FISA gave Prost and Senna an official warning, Prost also receiving a suspended one-race ban for bringing the sport into disrepute. This followed disparaging and inflammatory comments about Senna in a post-race TV interview. *Plus ça change.*

POLE POSITION Senna, McLaren-Honda, 1m 16.147s (1.232s), 187.595kph, 116.566mph
LAPS 77 x 3.968 km, 2.466 miles
DISTANCE 305.536 km, 189.851 miles
STARTERS/FINISHERS 26/17
WEATHER Cloudy with sunny intervals, hot, dry
LAP LEADERS Senna 1-77 (77)
WINNER'S LAPS 1-77 P1
FASTEST LAP B Gachot, Jordan-Ford, 1m 21.547s (lap 71), 175.173kph, 108.847mph
CHAMPIONSHIP Senna 61, Mansell 49, Patrese 32, Berger 22, Prost 21

Pos	Driver	Car	Time/gap	Grid	Stops	Tyres
1	A Senna	McLaren-Honda	1h 49m 12.796s	1	0	G
2	N Mansell	Williams-Renault	−4.599s	3	0	G
3	R Patrese	Williams-Renault	−15.594s	2	0	G
4	G Berger	McLaren-Honda	−21.856s	5	0	G
5	J Alesi	Ferrari	−31.389s	6	0	G
6	I Capelli	Leyton House-Ilmor	−1 lap	9	1	G

BELGIAN GP Spa Francorchamps

25 August 1991   **Race 511**

Ayrton Senna

McLaren-Honda MP4/6 209.883kph, 130.415mph

Michael Schumacher made his F1 debut with Jordan, qualifying P7. In a gripping race, Senna led Mansell until his lap 15 tyre stop. It was a poor one, Mansell rejoining from his own 5s clear and going away. But around half-distance electrics put him out and Alesi's non-stopping Ferrari took over his lead, Senna close behind. On lap 27 gearbox issues lost Senna 9s to the Ferrari, and surely Alesi's time had come, only for the Ferrari engine to fail four laps later. Senna held on for the win, fortunate for a third time that Patrese, penalised to the back of the grid, also suffered late gearbox problems. Another hard-luck story was de Cesaris, so nearly giving Jordan their first podium, dropping out from P2 with three laps left.

POLE POSITION Senna, McLaren-Honda, 1m 47.811s (1.010s), 231.739kph, 143.996mph
LAPS 44 x 6.940 km, 4.312 miles
DISTANCE 305.360 km, 189.742 miles
STARTERS/FINISHERS 26/13
WEATHER Cloudy with sunny intervals, warm, dry
LAP LEADERS Senna 1-14, 31-44 (28); N Mansell, Williams-Renault 15-16, 18-21 (6); Piquet 17 (1); J Alesi, Ferrari 22-30 (9)
WINNER'S LAPS 1-14 P1, 15 P2, 16-17 P5, 18-21 P3, 22-30 P2, 31-44 P1
FASTEST LAP Moreno, Benetton-Ford, 1m 55.161s (lap 40), 216.948kph, 134.806mph
CHAMPIONSHIP Senna 71, Mansell 49, Patrese 34, Berger 28, Piquet 22

Pos	Driver	Car	Time/gap	Grid	Stops	Tyres
1	A Senna	McLaren-Honda	1h 27m 17.669s	1	1	G
2	G Berger	McLaren-Honda	−1.901s	4	1	G
3	N Piquet	Benetton-Ford	−32.176s	6	1	P
4	R Moreno	Benetton-Ford	−37.310s	8	2	P
5	R Patrese	Williams-Renault	−57.187s	17	1	G
6	M Blundell	Brabham-Yamaha	−1m 40.035s	13	1	P

TOP **100** RACE

ITALIAN GP Monza

8 September 1991   **Race 512**

Nigel Mansell

Williams-Renault FW14 236.749kph, 147.109mph

Mansell renewed his title challenge by conclusively beating Senna into second place at Monza. Senna from pole led Mansell for the first 18 laps. Pressurising intently but unable to pass, Mansell let his charging teammate have a try, but, within a lap of finally passing Senna, Patrese's gearbox hesitated and pitched him off. By now Mansell's tyres had cleaned up and he mounted another assault, six laps of heart-in-mouth F1 combat culminating in his pass at the Ascari chicane. Senna immediately pitted to replace flat-spotted tyres, regaining P2 by passing Schumacher, Berger and finally Prost. Schumacher finished a remarkable P5, but driving for Benetton, not Jordan. In only his second F1 appearance he out-qualified and out-raced teammate Piquet.

POLE POSITION Senna, McLaren-Honda, 1m 21.114s (0.133s), 257.415kph, 159.951mph
LAPS 53 x 5.800 km, 3.604 miles
DISTANCE 307.400 km, 191.010 miles
STARTERS/FINISHERS 26/16
WEATHER Overcast, warm, dry
LAP LEADERS Senna 1-25, 27-33 (32); R Patrese, Williams-Renault 26 (1); Mansell 34-53 (20)
WINNER'S LAPS 1-18 P2, 19-26 P3, 27-33 P2, 34-53 P1
FASTEST LAP Senna, McLaren-Honda, 1m 26.061s (lap 41), 242.619kph, 150.756mph
CHAMPIONSHIP Senna 77, Mansell 59, Patrese 34, Berger 31, Prost 25

Pos	Driver	Car	Time/gap	Grid	Stops	Tyres
1	N Mansell	Williams-Renault	1h 17m 54.319s	2	0	G
2	A Senna	McLaren-Honda	−16.262s	1	1	G
3	A Prost	Ferrari	−16.829s	5	0	G
4	G Berger	McLaren-Honda	−27.719s	3	0	G
5	M Schumacher	Benetton-Ford	−34.463s	7	0	P
6	N Piquet	Benetton-Ford	−45.600s	8	1	P

PORTUGUESE GP Estoril

22 September 1991   Race 513

Riccardo Patrese

Williams-Renault FW14 193.626kph, 120.314mph

Patrese a phenomenal pole-lap in the spare car from Berger, Senna and Mansell, the last aggressively muscling past the McLarens by the second corner to chase after him. On lap 18, in the interests of his championship chances, Nigel was waved through, but within 13 laps it all went dreadfully wrong at the tyre stop. Mansell was released before the rear-right was secure, the wheel bouncing away almost immediately he exited his pit. In a tragicomedy F1 cameo his pit crew restored the errant wheel and Mansell drove 20 flat-out laps before he was shown the black flag, disqualified because his car had been worked on outside the designated pit area. Patrese went on to win from Senna, adding yet another six to his now 24-point lead.

POLE POSITION Patrese, Williams-Renault, 1m 13.001s (0.220s), 214.518kph, 133.295mph
LAPS 71 x 4.350 km, 2.703 miles
DISTANCE 308.850 km, 191.910 miles
STARTERS/FINISHERS 26/17
WEATHER Sunny, hot, dry
LAP LEADERS Patrese 1-17, 30-71 (59); Mansell 18-29 (12)
WINNER'S LAPS 1-17 P1, 18-29 P2, 30-71 P1
FASTEST LAP N Mansell, Williams-Renault, 1m 18.179s (lap 36), 200.310kph, 124.467mph
CHAMPIONSHIP Senna 83, Mansell 59, Patrese 44, Berger 31, Piquet 25

Pos	Driver	Car	Time/gap	Grid	Stops	Tyres
1	R Patrese	Williams-Renault	1h 35m 42.304s	1	1	G
2	A Senna	McLaren-Honda	−20.941s	3	1	G
3	J Alesi	Ferrari	−53.554s	6	1	G
4	P Martini	Minardi-Ferrari	−1m 3.498s	8	1	G
5	N Piquet	Benetton-Ford	−1m 10.033s	11	2	P
6	M Schumacher	Benetton-Ford	−1m 16.552s	10	2	P

SPANISH GP Cataluña

29 September 1991   Race 514

Nigel Mansell

Williams-Renault FW14 187.586kph, 116.561mph

Mansell's fifth win kept his title hopes alive, particularly as Senna only mustered fifth. Out-qualified by pole-man Berger, this was a strangely subdued Senna display, which included a wild lap 13 spin, although his earlier lap 5 wheel-to-wheel run-in with Mansell down the long main straight, millimetres apart, encapsulated the fierceness of their championship battle, as had their exchange in the drivers' briefing that morning. The early race action was spiced up by a wet track, the switch to slicks around lap 9, after which Berger still led Mansell from Schumacher and Prost, both of whom had switched early to slicks. On lap 21 Mansell made a lurid pass for the lead and that was that, Berger deserving more than a dnf, Prost finishing P2.

POLE POSITION G Berger, McLaren-Honda, 1m 18.751s (0.219s), 217.003kph, 134.839mph
LAPS 65 x 4.747 km, 2.950 miles
DISTANCE 308.555 km, 191.727 miles
STARTERS/FINISHERS 26/17
WEATHER Overcast, cold, wet then drying
LAP LEADERS G Berger, McLaren-Honda 1-8, 12-20 (17); Mansell 9, 21-65 (46); Patrese 10 (1); Senna 11 (1)
WINNER'S LAPS 1 P4, 2-4 P3, 5-8 P2, 9 P1, 10 P5, 11-12 P3, 13-20 P2, 21-65 P1
FASTEST LAP Patrese, Williams-Renault, 1m 22.837s (lap 63), 206.299kph, 128.188mph
CHAMPIONSHIP Senna 85, Mansell 69, Patrese 48, Prost 31, Berger 31

Pos	Driver	Car	Time/gap	Grid	Stops	Tyres
1	N Mansell	Williams-Renault	1h 38m 41.541s	2	1	G
2	A Prost	Ferrari	−11.331s	6	1	G
3	R Patrese	Williams-Renault	−15.909s	4	1	G
4	J Alesi	Ferrari	−22.772s	7	2	G
5	A Senna	McLaren-Honda	−1m 2.402s	3	1	G
6	M Schumacher	Benetton-Ford	−1m 19.468s	5	2	P

JAPANESE GP Suzuka

20 October 1991   Race 515

Gerhard Berger

McLaren-Honda MP4/6 202.298kph, 125.702mph

For the fifth season Suzuka decided the title fight. For the fourth season Senna was at its epicentre. For the third season unseemly events produced a surprise winner. Having besmirched F1 12 months ago, Senna misguidedly repeated the felony, gifting a glaringly hollow victory to teammate Berger. This 'noble gesture' was only made once he knew the championship was his. On lap 10, Senna leading, the Williams front wing beneath the McLaren's rear, Mansell ran wide at turn one and became marooned in the sand trap, complaining later of a 'long' brake pedal. Rather than delight in his third title in four years, Senna launched a foul-mouthed tirade against recently deposed FISA president Balestre, blaming him for the collision with Prost in 1990.

POLE POSITION Berger, McLaren-Honda, 1m 34.700s (0.198s), 222.919kph, 138.515mph
LAPS 53 x 5.864 km, 3.644 miles
DISTANCE 310.792 km, 193.117 miles
STARTERS/FINISHERS 26/11
WEATHER Sunny, warm, dry
LAP LEADERS Berger 1-17, 53 (18); Senna 18-21, 24-52 (33); Patrese 22-23 (2)
WINNER'S LAPS 1-17 P1, 18-19 P2, 20-23 P3, 24-52 P2, 53 P1
FASTEST LAP Senna, McLaren-Honda, 1m 41.532s (lap 39), 207.919kph, 129.915mph
CHAMPIONSHIP Senna 91, Mansell 69, Patrese 52, Berger 41, Prost 34

Pos	Driver	Car	Time/gap	Grid	Stops	Tyres
1	G Berger	McLaren-Honda	1h 32m 10.695s	1	1	G
2	A Senna	McLaren-Honda	−0.344s	2	1	G
3	R Patrese	Williams-Renault	−56.731s	5	1	G
4	A Prost	Ferrari	−1m 20.761s	4	1	G
5	M Brundle	Brabham-Yamaha	−1 lap	19	1	P
6	S Modena	Tyrrell-Honda	−1 lap	14	1	P

<table>
<tr><td>Round 16/16</td><td colspan="2">AUSTRALIAN GP Adelaide</td><td colspan="2">Ayrton Senna</td></tr>
<tr><td></td><td>3 November 1991</td><td align="right">Race 516</td><td colspan="2">McLaren-Honda MP4/6 129.170kph, 80.262mph</td></tr>
</table>

Morbidelli was entered alongside Alesi in Ferrari No27, Prost fired by the Scuderia. Senna's seventh win of the season, his 33rd career victory, was the shortest GP on record: 14 laps, 25 minutes. The race was started in torrential rain that soon became a deluge, yellow-flag incidents all around the circuit. From a record 60th pole Senna led Berger and Mansell, but it was only when these two, driving in zero visibility, crashed that the race was belatedly halted, Martini's wrecked Minardi still littering the main straight. In hindsight most agreed the dangerous farce should never have been started, the race abandoned 65 minutes after it was red-flagged, half-points awarded. McLaren beat Williams to a fourth consecutive constructors' championship.

POLE POSITION Senna, McLaren-Honda, 1m 14.041s (0.344s), 183.790kph, 114.202mph
LAPS 14 x 3.780 km, 2.349 miles (Scheduled for 81 laps but stopped due to rain)
DISTANCE 52.920 km, 32.883 miles (Minimum distance incomplete; half points awarded)
STARTERS/FINISHERS 26/20
WEATHER Overcast, humid, heavy rain
LAP LEADERS Senna 1-14 (14)
WINNER'S LAPS 1-14 P1
FASTEST LAP Berger, McLaren-Honda, 1m 41.141s (lap 14), 134.545kph, 83.602mph
CHAMPIONSHIP Senna 96, Mansell 72, Patrese 53, Berger 43, Prost 34

Pos	Driver	Car	Time/gap	Grid	Stops	Tyres
1	A Senna	McLaren-Honda	24m 34.899s	1	0	G
2	N Mansell	Williams-Renault	−1.259s	3	0	G
3	G Berger	McLaren-Honda	−5.120s	2	0	G
4	N Piquet	Benetton-Ford	−30.103s	5	0	P
5	R Patrese	Williams-Renault	−50.537s	4	0	G
6	G Morbidelli	Ferrari	−51.069s	8	0	G

1991 CHAMPIONSHIP FACTS AND FOLKLORE

- Modifications to wing dimensions front and rear plus more rigorous chassis crash-testing were the main revisions to technical regulations, but the most significant changes affected the sporting rulebook.
- One was the introduction of the stop-go penalty, another the points structure. Points for a win increased from nine to ten. Drivers' and constructors' championship points become 10, 6, 4, 3, 2, 1 to the top six finishers, with both championships brought into line, all 16 races now counting for the drivers' title.
- New racetracks were used in France and Spain, the Cataluña circuit near Barcelona and Magny-Cours south of Paris, the seventh venue for the French GP.
- The 1991 German Grand Prix was the first held within a reunified Germany. German Reunification had occurred on 3 October 1990, three months after the previous Grand Prix.
- Up against reigning champions Senna, McLaren and Honda, Mansell, Williams and Renault could hardly afford to give away one win, let alone two. Mansell's retirement with a dead engine on the final lap of the fifth round in Canada was bad enough, but the wheel-nut fiasco in Portugal, with just three more races to run, was the death knell for their championship aspirations.
- Williams were simply not yet ready to take the honours, but were building a formidable team, three key elements being exclusive use of Renault's excellent engine, Nigel Mansell's second coming, rejoining from Ferrari to lead the team, and Adrian Newey bringing fresh aero thinking on the design front.
- Renault's new RS3 series engine had the top-end power previous versions had lacked and but for failing one mile short in Canada would have powered just as many race victories as Honda. At Monza the 67° V10 produced a staggering 750bhp at 14,000rpm.
- Mansell made a tentative start to the season, initially out-performed by teammate Patrese, only fully into his stride with his attack on Prost at Monaco. Even so, his first win of the season didn't come until round seven. It was the 17th of his career, Mansell thereby breaking the record of GP victories for an English driver held by Stirling Moss for 30 years.
- As Williams sought to emulate Ferrari's paddle-shift gearbox advantage, gearbox gremlins were rife and cost them many points. But one of the many advantages of the electronic system, once reliable, was exemplified by Senna's flip in practice at Mexico City. He 'lost it' mid-corner because he was controlling the steering wheel with one hand, the other changing gear conventionally.
- Honda's new V12 won half the 16 championship rounds but Senna was rarely content with it, considering his successes more to do with the failure of others. However, four wins from the first four races was a record even Ascari supremacy hadn't matched.
- The lowest point for the team was Senna running dry in successive races, in Britain and in Germany. By then the Renault V10 was clearly in the ascendancy and with 'rocket' fuels or special brews prevalent in 1991, Shell introduced a new fuel for high-speed Silverstone and Hockenheim. This brew was physically heavier than normal, and to save weight Honda twice made a marginal fuel-load decision.
- At the very next race in Hungary Senna won decisively. It was an incredible demonstration of Honda might and desire. In little more than a month the Japanese manufacturer produced an entirely new V12 featuring hydraulically controlled variable length induction trumpets.
- Designed to improve torque and produce a better power curve and engine flexibility, the technology was active, trumpet height matched to throttle movement, the unit producing some 725bhp at 14,800rpm.
- Hungary was the turning point for the McLaren Honda season, but just six days before the Hungaroring triumph founder Soichiro Honda died at the age of 84. Whether two wheels or four, here was a man who believed that racing improves the breed.
- Tyrrell inherited the now Mugen-run V10 Hondas and with Braun title sponsorship much was expected but little achieved.
- By the end of last season Maranello had the measure of McLaren, but in 1991 Ferrari was disastrous, Prost not winning a race for the first time since his 1980 rookie season, ultimately ejected by the team before the final race.
- Prost considered Ferrari rudderless, lacking leadership, and

RACE 514, Spanish GP: Senna's wheel-to-wheel run-in with Mansell down the long main straight encapsulated the intensity of their championship battle.

substantiating that opinion was that when team boss Cesare Fiorio was finally fired in May, much to Prost's approval, a triumvirate took his place, much to his dismay. From France the revised 'high-nose' 643 was an improvement but not the solution, and with all seats taken at McLaren and Williams, Prost took a sabbatical for 1992.

■ Alesi's first Ferrari year was disappointing, still error-prone but the previous sparkle replaced by desperation. In Spain he became the first driver to receive a stop-go penalty, the offence 'dangerous driving'. Out-qualified 13-2 by Prost, only once – at Spa – did he threaten the top step of the rostrum.

■ Besides one lucky win for Piquet, Benetton only made headlines for dubious reasons. In Jordan's very promising debut year, unusual circumstances mid-season caused Eddie Jordan to spot and enter an unknown German driver, one

Michael Schumacher. He made such a sensation on debut that by the next race, piranha Benetton had purloined their new young star from minnow Jordan. Ron Dennis commiserated with Eddie Jordan, 'Welcome to the Piranha Club' he said.

■ A driver who made a rather less controversial debut was Mika Häkkinen, somehow managing to qualify a Lotus-Judd P13 on debut.

■ The incident that led to Schumacher's recruitment by Jordan was a two-month prison sentence for one of his drivers, Bertrand Gachot. His punishment was for the use of a CS gas spray in a traffic altercation with a London cab driver.

■ Benetton experienced a season of political upheaval that saw John Barnard depart and Tom Walkinshaw arrive. Also, at the end of the season, Nelson Piquet retired from GP racing. His fortuitous final victory in Canada was his 23rd, departing the scene with three world championships, one of just 11 multiple title holders.

▪ Leyton House used a V10 from new-to-F1 engine builder Ilmor, while Footwork (née Arrows) brought their association with Porsche to an end after Mexico following a string of dnqs for the Footwork-Porsche. After the enormous success of their V6 turbo, the Porsche V12 project was a huge disappointment.

▪ In Brazil, race 502, Goodyear celebrated their 250th race victory. At the other end of the scale, Piquet's win for Benetton was Pirelli's 45th. It was the Italian company's last victory for 20 years, until they returned as exclusive tyre supplier to F1 in 2011.

▪ In the FISA presidential election in October, Max Mosley defeated Jean-Marie Balestre. His departure presented Senna with an opportunity at the Suzuka press conference to vehemently criticise the volatile, autocratic Frenchman and blame him for the accident with Prost in 1990. The newly crowned world champion then went on to admit culpability for deliberately ramming Prost.

Championship ranking	Championship points	Driver nationality	1991 Drivers Championship		Races contested	Race victories	Podiumse excl. victories	Races led	Lights to flag victories	Laps led	Poles	Fastest laps	Triple Crowns
			Driver	Car									
1	96	BRA	Ayrton Senna	McLaren-Honda	16	7	5	10	5	467	8	2	
2	72	GBR	Nigel Mansell	Williams-Renault	16	5	4	9	1	296	2	6	1
3	53	ITA	Riccardo Patrese	Williams-Renault	16	2	6	6		125	4	2	
4	43	AUT	Gerhard Berger	McLaren-Honda	16	1	5	2		35	2	2	
5	34	FRA	Alain Prost	Ferrari	14		5	1		44		1	
6	26.5	BRA	Nelson Piquet	Benetton-Ford	16	1	2	2		2			
7	21	FRA	Jean Alesi	Ferrari	16		3	2		11		1	
8	10	ITA	Stefano Modena	Tyrrell-Honda	16		1						
9	9	ITA	Andrea de Cesaris	Jordan-Ford	15								
10	8	BRA	Roberto Moreno	Benetton-Ford (11) Jordan-Ford (2) Minardi-Ferrari (1)	14							1	
11	6	ITA	Pierluigi Martini	Minardi-Ferrari	16								
12	4	FIN	J J Lehto	Dallara-Judd	16		1						
13	4	FRA	Bertrand Gachot	Jordan-Ford	10							1	
13	4	GER	Michael Schumacher	Jordan-Ford (1) Benetton-Ford (5)	6								
15	2	JPN	Satoru Nakajima	Tyrrell-Honda	16								
15	2	FIN	Mika Häkkinen	Lotus-Judd	15								
15	2	GBR	Martin Brundle	Brabham-Yamaha	14								
18	1	JPN	Aguri Suzuki	Lola-Ford	11								
18	1	GBR	Julian Bailey	Lotus-Judd	1								
18	1	ITA	Emanuele Pirro	Dallara-Judd	13								
18	1	FRA	Éric Bernard	Lola-Ford	13								
18	1	ITA	Ivan Capelli	Leyton House-Ilmor	14								
18	1	GBR	Mark Blundell	Brabham-Yamaha	14								
24	0.5	ITA	Gianni Morbidelli	Minardi-Ferrari (15) Ferrari (1)	16								

Championship ranking	Championship points	Team/Marque nationality	1991 Constructors Championship		Engine maker nationality	Races contested	Race victories	1-2 finishes	Podiums excl. victories	Races led	Laps led	Poles	Fastest laps
			Chassis	Engine									
1	139	GBR	McLaren MP4-6	Honda 3.5 V12	JPN	16	8	3	10	10	502	10	4
2	125	GBR	Williams FW14	Renault 3.5 V10	FRA	16	7	2	10	11	421	6	8
3	55.5	ITA	Ferrari 642, 643	Ferrari 3.5 V12	ITA	16			8	3	55		2
4	38.5	GBR	Benetton B191, B190B	Ford Cosworth 3.5 V8	GBR	16	1		2	2	2		1
5	13	IRL	Jordan 191	Ford Cosworth 3.5 V8	GBR	16							1
6	12	GBR	Tyrrell 020	Honda 3.5 V10	JPN	16			1				
7	6	ITA	Minardi 191	Ferrari 3.5 V12	ITA	16							
8	5	ITA	Dallara BMS191	Judd 3.5 V8	GBR	16			1				
9	3	GBR	Lotus 102B	Judd 3.5 V8	GBR	16							
9	3	GBR	Brabham BT60Y, BT59Y	Yamaha 3.5 V12	JPN	16							
11	2	GBR	Lola 91	Ford Cosworth 3.5 V8	GBR	15							
12	1	JPN	Leyton House CG911	Ilmor 3.5 V10	GBR	16							

1992

Mansell by a mile

THE TALE OF THE TITLE

- Having come so close on previous occasions, Nigel Mansell was world drivers' champion at last.
- His championship crown was a long time coming, taking a record 176 races in his 13th active season.
- But this time he wrapped up the title in dominant style with five rounds of the championship remaining.
- His haul of nine race wins including the opening five of the season brought records tumbling.
- Williams-Renault were also decisive champions with ten race victories, including six team 1-2 finishes.
- The victorious Williams FW14B utilised electronics for suspension, gearbox and traction control.
- McLaren-Honda fashioned five victories from the Williams cast-offs, Senna denying Mansell at Monaco.
- After six preceding championship years, Honda announced their withdrawal at the end of the season.
- With Ferrari nowhere, Benetton emerged as the third force on the F1 grid.
- Twelve months after his Spa debut, Benetton's Michael Schumacher took his first race victory
- Mansell, Prost and Senna vied for a 1993 Williams seat, Senna pledging, 'I'll drive for nothing.'
- Ultimately Prost replaced USA-bound Mansell while the year ended with Senna's future still uncertain.
- And not forgetting: Red Five.

THE CHASE FOR THE CHAMPIONSHIP

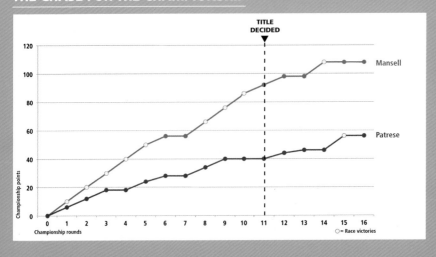

Williams-Renault FW14B

<table>
<tr><td>**Round 1/16**</td><td colspan="2">**SOUTH AFRICAN GP** Kyalami</td></tr>
<tr><td></td><td>**1 March 1992**</td><td>**Race 517**</td></tr>
</table>

Nigel Mansell
Williams-Renault FW14B 190.248kph, 118.215mph

Mansell's season got off to a flyer. From first practice at the new Kyalami circuit he was the man to beat, easily quickest in every session and annexing pole 0.74s up on Senna, 1.5s on Patrese. The Williams-Renault FW14B with 'active ride' suspension clearly had the measure of the rest, at least with Mansell at the wheel. Teammate Patrese lined up behind the McLarens, although traction control put that right by the first corner. There he stayed to complete a 1-2 team finish, pressed by Senna but way behind his rampant team leader. Mansell led every lap, pulling out 25–30s, maintaining it, then finishing with a fastest-lap flourish two laps from the end. The only hope for Senna, third, and Schumacher, fourth, was that their 1992 cars were yet to come.

POLE POSITION Mansell, Williams-Renault, 1m 15.486s (0.741s), 203.211kph, 126.270mph
LAPS 72 x 4.261 km, 2.648 miles
DISTANCE 306.792 km, 190.632 miles
STARTERS/FINISHERS 26/13
WEATHER Overcast, warm, dry
LAP LEADERS Mansell 1-72 (72)
WINNER'S LAPS 1-72 P1
FASTEST LAP Mansell, Williams-Renault, 1m 17.578s (lap 70), 197.731kph, 122.865mph
CHAMPIONSHIP Mansell 10, Patrese 6, Senna 4, Schumacher 3, Berger 2

Pos	Driver	Car	Time/gap	Grid	Stops	Tyres
1	N Mansell	Williams-Renault	1h 36m 45.320s	1	0	G
2	R Patrese	Williams-Renault	−24.360s	4	0	G
3	A Senna	McLaren-Honda	−34.675s	2	0	G
4	M Schumacher	Benetton-Ford	−47.863s	6	0	G
5	G Berger	McLaren-Honda	−1m 13.634s	3	0	G
6	J Herbert	Lotus-Ford	−1 lap	11	0	G

<table>
<tr><td>**Round 2/16**</td><td colspan="2">**MEXICAN GP** Mexico City</td></tr>
<tr><td></td><td>**22 March 1992**</td><td>**Race 518**</td></tr>
</table>

Nigel Mansell
Williams-Renault FW14B 199.176kph, 123.762mph

For a second year Senna crashed heavily in practice, losing control over a bump. Initially it looked far worse than severe bruising. Williams were very strong in Mexico last year, starting and finishing 1-2, Patrese in the ascendant. But this year Mansell was clearly at the top of his game, bursting with self-belief and energy. For the first 25 laps Patrese kept the gap between 2–4s, the pair trading fastest laps, but over the next 25 Mansell's relentless lappery stretched it to 15. In the 'B' race, the Benettons out-qualified the McLarens but Senna led Schumacher until the McLaren transmission failed after 11 laps. Brundle and Berger fought over fourth, the McLaren eventually getting by on lap 43, the Benetton out soon afterwards with overheating.

POLE POSITION Mansell, Williams-Renault, 1m 16.346s (0.016s), 208.487kph, 129.535mph
LAPS 69 x 4.421 km, 2.747 miles
DISTANCE 305.049 km, 189.549 miles
STARTERS/FINISHERS 26/13
WEATHER Cloudy with sunny intervals, hot, dry
LAP LEADERS Mansell 1-69 (69)
WINNER'S LAPS 1-69 P1
FASTEST LAP Berger, McLaren-Honda, 1m 17.711s (lap 60), 204.805kph, 127.260mph
CHAMPIONSHIP Mansell 20, Patrese 12, Schumacher 7, Berger 5, Senna 4

Pos	Driver	Car	Time/gap	Grid	Stops	Tyres
1	N Mansell	Williams-Renault	1h 31m 53.587s	1	0	G
2	R Patrese	Williams-Renault	−12.971s	2	0	G
3	M Schumacher	Benetton-Ford	−21.429s	3	0	G
4	G Berger	McLaren-Honda	−33.347s	5	0	G
5	A de Cesaris	Tyrrell-Ilmor	−1 lap	11	0	G
6	M Häkkinen	Lotus-Ford	−1 lap	18	0	G

BRAZILIAN GP Interlagos
5 April 1992   Race 519

Nigel Mansell
Williams-Renault FW14B 190.209kph, 118.191mph

McLaren brought their new car to Interlagos. Senna qualified it P3, over 2s behind Mansell's pole. New car issues truncated their debut race, Berger out after four laps, Senna after 17 from P3. A poor start gave Patrese the initiative, Mansell doing everything to wrest the lead, but he had to wait until the tyre stops. Once in front, Mansell forged ahead to another Williams 1-2, their hat-trick. With Senna's departure Schumacher again finished 'best of the rest', although by the end he was a lap down. Immediately behind Schumacher, Brundle again fought over P4 until on lap 25 he and Alesi touched and spun. Alesi recovered to finish fourth, Capelli next in the second Ferrari. After three rounds Mansell had 30 points, defending champion Senna four.

POLE POSITION Mansell, Williams-Renault, 1m 15.703s (1.191s), 205.672kph, 127.799mph
LAPS 71 x 4.325 km, 2.687 miles
DISTANCE 307.075 km, 190.808 miles
STARTERS/FINISHERS 26/10
WEATHER Sunny, hot, dry
LAP LEADERS Patrese 1-31 (31); Mansell 32-71 (40)
WINNER'S LAPS 1-31 P2, 32-71 P1
FASTEST LAP Patrese, Williams-Renault, 1m 19.490s (lap 34), 195.874kph, 121.710mph
CHAMPIONSHIP Mansell 30, Patrese 18, Schumacher 11, Berger 5, Senna 4

Pos	Driver	Car	Time/gap	Grid	Stops	Tyres
1	N Mansell	Williams-Renault	1h 36m 51.856s	1	1	G
2	R Patrese	Williams-Renault	−29.330s	2	1	G
3	M Schumacher	Benetton-Ford	−1 lap	5	0	G
4	J Alesi	Ferrari	−1 lap	6	1	G
5	I Capelli	Ferrari	−1 lap	11	1	G
6	M Alboreto	Footwork-Mugen Honda	−1 lap	14	0	G

SPANISH GP Cataluña
3 May 1992   Race 520

Nigel Mansell
Williams-Renault FW14B 159.353kph, 99.017mph

The Williams roadshow continued. Mansell's pole was a whole second quicker than the next man, Schumacher in the new Benetton, not Patrese. But in wet race conditions Williams' traction control rocketed Patrese from P4 to shadow Mansell, which is how they might have finished if the Italian hadn't tripped over a backmarker on lap 22. With the McLaren pair unable to engage with Schumacher, the race order looked set. Alesi had other ideas. A lightning start from P8 had him well placed until nurfed off by Berger on lap 13. On lap 33 Alesi bolted-on fresh wets, and after dispensing with Capelli and Berger set off after Senna. In two laps the flying Ferrari made up 14s, and under pressure, three from the end, the world champion spun out.

POLE POSITION Mansell, Williams-Renault, 1m 20.190s (1.005s), 213.109kph, 132.420mph
LAPS 65 x 4.747 km, 2.950 miles
DISTANCE 308.555 km, 191.727 miles
STARTERS/FINISHERS 26/12
WEATHER Overcast, cold, wet
LAP LEADERS Mansell 1-65 (65)
WINNER'S LAPS 1-65 P1
FASTEST LAP Mansell, Williams-Renault, 1m 42.503s (lap 10), 166.719kph, 103.594mph
CHAMPIONSHIP Mansell 40, Patrese 18, Schumacher 17, Berger 8, Alesi 7

Pos	Driver	Car	Time/gap	Grid	Stops	Tyres
1	N Mansell	Williams-Renault 1h 56m 10.674s		1	0	G
2	M Schumacher	Benetton-Ford	−23.914s	2	0	G
3	J Alesi	Ferrari	−26.462s	8	1	G
4	G Berger	McLaren-Honda	−1m 20.647s	7	0	G
5	M Alboreto	Footwork-Mugen Honda	−1 lap	16	0	G
6	P Martini	Dallara-Ferrari	−2 laps	13	0	G

SAN MARINO GP Imola
17 May 1992   Race 521

Nigel Mansell
Williams-Renault FW14B 204.596kph, 127.130mph

Winning five from five, Mansell beat Senna's record established only last year. Once again his pole margin was a second, the pattern of the race familiar. Patrese kept Mansell in sight until the tyre stops, after which Mansell powered on and Patrese settled back, perversely setting the fastest lap on his final tour, the race long since lost. The Noah's Ark grid had formed up Williams, McLaren, Benetton, Ferrari and stayed that way for 18 laps. Schumacher spun out trying to oust teammate Brundle from fifth, while, as others pitted, non-stop Alesi claimed P3, holding the McLarens at bay for a while. On lap 40 Senna slipstreamed past at Tosa, Berger tried to follow, Ferrari and McLaren colliding, both out. This elevated Brundle to fourth.

POLE POSITION Mansell, Williams-Renault, 1m 21.842s (1.053s), 221.695kph, 137.755mph
LAPS 60 x 5.040 km, 3.132 miles
DISTANCE 302.400 km, 187.903 miles
STARTERS/FINISHERS 26/14
WEATHER Sunny, hot, dry
LAP LEADERS Mansell 1-60 (60)
WINNER'S LAPS 1-60 P1
FASTEST LAP Patrese, Williams-Renault, 1m 26.100s (lap 60), 210.732kph, 130.943mph
CHAMPIONSHIP Mansell 50, Patrese 24, Schumacher 17, Berger 8, Senna 8

Pos	Driver	Car	Time/gap	Grid	Stops	Tyres
1	N Mansell	Williams-Renault	1h 28m 40.927s	1	1	G
2	R Patrese	Williams-Renault	−9.451s	2	1	G
3	A Senna	McLaren-Honda	−48.984s	3	1	G
4	M Brundle	Benetton-Ford	−53.007s	6	1	G
5	M Alboreto	Footwork-Mugen Honda	−1 lap	9	0	G
6	P Martini	Dallara-Ferrari	−1 lap	15	0	G

McLaren-Honda MP4/7A

MONACO GP Monte Carlo

31 May 1992   **Race 522**

Ayrton Senna

McLaren-Honda MP4/7A 140.329kph, 87.196mph

Round six, the Monte Carlo street circuit. So far Mansell had won every race from pole and here it was exactly the same story, until lap 70 of 78. After a sideways moment in the tunnel, he dived for the pits with a suspected puncture. The stop wasn't quick, Mansell rejoining immediately behind Senna, now leading. In the much faster car, Mansell almost drove over the top of Senna in his efforts to overtake, darting left then right to outmanoeuvre or force an error. But Senna knew Monaco far too well, holding his line to become five-times winner, equalling Graham Hill's record of 22 years' standing. Once Alesi's Ferrari was out Schumacher zeroed in on Patrese's P3, putting him under intense pressure for 30 laps. But to no avail – after all, this was Monaco.

POLE POSITION Mansell, Williams-Renault, 1m 19.495s (0.873s), 150.711kph, 93.648mph
LAPS 78 x 3.328 km, 2.068 miles
DISTANCE 259.584 km, 161.298 miles
STARTERS/FINISHERS 26/12
WEATHER Cloudy with sunny intervals, warm, dry
LAP LEADERS Mansell 1-70 (70), Senna 71-78 (8)
WINNER'S LAPS 1-70 P2, 71-78 P1
FASTEST LAP Mansell, Williams-Renault, 1m 21.598s (lap 74), 146.827kph, 91.234mph
CHAMPIONSHIP Mansell 56, Patrese 28, Schumacher 20, Senna 18, Berger 8

TOP 100 RACE

Pos	Driver	Car	Time/gap	Grid	Stops	Tyres
1	A Senna	McLaren-Honda	1h 50m 59.372s	3	0	G
2	N Mansell	Williams-Renault	−0.215s	1	1	G
3	R Patrese	Williams-Renault	−31.843s	2	0	G
4	M Schumacher	Benetton-Ford	−39.294s	6	0	G
5	M Brundle	Benetton-Ford	−1m 21.347s	7	1	G
6	B Gachot	Larrousse-Lamborghini	−1 lap	15	0	G

CANADIAN GP Montréal

14 June 1992   **Race 523**

Gerhard Berger

McLaren-Honda MP4/7A 188.805kph, 117.318mph

A new Honda V12 helped Senna to his first pole, from which he led Mansell in an 11-car crocodile. On lap 15, in a lunging, botched pass, Mansell eliminated himself, although in his opinion 'Senna pushed me off'. In the resultant mêleé Berger crucially got ahead of Patrese, which became the lead when Senna's electronics packed up on lap 38. Patrese trailed Berger by a couple of seconds but on lap 43 ground to a halt, gearbox. Brundle, who had nipped past Schumacher in traffic on lap 39, now held P2. He lasted just two laps before transmission failure put him out too. From there it was plain sailing for Berger, Schumacher unable to close and Alesi finishing a distant third through survival rather than speed. Wendlinger impressed with P4 for March-Ilmor.

POLE POSITION A Senna, McLaren-Honda, 1m 19.775s (0.097s), 199.912kph, 124.220mph
LAPS 69 x 4.430 km, 2.753 miles
DISTANCE 305.670 km, 189.935 miles
STARTERS/FINISHERS 26/14
WEATHER Cloudy with sunny intervals, hot, dry
LAP LEADERS Senna 1-37 (37); Berger 38-69 (32)
WINNER'S LAPS 1-14 P4, 15-37 P2, 38-69 P1
FASTEST LAP Berger, McLaren-Honda, 1m 22.325s (Lap 61), 193.720kph, 120.372mph
CHAMPIONSHIP Mansell 56, Patrese 28, Schumacher 26, Senna 18, Berger 18

Pos	Driver	Car	Time/gap	Grid	Stops	Tyres
1	G Berger	McLaren-Honda	1h 37m 8.299s	4	0	G
2	M Schumacher	Benetton-Ford	−12.401s	5	0	G
3	J Alesi	Ferrari	−1m 7.327s	8	0	G
4	K Wendlinger	March-Ilmor	−1 lap	12	0	G
5	A de Cesaris	Tyrrell-Ilmor	−1 lap	14	0	G
6	E Comas	Ligier-Renault	−1 lap	22	0	G

Round 8/16	**FRENCH GP** Magny-Cours		**Nigel Mansell**	

FRENCH GP Magny-Cours
5 July 1992   Race 524

Nigel Mansell
Williams-Renault FW14B 179.283kph, 111.401mph

Red-flagged for rain after 18 laps, the restarted race was decided on aggregate. At both starts Patrese led Mansell from an all-Williams front row, on the second occasion peevishly waving him though in protest against alleged Williams team orders. In the first part Schumacher took Senna out in a first-corner clash and in the second accounted for himself in exactly the same way. Benetton teammate Brundle performed rather better, finishing P3 for his first (official) podium visit. For part two the grid had restarted on slicks, but when the rain returned around lap 44, Alesi, until his engine blew, starred with a spectacular display of wet-weather driving on slicks. The forward momentum at Team Lotus persisted, Häkkinen P4 and Herbert P6.

POLE POSITION Mansell, Williams-Renault, 1m 13.864s (0.468), 207.137kph, 128.709mph
LAPS 69 x 4.250 km, 2.641 miles (72 lap race interrupted due to rain. Result aggregate of 18 + 51 laps)
DISTANCE 293.250 km, 182.217 miles
STARTERS/FINISHERS 26/11
WEATHER Overcast, warm, dry then wet
LAP LEADERS (On the road) Patrese 1-19 (19); Mansell 20-69 (50)
WINNER'S LAPS 1-19 P2, 20-69 P1
FASTEST LAP Mansell, Williams-Renault, 1m 17.070s (lap 37), 198.521kph, 123.355mph
CHAMPIONSHIP Mansell 66, Patrese 34, Schumacher 26, Senna 18, Berger 18

Pos	Driver	Car	Time/gap	Grid	Stops	Tyres
1	N Mansell	Williams-Renault	1h 38m 8.459s	1	1	G
2	R Patrese	Williams-Renault	−46.447s	2	1	G
3	M Brundle	Benetton-Ford	−1m 12.579s	7	1	G
4	M Häkkinen	Lotus-Ford	−1 lap	11	1	G
5	E Comas	Ligier-Renault	−1 lap	10	1	G
6	J Herbert	Lotus-Ford	−1 lap	12	1	G

BRITISH GP Silverstone
12 July 1992   Race 525

Nigel Mansell
Williams-Renault FW14B 215.828kph, 134.109mph

Mansell magic, utterly dominant in qualifying and the race. In the opening four laps his lead over Patrese, sore from a practice prang, read 3.2s, 5.9s, 7.9s, 10.1s. That day at Silverstone Mansell mania erupted with a highly dangerous track invasion before all cars had duly finished. Adding to the crowd's fervour, Martin Brundle held P3 every lap of the way in a battle with Senna reminiscent of their F3 days. Senna eventually got by on lap 53 then immediately coasted into retirement, transmission. In another McLaren/Benetton duel, Berger fought closely with Schumacher for much of the second half, only losing P4 on the final lap when the Honda let go. Neatly driving a pink and blue Brabham-Judd, Damon Hill debuted, finishing four laps down.

POLE POSITION Mansell, Williams-Renault, 1m 18.965s (1.919s), 238.252kph, 148.043mph
LAPS 59 x 5.226 km, 3.247 miles
DISTANCE 308.334 km, 191.590 miles
STARTERS/FINISHERS 26/17
WEATHER Cloudy with sunny intervals, hot, dry
LAP LEADERS Mansell 1-59 (59)
WINNER'S LAPS 1-59 P1
FASTEST LAP Mansell, Williams-Renault, 1m 22.539s (lap 57), 227.936kph, 141.633mph
CHAMPIONSHIP Mansell 76, Patrese 40, Schumacher 29, Berger 20, Senna 18

Pos	Driver	Car	Time/gap	Grid	Stops	Tyres
1	N Mansell	Williams-Renault	1h 25m 42.991s	1	1	G
2	R Patrese	Williams-Renault	−39.094s	2	0	G
3	M Brundle	Benetton-Ford	−43.395s	6	0	G
4	M Schumacher	Benetton-Ford	−53.267s	4	1	G
5	G Berger	McLaren-Honda	−55.795s	5	1	G
6	M Häkkinen	Lotus-Ford	−1m 20.138s	9	0	G

GERMAN GP Hockenheim
26 July 1992   Race 526

Nigel Mansell
Williams-Renault FW14B 234.798kph, 145.897mph

From the front row the Williams duo pulled away, Patrese leading briefly during Mansell's tyre stop. It also dropped Mansell behind Senna, figuring his only chance was a non-stop run. The McLaren proved hard to pass, Mansell accomplishing it by straightlining the Ostkurve chicane, a ploy fortunate to go unpenalised. When Patrese pitted for tyres Mansell retook the lead, but the stop put him behind Schumacher, also on a non-stop strategy. In front of his home crowd Schumacher held Patrese at bay for many laps, but once by he set off after Senna only to spin out on the final lap attempting a pass in the stadium. Patrese's no-score meant Mansell's championship was suddenly in sight, whereas despite his P2 Senna was no longer a title contender.

POLE POSITION Mansell, Williams-Renault, 1m 37.960s (0.550s), 250.449kph, 155.622mph
LAPS 45 x 6.815 km, 4.235 miles
DISTANCE 306.675 km, 190.559 miles
STARTERS/FINISHERS 26/16
WEATHER Cloudy with sunny intervals, hot, dry
LAP LEADERS Mansell 1-14, 20-45 (40); Patrese 15-19 (5)
WINNER'S LAPS 1-14 P1, 15-18 P3, 19 P2, 20-45 P1
FASTEST LAP R Patrese, Williams-Renault, 1m 41.591s (lap 36), 241.498kph, 150.060mph
CHAMPIONSHIP Mansell 86, Patrese 40, Schumacher 33, Senna 24, Berger 20

Pos	Driver	Car	Time/gap	Grid	Stops	Tyres
1	N Mansell	Williams-Renault	1h 18m 22.032s	1	1	G
2	A Senna	McLaren-Honda	−4.500s	3	0	G
3	M Schumacher	Benetton-Ford	−34.462s	6	0	G
4	M Brundle	Benetton-Ford	−36.959s	9	0	G
5	J Alesi	Ferrari	−1m 12.607s	5	0	G
6	E Comas	Ligier-Renault	−1m 36.498s	7	0	G

<table>
<tr><td>**Round 11/16**</td><td>**HUNGARIAN GP** Hungaroring</td><td>**Ayrton Senna**</td></tr>
</table>

Round 11/16	**HUNGARIAN GP** Hungaroring	**Ayrton Senna**
	16 August 1992 Race 527	McLaren-Honda MP4/7A 172.424kph, 107.139mph

After eight victories from the preceding ten rounds there was a certain irony that Mansell landed his championship with a mere P2 finish. Out-qualified by Patrese, Mansell found himself behind both McLarens after the start, bottled up behind first Berger, then Senna. Meanwhile pole-man Patrese had cleared off, establishing a 30s lead until inexplicably, around half-distance, he spun it all away. Now P2, the championship was Nigel's and any incentive to take on Senna evaporated. But there was still a twist. On lap 61 Mansell rushed into the pits with a puncture, then scythed back past Häkkinen, Brundle and Berger to regain the required six points and with them the title. So Senna won this battle, but Mansell had won the war.

POLE POSITION R Patrese, Williams-Renault, 1m 15.476s (0.167s), 189.263kph, 117.602mph
LAPS 77 x 3.968 km, 2.466 miles
DISTANCE 305.536 km, 189.851 miles
STARTERS/FINISHERS 26/11
WEATHER Cloudy with sunny intervals, hot, dry
LAP LEADERS Patrese 1-38 (38); Senna 39-77 (39)
WINNER'S LAPS 1-38 P2, 39-77 P1
FASTEST LAP Mansell, Williams-Renault, 1m 18.308s (lap 63), 182.418kph, 113.349mph
CHAMPIONSHIP Mansell 92, Patrese 40, Senna 34, Schumacher 33, Berger 24

Pos	Driver	Car	Time/gap	Grid	Stops	Tyres
1	A Senna	McLaren-Honda	1h 46m 19.216s	3	1	G
2	N Mansell	Williams-Renault	−40.139s	2	1	G
3	G Berger	McLaren-Honda	−50.782s	5	0	G
4	M Häkkinen	Lotus-Ford	−54.313s	16	0	G
5	M Brundle	Benetton-Ford	−57.498s	6	0	G
6	I Capelli	Ferrari	−1 lap	10	0	G

Benetton-Ford B192

Round 12/16	**BELGIAN GP** Spa Francorchamps	**Michael Schumacher**
	30 August 1992 Race 528	Benetton-Ford B192 191.429kph, 118.948mph

One year after his debut Schumacher won his first GP. In changeable weather conditions Senna, Patrese and Mansell led as they ducked and dived between pit stops – slicks, to wets, back to slicks. On lap 30, Schumacher, holding P4, ran off the road and as his teammate went by he observed that Brundle's tyres were blistered. Schumacher immediately made a smart if fortuitous switch to slicks whereas leader Mansell, forced to wait an extra lap because Patrese had pitted, finally made his switch three laps after the German. With 11 to go he rejoined 5s behind the new race leader, Schumacher. A thrilling finish was thwarted when Mansell lost power with a broken exhaust, although a 2-3 result secured the constructors' title for Williams.

POLE POSITION Mansell, Williams-Renault, 1m 50.545s (2.198s), 227.115kph, 141.123mph
LAPS 44 x 6.974 km, 4.333 miles
DISTANCE 306.856 km, 190.671 miles
STARTERS/FINISHERS 26/18
WEATHER Overcast, cold, changeable, dry, wet, dry
LAP LEADERS Senna 1, 7-10 (5); Mansell 2-3, 11-33 (25); Patrese 4-6 (3); Schumacher 34-44 (11)
WINNER'S LAPS 1-14 P1, 15 P2, 16-17 P5, 18-21 P3, 22-30 P2, 31-44 P1
FASTEST LAP Schumacher, Benetton-Ford, 1m 53.791s (lap 39), 220.636kph, 137.097mph
CHAMPIONSHIP Mansell 98, Patrese 44, Schumacher 43, Senna 36, Berger 24

Pos	Driver	Car	Time/gap	Grid	Stops	Tyres
1	M Schumacher	Benetton-Ford	1h 36m 10.721s	3	2	G
2	N Mansell	Williams-Renault	−36.595s	1	2	G
3	R Patrese	Williams-Renault	−43.897s	4	2	G
4	M Brundle	Benetton-Ford	−46.059s	9	2	G
5	A Senna	McLaren-Honda	−1m 8.369s	2	2	G
6	M Häkkinen	Lotus-Ford	−1m 10.030s	8	2	G

ITALIAN GP Monza

13 September 1992 Race 529

Ayrton Senna

McLaren-Honda MP4/7A 235.689kph, 146.450mph

Off-track, Mansell's negotiations with Williams finally broke down, Nigel announcing his F1 retirement. On-track, he took pole and drove into the distance. On lap 20, 15s ahead, he slowed abruptly to allow Patrese through, his teammate desperate for a Monza victory and fighting for runner-up in the championship. To exhibit his largesse, Mansell shadowed Patrese closely. On lap 42 Mansell and six laps later Patrese suffered hydraulics failures, the heartbroken Italian 10s ahead of Senna at the time. Senna gratefully picked up the pieces while his teammate finished P4 having started from the pit lane. The Benettons finished 2-3, Brundle's P2 his best-ever result, the team retaining a small lead over McLaren in the constructors' table.

POLE POSITION N Mansell, Williams-Renault, 1m 22.221s (0.601s), 253.950kph, 157.797mph
LAPS 53 x 5.800 km, 3.604 miles
DISTANCE 307.400 km, 191.010 miles
STARTERS/FINISHERS 26/11
WEATHER Cloudy with sunny intervals, hot, dry
LAP LEADERS Mansell 1-19 (19); Patrese 20-47 (28); Senna 48-53 (6)
WINNER'S LAPS 1-13 P2, 14-41 P3, 42-47 P2, 48-53 P1
FASTEST LAP N Mansell, Williams-Renault, 1m 26.119 (lap 39), 242.455kph, 150.655mph
CHAMPIONSHIP Mansell 98, Schumacher 47, Senna 46, Patrese 46, Berger 27

Pos	Driver	Car	Time/gap	Grid	Stops	Tyres
1	A Senna	McLaren-Honda	1h 18m 15.349s	2	0	G
2	M Brundle	Benetton-Ford	−17.050s	9	0	G
3	M Schumacher	Benetton-Ford	−24.373s	6	1	G
4	G Berger	McLaren-Honda	−1m 25.490s	5	1	G
5	R Patrese	Williams-Renault	−1m 33.158s	4	0	G
6	A de Cesaris	Tyrrell-Ilmor	−1 lap	21	0	G

PORTUGUESE GP Estoril

27 September 1992 Race 530

Nigel Mansell

Williams-Renault FW14B 195.521kph, 121.491mph

Mansell, in a race of his own, eclipsed Senna's 1988 record with his ninth win. Teammate Patrese, however, was involved in a sickening aerial accident. A problem with a jack during his pit stop dropped Patrese behind both McLarens. Completing lap 43 looking to pass, tucked tight under the McLaren rear wing, Berger without warning slowed to enter the pits. Wheels touched, launching the Williams vertically skywards. Patrese was miraculously unhurt but furious that Berger had not signalled his intent. There was also anger from Senna, directed at Prost following firm news that Williams had signed the Frenchman for 1993. His mood would not have been helped by a troubled race into third, teammate Berger P2 despite the earlier Patrese incident.

POLE POSITION Mansell, Williams-Renault, 1m 13.041s (0.631s), 214.400kph, 133.222mph
LAPS 71 x 4.350 km, 2.703 miles
DISTANCE 308.850 km, 191.910 miles
STARTERS/FINISHERS 26/14
WEATHER Cloudy with sunny intervals, warm, dry
LAP LEADERS Mansell 1-71 (71)
WINNER'S LAPS 1-71 P1
FASTEST LAP Senna, McLaren-Honda, 1m 16.272s (lap 66), 205.318kph, 127.579mph
CHAMPIONSHIP Mansell 108, Senna 50, Schumacher 47, Patrese 46, Berger 33

Pos	Driver	Car	Time/gap	Grid	Stops	Tyres
1	N Mansell	Williams-Renault	1h 34m 46.659s	1	0	G
2	G Berger	McLaren-Honda	−37.533s	3	2	G
3	A Senna	McLaren-Honda	−1 lap	6	4	G
4	M Brundle	Benetton-Ford	−1 lap	8	1	G
5	M Häkkinen	Lotus-Ford	−1 lap	11	1	G
6	M Alboreto	Footwork-Mugen Honda	−1 lap	10	1	G

JAPANESE GP Suzuka

25 October 1992 Race 531

Riccardo Patrese

Williams-Renault FW14B 200.168kph, 124.379mph

Mansell made a mockery of the Japanese GP, establishing a 20s lead over the first 35 laps and then virtually coming to a standstill to let his teammate by. Thankfully Patrese's victory, his first of the season, became bona fide when Mansell suffered his second mechanical failure of the season, an engine blow-up on lap 44. At their home circuit only one Honda-powered McLaren finished, Berger taking second despite two pit stops. Senna lost one Honda V12 in the warm-up and another on lap 3. Despite food poisoning Brundle's fine form for Benetton continued with third from a P13. His teammate retired with gearbox trouble on lap 13 when lying third, and after an absence of ten years Jan Lammers returned to a F1 cockpit.

POLE POSITION N Mansell, Williams-Renault, 1m 37.360s (0.859s), 216.828kph, 134.731mph
LAPS 53 x 5.864 km, 3.644 miles
DISTANCE 310.792 km, 193.117 miles
STARTERS/FINISHERS 26/15
WEATHER Cloudy, warm, dry
LAP LEADERS Mansell 1-35 (35); Patrese 37-53 (18)
WINNER'S LAPS 1-35 P2, 37-53 P1
FASTEST LAP N Mansell, Williams-Renault, 1m 40.646s (lap 44), 209.749kph, 130.332mph
CHAMPIONSHIP Mansell 108, Patrese 56, Senna 50, Schumacher 47, Berger 39

Pos	Driver	Car	Time/gap	Grid	Stops	Tyres
1	R Patrese	Williams-Renault	1h 33m 9.553s	2	1	G
2	G Berger	McLaren-Honda	−13.729s	4	2	G
3	M Brundle	Benetton-Ford	−1m 15.503s	13	2	G
4	A de Cesaris	Tyrrell-Ilmor	−1 lap	9	1	G
5	J Alesi	Ferrari	−1 lap	15	0	G
6	C Fittipaldi	Minardi-Lamborghini	−1 lap	12	1	G

AUSTRALIAN GP Adelaide

8 November 1992   **Race 532**

Gerhard Berger

McLaren-Honda MP4/7A 171.829kph, 106.770mph

The newly crowned champion's final F1 race was a titanic struggle for the lead with Senna until, on lap 19, they collided at the hairpin. Senna claimed he was 'brake-tested', Mansell he was 'pushed off'. Behind these two Berger, his final appearance for McLaren, drove an aggressive race pressurising Patrese and crucially taking fresh tyres well before Schumacher, who was badly advised by his pit. Despite engine failure on lap 51 when leading, Patrese finished championship runner-up from Schumacher and Senna. The Benetton pair finished 2-3 but were pipped by McLaren for constructors' runner-up although, uniquely, Benetton scored points in every championship round. So Mansell departed F1 and Senna looked to be heading the same way.

POLE POSITION N Mansell, Williams-Renault, 1m 13.732s (0.470s), 184.560kph, 114.680mph
LAPS 81 x 3.780 km, 2.349 miles
DISTANCE 306.180 km, 190.251 miles
STARTERS/FINISHERS 26/13
WEATHER Overcast, warm, dry
LAP LEADERS Mansell 1-18 (18); R Patrese, Williams-Renault 19-50 (32); Berger 51-81 (31)
WINNER'S LAPS 1-2 P5, 3-18 P4, 19-34 P2, 35-42 P3, 43-50 P2, 51-81 P1
FASTEST LAP Schumacher, Benetton-Ford, 1m 16.078s (lap 68), 178.869kph, 111.144mph
CHAMPIONSHIP Mansell 108, Patrese 56, Schumacher 53, Senna 50, Berger 49

Pos	Driver	Car	Time/gap	Grid	Stops	Tyres
1	G Berger	McLaren-Honda	1h 46m 54.786s	4	1	G
2	M Schumacher	Benetton-Ford	−0.741s	5	1	G
3	M Brundle	Benetton-Ford	−54.156s	8	1	G
4	J Alesi	Ferrari	−1 lap	6	0	G
5	T Boutsen	Ligier-Renault	−1 lap	22	0	G
6	S Modena	Jordan-Yamaha	−1 lap	15	0	G

1992 CHAMPIONSHIP FACTS AND FOLKLORE

- After a seven-year absence the 16-race calendar included Kyalami, sporting and other sanctions gradually easing as apartheid began to lift in South Africa. The circuit was virtually new, only Sunset and Clubhouse bends surviving intact.
- As a nod towards the upcoming Summer Games, the Barcelona race was billed as The Olympic GP, while Mexico City hosted a GP for the final time.
- After Pirelli's withdrawal Goodyear equipped all teams, and without 'tyre wars', qualifying rubber vanished again in 1992, while FISA announced stricter fuel controls before the Hungarian GP in an endeavour to reduce the significant horsepower gain from 'rocket fuel' concoctions.
- It had been on the cards the previous season, but 1992 saw the Williams/Head/Newey/Renault/Mansell package come to fruition, the combination stitching up both championships before the end of August.
- Mansell won the title with five rounds still remaining, a new and astonishing record, while nine race victories in a season topped Senna's 1988 yardstick.
- His five race victories in a row from the start of the season beat Senna's benchmark of last year, although Ascari's string of seven in 1952–53 (or nine excluding the Indy 500, in which Alberto did not participate) remained the all-time record for unbroken race wins.
- It was the first championship for Renault in their 14th season of championship participation, nine years as a team, five as engine supplier.
- The superiority of the Williams-Renault FW14B was at times staggering, taking pole in all but one of the 16 rounds, winning ten of them and leading over 80% of the 1,036 laps raced during the season.
- It brought Mansell a highly deserved championship after his previous near-misses. He became the seventh world champion from Britain, 16 years since Hunt's title, the longest interval yet.
- In Britain his unprecedented and tabloid-hyped early-season success meant that Silverstone attracted a different type of follower to the regular F1 fans. It culminated in what was termed Mansell mania, an epithet for mass crowd hysteria.
- The image of the season was Mansell's frenetic attempts to overtake Senna at Monaco. Although he failed, it somehow encapsulated the out-and-out superiority of his machinery and the splendid brio of the driver at the top of his game.
- The superiority of the Williams-Renault package was such that the world's three top drivers squabbled over the two seats available for 1993.
- The original line-up was to be incumbent Mansell joined by Prost returning from sabbatical, but Mansell was neither enamoured with the prospect of resuming an affiliation with Prost nor the deal on offer. Negotiations broke down and Mansell stalked off to Indycars. Including the ill-fated Jochen Rindt, Mansell became the fourth champion not to defend his title.
- Once Senna realised Prost was angling for the plum ride for 1993 he tried everything he knew to gain the seat alongside him, even offering to drive for nothing. It was to no avail. Prost, described as a coward by Senna, would not countenance the renewal of their torrid association.
- Senna was left with four options: retirement, a sabbatical, Indycars, or McLaren without Honda engines.
- Honda had provisionally notified partners McLaren of their intention to withdraw in mid-1991, so it would be unfair to conclude that the decision came from their 1992 trouncing by Renault. But it was unfortunate that after six successive championship seasons their participation ended on a downbeat.
- There was no lack of commitment this season, Honda introducing a new V12 in Brazil that was lighter, more compact, with pneumatic valves and a more aero-friendly V-configuration, widened to 75°, plus fly-by-wire throttle control.
- McLaren-Honda picked up five victories this season, which raised Honda's race-win tally since re-entering F1 as an engine supplier in 1983 to 68 victories from 151 races.
- Under the auspices of the company formed by Honda's son, Mugen Honda began to supply customer V10s in 1992, Footwork enjoying four points-scoring races with the power unit.
- With three race victories for Senna and two for Berger, McLaren's season was humble by recent standards and ended in some disarray with no engine deal, uncertainty over Senna's future, and Berger off to Ferrari.

RACE 524, French GP: Red-flagged for rain after 18 laps, the restarted race was decided on aggregate, Mansell claiming his sixth victory from eight races.

■ Ron Dennis searched diligently for a replacement for Honda, working especially hard to acquire a Renault deal via Ligier, but finished up with a customer supply of the Ford HB engine. These engines would always be one development step behind the works units supplied to Benetton, hardly a spur to Senna for another year at McLaren.

■ Despite increasing EU pressure on tobacco advertising, McLaren's sponsor Marlboro celebrated 20 years in F1. They had begun with BRM but their red and white livery soon became emblematic of McLaren.

■ The use of electronic 'driver aids' or 'gizmos' such as active suspension, traction control and anti-lock brakes were becoming increasingly commonplace and McLaren were no exception, introducing the first fully-automatic gearbox in F1.

■ Benetton had no such gizmos but finished a close third behind McLaren in the constructors' battle. The Ross Brawn-designed Benetton B192 was an effective machine and the abstemious fuel consumption of the Ford Cosworth HB V8 invariably allowed it to go to the start-line with a weight advantage.

■ The team scored points in all 16 rounds and Schumacher finished third in the drivers' championship behind the Williams pair, winning his first GP at Spa, where he had debuted for Jordan last year.

Towards the end of 1991 after a period of 15 years Luca di Montezemolo returned as president at Ferrari. This was the first step in rebuilding the Scuderia, rudderless since Enzo Ferrari's death in 1988, having in the unsuccessful interim been managed rather then led by FIAT 'suits'. Harvey Postlethwaite returned as technical director, later joined by John Barnard.

The Brabham name, once a giant of F1, vanished during 1992, by now a caricature of its former glory. The team failed to show at Spa, which would have been their 400th championship participation. In its two triumphant periods under Sir Jack and later Bernie Ecclestone the marque won 35 races, bringing two championships to Piquet and one each to Brabham and Hulme.

Sorrowfully, 1992 saw the death of 1967 world champion Denny Hulme at the early age of 56, the first former champion to die of natural causes.

The Brabham team's final death throes was notable only for two of its drivers. Giovanna Amati became the fifth and (to date) final female to enter the F1 world championship, although in each of her three attempts to qualify she failed. Damon Hill, son of twice world champion Graham, qualified twice from eight attempts, making his F1 debut at Silverstone.

Another great F1 name, Team Lotus, also signalling terminal symptoms, rallied in 1992 under the stewardship of Peter Collins and Peter Wright. Drivers Häkkinen and Herbert picked up points on eight occasions, Häkkinen increasingly catching the eye.

At Suzuka diminutive Dutchman Jan Lammers set an unusual record, returning to race F1 after an absence of ten years and three months or 162 GPs. In the intervening years he competed in many forms of motorsport, including victory at Le Mans.

Championship ranking	Championship points	Driver nationality	1992 Drivers Championship Driver	Car	Races contested	Race victories	Podiumse excl. victories	Races led	Lights to flag victories	Laps led	Poles	Fastest laps	Triple Crowns
1	108	GBR	Nigel Mansell	Williams-Renault	16	9	3	14	6	693	14	8	4
2	56	ITA	Riccardo Patrese	Williams-Renault	16	1	8	8		174	1	3	
3	53	GER	Michael Schumacher	Benetton-Ford	16	1	7	1		11		2	
4	50	BRA	Ayrton Senna	McLaren-Honda	16	3	4	5		95	1	1	
5	49	AUT	Gerhard Berger	McLaren-Honda	16	2	3	2		63		2	
6	38	GBR	Martin Brundle	Benetton-Ford	16		5						
7	18	FRA	Jean Alesi	Ferrari	16		2						
8	11	FIN	Mika Häkkinen	Lotus-Ford	15								
9	8	ITA	Andrea de Cesaris	Tyrrell-Ilmor	16								
10	6	ITA	Michele Alboreto	Footwork-Mugen Honda	16								
11	4	FRA	Erik Comas	Ligier-Renault	15								
12	3	AUT	Karl Wendlinger	March-Ilmor	14								
13	3	ITA	Ivan Capelli	Ferrari	14								
14	2	BEL	Thierry Boutsen	Ligier-Renault	16								
15	2	ITA	Pierluigi Martini	Dallara-Ferrari	16								
15	2	GBR	Johnny Herbert	Lotus-Ford	16								
17	1	FRA	Bertrand Gachot	Larrousse-Lamborghini	16								
17	1	BRA	Christian Fittipaldi	Minardi-Lamborghini	10								
17	1	ITA	Stefano Modena	Jordan-Yamaha	12								

Championship ranking	Championship points	Team/Marque nationality	1992 Constructors Championship Chassis	Engine	Engine maker nationality	Races contested	Race victories	1-2 finishes	Podiums excl. victories	Races led	Laps led	Poles	Fastest laps
1	164	GBR	Williams FW14B	Renault 3.5 V10	FRA	16	10	6	11	15	867	15	11
2	99	GBR	McLaren MP4-7A, MP4-6B	Honda 3.5 V12	JPN	16	5		7	6	158	1	3
3	91	GBR	Benetton B192, B191B	Ford Cosworth 3.5 V8	GBR	16	1		12	1	11		2
4	21	ITA	Ferrari F92A, F92AT	Ferrari 3.5 V12	ITA	16			2				
5	13	GBR	Lotus 107, 102D	Ford Cosworth 3.5 V8	GBR	16							
6	8	GBR	Tyrrell 020B	Ilmor 3.5 V10	GBR	16							
7	6	GBR	Footwork FA13	Mugen Honda 3.5 V10	JPN	16							
7	6	FRA	Ligier JS37	Renault 3.5 V10	FRA	16							
9	3	GBR	March CG911	Ilmor 3.5 V10	GBR	16							
10	2	ITA	Dallara BMS192	Ferrari 3.5 V12	ITA	16							
11	1	FRA	Larrousse LC92	Lamborghini 3.5 V12	ITA	16							
11	1	ITA	Minardi M192, M191B	Lamborghini 3.5 V12	ITA	16							
11	1	IRL	Jordan 192	Yamaha 3.5 V12	JPN	16							

1993

Prost's come-back trail

THE TALE OF THE TITLE

■ As predicted, Alain Prost and Williams-Renault ruled the 1993 championships.
■ Of Prost's seven race victories, a four-in-a-row sequence mid-season put the title beyond doubt.
■ Up to then Senna matched him win for win, finally adding a further five to his and McLaren's tally.
■ These included a record sixth Monaco victory and McLaren's 104th race win, a Ferrari-topping total.
■ Until mid-season Senna drove for McLaren on a freelance basis, then signed with Williams for 1994.
■ Schumacher was victorious only once, despite Benetton's preferential treatment by Ford over McLaren.
■ The surprise package was Damon Hill, making history as the first second-generation GP winner.
■ Hill's hat-trick contributed towards another Williams-Renault constructors' title with ten race victories.
■ Fifteen poles was also indicative of Williams-Renault superiority, but a single 1-2 finish hinted at certain frailties.
■ Electronic 'driver aids' proliferated, FISA's move to outlaw them raising tensions with certain teams.
■ Yet again there would be no defence of the title, four-times champion Prost announcing his retirement.
■ And not forgetting: Senna's Donington lap.

THE CHASE FOR THE CHAMPIONSHIP

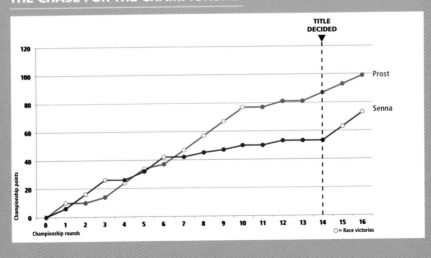

Williams-Renault FW15C

Round 1/16	**SOUTH AFRICAN GP** Kyalami							**Alain Prost**
	14 March 1993					Race 533		Williams-Renault FW15C 186.403kph, 115.825mph

Prost versus Senna resumed with a vengeance; vying for pole they finished 1.5s quicker than Schumacher in P3. Pole-man Prost started badly, lost another place when teammate Hill spun at turn one, which left the top three of the grid engaged in a terrific dice for the first 24 laps. Prost got the better of Schumacher on lap 13 and after a scrap relieved Senna of the lead on lap 24, pulling away to win by almost a lap. Senna and Schumacher battled over P2 until the German spun out on lap 40 when he clipped the McLaren attempting a pass. The race ended in a thunderstorm, just five cars still running. Notable finishers were returnee Mark Blundell, P3 in the Ligier-Renault, and an auspicious debut for Sauber, Lehto qualifying P6 and finishing P5.

POLE POSITION Prost, Williams-Renault, 1m 15.696s (0.088s), 202.647kph, 125.919mph
LAPS 72 x 4.261 km, 2.648 miles
DISTANCE 306.792 km, 190.632 miles
STARTERS/FINISHERS 26/7
WEATHER Overcast, warm, late rain
LAP LEADERS Senna 1-23 (23); Prost 24-72 (49)
WINNER'S LAPS 1-12 P3, 13-23 P2, 24-72 P1
FASTEST LAP Prost, Williams-Renault, 1m 19.492s (lap 40), 192.970kph, 119.906mph
CHAMPIONSHIP Prost 10, Senna 6, Blundell 4, Fittipaldi 3, Lehto 2

Pos	Driver	Car	Time/gap	Grid	Stops	Tyres
1	A Prost	Williams-Renault	1h 38m 45.082s	1	1	G
2	A Senna	McLaren-Ford	–1m 19.824s	2	1	G
3	M Blundell	Ligier-Renault	–1 lap	8	1	G
4	C Fittipaldi	Minardi-Ford	–1 lap	13	0	G
5	J J Lehto	Sauber-Ilmor	–2 laps	6	2	G
6r	G Berger	Ferrari	–3 laps	15	1	G

Round 2/16	**BRAZILIAN GP** Interlagos							**Ayrton Senna**
	28 March 1993					Race 534		McLaren-Ford MP4/8 165.601kph, 102.900mph

The Andretti/Berger first corner prang was a let-off for drivers and spectators alike. For 25 laps the race was a Williams romp until a deluge changed everything. Prost exited by aquaplaning into an accident-damaged car that littered the track, while Hill's resultant lead was eradicated by the Safety Car. The rain stopped quickly, the track began to dry, and Senna took the lead just as Hill rejoined from his switch back to slicks. So despite serving a stop-go penalty for a yellow flag transgression, divine providence had intervened in the shape of weather and the SC to assist Senna to a famous home victory and head Prost in the points table. Thanks to an early switch back to slicks, Herbert was heading for the podium until Schumacher pipped him three laps out.

POLE POSITION A Prost, Williams-Renault, 1m 15.866s (1.191s), 205.230kph, 127.524mph
LAPS 71 x 4.325 km, 2.687 miles
DISTANCE 307.075 km, 190.808 miles
STARTERS/FINISHERS 25/12
WEATHER Overcast, warm, dry then wet mid race
LAP LEADERS Prost 1-29 (29); Hill 30-41 (12); Senna 42-71 (30); SC 29-35 (7)
WINNER'S LAPS 1-10 P2, 11-23 P3, 24-27 P4, 28 P5, 29 P4, 30-40 P2, 41 P3, 42-71 P1
FASTEST LAP Schumacher, Benetton-Ford, 1m 20.024s (lap 61), 194.567kph, 120.898mph
CHAMPIONSHIP Senna 16, Prost 10, Hill 6, Blundell 6, Schumacher 4

Pos	Driver	Car	Time/gap	Grid	Stops	Tyres
1	A Senna	McLaren-Ford	1h 51m 15.485s	3	3	G
2	D Hill	Williams-Renault	–16.625s	2	2	G
3	M Schumacher	Benetton-Ford	–45.436s	4	2	G
4	J Herbert	Lotus-Ford	–46.557s	12	2	G
5	M Blundell	Ligier-Renault	–52.127s	10	2	G
6	A Zanardi	Lotus-Ford	–1 lap	15	2	G

McLaren-Ford MP4/8

Round 3/16	**EUROPEAN GP** Donington					
	11 April 1993				**Race 535**	

Starting P4 in pouring rain, Senna completed lap 1 in the lead. He dealt with Schumacher at Redgate, fast-starting Wendlinger around the outside of Craner Curves, Hill at Coppice and leader Prost at the Melbourne hairpin. Blending skill with strategy, Senna annihilated the Williams pair, both way ahead in dry qualifying. Track conditions fluctuated with each rain-squall, a record 63 pit stops as drivers switched between wets and slicks. Senna, optimally, made four stops plus – his pit crew unprepared – one drive-through. Hill made six stops to finish an unlapped second, while P3 went to the lapped Prost, who made seven on laps 19, 22, 33, 38, 48, 53 and 69. The other Brazilian star turn was rookie Barrichello, P3 with six to go when his Jordan failed.

Ayrton Senna
McLaren-Ford MP4/8 165.603kph, 102.901mph

POLE POSITION Prost, Williams-Renault, 1m 10.458s (0.304s), 205.552kph, 127.724mph
LAPS 76 x 4.023 km, 2.500 miles
DISTANCE 305.748 km, 189.983 miles
STARTERS/FINISHERS 25/11
WEATHER Overcast, cool, persistent rain showers
LAP LEADERS Senna 1-18, 20-34, 39-76 (71); Prost 19, 35-38 (5)
WINNER'S LAPS 1-18 P1, 19 P2, 20-34 P1, 35-38 P2, 39-76 P1
FASTEST LAP Senna, McLaren-Honda, 1m 18.029s (lap 57), 185.608kph, 115.331mph
CHAMPIONSHIP Senna 26, Prost 14, Hill 12, Blundell 6, Herbert 6

Pos	Driver	Car	Time/gap	Grid	Stops	Tyres
1	A Senna	McLaren-Ford	1h 50m 46.570s	4	5	G
2	D Hill	Williams-Renault	–1m 23.199s	2	6	G
3	A Prost	Williams-Renault	–1 lap	1	7	G
4	J Herbert	Lotus-Ford	–1 lap	11	1	G
5	R Patrese	Benetton-Ford	–2 laps	10	4	G
6	F Barbazza	Minardi-Ford	–2 laps	20	2	G

TOP **100** RACE

Round 4/16	**SAN MARINO GP** Imola					
	25 April 1993				**Race 536**	

Freelancer Senna, 'pissed off' by Ford's refusal to supply their latest engine, was almost a no-show. Arriving late direct from Brazil he shunted three times in practice to qualify behind the Williams pair and Schumacher, powered by the engine he craved. On a wet track Prost made a slow start from pole, so it was Hill leading his first GP and going away. Behind him, Senna and Prost slugged it out. Once overtaken on lap 8, Senna pitted for slicks, briefly bouncing ahead again. But by staying on wets too long Hill's 20s lead evaporated and on lap 12, exiting Tosa, Prost took Senna and Hill in a single incisive move and drove away to win. Neither Hill nor Senna finished, so, with two race wins apiece, Prost narrowed the points gap to Senna.

Alain Prost
Williams-Renault FW15C 197.625kph, 122.799mph

POLE POSITION Prost, Williams-Renault, 1m 22.070s (0.098s), 221.080kph, 137.372mph
LAPS 61 x 5.040 km, 3.132 miles
DISTANCE 307.440 km, 191.034 miles
STARTERS/FINISHERS 25/9
WEATHER Overcast, cool, wet initially, drying later
LAP LEADERS Hill 1-11 (11); Prost 12-61 (50)
WINNER'S LAPS 1-6 P3, 7-9 P2, 10-11 P3, 12-61 P1
FASTEST LAP Prost, Williams-Renault, 1m 26.128s (lap 42), 210.663kph, 130.900mph
CHAMPIONSHIP Senna 26, Prost 24, Hill 12, Schumacher 10, Blundell 6

Pos	Driver	Car	Time/gap	Grid	Stops	Tyres
1	A Prost	Williams-Renault	1h 33m 20.413s	1	1	G
2	M Schumacher	Benetton-Ford	–32.410s	3	1	G
3	M Brundle	Ligier-Renault	–1 lap	10	1	G
4r	J J Lehto	Sauber-Ilmor	–2 laps	16	1	G
5	P Alliot	Larrousse-Lamborghini	–2 laps	14	1	G
6	F Barbazza	Minardi-Ford	–2 laps	25	1	G

Round 5/16	**SPANISH GP** Cataluña **9 May 1993** **Race 537**	**Alain Prost** Williams-Renault FW15C 200.227kph, 124.415mph

The front row Williams pair made it a race of their own, Hill beating Prost away to lead the first ten laps. Even when he got by, Prost couldn't pull away, hampered by a severe vibration that was sapping the older man's stamina. Hill's car was fine and with no team orders it looked that the race might go his way, 25 years since father Graham's famous 1968 Spanish victory. But with 25 laps left Hill's Renault let go and Prost could now stroke it home well ahead of Senna and Schumacher, his championship lead restored. For the fourth time the 'customer' McLaren beat the 'works' Benetton, but despairing for the Ford-powered teams was that Prost hadn't stopped for tyres. The Andretti McLaren made its first finish, fifth but at least in the points.

POLE POSITION Prost, Williams-Renault, 1m 17.809s (0.537s), 219.630kph, 136.472mph
LAPS 65 x 4.747 km, 2.950 miles
DISTANCE 308.555 km, 191.727 miles
STARTERS/FINISHERS 25/14
WEATHER Cloudy with sunny intervals, warm, dry
LAP LEADERS Hill 1-10 (10); Prost 11-65 (55)
WINNER'S LAPS 1-10 P2, 11-65 P1
FASTEST LAP Schumacher, Benetton-Ford, 1m 20.898s (lap 61), 211.006kph, 131.113mph
CHAMPIONSHIP Prost 34, Senna 32, Schumacher 14, Hill 12, Blundell 6

Pos	Driver	Car	Time/gap	Grid	Stops	Tyres
1	A Prost	Williams-Renault 1h 32m 27.685s		1	0	G
2	A Senna	McLaren-Ford	–16.873s	3	1	G
3	M Schumacher	Benetton-Ford	–27.125s	4	1	G
4	R Patrese	Benetton-Ford	–1 lap	5	0	G
5	M Andretti	McLaren-Ford	–1 lap	7	1	G
6	G Berger	Ferrari	–2 laps	11	1	G

Round 6/16	**MONACO GP** Monte Carlo **23 May 1993** **Race 538**	**Ayrton Senna** McLaren-Ford MP4/8 138.837kph, 86.269mph

In winning his sixth Monaco GP, Senna surpassed Graham Hill's 24-year record. Unusually he qualified only P3, suffering a damaged thumb after a heavy shunt at Ste Devote on the wet Thursday morning. This injury perhaps explained why in the race he steadily fell away from pole-man Prost chased by Schumacher, the Benetton at last equipped with traction control. But Prost was deemed to have jumped the start and on lap 12 served a 10s stop-go, rejoining a lapped P22 after stalling twice. Schumacher's comfortable lead over Senna lasted until lap 32 when he retired with hydraulics failure. Hill finished behind Senna despite being clouted by Berger at the chicane seven laps from home. Alesi's Ferrari completed the podium, Prost a fighting fourth.

POLE POSITION Prost, Williams-Renault, 1m 20.557s (0.633s), 148.725kph, 92.413mph
LAPS 78 x 3.328 km, 2.068 miles
DISTANCE 259.584 km, 161.298 miles
STARTERS/FINISHERS 25/14
WEATHER Cloudy, warm, dry
LAP LEADERS Prost 1-11 (11); Schumacher 12-32 (21); Senna 33-78 (46)
WINNER'S LAPS 1-11 P3, 12-32 P2, 33-78 P1
FASTEST LAP Prost, Williams-Renault, 1m 23.604s (lap 52), 143.304kph, 89.045mph
CHAMPIONSHIP Senna 42, Prost 37, Hill 18, Schumacher 14, Blundell 6

Pos	Driver	Car	Time/gap	Grid	Stops	Tyres
1	A Senna	McLaren-Ford	1h 52m 10.947s	3	1	G
2	D Hill	Williams-Renault	–52.118s	4	0	G
3	J Alesi	Ferrari	–1m 3.362s	5	0	G
4	A Prost	Williams-Renault	–1 lap	1	1	G
5	C Fittipaldi	Minardi-Ford	–2 laps	17	0	G
6	M Brundle	Ligier-Renault	–2 laps	13	1	G

Round 7/16	**CANADIAN GP** Montréal **13 June 1993** **Race 539**	**Alain Prost** Williams-Renault FW15C 189.667kph, 117.853mph

Prost won from his seventh consecutive pole, building a 10s gap then sitting on it. Hill led the first five laps but once by no one could live with Prost's pace. Behind, Hill comfortably held Senna at bay until a botched tyre change dropped him to fourth, eventually finishing third. Thankfully, the race was kept alive by Schumacher and Senna's battle over P2. It began unusually, Schumacher making a dreadful start, dropping to seventh from P3, while Senna rocketed up to fourth on lap 1 and third by lap 2 from his lowly P8 grid slot, his poorest qualification in a McLaren. Over 50 laps Schumacher nibbled away at the 8s deficit to Senna, a potentially thrilling finish marred when Senna's alternator broke seven laps from the end.

POLE POSITION Prost, Williams-Renault, 1m 18.987s (0.504s), 201.907kph, 125.459mph
LAPS 69 x 4.430 km, 2.753 miles
DISTANCE 305.670 km, 189.935 miles
STARTERS/FINISHERS 25/18
WEATHER Cloudy with sunny intervals, hot, dry
LAP LEADERS Hill 1-5 (5); Prost 6-69 (64)
WINNER'S LAPS 1-5 P2, 6-69 P1
FASTEST LAP Schumacher, Benetton-Ford, 1m 21.500s (Lap 57), 195.681kph, 121.591mph
CHAMPIONSHIP Prost 47, Senna 42, Hill 22, Schumacher 20, Brundle 7

Pos	Driver	Car	Time/gap	Grid	Stops	Tyres
1	A Prost	Williams-Renault	1h 36m 41.822s	1	1	G
2	M Schumacher	Benetton-Ford	–14.527s	3	1	G
3	D Hill	Williams-Renault	–52.685s	2	1	G
4	G Berger	Ferrari	–1 lap	5	1	G
5	M Brundle	Ligier-Renault	–1 lap	7	1	G
6	K Wendlinger	Sauber-Ilmor	–1 lap	9	1	G

| Round 8/16 | **FRENCH GP** Magny-Cours | | | | | | **Alain Prost** |
| | **4 July 1993** | | | **Race 540** | | | Williams-Renault FW15C 186.231kph, 115.718mph |

Not a great race, although the French crowd went home pleased. On the grid Renault-engined cars started 1-2-3-4, the last two a pair of Ligiers. And for the first 20 laps that's how the four remained until Blundell's Ligier was punted off passing a backmarker. Brundle's sister car kept P3 for 46 laps but ultimately gave best to the race-long Schumacher/Senna squabble. Benetton resolved this strategically with a second tyre stop, using fresher rubber to catch and pass the tyre-worn McLaren nine laps from the finish. So in France a Frenchman led home a Williams-Renault 1-2, the team's first of the season. From his maiden pole Hill only narrowly lost his lead at the stops, dutifully finishing on Prost's tail, hoping maybe for a return complement at Silverstone.

POLE POSITION Hill, Williams-Renault, 1m 14.382s (0.142), 205.695kph, 127.813mph
LAPS 72 x 4.250 km, 2.641 miles
DISTANCE 306.000 km, 190.140 miles
STARTERS/FINISHERS 25/16
WEATHER Cloudy with sunny intervals, hot, dry
LAP LEADERS Hill 1-26 (26); Prost 27-72 (46)
WINNER'S LAPS 1-26 P2, 27-72 P1
FASTEST LAP Schumacher, Benetton-Ford, 1m 19.256s (lap 47), 193.045kph, 119.953mph
CHAMPIONSHIP Prost 57, Senna 45, Hill 28, Schumacher 24, Brundle 9

Pos	Driver	Car	Time/gap	Grid	Stops	Tyres
1	A Prost	Williams-Renault	1h 38m 35.241s	2	1	G
2	D Hill	Williams-Renault	−0.342s	1	1	G
3	M Schumacher	Benetton-Ford	−21.209s	7	2	G
4	A Senna	McLaren-Ford	−32.405s	5	1	G
5	M Brundle	Ligier-Renault	−33.795s	3	2	G
6	M Andretti	McLaren-Ford	−1 lap	16	2	G

| Round 9/16 | **BRITISH GP** Silverstone | | | | | | **Alain Prost** |
| | **11 July 1993** | | | **Race 541** | | | Williams-Renault FW15C 216.030kph, 134.235mph |

Another tentative Prost start from pole had him trapped behind Senna for six laps. To the delight of the British crowd this enabled Hill to draw away to an 8s lead which he held, albeit narrowing, both through the tyre stops as well as a SC period, controversially deployed to retrieve a car supposedly abandoned unsafely. Racing resumed on lap 40, and with Prost now closed right up Hill put the hammer down, recording a big fastest lap on lap 41. Next time round, only 18 to go, his Renault let go spectacularly, a gushing plume of smoke followed by a blaze. Silverstone proved the turning point in the championship, Prost's hat-trick victory along with Senna's fuel-starved loss of third place abruptly opening a yawning 20-point deficit.

POLE POSITION Prost, Williams-Renault, 1m 19.006s (0.128s), 238.129kph, 147.966mph
LAPS 59 x 5.226 km, 3.247 miles
DISTANCE 308.334 km, 191.590 miles
STARTERS/FINISHERS 25/14
WEATHER Overcast, cool, dry
LAP LEADERS Hill 1-41 (41); Prost 42-59 (18); SC 37-39 (3)
WINNER'S LAPS 1-6 P3, 7-41 P2, 42-59 P1
FASTEST LAP Hill, Williams-Renault, 1m 22.515s (lap 41), 228.002kph, 141.674mph
CHAMPIONSHIP Prost 67, Senna 47, Schumacher 30, Hill 28, Patrese 9

Pos	Driver	Car	Time/gap	Grid	Stops	Tyres
1	A Prost	Williams-Renault	1h 25m 42.991s	1	1	G
2	M Schumacher	Benetton-Ford	−7.660s	3	1	G
3	R Patrese	Benetton-Ford	−1m 17.482s	5	1	G
4	J Herbert	Lotus-Ford	−1m 18.407s	7	1	G
5r	A Senna	McLaren-Ford	−1 lap	4	1	G
6	D Warwick	Footwork-Mugen Honda	−1 lap	8	1	G

| Round 10/16 | **GERMAN GP** Hockenheim | | | | | | **Alain Prost** |
| | **25 July 1993** | | | **Race 542** | | | Williams-Renault FW15C 233.861kph, 145.314mph |

Warwick's car flipped during the wet warm-up, trapped driver thankfully unscathed. Once again Prost won, but Hill starred, leading comfortably when a puncture robbed him on the penultimate lap; unlike many, Hill went the distance without a tyre change, but debris was thought the cause. Pole-man Prost had allowed Hill and Schumacher to get away at the start but on lap 6 took the Benetton and on lap 8 the lead. Almost at once he served a stop-go for missing the second chicane on lap 1, dubious because it was unavoidable. From P6 he regained P2 in six laps and ultimately his fourth successive win. Schumacher pleased the locals with P2, Senna storming back to P4 from a first lap spin when he toughed it out with Prost at the first chicane.

POLE POSITION Prost, Williams-Renault, 1m 38.748s (0.157s), 248.451kph, 154.380mph
LAPS 45 x 6.815 km, 4.235 miles
DISTANCE 306.675 km, 190.559 miles
STARTERS/FINISHERS 26/17
WEATHER Cloudy with sunny intervals, warm, dry
LAP LEADERS D Hill, Williams-Renault 1-7, 10-43 (41); Prost 8-9, 44-45 (4)
WINNER'S LAPS 1-5 P5, 6-7 P2, 8-9 P1, 10 P3, 11 P6, 12-13 P5, 14-15 P4, 16 P3, 17-43 P2, 44-45 P1
FASTEST LAP Schumacher, Benetton-Ford, 1m 41.859s (lap 40), 240.862kph, 149.665mph
CHAMPIONSHIP Prost 77, Senna 50, Schumacher 36, Hill 28, Patrese 11

Pos	Driver	Car	Time/gap	Grid	Stops	Tyres
1	A Prost	Williams-Renault	1h 18m 40.885s	1	1	G
2	M Schumacher	Benetton-Ford	−16.664s	3	2	G
3	M Blundell	Ligier-Renault	−59.349s	5	1	G
4	A Senna	McLaren-Ford	−1m 8.229s	4	2	G
5	R Patrese	Benetton-Ford	−1m 31.516s	7	1	G
6	G Berger	Ferrari	−1m 34.754s	9	0	G

Round 11/16	**HUNGARIAN GP** Hungaroring		**Damon Hill**
	15 August 1993	Race 543	Williams-Renault FW15C 170.292kph, 105.814mph

Building steadily towards a maiden victory here it was at last, a lights-to-flag win in Hill's 13th GP. Pole-sitter Prost stalled prior to the parade lap, starting from the back, while Senna (throttle) and Schumacher (fuel pump) went out before one-third-distance, neither looking a winner beforehand. But Hill did, and was, and while his task was eased by the opposition's failure, his was a copybook two-stop race performance. Patrese came second, his best result so far for Benetton, while Berger spent a typically forceful afternoon rewarded with a podium. Prost scythed from 26th to fourth in 19 laps but spent ten minutes in the pits with rear-wing trouble to finish 12th and last. But his 27-point championship lead stayed intact, with Hill now third.

POLE POSITION A Prost, Williams-Renault, 1m 14.631s (0.204s), 191.406kph, 118.934mph
LAPS 77 x 3.968 km, 2.466 miles
DISTANCE 305.536 km, 189.851 miles
STARTERS/FINISHERS 26/12
WEATHER Sunny, very hot, dry
LAP LEADERS Hill 1-77 (77)
WINNER'S LAPS 1-77 P1
FASTEST LAP A Prost, Williams-Renault, 1m 19.633s (lap 52), 179.383kph, 111.463mph
CHAMPIONSHIP Prost 77, Senna 50, Hill 38, Schumacher 36, Patrese 17

Pos	Driver	Car	Time/gap	Grid	Stops	Tyres
1	D Hill	Williams-Renault	1h 47m 39.098s	2	2	G
2	R Patrese	Benetton-Ford	–1m 11.915s	5	2	G
3	G Berger	Ferrari	–1m 18.042s	6	2	G
4	D Warwick	Footwork-Mugen Honda	–1 lap	9	1	G
5	M Brundle	Ligier-Renault	–1 lap	13	2	G
6	K Wendlinger	Sauber-Ilmor	–1 lap	17	2	G

Round 12/16	**BELGIAN GP** Spa Francorchamps		**Damon Hill**
	29 August 1993	Race 544	Williams-Renault FW15C 217.795kph, 135.331mph

There was carnage at Eau Rouge when Zanardi survived a 150mph practice accident. In the race Hill did it again, winning convincingly. Third on lap 1, he forced by the fast-starting Senna on the climb from Eau Rouge then lap by lap shadowed leader Prost, a good start from pole for once. Prost's second tyre stop on lap 30 was sluggish, and Hill, already on fresh rubber, pounced. On his rejoining lap Prost was also mugged at Les Combes by Schumacher, who now set off after Hill. But for an appalling start Schumacher might have won, recovering from ninth on lap 1 to fourth by lap 4, separating Senna from P3 on lap 14. But Ultimately Hill had Schumacher's measure, and with their ninth win this year Williams retained their constructors' trophy.

POLE POSITION Prost, Williams-Renault, 1m 47.571s (0.895s), 233.394kph, 145.024mph
LAPS 44 x 6.974 km, 4.333 miles
DISTANCE 306.856 km, 190.671 miles
STARTERS/FINISHERS 25/15
WEATHER Cloudy with sunny intervals, hot, dry
LAP LEADERS Prost 1-30 (30); Hill 31-44 (14)
WINNER'S LAPS 1 P3, 2-12 P2, 13 P3, 14-30 P2, 31-44 P1
FASTEST LAP Prost, Williams-Renault, 1m 51.095s (lap 41), 225.990kph, 140.424mph
CHAMPIONSHIP Prost 81, Senna 53, Hill 48, Schumacher 42, Patrese 18

Pos	Driver	Car	Time/gap	Grid	Stops	Tyres
1	D Hill	Williams-Renault	1h 24m 32.124s	2	2	G
2	M Schumacher	Benetton-Ford	–3.668s	3	2	G
3	A Prost	Williams-Renault	–14.988s	1	2	G
4	A Senna	McLaren-Ford	–1m 39.763s	5	1	G
5	J Herbert	Lotus-Ford	–1 lap	10	1	G
6	R Patrese	Benetton-Ford	–1 lap	8	1	G

Round 13/16	**ITALIAN GP** Monza		**Damon Hill**
	12 September 1993	Race 545	Williams-Renault FW15C 239.144kph, 148.597mph

Prost could seal his title at Monza, but after leading every lap his engine blew five short of the championship, bringing teammate Hill a victory hat-trick. Hill's lap 1 clash with Senna at the first chicane delayed them both, but while Senna retired on lap 9 following yet another collision, Hill picked-off those ahead, tigering from P9 on lap 1 to third behind Schumacher by lap 10. After the tyre stops, with Schumacher out, Hill made up the 20s gap in seven laps and was shadowing his team leader when Prost's engine failed without warning. Alesi brought joy to the *tifosi* with second but in the scramble for the line the Minardis touched, Christian Fittipaldi surviving a miraculous back-flip midair loop-the-loop. Andretti's podium held some poignancy.

POLE POSITION A Prost, Williams-Renault, 1m 21.179s (0.312s), 257.209kph, 159.822mph
LAPS 53 x 5.800 km, 3.604 miles
DISTANCE 307.400 km, 191.010 miles
STARTERS/FINISHERS 26/14
WEATHER Sunny, hot, dry
LAP LEADERS Prost 1-48 (48); Hill 49-53 (5)
WINNER'S LAPS 1 P9, 2 P8, 3-4 P7, 5 P5, 6-9 P4, 10-21 P3, 22-48 P2, 49-53 P1
FASTEST LAP Hill, Williams-Renault, 1m 23.575s (lap 45), 249.835kph, 155.241mph
CHAMPIONSHIP Prost 81, Hill 58, Senna 53, Schumacher 42, Patrese 20

Pos	Driver	Car	Time/gap	Grid	Stops	Tyres
1	D Hill	Williams-Renault	1h 17m 7.509s	2	1	G
2	J Alesi	Ferrari	–40.012s	3	1	G
3	M Andretti	McLaren-Ford	–1 lap	9	2	G
4	K Wendlinger	Sauber-Ilmor	–1 lap	15	1	G
5	R Patrese	Benetton-Ford	–1 lap	10	2	G
6	E Comas	Larrousse-Lamborghini	–2 laps	20	0	G

Benetton-Ford B193B

Round 14/16	**PORTUGUESE GP** Estoril						**Michael Schumacher**
	26 September 1993				Race 546		Benetton-Ford B193B 199.748kph, 124.118mph

On Friday Prost announced his retirement and Senna made known he was departing McLaren for Williams. Häkkinen's McLaren debut started well, out-qualifying Senna, but finished badly when he crashed out on lap 33. Problems relegated pole-man Hill to the back, his absence assisting Alesi to carve through from P5 and lead the opening 19 laps, chased closely by Senna until his engine blew. Now Prost led but Schumacher, making a tactically astute early tyre stop, took the lead during Prost's pit stop. Over the final 20 laps Schumacher's lead was rarely more then a second, but only a mistake, which never came, would change things, Prost more intent on securing his title. Hill came third, taking just 22 laps to reach P2 from dead last.

POLE POSITION Hill, Williams-Renault, 1m 11.494s (0.189s), 219.039kph, 136.105mph
LAPS 71 x 4.350 km, 2.703 miles
DISTANCE 308.850 km, 191.910 miles
STARTERS/FINISHERS 26/16
WEATHER Sunny, warm, dry, windy
LAP LEADERS Alesi 1-19 (19); Prost 20-29 (10); Schumacher 30-71 (42)
WINNER'S LAPS 1-19 P5, 20-21 P2, 22-29 P3, 30-71 P1
FASTEST LAP Hill, Williams-Renault, 1m 14.859s (lap 68), 209.193kph, 129.897mph
CHAMPIONSHIP Prost 87, Hill 62, Senna 53, Schumacher 52, Patrese 20

Pos	Driver	Car	Time/gap	Grid	Stops	Tyres
1	M Schumacher	Benetton-Ford	1h 32m 46.309s	6	1	G
2	A Prost	Williams-Renault	−0.982s	2	1	G
3	D Hill	Williams-Renault	−8.206s	1	1	G
4	J Alesi	Ferrari	−1m 7.605s	5	2	G
5	K Wendlinger	Sauber-Ilmor	−1 lap	13	1	G
6	M Brundle	Ligier-Renault	−1 lap	11	2	G

Round 15/16	**JAPANESE GP** Suzuka						**Ayrton Senna**
	24 October 1993				Race 547		McLaren-Ford MP4/8 185.612kph, 115.334mph

New champion Prost on pole, Senna alongside. Their closely matched race lasted until rain around lap 15. This played to Senna's strengths on track while Prost was delayed during his switch to wets, and that's how it ended. Häkkinen impressively qualified and finished third while Hill came fourth despite qualifying poorly and being clouted by Schumacher in their early dice with Berger. Fifth and sixth – their first points of the season – were the Jordans. Suzuka specialist and F1 debutant Eddie Irvine out-qualified teammate Barrichello and after a bullet start lay fifth on lap 1. On lap 34 leader Senna lapped him, but Irvine, engaged in a battle with Hill, briefly repassed Senna. Afterwards the Brazilian infamously attacked him, verbally and physically.

POLE POSITION Prost, Williams-Renault, 1m 37.154s (0.130s), 217.288kph, 135.017mph
LAPS 53 x 5.864 km, 3.644 miles
DISTANCE 310.792 km, 193.117 miles
STARTERS/FINISHERS 24/14
WEATHER Cloudy, warm, then cool and wet
LAP LEADERS Senna 1-13, 21-53 (46); Prost 14-20 (7)
WINNER'S LAPS 1-13 P1, 14-20 P2, 21-53 P1
FASTEST LAP Prost, Williams-Renault, 1m 41.176s (lap 53), 208.650kph, 129.649mph
CHAMPIONSHIP Prost 93, Hill 65, Senna 63, Schumacher 52, Patrese 20

Pos	Driver	Car	Time/gap	Grid	Stops	Tyres
1	A Senna	McLaren-Ford	1h 40m 27.912s	2	2	G
2	A Prost	Williams-Renault	−11.435s	1	2	G
3	M Häkkinen	McLaren-Ford	−26.129s	3	3	G
4	D Hill	Williams-Renault	−1m 23.538s	6	3	G
5	R Barrichello	Jordan-Hart	−1m 35.101s	12	2	G
6	E Irvine	Jordan-Hart	−1m 46.421s	8	2	G

AUSTRALIAN GP Adelaide

7 November 1993   Race 548

Ayrton Senna

McLaren-Ford MP4/8 173.183kph, 107.611mph

Senna's pole was Williams-Renault's only lapse of the season, Senna having the measure of the Williams pair here. Apart from Prost's brief lead during the initial tyre stops nothing would come between Senna and his farewell gift to McLaren, a victory that also brought the accolade 'most successful team in F1 championship history'. Hill's attempt to wrest second from Prost ended with a spin, but he still finished third in the race as well as the championship, behind Senna but ahead of Schumacher, the latter ending the season poorly with no points again. On the podium it was the end of an era, for Senna farewell to McLaren, for Prost au revoir to F1. In a display of reconciliation, Senna pulled Prost up beside him on the top step. Prost versus Senna was over.

POLE POSITION Senna, McLaren-Ford, 1m 13.371s (0.436s), 185.468kph, 115.245mph
LAPS 79 x 3.780 km, 2.349 miles
DISTANCE 298.620 km, 185.554 miles
STARTERS/FINISHERS 24/15
WEATHER Cloudy with sunny intervals, warm, dry
LAP LEADERS Senna 1-23, 29-79 (74); Prost 24-28 (5)
WINNER'S LAPS 1-23 P1, 24-28 P2, 29-79 P1
FASTEST LAP Hill, Williams-Renault, 1m 15.381s (lap 64), 180.523kph, 112.172mph
CHAMPIONSHIP Prost 99, Senna 73, Hill 69, Schumacher 52, Patrese 20

Pos	Driver	Car	Time/gap	Grid	Stops	Tyres
1	A Senna	McLaren-Ford	1h 43m 27.476s	1	2	G
2	A Prost	Williams-Renault	−9.259s	2	2	G
3	D Hill	Williams-Renault	−33.902s	3	2	G
4	J Alesi	Ferrari	−1 lap	7	1	G
5	G Berger	Ferrari	−1 lap	6	2	G
6	M Brundle	Ligier-Renault	−1 lap	8	2	G

1993 CHAMPIONSHIP FACTS AND FOLKLORE

■ The governing body implemented a package of measures designed to address safety and cost. These included smaller wings and narrower tyres, Goodyear still the exclusive provider.

■ The Safety Car concept was introduced, to be utilised whenever warranted by unfavourable track conditions, primarily caused by weather or accidents. The SC had first appeared 20 years before at the 1973 Canadian GP, but now it became a permanent feature, first deployed at the second round in Brazil.

■ The 16-round championship would be contested by 13 teams, March going bust and never making an appearance, while a new Swiss team, Sauber, joined the grid, their car powered by the Ilmor V10.

■ Sauber had formed a successful partnership with Mercedes-Benz to run the Silver Arrows team in sports car racing. Now they provided a first step for Mercedes-Benz to re-enter F1 after almost 40 years, Stuttgart providing technical assistance to Sauber via their part-ownership of Ilmor engines, which would be badged Mercedes in 1994.

■ It was something of a forgone conclusion that the 1993 titles would go to Prost and Williams, and so it transpired, although in the early part of the season Senna didn't make things at all easy for his rival.

■ By the sixth round at Monaco the two protagonists shared the race victories, Senna's successes including possibly 'the greatest lap ever raced' at the one and only championship GP to be held at Donington, and his sixth Monaco triumph, exceeding Graham Hill's 25-year record. It was astonishing to realise that the last time anyone but Senna or Prost won at Monaco was Keke Rosberg in 1983.

■ After this Prost won four on the trot, effectively putting the title out of Senna's reach, although following this burst of success he surprisingly failed to win again over the balance of the season – but his seven-race haul was more than enough to see off Senna with five race victories.

■ The second seat at Williams had finally gone to their test driver, Damon Hill, son of double world champion Graham. Damon took a hat-trick of wins, making history as the very first second-generation GP winner.

■ At Spa Renault celebrated their 50th GP victory. Renault's massive contribution to the continuing success of Williams should not be underestimated, although a glance at the modest achievements of the Renault-powered Ligiers confirmed that to succeed, a fine power unit needed a fine car.

■ Having taken a sabbatical in 1992, Prost had to adapt to the numerous electronic gizmos now adorning the Williams-Renault, the FW15C probably the most technologically sophisticated F1 racing car of all time. Electronics intervened between driver and car for engine, gearbox, suspension and brakes.

■ In February FISA announced that all such electronic gadgetry would be outlawed from next year and a highly charged political wrangle broke out, broadly Max Mosley supported by Bernie Ecclestone versus Ron Dennis and Frank Williams.

■ McLaren and Williams were particularly aggrieved because it was they who had invested the most time and money into the development of electronic gizmos. Ron and Frank were also incensed because of the shortness of the notice given for technical change, which contravened the statutes of the Concorde Agreement.

■ The rationale for the ban was threefold. First, electronic driver aids would increasingly dehumanise and therefore devalue the drivers' world championship. Second, the R&D necessary would massively escalate F1 costs. Third, their removal would somewhat re-level the playing field for the less wealthy teams, which were being left behind.

■ Banning this avenue of technological development in F1, a series that prided itself as the pinnacle of motorsport technology, was a paradox. But if allowed to let rip where would it end, and many supported Mosley's stand. A glimpse of where it might lead was McLaren's new groundbreaking send-receive telemetry system first used at Donington. Remote adjustments by engineers was regarded as the logical next step.

■ Mosley got his way by threatening to disqualify any car currently using traction control or active suspension, citing violation of extant rules with which few could argue. The message was simple, accept the 1994 electronics ban or they would be made illegal with immediate effect.

■ A major restructuring of the governing body took place in

RACE 535, European GP: Track conditions at Donington fluctuated with each
rain squall, but blending skill with strategy, Senna annihilated the Williams pair.

October. FISA was disbanded and the FIA resurrected to
control the governance of world motorsport. At its head sat
the recently elected president of the FIA, Max Mosley.

- At the beginning of the season Prost had been dragged in
front of the FIA world council to answer for remarks he had
made in a magazine article considered defamatory to F1. He
was exonerated but this and other factors caused him to fall
out of love with F1 during the year and he announced his
retirement in September. Four drivers' championships and a
record 51 victories from 199 races was a remarkable legacy.

- His departure finally brought the extraordinary saga of Prost
versus Senna to a conclusion. Over nine seasons they had
raced against one another in 140 GPs, Prost winning 35
times, Senna 38.

- But Senna would race on as, gizmos or no gizmos, he
wanted a seat at Williams for 1994 and Prost's absence
opened the way.

- In this his final season with McLaren, the team that had
brought him all three of his world titles, Senna was unwilling
to make a firm commitment, turning up to race on an ad hoc
basis, finally signing for the remainder of the season before
round eight in France.

- He was provided with the McLaren MP4/8 bristling with
gizmos but fitted with a customer Ford HB engine, one
development step behind the V8 supplied to Ford's works
team, Benetton. Senna and Dennis tried everything to break
down Benetton's inevitable resistance to engine parity, but
from Silverstone it was granted.

- Their case rested on some plain facts: by Monaco, round
six, Senna was leading the championship with three wins
and two podiums. By contrast, Benetton-Ford's lead driver,
Schumacher, had just three podiums to his name.

- From then on, strong mid-season development saw
Schumacher make the running, and it wasn't until McLaren
improved suspension software and aero – the team one of
the first to add barge boards/turning vanes – that the car
came good for two more end-of-season victories.

- In Brazil Senna had scored McLaren's 100th GP win, and
with his final victory in Australia McLaren became the most
successful team in world championship history, exceeding
Ferrari's 103 wins from 521 GPs. McLaren's 104 came from
394 championship races.

- Michael Andretti, Senna's teammate, had a dispiriting F1
sojourn, replaced from Estoril by Mika Häkkinen just as

the difficult MP4/8 was coming good, test driver Häkkinen promptly out-qualifying Senna. Andretti was the first American to drive in F1 since Eddie Cheever in 1989. The next would be Scott Speed in 2006.

■ In his final race Andretti stood on the podium at Monza, the place where father Mario and twin brother Aldo, aged 14, first caught F1 fever watching Ascari's Ferrari battle with Fangio's Mercedes at the 1954 GP.

■ Benetton's B193B debuted at Donington with a full range of gizmos apart from traction control. Cosworth were initially reluctant to expose Ford's latest Series VII HB engine, equipped with pneumatic valves, to the harshness of this methodology. This meant Benetton did not have the advantage of traction control until the sixth round at Monaco.

■ From then on Schumacher took over from Senna in taking the fight to Williams, winning in Estoril but finishing the season lamely with two dnfs.

■ Teammate Patrese seemed to lose his mojo in 1993, which was perhaps not entirely surprising in his 17th F1 season. He retired after participating in his record 256 GPs, winning six.

■ Benetton were one of two teams to look for something radical, experimenting with four-wheel steering, the rears deflecting a maximum of 5°. The other was Williams, which tested CVT (continuously variable transmission).

■ Ferrari endured a third successive winless season, a record 50 races since their last triumph. The rebuilding process continued with the arrival of Jean Todt as sporting director, formerly the highly successful boss of Peugeot Talbot Sport.

■ James Hunt, 1976 world champion and latter-day BBC television commentator, died of a heart attack at the early age of 45.

Championship ranking	Championship points	Driver nationality	1993 Drivers Championship		Races contested	Race victories	Podiumse excl. victories	Races led	Lights to flag victories	Laps led	Poles	Fastest laps	Triple Crowns
			Driver	Car									
1	99	FRA	Alain Prost	Williams-Renault	16	7	5	15		431	13	6	2
2	73	BRA	Ayrton Senna	McLaren-Ford	16	5	2	6		290	1	1	
3	69	GBR	Damon Hill	Williams-Renault	16	3	7	10	1	242	2	4	
4	52	GER	Michael Schumacher	Benetton-Ford	16	1	8	2		63		5	
5	20	ITA	Riccardo Patrese	Benetton-Ford	16		2						
6	16	FRA	Jean Alesi	Ferrari	16		2	1		19			
7	13	GBR	Martin Brundle	Ligier-Renault	16		1						
8	12	AUT	Gerhard Berger	Ferrari	16		1						
9	11	GBR	Johnny Herbert	Lotus-Ford	16								
10	10	GBR	Mark Blundell	Ligier-Renault	16		2						
11	7	USA	Michael Andretti	McLaren-Ford	13		1						
12	7	AUT	Karl Wendlinger	Sauber-Ilmor	16								
13	5	FIN	J J Lehto	Sauber-Ilmor	16								
13	5	BRA	Christian Fittipaldi	Minardi-Ford	14								
15	4	FIN	Mika Häkkinen	McLaren-Ford	3			1					
16	4	GBR	Derek Warwick	Footwork-Mugen Honda	16								
17	2	FRA	Philippe Alliot	Larrousse-Lamborghini	14								
17	2	BRA	Rubens Barrichello	Jordan-Hart	16								
19	2	ITA	Fabrizio Barbazza	Minardi-Ford	8								
20	1	ITA	Alessandro Zanardi	Lotus-Ford	11								
20	1	FRA	Erik Comas	Larrousse-Lamborghini	16								
20	1	GBR	Eddie Irvine	Jordan-Hart	2								

Championship ranking	Championship points	Team/Marque nationality	1993 Constructors Championship		Engine maker nationality	Races contested	Race victories	1-2 finishes	Podiums excl. victories	Races led	Laps led	Poles	Fastest laps
			Chassis	Engine									
1	168	GBR	Williams FW15C	Renault 3.5 V10	FRA	16	10	1	12	16	673	15	10
2	84	GBR	McLaren MP4-8	Ford Cosworth 3.5 V8	GBR	16	5		4	6	290	1	1
3	72	GBR	Benetton B193A, B193B	Ford Cosworth 3.5 V8	GBR	16	1		10	2	63		5
4	28	ITA	Ferrari F93A	Ferrari 3.5 V12	ITA	16			3	1	19		
5	23	FRA	Ligier JS39	Renault 3.5 V10	FRA	16			3				
6	12	GBR	Lotus 107B	Ford Cosworth 3.5 V8	GBR	16							
7	12	SUI	Sauber C12	Ilmor 3.5 V10	GBR	16							
8	7	ITA	Minardi M193	Ford Cosworth 3.5 V8	GBR	16							
9	4	GBR	Footwork FA14, FA13B	Mugen Honda 3.5 V10	JPN	16							
10	3	FRA	Larrousse LH93	Lamborghini 3.5 V12	ITA	16							
10	3	IRL	Jordan 193	Hart 3.5 V10	GBR	16							

1994

Schumacher's smash and grab

THE TALE OF THE TITLE

- May Day 1994 will forever be remembered for the death of Ayrton Senna.
- At Tamburello, possibly the greatest-ever F1 driver died in front of a live global TV audience.
- At Imola and then at Monaco a devastating sequence of accidents shook the very foundations of F1.
- From this turmoil Michael Schumacher emerged as the dominant figure, winning the 1994 championship.
- But the first German to be hailed world champion wore a tarnished crown.
- There were persistent allegations over Benetton's illegal use of traction control.
- Other rule violations led to disqualification from two races and exclusion from two more.
- And finally, after blowing it, there was Schumacher's cynical removal of Hill at the Adelaide showdown.
- The FIA's ban on driver aids and the readoption of refuelling both had a marked impact on 1994.
- With eight wins, Schumacher and tactician Ross Brawn revelled in 'fuel strategy'-inspired sprint racing.
- For the third successive season Williams-Renault lifted the constructors' trophy with seven victories.
- After four years Ferrari ended their win drought, while McLaren began theirs.
- And not forgetting: Verstappen's pit-stop fireball; 'the plank'.

THE CHASE FOR THE CHAMPIONSHIP

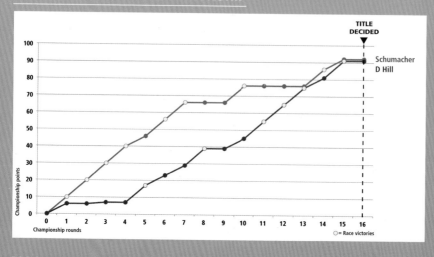

Benetton-Ford B194

Round 1/16	**BRAZILIAN GP** Interlagos	**Michael Schumacher**
	27 March 1994 Race 549	Benetton-Ford B194 192.632kph, 119.696mph

Schumacher stunned Brazil by winning the first round in Ayrton's backyard. From pole, Senna quickly pulled out 4s, Schumacher briefly held up by Alesi who beat him off the grid. Once by, the German closed the gap little by little until on lap 21 they simultaneously pitted for tyres and fuel. Slick pit-work had the Benetton out first, Schumacher eking out an 8s lead over the next 20 laps. Following a second stop on lap 44 Senna made his bid, closing the gap to 5s, until on lap 56, pushing very hard, the Williams spun broadside and stalled. Hill and Alesi, both lapped, completed the podium. Irvine was banned for one race, held responsible in an incident that saw Verstappen's car pitched into an alarming somersault.

POLE POSITION A Senna, Williams-Renault, 1m 15.962s (0.328s), 204.970kph, 127.363mph
LAPS 71 x 4.325 km, 2.687 miles
DISTANCE 307.075 km, 190.808 miles
STARTERS/FINISHERS 26/12
WEATHER Cloudy, warm, dry
LAP LEADERS A Senna 1-21 (21); Schumacher 22-71 (50)
WINNER'S LAPS 1 P3, 2-21 P2, 22-71 P1
FASTEST LAP Schumacher, Benetton-Ford, 1m 18.455s (lap 7), 198.457kph, 123.316mph
CHAMPIONSHIP Schumacher 10, Hill 6, Alesi 4, Barrichello 3, Katayama 2

Pos	Driver	Car	Time/gap	Grid	Stops	Tyres
1	M Schumacher	Benetton-Ford	1h 35m 38.759s	2	2	G
2	D Hill	Williams-Renault	−1 lap	4	1	G
3	J Alesi	Ferrari	−1 lap	3	2	G
4	R Barrichello	Jordan-Hart	−1 lap	14	2	G
5	U Katayama	Tyrrell-Yamaha	−2 laps	10	2	G
6	K Wendlinger	Sauber-Mercedes	−2 laps	7	2	G

Round 2/16	**PACIFIC GP** Aida	**Michael Schumacher**
	17 April 1994 Race 550	Benetton-Ford B194 173.924kph, 108.072mph

And Schumacher won round two as well, Senna out on lap 1. Too much wheelspin by the pole-sitter led to Häkkinen tagging Senna at the first corner. This spun the Williams which was then T-boned by Larini's Ferrari, subbing for the injured Alesi. After that it was a cruise for Schumacher. The next Williams put into a spin by Häkkinen's McLaren-Peugeot was Hill's, but undeterred he fought back from P9 such that when his transmission failed on lap 50 he was holding a solid P2. Häkkinen had retired from P2 as early as lap 19, so Berger's Ferrari finally took the spot, almost lapped. Barrichello followed fourth in Brazil with a podium for Jordan-Hart, the team's seven points one more than double world champions Williams had amassed to date.

POLE POSITION A Senna, Williams-Renault, 1m 10.218s (0.222s), 189.848kph, 117.967mph
LAPS 83 x 3.703 km, 2.301 miles
DISTANCE 307.349 km, 190.978 miles
STARTERS/FINISHERS 26/11
WEATHER Cloudy with sunny intervals, warm, dry
LAP LEADERS Schumacher 1-83 (83)
WINNER'S LAPS 1-83 P1
FASTEST LAP Schumacher, Benetton-Ford, 1m 14.023s (lap 10), 180.089kph, 111.903mph
CHAMPIONSHIP Schumacher 20, Barrichello 7, Hill 6, Berger 6, Alesi 4

Pos	Driver	Car	Time/gap	Grid	Stops	Tyres
1	M Schumacher	Benetton-Ford	1h 46m 1.693s	2	2	G
2	G Berger	Ferrari	−1m 15.300s	5	2	G
3	R Barrichello	Jordan-Hart	−1 lap	8	2	G
4	C Fittipaldi	Footwork-Ford	−1 lap	9	2	G
5	H-H Frentzen	Sauber-Mercedes	−1 lap	11	2	G
6	E Comas	Larrousse-Ford	−3 laps	16	2	G

Round 3/16	**SAN MARINO GP** Imola				
	1 May 1994			**Race 551**	

It started on Friday. Barrichello survived a terrifying smash at Variante Bassa. Saturday qualifying saw rookie Ratzenberger die at the 200mph Villeneuve Kink. By race-day, May Day, the tension was palpable, Senna questioning his motivation to race. From his 65th pole he led, but a start-line accident, spectators injured, immediately brought out the SC. On lap 6 racing resumed, but next time round Senna's Williams unaccountably speared off at Tamburello, striking the barriers forcibly. Red flag. On departure of the emergency helicopter the race restarted, but the Imola nightmare wasn't yet over, an errant wheel injuring pit-lane mechanics. Schumacher won but the world still held its breath. Later the news broke: Senna was dead.

Michael Schumacher
Benetton-Ford B194 198.233kph, 123.177mph

POLE POSITION A Senna, Williams-Renault, 1m 21.548s (0.337s), 222.494kph, 138.252mph
LAPS 58 x 5.040 km, 3.132 miles (61 lap race interrupted due to accident. Result aggregate of 5 + 53 laps)
DISTANCE 292.320 km, 181.639 miles
STARTERS/FINISHERS 25/13
WEATHER Cloudy with sunny intervals, hot, dry
LAP LEADERS (On the road) Senna 1-5 (5); G Berger, Ferrari 6-14 (9); Häkkinen 15-18 (4); Larini 19-23 (5); Schumacher 24-58 (35); SC 1-5 (5)
WINNER'S LAPS 1-12 P2, 13 P7, 14-15 P8, 16 P7, 17, P5, 18, P4, 19 P3, 20-23 P2, 24-58 P1
FASTEST LAP Hill, Williams-Renault, 1m 24.335s (lap 10), 215.141kph, 133.683mph
CHAMPIONSHIP Schumacher 30, Hill 7, Barrichello 7, Berger 6, Larini 6

Pos	Driver	Car	Time/gap	Grid	Stops	Tyres
1	M Schumacher	Benetton-Ford	1h 28m 28.642s	2	3	G
2	N Larini	Ferrari	−54.942s	6	1	G
3	M Häkkinen	McLaren-Peugeot	−1m 10.679s	8	2	G
4	K Wendlinger	Sauber-Mercedes	−1m 13.658s	10	2	G
5	U Katayama	Tyrrell-Yamaha	−1 lap	9	2	G
6	D Hill	Williams-Renault	−1 lap	4	2	G

Round 4/16	**MONACO GP** Monte Carlo				
	15 May 1994			**Race 552**	

At Monaco two weeks later the absence of the six-time winner was like a cloud, and further gloom descended when Karl Wendlinger crashed heavily at the chicane on Thursday morning, sustaining comatose head injuries from which he mercifully eventually recovered. By winning from his first-ever pole in such dominant style, Schumacher effectively assumed Senna's mantle as 'the man to beat'. The sprint-stop-sprint racing brought about by the resumption of refuelling seemed made for him. Two of the fancied runners, Häkkinen and Hill, tangled at Ste Devote, both out on lap 1, so the Ferraris gave chase to Schumacher for much of the race. But as the Ferrari challenge faded Brundle came through on lap 51 to bring McLaren-Peugeot an encouraging P2.

Michael Schumacher
Benetton-Ford B194 141.690kph, 88.042mph

POLE POSITION Schumacher, Benetton-Ford, 1m 18.560s (0.928s), 152.505kph, 94.762mph
LAPS 78 x 3.328 km, 2.068 miles
DISTANCE 259.584 km, 161.298 miles
STARTERS/FINISHERS 24/11
WEATHER Cloudy with sunny intervals, warm, dry
LAP LEADERS Schumacher 1-78 (78)
WINNER'S LAPS 1-78 P1
FASTEST LAP Schumacher, Benetton-Ford, 1m 21.076s (lap 35), 147.772kph, 91.822mph
CHAMPIONSHIP Schumacher 40, Berger 10, Hill 7, Barrichello 7, Larini 6

Pos	Driver	Car	Time/gap	Grid	Stops	Tyres
1	M Schumacher	Benetton-Ford	1h 49m 55.372s	1	2	G
2	M Brundle	McLaren-Peugeot	−37.278s	8	2	G
3	G Berger	Ferrari	−1m 16.824s	3	2	G
4	A de Cesaris	Jordan-Hart	−1 lap	14	1	G
5	A Alesi	Ferrari	−1 lap	5	2	G
6	M Alboreto	Minardi-Ford	−1 lap	12	1	G

Round 5/16	**SPANISH GP** Cataluña				
	29 May 1994			**Race 553**	

In the Imola aftermath nine teams boycotted first practice, protesting against FIA changes, the drivers insisting on a temporary tyre chicane. Reminiscent of his father's 1968 Spanish victory in lamentably similar circumstances, Damon Hill won for the beleaguered Williams team. Not that this seemed likely at the outset, Schumacher streaking away from pole until hobbled by his gearbox from lap 23. Stuck in fifth gear, Schumacher's display was extraordinary, restricting Hill's lead to around 10s and successfully negotiating his second pit stop to finish second. Häkkinen, on a three-stop, was the first to wrest the lead from the crippled Benetton, but when the Peugeot blew on lap 48, Hill's two-stop strategy unwound with victory. Coulthard made his Williams debut.

Damon Hill
Williams-Renault FW16 192.366kph, 119.531mph

POLE POSITION Schumacher, Benetton-Ford, 1m 21.908s (0.651s), 208.638kph, 129.642mph
LAPS 65 x 4.747 km, 2.950 miles
DISTANCE 308.555 km, 191.727 miles
STARTERS/FINISHERS 25/11
WEATHER Cloudy with sunny intervals, hot, dry
LAP LEADERS Schumacher 1-22, 41-45 (27); M Häkkinen, McLaren-Peugeot 23-30 (8); Hill 31-40, 46-65 (30)
WINNER'S LAPS 1-19 P2, 20 P4, 21-23 P3, 24-30 P2, 31-40 P1, 41 P2, 42-45 P3, 46-65 P1
FASTEST LAP Schumacher, Benetton-Ford, 1m 25.155s (lap 18), 200.683kph, 124.699mph
CHAMPIONSHIP Schumacher 46, Hill 17, Berger 10, Alesi 9, Barrichello 7

Pos	Driver	Car	Time/gap	Grid	Stops	Tyres
1	D Hill	Williams-Renault	1h 36m 14.374s	2	2	G
2	M Schumacher	Benetton-Ford	−24.166s	1	2	G
3	M Blundell	Tyrrell-Yamaha	−1m 26.969s	11	2	G
4	J Alesi	Ferrari	−1 lap	6	2	G
5	P Martini	Minardi-Ford	−1 lap	18	2	G
6	E Irvine	Jordan-Hart	−1 lap	13	3	G

Williams-Renault FW16

Round 6/16	**CANADIAN GP** Montréal						
	12 June 1994				**Race 554**		

Michael Schumacher
Benetton-Ford B194 176.243kph, 109.513mph

In the wake of further post-Imola rule changes, Ferrari enjoyed a resurgence. At Montréal it would have been fitting for Ferrari No27 to snatch pole, but although both Ferraris out-qualified the Williams-Renaults, Schumacher nabbed P1 and in the race disappeared up the road in the customary manner. Once Hill had made his way past his unobliging new teammate Coulthard and Berger's Ferrari, he set off after Alesi, closing down the 10s gap over the next 15 laps and then decisively passing when the Ferrari was first to pit around half-distance. Hill finished a convincing second ahead of the Ferraris but totally eclipsed by the one-stopping Benetton. With five wins and one second, Schumacher's championship lead over Hill was now 33 points.

POLE POSITION Schumacher, Benetton-Ford, 1m 26.178s (0.099s), 185.894kph, 115.509mph
LAPS 69 x 4.450 km, 2.765 miles
DISTANCE 307.050 km, 190.792 miles
STARTERS/FINISHERS 26/15
WEATHER Cloudy, warm, brief shower mid-race
LAP LEADERS Schumacher 1-69 (69)
WINNER'S LAPS 1-69 P1
FASTEST LAP Schumacher, Benetton-Ford, 1m 28.927s (Lap 31), 180.147kph, 111.939mph
CHAMPIONSHIP Schumacher 56, Hill 23, Berger 13, Alesi 13, Barrichello 7

Pos	Driver	Car	Time/gap	Grid	Stops	Tyres
1	M Schumacher	Benetton-Ford	1h 44m 31.887s	1	1	G
2	D Hill	Williams-Renault	−39.660s	4	1	G
3	J Alesi	Ferrari	−1m 13.388s	2	1	G
4	G Berger	Ferrari	−1m 15.609s	3	2	G
5	D Coulthard	Williams-Renault	−1 lap	5	1	G
6	J J Lehto	Benetton-Ford	−1 lap	16	1	G

Round 7/16	**FRENCH GP** Magny-Cours						
	3 July 1994				**Race 555**		

Michael Schumacher
Benetton-Ford B194 186.216kph, 115.709mph

Mansell made a guest appearance for Williams, taking Coulthard's seat and qualifying P2 to Hill's pole in an exciting qualifying session. The way Schumacher rocketed from row two to win the first corner reinforced growing concerns about Benetton's illegal use of traction-control. Hill tenaciously ran with Schumacher until the first stop, when they pitted simultaneously. Schumacher's stop was 2.3s faster and the Benetton now pulled out a 10s lead over 17 laps before diving for the pits again, and yet again after another 17 laps. The three-stop strategy worked superbly, Schumacher's winning margin over two-stopping Hill 12s. Mansell lost a possible podium when his transmission failed on lap 44, leaving Berger's Ferrari to come home a lonely third.

POLE POSITION Hill, Williams-Renault, 1m 16.282s (0.077), 200.571kph, 124.629mph
LAPS 72 x 4.250 km, 2.641 miles
DISTANCE 306.000 km, 190.140 miles
STARTERS/FINISHERS 26/11
WEATHER Cloudy with sunny intervals, very hot, dry
LAP LEADERS Schumacher 1-37, 45-72 (65); Hill 38-44 (7)
WINNER'S LAPS 1-37 P1, 38-44 P2, 45-72 P1
FASTEST LAP Hill, Williams-Renault, 1m 19.678s (lap 4), 192.022kph, 119.317mph
CHAMPIONSHIP Schumacher 66, Hill 29, Berger 17, Alesi 13, Barrichello 7

Pos	Driver	Car	Time/gap	Grid	Stops	Tyres
1	M Schumacher	Benetton-Ford	1h 38m 35.704s	3	3	G
2	D Hill	Williams-Renault	−12.642s	1	2	G
3	G Berger	Ferrari	−52.765s	5	2	G
4	H-H Frentzen	Sauber-Mercedes	−1 lap	10	2	G
5	P Martini	Minardi-Ford	−2 laps	16	2	G
6	A de Cesaris	Sauber-Mercedes	−2 laps	11	2	G

Round 8/16	**BRITISH GP** Silverstone						**Damon Hill**
	10 July 1994					Race 556	Williams-Renault FW16 202.143kph, 125.606mph

Events at and arising from Silverstone transformed the season. On the parade lap around the heavily revised circuit, Schumacher illegally overtook pole-sitter Hill, and after an aborted start did it yet again. He then failed to serve the resultant stop-go time penalty within the prescribed time and next ignored the ensuing black flag. On lap 27 he eventually served the 5s stop-go, losing the lead to Hill and settling for second. But it was not clear-cut that the penalty alone denied Schumacher victory. Hill pipped Schumacher to pole by 0.003s, led until the first pit stop and was still in a fighting P2 when Schumacher took his penalty. Receiving his trophy from Princess Diana, Hill was elated, British GP success something which had eluded his illustrious father.

POLE POSITION Hill, Williams-Renault, 1m 24.960s (0.003s), 214.279kph, 133.147mph
LAPS 60 x 5.057 km, 3.142 miles
DISTANCE 303.420 km, 188.536 miles
STARTERS/FINISHERS 25/15
WEATHER Cloudy with sunny intervals, hot, dry
LAP LEADERS Hill 1-14, 27-60 (48); M Schumacher, Benetton-Ford 15-17, 22-26 (8); G Berger, Ferrari 18-21 (4)
WINNER'S LAPS 1-14 P1, 15 P2, 16-21 P3, 22-26 P2, 37-60 P1
FASTEST LAP Hill, Williams-Renault, 1m 27.100s (lap 11), 209.014kph, 129.876mph
CHAMPIONSHIP Schumacher 66, Hill 39, Alesi 19, Berger 17, Barrichello 10

Pos	Driver	Car	Time/gap	Grid	Stops	Tyres
1	D Hill	Williams-Renault	1h 30m 3.640s	1	2	G
2	J Alesi	Ferrari	–1m 8.128s	4	1	G
3	M Häkkinen	McLaren-Peugeot	–1m 40.659s	5	1	G
4	R Barrichello	Jordan-Hart	–1m 41.751s	6	2	G
5	D Coulthard	Williams-Renault	–1 lap	7	2	G
6	U Katayama	Tyrrell-Yamaha	–1 lap	8	2	G

Ferrari 412T1B

Round 9/16	**GERMAN GP** Hockenheim						**Gerhard Berger**
	31 July 1994					Race 557	Ferrari 412T1B 222.970kph, 138.548mph

Berger's victory from pole ended Ferrari's four-year, 58-race win-drought. And although Ligiers finished 2-3, it was a worthy victory, the very fleet Ferrari keeping the Benetton behind until Schumacher's engine failed on lap 19, his first retirement. Already under a suspended ban for his last corner collision with Barrichello at Silverstone, Häkkinen was banned one race for triggering a first-corner incident that eliminated 11 cars. Hill, having survived this carnage, lost the perfect opportunity to make up ground on Schumacher with his own costly first lap indiscretion, tangling with Katayama. But this race will long be remembered for the damning FIA report on Benetton's launch control, and Verstappen's pit-stop fireball, mercifully inconsequential.

POLE POSITION Berger, Ferrari, 1m 43.582s (0.430s), 237.133kph, 147.348mph
LAPS 45 x 6.823 km, 4.240 miles
DISTANCE 307.035 km, 190.783 miles
STARTERS/FINISHERS 26/8
WEATHER Cloudy with sunny intervals, hot, dry
LAP LEADERS G Berger 1-45 (45)
WINNER'S LAPS 1-45 P1
FASTEST LAP D Coulthard, Williams-Renault, 1m 46.211s (lap 11), 231.264kph, 143.701mph
CHAMPIONSHIP Schumacher 66, Hill 39, Berger 27, Alesi 19, Barrichello 10

Pos	Driver	Car	Time/gap	Grid	Stops	Tyres
1	G Berger	Ferrari	1h 22m 37.272s	1	1	G
2	O Panis	Ligier-Renault	–54.779s	12	1	G
3	E Bernard	Ligier-Renault	–1m 5.042s	14	1	G
4	C Fittipaldi	Footwork-Ford	–1m 21.609s	17	1	G
5	G Morbidelli	Footwork-Ford	–1m 30.544s	16	2	G
6	E Comas	Larrousse-Ford	–1m 45.445s	22	1	G

HUNGARIAN GP Hungaroring

14 August 1994   **Race 558**

Michael Schumacher

Benetton-Ford B194 169.737kph, 105.470mph

For his Silverstone black flag transgressions Schumacher had been disqualified, the FIA adding a two-race ban suspended pending appeal. They were also probing teammate Verstappen's pit fire. In the meantime Schumacher stormed to another pole and delivered a textbook three-stop race-winning strategy. In typical Hungaroring traffic conditions, two-stopping Hill and Williams simply had no answer. Schumacher was beaten off the line by Hill but swept by the Williams on the outside of turn one, only losing the lead again for nine laps after his first pit stop. Even after being docked his Silverstone points, Schumacher's advantage was still 31. Verstappen took third when, yards from the flag, the alternator in Brundle's McLaren failed cruelly.

POLE POSITION Schumacher, Benetton-Ford, 1m 18.258s (0.566s), 182.534kph, 113.422mph
LAPS 77 x 3.968 km, 2.466 miles
DISTANCE 305.536 km, 189.851 miles
STARTERS/FINISHERS 26/14
WEATHER Cloudy with sunny intervals, hot, dry
LAP LEADERS Schumacher 1-16, 26-77 (68); Hill 17-25 (9)
WINNER'S LAPS 1-16 P1, 17-25 P2, 26-77 P1
FASTEST LAP Schumacher, Benetton-Ford, 1m 20.881s (lap 5), 176.615kph, 109.743mph
CHAMPIONSHIP Schumacher 76, Hill 45, Berger 27, Alesi 19, Barrichello 10

Pos	Driver	Car	Time/gap	Grid	Stops	Tyres
1	M Schumacher	Benetton-Ford	1h 48m 0.185s	1	3	G
2	D Hill	Williams-Renault	−20.827s	2	2	G
3	J Verstappen	Benetton-Ford	−1m 10.329s	12	2	G
4r	M Brundle	McLaren-Peugeot	−1 lap	6	2	G
5	M Blundell	Tyrrell-Yamaha	−1 lap	11	1	G
6	O Panis	Ligier-Renault	−1 lap	9	2	G

BELGIAN GP Spa Francorchamps

28 August 1994   **Race 559**

Damon Hill

Williams-Renault FW16B 208.170kph, 129.351mph

In the post-Imola uneasiness, a chicane was added at the entry to Eau Rouge. Barrichello made the most of changeable conditions in qualifying to become the youngest-ever pole-winner. Five hours after Schumacher's eighth win this season he was disqualified, Hill the beneficiary; the Benetton's 'plank', a post-Imola measure to increase ride-height/reduce downforce, was worn excessively. Benetton claimed it was the consequence of his fortuitously uneventful spin exiting Pouhon on lap 19. The stewards disagreed. Besides the spin, it was a routine two-stop for Schumacher whereas Hill contended with rookie teammate Coulthard, who got ahead at their first stop and stayed there for a further 24 frustrating laps until pitting on lap 36 to fix a rear wing failure.

POLE POSITION R Barrichello, Jordan-Hart, 2m 21.163s (0.331s), 178.542kph, 110.941mph
LAPS 44 x 7.001 km, 4.350 miles
DISTANCE 308.044 km, 191.410 miles
STARTERS/FINISHERS 26/13
WEATHER Cloudy with sunny intervals, warm, dry
LAP LEADERS (On the road) M Schumacher, Benetton-Ford 1-28, 30-44 (43); Coulthard 29 (1)
WINNER'S LAPS 1-2 P4, 3-11 P2, 12 P3, 13-17 P4, 18-36 P3, 37-44 P2 (Schumacher finished first but was disqualified for excessive 'plank' wear)
FASTEST LAP Hill, Williams-Renault, 1m 57.117s (lap 41), 215.200kph, 133.719mph
CHAMPIONSHIP Schumacher 76, Hill 55, Berger 27, Alesi 19, Häkkinen 14

Pos	Driver	Car	Time/gap	Grid	Stops	Tyres
1	D Hill	Williams-Renault	1h 28m 47.170s	3	2	G
2	M Häkkinen	McLaren-Peugeot	−51.381s	8	2	G
3	J Verstappen	Benetton-Ford	−1m 10.453s	6	2	G
4	D Coulthard	Williams-Renault	−1m 45.787s	7	3	G
5	M Blundell	Tyrrell-Yamaha	−1 lap	12	2	G
6	G Morbidelli	Footwork-Ford	−1 lap	14	1	G

ITALIAN GP Monza

11 September 1994   **Race 560**

Damon Hill

Williams-Renault FW16B 236.322kph, 146.844mph

With Schumacher absent, his two-race Silverstone ban upheld, Hill compounded the penalty with victory. A one-time 37-point lead was slashed to 11. An all-scarlet front row made *tifosi* hearts pound but a chaotic first corner brought out a red flag and cruelly knocked out Herbert's Lotus-Mugen from P4. From his maiden pole Alesi pulled away, on lap 15 pitting 11s ahead of teammate Berger. The despairing Alesi never left the pits. Gearbox. Berger on a one-stop and suffering from a big off during warm-up now led, but pit-stop complications converted a 2s advantage over the Williams-Renault pair into a 10s deficit. For Hill it was now a cruise to the finish, but Berger's late-race pressure gained some reward when Coulthard ran out of fuel.

POLE POSITION J Alesi, Ferrari, 1m 23.844s (0.134s), 249.033kph, 154.743mph
LAPS 53 x 5.800 km, 3.604 miles
DISTANCE 307.400 km, 191.010 miles
STARTERS/FINISHERS 26/10
WEATHER Cloudy with sunny intervals, hot, dry
LAP LEADERS Alesi 1-14 (14); Berger 15-23 (9); Hill 24, 29-53 (26); Coulthard 25, 27-28 (3); Häkkinen 26 (1)
WINNER'S LAPS 1-14 P3, 15-23 P2, 24 P1, 25-26 P3, 27-28 P2, 29-53 P1
FASTEST LAP Hill, Williams-Renault, 1m 25.930 (lap 24), 242.988kph, 150.986mph
CHAMPIONSHIP Schumacher 76, Hill 65, Berger 33, Alesi 19, Häkkinen 18

Pos	Driver	Car	Time/gap	Grid	Stops	Tyres
1	D Hill	Williams-Renault	1h 18m 2.754s	3	1	G
2	G Berger	Ferrari	−4.930s	2	1	G
3	M Häkkinen	McLaren-Peugeot	−25.640s	7	1	G
4	R Barrichello	Jordan-Hart	−50.634s	16	1	G
5	M Brundle	McLaren-Peugeot	−1m 25.575s	15	1	G
6r	D Coulthard	Williams-Renault	−1 lap	5	1	G

Round 13/16	**PORTUGUESE GP** Estoril					**Damon Hill**

25 September 1994 **Race 561**

Williams-Renault FW16B 183.589kph, 114.077mph

In qualifying Hill's car was pitched skywards by a spinning Irvine, landing upside down. Until transmission trouble, Berger led the first eight laps from another Ferrari pole after which Coulthard pulled away from an oversteering Hill. On his second set of tyres Hill's handling improved and on lap 28 he nipped past Coulthard in traffic. Until colliding with a backmarker mid-race, P3 looked the property of Alesi, although the impressive Frentzen's Sauber-Mercedes had threatened. Finally Häkkinen gave McLaren-Peugeot another podium. Coulthard's first podium completed a team 1-2, Williams taking the lead from Benetton in the constructors' championship while Hill's hat-trick victory reduced Schumacher's championship advantage to a single point.

POLE POSITION G Berger, Ferrari, 1m 20.608s (0.158s), 194.720kph, 120.993mph
LAPS 71 x 4.360 km, 2.709 miles
DISTANCE 309.560 km, 192.352 miles
STARTERS/FINISHERS 26/16
WEATHER Cloudy with sunny intervals, warm, dry
LAP LEADERS Berger 1-7 (7); Coulthard 8-17, 26-27 (12); Hill 18, 28-71 (45); J Alesi, Ferrari 19-22 (4); Barrichello 23-25 (3)
WINNER'S LAPS 1-7 P3, 8-17 P2, 18 P1, 19 P2, 20-23 P5, 24-25 P3, 26-27 P2, 28-71 P1
FASTEST LAP Coulthard, Williams-Renault, 1m 22.446s (lap 12), 190.379kph, 118.296mph
CHAMPIONSHIP Schumacher 76, Hill 75, Berger 33, Häkkinen 22, Alesi 19

Pos	Driver	Car	Time/gap	Grid	Stops	Tyres
1	D Hill	Williams-Renault	1h 41m 10.165s	2	2	G
2	D Coulthard	Williams-Renault	–0.603s	3	2	G
3	M Häkkinen	McLaren-Peugeot	–20.193s	4	2	G
4	R Barrichello	Jordan-Hart	–28.003s	8	1	G
5	J Verstappen	Benetton-Ford	–29.385s	10	2	G
6	M Brundle	McLaren-Peugeot	–52.702s	7	2	G

Round 14/16	**EUROPEAN GP** Jerez de la Frontera					**Michael Schumacher**

16 October 1994 **Race 562**

Benetton-Ford B194 182.507kph, 113.405mph

Schumacher returned from banishment and Mansell replaced Coulthard for the rest of the season. From the front row the two title contenders quickly made the race their own. Hill led from P2 but a first refuelling stop glitch upset race strategy. Initially unaware he was short-filled by ten laps, Hill allowed Schumacher to get away too far in the second stint. Then, using Mansell's rig at his second stop, he was tanked up to finish the race 34-laps hence, his fuel-laden car unable to nimbly deal with traffic. Schumacher's comparatively adroit three-stop victory reinstated his points lead to five over the disappointed Hill. Mansell made a scrappy return, never higher than P4, eventually spinning out on lap 47. Häkkinen recorded his fourth successive podium.

POLE POSITION Schumacher, Benetton-Ford, 1m 22.762s (0.130s), 192.610kph, 119.682mph
LAPS 69 x 4.428 km, 2.751 miles
DISTANCE 305.532 km, 189.849 miles
STARTERS/FINISHERS 26/19
WEATHER Cloudy with sunny intervals, hot, dry
LAP LEADERS Hill 1-17, 33-34 (19); Schumacher 18-32, 35-69 (50)
WINNER'S LAPS 1-17 P2, 18-32 P1, 33-34 P2, 35-69 P1
FASTEST LAP Schumacher, Benetton-Ford, 1m 25.040s (lap 17), 187.450kph, 116.476mph
CHAMPIONSHIP Schumacher 86, Hill 81, Berger 35, Häkkinen 26, Alesi 19

Pos	Driver	Car	Time/gap	Grid	Stops	Tyres
1	M Schumacher	Benetton-Ford	1h 40m 26.689s	1	3	G
2	D Hill	Williams-Renault	–24.689s	2	2	G
3	M Häkkinen	McLaren-Peugeot	–1m 9.648s	9	2	G
4	E Irvine	Jordan-Hart	–1m 18.446s	10	2	G
5	G Berger	Ferrari	–1 lap	6	2	G
6	H-H Frentzen	Sauber-Mercedes	–1 lap	4	1	G

Round 15/16	**JAPANESE GP** Suzuka					**Damon Hill**

6 November 1994 **Race 563**

Williams-Renault FW16B 151.796kph, 94.322mph

Atrocious rain, accidents and injury to a marshal eventually produced a red flag after 13 laps, Hill 7s behind Schumacher. From a SC rolling start the race restarted over 37 laps, decided on aggregate. After five laps Schumacher dived for the pits, Hill continuing for another seven and keeping the lead during his stop. It took Schumacher ten laps to narrow the 7s gap and regain the lead, but within five, lap 40, he made his second stop. It soon became clear Hill would not stop again and on rejoining Schumacher needed to gain 15s in ten laps. On the still-wet track Hill skilfully and resolutely defended his shrinking lead, this thrilling victory setting up an Adelaide showdown. In a race-long battle for P3, Mansell won on the road, Alesi on lapsed time.

POLE POSITION Schumacher, Benetton-Ford, 1m 37.209s (0.487s), 217.165kph, 134.940mph
LAPS 50 x 5.864 km, 3.644 miles (53 lap race interrupted due to accident. Result aggregate of 13 + 37 laps)
DISTANCE 293.200 km, 182.186 miles
STARTERS/FINISHERS 26/13
WEATHER Overcast, cold, very wet
LAP LEADERS (On the road) Schumacher 1-18, 36-40 (23); Hill 19-35, 41-50 (27); SC 3-9, 14-15 (9)
WINNER'S LAPS 1-18 P2, 19-35 P1, 36-40 P2, 41-50 P1
FASTEST LAP Hill, Williams-Renault, 1m 56.597s (lap 24), 181.054kph, 112.502mph
CHAMPIONSHIP Schumacher 92, Hill 91, Berger 35, Häkkinen 26, Alesi 23

Pos	Driver	Car	Time/gap	Grid	Stops	Tyres
1	D Hill	Williams-Renault	1h 55m 53.532s	2	1	G
2	M Schumacher	Benetton-Ford	–3.365s	1	2	G
3	J Alesi	Ferrari	–52.045s	7	1	G
4	N Mansell	Williams-Renault	–56.074s	4	1	G
5	E Irvine	Jordan-Hart	–1m 42.107s	6	1	G
6	H-H Frentzen	Sauber-Mercedes	–1m 59.863s	3	1	G

AUSTRALIAN GP Adelaide
13 November 1994   Race 564

Nigel Mansell
Williams-Renault FW16B 170.323kph, 105.834mph

In a failed attempt to regain pole from Mansell, Schumacher crashed. At the lights, the championship contenders streaked ahead, lap upon lap putting on a mesmeric shoot-out display. After 18 they entered and left the pits as one, Williams matching the Benetton three-stop strategy for the first time. On lap 35, separated by a mere 1.5s, Hill's relentless pursuit pressured Schumacher into a mistake, the Benetton striking the barrier. Aware that a Hill dnf would deliver the championship by a single point, the German cynically drove his damaged car back onto the racing line and into the path of the chasing Williams, eliminating both. Mansell won the race narrowly from Berger but, aptly after all the doubts, Benetton were denied the constructors' cup.

POLE POSITION Mansell, Williams-Renault, 1m 16.179s (0.018s), 178.631kph, 110.997mph
LAPS 81 x 3.780 km, 2.349 miles
DISTANCE 306.180 km, 190.251 miles
STARTERS/FINISHERS 26/12
WEATHER Overcast, warm, dry
LAP LEADERS Schumacher 1-35 (35); Mansell 36-53, 64-81 (36); Berger 54-63 (10)
WINNER'S LAPS 1-14 P5, 15-20 P4, 21-25 P3, 26-27 P6, 28-33 P4, 34-35 P3, 36-53 P1, 54-63, P2, 64-81 P1
FASTEST LAP M Schumacher, Benetton-Ford, 1m 17.140s (lap 29), 176.406kph, 109.614mph
CHAMPIONSHIP Schumacher 92, Hill 91, Berger 41, Häkkinen 26, Alesi 24

Pos	Driver	Car	Time/gap	Grid	Stops	Tyres
1	N Mansell	Williams-Renault	1h 47m 51.480s	1	2	G
2	G Berger	Ferrari	–2.511s	11	2	G
3	M Brundle	McLaren-Peugeot	–52.487s	9	2	G
4	R Barrichello	Jordan-Hart	–1m 10.530s	5	3	G
5	O Panis	Ligier-Renault	–1 lap	12	3	G
6	J Alesi	Ferrari	–1 lap	8	3	G

1994 CHAMPIONSHIP FACTS AND FOLKLORE

- Tragedy, controversy and even the whiff of scandal stalked 1994, another 16-round championship season.
- Kyalami dropped off the calendar, eliminating Africa from the world championship for the foreseeable future, while a second race was help in Japan, the first of two successive Pacific GPs held at Aida.
- Fourteen teams lined up for round one, Lola BMS Scuderia Italia replaced by newcomers Simtek and Pacific.
- Tyres remained the exclusive province of Goodyear, Akron celebrating their 300th GP victory in Spain.
- The FIA introduced two radical regulation changes. First, for the first time since 1983 refuelling was permitted. Second, with the exception of semi-auto gearboxes, all electronic driver aids were outlawed including 'traction control' and its first cousin 'launch control'.
- It might have been expected that Williams, the most successful exponents of the now illegal electronic gizmos, would be most affected by this ban, and was the most obvious reason to explain why initially the FW16 proved a handful even for their new number one driver Ayrton Senna.
- Benetton on the other hand fielded an extremely well-sorted car equipped with Ford's latest V8 power unit. The Ford HB had won the final three rounds of 1993 and now, via Cosworth, Ford introduced the more powerful Zetec-R, revving up to an astonishing 14,500rpm and delivering 740bhp.
- Over a flying lap the Williams-Renault was able to reinstate Senna's peerless pole-winning record, the first time he had set successive poles since 1991, but following the two opening GPs of the season Schumacher's Benetton had won twice and Senna had yet to score.
- Round three was the San Marino GP at Imola.
- 1 May 1994 will forever be etched in the mind for those with even the vaguest interest in motorsport. Twelve years had passed without a fatality at a GP meeting and suddenly here were two, one of them Senna. In a cataclysmic sequence of disaster Roland Ratzenberger had been killed the previous day, and less than two weeks later, at Monaco, Karl Wendlinger lay critically ill in a coma.
- In the aftermath of the Imola/Monaco accidents, with the world's press baying for a scapegoat, the FIA forced through

a raft of instant changes in the name of safety. These largely addressed a reduction in downforce and of engine power plus more forgiving chassis handling, and were phased over ten weeks and three races.
- At the Spanish GP on 27 May, a reduction in downforce was achieved due to changes to front wing and diffuser.
- Proposals from Canada on 10 June included lateral cockpit head protection; a 25kg increase in weight; removal of airboxes; pump fuel replacing exotic brews, and strengthened lower front wishbones.
- And from 29 July at the German GP, a stepped flat bottom was introduced by the attachment of a 10mm wooden 'skid-block'. This measure, which quickly became known as 'the plank', served to increase ride-height and therefore reduce downforce.
- In addition, following pressure from the resurrected GPDA, many circuits were modified, as well as lower speed limits being imposed in the pit lane.
- Silverstone was redesigned extensively; a chicane added in Montréal; tightened chicanes at Hockenheim, while Eau Rouge was totally emasculated. Thankfully the latter was just for one year – after all, only the previous autumn Senna himself had declared that Eau Rouge was one of the very reasons he did what he did.
- Mosley's package of measures, described as knee-jerk in some quarters, were by no means universally popular. They raised many dissenting voices among the teams, opposition led notably by Ron Dennis and Flavio Briatore, leading to various compromises, especially to the proposed structural modifications around the cockpit area.
- But for Briatore and Benetton there was another quite separate *tsunami* rolling towards them with a San Marino epicentre. At Imola the FIA seized the black boxes from the top three finishers, investigation revealing traction control hidden deep in Benetton's system.
- FIA technical delegate Charlie Whiting's report concluded, 'In the circumstances, I am not satisfied that car number 5 complied with the regulations at all times during the San Marino GP.'
- The FIA's difficulty was that there was no hard evidence, and the problem of unequivocal evidence had always produced

RACE 551, San Marino GP: Following the SC, racing resumed on lap six, but next time around the lead Williams unaccountably speared off at Tamburello, striking the barriers forcibly.

a certain amount of scepticism surrounding the FIA's technology ban in relation to its ability to police and enforce it, especially traction and launch control.

- In a 45-minute statement Benetton's Ross Brawn refuted the allegations, explaining how this illegal gizmo was simply a legacy from last year. In response the FIA stipulated that in future no disabled electronic driver aids should remain embedded in a team's computer software. There seemed to be little other action they could take.

- Or was there? Having already fined Benetton $100,000 for the tardy release of their software source codes, an extraordinary meeting of the World Motorsports Council on 26 July fined Benetton a further $500,000 and banned Schumacher from two races.

- These, some might regard as draconian, penalties were all ostensibly connected with the team's Silverstone 'black-flag' misdemeanours, Schumacher disqualified from this race too. But heinous as these infringements may have been, some felt the punishment disproportionate, perhaps intended to send a different message.

- What message the FIA were trying to send the next time Benetton appeared before them is difficult to fathom. Investigation into the cause of the fireball that, thankfully briefly, engulfed Verstappen's Benetton during his Hockenheim fuel stop was revealing. It proved to be the consequence of the illegal removal of a filter from their fuel rig by Benetton. This action would increase flow-rate, saving 1s in an 8s fuel stop. Benetton pleaded guilty, offered some circumstantial evidence and, to the astonishment of the F1 community, escaped further punishment.

- But at Spa, the race prior to Schumacher's two-race suspension, he was disqualified for excess wear to 'the plank'. As a result of these two disqualifications plus his two-race ban, he went to the finale in Australia just one point ahead of the dogged Damon Hill.

- In Adelaide, shortly before half-distance, Hill's close and relentless pursuit pressured Schumacher into a mistake. The Benetton clouted the barrier but, despite deranged steering, was still mobile, Schumacher cunningly positioning his car on the corner apex to impede or collide with the closely chasing Hill. A collision ensued, both cars were eliminated and Schumacher became the first German world champion.

- Nigel Mansell, drafted in by Williams to support Hill's title chances in the final three races of the season, went on to win in Australia and posted his final tally at a remarkable 33 race victories.

- The two Williams victories that rounded out the season brought the team another constructors' title but this was scant compensation in a year burning with bright anticipation that so quickly deteriorated into a horror story. In 1983 Frank had given Ayrton his first F1 test and somehow it seemed so right that they now had the opportunity to race together. But now the great Brazilian driver had come to grief at the wheel of one of his cars. Hard to bear.

- Theories abounded as to why Senna failed to negotiate Tamburello, but no categorical rationale was ever advanced. The Williams barely deviated as it left the road, decelerating from 190mph to 135mph before impacting forcefully with a concrete barrier surrounding the corner.

- The autopsy concluded that any one of three head injuries might have caused the fatality, including the penetration of his helmet by a suspension part.

- At the fifth round, Hill's very welcome Spanish GP victory for Williams echoed his father's similar victory for Lotus 26 years before in the aftermath of Jim Clark's death.

- So close to the start of only his second full season, leading a top-flight F1 team was a heavy burden for Hill to shoulder, but he acquitted himself extremely well on and off track.

- After a lone entry at Monaco, Hill was joined from Spain by Williams tester and rookie David Coulthard for eight races, the other four by Mansell. Whether matched against youth or experience, there was rarely any ambiguity over who was the Williams number one. It was Hill.

- His and Coulthard's 1-2 finish for Williams in Portugal was the first for British drivers since Graham Hill and Piers Courage at Monaco 1969.

- McLaren switched to Peugeot engines for 1994, and, despite eight podiums between drivers Häkkinen and Brundle, never looked race winners, the first time the team had failed to win in its 14 years under Ron Dennis. But for 1995 an engine partnership with Mercedes-Benz was already in place, a relationship that endures to this day.

- A certain wildness in Häkkinen's driving resulted in a one-race ban, after which he settled into delivering strong results consistently.

- Another to receive a ban was Eddie Irvine, and when he and Eddie Jordan appealed the decision his suspension was increased from one race to three. This time the FIA's message was very clear.

- In May yet another near catastrophe occurred during Silverstone testing. The rear wing detached from Lamy's Lotus, the car vaulting the three-metre spectator fence to land in the entrance to a spectator tunnel.
- Lotus scored not a single point in 1994 and 37 years after their debut and seven after Senna brought them a final victory, Team Lotus went into administration and bowed out of the GP scene.
- Another end of season farewell came from Andrea de Cesaris. He had made his GP debut way back in 1980 and completed his career second only to Patrese's 256 on the all-time GP starts list. But Andrea's 208 also set an unenviable record that he holds to this day: most GPs without a win.
- Flavio Briatore and Tom Walkinshaw with support from the Benetton group bought out Ligier and with it their supply of Renault engines. This association would eventually lead to the acquisition of the team by Renault in 2002 for their full-scale return to GP racing. In the shorter term it would provide new world champion Michael Schumacher with Renault power for 1995.

Championship ranking	Championship points	Driver nationality	1994 Drivers Championship		Races contested	Race victories	Podiumse excl. victories	Races led	Lights to flag victories	Laps led	Poles	Fastest laps	Triple Crowns
			Driver	Car									
1	92	GER	Michael Schumacher	Benetton-Ford	14	8	2	13	3	629	6	8	4
2	91	GBR	Damon Hill	Williams-Renault	16	6	5	8		216	2	6	1
3	41	AUT	Gerhard Berger	Ferrari	16	1	5	6	1	84	2		
4	26	FIN	Mika Häkkinen	McLaren-Peugeot	15		6	3		13			
5	24	FRA	Jean Alesi	Ferrari	14		4	2		18	1		
6	19	BRA	Rubens Barrichello	Jordan-Hart	15		1	1		3	1		
7	16	GBR	Martin Brundle	McLaren-Peugeot	16		2						
8	14	GBR	David Coulthard	Williams-Renault	8		1	3		16		2	
9	13	GBR	Nigel Mansell	Williams-Renault	4	1		1		36	1		
10	10	NLD	Jos Verstappen	Benetton-Ford	10		2						
11	9	FRA	Olivier Panis	Ligier-Renault	16		1						
12	8	GBR	Mark Blundell	Tyrrell-Yamaha	16		1						
13	7	GER	Heinz-Harald Frentzen	Sauber-Mercedes	15								
14	6	ITA	Nicola Larini	Ferrari	2		1	1		5			
15	6	BRA	Christian Fittipaldi	Footwork-Ford	16								
16	6	GBR	Eddie Irvine	Jordan-Hart	12								
17	5	JPN	Ukyo Katayama	Tyrrell-Yamaha	16								
18	4	FRA	Éric Bernard	Ligier-Renault (13) Lotus-Mugen Honda (1)	14		1						
19	4	AUT	Karl Wendlinger	Sauber-Mercedes	3								
19	4	ITA	Andrea de Cesaris	Jordan-Hart (2) Sauber-Mercedes (9)	11								
21	4	ITA	Pierluigi Martini	Minardi-Ford	16								
22	3	ITA	Gianni Morbidelli	Footwork-Ford	16								
23	2	FRA	Erik Comas	Larrousse-Ford	15								
24	1	ITA	Michele Alboreto	Minardi-Ford	16								
24	1	FIN	J J Lehto	Benetton-Ford (6) Sauber-Mercedes (2)	8								
-	0	BRA	Ayrton Senna	Williams-Renault	3			2		26	3		

Championship ranking	Championship points	Team/Marque nationality	1994 Constructors Championship		Engine maker nationality	Races contested	Race victories	1-2 finishes	Podiums excl. victories	Races led	Laps led	Poles	Fastest laps
			Chassis	Engine									
1	118	GBR	Williams FW16, FW16B	Renault 3.5 V10	FRA	16	7	1	6	12	294	6	8
2	103	GBR	Benetton B194	Ford Cosworth 3.5 V8	GBR	16	8		4	13	629	6	8
3	71	ITA	Ferrari 412T1, 412T1B	Ferrari 3.5 V12	ITA	16	1		10	6	107	3	
4	42	GBR	McLaren MP4-9	Peugeot 3.5 V10	FRA	16			8	3	13		
5	28	IRL	Jordan 194	Hart 3.5 V10	GBR	16			1	1	3	1	
6	13	FRA	Ligier JS39B	Renault 3.5 V10	FRA	16			2				
7	13	GBR	Tyrrell 022	Yamaha 3.5 V10	JPN	16			1				
8	12	SUI	Sauber C13	Mercedes-Benz 3.5 V10	GER	16							
9	9	GBR	Footwork FA15	Ford Cosworth 3.5 V8	GBR	16							
10	5	ITA	Minardi M194, M193B	Ford Cosworth 3.5 V8	GBR	16							
11	2	FRA	Larrousse LH94	Ford Cosworth 3.5 V8	GBR	16							

1995

Schumacher supremacy

THE TALE OF THE TITLE

- Michael Schumacher became the sixth and youngest-ever 'back-to-back' champion.
- The domineering German won nine races in the season, equalling Nigel Mansell's 1992 record.
- Eleven race victories brought a savvy Benetton-Renault team a deserved constructors' title.
- The French V10 engine powered all but one winner of the 17-round championship.
- Five race victories from 12 poles suggested under-achievement by Williams-Renault.
- Car reliability, driver error and race strategy, Williams lost out to Benetton on numerous fronts.
- Damon Hill again proved Schumacher's sternest opposition, taking runner-up spot with a four-race win tally.
- But four controversial on-track clashes caused their rivalry to become increasingly embittered.
- Herbert and Coulthard, number two drivers at Benetton and Williams, each scored maiden GP victories.
- The only other victor was Ferrari, an emotional one-and-only GP success for Jean Alesi in Canada.
- In another barren McLaren season, Mansell was squeezed out and Mika Häkkinen survived serious injury.
- And not forgetting: F1 mourns Fangio.

THE CHASE FOR THE CHAMPIONSHIP

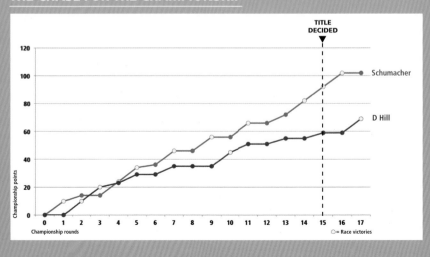

Benetton-Renault B195

| Round 1/17 | **BRAZILIAN GP** Interlagos | | |
| | **26 March 1995** | | **Race 565** |

With Williams and Benetton now both sporting the Renault V10, Hill comfortably took pole. In pre-season testing the FW17 appeared sorted, the B195 troublesome. Hill lost out at the start but tracked the Benetton easily until on lap 17 it peeled off for the first of three stops. Hill, on a two-stop, went three more laps before pitting, rejoined still in the lead, then eased away even though he was to make one stop less. But on lap 31 a rear pushrod broke, the wheels locked, and Hill spun off. So Schumacher won from Coulthard until, some hours later, both were disqualified for fuel irregularities. Berger's Ferrari, starting P5 and finishing a lapped P3, was awarded victory. Three weeks later, the drivers were reinstated on appeal but not the teams' points.

Pos	Driver	Car	Time/gap	Grid	Stops	Tyres
1	M Schumacher	Benetton-Renault	1h 38m 34.154s	2	3	G
2	D Coulthard	Williams-Renault	−8.060s	3	2	G
3	G Berger	Ferrari	−1 lap	5	2	G
4	M Häkkinen	McLaren-Mercedes	−1 lap	7	2	G
5	J Alesi	Ferrari	−1 lap	6	2	G
6	M Blundell	McLaren-Mercedes	−1 lap	9	2	G

Michael Schumacher
Benetton-Renault B195 186.919kph, 116.146mph

POLE POSITION D Hill, Williams-Renault, 1m 20.081s (0.301s), 194.428kph, 120.812mph
LAPS 71 x 4.325 km, 2.687 miles
DISTANCE 307.075 km, 190.808 miles
STARTERS/FINISHERS 25/10
WEATHER Overcast, warm, dry
LAP LEADERS Schumacher 1-17, 31-35, 47-71 (47); Hill 18-21, 23-30 (12); Coulthard 22, 36-46 (12)
WINNER'S LAPS 1-17 P1, 18 P3, 19 P5, 20-22 P4, 23-30 P2, 31-35 P1, 36-46 P2, 47-71 P1
FASTEST LAP Schumacher, Benetton-Renault, 1m 20.921s (lap 51), 192.409kph, 119.558mph
CHAMPIONSHIP Schumacher 10, Coulthard 6, Berger 4, Häkkinen 3, Alesi 2

| Round 2/17 | **ARGENTINEAN GP** Buenos Aires No 6 | | |
| | **5 April 1995** | | **Race 566** |

Coulthard claimed his maiden pole, both Williams drivers out-qualifying Schumacher's twitchy Benetton. At the start, the track damp, all hell broke loose when Alesi spun, the race stopped. From the restart Coulthard quickly pulled 4s on Schumacher but on lap 6 throttle electronics put paid to the Scotsman's victory bid. Once Hill carved past Schumacher in a great move on lap 11 there was only going to be one winner. Coulthard apart, Alesi was Hill's greatest threat, his two-stop Ferrari leading eight laps after Hill's first of three stops. He finished 6s adrift, the most competitive Ferrari showing in a while. Pat Symonds tried switching from two stops to three, but for Schumacher and Herbert 3-4 was the best Benetton could summon.

Pos	Driver	Car	Time/gap	Grid	Stops	Tyres
1	D Hill	Williams-Renault	1h 53m 14.532s	2	3	G
2	J Alesi	Ferrari	−6.407s	6	2	G
3	M Schumacher	Benetton-Renault	−33.376s	3	3	G
4	J Herbert	Benetton-Renault	−1 lap	11	2	G
5	H-H Frentzen	Sauber-Ford	−2 laps	9	1	G
6	G Berger	Ferrari	−2 laps	8	2	G

Damon Hill
Williams-Renault FW17 162.385kph, 100.902mph

POLE POSITION D Coulthard, Williams-Renault, 1m 53.241s (0.816s), 135.396kph, 84.131mph
LAPS 72 x 4.259 km, 2.646 miles (Race restarted for scheduled 72 laps following accident)
DISTANCE 306.482 km, 190.439 miles
STARTERS/FINISHERS 26/9
WEATHER Overcast, warm, dry
LAP LEADERS Coulthard 1-5 (5); Schumacher 6-10, 17 (6); Hill 11-16, 26-72 (53); Alesi 18-25 (8)
WINNER'S LAPS 1-5 P3, 6-10 P2, 11-16 P1, 17 P3, 18-25 P2, 26-72 P1
FASTEST LAP Schumacher, Benetton-Renault, 1m 30.522s (lap 55), 169.377kph, 105.246mph
CHAMPIONSHIP Schumacher 14, Hill 10, Alesi 8, Coulthard 6, Berger 5

Williams-Renault FW17

<table>
<tr><td>**Round 3/17**</td><td>**SAN MARINO GP** Imola
30 April 1995</td><td>**Race 567**</td></tr>
</table>

Damon Hill

Williams-Renault FW17 181.921kph, 113.041mph

Twelve months on, Imola produced a good race but drama surrounded Schumacher. On the plus side, his Interlagos victory had been reinstated, but on the other, FIA President Mosley publicly rebuked the world champion over the 'heavy helmet' pre-season weigh-in scam. And on track he crashed out on lap 10 while battling with the Williams duo and Berger. He had just switched from wets to slicks. A smart early swap to slicks now gave Berger P1 until delayed by a pit-stop stall. So on lap 22 the fierce Hill-Coulthard-Alesi tussle became a scrap for the lead. Following the second pit stops Hill took command and won, but Coulthard fell to fourth with a spin and a pit-lane speeding penalty. The Ferraris came 2-3 while Mansell debuted for McLaren.

POLE POSITION M Schumacher, Benetton-Renault, 1m 27.274s (0.008s), 201.915kph, 125.465mph
LAPS 63 x 4.895 km, 3.042 miles
DISTANCE 308.385 km, 191.622 miles
STARTERS/FINISHERS 26/16
WEATHER Overcast, cool, damp then drying
LAP LEADERS Schumacher 1-9 (9); Coulthard 10 (1); Berger 11-21 (11); Hill 22-63 (42)
WINNER'S LAPS 1-5 P4, 6-9 P3, 10 P4, 11 P3, 12-21 P2, 22-63 P1
FASTEST LAP Berger, Ferrari, 1m 29.568s (lap 57), 196.744kph, 122.251mph
CHAMPIONSHIP Hill 20, Schumacher 14, Alesi 14, Coulthard 9, Berger 9

Pos	Driver	Car	Time/gap	Grid	Stops	Tyres
1	D Hill	Williams-Renault	1h 41m 42.552s	4	3	G
2	J Alesi	Ferrari	−18.510s	5	3	G
3	G Berger	Ferrari	−43.116s	2	3	G
4	D Coulthard	Williams-Renault	−51.890s	3	4	G
5	M Häkkinen	McLaren-Mercedes	−1 lap	6	2	G
6	H-H Frentzen	Sauber-Ford	−1 lap	14	2	G

<table>
<tr><td>**Round 4/17**</td><td>**SPANISH GP** Cataluña
17 May 1995</td><td>**Race 568**</td></tr>
</table>

Michael Schumacher

Benetton-Renault B195 195.320kph, 121.367mph

In Spain the waywardness of the Benetton chassis apparent for the opening three rounds had been sorted. It enabled Schumacher to rediscover his form with a strong pole, then lead all the way to finish comfortably ahead of teammate Johnny Herbert, the latter's first podium in six years. While Benetton progressed Williams lost ground, qualifying behind the Ferraris. A close conflict for P2 was developing nicely between Alesi and Hill when the V12 failed on lap 25, Ferrari's first retirement of the season. Coulthard lost P3 with gearbox trouble with 11 laps to go but Hill's departure was cruel, denied second place with hydraulics failure on his final lap. One point now separated Schumacher from Hill. Mansell made his second and final appearance for McLaren.

POLE POSITION Schumacher, Benetton-Renault, 1m 21.452s (0.600s), 208.923kph, 129.819mph
LAPS 65 x 4.727 km, 2.937 miles
DISTANCE 307.114 km, 190.832 miles
STARTERS/FINISHERS 25/15
WEATHER Cloudy with sunny intervals, warm, dry
LAP LEADERS Schumacher 1-65 (65)
WINNER'S LAPS 1-65 P1
FASTEST LAP Hill, Williams-Renault, 1m 24.531s (lap 46), 201.313kph, 125.090mph
CHAMPIONSHIP Schumacher 24, Hill 23, Alesi 14, Berger 13, Coulthard 9

Pos	Driver	Car	Time/gap	Grid	Stops	Tyres
1	M Schumacher	Benetton-Renault	1h 34m 20.507s	1	2	G
2	J Herbert	Benetton-Renault	−51.988s	7	2	G
3	G Berger	Ferrari	−1m 5.237s	3	3	G
4	D Hill	Williams-Renault	−2m 1.749s	5	2	G
5	E Irvine	Jordan-Peugeot	−1 lap	6	3	G
6	O Panis	Ligier-Mugen Honda	−1 lap	15	2	G

MONACO GP Monte Carlo
28 May 1995   Race 569

Michael Schumacher
Benetton-Renault B195 137.603kph, 85.503mph

Despite a towering pole by Hill, on race day Williams got their strategy hopelessly wrong by opting for a two-stop, Schumacher afterwards claiming that he had known, had been informed. Anyway, even with his 25kg one-stop fuel load penalty, in race trim Schumacher was easily able to shadow Hill. Once the Williams pitted on lap 23 the Benetton was away, a demoralising 30s+ ahead by the finish. In another restarted race Coulthard ran third for the first 16 laps until his gearbox packed up. This released Alesi who reaffirmed Hill's hopeless stratagem by staying ahead of him after his single stop. But Alesi was out of luck, crashing out on lap 41 avoiding a spinning backmarker. Berger, driving the T-car, came third, his fourth podium in five races.

POLE POSITION Hill, Williams-Renault, 1m 21.952s (0.790s), 146.192kph, 90.840mph
LAPS 78 x 3.328 km, 2.068 miles (Race restarted for scheduled 78 laps following accident)
DISTANCE 259.584 km, 161.298 miles
STARTERS/FINISHERS 26/10
WEATHER Cloudy with sunny intervals, warm, dry
LAP LEADERS Hill 1-23 (23); Schumacher 24-35, 37-78 (54); Alesi 36 (1)
WINNER'S LAPS 1-78 P1
FASTEST LAP J Alesi, Ferrari, 1m 24.621s (lap 36), 141.581kph, 87.975mph
CHAMPIONSHIP Schumacher 34, Hill 29, Berger 17, Alesi 14, Herbert 12

Pos	Driver	Car	Time/gap	Grid	Stops	Tyres
1	M Schumacher	Benetton-Renault	1h 53m 11.258s	2	1	G
2	D Hill	Williams-Renault	−34.817s	1	2	G
3	G Berger	Ferrari	−1m 11.447s	4	2	G
4	J Herbert	Benetton-Renault	−1 lap	7	1	G
5	M Blundell	McLaren-Mercedes	−1 lap	10	2	G
6	H-H Frentzen	Sauber-Ford	−2 laps	14	2	G

Ferrari 412T2

CANADIAN GP Montréal
11 June 1995   Race 570

Jean Alesi
Ferrari 412T2 172.296kph, 107.060mph

At his 91st attempt Jean Alesi's losing streak finally ended. Until lap 58 a creditable P2 seemed likely behind pole-sitter and runaway leader Schumacher, but the Benetton's remorseless progress had been abruptly curtailed by a gearbox electronics glitch. An emotional Alesi swept by to reel off the final dozen laps, happy to later confess he crossed the line in tears. It was his 31st birthday and he was driving Ferrari No27 at the Circuit Gilles Villeneuve. Alesi crucially took teammate Berger on lap 2 and Hill for second on lap 17. With Häkkinen taking out Herbert at the start, Coulthard a lap 2 spinner, and Hill's gearbox-induced dnf on lap 50 when P3, further joy spread along the pit lane when Barrichello and Irvine brought Jordan their first-ever podiums.

POLE POSITION Schumacher, Benetton-Renault, 1m 27.661s (0.378s), 181.928kph, 113.045mph
LAPS 68 x 4.430 km, 2.753 miles (Race scheduled for 69 laps but declared at 68 due to crowd invasion)
DISTANCE 301.240 km, 187.182 miles
STARTERS/FINISHERS 24/11
WEATHER Overcast, warm, dry
LAP LEADERS Schumacher 1-57 (57); Alesi 58-68 (11)
WINNER'S LAPS 1 P5, 2-16 P3, 17-33 P2, 34 P3, 35-57 P2, 58-68 P1
FASTEST LAP Schumacher, Benetton-Renault, 1m 29.174s (Lap 67), 178.841kph, 111.127mph
CHAMPIONSHIP Schumacher 36, Hill 29, Alesi 24, Berger 17, Herbert 12

Pos	Driver	Car	Time/gap	Grid	Stops	Tyres
1	J Alesi	Ferrari	1h 46m 31.333s	5	1	G
2	R Barrichello	Jordan-Peugeot	−31.477s	9	1	G
3	E Irvine	Jordan-Peugeot	−35.980s	8	1	G
4	O Panis	Ligier-Mugen Honda	−41.314s	11	1	G
5	M Schumacher	Benetton-Renault	−44.676s	1	2	G
6	G Morbidelli	Footwork-Hart	−1 lap	13	1	G

FRENCH GP Magny-Cours

2 July 1995 — Race 571

Michael Schumacher
Benetton-Renault B195 186.332kph, 115.781mph

Hill got the better of Schumacher in qualifying, but the race was a different story. The title rivals quickly broke away, Hill leading, Schumacher probing for a way past. On lap 19 Schumacher pitted two laps sooner, but when Hill rejoined the Benetton was a miraculous 8s up the road. This was the most visible occurrence so far of the F1 'sleight of hand' that strategist Brawn and driver Schumacher would play time and again in forthcoming years. In and out laps; the stop itself; laps on fresh rubber, all these contributed, and in this case the timing too, Hill baulked 2s encountering traffic. Ferrari had a poor weekend, but in the team's 300th and home GP Brundle's Ligier-Mugen screamed across the line P4, nose-to-tail with Coulthard's Williams.

POLE POSITION Hill, Williams-Renault, 1m 17.225s (0.287), 198.122kph, 123.108mph
LAPS 72 x 4.250 km, 2.641 miles
DISTANCE 305.814 km, 190.024 miles
STARTERS/FINISHERS 24/16
WEATHER Cloudy, warm, dry
LAP LEADERS Hill 1-21 (21); Schumacher 22-72 (51)
WINNER'S LAPS 1-19 P2, 20 P3, 21 P2, 22-72 P1
FASTEST LAP Schumacher, Benetton-Renault, 1m 20.218s (lap 51), 190.730kph, 118.514mph
CHAMPIONSHIP Schumacher 46, Hill 35, Alesi 26, Berger 17, Coulthard 13

Pos	Driver	Car	Time/gap	Grid	Stops	Tyres
1	M Schumacher	Benetton-Renault	1h 38m 28.429s	2	2	G
2	D Hill	Williams-Renault	−31.309s	1	2	G
3	D Coulthard	Williams-Renault	−1m 2.826s	3	2	G
4	M Brundle	Ligier-Mugen Honda	−1m 3.293s	9	3	G
5	J Alesi	Ferrari	−1m 17.869s	4	2	G
6	R Barrichello	Jordan-Peugeot	−1 lap	5	3	G

BRITISH GP Silverstone

16 July 1995 — Race 572

Johnny Herbert
Benetton-Renault B195 195.682kph, 121.592mph

After Schumacher's 'brake-testing' accusation of Hill in France, controversy resurfaced at Silverstone. Hill led from a jubilant pole, Alesi's bullet start trapping Schumacher in P3 until lap 18. On lap 22 Hill stopped 18s ahead, and again on lap 41, plus 25s. It was going to be close, but on rejoining the one-stopping Schumacher was just ahead. But Hill was on fresh tyres, and at Silverstone. On lap 45 at Priory Schumacher left a gap and Hill's passing attempt eliminated them both. But a Benetton still led from a Williams, and four laps later Coulthard made a mirror image pass of Herbert at Priory without contact. The crowd was ecstatic, a first-time British winner at home was guaranteed. A pit-lane speeding penalty for Coulthard settled it.

POLE POSITION D Hill, Williams-Renault, 1m 28.124s (0.273s), 206.586kph, 128.367mph
LAPS 61 x 5.057 km, 3.142 miles
DISTANCE 308.477 km, 191.679 miles
STARTERS/FINISHERS 24/12
WEATHER Cloudy, warm, dry, windy
LAP LEADERS Hill 1-22, 32-41 (32); M Schumacher, Benetton-Renault 23-31, 42-45 (13); Herbert 46-48, 51-61 (14); Coulthard 49-50 (2)
WINNER'S LAPS 1-14 P5, 15-17 P4, 18-39 P3, 40-43 P4, 44-45 P3, 46-48 P1, 49-50 P2, 51-61 P1
FASTEST LAP D Hill, Williams-Renault, 1m 25.752s (lap 37), 202.838kph, 126.038mph
CHAMPIONSHIP Schumacher 46, Hill 35, Alesi 32, Herbert 22, Coulthard 17

Pos	Driver	Car	Time/gap	Grid	Stops	Tyres
1	J Herbert	Benetton-Renault	1h 34m 35.093s	5	2	G
2	J Alesi	Ferrari	−16.479s	6	2	G
3	D Coulthard	Williams-Renault	−23.888s	3	3	G
4	O Panis	Ligier-Mugen Honda	−1m 33.168s	13	3	G
5	M Blundell	McLaren-Mercedes	−1m 48.172s	10	2	G
6	H-H Frentzen	Sauber-Ford	−1 lap	12	1	G

GERMAN GP Hockenheim

30 July 1995 — Race 573

Michael Schumacher
Benetton-Renault B195 222.120kph, 138.019mph

On Schumacher's home turf Hill led from another triumphant pole. Lap 2, leading Schumacher by 2s, he entered turn one and spun off. With his team leader in the tyre-wall, Coulthard posed the only threat to Schumacher but it never materialised. Due to their differing refuelling strategies Coulthard did lead for four laps, but Schumacher was always in total control. Last year's winner Berger enlivened a dull race. Following a jumped-start penalty he charged back from 14th to secure yet another podium. On lap 33 engine maladies ended a highly impressive P3 performance by Häkkinen for McLaren-Mercedes, while earlier on the Peugeot ended another fine Barrichello drive for Jordan. Now 21 points in arrears, Hill's title aims looked bleak.

POLE POSITION D Hill, Williams-Renault, 1m 44.385s (0.080s), 235.309kph, 146.215mph
LAPS 45 x 6.823 km, 4.240 miles
DISTANCE 307.022 km, 190.775 miles
STARTERS/FINISHERS 24/9
WEATHER Sunny, hot, dry
LAP LEADERS Hill 1 (1); Schumacher 2-19, 24-45 (40); Coulthard 20-23 (4)
WINNER'S LAPS 1 P2, 2-19 P1, 20 P3, 21-23 P2, 24-45 P1
FASTEST LAP Schumacher, Benetton-Renault, 1m 48.824s (lap 22), 225.711kph, 140.250mph
CHAMPIONSHIP Schumacher 56, Hill 35, Alesi 32, Herbert 25, Coulthard 23

Pos	Driver	Car	Time/gap	Grid	Stops	Tyres
1	M Schumacher	Benetton-Renault	1h 22m 56.043s	2	2	G
2	D Coulthard	Williams-Renault	−5.988s	3	1	G
3	G Berger	Ferrari	−1m 8.097s	4	2	G
4	J Herbert	Benetton-Renault	−1m 23.436s	9	1	G
5	J-C Boullion	Sauber-Ford	−1 lap	14	1	G
6	A Suzuki	Ligier-Mugen Honda	−1 lap	18	2	G

HUNGARIAN GP Hungaroring

13 August 1995   Race 574

Damon Hill
Williams-Renault FW17 172.248kph, 107.030mph

Hill's lights-to-flag win from another pole gained further importance when Schumacher lost a certain P2. Front-row sitting Coulthard had no answer to Hill's early pace, Damon going away by a second a lap. After 13 laps Schumacher passed Coulthard and four later made his first fuel stop. But in another nine he was back for more owing to a fuel-rig problem. It is doubtful Schumacher could have beaten Hill that day, but with a compromised fuel/tyre strategy it was unachievable. In any case, four laps from the flag he retired with fuel pump trouble. So Coulthard took P2 while this time the Peugeot in Barrichello's Jordan waited until the final lap before it died, donating another P3 to Berger. Hill's victory slashed Schumacher's lead to 11 points.

POLE POSITION Hill, Williams-Renault, 1m 16.982s (0.384s), 185.560kph, 115.302mph
LAPS 77 x 3.968 km, 2.466 miles
DISTANCE 305.536 km, 189.851 miles
STARTERS/FINISHERS 24/13
WEATHER Cloudy with sunny intervals, hot, dry
LAP LEADERS Hill 11-77 (77)
WINNER'S LAPS 1-77 P1
FASTEST LAP Hill, Williams-Renault, 1m 20.247s (lap 34), 178.010kph, 110.611mph
CHAMPIONSHIP Schumacher 56, Hill 45, Alesi 32, Coulthard 29, Herbert 28

Pos	Driver	Car	Time/gap	Grid	Stops	Tyres
1	D Hill	Williams-Renault	1h 46m 25.721s	1	3	G
2	D Coulthard	Williams-Renault	–33.398s	2	3	G
3	G Berger	Ferrari	–1 lap	4	3	G
4	J Herbert	Benetton-Renault	–1 lap	9	3	G
5	H-H Frentzen	Sauber-Ford	–1 lap	11	2	G
6	O Panis	Ligier-Mugen Honda	–1 lap	10	3	G

BELGIAN GP Spa Francorchamps

27 August 1995   Race 575

Michael Schumacher
Benetton-Renault B195 190.204kph, 118.187mph

A weather-disrupted grid had Hill P8, Schumacher P16, yet by lap 15 they were vying for the lead. On lap 21 leader Hill stopped for wets, Schumacher remarkably staying on slicks. When the much quicker Hill came to retake the lead on the still wet surface, Schumacher employed dubious blocking tactics plus a blatant shove. Afterwards he received a suspended race ban for these improper tactics but in the race it worked out perfectly, as the rain stopped, forcing Hill back to slicks. More rain brought the SC, but when they switched back to wets a speeding penalty for Hill ruled out a close finish. Despite a quick spin, Hill eventually salvaged P2 by overtaking Brundle on the final lap. During a refuelling stop Irvine's Jordan was briefly engulfed in flames.

POLE POSITION G Berger, Ferrari, 1m 54.392s (0.239s), 219.476kph, 136.377mph
LAPS 44 x 6.974 km, 4.333 miles
DISTANCE 306.856 km, 190.671 miles
STARTERS/FINISHERS 24/14
WEATHER Overcast, warm, dry then intermittent rain
LAP LEADERS J Herbert, Benetton-Renault 1, 4-5 (3); J Alesi, Ferrari 2-3 (2); Coulthard 6-13 (8); Hill 14-15, 19-21, 24 (6); Schumacher 16-18, 22-23, 25-44 (25); SC 29-31 (3)
WINNER'S LAPS 1 P13, 2 P10, 3 P8, 4-5 P7, 6-10 P5, 11-13 P4, 14 P3, 15 P2, 16-18 P1, 19-20 P2, 22-23 P1, 24 P2, 25-44 P1
FASTEST LAP D Coulthard, Williams-Renault, 1m 53.412s (lap 11), 221.373kph, 137.555mph
CHAMPIONSHIP Schumacher 66, Hill 51, Alesi 32, Coulthard 29, Herbert 28

Pos	Driver	Car	Time/gap	Grid	Stops	Tyres
1	M Schumacher	Benetton-Renault	1h 28m 47.170s	16	2	G
2	D Hill	Williams-Renault	–19.493s	8	5	G
3	M Brundle	Ligier-Mugen Honda	–24.998s	13	1	G
4	H-H Frentzen	Sauber-Ford	–26.972s	10	2	G
5	M Blundell	McLaren-Mercedes	–33.772s	6	4	G
6	R Barrichello	Jordan-Peugeot	–39.674s	12	3	G

ITALIAN GP Monza

10 September 1995   Race 576

Johnny Herbert
Benetton-Renault B195 233.814kph, 145.286mph

Yet more controversy; for the third time in five races, Hill and Schumacher made car-on-car contact. On lap 24, running 2-3 behind Berger, Hill mis-braked lapping a backmarker, rear-punted Schumacher at the second chicane, both spinning out. Although Schumacher probably braked early, Hill got the suspended ban. Coulthard converted pole but with a 3s lead departed with wheel-bearing failure on lap 13. Suddenly a Ferrari 1-2 at Monza was in prospect. Berger's slow pit stop let Alesi ahead, the red cars triumphantly just 1s apart. But on lap 33 Alesi's on-car camera flew off, luckily only damaging Berger's front suspension. And with eight to go a wheel bearing denied a distraught Alesi a second victory, handing Johnny Herbert his.

POLE POSITION D Coulthard, Williams-Renault, 1m 24.462s (0.564s), 245.933kph, 152.816mph
LAPS 53 x 5.770 km, 3.585 miles (Race restarted for scheduled 53 laps following accident)
DISTANCE 305.772 km, 189.998 miles
STARTERS/FINISHERS 24/10
WEATHER Cloudy with sunny intervals, warm, dry
LAP LEADERS Coulthard 1-13 (13); Berger 14-24 (11); J Alesi, Ferrari 25, 30-45 (17); R Barrichello, Jordan-Peugeot 26 (1); Häkkinen 27 (1); Herbert 28-29, 46-53 (10)
WINNER'S LAPS 1-2 P6, 3 P7, 4-13 P8, 14-23 P7, 24 P5, 25 P4, 26 P3, 27 P2, 28-29 P1, 30-32 P3, 33-45 P2, 46-53 P1
FASTEST LAP G Berger, Ferrari, 1m 26.419 (lap 24), 240.363kph, 149.355mph
CHAMPIONSHIP Schumacher 66, Hill 51, Herbert 38, Alesi 32, Coulthard 29

Pos	Driver	Car	Time/gap	Grid	Stops	Tyres
1	J Herbert	Benetton-Renault	1h 18m 27.916s	8	1	G
2	M Häkkinen	McLaren-Mercedes	–17.779s	7	1	G
3	H-H Frentzen	Sauber-Ford	–24.321s	10	1	G
4	M Blundell	McLaren-Mercedes	–28.223s	9	1	G
5	M Salo	Tyrrell-Yamaha	–1 lap	16	2	G
6	J-C Boullion	Sauber-Ford	–1 lap	14	1	G

PORTUGUESE GP Estoril
24 September 1995   Race 577

David Coulthard
Williams-Renault FW17 182.319kph, 113.288mph

For the second straight race Coulthard was on pole and a red flag assisted his cause. At Monza he spun on the parade lap but rejoined the restarted race. This time Hill beat Schumacher to P2 at the first start but not the second. If Hill had been comfortably tracking Coulthard, the Scot would have forfeited his maiden win for Hill's title cause, but after 18 laps trapped behind Schumacher Hill elected to switch to a two-stop, his only hope. He duly got ahead, but ten laps on worn tyres made him easy prey for the three-stop Benetton, Schumacher's points advantage now unassailable. Coulthard's first victory was textbook, beating Schumacher on merit. The season's fourth red flag was for Katayama, extricated unconscious from his inverted Tyrrell but OK.

POLE POSITION Coulthard, Williams-Renault, 1m 20.537s (0.368s), 194.891kph, 121.100mph
LAPS 71 x 4.360 km, 2.709 miles (Race restarted for scheduled 71 laps following accident)
DISTANCE 309.545 km, 192.342 miles
STARTERS/FINISHERS 24/17
WEATHER Cloudy with sunny intervals, warm, dry
LAP LEADERS Coulthard 1-38, 44-71 (66); Hill 39-43 (5)
WINNER'S LAPS 1-38 P1, 39-43 P2, 44-71 P1
FASTEST LAP Coulthard, Williams-Renault, 1m 23.220s (lap 2), 188.608kph, 117.196mph
CHAMPIONSHIP Schumacher 72, Hill 55, Coulthard 39, Herbert 38, Alesi 34

Pos	Driver	Car	Time/gap	Grid	Stops	Tyres
1	D Coulthard	Williams-Renault	1h 41m 52.145s	1	3	G
2	M Schumacher	Benetton-Renault	–7.248s	3	3	G
3	D Hill	Williams-Renault	–22.121s	2	2	G
4	G Berger	Ferrari	–1m 24.879s	4	3	G
5	J Alesi	Ferrari	–1m 25.429s	7	2	G
6	H-H Frentzen	Sauber-Ford	–1 lap	5	2	G

EUROPEAN GP Nürburgring
1 October 1995   Race 578

Michael Schumacher
Benetton-Renault B195 183.180kph, 113.823mph

In wet but drying conditions Alesi gambled on slicks and a one-stop strategy, taking the lead on lap 13 when the leaders pitted for slicks, and retaining it when he made his lap 34 stop. That same lap Schumacher made his second stop, rejoining 29s behind, and on lap 52 his third, with 22s to find in 15 laps. Posting repeated fastest laps he didn't need 15, the *coup de grâce* when it came on lap 65 of 67 utterly ruthless, insisting on co-operation from his opponent, 'I pass or we crash'. But Alesi didn't resist, even he acquiesced. Pole-man Coulthard came P3 using the spare after spinning off in the warm-up, while Hill had a miserable time, tangling with Schumacher, losing his nosecone battling Alesi, and eventually crashing out on lap 58 playing catch-up.

POLE POSITION Coulthard, Williams-Renault, 1m 18.738s (0.234s), 129.435kph, 119.682mph
LAPS 67 x 4.556 km, 2.831 miles (Scheduled for 68 laps but reduced after aborted start)
DISTANCE 305.252 km, 189.675 miles
STARTERS/FINISHERS 24/19
WEATHER Overcast, cold, wet
LAP LEADERS Coulthard 1-12 (12); Alesi 13-64 (52); Schumacher 65-67 (3)
WINNER'S LAPS 1-11 P2, 12-14 P4, 15-20 P3, 21-33 P2, 34 P3, 35-38 P4, 39-40 P3, 41-64 P2, 65-67 P1
FASTEST LAP Schumacher, Benetton-Renault, 1m 21.180s (lap 57), 202.039kph, 125.542mph
CHAMPIONSHIP Schumacher 82, Hill 55, Coulthard 43, Herbert 40, Alesi 40

Pos	Driver	Car	Time/gap	Grid	Stops	Tyres
1	M Schumacher	Benetton-Renault	1h 39m 59.044s	3	3	G
2	J Alesi	Ferrari	–2.684s	6	1	G
3	D Coulthard	Williams-Renault	–35.382s	1	2	G
4	R Barrichello	Jordan-Peugeot	–1 lap	11	2	G
5	J Herbert	Benetton-Renault	–1 lap	7	3	G
6	E Irvine	Jordan-Peugeot	–1 lap	5	2	G

PACIFIC GP Aida
22 October 1995   Race 579

Michael Schumacher
Benetton-Renault B195 169.442kph, 105.287mph

With the rest trapped behind Alesi, Coulthard from his fourth straight pole decided his useful lead permitted a switch from three stops to two. Bad mistake. Benetton saw a glimmer for strategic advantage and, as if by magic, from his third stop on lap 60 Schumacher resumed 4s up on the incredulous Scotsman. Third on the grid yet first past the flag, Schumacher's contribution was priceless, emphasised by Herbert's P6 result from P7 start. But the whole Benetton team were operating supremely, for example saving three new tyre sets for race-day on the gripless Aida surface. There were further on and off track altercations with Hill, who came in third hampered by a refuelling rig issue, but it was Schumacher's race and with it his second championship.

POLE POSITION Coulthard, Williams-Renault, 1m 14.013s (0.200s), 180.114kph, 111.918mph
LAPS 83 x 3.703 km, 2.301 miles
DISTANCE 307.349 km, 190.978 miles
STARTERS/FINISHERS 24/17
WEATHER Cloudy with sunny intervals, warm, dry
LAP LEADERS Coulthard 1-49 (49); Schumacher 50-83 (34)
WINNER'S LAPS 1-4 P5, 5-20 P4, 21-49 P2, 50-83 P1
FASTEST LAP Schumacher, Benetton-Renault, 1m 16.374s (lap 40), 174.546kph, 108.458mph
CHAMPIONSHIP Schumacher 92, Hill 59, Coulthard 49, Alesi 42, Herbert 41

Pos	Driver	Car	Time/gap	Grid	Stops	Tyres
1	M Schumacher	Benetton-Renault	1h 48m 49.972s	3	3	G
2	D Coulthard	Williams-Renault	–14.920s	1	2	G
3	D Hill	Williams-Renault	–48.333s	2	3	G
4	G Berger	Ferrari	–1 lap	5	3	G
5	J Alesi	Ferrari	–1 lap	4	3	G
6	J Herbert	Benetton-Renault	–1 lap	7	3	G

JAPANESE GP Suzuka

29 October 1995   Race 580

Michael Schumacher

Benetton-Renault B195 192.349kph, 119.521mph

The new double champion's ninth victory equalled Mansell's 1992 winning spree and assured Benetton the constructors' title. Starting on a wet track from only his fourth pole this year, Schumacher led a feisty Alesi who at least cast some doubt over the outcome. Trying to minimise the disadvantage of a stop-go for a jumped start, Alesi gambled on slicks early and despite a lurid spin overtaking a backmarker, zeroed in on leader Schumacher, now slick-shod too. But on lap 25 a Ferrari driveshaft bearing failed. The Williams nightmare began on lap 37. Hill spun from P2 at Spoon, repeating the trick permanently on lap 40. On lap 39 Coulthard copied Hill then beached at 130R, having spun on gravel expelled from his sidepods as he braked.

POLE POSITION Schumacher, Benetton-Renault, 1m 38.023s (0.865s), 215.361kph, 133.820mph
LAPS 53 x 5.864 km, 3.644 miles
DISTANCE 310.588 km, 192.989 miles
STARTERS/FINISHERS 23/12
WEATHER Overcast, cold, wet then drying
LAP LEADERS Schumacher 1-10, 12-31, 36-53 (48); Häkkinen 11 (1); D Hill, Williams-Renault 32-35 (4)
WINNER'S LAPS 1-10 P1, 11 P2, 12-31 P1, 32-35 P2, 36-53 P1
FASTEST LAP Schumacher, Benetton-Renault, 1m 42.976s (lap 33), 205.003kph, 127.383mph
CHAMPIONSHIP Schumacher 102, Hill 59, Coulthard 49, Herbert 45, Alesi 42

Pos	Driver	Car	Time/gap	Grid	Stops	Tyres
1	M Schumacher	Benetton-Renault	1h 36m 52.930s	1	2	G
2	M Häkkinen	McLaren-Mercedes	−19.337s	3	2	G
3	J Herbert	Benetton-Renault	−1m 23.804s	9	3	G
4	E Irvine	Jordan-Peugeot	−1m 42.136s	7	3	G
5	O Panis	Ligier-Mugen Honda	−1 lap	11	2	G
6	M Salo	Tyrrell-Yamaha	−1 lap	12	2	G

AUSTRALIAN GP Adelaide

12 November 1995   Race 581

Damon Hill

Williams-Renault FW17B 168.129kph, 104.471mph

When he crashed heavily during practice with rear tyre failure, Mika Häkkinen was flown to hospital in a coma, mercifully to make a complete recovery. In the race Hill had the final word, winning by an astonishing two whole laps as his adversaries self-destructed. Coulthard got the better of pole-man Hill at the start but in his Williams finale ignominiously crashed from the lead into the pit-lane wall on lap 19. It got even better for Hill on lap 23 when Schumacher, joining Ferrari, clashed with Alesi, departing Ferrari, eliminating one another. Berger, lap 34, Frentzen's Sauber, lap 39, and Herbert, lap 69, each suffered mechanical failures when holding P2. Panis in a smoking Ligier-Mugen finally took the place from Morbidelli's Footwork-Hart.

POLE POSITION Hill, Williams-Renault, 1m 15.505s (0.123s), 180.226kph, 111.988mph
LAPS 81 x 3.780 km, 2.349 miles
DISTANCE 306.180 km, 190.251 miles
STARTERS/FINISHERS 22/8
WEATHER Cloudy with sunny intervals, warm, dry
LAP LEADERS D Coulthard, Williams-Renault 1-19 (19); M Schumacher, Benetton-Renault 20-21 (2); Hill 22-81 (60)
WINNER'S LAPS 1-18 P2, 19 P3, 20-21 P2, 22-81 P1
FASTEST LAP Hill, Williams-Renault, 1m 17.943s (lap 16), 174.589kph, 108.485mph
CHAMPIONSHIP Schumacher 102, Hill 69, Coulthard 49, Herbert 45, Alesi 42

Pos	Driver	Car	Time/gap	Grid	Stops	Tyres
1	D Hill	Williams-Renault	1h 49m 15.946s	1	3	G
2	O Panis	Ligier-Mugen Honda	−2 laps	12	3	G
3	G Morbidelli	Footwork-Hart	−2 laps	13	2	G
4	M Blundell	McLaren-Mercedes	−2 laps	10	2	G
5	M Salo	Tyrrell-Yamaha	−3 laps	14	2	G
6	P Lamy	Minardi-Ford	−3 laps	17	2	G

1995 CHAMPIONSHIP FACTS AND FOLKLORE

- Further post-Imola measures to slow cornering and straight-line speeds became effective for 1995 starting with engine capacity, cut from 3.5 to 3.0 litres.
- A further downforce reduction to circa 60% of pre-Imola levels was achieved through smaller wing area, lowered rear wing and a fully stepped bottom.
- There now had to be a 50mm step running down the centreline of the flat underside of the car from behind the front wheels to the rear axle. To that was fixed the 10mm 'plank' introduced last year.
- Although fly-by-wire throttles and electronic clutches were now permitted, these new cars demanded more skill and finesse from the driver.
- Changes specific to driver safety included higher cockpit sides, a larger cockpit opening, and more stringent chassis crash tests.
- For the first time since 1977 the championship would be decided over 17 rounds, Argentina returning to the calendar, last seen on the schedule in 1981.

- Later in the year Argentina and the world of F1 mourned the passing of their great champion Juan Manuel Fangio at the age of 84, his formidable winning strike rate and five world titles still marking him out as probably the greatest GP driver of all time.
- At the other end of the GP spectrum, Giancarlo Baghetti died aged 60 with just one GP triumph to his name. But what a triumph that French GP victory in 1961 was. Baghetti became the only driver to win a championship race on debut, Farina's 1950 Silverstone victory excepted.
- Following the smash-and-grab manner by which he took his first championship, Michael Schumacher and Benetton quite extraordinarily chose to again court controversy from the very first championship round in Brazil.
- In an endeavour to bring equanimity to the vexed question of driver weights – that lighter F1 drivers hold an advantage over their weightier brethren – the FIA revised the regulations. From a 515kg minimum weight limit for the car excluding driver, this year the limit was 595kg *including* driver.

RACE 579, Pacific GP: Schumacher's contribution was priceless, but the whole Benetton team were operating supremely, this victory bringing back-to-back drivers' championships.

■ On the Thursday before the first race the drivers plus their racing gear were weighed. Four drivers registered significantly heavier than last year, 8kg in the case of world champion Michael Schumacher. This equated to a performance advantage of 0.2s per lap around Interlagos, 14s over the race distance.

■ These four were re-weighed after the race and all matched their pre-race weight except Schumacher, who was 5.5kg lighter. For Schumacher the 'heavy helmet' allegation was personally damning, as whereas he could plead 'no knowledge; no involvement' to other Benetton transgressions, if true Schumacher was clearly party to this premeditated and grubby attempt to cheat.

■ Although Mosley publicly vilified Schumacher over the 'heavy helmet' scandal, no action ensued, Schumacher's attitude being that he was increasingly frustrated by accusations of foul play and was even quoted as considering a move to Indycars.

■ But controversy didn't end there. A number of incidents and clashes, notably between Schumacher and Hill, led to the FIA publishing a clarification on overtaking, the emphasis being that the manoeuvre should not deliberately endanger or deliberately obstruct another driver, pretty much summing up Schumacher's intimidatory tactics at Spa, the Nürburgring and elsewhere. Further, when similar treatment was dished out to him Schumacher was first to complain.

■ But setting aside these unwelcome tendencies, Schumacher put on some phenomenal driving displays this year and at times was simply unbeatable, winning nine times to equal Mansell's recent record, and at the age of 26 become the youngest-ever back-to-back champion.

■ One surprising statistic was that at Hockenheim Schumacher became the first German to win his home GP since the championship began.

■ His team, Benetton, switching from Ford to Renault engine supply, made a slow start to the season, taking time to get the new package au pointe. It virtually gave Williams and Hill a three-race start, an opportunity they only partially grasped, after which the Benetton B195 won 11 of the remaining 14 races.

■ Clearly Williams and Benetton both had the engine of the moment, the 3-litre Renault RS7. The 67° V10 produced 750bhp at 14,300rpm, winning all but one race, pundits generally agreeing that Williams had the quicker car, introducing significant developments with a 'B' version of the FW17 to maintain its chassis advantage in the latter part of the season.

■ Williams-Renault won five races and actually led more laps than Benetton, but although Hill's tally of four gave him another championship runner-up spot, his was a less convincing display than the previous year.

■ But it would be unjust to blame Hill alone for the litany of squandered opportunities at Williams, Schumacher and Benetton beating Hill, Coulthard, indeed, the entire Williams team, not so much on speed as on skill, strategy and preparation.

■ Hill had the final word, winning in Adelaide by an astonishing two complete laps as his adversaries self-destructed, so matching Stewart's equally extraordinary feat at Montjuïc in 1969.

■ Johnny Herbert and David Coulthard, number two drivers at Benetton and Williams, scored their maiden GP victories,

DC's error-strewn season coming good too late to prevent his 1996 seat being taken by Jacques Villeneuve.

- In a season with several dramatic incidents, including four GPs red-flagged and seven affected by rain, Ferrari was the only other team to win.
- Jean Alesi recorded his one and only GP victory in Canada, this win reinstating Ferrari at the top of the all-time list with 105 race victories to McLaren's 104. Ferrari was never to be headed again.
- Canada was also notable as the final GP win for a V12 engine. It was somehow fitting it should be a Ferrari V12, the Scuderia championing this configuration over the decades, but even they had to bow to the inevitable by building their first V10.
- For 1996 this new motor would be installed in John Barnard's latest creation for Ferrari's new lead driver, one Michael Schumacher, enticed by the fresh challenge and a retainer of $25 million a year over three years.
- McLaren began the season with their fourth new engine supplier in as many seasons, while after a brief flirtation as a McLaren-Mercedes driver Nigel Mansell concluded his F1 career on a downbeat note. In a disappointing pre-season test

session one of a range of issues was that he found the MP4/10 simply too much of a squeeze. His McLaren race debut was postponed for the two opening races while they built him a roomier monocoque, but after two lacklustre appearances Mansell parted company with Ron Dennis, to be replaced by Mark Blundell.

- In the final round in Australia his teammate Mika Häkkinen was seriously injured, but recovered to take his place on the grid for the first round the following season.
- Controversy surrounded the Ligier JS41, rival team owners complaining that the chassis was a copycat Benetton B195, Walkinshaw and Briatore the common factors. The Ligier quickly became known as 'the French Benetton'.
- Red Bull entered F1 as title sponsor for Sauber but Larrousse and Simtek both folded, the former not starting the season, the latter not finishing it. Pacific joined them shortly after the season ended.
- Schumacher's move to Ferrari triggered F1 musical chairs. Irvine joined Schumacher from Jordan; champions Benetton signed Ferrari pair Berger and Alesi; Coulthard joined Häkkinen at McLaren, and by joining Hill at Williams, Indy-star Jacques Villeneuve was recruited as the new Schumacher antidote.

Championship ranking	Championship points	Driver nationality	1995 Drivers Championship		Races contested	Race victories	Podiumse excl. victories	Races led	Lights to flag victories	Laps led	Poles	Fastest laps	Triple Crowns
			Driver	Car									
1	102	GER	Michael Schumacher	Benetton-Renault	17	9	2	14	1	454	4	8	1
2	69	GBR	Damon Hill	Williams-Renault	17	4	5	12	1	336	7	4	2
3	49	GBR	David Coulthard	Williams-Renault	17	1	7	11		191	5	2	1
4	45	GBR	Johnny Herbert	Benetton-Renault	17	2	2	3		27			
5	42	FRA	Jean Alesi	Ferrari	17	1	4	6		91		1	
6	31	AUT	Gerhard Berger	Ferrari	17		6	2		22	1	2	
7	17	FIN	Mika Häkkinen	McLaren-Mercedes	15		2	2		2			
8	16	FRA	Olivier Panis	Ligier-Mugen Honda	17		1						
9	15	GER	Heinz-Harald Frentzen	Sauber-Ford	17		1						
10	13	GBR	Mark Blundell	McLaren-Mercedes	15								
11	11	BRA	Rubens Barrichello	Jordan-Peugeot	17		1	1		1			
12	10	GBR	Eddie Irvine	Jordan-Peugeot	17		1						
13	7	GBR	Martin Brundle	Ligier-Mugen Honda	11		1						
14	5	ITA	Gianni Morbidelli	Footwork-Hart	10		1						
15	5	FIN	Mika Salo	Tyrrell-Yamaha	17								
16	3	FRA	Jean-Christophe Boullion	Sauber-Ford	11								
17	1	JPN	Aguri Suzuki	Ligier-Mugen Honda	5								
17	1	POR	Pedro Lamy	Minardi-Ford	8								

Championship ranking	Championship points	Team/Marque nationality	1995 Constructors Championship		Engine maker nationality	Races contested	Race victories	1-2 finishes	Podiums excl. victories	Races led	Laps led	Poles	Fastest laps
			Chassis	Engine									
1	137	GBR	Benetton B195	Renault 3.0 V10	FRA	17	11	1	4	16	481	4	8
2	112	GBR	Williams FW17, FW17B	Renault 3.0 V10	FRA	17	5	1	12	16	527	12	6
3	73	ITA	Ferrari 412T2	Ferrari 3.0 V12	ITA	17	1		10	7	113	1	3
4	30	GBR	McLaren MP4-10, MP4-10B, MP410C	Mercedes-Benz 3.0 V10	GER	17			2	2	2		
5	24	FRA	Ligier JS41	Mugen Honda 3.0 V10	JPN	17			2				
6	21	IRL	Jordan 195	Peugeot 3.0 V10	FRA	17			2	1	1		
7	18	SUI	Sauber C14	Ford Cosworth 3.0 V8	GBR	17			1				
8	5	GBR	Footwork FA16	Hart 3.0 V8	GBR	17			1				
9	5	GBR	Tyrrell 023	Yamaha 3.0 V10	JPN	17							
10	1	ITA	Minardi M195	Ford Cosworth 3.0 V8	GBR	17							

1996

Damon's dynasty destiny

THE TALE OF THE TITLE

- The singularity of Damon Hill's championship was twofold.
- First, 34 years after Graham Hill's first title, Damon uniquely matched his father's achievement.
- Second, he won by vanquishing another second-generation driver, Jacques Villeneuve, son of F1 star Gilles.
- Although a F1 rookie, reigning ChampCar champion and Indy 500 victor Villeneuve was no novice.
- Their intra-Williams battle went down to the wire, Hill bagging eight race victories, Villeneuve four.
- With pole and near victory in his first race, Villeneuve's was the most successful rookie season on record.
- With 12 race victories Williams-Renault dominated the constructors' championship.
- After a derisory two wins from the previous five seasons, the Ferrari renaissance truly began.
- Powered by their new megabucks V10 and led by their new megabucks driver, Maranello won three times.
- Michael Schumacher's first victory for the Scuderia in Spain was one of the great wet-weather drives.
- Without Schumacher, last year's champions Benetton-Renault did not conjure a single victory.
- But after a 15-season drought Ligier won again with an epic Monaco triumph by Olivier Panis.
- For McLaren it was another moribund year, but with clear signs of a brighter future.
- And not forgetting: 1-2-3-4-5 red lights start races.

THE CHASE FOR THE CHAMPIONSHIP

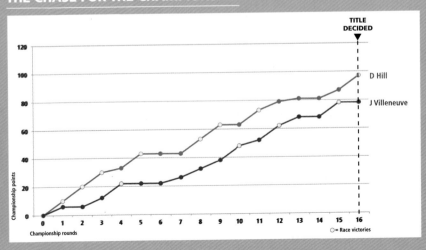

Williams-Renault FW18

AUSTRALIAN GP Melbourne
10 March 1996   Race 582

Damon Hill
Williams-Renault FW18 198.736kph, 123.489mph

The first GP at Albert Park was restarted after Brundle endured a violent 165mph barrel-rolling smash, climbing unhurt from an upturned Jordan. New Williams signing and F1 rookie Jacques Villeneuve sensationally annexed pole and led confidently. Team-leader Hill shadowed him awaiting a mistake. It came on lap 34. Soon after their only pit stops, Villeneuve, still leading but heavy with fuel, briefly skated off track under braking. He didn't forfeit his lead but kerbed an oil line, such that five from the end he had to back-off to save his oil-starved engine. Schumacher's Ferrari stayed with the Williams pair for the first 20 laps but fell away with brake trouble, teammate Irvine, who had out-qualified him, completing the podium.

POLE POSITION Villeneuve, Williams-Renault, 1m 32.371s (0.138s), 206.636kph, 128.398mph
LAPS 58 x 5.302 km, 3.295 miles (Race restarted for scheduled 58 laps following accident)
DISTANCE 307.516 km, 191.082 miles
STARTERS/FINISHERS 20/11
WEATHER Sunny, hot, dry
LAP LEADERS Villeneuve 1-29, 33-53 (50); Hill 30-32, 54-58 (8)
WINNER'S LAPS 1-29 P2, 30-32 P1, 33-53 P2, 54-58 P1
FASTEST LAP Villeneuve, Williams-Renault, 1m 33.421s (lap 27), 204.313kph, 126.955mph
CHAMPIONSHIP Hill 10, Villeneuve 6, Irvine 4, Berger 3, Häkkinen 2

Pos	Driver	Car	Time/gap	Grid	Stops	Tyres
1	D Hill	Williams-Renault	1h 32m 50.491s	2	1	G
2	J Villeneuve	Williams-Renault	–38.020s	1	1	G
3	E Irvine	Ferrari	–1m 2.571s	3	2	G
4	G Berger	Benetton-Renault	–1m 17.037s	7	2	G
5	M Häkkinen	McLaren-Mercedes	–1m 35.071s	5	1	G
6	M Salo	Tyrrell-Yamaha	–1 lap	10	2	G

BRAZILIAN GP Interlagos
31 March 1996   Race 583

Damon Hill
Williams-Renault FW18 167.673kph, 104.188mph

In the face of atrocious weather the race might have become a total lottery, but pole-sitter Hill drew away smoothly and strongly from a battling group of six. Until lap 26 this was led by Villeneuve, who spun out dicing with Alesi's Benetton-Renault. Despite a brief spin of his own, once released Alesi began to close the gap. But besides a couple of laps during his pit stop for slicks, Hill's lead was never under any undue threat. He won comfortably from Alesi, who, following an over-zealous accident in Australia, was driving under a strict edict from his new team, 'Finish.' Schumacher was never in the hunt for victory, coming home a lapped P3, but Barrichello's Jordan-Peugeot qualified on the front row and for a while raced strongly near the front.

POLE POSITION Hill, Williams-Renault, 1m 18.111s (0.981s), 199.331kph, 123.859mph
LAPS 71 x 4.325 km, 2.687 miles
DISTANCE 307.075 km, 190.808 miles
STARTERS/FINISHERS 22/12
WEATHER Overcast, warm, heavy rain, drying later
LAP LEADERS Hill 1-39, 43-71 (68); Alesi 40-42 (3)
WINNER'S LAPS 1-39 P1, 40-42 P2, 43-71 P1
FASTEST LAP Hill, Williams-Renault, 1m 21.547s (lap 65), 190.932kph, 118.640mph
CHAMPIONSHIP Hill 20, Villeneuve 6, Alesi 6, Häkkinen 5, Irvine 4

Pos	Driver	Car	Time/gap	Grid	Stops	Tyres
1	D Hill	Williams-Renault	1h 49m 52.976s	1	1	G
2	J Alesi	Benetton-Renault	–17.982s	5	1	G
3	M Schumacher	Ferrari	–1 lap	4	2	G
4	M Häkkinen	McLaren-Mercedes	–1 lap	7	2	G
5	M Salo	Tyrrell-Yamaha	–1 lap	11	2	G
6	O Panis	Ligier-Mugen Honda	–1 lap	15	2	G

Round 3/16	**ARGENTINEAN GP** Buenos Aires No 6		**Damon Hill**
	7 April 1996	**Race 584**	Williams-Renault FW18 160.013kph, 99.428mph

Hill's winning roll continued with a lights-to-flag two-stop victory from pole. From the front row Schumacher posed his only threat but a diminishing one, his vain chase renewed when a mid-race SC closed up the field. Hill was again able to ease cleanly away until, ironically, Schumacher's Ferrari suffered terminal rear wing damage from accident debris flung up by the Williams. The Benetton pair now looked good for second until problems intervened, so aided by the SC Villeneuve did well to make it a Williams 1-2, salvaging P2 after a poor start dropped him to P9. The SC was to deal with the inverted Ligier of Pedro Dinez, a flash fire due to a sticking fuel valve turning the scene into an inferno, renewing the disquiet many felt about refuelling.

POLE POSITION Hill, Williams-Renault, 1m 30.346s (0.252s), 169.707kph, 105.451mph
LAPS 72 x 4.259 km, 2.646 miles
DISTANCE 306.484 km, 190.440 miles
STARTERS/FINISHERS 22/10
WEATHER Sunny, warm, dry
LAP LEADERS Hill 1-72 (72); SC 29-33
WINNER'S LAPS 1-72 P1
FASTEST LAP Alesi, Benetton-Renault, 1m 29.413s (lap 66), 171.478kph, 106.552mph
CHAMPIONSHIP Hill 30, Villeneuve 12, Alesi 10, Irvine 6, Häkkinen 5

Pos	Driver	Car	Time/gap	Grid	Stops	Tyres
1	D Hill	Williams-Renault	1h 54m 55.322s	1	2	G
2	J Villeneuve	Williams-Renault	−12.167s	3	2	G
3	J Alesi	Benetton-Renault	−14.754s	4	2	G
4	R Barrichello	Jordan-Peugeot	−55.131s	6	1	G
5	E Irvine	Ferrari	−1m 4.991s	10	2	G
6	J Verstappen	Footwork-Hart	−1m 8.913s	7	2	G

Round 4/16	**EUROPEAN GP** Nürburgring		**Jacques Villeneuve**
	28 April 1996	**Race 585**	Williams-Renault FW18 196.006kph, 121.793mph

Initially rookie Villeneuve led comfortably, but by half-distance Schumacher, recovering from a slow start, had reeled him in. Over the final 15 laps Villeneuve was given a stern examination by a world champion at his home circuit in search of his first Ferrari victory. With two laps to go and backmarkers to negotiate the Ferrari came within 0.211s, but JV coolly held his nerve, the final margin 0.762s for an impressive maiden victory. Championship leader Hill's chance of a fifth consecutive victory went awry from the start and simply got worse. In a frantic last-lap assault on P3, Hill finished just behind Coulthard, his first podium for McLaren-Mercedes, but immediately ahead of Barrichello's quick Jordan-Peugeot, less than a second covering all three.

POLE POSITION Hill, Williams-Renault, 1m 18.941s (0.780s), 207.770kph, 129.103mph
LAPS 67 x 4.556 km, 2.831 miles
DISTANCE 305.252 km, 189.675 miles
STARTERS/FINISHERS 20/13
WEATHER Cloudy, warm, dry
LAP LEADERS Villeneuve 1-67 (67)
WINNER'S LAPS 1-67 P1
FASTEST LAP Hill, Williams-Renault, 1m 21.363s (lap 55), 201.585kph, 125.259mph
CHAMPIONSHIP Hill 33, Villeneuve 22, Alesi 10, Schumacher 10, Irvine 6

Pos	Driver	Car	Time/gap	Grid	Stops	Tyres
1	J Villeneuve	Williams-Renault	1h 33m 26.473s	2	2	G
2	M Schumacher	Ferrari	−0.762s	3	2	G
3	D Coulthard	McLaren-Mercedes	−32.834s	6	2	G
4	D Hill	Williams-Renault	−33.511s	1	2	G
5	R Barrichello	Jordan-Peugeot	−33.713s	5	2	G
6	M Brundle	Jordan-Peugeot	−55.567s	11	2	G

TOP **100** RACE

Round 5/16	**SAN MARINO GP** Imola		**Damon Hill**
	5 May 1996	**Race 586**	Williams-Renault FW18 193.760kph, 120.397mph

With Schumacher on pole, a fourth win from five races by Hill was no forgone conclusion. But it wasn't the Ferrari that led the first 19 laps but a fast-starting Coulthard from P3, the first time a McLaren-Mercedes had led on merit. In many ways Coulthard's intervention assisted Hill by limiting Schumacher's opportunity to make a decisive break from the front, but in any case Williams had out-manoeuvred Ferrari strategically by fuelling Hill for a long first stop. From this he rejoined P1, a lead he held comfortably to the finish. For Villeneuve, a first-lap tangle with a wayward Alesi put them both out of contention, Berger finishing a distant P3 for champions Benetton-Renault, Briatore beginning to ask questions of his new driver pairing.

POLE POSITION Schumacher, Ferrari, 1m 26.890s (0.215s), 202.683kph, 125.942mph
LAPS 63 x 4.892 km, 3.040 miles
DISTANCE 308.196 km, 191.504 miles
STARTERS/FINISHERS 21/11
WEATHER Cloudy with sunny intervals, warm, dry
LAP LEADERS D Coulthard 1-19 (19); Schumacher 20 (1); Hill 21-63 (43)
WINNER'S LAPS 1 P2, 2-19 P3, 20 P2, 21-63 P1
FASTEST LAP Hill, Williams-Renault, 1m 28.931s (lap 49), 198.032kph, 123.051mph
CHAMPIONSHIP Hill 43, Villeneuve 22, Schumacher 16, Alesi 11, Irvine 9

Pos	Driver	Car	Time/gap	Grid	Stops	Tyres
1	D Hill	Williams-Renault	1h 35m 26.156s	2	2	G
2	M Schumacher	Ferrari	−16.460s	1	2	G
3	G Berger	Benetton-Renault	−46.891s	7	2	G
4	E Irvine	Ferrari	−1m 1.583s	6	2	G
5	R Barrichello	Jordan-Peugeot	−1m 18.490s	9	2	G
6	J Alesi	Benetton-Renault	−1 lap	5	3	G

Ligier-Mugen Honda JS43

MONACO GP Monte Carlo
19 May 1996   **Race 587**

Olivier Panis
Ligier-Mugen Honda JS43 124.014kph, 77.059mph

On a wet surface Schumacher was beaten away from pole by Hill and within a minute had sensationally crashed out between Loews and Portier. Hill drew away from Alesi, then a long gap to a throng headed by Irvine. With a 26s lead, and having switched to slicks on lap 28, Hill's Renault blew on lap 41. For near on 20 laps it was now Alesi's race, but on lap 60 he too retired, a broken rear spring. The third and final leader of this bizarre race, from a P14 grid slot, was Olivier Panis and his Ligier-Mugen. Of 21 starters, just four were running at the finish, 14 retirements due to accidents. In difficult conditions, the race ending three laps early at the two-hour mark, Panis drove magnificently, and to his eternal credit the other finishers both started ahead of him.

POLE POSITION M Schumacher, Ferrari, 1m 20.356s (0.510s), 149.096kph, 92.644mph
LAPS 75 x 3.328 km, 2.068 miles (Scheduled for 78 laps but stopped after two hours)
DISTANCE 249.600 km, 155.094 miles
STARTERS/FINISHERS 21/7
WEATHER Overcast, warm, rain, drying later
LAP LEADERS D Hill, Williams-Renault 1-27, 30-40 (38); Alesi 28-29, 41-59 (21); Panis 60-75 (16)
WINNER'S LAPS 1-6 P12, 7-9 P11, 10-15 P10, 16-17 P9, 18-24 P8, 25-27 P7, 28 P9, 29 P6, 30-35 P4, 36-40 P3, 41-59 P2, 60-75 P1
FASTEST LAP J Alesi, Benetton-Renault, 1m 25.205s (lap 59), 140.611kph, 87.372mph
CHAMPIONSHIP Hill 43, Villeneuve 22, Schumacher 16, Panis 11, Alesi 11

Pos	Driver	Car	Time/gap	Grid	Stops	Tyres
1	O Panis	Ligier-Mugen Honda	2h 0m 45.629s	14	1	G
2	D Coulthard	McLaren-Mercedes	−4.828s	5	1	G
3	J Herbert	Sauber-Ford	−37.503s	13	1	G
4	H-H Frentzen	Sauber-Ford	−1 lap	9	3	G
5r	M Salo	Tyrrell-Yamaha	−5 laps	11	1	G
6r	M Häkkinen	McLaren-Mercedes	−5 laps	8	1	G

SPANISH GP Cataluña
2 June 1996   **Race 588**

Michael Schumacher
Ferrari F310 153.785kph, 95.558mph

After his Monaco faux pas, the reigning champion claimed his first Ferrari victory with one of the great wet-weather drives. He almost stalled on the grid, dropping way behind, but recovered to P6 after one lap. On lap 12 he overtook Alesi for P2 then leader Villeneuve. 'He left me standing,' Villeneuve shrugged afterwards, the Ferrari going away at a rate of 4s a lap. At its extreme Schumacher's lead was over a minute. On lap 37 Alesi got ahead of Villeneuve during the pit stops, both drivers doing well to remain on the same lap as the mesmeric Michael. Only six cars completed the two-hour ordeal, their drivers wet and cold from the teeming rain. Pole-sitter Hill got his wet race set-up badly wrong, going off for a third and final time on lap 11.

POLE POSITION D Hill, Williams-Renault, 1m 20.650s (0.434s), 211.000kph, 131.110mph
LAPS 65 x 4.727 km, 2.937 miles
DISTANCE 307.114 km, 190.832 miles
STARTERS/FINISHERS 20/6
WEATHER Overcast, warm, torrential rain
LAP LEADERS Villeneuve 1-11 (11); Schumacher 12-65 (54)
WINNER'S LAPS 1 P6, 2-3 P5, 4 P4, 5-8 P3, 9-11 P2, 12-65 P1
FASTEST LAP Schumacher, Ferrari, 1m 45.517s (lap 14), 161.234kph, 100.211mph
CHAMPIONSHIP Hill 43, Schumacher 26, Villeneuve 26, Alesi 17, Panis 11

Pos	Driver	Car	Time/gap	Grid	Stops	Tyres
1	M Schumacher	Ferrari	1h 59m 49.307s	3	2	G
2	J Alesi	Benetton-Renault	−45.302s	4	1	G
3	J Villeneuve	Williams-Renault	−48.388s	2	1	G
4	H-H Frentzen	Sauber-Ford	−1 lap	11	1	G
5	M Häkkinen	McLaren-Mercedes	−1 lap	10	1	G
6	P Diniz	Ligier-Mugen Honda	−2 laps	17	1	G

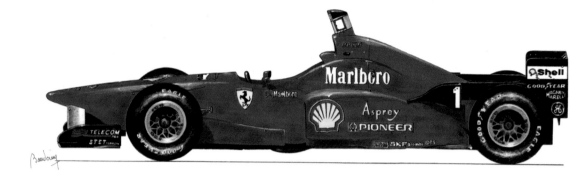

Ferrari F310

Round 8/16	**CANADIAN GP** Montréal						**Damon Hill**
	16 June 1996				**Race 589**		Williams-Renault FW18 190.541kph, 118.397mph

Willed on by a capacity crowd, Circuit Gilles Villeneuve was a track Jacques knew and a race he wanted. But by ousting Villeneuve from pole by .002s in a last-ditch effort, and then keeping his heavier-fuelled teammate at bay at the start, Hill had done most of the hard work by the first corner. To cover the strategic bases and neutralise the Schumacher threat, Williams had Hill on two stops, Villeneuve on one. In the event, Schumacher, who qualified P3, started from the back of the grid when the V10 failed to fire up. Hill easily won the intra-Williams strategy battle, rejoining from his second stop 12s ahead. Emphasising Williams superiority, Alesi's similarly Renault-powered Benetton held P3 throughout but finished 50s back.

POLE POSITION Hill, Williams-Renault, 1m 21.059s (0.020s), 196.345kph, 122.004mph
LAPS 69 x 4.421 km, 2.747 miles
DISTANCE 305.049 km, 189.549 miles
STARTERS/FINISHERS 22/8
WEATHER Sunny, warm, dry
LAP LEADERS Hill 1-27, 36-69 (61); Villeneuve 28-35 (8)
WINNER'S LAPS 1-27 P1, 28-35 P2, 36-69 P1
FASTEST LAP Villeneuve, Williams-Renault, 1m 21.916s (Lap 67), 194.291kph, 120.727mph
CHAMPIONSHIP Hill 53, Villeneuve 32, Schumacher 26, Alesi 21, Coulthard 13

Pos	Driver	Car	Time/gap	Grid	Stops	Tyres
1	D Hill	Williams-Renault	1h 36m 3.465s	1	2	G
2	J Villeneuve	Williams-Renault	−4.183s	2	1	G
3	J Alesi	Benetton-Renault	−54.656s	4	1	G
4	D Coulthard	McLaren-Mercedes	−1m 3.673s	10	1	G
5	M Häkkinen	McLaren-Mercedes	−1 lap	6	1	G
6	M Brundle	Jordan-Peugeot	−1 lap	9	2	G

Round 9/16	**FRENCH GP** Magny-Cours						**Damon Hill**
	30 June 1996				**Race 590**		Williams-Renault FW18 190.183kph, 118.174mph

Schumacher edged Hill from pole but, after the frustrations of Montréal, unreliability struck again, on the formation lap, the V10 spraying its oil on to track and the following Hill's visor. This was largely Hill's biggest problem of the day, as with Villeneuve qualifying back in P6 he cantered to his sixth victory of the season and a 25-point championship lead. Villeneuve did well to make it another Williams 1-2, taking Berger on lap 1, getting ahead of Häkkinen at the first pit stop, and overtaking Alesi for P2 at half-distance. Once Villeneuve had completed this passage through the field there was little interest, the other drivers in the top six finishing in grid order. As it was France, perhaps the spectators took something from Alesi's podium and a Renault 1-2-3-4.

POLE POSITION M Schumacher, Ferrari, 1m 15.898s (0.069), 201.344kph, 125.110mph
LAPS 72 x 4.250 km, 2.641 miles
DISTANCE 305.814 km, 190.024 miles
STARTERS/FINISHERS 21/12
WEATHER Cloudy with sunny intervals, warm, dry
LAP LEADERS Hill 1-27, 31-72 (69); Villeneuve 28-30 (3)
WINNER'S LAPS 1-27 P1, 28-30 P2, 31-72 P1
FASTEST LAP Villeneuve, Williams-Renault, 1m 18.610s (lap 48), 194.631kph, 120.939mph
CHAMPIONSHIP Hill 63, Villeneuve 38, Schumacher 26, Alesi 25, Coulthard 14

Pos	Driver	Car	Time/gap	Grid	Stops	Tyres
1	D Hill	Williams-Renault	1h 36m 28.795s	2	2	G
2	J Villeneuve	Williams-Renault	−8.127s	6	1	G
3	J Alesi	Benetton-Renault	−46.442s	3	2	G
4	G Berger	Benetton-Renault	−46.859s	4	2	G
5	M Häkkinen	McLaren-Mercedes	−1m 2.774s	5	2	G
6	D Coulthard	McLaren-Mercedes	−1 lap	7	2	G

| Round 10/16 | **BRITISH GP** Silverstone | | | | | | | **Jacques Villeneuve** |
| | **14 July 1996** | | | | **Race 591** | | | Williams-Renault FW18 199.576kph, 124.011mph |

Illustrating just how quickly championship fortunes change, a loose wheel-nut put Hill out of his home GP on lap 25, and a Villeneuve victory slashed his championship lead. A 90,000 crowd came to see Hill win from pole, but they were to be disappointed, Hill engulfed at the start then running P4 trapped behind Alesi and Häkkinen until his exit. Villeneuve, from alongside Hill, sailed rapidly away to an unchallenged victory. Unchallenged on the track, that is, Benetton later protesting the Williams front-wing endplates, their objection rejected after three hours' deliberation to leave Berger's Benetton P2 but inter-team relationships strained. For the third race running neither Ferrari finished and for the second in succession neither completed lap 6.

POLE POSITION D Hill, Williams-Renault, 1m 26.875s (0.195s), 210.177kph, 130.598mph
LAPS 61 x 5.072 km, 3.152 miles
DISTANCE 309.392 km, 192.247 miles
STARTERS/FINISHERS 20/11
WEATHER Cloudy with sunny intervals, warm, dry
LAP LEADERS Villeneuve 1-23, 31-61 (54); Alesi 24-30 (7)
WINNER'S LAPS 1-23 P1, 24-30 P2, 31-61 P1
FASTEST LAP Villeneuve, Williams-Renault, 1m 29.288s (lap 21), 204.497kph, 127.069mph
CHAMPIONSHIP Hill 63, Villeneuve 48, Schumacher 26, Alesi 25, Berger 16

Pos	Driver	Car	Time/gap	Grid	Stops	Tyres
1	J Villeneuve	Williams-Renault	1h 33m 0.874s	2	2	G
2	G Berger	Benetton-Renault	–19.026s	7	1	G
3	M Häkkinen	McLaren-Mercedes	–50.830s	4	2	G
4	R Barrichello	Jordan-Peugeot	–1m 6.716s	6	2	G
5	D Coulthard	McLaren-Mercedes	–1m 22.507s	9	2	G
6	M Brundle	Jordan-Peugeot	–1 lap	8	3	G

| Round 11/16 | **GERMAN GP** Hockenheim | | | | | | | **Damon Hill** |
| | **28 July 1996** | | | | **Race 592** | | | Williams-Renault FW18 225.409kph, 140.063mph |

An anti-climatic ending when Berger's Renault expired spectacularly three laps from a superb and exciting victory. Until that moment it had been some race. Not for the first time pole-man Hill made it hard for himself at the off, both one-stopping Benettons getting ahead, which was bad news for the two-stopping Williams driver. For 20 laps the three Renault-powered cars blasted round Hockenheim in close proximity, Hill first to stop as expected. A scintillating middle stint by Hill got him ahead of one Benetton, Alesi's, and right up behind the other, but to pass Berger would have had to make a mistake or blow up, which he did. Villeneuve started P6 to finish P3 once he got the better of Schumacher at his mid-race stop, Schumacher a desultory P4.

POLE POSITION Hill, Williams-Renault, 1m 43.912s (0.387s), 236.380kph, 146.880mph
LAPS 45 x 6.823 km, 4.240 miles
DISTANCE 307.022 km, 190.775 miles
STARTERS/FINISHERS 19/13
WEATHER Cloudy with sunny intervals, hot, dry
LAP LEADERS G Berger, Benetton-Renault 1-23, 35-42 (31); Hill 24-34, 43-45 (14)
WINNER'S LAPS 1-20 P3, 21 P5, 22 P4, 23 P3, 24-34 P1, 35-42 P2, 43-45 P1
FASTEST LAP Hill, Williams-Renault, 1m 46.504s (lap 26), 230.627kph, 143.306mph
CHAMPIONSHIP Hill 73, Villeneuve 52, Alesi 31, Schumacher 29, Coulthard 18

Pos	Driver	Car	Time/gap	Grid	Stops	Tyres
1	D Hill	Williams-Renault	1h 21m 43.417s	1	2	G
2	J Alesi	Benetton-Renault	–11.452s	5	1	G
3	J Villeneuve	Williams-Renault	–33.926s	6	1	G
4	M Schumacher	Ferrari	–41.517s	3	1	G
5	D Coulthard	McLaren-Mercedes	–42.196s	7	2	G
6	R Barrichello	Jordan-Peugeot	–1m 42.099s	9	1	G

TOP **100** RACE

| Round 12/16 | **HUNGARIAN GP** Hungaroring | | | | | | | **Jacques Villeneuve** |
| | **11 August 1996** | | | | **Race 593** | | | Williams-Renault FW18 172.372kph, 107.107mph |

From pole Schumacher led 18 laps, but at the first stops Villeneuve took command. Once more Hill spoilt his chances with a poor start, trapped behind Alesi's P3 Benetton for many laps. But on lap 31 Alesi made a mistake and Hill set about the 30s+ gap to JV. A tactically astute long third stint got him past Schumacher and a wheel-change glitch for Villeneuve soon had Hill on the leader's tail. But JV had previously shown ability to soak up pressure and at the flag led another 1-2 by less than a second. With Schumacher's dnf the destiny of the drivers' title was now an all-Williams affair, and with the constructors' title now safely locked away it would be a four-race shoot-out, Hill the clear favourite with his 17-point advantage.

POLE POSITION M Schumacher, Ferrari, 1m 17.129s (0.053s), 185.206kph, 115.082mph
LAPS 77 x 3.968 km, 2.466 miles
DISTANCE 305.536 km, 189.851 miles
STARTERS/FINISHERS 20/10
WEATHER Sunny, hot, dry
LAP LEADERS Schumacher 1-18 (18); Villeneuve 19-21, 25-58, 64-77 (51); Hill 22-24, 59-63 (8)
WINNER'S LAPS 1-18 P2, 19-21 P1, 22-24 P2, 25-58 P1, 59-63 P2, 64-77 P1
FASTEST LAP Hill, Williams-Renault, 1m 20.093s (lap 67), 178.352kph, 110.823mph
CHAMPIONSHIP Hill 79, Villeneuve 62, Alesi 35, Schumacher 29, Häkkinen 19

Pos	Driver	Car	Time/gap	Grid	Stops	Tyres
1	J Villeneuve	Williams-Renault	1h 46m 21.134s	3	3	G
2	D Hill	Williams-Renault	–0.771s	2	3	G
3	J Alesi	Benetton-Renault	–1m 24.212s	5	2	G
4	M Häkkinen	McLaren-Mercedes	–1 lap	7	2	G
5	O Panis	Ligier-Mugen Honda	–1 lap	11	2	G
6	R Barrichello	Jordan-Peugeot	–2 laps	13	2	G

BELGIAN GP Spa Francorchamps
25 August 1996 Race 594

Michael Schumacher
Ferrari F310 208.442kph, 129.520mph

The race outcome largely turned on a lap 14 SC, deployed for three laps when Verstappen had a big accident exiting Stavelot. Whereas Ferrari called in the chasing Schumacher, leader Villeneuve stayed out due to a radio glitch. This wrong-footed Hill's imminent stop and, net-net, in the SC queue Schumacher was now ahead of Villeneuve and Hill was down at P13. The McLaren pair led briefly, but once they made their one stop the final 20 laps was all MS versus JV, Schumacher on a familiar track which has been good to him, Villeneuve on a track learnt from a computer game. Try as he might, a disappointed Villeneuve simply could not get ahead of Schumacher, whereas a relieved Hill salvaged P5, still 13 points to the good.

POLE POSITION Villeneuve, Williams-Renault, 1m 50.574s (0.406s), 226.859kph, 140.964mph
LAPS 44 x 6.968 km, 4.330 miles
DISTANCE 306.592 km, 190.507 miles
STARTERS/FINISHERS 19/10
WEATHER Overcast, warm, damp at first then dry
LAP LEADERS Villeneuve 1-14, 30-32 (17); D Coulthard, McLaren-Mercedes 15-21 (7); Häkkinen 22-23 (2); Schumacher 24-29, 33-44 (18); SC 15-17 (3)
WINNER'S LAPS 1-13 P2, 14 P3, 15 P4, 16-21 P3, 22-23 P2, 24-29 P1, 30-32 P2, 33-44 P1
FASTEST LAP Berger, Benetton-Renault, 1m 53.067s (lap 42), 221.857kph, 137.856mph
CHAMPIONSHIP Hill 81, Villeneuve 68, Schumacher 39, Alesi 38, Häkkinen 23

Pos	Driver	Car	Time/gap	Grid	Stops	Tyres
1	M Schumacher	Ferrari	1h 28m 15.125s	3	2	G
2	J Villeneuve	Williams-Renault	−5.602s	1	2	G
3	M Häkkinen	McLaren-Mercedes	−15.710s	6	1	G
4	J Alesi	Benetton-Renault	−19.125s	7	2	G
5	D Hill	Williams-Renault	−29.179s	2	2	G
6	G Berger	Benetton-Renault	−29.896s	5	2	G

ITALIAN GP Monza
8 September 1996 Race 595

Michael Schumacher
Ferrari F310 236.034kph, 146.665mph

News broke that Williams had sacked Hill for 1997. Hill took pole from Villeneuve yet neither added to their points due to tyre problems. Not their own tyres, but by glancing the temporary linked-tyre stacks marking chicanes. These were to prevent cars dangerously straightlining recently lowered kerbs. During the race almost every car, including winner Schumacher, clouted these bizarre tyre 'kerbs', but some paid more dearly than others. Race leader Hill threw it away on lap 5, which made Villeneuve's similar misjudgement on lap 2 even more costly in their battle for points. The race was a straight fight between Alesi and Schumacher, the Ferrari taking the lead at the mid-race tyre stop for the Scuderia's first home victory in eight years.

POLE POSITION D Hill, Williams-Renault, 1m 24.204s (0.317s), 246.686kph, 153.284mph
LAPS 53 x 5.770 km, 3.585 miles
DISTANCE 305.772 km, 189.998 miles
STARTERS/FINISHERS 20/10
WEATHER Sunny, hot, dry
LAP LEADERS Hill 1-5 (5); Alesi 6-30 (25); Schumacher 31-53 (23)
WINNER'S LAPS 1 P6, 2-3 P4, 4-5 P3, 6-30 P2, 31-53 P1
FASTEST LAP Schumacher, Ferrari, 1m 26.110 (lap 50), 241.225kph, 149.891mph
CHAMPIONSHIP Hill 81, Villeneuve 68, Schumacher 49, Alesi 44, Häkkinen 27

Pos	Driver	Car	Time/gap	Grid	Stops	Tyres
1	M Schumacher	Ferrari	1h 17m 43.642s	3	1	G
2	J Alesi	Benetton-Renault	−18.265s	6	1	G
3	M Häkkinen	McLaren-Mercedes	−1m 6.635s	4	2	G
4	M Brundle	Jordan-Peugeot	−1m 25.217s	9	1	G
5	R Barrichello	Jordan-Peugeot	−1m 25.475s	10	1	G
6	P Diniz	Ligier-Mugen Honda	−1 lap	14	1	G

PORTUGUESE GP Estoril
22 September 1996 Race 596

Jacques Villeneuve
Williams-Renault FW18 182.423kph, 113.353mph

By leading in a sixth Williams 1-2, Villeneuve guaranteed a Suzuka showdown. Hill beat Villeneuve to pole by 0.009s and pulled away at the start. With Villeneuve pinned behind Alesi and Schumacher it looked to be game over. Villeneuve's superb victory drive began on lap 16 with a heart-stopping move on Schumacher. At the Senna Curve JV audaciously drove around the outside of the Ferrari and then set off after Alesi, who he passed in the pits, leaving 48 laps to make up 10s on Hill and find a way past. By lap 40 the two were together but passing was another thing, so Villeneuve bided his time until their third and final stop, stunning Hill and his pit crew by rejoining just ahead. That day the French-Canadian was irresistible.

POLE POSITION Hill, Williams-Renault, 1m 20.330s (0.009s), 195.393kph, 121.412mph
LAPS 70 x 4.360 km, 2.709 miles
DISTANCE 305.200 km, 189.642 miles
STARTERS/FINISHERS 20/16
WEATHER Cloudy with sunny intervals, warm, dry
LAP LEADERS Hill 1-17, 22-33, 36-48 (42); Alesi 18-21 (4); Villeneuve 34-35, 49-70 (24)
WINNER'S LAPS 1-15 P4, 16-17 P3, 18 P2, 19 P7, 20 P4, 21-22 P3, 23-33 P2, 34-35 P1, 36-48 P2, 49-70 P1
FASTEST LAP Villeneuve, Williams-Renault, 1m 22.873s (lap 37), 189.398kph, 117.687mph
CHAMPIONSHIP Hill 87, Villeneuve 78, Schumacher 53, Alesi 47, Häkkinen 27

Pos	Driver	Car	Time/gap	Grid	Stops	Tyres
1	J Villeneuve	Williams-Renault	1h 40m 22.915s	2	3	G
2	D Hill	Williams-Renault	−19.966s	1	3	G
3	M Schumacher	Ferrari	−53.765s	4	3	G
4	J Alesi	Benetton-Renault	−55.109s	3	2	G
5	E Irvine	Ferrari	−1m 27.389s	6	2	G
6	G Berger	Benetton-Renault	−1m 33.141s	5	2	G

JAPANESE GP Suzuka
13 October 1996   Race 597

Damon Hill
Williams-Renault FW18 197.520kph, 122.733mph

Ironic was not the only word that sprung to mind when, with a lights-to-flag victory, Damon Hill won the drivers' championship for himself and his now erstwhile team. Villeneuve never featured, wasting pole with an atrocious start which dropped him to P6, never rising above P4, and finally crashing out on lap 36 when a rear wheel came adrift shortly after his second pit stop. That moment Hill became the new world champion, celebrating his immense achievement on the podium with Schumacher and Häkkinen, who had fought closely for P2 throughout much of the race. Although the championship went to the wire, the final points table now more suitably reflected Hill's authority over the season's campaign, the winner of eight races to JV's four.

POLE POSITION J Villeneuve, Williams-Renault, 1m 38.909s (0.461s), 213.432kph, 132.621mph
LAPS 52 x 5.864 km, 3.644 miles
DISTANCE 304.718 km, 189.343 miles
STARTERS/FINISHERS 19/13
WEATHER Sunny, warm, dry
LAP LEADERS Hill 1-52 (52)
WINNER'S LAPS 1-52 P1
FASTEST LAP J Villeneuve, Williams-Renault, 1m 44.043s (lap 34), 202.900kph, 126.077mph
CHAMPIONSHIP Hill 97, Villeneuve 78, Schumacher 59, Alesi 47, Häkkinen 31

Pos	Driver	Car	Time/gap	Grid	Stops	Tyres
1	D Hill	Williams-Renault	1h 32m 33.791s	2	2	G
2	M Schumacher	Ferrari	−1.883s	3	2	G
3	M Häkkinen	McLaren-Mercedes	−3.212s	5	2	G
4	G Berger	Benetton-Renault	−26.526s	4	3	G
5	M Brundle	Jordan-Peugeot	−1m 7.120s	10	2	G
6	H-H Frentzen	Sauber-Ford	−1m 21.186s	7	2	G

1996 CHAMPIONSHIP FACTS AND FOLKLORE

- In a comparatively quiet year politically, attention centred on the new 1997–2001 Concorde Agreement. McLaren, Williams and Tyrrell refused to sign, unhappy with the direction F1 was taking and the financial arrangements on offer.

- Their stand-off appeared to have misfired when the FIA came to terms with the other teams, including Ferrari, and were then unwilling to allow the three dissidents back into the F1 'club'.

- Entry into F1 would be restricted to a maximum of 12 team franchises.

- 1996 F1 cars looked a bit different with the adoption of mandatory removable safety padding surrounding the cockpit, its increased height significantly improving head protection laterally.

- Aerodynamically-shaped suspension parts made a gradual appearance but were banned by the end of the year.

- Car numbering would now be based on team performance in the constructors' championship the previous season, although the drivers' champion would retain number 1. Thus Ferrari, not Benetton held the coveted number 1 for 1996.

- Goodyear's tyre monopoly continued for a fifth season but Japanese manufacturer Bridgestone laid plans for entry in 1997.

- To enhance the TV spectacle, qualifying was restricted to one hour on the Saturday while the 107% rule weeded out the no-hopers – any car timed over 7% outside the pole lap would not start the race.

- The red-and-green lights starting system was replaced by the current procedure of five red lights illuminated sequentially and then extinguished as one to release the grid.

- In a 16-race championship schedule, Melbourne took over from Adelaide, the Australian GP shifting from its traditional end of year spot to become the season opener.

- 1996 saw Damon Hill show that, like his father before him, he too could put together a championship year, any susceptibility to the occasional error more than compensated by resolute tenacity coupled with intrinsic skill.

- His new teammate at Williams-Renault, the highly rated Jacques Villeneuve, was also the son of a famous F1 father. When the French-Canadian took pole and nearly won his debut race it looked as though Hill would have his hands more than full.

- At 36 Hill knew this was his last title chance and he prepared thoroughly. His campaign strategy was to make a fast start and then sit on his points lead. Three races, three wins was exactly what he was looking for although, as it turned out, the contest was not decided until the final race.

- Hill, the eighth British title-holder, was a deserving champion by any measure. Against his two chief rivals Villeneuve and Schumacher, the stats read, Hill shown first, poles: 9-3-4; races led: 12-9-5; laps led: 480-285-114; and race wins: 8-4-3. Decisive.

- Although a top-flight monoposto racer, F1 cars, tracks, and standing starts were unfamiliar territory for Villeneuve, and for a first season he did extremely well. It began by emulating Andretti, 1968 for Lotus, and Reutemann, 1972 for Brabham, by winning pole on debut, but in his case without the 'home GP' stimulus the other two enjoyed.

- But undoubtedly his best race, of which father Gilles would have been immensely proud, was his mighty victory in Portugal to keep his championship hopes alive, his pass of Schumacher undoubtedly the move of the year.

- This year combining reliability with superior speed, another 12 race victories brought Williams-Renault their fourth constructors' title in five years to equal the record total of eight held by Ferrari since the constructors' trophy began in 1958.

- Yet despite all this success Williams released Hill at the end of four years, during which period he had won 21 races from 65 starts, an extraordinary one-in-three strike rate over four seasons in which he had competed against the likes of Prost, Senna, Schumacher and now Villeneuve.

- Surprisingly, for 1997 Hill took his 'number 1' to emblazon the nose of a Bridgestone-shod Arrows-Yamaha, apparently impressed by the potential of the package and the Leafield set-up of new team owner Tom Walkinshaw.

- After a miserable record of two solitary wins over the preceding five years, Jean Todt now had Michael Schumacher to spearhead Luca di Montezemolo's master-plan to restore the Italian marque to former glories. There was no shortage of cash thanks to the patronage of Gianni

Championship ranking	Championship points	Driver nationality	1996 Drivers Championship		Races contested	Race victories	Podiumse excl. victories	Races led	Lights to flag victories	Laps led	Poles	Fastest laps	Triple Crowns
			Driver	Car									
1	97	GBR	Damon Hill	Williams-Renault	16	8	2	12	2	480	9	5	2
2	78	CAN	Jacques Villeneuve	Williams-Renault	16	4	7	9	1	285	3	6	
3	59	GER	Michael Schumacher	Ferrari	15	3	5	5		114	4	2	
4	47	FRA	Jean Alesi	Benetton-Renault	16		8	5		60		2	
5	31	FIN	Mika Häkkinen	McLaren-Mercedes	16		4	1		2			
6	21	AUT	Gerhard Berger	Benetton-Renault	16		2	1		31		1	
7	18	GBR	David Coulthard	McLaren-Mercedes	16		2	2		26			
8	14	BRA	Rubens Barrichello	Jordan-Peugeot	16								
9	13	FRA	Olivier Panis	Ligier-Mugen Honda	16	1		1		16			
10	11	GBR	Eddie Irvine	Ferrari	16		1						
11	8	GBR	Martin Brundle	Jordan-Peugeot	16								
12	7	GER	Heinz-Harald Frentzen	Sauber-Ford	16								
13	5	FIN	Mika Salo	Tyrrell-Yamaha	16								
14	4	GBR	Johnny Herbert	Sauber-Ford	16		1						
15	2	BRA	Pedro Diniz	Ligier-Mugen Honda	16								
16	1	NLD	Jos Verstappen	Footwork-Hart	16								

RACE 583, Brazilian GP: In the face of atrocious weather the race might have become a total lottery, but pole-sitter Hill drew away smoothly and strongly from a battling group of six.

RACE 584, Argentinean GP: Uniquely, two second-generation F1 drivers, Damon Hill (right), son of Graham, and Gilles Villeneuve's son, Jacques, fought over the 1996 championship; they are shown here following their second of six team 1–2 finishes.

Agnelli of FIAT and increasing commitment from Philip Morris through Marlboro. Agnelli memorably expressed his personal confidence in their new driver: 'If Ferrari doesn't win with Schumacher, it will be our fault.'

- The recovery process began with three wins for the new V10-powered car, but the F310 was a troublesome design, resulting in John Barnard's tenure at Ferrari coming under pressure, especially with the arrival of Ross Brawn from Benetton in December.

- In Spain that great leveller, rain, allowed Schumacher to overcome the constraints of his equipment and conspicuously demonstrate his genius, but one that got away was Monaco, crashing on the opening lap after taking pole. In a race of attrition, Olivier Panis came through to win for Ligier, their first success in 15 seasons, his one and only. It also introduced Mugen Honda to the winners' list for F1 engine suppliers.

- Speculation about Ligier's reinvention as an all-French team was at the crux of Tom Walkinshaw's abandonment of his interests and switching his attention to Arrows (née Footwork), taking over Jackie Oliver's operation and moving to new headquarters at Leafield.

- The F1 landscape was changing, McLaren contributing by ending the longest title sponsorship in F1 history. Their 22 years with Marlboro had begun in 1974, 96 of McLaren's 104 race victories made in the well-known red and white colours, the iconic partnership spawning nine drivers' titles.

- McLaren had also wooed Adrian Newey from Williams, but not before he and Patrick Head had completed design work for the 1997 FW19. However, one sensed a shifting in the balance of power between Williams, McLaren and Ferrari, especially with Renault threatening withdrawal after 1997, while Benetton's brief period in the ascendancy seemed to have come and gone.

- But then there was the Blue Oval. Ford's 'works' team, Sauber, received a new V10 for 1996 but the engine and results were disappointing. For 1997 Ford announced that a new V10 would be built by Cosworth for exclusive use by their new team, Stewart Grand Prix. Was this the initiative even Agnelli feared?

Championship ranking	Championship points	Team/Marque nationality	1996 Constructors Championship		Engine maker nationality	Races contested	Race victories	1-2 finishes	Podiums excl. victories	Races led	Laps led	Poles	Fastest laps
			Chassis	Engine									
1	175	GBR	Williams FW18	Renault 3.0 V10	FRA	16	12	6	9	16	765	12	11
2	70	ITA	Ferrari F310	Ferrari 3.0 V10	ITA	16	3		6	5	114	4	2
3	68	ITA	Benetton B196	Renault 3.0 V10	FRA	16			10	6	91		3
4	49	GBR	McLaren MP4-11, MP4-11B	Mercedes-Benz 3.0 V10	GER	16			6	2	28		
5	22	IRL	Jordan 196	Peugeot 3.0 V10	FRA	16							
6	15	FRA	Ligier JS43	Mugen Honda 3.0 V10	JPN	16	1		1	16			
7	11	SUI	Sauber C15	Ford Cosworth 3.0 V10	GBR	16			1				
8	5	GBR	Tyrrell 024	Yamaha 3.0 V10	JPN	16							
9	1	GBR	Footwork FA17	Hart 3.0 V8	GBR	16							

1997

Jacques jubilant, Michael vilified

THE TALE OF THE TITLE

- The 1997 championship quickly became a battle between Jacques Villeneuve and Michael Schumacher.
- Swinging first one way then the other, their titanic struggle came to the final round at Jerez.
- There, on the brink of defeat by fair means, Schumacher reverted to type and chose foul, ramming JV.
- But this time his ploy failed and Villeneuve justly won, exceeding Schumacher 7-5 in race victories.
- As well as plumbing the depths, Schumacher reached the heights, *regenmeister* at Monaco and Spa.
- Whilst ultimately deserving, JV found the championship journey 'the most difficult season of my life'.
- Williams took a record ninth constructors' title, their fifth in six seasons.
- For the departing Engins Renault, it was a sixth straight championship.
- Williams-Renault won another eight races to Ferrari's five, McLaren's three and Benetton just one.
- Retiree Berger delivered Benetton's swansong victory, Gerhard one of six winning drivers.
- Defending champion Damon Hill so nearly made it seven with his near-miss for Arrows-Yamaha in Hungary.
- In rather contrived circumstances at the final round, Häkkinen became a race-winner at last after 96 starts.
- With engine partner Mercedes-Benz, McLaren re-emerged as a renewed force for constructors' honours.
- And not forgetting: Mercedes, winners again after 42 years; Stewart and Prost back as team owners.

THE CHASE FOR THE CHAMPIONSHIP

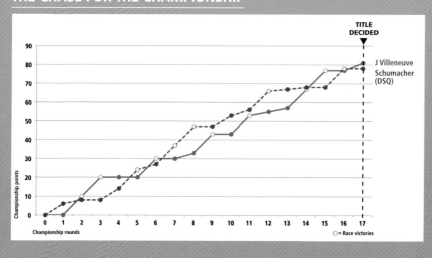

McLaren-Mercedes MP4/12

Round 1/17	**AUSTRALIAN GP** Melbourne 9 March 1997	**Race 598**

David Coulthard

McLaren-Mercedes MP4/12 203.926kph, 126.714mph

Flying in the face of pre-season conventional wisdom, round one went to Coulthard, McLaren's first win since Senna in 1993. An overambitious Irvine eliminated dominant pole-sitter Villeneuve at the first corner, so Frentzen, Hill's replacement at Williams, quickly established a significant lead over Coulthard and Schumacher, dictated by their differing strategies. Frentzen's fumbled second stop enabled one-stoppers Coulthard and Schumacher to get ahead, the three racing closely for ten laps. On lap 51 it became just two when the Ferrari made an unexpected splash-and-dash, the matter finally settled in leader Coulthard's favour when a Williams disc-brake exploded with two to go. Champion Hill's Arrows went out on the warm-up lap.

POLE POSITION J Villeneuve, Williams-Renault, 1m 29.369s (1.754s), 213.577kph, 132.711mph
LAPS 58 x 5.302 km, 3.295 miles
DISTANCE 307.516 km, 191.082 miles
STARTERS/FINISHERS 21/10
WEATHER Cloudy with sunny intervals, warm, dry
LAP LEADERS Frentzen 1-17, 33-39 (24); Coulthard 18-32, 40-58 (34)
WINNER'S LAPS 1-17 P2, 18-32 P1, 33 P4, 34 P3, 35-39 P2, 40-58 P1
FASTEST LAP H-H Frentzen, Williams-Renault, 1m 30.585s (lap 36), 210.710kph, 130.929mph
CHAMPIONSHIP Coulthard 10, M Schumacher 6, Häkkinen 4, Berger 3, Panis 2

Pos	Driver	Car	Time/gap	Grid	Stops	Tyres
1	D Coulthard	McLaren-Merced	es1h 30m 28.718s	4	1	G
2	M Schumacher	Ferrari	–20.046s	3	2	G
3	M Häkkinen	McLaren-Mercedes	–22.177s	6	1	G
4	G Berger	Benetton-Renault	–22.841s	10	1	G
5	O Panis	Prost-Mugen Honda	–1m 0.308s	9	2	B
6	N Larini	Sauber-Petronas	–1m 36.040s	13	1	G

Round 2/17	**BRAZILIAN GP** Interlagos 30 March 1997	**Race 599**

Jacques Villeneuve

Williams-Renault FW19 192.905kph, 119.866mph

For the second race running championship favourite Villeneuve was out at turn one, this time coming off second best to Schumacher. Fortuitously the race was restarted and this time he made no mistake from pole to lead all but three laps during his second stop. Throughout he was tracked by Berger, but the Benetton had lost too much time getting past Häkkinen and Schumacher in the early stages to seriously pressure Villeneuve. Häkkinen passed a gripless Schumacher to finish P4, but by using Bridgestones which enabled a competitive one-stop strategy, Panis in a Prost (née Ligier) wound up third. Frentzen's stock at Williams plummeted by qualifying P8 and finishing P9, the team mystified by his performance. Hill's Arrows at one time held P3.

POLE POSITION Villeneuve, Williams-Renault, 1m 16.004s (0.590s), 203.294kph, 126.321mph
LAPS 72 x 4.292 km, 2.667 miles (Race restarted for scheduled 72 laps following accidents)
DISTANCE 309.024 km, 192.019 miles
STARTERS/FINISHERS 22/18
WEATHER Overcast, humid, dry
LAP LEADERS Villeneuve 1-45, 49-72 (69); Berger 46-48 (3)
WINNER'S LAPS 1-45 P1, 46-48 P2, 49-72 P1
FASTEST LAP Villeneuve, Williams-Renault, 1m 18.397s (lap 28), 197.089kph, 122.466mph
CHAMPIONSHIP Coulthard 10, Villeneuve 10, Berger 9, M Schumacher 8, Häkkinen 7

Pos	Driver	Car	Time/gap	Grid	Stops	Tyres
1	J Villeneuve	Williams-Renault	1h 36m 06.990s	1	2	G
2	G Berger	Benetton-Renault	–4.190s	3	2	G
3	O Panis	Prost-Mugen Honda	–15.870s	5	1	B
4	M Häkkinen	McLaren-Mercedes	–33.033s	4	2	G
5	M Schumacher	Ferrari	–33.731s	2	2	G
6	J Alesi	Benetton-Renault	–34.020s	6	2	G

Round 3/17	**ARGENTINEAN GP** Buenos Aires No 6	**Jacques Villeneuve**
	13 April 1997 Race 600	Williams-Renault FW19 164.155kph, 102.002mph

Michael Schumacher eliminated himself in yet more first-corner mayhem and brought out the SC. Implementing a unique four-stint strategy Villeneuve led all but six laps, but two-stop Irvine chased him down to finish under a second behind, silencing mounting Italian press criticism. With eight laps left it seemed the Ferrari must win, yet, despite feeling unwell and a gearbox malfunction, a straight-line speed advantage kept Villeneuve ahead in a thrilling climax. Frentzen retired early with clutch trouble while Panis qualified the Prost P3, and was P2 on lap 18 when hydraulics caused retirement. In his third race, rookie Ralf Schumacher drove superbly from P9 on lap 2 to a P3 podium, only tarnished by punting off Jordan teammate Fisichella in a muscular pass.

POLE POSITION Villeneuve, Williams-Renault, 1m 24.473s (0.798s), 181.506kph, 112.783mph
LAPS 72 x 4.259 km, 2.646 miles
DISTANCE 306.502 km, 190.452 miles
STARTERS/FINISHERS 22/10
WEATHER Cloudy with sunny intervals, hot, dry
LAP LEADERS Villeneuve 1-38, 45-72 (66); Irvine 39-44 (6); SC 2-4 (3)
WINNER'S LAPS 1-38 P1, 39 P3, 40-44 P2, 45-72 P1
FASTEST LAP Berger, Benetton-Renault, 1m 27.981s (lap 63), 174.269kph, 108.286mph
CHAMPIONSHIP Villeneuve 20, Coulthard 10, Berger 10, Häkkinen 9, M Schumacher 8

Pos	Driver	Car	Time/gap	Grid	Stops	Tyres
1	J Villeneuve	Williams-Renault	1h 52m 1.715s	1	3	G
2	E Irvine	Ferrari	–0.979s	7	2	G
3	R Schumacher	Jordan-Peugeot	–12.089s	6	1	G
4	J Herbert	Sauber-Petronas	–29.919s	8	2	G
5	M Häkkinen	McLaren-Mercedes	–30.351s	17	1	G
6	G Berger	Benetton-Renault	–31.393s	12	1	G

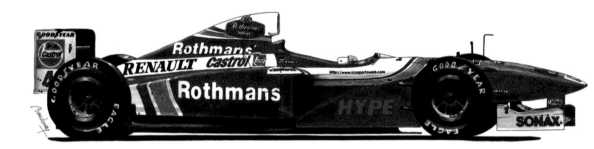

Williams-Renault FW19

Round 4/17	**SAN MARINO GP** Imola	**Heinz-Harald Frentzen**
	27 April 1997 Race 601	Williams-Renault FW19 201.509kph, 125.212mph

For his maiden victory, H-H Frentzen led home a German 1-2, the first since 1939, winning a close race with M. Schumacher. From pole, Villeneuve initially led Schumacher who had outgunned H-H at the start, but the first stops held the key. Frentzen was the last of the three to pit, quick lappery bringing him out P1, the Ferrari remaining the sandwich filling, the Williams pair switching places. Villeneuve dropped away into retirement with more gearbox ailments but Frentzen drove a strong second stint, pulling out 5s, enough to stave off Schumacher after their second stops and save the day for Williams. Ferrari and Jordan duelled race-long over what would be third, Irvine scoring a successive podium, Fisichella his first points.

POLE POSITION J Villeneuve, Williams-Renault, 1m 23.303s (0.343s), 213.053kph, 132.385mph
LAPS 62 x 4.930 km, 3.063 miles
DISTANCE 305.660 km, 189.928 miles
STARTERS/FINISHERS 21/11
WEATHER Cloudy with sunny intervals, warm, dry
LAP LEADERS Villeneuve 1-25 (25); Frentzen 26-43, 45-62 (36); M Schumacher 44 (1)
WINNER'S LAPS 1-23 P3, 24-25 P2, 26-43 P1, 44 P2, 45-62 P1
FASTEST LAP Frentzen, Williams-Renault, 1m 25.531s (lap 42), 207.503kph, 128.937mph
CHAMPIONSHIP Villeneuve 20, M Schumacher 14, Coulthard 10, Frentzen 10, Irvine 10

Pos	Driver	Car	Time/gap	Grid	Stops	Tyres
1	H-H Frentzen	Williams-Renault	1h 31m 0.673s	2	2	G
2	M Schumacher	Ferrari	–1.237s	3	2	G
3	E Irvine	Ferrari	–1m 18.343s	9	2	G
4	G Fisichella	Jordan-Peugeot	–1m 23.388s	6	2	G
5	J Alesi	Benetton-Renault	–1 lap	14	1	G
6	M Häkkinen	McLaren-Mercedes	–1 lap	8	1	G

Ferrari F310B

MONACO GP Monte Carlo

11 May 1997   Race 602

Michael Schumacher

Ferrari F310B 104.264kph, 64.787mph

Apart from a late race escape-road incident at Ste Devote in the treacherously wet conditions, a virtuoso performance by Schumacher took him ahead of Villeneuve in the championship for the first time. Neither Williams driver finished, completely out of the running anyway when the team inexplicably started both cars on slicks. Schumacher, on intermediates, led by 27s after just six laps and despite his brief pirouette had doubled it by the finish, which came 16 laps early at the two-hour cut-off. To the unbridled joy of Jackie, Barrichello delivered Stewart-Ford an incredible podium in their fifth race, from P10 to P2 in six laps. Irvine finished third from P15, while Panis came next, adding substance to his surprise Monaco victory last year.

POLE POSITION H-H Frentzen, Williams-Renault, 1m 18.216s (0.019s), 154.924kph, 96.266mph
LAPS 62 x 3.366 km, 2.092 miles
DISTANCE 208.692 km, 129.675 miles
STARTERS/FINISHERS 22/10
WEATHER Overcast, cold, rain
LAP LEADERS M Schumacher 1-62 (62)
WINNER'S LAPS 1-62 P1
FASTEST LAP M Schumacher, Ferrari, 1m 53.315s (lap 26), 106.937kph, 66.448mph
CHAMPIONSHIP M Schumacher 24, Villeneuve 20, Irvine 14, Coulthard 10, Frentzen 10

Pos	Driver	Car	Time/gap	Grid	Stops	Tyres
1	M Schumacher	Ferrari	2h 0m 5.654s	2	1	G
2	R Barrichello	Stewart-Ford	−53.306s	10	1	B
3	E Irvine	Ferrari	−1m 22.108s	15	1	G
4	O Panis	Prost-Mugen Honda	−1m 44.402s	12	1	B
5	M Salo	Tyrrell-Ford	−1 lap	14	0	G
6	G Fisichella	Jordan-Peugeot	−1 lap	4	1	G

SPANISH GP Cataluña

25 May 1997   Race 603

Jacques Villeneuve

Williams-Renault FW19 200.314kph, 124.469mph

Goodyear admitted later that on this abrasive track they had gone too soft, heavy tyre-wear creating havoc for most of the Goodyear runners and enabling the Bridgestone-shod Prost of Olivier Panis to almost win from P12. Almost. Barring his way was Villeneuve's Williams, one of very few Goodyear-equipped cars – including Schumacher who finished P4, and his teammate H-H Frentzen P8 – to complete the distance with only two stops, faster over the race distance by a mere 5.804s than Panis' similar strategy. This was a different JV victory, thoughtfully planned and patiently driving on rails to save the tyres. A new engine bounced McLaren-Mercedes, invisible of late, back towards the front of the grid, P3 and P5, to reliably finish P6 and P7.

POLE POSITION Villeneuve, Williams-Renault, 1m 16.525s (0.266s), 222.421kph, 138.206mph
LAPS 64 x 4.728 km, 2.938 miles (Scheduled for 65 laps but reduced after aborted start)
DISTANCE 302.469 km, 187.946 miles
STARTERS/FINISHERS 22/15
WEATHER Cloudy with sunny intervals, warm, dry
LAP LEADERS Villeneuve 1-20, 22-45, 47-64 (62); Alesi 21 (1); M Schumacher 46 (1)
WINNER'S LAPS 1-20 P1, 21 P2, 22-45 P1, 46 P2, 47-64 P1
FASTEST LAP G Fisichella, Jordan-Peugeot, 1m 22.242s (lap 20), 206.959kph, 128.599mph
CHAMPIONSHIP Villeneuve 30, M Schumacher 27, Panis 15, Irvine 14, Coulthard 11

Pos	Driver	Car	Time/gap	Grid	Stops	Tyres
1	J Villeneuve	Williams-Renault	1h 30m 35.896s	1	2	G
2	O Panis	Prost-Mugen Honda	−5.804s	12	2	B
3	J Alesi	Benetton-Renault	−12.534s	4	2	G
4	M Schumacher	Ferrari	−17.979s	7	3	G
5	J Herbert	Sauber-Petronas	−27.986s	10	3	G
6	D Coulthard	McLaren-Mercedes	−29.744s	3	3	G

CANADIAN GP Montréal

15 June 1997 Race 604

Michael Schumacher

Ferrari F310B 184.404kph, 114.583mph

On lap 52, holding P7, Panis crashed heavily at turn five sustaining leg injuries serious enough that after two SC laps the race was halted 15 laps prematurely. If leader Coulthard had pitted for tyres just one lap later he would have been declared the winner rather than, as he was, stalled in his pit. So despite being soundly beaten by Coulthard on pace and on strategy, pole-man Schumacher won to take a useful points lead. Benetton fought Jordan in a close battle over what became second, Alesi beating Fisichella, while Williams had a dreadful day. Villeneuve embarrassingly spun out of his home GP on lap 2 at the notorious last chicane. Frentzen's race began and ended P4. World champion Hill made the finish for the first time, P9.

Pos	Driver	Car	Time/gap	Grid	Stops	Tyres
1	M Schumacher	Ferrari	1h 17m 40.646s	1	3	G
2	J Alesi	Benetton-Renault	–2.565s	8	2	G
3	G Fisichella	Jordan-Peugeot	–3.219s	6	2	G
4	H-H Frentzen	Williams-Renault	–3.768s	4	3	G
5	J Herbert	Sauber-Petronas	–4.716s	13	2	G
6	S Nakano	Prost-Mugen Honda	–36.701s	19	1	B

POLE POSITION M Schumacher, Ferrari, 1m 18.095s (0.013s), 203.797kph, 126.634mph
LAPS 54 x 4.421 km, 2.747 miles (Race scheduled for 69 laps but stopped due to accident.)
DISTANCE 238.734 km, 148.342 miles
STARTERS/FINISHERS 22/11
WEATHER Sunny, hot, dry
LAP LEADERS M Schumacher 1-27, 40-43, 52-54 (34); Coulthard 28-39, 44-51 (20); SC 7-9 (3)
WINNER'S LAPS 1-27 P1, 28-39 P2, 40-43 P1, 44-51 P2, 52-54 P1
FASTEST LAP D Coulthard, McLaren-Mercedes, 1m 19.635s (Lap 37), 199.856kph, 124.185mph
CHAMPIONSHIP M Schumacher 37, Villeneuve 30, Panis 15, Irvine 14, Frentzen 13

FRENCH GP Magny-Cours

29 June 1997 Race 605

Michael Schumacher

Ferrari F310B 185.638kph, 115.351mph

The order at the end of the first lap was Schumacher, Frentzen, Irvine, Villeneuve. And 72 laps later it was no different. The race was almost that dreary, but not quite. Rain made for a frenetic final few laps, the leader briefly visiting the gravel trap, having elected to stay on slicks, but it didn't alter the finishing order. On pole for the second race running, Schumacher's Ferrari won the race on merit, an impression reinforced by Irvine's P3 performance. Much to their consternation, Williams had no answers, Villeneuve spinning at the final corner trying to catch and pass Irvine. At the halfway mark Schumacher's championship points lead was appreciable, while JV's recent form, outspoken remarks and new blonde hairdo were raising eyebrows.

Pos	Driver	Car	Time/gap	Grid	Stops	Tyres
1	M Schumacher	Ferrari	1h 38m 50.492s	1	2	G
2	H-H Frentzen	Williams-Renault	–23.537s	2	2	G
3	E Irvine	Ferrari	–1m 14.801s	5	3	G
4	J Villeneuve	Williams-Renault	–1m 21.784s	4	3	G
5	J Alesi	Benetton-Renault	–1m 22.735s	8	3	G
6	R Schumacher	Jordan-Peugeot	–1m 29.871s	3	3	G

POLE POSITION M Schumacher, Ferrari, 1m 14.548s (0.201), 205.236kph, 127.528mph
LAPS 72 x 4.250 km, 2.641 miles
DISTANCE 305.814 km, 190.024 miles
STARTERS/FINISHERS 22/12
WEATHER Overcast, warm, dry first then wet
LAP LEADERS M Schumacher 1-22, 24-46, 48-72 (70); Frentzen 23, 47 (2)
WINNER'S LAPS 1-22 P1, 23 P2, 24-46 P1, 47 P2, 48-72 P1
FASTEST LAP M Schumacher, Ferrari, 1m 17.910s (lap 37), 196.380kph, 122.025mph
CHAMPIONSHIP M Schumacher 47, Villeneuve 33, Frentzen 19, Irvine 18, Panis 15

BRITISH GP Silverstone

13 July 1997 Race 606

Jacques Villeneuve

Williams-Renault FW19 206.702kph, 128.439mph

With an aborted start and a SC period, the race proper began on lap 5. Schumacher from P4 closely pursued Villeneuve from pole, the rest vanishing in their mirrors. But a loose wheel hindered Villeneuve's first stint and a consequential 34s pit stop dropped him to P7. This left Schumacher way ahead on his own until soon after half-distance a Ferrari wheel-bearing failed. Victory now lay between the fast-recovering Villeneuve and Häkkinen, a one-stop bringing him into the reckoning. But the Finn's overdue first win went up in smoke along with his Mercedes motor seven laps short. Having cheered Schumacher's earlier retirement, the crowd gave voice again when Hill scored his first point since landing the championship. Frentzen lasted but two laps.

Pos	Driver	Car	Time/gap	Grid	Stops	Tyres
1	J Villeneuve	Williams-Renault	1h 28m 1.665s	1	2	G
2	J Alesi	Benetton-Renault	–10.205s	11	1	G
3	A Wurz	Benetton-Renault	–11.296s	8	1	G
4	D Coulthard	McLaren-Mercedes	–31.229s	6	1	G
5	R Schumacher	Jordan-Peugeot	–31.880s	5	2	G
6	D Hill	Arrows-Yamaha	–1m 13.552s	12	2	B

POLE POSITION Villeneuve, Williams-Renault, 1m 21.598s (0.134s), 226.770kph, 140.909mph
LAPS 59 x 5.140 km, 3.194 miles
DISTANCE 303.260 km, 188.437 miles
STARTERS/FINISHERS 22/11
WEATHER Sunny, warm, dry
LAP LEADERS Villeneuve 1-22, 38-44, 53-59 (36); M Schumacher 23-37 (15); M Häkkinen, McLaren-Mercedes 45-52 (8); SC 2-4 (3)
WINNER'S LAPS 1-22 P1, 23-27 P7, 28-29 P6, 30-33 P5, 34-35 P4, 36-37 P3, 38-44 P1, 45-52 P2, 53-59 P1
FASTEST LAP M Schumacher, Ferrari, 1m 24.475s (lap 34), 219.047kph, 136.110mph
CHAMPIONSHIP M Schumacher 47, Villeneuve 43, Alesi 21, Frentzen 19, Irvine 18

Benetton-Renault B197

<table>
<tr><td>**Round 10/17**</td><td colspan="4">**GERMAN GP** Hockenheim
27 July 1997   **Race 607**</td></tr>
</table>

Round 10/17	**GERMAN GP** Hockenheim			**Race 607**

27 July 1997

After his near-miss last year, Berger's Benetton-Renault won handsomely. Returning from a three-race health lay-off and grieving his father, Berger won from pole. Rookie Fisichella's Jordan-Peugeot lined up alongside, these two dominating the classic Hockenheim forest blast, Jordan favouring a one-stop, Benetton two. There was still little to choose between them as Berger resumed from his second stop still leading, but with seven to go a puncture finished Fisichella's superb challenge. His retirement handed Schumacher P2 and a ten-point championship advantage over Villeneuve. The Williams cars qualified on rows three and five. Frentzen collided with Irvine at the first corner, eliminating both. JV spun off on lap 33 when disputing P5 with Trulli's Prost.

Pos	Driver	Car	Time/gap	Grid	Stops	Tyres
1	G Berger	Benetton-Renau	lt1h 20m 59.046s	1	2	G
2	M Schumacher	Ferrari	–17.527s	4	2	G
3	M Häkkinen	McLaren-Mercedes	–24.770s	3	1	G
4	J Trulli	Prost-Mugen Honda	–27.165s	11	1	B
5	R Schumacher	Jordan-Peugeot	–29.995s	7	1	G
6	J Alesi	Benetton-Renault	–34.717s	6	2	G

Gerhard Berger
Benetton-Renault B197 227.477kph, 141.348mph

POLE POSITION Berger, Benetton-Renault, 1m 41.873s (0.023s), 241.111kph, 149.820mph
LAPS 45 x 6.823 km, 4.240 miles
DISTANCE 307.035 km, 190.783 miles
STARTERS/FINISHERS 22/11
WEATHER Cloudy with sunny intervals, hot, dry
LAP LEADERS Berger 1-17, 25-45 (38); G Fisichella, Jordan-Peugeot 18-24 (7)
WINNER'S LAPS 1-17 P1, 18 P4, 19-21 P3, 22-24 P2, 25-45 P1
FASTEST LAP Berger, Benetton-Renault, 1m 45.747s (lap 9), 232.278kph, 144.331mph
CHAMPIONSHIP M Schumacher 53, Villeneuve 43, Alesi 22, Berger 20, Frentzen 19

Round 11/17	**HUNGARIAN GP** Hungaroring			**Race 608**

10 August 1997

Two miles short of a famous victory, the reigning champion's Arrows-Yamaha was overtaken by former Williams teammate Villeneuve. Hill's underpowered car was superbly set-up and beautifully driven, his 35s lead enough to keep him ahead for two laps once hobbled by hydraulics failure, but not the very last. Hill had brilliantly qualified his Bridgestone-shod car third, closely pursued pole-man Schumacher for ten laps, then barged past into the lead. After that his only challenge to certain victory came ironically from Frentzen, the lone front-runner to opt for harder Goodyears, their softer rubber blistering badly on a baking day. But H-HF's nightmare season continued. Pitting from the lead on lap 29, a broken fuel filler valve kept him there.

Pos	Driver	Car	Time/gap	Grid	Stops	Tyres
1	J Villeneuve	Williams-Renault	1h 45m 47.149s	2	2	G
2	D Hill	Arrows-Yamaha	–9.079s	3	2	B
3	J Herbert	Sauber-Petronas	–20.445s	10	2	G
4	M Schumacher	Ferrari	–30.501s	1	3	G
5	R Schumacher	Jordan-Peugeot	–30.715s	14	2	G
6	S Nakano	Prost-Mugen Honda	–41.512s	16	2	B

Jacques Villeneuve
Williams-Renault FW19 173.295kph, 107.681mph

POLE POSITION M Schumacher, Ferrari, 1m 14.672s (0.187s), 191.300kph, 118.869mph
LAPS 77 x 3.968 km, 2.466 miles
DISTANCE 305.536 km, 189.851 miles
STARTERS/FINISHERS 22/13
WEATHER Sunny, hot, dry
LAP LEADERS M Schumacher 1-10 (10); D Hill 11-25, 30-76 (62); Frentzen 26-29 (4); Villeneuve 77 (1)
WINNER'S LAPS 1-6 P5, 7-12 P4, 13 P3, 14-23 P2, 24 P3, 25-26 P4, 27-29 P3, 30-76 P2, 77 P1
FASTEST LAP H-H Frentzen, Williams-Renault, 1m 18.372s (lap 25), 182.269kph, 113.257mph
CHAMPIONSHIP M Schumacher 56, Villeneuve 53, Alesi 22, Berger 20, Frentzen 19

BELGIAN GP Spa Francorchamps

24 August 1997   **Race 609**

Michael Schumacher

Ferrari F310B 196.149kph, 121.882mph

After a sudden rainstorm, the track awash, the race started behind the Safety Car, a GP first. But the rain stopped, three SC laps cleared the track of standing water, and Schumacher's gamble on intermediates rather than the widely favoured wets seemed inspired. Lap 4, the first racing lap, finished in grid order, Villeneuve, Alesi, Schumacher, but by the end of lap 5 Schumacher was ahead by 6s, building successively to 17, 23, 28. By lap 12 it was 65s, game over. Fisichella made the same tyre gamble and after Alesi faded from contention brought Jordan-Peugeot the P2 they had so deserved at Hockenheim. The Williams pair, fastest once the track dried, came P3 and P5, Häkkinen's McLaren later disqualified from P3 for a fuel infringement.

POLE POSITION Villeneuve, Williams-Renault, 1m 49.450s (0.309s), 229.189kph, 142.412mph
LAPS 44 x 6.968 km, 4.330 miles
DISTANCE 306.577 km, 190.498 miles
STARTERS/FINISHERS 22/15
WEATHER Overcast, warm, wet at first then dry
LAP LEADERS Villeneuve 1-4 (4); M Schumacher 5-44 (40); SC 1-3 (3)
WINNER'S LAPS 1-4 P3, 5-44 P1
FASTEST LAP Villeneuve, Williams-Renault, 1m 52.692s (lap 43), 222.596kph, 138.315mph
CHAMPIONSHIP M Schumacher 66, Villeneuve 55, Frentzen 23, Alesi 22, Berger 21

Pos	Driver	Car	Time/gap	Grid	Stops	Tyres
1	M Schumacher	Ferrari	1h 33m 46.717s	3	2	G
2	G Fisichella	Jordan-Peugeot	−26.753s	4	2	G
3	H-H Frentzen	Williams-Renault	−32.147s	5	2	G
4	J Herbert	Sauber-Petronas	−39.025s	7	2	G
5	J Villeneuve	Williams-Renault	−42.103s	11	3	G
6	G Berger	Benetton-Renault	−1m 3.741s	1	3	G

ITALIAN GP Monza

7 September 1997   **Race 610**

David Coulthard

McLaren-Mercedes MP4/12 238.036kph, 147.909mph

A scintillating start from P5 to shadow front-row pair Alesi and Frentzen during the first stint, plus a super-fast single stop by the McLaren pit crew, brought Coulthard another victory. Just 6.4s covered the top five finishers, storming around Monza in close company, but was it racing, the only significant pass accomplished in the pits? This was on lap 32 when Coulthard followed leader Alesi in, made up time during entry and the stop itself, and rejoined ahead. The Ferraris were strangely uncompetitive, especially for Monza, qualifying on row five. Schumacher managed to finish P6, thankful to drop only one point to Villeneuve, who was beaten by Fisichella to P4. In the title battle, Schumacher retained an invaluable ten-point advantage.

POLE POSITION Alesi, Benetton-Renault, 1m 22.990s (0.052s), 250.295kph, 155.526mph
LAPS 53 x 5.770 km, 3.585 miles
DISTANCE 305.785 km, 190.006 miles
STARTERS/FINISHERS 22/14
WEATHER Sunny, hot, dry
LAP LEADERS Alesi 1-31 (31); Häkkinen 32-33 (2); M Schumacher 34 (1); Coulthard 35-53 (19)
WINNER'S LAPS 1-28 P3, 29-31 P2, 32-33 P4, 34 P2, 35-53 P1
FASTEST LAP M Häkkinen, McLaren-Mercedes, 1m 24.808 (lap 49), 244.929kph, 152.192mph
CHAMPIONSHIP M Schumacher 67, Villeneuve 57, Alesi 28, Frentzen 27, Coulthard 24

Pos	Driver	Car	Time/gap	Grid	Stops	Tyres
1	D Coulthard	McLaren-Mercedes	1h 17m 4.609s	6	1	G
2	J Alesi	Benetton-Renault	−1.937s	1	1	G
3	H-H Frentzen	Williams-Renault	−4.343s	2	1	G
4	G Fisichella	Jordan-Peugeot	−5.871s	3	1	G
5	J Villeneuve	Williams-Renault	−6.416s	4	1	G
6	M Schumacher	Ferrari	−11.481s	9	1	G

AUSTRIAN GP A1-Ring

21 September 1997   **Race 611**

Jacques Villeneuve

Williams-Renault FW19 210.228kph, 130.630mph

A Bridgestone gripped the slippery new track better than a Goodyear, promoting some of the less fancied runners up the grid to influence the race. Leader Häkkinen's Mercedes blew before even completing lap 1, allowing Trulli's Prost to waltz away, only conceding P1 to pole-man Villeneuve at the halfway stops. JV made it harder on himself by getting trapped behind Barrichello's Stewart for 23 laps, but once by he quickly closed down the shock leader. When still P2, engine trouble ended Trulli's spirited drive on lap 58. Despite still being well off the pace, Schumacher dragged his Ferrari up from P9 to a likely podium, only to receive a stop-go for passing under a yellow, eventually overtaking Hill for the final point just two laps from the finish.

POLE POSITION Villeneuve, Williams-Renault, 1m 10.304s (0.094s), 221.364kph, 137.549mph
LAPS 71 x 4.323 km, 2.686 miles
DISTANCE 306.933 km, 190.719 miles
STARTERS/FINISHERS 21/14
WEATHER Sunny, hot, dry
LAP LEADERS J Trulli, Prost-Mugen Honda 1-37 (37); Villeneuve 38-40, 44-71 (31); M Schumacher 41-42 (2); Coulthard 43 (1)
WINNER'S LAPS 1-23 P3, 24-37 P2, 38-40 P1, 41-42 P4, 43 P2, 44-71 P1
FASTEST LAP Villeneuve, Williams-Renault, 1m 11.814s (lap 36), 216.709kph, 134.657mph
CHAMPIONSHIP M Schumacher 68, Villeneuve 67, Frentzen 31, Coulthard 30, Alesi 28

Pos	Driver	Car	Time/gap	Grid	Stops	Tyres
1	J Villeneuve	Williams-Renault	1h 27m 25.999s	1	1	G
2	D Coulthard	McLaren-Mercedes	−2.909s	10	1	G
3	H-H Frentzen	Williams-Renault	−3.962s	4	1	G
4	G Fisichella	Jordan-Peugeot	−12.127s	14	1	G
5	R Schumacher	Jordan-Peugeot	−31.859s	11	1	G
6	M Schumacher	Ferrari	−33.410s	9	2	G

Round 15/17	**LUXEMBOURG GP** Nürburgring	**Jacques Villeneuve**
	28 September 1997 Race 612	Williams-Renault FW19 200.232kph, 124.419mph

Häkkinen's 94th race start brought his maiden pole. And with teammate Coulthard slotting-in behind after another barely credible start from P6, a McLaren 1-2 looked a certainty. But at two-thirds-distance, within moments of one another, their Mercedes motors blew. It gifted Villeneuve an easy victory, the championship significance accentuated by events earlier. Trying to win the race at the first corner, brother Ralf became airborne and literally dropped in on his sibling, putting out both Schumachers and teammate Fisichella, who had qualified P4. Afterwards Michael was sanguine about his brother's role in a possibly title-deciding fracas. Renault power finished 1-2-3-4, Frentzen recovering to P3 after inadvertently switching off his ignition.

POLE POSITION M Häkkinen, McLaren-Mercedes, 1m 16.602s (0.089s), 214.114kph, 133.045mph
LAPS 67 x 4.556 km, 2.831 miles
DISTANCE 305.235 km, 189.664 miles
STARTERS/FINISHERS 22/10
WEATHER Sunny, warm, dry
LAP LEADERS Häkkinen 1-28, 32-43 (40); D Coulthard, McLaren-Mercedes 29-31 (3); Villeneuve 44-67 (24)
WINNER'S LAPS 1-42 P3, 43 P2, 44-67 P1
FASTEST LAP Frentzen, Williams-Renault, 1m 18.805s (lap 32), 208.128kph, 129.325mph
CHAMPIONSHIP Villeneuve 77, M Schumacher 68, Frentzen 35, Alesi 34, Coulthard 30

Pos	Driver	Car	Time/gap	Grid	Stops	Tyres
1	J Villeneuve	Williams-Renault	1h 31m 27.843s	2	2	G
2	J Alesi	Benetton-Renault	–11.770s	10	2	G
3	H-H Frentzen	Williams-Renault	–13.480s	3	2	G
4	G Berger	Benetton-Renault	–16.416s	7	2	G
5	P Diniz	Arrows-Yamaha	–43.147s	15	1	B
6	O Panis	Prost-Mugen Honda	–43.750s	11	1	B

Round 16/17	**JAPANESE GP** Suzuka	**Michael Schumacher**
	12 October 1997 Race 613	Ferrari F310B 207.507kph, 128.939mph

A yellow flag incident barred Villeneuve from starting. Under appeal he was permitted but points were likely to be erased, and duly were when Williams rescinded their plea. So his race strategy was to hold Schumacher up in the hope that other drivers might get ahead and reduce his points potential. But Ferrari, competitiveness restored with a new flexing front wing, outsmarted Williams. JV led a convoy from pole but Suzuka expert Irvine was tasked to get ahead, doing so on lap 3 to lead his first GP. A 12s gap kept him ahead at the first stop when Schumacher crucially beat JV out of the pits. Eddie then gifted Michael the lead and victory. From his P6 grid-slot H-HF was unable to help JV's cause, but a P2 result brought Williams the constructors' title.

POLE POSITION J Villeneuve, Williams-Renault, 1m 36.071s (0.062s), 219.737kph, 136.539mph
LAPS 53 x 5.864 km, 3.644 miles
DISTANCE 310.596 km, 192.987 miles
STARTERS/FINISHERS 21/13
WEATHER Cloudy with sunny intervals, warm, dry
LAP LEADERS Villeneuve 1-2, 17-20 (6); Irvine 3-16, 22-24 (17); Frentzen 21, 34-37 (5); M Schumacher 25-33, 38-53 (25)
WINNER'S LAPS 1 P2, 2-16 P3, 17-18 P2, 19-20 P5, 21 P3, 22-24 P2, 25-33 P1, 34-37 P2, 38-53 P1
FASTEST LAP Frentzen, Williams-Renault, 1m 38.942s (lap 48), 213.361kph, 132.577mph
CHAMPIONSHIP M Schumacher 78, Villeneuve 77, Frentzen 41, Alesi 36, Coulthard 30

Pos	Driver	Car	Time/gap	Grid	Stops	Tyres
1	M Schumacher	Ferrari	1h 29m 48.446s	2	2	G
2	H-H Frentzen	Williams-Renault	–1.378s	6	2	G
3	E Irvine	Ferrari	–26.384s	3	2	G
4	M Häkkinen	McLaren-Mercedes	–27.129s	4	2	G
5	J Alesi	Benetton-Renault	–40.403s	1	3	G
6	J Herbert	Sauber-Petronas	–41.630s	7	2	G

Round 17/17	**EUROPEAN GP** Jerez de la Frontera	**Mika Häkkinen**
	26 October 1997 Race 614	McLaren-Mercedes MP4/12 185.240kph, 115.103mph

With one point separating the title contenders, it came down to a winner-takes-all shoot-out. Villeneuve took pole but Schumacher, from alongside, rocketed away at the start. Now Villeneuve had to pass. Lap 48, just after their second stops, Villeneuve caught Schumacher napping and dived alongside to claim the slow right-hander. Alert to his crucial one-point advantage, Schumacher deliberately rammed Villeneuve but ended up in the gravel himself. A points finish essential, JV coaxed his damaged car the remaining 22 laps, steadily losing his 15s lead. Recognising P3 was enough, a little Williams/McLaren collision meant Villeneuve did not resist the closing McLaren pair that overtook on the final lap, Coulthard handing Häkkinen his maiden win.

POLE POSITION Villeneuve, Williams-Renault, 1m 21.072s (0.000s), 196.625kph, 122.177mph
LAPS 69 x 4.428 km, 2.751 miles
DISTANCE 305.532 km, 189.849 miles
STARTERS/FINISHERS 22/17
WEATHER Cloudy with sunny intervals, warm, dry
LAP LEADERS M Schumacher, Ferrari 1-21, 28-42, 45-47 (39); Villeneuve 22, 43-44, 48-68 (24); Frentzen 23-27 (5); Häkkinen 69 (1)
WINNER'S LAPS 1-21 P4, 22 P3, 23-25 P2, 26 P5, 27-28 P6, 29-43 P4, 44 P7, 45-46 P6, 47 P5, 48-66 P3, 67-68 P2, 69 P1
FASTEST LAP Frentzen, Williams-Renault, 1m 23.135s (lap 30), 191.745kph, 119.145mph
CHAMPIONSHIP Villeneuve 81, Frentzen 42, Coulthard 36, Alesi 36, Berger 27

Pos	Driver	Car	Time/gap	Grid	Stops	Tyres
1	M Häkkinen	McLaren-Mercedes	1h 38m 57.771s	5	2	G
2	D Coulthard	McLaren-Mercedes	–1.654s	6	2	G
3	J Villeneuve	Williams-Renault	–1.803s	1	2	G
4	G Berger	Benetton-Renault	–1.919s	8	2	G
5	E Irvine	Ferrari	–3.789s	7	2	G
6	H-H Frentzen	Williams-Renault	–4.537s	3	2	G

- On the safety front, lessons learned from Mika Häkkinen's 1995 accident translated into partially collapsing steering columns and padded steering-wheel bosses. Changes to the mountings reduced the chances of front suspension members or wheels striking a driver in an accident. An impact-absorbing structure fitted to the gearbox addressed rear impact protection.
- Third wings fitted to engine covers were outlawed but the regulations did not prevent unsightly X-wings sprouting on the Tyrrell during the season.
- With obligatory circuit modifications incomplete, Estoril was rescheduled to October, but further disputes finally killed off the Portuguese GP, a final round at Jerez replacing it on the calendar.
- Austria returned in the guise of the A1-Ring. This shortened circuit, broadly based on the former Österreichring, brought the championship trail up to 17 races.
- Tyre wars resumed and lap times tumbled as Bridgestone entered GP racing. The Japanese tyre company supported five of the lesser teams, three P2s the end product. For Goodyear, Villeneuve's Spanish victory was win number 350.
- With reigning champion Hill's controversial departure to Arrows, Jacques Villeneuve was firm pre-season favourite, particularly on the evidence of the Williams team's showing in winter testing. The sages were wrong.
- Going into the final round, Ferrari's Michael Schumacher led the championship from Villeneuve, but by a single point. Two-thirds through the race, Villeneuve made his bid for the lead and the championship, drawing alongside Schumacher in a well-judged overtaking manoeuvre. Facing defeat, Schumacher turned his car in, deliberately colliding with Villeneuve.
- Whereas in the similar circumstances of 1994 there had been a modicum of doubt over his collision with Hill, Schumacher's coming together with Villeneuve three years later was an unashamed attempt to take his rival out of the race and out of championship contention.
- The fact that his action failed and Villeneuve and Williams-Renault went on to clinch deserved titles took nothing away from the enormity of Schumacher's deed. It was astonishing that the punishment meted out by the FIA was entirely retrospective, although in the minds of many Schumacher's reputation and future standing in the sport would forever be blighted.
- The FIA disqualified Schumacher from the 1997 championship, hardly an onerous punishment since he had failed to win in any case, also allowing his results to stand along with his five race victories.
- The champion, moral and otherwise, was Jacques Villeneuve, he and the entire Williams team for that matter making heavy weather of their task with some unforced errors. Nonetheless, to become world champion by the end of only a second season in F1 was a remarkable achievement for a quick and determined racer who followed Damon Hill as another second-generation F1 driver to conquer the summit. Time would show that having been victorious 11 times in just 33 GP starts, JV would never win again in a further 130 attempts, or even add to his 13 pole positions. [His] final pole was at the European GP showdown at Jerez [where], uncannily, Villeneuve, Schumacher and Frentzen [set] identical qualifying times to 1/1,000th second, 1m [...]
- 1997 was the first year ITV had supplanted F1 television broadcaster the BBC, one fresh

- aspect explored being the professional relationship in contemporary F1 between a driver and his race engineer, Villeneuve with Jock Clear in this case.
- Villeneuve's Silverstone victory marked Williams' 100th GP triumph at the place their success began in 1979, 18 seasons and 285 races before.
- Villeneuve was the team's seventh drivers' champion, and their ninth constructors' trophy even placed them ahead of Ferrari.
- But there were pressures too. Throughout the year the Senna accident trial, entering its fourth year, rumbled on in Italy, F1 breathing a deep sigh of relief when Patrick Head and Adrian Newey were finally acquitted of all charges, specifically those relating to a steering redesign.
- Another pressure on Williams was that after nine seasons together engine partner Renault was to bow out, although V10 supply on a customer basis would continue for Williams and Benetton in 1998 via Renault associate Mecachrome.

- Renault considered that having played a major role in securing 11 of the last 12 F1 titles, and equalling Honda's six successive championships as an engine supplier, there wasn't much else to prove for the present. Over nine seasons their V10 had powered 75 winners from 146 races.
- But *plus ça change*, or whatever the German equivalent is. At the Frankfurt Motor Show BMW announced their return to F1 as engine supplier to Williams from 2000.
- During the year Honda also announced their imminent F1 return, but disclosed no details.
- At Benetton Dave Richards replaced Briatore from the Nürburgring, the German circuit hosting the first of just two Luxembourg GPs. Earlier at Hockenheim, Gerhard Berger, who was to retire at season end, won his tenth and last GP, which also marked a final victory for the Benetton team, who had lost Ross Brawn and Rory Byrne to Ferrari.
- Unlike their lead driver, Ferrari was not excluded and once more finished runner-up in the constructors' championship, but this time with five race victories, a surfeit of riches not seen since 1990.
- Ferrari also became an engine supplier in 1997, providing their V10 to Sauber, badged Petronas. Considering Enzo's *garagistas'* opinion, it was enough to make the *Commendatore* turn in his grave.
- John Barnard left Ferrari and joined Arrows from May as part of Walkinshaw's plans, along with a specially commissioned V10 from Brian Hart, to retain Hill for 1998. But Hill had had his fill of latent promise and moved to Jordan, a team which was at least closer to delivering its potential, especially fitted with a brand new Mugen engine, a further signal of Honda's renewed F1 interest.

RACE 614, European GP: On lap 48 Villeneuve (3) caught Schumacher (5) napping and dived alongside. Alert to his crucial one-point advantage, Schumacher deliberately rammed the Williams.

- Jordan were now a seasoned unit and regular points scorers, Argentina the team's 100th GP, which they celebrated with a podium, rookie Ralf Schumacher at 21 the youngest podium winner.
- Damon Hill's near-miss at the Hungaroring was the closest Arrows had ever got to victory in their up to then 299 race, 20-year GP history. It would also have been the first for Yamaha in their nine-year F1 involvement, as well as for tyre supplier Bridgestone.
- On 1 August Adrian Newey officially began work at McLaren. It was not entirely unrelated that Häkkinen's performances began to improve as he found more confidence in the MP4/12, his maiden win finally coming at his 96th attempt.
- After three fruitless seasons McLaren bagged three race victories, triumphs which returned engine partner Mercedes-Benz to the winners' circle for the first time since 1955.
- Responding to a rule clarification requested by McLaren, around mid-season the FIA loosened its rules for fly-by-wire throttles. This and some remarkable grid-starts, especially by McLaren and Ferrari drivers, raised questions over the potential abuse of this technology to reinstate traction control illegally through the back door.
- Without question, and flying in the face of the 1994 ban, electronics were creeping back into F1, not only throttle control, but brake balance and active differentials too.
- Other politically charged issues in 1997 concerned the Concorde Agreement, the public flotation of F1, and tobacco sponsorship.
- Lola withdrew after just one race, their GP team going into liquidation, but 1997 also saw two former multiple drivers' champions return to GP racing as principals of their eponymous teams. Alain Prost acquired and renamed Ligier, while Jackie Stewart reinvigorated Ford's F1 aspirations as engine suppliers and backers of his new GP team.
- Prost's lead driver Olivier Panis missed seven races following a major accident at Montréal, that race the first GP to finish behind the Safety Car.

Championship ranking	Championship points	Driver nationality	1997 Drivers Championship		Races contested	Race victories	Podiumse excl. victories	Races led	Lights to flag victories	Laps led	Poles	Fastest laps	Triple Crowns
			Driver	Car									
1	81	CAN	Jacques Villeneuve	Williams-Renault	17	7	1	11		348	10	3	2
2	42	GER	Heinz-Harald Frentzen	Williams-Renault	17	1	6	6		76	1	6	
3	36	GBR	David Coulthard	McLaren-Mercedes	17	2	2	5		77		1	
4	36	FRA	Jean Alesi	Benetton-Renault	17		5	2		32	1		
5	27	AUT	Gerhard Berger	Benetton-Renault	14	1	1	2		41	1	2	1
6	27	FIN	Mika Häkkinen	McLaren-Mercedes	17	1	2	4		51	1	1	
7	24	GBR	Eddie Irvine	Ferrari	17		5	2		23			
8	20	ITA	Giancarlo Fisichella	Jordan-Peugeot	17		2	1		7		1	
9	16	FRA	Olivier Panis	Prost-Mugen Honda	10		2						
10	15	GBR	Johnny Herbert	Sauber-Petronas	17		1						
11	13	GER	Ralf Schumacher	Jordan-Peugeot	17		1						
12	7	GBR	Damon Hill	Arrows-Yamaha	16		1	1		62			
13	6	BRA	Rubens Barrichello	Stewart-Ford	17		1						
14	4	AUT	Alexander Wurz	Benetton-Renault	3		1						
15	3	ITA	Jarno Trulli	Minardi-Ford (6) Prost-Mugen Honda (7)	13			1		37			
16	2	FIN	Mika Salo	Tyrrell-Ford	17								
16	2	BRA	Pedro Diniz	Arrows-Yamaha	17								
18	2	JPN	Shinji Nakano	Prost-Mugen Honda	17								
19	1	ITA	Nicola Larini	Sauber-Petronas	5								
DSQ	(78)	GER	Michael Schumacher	Ferrari	17	5	3	12	1	300	3	3	1

Championship ranking	Championship points	Team/Marque nationality	1997 Constructors Championship		Engine maker nationality	Races contested	Race victories	1-2 finishes	Podiums excl. victories	Races led	Laps led	Poles	Fastest laps
			Chassis	Engine									
1	123	GBR	Williams FW19	Renault 3.0 V10	FRA	17	8		7	13	424	11	9
2	102	ITA	Ferrari F310B	Ferrari 3.0 V10	ITA	17	5		8	13	323	3	3
3	67	ITA	Benetton B197	Renault 3.0 V10	FRA	17	1		7	4	73	2	2
4	63	GBR	McLaren MP4-12	Mercedes-Benz 3.0 V10	GER	17	3	1	4	7	128	1	2
5	33	IRL	Jordan 197	Peugeot 3.0 V10	FRA	17			3	1	7		1
6	21	FRA	Prost JS45	Mugen Honda 3.0 V10	JPN	17			2	1	37		
7	16	SUI	Sauber C16	Petronas 3.0 V10	ITA	17			1				
8	9	GBR	Arrows A18	Yamaha 3.0 V10	JPN	17			1	1	62		
9	6	GBR	Stewart SF1	Ford Cosworth 3.0 V10	GBR	17			1				
10	2	GBR	Tyrrell 025	Ford Cosworth 3.0 V8	GBR	17							

1998

Mika's Finnish-ing flourish

THE TALE OF THE TITLE

- Sweeping rule changes gave F1 cars a distinctive new 'skinny' look with narrowed track and grooved tyres.
- With Renault demoting Williams and Benetton to customer status, prospects for Ferrari looked good.
- But the Scuderia quickly learnt that mastery of the new technical regs lay with McLaren and Bridgestone.
- Five wins from the first six races put McLaren-Mercedes and Häkkinen on course for championship glory.
- But Goodyear enhancements, Schumacher brilliance and a slice of, let's say, lady luck kept the title race open.
- But finally Häkkinen landed two decisive blows to leave Schumacher and Ferrari on the canvas.
- With eight and nine race victories respectively, Häkkinen and McLaren-Mercedes were worthy champions.
- After five wilderness years McLaren were back, champions in their fourth year with partners Mercedes.
- The new drivers' champion deservedly won on track, and off-track offered controlled poise and graciousness.
- By contrast, 'flawed genius' again described Schumacher's season, brilliance tarnished by ruthless arrogance.
- Defending champions Villeneuve and Williams failed to win a race, two podiums their campaign highlights.
- The Jordan team were the first new winners in 12 seasons, Hill's Spa win, his 22nd, disproving doubters again.
- And not forgetting: farewell to Goodyear and to Tyrrell.

THE CHASE FOR THE CHAMPIONSHIP

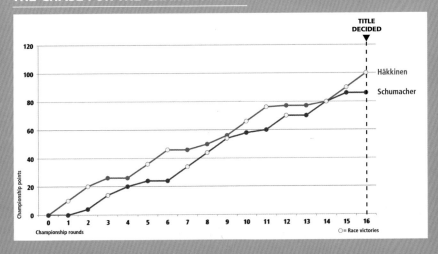

Round 1/16	**AUSTRALIAN GP** Melbourne				
	8 March 1998			**Race 615**	

Mika Häkkinen

McLaren-Mercedes MP4/13 201.101kph, 124.959mph

Effortlessly stitching-up the front row, McLaren had visibly adapted best to the radical new regulations. Apart from a first-corner attack by Schumacher on Coulthard before his Ferrari blew on lap 5, within ten laps the McLarens were touring round in formation 30s up on world champion Villeneuve's Williams-Mecachrome, lapping the entire field well before the chequer. A communication glitch caused leader Häkkinen a needless pit visit on lap 36, dropping him to P2. His recovery drive was entertaining if daunting, a fastest lap nearly 2s better than any non-McLaren driver. Under a pre-race agreement Coulthard stepped aside two laps from the flag. Aghast at McLaren's superiority, reaction to this was incensed. Mika's second was Bridgestone's first.

POLE POSITION Häkkinen, McLaren-Mercedes, 1m 30.010s (0.043s), 212.096kph, 131.791mph
LAPS 58 x 5.303 km, 3.295 miles
DISTANCE 307.574 km, 191.118 miles
STARTERS/FINISHERS 22/9
WEATHER Sunny, warm, dry
LAP LEADERS Häkkinen 1-23, 25-35, 56-58 (37); Coulthard 24, 36-55 (21)
WINNER'S LAPS 1-23 P1, 24 P2, 25-35 P1, 36-55 P2, 56-58 P1
FASTEST LAP Häkkinen, McLaren-Mercedes, 1m 31.649s (lap 39), 208.303kph, 129.434mph
CHAMPIONSHIP Häkkinen 10, Coulthard 6, Frentzen 4, Irvine 3, Villeneuve 2

Pos	Driver	Car	Time/gap	Grid	Stops	Tyres
1	M Häkkinen	McLaren-Mercedes	1h 31m 45.996s	1	3	B
2	D Coulthard	McLaren-Mercedes	−0.702s	2	2	B
3	H-H Frentzen	Williams-Mecachrome	−1 lap	6	1	G
4	E Irvine	Ferrari	−1 lap	8	1	G
5	J Villeneuve	Williams-Mecachrome	−1 lap	4	1	G
6	J Herbert	Sauber-Petronas	−1 lap	5	1	G

McLaren-Mercedes MP4/13

Round 2/16	**BRAZILIAN GP** Interlagos				
	29 March 1998			**Race 616**	

Mika Häkkinen

McLaren-Mercedes MP4/13 190.763kph, 118.535mph

With another dominant 1-2, McLaren-Mercedes remained invincible despite the banning of their controversial 'brake-steer' system. In qualifying and the race Häkkinen always held the edge over Coulthard, his hat-trick victory the first fully merited win, the other two donations. It truly was two quite separate races, Schumacher finishing P3 a full minute behind the McLarens. Wurz enlivened 'Race B' with a well-driven one-stop race, beating two-stopper Frentzen but falling just short of Schumacher's two-stop strategy. As late as lap 54 these three were little more than a second apart as their strategies unwound. At least Schumacher had opened his account, but already trailed Häkkinen by 16 points. Champions Villeneuve and Williams looked out of it.

POLE POSITION Häkkinen, McLaren-Mercedes, 1m 17.092s (0.665s), 200.425kph, 124.539mph
LAPS 72 x 4.292 km, 2.667 miles
DISTANCE 309.024 km, 192.019 miles
STARTERS/FINISHERS 22/11
WEATHER Overcast, humid, dry
LAP LEADERS Häkkinen 1-72 (72)
WINNER'S LAPS 1-72 P1
FASTEST LAP Häkkinen, McLaren-Mercedes, 1m 19.337s (lap 64), 194.754kph, 121.015mph
CHAMPIONSHIP Häkkinen 20, Coulthard 12, Frentzen 6, M Schumacher 4, Irvine 3

Pos	Driver	Car	Time/gap	Grid	Stops	Tyres
1	M Häkkinen	McLaren-Mercedes	1h 37m 11.74/s	1	1	B
2	D Coulthard	McLaren-Mercedes	−1.102s	2	1	B
3	M Schumacher	Ferrari	−1m 0.550s	4	2	G
4	A Wurz	Benetton-Playlife	−1m 7.473s	5	1	B
5	H-H Frentzen	Williams-Mecachrome	−1 lap	3	2	G
6	G Fisichella	Benetton-Playlife	−1 lap	7	1	B

Ferrari F300

Round 3/16	ARGENTINEAN GP Buenos Aires No 6						Michael Schumacher

12 April 1998   **Race 617**   **Ferrari F300** 169.304kph, 105.201mph

Firing a warning shot to McLaren and Bridgestone, wider Goodyear fronts transformed Ferrari competitiveness and breathed life into Schumacher's season and the championship battle. For pole-sitter Coulthard it was a victory opportunity lost, running wide on lap 5 while leading. The watchful Schumacher pounced, elbowing the Scotsman into a spin in a typically ruthless, even dubious move. The race was now Schumacher versus Häkkinen, two stops versus one. Eight laps from the finish it rained, leader Schumacher visiting the gravel trap. But for a lacklustre drive Häkkinen might have taken advantage of this error. Irvine and Wurz disputed P3 closely enough to make contact, Alex spinning it away in the rain on lap 66.

POLE POSITION Coulthard, McLaren-Mercedes, 1m 25.852s (0.399s), 178.591kph, 110.971mph
LAPS 72 x 4.259 km, 2.646 miles
DISTANCE 306.449 km, 190.419 miles
STARTERS/FINISHERS 22/15
WEATHER Overcast, cool, dry then late rain
LAP LEADERS Coulthard 1-4 (4); M Schumacher 5-28, 43-72 (54); Häkkinen 29-42 (14)
WINNER'S LAPS 1 P3, 2-4 P2, 5-28 P1, 29-42 P2, 43-72 P1
FASTEST LAP Wurz, Benetton-Playlife, 1m 28.179s (lap 39), 173.878kph, 108.043mph
CHAMPIONSHIP Häkkinen 26, M Schumacher 14, Coulthard 13, Irvine 7, Frentzen 6

Pos	Driver	Car	Time/gap	Grid	Stops	Tyres
1	M Schumacher	Ferrari	1h 48m 36.175s	2	2	G
2	M Häkkinen	McLaren-Mercedes	−22.898s	3	1	B
3	E Irvine	Ferrari	−57.745s	4	2	G
4	A Wurz	Benetton-Playlife	−1m 8.134s	8	1	B
5	J Alesi	Sauber-Petronas	−1m 18.286s	11	2	G
6	D Coulthard	McLaren-Mercedes	−1m 19.751s	1	1	B

Round 4/16	SAN MARINO GP Imola						David Coulthard

26 April 1998   **Race 618**   **McLaren-Mercedes MP4/13** 194.117kph, 120.619mph

Following his Argentinean lament, Coulthard silenced his critics on Ferrari turf with a fine lights-to-flag victory from pole. In his first of three stints Coulthard pulled out over 20s on Schumacher, also on a two-stop, which was enough to provide a cushion when a late-race overheating problem slowed his progress, presenting Schumacher's pursuing Ferrari with a sniff off victory. But Coulthard kept his cool and suddenly his championship aspirations were restored, especially as teammate Häkkinen had retired from P2 with gearbox failure on lap 17. Villeneuve and Irvine fought a race-long tussle for P3 that went to the Ferrari, but the Scuderia still trailed McLaren in the points race. The top three drivers, however, were only six apart.

POLE POSITION Coulthard, McLaren-Mercedes, 1m 25.973s (0.102s), 206.436kph, 128.274mph
LAPS 62 x 4.930 km, 3.063 miles
DISTANCE 305.443 km, 189.794 miles
STARTERS/FINISHERS 22/11
WEATHER Sunny, warm, dry
LAP LEADERS Coulthard 1-62 (62)
WINNER'S LAPS 1-62 P1
FASTEST LAP M Schumacher, Ferrari, 1m 29.345s (lap 48), 198.645kph, 123.433mph
CHAMPIONSHIP Häkkinen 26, Coulthard 23, M Schumacher 20, Irvine 11, Frentzen 8

Pos	Driver	Car	Time/gap	Grid	Stops	Tyres
1	D Coulthard	McLaren-Mercedes	1h 34m 24.593s	1	2	B
2	M Schumacher	Ferrari	−4.554s	3	2	G
3	E Irvine	Ferrari	−51.775s	4	2	G
4	J Villeneuve	Williams-Mecachrome	−54.590s	6	2	G
5	H-H Frentzen	Williams-Mecachrome	−1m 17.476s	8	2	G
6	J Alesi	Sauber-Petronas	−1 lap	12	2	G

SPANISH GP Cataluña

10 May 1998   **Race 619**

Mika Häkkinen

McLaren-Mercedes MP4/13 196.863kph, 122.325mph

Even the Ferraris sported X-wings at Imola and when the FIA didn't obtain unanimous agreement from the teams, they were banned on safety grounds from Spain. The three championship contenders qualified and finished in championship order, so not a riveting race this one. The McLarens had the measure of Schumacher, and Häkkinen had the measure of Coulthard. Fisichella stirred up the 'F1 overtaking crisis' debate with his clash with Irvine on lap 29, for which he received a fine, despite veraciously claiming to be the innocent party. Benetton-Playlife teammate Wurz added to his growing reputation with another P4, his third from five races. Barrichello's P5 finish brought Stewart their first points since Monaco last year.

POLE POSITION Häkkinen, McLaren-Mercedes, 1m 20.262s (0.734s), 212.065kph, 131.771mph
LAPS 65 x 4.728 km, 2.938 miles
DISTANCE 307.196 km, 190.883 miles
STARTERS/FINISHERS 21/16
WEATHER Sunny, hot, dry
LAP LEADERS Häkkinen 1-26, 28-45, 47-65 (63); Coulthard 27, 46 (2)
WINNER'S LAPS 1-26 P1, 27 P2, 28-45 P1, 46 P2, 47-65 P1
FASTEST LAP Häkkinen, McLaren-Mercedes, 1m 24.275s (lap 25), 201.967kph, 125.497mph
CHAMPIONSHIP Häkkinen 36, Coulthard 29, M Schumacher 24, Irvine 11, Wurz 9

Pos	Driver	Car	Time/gap	Grid	Stops	Tyres
1	M Häkkinen	McLaren-Mercedes	1h 33m 37.621s	1	2	B
2	D Coulthard	McLaren-Mercedes	−9.439s	2	2	B
3	M Schumacher	Ferrari	−47.095s	3	3	G
4	A Wurz	Benetton-Playlife	−1m 2.538s	5	2	B
5	R Barrichello	Stewart-Ford	−1 lap	9	2	B
6	J Villeneuve	Williams-Mecachrome	−1 lap	10	2	G

MONACO GP Monte Carlo

24 May 1998   **Race 620**

Mika Häkkinen

McLaren-Mercedes MP4/13 141.458kph, 87.898mph

Häkkinen put in a faultless start-to-finish drive for his fourth win of the season, and with neither championship rival scoring increased his points lead to 17. Coulthard's Mercedes blew on lap 18 when closely chasing in second while Schumacher finished down the field after a lengthy suspension repair. This followed a wheel-banging episode with Wurz over P2. It began when Schumacher got by at Loews on lap 38, was immediately repassed by Wurz, who then went wide at Portiers where their clash occurred. Consequentially, on lap 42 Wurz suffered a nasty pin-balling crash exiting the tunnel. Fisichella started P3 and with Coulthard's departure finished runner-up. Using their own V10 engines, Arrows came in P4 and P6.

POLE POSITION Häkkinen, McLaren-Mercedes, 1m 19.798s (0.339s), 151.898kph, 94.385mph
LAPS 78 x 3.366 km, 2.092 miles
DISTANCE 262.626 km, 163.188 miles
STARTERS/FINISHERS 21/12
WEATHER Sunny, hot, dry
LAP LEADERS Häkkinen 1-78 (78)
WINNER'S LAPS 1-78 P1
FASTEST LAP Häkkinen, McLaren-Mercedes, 1m 22.948s (lap 29), 146.130kph, 90.801mph
CHAMPIONSHIP Häkkinen 46, Coulthard 29, M Schumacher 24, Irvine 15, Wurz 9

Pos	Driver	Car	Time/gap	Grid	Stops	Tyres
1	M Häkkinen	McLaren-Mercedes	1h 51m 23.595s	1	1	B
2	G Fisichella	Benetton-Playlife	−11.475s	3	1	B
3	E Irvine	Ferrari	−41.378s	7	1	G
4	M Salo	Arrows	−1m 0.363s	8	1	B
5	J Villeneuve	Williams-Mecachrome	−1 lap	13	1	G
6	P Diniz	Arrows	−1 lap	12	1	B

CANADIAN GP Montréal

7 June 1998   **Race 621**

Michael Schumacher

Ferrari F300 181.296kph, 112.652mph

A post-race protest by Williams voiced mounting indignation over Schumacher's ruthless driving. As he rejoined the track from his first pit stop, Frentzen, approaching the pit exit at 180mph was barged off. For this Schumacher received a stop-go. But he still won, beating Fisichella with a devastating 15-lap sprint after serving his penalty. Schumacher's task was assisted by mechanical woes for McLaren, both out within 18 laps, and no less than three SC deployments. There was also carnage both at the start, Wurz's spectacular triple roll, and the restart, Trulli's Prost landing atop Alesi's Sauber, Ralf Schumacher the catalyst for both incidents. At his home GP Villeneuve made a stronger showing, but in a desperate lunge for the lead out-braked himself.

POLE POSITION D Coulthard, McLaren-Mercedes, 1m 18.213s (0.069s), 203.490kph, 126.443mph
LAPS 69 x 4.421 km, 2.747 miles (Race restarted for scheduled 69 laps following accident)
DISTANCE 305.049 km, 189.549 miles
STARTERS/FINISHERS 22/10
WEATHER Overcast, cool, dry
LAP LEADERS Coulthard 1-18 (18); M Schumacher 19, 44-69 (27); Fisichella 20-43 (24); SC 1-5, 15-17, 20-22 (11)
WINNER'S LAPS 1-18 P2, 19 P1, 20-22 P3, 23-34 P2, 35-37 P3, 38-43 P2, 44-69 P1
FASTEST LAP M Schumacher, Ferrari, 1m 19.379s (Lap 48), 200.501kph, 124.586mph
CHAMPIONSHIP Häkkinen 46, M Schumacher 34, Coulthard 29, Irvine 19, Fisichella 13

Pos	Driver	Car	Time/gap	Grid	Stops	Tyres
1	M Schumacher	Ferrari	1h 40m 57.355s	3	3	G
2	G Fisichella	Benetton-Playlife	−16.662s	4	1	B
3	E Irvine	Ferrari	−1m 0.059s	8	3	G
4	A Wurz	Benetton-Playlife	−1m 3.232s	11	1	B
5	R Barrichello	Stewart-Ford	−1m 21.513s	13	2	B
6	J Magnussen	Stewart-Ford	−1 lap	20	1	B

FRENCH GP Magny-Cours

28 June 1998   Race 622

Michael Schumacher

Ferrari F300 190.963kph, 118.659mph

Ferrari's first 1-2 in eight years put the Scuderia and Schumacher back into championship contention. France was a straight fight between McLaren and Ferrari, and McLaren lost. Or did luck simply abandon them? At the aborted first start Häkkinen made a perfect getaway from pole only to be beaten away by both Ferraris at the second. This allowed Irvine to bottle-up the McLaren duo while Schumacher made his escape. On lap 19, with Schumacher's lead 14s, Häkkinen briefly got ahead of Irvine, then promptly spun. He was back pressurising over the closing 15 laps, but Irvine held on. Coulthard's championship campaign suffered another setback, making four stops due to refuelling rig problems. A more upbeat Villeneuve qualified P5 to finish P4.

POLE POSITION Häkkinen, McLaren-Mercedes, 1m 14.929s (0.230), 204.193kph, 126.880mph
LAPS 71 x 4.250 km, 2.641 miles (72 lap race interrupted due to stalled car. Restarted over 71 laps)
DISTANCE 301.564 km, 187.383 miles
STARTERS/FINISHERS 22/17
WEATHER Cloudy with sunny intervals, hot, dry
LAP LEADERS M Schumacher 1-22, 24-71 (70); Irvine 23 (1)
WINNER'S LAPS 1-22 P1, 23 P2, 24-71 P1
FASTEST LAP Coulthard, McLaren-Mercedes, 1m 17.523s (lap 59), 197.360kph, 122.634mph
CHAMPIONSHIP Häkkinen 50, M Schumacher 44, Coulthard 30, Irvine 25, Wurz 14

Pos	Driver	Car	Time/gap	Grid	Stops	Tyres
1	M Schumacher	Ferrari	1h 34m 46.026s	2	2	G
2	E Irvine	Ferrari	−19.575s	4	2	G
3	M Häkkinen	McLaren-Mercedes	−19.747s	1	2	B
4	J Villeneuve	Williams-Mecachrome	−1m 6.965s	5	2	G
5	A Wurz	Benetton-Playlife	−1 lap	10	3	B
6	D Coulthard	McLaren-Mercedes	−1 lap	3	4	B

BRITISH GP Silverstone

12 July 1998   Race 623

Michael Schumacher

Ferrari F300 172.810kph, 107.379mph

More controversy surrounded Schumacher's hat-trick, notoriously winning while stationery in the pits serving a stop-go penalty. Häkkinen led superbly in the wet until conditions became so dire that even the leader engaged in a high-speed spin across the grass. Correctly, if too late for Mika, the SC was deployed. This negated Häkkinen's 40s lead over Schumacher, and with his front wing damaged by the off, any prospect of victory had gone. But a penalty for Schumacher for passing under yellow might have altered things. However, malimplementation by the stewards caused a confusing and unsatisfactory result, but one which withstood McLaren's post-race protest. Coulthard spun out on lap 37, extremely unhappy with his team over tyre choice.

POLE POSITION Häkkinen, McLaren-Mercedes, 1m 23.271s (0.449s), 222.214kph, 138.078mph
LAPS 60 x 5.140 km, 3.194 miles
DISTANCE 308.296 km, 191.566 miles
STARTERS/FINISHERS 22/9
WEATHER Overcast, cold, windy, dry at first then heavy rain
LAP LEADERS Häkkinen 1-50 (50); M Schumacher 51-60 (10); SC 45-49 (5)
WINNER'S LAPS 1-4 P2, 5-19 P3, 20-21 P5, 22-37 P3, 38-50 P2, 51-60 P1
FASTEST LAP M Schumacher, Ferrari, 1m 35.704s (lap 12), 193.346kph, 120.140mph
CHAMPIONSHIP Häkkinen 56, M Schumacher 54, Coulthard 30, Irvine 29, Wurz 17

Pos	Driver	Car	Time/gap	Grid	Stops	Tyres
1	M Schumacher	Ferrari	1h 47m 2.450s	2	2	G
2	M Häkkinen	McLaren-Mercedes	−22.465s	1	2	B
3	E Irvine	Ferrari	−29.199s	5	2	G
4	A Wurz	Benetton-Playlife	−1 lap	11	2	B
5	G Fisichella	Benetton-Playlife	−1 lap	10	2	B
6	R Schumacher	Jordan-Mugen Honda	−1 lap	21	3	G

AUSTRIAN GP A1-Ring

26 July 1998   Race 624

Mika Häkkinen

McLaren-Mercedes MP4/13 202.777kph, 126.000mph

Changeable qualifying weather had Fisichella and Alesi on row one, but once Häkkinen resisted the initial pressure from the more lightly fuelled Schumacher Ferrari there was never doubt about the winner. In a rare mistake on lap 17, Schumacher lost his front wing in a bucking off-course excursion, subsequently making a fighting recovery drive to P3. Similarly Coulthard, following his Silverstone disappointment, stormed incisively from dead last to P2, having been the innocent victim in a first-lap mêleé that brought out the SC. So a 1-2 result put Häkkinen and McLaren back in charge of the championships. Ferrari finished 3-4, Irvine's car developing 'brake problems' during his final stint, forcing him to cede P3 to Schumacher.

POLE POSITION G Fisichella, Benetton-Playlife, 1m 29.598s (0.719s), 173.535kph, 107.830mph
LAPS 71 x 4.319 km, 2.684 miles
DISTANCE 306.649 km, 190.543 miles
STARTERS/FINISHERS 22/12
WEATHER Sunny, hot, dry
LAP LEADERS Häkkinen 1-34, 37-71 (69); Coulthard 35-36 (2); SC 1-3 (3)
WINNER'S LAPS 1-34 P1, 35-36 P2, 37-71 P1
FASTEST LAP Coulthard, McLaren-Mercedes, 1m 12.878s (lap 30), 213.348kph, 132.569mph
CHAMPIONSHIP Häkkinen 66, M Schumacher 58, Coulthard 36, Irvine 32, Wurz 17

Pos	Driver	Car	Time/gap	Grid	Stops	Tyres
1	M Häkkinen	McLaren-Mercedes	1h 34m 46.026s	3	1	B
2	D Coulthard	McLaren-Mercedes	−5.289s	14	1	B
3	M Schumacher	Ferrari	−39.092s	4	2	G
4	E Irvine	Ferrari	−43.976s	8	2	G
5	R Schumacher	Jordan-Mugen Honda	−50.654s	9	2	G
6	J Villeneuve	Williams-Mecachrome	−53.202s	11	1	G

Round 11/16	**GERMAN GP** Hockenheim
	2 August 1998 **Race 625**

GERMAN GP Hockenheim
2 August 1998   Race 625

Mika Häkkinen
McLaren-Mercedes MP4/13 227.997kph, 141.671mph

Adopting low downforce configuration for the Hockenheim thrash, Ferrari found themselves off the pace, Schumacher qualifying P9 and finishing P5 to the chagrin of the home crowd. But for others things looked up. Villeneuve's Williams qualified and finished P3, the purple-haired champion claiming his first podium of the season after 11 rounds. The progressive Jordan-Mugen Honda team celebrated a double-points finish, Hill beating both Schumachers home. But this was all happening behind the McLaren pair, rarely more than a second apart. Despite last-minute fuel rig worries requiring Mika to drive abstemiously and David to play rear-gunner, back-to-back 1-2 finishes totally changed the face of the championship within just seven days.

POLE POSITION Häkkinen, McLaren-Mercedes, 1m 41.838s (0.509s), 241.194kph, 149.872mph
LAPS 45 x 6.823 km, 4.240 miles
DISTANCE 307.035 km, 190.783 miles
STARTERS/FINISHERS 21/16
WEATHER Cloudy with sunny intervals, hot, dry
LAP LEADERS Häkkinen 1-25, 28-45 (43); Coulthard 26-27 (2)
WINNER'S LAPS 1-25 P1, 26-27 P2, 28-45 P1
FASTEST LAP Coulthard, McLaren-Mercedes, 1m 46.116s (lap 17), 231.471kph, 143.830mph
CHAMPIONSHIP Häkkinen 76, M Schumacher 60, Coulthard 42, Irvine 32, Wurz 17

Pos	Driver	Car	Time/gap	Grid	Stops	Tyres
1	M Häkkinen	McLaren-Mercedes	1h 34m 46.026s	1	1	B
2	D Coulthard	McLaren-Mercedes	−0.426s	2	1	B
3	J Villeneuve	Williams-Mecachrome	−2.577s	3	1	G
4	D Hill	Jordan-Mugen Honda	−7.185s	5	1	G
5	M Schumacher	Ferrari	−12.613s	9	1	G
6	R Schumacher	Jordan-Mugen Honda	−29.738s	4	2	G

HUNGARIAN GP Hungaroring
Round 12/16   **16 August 1998**   Race 626

Michael Schumacher
Ferrari F300 174.062kph, 108.157mph

Ferrari bounced back from their Hockenheim doldrums with a 'how did they do that?' Schumacher/Brawn victory. Trapped behind Villeneuve at their first stop, Brawn chose a radical three-stop. At stop two Brawn advised: '19 laps to pick up 25s.' Despite a brief off on lap 52, Schumacher obliged brilliantly. Tactical blunders by McLaren, plus Goodyear performance outstripping Bridgestone, made his third stop a comparative formality, rejoining 5s ahead. Schumacher's sensational victory over Häkkinen's troubled one-point finish revitalised the championship chase. Former champions Villeneuve and Hill finished 3-4 from Coulthard, who was unable to stay with Schumacher when Mika fell away with a mysterious handling problem.

POLE POSITION Häkkinen, McLaren-Mercedes, 1m 16.973s (0.158s), 185.769kph, 115.432mph
LAPS 77 x 3.972 km, 2.468 miles
DISTANCE 305.844 km, 190.043 miles
STARTERS/FINISHERS 21/16
WEATHER Cloudy with sunny intervals, hot, dry
LAP LEADERS Häkkinen 1-46 (46); M Schumacher 47-77 (31)
WINNER'S LAPS 1-25 P3, 26-30 P4, 31-44 P3, 45-46 P2, 47-77 P1
FASTEST LAP M Schumacher, Ferrari, 1m 19.286s (lap 60), 180.349kph, 112.064mph
CHAMPIONSHIP Häkkinen 77, M Schumacher 70, Coulthard 48, Irvine 32, Villeneuve 20

Pos	Driver	Car	Time/gap	Grid	Stops	Tyres
1	M Schumacher	Ferrari	1h 45m 25.550s	3	3	G
2	D Coulthard	McLaren-Mercedes	−9.433s	2	2	B
3	J Villeneuve	Williams-Mecachrome	−44.444s	6	2	G
4	D Hill	Jordan-Mugen Honda	−55.076s	4	2	G
5	H-H Frentzen	Williams-Mecachrome	−56.510s	7	2	G
6	M Häkkinen	McLaren-Mercedes	−1 lap	1	2	B

BELGIAN GP Spa Francorchamps
Round 13/16   **30 August 1998**   Race 627

Damon Hill
Jordan-Mugen Honda 198 177.229kph, 110.125mph

This wet-race classic began with a terrifying 13-car first-corner pile-up triggered by Coulthard's spin. At the restart Hill, having qualified P3, nabbed the lead for nine laps until Michael Schumacher, having already spun Häkkinen out, went by to establish an unassailable 37s lead. On lap 25 in zero visibility he shunted Coulthard in the process of lapping him, which restored Hill to the lead. Fascinatingly, this race exposed the collective Schumacher mind-set. Michael was livid with Coulthard for getting in his way, while Ralf, only in contention due to a second SC, was livid with his team, anxiously on the verge of their maiden victory, for not allowing him to race his team leader. There was unbounded joy in the Jordan pit and at Sauber too for Alesi's P3.

POLE POSITION M Häkkinen, McLaren-Mercedes, 1m 48.682s (0.163s), 230.809kph, 143.418mph
LAPS 44 x 6.968 km, 4.330 miles (Race restarted for scheduled 44 laps following multiple accident)
DISTANCE 306.577 km, 190.498 miles
STARTERS/FINISHERS 22/8
WEATHER Overcast, cold, heavy rain
LAP LEADERS Hill 1-7, 26-44 (26); M Schumacher 8-25 (18); SC 1-2, 29-32 (6)
WINNER'S LAPS 1-7 P1, 8-25 P2, 26-44 P1
FASTEST LAP M Schumacher, Ferrari, 2m 03.766s (lap 9), 202.679kph, 125.939mph
CHAMPIONSHIP Häkkinen 77, M Schumacher 70, Coulthard 48, Irvine 32, Villeneuve 20

Pos	Driver	Car	Time/gap	Grid	Stops	Tyres
1	D Hill	Jordan-Mugen Honda	1h 43m 47.407s	3	2	G
2	R Schumacher	Jordan-Mugen Honda	−0.932s	8	2	G
3	J Alesi	Sauber-Petronas	−7.240s	10	2	G
4	H-H Frentzen	Williams-Mecachrome	−32.243s	9	2	G
5	P Diniz	Arrows	−51.682s	16	1	B
6	J Trulli	Prost-Peugeot	−2 laps	13	1	B

TOP **100** RACE

Jordan-Mugen Honda 198

Round 14/16	**ITALIAN GP** Monza						**Michael Schumacher**

ITALIAN GP Monza
13 September 1998   Race 628

Michael Schumacher
Ferrari **F300** 237.591kph, 147.633mph

A dream Monza 1-2 for Ferrari plus a double debacle for McLaren left the title protagonists locked on equal points with two rounds to go. McLaren plucked defeat from the jaws of victory when on lap 17 dominant leader Coulthard's Mercedes erupted in a cloud of smoke so dense that the following Häkkinen briefly lifted, letting Schumacher by. Then, having sorted his initial handling issues, failing brakes caused Häkkinen to spin in the final stages as he closed in on Schumacher's lead, putting him down to P4. Schumacher, starting from pole, had given McLaren every chance by entering the first chicane P5. His successful chase of the McLarens began on lap 3 after dispensing first with Villeneuve's front row Williams and then his teammate's Ferrari.

POLE POSITION Schumacher, Ferrari, 1m 25.289s (0.272s), 243.548kph, 151.334mph
LAPS 53 x 5.770 km, 3.585 miles
DISTANCE 305.548 km, 189.859 miles
STARTERS/FINISHERS 22/13
WEATHER Cloudy with sunny intervals, warm, dry
LAP LEADERS Häkkinen 1-7, 32-34 (10); D Coulthard, McLaren-Mercedes 8-16 (9); M Schumacher 17-31, 35-53 (34)
WINNER'S LAPS 1-2 P4, 3-16 P3, 17-31 P1, 32-34 P2, 35-53 P1
FASTEST LAP Häkkinen, McLaren-Mercedes, 1m 25.139 (lap 45), 243.977kph, 151.601mph
CHAMPIONSHIP Häkkinen 80, M Schumacher 80, Coulthard 48, Irvine 38, Villeneuve 20

Pos	Driver	Car	Time/gap	Grid	Stops	Tyres
1	M Schumacher	Ferrari	1h 17m 9.672s	1	1	G
2	E Irvine	Ferrari	−37.977s	5	1	G
3	R Schumacher	Jordan-Mugen Honda	−41.152s	6	1	G
4	M Häkkinen	McLaren-Mercedes	−56.671s	3	1	B
5	J Alesi	Sauber-Petronas	−1m 1.872s	8	1	G
6	D Hill	Jordan-Mugen Honda	−1m 6.688s	14	2	G

Round 15/16	**LUXEMBOURG GP** Nürburgring						**Mika Häkkinen**

LUXEMBOURG GP Nürburgring
27 September 1998   Race 629

Mika Häkkinen
McLaren-Mercedes **MP4/13** 198.534kph, 123.364mph

Starting behind an all-red front row, Häkkinen and McLaren won on merit, driver and tactics. The decisive moments were Häkkinen's brave and brilliant pass of Irvine for P2 on lap 14, releasing him to close in on Schumacher before the first stops. Then the 'qualifying' laps he pumped in to gain full advantage from the smart McLaren 'long' first stop tactic that took him into a lead he was never to lose. It was a victory completely in contrast to the Monza debacle as well as highly reminiscent of Schumacher/Brawn themselves, the German utterly shell-shocked by losing such a crucial race from pole. McLaren were also successful in the 'B' race, Coulthard P3, Irvine P4. McLaren entered the finale one point short, Mika needing P2 to be certain.

POLE POSITION Schumacher, Ferrari, 1m 18.561s (0.346s), 208.775kph, 129.727mph
LAPS 67 x 4.556 km, 2.831 miles
DISTANCE 305.235 km, 189.664 miles
STARTERS/FINISHERS 22/16
WEATHER Overcast, cool, dry
LAP LEADERS M Schumacher 1-24 (24); Häkkinen 25-67 (43)
WINNER'S LAPS 1-13 P3, 14-24 P2, 25-67 P1
FASTEST LAP Häkkinen, McLaren-Mercedes, 1m 20.450s (lap 25), 203.873kph, 126.681mph
CHAMPIONSHIP Häkkinen 90, M Schumacher 86, Coulthard 52, Irvine 41, Villeneuve 20

Pos	Driver	Car	Time/gap	Grid	Stops	Tyres
1	M Häkkinen	McLaren-Mercedes	1h 32m 14.789s	3	2	B
2	M Schumacher	Ferrari	−2.211s	1	2	G
3	D Coulthard	McLaren-Mercedes	−34.163s	5	2	B
4	E Irvine	Ferrari	−58.182s	2	2	G
5	H-H Frentzen	Williams-Mecachrome	−1m 0.247s	7	2	G
6	G Fisichella	Benetton-Playlife	−1m 1.359s	4	2	B

JAPANESE GP Suzuka

1 November 1998
Race 630

Mika Häkkinen

McLaren-Mercedes MP4/13 205.229kph, 127.524mph

As last year's finale, Schumacher had a good chance of the title for himself and Ferrari, this time effectively needing to win. A brilliant pole secured his first key objective, but when it came to the race he blew it. Maybe the Nürburgring trouncing had got to him, or the five-week gap to think about it, or when an aborted first start also raised tension. Whichever, he stalled on the grid. When the field finally got away at the third attempt, Schumacher was last on the grid, his sensational recovery drive ending with a puncture on lap 31 when P3. From the moment of his retirement Häkkinen and McLaren-Mercedes were champions, their comfortable race victory an added bonus. Three years after his brush with death at Adelaide, Mika was champion.

POLE POSITION M Schumacher, Ferrari, 1m 36.293s (0.178s), 219.230kph, 136.224mph
LAPS 51 x 5.864 km, 3.644 miles (Scheduled for 53 laps but reduced after two aborted starts)
DISTANCE 298.868 km, 185.708 miles
STARTERS/FINISHERS 21/12
WEATHER Sunny, warm, dry
LAP LEADERS Häkkinen 1-51 (51)
WINNER'S LAPS 1-51 P1
FASTEST LAP M Schumacher, Ferrari, 1m 40.190s (lap 19), 210.703kph, 130.925mph
CHAMPIONSHIP Häkkinen 100, M Schumacher 86, Coulthard 56, Irvine 47, Villeneuve 21

Pos	Driver	Car	Time/gap	Grid	Stops	Tyres
1	M Häkkinen	McLaren-Mercedes	1h 27m 22.535s	2	2	B
2	E Irvine	Ferrari	−6.491s	4	3	G
3	D Coulthard	McLaren-Mercedes	−27.662s	3	2	B
4	D Hill	Jordan-Mugen Honda	−1m 13.491s	8	2	G
5	H-H Frentzen	Williams-Mecachrome	−1m 13.857s	5	2	G
6	J Villeneuve	Williams-Mecachrome	−1m 15.867s	6	1	G

1998 CHAMPIONSHIP FACTS AND FOLKLORE

■ A 10% decrease in car width (chassis/suspension) to 1.8m plus the replacement of slicks for harder, grooved tyres constituted radical new regulations aimed primarily at a substantial increase in lap times. In the event a far smaller reduction in speed was achieved than had been anticipated.
■ What the new regs unquestionably did produce was lower grip levels. This engendered an unforeseen increase in unforced driver errors, possibly compromising safety, and even greater difficulty in overtaking.

■ The 'F1 overtaking crisis' spawned an expert group tasked to investigate the phenomenon, but the rule-makers, the FIA, were not convinced there was a crisis. President Max Mosley implied that changes in race position created by pit stops were just as compelling as on-track passes, likening F1 to a 'game of chess'.
■ From the Spanish GP the FIA moved to ban the unsightly and potentially dangerous X-wings.
■ The withdrawal by Renault of their factory-supported

RACE 627, Belgian GP: There was unbounded joy on the Jordan pit wall when Damon Hill (his car barely visible) delivered the team's very first GP victory, the first newly-winning marque in 12 seasons.

RACE 630, Japanese GP: Häkkinen embraces Ron Dennis and Norbert Haug.
Three years after his brush with death at Adelaide, Mika was champion.

engine supply to Williams and Benetton may have given Schumacher and Ferrari reasons to be cheerful, that 1998 could at last be their year.

■ As it transpired, the McLaren 1-2 in the final race of 1997 was a sign of things to come. Despite, or rather because of, the radical rule changes, McLaren won five of the first six races of the new season, including three 1-2 finishes.

■ But a mid-season loss of McLaren momentum plus improvements from Goodyear enabled Schumacher and Ferrari to make a fight of it, and for the second year running they entered the final round with a chance to win the title.

■ But their challenge ended in a whimper, or more precisely, an engine-stall on the grid, Mika Häkkinen sweeping to championship glory. The Finn proved himself not only the dominant McLaren driver but also that he could take the fight to Schumacher on-track. A worthy champion, he won eight of the 16 championship rounds.

■ McLaren's first championships since Ayrton Senna seven years ago largely turned on four factors. Their Bridgestone gamble, Newey's long-wheelbase interpretation of the new chassis regs, a strong if not bullet-proof Mercedes motor, and Häkkinen's talent finally unfettered.

■ Competitors hoped their 'brake-steer' system – an extra pedal to brake one rear wheel to assist turn-in to and traction out of corners – was the foundation of McLaren's dominance at round one, but at round two it was banned and they still won comfortably. The Woking team even had time to construct an 'F1' two-seater.

■ Round one was Bridgestone's maiden win, and Goodyear's end-of-season withdrawal left the field open for the Japanese tyre company to become sole supplier to F1 for the following two seasons.

■ Ferrari along with Goodyear were on the back foot at the start of the season, but Goodyear's broader, squarer-shouldered fronts and Ferrari's circuit-specific wheelbase geometry turned things around. Mid-season they also introduced

reworked exhausts venting from the top of the chassis towards the rear wing.

■ Schumacher became the first Ferrari driver since Ascari in 1952 to win six races in a season, while this latest clutch of wins took him ahead of Stewart and Mansell to third in the all-time GP winners standings with 33 victories, behind only Prost and Senna.

■ Although 1998 was another lost championship, at Monza Ferrari celebrated participation in 600 GPs (from 628) with ever-strengthening belief that the future was red.

■ Following the Coulthard-induced team orders kerfuffle in Australia, the FIA used vaguely worded terms whereby any act 'prejudicial to the interests of competition' was outlawed. Then, after blatant Ferrari team orders in Austria, the FIA used weasel words to say that team orders were not banned per se.

■ When Schumacher tripped over Coulthard at a wet Spa, Damon Hill proved his worth to Jordan by bringing home their very first win. The enormity of this achievement was shown by the fact that Jordan was the first new winning marque since Benetton joined the winners' ranks back in 1986.

■ As one marque newly won, a formerly victorious marque ended. In November 1997 Ken Tyrrell had sold-up to British American Racing (BAR), although for 1998 the Tyrrell name remained, with Ken still in nominal control until he quit before the season began over driver choice.

■ Ken Tyrrell's 32-year association with F1 begat 23 championship race victories, three world titles for Jackie Stewart, one for his own car in 1971, plus a second team title in 1969 with Matra. The one blemish was the team's disqualification from the 1984 championship.

■ Tyrrell's F1 franchise went to what was to become known as the 'Brackley Team', as in subsequent years it morphed from BAR to Honda to Brawn to Mercedes.

■ BAR was a consortium led by Craig Pollock, Jacques

Villeneuve's manager, the team built around the 1997 world champion, with an Adrian Reynard-designed car, a Mecachrome engine and tobacco money, plus the self-proclaimed aim of winning its first race.

■ Back in the real world of 1998, Pat Symonds and Nick Wirth designed the Benetton B198, which was about on a par with the Williams FW20 without Adrian Newey, in that both teams used the same engine and neither car was a winner.

■ Benetton's incarnation of the Mecachrome 'customer' Renault V10 was badged Playlife, a Benetton brand name. But whatever the moniker, Briatore became the commercial intermediary between Mecachrome and its teams through his Supertec company, which made neither Williams nor Benetton particularly happy, especially when BAR were added as a third team.

■ Unable to agree future direction, Dave Richards walked out at Benetton before the season ended, Rocco Benetton the new team boss.

■ Arrows scored just six points, one more than Stewart-Ford. These two teams were first to race carbon-fibre gearboxes, although in 1996 John Barnard had innovated with a carbon fibre plus titanium Ferrari box.

■ Fitted with their own Brian Hart-designed V10, Arrows became the first single-name British marque since BRM, while Barnard departed Arrows for Prost.

■ Cosworth became a fully-owned Ford subsidiary through a circuitous route. Owners Vickers sold Rolls Royce plus Cosworth to VW, then Audi sold Cosworth to Ford, securing its F1 future.

■ On-track politics surrounded traction control, teams lobbying the FIA to lift the ban because it could not be policed, undetectable ways having been found to emulate its benefits through the engine ECU (electronic control unit).

■ Off-track, after two years of political wrangling the Concorde Agreement was finally signed (Sauber and Arrows apart) for the next ten years. This might have opened the way to the public flotation of F1, but there was still at least one impediment: the EU's investigation into the FIA's rights to be the sole sanctioning body.

■ Threatening a reduction in the number of European F1 races, the FIA won an exemption to the EU tobacco advertising ban until the end of 2006.

■ Although surely in no way related, Ecclestone's £1 million gift to the UK Labour Party in November 1997 was investigated. Bernie refused a voluntary appearance at the public inquiry into the generous political donation from F1.

■ On the less seamy side, manufacturer interest in F1 continued apace, Berger appointed competitions director for BMW and rumours of Toyota entering in 2001 to perhaps snatch the 12th F1 team franchise from Honda.

Championship ranking	Championship points	Driver nationality	1998 Drivers Championship		Races contested	Race victories	Podiumse excl. victories	Races led	Lights to flag victories	Laps led	Poles	Fastest laps	Triple Crowns
			Driver	Car									
1	100	FIN	Mika Häkkinen	McLaren-Mercedes	16	8	3	12	3	576	9	6	4
2	86	GER	Michael Schumacher	Ferrari	16	6	5	8		268	3	6	
3	56	GBR	David Coulthard	McLaren-Mercedes	16	1	8	8	1	120	3	3	
4	47	GBR	Eddie Irvine	Ferrari	16		8	1		1			
5	21	CAN	Jacques Villeneuve	Williams-Mecachrome	16		2						
6	20	GBR	Damon Hill	Jordan-Mugen Honda	16	1		1		26			
7	17	GER	Heinz-Harald Frentzen	Williams-Mecachrome	16		1						
8	17	AUT	Alexander Wurz	Benetton-Playlife	16							1	
9	16	ITA	Giancarlo Fisichella	Benetton-Playlife	16		2	1		24	1		
10	14	GER	Ralf Schumacher	Jordan-Mugen Honda	16		2						
11	9	FRA	Jean Alesi	Sauber-Petronas	16		1						
12	4	BRA	Rubens Barrichello	Stewart-Ford	16								
13	3	FIN	Mika Salo	Arrows	16								
14	3	BRA	Pedro Diniz	Arrows	16								
15	1	GBR	Johnny Herbert	Sauber-Petronas	16								
16	1	DNK	Jan Magnussen	Stewart-Ford	7								
17	1	ITA	Jarno Trulli	Prost-Peugeot	16								

Championship ranking	Championship points	Team/Marque nationality	1998 Constructors Championship		Engine maker nationality	Races contested	Race victories	1-2 finishes	Podiums excl. victories	Races led	Laps led	Poles	Fastest laps
			Chassis	Engine									
1	156	GBR	McLaren MP4-13	Mercedes-Benz 3.0 V10	GER	16	9	5	11	14	696	12	9
2	133	ITA	Ferrari F300	Ferrari 3.0 V10	ITA	16	6	2	13	8	269	3	6
3	38	GBR	Williams FW20	Mecachrome 3.0 V10	FRA	16			3				
4	34	IRL	Jordan 198	Mugen Honda 3.0 V10	JPN	16	1	1	2	1	26		
5	33	ITA	Benetton B198	Playlife 3.0 V10	FRA	16			2	1	24	1	1
6	10	SUI	Sauber C17	Petronas 3.0 V10	ITA	16			1				
7	6	GBR	Arrows A19	Arrows 3.0 V10	GBR	16							
8	5	GBR	Stewart SF2	Ford Cosworth 3.0 V10	GBR	16							
9	1	FRA	Prost AP01, AP01B	Peugeot 3.0 V10	FRA	16							

1999

Mika's double, Michael's trouble

THE TALE OF THE TITLE

- Mika Häkkinen became the seventh double champion, retaining his world drivers' crown with five race wins.
- Schumacher's challenge ended with a dramatic mid-season accident, missing seven rounds with a broken leg.
- But of those seven races, and despite his six poles, a variety of setbacks brought Häkkinen just one victory.
- So Eddie Irvine took up the Ferrari mantle, his four race wins keeping the championship in play to its finale.
- It was a season of fluctuating fortunes, innumerable blunders and races ranging from stupendous to stultifying.
- Pundits considered the boredom and the blunders shared the same root cause, hard, grooved tyres.
- Edgy narrow-track cars on Bridgestone 'control' tyres made drivers error-prone and overtaking more difficult.
- Ferrari's six wins fell one short of McLaren, better reliability bringing their first constructors' title since 1983.
- Jordan rose to an impressive third place, as did H-H Frentzen in the drivers' contest with his two victories.
- Jordan teammate Hill made a low-key departure from F1, clearly no longer relishing the challenge.
- In only their third season Stewart-Ford picked up a noteworthy if fortuitous first race victory.
- The team, now fully under Ford ownership, planned to bring the Jaguar name to GP racing next season.
- And not forgetting: BAR's hyped-up arrival.

THE CHASE FOR THE CHAMPIONSHIP

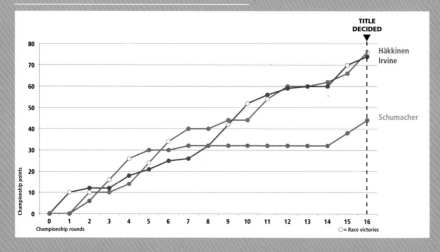

<table>
<tr><td></td></tr>
</table>

<table>
<tr>
<td>**Round 1/16**</td>
<td>**AUSTRALIAN GP** Melbourne
7 March 1999</td>
<td>**Eddie Irvine**
Ferrari F399 190.852kph, 118.590mph</td>
</tr>
</table>

McLaren's new car, dominant in qualifying and the early race, proved unreliable, Coulthard out on lap 13, leader Häkkinen soon afterwards following the first of two SCs. One was for Villeneuve, his BAR debut ending dramatically when the rear wing flew off, the second when Zanardi's Williams debut ended in the wall. The SCs aided recovery drives by Barrichello and M. Schumacher. Second row qualifiers, these two were both potential winners once the McLarens were out, but grid difficulties found them starting from the back. So when Irvine beat Frentzen away from the line he set up his maiden victory from his 86th start, a result only in doubt had he been forced to concede to Schumacher, but in an erratic drive P4 was as far as his teammate got.

POLE POSITION M Häkkinen, McLaren-Mercedes, 1m 30.462s (0.484s), 211.036kph, 131.132mph
LAPS 57 x 5.303 km, 3.295 miles
DISTANCE 302.271 km, 187.822 miles
STARTERS/FINISHERS 21/8
WEATHER Sunny, warm, dry
LAP LEADERS Häkkinen 1-17 (17); Irvine 18-57 (40); SC 16-17, 23-25 (5)
WINNER'S LAPS 1-13 P3, 14-17 P2, 18-57 P1
FASTEST LAP M Schumacher, Ferrari, 1m 32.112s (lap 55), 207.256kph, 128.783mph
CHAMPIONSHIP Irvine 10, Frentzen 6, R Schumacher 4, Fisichella 3, Barrichello 2

Pos	Driver	Car	Time/gap	Grid	Stops	Tyres
1	E Irvine	Ferrari	1h 35m 1.659s	6	1	B
2	H-H Frentzen	Jordan-Mugen Honda	–1.027s	5	1	B
3	R Schumacher	Williams-Supertec	–7.012s	8	1	B
4	G Fisichella	Benetton-Playlife	–33.418s	7	2	B
5	R Barrichello	Stewart-Ford	–54.698s	4	3	B
6	P de la Rosa	Arrows	–1m 24.317s	18	2	B

McLaren-Mercedes MP4/14

<table>
<tr>
<td>**Round 2/16**</td>
<td>**BRAZILIAN GP** Interlagos
11 April 1999</td>
<td>**Mika Häkkinen**
McLaren-Mercedes MP4/14 192.994kph, 119.921mph</td>
</tr>
</table>

When a gearbox glitch on lap 4 dropped Häkkinen from first to third, a Stewart-Ford led for the first time and, to local joy, Barrichello drove it. Brazilian euphoria lasted 23 laps before one-stoppers Schumacher and Häkkinen re-established command. Häkkinen, gears restored, leapfrogged Schumacher during the pit stop and that's how they finished. Coulthard might have won had he not stalled on the grid, while Barrichello lost P3 on lap 43 when the Ford V10 blew, leaving Frentzen to take another podium for Jordan even though he ran out of fuel. BAR's harsh F1 baptism continued, Zonta surviving a massive practice crash with only light injuries after hitting an unprotected barrier at over 100mph, while a fuel irregularity had JV starting from the back.

POLE POSITION Häkkinen, McLaren-Mercedes, 1m 16.568s (0.147s), 201.797kph, 125.391mph
LAPS 72 x 4.292 km, 2.667 miles
DISTANCE 308.994 km, 192.000 miles
STARTERS/FINISHERS 21/9
WEATHER Sunny, hot, dry
LAP LEADERS Häkkinen 1-3, 38-72 (38); R Barrichello, Stewart-Ford 4-26 (23); M Schumacher 27-37 (11)
WINNER'S LAPS 1-3 P1, 4-26 P3, 27-37 P2, 38-72 P1
FASTEST LAP Häkkinen, McLaren-Mercedes, 1m 18.448s (lap 70), 196.961kph, 122.386mph
CHAMPIONSHIP Irvine 12, Häkkinen 10, Frentzen 10, R Schumacher 7, M Schumacher 6

Pos	Driver	Car	Time/gap	Grid	Stops	Tyres
1	M Häkkinen	McLaren-Mercedes	1h 36m 3.785s	1	1	B
2	M Schumacher	Ferrari	–4.925s	4	1	B
3r	H-H Frentzen	Jordan-Mugen Honda	–1 lap	8	1	B
4	R Schumacher	Williams-Supertec	–1 lap	11	1	B
5	E Irvine	Ferrari	–1 lap	6	2	B
6	O Panis	Prost-Peugeot	–1 lap	12	3	B

Ferrari F399

SAN MARINO GP Imola
2 May 1999   Race 633

Michael Schumacher
Ferrari F399 195.481kph, 121.466mph

On lap 18 runaway leader Häkkinen spun off due to a self-confessed error, giving teammate and last year's winner a great chance to leap into title contention. But Coulthard could only finish a dismal P2 behind the flying Schumacher. Outsmarted tactically when Brawn switched to a two-stop; outgunned during Michael's short, sharp middle stint, and finally less able to deal with recalcitrant backmarkers, Imola was one that got away from Coulthard, from Häkkinen, from McLaren. Even though it was McLaren's loss, for Ferrari it was a much-needed victory, and on home soil, their first at Imola for 16 years. Barrichello reaffirmed the pace of the Stewart-Ford, five years on from those dire events at Tamburello, dedicating his podium to compatriot Senna.

POLE POSITION M Häkkinen, McLaren-Mercedes, 1m 26.362s (0.022s), 205.507kph, 127.696mph
LAPS 62 x 4.930 km, 3.063 miles
DISTANCE 305.428 km, 189.784 miles
STARTERS/FINISHERS 22/11
WEATHER Sunny, hot, dry
LAP LEADERS Häkkinen 1-17 (17); Coulthard 18-35 (18); M Schumacher 36-62 (27)
WINNER'S LAPS 1-17 P3, 18-35 P2, 36-62 P1
FASTEST LAP M Schumacher, Ferrari, 1m 28.547s (lap 45), 200.435kph, 124.545mph
CHAMPIONSHIP M Schumacher 16, Irvine 12, Häkkinen 10, Frentzen 10, R Schumacher 7

Pos	Driver	Car	Time/gap	Grid	Stops	Tyres
1	M Schumacher	Ferrari	1h 33m 44.792s	3	2	B
2	D Coulthard	McLaren-Mercedes	−4.265s	2	1	B
3	R Barrichello	Stewart-Ford	−1 lap	6	2	B
4	D Hill	Jordan-Mugen Honda	−1 lap	8	1	B
5	G Fisichella	Benetton-Playlife	−1 lap	16	1	B
6	J Alesi	Sauber-Petronas	−1 lap	13	3	B

MONACO GP Monte Carlo
16 May 1999   Race 634

Michael Schumacher
Ferrari F399 143.864kph, 89.394mph

Bumped from pole by the flying Finn in the dying moments of qualifying, Schumacher and Ferrari's chance of victory receded sharply. But on Sunday the more lightly fuelled Ferrari pair mugged the McLaren duo off the line and later Irvine relieved Häkkinen's malhandling car of P2 for a stirring Ferrari 1-2 victory, their first ever at Monaco. His 16th victory in red made Schumacher the most successful Ferrari race-winner ever, and against the odds the Scuderia and its drivers now led both championships handsomely. It was around half-distance that McLaren's race turned from disappointing to disastrous, Coulthard retiring from P4 with a gearbox oil leak, then Häkkinen losing 18s down the Mirabeau escape road. At least it wasn't Coulthard's oil.

POLE POSITION Häkkinen, McLaren-Mercedes, 1m 20.547s (0.064s), 150.486kph, 93.508mph
LAPS 78 x 3.367 km, 2.092 miles
DISTANCE 262.626 km, 163.188 miles
STARTERS/FINISHERS 22/9
WEATHER Sunny, hot, dry
LAP LEADERS M Schumacher 1-78 (78)
WINNER'S LAPS 1-78 P1
FASTEST LAP Häkkinen, McLaren-Mercedes, 1m 22.259s (lap 67), 147.354kph, 91.562mph
CHAMPIONSHIP M Schumacher 26, Irvine 18, Häkkinen 14, Frentzen 13, R Schumacher 7

Pos	Driver	Car	Time/gap	Grid	Stops	Tyres
1	M Schumacher	Ferrari	1h 49m 31.812s	2	1	B
2	E Irvine	Ferrari	−30.746s	4	2	B
3	M Häkkinen	McLaren-Mercedes	−37.483s	1	1	B
4	H-H Frentzen	Jordan-Mugen Honda	−54.009s	6	1	B
5	G Fisichella	Benetton-Playlife	−1 lap	9	1	B
6	A Wurz	Benetton-Playlife	−1 lap	10	1	B

SPANISH GP Cataluña
30 May 1999   Race 635

Following Schumacher's double victory McLaren needed to turn back the crimson tide in Spain, a task they duly accomplished with an emphatic 1-2. They were aided by a demon Villeneuve start from the third row, placing his BAR between the Ferraris and the escaping McLarens for 24 laps. This was a tedious, processional race that received widespread criticism, most of the blame heaped on the unloved narrow-track cars and hard, grooved tyres. JV failed to complete the distance, so after the McLaren duo followed by the Ferrari pair duly finished 1-2-3-4, Ralf Schumacher completed his third points finish for Williams from five starts. Modest results maybe, but piling massive pressure on his unfortunate teammate Zanardi's nightmare return to F1.

Pos	Driver	Car	Time/gap	Grid	Stops	Tyres
1	M Häkkinen	McLaren-Mercedes	1h 34m 13.665s	1	2	B
2	D Coulthard	McLaren-Mercedes	−6.238s	3	2	B
3	M Schumacher	Ferrari	−10.845s	4	2	B
4	E Irvine	Ferrari	−30.182s	2	2	B
5	R Schumacher	Williams-Supertec	−1m 27.208s	10	2	B
6	J Trulli	Prost-Peugeot	−1 lap	9	2	B

Mika Häkkinen
McLaren-Mercedes MP4/14 195.608kph, 121.546mph

POLE POSITION Häkkinen, McLaren-Mercedes, 1m 22.088s (0.131s), 207.348kph, 128.840mph
LAPS 65 x 4.728 km, 2.938 miles
DISTANCE 307.196 km, 190.883 miles
STARTERS/FINISHERS 22/12
WEATHER Cloudy with sunny intervals, hot, dry
LAP LEADERS Häkkinen 1-23, 27-44, 46-65 (61); Coulthard 24-26, 45 (4)
WINNER'S LAPS 1-23 P1, 24-26 P2, 27-44 P1, 45 P2, 46-65 P1
FASTEST LAP M Schumacher, Ferrari, 1m 24.982s (lap 29), 200.287kph, 124.453mph
CHAMPIONSHIP M Schumacher 30, Häkkinen 24, Irvine 21, Frentzen 13, Coulthard 12

CANADIAN GP Montréal
13 June 1999   Race 636

After the Barcelona bore we had the Canadian caper, three world champions coming to grief against the Turn 15 wall: Hill early on, Villeneuve later on, and on lap 29 leader Schumacher, who, having first administered the 'Schumacher chop' to Häkkinen, had led from pole. It was the first time Mika had been beaten to pole all season. In the treacherous conditions prescribed by low down-force plus 'wooden' tyres, the SC was deployed four times, the race even ending that way when Frentzen's brake disc disintegrated four laps short of another P2 finish. So Häkkinen won to regain the championship lead, Fisichella gave Benetton their best result of the season with P2, and despite a contretemps with Coulthard, Irvine finished a valuable P3 for Ferrari.

Pos	Driver	Car	Time/gap	Grid	Stops	Tyres
1	M Häkkinen	McLaren-Mercedes	1h 40m 57.355s	2	1	B
2	G Fisichella	Benetton-Playlife	−0.782s	7	1	B
3	E Irvine	Ferrari	−1.797s	3	1	B
4	R Schumacher	Williams-Supertec	−2.392s	13	1	B
5	J Herbert	Stewart-Ford	−2.805s	10	1	B
6	P Diniz	Sauber-Petronas	−3.711s	18	1	B

Mika Häkkinen
McLaren-Mercedes MP4/14 180.155kph, 111.943mph

POLE POSITION M Schumacher, Ferrari, 1m 19.298s (0.029s), 200.706kph, 124.713mph
LAPS 69 x 4.421 km, 2.747 miles
DISTANCE 305.049 km, 189.549 miles
STARTERS/FINISHERS 22/11
WEATHER Sunny, very hot, dry
LAP LEADERS M Schumacher 1-29 (29); Häkkinen 30-69 (40); SC 2, 5-7, 37-40, 68-69 (10)
WINNER'S LAPS 1-29 P2, 30-69 P1
FASTEST LAP Irvine, Ferrari, 1m 20.382s (Lap 62), 197.999kph, 123.031mph
CHAMPIONSHIP Häkkinen 34, M Schumacher 30, Irvine 25, Frentzen 13, Fisichella 13

FRENCH GP Magny-Cours
27 June 1999   Race 637

A mixed-up rain-affected grid and a race with 11 SC laps in torrential conditions, five race leaders and eight lead changes, four on track. Barrichello's Stewart led from pole and in three separate spells led 44 of the 72 laps to finally finish P3. On lap 6 Coulthard overtook him but his McLaren only lasted four more laps; on lap 38 Häkkinen tried but spun down to P7 in the wet; on lap 44 it was Schumacher's turn, but after 11 laps car problems restored Barrichello's lead. On lap 60 the recovering Häkkinen retook the lead, but when he and Rubens made their second fuel stops on lap 65 Frentzen's Jordan led. Having pitted on lap 22, surely H-HF had to stop again too? But no, he eked out those last litres to win with superior strategy and faultless driving.

Pos	Driver	Car	Time/gap	Grid	Stops	Tyres
1	H-H Frentzen	Jordan-Mugen Honda	1h 58m 24.343s	5	1	B
2	M Häkkinen	McLaren-Mercedes	−11.092s	14	2	B
3	R Barrichello	Stewart-Ford	−43.432s	1	2	B
4	R Schumacher	Williams-Supertec	−45.475s	16	2	B
5	M Schumacher	Ferrari	−47.881s	6	2	B
6	E Irvine	Ferrari	−48.901s	17	2	B

Heinz-Harald Frentzen
Jordan-Mugen Honda 199 154.965kph, 96.291mph

POLE POSITION Barrichello, Stewart-Ford, 1m 38.441s (0.440), 155.423kph, 96.575mph
LAPS 72 x 4.250 km, 2.641 miles
DISTANCE 305.814 km, 190.024 miles
STARTERS/FINISHERS 22/11
WEATHER Overcast, warm, dry then heavy rain
LAP LEADERS Barrichello 1-5, 10-43, 55-59 (44); Coulthard 6-9 (4); M Schumacher 44-54 (11); Häkkinen 60-65 (6); Frentzen 66-72 (7); SC 26-36 (11)
WINNER'S LAPS 1-9 P4, 10-13 P3, 14-24 P4, 25-37 P3, 38 P2, 39-54 P3, 55-56 P2, 57-64 P3, 65 P2, 66-72 P1
FASTEST LAP D Coulthard, McLaren-Mercedes, 1m 19.227s (lap 8), 193.115kph, 119.997mph
CHAMPIONSHIP Häkkinen 40, M Schumacher 32, Irvine 25, Frentzen 23, R Schumacher 15

BRITISH GP Silverstone

11 July 1999   **Race 638**

David Coulthard

McLaren-Mercedes MP4/14 199.970kph, 124.256mph

Lap 1 transformed the championship. Passing Irvine for P3 on the Hangar Straight, rear brake failure caused M. Schumacher to spear into the Stowe tyre barrier head-on, breaking his right leg. It was a needless accident, neither Ferrari driver informed that the race had already been red-flagged. At the restart Häkkinen led comfortably until, following a wheel problem at his first stop, his left rear parted company on lap 26. That same lap a pit-stop blunder cost new leader Irvine the lead to the already reshod Coulthard, and once ahead, despite the ever-present Ferrari threat, David grasped the opportunity to win his home GP. Behind Irvine, a strong drive by R. Schumacher gave Williams another podium, H-HF and Hill next up for Jordan.

Pos	Driver	Car	Time/gap	Grid	Stops	Tyres
1	D Coulthard	McLaren-Mercedes	1h 32m 30.144s	3	2	B
2	E Irvine	Ferrari	−1.829s	4	2	B
3	R Schumacher	Williams-Supertec	−27.411s	8	2	B
4	H-H Frentzen	Jordan-Mugen Honda	−27.789s	5	2	B
5	D Hill	Jordan-Mugen Honda	38.606s	6	2	B
6	P Diniz	Sauber-Petronas	−53.643s	12	2	B

POLE POSITION M Häkkinen, McLaren-Mercedes, 1m 24.804s (0.419s), 218.197kph, 135.581mph
LAPS 60 x 5.140 km, 3.194 miles (Race restarted for scheduled 60 laps following accident)
DISTANCE 308.296 km, 191.566 miles
STARTERS/FINISHERS 22/16
WEATHER Sunny, warm, dry
LAP LEADERS Häkkinen 1-24 (24); Irvine 25-26 (2); Coulthard 27-42, 46-60 (31); Frentzen 43-44 (2); Hill 45 (1); SC 1-2, 32 (3)
WINNER'S LAPS 1-25 P3, 26 P2, 27-42 P1, 43-45 P3, 46-60 P1
FASTEST LAP M Häkkinen, McLaren-Mercedes, 1m 28.309s (lap 28), 209.536kph, 130.200mph
CHAMPIONSHIP Häkkinen 40, M Schumacher 32, Irvine 32, Frentzen 26, Coulthard 22

AUSTRIAN GP A1-Ring

25 July 1999   **Race 639**

Eddie Irvine

Ferrari F399 208.587kph, 129.610mph

Dominant in qualifying, McLaren threw it away when Coulthard sent Häkkinen spinning with a misjudged pass at the second corner of the opening lap. Coulthard still led from Barrichello and Irvine, the first two making their single stop on laps 38 and 39. Now Irvine, long-fuelled under Ross Brawn's direction, took the lead and pumped out five storming laps such that he resumed still leading from his lap 44 stop. But to win he had to absorb enormous pressure from Coulthard's faster car over the remaining 26 laps, the pair finishing three-tenths apart. Häkkinen performed a glorious recovery, scything back through the field to P3, but on the podium McLaren faces were stony either side of the jubilant Eddie, now a mere two points shy of Mika.

Pos	Driver	Car	Time/gap	Grid	Stops	Tyres
1	E Irvine	Ferrari	1h 28m 12.438s	3	1	B
2	D Coulthard	McLaren-Mercedes	−0.313s	2	1	B
3	M Häkkinen	McLaren-Mercedes	−22.282s	1	1	B
4	H-H Frentzen	Jordan-Mugen Honda	−52.803s	4	1	B
5	A Wurz	Benetton-Playlife	−1m 6.358s	10	1	B
6	P Diniz	Sauber-Petronas	−1m 10.933s	16	2	B

POLE POSITION Häkkinen, McLaren-Mercedes, 1m 10.954s (0.199s), 219.113kph, 136.163mph
LAPS 71 x 4.319 km, 2.684 miles
DISTANCE 306.649 km, 190.543 miles
STARTERS/FINISHERS 22/15
WEATHER Overcast, warm, dry
LAP LEADERS Coulthard 1-39 (39); Irvine 40-71 (32)
WINNER'S LAPS 1-38 P3, 39 P2, 40-71 P1
FASTEST LAP Häkkinen, McLaren-Mercedes, 1m 12.107s (lap 39), 215.629kph, 133.986mph
CHAMPIONSHIP Häkkinen 44, Irvine 42, M Schumacher 32, Frentzen 29, Coulthard 28

GERMAN GP Hockenheim

1 August 1999   **Race 640**

Eddie Irvine

Ferrari F399 224.723kph, 139.637mph

For the third successive race Häkkinen was denied probable victory. Leading comfortably from pole, his routine lap 24 stop was a disaster due to a fuel-rig problem, dropping him to P4. Little more than a lap later he was out permanently when a high-speed rear-tyre burst pitched him heavily into the barriers. This left the Ferraris in control, Coulthard out of the running due to a stop-go for a missed chicane and an earlier stop to replace a damaged nosecone. The damage resulted from contact with Mika Salo's Ferrari, Schumacher's stand-in having a great race, assuming the lead after Häkkinen's departure then appositely waving Irvine by. This second consecutive victory, leading in a Ferrari 1-2, gave Irvine the championship lead from Häkkinen.

Pos	Driver	Car	Time/gap	Grid	Stops	Tyres
1	E Irvine	Ferrari	1h 21m 58.594s	5	1	B
2	M Salo	Ferrari	−1.007s	4	1	B
3	H-H Frentzen	Jordan-Mugen Honda	−5.195s	2	1	B
4	R Schumacher	Williams-Supertec	−12.809s	11	1	B
5	D Coulthard	McLaren-Mercedes	−16.823s	3	3	B
6	O Panis	Prost-Peugeot	−29.879s	7	2	B

POLE POSITION M Häkkinen, McLaren-Mercedes, 1m 42.950s (0.050s), 148.253mph
LAPS 45 x 6.823 km, 4.240 miles
DISTANCE 307.035 km, 190.783 miles
STARTERS/FINISHERS 22/11
WEATHER Cloudy with sunny intervals, very hot, dry
LAP LEADERS Häkkinen 1-24 (24); Salo 25 (1); Irvine 26-45 (20)
WINNER'S LAPS 1-5 P6, 6-10 P5, 11-20 P4, 21-22 P3, 23-24 P4, 25 P2, 26-45 P1
FASTEST LAP Coulthard, McLaren-Mercedes, 1m 45.270s (lap 43), 233.331kph, 144.985mph
CHAMPIONSHIP Irvine 52, Häkkinen 44, Frentzen 33, M Schumacher 32, Coulthard 30

HUNGARIAN GP Hungaroring

15 August 1999   Race 641

Mika Häkkinen

McLaren-Mercedes MP4/14 172.524kph, 107.202mph

Häkkinen didn't much care that his textbook win from pole made for a dull event. After three fruitless races he badly needed victory. And this time – his Ferrari's handling never fully to his liking – it was Irvine who dropped the ball, running wide 14 laps from the flag under pressure from Coulthard, enabling the Scot to deliver a welcome McLaren 1-2. After a poor start Coulthard had done well to bring himself into a position to attack Irvine, who still retained his championship lead, albeit narrowly. Hill's penultimate point came at the place of his first GP victory a mere six years and 98 races earlier, while teammate Frentzen delivered yet more valuable points for Jordan with P4, team and driver a solid third in their respective championships.

POLE POSITION Häkkinen, McLaren-Mercedes, 1m 18.156s (0.107s), 183.003kph, 113.713mph
LAPS 77 x 3.973 km, 2.469 miles
DISTANCE 305.921 km, 190.090 miles
STARTERS/FINISHERS 22/17
WEATHER Cloudy with sunny intervals, hot, dry
LAP LEADERS Häkkinen 1-77 (77)
WINNER'S LAPS 1-77 P1
FASTEST LAP Coulthard, McLaren-Mercedes, 1m 20.699s (lap 69), 177.236kph, 110.130mph
CHAMPIONSHIP Irvine 56, Häkkinen 54, Coulthard 36, Frentzen 36, M Schumacher 32

Pos	Driver	Car	Time/gap	Grid	Stops	Tyres
1	M Häkkinen	McLaren-Mercedes	1h 46m 23.536s	1	2	B
2	D Coulthard	McLaren-Mercedes	–9.706s	3	2	B
3	E Irvine	Ferrari	–27.228s	2	2	B
4	H-H Frentzen	Jordan-Mugen Honda	–31.815s	5	2	B
5	R Barrichello	Stewart-Ford	–43.808s	8	1	B
6	D Hill	Jordan-Mugen Honda	–55.726s	6	2	B

BELGIAN GP Spa Francorchamps

29 August 1999   Race 642

David Coulthard

McLaren-Mercedes MP4/14 214.595kph, 133.343mph

In qualifying, BAR drivers Villeneuve and Zonta crashed mightily at Eau Rouge. Another McLaren 1-2, but this one left the reigning champion and points leader less than thrilled about the absence of either team orders or teammate subservience. Despite Häkkinen's pole, Coulthard made the better start to claim a tyre-smoking La Source, the Finn culpable for some light contact between the two. Coulthard then ran a fast, clean race trailed by the disgruntled Häkkinen, perhaps waiting for his teammate to receive the call that never came. Off-the-pace Irvine qualified P6 and finished P4 behind prolific points scorer Frentzen. Also proving his points-scoring worth to Williams was Ralf Schumacher, while Damon delivered his final point, seventh of the season.

POLE POSITION Häkkinen, McLaren-Mercedes, 1m 50.329s (0.155s), 227.364kph, 141.277mph
LAPS 44 x 6.968 km, 4.330 miles
DISTANCE 306.577 km, 190.498 miles
STARTERS/FINISHERS 22/16
WEATHER Cloudy with sunny intervals, hot, dry
LAP LEADERS Coulthard 1-44 (44)
WINNER'S LAPS 1-44 P1
FASTEST LAP Häkkinen, McLaren-Mercedes, 1m 53.955s (lap 23), 220.129kph, 136.782mph
CHAMPIONSHIP Häkkinen 60, Irvine 59, Coulthard 46, Frentzen 40, M Schumacher 32

Pos	Driver	Car	Time/gap	Grid	Stops	Tyres
1	D Coulthard	McLaren-Mercedes	1h 25m 43.057s	2	2	B
2	M Häkkinen	McLaren-Mercedes	–10.469s	1	2	B
3	H-H Frentzen	Jordan-Mugen Honda	–33.433s	3	2	B
4	E Irvine	Ferrari	–44.848s	6	2	B
5	R Schumacher	Williams-Supertec	–48.067s	5	1	B
6	D Hill	Jordan-Mugen Honda	–54.916s	4	2	B

ITALIAN GP Monza

12 September 1999   Race 643

Heinz-Harald Frentzen

Jordan-Mugen Honda 199 237.938kph, 147.848mph

The image captured by an intrusive TV helicopter was painful: Mika Häkkinen, crouched in the trackside undergrowth, weeping with disappointment and frustration after an unforced error threw away yet another victory. With the race more then half-done and totally in his pocket he had spun-out at the first chicane. And Coulthard, never recovering from a poor first lap, wasn't there to pick up the pieces. McLaren's only saving grace was that Irvine's tribulations persisted, qualifying P8 and finishing P6, although the single point gave him a share of Mika's championship lead. So, from his front row slot alongside Häkkinen, Frentzen took his second victory of the season, and with four podiums and four points finishes moved into title contention.

POLE POSITION M Häkkinen, McLaren-Mercedes, 1m 22.432s (0.494s), 251.989kph, 156.579mph
LAPS 53 x 5.770 km, 3.585 miles
DISTANCE 305.548 km, 189.859 miles
STARTERS/FINISHERS 22/11
WEATHER Cloudy with sunny intervals, hot, dry
LAP LEADERS Häkkinen 1-29 (29); Frentzen 30-35, 37-53 (23); Salo 36 (1)
WINNER'S LAPS 1-29 P2, 30-35 P1, 36 P3, 37-53 P1
FASTEST LAP R Schumacher, Williams-Supertec, 1m 25.579 (lap 48), 242.723kph, 150.821mph
CHAMPIONSHIP Häkkinen 60, Irvine 60, Frentzen 50, Coulthard 48, M Schumacher 32

Pos	Driver	Car	Time/gap	Grid	Stops	Tyres
1	H-H Frentzen	Jordan-Mugen Honda	1h 17m 2.923s	2	1	B
2	R Schumacher	Williams-Supertec	–3.272s	5	1	B
3	M Salo	Ferrari	–11.932s	6	1	B
4	R Barrichello	Stewart-Ford	–17.630s	7	1	B
5	D Coulthard	McLaren-Mercedes	–18.142s	3	1	B
6	E Irvine	Ferrari	–27.402s	8	1	B

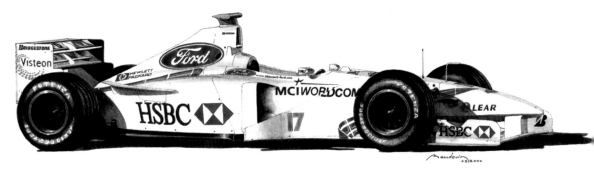

Stewart-Ford SF-3

Round 14/16	**EUROPEAN GP** Nürburgring		
	26 September 1999		**Race 644**

Johnny Herbert

Stewart-Ford SF-3 177.034kph, 110.004mph

Dinez's horrifying, somersaulting first lap crash released the SC for six laps. Then, H-HF's title bid for Jordan, which had begun with pole, continued for 32 leading laps. But having successfully beaten the chasing Coulthard away from their concurrent pit stop, electrical failure ended it. Changeable weather and resultant team blunders eliminated Häkkinen and Irvine from serious contention, while Coulthard and Fisichella spun out, and Ralf Schumacher punctured, all when leading. This, plus a timely call for wet tyres, set up victory for Herbert from P13 on the grid, the first for Stewart-Ford. Trulli brought Prost-Peugeot P2, but the lasting image was a champagne-soaked podium, Jackie Stewart flanked by drivers Herbert and Barrichello.

POLE POSITION H-H Frentzen, Jordan-Mugen Honda, 1m 19.910s (0.266s), 205.250kph, 127.537mph
LAPS 66 x 4.556 km, 2.831 miles (67 lap race interrupted due to accident. Restarted over 66 laps)
DISTANCE 300.679 km, 186.833 miles
STARTERS/FINISHERS 22/10
WEATHER Overcast, cold, dry then showers
LAP LEADERS Frentzen 1-32 (32); D Coulthard, McLaren-Mercedes 33-37 (5); R Schumacher 38-44, 49 (8); G Fisichella, Benetton-Playlife 45-48 (4); Herbert 50-66 (17); SC 2-7 (6)
WINNER'S LAPS 1-10 P13, 11-19 P12, 20 P9, 21 P8, 22-24 P7, 25-27 P8, 28 P7, 29-32 P6, 33-37 P5, 38-44 P3, 45-46 P2, 47 P3, 48 P4, 49 P2, 50-66 P1
FASTEST LAP Häkkinen, McLaren-Mercedes, 1m 21.282s (lap 64), 201.786kph, 125.384mph
CHAMPIONSHIP Häkkinen 62, Irvine 60, Frentzen 50, Coulthard 48, R Schumacher 33

Pos	Driver	Car	Time/gap	Grid	Stops	Tyres
1	J Herbert	Stewart-Ford	1h 41m 54.314s	14	2	B
2	J Trulli	Prost-Peugeot	-22.619s	10	3	B
3	R Barrichello	Stewart-Ford	-22.866s	15	1	B
4	R Schumacher	Williams-Supertec	-39.508s	4	3	B
5	M Häkkinen	McLaren-Mercedes	-1m 2.950s	3	2	B
6	M Gené	Minardi-Ford	-1m 5.154s	20	1	B

Round 15/16	**MALASIAN GP** Sepang		
	17 October 1999		**Race 645**

Eddie Irvine

Ferrari F399 192.682kph, 119.727mph

Making a mysteriously belated return, Michael Schumacher orchestrated a Ferrari 1-2 which left Häkkinen utterly bamboozled. The German's incredible speed superiority in qualifying and the race enabled him to dictate events on track, twice ceding the lead to Irvine as well as holding Häkkinen behind it. It wasn't pretty, but it was awesome. Unreliability curtailed Coulthard's short-lived effort to spoil the Maranello mayhem, which turned to Maranello misery a few hours after the race. Both Ferraris were disqualified for infringing precise barge-board dimensions, a shell-shocked Ross Brawn trying to explain the mistake under the harsh glare of the TV lights at the now dark circuit. Ferrari would appeal disqualification, but if it stood Häkkinen was champion.

POLE POSITION M Schumacher, Ferrari, 1m 39.688s (0.947s), 200.136kph, 124.359mph
LAPS 56 x 5.542 km, 3.444 miles
DISTANCE 310.352 km, 192.844 miles
STARTERS/FINISHERS 21/11
WEATHER Cloudy with sunny intervals, hot, humid, dry
LAP LEADERS M Schumacher 1-3, 26-28, 42-52 (17); Irvine 4-25, 29-41, 53-56 (39)
WINNER'S LAPS 1-3 P2, 4-25 P1, 26-27 P4, 28 P3, 29-41 P1, 42-47 P3, 48-52 P2, 53-56 P1
FASTEST LAP M Schumacher, Ferrari, 1m 40.267s (lap 25), 198.980kph, 123.641mph
CHAMPIONSHIP Irvine 70, Häkkinen 66, Frentzen 51, Coulthard 48, M Schumacher 38

Pos	Driver	Car	Time/gap	Grid	Stops	Tyres
1	E Irvine	Ferrari	1h 36m 38.494s	2	2	B
2	M Schumacher	Ferrari	-1.040s	1	1	B
3	M Häkkinen	McLaren-Mercedes	-9.743s	4	2	B
4	J Herbert	Stewart-Ford	-17.538s	5	1	B
5	R Barrichello	Stewart-Ford	-32.296s	6	2	B
6	H-H Frentzen	Jordan-Mugen Honda	-34.884s	14	2	B

JAPANESE GP Suzuka

31 October 1999   **Race 646**

Mika Häkkinen

McLaren-Mercedes MP4/14 204.086kph, 126.813mph

A week after their Sepang disqualification, an FIA Court of Appeal reinstated Ferrari, restoring Irvine's four-point advantage. So the championship would be decided at the final round, although it turned out to be a somewhat anti-climatic affair. Following a heavy qualifying accident, Irvine started from P5 to finish P3, while Häkkinen, needing victory, seized the lead from pole-sitter Schumacher at the start and won in style. The Ferrari was never far behind, but, whether by accident or design, didn't look like getting on terms, so race tension surrounded an unforced driver error, a pit-stop stumble, or McLaren reliability. But neither driver, car, team nor engine missed a beat, Ferrari disappointment tempered by their first constructors' title in 16 years.

POLE POSITION M Schumacher, Ferrari, 1m 37.470s (0.350s), 216.583kph, 134.579mph
LAPS 53 x 5.864 km, 3.644 miles
DISTANCE 310.596 km, 192.995 miles
STARTERS/FINISHERS 22/14
WEATHER Cloudy with sunny intervals, warm, dry
LAP LEADERS Häkkinen 1-19, 23-53 (50); M Schumacher 20-22 (3)
WINNER'S LAPS 1-19 P1, 20-22 P2, 23-53 P1
FASTEST LAP M Schumacher, Ferrari, 1m 41.319s (lap 31), 208.355kph, 129.466mph
CHAMPIONSHIP Häkkinen 70, Irvine 74, Frentzen 54, Coulthard 48, M Schumacher 44

Pos	Driver	Car	Time/gap	Grid	Stops	Tyres
1	M Häkkinen	McLaren-Mercedes	1h 31m 18.785s	2	2	B
2	M Schumacher	Ferrari	−5.015s	1	2	B
3	E Irvine	Ferrari	−1m 35.688s	5	2	B
4	H-H Frentzen	Jordan-Mugen Honda	−1m 38.635s	4	2	B
5	R Schumacher	Williams-Supertec	−1m 39.494s	9	2	B
6	J Alesi	Sauber-Petronas	−1 lap	10	2	B

1999 CHAMPIONSHIP FACTS AND FOLKLORE

- There was no new-found popularity for narrow-track cars and grooved tyres in their second season, indeed with a fourth groove added to the fronts and Bridgestone as sole supplier, tyres were harder and cars even less forgiving.
- New on the safety front were seats which could be removed with the driver in situ, and wheel tethers to reduce the danger from flying wheels, a legacy of the notorious 1998 Spa start-line pile-up.
- A number of heavy accidents in pre-season testing caused by rear wing failure appeared related to a cunning new development to reduce drag. By building in enough flexibility to the mountings, the rear wing would 'lean' backwards on the straights. This questionable innovation was controlled by a rear wing deflection test introduced from round two in Brazil.
- 1999 was another 16-round championship, Argentina departing while Malaysia joined the F1 circus with their first GP at Sepang, the first step in a massive push by Bernie Ecclestone towards a truly global F1 series through expansion especially in Asia and the Middle East.
- For a third consecutive year, Ferrari entered the final race with a strong chance of the drivers' title. Extraordinarily, circumstances had conspired whereby Eddie Irvine, their second driver, led the points race into the Suzuka finale. Maybe events had chosen him to lift the coveted championship for Ferrari for the first time in 20 years?
- But again they were thwarted, Mika Häkkinen taking the race to also become the seventh back-to-back champion in F1 history.
- Schumacher's aspirations had been fully on course at the British GP, the mid-point of the season, but a bizarre accident, possibly driver impetuosity, more probably car failure, put paid to his championship chances.
- His injury, a broken leg, sidelined Schumacher for seven races and should have made it an easy job for Häkkinen, but both team and driver made heavy weather of it and Irvine, with four race wins, remained a title challenger throughout the season.
- Another driver in contention until the latter stages of the championship battle was Heinz-Harald Frentzen, who secured two victories for Jordan-Mugen Honda, both

- driver and team having their most competitive season to date. Jordan easily beat constructors such as Williams and Benetton, while H-HF finished third in his championship ahead of Coulthard.
- Also driving for Jordan, Damon Hill retired at the end of a lacklustre final season. It is easy to underestimate his considerable achievements. In a comparatively short F1 career of just seven full seasons (115 starts) he won 22 race victories and a drivers' world championship.
- In a much-improved performance, Stewart-Ford in their third season also picked up a win at the Nürburgring. Now fully owned by the Blue Oval, next season the team would become Ford's instrument to bring the Jaguar name to GP racing for the first time.
- Jaguar Racing would be led my none other than Eddie Irvine, Rubens Barrichello taking his unenviable number two seat at Ferrari as Schumacher's highly paid slave.
- Schumacher's second of only two 1999 race wins, his Monaco victory, was still enough to make him the most prolific Ferrari race-winner, the pecking order: 16 Schumacher; 15 Lauda; 13 Ascari; 6 Gilles Villeneuve. Little did we then know that there were a further 56 Schumacher/Ferrari race victories still to come.
- This was a year when McLaren with 123 race wins at the outset should have repassed Ferrari's 125 all-time record tally, but at least Häkkinen's 11 pole positions took McLaren past the 100 mark in that respect.
- Mercedes took a 40% stake in McLaren, but other manufacturer involvement in F1 took a backward step when the Honda F1 car project was disbanded due to the death of designer Harvey Postlethwaite at the early age of 55.
- However, the engine project would proceed and 1999 newcomers BAR were linked to Honda horses for next season.
- BAR had a tumultuous first season on and off track. They went head-to-head with the FIA over duel branding rights, improperly wanting one car with Lucky Strike livery, the other in 555 colours. The FIA got their way and, further, called BAR to appear before the WMSC for referring the matter to the EU.
- BAR further fuelled their reputation for arrogance by then

fielding a pair of dual-liveried cars, Luckies one side, 555 the other, effectively cocking a snook at the F1 establishment.

■ There was recurrent rumour of intra-team management enmity at BAR, some massive car smashes in the early races, and the team that had pledged to win first time out failed to score even one championship point. Indeed, Villeneuve didn't finish a race until round 12. Arrogance or over-funded folly?

■ In January he became Sir Frank, but for a second year the most successful team of the decade, Williams, had a second winless season. But there were green shoots. A BMW-engined Williams hack was pounding around the test tracks of Europe, and 11 points finishes including three good podiums were delivered by their latest driver signing, Ralf Schumacher.

RACE 636, Canadian GP: Häkkinen became the seventh back-to-back champion, retaining his crown with five race wins, here on his way to number three in Montréal.

Championship ranking	Championship points	Driver nationality	1999 Drivers Championship		Races contested	Race victories	Podiumse excl. victories	Races led	Lights to flag victories	Laps led	Poles	Fastest laps	Triple Crowns
			Driver	Car									
1	76	FIN	Mika Häkkinen	McLaren-Mercedes	16	5	5	11	1	383	11	6	1
2	74	GBR	Eddie Irvine	Ferrari	16	4	5	5		133		1	
3	54	GER	Heinz-Harald Frentzen	Jordan-Mugen Honda	16	2	4	4		64	1		
4	48	GBR	David Coulthard	McLaren-Mercedes	16	2	4	7	1	145		3	
5	44	GER	Michael Schumacher	Ferrari	10	2	4	7	1	176	3	5	
6	35	GER	Ralf Schumacher	Williams-Supertec	16		3	1		8		1	
7	21	BRA	Rubens Barrichello	Stewart-Ford	16		3	2		67	1		
8	15	GBR	Johnny Herbert	Stewart-Ford	16	1		1		17			
9	13	ITA	Giancarlo Fisichella	Benetton-Playlife	16		1	1		4			
10	10	FIN	Mika Salo	BAR-Supertec (3) Ferrari (6)	9		2	2		2			
11	7	ITA	Jarno Trulli	Prost-Peugeot	15		1						
12	7	GBR	Damon Hill	Jordan-Mugen Honda	16		1			1			
13	3	AUT	Alexander Wurz	Benetton-Playlife	16								
14	3	BRA	Pedro Diniz	Sauber-Petronas	16								
15	2	FRA	Olivier Panis	Prost-Peugeot	16								
16	2	FRA	Jean Alesi	Sauber-Petronas	16								
17	1	ESP	Pedro de la Rosa	Arrows	16								
18	1	ESP	Marc Gené	Minardi-Ford	16								

Championship ranking	Championship points	Team/Marque nationality	1999 Constructors Championship		Engine maker nationality	Races contested	Race victories	1-2 finishes	Podiums excl. victories	Races led	Laps led	Poles	Fastest laps
			Chassis	Engine									
1	128	ITA	Ferrari F399	Ferrari 3.0 V10	ITA	16	6	3	11	12	311	3	6
2	124	GBR	McLaren MP4-14	Mercedes-Benz 3.0 V10	GER	16	7	3	9	14	528	11	9
3	61	IRL	Jordan 199	Mugen Honda 3.0 V10	JPN	16	2		4	4	65	1	
4	36	GBR	Stewart SF3	Ford Cosworth 3.0 V10	GBR	16	1		3	3	84	1	
5	35	GBR	Williams FW21	Supertec 3.0 V10	FRA	16			3	1	8		1
6	16	ITA	Benetton B199	Playlife 3.0 V10	FRA	16			1	1	4		
7	9	FRA	Prost AP02	Peugeot 3.0 V10	FRA	16			1				
8	5	SUI	Sauber C18	Petronas 3.0 V10	ITA	16							
9	1	GBR	Arrows A20	Arrows 3.0 V10	GBR	16							
9	1	ITA	Minardi M01	Ford Cosworth 3.0 V10	GBR	16							

RACE 804, Australian GP: Schumacher dominated the 'noughties' and compatriot Vettel the 'teenies', but the greatest F1 fairy-tale of all time was played out in 2009. Button's Brawn bonanza was straight out of Boy's Own, Jenson's first race with Brawn also producing their first win – the start of an incredible journey.

THE NOUGHTIES

Front-page news

A RED REVOLUTION, MOSLEY, MONEY AND MANUFACTURERS, EVEN SPYING AND SEX SCANDALS, THE F1 SOAP OPERA HAD THE LOT

2000

Ferrari and Schumacher, finally

THE TALE OF THE TITLE

- At last! For the first time since Jody Scheckter 21 years before, a Ferrari driver was crowned champion.
- At the penultimate round Schumacher finally deposed Häkkinen to clinch his third drivers' title.
- His tranche of nine race victories included the first three and the final four of the season.
- But in a barren mid-season spell, a 24-point advantage over Häkkinen slipped to a six-point deficit.
- A jaded early season behind him, a re-energised Häkkinen was on the cusp of a rare championship hat-trick.
- But Schumacher and the Ferrari 'family' – Brawn, Byrne, Todt, Montezemolo – fought back decisively.
- With Irvine gone to Jaguar, Barrichello joined the 'family' too, his reward an emotional maiden victory.
- With three wins, just one short of teammate Häkkinen, Coulthard enjoyed his most successful season to date.
- But Häkkinen defined the year with his winning pass of Schumacher at Spa, pure skill, courage, opportunism.
- By contrast, Schumacher marred his achievements, slated by fellow drivers for intimidatory driving tactics.
- Ferrari and McLaren dominated the season, winning all 17 races, Maranello retaining their constructors' title.
- Williams-BMW were best of the rest, but between the lot the also-rans led nine laps and won eight podiums.
- And not forgetting: marshal killed at Monza; red-wigged winners.

THE CHASE FOR THE CHAMPIONSHIP

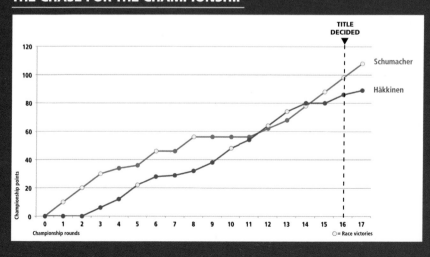

Ferrari F1 2000

Round 1/17	AUSTRALIAN GP Melbourne					
	12 March 2000				Race 647	

The first grid of the new Millennium suggested status quo for the top three teams: McLaren, Ferrari, Jordan pairing off like Noah's Ark. Come the finish only two of the six survived, both red, a Ferrari 1-2 reaffirming that success depends on speed with reliability. After both McLarens exited with Mercedes pneumatic valve trouble on laps 12 and 19, Schumacher won as he pleased. Afterwards he needled Ron Dennis by claiming he had been on course to win anyway, the gap a mere 2.7s when Mika retired. Barrichello's Ferrari debut was more fraught, trapped behind Frentzen until the Jordan also succumbed 20 laps further on. New engines from BMW and Honda made the finish, bringing a podium for Williams and for BAR their first-ever points.

Pos	Driver	Car	Time/gap	Grid	Stops	Tyres
1	M Schumacher	Ferrari	1h 34m 1.987s	3	1	B
2	R Barrichello	Ferrari	−11.415s	4	2	B
3	R Schumacher	Williams-BMW	−20.009s	11	1	B
4	J Villeneuve	BAR-Honda	−44.447s	8	1	B
5	G Fisichella	Benetton-Playlife	−45.165s	10	1	B
6	R Zonta	BAR-Honda	−46.468s	9	1	B

Michael Schumacher
Ferrari F1 2000 196.254kph, 121.947mph

POLE POSITION M Häkkinen, McLaren-Mercedes, 1m 30.556s (0.354s), 210.817kph, 130.996mph
LAPS 58 x 5.303 km, 3.295 miles
DISTANCE 307.574 km, 191.117 miles
STARTERS/FINISHERS 22/9
WEATHER Sunny, hot, dry
LAP LEADERS Häkkinen 1-18 (18); M Schumacher 19-29, 36-44, 46-58 (33); H-H Frentzen, Jordan-Mugen Honda 30-35 (6); Barrichello 45 (1); SC 8-10 (3)
WINNER'S LAPS 1-10 P3, 11-18 P2, 19-29 P1, 30-32 P3, 33-35 P2, 36-44 P1, 45 P2, 46-58 P1
FASTEST LAP Barrichello, Ferrari, 1m 31.481s (lap 41), 208.685kph, 129.671mph
CHAMPIONSHIP M Schumacher 10, Barrichello 6, R Schumacher 4, Villeneuve 3, Fisichella 2

Round 2/17	BRAZILIAN GP Interlagos					
	26 March 2000				Race 648	

Qualifying was a fiasco, red-flagged three times for collapsing advertising hoardings, Alesi's Prost struck at 170mph. Qualifying behind the McLarens once again, the two-stopping Ferraris soon got the better of their heavier one-stop opponents. Which strategy was superior looked too close to call, but was ultimately never tested, Häkkinen's engine on lap 30 and Coulthard's gearbox seeing to that. Unable to select any gear below fourth, Coulthard raced brilliantly to P2 only to be disqualified for a front wing infringement, McLaren yet to score a point this season. Coulthard's dsq and Barrichello's dnf promoted Fisichella's Benetton to P2, heading in the Jordan and Williams pairs. Jenson Button in his second race became the youngest-ever points-scorer.

Pos	Driver	Car	Time/gap	Grid	Stops	Tyres
1	M Schumacher	Ferrari	1h 31m 35.271s	3	2	B
2	G Fisichella	Benetton-Playlife	−39.898s	2	1	B
3	H-H Frentzen	Jordan-Mugen Honda	−42.268s	5	1	B
4	J Trulli	Jordan-Mugen Honda	−1m 12.780s	7	2	B
5	R Schumacher	Williams-BMW	−1 lap	12	1	B
6	J Button	Williams-BMW	−1 lap	11	1	B

Michael Schumacher
Ferrari F1 2000 200.403kph, 124.525mph

POLE POSITION M Häkkinen, McLaren-Mercedes, 1m 14.111s (0.174s), 209.313kph, 130.061mph
LAPS 71 x 4.309 km, 2.677 miles
DISTANCE 305.909 km, 190.083 miles
STARTERS/FINISHERS 20/10
WEATHER Cloudy with sunny intervals, hot, dry
LAP LEADERS Häkkinen 1, 23-29 (8); M Schumacher 2-20, 30-71 (61); R Barrichello, Ferrari 21-22 (2)
WINNER'S LAPS 1 P2, 2-20 P1, 21-22 P3, 23-29 P2, 30-71 P1
FASTEST LAP M Schumacher, Ferrari, 1m 14.755s (lap 48), 207.509kph, 128.941mph
CHAMPIONSHIP M Schumacher 20, Fisichella 8, Barrichello 6, R Schumacher 6, Frentzen 4

SAN MARINO GP Imola

9 April 2000   Race 649

Michael Schumacher
Ferrari F1 2000 200.043kph, 124.301mph

For a third time it was Häkkinen's pole, Schumacher's victory, and with a 24-point cushion over the Finn many considered the championship all but over. At least Mika made the finish, leading until his second stop on lap 44. By going four longer Schumacher used the pit stop to leapfrog ahead and reel off the final 18 laps. McLaren insisted they were not outsmarted tactically, losing due to Mika's car niggles, an engine electronics glitch and a debris-damaged floor. A savage chop by Schumacher at the start condemned Coulthard to 46 laps trailing Barrichello, the Brazilian slowed by a broken crotch-strap. DC eventually got by at the second stop to finish P3. The rest of the field was lapped, although Villeneuve drove the wheels off the BAR-Honda for P5.

POLE POSITION Häkkinen, McLaren-Mercedes, 1m 24.714s (0.091s), 209.632kph, 130.260mph
LAPS 62 x 4.933 km, 3.065 miles
DISTANCE 305.609 km, 189.897 miles
STARTERS/FINISHERS 22/15
WEATHER Overcast, warm, dry
LAP LEADERS Häkkinen 1-44 (44); M Schumacher 45-62 (18)
WINNER'S LAPS 1-44 P2, 45-62 P1
FASTEST LAP Häkkinen, McLaren-Mercedes, 1m 26.523s (lap 60), 205.249kph, 127.536mph
CHAMPIONSHIP M Schumacher 30, Barrichello 9, Fisichella 8, Häkkinen 6, R Schumacher 6

Pos	Driver	Car	Time/gap	Grid	Stops	Tyres
1	M Schumacher	Ferrari	1h 31m 39.776s	2	2	B
2	M Häkkinen	McLaren-Mercedes	−1.168s	1	2	B
3	D Coulthard	McLaren-Mercedes	−51.008s	3	2	B
4	R Barrichello	Ferrari	−1m 29.276s	4	2	B
5	J Villeneuve	BAR-Honda	−1 lap	9	2	B
6	M Salo	Sauber-Petronas	−1 lap	12	2	B

BRITISH GP Silverstone

23 April 2000   Race 650

David Coulthard
McLaren-Mercedes MP4/15 208.266kph, 129.410mph

Deep disquiet was caused in pre-race testing when Zonta's BAR hurdled the tyre barriers at Stowe. An Easter fixture in Britain produced a shameful quagmire for fans, rain-squalls for qualifying, but miraculously a dry race. From pole, heavily fuelled Barrichello led a six-car train – H-HF, DC, Mika, Jenson, Ralf – until only the one-stop McLarens remained. On lap 31 a tiny mistake at Becketts by the leader enabled Coulthard to make a bold outside pass at Stowe, Barrichello's race ending soon afterwards with duff hydraulics. In the closing laps Häkkinen chased down his gear-selection-troubled teammate, but fell 1.5s short. So McLaren 1-2 but damage limitation for Schumacher with P3. Elbowed to P8 at the start, he spent 31 laps behind the feisty Villeneuve.

POLE POSITION R Barrichello, Ferrari, 1m 25.703s (0.003s), 215.950kph, 134.185mph
LAPS 60 x 5.141 km, 3.195 miles
DISTANCE 308.356 km, 191.604 miles
STARTERS/FINISHERS 22/17
WEATHER Cloudy with sunny intervals, warm, dry
LAP LEADERS Barrichello 1-30, 33-35 (33); Coulthard 31-32, 42-60 (21); M Schumacher 36-38 (3); H-H Frentzen, Jordan-Mugen Honda 39-41 (3)
WINNER'S LAPS 1-23 P3, 24-30 P2, 31-32 P1, 33 P2, 34-35 P4, 36-38 P3, 39-41 P2, 42-60 P1
FASTEST LAP M Häkkinen, McLaren-Mercedes, 1m 26.217s (lap 56), 214.663kph, 133.385mph
CHAMPIONSHIP M Schumacher 34, Coulthard 14, Häkkinen 12, Barrichello 9, R Schumacher 9

Pos	Driver	Car	Time/gap	Grid	Stops	Tyres
1	D Coulthard	McLaren-Mercedes	1h 28m 50.108s	4	1	B
2	M Häkkinen	McLaren-Mercedes	−1.477s	3	1	B
3	M Schumacher	Ferrari	−19.917s	5	1	B
4	R Schumacher	Williams-BMW	−41.312s	7	2	B
5	J Button	Williams-BMW	−57.759s	6	2	B
6	J Trulli	Jordan-Mugen Honda	−1m 19.273s	11	1	B

SPANISH GP Cataluña

7 May 2000   Race 651

Mika Häkkinen
McLaren-Mercedes MP4/15 196.324kph, 121.990mph

A repeat 1-2 gave the world champion his first victory and McLaren hope in the championship, Schumacher dropping to P5 with a late puncture. However, Schumacher had pole-winning speed and race-leading pace up until a slow second stop. This resulted directly from injury to the official team refueller, Nigel Stepney, during a muffed first stop. Having failed to get ahead of Schumacher at the first round of stops, Häkkinen shadowed the Ferrari very closely during the second stint then pitted simultaneously and swiftly. If the Ferrari stop had not gone wrong it would have been incredibly close. Having recently survived a fatal air-crash, Coulthard's drive to P2 was highly courageous, overtaking both Schumachers on the way despite pain from cracked ribs.

POLE POSITION M Schumacher, Ferrari, 1m 20.974s (0.078s), 210.289kph, 130.668mph
LAPS 65 x 4.730 km, 2.939 miles
DISTANCE 307.323 km, 190.962 miles
STARTERS/FINISHERS 22/17
WEATHER Cloudy with sunny intervals, warm, dry
LAP LEADERS M Schumacher 1-23, 27-41 (38); Häkkinen 24-26, 42-65 (27)
WINNER'S LAPS 1-23 P2, 24-26 P1, 27-41 P2, 42-65 P1
FASTEST LAP Häkkinen, McLaren-Mercedes, 1m 24.470s (lap 28), 201.586kph, 125.260mph
CHAMPIONSHIP M Schumacher 36, Häkkinen 22, Coulthard 20, Barrichello 13, R Schumacher 12

Pos	Driver	Car	Time/gap	Grid	Stops	Tyres
1	M Häkkinen	McLaren-Mercedes	1h 33m 55.390s	2	2	B
2	D Coulthard	McLaren-Mercedes	−16.066s	4	2	B
3	R Barrichello	Ferrari	−29.112s	3	2	B
4	R Schumacher	Williams-BMW	−37.311s	5	2	B
5	M Schumacher	Ferrari	−47.983s	1	3	B
6	H-H Frentzen	Jordan-Mugen Honda	−1m 21.925s	8	2	B

McLaren-Mercedes MP4/15

| Round 6/17 | **EUROPEAN GP** Nürburgring | | | | | | | **Michael Schumacher** |
| | 21 May 2000 | | | Race 652 | | | | Ferrari F1 2000 179.540kph, 111.561mph |

As front-row pair Coulthard and Schumacher left the line, Häkkinen shot between them from P3, Schumacher having the brass neck to criticise his uncompromising manoeuvre. But rain on lap 10 forced Häkkinen to concede his lead to the more enterprising German. A much longer second stint appeared briefly to restore Häkkinen's initiative, but traffic eroded too much time and despite a spirited chase the race was Schumacher's. Despite taking pole Coulthard never threatened the two leaders, ending up a lapped third. With handling not to his liking DC was glad to narrowly beat Barrichello. Drive of the race was Pedro de la Rosa. Starting P14, by the finish he brought Arrows their first point of the season, fully deserved too.

POLE POSITION Coulthard, McLaren-Mercedes, 1m 17.529s (0.138s), 211.554kph, 131.454mph
LAPS 67 x 4.556 km, 2.831 miles
DISTANCE 305.235 km, 189.664 miles
STARTERS/FINISHERS 21/12
WEATHER Overcast, cold, dry then heavy rain
LAP LEADERS Häkkinen 1-10, 36-45 (20); M Schumacher 11-15, 17-35, 46-67 (46); Barrichello 16 (1)
WINNER'S LAPS 1-10 P2, 11-15 P1, 16 P3, 17-35 P1, 36-45 P2, 46-67 P1
FASTEST LAP M Schumacher, Ferrari, 1m 22.269s (lap 8), 199.365kph, 123.880mph
CHAMPIONSHIP M Schumacher 46, Häkkinen 28, Coulthard 24, Barrichello 16, R Schumacher 12

Pos	Driver	Car	Time/gap	Grid	Stops	Tyres
1	M Schumacher	Ferrari	1h 42m 0.307s	2	2	B
2	M Häkkinen	McLaren-Mercedes	−13.822s	3	2	B
3	D Coulthard	McLaren-Mercedes	−1 lap	1	2	B
4	R Barrichello	Ferrari	−1 lap	4	3	B
5	G Fisichella	Benetton-Playlife	−1 lap	7	2	B
6	P de la Rosa	Arrows-Supertec	−1 lap	12	2	B

| Round 7/17 | **MONACO GP** Monte Carlo | | | | | | | **David Coulthard** |
| | 4 June 2000 | | | Race 653 | | | | McLaren-Mercedes MP4/15 144.072kph, 89.522mph |

Led by Schumacher's Ferrari, the top five raced in grid order for 36 laps. Then Trulli's P2 Jordan dropped out with a broken gearbox, elevating Coulthard. By then the Ferrari was 35s ahead, although the Scot first stabilised then chipped away at the massive gap. But 20 laps later a satisfactory P2 became a sensational P1, Schumacher suffering a rare car failure when heat from a broken exhaust caused the rear suspension to fail. Jordan's grip on P2 now transferred to Frentzen, but just eight laps short he binned it at Ste Devote. So Barrichello and Fisichella joined Coulthard and Prince Rainier for the prize-giving. Jaguar scored their first-ever points, but on a day Michael did not score Mika had a difficult race and cut his deficit by only one point.

POLE POSITION M Schumacher, Ferrari, 1m 19.475s (0.271s), 152.651kph, 94.853mph
LAPS 78 x 3.370 km, 2.094 miles (Race restarted for scheduled 78 laps following accident)
DISTANCE 262.860 km, 163.333 miles
STARTERS/FINISHERS 22/10
WEATHER Sunny, hot, dry
LAP LEADERS M Schumacher 1-55 (55); Coulthard 56-78 (23)
WINNER'S LAPS 1-36 P3, 37-55 P2, 56-78 P1
FASTEST LAP Häkkinen, McLaren-Mercedes, 1m 21.571s (lap 57), 148.729kph, 92.416mph
CHAMPIONSHIP M Schumacher 46, Coulthard 34, Häkkinen 29, Barrichello 22, Fisichella 14

Pos	Driver	Car	Time/gap	Grid	Stops	Tyres
1	D Coulthard	McLaren-Mercedes	1h 49m 28.213s	3	1	B
2	R Barrichello	Ferrari	−15.889s	6	1	B
3	G Fisichella	Benetton-Playlife	−18.522s	8	1	B
4	E Irvine	Jaguar-Ford	−1m 5.924s	10	1	B
5	M Salo	Sauber-Petronas	−1m 20.775s	13	1	B
6	M Häkkinen	McLaren-Mercedes	−1 lap	5	1	B

CANADIAN GP Montréal
18 June 2000   Race 654

Michael Schumacher
Ferrari F1 2000 180.849kph, 112.375mph

Despite nursing a developing brake issue, Schumacher's fifth victory from eight races reinstated his crushing 20-plus points lead at the halfway mark. Schumacher won because, after a grid stall, the closely chasing Coulthard had to serve a stop-go on lap 14 for an illegal engine restart, dropping him out of contention. Schumacher won because Häkkinen got trapped behind a fast-starting Villeneuve for half the race. Schumacher won because when it rained, McLaren were too cautious in their switch to wets. And decisively, Schumacher won because Barrichello let him, relinquishing a first GP victory by dutifully backing-off. Rubens had made up 32s in the last 22 laps but, without regrets, elected to play the Ferrari 'family' game.

POLE POSITION M Schumacher, Ferrari, 1m 18.439s (0.098s), 202.904kph, 126.079mph
LAPS 69 x 4.421 km, 2.747 miles
DISTANCE 305.049 km, 189.549 miles
STARTERS/FINISHERS 22/16
WEATHER Overcast, warm, dry then heavy rain
LAP LEADERS M Schumacher 1-34, 43-69 (61); Barrichello 35-42 (8)
WINNER'S LAPS 1-34 P1, 35-42 P2, 43-69 P1
FASTEST LAP Häkkinen, McLaren-Mercedes, 1m 19.049s (Lap 37), 201.338kph, 125.106mph
CHAMPIONSHIP M Schumacher 56, Coulthard 34, Häkkinen 32, Barrichello 28, Fisichella 18

Pos	Driver	Car	Time/gap	Grid	Stops	Tyres
1	M Schumacher	Ferrari	1h 41m 12.313s	1	2	B
2	R Barrichello	Ferrari	−0.174s	3	2	B
3	G Fisichella	Benetton-Playlife	−15.365s	10	1	B
4	M Häkkinen	McLaren-Mercedes	−18.561s	4	2	B
5	J Verstappen	Arrows-Supertec	−52.202s	13	2	B
6	J Trulli	Jordan-Mugen Honda	−1m 1.687s	7	2	B

FRENCH GP Magny-Cours
2 July 2000   Race 655

David Coulthard
McLaren-Mercedes MP4/15 187.100kph, 116.259mph

Schumacher suffered his second car failure in three races, but not before being soundly beaten by Coulthard. A harsh first corner chop on Coulthard ensured Schumacher led from pole and also enabled Barrichello to get ahead. But Coulthard would not be denied. On lap 22 he overtook first one Ferrari, then the other on lap 40 to pull away to victory, but not before giving Schumacher the finger for deliberately driving him wide at Adelaide. Häkkinen eventually followed his more assertive teammate to bring about a McLaren 1-2, some speculating that DC's newfound forcefulness related to his recent near-death experience. Schumacher's engine failed on lap 59, but Barrichello's lasted for P3, Villeneuve beating Ralf and Trulli for best of the rest.

POLE POSITION M Schumacher, Ferrari, 1m 15.632s (0.102), 202.342kph, 125.730mph
LAPS 72 x 4.251 km, 2.641 miles
DISTANCE 305.886 km, 190.069 miles
STARTERS/FINISHERS 22/15
WEATHER Cloudy with sunny intervals, hot, dry
LAP LEADERS M Schumacher 1-24, 26-39 (38); D Coulthard, McLaren-Mercedes 25, 40-72 (34)
WINNER'S LAPS 1-21 P3, 22-24 P2, 25 P1, 26-39 P2, 40-72 P1
FASTEST LAP Coulthard, McLaren-Mercedes, 1m 19.479s (lap 28), 192.548kph, 119.644mph
CHAMPIONSHIP M Schumacher 56, Coulthard 44, Häkkinen 38, Barrichello 32, Fisichella 18

Pos	Driver	Car	Time/gap	Grid	Stops	Tyres
1	D Coulthard	McLaren-Mercedes	1h 38m 5.538s	2	2	B
2	M Häkkinen	McLaren-Mercedes	−14.748s	4	2	B
3	R Barrichello	Ferrari	−32.409s	3	2	B
4	J Villeneuve	BAR-Honda	−1m 1.322s	7	2	B
5	R Schumacher	Williams-BMW	−1m 3.981s	5	2	B
6	J Trulli	Jordan-Mugen Honda	−1m 15.605s	9	2	B

AUSTRIAN GP A1-Ring
16 July 2000   Race 656

Mika Häkkinen
McLaren-Mercedes MP4/15 208.792kph, 129.737mph

Häkkinen returned to form leading a dominant McLaren 1-2. From the front row the McLarens led all the way, and when pole-man Mika made his single stop on lap 38 his lead over David was 17s. Starting P4, Schumacher on a two-stop needed to get ahead of his heavier-fuelled teammate, the attempt to orchestrate this move causing a first corner fracas, Schumacher the casualty. In an attempt to contrive a red flag, he drove his crippled car back on to the track, but the SC was deployed instead. In the kerfuffle de la Rosa's Arrows ran a fine P3 for many laps, but by the flag Villeneuve finished best of the rest again. Schumacher's dnf closed up the drivers' points, though Ferrari kept their constructors' lead, McLaren docked ten points for a missing FIA seal.

POLE POSITION Häkkinen, McLaren-Mercedes, 1m 10.410s (0.385s), 221.184kph, 137.438mph
LAPS 71 x 4.326 km, 2.688 miles
DISTANCE 307.146 km, 190.852 miles
STARTERS/FINISHERS 22/12
WEATHER Cloudy with sunny intervals, hot, dry
LAP LEADERS Häkkinen 1-38, 43-71 (67); Coulthard 39-42 (4); SC 1-2 (2)
WINNER'S LAPS 1-38 P1, 39-42 P2, 43-71 P1
FASTEST LAP Coulthard, McLaren-Mercedes, 1m 11.783s (lap 67), 216.953kph, 134.809mph
CHAMPIONSHIP M Schumacher 56, Coulthard 50, Häkkinen 48, Barrichello 36, Fisichella 18

Pos	Driver	Car	Time/gap	Grid	Stops	Tyres
1	M Häkkinen	McLaren-Mercedes	1h 28m 15.818s	1	1	B
2	D Coulthard	McLaren-Mercedes	−12.535s	2	1	B
3	R Barrichello	Ferrari	−30.795s	3	1	B
4	J Villeneuve	BAR-Honda	−1 lap	7	1	B
5	J Button	Williams-BMW	−1 lap	18	1	B
6	M Salo	Sauber-Petronas	−1 lap	9	1	B

GERMAN GP Hockenheim
30 July 2000   Race 657

Rubens Barrichello
Ferrari F1 2000 215.340kph, 133.807mph

After a record 124 GP starts, Barrichello stood atop the podium openly weeping to the strains of the Brazilian national anthem. Starting P18 after a troubled qualifying, by lap 6 he was a brilliant P5 and P3 by lap 17, his first stop. On lap 26 the SC was deployed to apprehend a track-invading protester. This bizarre incident negated the massive 34s lead the two McLarens held over Barrichello. DC was unfortunate to lose out to the SC and after yet another, localised rain soon fell. Unlike most, including Mika, Rubens opted to stay out on slicks, pussyfooting through the wet stadium section, a gamble that won him the race. In another first-corner contretemps, Schumacher was punted off in front of his incredulous German fans. Button finished P4.

POLE POSITION Coulthard, McLaren-Mercedes, 1m 45.697s (1.366s), 232.456kph, 144.442mph
LAPS 45 x 6.825 km, 4.241 miles
DISTANCE 307.125 km, 190.839 miles
STARTERS/FINISHERS 22/12
WEATHER Cloudy, warm, dry then heavy rain later
LAP LEADERS Häkkinen 1-25, 28-35 (33); Coulthard 26-27 (2); Barrichello 36-45 (10); SC 27-28; 31 (3)
WINNER'S LAPS 1 P10, 2 P8, 3-4 P7, 5 P6, 6-11 P5, 12-14 P4, 15-17 P3, 18 P6, 19-24 P5, 25 P4, 26 P3, 27 P4, 28-34 P3, 35 P2, 36-45 P1
FASTEST LAP Barrichello, Ferrari, 1m 44.300s (lap 20), 235.570kph, 146.377mph
CHAMPIONSHIP M Schumacher 56, Coulthard 54, Häkkinen 54, Barrichello 46, Fisichella 18

Pos	Driver	Car	Time/gap	Grid	Stops	Tyres
1	R Barrichello	Ferrari	1h 25m 34.418s	18	2	B
2	M Häkkinen	McLaren-Mercedes	–7.452s	4	2	B
3	D Coulthard	McLaren-Mercedes	–21.168s	1	2	B
4	J Button	Williams-BMW	–22.685s	16	2	B
5	M Salo	Sauber-Petronas	–27.112s	15	2	B
6	P de la Rosa	Arrows-Supertec	–29.080s	5	2	B

HUNGARIAN GP Hungaroring
13 August 2000   Race 658

Mika Häkkinen
McLaren-Mercedes MP4/15 173.964kph, 108.097mph

Reigning champion Häkkinen's resurgence continued with another assertive win in energy-sapping heat. From the second row he blasted past his teammate, dived inside at the opening right-hander to sit it out with Schumacher, then led all but one pit-stop lap. Much to Ferrari chagrin, despite his strong pole Schumacher couldn't stay with him in race trim, the Finn steadily drawing out a lead that at one time reached over 30s. Coulthard pushed Schumacher hard for P2 but, unsurprisingly at this track, couldn't get by. Enhanced Williams aero and BMW horsepower had Ralf out-qualify Rubens for P4, although the Ferrari got ahead at the first stop. To the dismay of the Scuderia, for the first time Häkkinen and McLaren headed the points tables.

POLE POSITION M Schumacher, Ferrari, 1m 17.514s (0.372s), 184.611kph, 114.712mph
LAPS 77 x 3.975 km, 2.470 miles
DISTANCE 306.075 km, 190.186 miles
STARTERS/FINISHERS 22/16
WEATHER Cloudy with sunny intervals, very hot, dry
LAP LEADERS Häkkinen 1-31, 33-77 (76); Coulthard 32 (1)
WINNER'S LAPS 1-31 P1, 32 P2, 33-77 P1
FASTEST LAP Häkkinen, McLaren-Mercedes, 1m 20.028s (lap 33), 178.812kph, 111.109mph
CHAMPIONSHIP Häkkinen 64, M Schumacher 62, Coulthard 58, Barrichello 49, Fisichella 18

Pos	Driver	Car	Time/gap	Grid	Stops	Tyres
1	M Häkkinen	McLaren-Mercedes	1h 45m 33.869s	3	2	B
2	M Schumacher	Ferrari	–7.917s	1	2	B
3	D Coulthard	McLaren-Mercedes	–8.455s	2	2	B
4	R Barrichello	Ferrari	–44.157s	5	2	B
5	R Schumacher	Williams-BMW	–50.437s	4	2	B
6	H-H Frentzen	Jordan-Mugen Honda	–1m 8.099s	6	2	B

BELGIAN GP Spa Francorchamps
27 August 2000   Race 659

Mika Häkkinen
McLaren-Mercedes MP4/15 208.467kph, 129.536mph

Chasing Schumacher with four to go, Häkkinen got the better run out of Eau Rouge. Approaching Les Combes, Schumacher flicked left to pass backmarker Zonta. In a flash, in one of the great overtakes, Häkkinen dived to the right beneath them, three abreast. In their three-year struggle for supremacy it was awe-inspiring, deserving to be decisive. Häkkinen had led from pole, starting behind the SC on a wet track, but after switching to slicks a spin at Stavelot on lap 13 had given Schumacher a lead which, by the ferocity of the chop dealt to Mika on lap 40, he seemed loath to surrender. Until lap 41. So Schumachers finished 2-3 although on Saturday rookie Button caused a stir, his P3 grid-slot out-qualifying both Michael and teammate Ralf.

POLE POSITION Häkkinen, McLaren-Mercedes, 1m 50.646s (0.773s), 226.712kph, 140.872mph
LAPS 44 x 6.968 km, 4.330 miles
DISTANCE 306.592 km, 190.507 miles
STARTERS/FINISHERS 22/17
WEATHER Cloudy, warm, wet then drying
LAP LEADERS Häkkinen 1-12, 23-27, 41-44 (21); M Schumacher 13-22, 28-40 (23); SC 1 (1)
WINNER'S LAPS 1-12 P1, 13-22 P2, 23-27 P1, 28-40 P2, 41-44 P1
FASTEST LAP R Barrichello, Ferrari, 1m 53.803s (lap 30), 220.423kph, 136.965mph
CHAMPIONSHIP Häkkinen 74, M Schumacher 68, Coulthard 61, Barrichello 49, R Schumacher 20

Pos	Driver	Car	Time/gap	Grid	Stops	Tyres
1	M Häkkinen	McLaren-Mercedes	1h 28m 14.494s	1	2	B
2	M Schumacher	Ferrari	–1.104s	4	2	B
3	R Schumacher	Williams-BMW	–38.096s	6	2	B
4	D Coulthard	McLaren-Mercedes	–43.281s	5	2	B
5	J Button	Williams-BMW	–49.914s	3	2	B
6	H-H Frentzen	Jordan-Mugen Honda	–55.984s	8	2	B

TOP **100** RACE

ITALIAN GP Monza

10 September 2000   **Race 660**

Michael Schumacher

Ferrari F1 2000 210.286kph, 130.665mph

Post-race Schumacher broke into uncontrollable sobs, reflecting the pressure of conceding a seemingly invincible championship lead, now relieved by his first victory in almost three months. First-lap mayhem eliminated five cars including Coulthard and Barrichello, ending DC's chances for another year. In the second chicane incident de la Rosa somersaulted and wheels and debris flew, with fatal consequences for a marshal. Rather than a red flag, the race continued under the SC for 11 laps. In a race that at many levels was hard to savour, Schumacher always had the legs of Häkkinen. Ralf again finished P3 while teammate Button received an apology from big brother for erratic behaviour behind the SC that caused the rookie to spin off.

POLE POSITION M Schumacher, Ferrari, 1m 23.770s (0.027s), 248.953kph, 154.692mph
LAPS 53 x 5.793 km, 3.600 miles
DISTANCE 306.764 km, 190.614 miles
STARTERS/FINISHERS 22/12
WEATHER Sunny, hot, dry
LAP LEADERS M Schumacher 1-39, 43-53 (50); Häkkinen 40-42 (3); SC 1-11 (11)
WINNER'S LAPS 1-39 P1, 40-42 P2, 43-53 P1
FASTEST LAP Häkkinen, McLaren-Mercedes, 1m 25.595 (lap 50), 243.645kph, 151.394mph
CHAMPIONSHIP Häkkinen 80, M Schumacher 78, Coulthard 61, Barrichello 49, R Schumacher 24

Pos	Driver	Car	Time/gap	Grid	Stops	Tyres
1	M Schumacher	Ferrari	1h 27m 31.638s	1	1	B
2	M Häkkinen	McLaren-Mercedes	−3.810s	3	1	B
3	R Schumacher	Williams-BMW	−52.432s	7	1	B
4	J Verstappen	Arrows-Supertec	−59.938s	11	1	B
5	A Wurz	Benetton-Playlife	−1m 7.426s	13	1	B
6	R Zonta	BAR-Honda	−1m 9.293s	17	3	B

UNITED STATES GP Indianapolis

24 September 2000   **Race 661**

Michael Schumacher

Ferrari F1 2000 190.240kph, 118.210mph

For the first time in nine years, F1 was back in the USA. Barrichello 'towed' Schumacher around the Indy banking to clinch pole, but on a wet surface Coulthard made the better start, only to be penalised for his trouble. But not before their season-long feud over racing etiquette had reopened, Coulthard not making it easy for Schumacher to take the lead on lap 7. That same lap Häkkinen made an early switch to slicks, Michael delaying to lap 16 to rejoin 11s ahead of Mika, who began to close in quickly. But the massive crowd, estimated to be approaching 250,000, were denied a humdinger when, 4s behind, the Mercedes expired on lap 26. A Ferrari 1-2 and only two points for McLaren transformed the shape of the championship.

POLE POSITION M Schumacher, Ferrari, 1m 14.266s (0.126s), 203.204kph, 126.266mph
LAPS 73 x 4.192 km, 2.605 miles
DISTANCE 305.999 km, 190.139 miles
STARTERS/FINISHERS 22/15
WEATHER Cloudy, cool, damp then drying
LAP LEADERS Coulthard 1-6 (6); M Schumacher 7-73 (67)
WINNER'S LAPS 1-6 P2, 7-73 P1
FASTEST LAP Coulthard, McLaren-Mercedes, 1m 14.711s (lap 40), 201.994kph, 125.513mph
CHAMPIONSHIP M Schumacher 88, Häkkinen 80, Coulthard 63, Barrichello 55, R Schumacher 24

Pos	Driver	Car	Time/gap	Grid	Stops	Tyres
1	M Schumacher	Ferrari	1h 36m 30.883s	1	2	B
2	R Barrichello	Ferrari	−12.118s	4	2	B
3	H-H Frentzen	Jordan-Mugen Honda	−17.368s	7	2	B
4	J Villeneuve	BAR-Honda	−17.936s	8	2	B
5	D Coulthard	McLaren-Mercedes	−28.813s	2	3	B
6	R Zonta	BAR-Honda	−51.694s	12	2	B

JAPANESE GP Suzuka

8 October 2000   **Race 662**

Michael Schumacher

Ferrari F1 2000 207.315kph, 128.819mph

The pendulum swing back to Ferrari and Schumacher had been so rapid that suddenly an eighth race victory would settle it. Suzuka was an intense battle between the two double champions, Coulthard and Barrichello trailing in their wake. Schumacher won the pole but Häkkinen the start, successfully leading through the first of two stops. Soon afterwards, around lap 25, it began to drizzle. The outcome turned on an early second-stop call by McLaren on lap 37 to evade traffic, coinciding with intensifying drizzle just as Häkkinen rejoined on shiny new slicks. Before making his stop Schumacher banged in three frenzied laps on the slippery surface, his pit crew gained another 1.4s, the first Ferrari champion for 21 years exiting the pits still holding the lead.

POLE POSITION M Schumacher, Ferrari, 1m 35.825s (0.009s), 220.301kph, 136.889mph
LAPS 53 x 5.864 km, 3.644 miles
DISTANCE 310.596 km, 192.995 miles
STARTERS/FINISHERS 22/15
WEATHER Overcast, cool, dry at first then light rain later
LAP LEADERS Häkkinen 1-21, 25-36 (33); M Schumacher 22-23, 37-53 (19); Coulthard 24 (1)
WINNER'S LAPS 1-21 P2, 22-23 P1, 24 P3, 25-36 P2, 37-53 P1
FASTEST LAP Häkkinen, McLaren-Mercedes, 1m 39.189s (lap 26), 212.830kph, 132.246mph
CHAMPIONSHIP M Schumacher 98, Häkkinen 86, Coulthard 67, Barrichello 58, R Schumacher 24

Pos	Driver	Car	Time/gap	Grid	Stops	Tyres
1	M Schumacher	Ferrari	1h 29m 53.435s	1	2	B
2	M Häkkinen	McLaren-Mercedes	−1.837s	2	2	B
3	D Coulthard	McLaren-Mercedes	−1m 9.914s	3	2	B
4	R Barrichello	Ferrari	−1m 19.191s	4	2	B
5	J Button	Williams-BMW	−1m 25.694s	5	2	B
6	J Villeneuve	BAR-Honda	−1 lap	9	2	B

MALAYSIAN GP Sepang

22 October 2000   Race 663

Michael Schumacher

Ferrari F1 2000 194.199kph, 120.670mph

The new champion on pole, his predecessor alongside, the constructors' title still undecided. Before the gantry lights went out both moved a fraction. Häkkinen was penalised for breaking the light beam, Schumacher not. Before taking his punishment, Häkkinen ushered Coulthard into the lead, but an off-track excursion caused an early pit stop for DC which was all Schumacher needed, a blistering sequence of laps ensuring he led after his own first stop. In the closing laps Coulthard pressed the leader but could not prevent a fourth Ferrari victory on the trot, Schumacher's ninth this year. Their 1-3 finish sealed Ferrari's second consecutive constructors' title, Schumacher, Barrichello and Brawn celebrating on the podium wearing, er, fetching red wigs.

Pos	Driver	Car	Time/gap	Grid	Stops	Tyres
1	M Schumacher	Ferrari	1h 35m 54.235s	1	2	B
2	D Coulthard	McLaren-Mercedes	−0.732s	3	2	B
3	R Barrichello	Ferrari	−18.444s	4	2	B
4	M Häkkinen	McLaren-Mercedes	−35.269s	2	2	B
5	J Villeneuve	BAR-Honda	−1m 10.692s	6	2	B
6	E Irvine	Jaguar-Ford	−1m 12.568s	7	2	B

POLE POSITION M Schumacher, Ferrari, 1m 37.397s (0.463s), 204.881kph, 127.307mph
LAPS 56 x 5.543 km, 3.444 miles
DISTANCE 310.408 km, 192.879 miles
STARTERS/FINISHERS 22/13
WEATHER Overcast, very hot and humid, dry
LAP LEADERS Häkkinen 1-2 (2); Coulthard 3-17 (15); M Schumacher 18-24, 26-39, 42-56 (36); Barrichello 25, 40-41 (3); SC 1-2 (2)
WINNER'S LAPS 1-2 P3, 3-17 P2, 18-24 P1, 25 P2, 26-39 P1, 40-41 P2, 42-56 P1
FASTEST LAP Häkkinen, McLaren-Mercedes, 1m 38.543s (lap 34), 202.498kph, 125.827mph
CHAMPIONSHIP M Schumacher 108, Häkkinen 89, Coulthard 73, Barrichello 62, R Schumacher 24

2000 CHAMPIONSHIP FACTS AND FOLKLORE

■ Three charismatic names returned to GP racing in 2000. Indianapolis was reinstated as one of the 17 championship circuits – not the famous anticlockwise oval track, but a new clockwise road course which incorporated the banked turn four.

■ Other returnees were Honda and BMW, making their comeback via engine partnerships, supplying V10s to BAR and Williams respectively, ten cylinders now the ceiling in F1.

■ For a second season Bridgestone were the sole tyre supplier to the 11 F1 teams.

■ Having fought a losing battle in 1997, 1998 and 1999, Ferrari and Schumacher finally won in 2000. 1979, the last time a Ferrari driver was crowned, seemed – indeed was – an age away. It had been a long wait and few denied the Scuderia their moment of glory.

■ Michael Schumacher secured his third world title at the penultimate championship round for what appeared to be an overwhelming triumph. He finally amassed nine race victories, more than twice those of Häkkinen.

■ But the second half of the season began with a remarkable reversal in fortunes before the winning momentum returned by the end of the season.

■ Equalling his own record shared with Mansell, Schumacher's nine race-wins raised his personal tally to 44, now splitting Senna's 41 and Prost's record 51.

■ With Irvine's switch to Jaguar, Rubens Barrichello joined Schumacher at Ferrari and scored his maiden GP win in the wet at Hockenheim.

■ The design philosophy for the F1-2000 was to build a car much closer to the limits controlled by regulations and know-how, without compromising reliability, an objective largely accomplished. Ten race wins, an unprecedented Ferrari achievement, brought the reds a record tenth constructors' championship.

■ McLaren, the only other team to win races during the year, mounted a strong challenge, but reliability at critical moments blunted Häkkinen's challenge and his chances of a hat-trick of championships. The MP4-15 was the equal of the Ferrari, distinguished by ventilation funnels protruding from the sidepods, a feature unseen since the 1979 Shadow.

■ Häkkinen didn't relinquish his title easily either, but equally didn't attain top form until as late as round ten in Austria, after taking an overdue break from team duties and those of a world champion. In the three-year struggle for supremacy between these two multiple-champions, the pass of his nemesis for the lead and victory in Belgium was one of the great grand prix moments.

■ With three victories, only one short of the Finn's tally, Coulthard enjoyed his most successful season ever. He took full advantage of his teammate's early season doldrums, while others surmised a more steely ingredient in David's driving following his miraculous yet harrowing survival from a plane crash in which the two pilots lost their lives.

■ Whichever, Coulthard became a Monaco GP victor and joined Clark and Mansell as a back-to-back winner of his home GP.

■ Whether it was tears, sneers, or fears, DC's air crash was one of a number of occasions when F1 2000 showed its human face.

■ Under the public gaze of TV, both Ferrari drivers were totally overwhelmed by emotion at their moment of glory; Schumacher received frequent disdain from his peers, notably Coulthard, Villeneuve and Irvine, for his equally frequent chops and other on-track intimidation, while an anonymous French spectator also used the track, at Hockenheim, to protest his sacking by Mercedes after 20 years of service.

■ Of the remaining nine teams, only Williams appeared to be building towards a return to the winners' enclosure.

■ Their relationship with BMW, back after 13 years away, showed immense promise, and despite burning their fingers with Alex Zanardi from CART, for 2001 Williams were placing great store by another CART champion, Juan Pablo Montoya, hyped up to be the antidote to Schumachers, whether Michael or teammate Ralf.

■ Montoya's arrival at Williams for 2001 put Jenson Button out in the cold after what many regarded as an exceptional season from a 20-year-old rookie. In Brazil, his second race, he became the youngest ever points-winner, his first of seven points finishes. But more impressive still were his performances at the recognised 'drivers' circuits, where he out-qualified his esteemed teammate with P3 at Spa and P5 at Suzuka.

■ Another team recapturing forward momentum was Benetton, now fully Renault-owned. The Régie had reinstated Flavio Briatore as team principal, who brought in Mike Gascoyne from Jordan as technical director.

■ Renault began developing a new 111° wide-angle V10, while on the driver front Button would join Fisichella.

Championship ranking	Championship points	Driver nationality	Driver	Car	Races contested	Race victories	Podiumse excl. victories	Races led	Lights to flag victories	Laps led	Poles	Fastest laps	Triple Crowns
			2000 Drivers Championship										
1	108	GER	Michael Schumacher	Ferrari	17	9	3	14		548	9	2	
2	89	FIN	Mika Häkkinen	McLaren-Mercedes	17	4	7	12		352	5	9	
3	73	GBR	David Coulthard	McLaren-Mercedes	17	3	8	9		107	2	3	
4	62	BRA	Rubens Barrichello	Ferrari	17	1	8	7		58	1	3	
5	24	GER	Ralf Schumacher	Williams-BMW	17		3						
6	18	ITA	Giancarlo Fisichella	Benetton-Playlife	17		3						
7	17	CAN	Jacques Villeneuve	BAR-Honda	17								
8	12	GBR	Jenson Button	Williams-BMW	17								
9	11	GER	Heinz-Harald Frentzen	Jordan-Mugen Honda	17		2	2		9			
10	6	ITA	Jarno Trulli	Jordan-Mugen Honda	17								
11	6	FIN	Mika Salo	Sauber-Petronas	16								
12	5	NLD	Jos Verstappen	Arrows-Supertec	17								
13	4	GBR	Eddie Irvine	Jaguar-Ford	16								
14	3	BRA	Ricardo Zonta	BAR-Honda	17								
15	2	AUT	Alexander Wurz	Benetton-Playlife	17								
16	2	ESP	Pedro de la Rosa	Arrows-Supertec	17								

- Equipped with works Honda V10s, BAR had a much-improved second season, scoring points with a certain regularity but never reaching the podium. Lack of significant success could not be laid at the door of Villeneuve, who drove with gusto, despite becoming increasingly frustrated by lack of progress and the continued infighting within management circles.
- As too were engine partners Honda, marking their 200th GP at Monza, and strongly rumoured to be looking to take over BAR and form a full works effort in response to Toyota's 2002 arrival.
- Having each won races in 1999, Jordan and Jaguar, née Stewart, had an exceptionally disappointing 2000 season.

- Jordan plummeted from third to sixth in the constructors' championship, scoring the least points since 1993. On occasion the EJ10 showed a useful turn of speed, but reliability was awful, thought to result from excessive weight-saving, particularly the gearbox, to compensate for the ageing and overweight Mugen Honda V10. A works Honda engine deal for 2001 might restore the upward trend.
- It was soon clear that as the Stewart organisation was expanded to become Jaguar, it had added fat not muscle, and under the leadership of the unfortunate Neil Ressler, paddock sympathy for the overindulgent team was in short supply. The arrival of Bobby Rahal might change things in 2001.

RACE 663, Malaysian GP: Ferrari sealed their second consecutive constructors' title at the final round, Schumacher, Barrichello and Brawn celebrating by wearing, er, 'fetching' red wigs.

RACE 663, Malaysian GP: The Jaguar F1 team photocall at the end of their first year. Four further dismal seasons later Ford sold the team to Red Bull co-founder Dietrich Mateschitz and the rest, as they say, is history.

- The team scored just four championship points, all down to Irvine, Johnny Herbert departing F1 with a heavy prang caused by broken suspension at Sepang. 'I was carried into F1, and carried out again,' he quipped.
- Sauber signed a young Finnish driver named Kimi Räikkönen for 2001, raising questions over the criteria for the granting of F1 superlicences: he had only competed in 23 car races.
- When Schumacher's Ferrari gyrated on to wet grass during Silverstone practice, the rear wheels spun in vain until the fuel filler flap opened, Michael then able to rejoin the circuit without further difficulty. This and other suspicions led to a crackdown by the FIA. Their aim was to detect illegal control systems that could simulate traction control, hidden inside electronic software programs, including the pit-stop speed limiter.
- But accusation and counter-accusation remained rife, leaving the FIA little alternative. To provide a level playing field and be seen to do so, the FIA were forced to allow electronic gizmos to let rip. Traction control, fully automatic gearboxes and the like would be legalised from the 2001 Spanish GP.
- Although Max Mosley had won the stand-off between the FIA and the EU over anti-competition law, closer to home Ron Dennis was the most vociferous among certain team bosses to see Mosley ousted as FIA president in the upcoming 2001 elections, unhappy with his methods in various matters, not least the F1 financial structure.
- The FIA leased to SLEC the commercial rights to F1 for a further 100 years beyond the existing 2011 agreement, SLEC (an acronym from the name of his wife Slavica) being the F1 commercial rights holding company set up by Bernie Ecclestone in anticipation of flotation. By separating commercial from promotional activities, the FIA claimed to be complying with EU requirements.
- Ecclestone sold 50% of SLEC holdings to PE/VC companies Morgan Grenfell and Hellman and Friedman, who rapidly sold it on to German Media group EM.TV in March 2000.
- This spawned a response from an amalgam of five major motor manufacturers with F1 interests, Ford, DaimlerChrysler, Toyota, FIAT and BMW, later to form GPWC. The common purpose of these five was to secure better representation of the manufacturers in F1, improved financial conditions for the teams, stability for the championship, and maintenance of free-to-air television coverage. Their initial avenue was to purchase a one-third stake in SLEC from EM.TV.
- Echoing a less mercenary, more sporting F1 era, on 21 March 2000 Sir Stirling Moss became a motorsport knight, while two stalwarts of the 1950s/1960s GP scene took their leave during the year, BRM patron Sir Arthur Owen at the age of 85, and John Cooper of Cooper Cars aged 77.

Championship ranking	Championship points	Team/Marque nationality	2000 Constructors Championship		Engine maker nationality	Races contested	Race victories	1-2 finishes	Podiums excl. victories	Races led	Laps led	Poles	Fastest laps
			Chassis	Engine									
1	170	ITA	Ferrari F1-2000	Ferrari 3.0 V10	ITA	17	10	3	11	15	606	10	5
2	152	GBR	McLaren MP4-15	Mercedes-Benz 3.0 V10	GER	17	7	4	15	16	459	7	12
3	36	GBR	Williams FW22	BMW 3.0 V10	GER	17			3				
4	20	ITA	Benetton B200	Playlife 3.0 V10	FRA	17			3				
5	20	GBR	BAR 002	Honda 3.0 V10	JPN	17							
6	17	IRL	Jordan EJ10, EJ10B	Mugen Honda 3.0 V10	JPN	17			2	2	9		
7	7	GBR	Arrows A21	Supertec 3.0 V10	FRA	17							
8	6	SUI	Sauber C19	Petronas 3.0 V10	ITA	16							
9	4	GBR	Jaguar R1	Ford Cosworth 3.0 V10	GBR	17							

2001

Schumacher wins, rivals wilt

THE TALE OF THE TITLE

- Schumacher's second back-to-back championship also brought Ferrari a hat-trick of constructors' titles.
- With another nine-race haul he even surpassed Prost's career record, raising it to 54 GP victories.
- The other eight races were split between a fading McLaren-Mercedes and a rising Williams-BMW.
- Schumacher's younger brother Ralf opened his GP account with three wins for Williams.
- It was the team's first success in four years, but Williams, BMW and Michelin were far from ready for titles.
- Nor were McLaren and Coulthard, championship runners-up with two victories but already trailing by Monaco.
- Two victories aside, Häkkinen's season was compromised by deplorable reliability and sabbatical speculation.
- In a patchy yet formidable rookie season, the fifth race winner Montoya was unlucky to score just once.
- Besides these three teams, the crumbs – five P3s – went to BAR with two, Sauber, Jaguar and Benetton.
- Summing up, unless someone raised their game Ferrari and Schumacher were approaching invincibility.
- And not forgetting: tyre wars resumed; another marshall dies; electronic 'gizmos' legalised.

THE CHASE FOR THE CHAMPIONSHIP

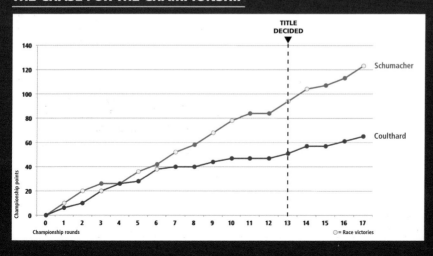

Ferrari F2001

Round 1/17	**AUSTRALIAN GP** Melbourne						**Michael Schumacher**
	4 March 2001					Race 664	Ferrari F2001 187.464kph, 116.485mph

A second fatality within five races marred round one. On lap 5 Villeneuve rammed Ralf Schumacher under braking, the BAR launched into a hurtling, wheel-shedding smash, and by sheer ill fate a flying wheel struck a marshal. After 10 SC laps Schumacher and Häkkinen resumed their scrap until the McLaren front suspension failed on lap 25, but for the first time since 1997 the fastest car at the season opener was not a McLaren. Coulthard did well to finish P2 from a P6 start whereas Barrichello, alongside pole-sitter Schumacher, had a scrappy race to P3. Of the rookies, Montoya qualified P11 but on lap 40 was in the points when the BMW blew. Räikkönen won a first point from P13, while Alonso did well just to finish for Minardi.

POLE POSITION M Schumacher, Ferrari, 1m 26.892s (0.371s), 209.707kph, 136.520mph
LAPS 58 x 5.303 km, 3.295 miles
DISTANCE 307.574 km, 191.117 miles
STARTERS/FINISHERS 22/14
WEATHER Cloudy with sunny intervals, hot, dry
LAP LEADERS M Schumacher 1-36, 41-58 (54); Coulthard 37-40 (4); SC 6-15 (10)
WINNER'S LAPS 1-36 P1, 37-38 P3, 39-40 P2, 41-58 P1
FASTEST LAP M Schumacher, Ferrari, 1m 28.214s (lap 34), 216.414kph, 134.474mph
CHAMPIONSHIP M Schumacher 10, Coulthard 6, Barrichello 4, Heidfeld 3, Frentzen 2

Pos	Driver	Car	Time/gap	Grid	Stops	Tyres
1	M Schumacher	Ferrari	1h 38m 26.533s	1	1	B
2	D Coulthard	McLaren-Mercedes	−1.718s	6	1	B
3	R Barrichello	Ferrari	−33.491s	2	1	B
4	N Heidfeld	Sauber-Petronas	−1m 11.419s	10	1	B
5	H-H Frentzen	Jordan-Honda	−1m 12.807s	4	1	B
6	K Räikkönen	Sauber-Petronas	−1m 24.143s	13	1	B

Round 2/17	**MALAYSIAN GP** Sepang						**Michael Schumacher**
	18 March 2001					Race 665	Ferrari F2001 170.030kph, 105.652mph

An inspired tyre choice plucked a Ferrari 1-2 from the jaws of defeat. Leading from the front row, on lap 3 both Ferraris skated off caught out by sudden rain, but luck held, rejoining the track P10 and P11. As the downpour intensified the SC circulated, the field pitting for wets. The Ferrari pit stops were farcical, Schumacher stacked behind Barrichello, stationary for 90s and 72s respectively. But they had opted for intermediates, a decision that enabled the pair to regain the lead on lap 16 as the storm passed and the track dried. Schumacher's sixth successive win from pole was perhaps his easiest. Behind DC's lonely P3, H-HF won a spirited race-long P4 battle from Ralf and Mika, Ralf recovering from a first corner nurf by Barrichello.

POLE POSITION M Schumacher, Ferrari, 1m 35.220s (0.099s), 209.565kph, 130.218mph
LAPS 55 x 5.543 km, 3.444 miles (Scheduled for 56 laps but reduced after aborted start)
DISTANCE 304.865 km, 189.434 miles
STARTERS/FINISHERS 22/13
WEATHER Hot and overcast, dry at first, heavy shower then drying
LAP LEADERS M Schumacher 1-2, 16-55 (42); J Trulli, Jordan-Honda 3 (1); Coulthard 4-15 (12); SC 4-10 (7)
WINNER'S LAPS 1-2 P1, 3 P7, 4 P4, 5-10 P11, 11 P9, 12 P6, 13-14 P3, 15 P2, 16-55 P1
FASTEST LAP Häkkinen, McLaren-Mercedes, 1m 40.962s (lap 48), 197.646kph, 122.812mph
CHAMPIONSHIP M Schumacher 20, Barrichello 10, Coulthard 10, Frentzen 5, Heidfeld 3

Pos	Driver	Car	Time/gap	Grid	Stops	Tyres
1	M Schumacher	Ferrari	1h 47m 34.801s	1	1	B
2	R Barrichello	Ferrari	−23.660s	2	1	B
3	D Coulthard	McLaren-Mercedes	−28.555s	8	1	B
4	H-H Frentzen	Jordan-Honda	−46.543s	9	2	B
5	R Schumacher	Williams-BMW	−48.233s	3	3	M
6	M Häkkinen	McLaren-Mercedes	−48.606s	4	1	B

Round 3/17	**BRAZILIAN GP** Interlagos				
	1 April 2001				**Race 666**

David Coulthard
McLaren-Mercedes MP4-16 185.373kph, 115.186mph

An all-Schumacher front row, Ralf out quickly in another collision with Barrichello. Häkkinen's grid stall caused a brief SC. On release, and despite the heavier fuel load, rookie Montoya sensationally blasted past Schumacher at turn one. For 25 laps these two plus Coulthard's McLaren raced closely until the two-stopping Schumacher peeled off. But the Columbian's fairytale ended on lap 38 when, with a 5s lead, a lapped Verstappen punted him off at turn one. Coulthard now led, lost it to Schumacher in the switch to wet tyres, but regained it finally on lap 50 with an epic three-abreast turn one pass on the soaking track, Michael around the outside of the backmarker, DC diving down the inside to take them both. The rest of the field were lapped.

POLE POSITION M Schumacher, Ferrari, 1m 13.780s (0.310s), 210.252kph, 130.645mph
LAPS 71 x 4.309 km, 2.677 miles
DISTANCE 305.909 km, 190.083 miles
STARTERS/FINISHERS 22/11
WEATHER Cloudy, hot, dry at first, heavy shower then drying
LAP LEADERS M Schumacher 1-2, 48-49 (4); J P Montoya, Williams-BMW 3-38 (36); Coulthard 39-47, 50-71 (31); SC 1-2 (2)
WINNER'S LAPS 1-24 P3, 25-38 P2, 39-47 P1, 48-49 P2, 50-71 P1
FASTEST LAP R Schumacher, Williams-BMW, 1m 15.693s (lap 38), 204.938kph, 127.343mph
CHAMPIONSHIP M Schumacher 26, Coulthard 20, Barrichello 10, Heidfeld 7, Frentzen 5

Pos	Driver	Car	Time/gap	Grid	Stops	Tyres
1	D Coulthard	McLaren-Mercedes	1h 39m 0.834s	5	2	B
2	M Schumacher	Ferrari	−16.164s	1	2	B
3	N Heidfeld	Sauber-Petronas	−1 lap	9	1	B
4	O Panis	BAR-Honda	−1 lap	11	2	B
5	J Trulli	Jordan-Honda	−1 lap	7	1	B
6	G Fisichella	Benetton-Renault	−1 lap	18	2	M

Williams-BMW FW23

Round 4/17	**SAN MARINO GP** Imola				
	15 April 2001				**Race 667**

Ralf Schumacher
Williams-BMW FW23 202.062kph, 125.556mph

A curious choice of hard Bridgestones had the Ferraris qualifying P4 and P6. In the drag off the line, Ralf Schumacher from P3 used BMW horses to power past the front-row McLaren duo, majestically sailing to his maiden victory and ending a 54-race win-drought for Williams. Car, driver, engine and tyres behaved flawlessly, pole-sitter Coulthard giving vain chase, the rest out of contention. On lap 24 M. Schumacher retired from P7 after a series of niggles, whereas Barrichello mugged Häkkinen at the first stop for P3. Montoya had a dismal event, finally retiring with clutch trouble on lap 48. Aside from the euphoria in the Williams-BMW and Michelin camps there was quiet satisfaction at McLaren, DC and Michael level and topping the points chase.

POLE POSITION Coulthard, McLaren-Mercedes, 1m 23.054s (0.228s), 213.822kph, 132.863mph
LAPS 62 x 4.933 km, 3.065 miles
DISTANCE 305.609 km, 189.897 miles
STARTERS/FINISHERS 22/12
WEATHER Sunny, warm, dry
LAP LEADERS R Schumacher 1-62 (62)
WINNER'S LAPS 1-62 P1
FASTEST LAP R Schumacher, Williams-BMW, 1m 25.524s (lap 27), 207.646kph, 129.026mph
CHAMPIONSHIP M Schumacher 26, Coulthard 26, Barrichello 14, R Schumacher 12, Heidfeld 7

Pos	Driver	Car	Time/gap	Grid	Stops	Tyres
1	R Schumacher	Williams-BMW	1h 30m 44.817s	3	2	M
2	D Coulthard	McLaren-Mercedes	−4.352s	1	2	B
3	R Barrichello	Ferrari	−34.766s	6	2	B
4	M Häkkinen	McLaren-Mercedes	−36.315s	2	2	B
5	J Trulli	Jordan-Honda	−1m 25.558s	5	2	B
6	H-H Frentzen	Jordan-Honda	−1 lap	9	2	B

Round 5/17	**SPANISH GP** Cataluña						**Michael Schumacher**
	29 April 2001					Race 668	Ferrari F2001 202.507kph, 125.833mph

The return of launch and traction control was partly responsible for car ailments delaying or eliminating many, notably Coulthard's dummy-grid stall. Shadowed by Häkkinen, M. Schumacher led much of the race from pole until after his second stop he dropped back due to severe tyre vibration. But a Häkkinen victory was denied in the cruellest possible way. Commencing the final lap holding a 40s lead over the Ferrari, the clutch exploded, his McLaren grinding to a halt half-a-mile short of the flag. With R. Schumacher sooner, and Barrichello later also out with technical problems, the rostrum had an unusual appearance. Joining Michael were Montoya and Villeneuve, each celebrating a first. Montoya's first podium from five starts, BAR's first from 38.

POLE POSITION M Schumacher, Ferrari, 1m 18.201s (0.085s), 217.746kph, 135.301mph
LAPS 65 x 4.730 km, 2.939 miles (Scheduled for 66 laps but reduced after aborted start)
DISTANCE 307.323 km, 190.962 miles
STARTERS/FINISHERS 22/16
WEATHER Cloudy with sunny intervals, warm, dry, windy
LAP LEADERS M Schumacher 1-22, 28-43, 65 (39); Häkkinen 23-27, 44-64 (26)
WINNER'S LAPS 1-22 P1, 23 P2, 24-25 P3, 26-27 P2, 28-43 P1, 44-64 P2, 65 P1
FASTEST LAP M Schumacher, Ferrari, 1m 21.151s (lap 25), 209.831kph, 130.383mph
CHAMPIONSHIP M Schumacher 36, Coulthard 28, Barrichello 14, R Schumacher 12, Heidfeld 8

Pos	Driver	Car	Time/gap	Grid	Stops	Tyres
1	M Schumacher	Ferrari	1h 31m 3.305s	1	2	B
2	J P Montoya	Williams-BMW	−40.737s	12	2	M
3	J Villeneuve	BAR-Honda	−49.625s	7	2	B
4	J Trulli	Jordan-Honda	−51.252s	6	2	B
5	D Coulthard	McLaren-Mercedes	−51.615s	3	3	B
6	N Heidfeld	Sauber-Petronas	−1m 1.892s	10	2	B

Round 6/17	**AUSTRIAN GP** A1-Ring						**David Coulthard**
	13 May 2001					Race 669	McLaren-Mercedes MP4-16 209.977kph, 130.474mph

Launch control malfunctions littered the grid, bringing out the SC, but not before the Williams-BMWs had blasted by pole-sitter M. Schumacher. But as his Michelins cycled through their 'graining' phase, Montoya soon headed a frustrated train led by M. Schumacher, R. Schumacher having departed on lap 10 with brake trouble. On lap 16 Schumacher tried a pass, JPM resisted and they both went off, Barrichello, Verstappen – having started P16 – and Coulthard going by. The Scotsman got ahead of the Ferrari driver by going longer at their late one-stop, but Barrichello, who had led more laps than anyone, didn't give up the chase until requested to back-off on the final lap and surrender P2 to the recovering M. Schumacher, Rubens mortified.

POLE POSITION M Schumacher, Ferrari, 1m 09.562s (0.124s), 223.880kph, 139.113mph
LAPS 71 x 4.326 km, 2.688 miles
DISTANCE 307.146 km, 190.852 miles
STARTERS/FINISHERS 22/11
WEATHER Cloudy with sunny intervals, warm, dry
LAP LEADERS J P Montoya, Williams-BMW 1-15 (15); Barrichello 16-46 (31); Coulthard 47-71 (25); SC 1-3 (3)
WINNER'S LAPS 1-4 P5, 5-9 P6, 10-15 P5 16-22 P3, 23-46 P2, 47-71 P1
FASTEST LAP Coulthard, McLaren-Mercedes, 1m 10.843s (lap 48), 219.832kph, 136.598mph
CHAMPIONSHIP M Schumacher 42, Coulthard 38, Barrichello 18, R Schumacher 12, Heidfeld 8

Pos	Driver	Car	Time/gap	Grid	Stops	Tyres
1	D Coulthard	McLaren-Mercedes	1h 27m 45.927s	7	1	B
2	M Schumacher	Ferrari	−2.190s	1	1	B
3	R Barrichello	Ferrari	−2.527s	4	1	B
4	K Räikkönen	Sauber-Petronas	−41.593s	9	1	B
5	O Panis	BAR-Honda	−53.775s	10	1	B
6	J Verstappen	Arrows-Asiatech	−1 lap	16	2	B

Round 7/17	**MONACO GP** Monte Carlo						**Michael Schumacher**
	27 May 2001					Race 670	Ferrari F2001 146.881kph, 91.268mph

Four points shy of M. Schumacher, pole at Monaco kept Coulthard's title ambitions very much alive. But on Sunday things unravelled. First another dummy-grid glitch put him to the back and then he spent half the race trapped behind Bernoldi's Arrows, fortunate in many ways to finally win points with P5. It was a 1-2 cakewalk for Ferrari, Montoya crashing out from P6 on lap 3 and Häkkinen, just as he began to trade fastest laps and put pressure on Schumacher, falling away on lap 13 to retire with steering issues. R. Schumacher was never in the hunt for victory, hydraulics putting him out on lap 57 when a distant P3, so with a clean fast drive from P5 Irvine gave Jaguar their first podium, joining his former teammates on the rostrum.

POLE POSITION Coulthard, McLaren-Mercedes, 1m 17.430s (0.201s), 156.683kph, 97.359mph
LAPS 78 x 3.370 km, 2.094 miles
DISTANCE 262.860 km, 163.333 miles
STARTERS/FINISHERS 22/10
WEATHER Sunny, hot, dry
LAP LEADERS M Schumacher 1-54, 60-78 (73); Barrichello 55-59 (5)
WINNER'S LAPS 1-54 P1, 55-59 P2, 60-78 P1
FASTEST LAP Coulthard, McLaren-Mercedes, 1m 19.424s (lap 68), 152.749kph, 94.914mph
CHAMPIONSHIP M Schumacher 52, Coulthard 40, Barrichello 24, R Schumacher 12, Heidfeld 8

Pos	Driver	Car	Time/gap	Grid	Stops	Tyres
1	M Schumacher	Ferrari	1h 47m 22.561s	2	1	B
2	R Barrichello	Ferrari	−0.431s	4	1	B
3	E Irvine	Jaguar-Ford	−30.698s	6	1	M
4	J Villeneuve	BAR-Honda	−32.454s	9	1	B
5	D Coulthard	McLaren-Mercedes	−1 lap	1	1	B
6	J Alesi	Prost-Acer	−1 lap	11	2	M

Round 8/17	**CANADIAN GP** Montréal		
	10 June 2001		**Race 671**

Ralf Schumacher
Williams-BMW FW23 193.629kph, 120.316mph

Despite Michael's pole and leading most of the way, it was Ralf Schumacher who headed the first-ever brotherly 1-2. From P2 Ralf hounded his elder sibling, but even with a BMW power advantage, overtake he could not. But once Michael pitted on lap 46 five blistering laps did it, the Michelins relishing the hot track. Resuming from his own stop, Ralf was 5s to the good and Michael accepted the race was over. Montoya dented his reputation and his Williams with a second successive unforced visit to the barriers, which brought out the SC when Barrichello, playing catch-up after an early spin, became involved in the incident too. Late engine failure for Coulthard denied the off-the-pace McLarens a 3-4 finish, P4 going to Räikkönen's Sauber.

POLE POSITION M Schumacher, Ferrari, 1m 15.782s (0.515s), 210.018kph, 130.499mph
LAPS 69 x 4.421 km, 2.747 miles
DISTANCE 305.049 km, 189.549 miles
STARTERS/FINISHERS 22/11
WEATHER Sunny, hot, dry
LAP LEADERS M Schumacher 1-45 (45); R Schumacher 46-69 (24); SC 21-23 (3)
WINNER'S LAPS 1-45 P2, 46-69 P1
FASTEST LAP R Schumacher, Williams-BMW, 1m 17.205s (Lap 50), 206.147kph, 128.094mph
CHAMPIONSHIP M Schumacher 58, Coulthard 40, Barrichello 24, R Schumacher 22, Heidfeld 8

Pos	Driver	Car	Time/gap	Grid	Stops	Tyres
1	R Schumacher	Williams-BMW	1h 34m 31.522s	2	1	M
2	M Schumacher	Ferrari	–20.235s	1	1	B
3	M Häkkinen	McLaren-Mercedes	–40.672s	8	1	B
4	K Räikkönen	Sauber-Petronas	–1m 8.116s	7	1	B
5	J Alesi	Prost-Acer	–1m 10.435s	16	1	M
6	P de la Rosa	Jaguar-Ford	–1 lap	14	2	M

Round 9/17	**EUROPEAN GP** Nürburgring		
	24 June 2001		**Race 672**

Michael Schumacher
Ferrari F2001 204.143kph, 126.849mph

As they accelerated away from the front row, Michael squeezed Ralf hard towards the pit wall, forcing him to lift. The move was excessive if not dangerous but no penalty ensued. It was Ralf who received the penalty. Livid with his brother's behaviour, the irate Ralf had been harrying his brother mercilessly for ten laps as their first stop loomed. But it was there the duel effectively ended, Ralf receiving a stop-go for crossing the white line as he exited the pits. Montoya made amends for recent indiscretions with a strong race to P2, so the Ferraris finished 1-5, Williams 2-4 and the very much third-best McLarens 3-6. Despite another podium for Coulthard, Schumacher's championship lead over the Scot was now a massive 24 points, the rest nowhere.

POLE POSITION M Schumacher, Ferrari, 1m 14.960s (0.266s), 218.804kph, 135.959mph
LAPS 67 x 4.556 km, 2.831 miles
DISTANCE 305.235 km, 189.664 miles
STARTERS/FINISHERS 22/15
WEATHER Sunny, warm, dry
LAP LEADERS M Schumacher 1-28, 30-67 (66); Montoya 29 (1)
WINNER'S LAPS 1-28 P1, 29 P2, 30-67 P1
FASTEST LAP Montoya, Williams-BMW, 1m 18.354s (lap 27), 209.326kph, 130.070mph
CHAMPIONSHIP M Schumacher 68, Coulthard 44, Barrichello 26, R Schumacher 25, Montoya 12

Pos	Driver	Car	Time/gap	Grid	Stops	Tyres
1	M Schumacher	Ferrari	1h 29m 42.724s	1	2	B
2	J P Montoya	Williams-BMW	–4.217s	3	2	M
3	D Coulthard	McLaren-Mercedes	–24.993s	5	1	B
4	R Schumacher	Williams-BMW	–33.345s	2	3	M
5	R Barrichello	Ferrari	–45.495s	4	1	B
6	M Häkkinen	McLaren-Mercedes	–1m 4.868s	6	1	B

Round 10/17	**FRENCH GP** Magny-Cours		
	1 July 2001		**Race 673**

Michael Schumacher
Ferrari F2001 196.093kph, 121.847mph

The Schumacher duel persisted, locking out the front row for the third race running, Ralf winning his maiden pole by .001s on his 26th birthday. His first stint established a narrow 3s lead, but at the first stop on lap 24 it all went wrong. First a slow pit stop due to a driver-induced error allowed brother Michael ahead, and then he lost a further 15s in almost as many laps due to a duff second set of Michelins, at their home race to boot. Ultimately he was fortunate to finish P2, first Coulthard looking good for that position until hit by a pit-lane speeding penalty, then Montoya until his BMW blew on lap 52. A switch by Ross Brawn to a three-stop strategy assisted Barrichello to P3 just ahead of Coulthard. Häkkinen didn't even get to start, gearbox failure.

POLE POSITION R Schumacher, Williams-BMW, 1m 12.989s (0.010), 209.669kph, 130.283mph
LAPS 72 x 4.251 km, 2.641 miles
DISTANCE 305.886 km, 190.069 miles
STARTERS/FINISHERS 21/17
WEATHER Sunny, hot, dry
LAP LEADERS R Schumacher 1-23 (23); M Schumacher 24-25, 31-45, 51-72 (39); Coulthard 26 (1); J P Montoya, Williams-BMW 27-30, 46-50 (9)
WINNER'S LAPS 1-23 P2, 24-25 P1, 26 P3, 27-30 P2, 31-45 P1, 46-50 P2, 51-72 P1
FASTEST LAP Coulthard, McLaren-Mercedes, 1m 16.088s (lap 53), 201.130kph, 124.977mph
CHAMPIONSHIP M Schumacher 78, Coulthard 47, R Schumacher 31, Barrichello 30, Montoya 12

Pos	Driver	Car	Time/gap	Grid	Stops	Tyres
1	M Schumacher	Ferrari	1h 33m 35.636s	2	2	B
2	R Schumacher	Williams-BMW	–10.399s	1	2	M
3	R Barrichello	Ferrari	–16.381s	8	3	B
4	D Coulthard	McLaren-Mercedes	–17.106s	3	3	B
5	J Trulli	Jordan-Honda	–1m 8.285s	5	2	B
6	N Heidfeld	Sauber-Petronas	–1 lap	9	2	B

BRITISH GP Silverstone
15 July 2001
Race 674

Mika Häkkinen
McLaren-Mercedes MP4-16 216.231kph, 134.360mph

After ten rounds Häkkinen had a mere nine points, his motivation in question due to horrendous car reliability plus talk of retirement or a sabbatical. But at Silverstone, Hakk was back! The McLaren wasn't good for pole, but a mistake by the heavier-fuelled M. Schumacher at Copse led to a brilliant lap 5 pass. Once by, two-stopping Mika pulled away from Michael by 2s per lap, and with a 30s advantage at his first stop on lap 20 it became increasingly clear that Ferrari's one-stop strategy was hopelessly wrong. But in the championship, Schumacher's only rival, Coulthard, fell further behind, first-corner contact leading to lap 2 suspension failure. JPM might have beaten Rubens for P3 if Ralf, on an alternate strategy, hadn't refused to let him by.

POLE POSITION M Schumacher, Ferrari, 1m 20.447s (0.082s), 230.059kph, 142.952mph
LAPS 60 x 5.141 km, 3.195 miles
DISTANCE 308.356 km, 191.604 miles
STARTERS/FINISHERS 21/16
WEATHER Cloudy with sunny intervals, warm, dry
LAP LEADERS M Schumacher 1-4 (4); Häkkinen 5-21, 25-60 (53); Montoya 22-24 (3)
WINNER'S LAPS 1-4 P2, 5-21 P1, 22-24 P2, 25-60 P1
FASTEST LAP Häkkinen, McLaren-Mercedes, 1m 23.405s (lap 34), 221.900kph, 137.882mph
CHAMPIONSHIP M Schumacher 84, Coulthard 47, Barrichello 34, R Schumacher 31, Häkkinen 19

Pos	Driver	Car	Time/gap	Grid	Stops	Tyres
1	M Häkkinen	McLaren-Mercedes	1h 25m 33.770s	2	2	B
2	M Schumacher	Ferrari	−33.646s	1	1	B
3	R Barrichello	Ferrari	−59.281s	6	1	B
4	J P Montoya	Williams-BMW	−1m 8.772s	8	2	M
5	K Räikkönen	Sauber-Petronas	−1 lap	7	2	B
6	N Heidfeld	Sauber-Petronas	−1 lap	9	2	B

GERMAN GP Hockenheim
29 July 2001
Race 675

Ralf Schumacher
Williams-BMW FW23 235.351kph, 146.240mph

The start was red-flagged when M. Schumacher crawled away from the grid with gear difficulties. Burti's Prost slammed into him, then launched skywards to land on Bernoldi's Arrows. A lucky escape. At the restart, Montoya's Williams-BMW led convincingly from his maiden pole followed by Ralf then the Ferraris. With a 10s lead he made his first and only stop, but a fuel-rig problem made it long, heat-soak during this delay causing the BMW to detonate two laps later. It left Ralf to romp to a commanding third victory, JPM still looking for his first. Despite a rare Ferrari retirement with fuel pressure on lap 23 Coulthard failed to claw back any points from M. Schumacher, neither Mercedes lasting the Hockenheim thrash, out on laps 13 and 27.

POLE POSITION J P Montoya, Williams-BMW, 1m 38.117s (0.019s), 250.415kph, 155.601mph
LAPS 45 x 6.825 km, 4.241 miles (Race restarted for scheduled 45 laps following accident)
DISTANCE 307.125 km, 190.839 miles
STARTERS/FINISHERS 22/10
WEATHER Cloudy with sunny intervals, very hot, dry
LAP LEADERS Montoya 1-22 (22); R Schumacher 23-45 (23)
WINNER'S LAPS 1-22 P2, 23-45 P1
FASTEST LAP J P Montoya, Williams-BMW, 1m 41.808s (lap 20), 241.336kph, 149.960mph
CHAMPIONSHIP M Schumacher 84, Coulthard 47, R Schumacher 41, Barrichello 40, Häkkinen 19

Pos	Driver	Car	Time/gap	Grid	Stops	Tyres
1	R Schumacher	Williams-BMW	1h 18m 17.873s	2	1	M
2	R Barrichello	Ferrari	−46.117s	6	2	B
3	J Villeneuve	BAR-Honda	−1m 2.806s	12	1	B
4	G Fisichella	Benetton-Renault	−1m 3.477s	17	1	M
5	J Button	Benetton-Renault	−1m 5.454s	18	1	M
6	J Alesi	Prost-Acer	−1m 5.950s	14	1	M

HUNGARIAN GP Hungaroring
19 August 2001
Race 676

Michael Schumacher
Ferrari F2001 180.348kph, 112.063mph

From a ninth pole, his seventh win of the season was a record-equalling 51st career victory. It brought with it a fourth world title for Michael Schumacher with four championship rounds remaining. Dominant in qualifying, loyal Rubens riding shotgun in the race, victory was never in question. Interest such as there was quickly transferred to the outcome between Coulthard and Barrichello, now vying for the championship runner-up spot. In the end, a 1-2 for Ferrari wrapped up the constructors' title too. In many ways the race summed up the season: Ferrari machinery in the ascendancy; Schumacher *über alles*; DC his most enduring rival; Mika's and McLaren's durability below par; the Williams-BMW-Michelin combo simply underbaked. Game, set, match.

POLE POSITION M Schumacher, Ferrari, 1m 14.059s (0.801s), 193.224kph, 120.064mph
LAPS 77 x 3.975 km, 2.470 miles
DISTANCE 306.075 km, 190.186 miles
STARTERS/FINISHERS 22/12
WEATHER Cloudy with sunny intervals, very hot, dry
LAP LEADERS M Schumacher 1-28, 33-52, 55-77 (71); Barrichello 29-30 (2); Coulthard 31-32, 53-54 (4)
WINNER'S LAPS 1-28 P1, 29-31 P3, 32 P2, 33-52 P1, 53 P3, 54 P2, 55-77 P1
FASTEST LAP Häkkinen, McLaren-Mercedes, 1m 16.723s (lap 51), 186.515kph, 115.895mph
CHAMPIONSHIP M Schumacher 94, Coulthard 51, Barrichello 46, R Schumacher 44, Häkkinen 21

Pos	Driver	Car	Time/gap	Grid	Stops	Tyres
1	M Schumacher	Ferrari	1h 41m 49.675s	1	2	B
2	R Barrichello	Ferrari	−3.363s	3	2	B
3	D Coulthard	McLaren-Mercedes	−3.940s	2	2	B
4	R Schumacher	Williams-BMW	−49.687s	4	2	M
5	M Häkkinen	McLaren-Mercedes	−1m 10.293s	6	3	B
6	N Heidfeld	Sauber-Petronas	−1 lap	7	2	B

BELGIAN GP Spa Francorchamps

2 September 2001   **Race 677**

Michael Schumacher

Ferrari F2001 221.050kph, 137.354mph

A lap 4 tangle with Irvine at 190mph Blanchimont resulted in Burti impacting a tyre-barrier almost head on, the Prost driver lucky to survive. The race restarted over a shortened distance, the four-times champion delivering a commanding display. This was assisted by the front row Williams pair eliminating themselves, pole-man Montoya stalling at the second start following an H-HF stall at the first, while R. Schumacher was ignominiously left stranded on his jacks for the post-Burti third start. The other factor was Fisichella's lightning third start in the Benetton, trapping Barrichello and the McLarens as Michael built a 20s lead. Coulthard did well to beat Fisi to P2, Mika a quiet P4, and Rubens P5 after clipping cones at the Bus Stop.

POLE POSITION J P Montoya, Williams-BMW, 1m 52.072s (0.887s), 223.827kph, 139.080mph
LAPS 36 x 6.968 km, 4.330 miles (44 lap race interrupted due to accident. Restarted over 36 laps)
DISTANCE 250.831 km, 155.859 miles
STARTERS/FINISHERS 22/13
WEATHER Overcast, warm, dry
LAP LEADERS M Schumacher 1-36 (36)
WINNER'S LAPS 1-36 P1
FASTEST LAP M Schumacher, Ferrari, 1m 49.748s (lap 3), 228.546kph, 142.012mph
CHAMPIONSHIP M Schumacher 104, Coulthard 57, Barrichello 48, R Schumacher 44, Häkkinen 24

Pos	Driver	Car	Time/gap	Grid	Stops	Tyres
1	M Schumacher	Ferrari	1h 08m 5.002s	3	2	B
2	D Coulthard	McLaren-Mercedes	−10.098s	9	2	B
3	G Fisichella	Benetton-Renault	−27.742s	8	2	M
4	M Häkkinen	McLaren-Mercedes	−36.087s	7	2	B
5	R Barrichello	Ferrari	−54.521s	5	2	B
6	J Alesi	Jordan-Honda	−59.684s	13	2	B

ITALIAN GP Monza

16 September 2001   **Race 678**

Juan Pablo Montoya

Williams-BMW FW23 239.103kph, 148.572mph

Friday practice began three days after 9/11. Saturday brought Zanardi's Lausitzring calamity. Paddock tension was palpable. Ferrari raced with black nosecones. The new champion proposed a first lap no-overtaking pact, Villeneuve's opposition snuffing out the idea. On Sunday Montoya won his maiden GP from his third pole in four races. Opposition came from the lighter-fuelled Barrichello whose potentially winning first-stint lead was negated by a refuelling hitch. The Ferrari got by Montoya on lap 9 when his Michelins blistered, but once they cleaned up and JPM adapted he regained his winning pace. The subdued Schumachers finished P3 and P4, both McLarens failing before lap 20. McLaren revealed Räikkönen would replace Häkkinen for 2002.

POLE POSITION J P Montoya, Williams-BMW, 1m 22.216s (0.312s), 253.658kph, 157.616mph
LAPS 53 x 5.793 km, 3.600 miles
DISTANCE 306.749 km, 190.605 miles
STARTERS/FINISHERS 22/13
WEATHER Cloudy with sunny intervals, warm, dry
LAP LEADERS Montoya 1-8, 20-28, 42-53 (29); Barrichello 9-19, 36-41 (17); R Schumacher 29-35 (7)
WINNER'S LAPS 1-8 P1, 9-19 P2, 20-28 P1, 29-35 P3, 36-41 P2, 42-53 P1
FASTEST LAP R Schumacher, Williams-BMW, 1m 25.073 (lap 39), 245.140kph, 152.323mph
CHAMPIONSHIP M Schumacher 107, Coulthard 57, Barrichello 54, R Schumacher 48, Häkkinen 24

Pos	Driver	Car	Time/gap	Grid	Stops	Tyres
1	J P Montoya	Williams-BMW	1h 16m 58.493s	1	1	M
2	R Barrichello	Ferrari	−5.175s	2	2	B
3	R Schumacher	Williams-BMW	−17.335s	4	1	M
4	M Schumacher	Ferrari	−24.991s	3	2	B
5	P de la Rosa	Jaguar-Ford	−1m 14.984s	10	1	M
6	J Villeneuve	BAR-Honda	−1m 22.469s	15	1	B

UNITED STATES GP Indianapolis

30 September 2001   **Race 679**

Mika Häkkinen

McLaren-Mercedes MP4-16 198.038kph, 123.056mph

The US GP went ahead, the mood lighter than expected as normality slowly returned post-9/11. Häkkinen won his penultimate race in vintage style. Demoted to start P4 for a pit-lane breach, Mika drove his well-balanced, one-stopping McLaren heavy and long, nursing his tyres. Initially P5, he was last to stop, but once ahead put the hammer down. Montoya's one-stopping Williams might have challenged for victory but retired on lap 39, while four laps from the end Barrichello suffered Ferrari's only race-engine failure of the season, losing a certain P2 and with it all but a slim chance of championship runner-up spot. A muted M. Schumacher finished P2, and as Coulthard succinctly put it, 'I went from seventh to third without passing anyone!'

POLE POSITION M Schumacher, Ferrari, 1m 11.708s (0.278s), 210.453kph, 130.770mph
LAPS 73 x 4.192 km, 2.605 miles
DISTANCE 306.016 km, 190.150 miles
STARTERS/FINISHERS 22/15
WEATHER Cloudy with sunny intervals, warm, dry
LAP LEADERS M Schumacher 1-4, 27-33, 36-38 (14); R Barrichello, Ferrari 5-26, 46-49 (26); Montoya 34-35 (2); Häkkinen 39-45, 50-73 (31)
WINNER'S LAPS 1-23 P5, 24-26 P4, 27-35 P3, 36-38 P2, 39-45 P1, 46-49 P2, 50-73 P1
FASTEST LAP J P Montoya, Williams-BMW, 1m 14.448s (lap 35), 202.707kph, 125.957mph
CHAMPIONSHIP M Schumacher 113, Coulthard 61, Barrichello 54, R Schumacher 48, Häkkinen 34

Pos	Driver	Car	Time/gap	Grid	Stops	Tyres
1	M Häkkinen	McLaren-Mercedes	1h 32m 42.840s	4	1	B
2	M Schumacher	Ferrari	−11.046s	1	1	B
3	D Coulthard	McLaren-Mercedes	−12.043s	7	1	B
4	J Trulli	Jordan-Honda	−57.423s	8	1	B
5	E Irvine	Jaguar-Ford	−1m 12.434s	14	2	M
6	N Heidfeld	Sauber-Petronas	−1m 12.996s	6	1	B

JAPANESE GP Suzuka

14 October 2001   Race 680

Michael Schumacher

Ferrari F2001 212.664kph, 132.144mph

M. Schumacher's 11th pole produced an unchallenged ninth victory. His opening laps on new Bridgestones were far too quick for Montoya's Williams, using scrubbed Michelins to reduce the debilitating 'graining' effect. Once his tyres 'came in' after some ten laps Montoya could hold the gap, but by then it was 10s. To beat Coulthard to runner-up spot, Ferrari tried to fix a win for Barrichello, but first he had to snatch P2 from Montoya. Screaming through 130R on lap 2, the lighter three-stop Ferrari exited well and into the chicane got a run down the inside of JPM. But on the straight the Williams out-dragged the Ferrari and, millimetres apart, retook P2 at turn one, Rubens' chance gone. So with P3, DC was a worthy if distant championship runner-up.

POLE POSITION M Schumacher, Ferrari, 1m 32.484s (0.700s), 228.065kph, 141.713mph
LAPS 53 x 5.859 km, 3.640 miles
DISTANCE 310.331 km, 192.831 miles
STARTERS/FINISHERS 22/17
WEATHER Cloudy with sunny intervals, warm, dry
LAP LEADERS M Schumacher 1-18, 24-36, 39-53 (46); Montoya 19-21, 37-38 (5); R Schumacher 22-23 (2)
WINNER'S LAPS 1-18 P1, 19-21 P4, 22-23 P3, 24-36 P1, 37 P3, 38 P2, 39-53 P1
FASTEST LAP R Schumacher, Williams-BMW, 1m 36.944s (lap 46), 217.573kph, 135.194mph
CHAMPIONSHIP M Schumacher 123, Coulthard 65, Barrichello 56, R Schumacher 49, Häkkinen 37

Pos	Driver	Car	Time/gap	Grid	Stops	Tyres
1	M Schumacher	Ferrari	1h 27m 33.298s	1	2	B
2	J P Montoya	Williams-BMW	–3.154s	2	2	M
3	D Coulthard	McLaren-Mercedes	–23.262s	7	2	B
4	M Häkkinen	McLaren-Mercedes	–35.539s	5	2	B
5	R Barrichello	Ferrari	–36.544s	4	3	B
6	R Schumacher	Williams-BMW	–37.122s	3	3	M

2001 CHAMPIONSHIP FACTS AND FOLKLORE

■ Electronic driver aids such as traction control, launch control and fully automatic gearboxes were permitted from the Spanish GP onwards. Unable to suppress ongoing suspicion or to adequately police potential lawbreakers, reinstatement was the only way the FIA could provide a level playing field, the argument being that what cannot be enforced cannot be banned.

■ Safety measures involved enlarged cockpit and chassis deformable structures and uprated loading tests for these and the roll-hoop. Wheel tethers were doubled-up, but even this added precaution could not save the life of an Australian marshal at the opening round.

■ Exotic metals, specifically beryllium, were banned in engine manufacture on health and cost grounds.

■ Between the German and Hungarian races a three-week summer break was introduced along with a testing ban, a measure to bring some respite to hard-pressed families during the long 30-week season.

■ Michelin returned to the GP racetracks after a 15-year absence, rekindling tyre wars with Bridgestone.

■ To compensate for the anticipated reduction in lap times due to the use of softer rubber, changes to front and rear wing regulations/dimensions were introduced, calculated to reduce downforce. It proved to be not nearly enough.

■ Tyre supplier and tyre choice became an ever more critical factor. Bridgestone, for example, enjoyed superiority in wet weather and fast corners, Michelin better under traction and braking, also thriving on hot track surfaces and high-speed circuits.

■ However, Michelins in particular suffered from tyre blistering and a phenomenon known as 'graining', a performance drop-off as tyres went through a traction degradation cycle lasting around ten laps.

■ Another factor influencing 2001 results was problems with the refuelling rigs. Supplier Intertechnique introduced a new kit with software-controlled delivery. Misprograming or software glitches took their toll at pit stops.

■ Under the auspices of the European Car Manufacturers Association, ECMA, the participating F1 manufacturers began to rattle their sabres with talk of a breakaway championship when the existing Concorde Agreement expired in 2008, although the F1 teams were unhappy they hadn't been notified of such a move.

■ This expression of fundamental discontent was triggered by the transfer of the F1 TV rights to the German media group Kirch; 50% owners EM.TV got into financial trouble, were bought out by Pay-TV Kirch Media Group who further increased their holding in SLEC to 75%.

■ Having pushed the design envelope last year, Ferrari's F-2001 was a highly effective logical development, fully a match for the McLaren MP4-16.

■ With their 11th drivers' championship Ferrari equalled McLaren's record, while Sepang was the Scuderia's 50th 1-2 finish.

■ At their 51st, round seven at Monaco, Schumacher broke Coulthard's early season challenge to streak away to his fourth world title, equalling Prost and just one short of Fangio's record.

■ Other records and milestones included, for the third time, a record-equalling nine race victories, these taking the German three ahead of Alain Prost's all-time career win-record of 51, established in 1993.

■ By the 17th and final championship round Schumacher had scored points in all but two races to produce a record points total in a single season, also exceeding Prost's career points record.

■ This also established a record 58-point gap to championship runner-up Coulthard, who with little more than half the Ferrari driver's points total still managed to retain the spot despite not adding to his two early season victories.

■ Schumacher's younger brother Ralf opened his GP account with three wins for Williams, so remarkably all but five of the 17 championship races were attributed to the one family, Ralf's Imola win the first by the brother of an existing winner.

■ Montréal was a Schumacher-fest, the brothers dominating qualifying and the race to create more F1 history, the first-ever brotherly 1-2.

■ Ralf's three and rookie Montoya's maiden victory were the first for Williams since Villeneuve's championship year in 1997, but the team and its two key suppliers BMW and Michelin were not yet ready to win championships.

■ Nevertheless, for the Williams-led triumvirate the Imola victory was a big moment. For Michelin it was success in their fourth race back after 17 years away, for BMW a win in

RACE 677, Belgian GP: Schumacher's commanding display at Spa was his eighth win of the season and his 52nd career victory, topping Alain Prost's record from 1993.

their 21st race since return. It was also BMW's first victory since their current competitions boss, Gerhard Berger, won for them and for Benetton at the 1986 Mexican GP.

■ At McLaren, the Australian GP marked their 100th race with Mercedes. After ending the 1990s with back-to-back championships, the Anglo-German combo had lost out to Ferrari in 2000 and it quickly became apparent that 2001 was unlikely to produce anything better.

■ Coulthard tried his utmost to mount a championship-winning campaign in a car no more than the equal of the Ferrari, while lead driver Häkkinen seemed to have lost his spark and began talking about a sabbatical year, ultimately taking full retirement at the end of the season.

■ Admittedly, Häkkinen's motivation was sorely tested by poor McLaren reliability, not winning a race until the 11th round of the championship at Silverstone.

■ The Renault team, still badged Benetton in 2001, vied with Jordan and BAR for best of the rest. But as one French team began to re-emerge, another departed. Prost went

bust, pulling out at the end of the season, a victim of the deepening world financial recession amplified by 9/11. By Suzuka there was increasing talk of an F1 cash crisis, of teams going bust and the need to control costs.

■ The Prost team endured a fraught final season. Luciano Burti suffered serious injuries from a crash in the Belgian GP, forced to sit out the rest of the season. He was replaced by Czech driver Tomáš Enge, one of a surprising five drivers to be fielded by the team in 2001.

■ For the final five races Frentzen joined Prost from Jordan in a direct swap with Alesi. It made no appreciable difference to the fortunes of either, Alesi's 13-year career ending with just a single race victory after 201 GPs. It might have been so different.

■ Bobby Rahal wooed Adrian Newey with a big money offer to leave McLaren for Jaguar, but Ron Dennis jumped straight in with a counter proposal. This extended Newey's McLaren deal by three years to mid-2005 but with stated responsibility for only the 2002 and 2003 cars. After that,

speculation went, McLaren would help Newey fulfil an ambition to design an America's Cup yacht-race winner.
- Purportedly Rahal had a signed agreement with Newey and was duly upset when his friend – their relationship going back to 1984 March days – reneged on the deal. But Rahal was out by Spa, marginalised by the Lauda/Irvine phalanx in the politically charged environment at Jaguar.
- The season had begun with the death of trackside marshal Graham Beveridge and there were to be many other sad moments in 2001.
- Five-times GP winner Michele Alboreto was killed testing a Le Mans Audi R8 at the Lausitzring.
- Vittorio Brambilla, nicknamed the Monza Gorilla, died of a heart attack aged 63, his wet-weather 1975 Austrian GP victory leaving an indelible entry in F1 folklore.
- Paul Morgan, co-founder of Ilmor Engineering, builders of the Mercedes-Benz GP engine, died in a plane crash.
- At the age of 77 Ken Tyrrell died in August, glad no doubt to have seen Sir Jackie Stewart become the third Formula 1 knight in 2001.
- Go-Go-Go became Stop-Stop-Stop when Murray Walker, the

voice of F1 television coverage in the UK, retired following the USA GP. Aged 76 he had spent over 50 years in the motorsport broadcasting business.
- The NYC twin towers was one of two disasters that stunned the Monza Paddock, the other an appalling accident to F1 refugee Alex Zanardi. After his desperately disappointing return to F1 with Williams in 1999, he had returned to Champ Cars, the series he had dominated with back-to-back championships in 1997–98.
- At the 16th round of the 2001 series held at the Lausitzring in Germany, he spun on to the racetrack from the pit-lane exit and was T-boned at 190mph, losing both his legs. His courageous return to touring car racing in 2003 and beyond was testament to an indomitable human spirit.
- Also on a forward-looking note, Fernando Alonso, Kimi Räikkönen and Juan Pablo Montoya made their debuts in 2001. The Columbian won his 15th race driving for Williams at Monza; Räikkönen was signed by McLaren to replace Häkkinen in 2002, and Alonso's grooming would next be a year spent as a Renault test driver.

Championship ranking	Championship points	Driver nationality	2001 Drivers Championship		Races contested	Race victories	Podiumse excl. victories	Races led	Lights to flag victories	Laps led	Poles	Fastest laps	Triple Crowns
			Driver	Car									
1	123	GER	Michael Schumacher	Ferrari	17	9	5	13	1	533	11	3	2
2	65	GBR	David Coulthard	McLaren-Mercedes	17	2	8	6		77	2	3	
3	56	BRA	Rubens Barrichello	Ferrari	17		10	5		81			
4	49	GER	Ralf Schumacher	Williams-BMW	17	3	2	6	1	141	1	5	
5	37	FIN	Mika Häkkinen	McLaren-Mercedes	16	2	1	3		110		3	
6	31	COL	Juan Pablo Montoya	Williams-BMW	17	1	3	9		122	3	3	
7	12	CAN	Jacques Villeneuve	BAR-Honda	17		2						
8	12	GER	Nick Heidfeld	Sauber-Petronas	17		1						
9	12	ITA	Jarno Trulli	Jordan-Honda	17			1		1			
10	9	FIN	Kimi Räikkönen	Sauber-Petronas	17								
11	8	ITA	Giancarlo Fisichella	Benetton-Renault	17		1						
12	6	GBR	Eddie Irvine	Jaguar-Ford	17		1						
13	6	GER	Heinz-Harald Frentzen	Jordan-Honda (10) Prost-Acer (5)	15								
14	5	FRA	Olivier Panis	BAR-Honda	17								
15	5	FRA	Jean Alesi	Prost-Acer (12) Jordan-Honda (5)	17								
16	3	ESP	Pedro de la Rosa	Jaguar-Ford	13								
17	2	GBR	Jenson Button	Benetton-Renault	17								
18	1	NLD	Jos Verstappen	Arrows-Asiatech	17								

Championship ranking	Championship points	Team/Marque nationality	2001 Constructors Championship		Engine maker nationality	Races contested	Race victories	1-2 finishes	Podiums excl. victories	Races led	Laps led	Poles	Fastest laps
			Chassis	Engine									
1	179	ITA	Ferrari F2001	Ferrari 3.0 V10	ITA	17	9	3	15	15	614	11	3
2	102	GBR	McLaren MP4-16	Mercedes-Benz 3.0 V10	GER	17	4		9	9	187	2	6
3	80	GBR	Williams FW23	BMW 3.0 V10	GER	17	4		5	11	263	4	8
4	21	SUI	Sauber C20	Petronas 3.0 V10	ITA	17			1				
5	19	IRL	Jordan EJ11	Honda 3.0 V10	JPN	17				1	1		
6	17	GBR	BAR 003	Honda 3.0 V10	JPN	17			2				
7	10	FRA	Benetton B201	Renault 3.0 V10	FRA	17			1				
8	9	GBR	Jaguar R2	Ford Cosworth 3.0 V10	GBR	17			1				
9	4	FRA	Prost AP04	Acer 3.0 V10	ITA	17							
10	1	GBR	Arrows A22	Asiatech 3.0 V10	FRA	17							

2002

Ferrari take the Michael

THE TALE OF THE TITLE

■ Michael Schumacher's fifth world championship equalled Fangio's extraordinary 1950s achievement.
■ If Ferrari dominated the preceding season, their 2002 superiority was overwhelmingly crushing.
■ Not since McLaren-Honda in 1988 had such pre-eminence existed, Ferrari winning 15 races, the rest two.
■ But in 1988 the racing was electrically charged due to the intra-team rivalry between Senna and Prost.
■ By contrast, Ferrari team orders – instigated as early as round six in Austria – made a mockery of GP racing.
■ And adding insult to injury, Schumacher clumsily attempted a staged dead-heat at Indianapolis.
■ Schumacher won the title before August, sooner than at any time before or since, six rounds remaining.
■ The best car, driver, race-tyres, plus bullet-proof reliability produced a new record 11 wins in the season.
■ Ferrari only failed to win two races, these going to Ralf Schumacher for Williams and Coulthard's McLaren.
■ For their fourth successive constructors' cup, Ferrari won as many points as all the other teams combined.
■ The Scuderia completed nine 1-2 team finishes and led 79% of all racing laps.
■ But Ferrari dominance and results manipulation hit TV audiences worldwide.
■ And with the global recession still biting, Arrows going bust resulted in the smallest grid in 20 years.
■ So despite the arrival of Toyota, by the end of 2002 F1 faced crisis, the FIA's mantra: 'Change or die'.
■ And not forgetting: no Hakk comeback.

THE CHASE FOR THE CHAMPIONSHIP

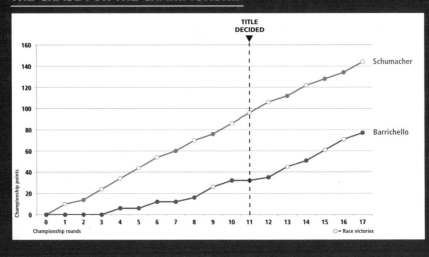

AUSTRALIAN GP Melbourne
3 March 2002 — Race 681

Michael Schumacher
Ferrari F2001 193.011kph, 119.932mph

First-corner mayhem eliminated eight cars, R. Schumacher's Williams terrifyingly launched over Barrichello's pole-sitting Ferrari. Following two SCs the race proper began on lap 12, surprise early leader Coulthard retiring instantly with gearbox trouble but wrong-footing M. Schumacher. Montoya took that chance to make a tyre-smoking pass for the lead, their encounter brief but thrilling. But once by on lap 17 the Ferrari's Bridgestones were decisive, the Michelin runners suffering from poor grip. On his McLaren debut Räikkönen finished P3 and home-boy Webber made a dream start with P5 for Minardi. The depleted field also brought debutants Toyota a first point, but all this happened well behind M. Schumacher, still driving last year's car.

POLE POSITION R Barrichello, Ferrari, 1m 25.843s (0.005s), 222.392kph, 138.188mph
LAPS 58 x 5.303 km, 3.295 miles
DISTANCE 307.574 km, 191.117 miles
STARTERS/FINISHERS 22/8
WEATHER Overcast, warm, dry
LAP LEADERS D Coulthard, McLaren-Mercedes 1-10 (10); M Schumacher 11, 17-58 (43); Montoya 12-16 (5); SC 1-5, 10-11 (7)
WINNER'S LAPS 1-5 P4, 6-8 P3, 9-10 P2, 11 P1, 12-16 P2, 17-58 P1
FASTEST LAP Räikkönen, McLaren-Mercedes, 1m 28.541s (lap 37), 215.615kph, 133.977mph
CHAMPIONSHIP M Schumacher 10, Montoya 6, Räikkönen 4, Irvine 3, Webber 2

Pos	Driver	Car	Time/gap	Grid	Stops	Tyres
1	M Schumacher	Ferrari	1h 35m 36.792s	2	1	B
2	J P Montoya	Williams-BMW	–18.627s	6	1	M
3	K Räikkönen	McLaren-Mercedes	–25.066s	5	2	M
4	E Irvine	Jaguar-Ford	–1 lap	19	1	M
5	M Webber	Minardi-Asiatech	–2 laps	18	1	M
6	M Salo	Toyota	–2 laps	14	2	M

MALAYSIAN GP Sepang
17 March 2002 — Race 682

Ralf Schumacher
Williams-BMW FW24 197.680kph, 122.833mph

From pole, M. Schumacher chopped inside. From P2 Montoya went for the outside. A battle of wills, neither would cede, first-corner contact inevitable. Schumacher lost a front wing, Montoya received a controversial stop-go. So Barrichello led R. Schumacher, but as the track got hotter and rubbered in, reaching 46°C, the Michelins on the Williams got quicker and quicker, the race decided well before Barrichello suffered a rare Ferrari engine failure on lap 40. And from P13 JPM recovered to bring Williams their first 1-2 since 1997. With the McLarens slow and unreliable, a last-lap suspension break denied Button his first podium. The beneficiary was M. Schumacher, P3 from P22 on completion of lap 1, and still using the 2001 car.

POLE POSITION M Schumacher, Ferrari, 1m 35.266s (0.231s), 209.464kph, 130.155mph
LAPS 56 x 5.543 km, 3.444 miles
DISTANCE 310.408 km, 192.879 miles
STARTERS/FINISHERS 22/13
WEATHER Cloudy, very hot, dry
LAP LEADERS R Barrichello, Ferrari 1-21, 32-35 (25); R Schumacher 22-31, 36-56 (31)
WINNER'S LAPS 1-21 P2, 22-31 P1, 32-35 P2, 36-56 P1
FASTEST LAP Montoya, Williams-BMW, 1m 38.049s (lap 38), 203.518kph, 126.461mph
CHAMPIONSHIP M Schumacher 14, Montoya 12, R Schumacher 10, Räikkönen 4, Irvine 3

Pos	Driver	Car	Time/gap	Grid	Stops	Tyres
1	R Schumacher	Williams-BMW	1h 34m 12.912s	4	1	M
2	J P Montoya	Williams-BMW	–39.699s	2	3	M
3	M Schumacher	Ferrari	–1m 1.794s	1	3	B
4	J Button	Renault	–1m 9.766s	8	1	M
5	N Heidfeld	Sauber-Petronas	–1 lap	7	2	B
6	F Massa	Sauber-Petronas	–1 lap	14	1	B

BRAZILIAN GP Interlagos
31 March 2002 — Race 683

Michael Schumacher
Ferrari F2002 200.098kph, 124.335mph

Williams, one-all with Ferrari, blew victory at round three. From pole Montoya's launch control hesitated, then reticently or fairly he conceded the lead to M. Schumacher at turn one. This enabled his more ruthless adversary to damagingly chop him at turn four, Montoya in quest of a new front wing. And second, wrongly believing Ferrari/Bridgestone were inescapably two-stopping, Ralf began to push too late, failing to take the lead at the pit stop. He harried Michael for the final 15 laps, but passing the new F2002 was something else. The McLarens fought the emerging Renaults over the placings, while from his P8 grid spot two-stop local hero Barrichello stormed to P1 in 14 laps, only for the hydraulics to fail after leading three laps.

POLE POSITION Montoya, Williams-BMW, 1m 13.780s (0.310s), 210.252kph, 130.645mph
LAPS 71 x 4.309 km, 2.677 miles
DISTANCE 305.909 km, 190.083 miles
STARTERS/FINISHERS 22/13
WEATHER Cloudy with sunny intervals, very hot, dry
LAP LEADERS M Schumacher 1-13, 17-39, 45-71 (63); R Barrichello, Ferrari 14-16 (3); R Schumacher 40-44 (5)
WINNER'S LAPS 1-13 P1, 14-16 P2, 17-39 P1, 40-44 P2, 45-71 P1
FASTEST LAP Montoya, Williams-BMW, 1m 16.079s (lap 60), 203.898kph, 126.697mph
CHAMPIONSHIP M Schumacher 24, R Schumacher 16, Montoya 14, Button 6, Räikkönen 4

Pos	Driver	Car	Time/gap	Grid	Stops	Tyres
1	M Schumacher	Ferrari	1h 31m 43.663s	2	1	B
2	R Schumacher	Williams-BMW	–0.588s	3	1	M
3	D Coulthard	McLaren-Mercedes	–59.110s	4	1	M
4	J Button	Renault	–1m 6.883s	7	1	M
5	J P Montoya	Williams-BMW	–1m 7.563s	1	2	M
6	M Salo	Toyota	–1 lap	10	1	M

Ferrari F2002

SAN MARINO GP Imola

14 April 2002   **Race 684**

Michael Schumacher

Ferrari F2002 205.613kph, 127.762mph

The Ferrari F2002's debut win in Brazil was unexpected, but here in Italy it simply blew the rest away. From pole, Michael had pulled nearly 20s on Ralf by half-distance, and once Barrichello had been eased past at the first stop, a Ferrari 1-2 was guaranteed. Both teams chose two-stops, by the finish Williams/Michelin personnel stunned by the margin of defeat, the rest despondent. The new Ferrari was a step forward, its Bridgestones working in perfect harmony now that McLaren had defected to Michelin. After four rounds Michael had only dropped six championship points. Behind Ferrari and Williams the McLarens qualified on row three, Räikkönen retiring, Coulthard a lapped P6 and beaten by Button in the Renault on pure race pace.

POLE POSITION M Schumacher, Ferrari, 1m 21.091s (0.064s), 218.998kph, 136.079mph
LAPS 62 x 4.933 km, 3.065 miles
DISTANCE 305.609 km, 189.897 miles
STARTERS/FINISHERS 21/11
WEATHER Cloudy, warm, dry
LAP LEADERS M Schumacher 1-31, 33-46, 48-62 (60); Barrichello 32, 47 (2)
WINNER'S LAPS 1-31 P1, 32 P2, 33-46 P1, 47 P2, 48-62 P1
FASTEST LAP Barrichello, Ferrari, 1m 24.170s (lap 38), 210.987kph, 131.101mph
CHAMPIONSHIP M Schumacher 34, R Schumacher 20, Montoya 17, Button 8, Barrichello 6

Pos	Driver	Car	Time/gap	Grid	Stops	Tyres
1	M Schumacher	Ferrari	1h 29m 10.789s	1	2	B
2	R Barrichello	Ferrari	−17.907s	2	2	B
3	R Schumacher	Williams-BMW	−19.755s	3	2	M
4	J P Montoya	Williams-BMW	−44.725s	4	2	M
5	J Button	Renault	−1m 23.395s	9	2	M
6	D Coulthard	McLaren-Mercedes	−1 lap	6	2	M

SPANISH GP Cataluña

28 April 2002   **Race 685**

Michael Schumacher

Ferrari F2002 203.753kph, 126.607mph

M. Schumacher got his problems out of the way prior to the race, forced to switch to the T-car during the morning warm-up, then driving from pole to an overwhelming victory, his hat-trick. His opponents were less fortunate: teammate Barrichello's gearbox failed ahead of the formation lap, the F2002 wheeled away; Räikkönen had a McLaren rear wing collapse on lap 4; brother Ralf made a damaging trip through the gravel on lap 23, putting him out of contention, while Montoya lost time when prematurely released at his second stop but at least managed a distant P2. Coulthard brought McLaren a welcome podium but no team or driver seemed capable of taking the fight to Schumacher, who already held a decisive championship lead.

POLE POSITION M Schumacher, Ferrari, 1m 16.364s (0.326s), 222.984kph, 138.556mph
LAPS 65 x 4.730 km, 2.939 miles
DISTANCE 307.327 km, 190.964 miles
STARTERS/FINISHERS 19/16
WEATHER Cloudy, warm, dry
LAP LEADERS M Schumacher 1-65 (65)
WINNER'S LAPS 1-65 P1
FASTEST LAP M Schumacher, Ferrari, 1m 20.355s (lap 49), 211.909kph, 131.675mph
CHAMPIONSHIP M Schumacher 44, Montoya 23, R Schumacher 20, Coulthard 9, Button 8

Pos	Driver	Car	Time/gap	Grid	Stops	Tyres
1	M Schumacher	Ferrari	1h 30m 29.981s	1	2	B
2	J P Montoya	Williams-BMW	−35.629s	4	2	M
3	D Coulthard	McLaren-Mercedes	−42.623s	7	2	M
4	N Heidfeld	Sauber-Petronas	−1m 6.696s	8	2	B
5	F Massa	Sauber-Petronas	−1m 18.973s	11	2	B
6	H-H Frentzen	Arrows-Ford	−1m 20.429s	10	2	B

Round 6/17	**AUSTRIAN GP** A1-Ring		**Michael Schumacher**

AUSTRIAN GP A1-Ring
28 April 2002 — Race 686

Michael Schumacher
Ferrari F2002 196.344kph, 122.003mph

As the grandstands prepared to acclaim Barrichello's decisive victory from pole over M. Schumacher, he surrendered victory to his team leader in the closing moments of the race. The outcry against these cynical Ferrari team orders was loud and immediate. Even the offending drivers looked suitably chastened on the podium, Ferrari boss Jean Todt unrepentant despite a summons to appear before the FIA. Between laps 23 and 36 there was a double SC period. The second incident looked horrific, rookie Sato fortunate to escape from a violent, explosive smash when his Jordan was T-boned at turn two by Heidfeld's out-of-control Sauber. This briefly allowed Ralf to get between the Ferraris, but it was a mirage, the Williams yet to stop.

POLE POSITION Barrichello, Ferrari, 1m 08.082s (0.282s), 228.747kph, 142.137mph
LAPS 71 x 4.326 km, 2.688 miles
DISTANCE 307.146 km, 190.852 miles
STARTERS/FINISHERS 22/12
WEATHER Cloudy, warm, dry
LAP LEADERS Barrichello 1-61, 63-70 (69); M Schumacher 62, 71 (2); SC 25-36 (12)
WINNER'S LAPS 1-24 P2, 25-27 P3, 28 P4, 29-31 P3, 32-33, P4, 34-46 P3, 47-61 P2, 62 P1, 63-70 P2, 71 P1
FASTEST LAP M Schumacher, Ferrari, 1m 09.298s (lap 68), 224.733kph, 139.643mph
CHAMPIONSHIP M Schumacher 54, Montoya 27, R Schumacher 23, Barrichello 12, Coulthard 10

Pos	Driver	Car	Time/gap	Grid	Stops	Tyres
1	M Schumacher	Ferrari	1h 33m 15.562s	3	2	B
2	R Barrichello	Ferrari	−0.182s	1	2	B
3	J P Montoya	Williams-BMW	−17.730s	4	1	M
4	R Schumacher	Williams-BMW	−18.448s	2	1	M
5	G Fisichella	Jordan-Honda	−49.965s	15	1	B
6	D Coulthard	McLaren-Mercedes	−50.672s	8	1	M

McLaren-Mercedes MP4/17

Round 7/17	**MONACO GP** Monte Carlo		**David Coulthard**

MONACO GP Monte Carlo
26 May 2002 — Race 687

David Coulthard
McLaren-Mercedes MP4-17 149.280kph, 92.758mph

Coulthard's second Monaco victory dealt Maranello its only genuine defeat of the season. But it did not signify a resurgence, the winding street circuit masking McLaren shortcomings while showcasing Michelin benefits. Beating pole-sitter Montoya into Ste Devote, Coulthard resisted the Columbian's close attentions for half the race, the Schumachers completing a close-fought four-car convoy. Of these Michael was first to pit, and once JPM's BMW failed on lap 47 and brother Ralf fell back with tyre issues the world champion made his victory bid. But DC just had the speed to hold his lead when he made his late stop, Michael exerting severe pressure for the final 27 laps. Only the Schumachers and the joyous Coulthard completed the distance.

POLE POSITION J P Montoya, Williams-BMW, 1m 16.676s (0.392s), 158.224kph, 98.316mph
LAPS 78 x 3.370 km, 2.094 miles
DISTANCE 262.860 km, 163.333 miles
STARTERS/FINISHERS 22/12
WEATHER Sunny, hot, dry
LAP LEADERS Coulthard 1-78 (78)
WINNER'S LAPS 1-78 P1
FASTEST LAP R Barrichello, Ferrari, 1m 18.023s (lap 68), 155.492kph, 96.619mph
CHAMPIONSHIP M Schumacher 60, R Schumacher 27, Montoya 27, Coulthard 20, Barrichello 12

Pos	Driver	Car	Time/gap	Grid	Stops	Tyres
1	D Coulthard	McLaren-Mercedes	1h 45m 39.055s	2	1	M
2	M Schumacher	Ferrari	−1.049s	3	1	B
3	R Schumacher	Williams-BMW	−1m 17.449s	4	2	M
4	J Trulli	Renault	−1 lap	7	1	M
5	G Fisichella	Jordan-Honda	−1 lap	11	1	B
6	H-H Frentzen	Arrows-Ford	−1 lap	12	2	B

CANADIAN GP Montréal
9 June 2002   Race 688

Michael Schumacher
Ferrari F2002 195.682kph, 121.591mph

Montoya's second consecutive pole ended the same way, engine failure. Seven seconds behind with 14 to go, his two-stop Williams was closing down M. Schumacher's leading, one-stop and tyre-blistered Ferrari at a rate indicating a very close finish. Then boom. Coulthard had qualified only P8 but superb launch control, a SC, good strategy and aggressive driving brought P2. Early leader Barrichello looked to have the beating of DC but cost himself a passing chance by strangely straight-lining the chicane in sympathy with Coulthard's own lap 60 error. Michael's sixth win from eight races and 43-point advantage turned attention to 'best of the rest'. Williams' woes and Coulthard's recent success was producing a really close championship battle – for second!

POLE POSITION J P Montoya, Williams-BMW, 1m 12.836s (0.182s), 215.547kph, 133.935mph
LAPS 70 x 4.361 km, 2.710 miles
DISTANCE 305.270 km, 189.686 miles
STARTERS/FINISHERS 22/15
WEATHER Overcast, hot, dry
LAP LEADERS Barrichello 1-25 (25); M Schumacher 26-37, 51-70 (32); Montoya 38-50 (13); SC 15-17 (3)
WINNER'S LAPS 1-13 P3, 14-25 P2, 26-37 P1, 38-50 P2, 51-70 P1
FASTEST LAP J P Montoya, Williams-BMW, 1m 15.960s (Lap 50), 206.682kph, 128.427mph
CHAMPIONSHIP M Schumacher 70, R Schumacher 27, Montoya 27, Coulthard 26, Barrichello 16

Pos	Driver	Car	Time/gap	Grid	Stops	Tyres
1	M Schumacher	Ferrari	1h 33m 36.111s	2	1	B
2	D Coulthard	McLaren-Mercedes	–1.132s	8	1	M
3	R Barrichello	Ferrari	–7.082s	3	2	B
4	K Räikkönen	McLaren-Mercedes	–37.563s	5	1	M
5	G Fisichella	Jordan-Honda	–42.812s	6	1	B
6	J Trulli	Renault	–48.948s	10	1	M

EUROPEAN GP Nürburgring
23 June 2002   Race 689

Rubens Barrichello
Ferrari F2002 194.741kph, 121.007mph

Williams, Ferrari, McLaren, Renault qualified in pairs, but on Sunday the Ferraris and their Bridgestones were in a league apart. Rubens made the better start, Michael briefly stuck behind brother Ralf, and by his first stop on lap 25 led Ralf in P3 by 40s. And this time he didn't get the call, so after 32 winless races Barrichello won Ferrari victory number two to join the throng intent on championship runner-up spot. But was it real or stage-managed? A Schumacher spin on lap 23 suggested it was a race, Barrichello's 0.294s winning margin indicating otherwise. In the 'other' contest, qualifying kings Williams rooted their Michelins in the race, Montoya's spin on bald tyres collecting the luckless Coulthard, Räikkönen first home for 'the rest'.

POLE POSITION J P Montoya, Williams-BMW, 1m 29.906s (0.009s), 206.055kph, 128.037mph
LAPS 60 x 5.146 km, 3.198 miles
DISTANCE 308.743 km, 191.844 miles
STARTERS/FINISHERS 22/16
WEATHER Overcast, warm, dry
LAP LEADERS Barrichello 1-60 (60)
WINNER'S LAPS 1-60 P1
FASTEST LAP M Schumacher, Ferrari, 1m 32.226s (lap 26), 200.871kph, 124.816mph
CHAMPIONSHIP M Schumacher 76, R Schumacher 30, Montoya 27, Barrichello 26, Coulthard 26

Pos	Driver	Car	Time/gap	Grid	Stops	Tyres
1	R Barrichello	Ferrari	1h 35m 7.426s	4	2	B
2	M Schumacher	Ferrari	–0.294s	3	2	B
3	K Räikkönen	McLaren-Mercedes	–46.435s	6	1	M
4	R Schumacher	Williams-BMW	–1m 6.963s	2	1	M
5	J Button	Renault	–1m 16.944s	8	2	M
6	F Massa	Sauber-Petronas	–1 lap	11	1	B

BRITISH GP Silverstone
7 July 2002   Race 690

Michael Schumacher
Ferrari F2002 201.649kph, 125.299mph

Montoya's fourth consecutive pole again didn't bring victory. With the track dry he just about kept M. Schumacher at bay, but once it rained, the pair both pitting on lap 13 for wets, Bridgestone intermediates were the only tyres to have. As a measure of their superiority, Barrichello, forced to start from the back, overtook Montoya for P2 on lap 18. Later they swapped places twice more in their spirited scrap, JPM finishing P3 behind the Ferraris, the only Michelin runner in the top six. McLaren's race was a comedy of errors, with chaotic pit stops and wrong tyre choices, the Räikkönen Mercedes blowing up on lap 44 when P10, Coulthard finishing two laps down. Ralf's race was also dismal but BAR-Honda scored their first points, P4 and P5.

POLE POSITION Montoya, Williams-BMW, 1m 18.998s (0.034s), 234.279kph, 145.574mph
LAPS 60 x 5.141 km, 3.195 miles
DISTANCE 308.356 km, 191.604 miles
STARTERS/FINISHERS 21/12
WEATHER Overcast, cool, intermittent showers
LAP LEADERS Montoya 1-15 (15); M Schumacher 16-60 (45)
WINNER'S LAPS 1-15 P2, 16-60 P1
FASTEST LAP Barrichello, Ferrari, 1m 23.083s (lap 58), 222.760kph, 138.417mph
CHAMPIONSHIP M Schumacher 86, Barrichello 32, Montoya 31, R Schumacher 30, Coulthard 26

Pos	Driver	Car	Time/gap	Grid	Stops	Tyres
1	M Schumacher	Ferrari	1h 31m 45.015s	3	3	B
2	R Barrichello	Ferrari	–14.578s	2	3	B
3	J P Montoya	Williams-BMW	–31.661s	1	2	M
4	J Villeneuve	BAR-Honda	–1 lap	9	2	B
5	O Panis	BAR-Honda	–1 lap	13	2	B
6	N Heidfeld	Sauber-Petronas	–1 lap	10	2	B

FRENCH GP Magny-Cours
21 July 2002 Race 691

Michael Schumacher
Ferrari F2002 199.135kph, 123.737mph

Four laps from victory he slid wide on oil at the Adelaide hairpin, M. Schumacher pounced, and Räikkönen's maiden win would have to wait. From his fifth consecutive pole Montoya led the first stint from M. Schumacher and Räikkönen, the Ferrari easily taking the lead at the first stop, home free until penalised a stop-go for crossing the pit-exit line. This dropped Michael back behind JPM and Kimi, and as the Williams challenge died with their tyres Räikkönen led, holding Schumacher until his hairpin mishap. A long second stint brought Coulthard into the picture but a drive-through ruled him out, although McLaren clearly outclassed Williams at Magny-Cours. His eighth race victory cemented Schumacher's fifth world title.

POLE POSITION Montoya, Williams-BMW, 1m 11.985s (0.023), 212.594kph, 132.100mph
LAPS 72 x 4.248 km, 2.640 miles
DISTANCE 305.886 km, 190.069 miles
STARTERS/FINISHERS 18/11
WEATHER Cloudy, hot, dry
LAP LEADERS Montoya 1-23, 36-42 (30); M Schumacher 24-25, 29-35, 68-72 (14); Coulthard 27-28, 50-54 (7); Räikkönen 26, 43-49, 55-67 (21)
WINNER'S LAPS 1-23 P2, 24-25 P1, 26 P2, 27 P3, 28 P2, 29-35 P1, 36-42 P3, 43-48 P2, 49-54 P3, 55-67 P2, 68-72 P1
FASTEST LAP Coulthard, McLaren-Mercedes, 1m 15.045s (lap 62), 203.925kph, 126.714mph
CHAMPIONSHIP M Schumacher 96, Montoya 34, Barrichello 32, R Schumacher 32, Coulthard 30

Pos	Driver	Car	Time/gap	Grid	Stops	Tyres
1	M Schumacher	Ferrari	1h 33m 35.636s	2	3	B
2	K Räikkönen	McLaren-Mercedes	−1.104s	4	2	M
3	D Coulthard	McLaren-Mercedes	−31.975s	6	2	M
4	J P Montoya	Williams-BMW	−40.675s	1	2	M
5	R Schumacher	Williams-BMW	−41.772s	5	3	M
6	J Button	Renault	−1 lap	7	3	M

GERMAN GP Hockenheim
28 July 2002 Race 692

Michael Schumacher
Ferrari F2002 209.262kph, 130.030mph

At the heavily revised Hockenheim circuit Schumacher recorded his 62nd race win, surprisingly his first German GP victory for Ferrari in six attempts. Ralf Schumacher presented a mild early threat to Michael's tyre-preserving drive from pole, but it was Montoya who eventually won the tussle for P2 between Barrichello and the resurgent Williams pair. With both McLarens strangely off the pace it still took ten laps for Montoya to regain the place Räikkönen had nabbed on the opening lap. By then he was well behind the leaders and his subsequent strong run would have only produced P4 if Rubens and Ralf had not suffered irksome delays: Barrichello's a refuelling problem; Ralf an extra stop to pump up leaking hydraulics late in the race.

POLE POSITION M Schumacher, Ferrari, 1m 14.389s (0.181s), 221.355kph, 137.544mph
LAPS 67 x 4.574 km, 2.842 miles
DISTANCE 306.458 km, 190.424 miles
STARTERS/FINISHERS 21/9
WEATHER Sunny, hot, dry
LAP LEADERS M Schumacher 1-26, 31-47, 49-67 (62); R Schumacher 27-29, 48 (4); Montoya 30 (1)
WINNER'S LAPS 1-26 P1, 27 P2, 28-29 P3, 30 P2, 31-47 P1, 48 P2, 49-67 P1
FASTEST LAP M Schumacher, Ferrari, 1m 16.462s (lap 44), 215.354kph, 133.815mph
CHAMPIONSHIP M Schumacher 106, Montoya 40, R Schumacher 36, Barrichello 35, Coulthard 32

Pos	Driver	Car	Time/gap	Grid	Stops	Tyres
1	M Schumacher	Ferrari	1h 27m 52.078s	1	2	B
2	J P Montoya	Williams-BMW	−10.503s	4	2	M
3	R Schumacher	Williams-BMW	−14.466s	2	3	M
4	R Barrichello	Ferrari	−23.195s	3	2	B
5	D Coulthard	McLaren-Mercedes	−1 lap	9	2	M
6	N Heidfeld	Sauber-Petronas	−1 lap	10	2	B

HUNGARIAN GP Hungaroring
18 August 2002 Race 693

Rubens Barrichello
Ferrari F2002 180.364kph, 112.073mph

Dominant in qualifying, a lights-to-flag demonstration run clinched Ferrari's fourth successive constructors' title. To meet the Scuderia's final imperative, a 1-2 in the drivers' championship, Barrichello was nominated winner, Schumacher in the closing stages accentuating the deceit by deliberately dropping back then making up 4s in one super-fast lap. So just by coasting, not racing each other, the Ferraris still destroyed the rest, only R. Schumacher remotely in the same race. Montoya qualified poorly and drove a scrappy race, going off the road trying to stave off Räikkönen. The McLarens qualified weakly in mid-field but raced strongly in the hotter conditions to finish P4 and P5 as Fisichella and Massa wilted, but no one troubled the Ferraris.

POLE POSITION Barrichello, Ferrari, 1m 13.333s (0.059s), 195.137kph, 121.253mph
LAPS 77 x 3.975 km, 2.470 miles
DISTANCE 306.069 km, 190.182 miles
STARTERS/FINISHERS 20/16
WEATHER Sunny, very hot, dry
LAP LEADERS Barrichello 1-32, 34-77 (76); R Schumacher 33 (1)
WINNER'S LAPS 1-32 P1, 33 P2, 34-77 P1
FASTEST LAP M Schumacher, Ferrari, 1m 16.207s (lap 72), 187.778kph, 116.680mph
CHAMPIONSHIP M Schumacher 112, Barrichello 45, R Schumacher 40, Montoya 40, Coulthard 34

Pos	Driver	Car	Time/gap	Grid	Stops	Tyres
1	R Barrichello	Ferrari	1h 41m 49.001s	1	2	B
2	M Schumacher	Ferrari	−0.434s	2	2	B
3	R Schumacher	Williams-BMW	−13.356s	3	2	M
4	K Räikkönen	McLaren-Mercedes	−29.479s	11	2	M
5	D Coulthard	McLaren-Mercedes	−37.800s	10	2	M
6	G Fisichella	Jordan-Honda	−1m 8.804s	5	2	B

BELGIAN GP Spa Francorchamps

1 September 2002   Race 694

Michael Schumacher
Ferrari F2002 225.970kph, 140.411mph

Remarkably, the soon to be six-time Spa winner started from pole for the first time. A perfect car set-up and tyre choice, Schumacher revelled in the circuit's fast sweeps, 26s ahead of Barrichello by lap 31. It was an awesome display, driving the first two stints flat out, eventually allowing Rubens to close up to 2s by the end. It was his tenth win in the season, a new record. After playing second fiddle in Hungary his message was clear to all. Räikkönen qualified P2 but lost out to Barrichello at the start and then to Montoya in a huge moment at Pouhon on lap 2, eventually out with a broken Mercedes. Coulthard raced strongly, pushing Montoya for P3, the position the Williams driver occupied throughout the race. And Irvine scored a point for Jaguar.

POLE POSITION M Schumacher, Ferrari, 1m 43.726s (0.424s), 241.663kph, 150.163mph
LAPS 44 x 6.963 km, 4.327 miles
DISTANCE 306.355 km, 190.360 miles
STARTERS/FINISHERS 20/12
WEATHER Cloudy with sunny intervals, warm, dry
LAP LEADERS M Schumacher 1-16, 18-44 (43); Barrichello 17 (1)
WINNER'S LAPS 1-16 P1, 17 P2, 18-44 P1
FASTEST LAP M Schumacher, Ferrari, 1m 47.176s (lap 15), 233.884kph, 145.329mph
CHAMPIONSHIP M Schumacher 122, Barrichello 51, Montoya 44, R Schumacher 42, Coulthard 37

Pos	Driver	Car	Time/gap	Grid	Stops	Tyres
1	M Schumacher	Ferrari	1h 21m 20.634s	1	2	B
2	R Barrichello	Ferrari	−1.977s	3	2	B
3	J P Montoya	Williams-BMW	−18.445s	5	2	M
4	D Coulthard	McLaren-Mercedes	−19.358s	6	2	M
5	R Schumacher	Williams-BMW	−56.440s	4	2	M
6	E Irvine	Jaguar-Ford	−1m 17.370s	8	2	M

ITALIAN GP Monza

15 September 2002   Race 695

Rubens Barrichello
Ferrari F2002 241.090kph, 149.806mph

Montoya's seventh pole was the fastest lap in F1 history, 161.170mph, but again no success for Williams, Ralf's BMW lasting four laps, Montoya running P3 until kerb-hopping chassis failure mid-race. The Williams pair quickly lost their initial lead over the Ferraris which recorded another dominant 1-2, or 2-1, as it was Barrichello's turn, claiming they were racing but with clear pointers to just another put-up job. The McLarens were accounted for by a lap 1 replacement nosecone for Coulthard, and another broken engine for Räikkönen on lap 30, running P4. Which left Jaguar to post their second-ever podium. Although Irvine was almost a lap in arrears, it was a strong performance, P5 in qualifying and never lower than P6 in the race.

POLE POSITION J P Montoya, Williams-BMW, 1m 20.264s (0.257s), 259.828kph, 161.449mph
LAPS 53 x 5.793 km, 3.600 miles
DISTANCE 306.719 km, 190.586 miles
STARTERS/FINISHERS 20/13
WEATHER Sunny, hot, dry
LAP LEADERS R Schumacher, Williams-BMW 1-3 (3); Montoya 4 (1); Barrichello 5-19, 29-53 (40); M Schumacher 20-28 (9)
WINNER'S LAPS 1-3 P3, 4 P2, 5-19 P1, 20-28 P2, 29-53 P1
FASTEST LAP R Barrichello, Ferrari, 1m 23.657 (lap 15), 249.289kph, 154.901mph
CHAMPIONSHIP M Schumacher 128, Barrichello 61, Montoya 44, R Schumacher 42, Coulthard 37

Pos	Driver	Car	Time/gap	Grid	Stops	Tyres
1	R Barrichello	Ferrari	1h 16m 19.982s	4	2	B
2	M Schumacher	Ferrari	−0.255s	2	1	B
3	E Irvine	Jaguar-Ford	−52.579s	5	1	M
4	J Trulli	Renault	−58.219s	11	1	M
5	J Button	Renault	−1m 7.770s	17	1	M
6	O Panis	BAR-Honda	−1m 8.491s	16	2	B

UNITED STATES GP Indianapolis

29 September 2002   Race 696

Rubens Barrichello
Ferrari F2002 201.475kph, 125.191mph

Ferrari's 1-2 hat-trick saw Barrichello win by 0.011s in a clumsily staged dead heat. Circulating in team order until the last lap, Schumacher invited Barrichello alongside at the final corner. Williams' embarrassment was quite different, their drivers colliding on lap 2 disputing P4, JPM recovering to fourth. An on-form Coulthard qualified and finished P3 with a well-executed one-stop strategy, Räikkönen suffering another mid-race engine failure on a day that dishonoured GP racing. It was not simply what occurred, Schumacher leading then 'taking a dive' to use boxing parlance, but also the venue, the historical Indy track where drivers had died in the name of motor racing, and in a country that reveres winners, not handouts to defeated rivals.

POLE POSITION M Schumacher, Ferrari, 1m 10.790s (0.268s), 213.182kph, 132.466mph
LAPS 73 x 4.192 km, 2.605 miles
DISTANCE 306.016 km, 190.150 miles
STARTERS/FINISHERS 20/16
WEATHER Sunny, warm, dry
LAP LEADERS M Schumacher 1-26, 29-48, 51-72 (68); Barrichello, Ferrari 27-28, 49-50, 73 (5)
WINNER'S LAPS 1-26 P2, 27-28 P1, 29-48 P2, 49-50 P1, 51-72 P2, 73 P1
FASTEST LAP Barrichello, Ferrari, 1m 12.738s (lap 27), 207.473kph, 128.918mph
CHAMPIONSHIP M Schumacher 134, Barrichello 71, Montoya 47, R Schumacher 42, Coulthard 41

Pos	Driver	Car	Time/gap	Grid	Stops	Tyres
1	R Barrichello	Ferrari	1h 31m 7.934s	2	2	B
2	M Schumacher	Ferrari	−0.011s	1	2	B
3	D Coulthard	McLaren-Mercedes	−7.799s	3	1	M
4	J P Montoya	Williams-BMW	−9.911s	4	1	M
5	J Trulli	Renault	−56.857s	8	1	M
6	J Villeneuve	BAR-Honda	−58.212s	7	2	B

Round 17/17	**JAPANESE GP** Suzuka						**Michael Schumacher**

Round 17/17 | **JAPANESE GP** Suzuka
13 October 2002   Race 697

Michael Schumacher
Ferrari F2002 212.644kph, 132.131mph

Allan McNish was fortunate to escape from a violent qualifying accident, his Toyota vaulting the barriers at 130R. Behind M. Schumacher's 11th victory and Ferrari's ninth 1-2, Räikkönen completed the podium, but only following the retirement from P3 of Coulthard early on, throttle on lap 7, and Ralf's later engine failure on lap 48. Montoya's unusually quiet race to P4 cemented his 'best-non-Ferrari-driver' championship status, but star of the show was rookie Takuma Sato. He wowed the partisan crowd by qualifying P7 and finishing fifth in the Jordan-Honda, his first points of the season. Honda produced special engines for their home race, Sato's exploits made ever more dramatic as one by one the other Honda-powered cars expired.

POLE POSITION M Schumacher, Ferrari, 1m 31.317s (0.432s), 229.481kph, 142.593mph
LAPS 53 x 5.821 km, 3.617 miles
DISTANCE 308.317 km, 191.579 miles
STARTERS/FINISHERS 19/11
WEATHER Sunny, hot, dry
LAP LEADERS M Schumacher 1-20, 22-53 (52); Barrichello 21 (1)
WINNER'S LAPS 1-20 P1, 21 P2, 22-53 P1
FASTEST LAP M Schumacher, Ferrari, 1m 36.125s (lap 15), 218.003kph, 135.461mph
CHAMPIONSHIP M Schumacher 144, Barrichello 77, Montoya 50, R Schumacher 42, Coulthard 41

Pos	Driver	Car	Time/gap	Grid	Stops	Tyres
1	M Schumacher	Ferrari	1h 26m 59.698s	1	2	B
2	R Barrichello	Ferrari	−0.507s	2	2	B
3	K Räikkönen	McLaren-Mercedes	−23.292s	4	2	M
4	J P Montoya	Williams-BMW	−36.275s	6	2	M
5	T Sato	Jordan-Honda	−1m 22.694s	7	2	B
6	J Button	Renault	−1 lap	10	2	M

2002 CHAMPIONSHIP FACTS AND FOLKLORE

- This year Michael Schumacher was not the prime factor in championship success but the prime beneficiary. At the heart of Ferrari's phenomenal 2002 landslide was the car. Remove Schumacher's 11 wins from the equation and Barrichello's Ferrari would still have dominated the season with nine victories.

- Outwardly similar to the F2001, the Ferrari F2002 was a complete redesign, but not fundamentally, changes made simply to bring the existing package closer to all-round perfection. New was a pocket-sized seven-speed gearbox, radical in having no dog-rings. Over a race distance smoother changes would save vital seconds, but there was no quantum technological leap in design.

- Ferrari's rivals expressed early-season discontent over possible rear wing and barge-board flexibility, believing this to be the F2002's 'unfair advantage', but that turned out to be a red herring, to coin a phrase.

- One performance factor of increasing magnitude was the Ferrari/Bridgestone relationship, ironically the consequence of McLaren joining Williams on Michelins for 2002. Ferrari suddenly became Bridgestone's only real chance of race and championship success, the needs of the Scuderia inevitably Bridgestone's growing primary concern.

- As Jean Todt frequently asserted, Ferrari domination was not the Scuderia's fault. Few disagreed, especially Williams and McLaren who had metered out similar treatment to Ferrari in bygone seasons.

- Where the majority parted company with Todt was not so much in substance but in style. Even allowing for Ferrari paranoia fed by Schumacher's 1999 Silverstone mishap, what happened in Austria and then again in at least three further GPs, including the Indianapolis sham, was unacceptable and damaging because, quite simply, it was not justifiable.

- Few find the concept of team orders difficult to accept if implemented with rational justification. Without good reason it is simply result-fixing, anathema in any and every sport. And the rationality behind team orders must reflect the simple fact that F1 exists today purely because it is a television sport. Team orders can never be justified purely on the grounds of what was regarded as acceptable in the era before TV ruled, when F1 was solely a spectator sport.

- The anger engendered by the Austrian GP team orders fiasco was that on this rare occasion Barrichello had manifestly bettered Schumacher on the day, and secondly, Schumacher was already holding a commanding points position for the title.

- A secondary consideration was that declining TV audiences brought about by viewers switching off, disenchanted by dull or 'fixed' races, could only exacerbate the extant F1 cash crisis.

- In this setting, Austria 2002 was the last straw for F1 disillusionment, and Todt and Schumacher, the latter with his 'unique' contract clauses, both behaved with typical arrogance and contempt, manipulating rather than having the confidence in themselves and those around them that they would and could win on merit.

- Some six weeks later the FIA failed F1 miserably. Ferrari appeared before the FIA World Council, most pundits expecting heavy punishment for bringing the sport into disrepute. Instead the FIA were unwilling to find against them, unable to separate the team-orders wheat from the team-orders chaff in the rule book.

- Ferrari was fined merely for failing to adhere to protocol at the podium ceremony, Schumacher, boos and jeers ringing in his ears, hoisting Barrichello on to the top step.

- When Schumacher, possibly inadvertently, also fixed the result at Indianapolis, some F1 historians compared it with the Parkes, Scarfiotti dead heat for Ferrari at the 1967 Syracuse GP. But that was a non-championship F1 race, in the pre-TV era, and a dead heat was only feasible because of the use of hand-timing to one tenth of a second.

- For Schumacher, 2002 set numerous records: record race wins in a season; record points in a season; another record winning points margin, only this time over his Ferrari teammate; the first driver to finish on the podium in all races in a season, and the first to finish every lap of the season. Remarkable.

- It was the extraordinary reliability allied to the speed of the F2002 that made Schumacher's season so formidable, Hockenheim on 29 July 2001 the last time Schumacher's car failed in a race. By contrast, Barrichello failed to even make the start on two occasions this year due to car maladies.

RACE 686, Austrian GP: The outcry against cynical Ferrari team orders was loud and immediate, even the offending drivers looking suitably chastened on the podium.

- By winning 15 races Ferrari equalled the astonishing feat of McLaren-Honda in 1988, Maranello's accomplishment only marginally less daunting because it was from 17 rounds rather than 16. Canada also happened to be Ferrari's 150th GP victory.
- But the Ferrari killer-stat was that this one team scored as many championship points as all the other ten teams added together, this dominance spurring the FIA to seek solutions in order to make F1 racing more entertaining in 2003.
- The fact was, despite the arrival of Toyota, GP racing was at a low ebb by the end of 2002. Predictable racing was causing world TV audiences to reach for the off switch, whilst the world economic recession bit again with Arrows following Prost into liquidation, fielding no further entries after Hockenheim.
- How to lance the F1 expenditure bubble suddenly became a pressing topic, the FIA advocating that unbridled spending by the 'haves' at the top end of the grid was making the existence of the teams propping up the grid financially unviable, that cost controls and cost-cutting measures were essential to guarantee a full and healthy grid.
- In parallel, talk of a breakaway series led by dissident manufacturers gathered further momentum when Kirch, owner of 75% of the F1 commercial rights-holding company SLEC, became insolvent and three creditor banks took control.

- With one race victory apiece in 2002 Williams and McLaren had a miserable time of it. The key shortage for the FW24 was downforce, for the MP4-17 horsepower. Their common problems were tyres – as Michelin could rarely provide rubber that suited both teams equally well – and reliability, neither team nor their engine suppliers a match for Ferrari robustness.
- Also, at least against Ferrari, BMW conceded the power advantage they enjoyed in 2001, although they were never in deficit, pushing engine speeds up to 19,000rpm by Monza to wring out 880 horses.
- Montoya's Monza pole was the fastest lap in F1 history, 161.170mph, it having taken 17 years to exceed Rosberg's 160.937mph Silverstone lap of 1985.
- Indeed, the Montoya/BMW/Michelin combo proved highly effective in qualifying, the equal to Schumacher/Ferrari/Bridgestone with seven poles apiece. It was what happened on Sunday where the difference lay.
- For the record, the final round at Suzuka was Schumacher's 50th pole as well as Bridgestone's 100th GP.
- McLaren's sole victory, where Coulthard brilliantly soaked up unremitting pressure from Montoya and Michael Schumacher, was also technically fascinating. Disappointed to qualify P2, DC was told not to worry by the

launch control technicians, he would lead at the first corner, and duly he did so. During the race McLaren took advantage of the recent regulation change allowing two-way telemetry between pit and car. Through this they fixed an oil problem, which a year ago might have been terminal for the smoking Mercedes V10.

■ Having taken the organic route to building an F1 team, Toyota in their inaugural season produced a strong engine but a middling chassis, axing Salo and McNish for a fresh driver line-up in year two.

■ Jaguar also had a driver clear-out, Webber and Pizzonia replacing de la Rosa and Irvine, Eddie bringing his nine-and-a-bit year career to a close having won four GPs from 146 starts.

■ Another departure was Arrows, so nearly a winner since their 1978 debut but ending up with the unenviable record of least successful marque to compete in the championship, winless after 382 GP attempts.

■ Mika Häkkinen's career record was far more imposing with his back-to-back drivers' championships and 20 race

victories from 161 starts. In July he announced that his sabbatical year had become full retirement from F1.

■ In their first season back, Renault fell further behind in the power-race with their innovative wide-angle engine but began to build a reputation for rocket-like standing starts from the grid.

■ Dave Richards became team principal at BAR and signed Button alongside JV for 2003, Jenson replaced by Alonso at Renault. Honda's relationship with BAR was further strengthened through an exclusive engine deal for 2003.

■ This left Jordan short of a motor, but in something of a coup Eddie Jordan landed a quasi-works Ford deal for 2003, patience at the Blue Oval wearing thin for the Jaguar project led by Niki Lauda. Incidentally, another Austrian was speculatively linked to Jaguar, Red Bull owner Dietrich Mateschitz.

■ Arguably the Dietrich Mateschitz of his day, R.R.C. (Rob) Walker died aged 84. Heir to the Scotch Whisky fortune, his privately entered Lotus and Cooper cars won nine *Grandes Épreuves* between 1958 and 1968, seven of those in the hands of Stirling Moss.

Championship ranking	Championship points	Driver nationality	2002 Drivers Championship		Races contested	Race victories	Podiumse excl. victories	Races led	Lights to flag victories	Laps led	Poles	Fastest laps	Triple Crowns
			Driver	Car									
1	144	GER	Michael Schumacher	Ferrari	17	11	17	13	1	558	7	7	4
2	77	BRA	Rubens Barrichello	Ferrari	15	4	10	11	1	307	3	5	
3	50	COL	Juan Pablo Montoya	Williams-BMW	17		7	6		65	7	3	
4	42	GER	Ralf Schumacher	Williams-BMW	17	1	6	5		44			
5	41	GBR	David Coulthard	McLaren- Mercedes	17	1	6	3	1	95		1	
6	24	FIN	Kimi Räikkönen	McLaren- Mercedes	17		4	1		21		1	
7	14	GBR	Jenson Button	Renault	17								
8	9	ITA	Jarno Trulli	Renault	17								
9	8	GBR	Eddie Irvine	Jaguar-Ford	17		1						
10	7	GER	Nick Heidfeld	Sauber-Petronas	17								
11	7	ITA	Giancarlo Fisichella	Jordan-Honda	16								
12	4	CAN	Jacques Villeneuve	BAR-Honda	17								
13	4	BRA	Felipe Massa	Sauber-Petronas	16								
14	3	FRA	Olivier Panis	BAR-Honda	17								
15	2	JPN	Takuma Sato	Jordan-Honda	17								
16	2	AUS	Mark Webber	Minardi-Asiatech	16								
17	2	FIN	Mika Salo	Toyota	17								
18	2	GER	Heinz-Harald Frentzen	Arrows-Ford (11) Sauber-Petronas (1)	12								

Championship ranking	Championship points	Team/Marque nationality	2002 Constructors Championship		Engine maker nationality	Races contested	Race victories	1-2 finishes	Podiums excl. victories	Races led	Laps led	Poles	Fastest laps
			Chassis	Engine									
1	221	ITA	Ferrari F2002, F2001	Ferrari 3.0 V10	ITA	17	15	9	12	16	865	10	12
2	92	GBR	Williams FW24	BMW 3.0 V10	GER	17	1	1	12	9	109	7	3
3	65	GBR	McLaren MP4-17	Mercedes-Benz 3.0 V10	GER	17	1		9	3	116		2
4	23	FRA	Renault R202	Renault 3.0 V10	FRA	17							
5	11	SUI	Sauber C21	Petronas 3.0 V10	ITA	17							
6	9	IRL	Jordan EJ12	Honda 3.0 V10	JPN	17							
7	8	GBR	Jaguar R3	Ford Cosworth 3.0 V10	GBR	17			1				
8	7	GBR	BAR 004	Honda 3.0 V10	JPN	17							
9	2	ITA	Minardi PS02	Asiatech 3.0 V10	FRA	16							
10	2	JPN	Toyota TF102	Toyota 3.0 V10	JPN	17							
11	2	GBR	Arrows A23	Ford Cosworth 3.0 V10	GBR	11							

2003

Schumacher 'scrapes in' 6-1

THE TALE OF THE TITLE

■ Following the one-sided 2002 championship, the FIA introduced measures to spice up the show.

■ To the extent of eight different race winners and the titles undecided until the final round, they worked.

■ Nevertheless, for the fourth year in succession Schumacher and Ferrari took championship honours.

■ With this, the German eclipsed Fangio to establish a new record of six drivers' world titles.

■ After their 2002 landslide the Bridgestone-shod Ferraris 'only' won half the 16 championship rounds.

■ Michelin-equipped Williams, with four race wins, and McLaren, with two, provided stern opposition.

■ Indeed, Räikkönen, profiting from the revised points system, went to the season finale with a title chance.

■ But with just one race victory, Kimi's first, it would have been a 6-1 travesty against Schumacher's six.

■ For Williams-BMW 2003 was an opportunity lost, in the hunt for both titles until the penultimate round.

■ It was a collective failure, the fault partly Williams, partly BMW, partly Michelin and partly their drivers.

■ By contrast, when Ferrari were on the ropes in Hungary the team showed immense profundity.

■ Together – and that was the key ingredient – the Scuderia won the final three rounds to secure both titles.

■ Alonso's Hungarian victory, the youngest-ever GP winner, signalled the resurgence of Renault.

■ Fisichella broke his duck with a bizarre victory in Brazil for Jordan, the team's fourth and final victory.

■ And not forgetting: one-lap qualifying; Silverstone track invader.

THE CHASE FOR THE CHAMPIONSHIP

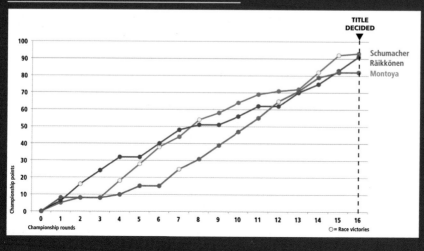

Round 1/16	**AUSTRALIAN GP** Melbourne						**David Coulthard**
	9 March 2003					**Race 698**	McLaren-Mercedes MP4-17D 194.868kph, 121.086mph

The first 20 laps were breathtaking. Single-shot qualifying had scrambled the grid, together with a wet track and differing tyre choices and fuel loads. Additionally, two SC periods assisted some, hindered others. Once things settled down, Räikkönen, Montoya and M. Schumacher all led but each lost time to costly error, the Columbian spinning away the lead on worn tyres with just ten laps to go. So Coulthard, starting P11 and plain last on lap 2, won by 8s from Montoya-Räikkönen-Schumacher, these three covered by less than a second. It was not Coulthard's finest win, but unlike his opposition his drive was mistake-free. It was his 13th GP victory and his seventh victorious season in succession.

POLE POSITION M Schumacher, Ferrari, 1m 27.173s (0.245s), 218.999kph, 136.080mph
LAPS 58 x 5.303 km, 3.295 miles
DISTANCE 307.574 km, 191.117 miles
STARTERS/FINISHERS 20/13
WEATHER Overcast, warm, wet then drying
LAP LEADERS M Schumacher 1-6, 42-45 (10); Montoya 7-16, 33-41, 46-47 (21); Räikkönen 17-32 (16); Coulthard 48-58 (11); SC 9-11, 18-20 (6)
WINNER'S LAPS 1 P10, 2-3 P20, 4 P18, 5 P17, 6 P15, 7 P12, 8-9 P8, 10-15 P7, 16 P6, 17-28 P3, 29-31 P2, 32-35 P5, 36-38 P4, 39-45 P3, 46-47 P2, 48-58 P1
FASTEST LAP Räikkönen, McLaren-Mercedes, 1m 27.724s (lap 32), 217.623kph, 135.225mph
CHAMPIONSHIP Coulthard 10, Montoya 8, Räikkönen 6, M Schumacher 5, Trulli 4

TOP **100** RACE

Pos	Driver	Car	Time/gap	Grid	Stops	Tyres
1	D Coulthard	McLaren-Mercedes	1h 34m 42.124s	11	2	M
2	J P Montoya	Williams-BMW	–8.675s	3	2	M
3	K Räikkönen	McLaren-Mercedes	–9.192s	15	2	M
4	M Schumacher	Ferrari	–9.482s	1	2	B
5	J Trulli	Renault	–38.801s	12	2	M
6	H-H Frentzen	Sauber-Petronas	–43.928s	4	2	B

McLaren-Mercedes MP4/17D

Round 2/16	**MALAYSIAN GP** Sepang						**Kimi Räikkönen**
	23 March 2003					**Race 699**	McLaren-Mercedes MP4-17D 201.629kph, 125.287mph

Alonso's first pole, Räikkönen's first victory. Lightly fuelled Alonso led but inevitably pitted early, lap 14, eventually finishing P3. Once ahead Räikkönen was never challenged, beating Barrichello by almost 40s. The key to Kimi's first GP success lay in his journey from P7 on the grid: of those drivers ahead, M. Schumacher and Trulli collided after the start at turn two; he got ahead of Barrichello in the mêlée; Coulthard dropped out from P2 on lap 2 with spark-box failure, and, having been out-qualified by Heidfeld's Sauber, the Finn put matters right by passing him into second just as teammate Coulthard stuttered to a halt. Qualifying P17, Ralf salvaged P4 for Williams, JPM in trouble from the start. Round 2: McLaren 2, Ferrari 0.

POLE POSITION F Alonso, Renault, 1m 37.044s (0.173s), 205.626kph, 127.770mph
LAPS 56 x 5.543 km, 3.444 miles
DISTANCE 310.408 km, 192.879 miles
STARTERS/FINISHERS 19/13
WEATHER Sunny, very hot, dry
LAP LEADERS Alonso 1-13 (13); Räikkönen 14-19, 23-56 (40); Barrichello 20-22 (3)
WINNER'S LAPS 1-2 P4, 3-13 P2, 14-19 P1, 20-22 P2, 23-56 P1
FASTEST LAP M Schumacher, Ferrari, 1m 36.412s (lap 45), 206.974kph, 128.608mph
CHAMPIONSHIP Räikkönen 16, Coulthard 10, Montoya 8, Barrichello 8, Alonso 8

Pos	Driver	Car	Time/gap	Grid	Stops	Tyres
1	K Räikkönen	McLaren-Mercedes	1h 32m 22.195s	7	2	M
2	R Barrichello	Ferrari	–39.286s	5	2	B
3	F Alonso	Renault	–1m 4.007s	1	2	M
4	R Schumacher	Williams-BMW	–1m 28.026s	17	2	M
5	J Trulli	Renault	–1 lap	2	2	M
6	M Schumacher	Ferrari	–1 lap	3	4	B

Jordan-Ford EJ13

Round 3/16	**BRAZILIAN GP** Interlagos						**Giancarlo Fisichella**
	6 April 2003			Race 700			Jordan-Ford EJ13 152.902kph, 95.009mph

The track awash, unsuitable 'one-choice' rain tyres, the race chaotic. But, gratefully, not catastrophic. Starting under the SC, a series of accidents caused three more deployments, the 'river' flowing across turn three collecting six aquaplaning victims including M. Schumacher. The race was red-flagged 17 laps early when Webber crashed and Alonso smashed into the wrecked Jaguar. Barrichello, from his first home GP pole, was denied the fairytale ending when fuel-feed halted him on lap 46. Coulthard also came close to victory, pitting for tyres while in the lead just one lap before the red flag was shown. So ultimately, although the reverse result had stood initially, Fisichella's won an eventful if bizarre race from Räikkönen. Round 3: Ferrari still 0.

POLE POSITION R Barrichello, Ferrari, 1m 13.807s (0.011s), 210.175kph, 130.597mph
LAPS 54 x 4.309 km, 2.677 miles (Race scheduled for 71 laps but following after accident)
DISTANCE 232.656 km, 144.566 miles
STARTERS/FINISHERS 20/10
WEATHER Overcast, hot, heavy rain drying later
LAP LEADERS Barrichello 1-8, 45-46 (10); Coulthard 9-10, 27-44, 47-52 (26); Räikkönen 11-26, 53 (17); Fisichella 54 (1); SC 1-8, 20-22, 28-29, 34-36 (16)
WINNER'S LAPS 1-6 P8, 7 P10, 8 P19, 9-15 P18, 16-17 P17, 18-19 P16, 20 P14, 21-22 P13, 23-24 P12, 25 P10, 26 P11, 27 P10, 28-29 P8, 30 P9, 31-32 P8, 33 P7, 34-41 P6, 42-46 P5, 47 P4, 48-52 P3, 53 P2, 54 P1
FASTEST LAP R Barrichello, Ferrari, 1m 22.032s (lap 46), 189.101kph, 117.502mph
CHAMPIONSHIP Räikkönen 24, Coulthard 15, Alonso 14, Fisichella 10, Trulli 9

TOP **100** RACE

Pos	Driver	Car	Time/gap	Grid	Stops	Tyres
1	G Fisichella	Jordan-Ford	1h 31m 17.748s	8	1	B
2	K Räikkönen	McLaren-Mercedes	−0.945s	4	1	M
3	F Alonso	Renault	−6.348s	10	4	M
4	D Coulthard	McLaren-Mercedes	−8.096s	2	2	M
5	H-H Frentzen	Sauber-Petronas	−8.642s	14	1	B
6	J Villeneuve	BAR-Honda	−16.054s	13	1	B

Round 4/16	**SAN MARINO GP** Imola						**Michael Schumacher**
	20 April 2003			Race 701			Ferrari F2002 207.894kph, 129.180mph

Ferrari's 2003 race-win crisis ended in poignant circumstances. Grieving the demise of their mother on Saturday night, the Schumacher brothers elected to race on Sunday and, from the seventh all-Schumacher front row, fought for the lead over the first 15 laps. Held up by Ralf's graining Michelins in those opening laps, Ross Brawn switched Michael to a three-stop, concerned about the pace of the two-stopping Räikkönen. It worked, Ferrari taking their first victory of the year. But the new scoring system kept Räikkönen, who finished second, well ahead in the points table. Ultimately Ralf lost his podium spot to Barrichello's Ferrari, but when eventually it was all over the Schumachers swiftly and sombrely departed the circuit.

POLE POSITION M Schumacher, Ferrari, 1m 22.327s (0.014s), 215.710kph, 134.036mph
LAPS 62 x 4.933 km, 3.065 miles
DISTANCE 305.609 km, 189.897 miles
STARTERS/FINISHERS 20/15
WEATHER Overcast, warm, dry
LAP LEADERS R Schumacher 1-15 (15); M Schumacher 16-18, 23-49, 51-62 (42); Räikkönen 19-22 (4); Barrichello 50 (1)
WINNER'S LAPS 1-15 P2, 16-18 P1, 19-21 P3, 22 P2, 23-49 P1, 50 P2, 51-62 P1
FASTEST LAP M Schumacher, Ferrari, 1m 22.491s (lap 17), 215.281kph, 133.770mph
CHAMPIONSHIP Räikkönen 32, Coulthard 19, M Schumacher 18, Alonso 17, Barrichello 14

Pos	Driver	Car	Time/gap	Grid	Stops	Tyres
1	M Schumacher	Ferrari	1h 28m 12.058s	1	3	B
2	K Räikkönen	McLaren-Mercedes	−1.882s	6	2	M
3	R Barrichello	Ferrari	−2.291s	3	3	B
4	R Schumacher	Williams-BMW	−8.803s	2	3	M
5	D Coulthard	McLaren-Mercedes	−9.411s	12	2	M
6	F Alonso	Renault	−43.689s	8	2	M

Round 5/16	**SPANISH GP** Cataluña							**Michael Schumacher**
	4 May 2003					**Race 702**		Ferrari F2003-GA 196.619kph, 122.174mph

At his home GP, Alonso made a rocket start from P3 to almost jump the front row Ferraris. Meanwhile Räikkönen, starting last having blown his one-shot qualifying lap, shunted Pizzonia's stalled Jaguar on the grid, bringing out the SC. Once the track was clear Alonso's superb race pace dealt with Barrichello at the first round of stops and kept pressure on Schumacher such that Michael was thankful Ferrari had debuted their new, faster F2003-GA. Coulthard and Trulli put paid to their races with a first-lap tangle and the Williams pair never looked like winners, finishing fourth and fifth. But Schumacher's second victory and Räikkönen's dnf slashed the points deficit to just four, and now Alonso too was joining in the championship fray.

POLE POSITION M Schumacher, Ferrari, 1m 17.762s (0.258s), 218.975kph, 136.065mph
LAPS 65 x 4.730 km, 2.939 miles
DISTANCE 307.324 km, 190.962 miles
STARTERS/FINISHERS 20/12
WEATHER Sunny, hot, dry
LAP LEADERS M Schumacher 1-18, 21-35, 38-49, 51-65 (60); Barrichello 19-20 (2); Alonso 36-37, 50 (3); SC 1-5 (5)
WINNER'S LAPS 1-18 P1, 19-20 P2, 21-35 P1, 36 P4, 37 P2, 38-49 P1, 50 P3, 51-65 P1
FASTEST LAP Barrichello, Ferrari, 1m 20.143s (lap 52), 212.470kph, 132.023mph
CHAMPIONSHIP Räikkönen 32, M Schumacher 28, Alonso 25, Barrichello 20, Coulthard 19

Pos	Driver	Car	Time/gap	Grid	Stops	Tyres
1	M Schumacher	Ferrari	1h 33m 46.933s	1	2	B
2	F Alonso	Renault	−5.716s	3	2	M
3	R Barrichello	Ferrari	−18.001s	2	2	B
4	J P Montoya	Williams-BMW	−1m 2.022s	9	2	M
5	R Schumacher	Williams-BMW	−1 lap	7	2	M
6	C da Matta	Toyota	−1 lap	13	3	M

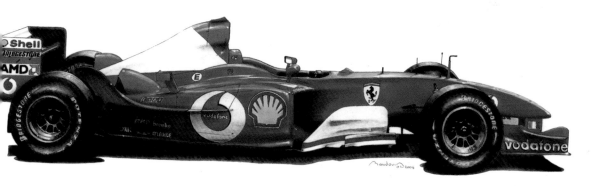

Ferrari F2003-GA

Round 6/16	**AUSTRIAN GP** A1-Ring							**Michael Schumacher**
	18 May 2003					**Race 703**		Ferrari F2003-GA 213.003kph, 132.354mph

Following two restarts and a first-lap SC, Schumacher shot into an increasing lead until a sharp shower closed-up the field. Then the Ferrari fuel-rigs misbehaved, Schumacher coolly sitting out a terrifying flash fire. He rejoined third, now behind his earlier pursuers, Montoya and Räikkönen. But shortly before half-distance he regained the lead as almost simultaneously he swept past Räikkönen just as leader Montoya's engine blew, the three race-starts more than the BMW could withstand. Over the final eight laps Räikkönen received close attention from Barrichello, but he managed to resist and so the Finn held on to his second place and, despite Schumacher's hat-trick, his narrow points lead in the championship. Button finished P4 for BAR.

POLE POSITION M Schumacher, Ferrari, 1m 09.150s (0.039s), 225.214kph, 139.942mph
LAPS 69 x 4.326 km, 2.688 miles (Scheduled for 71 laps but reduced after two aborted starts)
DISTANCE 298.494 km, 185.476 miles
STARTERS/FINISHERS 20/13
WEATHER Cloudy, warm, dry then occasional light showers
LAP LEADERS M Schumacher 1-23, 32-42, 51-69 (53); J P Montoya, Williams-BMW 24-31 (8); Räikkönen 43-49 (7); Barrichello 50 (1); SC 2-4 (3)
WINNER'S LAPS 1-23 P1, 24-31 P3, 32-42 P1, 43-49 P3, 50 P2, 51-69 P1
FASTEST LAP M Schumacher, Ferrari, 1m 08.337s (lap 41), 227.894kph, 141.607mph
CHAMPIONSHIP Räikkönen 40, M Schumacher 38, Barrichello 26, Alonso 25, Coulthard 23

Pos	Driver	Car	Time/gap	Grid	Stops	Tyres
1	M Schumacher	Ferrari	1h 24m 4.888s	1	2	B
2	K Räikkönen	McLaren-Mercedes	−3.362s	2	2	M
3	R Barrichello	Ferrari	−3.951s	5	2	B
4	J Button	BAR-Honda	−42.243s	7	2	B
5	D Coulthard	McLaren-Mercedes	−59.750s	14	2	M
6	R Schumacher	Williams-BMW	−1 lap	10	2	M

Williams-BMW FW25

Round 7/16	**MONACO GP** Monte Carlo						**Juan Pablo Montoya**
	1 June 2003					**Race 704**	Williams-BMW FW25 152.772kph, 94.928mph

Jenson Button was stretchered away concussed after a massive crash at the chicane during practice. Unlike last year when seven Williams poles begat a single race victory, the team's first pole of the season was suitably converted, but not by pole-sitter Ralf. Montoya, from P3, the clean side of the grid, overtook Räikkönen to chase his teammate and then seize the lead during the first round of pit stops as R. Schumacher sank to finish fourth with tyre pressure and balance problems. Once ahead, Montoya, polished and relentless, saw off heavy pressure from Räikkönen over the final stint to end Williams' 20-year Monaco victory drought. From his P5 grid slot M. Schumacher did well to finish a strong third.

POLE POSITION R Schumacher, Williams-BMW, 1m 15.259s (0.036s), 159.768kph, 99.275mph
LAPS 78 x 3.340 km, 2.075 miles
DISTANCE 260.520 km, 161.880 miles
STARTERS/FINISHERS 19/13
WEATHER Cloudy with sunny intervals, warm, dry
LAP LEADERS R Schumacher 1-20 (20); Montoya 21-22, 31-48, 59-78 (40); Trulli 25-26 (2); Räikkönen 23-24, 49-52 (6); M Schumacher 27-30, 53-58 (10); SC 2-4 (3)
WINNER'S LAPS 1-20 P2, 21-22 P1, 23-24 P7, 25-26 P6, 27-28 P4, 29 P3, 30 P2, 31-48 P1, 49-52 P3, 53-58 P2, 59-78 P1
FASTEST LAP Räikkönen, McLaren-Mercedes, 1m 14.545s (lap 49), 161.298kph, 100.226mph
CHAMPIONSHIP Räikkönen 48, M Schumacher 44, Alonso 29, Barrichello 27, Montoya 25

Pos	Driver	Car	Time/gap	Grid	Stops	Tyres
1	J P Montoya	Williams-BMW	1h 42m 19.010s	3	2	M
2	K Räikkönen	McLaren-Mercedes	−0.602s	2	2	M
3	M Schumacher	Ferrari	−1.720s	5	2	B
4	R Schumacher	Williams-BMW	−28.518s	1	2	M
5	F Alonso	Renault	−36.251s	8	2	M
6	J Trulli	Renault	−40.972s	4	2	M

Round 8/16	**CANADIAN GP** Montréal						**Michael Schumacher**
	15 June 2003					**Race 705**	Ferrari F2003-GA 200.777kph, 124.757mph

Ralf Schumacher's second consecutive pole produced a Williams front-row lockout. But Montoya's lap 2 spin put paid to any team tactics and enabled Michael to harry brother Ralf. Over the entire 70 laps the brothers were never separated by more than a second, but it was on the critical pit-stop laps that Michael could produce the super-fast lappery which made all the difference. He fired in the one extra at the first stop to take the lead, and two at the second to keep it. Montoya recovered to a close third whereas Räikkönen's sixth was damage limitation, having spun-out in qualifying yet again. So Schumacher's fourth victory gave him the championship lead for the first time this season. Alonso's strong P4 kept him third in the points table.

POLE POSITION R Schumacher, Williams-BMW, 1m 15.529s (0.394s), 129.159mph
LAPS 70 x 4.361 km, 2.710 miles
DISTANCE 305.270 km, 189.686 miles
STARTERS/FINISHERS 20/11
WEATHER Cloudy, warm, dry, windy
LAP LEADERS R Schumacher 1-19 (19); M Schumacher 20, 26-48, 55-70 (40); Alonso 21-25, 49-54 (11)
WINNER'S LAPS 1 P3, 2-19 P2, 20 P1, 21-25 P2, 26-48 P1, 49-54 P2, 55-70 P1
FASTEST LAP Alonso, Renault, 1m 16.040s (Lap 53), 206.465kph, 128.291mph
CHAMPIONSHIP M Schumacher 54, Räikkönen 51, Alonso 34, R Schumacher 33, Montoya 31

Pos	Driver	Car	Time/gap	Grid	Stops	Tyres
1	M Schumacher	Ferrari	1h 31m 13.591s	3	2	B
2	R Schumacher	Williams-BMW	−0.784s	1	2	M
3	J P Montoya	Williams-BMW	−1.355s	2	2	M
4	F Alonso	Renault	−4.481s	4	2	M
5	R Barrichello	Ferrari	−1m 4.261s	5	2	B
6	K Räikkönen	McLaren-Mercedes	−1m 10.502s	20	1	M

Round 9/16	**EUROPEAN GP** Nürburgring				**Ralf Schumacher**		
	29 June 2003			Race 706	Williams-BMW FW25 195.633kph, 121.561mph		

Räikkönen bounced straight back with a brilliant pole, his first in 26 starts for McLaren. It would likely have resulted in a second victory had not his Mercedes motor blown on lap 26 when in a comfortable lead. This left the way open for the other German engine supplier to win on home turf, powering the Williams of an on-form Ralf Schumacher. The Williams duo conspired to spoil M. Schumacher's afternoon, Ralf demoting his brother at the first corner and then, 43 laps later, Montoya causing Michael to spin with an audacious overtaking move around the outside at the hairpin. A Williams 1-2 plus Schumacher's eventual fifth and Räikkönen's dnf gave the championship battle a new perspective, the Williams duo entering the contest at last.

POLE POSITION K Räikkönen, McLaren-Mercedes, 1m 31.523s (0.032s), 202.493kph, 125.824mph
LAPS 60 x 5.148 km, 3.199 miles
DISTANCE 308.863 km, 191.919 miles
STARTERS/FINISHERS 20/15
WEATHER Cloudy, warm, dry
LAP LEADERS Räikkönen 1-16, 22-25 (30); R Schumacher 17-21, 26-60 (30)
WINNER'S LAPS 1-16 P2, 17-21 P1, 22-25 P2, 26-60 P1
FASTEST LAP K Räikkönen, McLaren-Mercedes, 1m 32.621s (lap 14), 200.092kph, 124.332mph
CHAMPIONSHIP M Schumacher 58, Räikkönen 51, R Schumacher 43, Montoya 39, Alonso 39

Pos	Driver	Car	Time/gap	Grid	Stops	Tyres
1	R Schumacher	Williams-BMW	1h 34m 43.622s	3	2	M
2	J P Montoya	Williams-BMW	−16.821s	4	2	M
3	R Barrichello	Ferrari	−39.673s	5	2	B
4	F Alonso	Renault	−1m 5.731s	8	2	M
5	M Schumacher	Ferrari	−1m 6.162s	2	2	B
6	M Webber	Jaguar-Ford	−1 lap	11	2	M

Round 10/16	**FRENCH GP** Magny-Cours				**Ralf Schumacher**		
	6 July 2003			Race 707	Williams-BMW FW25 203.866kph, 123.676mph		

Indeed, when Williams repeated their 1-2 trick a week later the championship genuinely took on the shape of a four-way battle. From pole, Ralf led sublimely from lights to flag to comfortably beat his teammate. In fairness, Montoya only finally accepted defeat once he fell well short in trying to jump the German at the third stop. With the top five finishing in grid order this was hardly an enthralling race, although the predictable result disguises the fact that M. Schumacher, starting P3, ran most of the race in fifth behind the McLarens. But as the Woking pair slowed with problems, a long third stint by Ferrari restored grid equilibrium. At their home race Renault proved disappointing. Qualifying P6 and P7, neither Renault V10 made the finish.

POLE POSITION R Schumacher, Williams-BMW, 1m 15.019s (0.117), 211.674kph, 131.528mph
LAPS 70 x 4.411 km, 2.741 miles
DISTANCE 308.586 km, 191.746 miles
STARTERS/FINISHERS 20/16
WEATHER Cloudy with sunny intervals, hot, dry
LAP LEADERS R Schumacher 1-70 (70)
WINNER'S LAPS 1-70 P1
FASTEST LAP Montoya, Williams-BMW, 1m 15.512s (lap 36), 210.292kph, 130.670mph
CHAMPIONSHIP M Schumacher 64, Räikkönen 56, R Schumacher 53, Montoya 47, Barrichello 39

Pos	Driver	Car	Time/gap	Grid	Stops	Tyres
1	R Schumacher	Williams-BMW	1h 30m 49.213s	1	3	M
2	J P Montoya	Williams-BMW	−13.813s	2	3	M
3	M Schumacher	Ferrari	−19.568s	3	3	B
4	K Räikkönen	McLaren-Mercedes	−38.047s	4	3	M
5	D Coulthard	McLaren-Mercedes	−40.289s	5	3	M
6	M Webber	Jaguar-Ford	−1m 6.380s	9	3	M

Round 11/16	**BRITISH GP** Silverstone				**Rubens Barrichello**		
	20 July 2003			Race 708	Ferrari F2003-GA 208.757kph, 129.716mph		

Gambling on new-spec Bridgestones, Barrichello started from pole, but the opening lap went poorly. He was still third after a brief SC, but after its second appearance, to detain a crazy track-invader, the picture changed. When released on lap 16 Rubens found himself eighth in a SC-generated snake headed by two Toyotas. By lap 31, overtaking in inspired fashion, he lay 10s behind leader Räikkönen. On lap 42, following the second pit stops, Rubens delivered the *coup de grâce* on Kimi, a move which started at Stowe and finished at Bridge. Six laps later Montoya also demoted Räikkönen, the Columbian's drive almost as amazing as the sensational winner. That day there were 17 overtakes for points-paying positions and plenty more besides. A F1 classic.

POLE POSITION Barrichello, Ferrari, 1m 21.209s (0.172s), 227.900kph, 141.611mph
LAPS 60 x 5.141 km, 3.195 miles
DISTANCE 308.356 km, 191.604 miles
STARTERS/FINISHERS 20/17
WEATHER Cloudy, warm, dry
LAP LEADERS Trulli 1-12 (12); C da Matta, Toyota 13-29 (17); Räikkönen 30-35, 40-41 (8); Barrichello 36-39, 42-60 (23); SC 6-7, 12-15 (6)
WINNER'S LAPS 1-10 P3, 11-12 P2, 13-15 P8, 16 P7, 17-25 P6, 26-27 P5, 28-29 P4, 30 P3, 31-35 P2, 36-39 P1, 40-41 P2, 42-60 P1
FASTEST LAP Barrichello, Ferrari, 1m 22.236s (lap 38), 225.054kph, 139.843mph
CHAMPIONSHIP M Schumacher 69, Räikkönen 62, Montoya 55, R Schumacher 53, Barrichello 49

Pos	Driver	Car	Time/gap	Grid	Stops	Tyres
1	R Barrichello	Ferrari	1h 28m 37.554s	1	2	B
2	J P Montoya	Williams-BMW	−5.462s	7	2	M
3	K Räikkönen	McLaren-Mercedes	−10.676s	3	2	M
4	M Schumacher	Ferrari	−25.648s	5	2	B
5	D Coulthard	McLaren-Mercedes	−36.827s	12	2	M
6	J Trulli	Renault	−43.067s	2	2	M

GERMAN GP Hockenheim

3 August 2003   **Race 709**

Juan Pablo Montoya

Williams-BMW FW25 207.036kph, 128.646mph

Räikkönen a brilliant start from the third row; Ralf Schumacher a tardy getaway from P2. By turn one Barrichello became the unwitting meat in their 150mph sandwich, the violent clash eliminating all three cars, Räikkönen into the barriers. Making good use of his pole Montoya was well clear of the carnage, and once released by the SC sailed away to an unchallenged 65s victory. Behind, Schumacher's Ferrari fought with the Renault pair, ultimately getting the better of them only for a late puncture to lose a certain second place. Coulthard was the beneficiary, having passed an oversteering Trulli with seven to go. With his second win Montoya was now a genuine title contender, having dropped just ten points in the last six rounds.

POLE POSITION Montoya, Williams-BMW, 1m 15.167s (0.018s), 219.064kph, 136.120mph
LAPS 67 x 4.574 km, 2.842 miles
DISTANCE 306.458 km, 190.424 miles
STARTERS/FINISHERS 20/13
WEATHER Sunny, very hot, dry
LAP LEADERS Montoya 1-17, 19-67 (66); Alonso 18 (1); SC 1-3 (3)
WINNER'S LAPS 1-17 P1, 18 P2, 19-67 P1
FASTEST LAP Montoya, Williams-BMW, 1m 14.917s (lap 14), 219.795kph, 136.574mph
CHAMPIONSHIP M Schumacher 71, Montoya 65, Räikkönen 62, R Schumacher 53, Barrichello 49

Pos	Driver	Car	Time/gap	Grid	Stops	Tyres
1	J P Montoya	Williams-BMW	1h 28m 48.769s	1	3	M
2	D Coulthard	McLaren-Mercedes	−1m 5.459s	10	2	M
3	J Trulli	Renault	−1m 9.060s	4	2	M
4	F Alonso	Renault	−1m 9.344s	8	2	M
5	O Panis	Toyota	−1 lap	7	3	M
6	C da Matta	Toyota	−1 lap	9	3	M

Renault R23B

HUNGARIAN GP Hungaroring

24 August 2003   **Race 710**

Fernando Alonso

Renault R23B 185.810kph, 115.458mph

With victory in his 30th race Fernando Alonso became the youngest GP winner of all time at just 22. It was a scintillating display, Renault's 13th victory, the result never in question from his rocket-ship getaway from pole to the moment he led the lapped Michael Schumacher across the line 99 minutes later. Webber's Jaguar provided some assistance, qualifying a creditable P3 and behaving like a mobile chicane for the opening 12 laps, during which Alonso gained 20s over the pack. The Ferraris were nowhere, Barrichello suffering suspension failure and Schumacher starting and finishing eighth. So with Räikkönen P2 and Montoya P3 despite a late spin, just two points covered the top three title contenders with only three rounds remaining.

POLE POSITION Alonso, Renault, 1m 21.688s (0.256s), 193.071kph, 119.969mph
LAPS 70 x 4.381 km, 2.722 miles
DISTANCE 306.663 km, 190.552 miles
STARTERS/FINISHERS 20/13
WEATHER Sunny, very hot, dry
LAP LEADERS Alonso 1-13, 15-70 (69); Räikkönen 14 (1)
WINNER'S LAPS 1-13 P1, 14 P2, 15-70 P1
FASTEST LAP Montoya, Williams-BMW, 1m 22.095s (lap 37), 192.7114ph, 119.374mph
CHAMPIONSHIP M Schumacher 72, Montoya 71, Räikkönen 70, R Schumacher 58, Alonso 54

Pos	Driver	Car	Time/gap	Grid	Stops	Tyres
1	F Alonso	Renault	1h 39m 1.460s	1	3	M
2	K Räikkönen	McLaren-Mercedes	−16.768s	7	3	M
3	J P Montoya	Williams-BMW	−34.537s	4	3	M
4	R Schumacher	Williams-BMW	−35.620s	2	3	M
5	D Coulthard	McLaren-Mercedes	−56.535s	9	2	M
6	M Webber	Jaguar-Ford	−1m 12.643s	3	3	M

ITALIAN GP Monza

14 September 2003   Race 711

Michael Schumacher
Ferrari F2003-GA 247.585kph, 153.843mph

In the last five races M. Schumacher had led not once, lapped in the last two. These stark facts made his and Ferrari's victory at Monza simply superb. Michael's eulogy at the post-race conference verged on insufferable but it was one of his greatest victories, his 50th for the Scuderia and an astonishing resurgence for the team following the humiliation of Budapest. The pole position; the scrubbed front tyres; the skinny aero set-up; the fuel levels; the pit stops, all superbly conceived and executed. And a truly sublime drive, from seeing off Montoya on the first lap to breaking his challenge in traffic. This was the stuff of championships. Yet Montoya P2 and Räikkönen P4 had by no means conceded. After a testing accident, Gené subbed for Ralf.

POLE POSITION M Schumacher, Ferrari, 1m 20.963s (0.051s), 257.584kph, 160.055mph
LAPS 53 x 5.793 km, 3.600 miles
DISTANCE 306.719 km, 190.586 miles
STARTERS/FINISHERS 20/13
WEATHER Sunny, hot, dry
LAP LEADERS M Schumacher 1-15, 17-53 (52); Montoya 16 (1)
WINNER'S LAPS 1-15 P1, 16 P2, 17-53 P1
FASTEST LAP M Schumacher, Ferrari, 1m 21.832 (lap 14), 254.848kph, 158.356mph
CHAMPIONSHIP M Schumacher 82, Montoya 79, Räikkönen 75, R Schumacher 58, Barrichello 55

Pos	Driver	Car	Time/gap	Grid	Stops	Tyres
1	M Schumacher	Ferrari	1h 14m 19.838s	1	2	B
2	J P Montoya	Williams-BMW	−5.294s	2	2	M
3	R Barrichello	Ferrari	−11.835s	3	2	B
4	K Räikkönen	McLaren-Mercedes	−12.834s	4	2	M
5	M Gené	Williams-BMW	−27.891s	5	2	M
6	J Villeneuve	BAR-Honda	−1 lap	10	2	B

UNITED STATES GP Indianapolis

28 September 2003   Race 712

Michael Schumacher
Ferrari F2003-GA 196.164kph, 121.891mph

Rather abruptly the championship was effectively over: Schumacher an exuberant race-winner; Räikkönen, by finishing P2, hanging on by his fingertips, but Montoya blowing his bid with P6. The race between Räikkönen and Schumacher turned on tyre performance. Over the initial dry then damp conditions, Räikkönen's Michelins re-emphasised the Finn's pole position. But once the rain intensified, Schumacher's Bridgestones were unstoppable, amply demonstrated by Button's similarly clad BAR-Honda leading laps 23–37. As for Montoya, a typically impetuous overtaking clash with Barrichello on lap 2 led to a championship-losing drive-through penalty. On such split-second judgements are championships won … or lost.

POLE POSITION Räikkönen, McLaren-Mercedes, 1m 11.670s (0.124s), 210.565kph, 130.839mph
LAPS 73 x 4.192 km, 2.605 miles
DISTANCE 306.016 km, 190.150 miles
STARTERS/FINISHERS 20/11
WEATHER Cloudy, cold, dry then rain
LAP LEADERS Räikkönen 1-18 (18); M Schumacher 19, 38-47, 49-73 (36); M Webber, Jaguar-Ford 20-21 (2); D Coulthard, McLaren-Mercedes 22 (1); J Button 23-37 (15); Frentzen 48 (1)
WINNER'S LAPS 1-4 P4, 5-6 P3, 7-14 P6, 15-16 P5, 17 P3, 18 P2, 19 P1, 20 P5, 21 P11, 22 P8, 23 P7, 24-25 P6, 26-27 P4, 28-32 P3, 33-37 P2, 38-47 P1, 48 P2, 49-73 P1
FASTEST LAP M Schumacher, Ferrari, 1m 11.473s (lap 13), 211.145kph, 131.200mph
CHAMPIONSHIP M Schumacher 92, Räikkönen 83, Montoya 82, R Schumacher 58, Barrichello 55

Pos	Driver	Car	Time/gap	Grid	Stops	Tyres
1	M Schumacher	Ferrari	1h 33m 35.997s	7	3	B
2	K Räikkönen	McLaren-Mercedes	−18.258s	1	3	M
3	H-H Frentzen	Sauber-Petronas	−37.964s	15	2	B
4	J Trulli	Renault	−48.329s	10	3	M
5	N Heidfeld	Sauber-Petronas	−56.403s	13	3	B
6	J P Montoya	Williams-BMW	−1 lap	4	4	M

JAPANESE GP Suzuka

12 October 2003   Race 713

Rubens Barrichello
Ferrari F2003-GA 216.611kph, 134.596mph

Despite the destiny of the championship seemingly assured, doubt remained to the end. Uncertainty stemmed from the championship leader qualifying 14th in damp conditions, dropping to dead last on lap 7 with nosecone damage from a clash with Sato, and only reaching the P8 necessary to claim his decisive championship point with 13 laps to go. Even then he survived a second incident with brother Ralf on lap 41. Until then there was just that faint chance that race-leader Barrichello might not finish and enable the vainly chasing Räikkönen to snatch an unlikely win and an even more unlikely championship. But in reality, once Montoya, lap 9, and Alonso, lap 17, succumbed to mechanical failure Barrichello was unchallenged.

POLE POSITION Barrichello, Ferrari, 1m 31.713s (0.699s), 227.941kph, 141.636mph
LAPS 53 x 5.807 km, 3.608 miles
DISTANCE 307.573 km, 191.117 miles
STARTERS/FINISHERS 20/16
WEATHER Overcast, warm, light rain
LAP LEADERS J P Montoya, Williams-BMW 1-8 (8); Barrichello 9-12, 17-40, 42-53 (40); Räikkönen 13 (1); Button 14-16 (3); Coulthard 41 (1)
WINNER'S LAPS 1-8 P2, 9-12 P1, 13 P4, 14 P3, 15-16 P2, 17-40 P1, 41 P2, 42-53 P1
FASTEST LAP R Schumacher, Williams-BMW, 1m 33.408s (lap 43), 223.805kph, 139.066mph
CHAMPIONSHIP M Schumacher 93, Räikkönen 91, Montoya 82, Barrichello 65, R Schumacher 58

Pos	Driver	Car	Time/gap	Grid	Stops	Tyres
1	R Barrichello	Ferrari	1h 25m 11.743s	1	3	B
2	K Räikkönen	McLaren-Mercedes	−11.085s	8	2	M
3	D Coulthard	McLaren-Mercedes	−11.614s	7	3	M
4	J Button	BAR-Honda	−33.106s	9	2	B
5	J Trulli	Renault	−34.269s	19	3	M
6	T Sato	BAR-Honda	−51.692s	13	2	B

2003 CHAMPIONSHIP FACTS AND FOLKLORE

- 2003 saw the introduction of an important new safety measure. The HANS device, standing for 'head and neck support', became compulsory wear for drivers. The device fitted over the shoulders with belts/chords attached to the back of the driver's helmet.
- In an effort to shake up the grid, one-by-one 'single-shot' qualifying would take place on Saturday, each driver making a single flying qualifying lap in the reverse order of Friday free-practice times.
- Further, by banning refuelling between qualifying and the start of the race, cars held overnight in *parc fermé* conditions, grid order would be further influenced by the fuel strategy adopted for the race.
- As well as mixing up the grid to improve the show, this move also addressed the FIA's dual imperative, cost reduction. At a stroke it eliminated the expensive practice of fielding special qualifying cars/engines, spare cars also no longer allowed except in the case of serious damage.
- Additionally an optional extra two hours of testing on Friday morning was on offer while the traditional Sunday morning warm-up was replaced with a 15-minute session before Saturday qualifying.
- The Friday testing option was a way to wean teams away from the costly practice of virtually unlimited testing during the season conducted by separate test teams operated in parallel with the race teams. Teams could now choose the alternative Friday morning scenario as long as testing during the rest of the season was limited to 20 car-days.
- As a further incentive, the 'Friday testers' could select their two types of tyres for the weekend after their Friday test session, the rest making their selection before Thursday scrutineering. For 2003 Renault, Jordan and Minardi chose the Friday testing route.
- To keep the championship alive for as long as possible, the points scoring system was changed to 10 points for a win, 8 for second place, then 6, 5, 4, 3, 2, 1 down to eighth place, substantially reducing the weighting attached to race victories.
- Initially the FIA also threatened to ban electronic 'driver aids' for 2003 but it didn't happen, the threat used as a negotiating ploy with the manufacturers to supply affordable engine packages to independent teams for 2004.
- But the major car manufacturers, now represented by the GPWC, weren't going to be pushed around and took a step closer towards bringing alive their threat of a breakaway series from 2008. The GPWC obtained the signatures of all ten team principles on a memorandum of intent promising long-term stability and increased team payments in a more transparent commercial environment. Amen.
- After the monotony of last year, 2003 turned out to be a far more combative season, although precisely to what extent this was the FIA's regulatory measures rather than divine providence is open to debate, 2004 siding with the latter. Anyway, eight different winning drivers was remarkable, only exceeded in 1982 with 11, and 1975 with nine.
- The same ten teams which contested the final races of last season lined up for 2003, a 16-round championship due to the lamentable absence of Spa, dropped from the calendar over conflicts concerning tobacco advertising.
- The third round, Brazil, marked the 700th F1 world championship race, of which 109 were rain-affected, 156 flag-to-flag victories, and 190 1-2 team finishes.
- The closeness of both championship contests was apparent from the 2003 points tables, 11 points separating the top three drivers, 16 the top three teams.
- McLaren got off to a flyer, giving the rest a jolt by picking up a pair of victories at the first two rounds, after which there were no more wins although Räikkönen scored regular big points, including a record-equalling seven P2s, to stay in contention till the end.
- Although he won the opening round, Coulthard had a weak season, never able to master single-shot qualifying.
- McLaren's season was also held back by reliability and other problems with their new car, the supposedly radical MP4-18. It even repeatedly failed the FIA side-impact test and in the end never raced.
- Until the fifth round, reliability issues also delayed the first appearance of Ferrari's new car, the F2003-GA, the GA suffix in recognition of Gianni Agnelli, the FIAT boss who had died in January aged 82. This tribute to Agnelli was made in recognition of the powerful personal support he had provided to the 1990s Ferrari revival under Luca di Montezemolo.
- Ferrari failed to resume their 2002 winning ways until the fourth round, Australia the first time for 54 races that a Ferrari driver had not stood on the podium. There was then a winning flurry followed by another lull, during which period Räikkönen and Montoya closed in on Schumacher.
- In Hungary Ferrari appeared to be down and out, Schumacher lapped by winner Alonso and three points covering the top three in the championship.
- There was then an incident that, in the eyes of the Michelin runners, branded Ferrari poor losers, although it probably had the desired effect of destabilising the Michelin teams. Despite unchanged moulds over three years, Ferrari protested the legality of the 270mm contact patch on Michelin front tyres. As a result the FIA changed their measurement protocol, forcing Michelin to revise their tyres for Monza to ensure they met the new measurement criteria.
- But despite the gamesmanship, the Scuderia showed great strength in depth by working as a unit to win the final three rounds of the championship and deservedly secure both titles.
- Michael Schumacher's remarkable Monza victory was the fastest GP of all time. His average speed of 153.843mph exceeded the 150.755mph established by Peter Gethin's BRM on the 1971 pre-chicane track layout 32 years before.
- Speaking of BRM, Tony Rudd, their chief engineer during the 1960s glory days, died aged 80.
- Ferrari's fourth consecutive drivers' title equalled McLaren's 1988–91 sequence with Senna and Prost, while a fifth successive constructors' title now surpassed the McLaren-Honda record of that time.
- But the Williams-BMW team would reflect on 2003 with the greatest regret of opportunity missed. With two wins for each driver and numerous other podium finishes, they were in the hunt for both titles until the US GP, the penultimate round.
- Of the leading teams, the Williams FW25 was the only new

RACE 711, Italian GP: Monza was one of Schumacher's greatest victories, his 50th for the Scuderia, bouncing back after failing in the previous five races to lead even one lap.

car at Melbourne, but as a team they didn't come truly alive until Monaco, round seven, ruinously late.

■ During the season BMW reached the 300 bhp-per-litre 'holy grail' and extended their contract with Williams until the end of 2009, but there were signs that cracks were opening in relationships between team and engine supplier, even between team and drivers, Montoya announcing his departure to McLaren for 2005.

■ Towards the end of the season the FIA's stance on 'team orders' shifted, with a statement that their blatant imposition would not be accepted as the championship reached its climax.

■ So it was McLaren's Kimi Räikkönen who took the championship down to the wire, but if it had led to a world title it would have been farcical, the revised points system differentiating six Schumacher race victories to Räikkönen's one by 10 points within a 158 winning points total. Ludicrous.

■ Flavio Briatori's controversial decision to replace Button with Alonso for 2003 looked like a good call when the Spaniard took his first pole in Malaysia, the youngest ever. He also stole the youngest race leader mantle from Rubens, who had held both benchmarks for some nine years since the 1994 Belgian GP.

■ Then in Hungary, at 22 years 26 days, Alonso became the youngest-ever GP winner, eclipsing Bruce McLaren's long-standing landmark from 1959.

■ Malaysia was the first Renault pole since the 1984 French GP, and the Hungarian victory their first win as a constructor since Alain Prost 20 years and 10 days earlier, Austria 1983.

■ After 109 starts Giancarlo Fisichella won his first GP victory in Brazil for Jordan-Ford. In their 200th GP start it was the team's fourth and final victory.

■ It was also the final F1 victory for engine supplier Ford. In association with Cosworth, their championship race victory tally was 176, 155 accounted for by the remarkable DFV series. By comparison, Ferrari engines had reached 167 GP victories, Renault 96.

Championship ranking	Championship points	Driver nationality	2003 Drivers Championship		Races contested	Race victories	Podiumse excl. victories	Races led	Lights to flag victories	Laps led	Poles	Fastest laps	Triple Crowns
			Driver	Car									
1	93	GER	Michael Schumacher	Ferrari	16	6	2	8		303	5	5	3
2	91	FIN	Kimi Räikkönen	McLaren-Mercedes	16	1	9	11		138	2	3	
3	82	COL	Juan Pablo Montoya	Williams-BMW	16	2	7	6		144	1	3	1
4	65	BRA	Rubens Barrichello	Ferrari	16	2	6	7		80	3	3	1
5	58	GER	Ralf Schumacher	Williams-BMW	15	2	1	5	1	164	3	1	
6	55	ESP	Fernando Alonso	Renault	16	1	3	5		97	2	1	
7	51	GBR	David Coulthard	McLaren-Mercedes	16	1	2	4		39			
8	33	ITA	Jarno Trulli	Renault	16		1	2		14			
9	17	GBR	Jenson Button	BAR-Honda	15			2		18			
10	17	AUS	Mark Webber	Jaguar-Ford	16			1		2			
11	13	GER	Heinz-Harald Frentzen	Sauber-Petronas	16		1	1		1			
12	12	ITA	Giancarlo Fisichella	Jordan-Ford	16	1		1		1			
13	10	BRA	Cristiano da Matta	Toyota	16			1		17			
14	6	GER	Nick Heidfeld	Sauber-Petronas	16								
15	6	FRA	Olivier Panis	Toyota	16								
16	6	CAN	Jacques Villeneuve	BAR-Honda	14								
17	4	ESP	Marc Gené	Williams-BMW	1								
18	3	JPN	Takuma Sato	BAR-Honda	1								
19	1	IRL	Ralph Firman	Jordan-Ford	14								
20	1	GBR	Justin Wilson	Minardi-Ford (11) Jaguar-Ford (5)	16								

Championship ranking	Championship points	Team/Marque nationality	2003 Constructors Championship		Engine maker nationality	Races contested	Race victories	1-2 finishes	Podiums excl. victories	Races led	Laps led	Poles	Fastest laps
			Chassis	Engine									
1	158	ITA	Ferrari F2003-GA, F2002	Ferrari 3.0 V10	ITA	16	8		8	12	383	8	8
2	144	GBR	Williams FW25	BMW 3.0 V10	GER	16	4	2	8	10	308	4	4
3	142	GBR	McLaren MP4-17D	Mercedes-Benz 3.0 V10	GER	16	2		11	11	177	2	3
4	88	FRA	Renault R23, R23B	Renault 3.0 V10	FRA	16	1		4	7	111	2	1
5	26	GBR	BAR 005	Honda 3.0 V10	JPN	16				2	18		
6	19	SUI	Sauber C22	Petronas 3.0 V10	ITA	16			1	1	1		
7	18	GBR	Jaguar R4	Ford Cosworth 3.0 V10	GBR	16				1	2		
8	16	JPN	Toyota TF103	Toyota 3.0 V10	JPN	16				1	17		
9	13	IRL	Jordan EJ13	Ford Cosworth 3.0 V10	GBR	16	1			1	1		

2004

Schumacher's seventh heaven

THE TALE OF THE TITLE

- Ferrari's dip in competitiveness last season proved short-lived, 2004 witnessing a return to total supremacy.
- A record fifth drivers' championship on the trot brought Schumacher an unprecedented seventh title.
- Ferrari's 14th overall and sixth successive constructors' cup took them five ahead of nearest rival Williams.
- In a season comprising an unparalleled 18 rounds, Ferrari won yet another 15 race victories.
- And Schumacher raised his own record for individual wins in a season to an astonishing 13.
- He was victorious in 12 of the first 13 rounds of the championship, his only stumble at Monaco.
- Eight Ferrari 1-2 finishes and two further Barrichello victories vividly illustrated their performance advantage.
- Using bespoke Bridgestone tyres, the Scuderia was only beaten three times by the Michelin teams.
- At Monaco Jarno Trulli won for the improving Renault team, even though Briatori later fired him.
- For Räikkönen to win at Spa, McLaren had to produce a radically revised 'B' version of the MP4-19.
- And Williams had to ditch the ineffective 'walrus' nose to give Montoya a winning steed at the Brazil finale.
- In the constructors', Williams and McLaren finished behind Renault as well as surprise package BAR-Honda.
- Jenson Button delivered nine podiums for BAR-Honda, but the Michelin team rarely looked outright winners.
- Neither did Jaguar with a meagre ten points, after five years Ford announcing the team's withdrawal from F1.
- And not forgetting: Friday drivers; Buttongate.

THE CHASE FOR THE CHAMPIONSHIP

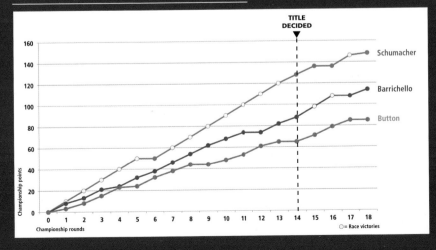

Ferrari F2004

Round 1/18	**AUSTRALIAN GP** Melbourne						**Michael Schumacher**
	7 March 2004					**Race 714**	Ferrari F2004 219.011kph, 136.087mph

Nothing during winter testing had prepared F1 for the shocking 1-2 rout inflicted by Ferrari in the season opener. Dominating practice, the red cars qualified 0.8s ahead of last year and 0.5 up on the rest. Neither was headed in their lights-to-flag team demonstration run, both drivers recording race laps almost 1s faster than their closest opposition, Fernando Alonso. Some surmised that it was a freak result, Ferrari's use of quasi-bespoke Bridgestone tyres fortuitously combining with cool temperatures and the particular characteristics of the Melbourne track. Wait until Sepang, they counselled. In any case, McLaren's new car was off the pace and driver in-fighting had cost Williams dearly. At least that was true.

POLE POSITION M Schumacher, Ferrari, 1m 24.408s (0.074s), 226.172kph, 140.537mph
LAPS 58 x 5.303 km, 3.295 miles
DISTANCE 307.574 km, 191.117 miles
STARTERS/FINISHERS 20/14
WEATHER Cloudy, warm, dry
LAP LEADERS M Schumacher 1-58 (58)
WINNER'S LAPS 1-58 P1
FASTEST LAP M Schumacher, Ferrari, 1m 24.125s (lap 29), 226.933kph, 141.010mph
CHAMPIONSHIP M Schumacher 10, Barrichello 8, Alonso 6, R Schumacher 5, Montoya 4

Pos	Driver	Car	Time/gap	Grid	Stops	Tyres
1	M Schumacher	Ferrari	1h 24m 15.757s	1	3	B
2	R Barrichello	Ferrari	–13.605s	2	3	B
3	F Alonso	Renault	–34.673s	5	3	M
4	R Schumacher	Williams-BMW	–1m 0.423s	8	3	M
5	J P Montoya	Williams-BMW	–1m 8.536s	3	3	M
6	J Button	BAR-Honda	–1m 10.598s	4	3	M

Round 2/18	**MALAYSIAN GP** Sepang						**Michael Schumacher**
	21 March 2004					**Race 715**	Ferrari F2004 204.384kph, 126.998mph

Schumacher won again from pole, but at least this was a race. Intermittent dampness around the track initially favoured Michelin runners. This enabled Montoya from P4 to overtake Barrichello on lap 2 and briefly attack Schumacher until, as the track dried, the world champion assumed control. Mark Webber's Jaguar had split the Ferraris by qualifying on the front row, but his race was effectively over when the anti-stall kicked in as the lights went out. The other surprise package was Button's BAR-Honda. Quick qualifying pace brought P6 but even better race pace resulted in Jenson's first-ever podium in his 68th race. Barrichello came fourth, and Coulthard's sixth in a Renault sandwich provided at least some encouragement for McLaren.

POLE POSITION M Schumacher, Ferrari, 1m 33.074s (0.641s), 214.397kph, 133.220mph
LAPS 56 x 5.543 km, 3.444 miles
DISTANCE 310.408 km, 192.879 miles
STARTERS/FINISHERS 20/16
WEATHER Overcast, very hot, dry
LAP LEADERS M Schumacher 1-9, 13-26, 28-56 (52); Montoya 10-12 (3); Barrichello 27 (1)
WINNER'S LAPS 1-9 P1, 10 P7, 11-12 P3, 13-26 P1, 27 P2, 28-56 P1
FASTEST LAP Montoya, Williams-BMW, 1m 34.223s (lap 28), 211.782kph, 131.596mph
CHAMPIONSHIP M Schumacher 20, Barrichello 13, Montoya 12, Button 9, Alonso 8

Pos	Driver	Car	Time/gap	Grid	Stops	Tyres
1	M Schumacher	Ferrari	1h 31m 7.490s	1	3	B
2	J P Montoya	Williams-BMW	–5.022s	4	3	M
3	J Button	BAR-Honda	–11.568s	6	3	M
4	R Barrichello	Ferrari	–13.616s	3	3	B
5	J Trulli	Renault	–37.360s	8	3	M
6	D Coulthard	McLaren-Mercedes	–53.098s	9	3	M

BAHRAIN GP Sakhir
4 April 2004
Race 716

Michael Schumacher
Ferrari F2004 208.976kph, 129.852mph

Ferraris, Williams and BAR-Hondas paired-up on the grid to fill the first three rows for the inaugural Bahrain GP. For the third successive race, M. Schumacher duly converted pole into victory. By lap 11 the gap to his teammate was around 10s, half won on the road, the rest a troublesome wheel-nut during Barrichello's first stop. Thereafter he controlled his lead, Michael's 73rd victory that clear-cut. Montoya could offer no challenge to either Ferrari, losing a certain third when the Williams' hydraulics began to fail towards the end. So Button, having jumped Trulli at the third stop, scored another podium. From a lowly start Alonso did well to finish P6 whereas McLaren's nightmare endured, neither car featuring and both exiting early.

POLE POSITION M Schumacher, Ferrari, 1m 30.139s (0.173s), 216.345kph, 134.431mph
LAPS 57 x 5.417 km, 3.366 miles
DISTANCE 308.523 km, 191.707 miles
STARTERS/FINISHERS 20/17
WEATHER Cloudy, hot, dry then light rain
LAP LEADERS M Schumacher 1-9, 12-24, 28-41, 44-57 (50); Barrichello 10, 25-27, 42-43 (6); Button, 11 (1)
WINNER'S LAPS 1-9 P1, 10 P6, 11 P2, 12-24 P1, 25-26 P3, 27 P2, 28-41 P1, 42-43 P2, 44-57 P1
FASTEST LAP M Schumacher, Ferrari, 1m 30.252s (lap 7), 216.074kph, 134.263mph
CHAMPIONSHIP M Schumacher 30, Barrichello 21, Button 15, Montoya 12, Alonso 11

Pos	Driver	Car	Time/gap	Grid	Stops	Tyres
1	M Schumacher	Ferrari	1h 28m 34.875s	1	3	B
2	R Barrichello	Ferrari	−1.367s	2	3	B
3	J Button	BAR-Honda	−26.687s	6	3	M
4	J Trulli	Renault	−32.214s	7	3	M
5	T Sato	BAR-Honda	−52.460s	5	3	M
6	F Alonso	Renault	−53.156s	16	3	M

SAN MARINO GP Imola
25 April 2004
Race 717

Michael Schumacher
Ferrari F2004 212.405kph, 131.983mph

A new pole-sitter, Jenson Button, M. Schumacher alongside. Blasting from the grid, Button was 2.7s ahead on lap 1, the Ferrari's Bridgestones slow to warm up. On lap 2 Montoya saw his chance to attack the sluggish Ferrari, the German ruthlessly defending to leave the Columbian seething. Then abruptly the true race performance of the Ferrari's tyres kicked in, reeling in the BAR-Honda and, as Jenson pitted on lap 9, letting rip with two explosive laps which turned a 1s deficit into a 5s lead. Game over. Montoya trailed in third, complaining that Williams were no longer even 'best of the rest', but perhaps conveniently overlooking that McLaren, the team he would join next year, remained even deeper in the mire.

POLE POSITION Button, BAR-Honda, 1m 19.753s (0.258s), 222.672kph, 138.362mph
LAPS 62 x 4.933 km, 3.065 miles
DISTANCE 305.609 km, 189.897 miles
STARTERS/FINISHERS 20/16
WEATHER Sunny, warm, dry
LAP LEADERS Button 1-8 (8); M Schumacher 9-62 (54)
WINNER'S LAPS 1-8 P2, 9-62 P1
FASTEST LAP M Schumacher, Ferrari, 1m 20.411s (lap 10), 220.850kph, 137.230mph
CHAMPIONSHIP M Schumacher 40, Barrichello 24, Button 23, Montoya 18, Alonso 16

Pos	Driver	Car	Time/gap	Grid	Stops	Tyres
1	M Schumacher	Ferrari	1h 26m 19.670s	2	3	B
2	J Button	BAR-Honda	−9.702s	1	3	M
3	J P Montoya	Williams-BMW	−21.617s	3	3	M
4	F Alonso	Renault	−23.654s	6	3	M
5	J Trulli	Renault	−36.216s	9	3	M
6	R Barrichello	Ferrari	−36.683s	4	3	B

SPANISH GP Cataluña
9 May 2004
Race 718

Michael Schumacher
Ferrari F2004 209.205kph, 129.994mph

Jarno Trulli made a humdinger start from row two to lead M. Schumacher, back on customary pole, over the opening laps. Under no immediate threat from behind, Schumacher took the safe option, electing to do his overtaking in the pits. On lap 11 he duly rejoined ahead of the Renault driver but behind the two-stopping Barrichello. Rubens' alternate strategy from a P5 grid-slot got him ahead of Trulli by the finish, these three comprising the podium. Breezy qualifying conditions put Button out of contention, but teammate Sato reaffirmed BAR-Honda potential by qualifying P3, finishing fifth. Alonso, another victim of the gusting wind, made up ground from P8 to finish fourth. McLaren remained off the pace, Williams hobbled by brake issues.

POLE POSITION M Schumacher, Ferrari, 1m 15.022s (0.617s), 222.030kph, 137.964mph
LAPS 66 x 4.627 km, 2.875 miles
DISTANCE 305.256 km, 189.677 miles
STARTERS/FINISHERS 20/13
WEATHER Sunny, hot, dry
LAP LEADERS Trulli 1-8 (8); M Schumacher 9-10, 18-66 (51); Barrichello 11-17 (7)
WINNER'S LAPS 1-8 P2, 9-10 P1, 11 P3, 12-17 P2, 18-66 P1
FASTEST LAP M Schumacher, Ferrari, 1m 17.450s (lap 12), 215.070kph, 133.639mph
CHAMPIONSHIP M Schumacher 50, Barrichello 32, Button 24, Alonso 21, Trulli 21

Pos	Driver	Car	Time/gap	Grid	Stops	Tyres
1	M Schumacher	Ferrari	1h 27m 32.841s	1	3	B
2	R Barrichello	Ferrari	−13.290s	5	2	B
3	J Trulli	Renault	−32.294s	4	3	M
4	F Alonso	Renault	−32.952s	8	3	M
5	T Sato	BAR-Honda	−42.327s	3	3	M
6	R Schumacher	Williams-BMW	−1m 13.804s	6	3	M

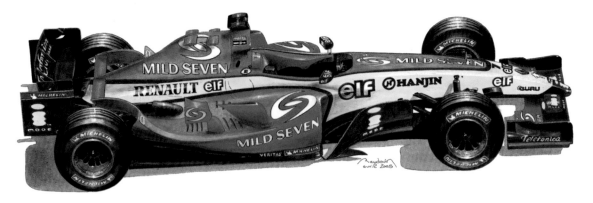

Renault R24

MONACO GP Monte Carlo
23 May 2004

Race 719

Jarno Trulli
Renault R24 145.880kph, 90.646mph

Jarno Trulli's first pole, Button next up, these two destined to finish first and second just metres apart following a dramatic race of incident and excitement. The excitement peaked in the closing dozen laps as Button chased down Trulli's 5s advantage in a bid to beat the Italian to that elusive first-ever GP victory. A SC incident began as early as lap 2, the smokescreen from Sato's detonated Honda blinding Fisichella such that he slammed into Coulthard's McLaren and flipped. Later, on lap 41, Alonso crashed out of second as he attempted to lap R. Schumacher in the tunnel. Ironically, four laps later a not dissimilar fate befell M. Schumacher, then leading, tangling with Montoya's Williams while still under SC conditions.

POLE POSITION Trulli, Renault, 1m 13.985s (0.411s), 162.519kph, 100.985mph
LAPS 77 x 3.340 km, 2.075 miles (Scheduled for 78 laps but reduced after aborted start)
DISTANCE 257.180 km, 159.804 miles
STARTERS/FINISHERS 20/10
WEATHER Sunny, warm, dry
LAP LEADERS Trulli 1-23, 26-42, 46-77 (72); F Alonso, Renault 24 (1); M Schumacher 25, 43-45 (4); SC 4-7, 44-46 (7)
WINNER'S LAPS 1-23 P1, 24 P3, 25 P2, 26-42 P1, 43-45 P2, 46-77 P1
FASTEST LAP M Schumacher, Ferrari, 1m 14.439s (lap 23), 161.528kph, 100.369mph
CHAMPIONSHIP M Schumacher 50, Barrichello 38, Button 32, Trulli 31, Montoya 23

Pos	Driver	Car	Time/gap	Grid	Stops	Tyres
1	J Trulli	Renault	1h 45m 46.601s	1	2	M
2	J Button	BAR-Honda	−0.497s	2	2	M
3	R Barrichello	Ferrari	−1m 15.766s	6	2	B
4	J P Montoya	Williams-BMW	−1 lap	9	2	M
5	F Massa	Sauber-Petronas	−1 lap	16	2	B
6	C da Matta	Toyota	−1 lap	15	2	M

TOP **100** RACE

EUROPEAN GP Nürburgring
30 May 2004

Race 720

Michael Schumacher
Ferrari F2004 200.159kph, 124.373mph

From pole, Michael Schumacher drove seven successive fastest laps. On the eighth he pitted 17s ahead of Räikkönen in second. Once the first pit-stop sequence had played out he completed another routine victory, never again headed and finishing 15s in front of his two-stopping teammate in second. His total dominance seemed to proclaim: 'Monaco? It was just a blip.' Button completed the podium but teammate Sato out-qualified and outraced him until forced to give up P2 15 laps out due to an altercation with Barrichello. Soon afterwards Sato was out with Honda maladies. Renault finished 4-5; the Williams pair ran into one another at the first turn, and by lap 25 both Mercedes engines had expired in the improving McLarens.

POLE POSITION M Schumacher, Ferrari, 1m 28.351s (0.635s), 209.763kph, 130.341mph
LAPS 60 x 5.148 km, 3.199 miles
DISTANCE 308.863 km, 191.919 miles
STARTERS/FINISHERS 20/15
WEATHER Cloudy with sunny intervals, warm, dry
LAP LEADERS M Schumacher 1-8, 16-60 (53); Alonso 9 (1); T Sato, BAR-Honda 10-11 (2); Barrichello 12-15 (4)
WINNER'S LAPS 1-8 P1, 9 P6, 10 P5, 11-12 P3, 13-15 P2, 16-60 P1
FASTEST LAP M Schumacher, Ferrari, 1m 29.468s (lap 7), 207.144kph, 128.714mph
CHAMPIONSHIP M Schumacher 60, Barrichello 46, Button 38, Trulli 36, Alonso 25

Pos	Driver	Car	Time/gap	Grid	Stops	Tyres
1	M Schumacher	Ferrari	1h 32m 35.101s	1	3	B
2	R Barrichello	Ferrari	−17.898s	7	2	B
3	J Button	BAR-Honda	−22.533s	5	3	M
4	J Trulli	Renault	−53.673s	3	3	M
5	F Alonso	Renault	−1m 0.987s	6	3	M
6	G Fisichella	Sauber-Petronas	−1m 13.448s	18	2	B

Round 8/18	**CANADIAN GP** Montréal						**Michael Schumacher**
	13 June 2004					**Race 721**	Ferrari F2004 207.165kph, 128.727mph

Ralf Schumacher a superb pole, his brother on the third row. Ralf drove a fast, faultless race but ended up second to his brother. How? Superior strategy maybe, Ralf three-stopping, Michael two, but on paper little to choose. So it was performance, especially when Michael's strategy gave him free air between laps 33–46. Here the now leading Ferrari gained the crucial time to rejoin still ahead at their final stops, Michael lap 47, Ralf lap 48. Post-qualifying, Renault had looked well placed for success, but both cars went out with driveshaft failure. Massa survived a huge shunt in the closing stages when his Sauber's rear suspension collapsed, and subsequently Ralf lost his P2 when the Williams team was disqualified for brake-duct irregularities!

POLE POSITION R Schumacher, Williams-BMW, 1m 12.275s (0.066s), 217.220kph, 134.974mph
LAPS 70 x 4.361 km, 2.710 miles
DISTANCE 305.270 km, 189.686 miles
STARTERS/FINISHERS 20/10
WEATHER Sunny, warm, dry
LAP LEADERS R Schumacher 1-14, 19-32, 47 (29); F Alonso, Renault 15-16 (2); M Schumacher 17-18, 33-46, 48-70 (39)
WINNER'S LAPS 1-12 P5, 13-14 P3, 15-16 P2, 17-18 P1, 19-30 P3, 31-32 P2, 33-46 P1, 47 P2, 48-70 P1
FASTEST LAP Barrichello, Ferrari, 1m 13.622s (Lap 68), 213.246kph, 132.505mph
CHAMPIONSHIP M Schumacher 70, Barrichello 54, Button 44, Trulli 36, Alonso 25

Pos	Driver	Car	Time/gap	Grid	Stops	Tyres
1	M Schumacher	Ferrari	1h 28m 24.803s	6	2	B
2	R Barrichello	Ferrari	−5.108s	1	2	B
3	J Button	BAR-Honda	−20.409s	7	3	M
4	G Fisichella	Sauber-Petronas	−1 lap	2	2	B
5	K Räikkönen	McLaren-Mercedes	−1 lap	4	5	M
6	D Coulthard	McLaren-Mercedes	−1 lap	11	3	M

Round 9/18	**UNITED STATES GP** Indianapolis						**Michael Schumacher**
	20 June 2004					**Race 722**	Ferrari F2004 182.698kph, 113.524mph

When a rear tyre deflated on lap 9 Ralf Schumacher made a massive 78g impact with the concrete wall at the fast, banked final turn. Despite anxiety over his concussed brother, out for six races with damaged vertebrae, it was business as usual for Michael. Ironically, the ensuing SC was Michael's chance to outgun pole-sitter Barrichello at the restart, although Rubens ran him close with a long second stint. Joining the Ferrari drivers on the podium was Takuma Sato who had also qualified an excellent third. Trulli drove a stormer to P4 from last place, while Alonso's Renault, from a P9 start, was third at turn one but out with a puncture by lap 8. After a dummy-grid irregularity the stewards took until lap 58 to black-flag Montoya!

POLE POSITION Barrichello, Ferrari, 1m 10.223s (0.177s), 214.903kph, 133.535mph
LAPS 73 x 4.192 km, 2.605 miles
DISTANCE 306.016 km, 190.150 miles
STARTERS/FINISHERS 20/9
WEATHER Sunny, warm, dry
LAP LEADERS Barrichello 1-5, 42-50 (14); M Schumacher 6-41, 51-73 (59); SC 1-5, 11-19 (14)
WINNER'S LAPS 1-5 P2, 6-41 P1, 42 P2, 43-45 P3, 46-50 P2, 51-73 P1
FASTEST LAP Barrichello, Ferrari, 1m 10.399s (lap 7), 214.366kph, 133.201mph
CHAMPIONSHIP M Schumacher 80, Barrichello 62, Button 44, Trulli 41, Alonso 25

Pos	Driver	Car	Time/gap	Grid	Stops	Tyres
1	M Schumacher	Ferrari	1h 40m 29.914s	2	2	B
2	R Barrichello	Ferrari	−2.950s	1	2	B
3	T Sato	BAR-Honda	−22.036s	3	2	M
4	J Trulli	Renault	−34.544s	20	2	M
5	O Panis	Toyota	−37.534s	8	2	M
6	K Räikkönen	McLaren-Mercedes	−1 lap	7	3	M

Round 10/18	**FRENCH GP** Magny-Cours						**Michael Schumacher**
	4 July 2004					**Race 723**	Ferrari F2004 205.035kph, 127.403mph

A Renault on pole, a Ferrari alongside. Could Alonso bring joy to the locals and keep Schumacher behind? He managed it for half the race but not the half that mattered. The short pit lane here presented a four-stop strategy option to Ferrari, and Renault fell for it, mirroring Ferrari's short-fuelling tactics until they realised, too late, that Brawn was planning a fourth. Adding insult to injury, Barrichello snatched third from the second Renault on the final lap. Montoya, in discomfort following a hefty practice shunt, was never in the picture, but Coulthard qualified the heavily revised McLaren third, he and Räikkönen finishing on the same lap as the winner and, a season's first, both scoring points. Button added P5 to his remarkable finishing record.

POLE POSITION Alonso, Renault, 1m 13.698s (0.273), 215.468kph, 133.886mph
LAPS 70 x 4.411 km, 2.741 miles
DISTANCE 308.586 km, 191.746 miles
STARTERS/FINISHERS 20/18
WEATHER Sunny, hot, dry
LAP LEADERS Alonso 1-32, 43-46 (36); M Schumacher 33-42, 47-70 (34)
WINNER'S LAPS 1-11 P2, 12 P8 13 P6, 14 P4, 15-29 P2, 30 P5, 31 P4, 32 P2, 33-42 P1, 43-46 P2, 47-70 P1
FASTEST LAP M Schumacher, Ferrari, 1m 15.377s (lap 32), 210.669kph, 130.904mph
CHAMPIONSHIP M Schumacher 90, Barrichello 68, Button 48, Trulli 46, Alonso 33

Pos	Driver	Car	Time/gap	Grid	Stops	Tyres
1	M Schumacher	Ferrari	1h 30m 18.133s	2	4	B
2	F Alonso	Renault	−8.329s	1	3	M
3	R Barrichello	Ferrari	−31.622s	10	3	B
4	J Trulli	Renault	−32.082s	5	3	M
5	J Button	BAR-Honda	−32.484s	4	3	M
6	D Coulthard	McLaren-Mercedes	−35.520s	3	3	M

BRITISH GP Silverstone

11 July 2004   Race 724

Michael Schumacher
Ferrari F2004 218.403kph, 135.709mph

In its second outing the revised McLaren took pole, Räikkönen building a useful gap over Barrichello's similarly fuelled Ferrari in the first stint. Dubious about pole, Ferrari had put Schumacher on the alternate two-stop strategy and by going longer and firing in super-fast laps when those ahead pitted, Schumacher assumed a lead on lap 12 he would never lose. But it wasn't quite that simple. On lap 39 Trulli suffered a massive and mysterious accident exiting Bridge, the SC presenting Kimi with a free pit stop. But when the SC pulled off Schumacher was protected from a pumped-up Finn on fresh Michelins by two backmarkers, disappointingly removing the piquancy from their closing laps duel. Barrichello made the podium, Button P4.

POLE POSITION Räikkönen, McLaren-Mercedes, 1m 18.233s (0.072s), 236.570kph, 146.998mph
LAPS 60 x 5.141 km, 3.195 miles
DISTANCE 308.356 km, 191.604 miles
STARTERS/FINISHERS 20/16
WEATHER Overcast, warm, dry
LAP LEADERS Räikkönen 1-11 (11); M Schumacher 12-60 (49); SC 41-45 (5)
WINNER'S LAPS 1-9 P4, 10 P3, 11 P2, 12-60 P1
FASTEST LAP M Schumacher, Ferrari, 1m 18.739s (lap 14), 235.049kph, 146.053mph
CHAMPIONSHIP M Schumacher 100, Barrichello 74, Button 53, Trulli 46, Alonso 33

Pos	Driver	Car	Time/gap	Grid	Stops	Tyres
1	M Schumacher	Ferrari	1h 24m 42.700s	4	2	B
2	K Räikkönen	McLaren-Mercedes	−2.130s	1	3	M
3	R Barrichello	Ferrari	−3.114s	2	3	B
4	J Button	BAR-Honda	−10.683s	3	3	M
5	J P Montoya	Williams-BMW	−12.173s	7	3	M
6	G Fisichella	Sauber-Petronas	−12.888s	20	2	B

GERMAN GP Hockenheim

25 July 2004   Race 725

Michael Schumacher
Ferrari F2004 215.852kph, 134.124mph

With Schumacher on pole only one result was possible. The home crowd hoped so and duly got their wish. But what if Räikkönen's rear wing hadn't failed, pitching him into the barriers on lap 13 when the McLaren had been snapping at the Ferrari's rear Bridgestones? What if the fast-starting Alonso's pace hadn't been compromised by a piece of debris lodged in the Renault's bargeboard? But especially, what if Button hadn't received a ten-place engine-change grid penalty and instead started third? By lap 15 Button's long opening stint vaulted him to fifth after which he just kept flying. On lap 52 he separated Alonso from second place despite a broken strap requiring him to hold on to his helmet along the straights. *Boy's Own* stuff.

POLE POSITION M Schumacher, Ferrari, 1m 13.306s (0.362s), 224.625kph, 139.576mph
LAPS 66 x 4.574 km, 2.842 miles (Scheduled for 67 laps but reduced after aborted start)
DISTANCE 301.884 km, 187.582 miles
STARTERS/FINISHERS 20/17
WEATHER Sunny, hot, dry
LAP LEADERS M Schumacher 1-10, 15-28, 35-47, 51-66 (53); Räikkönen 11 (1); Button 12-14, 30-34, 48-50 (11); Alonso 29 (1)
WINNER'S LAPS 1-10 P1, 11 P5, 12 P3, 13-14 P2, 15-28 P1, 29 P3, 30-34 P2, 35-47 P1, 48-50 P2, 51-66 P1
FASTEST LAP K Räikkönen, McLaren-Mercedes, 1m 13.780s (lap 10), 223.182kph, 138.679mph
CHAMPIONSHIP M Schumacher 110, Barrichello 74, Button 61, Trulli 46, Alonso 39

Pos	Driver	Car	Time/gap	Grid	Stops	Tyres
1	M Schumacher	Ferrari	1h 23m 54.848s	1	3	B
2	J Button	BAR-Honda	−8.388s	13	3	M
3	F Alonso	Renault	−16.060s	5	3	M
4	D Coulthard	McLaren-Mercedes	−19.231s	4	3	M
5	J P Montoya	Williams-BMW	−23.055s	2	3	M
6	M Webber	Jaguar-Ford	−41.108s	11	3	M

HUNGARIAN GP Hungaroring

15 August 2004   Race 726

Michael Schumacher
Ferrari F2004 192.798kph, 119.799mph

Just as round one in Melbourne five months earlier, Ferrari's opposition departed Budapest stunned. It wasn't the 1-2 qualifying, or that neither car was headed by a competitor during their lights-to-flag team demonstration. Once again it was that in racing trim, the Ferrari/Bridgestone combo could deliver laps 1s quicker than the next best, who, as in Melbourne, was Fernando Alonso, finishing almost a minute behind winner Schumacher. The German ace's 12th win from 13 races established a new benchmark for a single season and also brought Ferrari the 2004 constructors' championship. Montoya ran strongly, up from seventh to fourth, whereas the BAR pair both lost places. McLaren's excuse was poor tyre choice.

POLE POSITION M Schumacher, Ferrari, 1m 19.146s (0.177s), 199.272kph, 123.822mph
LAPS 70 x 4.381 km, 2.722 miles
DISTANCE 306.663 km, 190.552 miles
STARTERS/FINISHERS 20/15
WEATHER Cloudy with sunny intervals, hot, dry
LAP LEADERS M Schumacher 1-70 (70)
WINNER'S LAPS 1-70 P1
FASTEST LAP M Schumacher, Ferrari, 1m 19.071s (lap 29), 199.461kph, 123.939mph
CHAMPIONSHIP M Schumacher 120, Barrichello 82, Button 65, Trulli 46, Alonso 45

Pos	Driver	Car	Time/gap	Grid	Stops	Tyres
1	M Schumacher	Ferrari	1h 35m 26.131s	1	3	B
2	R Barrichello	Ferrari	−4.696s	2	3	B
3	F Alonso	Renault	−44.599s	5	3	M
4	J P Montoya	Williams-BMW	−1m 2.613s	7	3	M
5	J Button	BAR-Honda	−1m 7.439s	4	3	M
6	T Sato	BAR-Honda	−1 lap	3	3	M

McLaren-Mercedes MP4-19B

BELGIAN GP Spa Francorchamps

29 August 2004   **Race 727**

Kimi Räikkönen

McLaren-Mercedes MP4-19B 198.898kph, 123.590mph

The seven race-winning spell cast over F1 by M. Schumacher since Monaco had to break sometime. A first-corner fracas eliminated four cars but propelled Räikkönen from his P10 grid slot to fifth behind Schumacher. At the SC restart Kimi overtook him magnificently entering Eau Rouge, and by quarter-distance – once the Renault challenge had evaporated – he was in the lead. But a second SC on lap 30 gave Schumacher, now P2, a free pit stop and eradicated Kimi's 12s advantage. But the Finn always had the pace for victory, his second, and his and McLaren's first for 27 races. It was an admirable return to form but far too little far too late to prevent Michael's fifth consecutive drivers' title. Neither Williams finished in a race of high attrition.

POLE POSITION J Trulli, Renault, 1m 56.232s (0.072s), 216.064kph, 134.256mph
LAPS 44 x 6.976 km, 4.335 miles
DISTANCE 306.927 km, 190.716 miles
STARTERS/FINISHERS 20/11
WEATHER Cloudy with sunny intervals, warm, dry
LAP LEADERS Trulli 1-9 (9); F Alonso, Renault 10-11 (2); Räikkönen 12-13, 17-29, 31-44 (29); J P Montoya, Williams-BMW 14 (1); M Schumacher 15, 30 (2); A Pizzonia, Williams-BMW 16 (1); SC 1-4, 30-34, 40-41 (11)
WINNER'S LAPS 1-4 P5, 5 P4, 6-9 P3, 10-11 P2, 12-13 P1, 14-15 P4, 16 P3, 17-29 P1, 30 P2, 31-44 P1
FASTEST LAP Räikkönen, McLaren-Mercedes, 1m 45.108s (lap 42), 238.931kph, 148.465mph
CHAMPIONSHIP M Schumacher 128, Barrichello 88, Button 65, Trulli 46, Alonso 45

Pos	Driver	Car	Time/gap	Grid	Stops	Tyres
1	K Räikkönen	McLaren-Mercedes	1h 32m 35.274s	10	2	M
2	M Schumacher	Ferrari	−3.132s	2	2	B
3	R Barrichello	Ferrari	−4.371s	6	3	B
4	F Massa	Sauber-Petronas	−12.504s	8	4	B
5	G Fisichella	Sauber-Petronas	−14.104s	5	2	B
6	C Klien	Jaguar-Ford	−14.614s	13	3	M

ITALIAN GP Monza

12 September 2004   **Race 728**

Rubens Barrichello

Ferrari F2004 244.374kph, 151.847mph

It looked all over for Maranello at Monza. Schumacher spun on lap 1, and five later pole-sitter and race leader Barrichello pitted, intermediates the wrong choice on a drying track. Both were now mired in mid-field while Alonso and especially Button looked very racy up front. The Ferraris' eventual 1-2 finish demonstrated simply immense superiority, reeling-in Button's BAR-Honda at a second a lap. Barrichello took victory, completing his third stop just before the two-stopping Schumacher caught him. Button was a chastened third, teammate Sato next, and with Alonso spinning away a certain podium Renault surrendered runner-up spot to BAR-Honda in the constructors' championship. Minardi had to deal smartly with an alarming refuelling fire.

POLE POSITION Barrichello, Ferrari, 1m 20.089s (0.531s), 260.395kph, 161.802mph
LAPS 53 x 5.793 km, 3.600 miles
DISTANCE 306.719 km, 190.586 miles
STARTERS/FINISHERS 20/15
WEATHER Overcast, warm, wet first then drying
LAP LEADERS Barrichello 1-4, 37-53 (21); F Alonso, Renault 5-10 (6); Button 11-34 (24); M Schumacher 35-36 (2)
WINNER'S LAPS 1-4 P1, 5 P3, 6-10 P9, 11 P10, 12 P9, 13 P8, 14-15 P6, 16-29 P4, 30-33 P6, 34 P3, 35-36 P2, 37-53 P1
FASTEST LAP Barrichello, Ferrari, 1m 21.046s (lap 41), 257.320kph, 159.892mph
CHAMPIONSHIP M Schumacher 136, Barrichello 98, Button 71, Trulli 46, Alonso 45

Pos	Driver	Car	Time/gap	Grid	Stops	Tyres
1	R Barrichello	Ferrari	1h 15m 18.448s	1	3	B
2	M Schumacher	Ferrari	−1.347s	3	2	B
3	J Button	BAR-Honda	−10.197s	6	2	M
4	T Sato	BAR-Honda	−15.370s	5	2	M
5	J P Montoya	Williams-BMW	−32.352s	2	2	M
6	D Coulthard	McLaren-Mercedes	−33.439s	10	1	M

Round 16/18	**CHINESE GP** Shanghai					
	26 September 2004				**Race 729**	

With his team leader strangely off the boil, Barrichello won back-to-back victories at the inaugural Chinese GP. Schumacher's woes began by spinning off in qualifying, then an early collision in the race followed by a later spin and puncture, P12 his worst-ever F1 finish. Meanwhile his teammate made the running from pole position, seeing off genuine challenges from both Räikkönen and Button. From his front-row start Räikkönen chased Barrichello hard for half the race but failed to leapfrog the Ferrari with a short-fuelled second-stop gamble which also handed Button second, Jenson's two-stop from P3 looking particularly threatening mid-race. Ralf returned for Williams and Villeneuve replaced Trulli at Renault, neither in the points.

Pos	Driver	Car	Time/gap	Grid	Stops	Tyres
1	R Barrichello	Ferrari	1h 29m 12.420s	1	3	B
2	J Button	BAR-Honda	−1.035s	3	2	M
3	K Räikkönen	McLaren-Mercedes	−1.469s	2	3	M
4	F Alonso	Renault	−32.510s	6	2	M
5	J P Montoya	Williams-BMW	−45.193s	10	2	M
6	T Sato	BAR-Honda	−54.791s	18	2	M

Rubens Barrichello

Ferrari F2004 205.185kph, 127.496mph

POLE POSITION Barrichello, Ferrari, 1m 34.012s (0.166s), 208.735kph, 129.702mph
LAPS 56 x 5.451 km, 3.387 miles
DISTANCE 305.066 km, 189.559 miles
STARTERS/FINISHERS 20/16
WEATHER Cloudy with sunny intervals, hot, dry
LAP LEADERS Barrichello 1-12, 16-29, 36-56 (47); Button 13-14, 30-35 (8); R Schumacher, Williams-BMW 15 (1)
WINNER'S LAPS 1-12 P1, 13 P4, 14 P3, 15 P2, 16-29 P1, 30-35 P2, 36-56 P1
FASTEST LAP M Schumacher, Ferrari, 1m 32.238s (lap 55), 212.749kph, 132.196mph
CHAMPIONSHIP M Schumacher 136, Barrichello 108, Button 79, Alonso 50, Trulli 46

Round 17/18	**JAPANESE GP** Suzuka					
	10 October 2004				**Race 730**	

Threat of a typhoon postponed qualifying to Sunday morning, enabling the world champion to display a supreme return to form all in the one day. Schumacher annexed pole on a drying track and a few hours later simply walked away in the dry race, able to execute all three pit stops without once being headed, storming to a record 13th victory in a season. Ralf, starting alongside, completed their fifth brotherly 1-2 with a faultless if futile drive. The BAR-Hondas, especially Sato, pleased the locals with third and fourth, Button's tenth podium, and Trulli made a Japanese debut for Toyota. Making penultimate appearances, Jaguar qualified P3 although Webber dnf-ed, and Coulthard's 149th race for McLaren ended in a collision with Barrichello.

Pos	Driver	Car	Time/gap	Grid	Stops	Tyres
1	M Schumacher	Ferrari	1h 24m 26.985s	1	3	B
2	R Schumacher	Williams-BMW	−14.098s	2	3	M
3	J Button	BAR-Honda	−19.662s	5	2	M
4	T Sato	BAR-Honda	−31.781s	4	3	M
5	F Alonso	Renault	−37.767s	11	2	M
6	K Räikkönen	McLaren-Mercedes	−39.362s	12	2	M

Michael Schumacher

Ferrari F2004 218.524kph, 135.785mph

POLE POSITION M Schumacher, Ferrari, 1m 33.542s (0.490s), 223.484kph, 138.867mph
LAPS 53 x 5.807 km, 3.608 miles
DISTANCE 307.573 km, 191.117 miles
STARTERS/FINISHERS 20/16
WEATHER Sunny, hot, dry
LAP LEADERS M Schumacher 1-53 (3)
WINNER'S LAPS 1-53 P1
FASTEST LAP R Barrichello, Ferrari, 1m 32.730s (lap 30), 225.441kph, 140.083mph
CHAMPIONSHIP M Schumacher 146, Barrichello 108, Button 85, Alonso 54, Montoya 48

Williams-BMW FW26

Round 18/18	**BRAZILIAN GP** Interlagos		**Juan Pablo Montoya**
	24 October 2004	Race 731	Williams-BMW FW26 208.517kph, 129.566mph

At his home race Rubens took a hat-trick pole while Schumacher crashed out, consigned to the T-car and a grid penalty. A wet start, a breathless opening sequence, Räikkönen leading initially but Barrichello overtaking him on lap 4 with a classic turn one move. In the early rush for dry tyres Rubens lost ground, but crucially Montoya passed Räikkönen at turn four, the pair having spectacularly exited the pits side by side. Meanwhile Alonso led, his risky dry-tyre gamble paying off to finish P4. But victory lay between JPM and Kimi, next season's McLaren teammates. It was close, but the Columbian never made a slip. But just as with McLaren's improved mid-season form, the Williams revival came too late, the titles long-since decided.

POLE POSITION Barrichello, Ferrari, 1m 10.646s (0.204s), 219.579kph, 136.440mph
LAPS 71 x 4.309 km, 2.677 miles
DISTANCE 305.909 km, 190.083 miles
STARTERS/FINISHERS 20/10
WEATHER Overcast, warm, light rain then drying
LAP LEADERS Räikkönen 1-3, 29, 51-55 (9); Barrichello 4-5 (2); F Massa, Sauber-Petronas 6-7 (2); Alonso 8-18 (11); Montoya 19-28, 30-50, 56-71 (47)
WINNER'S LAPS 1 P5, 2-4 P3, 5 P4, 6 P9, 7 P3, 8-18 P2, 19-28 P1, 29 P2, 30-50 P1, 51-55 P2, 56-71 P1
FASTEST LAP Montoya, Williams-BMW, 1m 11.473s (lap 49), 217.038kph, 134.862mph
CHAMPIONSHIP M Schumacher 148, Barrichello 114, Button 85, Alonso 59, Montoya 58

Pos	Driver	Car	Time/gap	Grid	Stops	Tyres
1	J P Montoya	Williams-BMW	1h 28m 1.451s	2	3	M
2	K Räikkönen	McLaren-Mercedes	−1.022s	3	3	M
3	R Barrichello	Ferrari	−24.099s	1	3	B
4	F Alonso	Renault	−48.908s	8	2	M
5	R Schumacher	Williams-BMW	−49.740s	7	3	M
6	T Sato	BAR-Honda	−50.248s	6	3	M

2004 CHAMPIONSHIP FACTS AND FOLKLORE

- An unprecedented 18-race GP calendar with the addition of two new countries, indeed two new global regions, Bahrain in the Middle East and Shanghai in China, the latter the 25th different country to host a championship round.
- Spa was restored to the championship, replacing the A1-Ring, while Interlagos was switched to the end of the season, the finale.
- The FIA announced major revisions to the three-day GP weekend schedule. Friday would consist of two 60-minute free practice sessions during which all teams except those which finished in the top four of the constructors' championship last season could run a third car driven by a specifically nominated driver, 'Friday drivers'. Tyre choice for qualifying and the race must be made by 9am Saturday.
- On Saturday following two morning 45-minute free-practice sessions qualifying would now be held in two parts run consecutively. In the first part each car would make a single timed flying lap in the finishing order of the preceding race and with no fuel restrictions. The reverse order of part one would decide the running order for part two with race fuel and race settings, as last year. The single timed flying lap in part two would determine the final starting grid.
- As before, cars would be held in parc fermé until Sunday's race.
- In an endeavour to control costs and rein in performance, teams were restricted to one engine per car per GP weekend. If a replacement was required before the race, the car/driver in question forfeited a ten-place grid penalty.
- Launch control and fully automatic gearboxes were outlawed, but not traction control.
- During the year the FIA became increasingly tough on cost-cutting and, on the grounds of safety, measures to control lap speeds. They announced a raft of proposals for introduction by 2008 or sooner, including downsizing engines to 2.4-litre V8s, plus restrictions on testing, and the introduction of control tyres. Ferrari, the team with by far the biggest F1 budget, was instrumental in opposing ratification of such initiatives.
- Barrichello's Monza pole was the fastest-ever official F1 qualifying lap, 161.820mph. Montoya went even faster in

the first pre-qualifying run, 162.968mph, the fastest lap ever recorded in F1.
- The 2004 season held remarkable parallels with 2002, as Ferrari had their 'steamroller' working perfectly again. No doubt in Italy and Germany this was a source of enormous delight, but for less partisan devotees of F1 it was tedious.
- Comparison of Ferrari's key stats make the point, 2002 shown first: races contested 17/18; race victories 15/15; 1-2 finishes 9/8; podiums 27/29; championship points 221/262; percentage laps led 79/77; poles 10/12; fastest laps 12/14.
- An unprecedented sixth consecutive constructors' championship placed Ferrari on a different plateau to their rivals, Ferrari 14, Williams 9, McLaren 8.
- Similarly, with his unprecedented fifth consecutive drivers' title Schumacher was now out on his own with seven to Fangio's five and Prost's four.
- Schumacher also raised his own record for individual wins in a year to an astonishing 13. This included the first five of the season, equalling Mansell's 1992 achievement, and after a stumble at Monaco – where Jarno Trulli became a first-time winner for Renault – he reeled off a further seven straight victories!
- Schumacher's astonishing race-winning spree in 2004 raised his personal record to 83 and his Ferrari victories to 64.
- Michael's Canadian victory was the first time a driver had won the same GP for a seventh time, a feat he repeated in France. His victory at Magny-Cours was the first four-stop win since Ayrton Senna's epic wet-weather drive at Donington Park in 1993.
- As in 2002, Schumacher's teammate Rubens Barrichello was championship runner-up. His Italian GP victory was the first time Ferrari had completed a Monza hat-trick, matching Lotus in 1972–74.
- Monza was one of two Barrichello victories, while eight team 1-2 finishes suggested Ferrari with their bespoke Bridgestone tyres had a clear performance advantage over their Michelin-shod opposition.
- In truth this was probably as much to do with the abject failure of the usual suspects, McLaren and Williams, which could only muster one win apiece to finish fifth and fourth in the championship.

RACE 730, Japanese GP: Having already clinched his fifth successive world title, his seventh in all, at Suzuka Schumacher stormed to a record 13th victory in a season.

■ A measure of their weakness was that Jenson Button and Bar-Honda, now also on Michelins, emerged runners-up to Ferrari and their drivers in the respective championships, having provided more consistent opposition to the Italian team throughout the season without ever looking like true winners.

■ It was a curious season for Button, visiting the podium on ten occasions yet not finally breaking into the winners' circle, while off-track he was at the centre of conflict, the contracts recognition board coming out in favour of BAR in their tug-of-love with Williams over JB's future.

■ Button's teammate Takuma Sato had a promising season, his fine qualifying performance at the Nürburgring the first and only time a Japanese driver had qualified on the front row.

■ France might have hoped for more in 2004. Following Olivier Panis' decision to retire and become a test driver, at Interlagos no French driver contested a GP for the first time since 1967, while the Renault team were another to underperform.

■ Renault's Monaco victory was well taken but after a strong start they allowed BAR to finally get the better of them in the constructors' championship. They ditched the wide-angle engine for a narrow-angle 72° version, their design philosophy continuing to emphasise traction and providing scintillating grid getaways and acceleration from low-speed corners even without launch control.

■ Their melange was a combination of rear-weight bias, a high-torque engine and heavy-duty transmission, but as yet it wasn't delivering the desired results.

■ The McLaren Technology centre at Woking was officially opened by the Queen, preoccupation with this massive project providing perhaps one reason for the team's poor recent form. A second could be found at Brixworth, the power and reliability of Mercedes engines again falling short.

■ At Williams, in the face of their disappointing season, Patrick Head stepped aside as technical director, making way for Sam Michael. On the driver front, Ralf Schumacher joined Trulli at Toyota, Montoya already Woking-bound.

■ In September Ford announced its withdrawal from F1 and put Jaguar and Cosworth up for sale. US Champ Car series co-owners Kevin Kalkhoven and Gerald Forsythe purchased the legendary engine manufacturer and Jaguar would become Red Bull Racing from 2005.

■ F1 politics rumbled on during the year. An MOU (memorandum of understanding) was agreed between the manufacturer-supported GPWC (GP World Championship), the teams, Bernie Ecclestone and the banks holding the bankrupt Kirch shares in SLEC. The hope was that this was the first step in a more equitable division of F1's commercial-rights income.

■ The tranquillity didn't last. Later in the year the banks took out a high court action against Ecclestone, claiming he had deprived them of their voting rights and not delivered on the MOU. Threat of a breakaway F1 series returned.

■ Max Mosley, President of the FIA, shocked the F1 world by announcing that after 12 years he would step down in October. A week later he declared that having been begged to stay on, he might after all stand at the 2005 presidential election, but very much on his own terms.

■ Louis Stanley died at the grand old age of 92. Largely associated with leadership at BRM, his contribution to driver safety, particularly the International GP Medical Service, should also be recognised.

Championship ranking	Championship points	Driver nationality	2004 Drivers Championship Driver	Car	Races contested	Race victories	Podiumse excl. victories	Races led	Lights to flag victories	Laps led	Poles	Fastest laps	Triple Crowns
1	148	GER	Michael Schumacher	Ferrari	18	13	2	16	3	683	8	10	5
2	114	BRA	Rubens Barrichello	Ferrari	18	2	12	8		102	4	4	1
3	85	GBR	Jenson Button	BAR-Honda	18		10	5		52	1		
4	59	ESP	Fernando Alonso	Renault	18		4	8		60	1		
5	58	COL	Juan Pablo Montoya	Williams-BMW	18	1	2	3		51		2	
6	46	ITA	Jarno Trulli	Renault (15) Toyota (2)	17	1	1	3		89	2		
7	45	FIN	Kimi Räikkönen	McLaren-Mercedes	18	1	3	4		50	1	2	
8	34	JPN	Takuma Sato	BAR-Honda	18		1	1		2			
9	24	GER	Ralf Schumacher	Williams-BMW	12		1	2		30	1		
10	24	GBR	David Coulthard	McLaren-Mercedes	18								
11	22	ITA	Giancarlo Fisichella	Sauber-Petronas	18								
12	12	BRA	Felipe Massa	Sauber-Petronas	18		1			2			
13	7	AUS	Mark Webber	Jaguar-Ford	18								
14	6	FRA	Olivier Panis	Toyota	17								
15	6	BRA	Antônio Pizzonia	Williams-BMW	4		1			1			
16	3	AUT	Christian Klien	Jaguar-Ford	18								
17	3	BRA	Cristiano da Matta	Toyota	12								
18	3	GER	Nick Heidfeld	Jordan-Ford	18								
19	2	GER	Timo Glock	Jordan-Ford	4								
20	1	HUN	Zsolt Baumgartner	Minardi-Ford	18								

Championship ranking	Championship points	Team/Marque nationality	2004 Constructors Championship Chassis	Engine	Engine maker nationality	Races contested	Race victories	1-2 finishes	Podiums excl. victories	Races led	Laps led	Poles	Fastest laps
1	262	ITA	Ferrari F2004	Ferrari 3.0 V10	ITA	18	15	8	14	18	785	12	14
2	119	GBR	BAR 006	Honda 3.0 V10	JPN	18			11	6	54	1	
3	105	FRA	Renault R24	Renault 3.0 V10	FRA	18	1		5	9	149	3	
4	88	GBR	Williams FW26	BMW 3.0 V10	GER	18	1		3	6	82	1	2
5	69	GBR	McLaren MP4-19, MP4-19B	Mercedes-Benz 3.0 V10	GER	18	1		3	4	50	1	2
6	34	SUI	Sauber C23	Petronas 3.0 V10	ITA	18				1	2		
7	10	GBR	Jaguar R5, R5B	Ford Cosworth 3.0 V10	GBR	18							
8	9	JPN	Toyota TF104, T104B	Toyota 3.0 V10	JPN	18							
9	5	IRL	Jordan EJ14	Ford Cosworth 3.0 V10	GBR	18							
10	1	ITA	Minardi PS04B	Ford Cosworth 3.0 V10	GBR	18							

2005

Fernando's highway

THE TALE OF THE TITLE

■ Ferrari supremacy ended with startling suddenness, Fernando Alonso becoming the youngest-ever champion.

■ At 24 years 58 days the Spaniard eclipsed Emerson Fittipaldi's long-standing record from 1972.

■ Renault and Alonso put together a brilliant campaign, blitzing the first four rounds before rivals hit their stride.

■ From there Alonso's quick, dependable Renault was always in control, Räikkönen forced to play catch-up.

■ Despite seven race victories, Kimi's faster but fragile McLaren-Mercedes never quite got on terms.

■ Alonso matched Kimi's seven but McLaren won more, three of their ten supplied by an erratic Montoya.

■ Even so, McLaren also lost the constructors' title despite their technical innovation, the seamless shift gearbox.

■ But what of the Italian team that had hitherto held mastery over 21st-century GP racing?

■ First, the abruptness of their change in fortune underscored Ferrari's uncanny achievements since 2000.

■ Second, within the F1 performance mix it vividly illustrated the extent of the black art of tyre optimisation.

■ This was accentuated by the new tyre regulation requiring one set to last throughout qualifying and the race.

■ Within this new order, Ferrari's Bridgestones were far less proficient than their Michelin-shod rivals.

■ Apart from the charade known as the US GP, Ferrari failed to win any races in 2005.

■ At Indy Michelin dropped the ball badly, their tyres deemed unsafe, only six Bridgestone runners taking part.

■ And not forgetting: BAR's ban.

THE CHASE FOR THE CHAMPIONSHIP

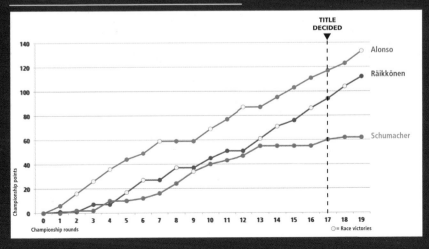

| Round 1/19 | **AUSTRALIAN GP** Melbourne | | **Giancarlo Fisichella** |

Round 1/19	AUSTRALIAN GP Melbourne
	6 March 2005 Race 732

AUSTRALIAN GP Melbourne
Round 1/19
6 March 2005 — Race 732

Giancarlo Fisichella
Renault R25 215.167kph, 133.699mph

Wet-dry-wet qualifying left the leading lights scattered through the grid, but for Fisichella it worked perfectly. From pole, the Italian drove his Renault immaculately, his principle rivals needing to surge through the field to get on terms. Barrichello came closest from his P11 grid spot, but the drive of the race was Alonso. The sister Renault started from row seven, Alonso convinced that but for time lost behind Villeneuve's Sauber he was good for P2. The world champion, from the back row following an engine change, worked his way up to eighth, only to collide with Heidfeld on lap 42. The McLaren pair had scrappy races, Räikkönen starting from the pit lane after stalling and causing a restart. In his first race for Red Bull, Coulthard finished fourth.

POLE POSITION Fisichella, Renault, 3m 01.460s (2.969s), 210.413kph, 130.744mph
LAPS 57 x 5.303 km, 3.295 miles (Scheduled for 58 laps but reduced after aborted start)
DISTANCE 302.271 km, 187.822 miles
STARTERS/FINISHERS 20/17
WEATHER Overcast, warm, dry
LAP LEADERS Fisichella 1-23, 25-42, 45-57 (54); Barrichello 24 (1); Alonso 43-44 (2)
WINNER'S LAPS 1-23 P1, 24 P2, 25-42 P1, 43-44 P2, 45-57 P1
FASTEST LAP Alonso, Renault, 1m 25.683s (lap 24), 222.807kph, 138.446mph
CHAMPIONSHIP Fisichella 10, Barrichello 8, Alonso 6, Coulthard 5, Webber 4

Pos	Driver	Car	Time/gap	Grid	Stops	Tyres
1	G Fisichella	Renault	1h 24m 17.336s	1	2	M
2	R Barrichello	Ferrari	−5.553s	11	2	B
3	F Alonso	Renault	−6.712s	13	2	M
4	D Coulthard	Red Bull-Cosworth	−16.131s	5	2	M
5	M Webber	Williams-BMW	−16.908s	3	2	M
6	J P Montoya	McLaren-Mercedes	−35.033s	9	2	M

Renault R25

MALAYSIAN GP Sepang
Round 2/19
20 March 2005 — Race 733

Fernando Alonso
Renault R25 203.407kph, 126.392mph

With their Bridgestones suffering from lack of grip in the heat, the Ferraris qualified 12th and 13th. By contrast, the Renaults lined up first and third, separated by Jarno Trulli's Toyota. Alonso had little difficulty in winning from pole, but surprisingly Trulli was still second at the finish, Toyota's very first podium, albeit trailing the victorious Renault at some distance. Webber was on course for his first podium too, but a lap 36 collision with Fisichella put paid to that, allowing Williams-BMW teammate Heidfeld to gain the podium. McLaren still couldn't get their season started, Montoya compromising his race with a qualifying slip to finish fourth, and a faulty valve leading to rear-tyre failure for Räikkönen. Renault 2, The Rest 0.

POLE POSITION Alonso, Renault, 3m 07.672s (0.253s), 212.656kph, 132.138mph
LAPS 56 x 5.543 km, 3.444 miles
DISTANCE 310.408 km, 192.879 miles
STARTERS/FINISHERS 20/13
WEATHER Sunny, very hot, dry
LAP LEADERS Alonso 1-21, 25-40, 43-56 (51); G Fisichella, Renault 22 (1); Räikkönen 23-24 (2); Trulli 41-42 (2)
WINNER'S LAPS 1-21 P1, 22 P4, 23-24 P2, 25-40 P1, 41-42 P2, 43-56 P1
FASTEST LAP K Räikkönen, McLaren-Mercedes, 1m 35.483s (lap 23), 208.987kph, 129.859mph
CHAMPIONSHIP Alonso 16, Fisichella 10, Trulli 8, Barrichello 8, Montoya 8

Pos	Driver	Car	Time/gap	Grid	Stops	Tyres
1	F Alonso	Renault	1h 31m 33.736s	1	2	M
2	J Trulli	Toyota	−24.327s	2	2	M
3	N Heidfeld	Williams-BMW	−32.188s	10	2	M
4	J P Montoya	McLaren-Mercedes	−41.631s	11	2	M
5	R Schumacher	Toyota	−51.854s	5	2	M
6	D Coulthard	Red Bull-Cosworth	−1m 12.543s	8	2	M

<table>
<tr><td></td><td colspan="2">BAHRAIN GP Sakhir
3 April 2005   Race 734</td></tr>
</table>

	BAHRAIN GP Sakhir	
Round 3/19	3 April 2005	**Race 734**

Despite a reinvigorated challenge from Ferrari, Alonso delivered a Renault hat-trick, their very first as a constructor. Armed with the new F2005, Schumacher was alongside pole-sitter Alonso and chased him hard for 11 laps until a hydraulic glitch in the hastily introduced car put him out, his first mechanical retirement in four years. Renault too suffered unreliability, Fisichella's engine lasting just three laps. Trulli underlined Toyota's potential with another drive to second place, his teammate Ralf Schumacher fourth. From a poor P9 in qualifying Räikkönen drove strongly to third, while de la Rosa, subbing for Montoya sidelined through injury, came in fifth. The BAR-Honda nightmare persisted and would get very much worse. Renault 3, The Rest 0.

Fernando Alonso
Renault R25 207.082kph, 128.675mph

POLE POSITION Alonso, Renault, 3m 01.902s (0.455s), 214.216kph, 133.108mph
LAPS 57 x 5.412 km, 3.363 miles
DISTANCE 308.238 km, 191.530 miles
STARTERS/FINISHERS 19/13
WEATHER Sunny, very hot, dry
LAP LEADERS Alonso 1-20, 22-41, 43-57 (55); Trulli 21, 42 (2)
WINNER'S LAPS 1-20 P1, 21 P3, 22-41 P1, 42 P2, 43-57 P1
FASTEST LAP de la Rosa, McLaren-Mercedes, 1m 31.447s (lap 43), 213.054kph, 132.386mph
CHAMPIONSHIP Alonso 26, Trulli 16, Fisichella 10, R Schumacher 9, Coulthard 9

Pos	Driver	Car	Time/gap	Grid	Stops	Tyres
1	F Alonso	Renault	1h 29m 18.531s	1	2	M
2	J Trulli	Toyota	−13.409s	3	2	M
3	K Räikkönen	McLaren-Mercedes	−32.063s	9	2	M
4	R Schumacher	Toyota	−53.372s	6	2	M
5	P de la Rosa	McLaren-Mercedes	−1m 4.988s	8	2	M
6	M Webber	Williams-BMW	−1m 14.701s	5	2	M

	SAN MARINO GP Imola	
Round 4/19	24 April 2005	**Race 735**

For eight laps Räikkönen led from pole, pulling out a handy lead over the chasing Alonso. On the ninth the driveshaft let go. Now it was easy for Fernando, Button stalking but not contesting. But Schumacher was to unleash an astonishing challenge. Starting P13 due to a qualifying error, then becalmed in traffic until the first pit stops, once in clean air he reeled-in Alonso, neutralising his over-30s lead in as many laps. The final 11 were gripping, the pair tied together, champion persistently pressurising, pretender successfully resisting. At post-race scrutineering a weight irregularity placed Button's podium in doubt. Cleared by the stewards, BAR-Honda was summoned to an FIA court the following week to explain. Renault 4, The Rest 0.

Fernando Alonso
Renault R25 209.085kph, 129.920mph

POLE POSITION K Räikkönen, McLaren-Mercedes, 2m 42.880s (0.561s), 218.059kph, 135.496mph
LAPS 62 x 4.933 km, 3.065 miles
DISTANCE 305.609 km, 189.897 miles
STARTERS/FINISHERS 20/15
WEATHER Overcast, warm, dry
LAP LEADERS Räikkönen 1-8 (8); Alonso 9-23, 25-42, 50-62 (46); J Button, BAR-Honda 24, 43-46 (5); M Schumacher 47-49 (3)
WINNER'S LAPS 1-8 P2, 9-23 P1, 24 P2, 25-42 P1, 43-48 P3, 49 P2, 50-62 P1
FASTEST LAP M Schumacher, Ferrari, 1m 21.858s (lap 48), 216.946kph, 134.804mph
CHAMPIONSHIP Alonso 36, Trulli 20, Fisichella 10, M Schumacher 10, Heidfeld 9

Pos	Driver	Car	Time/gap	Grid	Stops	Tyres
1	F Alonso	Renault	1h 27m 41.921s	2	2	M
2	M Schumacher	Ferrari	−0.215s	13	2	B
3	A Wurz	McLaren-Mercedes	−27.554s	7	2	M
4	J Villeneuve	Sauber-Petronas	−1m 4.442s	11	2	M
5	J Trulli	Toyota	−1m 10.258s	5	2	M
6	N Heidfeld	Williams-BMW	−1m 11.282s	8	2	M

McLaren-Mercedes MP4-20

SPANISH GP Cataluña
8 May 2005
Race 736

Kimi Räikkönen
McLaren-Mercedes MP4-20 209.844kph, 130.392mph

Following a first-lap SC to clear stalled Minardis, a pulverising opening stint from pole saw Räikkönen fulfil the promise of Imola. Leading lights-to-flag he finished almost half a minute up the road from the chasing Alonso. The crushing defeat for the Spaniard on home turf was only compensated by the minor impact it made on his massive early points lead over the Finn. A promising front-row berth for Webber's Williams-BMW produced little, nor did Montoya's return to the McLaren cockpit. M. Schumacher seemed well-placed for a podium charge after another long first stint from P8, but retired with tyre trouble, while brother Ralf had a race-long intra-team duel with Trulli, who delivered another Toyota podium despite a pits flash fire.

POLE POSITION Räikkönen, McLaren-Mercedes, 2m 31.421s (0.247s), 220.011kph, 136.708mph
LAPS 66 x 4.627 km, 2.875 miles
DISTANCE 305.256 km, 189.677 miles
STARTERS/FINISHERS 18/13
WEATHER Sunny, warm, dry
LAP LEADERS Räikkönen 1-66 (66); SC 1-2 (2)
WINNER'S LAPS 1-66 P1
FASTEST LAP Fisichella, Renault, 1m 15.651s (lap 66), 220.213kph, 136.835mph
CHAMPIONSHIP Alonso 44, Trulli 26, Räikkönen 17, Fisichella 14, R Schumacher 14

Pos	Driver	Car	Time/gap	Grid	Stops	Tyres
1	K Räikkönen	McLaren-Mercedes	1h 27m 16.830s	1	2	M
2	F Alonso	Renault	−27.652s	3	2	M
3	J Trulli	Toyota	−45.947s	5	2	M
4	R Schumacher	Toyota	−46.719s	4	2	M
5	G Fisichella	Renault	−57.936s	6	2	M
6	M Webber	Williams-BMW	−1m 8.542s	2	2	M

MONACO GP Monte Carlo
22 May 2005
Race 737

Kimi Räikkönen
McLaren-Mercedes MP4-20 148.501kph, 92.275mph

A second crushing triumph laid down Räikkönen's title challenge. He also took a bite out of Alonso's points lead, the championship leader P4. Again, Kimi led all the way from pole, making just one stop and staying out during the laps 25–28 SC, deployed to disentangle cars from a Minardi-inspired Mirabeau grid-lock. The SC pit stop killed the Renault challenge, their rear Michelins, already worn from chasing Räikkönen, never regaining operating temperature. Alonso fell prey to both Williams on harder rubber. The second McLaren finished fifth, Montoya starting P18 after being found guilty of brake-testing Ralf S. in practice. Michael S. gave further evidence that much of Ferrari/Bridgestone's difficulties lay in qualifying rather than race pace.

POLE POSITION Räikkönen, McLaren-Mercedes, 2m 30.323s (0.083s), 159.975kph, 99.404mph
LAPS 78 x 3.340 km, 2.075 miles
DISTANCE 260.520 km, 161.880 miles
STARTERS/FINISHERS 18/14
WEATHER Cloudy with sunny intervals, warm, dry
LAP LEADERS Räikkönen 1-78 (78); SC 25-28 (4)
WINNER'S LAPS 1-78 P1
FASTEST LAP M Schumacher, Ferrari, 1m 15.842s (lap 40), 158.540kph, 98.512mph
CHAMPIONSHIP Alonso 49, Räikkönen 27, Trulli 26, Webber 18, Heidfeld 17

Pos	Driver	Car	Time/gap	Grid	Stops	Tyres
1	K Räikkönen	McLaren-Mercedes	1h 45m 15.556s	1	1	M
2	N Heidfeld	Williams-BMW	−13.877s	6	2	M
3	M Webber	Williams-BMW	−18.484s	3	2	M
4	F Alonso	Renault	−36.487s	2	1	M
5	J P Montoya	McLaren-Mercedes	−36.647s	16	1	M
6	R Schumacher	Toyota	−37.177s	18	1	M

EUROPEAN GP Nürburgring
29 May 2005
Race 738

Fernando Alonso
Renault R25 198.555kph, 123.377mph

Seven days after Monaco, Räikkönen's on a hat-trick. Despite 25 laps of intensifying vibration from a flat-spotted tyre, Kimi retains his fast-shrinking lead going into the final lap. Sensationally, the front suspension breaks, the tethered wheel flailing violently. McLaren's gamble for outright victory has failed. Alonso sweeps by to win. A potential 3-3 becomes 4-2. Twelve points are lost. If there was a defining moment in the destiny of the 2005 championship, this was it. Alonso is elated. His relentless race chase of Räikkönen pushed the McLaren driver into the two errors that led to his downfall. Pole-sitter Heidfeld takes second, Barrichello third, then Coulthard's Red Bull leading in the other Ferrari. BAR-Honda's post-ban return is downbeat.

POLE POSITION Heidfeld, Williams-BMW, 1m 30.081s (0.116s), 205.734kph, 127.838mph
LAPS 59 x 5.148 km, 3.199 miles (Scheduled for 60 laps but reduced after aborted start)
DISTANCE 303.715 km, 188.730 miles
STARTERS/FINISHERS 20/18
WEATHER Cloudy with sunny intervals, hot, dry
LAP LEADERS K Räikkönen, McLaren-Mercedes 1-18, 24-29, 31-43, 48-58 (48); Coulthard 19 (1); Alonso 20-23, 44-47, 59 (9); Heidfeld 30 (1)
WINNER'S LAPS 1-7 P5, 8-12 P4, 13-18 P3, 19 P2, 20-23 P1, 24-31 P3, 32-43 P2, 44-47 P1, 48 P4, 49-50 P3, 51-58 P2, 59 P1
FASTEST LAP Alonso, Renault, 1m 30.711s (lap 44), 204.305kph, 126.950mph
CHAMPIONSHIP Alonso 59, Räikkönen 27, Trulli 27, Heidfeld 25, Webber 18

Pos	Driver	Car	Time/gap	Grid	Stops	Tyres
1	F Alonso	Renault	1h 31m 46.648s	6	2	M
2	N Heidfeld	Williams-BMW	−16.567s	1	3	M
3	R Barrichello	Ferrari	−18.549s	7	3	B
4	D Coulthard	Red Bull-Cosworth	−31.588s	12	3	M
5	M Schumacher	Ferrari	−50.445s	10	2	B
6	G Fisichella	Renault	−51.932s	9	2	M

CANADIAN GP Montréal

12 June 2005   Race 739

Räikkönen after the Nürburgring needed luck, and got it when a lap 48 SC went badly for his teammate then leading, McLaren missing the ideal moment to call-in Montoya. The chief beneficiary was Räikkönen, another to benefit M. Schumacher, the SC erasing a 30s deficit, Kimi just keeping the Ferrari at bay in the closing laps. The SC was deployed to remove pole-sitter Button's stricken BAR, crashing on lap 47 on course for a likely podium. But Renault would suffer most acutely the pain of opportunity lost, both cars out when leading. Fisichella on lap 32 with hydraulics, then six laps later Alonso hit the turn five wall under pressure from Montoya, his one mistake of the season. Later JPM was black-flagged for ignoring the pit-lane red light.

Pos	Driver	Car	Time/gap	Grid	Stops	Tyres
1	K Räikkönen	McLaren-Mercedes	1h 32m 9.290s	7	2	M
2	M Schumacher	Ferrari	−1.137s	2	2	B
3	R Barrichello	Ferrari	−40.483s	20	3	B
4	F Massa	Sauber-Petronas	−55.139s	11	3	M
5	M Webber	Williams-BMW	−55.779s	14	0	M
6	R Schumacher	Toyota	−1 lap	10	2	M

Kimi Räikkönen

McLaren-Mercedes MP4-20 198.754kph, 123.500mph

POLE POSITION J Button, BAR-Honda, 1m 15.217s (0.258s), 208.724kph, 129.695mph
LAPS 70 x 4.361 km, 2.710 miles
DISTANCE 305.270 km, 189.686 miles
STARTERS/FINISHERS 20/11
WEATHER High cloud, warm, dry
LAP LEADERS G Fisichella, Renault 1-32 (32); F Alonso, Renault 33-38 (6); J P Montoya, McLaren-Mercedes 39-48 (10); Räikkönen 49-70 (32); SC 48-51 (4)
WINNER'S LAPS 1-14 P5, 15-32 P4, 33-38 P3, 39-48 P2, 49-70 P1
FASTEST LAP Räikkönen, McLaren-Mercedes, 1m 14.384s (Lap 23), 211.061kph, 131.148mph
CHAMPIONSHIP Alonso 59, Räikkönen 37, Trulli 27, Heidfeld 25, M Schumacher 24

UNITED STATES GP Indianapolis

19 June 2005   Race 740

Indy's long banked final corner, turn 13, placed exceptional loads on the left rear. On Friday, Ralf Schumacher experienced a horror 2004 déjà vu, crashing heavily at said corner due to failure of said tyre. A bewildering Saturday ensued, Michelin announcing their tyres unsafe to race on Sunday morning. Attempts by the organisers to insert a temporary chicane had been vetoed by the FIA, and Ferrari. So after the parade lap the Michelin runners retired en masse, the three Bridgestone teams taking the grid. The crowd were first bemused, later incensed. Ninety farcical minutes later came an inevitable Ferrari 1-2, Schumacher snatching victory in a close contest as he exited the pits for the second time. The crowd pelted the track in disgust.

Pos	Driver	Car	Time/gap	Grid	Stops	Tyres
1	M Schumacher	Ferrari	1h 40m 29.914s	5	2	B
2	R Barrichello	Ferrari	−1.522s	7	2	B
3	T Monteiro	Jordan-Toyota	−1 lap	17	2	B
4	N Karthikeyan	Jordan-Toyota	−1 lap	19	2	B
5	C Albers	Minardi-Cosworth	−2 laps	18	2	B
6	P Friesacher	Minardi-Cosworth	−2 laps	20	2	B

Michael Schumacher

Ferrari F2005 204.648kph, 127.162mph

POLE POSITION J Trulli, Renault, 1m 10.625s (0.069s), 213.680kph, 132.775mph
LAPS 73 x 4.192 km, 2.605 miles
DISTANCE 306.016 km, 190.150 miles
STARTERS/FINISHERS 6/6
WEATHER Overcast, warm, dry
LAP LEADERS M Schumacher 1-26, 49-73 (51); Barrichello 27-48 (22)
WINNER'S LAPS 1-26 P1, 27-48 P2, 49-73 P1
FASTEST LAP M Schumacher, Ferrari, 1m 11.497s (lap 48), 211.074kph, 131.156mph
CHAMPIONSHIP Alonso 59, Räikkönen 37, M Schumacher 34, Barrichello 29, Trulli 27

FRENCH GP Magny-Cours

3 July 2005   Race 741

Fernando Alonso was untouchable, bringing Régie Renault their first home win since 1983. He led every lap from pole, Trulli's front-row sharing Toyota assisting by holding the pack at bay during the opening stint. Fortune also smiled in practice with his closest title rival's ten-place grid penalty following a blown Mercedes. That Räikkönen finished second from a heavy-fuelled P13 vividly demonstrated how different things might have been. Montoya too looked good for a podium until lap 46 hydraulics failure, M. Schumacher taking his place on the podium from his P3 start. So in the points table at the halfway point, Alonso had still lost very little to Räikkönen of the massive advantage he had accrued with his scintillating start to the season.

Pos	Driver	Car	Time/gap	Grid	Stops	Tyres
1	F Alonso	Renault	1h 31m 22.233s	1	3	M
2	K Räikkönen	McLaren-Mercedes	−11.805s	13	2	M
3	M Schumacher	Ferrari	−1m 21.914s	3	3	B
4	J Button	BAR-Honda	−1 lap	7	2	M
5	J Trulli	Toyota	−1 lap	2	2	M
6	G Fisichella	Renault	−1 lap	6	3	M

Fernando Alonso

Renault R25 202.638kph, 125.914mph

POLE POSITION Alonso, Renault, 1m 14.412s (0.109), 213.401kph, 132.601mph
LAPS 70 x 4.411 km, 2.741 miles
DISTANCE 308.586 km, 191.746 miles
STARTERS/FINISHERS 20/15
WEATHER Sunny, hot, dry
LAP LEADERS Alonso 1-70 (70)
WINNER'S LAPS 1-70 P1
FASTEST LAP Räikkönen, McLaren-Mercedes, 1m 16.423s (lap 25), 207.785kph, 129.112mph
CHAMPIONSHIP Alonso 69, Räikkönen 45, M Schumacher 40, Trulli 31, Barrichello 29

Round 11/19	**BRITISH GP** Silverstone
	10 July 2005 **Race 742**

Juan Pablo Montoya
McLaren-Mercedes MP4-20 218.968kph, 136.060mph

Montoya's problematic first season for McLaren came good at last. A forceful start from P3 took him past pole-man Alonso, the two side-by-side through Maggotts/Becketts. JPM never put a wheel wrong, although Alonso, shadowing him all the way, was convinced he would prevail through a long second stint, a strategy ultimately thwarted by heavy traffic. So he settled for second, happy to finish ahead of Räikkönen, who came through to beat Fisichella's Renault into third from a P12 grid-slot, legacy of another Mercedes malfunction in practice. Button's front row start energised the partisan crowd, but he didn't have the race pace to beat the McLarens and the Renaults, only good for fifth ahead of two Ferraris and the Toyota pair.

POLE POSITION Alonso, Renault, 1m 19.905s (0.302s), 231.620kph, 143.922mph
LAPS 60 x 5.141 km, 3.195 miles
DISTANCE 308.356 km, 191.604 miles
STARTERS/FINISHERS 20/19
WEATHER Sunny, hot, dry
LAP LEADERS Montoya 1-21, 26-44, 50-60 (51); Alonso 22-23, 45-49 (7); Fisichella 24-25 (2); SC 1-2 (2)
WINNER'S LAPS 1-21 P1, 22 P2, 23 P3, 24-25 P2, 26-44 P1, 45-46 P3, 47-49 P2, 50-60 P1
FASTEST LAP Räikkönen, McLaren-Mercedes, 1m 20.502s (lap 60), 229.902kph, 142.855mph
CHAMPIONSHIP Alonso 77, Räikkönen 51, M Schumacher 43, Barrichello 31, Trulli 31

Pos	Driver	Car	Time/gap	Grid	Stops	Tyres
1	J P Montoya	McLaren-Mercedes	1h 24m 29.588s	3	2	M
2	F Alonso	Renault	–2.739s	1	2	M
3	K Räikkönen	McLaren-Mercedes	–14.436s	12	2	M
4	G Fisichella	Renault	–17.914s	6	2	M
5	J Button	BAR-Honda	–40.264s	2	2	M
6	M Schumacher	Ferrari	–1m 15.322s	9	2	B

Round 12/19	**GERMAN GP** Hockenheim
	24 July 2005 **Race 743**

Fernando Alonso
Renault R25 212.629kph, 132.122mph

'Kimi's pain is Fernando's gain' roared the *Autosport* banner headline. Equally it could have read, 'Cheap part, expensive consequences', the poorly-tightened component in the McLaren hydraulics supposedly costing a tenner. It failed on lap 35, Räikkönen, from pole, leading the race and Alonso by 10s. The other McLaren also created a storyline, Montoya starting dead last after a final-corner spin in qualifying when ahead of his teammate on the clock. His drive to P2 made F1 history, improving on the five drivers who had previously attained P3 from those same humble beginnings. Button completed the podium. With seven rounds left the championship wasn't over, but Alonso, a sixth win and 36-point lead, was making it look that way.

POLE POSITION K Räikkönen, McLaren-Mercedes, 1m 14.320s (0.439s), 221.560kph, 137.672mph
LAPS 67 x 4.574 km, 2.842 miles
DISTANCE 306.458 km, 190.424 miles
STARTERS/FINISHERS 20/18
WEATHER Overcast, warm, dry
LAP LEADERS Räikkönen 1-35 (35); Alonso 36-67 (32)
WINNER'S LAPS 1-35 P2, 36-67 P1
FASTEST LAP K Räikkönen, McLaren-Mercedes, 1m 14.875s (lap 24), 219.924kph, 136.655mph
CHAMPIONSHIP Alonso 87, Räikkönen 51, M Schumacher 47, Montoya 34, Barrichello 31

Pos	Driver	Car	Time/gap	Grid	Stops	Tyres
1	F Alonso	Renault	1h 26m 28.599s	3	2	M
2	J P Montoya	McLaren-Mercedes	– 22.569s	20	2	M
3	J Button	BAR-Honda	–24.422s	2	2	M
4	G Fisichella	Renault	–50.587s	4	2	M
5	M Schumacher	Ferrari	–51.690s	5	2	B
6	R Schumacher	Toyota	–52.242s	12	2	M

Round 13/19	**HUNGARIAN GP** Hungaroring
	31 July 2005 **Race 744**

Kimi Räikkönen
McLaren-Mercedes MP4-20 188.859kph, 117.352mph

But that's the beauty of the F1 world championship. Just one week later Räikkönen had won back all those points lost in Germany. Alonso's race was destroyed by a turn one altercation, the penalty for a P6 start having run wide in qualifying. Räikkönen, by contrast, was given a leg-up from P4 by his two-stopping teammate, aware that Kimi was on a three-stopper. But the man who easily took pole, leading almost as many laps as winner Räikkönen to eventually finish second, was Michael Schumacher, evidence of a tremendous effort by Ferrari and Bridgestone. But what of the magnanimous team player Montoya, convinced his two-stop strategy would win through? Up to lap 41 it might well have done, if a McLaren driveshaft had held together.

POLE POSITION M Schumacher, Ferrari, 1m 19.882s (0.897s), 197.436kph, 122.681mph
LAPS 70 x 4.381 km, 2.722 miles
DISTANCE 306.663 km, 190.552 miles
STARTERS/FINISHERS 20/14
WEATHER Sunny, very hot, dry
LAP LEADERS M Schumacher 1-15, 23-35 (28); J P Montoya, McLaren-Mercedes 16-22, 38-40 (10); Räikkönen 36-37, 41-70 (32)
WINNER'S LAPS 1-11 P2, 12-13 P5, 14-15 P4, 16-22 P3, 23-35 P2, 36-37 P1, 38-40 P2, 41-70 P1
FASTEST LAP Räikkönen, McLaren-Mercedes, 1m 21.219s (lap 40), 194.186kph, 120.662mph
CHAMPIONSHIP Alonso 87, Räikkönen 61, M Schumacher 55, Trulli 36, Montoya 34

Pos	Driver	Car	Time/gap	Grid	Stops	Tyres
1	K Räikkönen	McLaren-Mercedes	1h 37m 25.552s	4	3	M
2	M Schumacher	Ferrari	–35.581s	1	3	B
3	R Schumacher	Toyota	–36.129s	5	3	M
4	J Trulli	Toyota	–54.221s	3	3	M
5	J Button	BAR-Honda	–58.832s	8	2	M
6	N Heidfeld	Williams-BMW	–1m 8.375s	12	2	M

Round 14/19	**TURKISH GP** Istanbul					
	21 August 2005				Race 745	

Turkey's first GP was a McLaren vs Renault affair, the remainder bystanders. With two laps to go McLaren had it in the bag, Räikkönen home free leading as he pleased from pole, 20s plus up the road. From his P4 start Montoya had slotted into P2 on lap 15, jumping the two short-fuelled Renaults at the first stops. Rejoining from his second and final stop, Montoya was 15s to the good over Alonso although his pace was compromised by a flat-spotted tyre. The never-say-die Spaniard began reeling him in. Under pressure, JPM tangled with a backmarker and two laps from the flag his damaged car spun away the first McLaren 1-2 finish in five years. Worse, with the championship running out of races it gifted two extra points to Alonso.

Kimi Räikkönen
McLaren-Mercedes MP4-20 219.496kph, 136.389mph

POLE POSITION Räikkönen, McLaren-Mercedes, 1m 26.797s (0.242s), 221.399kph, 137.571mph
LAPS 58 x 5.338 km, 3.317 miles
DISTANCE 309.396 km, 192.250 miles
STARTERS/FINISHERS 20/15
WEATHER Sunny, hot, dry
LAP LEADERS Räikkönen 1-58 (58)
WINNER'S LAPS 1-58 P1
FASTEST LAP Montoya, McLaren-Mercedes, 1m 24.770s (lap 39), 226.693kph, 140.861mph
CHAMPIONSHIP Alonso 95, Räikkönen 71, M Schumacher 55, Montoya 40, Trulli 39

Pos	Driver	Car	Time/gap	Grid	Stops	Tyres
1	K Räikkönen	McLaren-Mercedes	1h 24m 34.454s	1	2	M
2	F Alonso	Renault	−18.609s	3	2	M
3	J P Montoya	McLaren-Mercedes	−19.635s	4	2	M
4	G Fisichella	Renault	−37.973s	2	2	M
5	J Button	BAR-Honda	−39.304s	13	2	M
6	J Trulli	Toyota	−55.420s	5	2	M

Round 15/19	**ITALIAN GP** Monza					
	4 September 2005				Race 746	

The longest reign in F1 championship history ended when Ferrari failed to score any points at Monza. With another second place, Alonso's grip on the crown strengthened, sole rival Räikkönen fourth after a tough weekend. Yet another Mercedes failure had rendered a superb Kimi pole a penalised P11, but with half-distance approaching he had climbed to second behind his teammate. Then a rear Michelin delaminated in Parabolica, condemning him to a slow recovery lap. And finally he spun when tigering to snatch a podium from Fisichella to finish P4. Promoted to pole by Räikkönen's engine penalty, Montoya controlled the race until the final stint when tyre issues gave Alonso hope that the tortoise might yet again beat the hare.

Juan Pablo Montoya
McLaren-Mercedes MP4-20 247.096kph, 153.539mph

POLE POSITION Montoya, McLaren-Mercedes, 1m 21.054s (0.265s), 257.295kph, 159.876mph
LAPS 53 x 5.793 km, 3.600 miles
DISTANCE 306.719 km, 190.586 miles
STARTERS/FINISHERS 20/20
WEATHER Sunny, hot, dry
LAP LEADERS Montoya 1-53 (53)
WINNER'S LAPS 1-53 P1
FASTEST LAP Räikkönen, McLaren-Mercedes, 1m 21.504 (lap 51), 255.874kph, 158.993mph
CHAMPIONSHIP Alonso 103, Räikkönen 76, M Schumacher 55, Montoya 50, Trulli 43

Pos	Driver	Car	Time/gap	Grid	Stops	Tyres
1	J P Montoya	McLaren-Mercedes	1h 14m 28.659s	1	2	M
2	F Alonso	Renault	−2.479s	2	2	M
3	G Fisichella	Renault	−17.975s	8	2	M
4	K Räikkönen	McLaren-Mercedes	−22.775s	11	2	M
5	J Trulli	Toyota	−33.786s	5	2	M
6	R Schumacher	Toyota	−43.925s	9	2	M

Round 16/19	**BELGIAN GP** Spa Francorchamps					
	11 September 2005				Race 747	

The front row a McLaren lockout, Montoya an imperious pole. The lengthy lap distance plus a slowly drying track made the timing of the switch to dry tyres critical. A lap 11 SC presented an opportunity. The leading McLarens took fuel only, but many switched tyres also and lost out, notably Trulli's Toyota running a strong P3. But Toyota were still in it, an early pit call had teammate Ralf S. splitting the McLarens once racing resumed. Toyota's maiden win was never so close but any chance was blown on lap 24, the team now switching Ralf to dries prematurely. This allowed McLaren to make the inevitable positional 'switch' during their final stop and cruise home 1-2. Until JPM tangled with a backmarker, gifting two extra points to Alonso.

Kimi Räikkönen
McLaren-Mercedes MP4-20 204.568kph, 127.113mph

POLE POSITION J P Montoya, McLaren-Mercedes, 1m 46.391s (0.049s), 236.050kph, 146.675mph
LAPS 44 x 6.976 km, 4.335 miles
DISTANCE 306.927 km, 190.716 miles
STARTERS/FINISHERS 20/15
WEATHER Overcast, warm, wet
LAP LEADERS Montoya 1-32 (32); Räikkönen 33-44 (12); SC 11-13 (3)
WINNER'S LAPS 1-11 P2, 12-13 P4, 14-23 P3, 24-32 P2, 33-44 P1
FASTEST LAP R Schumacher, Toyota, 1m 51.453s (lap 43), 225.329kph, 140.013mph
CHAMPIONSHIP Alonso 111, Räikkönen 86, M Schumacher 55, Montoya 50, Trulli 43

Pos	Driver	Car	Time/gap	Grid	Stops	Tyres
1	K Räikkönen	McLaren-Mercedes	1h 30m 1.295s	2	2	M
2	F Alonso	Renault	−28.394s	4	2	M
3	J Button	BAR-Honda	−32.077s	8	3	M
4	M Webber	Williams-BMW	−1m 9.167s	9	4	M
5	R Barrichello	Ferrari	−1m 18.136s	12	3	B
6	J Villeneuve	Sauber-Petronas	−1m 27.435s	14	1	M

BRAZILIAN GP Interlagos

25 September 2005   Race 748

Juan Pablo Montoya

McLaren-Mercedes MP4-20 205.439kph, 127.654mph

Having threatened for a while, McLaren delivered a 1-2. But Fernando delivered a championship. He didn't need to win, and probably couldn't beat McLaren that day anyway. Six points would guarantee the title. Alonso's perfect pole in qualifying, compared with Räikkönen's spoilt P5 lap, suggested the 24-year-old Spaniard had his head together. So too in the race, Kimi a low-key effort which seemed to acknowledge defeat at all levels, Montoya still hungry to beat his teammate. Following a first-lap contretemps eliminating Coulthard and effectively both Williams, Montoya relieved Alonso of the lead at the SC restart and raced hard to the finish from Kimi then the new champion. For beleaguered Ferrari, P4 and P6 was their best for a while.

POLE POSITION Alonso, Renault, 1m 11.988s (0.157s), 215.485kph, 133.897mph
LAPS 71 x 4.309 km, 2.677 miles
DISTANCE 305.909 km, 190.083 miles
STARTERS/FINISHERS 20/15
WEATHER Overcast, warm, light rain, damp then dry
LAP LEADERS Alonso 1-2 (2); Montoya 3-28, 32-54, 60-71 (61); Räikkönen 29-31, 55-59 (8); SC 1-2 (2)
WINNER'S LAPS 1-2 P2, 3-28 P1, 29-31 P2, 32-54 P1, 55-59 P2, 60-71 P1
FASTEST LAP Räikkönen, McLaren-Mercedes, 1m 12.268s (lap 8), 214.651kph, 133.378mph
CHAMPIONSHIP Alonso 117, Räikkönen 94, Montoya 60, M Schumacher 60, Fisichella 45

Pos	Driver	Car	Time/gap	Grid	Stops	Tyres
1	J P Montoya	McLaren-Mercedes	1h 29m 20.574s	2	2	M
2	K Räikkönen	McLaren-Mercedes	−2.527s	5	2	M
3	F Alonso	Renault	−24.840s	1	2	M
4	M Schumacher	Ferrari	−35.668s	7	2	B
5	G Fisichella	Renault	−40.218s	3	2	M
6	R Barrichello	Ferrari	−1m 9.173s	9	2	B

JAPANESE GP Suzuka

9 October 2005   Race 749

Kimi Räikkönen

McLaren-Mercedes MP4-20 207.266kph, 128.790mph

Wet qualifying, a mixed-up grid: Fernando P16, Kimi P17. At the start a lengthy SC bunched the field and triggered two momentous drives. First Räikkönen: lap 1, P12; lap 14, P7, M. Schumacher-Alonso-Räikkönen thundering around Suzuka in echelon; lap 30, shortly after their first stops passes Schumacher for P4; lap 45, his second stop from the lead to rejoin 5s behind Fisichella with eight laps to go; final lap, miraculously passes Fisichella to win. Second Alonso: some say that but for an unwarranted penalty costing time and position his race from P16 even eclipsed Räikkönen's, just as potent and committed and superbly highlighted by his first of two passes on Schumacher around the outside of 130R, the king he had so recently deposed.

POLE POSITION R Schumacher, Toyota, 1m 46.106s (0.035s), 197.021kph, 122.424mph
LAPS 53 x 5.807 km, 3.608 miles
DISTANCE 307.573 km, 191.117 miles
STARTERS/FINISHERS 20/17
WEATHER Cloudy with sunny intervals, warm, dry, stiff breeze
LAP LEADERS R Schumacher 1-12 (12); Fisichella 13-20, 27-38, 46-52 (27); Button 21-22, 39-40 (4); Coulthard 23 (1); M Schumacher, Ferrari 24-26 (3); Räikkönen 41-45, 53 (6); SC 2-7 (6)
WINNER'S LAPS 1-7 P12, 8 P11, 9 P10, 10-13 P9, 14-20 P7, 21-22 P6, 23 P4, 24-26 P2, 27-28 P6, 29 P5, 30-38 P4, 39-40 P4, 41-45 P1, 46-52 P2, 53 P1
FASTEST LAP Räikkönen, McLaren-Mercedes, 1m 31.540s (lap 44), 228.372kph, 141.904mph
CHAMPIONSHIP Alonso 123, Räikkönen 104, M Schumacher 62, Montoya 60, Fisichella 53

TOP **100** RACE

Pos	Driver	Car	Time/gap	Grid	Stops	Tyres
1	K Räikkönen	McLaren-Mercedes	1h 29m 2.212s	17	2	M
2	G Fisichella	Renault	−1.633s	3	2	M
3	F Alonso	Renault	−17.476s	16	2	M
4	M Webber	Williams-BMW	−22.274s	7	2	M
5	J Button	BAR-Honda	−29.507s	2	2	M
6	D Coulthard	Red Bull-Cosworth	−31.601s	6	2	M

CHINESE GP Shanghai

16 October 2005   Race 750

Fernando Alonso

Renault R25 183.234kph, 113.857mph

'We are the champions,' sang Fernando on his wind-down lap, unquestionably elated to match Räikkönen's seven race wins. Räikkönen's superlative Suzuka victory had kept the constructors' title in play, just two points in it. Perhaps two SC periods, the second a massively destructive shunt for Karthikeyan, had upset McLaren race strategy? Maybe, but post-race Renault claimed they had duped McLaren, fitting V10 screamers in a win-or-bust stratagem. In qualifying it looked plausible, Renault 1-2, McLaren 3-5 on similar fuel loads. In the race it looked certain, Alonso in control, Räikkönen beaten. But in the end the number two drivers' settled it, Fisichella a tactically savvy fourth, Montoya a broken Mercedes. Summed it up really.

POLE POSITION Alonso, Renault, 1m 34.080s (0.321s), 208.584kph, 129.608mph
LAPS 56 x 5.451 km, 3.387 miles
DISTANCE 305.066 km, 189.559 miles
STARTERS/FINISHERS 20/16
WEATHER Sunny, warm, dry
LAP LEADERS Alonso 1-56 (56); SC 19-24, 30-34 (11)
WINNER'S LAPS 1-56 P1
FASTEST LAP Räikkönen, McLaren-Mercedes, 1m 33.242s (lap 56), 210.458kph, 130.773mph
CHAMPIONSHIP Alonso 133, Räikkönen 112, M Schumacher 62, Montoya 60, Fisichella 58

Pos	Driver	Car	Time/gap	Grid	Stops	Tyres
1	F Alonso	Renault	1h 39m 53.618s	1	2	M
2	K Räikkönen	McLaren-Mercedes	−4.015s	3	2	M
3	R Schumacher	Toyota	−25.376s	9	2	M
4	G Fisichella	Renault	−26.114s	2	3	M
5	C Klien	Red Bull-Cosworth	−31.839s	14	2	M
6	F Massa	Sauber-Petronas	−36.400s	11	2	M

2005 CHAMPIONSHIP FACTS AND FOLKLORE

- In a season of political turbulence the starting point must be the continuing unrest between the FIA and FOM on the one hand and the manufacturers and teams on the other. Essentially the F1 participants, represented by GPWC and threatening a breakaway series, were unhappy with the F1 organisers, Max and Bernie.
- The primary issue remained more equitable distribution of F1 revenues as the renegotiation of the 2008 Concorde Agreement loomed. But as Max Mosley, with scant regard for protocol, bulldozed through regulations addressing costs and safety in an increasingly hostile climate, rule-making transparency and improved governance protocol also became of mounting importance.
- Bernie played two potent cards during the year. In January he persuaded Ferrari to rejoin FIA/FOM, causing a massive fissure in the strength and unity of GPWC. At year's end Ecclestone sold most of SLEC to CVC Capital Partners, neatly moving the 'ownership' goalposts.
- The GPWC-aligned teams were exceedingly unhappy when it became known that as the first signatory to the 2008–12 Concorde Agreement, Ferrari would receive special financial and other advantages.
- Mosley's methods were just as devious but more opportunistic, and certainly more bellicose. His battleground was Indy-gate.
- On the fast, banked turns of Indianapolis, Michelin found they had brought tyres unsuitable to cope safely with the high G-forces. Instead of supporting Bernie to find a way to put the show on the road for the paying public and the TV viewers, the FIA took an intransigent position and, further, rather than cancel the race allowed a travesty of a GP to take place.
- The FIA then censured the Michelin teams for the Indy tyre fiasco, threatening bans, which put on the back foot the team principals keen to see Mosley unseated at the October FIA presidential election.
- In the end Mosley was re-elected unopposed, the bans threatened by the FIA did not come to pass, and a form of peace broke out. But the Indy-gate affair was a distasteful scandal, reflecting badly on all those responsible for 'the show' who chose to play their power games at the expense of the punters.
- As an event it certainly flew in the face of the survey conducted by the FIA to ascertain the wishes of the F1 fans: 93,000 respondents participated and 94% of them summed it up in two words, 'more overtaking'.
- The 2005 championship calendar reached 19 races for the first time with the addition of Turkey, staging a GP at a new unusually anticlockwise track close to Istanbul. China was championship race number 750.
- During the course of 2005, no less than five of the ten GP teams changed ownership.
- At the start of the season, the woefully disappointing Jaguar team had morphed into Red Bull Racing.
- Although the disappearance of Jaguar represented a pull-out by Ford, manufacturer involvement continued to increase with BAR,

after 117 races, and Sauber, after 215, bowing out to become the Honda and BMW works teams for the following season.

- In September the Minardi name disappeared after 340 races, acquired by Dietrich Mateschitz as a Red Bull 'B' team, to be renamed Scuderia Toro Rosso from 2006.
- Eddie Jordan sold his eponymous team to Alex Shnaider's Midland conglomerate, which retained the Jordan moniker during 2005. Of these five teams, only Jordan had won GPs, four from 250 races.
- Regulation changes for 2005 included a hefty 20–25% reduction in downforce by raising the front wing, bringing the rear wing forward and reducing the height of the diffuser.
- Engines were now required to last two consecutive race weekends, a ten-place grid penalty incurred if changed. Despite the two-race durability requirement, in their final season the best of the 3-litre V10 F1 engines produced well over 300bhp per litre, even 1,000 bhp mooted.
- Just two sets of harder, 'long-life' tyres were permitted for each car per weekend, and with tyres now required to last for qualifying and the entire race, pit stops would continue for refuelling purposes only.
- Single-shot qualifying also continued, the grid to be formed by aggregate times from a Saturday and a Sunday morning qualifying session. This proved so unpopular that the aggregate times concept was dropped from round seven, the Nürburgring, replaced by Saturday-only single-shot qualifying based on the reverse finishing order of the previous GP.
- The 2005 season was remarkable not only for the Renault/ Alonso success but for the Ferrari/Schumacher failure. How

could a team and driver which up to now had dominated the 21st century form of GP racing – short dynamic sprints punctuated by tactically savvy pit stops – score just one race victory, and that a bogus sham? How could ten championships and 48 GP victories suddenly become one ill-famed race win?

- It would be too easy to explain Ferrari's fall from grace by pointing the finger at tyres, to assume it was entirely Bridgestone's failure to deliver a tyre that could cope with the new 'long-life' regulations, but it was more complex than that.
- Ferrari's performance shortfall also lay in their inability to successfully respond to the major aero changes associated with the significant downforce reduction prescribed for 2005. In addition, it was not the change in tyre regs per se, but Ferrari's quasi-exclusivity with Bridgestone which had come back to bite them.
- In times of rule stability, supplier exclusivity could be a powerful advantage. In times of change it could spell isolation; of insularity compromising the quality and quantity of tyre-testing feedback.
- And finally, the Ferrari F2005 was the first since 1997 not to be designed by Rory Byrne under the technical direction of Ross Brawn. Ross was still there but Aldo Costa took charge of design, Byrne in support.
- So by winning just one race, the farce known as the 2005 US GP, Schumacher had to settle for lesser records and milestones than usual, in Canada exceeding Coulthard's record number of starts for a single team, 150 for McLaren.
- 33 years had passed since Emerson Fittipaldi became the youngest world champion of all time but now the accolade changed hands. At 24 years and 58 days Fernando Alonso was both the youngest-ever and the first from Spain.
- Renault and Alonso put together a brilliant championship-winning campaign, bringing Renault their first championship success in eight years and meaningfully the very first as a fully-fledged constructor. Alonso's Bahrain victory was the 100th for Renault engines.
- The philosophy, concept and implementation of the whole Renault R25 package was superb, the engine shop in Vivry, France, and the chassis and racing operation in Enstone, Oxfordshire, fully integrated along with a team spirit and belief second to none.
- Alonso's fast, faultless, attacking driving did the rest, best exemplified at the Nürburgring. Fernando's relentless pushing of the leader caused Kimi to make a race-losing error. The sequence began when Räikkönen ran across the grass, breaking a bargeboard. This in turn led to the flat-spotted tyre, the extreme vibration, and finally the resultant disintegration of the front suspension on the final lap. In that single moment 14 points changed hands.
- It must have been tough for McLaren to win ten races and come away with neither championship, but almost out of contention after the first four rounds, McLaren were forced to adopt an all-out attacking strategy with its associated risks.
- The MP4-20 was the last 'Newey' McLaren, after nine years Adrian moving on to join Red Bull Racing for 2006. It was the most effective McLaren since the 1998–99 championship-winning cars, but four engine-change grid penalties for Räikkönen and another for Montoya said much if not all about McLaren's lost titles.

RACE 738, European GP: Moments after the defining moment in the destiny of the 2005 world championship, Alonso sweeps by to win at the Nürburgring.

- Monaco was actually the 200th race for a Mercedes engine, 45 having culminated in victory. Before the start of that race, the 62nd Grand Prix de Monaco, tribute was paid to the recently deceased Prince Rainier. Twice Monaco GP winner Maurice Trintignant also died in 2005. He was 87.
- Montoya missed two races after fracturing a shoulder blade in a motocross accident. It was hard to guess if Ron Dennis' wrath was greater for the squandered championship points or Juan's initial explanation, 'a tennis injury'.
- BAR-Honda were disqualified at Imola and served a further two-race ban for running their car underweight. A catch-tank in their pressurised fuel-feed system, supposedly there to improve fuel pick-up, meant that when weighed dry the car was under the 600kg weight limit.
- The BAR vs Williams tug of love for Jenson Button's services for 2006 resurfaced, BAR's case not helped by their ban, Williams'
- claim compromised by the loss of BMW engines. Button took the matter into his own hands, personally contributing £16m of the payment made by BAR-Honda to Williams.
- In a winless season, their first with Mark Webber but their last with BMW, Hockenheim marked Williams' 500th GP as a constructor.
- Heidfeld's Nürburgring pole for Williams-BMW, his one and only, was also a first for a German driver in Germany powered by a German engine.
- Toyota did well to beat Williams into fourth pace in the constructors' championship, while Red Bull scored nearly as many points in their first season as Jaguar had in the preceding five.
- Portugal's Tiego Monteiro finished all but one race, 18, a rookie record which beat 14 by Panis in 1994 and by Klien in 2004. Monteiro also took the podium at that ugly episode at Indianapolis.

Championship ranking	Championship points	Driver nationality	2005 Drivers Championship Driver	Car	Races contested	Race victories	Podiumse excl. victories	Races led	Lights to flag victories	Laps led	Poles	Fastest laps	Triple Crowns
1	133	ESP	Fernando Alonso	Renault	18	7	8	11	2	336	6	2	
2	112	FIN	Kimi Räikkönen	McLaren-Mercedes	18	7	5	12	3	375	5	10	
3	62	GER	Michael Schumacher	Ferrari	19	1	4	4		85	1	3	
4	60	COL	Juan Pablo Montoya	McLaren-Mercedes	16	3	2	6	1	217	2	1	
5	58	ITA	Giancarlo Fisichella	Renault	18	1	2	5		116	1	1	
6	45	GER	Ralf Schumacher	Toyota	18		2	1		12	1	1	
7	43	ITA	Jarno Trulli	Toyota	18		3	2		4	1		
8	38	BRA	Rubens Barrichello	Ferrari	19		4	2		23			
9	37	GBR	Jenson Button	BAR-Honda	16		2	2		9	1		
10	36	AUS	Mark Webber	Williams-BMW	18		1						
11	28	GER	Nick Heidfeld	Williams-BMW	13		3	1		1	1		
12	24	GBR	David Coulthard	Red Bull-Cosworth	18			2		2			
13	11	BRA	Felipe Massa	Sauber-Petronas	18								
14	9	CAN	Jacques Villeneuve	Sauber-Petronas	18								
15	9	AUT	Christian Klien	Red Bull-Cosworth	13								
16	7	POR	Tiago Monteiro	Jordan-Toyota	19		1						
17	6	AUT	Alexander Wurz	McLaren-Mercedes	1		1						
18	5	IND	Narain Karthikeyan	Jordan-Toyota	19								
19	4	NLD	Christijan Albers	Minardi-Cosworth	19								
20	4	ESP	Pedro de la Rosa	McLaren-Mercedes	1							1	
21	3	AUT	Patrick Friesacher	Minardi-Cosworth	11								
22	2	BRA	Antônio Pizzonia	Williams-BMW	5								
23	1	JPN	Takuma Sato	BAR-Honda	15								
24	1	ITA	Vitantonio Liuzzi	Red Bull-Cosworth	4								

Championship ranking	Championship points	Team/Marque nationality	2005 Constructors Championship Chassis	Engine	Engine maker nationality	Races contested	Race victories	1-2 finishes	Podiums excl. victories	Races led	Laps led	Poles	Fastest laps
1	191	FRA	Renault R25	Renault 3.0 V10	FRA	18	8		10	12	452	7	3
2	182	GBR	McLaren MP4-20	Mercedes-Benz 3.0 V10	GER	18	10	1	8	14	592	7	12
3	100	ITA	Ferrari F2005, F2004M	Ferrari 3.0 V10	ITA	19	1	1	8	5	108	1	3
4	88	JPN	Toyota TF105, TF105B	Toyota 3.0 V10	JPN	18			5	3	16	2	1
5	66	GBR	Williams FW27	BMW 3.0 V10	GER	18			4	1	1	1	
6	38	GBR	BAR 007	Honda 3.0 V10	JPN	18			2	2	9	1	
7	34	AUT	Red Bull RB1	Cosworth 3.0 V10	GBR	18				2	2		
8	20	SUI	Sauber C24	Petronas 3.0 V10	ITA	18							
9	12	GBR	Jordan EJ15, EJ15B	Toyota 3.0 V10	JPN	19			1				
10	7	ITA	Minardi PS05, PS04B	Cosworth 3.0 V10	GBR	19							

2006

Alonso 'retires' Schumacher

THE TALE OF THE TITLE

- Renault was still the team to beat, Fernando Alonso dropping just six points in the first half of the season.
- With tyre changing resumed, Ferrari/Bridgestone displaced McLaren as Renault's nearest challenger.
- Montréal was the summit of Renault superiority, Alonso leading Schumacher by 25 points.
- From then on the reigning world champion was up against Michael on track and Machiavelli off it.
- Not only had Bridgestone come on strong, but out of the blue the FIA outlawed mass dampers.
- Alonso's big points lead was wiped out, he and Schumacher dead level with two races to run.
- But at Suzuka fate smiled on Fernando, Schumacher suffering his first engine failure in six years.
- After delay at the Interlagos showdown, Schumacher put on a memorable 'farewell' drive.
- But being Schumacher, he even besmirched his final season with his Rascasse 'dirty trick' at Monaco.
- It was a finely balanced contest, Alonso seven, Schumacher seven; Renault eight, Ferrari nine; Michelin nine, Bridgestone nine.
- Honda also won their first success as a team for 39 years, also ending Button's 113-race win-drought.
- Felipe Massa too became a first-time winner in his inaugural season as a Ferrari driver.
- Not since 1995 had McLaren failed to land a race victory, perhaps already missing the Newey factor.
- But the season belonged to Alonso, the man who 'retired' Schumacher.
- And not forgetting: V8s replace V10s; wheel frisbees; the final 'tyre wars'.

THE CHASE FOR THE CHAMPIONSHIP

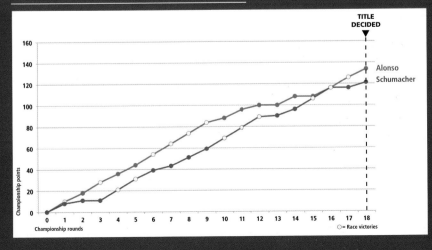

Renault R26

Round 1/18	**BAHRAIN GP** Sakhir					
	12 March 2006					Race 751

Fernando Alonso
Renault R26 206.018kph, 128.014mph

The revised tyre regulations produced a different challenger in Ferrari, but not a different winner in Renault. Alonso and Schumacher engaged in an enthralling opening-race duel, so closely matched it came down to line versus momentum: Alonso's inside line as he rejoined from his second stop, Schumacher's hurtling momentum as he stormed towards the pit exit. Line just took it, and kept it for the remaining 17 laps. In the absence of on-track overtaking this was next best. But round one held yet more future promise, Räikkönen's McLaren finishing third having started last; the Honda Racing Team marking their return with P4, and, having switched to Cosworth and Bridgestone, both Williamses taking points, rookie Nico Rosberg posting fastest lap.

POLE POSITION M Schumacher, Ferrari, 1m 31.431s (0.047s), 213.091kph, 132.408mph
LAPS 57 x 5.412 km, 3.363 miles
DISTANCE 308.238 km, 191.530 miles
STARTERS/FINISHERS 22/18
WEATHER Sunny, warm, dry, breezy
LAP LEADERS M Schumacher 1-15, 24-35 (27); Alonso 16-19, 36-39, 41-57 (25); Montoya 20-23 (4); Button 40 (1)
WINNER'S LAPS 1-15 P2, 16-19 P1, 20-23 P3, 24-35 P2, 36-39 P1, 40 P2, 41-57 P1
FASTEST LAP N Rosberg, Williams-Cosworth, 1m 32.408s (lap 42), 210.838kph, 131.009mph
CHAMPIONSHIP Alonso 10, M Schumacher 8, Räikkönen 6, Button 5, Montoya 4

Pos	Driver	Car	Time/gap	Grid	Stops	Tyres
1	F Alonso	Renault	1h 29m 46.205s	4	2	M
2	M Schumacher	Ferrari	−1.246s	1	2	B
3	K Räikkönen	McLaren-Mercedes	−19.360s	22	1	M
4	J Button	Honda	−19.992s	3	2	M
5	J P Montoya	McLaren-Mercedes	−37.048s	5	2	M
6	M Webber	Williams-Cosworth	−41.932s	7	2	B

Round 2/18	**MALAYSIAN GP** Sepang					
	19 March 2006					Race 752

Giancarlo Fisichella
Renault R26 205.397kph, 127.628mph

A Renault 1-2 headed by Fisichella from pole, his third race victory. Alonso's race to second was more eventful, starting from an over-fuelled P7 due to a fuel-rig glitch in Q3 of the new qualifying procedure. A rocket start and a superb turn one outside move had him third, passing the Williams and McLaren pairs. Heavy with fuel, Alonso lost 15s in his first stint to Button's P2 Honda ahead, but got the hammer down and passed him at the second round of stops. Räikkönen was knocked off at the first corner, Montoya's McLaren finished fourth followed by the two Ferraris, both compromised by engine-change grid penalties. Both Williams were out by lap 15 although Rosberg had been an eye-catching P3 in qualifying.

POLE POSITION Fisichella, Renault, 1m 33.840s (0.146s), 212.647kph, 132.132mph
LAPS 56 x 5.543 km, 3.444 miles
DISTANCE 310.408 km, 192.879 miles
STARTERS/FINISHERS 22/14
WEATHER Overcast, hot, dry
LAP LEADERS Fisichella 1-17, 27-38, 44-56 (42); Alonso 20-26, 39-43 (12); Button 18-19 (2)
WINNER'S LAPS 1-17 P1, 18-19 P3, 20-26 P2, 27-38 P1, 39-43 P2, 44-56 P1
FASTEST LAP Alonso, Renault, 1m 34.803s (lap 45), 210.487kph, 130.791mph
CHAMPIONSHIP Alonso 18, M Schumacher 11, Button 11, Fisichella 10, Montoya 9

Pos	Driver	Car	Time/gap	Grid	Stops	Tyres
1	G Fisichella	Renault	1h 30m 40.529s	1	2	M
2	F Alonso	Renault	−4.585s	8	2	M
3	J Button	Honda	−9.631s	2	2	M
4	J P Montoya	McLaren-Mercedes	−39.351s	6	2	M
5	F Massa	Ferrari	−43.254s	16	1	B
6	M Schumacher	Ferrari	−43.854s	4	2	B

<table>
<tr><td>

Round 3/18

</td><td>

AUSTRALIAN GP Melbourne
2 April 2006   Race 753

</td><td>

Fernando Alonso
Renault R26 191.990kph, 119.297mph

</td></tr>
</table>

A deferred race date, Autumnal cool playing havoc with tyre temperatures, four SCs partly the consequence, two earlier, two later. Honda was particularly affected, Button sliding down the field from pole, the final ignominy a blown engine on the final lap. Renault's canny Michelin choice enabled Alonso to out-drag Button at the first SC restart, Räikkönen repeating the trick at the second. The third was triggered by M. Schumacher crashing out, as did Montoya later, many ill at ease on cold rubber. Save Alonso, leading every lap bar six. Despite SC bunching, Räikkönen never pressured him, partly due to problems arising from a flat-spotted tyre. On lap 21 Webber became the first Australian to lead his home GP. Next lap his gearbox failed.

POLE POSITION J Button, Honda, 1m 25.229s (0.406s), 223.994kph, 139.183mph
LAPS 57 x 5.303 km, 3.295 miles (Scheduled for 58 laps but reduced after aborted start)
DISTANCE 302.271 km, 187.822 miles
STARTERS/FINISHERS 22/13
WEATHER Cloudy, warm, dry
LAP LEADERS Button 1-3 (3); Alonso 4-19, 23-57 (51); Räikkönen 20 (1); M Webber, Williams-Cosworth 21-22 (2); SC 1-3, 8-9, 34-40 (12)
WINNER'S LAPS 1-3 P2, 4-19 P1, 20 P3, 21-22 P2, 23-57 P1
FASTEST LAP Räikkönen, McLaren-Mercedes, 1m 26.045s (lap 57), 221.869kph, 137.864mph
CHAMPIONSHIP Alonso 28, Fisichella 14, Räikkönen 14, M Schumacher 11, Button 11

Pos	Driver	Car	Time/gap	Grid	Stops	Tyres
1	F Alonso	Renault	1h 34m 27.870s	3	2	M
2	K Räikkönen	McLaren-Mercedes	−1.829s	4	2	M
3	R Schumacher	Toyota	−24.824s	6	3	B
4	N Heidfeld	BMW	−31.032s	8	2	M
5	G Fisichella	Renault	−38.421s	2	2	M
6	J Villeneuve	BMW	−49.554s	19	1	M

Ferrari 248 F1

<table>
<tr><td>

Round 4/18

</td><td>

SAN MARINO GP Imola
23 April 2006   Race 754

</td><td>

Michael Schumacher
Ferrari 248 F1 202.322kph, 125.717mph

</td></tr>
</table>

Four cars pulled away, Schumacher, Button, Massa, Alonso, Ferrari's pole due to engine work and Bridgestone's single-lap pace. Race pace was also strong in the first stint, Michael gaining 13s on Alonso, albeit assisted by a teammate buffer. The second stint on un-scrubbed Bridgestones was quite different, graining allowing Alonso to close down the leader rapidly. But catching is one thing, passing another, especially at Imola. Held up by Schumacher but unable to pass, Renault opted to pit Alonso first for the final stops. The gamble failed. Schumacher unleashed an almighty in-lap that bought him a crucial 1.6s. Game over. Montoya completed the podium while Honda qualifying pace again flattered race performance.

POLE POSITION M Schumacher, Ferrari, 1m 22.795s (0.193s), 215.621kph, 133.980mph
LAPS 62 x 4.959 km, 3.081 miles
DISTANCE 307.221 km, 190.898 miles
STARTERS/FINISHERS 22/16
WEATHER Sunny, hot, dry
LAP LEADERS M Schumacher 1-20, 26-42, 45-62 (55); Alonso 21-25 (5); Montoya 43-44 (2); SC 1-2 (2)
WINNER'S LAPS 1-20 P1, 21-25 P2, 26-42 P1, 43-44 P2, 45-62 P1
FASTEST LAP Alonso, Renault, 1m 24.569s (lap 23), 211.098kph, 131.171mph
CHAMPIONSHIP Alonso 36, M Schumacher 21, Räikkönen 18, Fisichella 15, Montoya 15

Pos	Driver	Car	Time/gap	Grid	Stops	Tyres
1	M Schumacher	Ferrari	1h 31m 6.486s	1	2	B
2	F Alonso	Renault	−2.096s	5	2	M
3	J P Montoya	McLaren-Mercedes	−15.868s	7	2	M
4	F Massa	Ferrari	−17.096s	4	2	M
5	K Räikkönen	McLaren-Mercedes	−17.524s	8	2	M
6	M Webber	Williams-Cosworth	−37.739s	10	2	B

| Round 5/18 | **EUROPEAN GP** Nürburgring | | | **Michael Schumacher** |

| | 7 May 2006 | | Race 755 | Ferrari 248 F1 193.080kph, 119.974mph |

The duel between the reigning champion and the seven-times champion resumed, youth winning Saturday, experience the day that mattered. Maintaining grid order, over the first 38 laps they were locked in combat, the gap once briefly greater than 2s. Alonso knew Schumacher was fuelled longer for the second stint, pushing his car to make a decisive break. To no avail, that afternoon Bridgestone held all the aces, once in free air Michael gaining 7s in five laps. It also brought Massa his maiden podium, the two jubilant drivers aware of the significance of a 1-3 result to Maranello's championship prospects. But just 4.879s covered the top four, Räikkönen up tight behind Massa, so it wasn't a landslide victory for the Scuderia.

POLE POSITION Alonso, Renault, 1m 28.819s (0.209s), 206.334kph, 128.210mph
LAPS 60 x 5.148 km, 3.199 miles
DISTANCE 308.863 km, 191.919 miles
STARTERS/FINISHERS 22/13
WEATHER Cloudy with sunny intervals, warm, dry, breezy
LAP LEADERS Alonso 1-16, 24-37 (30); M Schumacher 17-18, 38-41, 45-60 (22); Räikkönen 19-23, 42-44 (8); SC 2-3 (2)
WINNER'S LAPS 1-16 P2, 17-18 P1, 19-20 P4, 21-23 P3, 24-37 P2, 38-41 P1, 42-44 P2, 45-60 P1
FASTEST LAP M Schumacher, Ferrari, 1m 32.099s (lap 39), 201.226kph, 125.037mph
CHAMPIONSHIP Alonso 44, M Schumacher 31, Räikkönen 23, Fisichella 18, Massa 15

Pos	Driver	Car	Time/gap	Grid	Stops	Tyres
1	M Schumacher	Ferrari	1h 35m 58.765s	2	2	B
2	F Alonso	Renault	−3.751s	1	2	M
3	F Massa	Ferrari	−4.447s	3	2	B
4	K Räikkönen	McLaren-Mercedes	−4.879s	5	2	M
5	R Barrichello	Honda	−1m 12.586s	4	2	M
6	G Fisichella	Renault	−1m 14.116s	11	2	M

| Round 6/18 | **SPANISH GP** Cataluña | | | **Fernando Alonso** |

| | 14 May 2006 | | Race 756 | Renault R26 212.074kph, 131.777mph |

The duel continued. As King Juan Carlos, in front of 131,000 adoring countrymen, presented the trophy to the first Spaniard to win his home GP, Schumacher's expression conveyed it all. It seemed to say, 'Despite back-to-back Ferrari victories harking back to 2000 and 2004, this year feels very different.' In the sense that the Renault pair had utterly pulverised the Ferrari duo, he was absolutely correct. Alonso/Renault represented a level of competition not felt since McLaren/Häkkinen seven years before. So Alonso beat Schumacher and Fisichella beat Massa. And Räikkönen made a ballistic start from ninth to fifth, but that's where he stayed, confirming the growing feeling that there really were only two teams in contention for championship honours.

POLE POSITION Alonso, Renault, 1m 14.648s (0.061s), 223.143kph, 138.654mph
LAPS 66 x 4.627 km, 2.875 miles
DISTANCE 305.256 km, 189.677 miles
STARTERS/FINISHERS 22/17
WEATHER Sunny, hot, dry
LAP LEADERS Alonso 1-17, 24-40, 47-66 (54); Fisichella 18 (1); M Schumacher 19-23, 41-46 (11)
WINNER'S LAPS 1-17 P1, 18 P4, 19 P3, 20-23 P2, 24-40 P1, 41-46 P2, 47-66 P1
FASTEST LAP Massa, Ferrari, 1m 16.648s (lap 42), 217.320kph, 135.037mph
CHAMPIONSHIP Alonso 54, M Schumacher 39, Räikkönen 27, Fisichella 24, Massa 20

Pos	Driver	Car	Time/gap	Grid	Stops	Tyres
1	F Alonso	Renault	1h 26m 21.759s	1	2	M
2	M Schumacher	Ferrari	−18.502s	3	2	B
3	G Fisichella	Renault	−23.951s	2	2	M
4	F Massa	Ferrari	−29.859s	4	2	B
5	K Räikkönen	McLaren-Mercedes	−56.875s	9	2	M
6	J Button	Honda	−58.347s	8	2	M

| Round 7/18 | **MONACO GP** Monte Carlo | | | **Fernando Alonso** |

| | 28 May 2006 | | Race 757 | Renault R26 150.707kph, 93.645mph |

Having snatched provisional pole in Q3, Schumacher sickened the F1 community by feigning an off at Rascasse, the resultant yellow spoiling Alonso's final qualifying run. Wide-eyed innocence compounded the felony, the stewards relegating M. Schumacher to the back of the grid. So Alonso started first and remained there apart from his first pit stop. During this single lap the other front-row man Webber led, but his challenge fell apart on lap 48, his Williams ablaze. Bizarrely, two laps later the same fate befell Alonso's other chief adversary, Räikkönen. Webber had provoked the SC so Montoya, now P2, had to negotiate a string of backmarkers before engaging Alonso, by which time he was 10s behind. Coulthard gave RBR a first podium.

POLE POSITION Alonso, Renault, 1m 13.962s (0.120s), 162.569kph, 101.015mph
LAPS 78 x 3.340 km, 2.075 miles
DISTANCE 260.520 km, 161.880 miles
STARTERS/FINISHERS 22/17
WEATHER Cloudy with sunny intervals, warm, dry
LAP LEADERS Alonso 1-23, 25-78 (77); M Webber, Williams-Cosworth 24 (1); SC 49-52 (4)
WINNER'S LAPS 1-23 P1, 24 P2, 25-78 P1
FASTEST LAP M Schumacher, Ferrari, 1m 15.143s (lap 74), 160.014kph, 99.429mph
CHAMPIONSHIP Alonso 64, M Schumacher 43, Fisichella 27, Räikkönen 27, Montoya 23

Pos	Driver	Car	Time/gap	Grid	Stops	Tyres
1	F Alonso	Renault	1h 43m 43.116s	1	2	M
2	J P Montoya	McLaren-Mercedes	−14.567s	4	2	M
3	D Coulthard	Red Bull-Ferrari	−52.298s	7	1	M
4	R Barrichello	Honda	−53.337s	5	2	M
5	M Schumacher	Ferrari	−53.830s	22	1	B
6	G Fisichella	Renault	−1m 2.072s	9	2	M

BRITISH GP Silverstone
11 June 2006   **Race 758**

Fernando Alonso
Renault R26 215.468kph, 133.886mph

Alonso's pole was a massive 0.32s up on title rival Schumacher in P3, suggesting highly contrasting fuel strategies. And there were other clear clues of Alonso's light fuel load: effortlessly beating Räikkönen's McLaren from the front row; keeping him at bay following the almost immediate SC restart; pulling away during the first stint. Until lap 18, that is. It was then that Schumacher pitted, and one lap later so did Räikkönen. Alonso didn't refuel until lap 22, a measure of his phenomenal pole lap, an astute choice of tyres and Renault's all-round superiority. Michael got the better of Kimi at the second stop of an otherwise processional race, made worse for the partisan crowd by woeful performances from Button and Coulthard.

POLE POSITION Alonso, Renault, 1m 20.253s (0.144s), 230.615kph, 143.297mph
LAPS 60 x 5.141 km, 3.195 miles
DISTANCE 308.356 km, 191.604 miles
STARTERS/FINISHERS 22/18
WEATHER Cloudy with sunny intervals, hot, dry
LAP LEADERS Alonso 1-44, 46-60 (59); Fisichella 45 (1); SC 1-3 (3)
WINNER'S LAPS 1-44 P1, 45 P2, 46-60 P1
FASTEST LAP Alonso, Renault, 1m 21.599s (lap 21), 226.811kph, 140.934mph
CHAMPIONSHIP Alonso 74, M Schumacher 51, Räikkönen 33, Fisichella 32, Montoya 26

Pos	Driver	Car	Time/gap	Grid	Stops	Tyres
1	F Alonso	Renault	1h 25m 51.927s	1	2	M
2	M Schumacher	Ferrari	–13.951s	3	2	B
3	K Räikkönen	McLaren-Mercedes	–18.672s	2	2	M
4	G Fisichella	Renault	–19.976s	4	2	M
5	F Massa	Ferrari	–31.559s	9	2	B
6	J P Montoya	McLaren-Mercedes	–1m 4.769s	8	2	M

CANADIAN GP Montréal
25 June 2006   **Race 759**

Fernando Alonso
Renault R26 193.572kph, 120.281mph

Round nine, Montréal, the halfway point of the season. It brought Renault their seventh victory of the season, for Alonso his fourth in succession from pole. His championship lead over Schumacher was now a massive 25 points. It might have been 27 but for Schumacher nabbing second from a clutch-troubled Räikkönen on the penultimate lap, Michael smelling an opportunity when a late SC eradicated his 18s deficit to Kimi. Over the first two-thirds of the race Räikkönen had given Alonso a hard time and might well have won the day but for the dragging clutch which lost him around 12s during his two stops. His teammate Montoya's nightmare season persisted, crashing out on lap 13.

POLE POSITION Alonso, Renault, 1m 14.942s (0.236s), 209.490kph, 130.171mph
LAPS 70 x 4.361 km, 2.710 miles
DISTANCE 305.270 km, 189.686 miles
STARTERS/FINISHERS 22/15
WEATHER Sunny, hot, dry
LAP LEADERS Alonso 1-22, 25-49, 53-70 (65); Räikkönen 23-24, 50-52 (5); SC 2-3, 60-63 (6)
WINNER'S LAPS 1-22 P1, 23-24 P2, 25-49 P1, 50-52 P2, 53-70 P1
FASTEST LAP Räikkönen, McLaren-Mercedes, 1m 15.841s (Lap 22), 207.006kph, 128.628mph
CHAMPIONSHIP Alonso 84, M Schumacher 59, Räikkönen 39, Fisichella 37, Massa 28

Pos	Driver	Car	Time/gap	Grid	Stops	Tyres
1	F Alonso	Renault	1h 34m 37.308s	1	2	M
2	M Schumacher	Ferrari	–2.111s	5	2	B
3	K Räikkönen	McLaren-Mercedes	–8.813s	3	2	M
4	G Fisichella	Renault	–15.679s	2	3	M
5	F Massa	Ferrari	–25.172s	10	1	B
6	J Trulli	Toyota	–1 lap	4	2	B

UNITED STATES GP Indianapolis
2 July 2006   **Race 760**

Michael Schumacher
Ferrari 248 F1 194.117kph, 120.619mph

The Schumacher-led Ferrari 1-2 was his fifth Indy victory in seven years. Ferrari superiority in qualifying, 1.088s, and in the race was overwhelming, due entirely to, yes, tyres. After last year's fiasco Michelin went ultra-conservative, Bridgestone ultra-aggressive, desperate to recover championship momentum. Which was accomplished to the tune of six points. Alonso qualified and finished P5, his poorest result of the year, outpaced all weekend by teammate Fisichella. It might well have been worse for Fernando but for the first-lap carnage. Seven cars were eliminated in separate incidents at turns one and two. In the latter, Heidfeld's BMW triple barrel-rolled and Montoya took out teammate Räikkönen. The mercurial Columbian never drove F1 again.

POLE POSITION M Schumacher, Ferrari, 1m 10.832s (0.603s), 213.056kph, 132.386mph
LAPS 73 x 4.192 km, 2.605 miles
DISTANCE 306.016 km, 190.150 miles
STARTERS/FINISHERS 22/9
WEATHER Sunny, very hot, dry
LAP LEADERS Massa 1-29 (29); Alonso 30 (1); M Schumacher 31-73 (43); SC 1-6 (6)
WINNER'S LAPS 1-28 P2, 29 P4, 30 P3, 31-73 P1
FASTEST LAP M Schumacher, Ferrari, 1m 12.719s (lap 56), 207.527kph, 128.951mph
CHAMPIONSHIP Alonso 88, M Schumacher 69, Fisichella 43, Räikkönen 39, Massa 36

Pos	Driver	Car	Time/gap	Grid	Stops	Tyres
1	M Schumacher	Ferrari	1h 34m 35.199s	1	2	B
2	F Massa	Ferrari	–7.984s	2	2	B
3	G Fisichella	Renault	–16.595s	3	2	M
4	J Trulli	Toyota	–23.604s	22	1	B
5	F Alonso	Renault	–28.410s	5	2	M
6	R Barrichello	Honda	–36.516s	4	2	M

Round 11/18	**FRENCH GP** Magny-Cours **16 July 2006** **Race 761**	**Michael Schumacher** Ferrari 248 F1 200.967kph, 124.875mph

In hot race-day conditions, Schumacher's Ferrari again trounced Alonso's Renault, assisted by teammate Massa. Felipe's P2 on the all-red front row created the opportunity to keep Alonso, P3, at bay during the first stint as his team-leader, on fast but fragile Bridgestones, escaped up the road. Felipe did the perfect job. Alonso knew what to expect, trying everything to take Massa at the start. Once that failed Renault went for championship damage limitation, feigning a matching three-stop but switching to two. Massa was mugged. This was a Bridgestone weekend as the strong pace of Toyota confirmed, qualifying 4-5, where they might have finished had Trulli's brakes lasted. In the event, for Alonso, the loss of two points was a result.

POLE POSITION M Schumacher, Ferrari, 1m 15.493s (0.017), 210.345kph, 130.702mph
LAPS 70 x 4.411 km, 2.741 miles
DISTANCE 308.586 km, 191.746 miles
STARTERS/FINISHERS 22/16
WEATHER Sunny, very hot, dry
LAP LEADERS M Schumacher 1-18, 23-38, 42-70 (63); J Trulli, Toyota 19-20 (2); R Schumacher 21-22 (2); Alonso 39-41 (3)
WINNER'S LAPS 1-18 P1, 19-20 P3, 21-22 P2, 23-38, 39-41 P2, 42-70 P1
FASTEST LAP M Schumacher, Ferrari, 1m 17.111s (lap 46), 205.931kph, 127.960mph
CHAMPIONSHIP Alonso 96, M Schumacher 79, Fisichella 46, Räikkönen 43, Massa 42

Pos	Driver	Car	Time/gap	Grid	Stops	Tyres
1	M Schumacher	Ferrari	1h 32m 7.803s	1	3	B
2	F Alonso	Renault	−10.131s	3	2	M
3	F Massa	Ferrari	−22.546s	2	3	B
4	R Schumacher	Toyota	−27.212s	5	2	B
5	K Räikkönen	McLaren-Mercedes	−33.006s	6	3	M
6	G Fisichella	Renault	−45.265s	7	2	M

Round 12/18	**GERMAN GP** Hockenheim **30 July 2006** **Race 762**	**Michael Schumacher** Ferrari 248 F1 209.277kph, 130.039mph

But in Germany a further six points shifted to Ferrari. Events influencing these results began in Paris, the FIA banning mass dampers. Renault, their car conceived around these devices, protested but chose to race without them. They qualified P5 and P7 to finish fifth and sixth, troubled by blistering Michelins. By contrast, Ferrari scored another Schumacher-led 1-2, neither car headed or separated by much after displacing Räikkönen. The Finn had brought McLaren their first pole of the season, and appeared a threat until it transpired that his qualifying speed resulted from being lightly fuelled due to a fuel-sensor glitch. He and Button, each struggling at different times, disputed the final podium place, Kimi finishing the stronger.

POLE POSITION K Räikkönen, McLaren-Mercedes, 1m 14.070s (0.135s), 222.308kph, 138.135mph
LAPS 67 x 4.574 km, 2.842 miles
DISTANCE 306.458 km, 190.424 miles
STARTERS/FINISHERS 22/12
WEATHER Sunny, very hot, dry
LAP LEADERS Räikkönen 1-9 (9); M Schumacher 10-67 (58)
WINNER'S LAPS 1-9 P2, 10-67 P1
FASTEST LAP M Schumacher, Ferrari, 1m 16.357s (lap 17), 215.650kph, 133.999mph
CHAMPIONSHIP Alonso 100, M Schumacher 89, Massa 50, Fisichella 49, Räikkönen 49

Pos	Driver	Car	Time/gap	Grid	Stops	Tyres
1	M Schumacher	Ferrari	1h 27m 51.693s	2	2	B
2	F Massa	Ferrari	−0.720s	3	2	B
3	K Räikkönen	McLaren-Mercedes	−13.206s	1	3	M
4	J Button	Honda	−18.898s	4	2	M
5	F Alonso	Renault	−23.707s	7	2	M
6	G Fisichella	Renault	−24.814s	5	2	M

Round 13/18	**HUNGARIAN GP** Hungaroring **6 August 2006** **Race 763**	**Jenson Button** Honda RA106 163.773kph, 101.764mph

The first wet race in 21-years of the Hungarian GP was special. First Räikkönen led from another pole, building a 20s lead during his first stint, then tripping over a backmarker on lap 25. Alonso led from lap 18 to 51, at which point a switch to dries went disastrously wrong, the championship leader on three wheels soon after the stop. This left Button to complete the final 18 laps and his maiden victory, having started P14 after an engine-change penalty. On Michelin intermediates, Button, and Alonso from a penalised P15, carved through the field to be running fourth and third by lap 7, the ever-present Button there to pick up the pieces after the McLaren and Renault misdemeanours. Schumacher scored a lucky point.

POLE POSITION K Räikkönen, McLaren-Mercedes, 1m 19.599s (0.287s), 198.138kph, 123.117mph
LAPS 70 x 4.381 km, 2.722 miles
DISTANCE 306.663 km, 190.552 miles
STARTERS/FINISHERS 20/14
WEATHER Cloudy, cool, intermittent heavy rain
LAP LEADERS K Räikkönen, McLaren-Mercedes 1-17 (17); F Alonso, Renault 18-51 (34); J Button, 52-70 (19); SC 27-31 (5)
WINNER'S LAPS 1 P11, 2 P9, 3 P8, 4-5 P7, 6 P5, 7-16 P4, 17 P3, 18-25 P4, 26 P3, 27-51 P2, 52-70 P1
FASTEST LAP Massa, Ferrari, 1m 23.516s (lap 65), 188.845kph, 117.343mph
CHAMPIONSHIP Alonso 100, M Schumacher 90, Massa 52, Fisichella 49, Räikkönen 49

Pos	Driver	Car	Time/gap	Grid	Stops	Tyres
1	J Button	Honda	1h 52m 20.941s	14	3	M
2	P de la Rosa	McLaren-Mercedes	−30.837s	4	3	M
3	N Heidfeld	BMW	−43.822s	10	2	M
4	R Barrichello	Honda	−45.205s	3	3	M
5	D Coulthard	Red Bull-Ferrari	−1 lap	12	2	M
6	R Schumacher	Toyota	−1 lap	6	2	B

Honda RA106

TURKISH GP Istanbul

27 August 2006   **Race 764**

Felipe Massa

Ferrari 248 F1 208.930kph, 129.823mph

Back-to-back maiden victories, first Button now Massa. This victory hung on the race-long battle between the title contenders, and, fortunately for Felipe, Alonso took the honours. Not that victory wasn't fully deserved, Massa driving fast and well from pole. It began to unravel for Michael when, due to an error, he qualified P2 and, consequently, when the SC was triggered on lap 13 he was forced to queue behind his still-leading teammate in the rush for the pits. This allowed Alonso to get ahead, then an off at turn eight helped Fernando to get away. But over the closing 14 laps Schumacher, now in the quicker car, put Alonso under the most intense pressure imaginable, but he defended valiantly to steal back invaluable points against the odds.

POLE POSITION Massa, Ferrari, 1m 26.907s (0.377s), 221.119kph, 137.396mph
LAPS 58 x 5.338 km, 3.317 miles
DISTANCE 309.396 km, 192.250 miles
STARTERS/FINISHERS 22/15
WEATHER Sunny, very hot, dry
LAP LEADERS Massa 1-39, 44-58 (54); M Schumacher 40-43 (4); SC 14-16 (3)
WINNER'S LAPS 1-39 P1, 40-43 P2, 44-58 P1
FASTEST LAP M Schumacher, Ferrari, 1m 28.005s (lap 55), 218.360kph, 135.683mph
CHAMPIONSHIP Alonso 108, M Schumacher 96, Massa 62, Fisichella 52, Räikkönen 49

Pos	Driver	Car	Time/gap	Grid	Stops	Tyres
1	F Massa	Ferrari	1h 28m 51.082s	1	2	B
2	F Alonso	Renault	−5.575s	3	2	M
3	M Schumacher	Ferrari	−5.656s	2	2	B
4	J Button	Honda	−12.334s	6	2	M
5	P de la Rosa	McLaren-Mercedes	−45.908s	11	1	M
6	G Fisichella	Renault	−46.594s	4	2	M

ITALIAN GP Monza

10 September 2006   **Race 765**

Michael Schumacher

Ferrari 248 F1 245.814kph, 152.742mph

Already destabilised by the mass damper ban, Renault's next hurdle was a dubious qualifying penalty, Alonso supposedly impeding Massa. Relegated to a P10 start Alonso had to push his car to the limit, but just as he snatched third place with ten laps remaining his over-stressed engine blew. From pole Räikkönen initially led Schumacher, but once leapfrogged on lap 15 was unable to get back on terms. So one way or another Schumacher and Ferrari were right back in the title race. Ferrari chose Monza to announce their 2007 driver line-up: the race-winner Schumacher would retire, his seat taken by the driver he beat into second, Kimi Räikkönen. In his third race for BMW Kubica led briefly and promisingly gained his first podium.

POLE POSITION Räikkönen, McLaren-Mercedes, 1m 21.484s (0.002s), 255.937kph, 159.031mph
LAPS 53 x 5.793 km, 3.600 miles
DISTANCE 306.719 km, 190.586 miles
STARTERS/FINISHERS 22/17
WEATHER Sunny, hot, dry
LAP LEADERS Räikkönen 1-14 (14); M Schumacher 15-17, 23-53 (34); Kubica 18-22 (5)
WINNER'S LAPS 1-14 P2, 15-17 P1, 18-19 P6, 20 P4, 21 P3, 22 P2, 23-53 P1
FASTEST LAP Räikkönen, McLaren-Mercedes, 1m 22.559 (lap 13), 252.604kph, 156.961mph
CHAMPIONSHIP Alonso 108, M Schumacher 106, Massa 62, Fisichella 57, Räikkönen 57

Pos	Driver	Car	Time/gap	Grid	Stops	Tyres
1	M Schumacher	Ferrari	1h 14m 51.975s	2	2	B
2	K Räikkönen	McLaren-Mercedes	−8.046s	1	2	M
3	R Kubica	BMW	−26.414s	6	2	M
4	G Fisichella	Renault	−32.045s	9	1	M
5	J Button	Honda	−32.685s	5	2	M
6	R Barrichello	Honda	−42.409s	8	1	M

CHINESE GP Shanghai

1 October 2006 **Race 766**

Michael Schumacher

Ferrari 248 F1 187.644kph, 116.597mph

Schumacher's 91st career victory was his seventh of the season. Somehow, he and Ferrari had clawed back 25 points on Alonso and Renault since Montréal. The grid had not pointed to a Maranello victory, with Renaults 1-2, Hondas 3-4 and Ferraris 6-20. Inclement race conditions initially favoured the Michelin intermediates, Alonso pulling 25s on Schumacher in the first stint. But as the track dried tyre performances swung drastically during the second stint, Michael retrieving all the lost time. Fernando's victory chances ended with a muffed change to dries, but Fisichella was still leading for Renault. But on lap 42 Schumacher got ahead at the final stops, and six later Alonso also slipped by for P2. Their points were now even with two races to run.

Pos	Driver	Car	Time/gap	Grid	Stops	Tyres
1	M Schumacher	Ferrari	1h 37m 32.747s	6	2	B
2	F Alonso	Renault	–3.121s	1	2	M
3	G Fisichella	Renault	–44.197s	2	3	M
4	J Button	Honda	–1m 12.056s	4	2	M
5	P de la Rosa	McLaren-Mercedes	–1m 17.137s	7	2	M
6	R Barrichello	Honda	–1m 19.131s	3	2	M

POLE POSITION Alonso, Renault, 1m 44.360s (0.632s), 188.037kph, 116.840mph
LAPS 56 x 5.451 km, 3.387 miles
DISTANCE 305.066 km, 189.559 miles
STARTERS/FINISHERS 22/16
WEATHER Overcast, warm, rain then drying
LAP LEADERS Alonso 1-22, 24-29 (28); Fisichella 23, 30-41 (13); M Schumacher 42-56 (15)
WINNER'S LAPS 1-7 P6, 8-12 P5, 13-16 P4, 17-30 P3, 31-41 P2, 42-56 P1
FASTEST LAP Alonso, Renault, 1m 37.586s (lap 49), 201.090kph, 124.952mph
CHAMPIONSHIP M Schumacher 116, Alonso 116, Fisichella 63, Massa 62, Räikkönen 57

JAPANESE GP Suzuka

8 October 2006 **Race 767**

Fernando Alonso

Renault R26 219.982kph, 136.690mph

At Suzuka the pendulum swung again when, just as at Monza, ten points changed hands, Alonso victor, Schumacher vanquished, a Brazilian showdown now in prospect. They drew up on the grid in pairs, Ferrari, Toyota, Renault, Honda, Bridgestone filling the front two rows. Once Schumacher disposed of his pole-sitting teammate he appeared to be home free. But Alonso had other ideas, Michelins responding to the cooler race-day conditions. He took 14 laps to reach P2 from his P5 grid slot, chasing and harrying 5s behind, keeping up the pressure, waiting perhaps for fate to glance in his direction for a change. On lap 36 Schumacher's engine let go, Alonso sweeping past to his seventh win of the year.

Pos	Driver	Car	Time/gap	Grid	Stops	Tyres
1	F Alonso	Renault	1h 23m 53.413s	5	2	M
2	F Massa	Ferrari	–16.151s	1	2	B
3	G Fisichella	Renault	–23.953s	6	2	M
4	J Button	Honda	–34.101s	7	2	M
5	K Räikkönen	McLaren-Mercedes	–43.596s	11	1	M
6	J Trulli	Toyota	–46.717s	4	2	B

POLE POSITION F Massa, Ferrari, 1m 46.106s (0.112s), 233.319kph, 144.977mph
LAPS 53 x 5.807 km, 3.608 miles
DISTANCE 307.573 km, 191.117 miles
STARTERS/FINISHERS 22/18
WEATHER Cloudy with sunny intervals, warm, dry, windy
LAP LEADERS Massa 1-2 (2); M Schumacher, Ferrari 3-36 (34); Alonso 37-53 (17)
WINNER'S LAPS 1-12 P4, 13 P3, 14-15 P2, 16 P3, 17-36 P2, 37-53 P1
FASTEST LAP Alonso, Renault, 1m 32.676s (lap 14), 225.572kph, 140.165mph
CHAMPIONSHIP Alonso 126, M Schumacher 116, Massa 70, Fisichella 69, Räikkönen 61

BRAZILIAN GP Interlagos

22 October 2006 **Race 768**

Felipe Massa

Ferrari 248 F1 199.731kph, 124.107mph

They think it's all over: Schumacher needed victory, Alonso a point. Alonso qualified P4, Schumacher P10, a fuel pressure glitch. *It is now*: Schumacher punctures on lap 1, a brush with Fisichella. Many feel the display that followed was Michael at his classic best, a farewell virtuoso performance, a sequence of scintillating lappery culminating in the symbolic pass of successor Räikkönen on lap 69. Why was this man retiring? Maybe part of the answer finished P2, stripping Schumacher of one of his numerous titles, youngest double champion. Maybe another part finished first, winning his home GP on his first visit with Ferrari. Ferrari/Bridgestone had won another battle, but with both championships, Renault/Michelin had won the war.

Pos	Driver	Car	Time/gap	Grid	Stops	Tyres
1	F Massa	Ferrari	1h 31m 53.751s	1	2	B
2	F Alonso	Renault	–18.658s	4	2	M
3	J Button	Honda	–19.394s	14	2	M
4	M Schumacher	Ferrari	–24.094s	10	2	B
5	K Räikkönen	McLaren-Mercedes	–28.503s	2	2	M
6	G Fisichella	Renault	–30.287s	6	2	M

POLE POSITION Massa, Ferrari, 1m 10.680s (0.619s), 219.473kph, 136.374mph
LAPS 71 x 4.309 km, 2.677 miles
DISTANCE 305.909 km, 190.083 miles
STARTERS/FINISHERS 22/17
WEATHER Cloudy with sunny intervals, warm, dry
LAP LEADERS Massa 1-24, 27-71 (69); Alonso 25-26 (2); SC 2-6 (5)
WINNER'S LAPS 1-24 P1, 25 P3, 26 P2, 27-71 P1
FASTEST LAP M Schumacher, Ferrari, 1m 12.162s (lap 70), 214.966kph, 133.574mph
CHAMPIONSHIP Alonso 134, M Schumacher 121, Massa 80, Fisichella 72, Räikkönen 65

- Significant regulation changes affected engines, tyres and qualifying.
- The introduction of 2.4-litre V8s was a major initiative to reduce and contain engine power and cost. Cutting two cylinders and corresponding capacity decreased power to approx 750 bhp, while a development freeze eliminated the 'money no object', arms-race attitude adopted by the engine manufacturers.
- Homologated engine regulations would be brought forward, whereby the engine specification used at the 2006 Japanese GP, subject to returning to a maximum of 19,000rpm, would be used for 2007.
- By curbing exorbitant development costs, the engine manufacturers could now supply customer engines at lower cost, a move to promote successful coexistence between manufacturers with unlimited financial resources and independent F1 teams operating on more modest budgets.
- As another cost-cutting measure the teams agreed to a voluntary testing agreement, restricting testing to 30,000km per team, to apply in 2007.
- Tyre changing returned after only a single season away, the dubious sight of F1 cars struggling to finish GPs on worn-out tyres the explanation given, the reduction in engine size countering any performance gain. The tyre allowance was 14 sets per car over the GP weekend, seven for dry weather.
- 2006 was the very last 'tyre wars' season, and with Bridgestone back in contention they and Michelin produced a splendid final curtain, the initiative swinging back and forth to finish 9-9 in race victories.
- Another cost-cutting avenue had been the elimination of tyre testing by the appointment of a single supplier to F1, the FIA tendering for a F1 'control tyre' to be implemented

- from 2008. Disillusioned by the removal of competition, their *raison d'être* for F1 participation, in December 2005 Michelin announced their withdrawal from F1 from 2007.
- This left the way open for the appointment of Bridgestone as exclusive supplier, effectively from 2007.
- Although Toyota and Williams had joined the Bridgestone camp, at Montréal Michelin beat their rival to 100 race victories, the Japanese manufacturer reaching their ton just three races later. Both tyre companies still lay well behind Goodyear's 368 wins.
- It was regrettable that Édouard Michelin, CEO and great grandson of the founder, lost his life in a drowning accident prior to his company reaching the 100th F1 landmark and successive championships.
- Others to depart were Cosworth founder Keith Ducksworth, 72, shortly before Christmas 2005; 12 months later driver Clay Regazzoni aged 67, and in the spring driver Johnny Servoz-Gavin at the age of 64.
- After three years the increasingly tedious single-shot qualifying was replaced by a more imaginative knockout version, rapidly hailed a success. Three separate segments, Q1, Q2 and Q3, were conducted over an hour, the slowest handful of cars eliminated in the first two sessions to take up their grid positions appropriately, but unrestricted over tyre or fuel choice.
- This preliminary elimination process built excitement towards Q3, a shoot-out between the final top ten survivors. But for Q3 participants, race tyres, settings and fuel-loads were stipulated, enforced by *parc fermé* conditions as before, although a controversial fuel burn and fuel credit system in Q3 was rapidly abolished.

RACE 768, Brazilian GP: Fernando Alonso celebrates with the Renault team at Interlagos having surplanted Schumacher as the youngest-ever back-to-back champion.

RACE 763, Hungarian GP: In Honda's first season back after 38 years as a fully-fledged F1 team, Jenson Button won his first and Honda's third ever race victory; here he makes one of three pit-stops in the changeable conditions.

- The FIA appointed Briton Tony Scott-Andrews to the new role of permanent chief steward.
- Bahrain took over as the season opener, Melbourne postponed to round three due to the Commonwealth Games, while financial instability dropped Spa from the calendar.
- A new team, Super Aguri, increased the 2006 grid to 22. Founded on Honda engines and support, the Super Aguri team was created as a vehicle for Japanese favourite Takuma Sato after he was supplanted in the works Honda team, to the dismay of the Japanese populace, by Rubens Barrichello.
- Former GP driver Aguri Suzuki did the impossible, getting a F1 team up and running in months by operating out of the former Arrows HQ at Leafield and utilising their ageing chassis technology.
- At the Hungarian GP Jenson Button won his first and Honda's third-ever race victory. It was Honda's first season back as a fully-fledged F1 team in 38 years.
- In September the Midland team, formerly Jordan, were purchased by Dutch performance car manufacturer Spyker, while scepticism was expressed over the status of Scuderia Toro Rosso. Was the team a genuine constructor or simply a customer team using a thinly disguised Red Bull chassis from the previous season?
- STR also received dispensation on the engine front. Cosworth produced a yowling 20,000rpm 2.4-litre V8 for Williams but also a restricted 3.0-litre V10 for Toro Rosso, originally a concession offered to cash-strapped Minardi. Revs were pegged at 16,700rpm and air induction to 77mm.
- Months before the 2006 season even began, Ron Dennis shook F1 by announcing that the reigning world champion would leave Renault and join McLaren from 2007. On the surface this bombshell didn't appear to disturb the equilibrium of the Enstone team, carrying on where they left off last season, Alonso unstoppable.
- In the first 11 rounds he scored six wins and four P2s, Fisichella adding a seventh victory.
- But at the 12th round, the day before Hockenheim first practice, the FIA moved to outlaw mass dampers on the grounds that they contravened the moveable aerodynamic device rule, also disregarding their overt use by Renault since Brazil 2005.
- Other teams were experimenting with mass dampers, but as the main exponent, Renault would be the most acutely affected by the removal of a device designed to neutralise vertical chassis movement and so optimise the tyre contact patch.
- Then at Monza, Alonso received a harsh five-place grid penalty for allegedly impeding Massa's Ferrari during Q3.
- So by hook or by crook, Schumacher and Alonso were level on points with just two championship rounds to run.
- But finally Renault and Alonso did it, and deservedly so, back-to-back champions both.
- In 2006, at the age of 37, Michael Schumacher entered his 16th F1 season, the 11th with Ferrari. With Alonso already ensconced at McLaren for 2007, retirement speculation mounted along with rumours that Ferrari had signed Räikkönen as insurance should Schumacher choose to retire.
- But Räikkönen would have no restraining orders in his contract, he and Schumacher having equal status. Schumacher's choice was to face one of the fastest of the new generation of drivers, or take retirement, a decision he announced at Monza.
- In his final season Schumacher acquired one of the few major F1 records not already in his possession, claiming Senna's record for poles, ironically at Imola. Michael's final key F1 stats were extraordinary: 68 poles, 91 wins, 76 fastest laps bringing seven championships. In France he also became the only driver to ever win the same GP eight times, all at Magny-Cours.
- But as always there was Schumacher's darker side, not only his Monaco monstrosity but also censured by fellow drivers at the Turkish GP drivers' briefing following questionable driving conduct in Hungary.

- At Hockenheim, regardless of the Schumacher decision, Ross Brawn announced he would take a sabbatical in 2007, whereas Rory Byrne pledged to remain in a consultative capacity until the end of 2008.
- During the year there was controversy over aero-elastic or flexi-wings, mainly directed at Ferrari and their straight-line speed advantage. From the Canadian GP a rear wing slot-gap separator was mandated.
- For the first time in 11 seasons McLaren failed to win a race, Monza marking their 200th race with Mercedes.
- With Alonso casting a deep shadow over the team's future, both McLaren drivers jumped ship, Räikkönen to Ferrari and Montoya, after an unconvincing half-season, prematurely walking out on F1 to return to the USA, rejoin Chip Ganassi and campaign in the NASCAR series.
- So not the happiest of seasons for McLaren to celebrate their 600th GP at the Nürburgring and their 40th anniversary at Monaco. In those 40 years since Bruce McLaren debuted the M2B the team had been victorious 148 times. Over the identical time-span, comparative stats were Ferrari 146 and Williams 113.

- The F1 political climate improved appreciably in 2006. The GPWC breakaway faction had morphed into the GPMA, which at the start of the year received a setback when a prominent member, Williams, joined Ferrari by transferring allegiance to the FIA/FOM.
- Mosley piled on pressure by imposing a deadline for the remaining GPMA-affiliated teams to submit their entries, and in May, at the Spanish GP, a memorandum of understanding was signed between CVC, FOM and the GPMA for 2008–12, the bottom line being that revenues distributed to teams would double. By November Mosley and the manufacturers also seemed to have found some form of 'peace in our time'.
- Rookie Scott Speed became the first US driver in F1 since Michael Andretti in 1993, while the career of 1997 champion Jacques Villeneuve ended six races prematurely, axed by BMW. Robert Kubica took his seat.
- Sebastian Vettel assumed Kubica's role as BMW test driver. In Turkey, aged 19 years and 53 days, Vettel became the youngest driver to take part in a GP meeting. On the Friday afternoon FP2 he grabbed the headlines by setting fastest lap of the 29 participants.

Championship ranking	Championship points	Driver nationality	2006 Drivers Championship Driver	Car	Races contested	Race victories	Podiumse excl. victories	Races led	Lights to flag victories	Laps led	Poles	Fastest laps	Triple Crowns
1	134	ESP	Fernando Alonso	Renault	18	7	7	15		463	6	5	1
2	121	GER	Michael Schumacher	Ferrari	18	7	5	11		366	4	7	2
3	80	BRA	Felipe Massa	Ferrari	18	2	5	4		154	3	2	
4	72	ITA	Giancarlo Fisichella	Renault	18	1	4	4		57	1		
5	65	FIN	Kimi Räikkönen	McLaren-Mercedes	18		6	6		54	3	3	
6	56	GBR	Jenson Button	Honda	18	1	2	4		25	1		
7	30	BRA	Rubens Barrichello	Honda	18								
8	26	COL	Juan Pablo Montoya	McLaren-Mercedes	10		2	2		6			
9	23	GER	Nick Heidfeld	BMW	18		1						
10	20	GER	Ralf Schumacher	Toyota	18		1	1		2			
11	19	ESP	Pedro de la Rosa	McLaren-Mercedes	8		1						
12	15	ITA	Jarno Trulli	Toyota	18			1		2			
13	14	GBR	David Coulthard	Red Bull-Ferrari	18		1						
14	7	AUS	Mark Webber	Williams-Cosworth	18			2		3			
15	7	CAN	Jacques Villeneuve	BMW	12								
16	6	POL	Robert Kubica	BMW	6		1	1		5			
17	4	GER	Nico Rosberg	Williams-Cosworth	18							1	
18	2	AUT	Christian Klien	Red Bull-Ferrari	15								
19	1	ITA	Vitantonio Liuzzi	Toro Rosso-Cosworth	18								

Championship ranking	Championship points	Team/Marque nationality	2006 Constructors Championship Chassis	Engine	Engine maker nationality	Races contested	Race victories	1-2 finishes	Podiums excl. victories	Races led	Laps led	Poles	Fastest laps
1	206	FRA	Renault R26	Renault 2.4 V8	FRA	18	8	1	11	15	520	7	5
2	201	ITA	Ferrari F248	Ferrari 2.4 V8	ITA	18	9	2	10	12	520	7	9
3	110	GBR	McLaren MP4-21	Mercedes-Benz 2.4 V8	GER	18			9	8	60	3	3
4	86	JPN	Honda RA106	Honda 2.4 V8	JPN	18	1		2	4	25	1	
5	36	GER	BMW F1.06	BMW 2.4 V8	GER	18			2	1	5		
6	35	JPN	Toyota TF106, TF106B	Toyota 2.4 V8	JPN	18			1	1	4		
7	16	AUT	Red Bull RB2	Ferrari 2.4 V8	ITA	18			1				
8	11	GBR	Williams FW28	Cosworth 2.4 V8	GBR	18				2	3		1
9	1	ITA	Toro Rosso STR-01	Cosworth 3.0 V10	GBR	18							

2007

Räikkönen pips the rookie

THE TALE OF THE TITLE

- Post-Schumacher, Ferrari won both championships, but attention centred on McLaren, on track and off.
- With fresh sponsors in Vodafone, champion Alonso and rookie Hamilton new drivers, the season held promise.
- But in an *annus horribilis*, McLaren were expelled from the constructors' title, and lost the drivers' by one point.
- For Alonso, rather than a third title with McLaren it ended with a hasty departure, his reputation tarnished.
- Through all this rancour, rookie Hamilton frequently outdrove his illustrious teammate and the Ferrari pair.
- The 22-year-old led the championship from May to October, finally losing the title by a single point.
- For Kimi to gain the two final points needed to beat Lewis, Ferrari were forced to impose team orders.
- That was how close a rookie came to becoming champion in his very first season.
- The 17 races were split 9-8 between Ferrari and McLaren, Massa adding three victories for Maranello.
- McLaren's eight were shared, Hamilton also mounting the podium on his first nine outings in GP racing.
- Bridgestone control tyres were a significant factor in their first year, many drivers taking time to adapt.
- Michelin's absence damaged the reigning double champions the most, Renault slipping down the grid.
- BMW became the third force, but neither they nor Renault came close to winning.
- But in the end, the Iceman cometh, Räikkönen pulling back 17 points on Hamilton in the final two rounds.
- And not forgetting: Stepneygate spy scandal; McLaren's $100 million fine.

THE CHASE FOR THE CHAMPIONSHIP

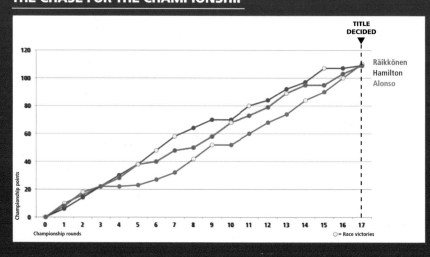

Ferrari F2007

Round 1/17	**AUSTRALIAN GP** Melbourne					Kimi Räikkönen		
	18 March 2007			Race 769		Ferrari F2007 215.893kph, 134.150mph		

Ferrari's pole verified winter testing, and Räikkönen's subsequent race performance was even more imposing. The Finnish Ferrari debutant, in the Scuderia's first season opener without Schumacher since 1995, also claimed fastest lap 1s better than the rest, and led all but six laps. Michael who? Four of the laps he did not lead were attributable to a rookie, Hamilton making his F1 debut for McLaren alongside the reigning champion. Alonso qualified and finished second, but spent most of the race tracking his impertinent teammate, only getting ahead at the second stop. Nonetheless, Lewis delighted in his debut podium. Heidfeld was next up for the impressive BMWs, Massa's weekend compromised by his Ferrari gearbox.

POLE POSITION Räikkönen, Ferrari, 1m 26.072s (0.421s), 221.800kph, 137.820mph
LAPS 58 x 5.303 km, 3.295 miles
DISTANCE 307.574 km, 191.118 miles
STARTERS/FINISHERS 22/17
WEATHER Sunny, warm, dry
LAP LEADERS Räikkönen 1-18, 23-42, 45-58 (52); Hamilton 19-22 (4); Alonso 43-44 (2)
WINNER'S LAPS 1-18 P1, 19 P3, 20 P4, 21 P3, 22 P2, 23-42 P1, 43-44 P2, 45-58 P1
FASTEST LAP Räikkönen, Ferrari, 1m 25.235s (lap 41), 223.978kph, 139.174mph
CHAMPIONSHIP Räikkönen 10, Alonso 8, Hamilton 6, Heidfeld 5, Fisichella 4

Pos	Driver	Car	Time/gap	Grid	Stops	Tyres
1	K Räikkönen	Ferrari	1h 25m 28.770s	1	2	B
2	F Alonso	McLaren-Mercedes	−7.242s	2	2	B
3	L Hamilton	McLaren-Mercedes	−18.595s	4	2	B
4	N Heidfeld	BMW	−38.763s	3	2	B
5	G Fisichella	Renault	−1m 6.469s	6	2	B
6	F Massa	Ferrari	−1m 6.805s	22	1	B

Round 2/17	**MALAYSIAN GP** Sepang					Fernando Alonso		
	8 April 2007			Race 770		McLaren-Mercedes MP4-22 201.893kph, 125.451mph		

While McLaren could advantageously idle their engine for prolonged intervals awaiting the pit-lane green in qualifying, Ferrari in contrast had to adopt cooling louvres and restrict revs to deal with the Sepang heat. Ferrari still qualified 1-3 to McLaren's 2-4, but within yards of the start the Woking pair were leading, Hamilton making a sensational move on Massa. Lewis next spent the first stint allowing Alonso to escape at the front, then made runner-up position his own with a strong drive in the second. His quest was assisted by Massa's clumsy attempt to repass him on lap 6, enabling Räikkönen and Heidfeld to get ahead and stay there. That afternoon Ferrari were both outwitted and outdriven by McLaren.

POLE POSITION Massa, Ferrari, 1m 35.043s (0.267s), 209.955kph, 130.459mph
LAPS 56 x 5.543 km, 3.444 miles
DISTANCE 310.408 km, 192.879 miles
STARTERS/FINISHERS 22/18
WEATHER Sunny, very hot, dry
LAP LEADERS Alonso 1-18, 22-40, 42-56 (52); Hamilton 19-20 (2); Heidfeld 21 (1); Räikkönen 41 (1)
WINNER'S LAPS 1-18 P1, 19-20 P3, 21 P2, 22-40 P1, 41 P2, 42-56 P1
FASTEST LAP Hamilton, McLaren-Mercedes, 1m 36.701s (lap 22), 206.355kph, 128.223mph
CHAMPIONSHIP Alonso 18, Räikkönen 16, Hamilton 14, Heidfeld 10, Massa 7

Pos	Driver	Car	Time/gap	Grid	Stops	Tyres
1	F Alonso	McLaren-Mercedes	1h 32m 14.930s	2	2	B
2	L Hamilton	McLaren-Mercedes	−17.557s	4	2	B
3	K Räikkönen	Ferrari	−18.339s	3	2	B
4	N Heidfeld	BMW	−33.777s	5	2	B
5	F Massa	Ferrari	−36.705s	1	2	B
6	G Fisichella	Renault	−1m 5.638s	12	2	B

Round 3/17	**BAHRAIN GP** Sakhir	
	15 April 2007	**Race 771**

Felipe Massa

Ferrari F2007 197.887kph, 122.961mph

Number two drivers qualified 1-2, lead drivers 3-4, fuel strategy not the only factor. Massa atoned for Sepang with a fine front-running performance, Hamilton keeping him honest throughout his first and final stints, only losing ground mid-race on less suitable rubber. Regardless of their differing strategies, Massa held the upper hand over Räikkönen in qualifying and the race, Kimi surrendering any opportunity for a better finish by losing out to Alonso on lap 1, trapped behind a dawdling champion for more than 20 laps. Discomfort with the car's feel, particularly under braking, accounted for Alonso's deficient speed, even Heidfeld's BMW getting the better of him mid-race with a great outside passing move at turn four.

POLE POSITION Massa, Ferrari, 1m 32.652s (0.283s), 210.283kph, 130.663mph
LAPS 57 x 5.412 km, 3.363 miles
DISTANCE 308.238 km, 191.530 miles
STARTERS/FINISHERS 22/16
WEATHER Sunny, hot, dry, windy
LAP LEADERS Massa 1-21, 24-40, 45-57 (51); Räikkönen 22-23 (2); Hamilton 41-44 (4); SC 1-3 (3)
WINNER'S LAPS 1-21 P1, 22 P5, 23 P3, 24-40 P1, 41 P5, 42-43 P3, 44 P2, 45-57 P1
FASTEST LAP Massa, Ferrari, 1m 34.067s (lap 42), 207.120kph, 128.699mph
CHAMPIONSHIP Alonso 22, Räikkönen 22, Hamilton 22, Massa 17, Heidfeld 15

Pos	Driver	Car	Time/gap	Grid	Stops	Tyres
1	F Massa	Ferrari	1h 33m 27.515s	1	2	B
2	L Hamilton	McLaren-Mercedes	−2.360s	2	2	B
3	K Räikkönen	Ferrari	−10.839s	3	2	B
4	N Heidfeld	BMW	−13.831s	5	2	B
5	F Alonso	McLaren-Mercedes	−14.426s	4	2	B
6	R Kubica	BMW	−45.529s	6	2	B

Round 4/17	**SPANISH GP** Cataluña	
	13 May 2007	**Race 772**

Felipe Massa

Ferrari F2007 198.102kph, 123.095mph

A repeat Massa-Hamilton 1-2 reinforced the notion of a four-way championship battle. Massa aced qualifying for the fifth time in six races, then shrugged off a bullying attempt by Alonso at the first corner, the world champion fortunate to rejoin fourth from the gravel-trap. Hamilton did to Räikkönen what Alonso failed to accomplish with Massa, the outcome of the race now set and never in doubt, Felipe just too quick that day. Räikkönen was out of luck, alternator on lap 9, as was Heidfeld's impressive opening to the season, gearbox gremlins intervening. But Kubica kept the BMW flag flying followed by Coulthard's Red Bull and Rosberg's Williams. A rookie now led the championship, pre-season favourite Kimi fourth.

POLE POSITION Massa, Ferrari, 1m 21.421s (0.030s), 205.819kph, 127.889mph
LAPS 65 x 4.655 km, 2.892 miles
DISTANCE 302.449 km, 187.933 miles
STARTERS/FINISHERS 22/14
WEATHER Hazy sun, hot, dry
LAP LEADERS Massa 1-19, 25-42, 48-65 (55); Hamilton 20-22, 43-47 (8); N Heidfeld, BMW 22-23 (2)
WINNER'S LAPS 1-19 P1, 20-21 P4, 22 P3, 23-24 P2, 25-42 P1, 43-47 P2, 48-65 P1
FASTEST LAP Massa, Ferrari, 1m 22.680s (lap 14), 202.685kph, 125.943mph
CHAMPIONSHIP Hamilton 30, Alonso 28, Massa 27, Räikkönen 22, Heidfeld 15

Pos	Driver	Car	Time/gap	Grid	Stops	Tyres
1	F Massa	Ferrari	1h 31m 36.230s	1	2	B
2	L Hamilton	McLaren-Mercedes	−6.790s	4	2	B
3	F Alonso	McLaren-Mercedes	−17.456s	2	2	B
4	R Kubica	BMW	−31.615s	5	2	B
5	D Coulthard	Red Bull-Renault	−58.331s	9	2	B
6	N Rosberg	Williams-Toyota	−59.538s	11	2	B

Round 5/17	**MONACO GP** Monte Carlo	
	27 May 2007	**Race 773**

Fernando Alonso

McLaren-Mercedes MP4-22 155.551kph, 96.655mph

At the street circuit Alonso reasserted himself. Or was it team orders? The race, as qualifying, was all about one team, McLaren. Put simply, Lewis was quicker 'round the houses', a fuel-adjusted 0.4s faster in Q3 but P2 on the grid due to 9kg more fuel. So how come Lewis' extra fuel-load never paid off, especially as Alonso lost several seconds when Trulli unlapped himself for six laps just before the first stop? Team orders was the answer, but so subtle Hamilton's unaccountably early call for fuel on lap 53 was barely discernable. But it sowed seeds of discontent between the drivers. Massa started and finished P3, but over a minute in arrears, while Räikkönen's Q2 faux pas at Rascasse produced one point for eighth place from his P16 start.

POLE POSITION Alonso, McLaren-Mercedes, 1m 15.726s (0.179s), 158.782kph, 98.663mph
LAPS 78 x 3.340 km, 2.075 miles
DISTANCE 260.520 km, 161.880 miles
STARTERS/FINISHERS 22/19
WEATHER Cloudy with sunny intervals, warm, dry
LAP LEADERS Alonso 1-25, 29-50, 53-78 (73); Hamilton 26-28, 51-52 (5)
WINNER'S LAPS 1-25 P1, 26-28 P2, 29-50 P1, 51-52 P2, 53-78 P1
FASTEST LAP Alonso, McLaren-Mercedes, 1m 15.284s (lap 44), 159.715kph, 99.242mph
CHAMPIONSHIP Alonso 38, Hamilton 38, Massa 33, Räikkönen 23, Heidfeld 18

Pos	Driver	Car	Time/gap	Grid	Stops	Tyres
1	F Alonso	McLaren-Mercedes	1h 40m 29.329s	1	2	B
2	L Hamilton	McLaren-Mercedes	−4.095s	2	2	B
3	F Massa	Ferrari	−1m 9.114s	3	2	B
4	G Fisichella	Renault	−1 lap	4	2	B
5	R Kubica	BMW	−1 lap	8	1	B
6	N Heidfeld	BMW	−1 lap	7	1	B

McLaren-Mercedes MP4-22

| Round 6/17 | CANADIAN GP Montréal | Lewis Hamilton |
| | 10 June 2007 Race 774 | McLaren-Mercedes MP4-22 175.799kph, 109.237mph |

From his first pole at a new-to-him and traditionally punishing circuit, Hamilton fully deserved his maiden victory. In an incident-packed, debris-strewn race with four SCs, Lewis consummately handled all the extra pressure and uncertainty while his rivals found the challenging circumstances more problematical. In an attempt to instantly rectify a qualifying error, Alonso lost out at the first corner, and later suffered a stop-go for pitting illegally during SC conditions; that or run out of fuel. Massa was disqualified for ignoring a pit-exit red, while Räikkönen battled to P5 with self-inflicted and other damage. Widespread relief was felt when Kubica survived a catastrophically violent smash on lap 26. Heidfeld and Wurz flanked Lewis on the podium.

POLE POSITION Hamilton, McLaren-Mercedes, 1m 15.707s (0.456s), 207.373kph, 128.855mph
LAPS 70 x 4.361 km, 2.710 miles
DISTANCE 305.270 km, 189.686 miles
STARTERS/FINISHERS 22/15
WEATHER Cloudy with sunny intervals, hot, dry
LAP LEADERS Hamilton 1-21, 25-70 (67); F Massa, Ferrari 22-24 (3); SC 23-26, 28-33, 51-54, 56-60 (19)
WINNER'S LAPS 1-21 P1, 22-24 P2, 25-70 P1
FASTEST LAP F Alonso, McLaren-Mercedes, 1m 16.367s (Lap 46), 205.580kph, 127.742mph
CHAMPIONSHIP Hamilton 48, Alonso 40, Massa 33, Räikkönen 27, Heidfeld 26

Pos	Driver	Car	Time/gap	Grid	Stops	Tyres
1	L Hamilton	McLaren-Mercedes	1h 44m 11.292s	1	2	B
2	N Heidfeld	BMW	−4.343s	3	2	B
3	A Wurz	Williams-Toyota	−5.325s	19	1	B
4	H Kovalainen	Renault	−6.729s	22	2	B
5	K Räikkönen	Ferrari	−13.007s	4	2	B
6	T Sato	Super Aguri-Honda	−16.698s	11	3	B

| Round 7/17 | UNITED STATES GP Indianapolis | Lewis Hamilton |
| | 17 June 2007 Race 775 | McLaren-Mercedes MP4-22 201.401kph, 125.145mph |

Hamilton cranked up McLaren intra-team rivalry by winning again, Alonso gesticulating to his pit in frustration after being denied the lead at turn one on lap 39. Apart from the start, this had been his one and only opportunity to attack, Hamilton briefly delayed by backmarkers during lap 38. Otherwise Alonso was held at arm's length, 2–4s back. McLaren were in a class of their own at Indy and Hamilton top of that class, holding sway over his teammate in qualifying and the race. The Ferraris started and finished 3-4, Räikkönen's chance of beating Massa vanishing at the start when he dropped behind Heidfeld and Kovalainen. Ferrari championship hopes were on the slide. They needed to do something, and fast.

POLE POSITION Hamilton, McLaren-Mercedes, 1m 12.331s (0.169s), 208.640kph, 129.642mph
LAPS 73 x 4.192 km, 2.605 miles
DISTANCE 306.016 km, 190.150 miles
STARTERS/FINISHERS 22/17
WEATHER Sunny, very hot, dry
LAP LEADERS Hamilton 1-20, 27-50, 52-73 (66); Alonso 21 (1); Kovalainen 22-26 (5); Massa 51 (1)
WINNER'S LAPS 1-20 P1, 21-22 P4, 23 P3, 24-26 P2, 27-50 P1, 51 P2, 52-73 P1
FASTEST LAP Räikkönen, Ferrari, 1m 13.117s (lap 49), 206.397kph, 128.250mph
CHAMPIONSHIP Hamilton 58, Alonso 48, Massa 39, Räikkönen 32, Heidfeld 26

Pos	Driver	Car	Time/gap	Grid	Stops	Tyres
1	L Hamilton	McLaren-Mercedes	1h 31m 9.965s	1	2	B
2	F Alonso	McLaren-Mercedes	−1.518s	2	2	B
3	F Massa	Ferrari	−12.842s	3	2	B
4	K Räikkönen	Ferrari	−15.422s	4	2	B
5	H Kovalainen	Renault	−41.402s	6	2	B
6	J Trulli	Toyota	−1m 6.703s	8	2	B

| Round 8/17 | **FRENCH GP** Magny-Cours | | | | | **Kimi Räikkönen** |
| | **1 July 2007** | | | **Race 776** | | Ferrari F2007 203.679kph, 126.560mph |

The Ferrari resurgence was immediate, the fast sweeping corners of the Nevers track suiting the F2007 and its erratic tyre behaviour. Ferrari dominance was such that which driver would win was about the only uncertainty. Massa took another pole, led most of the way, yet ended up second. A mistake in qualifying had Räikkönen P3, but from the clean side of the grid he beat Hamilton to turn one. His heavier fuel load did not leapfrog him ahead of Massa at the first stop, but at the second it worked, Felipe complaining of traffic. P3 consolidated Hamilton's championship lead, the BMW duo next up, Kubica returning after missing Indy. Alonso? Gearbox maladies in Q3 had him starting P10, and despite strenuous efforts P7 was the net result.

POLE POSITION Massa, Ferrari, 1m 15.034s (0.070), 211.632kph, 131.502mph
LAPS 70 x 4.411 km, 2.741 miles
DISTANCE 308.586 km, 191.746 miles
STARTERS/FINISHERS 22/17
WEATHER Overcast, warm, dry
LAP LEADERS Massa 1-19, 23-43 (40); Räikkönen 20-22, 44-70 (30)
WINNER'S LAPS 1-19 P2, 20-22 P1, 23-43 P2, 44-70 P1
FASTEST LAP Massa, Ferrari, 1m 16.099s (lap 42), 208.670kph, 129.662mph
CHAMPIONSHIP Hamilton 64, Alonso 50, Massa 47, Räikkönen 42, Heidfeld 30

Pos	Driver	Car	Time/gap	Grid	Stops	Tyres
1	K Räikkönen	Ferrari	1h 30m 54.200s	3	2	B
2	F Massa	Ferrari	−2.414s	1	2	B
3	L Hamilton	McLaren-Mercedes	−32.153s	2	3	B
4	R Kubica	BMW	−41.727s	4	2	B
5	N Heidfeld	BMW	−48.801s	7	2	B
6	G Fisichella	Renault	−52.210s	5	2	B

| Round 9/17 | **BRITISH GP** Silverstone | | | | | **Kimi Räikkönen** |
| | **8 July 2007** | | | **Race 777** | | Ferrari F2007 222.629kph, 138.335mph |

In the dying seconds Alonso went quickest, then Räikkönen, but it was Hamilton who snatched pole for his home GP. To the delight of the adoring crowd, he led his rivals away from the line to hold a narrow first stint lead. When he pitted two laps sooner than Räikkönen and four earlier than Alonso his low-fuel qualifying gamble was revealed, and now shuffled down to third those in the know knew it had failed. A muffed pit-stop and a poor second stint with tyre graining ended Lewis' least competitive showing of the season, albeit another podium. Fernando did well to make Kimi work for his victory, but Ferrari always had the measure of McLaren around Silverstone. Massa demonstrated it best, storming from a pit-lane start to P5 behind Kubica.

POLE POSITION Hamilton, McLaren-Mercedes, 1m 19.997s (0.102s), 231.353kph, 143.756mph
LAPS 59 x 5.141 km, 3.195 miles (Scheduled for 60 laps but reduced after aborted start)
DISTANCE 303.214 km, 188.408 miles
STARTERS/FINISHERS 22/16
WEATHER Cloudy with sunny intervals, warm, dry
LAP LEADERS Hamilton 1-15 (15); Räikkönen 16-17, 38-59 (24); Alonso 18-37 (20)
WINNER'S LAPS 1-15 P2, 16-17 P1, 18 P2, 19 P4, 20 P3, 21-37 P2, 38-59 P1
FASTEST LAP Räikkönen, Ferrari, 1m 20.638s (lap 17), 229.514kph, 142.614mph
CHAMPIONSHIP Hamilton 70, Alonso 58, Räikkönen 52, Massa 51, Heidfeld 33

Pos	Driver	Car	Time/gap	Grid	Stops	Tyres
1	K Räikkönen	Ferrari	1h 21m 43.074s	2	2	B
2	F Alonso	McLaren-Mercedes	−2.459s	3	2	B
3	L Hamilton	McLaren-Mercedes	−39.373s	1	2	B
4	R Kubica	BMW	−53.319s	5	2	B
5	F Massa	Ferrari	−54.063s	4	2	B
6	N Heidfeld	BMW	−56.336s	9	2	B

| Round 10/17 | **EUROPEAN GP** Nürburgring | | | | | **Fernando Alonso** |
| | **22 July 2007** | | | **Race 778** | | McLaren-Mercedes MP4-22 146.566kph, 91.072mph |

Hamilton's spellbinding run ended heavily and painfully in the tyre-barriers in Q3, the consequence of a collapsed front wheel. Starting tenth, he finished ninth, at one point craned out of a gravel-trap, his first no-score. Räikkönen also failed to score, hydraulics on lap 34. But that was just the half of it. First a biblical downpour, an inspired tyre-change call, a red flag and a SC restart all conspired to give debutant Winkelhock's Spyker the lead for six glorious laps. Then another downpour transformed Massa's racing certainty into an Alonso victory. Afterwards Massa was critical of Alonso's forceful wheel-banging pass five laps from the finish. Fernando didn't care. He'd won, and what's more, was now just two points shy of Lewis.

POLE POSITION K Räikkönen, Ferrari, 1m 31.450s (0.291s), 202.655kph, 125.923mph
LAPS 60 x 5.148 km, 3.199 miles
DISTANCE 308.863 km, 191.919 miles
STARTERS/FINISHERS 22/13
WEATHER Cloudy, cool, heavy rain, drying then rain
LAP LEADERS Räikkönen 1 (1); M Winkelhock, Spyker-Ferrari 2-7 (6); Massa 8-12, 14-55 (47); Coulthard 13 (1); Alonso 56-60 (5); SC 3-7 (5)
WINNER'S LAPS 1-7 P3, 8-12 P2, 13 P4, 14-55 P2, 56-60 P1
FASTEST LAP Massa, Ferrari, 1m 32.853s (lap 34), 199.592kph, 124.021mph
CHAMPIONSHIP Hamilton 70, Alonso 68, Massa 59, Räikkönen 52, Heidfeld 36

Pos	Driver	Car	Time/gap	Grid	Stops	Tyres
1	F Alonso	McLaren-Mercedes	2h 6m 26.358s	2	4	B
2	F Massa	Ferrari	−8.155s	3	4	B
3	M Webber	Red Bull-Renault	−1m 5.674s	6	4	B
4	A Wurz	Williams-Toyota	−1m 5.937s	12	4	B
5	D Coulthard	Red Bull-Renault	−1m 13.656s	20	4	B
6	N Heidfeld	BMW	−1m 20.298s	4	6	B

HUNGARIAN GP Hungaroring
5 August 2007   **Race 779**

Lewis Hamilton
McLaren-Mercedes MP4-22 191.897kph, 119.239mph

In Q3 Hamilton failed to comply with a prearrangement to concede to Alonso during the fuel-burn laps. In retaliation Alonso held the stacked Hamilton in the pits such that he could not complete his final hot qualifying lap. The stewards docked McLaren their constructors' points and Alonso five grid places, handing Hamilton pole. These events led to a serious rift between Alonso, Hamilton and Dennis. As for the race, Hamilton sprung into an immediate lead and was never headed. Räikkönen from P3 outgunned Heidfeld for second but around the Hungaroring could never find a way past Hamilton. Heidfeld completed the podium, Alonso fourth. A refuelling gaff saw Massa fail to qualify for Q3 and finish outside the points.

POLE POSITION Hamilton, McLaren-Mercedes, 1m 19.781s (0.478s), 197.686kph, 122.836mph (Alonso took pole with 1m 19.674s but received a five-place grid penalty)
LAPS 70 x 4.381 km, 2.722 miles
DISTANCE 306.663 km, 190.552 miles
STARTERS/FINISHERS 22/18
WEATHER Cloudy with sunny intervals, hot, dry
LAP LEADERS Hamilton 1-70 (70)
WINNER'S LAPS 1-70 P1
FASTEST LAP Räikkönen, Ferrari, 1m 20.047s (lap 70), 197.029kph, 122.428mph
CHAMPIONSHIP Hamilton 80, Alonso 73, Räikkönen 60, Massa 59, Heidfeld 42

Pos	Driver	Car	Time/gap	Grid	Stops	Tyres
1	L Hamilton	McLaren-Mercedes	1h 35m 52.991s	1	2	B
2	K Räikkönen	Ferrari	−0.715s	3	2	B
3	N Heidfeld	BMW	−43.129s	2	3	B
4	F Alonso	McLaren-Mercedes	−44.858s	6	2	B
5	R Kubica	BMW	−47.616s	7	3	B
6	R Schumacher	Toyota	−50.669s	5	2	B

TURKISH GP Istanbul
26 August 2007   **Race 780**

Felipe Massa
Ferrari F2007 214.108kph, 133.041mph

In a reprise of his breakthrough victory 12 months earlier, Massa again won from pole at Istanbul Park. Räikkönen chased him all the way, subsequently admitting, 'It's boring sitting behind another car; you can't pass in F1 these days.' After a mistake in qualifying Räikkönen started P3, but used his clean-side grid advantage to beat Hamilton into turn one. Hamilton strove to keep the Ferraris in sight but on lap 43 it became immaterial. A front tyre delaminated, Lewis doing well to recover back to the pits and finish fifth. Hamilton's bad luck gifted Alonso a podium finish, reducing his points deficit to five, the Ferrari pair also closing up with five championship rounds to run.

POLE POSITION Massa, Ferrari, 1m 27.329s (0.044s), 220.050kph, 136.732mph
LAPS 58 x 5.338 km, 3.317 miles
DISTANCE 309.396 km, 192.250 miles
STARTERS/FINISHERS 22/21
WEATHER Sunny, very hot, dry
LAP LEADERS Massa 1-19, 22-42, 44-58 (55); Hamilton 20 (1); Kovalainen 21 (1); Alonso 43 (1)
WINNER'S LAPS 1-19 P1, 20 P3, 21 P2, 22-42 P1, 43 P2, 44-58 P1
FASTEST LAP Räikkönen, Ferrari, 1m 27.295s (lap 57), 220.136kph, 136.786mph
CHAMPIONSHIP Hamilton 84, Alonso 79, Massa 69, Räikkönen 68, Heidfeld 47

Pos	Driver	Car	Time/gap	Grid	Stops	Tyres
1	F Massa	Ferrari	1h 26m 42.161s	1	2	B
2	K Räikkönen	Ferrari	−2.275s	3	2	B
3	F Alonso	McLaren-Mercedes	−26.181s	4	2	B
4	N Heidfeld	BMW	−39.674s	6	2	B
5	L Hamilton	McLaren-Mercedes	−45.085s	2	2	B
6	H Kovalainen	Renault	−46.169s	7	2	B

ITALIAN GP Monza
9 September 2007   **Race 781**

Fernando Alonso
McLaren-Mercedes MP4-22 234.047kph, 145.430mph

As the Ferrari/McLaren spy saga gathered new momentum, the toxic paddock atmosphere surrounding the McLaren motorhome was hardly eased by the team's first-ever 1-2 finish in Ferrari's backyard. The McLaren drivers were dominant in qualifying and the race, but in a reversal of Indianapolis it was Alonso who always held the edge. Indeed, Hamilton lost ground in the second stint with a flat-spotted tyre, allowing the one-stopping Räikkönen to briefly jump him, but Lewis assertively restored the status quo next time round. A substantial off in Practice 3 gave Räikkönen a stiff neck and the spare F2007, but he was still easily able to see off the BMWs, once more best of the rest. Massa's rear suspension broke when third on lap 8.

POLE POSITION Alonso, McLaren-Mercedes, 1m 21.997s (0.037s), 255.937kph, 159.031mph
LAPS 53 x 5.793 km, 3.600 miles
DISTANCE 306.719 km, 190.586 miles
STARTERS/FINISHERS 22/17
WEATHER Sunny, hot, dry
LAP LEADERS Alonso 1-20, 26-53 (48); Räikkönen 21-25 (5); SC 3-6 (4)
WINNER'S LAPS 1-20 P1, 21 P5, 22-23 P3, 24-25 P2, 26-53 P1
FASTEST LAP Alonso, McLaren-Mercedes, 1m 22.871 (lap 51), 251.653kph, 156.370mph
CHAMPIONSHIP Hamilton 92, Alonso 89, Räikkönen 74, Massa 69, Heidfeld 52

Pos	Driver	Car	Time/gap	Grid	Stops	Tyres
1	F Alonso	McLaren-Mercedes	1h 18m 37.806s	2	2	B
2	L Hamilton	McLaren-Mercedes	−6.062s	3	2	B
3	K Räikkönen	Ferrari	−27.325s	1	1	B
4	N Heidfeld	BMW	−56.562s	5	2	B
5	R Kubica	BMW	−1m 0.558s	4	2	B
6	N Rosberg	Williams-Toyota	−1m 5.810s	9	1	B

Round 14/17	**BELGIAN GP** Spa Francorchamps					
	16 September 2007				**Race 782**	

Kimi Räikkönen
Ferrari F2007 229.174kph, 142.402mph

The Eiffel Mountains echoed to the ramifications of the spy scandal verdict. The expunging of the accused McLaren's points effectively handed the 2007 constructors' championship to the plaintiff, Ferrari. Adding to Ron's pain, Ferrari swept the McLaren challenge aside at Spa much as at Istanbul, this time Räikkönen doing the winning. It was the first all-red front row of the season but their third 1-2 result. For Kimi it was his third successive Spa triumph too, his decisive initial break offering Filipe not even a sniff of victory. Alonso led in the McLarens, the pair still topping the championship standings, separated by a mere two points. After an excruciating weekend, salvation for McLaren now only lay in securing the drivers' title.

POLE POSITION Räikkönen, Ferrari, 1m 45.994s (0.017s), 237.885kph, 147.814mph
LAPS 44 x 7.004 km, 4.532 miles
DISTANCE 308.053 km, 191.415 miles
STARTERS/FINISHERS 22/17
WEATHER Cloudy with sunny intervals, warm, dry
LAP LEADERS Räikkönen 1-15, 17-31, 33-44 (42); Massa 16, 32 (2)
WINNER'S LAPS 1-15 P1, 16 P2, 17-31 P1, 32 P2, 33-44 P1
FASTEST LAP Massa, Ferrari, 1m 48.036s (lap 34), 233.388kph, 145.021mph
CHAMPIONSHIP Hamilton 97, Alonso 95, Räikkönen 84, Massa 77, Heidfeld 56

Pos	Driver	Car	Time/gap	Grid	Stops	Tyres
1	K Räikkönen	Ferrari	1h 20m 39.066s	1	2	B
2	F Massa	Ferrari	−4.695s	2	2	B
3	F Alonso	McLaren-Mercedes	−14.343s	3	2	B
4	L Hamilton	McLaren-Mercedes	−23.615s	4	2	B
5	N Heidfeld	BMW	−51.879s	6	2	B
6	N Rosberg	Williams-Toyota	−1m 16.876s	5	2	B

Round 15/17	**JAPANESE GP** Fuji					
	30 September 2007				**Race 783**	

Lewis Hamilton
McLaren-Mercedes MP4-22 151.978kph, 94.435mph

And two weeks later McLaren's amazing rookie appeared to seal it. Hamilton's supreme victory began with a superb pole in typical Fuji conditions. With yet more rain and mist on Sunday, racing only began on lap 19 when the SC exited. Hamilton made his one stop on lap 28, not regaining the lead until lap 41 as different pit-stop strategies played out. That same lap Alonso crashed heavily, causing further SC laps. During these Hamilton controversially varied his pace, unwittingly causing strife between Red Bull's A and B teams, Vettel P3 ramming Webber P2. Kovalainen's P2 for Renault produced the first ever rookie 1-2 while Räikkönen, at one time P21 due to an enforced extra stop to remedy incorrect tyre selection, recovered remarkably to P3.

POLE POSITION Hamilton, McLaren-Mercedes, 1m 25.368s (0.070s), 192.423kph, 119.566mph
LAPS 67 x 4.563 km, 2.835 miles
DISTANCE 305.416 km, 189.777 miles
STARTERS/FINISHERS 22/18
WEATHER Overcast, cool, rain
LAP LEADERS Hamilton 1-28, 41-67 (55); S Vettel, Toro Rosso-Ferrari 29-31 (3); M Webber, Red Bull-Renault 32-36 (5); Kovalainen 37-39 (3); Fisichella 40 (1); SC 1-19, 43-48 (25)
WINNER'S LAPS 1-28 P1, 29-32 P3, 33 P2, 34-35 P4, 36 P6, 37-38 P4, 39 P3, 40 P2, 41-67 P1
FASTEST LAP Hamilton, McLaren-Mercedes, 1m 28.193s (lap 27), 186.259kph, 115.736mph
CHAMPIONSHIP Hamilton 107, Alonso 95, Räikkönen 90, Massa 80, Heidfeld 56

Pos	Driver	Car	Time/gap	Grid	Stops	Tyres
1	L Hamilton	McLaren-Mercedes	2h 0m 34.579s	1	2	B
2	H Kovalainen	Renault	−8.377s	11	2	B
3	K Räikkönen	Ferrari	−9.478s	3	2	B
4	D Coulthard	Red Bull-Renault	−20.297s	12	2	B
5	G Fisichella	Renault	−38.864s	10	2	B
6	F Massa	Ferrari	−49.042s	4	2	B

Round 16/17	**CHINESE GP** Shanghai					
	7 October 2007				**Race 784**	

Kimi Räikkönen
Ferrari F2007 186.826kph, 116.088mph

On lap 28, half-distance, Lewis Hamilton's inexorable journey towards F1 immortality was very much alive. From pole he was still leading, his first stop behind him. But on lap 30 it was over, his first dnf. Why oh why his team kept him out so long on badly worn intermediates simply beggars belief. When he eventually entered the now wet pit lane with tyres now showing the canvas, the F1 rookie, in only his 16th GP, went straight on into the gravel trap, 'driving on ice'. Worse, Räikkönen won the race, his fifth of the season, heading in Alonso from Massa. Vettel made some amends for his Fuji faux pas by finishing fourth for Toro Rosso. But with a useful points lead and one race to go, the championship was still Lewis' to lose, wasn't it?

POLE POSITION Hamilton, McLaren-Mercedes, 1m 35.908s (0.136s), 204.608kph, 127.137mph
LAPS 56 x 5.451 km, 3.387 miles
DISTANCE 305.066 km, 189.559 miles
STARTERS/FINISHERS 22/17
WEATHER Overcast, hot, light rain then drying
LAP LEADERS Hamilton 1-15, 20-28 (24); Räikkönen 16-19, 29-32, 34-56 (31); Kubica 33 (1)
WINNER'S LAPS 1-15 P2, 16-19 P1, 20-28 P2, 29-32 P1, 33 P2, 34-56 P1
FASTEST LAP Massa, Ferrari, 1m 37.454s (lap 56), 201.362kph, 125.121mph
CHAMPIONSHIP Hamilton 107, Alonso 103, Räikkönen 100, Massa 86, Heidfeld 58

Pos	Driver	Car	Time/gap	Grid	Stops	Tyres
1	K Räikkönen	Ferrari	1h 37m 58.395s	2	2	B
2	F Alonso	McLaren-Mercedes	−9.806s	4	2	B
3	F Massa	Ferrari	−12.891s	3	2	B
4	S Vettel	Toro Rosso-Ferrari	−53.509s	17	1	B
5	J Button	Honda	−1m 8.666s	10	2	B
6	V Liuzzi	Toro Rosso-Ferrari	−1m 13.673s	11	2	B

BRAZILIAN GP Interlagos
21 October 2007   **Race 785**

Kimi Räikkönen
Ferrari F2007 207.972kph, 129.228mph

Lewis didn't have to win in Brazil, just keep his rivals close. P2 beside pole-man Massa was a good start. Barged down to fourth at turn one by Räikkönen and Alonso wasn't so good. An off at turn four in a rash attempt to repass Alonso was bad, now eighth. But what occurred on lap seven was disastrous. Running P6, a mysterious gearbox electronics glitch left him stranded for 30s, after which, equally mysteriously, it cured itself. From P18 he recovered to finish P7, but still two places short of nirvana. The fairytale had ended. Up front the Ferraris streaked away from Alonso, the inevitable switch occurring during the second stops, which denied Massa home victory, but bestowed world champion status upon Kimi Räikkönen by a single point.

POLE POSITION Massa, Ferrari, 1m 11.931s (0.151s), 215.656kph, 134.002mph
LAPS 71 x 4.309 km, 2.677 miles
DISTANCE 305.909 km, 190.083 miles
STARTERS/FINISHERS 22/14
WEATHER Sunny, very hot, dry
LAP LEADERS Massa 1-19, 23-49 (46); Räikkönen 20-21, 50-71 (24); Alonso 22 (1)
WINNER'S LAPS 1-19 P2, 20-21 P1, 22 P3, 23-49 P2, 50-71 P1
FASTEST LAP Räikkönen, Ferrari, 1m 12.445s (lap 66), 214.126kph, 133.052mph
CHAMPIONSHIP Räikkönen 110, Hamilton 109, Alonso 109, Massa 94, Heidfeld 61

Pos	Driver	Car	Time/gap	Grid	Stops	Tyres
1	K Räikkönen	Ferrari	1h 28m 15.270s	3	2	B
2	F Massa	Ferrari	−1.493s	1	2	B
3	F Alonso	McLaren-Mercedes	−57.019s	4	2	B
4	N Rosberg	Williams-Toyota	−1m 2.848s	10	2	B
5	R Kubica	BMW	−1m 10.957s	7	3	B
6	N Heidfeld	BMW	−1m 11.317s	6	2	B

2007 CHAMPIONSHIP FACTS AND FOLKLORE

- Michelin's withdrawal effectively brought in 'control tyres' one year early. Bridgestone brought two compounds to each race, prime and option, the latter the softer of the two and identified by a white stripe in the centre tread groove of each tyre. Both types had to be used during the race and those in the top ten shoot-out were required to start the race on the same tyres used in qualifying.
- Teams accustomed to the characteristics of Michelin rubber, especially Renault, suffered from this change, as did the performance of certain drivers who found Bridgestone control tyres less in tune with their style.
- In their second year, the 2.4-litre V8s were rev-limited to 19,000rpm with engine specifications frozen for the next three years. Engine and gearbox penalties no longer applied to Friday practice sessions.
- Under revised Safety Car rules, when deployed the pit lane would remain closed while backmarkers unlapped themselves.
- The same 11 teams contested the 2007 championship, but independent engine supplier Cosworth found themselves out of F1 when Red Bull signed up with Renault, Toro Rosso took over RBR's Ferrari supply, and Williams switched to Toyota. It was the first time since 1963 that there would be no Cosworth presence in F1, but they'd be back.
- Super Aguri's new car reignited the customer car/B-team row, its appearance closely resembling last year's Honda. This year's Honda performed about as badly as its 'Earth-car' paint-job looked, Barrichello failing to score a single point with it.
- In a 17-race calendar, the venue for the Japanese GP switched to Fuji after 20 years at Suzuka and the Belgian GP at Spa was reinstated following intervention by local government.
- At the opening round in Melbourne the Scuderia got the post Schumacher/Brawn era off to a cracking start, Räikkönen's pole on Ferrari debut the first in 51 years – previously Fangio, Argentina 1956 – and his subsequent victory the first Ferrari debut win since Mansell in 1989.
- After the race McLaren questioned the legality of flexible floors, Ferrari's spring-loaded 'tea-tray' uppermost in their thoughts. The FIA ruled them in breach of the regulations but Kimi's victory still stood, which would prove significant.

- Also significant, perhaps, was McLaren's knowledge of the finer design details of the Ferrari F2007.
- Despite Ferrari's perceived 2007 advantage of longstanding familiarity with Bridgestone tyres, they spent the first half of the season struggling with tyre temperatures and single-lap pace. And despite his perfect Ferrari debut, Räikkönen too was overshadowed by Massa, Kimi taking many races to discover a chassis/tyre configuration that showcased his talents.
- But finally Räikkönen had a car under him he could appreciate, 'winning' the second half of the season and making up 17 points on Hamilton in the final two rounds to snatch the drivers' title from the team he led last season.
- Temporary doubt was cast on Räikkönen's last-gasp championship when McLaren threatened to appeal against the stewards' decision not to penalise certain cars that finished ahead of Hamilton for the use of illegally chilled fuel, but thought better of it.
- Räikkönen's 121-race wait for the championship crown was the second longest in history, only exceeded by Mansell's 1992 176-race spell.
- Beginning with Keke Rosberg in 1982 and followed by Mika Häkkinen in 1998–99, Kimi Räikkönen was the third world champion Finland had produced in the last three decades, a remarkable record for a tiny country in northern Europe. And all three shared a distinctive trait, each acknowledged as 'super-quick'.
- Equal with Räikkönen as pre-season favourite was double-champion Fernando Alonso, already on the threshold of greatness and looking for a third straight title which would take him there. Teamed with anyone else but Hamilton he probably would have carved out a special place in the F1 pantheon as 'the man to beat'.
- But to be a great 'man to beat' you can rarely be defeated without just cause, especially by your teammate, and absolutely not a rookie teammate. The comparative stats speak for themselves, Alonso first: 7-10 qualifying; 2-6 poles; 9-12 races led; 203-321 laps led; 4-4 race victories; 109-109 championship points.
- But for Alonso it was a double whammy. Not only was rookie Hamilton as good, as quick, he was also McLaren's blue-eyed

RACE 784, Chinese GP: Lap 30, and rookie Hamilton's journey towards F1 immortality is derailed. Why his team kept him out so long on badly worn tyres beggars belief.

boy, a prodigious talent nurtured by Ron Dennis from an early age to deliver exactly what he was achieving, race victories and championships.

■ Hamilton's phenomenal rookie season compared closely with that of Jacques Villeneuve in 1996, JV first: 3-6 poles; 9-12 races led; 285-321 laps led; 6-2 fastest laps; 11-12 podiums; 4-4 race victories.

■ JV won his fourth-ever GP, Hamilton his sixth, but in so doing Lewis became the youngest GP winner ever, pinching that particular badge of honour from, yes, you guessed it, Fernando Alonso.

■ By the Hungarian GP Alonso knew that his third championship was in jeopardy unless McLaren gave him the support and commitment he considered worthy of his number one driver status. As team management seemed disinclined to offer the necessary reassurances, he resorted to dubious means to obtain them.

■ With his on-track reputation already reeling, Alonso's next ethically challenged off-track step simply exacerbated his fall from grace. He threatened Ron Dennis that unless preferential treatment was forthcoming he would reveal incriminatory email evidence to the FIA in connection with the ongoing 'spy scandal'.

■ In June F1 had become embroiled in industrial espionage, a spying scandal principally involving the alleged passing of confidential documents and plans between Nigel Stepney at Ferrari and Mike Coughlan of McLaren.

■ The peripheral involvement of Honda also came to light, but at a 26 July WMSC meeting the FIA investigation cleared McLaren on the grounds that evidence was insufficient to suggest the championships had been negatively affected, but found the team in breach of the FIA's sporting code.

■ When no sanctions were imposed on McLaren, Ferrari's Jean Todt complained vociferously, requesting through his NSA an appeal of the WMSC decision. This was duly granted on 31 July.

■ On 5 August Alonso made his whistle-blower threat and from then on 'Stepneygate' became ugly and highly personal.

■ The FIA, Mosley, took McLaren, Dennis, to task over the new email evidence which appeared to counter the team's initial stance, positioning Coughlan as a rogue employee, denying knowledge of his activities or use of the Ferrari information. Mosley implied that dissemination within McLaren was far greater that the FIA had been led to believe. The FIA president also very publically refuted Dennis' account of how the existence of the new email evidence was brought to the attention of the governing body.

■ The upshot was that at a WMSC hearing in September, McLaren were fined a draconian $100 million and disqualified from the constructors' championship, a title they would have won by 14 points. McLaren drivers Alonso and Hamilton retained their points, however.

■ It is easy to overlook that Maranello was where the 'Stepneygate' spy scandal originated, yet corporately Ferrari was never chastised for their part, positioning themselves as the blameless and indignant plaintiffs. But if McLaren were responsible for Coughlan, Ferrari were equally responsible for Stepney – after all, there had been no Watergate-like break-in.

■ As early as February Ferrari management were at loggerheads with long-term employee Nigel Stepney, a member of staff in a position of considerable trust. Clearly they failed to recognise the developing situation or control the passing of sensitive information to McLaren, something which only came to light when, quite ludicrously, Coughlan's wife was spotted at a copy-shop near Woking in June.

■ In November the FIA announced that Renault had been summoned to answer charges of possession of confidential McLaren technical information. Allegedly an ex-employee took electronic files with him, 15 Renault employees aware of their existence. At a WMSC meeting in December, Renault was found guilty of breaching the International Sporting Code but went unpunished.

■ Following the massive success of back-to-back drivers' and constructors' championships in the last two years, Renault now had much more to show for their efforts in F1. Setting aside their 80 GP victories as engine supplier, their win tally had now doubled to a far more imposing 33 from 227 races.

■ But in 2007, without Michelin or Alonso, Renault were a shadow of their former selves. At the British GP the Régie celebrated 30 years since their championship debut with the RS01, 15 of those spent as a fully-fledged F1 team.

■ It was BMW in their second season with Sauber that made a quantum leap forward, moving ahead of Renault to become the third force behind Ferrari and McLaren.

■ Following his massive Canadian GP accident, BMW substituted Sebastian Vettel for Robert Kubica at the US GP. By finishing P8, Vettel at 19 years 349 days became the youngest points scorer in F1 history.

■ At the Nürburgring, German Marcus Winkelhock, son of former GP driver Manfred, qualified his Spyker last on the 22-car grid. Events conspired such that by lap 2 of the race he was leading, becoming only the eighth driver to do so on debut.

■ And the final German F1 driver story from 2007: one year on from Michael Schumacher's retirement, brother Ralf joined him. The inevitable comparison: Ralf six GP wins from 180 starts; Michael 91 from 249.

Championship ranking	Championship points	Driver nationality	2007 Drivers Championship		Races contested	Race victories	Podiums excl. victories	Races led	Lights to flag victories	Laps led	Poles	Fastest laps	Triple Crowns
			Driver	Car									
1	110	FIN	Kimi Räikkönen	Ferrari	17	6	6	10		212	3	6	1
2	109	GBR	Lewis Hamilton	McLaren-Mercedes	17	4	8	12	1	321	6	2	1
3	109	ESP	Fernando Alonso	McLaren-Mercedes	17	4	8	9		203	2	3	2
4	94	BRA	Felipe Massa	Ferrari	17	3	7	9		300	6	6	2
5	61	GER	Nick Heidfeld	BMW	17		2	2		3			
6	39	POL	Robert Kubica	BMW	16			1		1			
7	30	FIN	Heikki Kovalainen	Renault	17		1	3		9			
8	21	ITA	Giancarlo Fisichella	Renault	17			1		1			
9	20	GER	Nico Rosberg	Williams-Toyota	17								
10	14	GBR	David Coulthard	Red Bull-Renault	17			1		1			
11	13	AUT	Alexander Wurz	Williams-Toyota	16		1						
12	10	AUS	Mark Webber	Red Bull-Renault	17		1	1		5			
13	8	ITA	Jarno Trulli	Toyota	17								
14	6	GER	Sebastian Vettel	BMW (1) Toro Rosso-Ferrari (7)	8			1		3			
15	6	GBR	Jenson Button	Honda	17								
16	5	GER	Ralf Schumacher	Toyota	17								
17	4	JPN	Takuma Sato	Super Aguri-Honda	17								
18	3	ITA	Vitantonio Liuzzi	Toro Rosso-Ferrari	17								
19	1	GER	Adrian Sutil	Spyker-Ferrari	17								
-	0	GER	Markus Winkelhock	Spyker-Ferrari	1			1		6			

Championship ranking	Championship points	Team/Marque nationality	2007 Constructors Championship		Engine maker nationality	Races contested	Race victories	1-2 finishes	Podiums excl. victories	Races led	Laps led	Poles	Fastest laps
			Chassis	Engine									
1	204	ITA	Ferrari F2007	Ferrari 2.4 V8	ITA	17	9	6	13	19	512	9	12
2	101	GER	BMW F1.07	BMW 2.4 V8	GER	17			2	4	7		
3	51	FRA	Renault R27	Renault 2.4 V8	FRA	17			1	4	10		
4	33	GBR	Williams FW29	Toyota 2.4 V8	JPN	17			1				
5	24	AUT	Red Bull RB3	Renault 2.4 V8	FRA	17			1	2	6		
6	13	JPN	Toyota TF107	Toyota 2.4 V8	JPN	17							
7	8	ITA	Toro Rosso STR2	Ferrari 2.4 V8	ITA	17							
8	6	JPN	Honda RA107	Honda 2.4 V8	JPN	17							
9	4	JPN	Super Aguri SA07	Honda 2.4 V8	JPN	17							
10	1	NLD	Spyker F8-VII, F8-VIIB	Ferrari 2.4 V8	ITA	17				1	6		
DSQ	(218)	GBR	McLaren MP4-22	Mercedes-Benz 2.4 V8	GER	17	8	4	16	21	524	8	5

2008

Hamilton corners it

THE TALE OF THE TITLE

- Just a point short in his rookie season, Hamilton and McLaren again made heavy weather of it in 2008.
- Ferrari's Felipe Massa won the season finale and for precious seconds appeared to have taken the title.
- But 39s later Lewis crossed the line, having crucially passed Timo Glock on the final corner.
- That extra point was enough to win him the title and the mantle of youngest-ever world champion.
- The changing emotions in the Ferrari pit and Felipe's dignity in defeat provided powerful imagery.
- In another tumultuous season on track and off, four drivers and three teams fought for the crown.
- Lewis demonstrated brilliance, but laced with a brashness which led to the occasional costly goof.
- Reigning champion Räikkönen's season was too often compromised by poor qualifying performance.
- By contrast, Robert Kubica had an excellent year crowned by a first victory for him and for BMW.
- Misguidedly BMW switched focus to 2009, deciding future title prospects exceeded present opportunities.
- Hamilton's title was the first for McLaren since 1999, but Ferrari again won the constructors' trophy.
- Among five winning teams and seven winning drivers, Ferrari took eight race victories to McLaren's six.
- There were unexpected victories for Toro Rosso and two for Renault, one at the first Singapore night race.
- First-time winners were Kubica, Kovalainen and Vettel, the latter becoming the youngest-ever GP winner.
- And not forgetting: Mosley's spank-gate; Honda withdraw.

THE CHASE FOR THE CHAMPIONSHIP

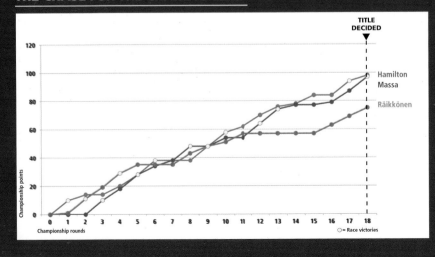

McLaren-Mercedes MP4-23

Round 1/18 — AUSTRALIAN GP Melbourne
16 March 2008 — Race 786

Lewis Hamilton
McLaren-Mercedes MP4-23 194.577kph, 120.905mph

Fuel-pump trouble consigned champions and favourites Räikkönen and Ferrari to a troubled P15 start. Hamilton, conversely, made the season opener look easy with pole and a comfortable victory. The race was a three-SC demolition derby, five cars out on lap 1 and just six running by the flag. The sensible place to be was out front, as Lewis' fast, unruffled display amply demonstrated. By contrast, the Ferrari drivers' races were error-strewn, ended ultimately by engine maladies. The BMWs qualified well, Heidfeld racing strongly to beat Rosberg's Williams to the podium. But for a bad SC break, McLaren debutant Kovalainen was heading for a 1-2, then on his final lap lost P4 to Alonso by inadvertently engaging the pit-lane speed limiter.

POLE POSITION Hamilton, McLaren-Mercedes, 1m 26.714s (0.155s), 220.158kph, 136.799mph
LAPS 58 x 5.303 km, 3.295 miles
DISTANCE 307.574 km, 191.118 miles
STARTERS/FINISHERS 22/8
WEATHER Sunny, hot, dry
LAP LEADERS Hamilton 1-17, 22-42, 47-58 (52); Kovalainen 18-21, 43-46 (8); SC 1-2, 27-30, 45-48 (10)
WINNER'S LAPS 1-17 P1, 18 P2, 19-20 P4, 21 P2, 22-42 P1, 43 P3, 44 P4, 45-46 P2, 47-58 P1
FASTEST LAP Kovalainen, McLaren-Mercedes, 1m 27.418s (lap 43), 218.385kph, 135.698mph
CHAMPIONSHIP Hamilton 10, Heidfeld 8, Rosberg 6, Alonso 5, Kovalainen 4

Pos	Driver	Car	Time/gap	Grid	Stops	Tyres
1	L Hamilton	McLaren-Mercedes	1h 34m 50.616s	1	2	B
2	N Heidfeld	BMW	−5.478s	5	2	B
3	N Rosberg	Williams-Toyota	−8.163s	7	2	B
4	F Alonso	Renault	−17.181s	11	2	B
5	H Kovalainen	McLaren-Mercedes	−18.014s	3	2	B
6	K Nakajima	Williams-Toyota	−1 lap	13	3	B

Round 2/18 — MALAYSIAN GP Sepang
23 March 2008 — Race 787

Kimi Räikkönen
Ferrari F2008 203.971kph, 126.742mph

Ferrari bounced back immediately from their poor opening form with a Massa-led front row. Räikkönen got ahead at the first stops to take a victory made easy when Massa spun out on lap 30, his mistake roundly criticised. So Kubica, his best finish to date, gave BMW their second successive runner-up spot, although the 20s margin to Räikkönen demonstrated the need for improved race pace. The McLarens started P8 and P9, both penalised five places for dawdling on the racing line in Q3. Returning to the pits in fuel-saving mode, they were unaware that others were still at qualifying pace, the speed differentials alarming. Kovalainen came third while Hamilton, delayed by a stubborn wheel-nut, finished fifth yet retained his championship lead.

POLE POSITION F Massa, Ferrari, 1m 35.748s (0.482s), 208.409kph, 129.499mph
LAPS 56 x 5.543 km, 3.444 miles
DISTANCE 310.408 km, 192.879 miles
STARTERS/FINISHERS 22/16
WEATHER Cloudy, hot, dry
LAP LEADERS Massa 1-16 (16); Räikkönen 17-18, 22-38, 44-56 (32); Kubica 19-21, 39-43 (8)
WINNER'S LAPS 1-16 P2, 17-18 P1, 19 P4, 20 P3, 21 P2, 22-38 P1, 39-43 P2, 44-56 P1
FASTEST LAP Heidfeld, BMW, 1m 35.366s (lap 55), 209.244kph, 130.018mph
CHAMPIONSHIP Hamilton 14, Räikkönen 11, Heidfeld 11, Kovalainen 10, Kubica 8

Pos	Driver	Car	Time/gap	Grid	Stops	Tyres
1	K Räikkönen	Ferrari	1h 31m 18.555s	2	2	B
2	R Kubica	BMW	−19.570s	4	2	B
3	H Kovalainen	McLaren-Mercedes	−38.450s	8	2	B
4	J Trulli	Toyota	−45.832s	3	2	B
5	L Hamilton	McLaren-Mercedes	−46.548s	9	2	B
6	N Heidfeld	BMW	−49.833s	5	2	B

Ferrari F2008

Round 3/18	**BAHRAIN GP** Sakhir				
	6 April 2008			**Race 788**	

Felipe Massa
Ferrari F2008 202.974kph, 126.122mph

The paddock was in uproar following recent newspaper allegations involving FIA President Max Mosley. On track, Massa silenced his critics with an emphatic victory, convincingly beating Räikkönen. Kubica had delivered BMW their first pole but too much wheelspin gave Massa, alongside, the initiative. From P4 Räikkönen took a further two laps to oust Kubica, by which time Massa's lead was 3s and, on a track he relishes, fully on course to kick-start his championship campaign. The impressive BMWs finished 3-4, Kubica only 5s shy of the winner. For Hamilton this was one to forget: a practice shunt; engaging anti-stall on the grid and finally tangling with Alonso. He limped home P13, slipping to third in the championship.

POLE POSITION Kubica, BMW, 1m 33.096s (0.027s), 209.280kph, 130.040mph
LAPS 57 x 5.412 km, 3.363 miles
DISTANCE 308.238 km, 191.530 miles
STARTERS/FINISHERS 22/19
WEATHER Hazy sun, hot, dry
LAP LEADERS Massa 1-39, 46-57 (51); Kubica 40-41 (2); Heidfeld 42-45 (4)
WINNER'S LAPS 1-39 P1, 40-41 P3, 42-45 P2, 46-57 P1
FASTEST LAP Kovalainen, McLaren-Mercedes, 1m 33.193s (lap 49), 209.062kph, 129.906mph
CHAMPIONSHIP Räikkönen 19, Heidfeld 16, Hamilton 14, Kubica 14, Kovalainen 14

Pos	Driver	Car	Time/gap	Grid	Stops	Tyres
1	F Massa	Ferrari	1h 31m 6.970s	2	2	B
2	K Räikkönen	Ferrari	−3.339s	4	2	B
3	R Kubica	BMW	−4.998s	1	2	B
4	N Heidfeld	BMW	−8.409s	6	2	B
5	H Kovalainen	McLaren-Mercedes	−26.789s	5	2	B
6	J Trulli	Toyota	−41.314s	7	2	B

Round 4/18	**SPANISH GP** Cataluña				
	27 April 2008			**Race 789**	

Kimi Räikkönen
Ferrari F2008 187.415kph, 116.454mph

Defending champion Räikkönen extended his lead to nine points, heading a successive Ferrari 1-2 from pole. In a largely processional event, Ferrari were far more dominant than suggested by the few seconds which ultimately covered the top four finishers. They were cruising, saving engines for Turkey. At his home race, Alonso created excitement among his followers by qualifying P2, but it was a low-fuel illusion, his race ending at half-distance with engine trouble when P5. Hamilton finished a solid third but on lap 21 teammate Kovalainen survived a 26g impact when a wheel-rim failed. Head-on at 145mph into the tyre wall, there was extensive frontal damage. Briefly unconscious, Heikki was helicoptered to hospital, fortunately unscathed.

POLE POSITION Räikkönen, Ferrari, 1m 21.813s (0.091s), 204.832kph, 127.276mph
LAPS 66 x 4.655 km, 2.892 miles
DISTANCE 307.104 km, 190.826 miles
STARTERS/FINISHERS 22/13
WEATHER Sunny, warm, dry
LAP LEADERS Räikkönen 1-20, 25-66 (62); Hamilton 21 (1); N Heidfeld, BMW 22-24 (3); SC 1-3, 33-28 (9)
WINNER'S LAPS 1-20 P1, 21 P5, 22-24 P2, 25-66 P1
FASTEST LAP Räikkönen, Ferrari, 1m 21.670s (lap 46), 205.191kph, 127.500mph
CHAMPIONSHIP Räikkönen 29, Hamilton 20, Kubica 19, Massa 18, Heidfeld 16

Pos	Driver	Car	Time/gap	Grid	Stops	Tyres
1	K Räikkönen	Ferrari	1h 38m 19.051s	1	2	B
2	F Massa	Ferrari	−3.228s	3	2	B
3	L Hamilton	McLaren-Mercedes	−4.187s	5	2	B
4	R Kubica	BMW	−5.694s	4	2	B
5	M Webber	Red Bull-Renault	−35.938s	7	2	B
6	J Button	Honda	−53.010s	13	2	B

TURKISH GP Istanbul
11 May 2008   Race 790

Felipe Massa
Ferrari F2008 213.808kph, 132.854mph

Two weeks later Kovalainen was not only race-fit, he qualified a place ahead of Hamilton and alongside Massa on pole. Felipe was in search of a Turkish hat-trick, and this he duly delivered with a commanding performance, Ferrari's fourth consecutive win. But this time Hamilton managed to separate the red cars, adopting an unusual three-stop strategy forced upon the team by the poor wear rates predicted over longer runs. Another contributory factor was that Räikkönen's race pace was slightly compromised by front-wing end-plate damage sustained in first corner contact with Kovalainen. Once Heikki replaced the rear tyre punctured by Kimi's wing, he displayed a race pace suggesting that Kimi may well have done Felipe a favour.

POLE POSITION Massa, Ferrari, 1m 27.617s (0.191s), 219.327kph, 136.283mph
LAPS 58 x 5.338 km, 3.317 miles
DISTANCE 309.396 km, 192.250 miles
STARTERS/FINISHERS 20/17
WEATHER Cloudy with sunny intervals, cool, dry
LAP LEADERS Massa 1-19, 22-23, 33-40, 46-58 (42); Räikkönen 20-21, 41-43 (5); Hamilton 24-32, 44-45 (11); SC 1-2 (2)
WINNER'S LAPS 1-19 P1, 20-21 P3, 22-23 P1, 24-32 P2, 33-40 P1, 41-43 P3, 44-45 P2, 46-58 P1
FASTEST LAP Räikkönen, Ferrari, 1m 26.506s (lap 20), 222.144kph, 138.034mph
CHAMPIONSHIP Räikkönen 35, Massa 28, Hamilton 28, Kubica 24, Heidfeld 20

Pos	Driver	Car	Time/gap	Grid	Stops	Tyres
1	F Massa	Ferrari	1h 26m 49.451s	1	2	B
2	L Hamilton	McLaren-Mercedes	–3.779s	3	3	B
3	K Räikkönen	Ferrari	–4.271s	4	2	B
4	R Kubica	BMW	–21.945s	5	2	B
5	N Heidfeld	BMW	–38.741s	9	2	B
6	F Alonso	Renault	–53.724s	7	2	B

MONACO GP Monte Carlo
25 May 2008   Race 791

Lewis Hamilton
McLaren-Mercedes MP4-23 126.170kph, 78.399mph

Pole at his bogey circuit added impetus to Massa's championship candidacy. On wets he led until a moment at Ste Devote on lap 16 let Kubica through. But there was a third contender for victory. Running P2 on lap 5, Hamilton swiped the unrelenting barriers, but by refuelling as well as replacing his punctured right rear he remained in contention, because, fortuitously, on lap 9 the SC was deployed. So when Massa pitted on lap 33, there was Hamilton to assume the lead and pull away, Kubica repeating the trick at Felipe's second stop. With ten laps to go, Räikkönen's tank-slapper rammed the luckless Sutil at the tunnel exit, the inconsolable German heading towards a best-ever P4 for Force India. Victory restored Hamilton's championship lead.

POLE POSITION Massa, Ferrari, 1m 15.787s (0.028s), 158.655kph, 98.584mph
LAPS 76 x 3.340 km, 2.075 miles (Scheduled for 78 laps but stopped after two hours)
DISTANCE 253.840 km, 157.729 miles
STARTERS/FINISHERS 20/14
WEATHER Overcast, warm, drizzle, wet then drying
LAP LEADERS Massa 1-15, 26-32 (22); Kubica 16-25 (10); Hamilton 33-76 (44); SC 9-10, 62-67 (8)
WINNER'S LAPS 1-5 P2, 6-7 P5, 8-13 P4, 14-25 P3, 26-32 P2, 33-76 P1
FASTEST LAP K Räikkönen, Ferrari, 1m 16.689s (lap 74), 156.789kph, 97.424mph
CHAMPIONSHIP Hamilton 38, Räikkönen 35, Massa 34, Kubica 32, Heidfeld 20

Pos	Driver	Car	Time/gap	Grid	Stops	Tyres
1	L Hamilton	McLaren-Mercedes	2h 0m 42.742s	3	2	B
2	R Kubica	BMW	–3.064s	5	2	B
3	F Massa	Ferrari	–4.811s	1	2	B
4	M Webber	Red Bull-Renault	–19.295s	9	1	B
5	S Vettel	Toro Rosso-Ferrari	–24.657s	19	1	B
6	R Barrichello	Honda	–28.408s	14	1	B

CANADIAN GP Montréal
8 June 2008   Race 792

Robert Kubica
BMW F1.08 189.987kph, 118.053mph

Hamilton, in irrepressible form, pulled away brilliantly from pole. On lap 18, 7s to the good over Kubica then Räikkönen, Lewis led a SC-induced charge for the pits. Taking on a hefty fuel-load, he left his pit now third. Too late he saw Kubica and Räikkönen stationary at the pit-lane exit stop-light, awaiting the SC to pass. Wheels locked, Lewis rammed Kimi eliminating both the leading championship contenders. With Massa delayed by a refuelling glitch, Kubica and BMW had their maiden victories sewn up. Indeed, it was a 1-2, the one-stopping Heidfeld hinting that but for team strategy duties he might have won. Coulthard was P3 for Red Bull, but 12 months after his appalling accident at the same circuit Kubica now led the championship.

POLE POSITION L Hamilton, McLaren-Mercedes, 1m 17.886s (0.612s), 201.571kph, 125.250mph
LAPS 70 x 4.361 km, 2.710 miles
DISTANCE 305.270 km, 189.686 miles
STARTERS/FINISHERS 20/13
WEATHER Cloudy with sunny intervals, hot, dry
LAP LEADERS Hamilton 1-18 (18); Heidfeld 19-28 (10); R Barrichello, Honda 29-35 (7); Coulthard 36 (1); Trulli 37-38 (2); Glock 39-41 (3); Kubica 42-70 (29); SC 18-21 (4)
WINNER'S LAPS 1-18 P2, 19 P9, 20-28 P10, 29 P9, 30 P8, 31-32 P7, 33-35 P6, 36 P5, 37-38 P3, 39-41 P2, 42-70 P1
FASTEST LAP K Räikkönen, Ferrari, 1m 17.387s (Lap 14), 202.871kph, 126.058mph
CHAMPIONSHIP Kubica 42, Hamilton 38, Massa 38, Räikkönen 35, Heidfeld 28

Pos	Driver	Car	Time/gap	Grid	Stops	Tyres
1	R Kubica	BMW	1h 36m 24.447s	1	2	B
2	N Heidfeld	BMW	–16.495s	3	1	B
3	D Coulthard	Red Bull-Renault	–23.352s	4	1	B
4	T Glock	Toyota	–42.627s	5	1	B
5	F Massa	Ferrari	–43.934s	9	3	B
6	J Trulli	Toyota	–47.775s	7	1	B

BMW F1.08

FRENCH GP Magny-Cours
Round 8/18
22 June 2008   Race 793

Felipe Massa
Ferrari F2008 201.608kph, 125.273mph

A third victory made Massa the fourth championship leader. The Ferraris were strong, qualifying 1-2 and then pulling away in tandem from the rest of the field. Hamilton might have hung on had he not started P13, a ten-place grid penalty for his Montréal blunder. In his endeavours to catch up he was deemed to have cut a corner in an overtaking move and given a drive-through. He finished out of the points. Back at the front, Räikkönen led comfortably until a sudden loss of power mid-race slowed his pace, a broken exhaust. Massa pounced on lap 39, leaving his teammate to nurse his crippled car home. Despite losing his tailpipe and other related damage, Kimi kept second from a slow but resolute Jarno Trulli, who qualified P4 and finished third.

POLE POSITION Räikkönen, Ferrari, 1m 16.449s (0.041), 207.714kph, 129.067mph
LAPS 70 x 4.411 km, 2.741 miles
DISTANCE 308.586 km, 191.746 miles
STARTERS/FINISHERS 20/19
WEATHER Cloudy, warm, dry then drizzle
LAP LEADERS Räikkönen 1-21, 24-38 (36); Massa 22-23, 39-70 (34)
WINNER'S LAPS 1-21 P2, 22-23 P1, 24-38 P2, 39-70 P1
FASTEST LAP Räikkönen, Ferrari, 1m 16.630s (lap 16), 207.224kph, 128.763mph
CHAMPIONSHIP Massa 48, Kubica 46, Räikkönen 43, Hamilton 38, Heidfeld 28

Pos	Driver	Car	Time/gap	Grid	Stops	Tyres
1	F Massa	Ferrari	1h 31m 50.245s	2	2	B
2	K Räikkönen	Ferrari	–17.984s	1	2	B
3	J Trulli	Toyota	–28.250s	4	2	B
4	H Kovalainen	McLaren-Mercedes	–28.929s	10	2	B
5	R Kubica	BMW	–30.512s	5	2	B
6	M Webber	Red Bull-Renault	–40.304s	6	2	B

BRITISH GP Silverstone
Round 9/18
6 July 2008   Race 794

Lewis Hamilton
McLaren-Mercedes MP4-23 186.585kph, 115.939mph

Having failed to score in two races, Hamilton bounced back at his home circuit. His imperious wet-weather performance made the rest look ordinary, championship rival Massa spinning repeatedly. A Kovalainen and Webber front row was unusual, Räikkönen and Hamilton next. But dire race-day weather had Webber spinning on lap 1 and leader Kovalainen conceding to his faster teammate soon after. Optimising his speed by using unique and varying lines, Hamilton finished over a minute ahead of the struggling field. That day there were many red faces, including the Ferrari pair and Kubica, but not Heidfeld and Barrichello who shared Hamilton's podium. At mid-season, just two points separated the four championship contenders.

POLE POSITION Kovalainen, McLaren-Mercedes, 1m 21.049s (0.505s), 228.350kph, 141.890mph
LAPS 60 x 5.141 km, 3.195 miles
DISTANCE 308.355 km, 191.603 miles
STARTERS/FINISHERS 20/13
WEATHER Overcast, cold, rain
LAP LEADERS Kovalainen 1-4 (4); Hamilton 5-21, 23-60 (55); Heidfeld 22 (1)
WINNER'S LAPS 1-4 P2, 5-21 P1, 22 P2, 23-60 P1
FASTEST LAP Räikkönen, Ferrari, 1m 32.150s (lap 18), 200.842kph, 124.797mph
CHAMPIONSHIP Hamilton 48, Massa 48, Räikkönen 48, Kubica 46, Heidfeld 36

Pos	Driver	Car	Time/gap	Grid	Stops	Tyres
1	L Hamilton	McLaren-Mercedes	1h 39m 9.440s	4	2	B
2	N Heidfeld	BMW	–1m 8.577s	5	2	B
3	R Barrichello	Honda	–1m 22.273s	16	3	B
4	K Räikkönen	Ferrari	–1 lap	3	2	B
5	H Kovalainen	McLaren-Mercedes	–1 lap	1	2	B
6	F Alonso	Renault	–1 lap	6	2	B

TOP 100 RACE

GERMAN GP Hockenheim

20 July 2008   Race 795

Lewis Hamilton

McLaren-Mercedes MP4-23 201.290kph, 125.076mph

For 34 laps of Hockenheim it was a Silverstone continuum, only in the dry, Hamilton in a class of his own. On lap 35 Glock's accident and the resultant SC triggered a remarkable finish. Wrongly, McLaren elected to keep Hamilton out during the seven SC laps. Renault, conversely, had just pitted one-stopping Piquet Jnr, so the SC propelled him from a dismal 12th to a brilliant third. When they eventually brought Lewis in on lap 50, he rejoined fifth yet still won: lap 52, he overtook Kovalainen for fourth, easy; lap 54, Heidfeld for third, a pit pass; lap 57, Massa for second, hobbled by brakes; lap 60, Nelsinho for the lead, sensible. Afterwards Ron Dennis apologised to Lewis for making his brilliant victory unnecessarily difficult. Massa finished P3.

POLE POSITION Hamilton, McLaren-Mercedes, 1m 15.666s (0.193s), 217.619kph, 135.222mph
LAPS 67 x 4.574 km, 2.842 miles
DISTANCE 306.458 km, 190.424 miles
STARTERS/FINISHERS 20/17
WEATHER Cloudy, warm, dry
LAP LEADERS Hamilton 1-18, 22-37, 39-50, 60-67 (54); Massa 19-20, 38 (3); Kovalainen 21 (1); Heidfeld 51-53 (3); Piquet 54-59 (6); SC 36-41 (6)
WINNER'S LAPS 1-18 P1, 19-20 P3, 21 P2, 22-37 P1, 38 P2, 39-50 P1, 51 P5, 52-53 P4, 54-56 P3, 57-59 P2, 60-67 P1
FASTEST LAP Heidfeld, BMW, 1m 15.987s (lap 52), 216.700kph, 134.651mph
CHAMPIONSHIP Hamilton 58, Massa 54, Räikkönen 51, Kubica 48, Heidfeld 41

Pos	Driver	Car	Time/gap	Grid	Stops	Tyres
1	L Hamilton	McLaren-Mercedes	1h 31m 20.874s	1	2	B
2	N Piquet	Renault	−5.586s	17	1	B
3	F Massa	Ferrari	−9.339s	2	2	B
4	N Heidfeld	BMW	−9.825s	12	2	B
5	H Kovalainen	McLaren-Mercedes	−12.411s	3	2	B
6	K Räikkönen	Ferrari	−14.483s	6	2	B

HUNGARIAN GP Hungaroring

3 August 2008   Race 796

Heikki Kovalainen

McLaren-Mercedes MP4-23 188.790kph, 117.309mph

With a front row lockout, McLaren looked set for victory. Massa, from P3, had other ideas, first rocketing past Kovalainen and then Hamilton around turn one. Could he keep Lewis behind at the stops? Yes at the first, and by the second Hamilton's challenge had been neutered by a puncture, finishing up P5. With Kovalainen 20s distant at tyre-conserving pace, Felipe had done it, beaten McLaren against the odds. Then bang! Engine failure with three laps to go. Kovalainen drove through the pall of smoke to his maiden victory, the 100th winner in world championship history. Glock was runner-up, his first podium; Räikkönen third following a Q3 error, while Kubica's gripless eighth dropped him further out of championship contention.

POLE POSITION Hamilton, McLaren-Mercedes, 1m 20.899s (0.241s), 194.954kph, 121.138mph
LAPS 70 x 4.381 km, 2.722 miles
DISTANCE 306.630 km, 190.531 miles
STARTERS/FINISHERS 20/18
WEATHER Sunny, hot, dry
LAP LEADERS Massa 1-18, 22-44, 49-67 (60); Hamilton 19 (1); Kovalainen 20-21, 45-48, 68-70 (9)
WINNER'S LAPS 1-18 P3, 19 P2, 20-21 P1, 22 P7, 23 P5, 24-25 P4, 26-40 P3, 41-44 P2, 45-48 P1, 49-50 P4, 51 P3, 52-67 P2, 68-70 P1
FASTEST LAP Räikkönen, Ferrari, 1m 21.195s (lap 61), 194.243kph, 120.697mph
CHAMPIONSHIP Hamilton 62, Räikkönen 57, Massa 54, Kubica 49, Heidfeld 41

Pos	Driver	Car	Time/gap	Grid	Stops	Tyres
1	H Kovalainen	McLaren-Mercedes	1h 37m 27.067s	2	2	B
2	T Glock	Toyota	−11.061s	5	2	B
3	K Räikkönen	Ferrari	−16.856s	6	2	B
4	F Alonso	Renault	−21.614s	7	2	B
5	L Hamilton	McLaren-Mercedes	−23.048s	1	2	B
6	N Piquet	Renault	−32.298s	10	2	B

EUROPEAN GP Valencia

24 August 2008   Race 797

Felipe Massa

Ferrari F2008 193.983kph, 120.536mph

Massa shrugged off his Hungaroring disappointment with pole at this brand new circuit. In the race, a succession of fastest laps in the first stint established a 5s margin to Hamilton, discomforted by a neck spasm, that would grow to 10s by the second pit stop. It was here that things almost went badly wrong, Massa's pit release deemed dangerous, but the stewards handed out a fine rather than a drive-through. Räikkönen's stop was really messy, Kimi misreading Ferrari's new lights release system, a refueller knocked down. His race, once again compromised in qualification, ended with an engine blow-up identical to Massa's in Hungary. It was a bland inaugural race, especially for the crowd, local favourite Alonso punted out on lap 1.

POLE POSITION Massa, Ferrari, 1m 38.989s (0.210s), 197.076kph, 122.457mph
LAPS 57 x 5.419 km, 3.367 miles
DISTANCE 308.883 km, 191.931 miles
STARTERS/FINISHERS 20/17
WEATHER Sunny, hot, dry
LAP LEADERS Massa 1-14, 20-36, 39-57 (50); Hamilton 15-16, 37-38 (4); Kubica 17 (1); Kovalainen 18-19 (2)
WINNER'S LAPS 1-14 P1, 15 P2, 16-17 P4, 18-19 P2, 20-36 P1, 37-38 P2, 39-57 P1
FASTEST LAP Massa, Ferrari, 1m 38.708s (lap 36), 197.637kph, 122.806mph
CHAMPIONSHIP Hamilton 70, Massa 64, Räikkönen 57, Kubica 55, Kovalainen 43

Pos	Driver	Car	Time/gap	Grid	Stops	Tyres
1	F Massa	Ferrari	1h 35m 32.339s	1	2	B
2	L Hamilton	McLaren-Mercedes	−5.611s	2	2	B
3	R Kubica	BMW	−37.353s	3	2	B
4	H Kovalainen	McLaren-Mercedes	−39.703s	5	2	B
5	J Trulli	Toyota	−50.684s	7	2	B
6	S Vettel	Toro Rosso-Ferrari	−52.625s	6	2	B

Round 13/18	**BELGIAN GP** Spa Francorchamps					
	7 September 2008					Race 798

Felipe Massa
Ferrari F2008 222.715kph, 138.389mph

Spa produced controversy on which the whole championship might have hinged. Hamilton won but was subsequently penalised 25s, handing victory to the cautious Massa, who from third had tracked the gripping race-long duel between Räikkönen and Hamilton. From the start Räikkönen was on a win or bust mission, taking Kovalainen and Massa on lap 1 and Hamilton when he spun on lap 2. During a late-race shower Hamilton closed in, getting ahead of Kimi by cutting the Bus Stop chicane. Despite obvious efforts to return track position to Räikkönen, who crashed out soon afterwards, the penalty was invoked two hours after the podium. 'Is F1 Fixed?' screamed Monday's headlines. The superb racing deserved a better outcome.

POLE POSITION Hamilton, McLaren-Mercedes, 1m 47.338s (0.340s), 234.906kph, 145.963mph
LAPS 44 x 7.004 km, 4.532 miles
DISTANCE 308.053 km, 191.415 miles
STARTERS/FINISHERS 20/18
WEATHER Cloudy, cold, showery
LAP LEADERS Hamilton 1, 43-44 (3); Räikkönen 2-12, 14-25, 29-42 (37); Massa 13, 26-28 (2) (On the road. Hamilton finished first but was penalised 25 seconds.)
WINNER'S LAPS 1-11 P3, 12 P2, 13 P1, 14 P5, 15 P4, 16-25 P3, 26-28 P1, 29-42 P3, 43-44 P2
FASTEST LAP K Räikkönen, Ferrari, 1m 47.930s (lap 24), 233.618kph, 145.164mph
CHAMPIONSHIP Hamilton 76, Massa 74, Kubica 58, Räikkönen 57, Heidfeld 49

Pos	Driver	Car	Time/gap	Grid	Stops	Tyres
1	F Massa	Ferrari	1h 22m 59.394s	2	2	B
2	N Heidfeld	BMW	−9.383s	5	3	B
3	L Hamilton	McLaren-Mercedes	−10.539s	1	2	B
4	F Alonso	Renault	−14.478s	6	3	B
5	S Vettel	Toro Rosso-Ferrari	−14.576s	10	2	B
6	R Kubica	BMW	−15.037s	8	2	B

Toro Rosso-Ferrari STR03

Round 14/18	**ITALIAN GP** Monza					
	14 September 2008					Race 799

Sebastian Vettel
Toro Rosso-Ferrari STR03 212.039kph, 131.755mph

A Toro Rosso on pole, the four championship contenders P6, P11, P14, P15. That's how a rainy Saturday disrupted the Monza grid, but it would sort itself out the following day. Not so. The unrelenting weather provided conditions ideal for Sebastian Vettel to confound the establishment and convert his first pole into a maiden victory, also inheriting the mantle of youngest GP winner. It was a masterly drive in treacherous conditions, beating Kovalainen's McLaren, starting alongside but never able to get on terms, by 12.5s. Seb's greater challenge might have come from the McLaren starting P15. On a one-stop, and fitted with extreme wets, Lewis' strategy required the rain to intensify as forecast, but the threatened storm passed the circuit by.

POLE POSITION Vettel, Toro Rosso-Ferrari, 1m 37.555s (0.076s), 213.774kph, 132.833mph
LAPS 53 x 5.793 km, 3.600 miles
DISTANCE 306.719 km, 190.586 miles
STARTERS/FINISHERS 20/19
WEATHER Overcast, cold, rain, drying later
LAP LEADERS Vettel 1-18, 23-53 (49); Kovalainen 19-22 (4); SC 1-2 (2)
WINNER'S LAPS 1-18 P1, 19-22 P4, 23-53 P1
FASTEST LAP K Räikkönen, Ferrari, 1m 28.047 (lap 53), 236.859kph, 147.178mph
CHAMPIONSHIP Hamilton 78, Massa 77, Kubica 64, Räikkönen 57, Heidfeld 53

Pos	Driver	Car	Time/gap	Grid	Stops	Tyres
1	S Vettel	Toro Rosso-Ferrari	1h 26m 47.494s	1	2	B
2	H Kovalainen	McLaren-Mercedes	−12.512s	2	2	B
3	R Kubica	BMW	−20.471s	11	1	B
4	F Alonso	Renault	−23.903s	8	1	B
5	N Heidfeld	BMW	−27.748s	10	1	B
6	F Massa	Ferrari	−28.816s	6	2	B

Renault R28

<table>
<tr><td>Round 15/18</td><td>SINGAPORE GP Marina Bay
28 September 2008   Race 800</td><td>Fernando Alonso
Renault R28 158.068kph, 98.219mph</td></tr>
</table>

For Renault, the first 'night race' was a fairytale. Starting P15, Alonso won. Going for a short-fuelled early stop, the victory opportunity turned on a timely lap 15 SC, catapulting him from last to fifth as the rest pitted. Bizarrely, the SC was triggered by the other Renault, Piquet going off at turn 17. The SC also negatively impacted many of Alonso's rivals: leader Massa released prematurely, mechanics bowled over, fuel spraying from the trailing broken hose; Räikkönen losing time stacked behind Massa; Rosberg and Kubica receiving stop-gos for entering the closed pits. From his fortuitous P5 on lap 18, to the lead on lap 34, Alonso overtook on track ... no one. The Red Sea had parted, or was it voodoo? There will always be sceptics.

Pos	Driver	Car	Time/gap	Grid	Stops	Tyres
1	F Alonso	Renault	1h 57m 16.304s	15	2	B
2	N Rosberg	Williams-Toyota	−2.957s	8	3	B
3	L Hamilton	McLaren-Mercedes	−5.917s	2	2	B
4	T Glock	Toyota	−8.155s	7	2	B
5	S Vettel	Toro Rosso-Ferrari	−10.268s	6	2	B
6	N Heidfeld	BMW	−11.101s	9	2	B

POLE POSITION F Massa, Ferrari, 1m 44.801s (0.664s), 174.055kph, 108.152mph
LAPS 61 x 5.067 km, 3.148 miles
DISTANCE 308.950 km, 191.973 miles
STARTERS/FINISHERS 20/15
WEATHER Dark, hot, dry
LAP LEADERS Massa 1-17 (17); Rosberg 18-28 (11); J Trulli, Toyota 29-33 (5); Alonso 34-61 (28); SC 15-19, 51-53 (8)
WINNER'S LAPS 1-8 P12, 9-12 P11, 13 P20, 14 P19, 15-16 P16, 17 P15, 18-26 P5, 27-28 P4, 29-33 P2, 34-61 P1
FASTEST LAP K Räikkönen, Ferrari, 1m 45.599s (lap 14), 172.740kph, 107.336mph
CHAMPIONSHIP Hamilton 84, Massa 77, Kubica 64, Räikkönen 57, Heidfeld 56

<table>
<tr><td>Round 16/18</td><td>JAPANESE GP Fuji
12 October 2008   Race 801</td><td>Fernando Alonso
Renault R28 202.788kph, 126.007mph</td></tr>
</table>

Hamilton's problems began when the lights went out. Beaten from pole by Räikkönen, he couldn't resist turn-one retaliation rather than focusing on Massa, his real championship rival, back in P5. His impetuous move pushed Kovalainen and the Ferraris wide, releasing Kubica, P6, and Alonso, P4, into a race-long tussle for victory. But the main title protagonists, Felipe and Lewis, hadn't finished yet, clashing again on lap 2 to finish seventh and 12th respectively after drive-throughs for their misdemeanours. So once Kovalainen's engine failed on lap 16, and with Räikkönen running a steering-damaged P3, the result lay between BMW and Renault, and for the second race in succession the double-champion got the verdict, Alonso simply flying.

Pos	Driver	Car	Time/gap	Grid	Stops	Tyres
1	F Alonso	Renault	1h 30m 21.892s	4	2	B
2	R Kubica	BMW	−5.283s	6	2	B
3	K Räikkönen	Ferrari	−6.400s	2	2	B
4	N Piquet	Renault	−20.570s	12	2	B
5	J Trulli	Toyota	−23.767s	7	2	B
6	S Vettel	Toro Rosso-Ferrari	−39.207s	9	2	B

POLE POSITION Hamilton, McLaren-Mercedes, 1m 18.404s (0.240s), 209.514kph, 130.185mph
LAPS 67 x 4.563 km, 2.835 miles
DISTANCE 305.416 km, 189.777 miles
STARTERS/FINISHERS 20/15
WEATHER Overcast, cold, dry
LAP LEADERS Kubica 1-16, 44-45 (18); Alonso 17-18, 29-43, 53-67 (32); Trulli 19-21, 49 (4); S Bourdais, Toro Rosso-Ferrari 22-24 (3); Piquet 25-28, 50-52 (7); Räikkönen 46-48 (3)
WINNER'S LAPS 1-16 P2, 17-18 P1, 19-21 P5, 22-23 P4, 24-25 P3, 26-28 P2, 29-43 P1, 44-46 P6, 47-48 P5, 49-50 P4, 51-52 P2, 53-67 P1
FASTEST LAP F Massa, Ferrari, 1m 18.436s (lap 55), 209.456kph, 130.150mph
CHAMPIONSHIP Hamilton 84, Massa 79, Kubica 72, Räikkönen 63, Heidfeld 56

CHINESE GP Shanghai
9 October 2008   Race 802

Lewis Hamilton
McLaren-Mercedes MP4-23 199.049kph, 123.683mph

At the circuit where his championship challenge began to unravel last year, without a victory to his name in the last six races, and severely criticised for his Fuji follies, Hamilton was under pressure in China. His response was an inch-perfect pole lap, a clean start, and a fast faultless drive to victory. He just drove away from the two Ferraris immediately behind him on the grid, Räikkönen ahead: 4s by the first stop; 10s by the second, 15s at the finish. Only by the end Massa was second, Ferrari doing the swap on lap 49 to give their championship contender his best chance at the Interlagos showdown. Hamilton's dominant win in the penultimate round in China had all but sealed his championship, so it seemed.

POLE POSITION Hamilton, McLaren-Mercedes, 1m 36.303s (0.342s), 203.769kph, 126.616mph
LAPS 56 x 5.451 km, 3.387 miles
DISTANCE 305.066 km, 189.559 miles
STARTERS/FINISHERS 20/17
WEATHER Overcast, hot, dry
LAP LEADERS Hamilton 1-15, 19-56 (53); H Kovalainen, McLaren-Mercedes 16-18 (3)
WINNER'S LAPS 1-15 P1, 16 P3, 17-18 P2, 19-56 P1
FASTEST LAP Hamilton, McLaren-Mercedes, 1m 36.525s (lap 13), 203.722kph, 126.587mph
CHAMPIONSHIP Hamilton 94, Massa 87, Kubica 75, Räikkönen 69, Heidfeld 60

Pos	Driver	Car	Time/gap	Grid	Stops	Tyres
1	L Hamilton	McLaren-Mercedes	1h 31m 57.403s	1	2	B
2	F Massa	Ferrari	−14.925s	3	2	B
3	K Räikkönen	Ferrari	−16.445s	2	2	B
4	F Alonso	Renault	−18.370s	4	2	B
5	N Heidfeld	BMW	−28.923s	9	2	B
6	R Kubica	BMW	−33.219s	11	2	B

BRAZILIAN GP Interlagos
2 November 2008   Race 803

Felipe Massa
Ferrari F2008 194.865kph, 121.083mph

The final showdown, Massa needing a home victory, Hamilton P5 or better. Massa duly won superbly whereas McLaren chose an ultra-conservative strategy that appeared to backfire badly when rain caused a late-race switch to wets for all but the Toyotas. With three laps to go Vettel overtook Hamilton, demoting him to a championship-losing P6. Unable to retake Vettel McLaren had blown it, but on the final corner of the last breathtaking lap Lewis overtook Timo Glock for P5, the Toyotas now scrabbling on their dry-tyres gamble, to deny Massa and win the title by a single point. Television provided unforgettable human images: Felipe's father, euphoric one moment, frozen in disbelief the next, and his son's dignified disappointment in defeat.

POLE POSITION Massa, Ferrari, 1m 12.368s (0.369s), 214.354kph, 133.193mph
LAPS 71 x 4.309 km, 2.677 miles
DISTANCE 305.909 km, 190.083 miles
STARTERS/FINISHERS 20/18
WEATHER Cloudy, hot, showers at start and finish
LAP LEADERS Massa 1-9, 12-38, 44-71 (64); J Trulli, Toyota 10-11 (2); Alonso 39-40 (2); Räikkönen 41-43 (3); SC 1-4 (4)
WINNER'S LAPS 1-9 P1, 10-11 P4, 12-38 P1, 39-40 P4, 41-43 P2, 44-71 P1
FASTEST LAP Massa, Ferrari, 1m 13.736s (lap 36), 210.377kph, 130.723mph
CHAMPIONSHIP Hamilton 98, Massa 97, Räikkönen 75, Kubica 75, Alonso 61

Pos	Driver	Car	Time/gap	Grid	Stops	Tyres
1	F Massa	Ferrari	1h 34m 11.435s	1	3	B
2	F Alonso	Renault	−13.298s	6	3	B
3	K Räikkönen	Ferrari	−16.235s	3	3	B
4	S Vettel	Toro Rosso-Ferrari	−38.011s	7	4	B
5	L Hamilton	McLaren-Mercedes	−38.907s	4	3	B
6	T Glock	Toyota	−44.368s	10	2	B

TOP 100 RACE

2008 CHAMPIONSHIP FACTS AND FOLKLORE

- In advance of swingeing changes tabled for 2009, major rule changes were few but significant.
- Traction control, including launch control and engine braking, was banned for the second and final time. The means was a standard ECU (electronic control unit) common to all teams, so eliminating any possibility of concealed programs within their own engine management systems.
- In the first season that Bridgestone officially became the sole supplier of the F1 control tyre, teams were required to use at least two compounds during each race, the softer option delineated by a white stripe around the tread.
- Gearboxes now had to last four races, failure invoking a five-place grid penalty, while spare cars were banned, as were exotic materials in car manufacture.
- Strict limits were placed on the amount of CFD (computational fluid dynamics) and wind-tunnel testing permitted each year.
- In qualifying Q3 was shortened to ten minutes and, with no subsequent 'fuel-credit' top-up, eliminated the controversial fuel-burn phase. A 5.75% bio-fuels content was introduced to F1 fuels.
- Spyker (née Jordan, née Midland) became Force India, but Super Aguri lasted just four races into the season before withdrawing due to financial difficulties in the face of the global recession.
- For the first time in 40 years, since Gold Leaf Team Lotus began the sponsorship genre in 1968, no tobacco branding appeared on F1 cars.
- The 18-round championship calendar included the 800th championship race. This was the inaugural F1 'night race', staged around a Singapore street circuit, the arrangement intended to boost the important TV audiences in Europe by transmitting early-morning live coverage at a more social hour.
- A second Spanish race was run for the first time. Designated the European Grand Prix, it was held at a new dockside circuit in Valencia.
- In 2000, after a nine-year absence, Indianapolis had

RACE 803, Brazilian GP: On the final corner of the last breathtaking lap Lewis overtook Timo Glock for P5 to deny Massa the title by a single point.

resurrected the US Grand Prix, but this year it was gone, while the unloved Magny-Cours staged the final French GP, at least for the foreseeable future.

■ And 2009 would be the final GP at Silverstone, Bernie Ecclestone mischievously announcing a new ten-year deal with Donington on the weekend of the British GP.

■ Having contrived to lose the championship by one point in his rookie season, this time a single point brought Lewis Hamilton the drivers' title, and highly deserved it was too in one of the most competitively fought championships for years.

■ Twenty highly impressive points in July gave Lewis a winning platform from which he managed to hold sway through the second half of the season despite various challenges and setbacks, most notably at Spa where he won on the road but was later controversially handed a time penalty which gifted Massa the race victory.

■ By the final race in Brazil the four-way title fight had turned into a two-horse race with Massa, and it was there Hamilton and McLaren almost blew their near impregnable championship position.

■ In the most agonising ending to a championship and possibly to a race, it is now enshrined in F1 folklore that on the final corner of the final lap Hamilton fortuitously encountered Timo Glock's Toyota, struggling with cold slicks on a wet surface, Lewis' pass denying Massa the title by a single point.

■ Between Massa crossing the winning line and Hamilton overtaking Glock it looked as though the amiable Brazilian inspired by his trusty race engineer Rob Smedley had done it, those 20 brief seconds capturing some of the most emotive TV pictures of the season.

■ Almost visibly, ecstatic jubilation swept out of the Ferrari pit in search of the McLaren garage, realisation beginning to dawn on their supporters that the team had landed their first drivers' championship since 1999, their 12th ever.

■ From the 19 British drivers who have won GP races, Lewis Hamilton was the eighth world champion and, at the age of 23 years 9 months 26 days, the youngest of all time. His China victory was the 200th by a British driver, including the Moss/ Brooks 1957 shared win.

■ 2008 was the first season that Stefano Domenicali took the helm at Ferrari, Jean Todt stepping down from the bridge at

Maranello amid growing rumours of the Frenchman running for office as FIA president.

■ An eighth constructors' championship from the last ten years was some consolation for the Scuderia, but the drivers' title undoubtedly went to the right man, Hamilton up against a Ferrari F2008 which on balance had the legs of the McLaren MP4-23, and especially once the slings and arrows of outrageous fortune had been discounted.

■ Reigning champion Räikkönen's disappointing season started strongly but was destroyed by four successive no-score races, by no means all attributable to car and team. Ten fastest laps, matching his own record of 2005 and Schumacher's of 2004, indicated that once new-tyre understeer he so disliked wore off, he could be the fastest car on track.

■ Ferrari developed a pit-lights system to replace the 'lollipop' man. There were some inevitable but costly teething troubles as the team adapted, most dramatic the premature release of Massa at Singapore, the broken refuelling hose flailing behind Felipe as he powered down the pit lane. Having run the length of the pit lane to detach it from the car, a sight to behold was the forlorn mechanics marching back carrying their 'trophy'.

■ For much of the season the fourth driver in genuine title contention was BMW's Robert Kubica, leading the championship following his worthy if opportune round seven victory at Montréal. If the team had listened to their driver and kept pushing to the end of the season, who knows the eventual outcome.

■ Instead, perhaps intoxicated by that first victory and deceived by the success of their lock-step march towards championship glory, BMW elected to switch attention to 2009. How wrong can you be?

■ Back with Renault for 2008 after his bruising McLaren sojourn, Fernando Alonso won two races against the odds. One of these, the Singapore GP, seemed almost too good to be true. Alonso, from a P15 grid-slot, was fuelled for a nonsensically short first stop, but within three laps it became a remarkable winning strategy due to a SC.

■ Bizarrely the SC had been triggered by his beleaguered teammate, Nelsinho Piquet, son of the three-times champion, who's future at Renault was in question. But at least on this occasion his turn 17 error brought victory to his team.

- Alonso not only lost the mantle of youngest-ever world champion to Hamilton, but also youngest race winner to Vettel after his remarkable Monza victory aged 21 years 2 months 11 days. Alonso had now relinquished the 'youngest' accolade to Vettel for: pole, points scorer, podium, race leader and race winner.
- Almost wholly thanks to Vettel, Red Bull 'B-team' Toro Rosso beat the 'A-team' in the constructors' championship, Mark Webber scoring 21 points to Sebastian's 35, although Webber was possibly denied victory in Singapore when his gearbox selected two gears, this electronics glitch blamed on static from a passing tram.
- Red Bull driver David Coulthard retired at season's end, after a 246-race, 14-year career that included 13 race victories.
- At Istanbul Honda driver Rubens Barrichello exceeded Riccardo Patrese's GP starts record of 256.
- Following his sabbatical year, Ross Brawn took over from Nick Fry as team principal at Honda, Fry remaining as CEO. But in December, in the face of the global financial crisis and ensuing worldwide collapse in car sales, Honda withdrew after another miserable season that had seen them finish last in the constructors' championship.
- 2008 was the last year before introduction of tighter restrictions on aero appendages, cars simply bristling with add-ons. Most evident were BMW's horns and Honda's antlers atop the nose, and the 'shark fin' engine cover pioneered by Red Bull.
- In March a UK Sunday tabloid exposed a sado-masochistic sex scandal with Nazi undertones involving FIA President Max Mosley. Mosley resisted calls for his resignation, and despite the deepening scandal circumspectly followed FIA protocol. This led to a confidence vote conducted at the FIA general assembly meeting held on 3 June, which he won.
- In July Mosley was also successful in his High Court action against the News of the World newspaper for invasion of privacy. By judiciously choosing his moments to reappear in public, Mosley gradually resumed his FIA duties, and in December stated that he would complete his term as President, due to terminate in October 2009, but would not seek re-election.
- In August FOTA (Formula One Teams Association) was formed, representing all ten F1 teams under the leadership of Ferrari president, Luca di Montezemolo. Between the FIA and FOM, FOTA's purpose was to provide a constructive third 'leg' in how F1 was run, as well as a platform for the teams to represent themselves as a unified force.

Championship ranking	Championship points	Driver nationality	2008 Drivers Championship		Races contested	Race victories	Podiums excl. victories	Races led	Lights to flag victories	Laps led	Poles	Fastest laps	Triple Crowns
			Driver	Car									
1	98	GBR	Lewis Hamilton	McLaren-Mercedes	18	5	5	11		294	7	1	1
2	97	BRA	Felipe Massa	Ferrari	18	6	4	11		363	6	3	2
3	75	FIN	Kimi Räikkönen	Ferrari	18	2	7	7		178	2	10	1
4	75	POL	Robert Kubica	BMW	18	1	6	6		68	1		
5	61	ESP	Fernando Alonso	Renault	18	2	1	3		62			
6	60	GER	Nick Heidfeld	BMW	18		4	5		21		2	
7	53	FIN	Heikki Kovalainen	McLaren-Mercedes	18	1	2	7		31	1	2	
8	35	GER	Sebastian Vettel	Toro Rosso-Ferrari	18	1		1		49	1		
9	31	ITA	Jarno Trulli	Toyota	18		1	3		13			
10	25	GER	Timo Glock	Toyota	18		1	1		3			
11	21	AUS	Mark Webber	Red Bull-Renault	18								
12	19	BRA	Nelsinho Piquet	Renault	18		1	2		13			
13	17	GER	Nico Rosberg	Williams-Toyota	18		2	1		11			
14	11	BRA	Rubens Barrichello	Honda	18		1	1		7			
15	9	JPN	Kazuki Nakajima	Williams-Toyota	18								
16	8	GBR	David Coulthard	Red Bull-Renault	18		1	1		1			
17	4	FRA	Sébastien Bourdais	Toro Rosso-Ferrari	18			1		3			
18	3	GBR	Jenson Button	Honda	18								

Championship ranking	Championship points	Team/Marque nationality	2008 Constructors Championship		Engine maker nationality	Races contested	Race victories	1-2 finishes	Podiums excl. victories	Races led	Laps led	Poles	Fastest laps
			Chassis	Engine									
1	172	ITA	Ferrari F2008	Ferrari 2.4 V8	ITA	18	8	3	11	18	541	8	13
2	151	GBR	McLaren MP4-23	Mercedes-Benz 2.4 V8	GER	18	6		7	18	325	8	3
3	135	GER	BMW F1.08	BMW 2.4 V8	GER	18	1		10	11	89	1	2
4	80	FRA	Renault R28	Renault 2.4 V8	FRA	18	2		2	5	75		
5	56	JPN	Toyota TF108	Toyota 2.4 V8	JPN	18			2	4	16		
6	39	ITA	Toro Rosso STR3, STR2B	Ferrari 2.4 V8	ITA	18	1		2		52	1	
7	29	AUT	Red Bull RB4	Renault 2.4 V8	FRA	18			1	1	1		
8	26	GBR	Williams FW30	Toyota 2.4 V8	JPN	18			2	1	11		
9	14	JPN	Honda RA108	Honda 2.4 V8	JPN	18			1	1	7		

2009

Button's Brawn bonanza

THE TALE OF THE TITLE

- In the greatest-ever F1 fairytale, the team formerly known as Honda won both championships in 2009.
- Rescued from oblivion, Brawn GP rose phoenix-like to utterly dominate the first half of the season.
- Jenson Button brilliantly won six of the first seven races, then didn't win again over the remaining ten.
- By the end Red Bull had the fastest car, winning the last three races, Vettel championship runner-up.
- But no one mounted a sustained attack on Button who, wobbles aside, finally sealed the title with aplomb.
- Despite the double-diffuser dispute, Brawn with eight victories were deservedly constructors' champions.
- Red Bull were also first-time winners, as was Webber, the squad serving notice of intent with six wins.
- Usual suspects Ferrari and McLaren exploited the KERS opportunity most effectively to keep in the hunt.
- McLaren performed one of the most remarkable turnarounds in form, from also-ran to race winner.
- Toyota just couldn't quite discover that last winning ingredient, they and BMW gone by season's end.
- Force India and Renault enjoyed flashes of promise, while the Williams performance flattered to deceive.
- The Brawn phenomenon was a one-year wonder, morphing into Mercedes GP for the 2010 season.
- And in a bizarre link to Massa's nasty accident, one 'Silver Arrow' pilot would be Michael Schumacher.
- But what of the new champion? Jenson would join outgoing champion Lewis in a McLaren dream team.
- And not forgetting: F1 facelift spawns diffuser row; KERS arrives, slicks return; lie-gate and crash-gate.

THE CHASE FOR THE CHAMPIONSHIP

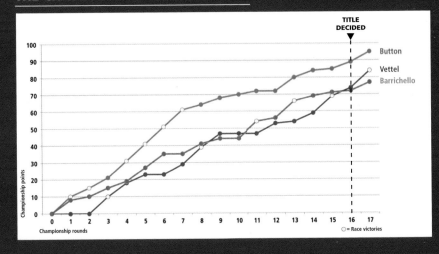

AUSTRALIAN GP Melbourne

29 March 2009 **Race 804**

Jenson Button

Brawn-Mercedes BGP 001 195.775kph, 121.650mph

Debutants Brawn GP qualified and finished 1-2, Button leading every lap from pole. On lap 1 Jenson pulled out 3.9s, but concerned about reliability maintained an easy 5s cushion to Vettel's Red Bull with performance in hand. It was only near the end that Kubica on prime tyres posed a threat to Button on options, but on lap 56 Vettel, struggling on his options, refused to surrender P2 to the faster BMW and they touched, putting both cars out. This benefitted Barrichello's Brawn, which after a disastrous start had recovered from P8. Mid-race Massa and Räikkönen ran P3 and P5, but neither Ferrari finished. In his first race as champion, from a troubled P15 grid-slot, Hamilton drove strongly to P4, but later was disqualified for misleading the stewards.

POLE POSITION Button, Brawn-Mercedes, 1m 26.202s (0.303s), 221.465kph, 137.611mph
LAPS 58 x 5.303 km, 3.295 miles
DISTANCE 307.574 km, 191.118 miles
STARTERS/FINISHERS 20/15
WEATHER Sunny, warm, dry
LAP LEADERS Button 1-58 (58); SC 19-24, 56-58 (9)
WINNER'S LAPS 1-58 P1
FASTEST LAP Rosberg, Williams-Toyota, 1m 27.706s (lap 48), 217.668kph, 135.253mph
CHAMPIONSHIP Button 10, Barrichello 8, Trulli 6, Glock 5, Alonso 4

Pos	Driver	Car	Time/gap	Grid	Stops	Tyres
1	J Button	Brawn-Mercedes	1h 34m 15.784s	1	2	B
2	R Barrichello	Brawn-Mercedes	−0.807s	2	2	B
3	J Trulli	Toyota	−1.604s	19	2	B
4	T Glock	Toyota	−4.435s	20	2	B
5	F Alonso	Renault	−4.879s	10	2	B
6	N Rosberg	Williams-Toyota	−5.722s	5	2	B

Brawn-Mercedes BGP 001

MALAYSIAN GP Sepang

5 April 2009 **Race 805**

Jenson Button

Brawn-Mercedes BGP 001 185.730kph, 115.408mph

From P4 Rosberg catapulted his Williams into the lead from Trulli, then Button, who crucially passed Alonso, his heavy-fuelled Renault plus KERS a 'mobile blockade' enabling these three to break away. Last to pit for tyres, with two stunning laps Button leapfrogged Rosberg and Trulli, but then rain presaged the impending thunderstorm. During this phase Glock, uniquely on intermediates not wets, rocketed from P11 to P2 in six laps, switching just before the race was stopped early, the now monsoon conditions impossible. This let one-stopping Heidfeld into a lucky P2. Most made several stops – wets-inters-wets – not least Button, but once in P1 he impressed while others struggled, Rosberg especially disappointing, losing time on in-and-out laps for P8.

POLE POSITION Button, Brawn-Mercedes, 1m 35.181s (0.092s), 209.651kph, 130.271mph
LAPS 31 x 5.543 km, 3.444 miles (Scheduled for 56 laps but stopped due to rain)
DISTANCE 171.833 km, 106.722 miles (Minimum distance incomplete; half points awarded)
STARTERS/FINISHERS 20/18
WEATHER Overcast, hot and humid, rain, sometimes torrential
LAP LEADERS N Rosberg, Williams-Toyota 1-15 (15); Trulli 16 (1); Button 17-19, 21-31 (14); Barrichello 20 (1)
WINNER'S LAPS 1-15 P3, 16 P2, 17-19 P1, 20 P2, 21-31 P1
FASTEST LAP Button, Brawn-Mercedes, 1m 36.641s (lap 18), 206.483kph, 128.303mph
CHAMPIONSHIP Button 15, Barrichello 10, Trulli 8.5, Glock 8, Heidfeld 4

Pos	Driver	Car	Time/gap	Grid	Stops	Tyres
1	J Button	Brawn-Mercedes	55m 30.622s	1	4	B
2	N Heidfeld	BMW	−22.722s	10	1	B
3	T Glock	Toyota	−23.513s	3	3	B
4	J Trulli	Toyota	−46.173s	2	4	B
5	R Barrichello	Brawn-Mercedes	−47.360s	8	4	B
6	M Webber	Red Bull-Renault	−52.333s	5	4	B

Red Bull-Renault RB5

Round 3/17	**CHINESE GP** Shanghai					
	19 April 2009				Race 806	

On lap 8 the SC pulled off and the race got under way, Red Bulls leading Brawns on the streaming surface. Sepang had hinted it, but in the wet the Red Bulls were in a totally different class, Vettel's great pole also bringing enhanced front-running visibility. On lap 18 a second SC helped the heavier-fuelled Button divide the Red Bulls. It also almost did for Vettel when Buemi's STR rear-ended him, an ironic reprise of his own Fuji '07 rookie gaff. On lap 40 Button led but it was a pit-stop sequence mirage, RBR unbeatable in the prevailing weather, Buemi illustrating the RBR/STR chassis advantage with P8. So the Red Bull pair beat the Brawn pair beat the McLaren pair, the latter a good effort after qualifying midfield. The Ferrari pair had yet to score.

Pos	Driver	Car	Time/gap	Grid	Stops	Tyres
1	S Vettel	Red Bull-Renault	1h 57m 43.485s	1	2	B
2	M Webber	Red Bull-Renault	–10.970s	3	2	B
3	J Button	Brawn-Mercedes	–44.975s	5	2	B
4	R Barrichello	Brawn-Mercedes	–1m 3.704s	4	2	B
5	H Kovalainen	McLaren-Mercedes	–1m 5.102s	12	1	B
6	L Hamilton	McLaren-Mercedes	–1m 11.866s	9	1	B

Sebastian Vettel
Red Bull-Renault RB5 155.480kph, 96.611mph

POLE POSITION Vettel, Red Bull-Renault, 1m 36.184s (0.197s), 204.021kph, 126.772mph
LAPS 56 x 5.451 km, 3.387 miles
DISTANCE 305.066 km, 189.559 miles
STARTERS/FINISHERS 20/17
WEATHER Overcast, warm, rain
LAP LEADERS Vettel 1-15, 20-37, 41-56 (49); Button 16-19, 40 (5); Webber 38-39 (2); SC 1-8, 19-22 (12)
WINNER'S LAPS 1-15 P1, 16-19 P3, 20-37 P1, 38-39 P3, 40 P2, 41-56 P1
FASTEST LAP Barrichello, Brawn-Mercedes, 1m 52.592s (lap 42), 174.289kph, 108.298mph
CHAMPIONSHIP Button 21, Barrichello 15, Vettel 10, Glock 10, Webber 9.5

Round 4/17	**BAHRAIN GP** Sakhir					
	26 April 2009				Race 807	

Toyota locked out the front row, yet rather than a maiden victory breakthrough P3 and P7 was the dispiriting result. Yes they were lightly fuelled, pitting early, but tyre strategy was their undoing, curiously opting for the harder prime in the second stint, which ended the challenge of initial leader Glock and compromised that of pole-man Trulli. Button won the race by crucially overtaking Hamilton at turn one on lap 2. This enabled him to stay in touch with the fleeing Toyotas and then leapfrog into the lead with his longer first stint. Vettel went even longer but didn't jump Trulli for P2 until their second stops. From his modest P6 Barrichello's three-stop didn't work, invariably bottled up, never incisive, out-qualified and beaten by Hamilton to P4.

Pos	Driver	Car	Time/gap	Grid	Stops	Tyres
1	J Button	Brawn-Mercedes	1h 31m 48.182s	4	2	B
2	S Vettel	Red Bull-Renault	7.187s	3	2	B
3	J Trulli	Toyota	–9.170s	1	2	B
4	L Hamilton	McLaren-Mercedes	–22.096s	5	2	B
5	R Barrichello	Brawn-Mercedes	–37.779s	6	3	B
6	K Räikkönen	Ferrari	–42.057s	10	2	B

Jenson Button
Brawn-Mercedes BGP 001 201.456kph, 125.179mph

POLE POSITION Trulli, Toyota, 1m 33.431s (0.281s), 208.530kph, 129.574mph
LAPS 57 x 5.412 km, 3.363 miles
DISTANCE 308.238 km, 191.530 miles
STARTERS/FINISHERS 20/19
WEATHER Sunny, very hot, dry
LAP LEADERS Glock, Toyota 1-10 (10); Trulli 11-12 (2); Button 13-15, 22-37, 41-57 (36); Vettel 16-19, 38-40 (7); K Räikkönen, Ferrari 20-21 (2)
WINNER'S LAPS 1 P4, 2-11 P3, 12 P2, 13-15 P1, 16-19 P3, 20-21 P2, 22-37 P1, 38-40 P2, 41-57 P1
FASTEST LAP Trulli, Toyota, 1m 34.556s (lap 10), 206.049kph, 128.033mph
CHAMPIONSHIP Button 31, Barrichello 19, Vettel 18, Trulli 14.5, Glock 12

SPANISH GP Cataluña
10 May 2009   Race 808

Jenson Button
Brawn-Mercedes BGP 001 189.336kph, 117.648mph

Brawn versus Red Bull in qualifying, Massa's P4 spoiling the symmetry. From P3 Barrichello got the better of pole-man Button at the start and after a SC looked set for victory, both on three-stops. So when he ended up P2 behind his victorious teammate – Button switched to a two-stop to avoid traffic – he was frustrated and angry, suspecting team prejudice. What he overlooked was Jenson's superb long second stint performance against his own second and third stints, when Rubens made poor use of his twin advantages of lighter fuel-load then fresher tyres. Near the end Barrichello's P2 even came under pressure from Webber. Vettel, trapped behind Massa for most of the race, was P4. On lap 64 winner Button lapped champion Hamilton.

POLE POSITION Button, Brawn-Mercedes, 1m 20.527s (0.133s), 208.104kph, 129.309mph
LAPS 66 x 4.655 km, 2.892 miles
DISTANCE 307.104 km, 190.826 miles
STARTERS/FINISHERS 20/14
WEATHER Cloudy with sunny intervals, warm, dry
LAP LEADERS Barrichello 1-19, 21-31, 49-50 (32); Massa 20 (1); Button 32-48, 51-66 (33); SC 1-5 (5)
WINNER'S LAPS 1-18 P2, 19 P6, 20 P5, 21-25 P3, 26-31 P2, 32-48 P1, 49-50 P2, 51-66 P1
FASTEST LAP Barrichello, Brawn-Mercedes, 1m 22.762s (lap 28), 202.484kph, 125.818mph
CHAMPIONSHIP Button 41, Barrichello 27, Vettel 23, Webber 15.5, Trulli 14.5

Pos	Driver	Car	Time/gap	Grid	Stops	Tyres
1	J Button	Brawn-Mercedes	1h 37m 19.202s	1	2	B
2	R Barrichello	Brawn-Mercedes	–13.056s	3	3	B
3	M Webber	Red Bull-Renault	–13.924s	5	2	B
4	S Vettel	Red Bull-Renault	–18.941s	2	2	B
5	F Alonso	Renault	–43.166s	8	2	B
6	F Massa	Ferrari	–50.827s	4	2	B

MONACO GP Monte Carlo
24 May 2009   Race 809

Jenson Button
Brawn-Mercedes BGP 001 155.166kph, 96.416mph

With Red Bull less competitive at Monaco, Ferrari took a shot at dethroning Brawn but couldn't prevent another 1-2. It was settled in qualifying, Räikkönen edging out Barrichello but not Button for pole, and then at the start Rubens getting the jump at Ste Devote, the tyre-friendly Brawns on the softer options unlike the other front runners. From lap 10 Jenson's lead ballooned by 15s as Barrichello suffered tyre graining, super-smooth Button immune. Misfortune aside the race was Button's, his only mistake forgetting to park by the Royal box, jogging back from the pits to collect his trophy. The Ferraris and Webber finished as one, Felipe sure P2 was his given the breaks, while Rosberg's P6 Williams left a feeling of potential unfulfilled.

POLE POSITION Button, Brawn-Mercedes, 1m 14.902s (0.025s), 160.529kph, 99.748mph
LAPS 78 x 3.340 km, 2.075 miles
DISTANCE 260.520 km, 161.880 miles
STARTERS/FINISHERS 20/15
WEATHER Sunny, hot, dry
LAP LEADERS Button 1-51, 53-78 (77); Räikkönen 52 (1)
WINNER'S LAPS 1-51 P1, 52 P2, 53-78 P1
FASTEST LAP Massa, Ferrari, 1m 15.154s (lap 50), 159.991kph, 99.414mph
CHAMPIONSHIP Button 51, Barrichello 35, Vettel 23, Webber 19.5, Trulli 14.5

Pos	Driver	Car	Time/gap	Grid	Stops	Tyres
1	J Button	Brawn-Mercedes	1h 40m 44.282s	1	2	B
2	R Barrichello	Brawn-Mercedes	–7.666s	3	2	B
3	K Räikkönen	Ferrari	–13.442s	2	2	B
4	F Massa	Ferrari	–15.110s	5	2	B
5	M Webber	Red Bull-Renault	–15.730s	8	2	B
6	N Rosberg	Williams-Toyota	–33.586s	6	2	B

TURKISH GP Istanbul
7 June 2009   Race 810

Jenson Button
Brawn-Mercedes BGP 001 214.823kph, 133.485mph

Turkey was Button's sixth victory from seven races, but also proved that the extensive regulation changes had not fundamentally improved the F1 overtaking issue. Following Monaco it was back to Brawn vs RBR, Vettel knowing that despite his lighter-fuelled pole only a perfect race could beat Button. But on the first lap a wind direction change unsettled the car and a tank-slapper at turn ten let the astonished Button by. At his first of two stops the Brawn rejoined 5s ahead, the three-stopping Vettel quickly reeling him in but simply unable to overtake, aggravated by a shorter seventh gear. Indeed this time-loss allowed the two-stopping Webber ahead of the exasperated German, his points total now less than half the soaring Button's near perfect score.

POLE POSITION Vettel, Red Bull-Renault, 1m 28.316s (0.105s), 217.591kph, 135.204mph
LAPS 58 x 5.338 km, 3.317 miles
DISTANCE 309.396 km, 192.250 miles
STARTERS/FINISHERS 20/18
WEATHER Sunny, hot, dry
LAP LEADERS Button 1-17, 19-58 (57); Webber 18 (1)
WINNER'S LAPS 1-17 P1, 18 P3, 19-58 P1
FASTEST LAP Button, Brawn-Mercedes, 1m 27.579s (lap 40), 219.422kph, 136.343mph
CHAMPIONSHIP Button 61, Barrichello 35, Vettel 29, Webber 27.5, Trulli 19.5

Pos	Driver	Car	Time/gap	Grid	Stops	Tyres
1	J Button	Brawn-Mercedes	1h 26m 24.848s	2	2	B
2	M Webber	Red Bull-Renault	–6.714s	4	2	B
3	S Vettel	Red Bull-Renault	–7.461s	1	3	B
4	J Trulli	Toyota	–27.843s	5	2	B
5	N Rosberg	Williams-Toyota	–31.539s	9	2	B
6	F Massa	Ferrari	–39.996s	7	2	B

Round 8/17	**BRITISH GP** Silverstone **21 June 2009** **Race 811**	**Sebastian Vettel** Red Bull-Renault RB5 223.385kph, 138.805mph

A large crowd assembled for the final GP at Silverstone and to watch JB make it seven wins from eight. They witnessed neither. Vettel in a revamped RB5 was too quick for everyone, including teammate Webber and the tyre-temperature-troubled Brawns. Seb's opening stint was reminiscent of Jim Clark in 1965, within ten laps the rampant leader rounding Copse as the rest hove into sight at Woodcote. On lap 19 the chasing Barrichello made his first stop, the gap doubling to 40s by the end, Rubens also relegated from P2 by the sister RB5. What of the championship leader? In cool weather Button's smooth style along with the tyre-friendly Brawn chassis, usually assets, became a liability, qualifying and finishing P6, the crowd deflated.

POLE POSITION Vettel, Red Bull-Renault, 1m 19.509s (0.347s), 232.773kph, 144.638mph
LAPS 60 x 5.141 km, 3.195 miles
DISTANCE 308.355 km, 191.603 miles
STARTERS/FINISHERS 20/18
WEATHER Overcast, cool, dry
LAP LEADERS Vettel 1-44, 48-60 (57); Webber 45-47 (3)
WINNER'S LAPS 1-44 P1, 45-47 P2, 48-60 P1
FASTEST LAP Vettel, Red Bull-Renault, 1m 20.735s (lap 16), 229.238kph, 142.442mph
CHAMPIONSHIP Button 64, Barrichello 41, Vettel 39, Webber 35.5, Trulli 21.5

Pos	Driver	Car	Time/gap	Grid	Stops	Tyres
1	S Vettel	Red Bull-Renault	1h 22m 49.328s	1	2	B
2	M Webber	Red Bull-Renault	−15.188s	3	2	B
3	R Barrichello	Brawn-Mercedes	−41.175s	2	2	B
4	F Massa	Ferrari	−45.043s	11	2	B
5	N Rosberg	Williams-Toyota	−45.915s	7	2	B
6	J Button	Brawn-Mercedes	−46.285s	6	2	B

Round 9/17	**GERMAN GP** Nürburgring **12 July 2009** **Race 812**	**Mark Webber** Red Bull-Renault RB5 191.598kph, 119.053mph

Webber's first pole and first victory, although at turn one he appeared to have blown it, penalised for a barge into Barrichello. He also inadvertently punctured Hamilton's improving, KERS-assisted McLaren with his front wing. But a blend of fast, determined driving and lucky breaks produced a remarkable victory. Besides the Lewis incident, his first break was that 11 laps passed before the stewards acted, and with Kovalainen's McLaren holding up the chasing field he was still ahead after serving the drive-through. Then Rubens got badly trapped behind Massa, eventually finishing P6 behind Button and extremely upset with his team. But finally, having fallen to P8 at his own first pit stop, the seas parted as those ahead pitted, Mark resuming P1 on lap 32.

POLE POSITION Webber, Red Bull-Renault, 1m 32.230s (0.127s), 200.941kph, 124.858mph
LAPS 60 x 5.148 km, 3.199 miles
DISTANCE 308.863 km, 191.919 miles
STARTERS/FINISHERS 20/18
WEATHER Cloudy with sunny intervals, warm, dry
LAP LEADERS Barrichello 1-14, 25-31 (21); Webber 15-19, 32-43, 45-60 (33); Massa 20-24 (5); Vettel 44 (1)
WINNER'S LAPS 1-14 P2, 15-19 P1, 20-21 P8, 22 P7, 23-24 P6, 25 P5, 26-27 P4, 28 P3, 29-31 P1, 32-43 P1, 44 P2, 45-60 P1
FASTEST LAP F Alonso, Renault, 1m 33.365s (lap 49), 198.498kph, 123.341mph
CHAMPIONSHIP Button 68, Vettel 47, Webber 45.5, Barrichello 44, Massa 22

Pos	Driver	Car	Time/gap	Grid	Stops	Tyres
1	M Webber	Red Bull-Renault	1h 36m 43.310s	1	3	B
2	S Vettel	Red Bull-Renault	−9.252s	4	2	B
3	F Massa	Ferrari	−15.906s	8	2	B
4	N Rosberg	Williams-Toyota	−21.099s	15	2	B
5	J Button	Brawn-Mercedes	−23.609s	3	3	B
6	R Barrichello	Brawn-Mercedes	−24.468s	2	3	B

Round 10/17	**HUNGARIAN GP** Hungaroring **26 July 2009** **Race 813**	**Lewis Hamilton** McLaren-Mercedes MP4-24 186.973kph, 116.180mph

In Q2 Felipe Massa survived a freak accident, struck by an errant 700g suspension spring at 162mph. Unconscious, skull fractured, he ploughed virtually head-on into the tyre barriers. In Q3 the timing screens blanked, Alonso declared pole-sitter. He led the opening laps, pitted on 12 but was out after 13 in a three-wheeled Renault. The Red Bulls qualified behind Alonso, Vettel suffering terminal suspension damage in a turn one KERS/non-KERS mêleé, then Webber overtaken by a resurgent Hamilton on lap 5 with a brilliant KERS-assisted pass, after which the winner was never in doubt. Button qualified P8, finished P7, but with Seb's no-score Webber became his closest points rival. Rubens finished P10, Q2 ruined by an errant spring.

POLE POSITION F Alonso, Renault, 1m 21.569s (0.038s), 193.352kph, 120.143mph
LAPS 70 x 4.381 km, 2.722 miles
DISTANCE 306.630 km, 190.531 miles
STARTERS/FINISHERS 19/16
WEATHER Cloudy with sunny intervals, warm, dry
LAP LEADERS Alonso 1-11 (11); Hamilton 12-20, 22-70 (58); Kovalainen 21 (1)
WINNER'S LAPS 1-4 P3, 5-11 P2, 12-20 P1, 21 P3, 22-70 P1
FASTEST LAP Webber, Red Bull-Renault, 1m 21.931s (lap 65), 192.498kph, 119.613mph
CHAMPIONSHIP Button 70, Webber 51.5, Vettel 47, Barrichello 44, Rosberg 25.5

Pos	Driver	Car	Time/gap	Grid	Stops	Tyres
1	L Hamilton	McLaren-Mercedes	1h 38m 23.876s	4	2	B
2	K Räikkönen	Ferrari	−11.529s	7	2	B
3	M Webber	Red Bull-Renault	−16.886s	3	2	B
4	N Rosberg	Williams-Toyota	−26.967s	5	2	B
5	H Kovalainen	McLaren-Mercedes	−34.392s	6	2	B
6	T Glock	Toyota	−35.237s	13	2	B

McLaren-Mercedes MP4-24

Round 11/17	**EUROPEAN GP** Valencia					
	23 August 2009					Race 814

Rubens Barrichello
Brawn-Mercedes BGP 001 193.344kph, 120.138mph

The Brawns basked in the Spanish sun, Barrichello's P3 a fuel-adjusted pole. But Valencia also suited the revitalised McLarens, unlikely to be beaten from their front-row slots with KERS. Kovalainen's job would be to hold Rubens up and let Hamilton build a winning lead. The Brawn strategy was to hang on to the lighter-fuelled McLarens, go longer and vault past at the stops, and with Barrichello driving with relentless panache that is exactly how it played out. McLaren made it easier by screwing up their second stops, but the faster car beat them, not their blunder. Button's below-par performance brought two points on a day the Red Bulls failed to score. Badoer replaced Massa, qualifying last, but Räikkönen brought Ferrari another podium.

POLE POSITION Hamilton, McLaren-Mercedes, 1m 39.498s (0.034s), 196.068kph, 121.831mph
LAPS 57 x 5.419 km, 3.367 miles
DISTANCE 308.883 km, 191.931 miles
STARTERS/FINISHERS 20/18
WEATHER Sunny, hot, dry
LAP LEADERS Hamilton 1-15, 21-36 (31); Kovalainen 16 (1); Barrichello 17-20, 37-57 (25)
WINNER'S LAPS 1-15 P3, 16 P2, 17-20 P1, 21-36 P2, 37-57 P1
FASTEST LAP T Glock, Toyota, 1m 38.683s (lap 55), 197.687kph, 122.837mph
CHAMPIONSHIP Button 72, Barrichello 54, Webber 51.5, Vettel 47, Rosberg 29.5

Pos	Driver	Car	Time/gap	Grid	Stops	Tyres
1	R Barrichello	Brawn-Mercedes	1h 35m 51.289s	3	2	B
2	L Hamilton	McLaren-Mercedes	−2.358s	1	2	B
3	K Räikkönen	Ferrari	−15.994s	6	2	B
4	H Kovalainen	McLaren-Mercedes	−20.032s	2	2	B
5	N Rosberg	Williams-Toyota	−20.870s	7	2	B
6	F Alonso	Renault	−27.744s	8	2	B

Ferrari F60

BELGIAN GP Spa Francorchamps

30 August 2009 — **Race 815**

Kimi Räikkönen

Ferrari F60 220.430kph, 136.969mph

A curious grid for a dry qualifying, Fisichella's Force India on pole, Trulli's Toyota, fuel-adjusted pole, alongside. Then in a fraught opening lap ending in a SC, four cars were sidelined, Button and Hamilton out at Les Combes, Trulli in for a new front wing. Without the SC, leader Fisichella might have broken away to win, instead he was vulnerable at the restart to Räikkönen's KERS-equipped Ferrari, which duly zapped past out of Radillon to set up a two-car duel for the rest of the race, Fisi chasing 1s in arrears. Starting P6, Räikkönen got himself into contention through dubious use of the large asphalt run-off at La Source on lap 1, but somehow evaded the wrath of the stewards. In the championship stakes, Button's rivals failed to capitalise on his dnf.

Pos	Driver	Car	Time/gap	Grid	Stops	Tyres
1	K Räikkönen	Ferrari	1h 23m 50.995s	6	2	B
2	G Fisichella	Force India-Mercedes	−0.939s	1	2	B
3	S Vettel	Red Bull-Renault	−3.875s	8	2	B
4	R Kubica	BMW	−9.966s	5	2	B
5	N Heidfeld	BMW	−11.276s	3	2	B
6	H Kovalainen	McLaren-Mercedes	−32.763s	15	1	B

POLE POSITION Fisichella, Force India-Mercedes, 1m 46.308s (0.087s), 237.182kph, 147.378mph
LAPS 44 x 7.004 km, 4.532 miles
DISTANCE 308.053 km, 191.415 miles
STARTERS/FINISHERS 20/14
WEATHER Cloudy with sunny intervals, cool, dry
LAP LEADERS Fisichella 1-4 (4); Räikkönen 5-14, 18-31, 36-44 (33); Vettel 15-16, 32-35 (6); N Rosberg, Williams-Toyota 17 (1); SC 1-4 (4)
WINNER'S LAPS 1-4 P2, 5-14 P1, 15-16 P3, 17 P2, 18-31 P1, 32 P3, 33-35 P2, 36-44 P1
FASTEST LAP Vettel, Red Bull-Renault, 1m 47.263s (lap 38), 235.070kph, 146.066mph
CHAMPIONSHIP Button 72, Barrichello 56, Vettel 53, Webber 51.5, Räikkönen 34

ITALIAN GP Monza

13 September 2009 — **Race 816**

Rubens Barrichello

Brawn-Mercedes BGP 001 241.000kph, 149.750mph

Force India quick again, Sutil P2 beside pole-man Hamilton. To beat the one-stopping Brawns, Lewis went for the notionally slower two-stop, relying on light fuel, track position, low downforce and clean air. His first stint was scintillating, pulling out 17s on Barrichello, on target to win. But the middle stint on harder primes went less well, rejoining behind the Brawns. From there he could no longer win, but on he charged intent on Button's P2, knowing KERS could squirt him past. The final lap, 1s behind and closing fast, Lewis crashed spectacularly at the first Lesmo, asking just too much of a car in super-skinny trim. So for Brawn a fourth points maximum while the Red Bulls scored one between them, qualifying mid-grid, short of Renault horses.

Pos	Driver	Car	Time/gap	Grid	Stops	Tyres
1	R Barrichello	Brawn-Mercedes	1h 16m 21.706s	5	1	B
2	J Button	Brawn-Mercedes	−2.866s	6	1	B
3	K Räikkönen	Ferrari	−30.664s	3	2	B
4	A Sutil	Force India-Mercedes	−31.131s	2	2	B
5	F Alonso	Renault	−59.182s	8	1	B
6	H Kovalainen	McLaren-Mercedes	−1m 0.693s	4	1	B

POLE POSITION L Hamilton, McLaren-Mercedes, 1m 24.066s (0.195s), 248.076kph, 154.147mph
LAPS 53 x 5.793 km, 3.600 miles
DISTANCE 306.719 km, 190.586 miles
STARTERS/FINISHERS 20/16
WEATHER Sunny, hot, dry
LAP LEADERS Hamilton 1-15, 30-34 (20); Räikkönen 16-19, 35-37 (7); Barrichello 20-29, 38-53 (26)
WINNER'S LAPS 1-15 P4, 16-17 P3, 18-19 P2, 20-29 P1, 30-34 P4, 35-37 P3, 38-53 P1
FASTEST LAP Sutil, Force India-Mercedes, 1m 24.739 (lap 36), 246.106kph, 152.923mph
CHAMPIONSHIP Button 80, Barrichello 66, Vettel 54, Webber 51.5, Räikkönen 40

SINGAPORE GP Marina Bay

27 September 2009 — **Race 817**

Lewis Hamilton

McLaren-Mercedes MP4-24 159.845kph, 98.323mph

Unharmed at Monza, Hamilton bounced back with his third pole in four races, this time fuelled heavier than most and thus able to control the race. Initially only Rosberg and Vettel could keep the flying McLaren in sight but their races were compromised by drive-throughs for pit infringements. A lap 20 SC before Rosberg had even served his penalty completely destroyed this season's best showing by Williams, while with Vettel's punishment and Webber ordered to return two places gained improperly, it was Glock and Alonso from the third row who shared the podium with Lewis. Unusually ragged, championship leader Button failed to make Q3 but raced superbly to P5, behind Vettel and ahead of Barrichello, shuffling closer to that elusive title.

Pos	Driver	Car	Time/gap	Grid	Stops	Tyres
1	L Hamilton	McLaren-Mercedes	1h 56m 6.337s	1	2	B
2	T Glock	Toyota	−9.634s	6	2	B
3	F Alonso	Renault	−16.624s	5	2	B
4	S Vettel	Red Bull-Renault	−20.261s	2	3	B
5	J Button	Brawn-Mercedes	−30.015s	11	2	B
6	R Barrichello	Brawn-Mercedes	−31.858s	9	2	B

POLE POSITION Hamilton, McLaren-Mercedes, 1m 47.891s (0.313s), 169.270kph, 105.179mph
LAPS 61 x 5.073 km, 3.152 miles
DISTANCE 309.316 km, 192.200 miles
STARTERS/FINISHERS 20/14
WEATHER Dark, hot, dry
LAP LEADERS Hamilton 1-46, 51-61 (57); Alonso 47-50 (4); SC 22-25 (4)
WINNER'S LAPS 1-46 P1, 47-50 P2, 51-61 P1
FASTEST LAP Alonso, Renault, 1m 48.240s (lap 53), 168.725kph, 104.841mph
CHAMPIONSHIP Button 84, Barrichello 69, Vettel 59, Webber 51.5, Räikkönen 40

JAPANESE GP Suzuka

4 October 2009 **Race 818**

Sebastian Vettel
Red Bull-Renault RB5 208.900kph, 129.804mph

Suzuka's fast sweeps suited Red Bull, Vettel making the most of it with pole, Webber the least of it, making a pit-lane start after crashing in FP3. Vettel saw off Hamilton's KERS-boosted challenge at the first corner and never looked back, his fourth victory of the season keeping his slim title hopes alive. Since his last win in Turkey four months ago, points leader Button had added just 24 in eight races, but extraordinarily had only lost 12 to his nearest rival. No one was offering a consistent challenge and here again, while Button was a drab P8, Barrichello finished a dismal P7. Both Brawns had yellow-flag grid penalties, but even so were way off the pace in qualifying and the race, only a late SC closing up the field. Trulli's Toyota beat Lewis for P2.

POLE POSITION Vettel, Red Bull-Renault, 1m 32.160s (0.060s), 226.835kph, 140.948mph
LAPS 53 x 5.807 km, 3.608 miles
DISTANCE 307.573 km, 191.117 miles
STARTERS/FINISHERS 19/17
WEATHER Sunny, warm, dry
LAP LEADERS Vettel 1-53 (53); SC 46-49 (4)
WINNER'S LAPS 1-53 P1
FASTEST LAP M Webber, Red Bull-Renault, 1m 32.569s (lap 50), 225.327kph, 140.150mph
CHAMPIONSHIP Button 85, Barrichello 71, Vettel 69, Webber 51.5, Räikkönen 45

Pos	Driver	Car	Time/gap	Grid	Stops	Tyres
1	S Vettel	Red Bull-Renault	1h 28m 20.443s	1	2	B
2	J Trulli	Toyota	−4.877s	2	2	B
3	L Hamilton	McLaren-Mercedes	−6.472s	3	2	B
4	K Räikkönen	Ferrari	−7.940s	5	2	B
5	N Rosberg	Williams-Toyota	−8.793s	7	2	B
6	N Heidfeld	BMW	−9.509s	4	2	B

BRAZILIAN GP Interlagos

18 October 2009 **Race 819**

Mark Webber
Red Bull-Renault RB5 198.675kph, 123.451mph

Rain mixed up the grid, Button P14, Vettel P15, Hamilton P17, Q3 even in doubt. But finally it gave a home pole to Rubens, the heavier-fuelled Webber alongside. Following a long SC to clean up the Sutil/Trulli/Alonso mess, the latter an innocent party, Rubens led Mark by 2–3s before pitting on lap 21. But due to the SC he rejoined mired in traffic, hope of victory gone. Webber stopped five laps later, never headed again. There were some great drives that day, Kubica, Hamilton, Vettel, but the race will forever be remembered as Button's championship race, the tortured soul from Saturday gone, the early-season Jenson back, reaching P2 within 25 laps with incisive passes, to finally finish P5 and as champion. Kobayashi debuted impressively.

POLE POSITION R Barrichello, Brawn-Mercedes, 1m 19.576s (0.092s), 194.938kph, 121.128mph
LAPS 71 x 4.309 km, 2.677 miles
DISTANCE 305.909 km, 190.083 miles
STARTERS/FINISHERS 20/14
WEATHER Cloudy with sunny intervals, hot, dry
LAP LEADERS Barrichello 1-20 (20); Webber 21-71 (51); SC 1-5 (5)
WINNER'S LAPS 1-20 P2, 21-71 P1
FASTEST LAP Webber, Red Bull-Renault, 1m 13.733s (lap 25), 210.386kph, 130.728mph
CHAMPIONSHIP Button 89, Vettel 74, Barrichello 72, Webber 61.5, Hamilton 49

Pos	Driver	Car	Time/gap	Grid	Stops	Tyres
1	M Webber	Red Bull-Renault	1h 32m 23.081s	2	2	B
2	R Kubica	BMW	−7.626s	8	2	B
3	L Hamilton	McLaren-Mercedes	−18.944s	17	2	B
4	S Vettel	Red Bull-Renault	−19.652s	15	2	B
5	J Button	Brawn-Mercedes	−29.005s	14	2	B
6	K Räikkönen	Ferrari	−33.340s	5	2	B

ABU DHABI GP Yas Marina

1 November 2009 **Race 820**

Sebastian Vettel
Red Bull-Renault RB5 194.789kph, 121.036mph

The first day-night race, a superb new facility, the race processional. With a stunning pole, Hamilton out-qualified both Red Bulls followed by the Brawn pair. But instead of running away with the race as expected, Hamilton was in trouble from the start with brake trouble, needing to work KERS hard to keep Vettel at bay during a troubled first stint. Shortly after his lap 17 stop the team had no option but to retire the McLaren, too dangerous to continue with a right-rear Brembo pad wearing at an alarming rate. With Lewis out Seb's victory became routine. The new world champion finished on a high with a podium, passing Barrichello on lap 1 and coming close to beating Webber for P2. From P12 Kobayashi drove a superb race to P6 for Toyota.

POLE POSITION L Hamilton, McLaren-Mercedes, 1m 40.948s (0.667), 198.066kph, 123.072mph
LAPS 55 x 5.554 km, 3.451 miles
DISTANCE 305.355 km, 189.739 miles
STARTERS/FINISHERS 20/18
WEATHER Sunny, hot, dry, dusk to dark
LAP LEADERS Hamilton 1-16 (16); Vettel 17-55 (39)
WINNER'S LAPS 1-16 P2, 17-55 P1
FASTEST LAP Vettel, Red Bull-Renault, 1m 40.279s (lap 54), 199.387kph, 123.894mph
CHAMPIONSHIP Button 95, Vettel 84, Barrichello 77, Webber 69.5, Hamilton 49

Pos	Driver	Car	Time/gap	Grid	Stops	Tyres
1	S Vettel	Red Bull-Renault	1h 34m 3.414s	2	2	B
2	M Webber	Red Bull-Renault	−17.857s	3	2	B
3	J Button	Brawn-Mercedes	−18.467s	5	2	B
4	R Barrichello	Brawn-Mercedes	−22.735s	4	2	B
5	N Heidfeld	BMW	−26.253s	8	2	B
6	K Kobayashi	Toyota	−28.343s	12	1	B

- The 2009 F1 regulations were as close to a clean sheet as had been seen in decades, featuring wholesale aero changes, the return of slick tyres, and the arrival of KERS.
- In order to clean-up aero as well as car aesthetics, the FIA created an exclusion zone for add-ons. This eliminated the majority of appendages that had increasingly disfigured F1 cars of late.
- The front wing was wider and lower and driver-adjustable by 3° three times per lap, the rear wing higher and narrower. These changes reduced downforce by 15% and therefore turbulence, the collective purpose being to clean-up the aero 'wake' affecting a following car and so assist overtaking.
- Another significant aero change was to the diffuser, longer, wider more rearward-mounted but giving a small increase in underbody downforce.
- For the first time since 1998 non-grooved or 'slick' tyres were back, although tyre sizes were unchanged, creating major challenges in balancing front and rear grip.
- Two tyre types would be allocated for each GP and both must be used during the race, but instead of adjacent tyre compounds, such as soft and medium, there would now be two steps between each type, *eg* soft and hard, to accentuate the tyre performance component in strategy. The softer option tyre would be identified by a green stripe at the top of the tyre wall.
- 'Kinetic energy recovery system' or KERS, with eco-friendly connotations for road cars, was another device available to the driver to assist overtaking, although naturally a defending driver with KERS could negate an attacking driver's usage. During a given lap, by pressing a button the driver could release, all at once or in 'squirts', an extra 80bhp surge for up to 6.7s, the charge replenished each lap.
- KERS incorporated a motor-generator in the car's transmission which harvested kinetic energy under braking, converting the mechanical energy into electrical energy. Once the electrical energy had been harnessed it was stored in a battery, to be released as mechanical energy when required.
- In 2009 four teams utilised KERS, Ferrari and McLaren throughout the season, Renault and BMW sporadically, mainly in the early races. Through FOTA it was agreed that for cost reasons a moratorium would be placed on the use of KERS in 2010.
- Many teams chose not to install KERS, significantly Brawn and Red Bull, considering that the trade-offs in weight distribution, higher centre of gravity and reliability did not offset the improved lap time or overtaking potential.
- Engines, now restricted to 18,000rpm, were limited to eight per car per season but could be used at will during practice, qualifying and the 17 races. An engine change after Saturday FP3 forfeited a ten-place grid penalty. The use of each additional engine over eight also triggered a ten-place grid penalty. As last year, gearboxes must last at least four races without incurring a five-place grid penalty.
- No testing would be permitted outside GP weekends apart from shakedown runs; no post-season testing until the new year, and overall testing distance restricted to 15,000km per team per calendar year.
- Wind tunnels would be restricted to a maximum 60% scale and an airspeed of 50 metres per second; car starting weights would be announced after qualifying, and stewards' decisions given greater transparency.
- Since 2007 the pit lane had been closed to prevent drivers pitting at the start of a SC period. To reduce the unfairness of lower-order cars potentially benefitting from this, as in Singapore and Germany last year, each driver had a minimum time allowance to reach the pits from their specific point on the track.
- Something else new was an Abu Dhabi GP, the 28th country to host a championship race. To be the first day/night race, starting in twilight and finishing under floodlights, it would conclude the 2009 17-race championship.
- This new waterfront venue, the Yas Marina circuit, was purpose-built, with a harbour backdrop and a unique pit-lane exit tunnel beneath the track.
- Without Montréal there was no fly-away to North America, France had also gone, and after two years at Fuji, Sujuka would host the Japanese GP.
- F1 fans in Britain sorrowfully prepared for the final race at Silverstone, but generally welcomed the return of UK TV coverage to the BBC for the first time since 1996.
- Of the ten participating teams the Honda name had gone but not the team from Brackley per se, now branded Brawn GP and retaining drivers Button and Barrichello.
- Over the winter Ross Brawn and Nick Fry managed to rescue the team through a management buy-out supported by a financial dowry from Honda, $40 million owed TV rights from FOM, Mercedes customer engines encouraged by FOTA, some sponsorship from Virgin, and much sacrifice and goodwill, not least from their drivers. The other side of the survival coin, cost-cutting, painfully shrunk the company from 720 to 450 staff.
- Under Brawn, in his first year as team principal, Honda had abandoned development of the hopeless 2008 car to focus attention on 2009. The thinking was to take full advantage of heavy Honda investment in CFD and an on-site wind tunnel and apply these resources to the radical new 2009 regulations. Such a fundamental shake-up with so many changes might hit a collective sweet spot and produce a surprise.
- Which is exactly how it was, the car late to testing due to the engine switch from Honda to Mercedes, but immediately quick out of the box.
- Brawn GP won first time out in Australia, but they, Toyota and Williams were protested for the way they had interpreted the regulations for their diffuser design. The dispute pivoted on whether the surfaces of the 'step plane' and the 'reference plane' be considered as one or independent of each other. If the latter an opening above the normal diffuser could be exploited, creating a double-decker diffuser with enhanced downforce benefits.
- The Melbourne stewards ruled double-diffusers legal, but the protesting teams appealed their decision, an FIA Court of Appeal set for 14 April. This placed the results from the first two races in question and also produced a conundrum for the teams, whether to begin development of their own double-diffuser or await the FIA verdict. Ultimately the FIA sided with the Melbourne stewards; double-diffusers were permissible.
- For some teams, especially Red Bull, which, with their V-section chassis and pull-rod rear suspension had applied a more fundamental rethink to the new regulations than many other designs, incorporating a double-diffuser on the RB5 was not a simple matter.
- However, it would be wrong to conclude that Brawn's early-season success could be solely ascribed to the double-diffuser. It was an important ingredient in a melange of

factors, not least Button's outstanding early form, his subsequent inability to deal with the tyre temperature problems which plagued the BGP 001 mid-season onwards, and of course the in-season car development 'arms race' between the teams, which the emaciated Brawn team were bound to lose.

■ The highly talented Button was deserving of the 2009 title, just as Brawn GP were worthy constructors' champions.

Because of the engine switch from Honda to Mercedes, Brawn may reasonably claim to be the only constructor to have won the title in their debut season. Certainly Brawn was the first constructor to win its debut race since Scheckter's first victory for Wolf in 1977.

■ By winning six of the first seven GPs of the season, Button joined distinguished company, namely Ascari in 1952, Fangio 1954, Clark 1965, and Michael Schumacher 1994

RACE 817, Singapore GP: The 2009 season belonged to Button and Brawn but one of the greatest in-season performance turnarounds was by McLaren and reigning champion Lewis Hamilton. In his second of two race victories Lewis became the first 'legitimate' winner of the Singapore night race.

- and 2004. He was the tenth British champion and together with Hamilton the first back-to-back British champions since Hill and Stewart in 1968–69 and the first back-to-back champions of the same nationality since Piquet and Senna in 1987–88.
- Button's Sepang victory was only the fifth GP for which half-points were awarded. A further ten laps were needed to complete the 75% race distance and trigger full points, but advancing darkness decreed otherwise.
- Barrichello's Valencia victory ended the sixth longest win-drought ever, 4 years 10 months 28 days, still well short of Patrese's 6-6-28 record.
- Vettel joining Webber was the final corner piece in the Red Bull jigsaw of talent, the youngster winning four races in 2009. Webber's first win after 130 races beat Barrichello's 123 record, elevating him from top of F1's nearly men. Recovering from a serious off-season leg injury, Mark was the first Australian to win a GP since Alan Jones in 1981.
- Red Bull's young drivers programme produced the youngest-ever GP driver when Spaniard Jaime Alguersuari took the start at the Hungaroring aged 19 years 4 months 3 days, beating Mike Thackwell's long-standing record from 1980 by nearly two months.
- At McLaren Martin Whitmarsh took over from Ron Dennis and in his first race as team principal faced a crisis, a scandal known as 'lie-gate'.
- At the first round in Australia, during a late-race SC, Trulli went wide on to the grass and Hamilton passed him. The team ordered Hamilton to wave Trulli through, for which Jarno was penalised 25s for passing Hamilton under yellow.
- In the subsequent stewards' enquiry, McLaren's sporting director Dave Ryan and driver Hamilton stated that they had not waved Trulli through, he had passed under yellow, so the penalty was upheld and McLaren gained a P3 podium.
- Trulli and Toyota were unhappy with this outcome and pushed for a review, which took place at the Malaysian GP the following weekend. Radio transmissions and other evidence exposed lies that had been repeated at the Sepang enquiry, essentially revealing that under instruction Hamilton had indeed waved Trulli through.
- Trulli's P3 was reinstated, Hamilton disqualified, and Dave Ryan, the scapegoat, fired. On the Friday at Sepang Hamilton made an emotional apology to the assembled press, squarely blaming Ryan for misleading him. Devastated by the slur on his good character, there was even suggestion that the Hamiltons, father and son, would leave McLaren, even depart F1.
- McLaren were ordered to appear at an FIA world council meeting on 29 April, and with the dust from the spy scandal barely settled no mercy was expected. Suspension from three championship rounds was the penalty, but in mitigation the punishment was suspended. Whitmarsh was able to plead that a new culture now existed at McLaren, pointing to his own appointment as team principal, the sacking of Dave Ryan, and the withdrawal of Ron Dennis from frontline involvement in the F1 team.
- Whitmarsh also had to deal with a new car, the MP4-24, which performed badly in pre-season testing and the early races. Hamilton scored just nine points in the first half of the season, but from Hungary, his first of two victories and the first for a KERS car, he accumulated 40 points, outscoring everyone else including Vettel and Barrichello. It was an extraordinary turnaround, demonstrating the prodigious power of McLaren's in-season car development capability.
- McLaren-Mercedes and Force India formed a technical partnership, the Silverstone-based team replacing their Ferrari engines with a McLaren-Mercedes drivetrain, engine, gearbox and, notionally, KERS, finding some success through the arrangement with their first podium.
- By the end of the season McLaren's relationship with Mercedes underwent substantial change when Mercedes purchased Brawn GP, selling their interests in McLaren. Eventually McLaren's future status would be as a customer, no longer effectively the Mercedes factory team.
- Mercedes GP, as the Brackley team would now be known, would recapture the derring-do of the 'Silver Arrows' back in the 1930s and 1950s, and their drivers for 2010 would both be German, Nico Rosberg and Michael Schumacher.
- The prospect of Schumacher returning to F1 resulted from Ferrari considering him as replacement for Felipe Massa, out for the remainder of the season following his unfortunate qualifying accident at the Hungaroring. It never happened because testing revealed that Schumacher was unfit due to a previous motorcycle neck injury.
- Ferrari then turned to test-driver Luca Badoer, who wretchedly gained the dubious distinction of being the only driver to qualify a Ferrari last on merit. So at Monza Italian Fisichella replaced Badoer, drafted in from Force India, but qualified P14 to Räikkönen's P3, and in his five Ferrari races never reached Q3 or scored a point.
- But by now the 'Schumacher return to F1' bandwagon was rolling fast, and for Mercedes the prospect of the great German champion renewing his immensely successful relationship with Ross Brawn in a Silver Arrow was a no-brainer.
- Much speculation surrounded new champion Button's position, ie was he pushed or did he jump, but whichever, Jenson departed for McLaren, the seventh reigning champion to jump ship to another team, Alonso the last in 2007.
- Alonso meanwhile had joined Ferrari, and as the Scuderia didn't actually have a seat vacant for him until 2011 Räikkönen had to go, the 2007 champion bought-out of his contract and off to rally driving in the WRC.
- Alonso was also tainted, if not tarnished, with the 'crash-gate' affair that resurfaced during 2009. When Renault dropped Nelsinho Piquet after Hungary, he testified to the FIA that the team had instructed him to deliberately crash at the 2008 Singapore GP, an action that directly led to teammate Alonso's victory.
- The FIA investigated, the evidence heard at a WMSC meeting on 21 September, the upshot being that Renault's team principal Flavio Briatore and director of engineering Pat Symonds received, respectively, a life-time and a five-year ban from FIA-sanctioned events.
- These unsavoury proceedings cast uncertainty over Renault's F1 future, but it was Toyota and BMW that would be missing from the 2010 grids.
- Anticipating a withdrawal by manufacturers due to the worsening world recession, during 2009 the FIA had sought to expand the grid from 10 to 13 teams, inviting applications and initially granting 2010 grid slots to Campos Meta/Dallara, Manor, and US F1. Campos eventually became HRT, Manor became Virgin and Lotus replaced US F1, which could not deliver on their promise, all three teams to be powered by Cosworth.
- Peter Sauber's team also weathered the maelstrom caused by BMW's withdrawal, so 12 teams would participate in 2010.

- The architect of all this, FIA president Max Mosley, did not survive, using his agreement to step down and not contest the 2009 FIA election as his final bargaining chip in successfully steering F1 along a cost-capped path which would attract new teams.
- FOTA wanted a new Concorde Agreement that also addressed the governance of F1. Rather than the FIA president dictating the majority of regulation changes, FOTA wanted the Technical Working Group, the TWG, to have a greater say. They also wanted reform of the FIA International Court of Appeal, and independent auditors, not those of the FIA, to scrutinise adherence to the proposed $40 million per team budget cap.
- In an attempt to divide and rule, the FIA had even revealed that since 1998 Ferrari had held a veto over technical rule changes, but even this didn't split FOTA unity, neither did Williams and Force India breaking ranks by lodging an entry for 2010 with the FIA. The removal of Mosley was more important to FOTA than any of that.
- The FIA versus FOTA, or rather brinkmanship between Mosley and di Montezemolo, continued throughout 2009, the absurdity being that in substance there were major areas of agreement – it was more in style, Mosley's autocratic style and vindictiveness, from whence discord sprang.
- By Monaco there was stalemate, while at Silverstone FOTA breakaway threats grew even louder, but in the end a new Concorde Agreement for 2009–12 was struck, Mosley stepped down, and in the October FIA presidency election Jean Todt, Mosley's anointed one, beat Ari Vatanan and so replaced Mosley, who had held the office for 16 tumultuous years.
- For many reasons 2009 was an extraordinary F1 season, but would be incomplete without remembering those who departed, namely Peter Arundell, Frank Gardner, Tony Maggs, Teddy Mayer, Tony Marsh, Jean Sage and Tom Wheatcroft.
- Tom Wheatcroft's death in December came soon after the announcement that the project to see the British GP transfer to Donington from 2010 had floundered; Silverstone would, after all, continue to host the event for a further 12 years.

Championship ranking	Championship points	Driver nationality	2009 Drivers Championship		Races contested	Race victories	Podiumse excl. victories	Races led	Lights to flag victories	Laps led	Poles	Fastest laps	Triple Crowns
			Driver	Car									
1	95	GBR	Jenson Button	Brawn-Mercedes	17	6	3	7	1	280	4	2	1
2	84	GER	Sebastian Vettel	Red Bull-Renault	17	4	4	7	1	212	4	3	1
3	77	BRA	Rubens Barrichello	Brawn-Mercedes	17	2	4	6		125	1	2	
4	69.5	AUS	Mark Webber	Red Bull-Renault	17	2	6	5		90	1	3	
5	49	GBR	Lewis Hamilton	McLaren-Mercedes	17	2	3	5		182	4		
6	48	FIN	Kimi Räikkönen	Ferrari	17	1	4	4		43			
7	34.5	GER	Nico Rosberg	Williams-Toyota	17			2		16		1	
8	32.5	ITA	Jarno Trulli	Toyota	17		3	2		3	1	1	
9	26	ESP	Fernando Alonso	Renault	17		1	2		15	1	2	
10	24	GER	Timo Glock	Toyota	14		2	1		10		1	
11	22	BRA	Felipe Massa	Ferrari	9		1	2		6		1	
12	22	FIN	Heikki Kovalainen	McLaren-Mercedes	17			2		2			
13	19	GER	Nick Heidfeld	BMW	17		1						
14	17	POL	Robert Kubica	BMW	17		1						
15	8	ITA	Giancarlo Fisichella	Force India-Mercedes (12) Ferrari (5)	17		1	1		4	1		
16	6	SUI	Sébastien Buemi	Toro Rosso-Ferrari	17								
17	5	GER	Adrian Sutil	Force India-Mercedes	17							1	
18	3	JPN	Kamui Kobayashi	Toyota	2								
19	2	FRA	Sébastien Bourdais	Toro Rosso-Ferrari	9								

Championship ranking	Championship points	Team/Marque nationality	2009 Constructors Championship		Engine maker nationality	Races contested	Race victories	1-2 finishes	Podiums excl. victories	Races led	Laps led	Poles	Fastest laps
			Chassis	Engine									
1	172	GBR	Brawn BGP 001	Mercedes-Benz 2.4 V8	GER	17	8	4	7	11	405	5	4
2	153.5	AUT	Red Bull RB5	Renault 2.4 V8	FRA	17	6	4	10	9	302	5	6
3	71	GBR	McLaren MP4-24	Mercedes-Benz 2.4 V8	GER	17	2		3	5	184	4	
4	70	ITA	Ferrari F60	Ferrari 2.4 V8	ITA	17	1		5	6	49		1
5	59.5	JPN	Toyota TF109	Toyota 2.4 V8	JPN	17			5	2	13	1	2
6	36	GER	BMW F1.09	BMW 2.4 V8	GER	17			2				
7	34.5	GBR	Williams FW31	Toyota 2.4 V8	JPN	17				2	16		1
8	26	FRA	Renault R29	Renault 2.4 V8	FRA	17		1	2	15	1	2	
9	13	IND	Force India VJM02	Mercedes-Benz 2.4 V8	GER	17			1	1	4	1	1
10	8	ITA	Toro Rosso STR4	Ferrari 2.4 V8	ITA	17							

2010

Vettel shows his mettle

THE TALE OF THE TITLE

■ In a closely contested championship, five drivers battled for honours for most of the season.
■ Driver victories were spread three for Jenson, four for Lewis and Mark, and five for Fernando and Seb.
■ Vettel eventually won, displaying great fortitude as others buckled to snatch the points lead at the last race.
■ Vettel also seized the 'youngest-ever' accolade from Hamilton, five months sooner but 27 races later.
■ Red Bull won the constructors' title at only their sixth attempt, Renault's seventh as an engine supplier.
■ The RB6 was the fastest car with a record-equalling 15 poles, although this 'only' produced nine victories.
■ But for car reliability and driver error, Vettel and Red Bull might well have wrapped things up sooner.
■ Webber and Alonso will each marvel at how they came to lose, both also susceptible to costly error.
■ Points leader Webber's muddy gyration at the inaugural Korean GP finished his challenge.
■ At the final round, a grim strategic blunder by Ferrari shattered a potent late title charge by Alonso.
■ Ferrari optimised their challenge with team orders, Red Bull's less dictatorial method also proving thorny.
■ At Istanbul, race leaders Webber and Vettel infamously collided, handing McLaren a 1-2 victory.
■ Michael Schumacher made a weak comeback with the equally disappointing Mercedes GP.
■ Overshadowed by team-mate Rosberg, only deplorable track conduct showed that it was the same driver.
■ And not forgetting: F-ducts and blown diffusers; three new teams.

THE CHASE FOR THE CHAMPIONSHIP

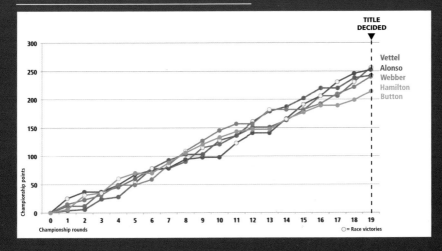

Ferrari F10

Round 1/19	**BAHRAIN GP** Sakhir **14 March 2010** **Race 821**	**Fernando Alonso** Ferrari F10 186.272kph, 115.744mph

In low-fuel qualifying trim Vettel beat the returning Felipe Massa to pole, but come Sunday would single-lap form be turned on its head by the new regulations? Disappointingly not, the turgid race boding poorly for the new 'no refuelling' era, little variation for the top eight qualifiers by the finish. Pole-sitter Vettel was on course for victory until, 16 laps from the flag, spark-plug failure caused a sudden power-loss, relegating him to P4. So Alonso, from a close but unthreatening P2, took the lead to win on his Ferrari debut from teammate Massa who he had passed at the first corner. Hamilton also overtook the hobbled Vettel, who successfully coaxed his car to the finish. Making their return debut, born-again Team Lotus brought both cars home.

POLE POSITION Vettel, Red Bull-Renault, 1m 54.101s (0.141s), 198.739kph, 123.490mph
LAPS 49 x 6.299 km, 3.910 miles
DISTANCE 308.405 km, 191.634 miles
STARTERS/FINISHERS 24/17
WEATHER Sunny, very hot, dry
LAP LEADERS Vettel 1-33 (33); Alonso 34-49 (16)
WINNER'S LAPS 1-16 P2, 17 P3, 18-33 P2, 34-49 P1
FASTEST LAP Alonso, Ferrari, 1m 58.287s (lap 45), 191.706kph, 119.121mph
CHAMPIONSHIP Alonso 25, Massa 18, Hamilton 15, Vettel 12, Rosberg 10

Pos	Driver	Car	Time/gap	Grid	Stops	Tyres
1	F Alonso	Ferrari	1h 39m 20.396s	3	1	B
2	F Massa	Ferrari	−16.099s	2	1	B
3	L Hamilton	McLaren-Mercedes	−23.182s	4	1	B
4	S Vettel	Red Bull-Renault	−38.799s	1	1	B
5	N Rosberg	Mercedes	−40.213s	5	1	B
6	M Schumacher	Mercedes	−44.163s	7	1	B

Round 2/19	**AUSTRALIAN GP** Melbourne **28 March 2010** **Race 822**	**Jenson Button** McLaren-Mercedes MP4-25 197.144kph, 122.500mph

Was Button's first McLaren win lucky, opportunistic, or simply brilliant? Lucky that only the Ferrari spun in his first-turn clash with Alonso; opportunistic that, overtaken by his teammate for P6, he immediately pitted to change his inters for slicks, and brilliant that by taking this bold gamble two laps before the rest he was vaulted from P19 to P2 in four laps. But victory still needed another roll of the dice as 5s ahead and easing away was Vettel, who had taken a superb pole in the first-ever all-Red Bull front row. It came on lap 26 when the left-front wheel broke on the RB6. Kubica brought Renault a welcome P2; Massa denied a podium to his recovering teammate Alonso, while Hamilton was lucky to finish P6 after being rear-ended by Webber.

POLE POSITION S Vettel, Red Bull-Renault, 1m 23.919s (0.116s), 227.490kph, 141.355mph
LAPS 58 x 5.303 km, 3.295 miles
DISTANCE 307.574 km, 191.118 miles
STARTERS/FINISHERS 24/14
WEATHER Cloudy, warm, damp at start, occasional drizzle
LAP LEADERS Vettel 1-8, 11-25 (23); Webber 9-10 (2); Button 26-58 (33); SC 1-4 (4)
WINNER'S LAPS 1-5 P6, 6-7 P19, 8 P12, 9 P4, 10 P3, 11-25 P2, 26-58 P1
FASTEST LAP M Webber, Red Bull-Renault, 1m 28.358s (lap 47), 216.061kph, 134.255mph
CHAMPIONSHIP Alonso 37, Massa 33, Button 31, Hamilton 23, Rosberg 20

Pos	Driver	Car	Time/gap	Grid	Stops	Tyres
1	J Button	McLaren-Mercedes	1h 33m 36.531s	4	1	B
2	R Kubica	Renault	−12.034s	9	1	B
3	F Massa	Ferrari	−14.488s	5	1	B
4	F Alonso	Ferrari	−16.304s	3	1	B
5	N Rosberg	Mercedes	−16.683s	6	1	B
6	L Hamilton	McLaren-Mercedes	−29.898s	11	2	B

McLaren-Mercedes MP4-25

Round 3/19	**MALAYSIAN GP** Sepang **4 April 2010** — **Race 823**	**Sebastian Vettel** Red Bull-Renault RB6 198.540kph, 123.367mph

In wet qualifying, McLaren and Ferrari's weather radar proved misleading, only Button making Q2. A brave choice of inters in Q3 brought Webber pole but at turn one he let his teammate get by on the inside, his only chance to regain the lead lost to an airgun problem during his tyre stop. The Ferraris and McLarens added some entertainment playing catch-up from the nether regions of the grid, but out front the Red Bulls were imperious. Behind them Rosberg had a lonely race to P3, bringing Mercedes GP their first podium. Three races, three winners from three different teams, the top six in the points table covered by just six points. But the underlying message was clear, reliability permitting, Red Bull – especially Vettel – had the legs of everyone.

POLE POSITION Webber, Red Bull-Renault, 1m 49.327s (1.346s), 182.523kph, 113.414mph
LAPS 56 x 5.543 km, 3.444 miles
DISTANCE 310.408 km, 192.879 miles
STARTERS/FINISHERS 24/17
WEATHER Cloudy, hot, dry
LAP LEADERS Vettel 1-22, 25-56 (54); Webber 23-24 (2)
WINNER'S LAPS 1-22 P1, 23-24 P2, 25-56 P1
FASTEST LAP Webber, Red Bull-Renault, 1m 37.054s (lap 53), 205.605kph, 127.757mph
CHAMPIONSHIP Massa 39, Alonso 37, Vettel 37, Button 35, Rosberg 35

Pos	Driver	Car	Time/gap	Grid	Stops	Tyres
1	S Vettel	Red Bull-Renault	1h 33m 48.412s	3	1	B
2	M Webber	Red Bull-Renault	−4.849s	1	1	B
3	N Rosberg	Mercedes	−13.504s	2	1	B
4	R Kubica	Renault	−18.589s	6	1	B
5	A Sutil	Force India-Mercedes	−21.059s	4	1	B
6	L Hamilton	McLaren-Mercedes	−23.471s	20	1	B

Round 4/19	**CHINESE GP** Shanghai **18 April 2010** — **Race 824**	**Jenson Button** McLaren-Mercedes MP4-25 171.541kph, 106.591mph

With rain threatening, most used a first lap SC to switch to inters. Rosberg, Button and Kubica did not, leading at the restart and extending it when the rest had to switch back to slicks. On lap 19, as rain finally fell, Button took the lead and next lap led the charge for inters. But a second SC slashed his massive advantage, Hamilton using this to charge past the Renaults and Rosberg and get Button in his sights 3s ahead. So, two rain aces in identical cars, same tyres, 17 laps. Lewis' tyres were first to show the strain, Button pulling out 10s at one time, both McLarens gripless by the time they crossed the line for a resounding 1-2. After Rosberg, Alonso was P4 despite a jump-start drive-through, while the front row Red Bulls never featured.

POLE POSITION Vettel, Red Bull-Renault, 1m 34.558s (0.248s), 207.529kph, 128.952mph
LAPS 56 x 5.451 km, 3.387 miles
DISTANCE 305.066 km, 189.559 miles
STARTERS/FINISHERS 24/17
WEATHER Overcast, warm, dry start then showers
LAP LEADERS Alonso 1-2 (2); Rosberg 3-18 (16); Button 19-56 (38); SC 1-3, 22-25 (7)
WINNER'S LAPS 1 P5, 2 P4, 3-18 P2, 19-56 P1
FASTEST LAP Hamilton, McLaren-Mercedes, 1m 42.061s (lap 13), 192.273kph, 119.473mph
CHAMPIONSHIP Button 60, Rosberg 50, Alonso 49, Hamilton 49, Vettel 45

Pos	Driver	Car	Time/gap	Grid	Stops	Tyres
1	J Button	McLaren-Mercedes	1h 46m 42.163s	5	2	B
2	L Hamilton	McLaren-Mercedes	−1.530s	6	4	B
3	N Rosberg	Mercedes	−9.484s	4	2	B
4	F Alonso	Ferrari	−11.869s	3	5	B
5	R Kubica	Renault	−22.213s	8	2	B
6	S Vettel	Red Bull-Renault	−33.310s	1	4	B

TOP **100** RACE

Red Bull-Renault RB6

Round 5/19	**SPANISH GP** Cataluña						**Mark Webber**
	9 May 2010				Race 825		Red Bull-Renault RB6 192.471kph, 119.596mph

Another Red Bull front row, peerless pole-sitter Webber almost a second up on Hamilton's P3 time, and this time a faultless run to victory bringing the Australian into championship consideration. Vettel's race was more arduous, bundled down to third by Hamilton when rejoining from a slow pit stop, then surrendering third to Alonso due to a severe brake problem, brilliantly nursing his car to the finish without touching his brakes in the final five laps. His efforts were rewarded when front-wheel failure caused Hamilton to crash on the penultimate lap, returning Vettel to P3. Schumacher produced a more upbeat performance, qualifying P6 to finish fourth by jumping Button in the pits and then fending off the championship points-leader for 50 laps.

POLE POSITION Webber, Red Bull-Renault, 1m 19.995s (0.106s), 209.488kph, 130.169mph
LAPS 66 x 4.655 km, 2.892 miles
DISTANCE 307.104 km, 190.826 miles
STARTERS/FINISHERS 24/19
WEATHER Cloudy with sunny intervals, warm, dry
LAP LEADERS Webber 1-66 (66)
WINNER'S LAPS 1-66 P1
FASTEST LAP L Hamilton, McLaren-Mercedes, 1m 24.357s (lap 59), 198.655kph, 123.439mph
CHAMPIONSHIP Button 70, Alonso 67, Vettel 60, Webber 53, Rosberg 50

Pos	Driver	Car	Time/gap	Grid	Stops	Tyres
1	M Webber	Red Bull-Renault	1h 35m 44.101s	1	1	B
2	F Alonso	Ferrari	−24.065s	4	1	B
3	S Vettel	Red Bull-Renault	−51.338s	2	2	B
4	M Schumacher	Mercedes	−1m 2.195s	6	1	B
5	J Button	McLaren-Mercedes	−1m 3.728s	5	1	B
6	F Massa	Ferrari	−1m 5.767s	9	1	B

Round 6/19	**MONACO GP** Monte Carlo						**Mark Webber**
	16 May 2010				Race 826		Red Bull-Renault RB6 141.814kph, 88.119mph

Webber's rare feat of two poles and wins in one week, heading a team 1-2, put the Red Bull pair joint top in the points table. Webber snatched pole by hundredths from Kubica, leading every lap in a race that saw little change in order. Overheating put Button out on lap 2, a side-pod inlet cover still in place, while Williams had an expensive weekend, Hülkenberg crashing in the tunnel on lap 1 and a drain cover putting Barrichello heavily into the wall at Massenet on lap 31. Following a major prang in FP3 Alonso started in the pit lane, made his mandatory tyre-change after one lap to finish an excellent P6, assisted by four SCs. In fact the race ended that way, Schumacher penalised for jumping Alonso at the last corner as the SC pulled into the pits.

POLE POSITION Webber, Red Bull-Renault, 1m 13.826s (0.294s), 162.869kph, 101.202mph
LAPS 78 x 3.340 km, 2.075 miles
DISTANCE 260.520 km, 161.880 miles
STARTERS/FINISHERS 24/15
WEATHER Cloudy with sunny intervals, warm, dry
LAP LEADERS Webber 1-78 (78); SC 1-6, 31-33, 44-45, 76-78 (13)
WINNER'S LAPS 1-78 P1
FASTEST LAP Vettel, Red Bull-Renault, 1m 15.192s (lap 71), 159.910kph, 99.364mph
CHAMPIONSHIP Webber 78, Vettel 78, Alonso 75, Button 70, Massa 61

Pos	Driver	Car	Time/gap	Grid	Stops	Tyres
1	M Webber	Red Bull-Renault	1h 50m 13.355s	1	1	B
2	S Vettel	Red Bull-Renault	−0.448s	3	1	B
3	R Kubica	Renault	−1.675s	2	1	B
4	F Massa	Ferrari	−2.666s	4	1	B
5	L Hamilton	McLaren-Mercedes	−4.363s	5	1	B
6	F Alonso	Ferrari	−6.341s	24	1	B

TURKISH GP Istanbul
30 May 2010   Race 827

Lewis Hamilton
McLaren-Mercedes MP4-25 209.066kph, 129.908mph

A broken roll-bar in Q3 hindered the faster Vettel, Webber taking pole, Hamilton alongside. There was no order change until on lap 16 Vettel jumped Hamilton for P2 at the stops. To guarantee fuel to finish, Webber was instructed to turn down his engine whereas Vettel, always following, wasn't so restricted and, coming under increasing pressure from Hamilton, made a sudden inside lunge for the lead on lap 40. The surprised Webber held his line, they collided and spun, Vettel out but Webber, after a nosecone replacement, regaining P3 behind the astonished McLaren pair. Drizzle in the closing stages enabled the McLarens to demonstrate how it should be done, on lap 48 Button passing around the outside at turn 12, Hamilton taking it back at turn two.

POLE POSITION Webber, Red Bull-Renault, 1m 26.295s (0.138s), 222.687kph, 138.371mph
LAPS 58 x 5.338 km, 3.317 miles
DISTANCE 309.396 km, 192.250 miles
STARTERS/FINISHERS 24/20
WEATHER Cloudy with sunny intervals, hot, dry, spitting rain
LAP LEADERS Webber 1-15, 18-39 (37); Button 16-17, 48 (3); Hamilton 40-47, 49-58 (18)
WINNER'S LAPS 1-15 P2, 16-17 P4, 18-39 P3, 40-47 P1, 48 P2, 49-58 P1
FASTEST LAP V Petrov, Renault, 1m 29.165s (lap 57), 215.519kph, 133.918mph
CHAMPIONSHIP Webber 93, Button 88, Hamilton 84, Alonso 79, Vettel 78

Pos	Driver	Car	Time/gap	Grid	Stops	Tyres
1	L Hamilton	McLaren-Mercedes	1h 28m 47.620s	2	1	B
2	J Button	McLaren-Mercedes	−2.645s	4	1	B
3	M Webber	Red Bull-Renault	−24.285s	1	2	B
4	M Schumacher	Mercedes	−31.110s	5	1	B
5	N Rosberg	Mercedes	−32.226s	6	1	B
6	R Kubica	Renault	−32.824s	7	1	B

CANADIAN GP Montréal
13 June 2010   Race 828

Lewis Hamilton
McLaren-Mercedes MP4-25 195.079kph, 121.216mph

Finally, in round eight, Red Bulls' 2010 stranglehold on pole was broken. Hamilton dominated Q1, Q2 and Q3, then in the race led home a second successive McLaren 1-2 in an action-packed race defined by high tyre degradation and, unusually for Montréal, no SCs. McLaren and Ferrari started on the super-soft options, Red Bull on the medium primes. Initial wear rates were acute, Lewis pitting on lap 7, Seb on lap 14, but in the first two-stop race of the year, dispensing of the softer rubber early looked the better strategy as the track rubbered-in. Following a grid penalty Webber found clean air by leaving his options for the final stint, but in the end McLaren number-crunching plus their F-duct produced the optimal result, Alonso a comfortable P3.

POLE POSITION Hamilton, McLaren-Mercedes, 1m 15.105s (0.268s), 209.035kph, 129.888mph
LAPS 70 x 4.361 km, 2.710 miles
DISTANCE 305.270 km, 189.686 miles
STARTERS/FINISHERS 24/19
WEATHER Sunny, warm, dry
LAP LEADERS Hamilton 1-6, 15-25, 50-70 (38); Vettel 7-13 (7); S Buemi, Toro Rosso-Ferrari 14 (1); Alonso 26-27 (2); Webber 28-49 (22)
WINNER'S LAPS 1-6 P1, 7-8 P8, 9-11 P6, 12 P5, 13 P4, 14 P3, 15-25 P1, 26 P5, 27 P3, 28-49 P2, 50-70 P1
FASTEST LAP R Kubica, Renault, 1m 16.972s (Lap 67), 203.965kph, 126.738mph
CHAMPIONSHIP Hamilton 109, Button 106, Webber 103, Alonso 94, Vettel 90

Pos	Driver	Car	Time/gap	Grid	Stops	Tyres
1	L Hamilton	McLaren-Mercedes	1h 33m 53.456s	1	2	B
2	J Button	McLaren-Mercedes	−2.254s	4	2	B
3	F Alonso	Ferrari	−9.214s	3	2	B
4	S Vettel	Red Bull-Renault	−37.817s	2	2	B
5	M Webber	Red Bull-Renault	−39.291s	7	2	B
6	N Rosberg	Mercedes	−56.084s	10	2	B

EUROPEAN GP Valencia
27 June 2010   Race 829

Sebastian Vettel
Red Bull-Renault RB6 184.420kph, 114.593mph

Red Bull regained qualifying form, but in the race, while Vettel led from pole, an horrific sequence unfolded for Webber. Barged down to P9 on lap 1, he made an early tyre stop which went badly, rejoining P19 behind Kovalainen. Urged to overtake by team radio, Webber misjudged it, struck the Lotus at 190.1mph, launching his car skywards, back-flipping first on to its nose, then roll-hoop, finally upright to thump the tyre-wall hard. Miraculously Webber stepped out, but the resultant SC reshaped the race. As it exited Hamilton braked, then just failed to race it to the SC line, the resultant drive-through ending his challenge to Vettel. The SC also ruined Ferrari's promising race, Alonso mistakenly incensed that Lewis had deliberately baulked him.

POLE POSITION Vettel, Red Bull-Renault, 1m 37.587s (0.075s), 199.907kph, 124.216mph
LAPS 57 x 5.419 km, 3.367 miles
DISTANCE 308.883 km, 191.931 miles
STARTERS/FINISHERS 24/21
WEATHER Sunny, hot, dry
LAP LEADERS Vettel 1-57 (57); SC 10-14 (5)
WINNER'S LAPS 1-57 P1
FASTEST LAP Button, McLaren-Mercedes, 1m 38.766s (lap 54), 197.521kph, 122.734mph
CHAMPIONSHIP Hamilton 127, Button 121, Vettel 115, Webber 103, Alonso 98

Pos	Driver	Car	Time/gap	Grid	Stops	Tyres
1	S Vettel	Red Bull-Renault	1h 40m 29.571s	1	1	B
2	L Hamilton	McLaren-Mercedes	−5.042s	3	1	B
3	J Button	McLaren-Mercedes	−12.658s	7	1	B
4	R Barrichello	Williams-Cosworth	−25.627s	9	1	B
5	R Kubica	Renault	−27.122s	6	1	B
6	A Sutil	Force India-Mercedes	−30.168s	13	1	B

Round 10/19 — BRITISH GP Silverstone

11 July 2010 — Race 830

Mark Webber
Red Bull-Renault RB6 217.088kph, 134.892mph

When Vettel's new front wing, worth a tenth or two, got damaged the team infuriated Webber by transferring his own new wing to Vettel's car, Vettel then shading Webber to pole by about the same margin. Without this angst maybe Webber would have been less assertive in winning the first corner from his slow-starting teammate, and then in turn Hamilton's front end-plate would not have glanced and punctured Vettel's rear tyre. Once again Red Bull had shot themselves in the foot, winning the race but adding only one more point than the McLaren pair, who still led the championship battle. 'Not bad for a number two driver,' quipped Webber as he took the flag. Despite another fruitless race, Alonso, 47 points adrift, still claimed to be a title contender.

POLE POSITION S Vettel, Red Bull-Renault, 1m 29.615s (0.143s), 236.652kph, 147.048mph
LAPS 52 x 5.891 km, 3.660 miles
DISTANCE 306.227 km, 190.281 miles
STARTERS/FINISHERS 24/20
WEATHER Sunny, warm, dry
LAP LEADERS Webber 1-52 (52); SC 28-30 (3)
WINNER'S LAPS 1-52 P1
FASTEST LAP F Alonso, Ferrari, 1m 30.874s (lap 52), 233.373kph, 145.012mph
CHAMPIONSHIP Hamilton 145, Button 133, Webber 128, Vettel 121, Alonso 98

Pos	Driver	Car	Time/gap	Grid	Stops	Tyres
1	M Webber	Red Bull-Renault	1h 24m 38.200s	2	1	B
2	L Hamilton	McLaren-Mercedes	−1.360s	4	1	B
3	N Rosberg	Mercedes	−21.307s	5	1	B
4	J Button	McLaren-Mercedes	−21.986s	14	1	B
5	R Barrichello	Williams-Cosworth	−31.456s	8	1	B
6	K Kobayashi	Sauber-Ferrari	−32.171s	12	1	B

Round 11/19 — GERMAN GP Hockenheim

25 July 2010 — Race 831

Fernando Alonso
Ferrari F10 209.788kph, 130.356mph

Another Vettel pole but narrowly from Alonso's Ferrari. But Vettel started badly, and as he and Alonso fought for the first corner Massa from P3 passed them both around the outside. During the first stint Massa on the super-softs held his own and his lead, but once on the harder primes Felipe was all locked wheels, struggling to get the fronts up to temperature. On lap 20 Alonso attempted a pass, after which he fell back a few seconds only to catch up quickly as though to prove he was faster. Around lap 40, Vettel, 5s back in P3, stepped up his pace, whereupon, 364 days after his Hungaroring near-death experience, Massa was advised, 'Fernando is faster than you,' letting Alonso ahead on lap 49. Another storm over team orders cost Ferrari a $100,000 fine.

POLE POSITION Vettel, Red Bull-Renault, 1m 13.791s (0.002s), 223.149kph, 138.658mph
LAPS 67 x 4.574 km, 2.842 miles
DISTANCE 306.458 km, 190.424 miles
STARTERS/FINISHERS 24/19
WEATHER Cloudy with sunny intervals, warm, dry
LAP LEADERS Massa 1-14, 23-48 (40); Button 15-22 (8); Alonso 49-67 (19)
WINNER'S LAPS 1-13 P2, 14 P4, 15-22 P3, 23-48 P2, 49-67 P1
FASTEST LAP Vettel, Red Bull-Renault, 1m 15.824s (lap 67), 217.166kph, 134.941mph
CHAMPIONSHIP Hamilton 157, Button 143, Webber 136, Vettel 136, Alonso 123

Pos	Driver	Car	Time/gap	Grid	Stops	Tyres
1	F Alonso	Ferrari	1h 27m 38.864s	2	1	B
2	F Massa	Ferrari	−4.196s	3	1	B
3	S Vettel	Red Bull-Renault	−5.121s	1	1	B
4	L Hamilton	McLaren-Mercedes	−26.896s	6	1	B
5	J Button	McLaren-Mercedes	−29.482s	5	1	B
6	M Webber	Red Bull-Renault	−43.606s	4	1	B

Round 12/19 — HUNGARIAN GP Hungaroring

1 August 2010 — Race 832

Mark Webber
Red Bull-Renault RB6 181.989kph, 113.083mph

Vettel pulled away rapidly from Alonso at the start, Webber third. On lap 15, with a 12s lead, the SC was deployed for track debris, Vettel leading the charge for tyres. Intent on jumping Alonso, Webber stayed out. Due to a radio fault Vettel received no warning of the SC restart, inexplicably following leader Webber way beyond the set distance, for which he received a drive-through. Webber meanwhile was disappearing fast, intent on fast lappery to make up time over Alonso for his impending tyre stop. This elated winner duly achieved, a delighted Alonso next then Vettel, distraught over the harsh penalty for one small lapse. Disputing P10, Schumacher caused universal disgust by almost putting Barrichello into the pit wall at 190mph.

POLE POSITION Vettel, Red Bull-Renault, 1m 18.773s (0.411s), 200.215kph, 124.407mph
LAPS 70 x 4.381 km, 2.722 miles
DISTANCE 306.630 km, 190.531 miles
STARTERS/FINISHERS 24/19
WEATHER Sunny, hot, dry
LAP LEADERS Vettel 1-15 (15); Webber 16-70 (55); SC 15-17 (3)
WINNER'S LAPS 1-14 P3, 15 P2, 16-70 P1
FASTEST LAP Vettel, Red Bull-Renault, 1m 22.362s (lap 70), 191.491kph, 118.987mph
CHAMPIONSHIP Webber 161, Hamilton 157, Vettel 151, Button 147, Alonso 141

Pos	Driver	Car	Time/gap	Grid	Stops	Tyres
1	M Webber	Red Bull-Renault	1h 41m 5.571s	2	1	B
2	F Alonso	Ferrari	−17.821s	3	1	B
3	S Vettel	Red Bull-Renault	−19.252s	1	1	B
4	F Massa	Ferrari	−27.474s	4	1	B
5	V Petrov	Renault	−1m 13.192s	7	1	B
6	N Hülkenberg	Williams-Cosworth	−1m 16.723s	10	1	B

Round 13/19	**BELGIAN GP** Spa Francorchamps	**Lewis Hamilton**
	29 August 2010 Race 833	McLaren-Mercedes MP4-25 207.509kph, 128.940mph

Championship leader Webber took pole from Hamilton but in the race Lewis soundly beat Mark and with *nil points* for Vettel, Button and Alonso, these two suddenly began to look like the title favourites. Alonso didn't complete lap 1, speared by Barrichello at the Bus Stop, a short, sharp shower causing many of the leaders to run wide. The Bus Stop on lap 16 was also the scene for another Vettel blunder, losing control and T-boning Button in a rash attempt to take P2 on the slick surface. Which moved Webber up to P3, having completed lap 1 P6 by triggering the anti-stall at the start. In late-race rain Hamilton survived a trip through the gravel at Rivage, and on lap 35, in a final stop for inters, Webber passed Kubica for P2 when Robert overshot his pit.

POLE POSITION Webber, Red Bull-Renault, 1m 45.778s (0.085s), 238.370kph, 148.116mph
LAPS 44 x 7.004 km, 4.532 miles
DISTANCE 308.053 km, 191.415 miles
STARTERS/FINISHERS 22/20
WEATHER Cloudy with sunny intervals, cool, intermittent showers
LAP LEADERS Hamilton 1-44 (44); SC 2-3, 38-40 (5)
WINNER'S LAPS 1-44 P1
FASTEST LAP Hamilton, McLaren-Mercedes, 1m 49.069s (lap 32), 231.178kph, 143.648mph
CHAMPIONSHIP Hamilton 182, Webber 179, Vettel 151, Button 147, Alonso 141

Pos	Driver	Car	Time/gap	Grid	Stops	Tyres
1	L Hamilton	McLaren-Mercedes	1h 29m 4.268s	2	2	B
2	M Webber	Red Bull-Renault	−1.571s	1	2	B
3	R Kubica	Renault	−3.493s	3	2	B
4	F Massa	Ferrari	−8.264s	6	2	B
5	A Sutil	Force India-Mercedes	−9.094s	8	2	B
6	N Rosberg	Mercedes	−12.359s	14	1	B

Round 14/19	**ITALIAN GP** Monza	**Fernando Alonso**
	12 September 2010 Race 834	Ferrari F10 240.849kph, 149.657mph

From his first Ferrari pole Alonso scored a Monza win for the Scuderia. Not that Button made it easy, leading for two-thirds of the race from P2 in the marginally slower McLaren. But at their single pit stop the relentless Spaniard went one lap further, his team producing a stunning 3.4s tyre change to pass Jenson, Fernando then extending his small advantage to win by 3s. On lap 1 Hamilton seriously dented his title hopes by leaving his nose inside Massa at the Roggia chicane, his suspension broken in the inevitable contact. Massa finished P3. At a circuit less suited to Red Bull they qualified P4 and P6 and there they finished, but in reverse order. Upwardly mobile was Vettel. By delaying his pit stop until the penultimate lap he beat Rosberg and Webber.

POLE POSITION Alonso, Ferrari, 1m 21.962s (0.122s), 254.444kph, 158.104mph
LAPS 53 x 5.793 km, 3.600 miles
DISTANCE 306.719 km, 190.586 miles
STARTERS/FINISHERS 24/20
WEATHER Sunny, warm, dry
LAP LEADERS Button 1-35 (35); Alonso 36, 39-53 (16); Massa 37-38 (2)
WINNER'S LAPS 1-35 P2, 36 P1, 37-38 P2, 39-53 P1
FASTEST LAP Alonso, Ferrari, 1m 24.139 (lap 52), 247.861kph, 154.014mph
CHAMPIONSHIP Webber 187, Hamilton 182, Alonso 166, Button 165, Vettel 163

Pos	Driver	Car	Time/gap	Grid	Stops	Tyres
1	F Alonso	Ferrari	1h 16m 24.572s	1	1	B
2	J Button	McLaren-Mercedes	−2.938s	2	1	B
3	F Massa	Ferrari	−4.223s	3	1	B
4	S Vettel	Red Bull-Renault	−28.196s	6	1	B
5	N Rosberg	Mercedes	−29.942s	7	1	B
6	M Webber	Red Bull-Renault	−31.276s	4	1	B

Round 15/19	**SINGAPORE GP** Marina Bay	**Fernando Alonso**
	26 September 2010 Race 835	Ferrari F10 157.422kph, 97.817mph

Five races left, five drivers from three teams still in the hunt. Q1 Alonso, Q2 Vettel, but crucially Q3 Alonso when Seb brushed a barrier. Alonso won the next crucial contest, the first corner, and the next when leader and follower pitted simultaneously on lap 29. For Vettel, pressure was the only remaining weapon, and over the final 16 he exerted it, lap after lap, to cross the line just 0.293s shy of the wily Fernando. The McLarens in P3 and P4 fell steadily away from the leading two, jumped by Webber at the halfway tyre stop following which there was a second SC. At the restart Hamilton got a run on Webber, they clashed and Lewis was out once again. Kubica made a stirring late recovery drive on fresh rubber, Kovalainen a fiery exit in the darkness.

POLE POSITION Alonso, Ferrari, 1m 45.390s (0.067s), 173.287kph, 107.675mph
LAPS 61 x 5.073 km, 3.152 miles
DISTANCE 309.316 km, 192.200 miles
STARTERS/FINISHERS 24/16
WEATHER Dark, warm, dry
LAP LEADERS Alonso 1-61 (61); SC 3-5, 32-35 (7)
WINNER'S LAPS 1-61 P1
FASTEST LAP Alonso, Ferrari, 1m 47.976s (lap 58), 169.137kph, 105.097mph
CHAMPIONSHIP Webber 202, Alonso 191, Hamilton 182, Vettel 181, Button 177

Pos	Driver	Car	Time/gap	Grid	Stops	Tyres
1	F Alonso	Ferrari	1h 57m 53.579s	1	1	B
2	S Vettel	Red Bull-Renault	−0.293s	2	1	B
3	M Webber	Red Bull-Renault	−29.141s	5	1	B
4	J Button	McLaren-Mercedes	−30.384s	4	1	B
5	N Rosberg	Mercedes	−49.394s	7	1	B
6	R Barrichello	Williams-Cosworth	−56.101s	6	1	B

JAPANESE GP Suzuka

10 October 2010   Race 836

Sebastian Vettel

Red Bull-Renault RB6 203.948kph, 126.727mph

With Saturday a washout, race-day morning qualifying was a Red Bull whitewash, as too the race, their order decided by Vettel's 0.068s advantage in Q3. The run to turn one produced four wrecked cars, while Kubica stole P2 from Webber, albeit briefly, the Renault's rear wheel parting company on the third SC lap. Choosing a hard-tyres gamble, Button led mid-race but could only finish P4, Hamilton next up. Starting P8 due to a gearbox penalty, Lewis was drastically hampered over the final 17 laps when his fresh gearbox shed gears. The fifth title contender, Alonso, finished P3 between the joyful Red Bull pair and the forlorn McLaren duo. Kobayashi, also on the Button strategy, enlivened the closing laps by scything from P12 to an exceptional P7.

POLE POSITION Vettel, Red Bull-Renault, 1m 30.785s (0.068s), 230.271kph, 143.083mph
LAPS 53 x 5.807 km, 3.608 miles
DISTANCE 307.471 km, 191.054 miles
STARTERS/FINISHERS 24/17
WEATHER Cloudy with sunny intervals, hot, dry
LAP LEADERS Vettel 1-24, 39-53 (39); Webber 25 (1); Button 26-38 (13); SC 1-6 (6)
WINNER'S LAPS 1-24 P1, 25 P3, 26-38 P2, 39-53 P1
FASTEST LAP Webber, Red Bull-Renault, 1m 33.474s (lap 53), 223.647kph, 138.968mph
CHAMPIONSHIP Webber 220, Alonso 206, Vettel 206, Hamilton 192, Button 189

Pos	Driver	Car	Time/gap	Grid	Stops	Tyres
1	S Vettel	Red Bull-Renault	1h 30m 27.323s	1	1	B
2	M Webber	Red Bull-Renault	−0.905s	2	1	B
3	F Alonso	Ferrari	−2.721s	4	1	B
4	J Button	McLaren-Mercedes	−13.522s	5	1	B
5	L Hamilton	McLaren-Mercedes	−39.595s	8	1	B
6	M Schumacher	Mercedes	−59.933s	10	1	B

KOREAN GP Yeongam

24 October 2010   Race 837

Fernando Alonso

Ferrari F10 109.997kph, 68.349mph

Would new circuit uncertainties alter the status quo? Not on the grid, a ninth RBR front-row lockout. But the race was something else. Teeming rain, a ten-minute delay; three exploratory SC laps, red flag; 49-minute delay; 13 SC laps, race started; lap 19, Webber from P2 dropping it on a greasy kerb, evading Alonso but eliminating Rosberg; race resumed after five SC laps, Vettel-gapping-Alonso-gapping-Hamilton; lap 32, three-lap SC closes up field; lap 42, 75% race-distance, full points available, but dusk falling; lap 46 Vettel's engine blows; lap 55, Alonso wins from Hamilton, his third victory from the last four races and points leader for the first time. Reigning champion Button finished P12 with brake issues, his title defence effectively over.

POLE POSITION S Vettel, Red Bull-Renault, 1m 35.585s (0.074s), 211.476kph, 131.405mph
LAPS 55 x 5.615 km, 3.489 miles (Race stopped after three laps due to rain. Restarted in finishing order for remaining 52 laps. Race time includes waiting period before restart)
DISTANCE 308.630 km, 191.774 miles
STARTERS/FINISHERS 24/15
WEATHER Overcast, cool, flooded, then wet but drying
LAP LEADERS Vettel 1-45 (45); Alonso 46-55 (10); SC 1-17, 20-23, 32-34 (24)
WINNER'S LAPS 1-18 P3, 19-32 P2, 33-34 P3, 35-45 P2, 46-55 P1
FASTEST LAP Alonso, Ferrari, 1m 50.257s (lap 42), 183.335kph, 113.919mph
CHAMPIONSHIP Alonso 231, Webber 220, Hamilton 210, Vettel 206, Button 189

Pos	Driver	Car	Time/gap	Grid	Stops	Tyres
1	F Alonso	Ferrari	2h 48m 20.810s	3	1	B
2	L Hamilton	McLaren-Mercedes	−14.999s	4	1	B
3	F Massa	Ferrari	−30.868s	6	1	B
4	M Schumacher	Mercedes	−39.688s	9	1	B
5	R Kubica	Renault	−47.734s	8	1	B
6	V Liuzzi	Force India-Mercedes	−53.571s	17	1	B

BRAZILIAN GP Interlagos

7 November 2010   Race 838

Sebastian Vettel

Red Bull-Renault RB6 196.944kph, 122.375mph

Rain-affected qualifying produced a maverick pole, Nico Hülkenberg bringing Williams their first since 2005, Cosworth's since 1999. The RB6s were by on lap 1, Alonso lap 7, Hamilton 14, the 'Hulk's' intrusion stringing out the five championship contenders by 25s. Not that it mattered, the Red Bulls untouchable, the team's fourth 1-2 a fitting way to clinch the constructors' championship. Although Webber was ahead on points going into the race, the team allowed Vettel to win, an inevitably contentious if crucial decision as things turned out. But by finishing P3 Alonso put himself in a very strong position for his third title, entering the finale shoot-out with a useful points lead. Hülkenberg's Williams finished a lapped P8.

POLE POSITION N Hülkenberg, Williams-Cosworth, 1m 14.470s (1.049s), 208.304kph, 129.434mph
LAPS 71 x 4.309 km, 2.677 miles
DISTANCE 305.909 km, 190.083 miles
STARTERS/FINISHERS 24/22
WEATHER Sunny, warm, dry
LAP LEADERS Vettel 1-24, 27-71 (69); Webber 25-26 (2); SC 51-55 (5)
WINNER'S LAPS 1-24 P1, 25-26 P2, 27-71 P1
FASTEST LAP Hamilton, McLaren-Mercedes, 1m 13.851s (lap 66), 210.049kph, 130.519mph
CHAMPIONSHIP Alonso 246, Webber 238, Vettel 231, Hamilton 222, Button 199

Pos	Driver	Car	Time/gap	Grid	Stops	Tyres
1	S Vettel	Red Bull-Renault	1h 33m 11.803s	2	1	B
2	M Webber	Red Bull-Renault	−4.243s	3	1	B
3	F Alonso	Ferrari	−6.807s	5	1	B
4	L Hamilton	McLaren-Mercedes	−14.634s	4	2	B
5	J Button	McLaren-Mercedes	−15.593s	11	2	B
6	N Rosberg	Mercedes	−35.320s	13	3	B

ABU DHABI GP Yas Marina

14 November 2010

Race 839

Sebastian Vettel

Red Bull-Renault RB6 183.923kph, 114.284mph

Vettel on pole but Alonso P3, crucially ahead of Webber, Alonso's title if it finished that way. At the start he dropped to P4, still OK even if Vettel won. Then SC, Schumacher having spun collecting Liuzzi. Significantly, Petrov pitted, switching from delicate options to durable primes, Webber misguidedly awaiting lap 11. On lap 15, still regarding Webber their primary threat, Ferrari lost the championship by pitting Alonso. He still led Webber but had forfeited track position, down in P12 behind Petrov. For 40 laps Alonso tried vainly to pass the rapid and error-free Renault with its prodigious straight-line speed, finishing a disenchanted P8. By winning the race Vettel took the points lead for the first time, celebrating his title with his two predecessors.

POLE POSITION Vettel, Red Bull-Renault, 1m 39.394s (0.031), 201.163kph, 124.996mph
LAPS 55 x 5.554 km, 3.451 miles
DISTANCE 305.355 km, 189.739 miles
STARTERS/FINISHERS 24/21
WEATHER Sunny, hot, dry, dusk to dark
LAP LEADERS Vettel.1-24, 40-55 (40); Button 25-39 (15); SC 1-5 (5)
WINNER'S LAPS 1-24 P1, 25-39 P2, 40-55 P1
FASTEST LAP Hamilton, McLaren-Mercedes, 1m 41.274s (lap 47), 197.428kph, 122.677mph
CHAMPIONSHIP Vettel 256, Alonso 252, Webber 242, Hamilton 240, Button 214

Pos	Driver	Car	Time/gap	Grid	Stops	Tyres
1	S Vettel	Red Bull-Renault	1h 39m 36.837s	1	1	B
2	L Hamilton	McLaren-Mercedes	–10.162s	2	1	B
3	J Button	McLaren-Mercedes	–11.047s	4	1	B
4	N Rosberg	Mercedes	–30.747s	9	1	B
5	R Kubica	Renault	–39.026s	11	1	B
6	V Petrov	Renault	–43.520s	10	1	B

2010 CHAMPIONSHIP FACTS AND FOLKLORE

■ Despite the withdrawal of BMW and Toyota, the 2010 grid numbered 24 cars, the largest since 1995 with the arrival of three new teams. The very late arrival in the case of the Hispania Racing Team (HRT) coming into being out of the former Campos project just weeks before the Bahrain opener.

■ But it was thanks to HRT that after 16 years the Senna name returned to the F1 grid, Ayrton's nephew Bruno one of four drivers used by the team during their first season.

■ Much was made by Virgin Racing's designer Nick Wirth of the fact that the car had been designed without the use of a wind tunnel, purely reliant on CFD. This claim and the team's credibility was further stretched when it was discovered the design incorporated a fuel tank too small to complete a GP distance.

■ Of the newcomers Team Lotus was a cut above, while Peter Sauber's eponymous team had survived abandonment by BMW, turning back to Ferrari for their engines, Williams replacing their Toyota units with Cosworth power.

■ Renault F1 continued under that name although the Enstone team had been acquired by investment firm Genii Capital, while Toro Rosso were no longer permitted to field a Red Bull clone, the team now required to design and construct their own chassis.

■ Brawn became Mercedes, the explanation for their poor showing being that the car was conceived after savage staff cuts and when management was preoccupied with saving the company and winning the championship. 2011 would be different.

■ For only the second time, the first occasion 2005, the championship would be decided over 19 rounds. Following various delays in completion, a new Hermann Tilke-designed circuit in South Korea was added to the calendar, the 29th country and the 68th venue. With their new 17-year deal, Silverstone continued to host the British GP, a new loop added to the GP 'Arena' circuit between Abby and Luffield and an impressive new pits complex under construction between Club and Abby.

■ As for the F1 regulations for 2010, for the first time since 1993 fuel stops were banned, although a minimum of one tyre stop remained mandatory.

■ Ending refuelling in the interests of lowering costs required cars to carry 200–230 litres or 150–170kg of fuel, some 60–70% more than under fuel-stopping regulations. Dry minimum car weight including driver and camera was also raised by 15kg to 620kg.

■ Especially when fuelled to the gunnels at the start and in the early race stages, this extra weight produced drastic differences in car handling and brake and tyre wear compared with the closing stages of the race.

■ This demanded a very different driver mindset by comparison with the sprint-replenish-sprint format dictated by the refuelling era. Some concern was expressed that F1 would become another form of endurance racing, victory dependant on preservation of fuel and tyres rather than outright speed.

■ With fuel equal to weight equal to performance loss, more emphasis was given to fuel-saving modes in engine mapping, and pit-stop strategy also required a rethink, cut from around 8s, when duration was controlled by the refuelling process, to about 3s, the time needed for a wheel change, wheel 'frisbees' having been banned.

■ As always, change to tyre regulations was also critical, Bridgestone in their final season required to produce front tyres narrower by 25mm and supply fewer dry-weather tyres, cut from 15 to 11 sets each GP weekend, six prime, five the softer option.

■ With the top ten drivers required to start the race on the tyre type selected for Q3, tyre strategy quickly became predictable in this first season without refuelling, most starting on the softer options necessary for Q3 competitiveness, then making a moderately early single stop to fit the more durable primes which would last the remainder of the race.

■ But at the highly eventful race in Montréal, peculiar circumstances caused both high tyre degradation and wider performance variation between prime and option tyres. Pirelli, the new F1 control tyres supplier, were requested to regard Montréal as the blueprint for their 2011 supply.

■ Another development widely welcomed was the appointment of a 'driver steward' for each race selected from a panel of ex-F1 drivers. They would assist the regular race stewards in their decision-taking process over incidents,

RACE 827, Turkish GP: As the title pressure mounted, Vettel showed great fortitude, and but for prior mishaps would have concluded matters sooner; this is the infamous collision with Webber at Istanbul.

contributing their knowledge and experience as a driver to make the fairest ruling.

■ The final major change in 2010 was to the championship points system, now extended to the top ten race finishers on the basis 25, 18, 15, 12, 10, 8, 6, 4, 2, 1, the idea being to emphasise winning rather than settling for a podium finish, and offer more teams the opportunity to score points. It was largely window dressing, in reality minimal change genuinely occurring in the weighting between points-paying positions.

■ Despite all of the above, something that did not change was that Red Bull Racing remained the team to beat, continuing into 2010 as they had ended last season with the fastest car, indubitably in qualifying, normally in race conditions given clean air.

■ Red Bull's continuing superiority, especially their conspicuous downforce advantage, caused other teams to speculate over rules adherence or interpretation, especially over ride-height and bodywork flexibility.

■ Conjecture had it that the RB6 incorporated illegal 'trick' suspension enabling the adoption of the same low front ride-height both when running light in qualifying and when heavy with fuel for the race. Or, others surmised, was this simply an inherent benefit derived from the basic attributes of the design, the super-efficiency of the front wing and upper-body surfaces making the diffuser's contribution, already compromised by pull-rod suspension, proportionally less important than on other designs? Whatever, after investigation the FIA's technical delegate Charlie Whiting was content on that front.

■ Where there was less certainty was over flexing bodywork, as from Spa and Monza respectively the FIA felt obliged to increase the deflection tests for front wings and the floor's leading edge 'tea-tray', one or the other or both of these appearing to flex advantageously under aerodynamic load.

■ Again, Red Bull subsequently had no difficulty passing FIA scrutineering, leaving sceptics to query if RBR had taken a technological leap forward in carbon fibre fabrication, able to produce rigidity under static test loads yet flexibility in racing conditions without compromising intrinsic structural strength.

■ But another factor that enabled the RB6 to be run with a raked tail-high, nose-down attitude without stalling the diffuser was the use of exhaust gas to energise the diffuser's flow. Exhaust-blown diffusers were not new, first used in 1983 by Renault but dropped because they made their car too pitch sensitive.

■ Not that other teams were not also looking to innovate. With KERS banned, or at least suspended for 2010, McLaren came up with a device that would not only enhance lap time but would prove beneficial in overtaking.

■ The blown rear wing, generically known by the McLaren moniker 'F-duct', collected airflow through an inlet duct on the chassis ahead of the driver. This was piped through the cockpit and up through the shark-fin on to the rear wing. The driver could control this airflow using his hand or knee to block/unblock a hole in the piping as it passed through the cockpit. This altered the airflow across the rear wing to induce stall, thereby reducing drag, so raising terminal speed on a straight by a useful 5–6kph.

- Although F-ducts and blown diffusers were tricky to incorporate as add-ons, most of the leading teams were sporting their own adaptations by mid-season, Ferrari enjoying the benefit of both developments.
- This is reflected in the fact that taking the British GP as the season's mid-point, Ferrari in round terms scored 60% of their points in the second half, McLaren just 40%. Although the MP4-25 benefitted from blown diffuser development in the latter part of the year, overall it was the slowest car of the leading teams, more reliant for their successes on a strong driver line-up, the first time two British world champions had been paired since Clark and Hill at Lotus in 1967.
- Red Bull scored an even 50% of their points in each half, and although fortunes between their two drivers fluctuated, the team's rate of development kept them highly competitive throughout the season, as 15 poles and leading 62% of the season's 1,129 racing laps indicated.
- Their 15 poles equalled the record number established in highly dominant seasons by McLaren, 1988 and 1989, and Williams, 1992 and 1993, another measure of the RB6's fundamental superiority, not fully exploited in race results through car and driver frailties.

- Ultimately Sebastian Vettel deserved his championship, and aged 23 years 4 months 11 days separated Lewis Hamilton from his 'youngest' mantle after only two seasons.
- The intra-team dynamic between drivers was a particularly fascinating aspect of the 2010 season, Vettel/Webber, Hamilton/Button, Schumacher/Rosberg and, not least, Alonso/Massa.
- After three Räikkönen/Massa years Ferrari craved leadership from the cockpit and Alonso brought them that and so nearly a championship. He was victorious also at their hallowed Monza, and only the fifth driver to win on their Ferrari debut: Fangio 1956, Baghetti 1961, Mansell 1989 and Räikkönen 2007.
- At the season opener in Bahrain, the 60th anniversary of the commencement of the F1 championship was celebrated, invitations sent to every former champion. Only Räikkönen and Piquet were absent, the other 18 providing the greatest-ever F1 photo-call, each of the six decades represented, Sir Jack Brabham, at almost 84, the embodiment of the 1950s.
- Peter Warr took part in the Bahrain celebrations but died in October aged 72. F1 also bade farewell in 2010 to Trevor Taylor, 74, and Tom Walkinshaw, 64.

Championship ranking	Championship points	Driver nationality	2010 Drivers Championship		Races contested	Race victories	Podiumse excl. victories	Races led	Lights to flag victories	Laps led	Poles	Fastest laps	Triple Crowns
			Driver	Car									
1	256	GER	Sebastian Vettel	Red Bull-Renault	19	5	5	10	2	382	10	3	
2	252	ESP	Fernando Alonso	Ferrari	19	5	5	7	1	126	2	5	2
3	242	AUS	Mark Webber	Red Bull-Renault	19	4	6	10	2	317	5	3	
4	240	GBR	Lewis Hamilton	McLaren-Mercedes	19	3	6	3	1	100	1	5	
5	214	GBR	Jenson Button	McLaren-Mercedes	19	2	5	7		145		1	
6	144	BRA	Felipe Massa	Ferrari	19		5	2		42			
7	142	GER	Nico Rosberg	Mercedes	19		3	1		16			
8	136	POL	Robert Kubica	Renault	19		3					1	
9	72	GER	Michael Schumacher	Mercedes	19								
10	47	BRA	Rubens Barrichello	Williams-Cosworth	19								
11	47	GER	Adrian Sutil	Force India-Mercedes	19								
12	32	JPN	Kamui Kobayashi	Sauber-Ferrari	19								
13	27	RUS	Vitaly Petrov	Renault	19							1	
14	22	GER	Nico Hülkenberg	Williams-Cosworth	19						1		
15	21	ITA	Vitantonio Liuzzi	Force India-Mercedes	19								
16	8	SUI	Sébastien Buemi	Toro Rosso-Ferrari	19			1		1			
17	6	ESP	Pedro de la Rosa	Sauber-Ferrari	13								
18	6	GER	Nick Heidfeld	Sauber-Ferrari	5								
19	5	ESP	Jaime Alguersuari	Toro Rosso-Ferrari	19								

Championship ranking	Championship points	Team/Marque nationality	2010 Constructors Championship		Engine maker nationality	Races contested	Race victories	1-2 finishes	Podiums excl. victories	Races led	Laps led	Poles	Fastest laps
			Chassis	Engine									
1	498	AUT	Red Bull RB6	Renault 2.4 V8	FRA	19	9	4	11	14	699	15	6
2	454	GBR	McLaren MP4-25	Mercedes-Benz 2.4 V8	GER	19	5	3	11	9	245	2	6
3	396	ITA	Ferrari F10	Ferrari 2.4 V8	ITA	19	5	2	10	7	168	1	5
4	214	GER	Mercedes MGP W01	Mercedes-Benz 2.4 V8	GER	19			3	1	16		
5	163	FRA	Renault R30	Renault 2.4 V8	FRA	19			3				2
6	69	GBR	Williams FW32	Cosworth 2.4 V8	GBR	19						1	
7	68	IND	Force India VJM03	Mercedes-Benz 2.4 V8	GER	19							
8	44	SUI	Sauber C29	Ferrari 2.4 V8	ITA	19							
9	13	ITA	Toro Rosso STR5	Ferrari 2.4 V8	ITA	19					1	1	

2011

Seb raises two fingers

THE TALE OF THE TITLE

- With 11 race victories, Sebastian Vettel dominated the 2011 championship in a manner seldom witnessed.
- In becoming the youngest-ever back-to-back champion he clinched his second title with four rounds to go.
- In his hands the RB7 could be unbeatable, as new records of 15 poles and 739 laps led in a season proved.
- Constructors' titleholders Red Bull-Renault won for a second time, taking 12 wins from 19 races.
- With six wins split between Button and Hamilton, McLaren battled hard but never achieved ascendancy.
- Ferrari remained a top-three team but rarely competed for outright victory, Alonso winning just once.
- Five drivers – Vettel, Webber, Button, Hamilton, Alonso – won all races and all but two of the other podiums.
- To improve 'the show' via more overtaking, Pirelli tyres plus DRS altered the dynamics of F1 racing.
- Emphasis on tyre management and strategy over raw pace led to a switch in driver fortunes at McLaren.
- Button in his bubble of contentment grew stronger; Hamilton's frustration and misery equal and opposite.
- Better overtaking potential spiced up the racing between midfield teams, producing a fascinating scrap.
- The Bahrain GP was a casualty of the Arab Spring but the Indian GP made a welcome first appearance.
- Williams endured their worst season in more than 30 years, scoring a meagre five championship points.
- After crashing out in a minor rally in Italy, Robert Kubica missed the entire season due to injury.
- And not forgetting: off-throttle hot and cold 'blowing'.

THE CHASE FOR THE CHAMPIONSHIP

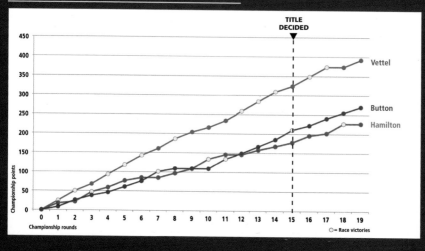

Red Bull-Renault RB7

Round 1/19	**AUSTRALIAN GP** Melbourne	**Sebastian Vettel**

27 March 2011   Race 840

Red Bull-Renault RB7 206.184kph, 128.117mph

Vettel's blistering pole lap mortified team-mate Webber at his home GP. The new champion made a storming KERS-free start, always in command of the chasing Hamilton for his 11th career victory. After McLaren defied poor winter testing form to qualify P2 and P4, a timid first corner condemned Button to 10 laps trapped behind Massa, DRS proving little help in their P5 dice. It ended in a drive-through for Button for passing off the track. Petrov starred for Renault with a strong podium drive from P6, many wondering where the missing Kubica might have finished. Webber ate four sets of the new Pirellis although two stops were the norm. Debutant Perez one-stopped his way to P8, but a technicality disqualified the Saubers, bringing rookie di Resta a point.

POLE POSITION S Vettel, Red Bull-Renault, 1m 23.529s (0.778s), 228.552kph, 142.016mph
LAPS 58 x 5.303 km, 3.295 miles
DISTANCE 307.574 km, 191.118 miles
STARTERS/FINISHERS 22/14
WEATHER Sunny, hot, dry
LAP LEADERS Vettel 1-13, 17-58 (55); Hamilton 14-16 (3)
WINNER'S LAPS 1-13 P1, 14 P3, 15 P4, 16 P2, 17-58 P1
FASTEST LAP F Massa, Ferrari, 1m 28.947s (lap 55), 214.631kph, 133.366mph
CHAMPIONSHIP Vettel 25, Hamilton 18, Petrov 15, Alonso 12, Webber 10

Pos	Driver	Car	Time/gap	Grid	Stops	Tyres
1	S Vettel	Red Bull-Renault	1h 29m 30.259s	1	2	P
2	L Hamilton	McLaren-Mercedes	−22.297s	2	2	P
3	V Petrov	Renault	−30.560s	6	2	P
4	F Alonso	Ferrari	−31.772s	5	3	P
5	M Webber	Red Bull-Renault	−38.171s	3	3	P
6	J Button	McLaren-Mercedes	−54.304s	4	2	P

Round 2/19	**MALAYSIAN GP** Sepang	**Sebastian Vettel**

10 April 2011   Race 841

Red Bull-Renault RB7 190.699kph, 118.495mph

Vettel just pipped Hamilton for pole, but it was Heidfeld's fast-starting P6 Renault which defined the race, slotting into P2 at the first corner, allowing Vettel to escape. The rain held off but Pirellis played a crucial role. Most three-stopped, this factor – plus variable race pace governed by relative prime/option performance – keeping the final result in doubt. Vettel's lead, never over 10s, enabled him to dictate to Heidfeld, then to Hamilton and finally Button who, never lower than P4, enjoyed a strong final stint on primes. Lewis lost out to Jenson in a slow second stop, later clipped by Alonso in a short, fraught dice for which both were penalised 20s. Webber almost snatched Heidfeld's podium, using four stops to recover from start-line KERS issues.

POLE POSITION Vettel, Red Bull-Renault, 1m 34.870s (0.104s), 210.338kph, 130.698mph
LAPS 56 x 5.543 km, 3.444 miles
DISTANCE 310.408 km, 192.879 miles
STARTERS/FINISHERS 24/17
WEATHER Overcast, hot, humid, dry
LAP LEADERS Vettel 1-13, 15-25, 27-56 (54); Alonso 14, 26 (2)
WINNER'S LAPS 1-13 P1, 14 P3, 15-25 P1, 26 P3, 27-56 P1
FASTEST LAP Webber, Red Bull-Renault, 1m 40.571s (lap 46), 198.415kph, 123.289mph
CHAMPIONSHIP Vettel 50, Button 26, Hamilton 22, Webber 22, Alonso 20

Pos	Driver	Car	Time/gap	Grid	Stops	Tyres
1	S Vettel	Red Bull-Renault	1h 37m 39.832s	1	3	P
2	J Button	McLaren-Mercedes	−3.261s	4	3	P
3	N Heidfeld	Renault	−25.075s	6	3	P
4	M Webber	Red Bull-Renault	−26.384s	3	4	P
5	F Massa	Ferrari	−36.958s	7	3	P
6	F Alonso	Ferrari	−57.248s	5	4	P

McLaren-Mercedes MP4-26

CHINESE GP Shanghai

17 April 2011

Race 842

Lewis Hamilton

McLaren-Mercedes MP4-26 188.758kph, 117.289mph

A single Q3 run saved Hamilton a new set of options for race day. Vettel, beaten from pole by the McLarens, switched to a two-stop as a result. At the first stops leader Button mistakenly entered the RBR pit, while an early call gave Rosberg P1 from Vettel. In his third stint Hamilton passed Button for P2, dropping to P4 at his final stop. Two assertive passes soon regained P2, 5s behind leader Vettel but on fresher rubber with 12 laps to go. On lap 52 Lewis pounced for a victory that had seemed inconceivable when the pit-crew were battling a pre-race fuel leak. Webber, starting P18, made little early progress, but on lap 40 bolted on fresh primes to gain 30s in 16 laps, finishing 2.3s shy of poleman Vettel…from P18, no SC, no rain! Massa out-qualified and out-raced Alonso.

POLE POSITION Vettel, Red Bull-Renault, 1m 33.706s (0.715s), 209.416kph, 130.125mph
LAPS 56 x 5.451 km, 3.387 miles
DISTANCE 305.066 km, 189.559 miles
STARTERS/FINISHERS 24/23
WEATHER Sunny, warm, hazy, dry
LAP LEADERS Button 1-13 (13); Hamilton 14, 52-56 (7); Alonso 15-16 (2); Rosberg 17-24, 40-51 (14); Vettel 25-30, 40-51 (18); Massa 31-33 (3)
WINNER'S LAPS 1-13 P2, 14 P1, 15 P3, 16 P7, 17-23 P5, 24-25 P4, 26 P8, 27-29 P6, 30-31 P5, 32-33 P4, 34-35 P3, 36-38 P2, 39-41 P4, 42-43 P3, 44-51 P2, 52-56 P1
FASTEST LAP Webber, Red Bull-Renault, 1m 38.993s (lap 42), 198.232kph, 123.176mph
CHAMPIONSHIP Vettel 68, Hamilton 47, Button 38, Webber 37, Alonso 26

Pos	Driver	Car	Time/gap	Grid	Stops	Tyres
1	L Hamilton	McLaren-Mercedes	1h 36m 58.226s	3	3	P
2	S Vettel	Red Bull-Renault	−5.198s	1	2	P
3	M Webber	Red Bull-Renault	−7.555s	18	3	P
4	J Button	McLaren-Mercedes	−10.000s	2	3	P
5	N Rosberg	Mercedes	−13.448s	4	3	P
6	F Massa	Ferrari	−15.840s	6	2	P

TURKISH GP Istanbul

8 May 2011

Race 843

Sebastian Vettel

Red Bull-Renault RB7 205.595kph, 127.751mph

In wet FP1 Vettel spun, car damage ending Friday running. But on Saturday a single Q3 run delivered a mighty pole. And on Sunday he made the race his own, 6s ahead after 10 laps, 9s by half distance, only the relentless Alonso exerting some late pressure. Qualifying P5, Alonso's race pace was the surprise, and Webber had to work hard to deliver Red Bull a 1–2 finish. From his promising P3 grid slot, Rosberg's Mercedes held P2 for the first four laps, but faded to a disappointing fifth. The McLarens ended up where they began, P4 and P6, Hamilton elbowed back at turn three and then suffering a slow wheel change, Button inadvisedly three-stopping. With most making four stops and plenty of DRS action, the race was entertaining, behind P1 that is.

POLE POSITION Vettel, Red Bull-Renault, 1m 25.049s (0.405s), 225.949kph, 140.398mph
LAPS 58 x 5.338 km, 3.317 miles
DISTANCE 309.396 km, 192.250 miles
STARTERS/FINISHERS 24/22
WEATHER Sunny, warm, dry
LAP LEADERS Vettel 1-11, 13-58 (57); Button 12 (1)
WINNER'S LAPS 1-11 P1, 12 P2, 13-58 P1
FASTEST LAP Webber, Red Bull-Renault, 1m 29.703s (lap 48), 214.226kph, 133.114mph
CHAMPIONSHIP Vettel 93, Hamilton 59, Webber 55, Button 46, Alonso 41

Pos	Driver	Car	Time/gap	Grid	Stops	Tyres
1	S Vettel	Red Bull-Renault	1h 30m 17.558s	1	4	P
2	M Webber	Red Bull-Renault	−8.807s	2	4	P
3	F Alonso	Ferrari	−10.075s	5	4	P
4	L Hamilton	McLaren-Mercedes	−40.232s	4	4	P
5	N Rosberg	Mercedes	−47.539s	3	4	P
6	J Button	McLaren-Mercedes	−59.431s	6	3	P

| Round 5/19 | **SPANISH GP** Cataluña | | | | | | **Sebastian Vettel** |

Round 5/19 — **SPANISH GP** Cataluña
22 May 2011 — Race 844 — **Sebastian Vettel**
Red Bull-Renault RB7 186.020kph, 115.587mph

Webber ended Vettel's five-pole run but was P3 at turn one, finishing P4. Leader at turn one was Alonso with a brilliant home-crowd inspired getaway. He kept Vettel behind for 18 laps, including the first stops, this pair plus Hamilton racing closely as they pulled away. At the second stops Seb and Lewis jumped Fernando, the Ferrari falling away to a lapped P5. Now it was a classic Vettel/Hamilton duel, nothing in it over the final 17-lap stint, Seb never making that crucial slip, his victory built also on superb pit-work and incisive post-stop passing. Another lively four-stop race proved that tyres were the overtaking factor, not DRS/KERS. Button's three-stop turned a disastrous P10 first lap into a podium, while Heidfeld came from last to P8.

POLE POSITION Webber, Red Bull-Renault, 1m 20.981s (0.200s), 206.937kph, 128.585mph
LAPS 66 x 4.655 km, 2.892 miles
DISTANCE 307.104 km, 190.826 miles
STARTERS/FINISHERS 24/21
WEATHER Sunny, hot, dry
LAP LEADERS Alonso 1-10, 12-18 (17); Hamilton 11, 19-23, 34-35, 48-49 (10); Vettel 24-33, 36-47, 50-66 (39)
WINNER'S LAPS 1-8 P2, 9 P4, 10 P6, 11 P3, 12-17 P2, 18-19 P4, 20-23 P2, 24-33 P1, 34-35 P2, 36-47 P1, 48-49 P2, 50-66 P1
FASTEST LAP Hamilton, McLaren-Mercedes, 1m 26.727s (lap 52), 193.227kph, 120.066mph
CHAMPIONSHIP Vettel 118, Hamilton 77, Webber 67, Button 61, Alonso 51

Pos	Driver	Car	Time/gap	Grid	Stops	Tyres
1	S Vettel	Red Bull-Renault	1h 39m 3.301s	2	4	P
2	L Hamilton	McLaren-Mercedes	−0.630s	3	4	P
3	J Button	McLaren-Mercedes	−35.697s	5	3	P
4	M Webber	Red Bull-Renault	−47.996s	1	4	P
5	F Alonso	Ferrari	−1 lap	4	4	P
6	M Schumacher	Mercedes	−1 lap	10	3	P

Round 6/19 — **MONACO GP** Monte Carlo
29 May 2011 — Race 845 — **Sebastian Vettel**
Red Bull-Renault RB7 120.574kph, 74.921mph

The result was shaped by two red flags and an SC, all mercifully inconsequential. An accident halted Q3, spoiling Hamilton's single run, his endeavours to come through the field resulting in two penalised collisions. Vettel led from pole but victory looked to be Button's when Red Bull fouled up their first pit-stops. On super-soft tyres Button pulled out 15s, all negated by an SC on lap 32, Vettel regaining P1 by non-stopping. Could one-stop Vettel really make his soft tyres last 62 laps and hold back two-stop Alonso and notably three-stop Button, both on much fresher rubber? But a late red flag ruined an enthralling climax. Restarted behind the SC over five laps, the final outcome was foregone, rules allowing the three victory contenders to change tyres.

POLE POSITION Vettel, Red Bull-Renault, 1m 13.556s (0.441s), 163.467kph, 101.574mph
LAPS 78 x 3.340 km, 2.075 miles
DISTANCE 260.520 km, 161.880 miles
STARTERS/FINISHERS 23/18
WEATHER Sunny, warm, dry
LAP LEADERS Vettel 1-15, 33-78 (61); Alonso 16 (1); Button 17-32 (16); SC 33-38, 69-73 (11)
WINNER'S LAPS 1-5 P1, 16 P2, 17 P3, 18-32 P2, 33-78 P1
FASTEST LAP Webber, Red Bull-Renault, 1m 16.234s (lap 78), 157.724kph, 98.005mph
CHAMPIONSHIP Vettel 143, Hamilton 85, Webber 79, Button 76, Alonso 69

Pos	Driver	Car	Time/gap	Grid	Stops	Tyres
1	S Vettel	Red Bull-Renault	2h 9m 38.373s	1	1	P
2	F Alonso	Ferrari	−1.138s	4	2	P
3	J Button	McLaren-Mercedes	−2.378s	2	3	P
4	M Webber	Red Bull-Renault	−23.101s	3	2	P
5	K Kobayashi	Sauber-Ferrari	−26.916s	12	1	P
6	L Hamilton	McLaren-Mercedes	−47.210s	9	3	P

Round 7/19 — **CANADIAN GP** Montréal
12 June 2011 — Race 846 — **Jenson Button**
McLaren-Mercedes MP4-26 74.864kph, 46.518mph

Vettel beat the Ferraris to pole, leading until the final lap when he half-spun under pressure from Button. Anticipating rain, the McLarens qualified P5 and P7, and wet it was with a two-hour delay mid-race and numerous SC outings, the start included. Once released, Hamilton clashed first with Webber and then with team-mate Button, race over for the rash Lewis. Button's damage check was the first of six pit visits, his second an SC speeding drive-through on lap 13, the fifth a lap 36 puncture after tangling with Alonso, who spun out. Now, in a 16-lap green-flag period, Button charged from 21st and last to P4, a final SC then closing up the field. Jenson, on option slicks as the racing line dried, passed Webber, Schumacher and finally Vettel for P1 when Seb slid wide.

POLE POSITION Vettel, Red Bull-Renault, 1m 13.014s (0.185s), 215.021kph, 133.608mph
LAPS 70 x 4.361 km, 2.710 miles
DISTANCE 305.270 km, 189.686 miles
STARTERS/FINISHERS 24/18
WEATHER Overcast, cool, wet then drying
LAP LEADERS Vettel 1-19, 21-69 (68); Massa 20 (1); Button 70 (1); SC 1-4, 8-12, 20-34, 37-40, 57-60 (32)
WINNER'S LAPS 1-5 P4, 6-7 P6, 8 P14, 9-12 P12, 13 P15, 14 P14, 15-16 P11, 17 P10, 18 P8, 19-20 P11, 21-24 P10, 25 P11, 26-33 P10, 34 P9, 35 P15, 36 P11, 37-40 P21, 41 P20, 42 P18, 43 P15, 44 P14, 45-48 P12, 49 P10, 50 P8, 51 P10, 52 P9, 53 P7, 54 P5, 55-63 P4, 64 P3, 65-69 P2, 70 P1
FASTEST LAP Button, McLaren-Mercedes, 1m 16.956s (Lap 69), 204.007kph, 126.764mph
CHAMPIONSHIP Vettel 161, Button 101, Webber 94, Hamilton 85, Alonso 69

Pos	Driver	Car	Time/gap	Grid	Stops	Tyres
1	J Button	McLaren-Mercedes	4h 4m 39.537s	7	6	P
2	S Vettel	Red Bull-Renault	−2.709s	1	3	P
3	M Webber	Red Bull-Renault	−13.828s	4	3	P
4	M Schumacher	Mercedes	−14.219s	8	4	P
5	V Petrov	Renault	−20.395s	10	2	P
6	F Massa	Ferrari	−33.225s	3	4	P

TOP 100 RACE

Round 8/19	**EUROPEAN GP** Valencia		**Sebastian Vettel**
	26 June 2011	**Race 847**	Red Bull-Renault RB7 186.068kph, 115.617mph

Valencia was always going to struggle to match the excitement of Montréal and so it proved. This was the first of a two-race FIA clampdown on blown diffuser embellishments which would curb Red Bull superiority, wouldn't it? Instead, on a circuit less than ideal for RBR, the team qualified 1–2 and finished 1–3, Vettel's sixth win from his seventh pole. It was a bit like Turkey: behind P1 it was an entertaining race. Alonso won his race-long scrap with Webber for P2, and at half distance – when the three leaders were running within 2–3s of each other – another Vettel victory was no certainty. The McLarens qualified P3 and P6, convinced that race day would prove far better. But in the hot conditions race pace was disappointing, neither happy with their tyres.

POLE POSITION Vettel, Red Bull-Renault, 1m 36.975s (0.188s), 201.169kph, 125.001mph
LAPS 57 x 5.419 km, 3.367 miles
DISTANCE 308.883 km, 191.931 miles
STARTERS/FINISHERS 24/24
WEATHER Sunny, hot, dry
LAP LEADERS Vettel 1-13, 15-57 (56); Massa 14 (1)
WINNER'S LAPS 1-13 P1, 14 P2, 15-57 P1
FASTEST LAP Vettel, Red Bull-Renault, 1m 41.852s (lap 53), 191.536kph, 119.015mph
CHAMPIONSHIP Vettel 186, Button 109, Webber 109, Hamilton 97, Alonso 87

Pos	Driver	Car	Time/gap	Grid	Stops	Tyres
1	S Vettel	Red Bull-Renault	1h 39m 36.169s	1	3	P
2	F Alonso	Ferrari	–10.891s	4	3	P
3	M Webber	Red Bull-Renault	–27.255	2	3	P
4	L Hamilton	McLaren-Mercedes	–46.190s	3	3	P
5	F Massa	Ferrari	–51.705s	5	3	P
6	J Button	McLaren-Mercedes	–1m 00.065s	6	3	P

Ferrari 150° Italia

Round 9/19	**BRITISH GP** Silverstone		**Fernando Alonso**
	10 July 2011	**Race 848**	Ferrari 150° Italia 207.155kph, 128.720mph

Friday's more stringent blown diffuser regulations were lifted, 'Valencia conditions' reinstated for the race and qualifying. This had Red Bull 1–2 and Ferrari 3–4, but McLaren 5–10. A pre-race shower saw the grid on 'inters', Vettel beating pole-man Webber away. Seb looked good for his seventh victory until on lap 26 a fumbled second pit-stop let Alonso and Hamilton through. Lewis gave the race sparkle, rocketing from P10 while the track was slick to overtake Alonso for P3 on lap 15. Later Lewis's stout defence of P2 allowed Alonso to escape from Vettel's clutches but as the track dried – and short of fuel – he fell back, fending off Massa on the line for P4. Just as Button's race might have come alive it ended on three wheels, a pit-stop gaff. At his first British GP, Paul di Resta qualified P6.

POLE POSITION Webber, Red Bull-Renault, 1m 30.399s (0.032s), 234.599kph, 145.773mph
LAPS 52 x 5.891 km, 3.660 miles
DISTANCE 306.227 km, 190.281 miles
STARTERS/FINISHERS 24/19
WEATHER Cloudy, cool, damp at start drying quickly
LAP LEADERS Vettel 1-27 (27); Alonso 28-52 (25)
WINNER'S LAPS 1-12 P3, 13 P4, 14 P3, 15-24 P4, 25-26 P3, 27 P2, 28-52 P1
FASTEST LAP F Alonso, Ferrari, 1m 34.908s (lap 41), 223.454kph, 138.848mph
CHAMPIONSHIP Vettel 204, Webber 124, Alonso 112, Hamilton 109, Button 109

Pos	Driver	Car	Time/gap	Grid	Stops	Tyres
1	F Alonso	Ferrari	1h 28m 41.196s	3	3	P
2	S Vettel	Red Bull-Renault	–16.511s	2	3	P
3	M Webber	Red Bull-Renault	–16.947s	1	3	P
4	L Hamilton	McLaren-Mercedes	–28.986s	10	3	P
5	F Massa	Ferrari	–29.010s	4	3	P
6	N Rosberg	Mercedes	–1m 00.665s	9	2	P

GERMAN GP Nürburgring

24 July 2011 Race 849

A superb Q3 lap had Hamilton on the front row splitting the Red Bulls. Out-gunning pole-man Webber off the damp grid, victory would not be denied. It showed when he went wide and Webber passed him on lap 12, Hamilton immediately retaking the lead at the following corner. And again on lap 32 when Alonso's later tyre stop got him ahead at the pit exit, Lewis simply drove around the outside to regain the lead at turn two. Which of these three would finally triumph turned on the performance of the harder primes in the final stint. In the cold conditions the McLaren pit-wall called it right for a superb win. Error-prone Vettel, never in the hunt for victory, beat Massa to P4 in a last-lap pit-stop shoot-out. Button's poor Q3 and start left him too much to do.

Lewis Hamilton

McLaren-Mercedes MP4-26 189.911kph, 118.005mph

POLE POSITION Webber, Red Bull-Renault, 1m 30.079s (0.055s), 205.739kph, 127.840mph
LAPS 60 x 5.148 km, 3.199 miles
DISTANCE 308.863 km, 191.919 miles
STARTERS/FINISHERS 24/20
WEATHER Cloudy, cold, slightly damp at start, otherwise dry
LAP LEADERS Hamilton 1-11, 13-16, 30, 33-50, 57-60 (38); Webber 12, 17-29, 54-56 (17); Alonso 31-32, 51-53 (5)
WINNER'S LAPS 1-11 P1, 12 P2, 13-16 P1, 17-29 P2, 30 P1, 31-32 P2, 33-50 P1, 51 P2, 52-53 P3, 54-56 P2, 57-60 P1
FASTEST LAP Hamilton, McLaren-Mercedes, 1m 34.302s (lap 59), 196.526kph, 122.116mph
CHAMPIONSHIP Vettel 216, Webber 139, Hamilton 134, Alonso 130, Button 109

Pos	Driver	Car	Time/gap	Grid	Stops	Tyres
1	L Hamilton	McLaren-Mercedes	1h 37m 30.334s	2	3	P
2	F Alonso	Ferrari	–3.980s	4	3	P
3	M Webber	Red Bull-Renault	–9.788s	1	3	P
4	S Vettel	Red Bull-Renault	–47.921s	3	3	P
5	F Massa	Ferrari	–52.252s	5	3	P
6	A Sutil	Force India-Mercedes	–1m 26.208s	8	2	P

HUNGARIAN GP Hungaroring

31 July 2011 Race 850

On a treacherously damp, greasy surface, cars twitching for adhesion, Vettel, back to pole-winning form, went wide on lap 5 and Hamilton was by. Early onto slicks, Button followed on lap 14, so McLarens were 1–2. Another shower saw Lewis spin at the chicane on lap 47, regaining the lead in wheel-to-wheel combat with Jenson as he too went wide. Crucially, on lap 52, Hamilton switched to inters while Button cannily stayed on slicks to win his 200th GP. On lap 56, back on slicks, Lewis served a drive-through for an unsafe spin-turn used to recover from his earlier rotation. Rejoining P6, he fought by Massa then Webber to take P4. But P2 increased Vettel's massive points lead, while di Resta finished an impressive P7 and Heidfeld retired a flaming Renault.

Jenson Button

McLaren-Mercedes MP4-26 172.416kph, 107.134mph

POLE POSITION Vettel, Red Bull-Renault, 1m 19.815s (0.163s), 197.601kph, 122.784mph
LAPS 70 x 4.381 km, 2.722 miles
DISTANCE 306.630 km, 190.531 miles
STARTERS/FINISHERS 24/20
WEATHER Overcast, warm, damp start, drying then rain later
LAP LEADERS Vettel 1-4, 28 (5); Hamilton 5-26, 29-40, 43-46, 51 (39); Button 27, 41-42, 47-50, 52-70 (26)
WINNER'S LAPS 1-10 P3, 11 P4, 12 P6, 13 P4, 14-26 P2, 27 P1, 28 P3, 29-40 P2, 41-42 P1, 43-46 P2, 47-50 P1, 51 P2, 52-70 P1
FASTEST LAP Massa, Ferrari, 1m 23.415s (lap 61), 189.073kph, 117.485mph
CHAMPIONSHIP Vettel 234, Webber 149, Hamilton 146, Alonso 145, Button 134

Pos	Driver	Car	Time/gap	Grid	Stops	Tyres
1	J Button	McLaren-Mercedes	1h 46m 42.337s	3	3	P
2	S Vettel	Red Bull-Renault	–3.588s	1	3	P
3	F Alonso	Ferrari	–19.819s	5	3	P
4	L Hamilton	McLaren-Mercedes	–48.338s	2	5	P
5	M Webber	Red Bull-Renault	–49.742s	6	5	P
6	F Massa	Ferrari	–1m 23.176s	4	4	P

BELGIAN GP Spa Francorchamps

28 August 2011 Race 851

Rosberg, from P5, led the first two laps, but after three defeats RBR delivered a crushing 1–2 victory, but not without anxiety. Despite Vettel's ninth pole, camber-induced blistering qualifying tyres offered a hard choice: a pitlane start on fresh rubber or a safety risk. Laps 4 and 5 pit-stops minimised the gamble, working out well for Vettel; a lap 12 SC compromised his lead but donated a free pit stop. On fresh rubber Seb was on his winning way. The SC was for a curious Hamilton/Kobayashi collision when disputing P4 on lap 12. Webber's P2 drive, having dropped to P8 at the start, demonstrated Red Bull superiority, but drive-of-the-day was Button's: he fell to P19 with a broken wing, then sliced through the field to P3. Schumacher, in his 20th anniversary race, finished P5 from dead last.

Sebastian Vettel

Red Bull-Renault RB7 213.066kph, 132.393mph

POLE POSITION Vettel, Red Bull-Renault, 1m 48.298s (0.432s), 232.824kph, 144.670mph
LAPS 44 x 7.004 km, 4.532 miles
DISTANCE 308.053 km, 191.415 miles
STARTERS/FINISHERS 24/19
WEATHER Cloudy, cool, dry
LAP LEADERS Rosberg 1-2, 6 (3); Vettel 3-5, 11-13, 18-30, 32-44 (32); Alonso 7, 14-17 (5); Hamilton 8-10 (3); Button 31 (1); SC 13-16 (4)
WINNER'S LAPS 1-2 P2, 3-5 P1, 6 P7, 7 P6, 8 P5, 9 P3, 10 P2, 11-13 P1, 14-16 P3, 17 P2, 18-30 P1, 31 P2, 32-44 P1
FASTEST LAP Webber, Red Bull-Renault, 1m 49.883s (lap 33), 229.465kph, 142.583mph
CHAMPIONSHIP Vettel 259, Webber 167, Alonso 157, Button 149, Hamilton 146

Pos	Driver	Car	Time/gap	Grid	Stops	Tyres
1	S Vettel	Red Bull-Renault	1h 26m 44.893s	1	3	P
2	M Webber	Red Bull-Renault	–3.741s	3	2	P
3	J Button	McLaren-Mercedes	–9.669s	13	3	P
4	F Alonso	Ferrari	–13.022s	8	2	P
5	M Schumacher	Mercedes	–47.464s	24	3	P
6	N Rosberg	Mercedes	–48.674s	5	2	P

ITALIAN GP Monza

11 September 2011   **Race 852**

Sebastian Vettel

Red Bull-Renault RB7 227.848kph, 141.578mph

Alonso led from row two, but car carnage at the first chicane – Liuzzi arrived sideways – released the SC. On resumption the race was defined: Webber and Massa clashed; Hamilton was caught napping by Schumacher, while Vettel bravely took Alonso around the outside of Curva Grande. This was vital for Seb: despite his mighty Monza pole, top speed was constrained by a short gear-ratio strategy only optimal for race leadership, as he imperiously demonstrated by steadily pulling away to victory. Schumacher's notoriously robust defence of P3 helped Button pass first Hamilton and then Michael too – something Lewis couldn't manage. Jenson then caught Alonso for P2, undercutting him at the second stops. Once free of the Schumacher 'chicane', Lewis almost caught Fernando for P3, the five world champions finishing 1–5.

POLE POSITION Vettel, Red Bull-Renault, 1m 22.275s (0.450s), 253.476kph, 157.503mph
LAPS 53 x 5.793 km, 3.600 miles
DISTANCE 306.719 km, 190.586 miles
STARTERS/FINISHERS 24/15
WEATHER Sunny, hot, dry
LAP LEADERS Alonso 1-4 (4); Vettel 5-53 (49); SC 1-3 (3)
WINNER'S LAPS 1-4 P2, 5-53 P1
FASTEST LAP Hamilton, McLaren-Mercedes, 1m 26.187 (lap 52), 241.971kph, 150.354mph
CHAMPIONSHIP Vettel 284, Alonso 172, Button 167, Webber 167, Hamilton 158

Pos	Driver	Car	Time/gap	Grid	Stops	Tyres
1	S Vettel	Red Bull-Renault	1h 20m 46.172s	1	2	P
2	J Button	McLaren-Mercedes	−9.590s	3	2	P
3	F Alonso	Ferrari	−16.909s	4	2	P
4	L Hamilton	McLaren-Mercedes	−17.417s	2	2	P
5	M Schumacher	Mercedes	−32.677s	8	2	P
6	F Massa	Ferrari	−42.993s	6	2	P

SINGAPORE GP Marina Bay

25 September 2011   **Race 853**

Sebastian Vettel

Red Bull-Renault RB7 155.810kph, 96.816mph

On his 11th pole, Vettel headed a paired grid – Red Bull, McLaren, Ferrari, Mercedes, Force India – then scampered away from Button at a second a lap, controlling a 10–20s lead. A mid-race SC, deployed for Schumacher's briefly aerial crash when he clouted Perez's rear tyre, barely affected matters. After a difficult start, Hamilton's lap 12 clash with Massa destroyed their races, Lewis receiving a drive-through as well as a fresh front wing. He did well to recover to P5, and later was the recipient of Massa's highly public post-race rancour. Webber and Alonso squabbled over the third podium step while di Resta brilliantly took P6. In the closing laps Button created excitement as he cut the gap until thwarted by traffic, but Sebastian was in command, now one point short of a second title.

POLE POSITION Vettel, Red Bull-Renault, 1m 44.381s (0.351s), 174.962kph, 108.716mph
LAPS 61 x 5.073 km, 3.152 miles
DISTANCE 309.316 km, 192.200 miles
STARTERS/FINISHERS 24/21
WEATHER Dark, hot, dry
LAP LEADERS Vettel 1-61 (61); SC 30-33 (4)
WINNER'S LAPS 1-61 P1
FASTEST LAP Button, McLaren-Mercedes, 1m 48.454s (lap 54), 168.392kph, 104.634mph
CHAMPIONSHIP Vettel 309, Button 185, Alonso 184, Webber 182, Hamilton 168

Pos	Driver	Car	Time/gap	Grid	Stops	Tyres
1	S Vettel	Red Bull-Renault	1h 59m 6.757s	1	3	P
2	J Button	McLaren-Mercedes	−1.737s	3	3	P
3	M Webber	Red Bull-Renault	−29.279s	2	3	P
4	F Alonso	Ferrari	−55.449s	5	3	P
5	L Hamilton	McLaren-Mercedes	−1m 7.766s	4	4	P
6	P di Resta	Force India-Mercedes	−1m 51.067s	10	2	P

JAPANESE GP Suzuka

9 October 2011   **Race 854**

Jenson Button

McLaren-Mercedes MP4-26 202.972kph, 126.121mph

In practice McLaren had the measure of Red Bull, but Vettel beat Button to pole by 0.009s and at the start ruthlessly chopped across to foil Jenson's run up the inside. While Hamilton chased the leader, the somewhat aggrieved Button bided his time, taking the lead from Vettel on lap 23 after a rapid second stop preceded by fast lappery. A mid-race SC to remove track debris – clashes between Webber/Schumacher and, bizarrely, Hamilton/Massa, neither incident penalised – allowed Button to demonstrate winning pace on the resumption. Indeed Alonso, about to lose his mantle as youngest back-to-back champion, also got ahead of Vettel at the third stops and stayed there once Seb accepted that a safe P3 guaranteed a second F1 world title at the age of 24.

POLE POSITION Vettel, Red Bull-Renault, 1m 30.466s (0.009s), 231.083kph, 143.588mph
LAPS 53 x 5.807 km, 3.608 miles
DISTANCE 307.471 km, 191.054 miles
STARTERS/FINISHERS 24/23
WEATHER Sunny, warm, dry
LAP LEADERS Vettel 1-9, 12-18 (16); Button 10, 19-20, 23-36, 41-53 (30); Massa 11, 22 (2); Alonso 21, 37 (2); Schumacher 38-40 (3); SC 24-27 (4)
WINNER'S LAPS 1-7 P3, 8-9 P2, 10 P1, 11 P3, 12-18 P2, 19-20 P1, 21 P4, 22 P2, 23-36 P1, 37 P3, 38-40 P2, 41-53 P1
FASTEST LAP Button, McLaren-Mercedes, 1m 36.568s (lap 52), 216.481kph, 134.515mph
CHAMPIONSHIP Vettel 324, Button 210, Alonso 202, Webber 194, Hamilton 178

Pos	Driver	Car	Time/gap	Grid	Stops	Tyres
1	J Button	McLaren-Mercedes	1h 30m 53.427s	2	3	P
2	F Alonso	Ferrari	−1.160s	5	3	P
3	S Vettel	Red Bull-Renault	−2.006s	1	3	P
4	M Webber	Red Bull-Renault	−8.071s	6	3	P
5	L Hamilton	McLaren-Mercedes	−24.268s	3	3	P
6	M Schumacher	Mercedes	−27.120s	8	3	p

Round 16/19	**KOREAN GP** Yeongam					
	16 October 2011				Race 855	

Sebastian Vettel

Red Bull-Renault RB7 188.893kph, 117.373mph

Even the first non-Red Bull pole of the season didn't bring troubled Hamilton joy, his disposition further soured when overtaken by Vettel on lap 1. But how the two teams might perform over race distance was uncertain, limited preparation time due to poor Friday weather producing divergent tyre strategies. But as Vettel edged away, the understeering Hamilton became embroiled in a 30-lap duel with Webber, passing and repassing, their spirited scrap allowing Seb to escape despite an SC. Behind these two, Button, bundled back to P8 at the start, menaced but never threatened and was reeled in during the closing stages by Alonso, once released from tracking team-mate Massa. And that was how it ended, P2–P5 just 3.6s apart but 12s behind the flying Vettel. Red Bull wrapped up the constructors' title.

POLE POSITION Hamilton, McLaren-Mercedes, 1m 35.820s (0.222s), 210.958kph, 131.083mph
LAPS 55 x 5.615 km, 3.489 miles
DISTANCE 308.630 km, 191.774 miles
STARTERS/FINISHERS 24/21
WEATHER Cloudy, warm, dry with spots of rain
LAP LEADERS Vettel 1-34, 37-55 (53); Alonso 35-36 (2); SC 17-20 (4)
WINNER'S LAPS 1-34 P1, 35-36 P2, 37-55 P1
FASTEST LAP Vettel, Red Bull-Renault, 1m 39.605s (lap 55), 202.941kph, 126.102mph
CHAMPIONSHIP Vettel 349, Button 222, Alonso 212, Webber 209, Hamilton 196

Pos	Driver	Car	Time/gap	Grid	Stops	Tyres
1	S Vettel	Red Bull-Renault	1h 38m 1.994s	2	2	P
2	L Hamilton	McLaren-Mercedes	−12.019s	1	2	P
3	M Webber	Red Bull-Renault	−12.477s	4	2	P
4	J Button	McLaren-Mercedes	−14.694s	3	2	P
5	F Alonso	Ferrari	−15.689s	6	2	P
6	F Massa	Ferrari	−25.133s	5	2	P

Round 17/19	**INDIAN GP** Buddh					
	30 October 2011				Race 856	

Sebastian Vettel

Red Bull-Renault RB7 203.513kph, 126.457mph

The first Indian GP, a welcome if smoggy, dusty affair on an admirable new circuit. Vettel's victory marked his first-ever grand slam, leading every lap from pole then exuberantly posting fastest lap on his final tour. Button alone kept him honest, blasting past Webber on lap 1 to stalk Vettel at 3–6s distance, catching in the pit-stops, losing on the track. At the second stop Alonso took Webber for the third podium step. Schumacher beat Rosberg in the Mercedes contest, while Sutil brought gratifying points to Force India at their home event. Hamilton's misery persisted: in qualifying he split the Red Bulls but was given a grid penalty for ignoring yellow; in the race he and Massa collided yet again, Felipe deemed the culprit, the haphazard Brazilian missing apexes to break his front suspension twice during the meeting.

POLE POSITION Vettel, Red Bull-Renault, 1m 24.178s (0.330s), 219.178kph, 136.191mph
LAPS 60 x 5.125 km, 3.185 miles
DISTANCE 307.249 km, 190.917 miles
STARTERS/FINISHERS 24/19
WEATHER Sunny, smoggy, hot, dry
LAP LEADERS Vettel 1-60 (60)
WINNER'S LAPS 1-60 P1
FASTEST LAP Vettel, Red Bull-Renault, 1m 27.249s (lap 60), 211.463kph, 131.397mph
CHAMPIONSHIP Vettel 374, Button 240, Alonso 227, Webber 221, Hamilton 202

Pos	Driver	Car	Time/gap	Grid	Stops	Tyres
1	S Vettel	Red Bull-Renault	1h 30m 35.002s	1	2	P
2	J Button	McLaren-Mercedes	8.433s	4	2	P
3	F Alonso	Ferrari	−24.301s	3	2	P
4	M Webber	Red Bull-Renault	−25.529s	2	2	P
5	M Schumacher	Mercedes	−1m 5.421s	11	2	P
6	N Rosberg	Mercedes	−1m 6.851s	7	2	P

Round 18/19	**ABU DHABI GP** Yas Marina					
	13 November 2011				Race 857	

Lewis Hamilton

McLaren-Mercedes MP4-26 188.494kph, 117.125mph

Despite Hamilton's indomitable practice form, Vettel stole pole to equal Mansell's season record of 14. Vettel pushed his fuel-laden car hard off the start to elude DRS reach, but the rear tyre deflated at turn two – his first retirement in 20 starts. The race, now Hamilton's to lose, was kept alive by the tenacious Alonso, from P5 muscling past Webber and Button on lap 1 and hanging on to exert mild pressure on Lewis at their second stops. Button battled Webber, spinner Massa, and a recalcitrant KERS for a gratifying if inconspicuous podium. Even without his team-mate's presence, Webber didn't improve on his P4 grid slot, a muffed tyre-change not helping but neither explaining his modest result. So Hamilton assuaged his 2011 misery while Rosberg's P6 and points finishes for the Force India pair were also notable.

POLE POSITION Vettel, Red Bull-Renault, 1m 38.481s (0.141), 203.027kph, 126.155mph
LAPS 55 x 5.554 km, 3.451 miles
DISTANCE 305.355 km, 189.739 miles
STARTERS/FINISHERS 24/20
WEATHER Dry and bright, hot then cooling quickly as darkness fell
LAP LEADERS Hamilton 1-16, 18-40, 44-55 (51); Webber 17 (1); Alonso 41-43 (3)
WINNER'S LAPS 1-16 P1, 17 P2, 18-40 P1, 41-43 P2, 44-55 P1
FASTEST LAP Webber, Red Bull-Renault, 1m 42.612s (lap 51), 194.854kph, 121.077mph
CHAMPIONSHIP Vettel 374, Button 255, Alonso 245, Webber 233, Hamilton 227

Pos	Driver	Car	Time/gap	Grid	Stops	Tyres
1	L Hamilton	McLaren-Mercedes	1h 37m 11.886s	2	2	P
2	F Alonso	Ferrari	−8.457s	5	2	P
3	J Button	McLaren-Mercedes	−25.881s	3	2	P
4	M Webber	Red Bull-Renault	−35.784s	4	3	P
5	F Massa	Ferrari	−50.578s	6	2	P
6	N Rosberg	Mercedes	−52.317s	7	2	P

Round 19/19	**BRAZILIAN GP** Interlagos		**Mark Webber**
	27 November 2011	Race 858	Red Bull-Renault RB7 198.876kph, 123.576mph

A blinding lap brought Seb a record 15th pole that exceeded Mansell's 1992 benchmark. By the time DRS was enabled, two scintillating laps had him well clear of the chasing Webber for a Red Bull demonstration run. But it was Webber who led the 1–2 team finish for his first win of the year. Vettel was hobbled by a gearbox oil leak, but brilliantly nursed his car to P2. The race-long struggle for P3 was more entertaining. When track debris caused Button to lift on lap 11, Alonso took him superbly around the outside at Laranjinha for third place. On options Alonso had his measure but in the final stint on harder primes Button was flying, reeling in 5s in even laps to reclaim P3 on lap 62. Never higher than P4, Hamilton retired on lap 33 with gearbox trouble.

POLE POSITION Vettel, Red Bull-Renault, 1m 11.918s (0.181s), 215.695kph, 134.027mph
LAPS 71 x 4.309 km, 2.677 miles
DISTANCE 305.909 km, 190.083 miles
STARTERS/FINISHERS 24/20
WEATHER Cloudy with sunny intervals, warm, dry
LAP LEADERS Vettel 1-16, 21-29, 38-39, 59 (28); Webber 17-18, 30-37, 40-58, 60-71 (41); Massa 19-20 (2)
WINNER'S LAPS 1-16 P2, 17-18 P1, 19-20 P3, 21-29 P2, 30-37 P1, 38-39 P2, 40-58 P1, 59 P2, 60-71 P1
FASTEST LAP Webber, Red Bull-Renault, 1m 15.324s (lap 71), 205.942kph, 127.972mph
CHAMPIONSHIP Vettel 392, Button 270, Webber 258, Alonso 257, Hamilton 227

Pos	Driver	Car	Time/gap	Grid	Stops	Tyres
1	M Webber	Red Bull-Renault	1h 32m 17.464s	2	3	P
2	S Vettel	Red Bull-Renault	−16.983s	1	3	P
3	J Button	McLaren-Mercedes	−27.638s	3	3	P
4	F Alonso	Ferrari	−35.048s	5	3	P
5	F Massa	Ferrari	−1m 6.733s	7	2	P
6	A Sutil	Force India-Mercedes	−1 lap	8	3	P

2011 CHAMPIONSHIP FACTS AND FOLKLORE

■ Although the essential shape and form of the season was much as last year – 12 teams competing over 19 championship rounds and no driver moves in the leading teams – the character of F1 racing perceptibly altered in 2011.

■ This was caused by the introduction of DRS, the return of KERS, and the replacement of Bridgestone by Pirelli. How much each contributed to a season of enhanced on-track entertainment was a matter of conjecture, as was the debate led by purists surrounding the rectitude of such artificiality.

■ The previous season's 'F-ducts' having been banned and moveable front wings dropped, DRS (Drag Reduction System) was introduced, and blatantly gave a chasing car a performance advantage over the one immediately ahead. DRS promised to overcome the obstacle of 'dirty air' that had so inhibited on-track overtaking for decades.

■ DRS, a cockpit-controlled device, 'feathered' an element of the rear wing to reduce drag. Terminal speed along a straight could benefit by some 7mph. In free practice and qualifying a driver could use DRS at will, but in the race it was enabled for one driver yet denied to another. It was this induced 'unfairness' which disturbed traditionalists concerned over its erosion of the intrinsic integrity of GP racing.

■ In race conditions the driver of a chasing car could open this rear-wing 'flap' in a prescribed DRS zone as long as he was within 1s of the car ahead at the DRS detection point. The detection, activation and de-activation points were marked on the track and cockpit display informed a driver when DRS became available. Five tracks were set up with two DRS zones.

■ On balance the DRS experiment was regarded as a qualified success although many believed Pirelli's contribution to the improved 'show' to be far greater.

■ New exclusive tyre supplier Pirelli were prepared to trade off the benefits of F1 exposure against the provision of tyres consciously designed to enhance 'the show'. They were roundly applauded for accepting the risk that their products might not always be showcased positively.

■ Pirelli's approach was to manufacture tyres of limited life with wider performance differentials between the four dry compounds – hard (silver), medium (white), soft (yellow), super-soft (red) – along with a tyre-degradation 'window',

whereby loss of performance was likened to 'falling off a cliff'. As before, two steps usually existed between prime and option tyres, both of which had to be used during the race.

■ Dry tyre allocation was further reduced by three sets to 11 per car/weekend, capped to six sets for qualifying and the race. This, coupled with multiple race stints, produced an abstemious attitude towards use of the softer and appreciably quicker option tyres, some teams saving sets for the race by electing not to make Q2 or Q1 runs.

■ With drivers now required to use four or even five sets of tyres in a race, the ability to 'manage' tyre longevity against sustained race speed in each stint became a key factor in race strategy. Further, as alternate strategies played out during different phases of the race, the performance variation between cars was accentuated. This resulted in a much higher incidence of on-track overtaking although many again felt it was all too contrived.

■ A by-product of stiffer, high-degradation tyres was excessive 'marbles' (chunks of rubber) off the racing line. Fortunately this trait rarely interfered with successful overtaking.

■ At the fourth championship round in Turkey a record 88 overtakes took place – almost bewildering for even the most seasoned F1 spectator. But this was the only race in which the new overtaking measures appeared to be verging on counter-productive.

■ Making its return, the KERS power booster was adopted by all but the 'newer' lower-order teams. Red Bull purported to have developed a compromise 'lite' version designed to save weight and assist packaging without compromising race starts.

■ Other changes were as follows: minimum car weight (including driver) was raised by 20kg to 640kg, with weight distribution mandated; the 107% qualifying rule was reinstated, albeit alleviated by the fact that it only applied within the context of slower Q1 times; gearbox life was increased from four to five races; a curfew was introduced to limit excessive work schedules by mechanics; and, whisper it, the regulation banning team orders was removed.

■ Which leaves diffusers. While the previous season's 'double diffusers' were banned, 'exhaust-blown diffusers' gained both in sophistication and significance. Variations on the theme became as wide-ranging as a Starbucks coffee menu: cold blown, hot blown, on-pedal, off-pedal, octopus exhaust (McLaren), front-exiting exhaust (Renault), and so on.

- By remodelling the exhaust system to direct outlet gases to the diffuser, exhaust-blown diffusers generated increased downforce by energising airflow through and around the venturi. By remapping engine electronics to cut fuel supply and ignition, most of this effect could be achieved even when the driver lifted the throttle, known as 'off-pedal blowing'.
- With 'hot-blowing', an ensuing refinement in 2011, during 'off-pedal' sequences some fuel was injected and the spark restored. But to kill the inevitable engine torque, the ignition timing was savagely retarded, combustion occurring in the exhaust system itself. Hot-blowing significantly increased the energy of exhaust gases, massively enhancing diffuser downforce but carrying with it a fuel consumption penalty of some 15%. But the net performance benefits were considerable.
- With its consequent heavy fuel consumption and costly engine reliability programmes, the FIA moved to ban 'exhaust-blown diffusers' mid-season. Later this was rescinded, a mid-season rule revision proving impossible to define fairly; but 'exhaust-blown diffusers' would be gone from 2012 and with them the displeasing 'coughing attacks' emitted from exhausts during mid-corner throttle overrun.
- The 2011 season began in Australia two weeks late after the planned Bahrain opener was initially postponed, then ultimately cancelled, due to unrest in the Gulf kingdom as the 'Arab Spring' escalated.
- Following the debut of South Korea last year, India was the newcomer with a Hermann Tilke-designed circuit 35km from New Delhi. The Buddh track pleased the drivers and was altogether a popular addition to the championship.

- Indian driver Narain Karthikeyan made history in Valencia when he became the first driver in a championship race to be classified 24th when all starters finished, F1 mechanical reliability reaching unparalleled levels.
- Due to extreme weather in Montréal there were record SC deployments and for rather bizarre reasons the race became the longest ever in time and slowest ever on record. It was won by Jenson Button when Vettel spun under pressure.
- Sebastian's 2011 campaign was not error-free although he confined most of his indiscretions to free practice. But as the season unfolded it became increasingly clear that while the RB7 was the class car, Vettel was the class act, his contribution bringing near invincibility to the team.
- Although a somewhat spurious calculation, eliminate Vettel from the contest and Webber would not have delivered Red Bull the drivers' title. Button would have been champ with seven race victories to Webber's three.
- At times Vettel displayed the qualifying supremacy of a Senna, the front running dominance of a Clark, the race-craft *sympatico* of a Prost, and the astute commitment of a Schumacher, the latter exemplified by his pre-season visit to Pirelli HQ, the only F1 driver to check out a new tyre supplier's response to a radically changed brief. This trait was also evident at the penultimate round after his one and only dnf, joining the RBR pit-wall to "see what I could learn".
- Vettel's Abu Dhabi puncture and retirement was never fully explained, some speculating it to be the downside risk of using exhaust gases to heat rear tyres, a ploy to ensure the crucial 1s gap was opened by the time DRS was deployed on lap 3. Certainly the team used wheel warmers – pre-heated hub-mounted metal cylinders – to reduce tyre heat dissipation.
- Vettel's string of 'youngest' landmarks was now headed by his back-to-back championships. At a mere 24 years and 98

RACE 848, British GP: At Silverstone Fernando Alonso gave a spirited demonstration of the Ferrari 375 which won the British GP at the very same circuit 60 years before. It was in celebration of the occasion when José Froilán González won the very first world championship race for Ferrari in 1951 (see pages 22 and 24).

RACE 854, Japanese GP: Having laid claim to the 'number one' gesture as his own, Sebastian Vettel inevitably raised two index fingers to proclaim his back-to-back championships, the youngest driver to achieve this.

days, he was a full year younger than predecessor Alonso in 2006. His two other notable 'in a season' records, 15 poles and 739 laps led, each supplanted Nigel Mansell from 1992.

■ It might be a stretch to suggest that a second season of Adrian Newey-inspired superiority at Red Bull led directly to a flurry of Technical Director sackings, but Pat Fry replaced Aldo Costa at Ferrari and Sam Michael departed Williams, his position effectively filled by Mike Coughlan, having served his expulsion period over the 2007 spy scandal. Costa and Michael were quickly snapped up by Mercedes GP and McLaren respectively.

■ Little argument remained that Red Bull continued to enjoy a downforce advantage, but from whence it came was the ongoing mystery. Ferrari's flexing, fluttering front wings in India suggested the Scuderia still suspected 'trick' carbon fibre overlay techniques to be one answer, a complex technology with myriad benefits if mastered.

■ McLaren seemed to have better answers to RBR supremacy than Maranello as their six race victories, three apiece for drivers Hamilton and Button, proved. The changing relationship between McLaren's drivers was one of the fascinations of the year, Lewis beaten in the championship by a team-mate for the first time.

■ Numerous issues seemed to pile up on Lewis and recede from Jenson in almost equal and opposite measure, even the fortunes of their love life and family affairs. Probably the most telling were tyres and mindset.

■ 'Looking after' sensitive Pirelli tyres was unnatural for 'racer' Hamilton yet idyllic for 'silky smooth' Button. Further, Jenson was entering his second year with McLaren, team and driver now more able to complement one another. For Hamilton it was his fifth McLaren year, and for the third in a row he had a car less than the very best he demanded.

■ Too frequently Hamilton had to endure Vettel driving off into the sunset winning titles and breaking records while he scrapped over lesser placings. The frustration began to show through a series of on-track clashes, especially with Massa, the Ferrari driver no doubt equally discontent about his waning fortunes.

■ In the Montréal paddock it even led Lewis to pay a visit to the Red Bull motorhome, the upshot being that Lewis, at the time of writing, would be out of contract with McLaren after 2012 while Button already has a new multi-year deal in his back pocket.

■ Five drivers – Vettel, Button, Hamilton, Alonso, Webber – from the top three teams dominated the podium this year. Renault were the only interlopers with two early P3s, but the Enstone squad's prospects were compromised by their technical cul-de-sac with exhaust-blown diffusers and the absence of Robert Kubica.

■ Due to lengthy recuperation following serious injury in a minor rally in February, Robert Kubica missed the entire season. His return to F1, latterly linked to Ferrari, is still uncertain while his team have signed Kimi Räikkönen for 2012 – meaning that a record six world champions would form up on 2012 grids.

- The Enstone team officially became Lotus for 2012 after the dispute over ownership of the iconic name was finally settled. The Team Lotus of 2010–11, led by Tony Fernandes, would become known as Caterham.

- Improved overtaking opportunities produced an entertaining championship squabble between the midfield teams: Renault was almost pipped by Force India for fifth, and Sauber held out to beat Toro Rosso to seventh.

- Mercedes GP remained stuck in fourth, neither midfield nor front runner, Schumacher showing improved form but still shaded by team-mate Rosberg.

- Managed by Lewis's father Anthony Hamilton, Force India's Paul di Resta was rookie of the year, but Sergio Perez (Sauber) also occasionally caught the eye.

- Sergio Perez was the first Mexican in F1 since Hector Rebaque in 1981 and Jerome d'Ambrosio (Virgin Racing) the first Belgian since Thierry Boutsen in 1993.

- As part of a Williams 2011 nightmare, reigning GP2 champion Pastor Maldonado had an F1 baptism from hell, contributing just one of the team's five points; the nadir was

reached when the Williams pair formed the back row of the Abu Dhabi grid.

- Following their stock market launch in March, Williams share values slumped; in May Sam Michael fell on his sword and the season end saw Patrick Head step away from the F1 scene.

- Motor racing people who died in 2011 included the following: Derek Gardner (79), six-wheeler Tyrrell designer; Jim Endruweit (83), Lotus mechanic in the Clark glory years; 1960s/70s privateer Pete Lovely (85); 1960 Indy 500 winner Jim Rathmann (83); 1971 Monza victor Peter Gethin (71); and Indycar champion and twice Indy 500 winner Dan Wheldon (33). The sad and violent deaths of Wheldon and MotoGP ace Marco Simoncelli on successive weekends in October was a shocking wake-up call for motorsport.

- In July at Silverstone the 60th anniversary of the first Ferrari world championship race win was celebrated. Spaniard Fernando Alonso gave a spirited demonstration of the very Ferrari 375 with which Argentinean José Froilán González won at the very same circuit in 1951; 830 races and 215 Ferrari victories later, Alonso fittingly went on to win the 2011 British GP.

Championship ranking	Championship points	Driver nationality	2011 Drivers Championship		Races contested	Race victories	Podiumse excl. victories	Races led	Lights to flag victories	Laps led	Poles	Fastest laps	Triple Crowns
			Driver	Car									
1	392	GER	Sebastian Vettel	Red Bull-Renault	19	11	6	17	2	739	15	3	2
2	270	GBR	Jenson Button	McLaren-Mercedes	19	3	9	7		88		3	
3	258	AUS	Mark Webber	Red Bull-Renault	19	1	9	3		59	3	7	
4	257	ESP	Fernando Alonso	Ferrari	19	1	9	11		68		1	
5	227	GBR	Lewis Hamilton	McLaren-Mercedes	19	3	3	7		150	1	3	
6	118	BRA	Felipe Massa	Ferrari	19			5		9		2	
7	89	GER	Nico Rosberg	Mercedes	19			2		17			
8	76	GER	Michael Schumacher	Mercedes	19			1		3			
9	42	GER	Adrian Sutil	Force India-Mercedes	19								
10	37	RUS	Vitaly Petrov	Renault	19		1						
11	34	GER	Nick Heidfeld	Renault	11		1						
12	30	JPN	Kamui Kobayashi	Sauber-Ferrari	19								
13	27	GBR	Paul Di Resta	Force India-Mercedes	19								
14	26	ESP	Jaime Alguersuari	Toro Rosso-Ferrari	19								
15	15	SUI	Sébastien Buemi	Toro Rosso-Ferrari	19								
16	14	MEX	Sergio Pérez	Sauber-Ferrari	17								
17	4	BRA	Rubens Barrichello	Williams-Cosworth	19								
18	2	BRA	Bruno Senna	Renault	8								
19	1	VEN	Pastor Maldonado	Williams-Cosworth	19								

Championship ranking	Championship points	Team/Marque nationality	2011 Constructors Championship		Engine maker nationality	Races contested	Race victories	1-2 finishes	Podiums excl. victories	Races led	Laps led	Poles	Fastest laps
			Chassis	Engine									
1	650	AUT	Red Bull RB7	Renault 2.4 V8	FRA	19	12	3	15	19	798	18	10
2	497	GBR	McLaren MP4-26	Mercedes-Benz 2.4 V8	GER	19	6		12	11	238	1	6
3	375	ITA	Ferrari 150° Italia	Ferrari 2.4 V8	ITA	19	1		9	13	77		3
4	165	GER	Mercedes MGP W02	Mercedes-Benz 2.4 V8	GER	19			3	20			
5	73	FRA	Renault R31	Renault 2.4 V8	FRA	19			2				
6	69	IND	Force India VJM04	Mercedes-Benz 2.4 V8	GER	19							
7	44	SUI	Sauber C30	Ferrari 2.4 V8	ITA	19							
8	41	ITA	Toro Rosso STR6	Ferrari 2.4 V8	ITA	19							
9	5	GBR	Williams FW33	Cosworth 2.4 V8	GBR	19							

Formula 1: All the non-championship races

This book tells the race-by-race story of the Formula 1 World Championship from its origins in 1950, but there have also been numerous non-championship Formula 1 races, many before 1950.

Going back to the dawn of motor racing, it is widely acknowledged that the first Grand Prix was held on *routes françaises* near Le Mans over two days in June 1906, following on from the pioneering city-to-city-races (1894–1903) and the Gordon Bennett Cup (1900–05). After the First World War the sport gained further popularity until the 1929 Wall Street Crash, and then was resurgent during the 1930s – a period known as the 'Golden Era' of Grand Prix racing.

For cars to participate in Grands Prix, entries were required to comply with certain technical regulations – normally engine capacity, weight or both – as defined by the governing body, the *CSI*. Following the Second World War a new set of rules was proposed for Grand Prix cars, *International Racing Formula A*, which quickly evolved into Formula 1. The first Formula 1 race was held on 1 September 1946 in Valentino Park, Turin.

Besides regulation, the CSI controlled the events calendar. The most important international Grands Prix were given preferential treatment and designated Grandes Épreuves (great trials). The nomenclature *Grande Épreuve* also identified the handful of races selected each season as championship rounds, for Grand Prix cars (1925–27) and Grand Prix drivers (1935–39).

Following the Second World War but before the Formula

1 World Championship for Drivers was formalised in 1950, Grandes Épreuves also provided the nucleus of races from which a forerunner award – 'My Driver of the Year' – was determined. This accolade went to Jean-Pierre Wimille in 1947 and 1948, and Alberto Ascari in 1949.

The 1947–49 Grandes Épreuves are suitably highlighted in the record of non-championship Formula 1 races that follows. With one exception (the 1948 *Formule Libre* Circuito del Garda), this list faithfully follows the Formula 1 races identified as such in Paul Sheldon's *A Record of Grand Prix and Voiturette Racing*. It is an eclectic mix, many truly of Grande Épreuve stature but others clearly not, such as races from the French national championship and a 15-minute thrash in 1956 described by Doug Nye as 'British teeny meeting dominated by Scott-Brown in now sorted B7'.

But the common denominator of these Formula 1 races is that they were held during those seminal years in parallel with the burgeoning World Championship series and largely featured the most up-to-date machinery available.

The final non-championship F1 race took place in 1983 and from then on Grand Prix racing and Formula 1 became one and the same. Incidentally, the South African national F1 championship (1960–75) and British national F1 championship (1978–80 and 1982) have been excluded as they relied mainly on cast-off equipment; historic F1 races have also been omitted.

Race	Date	Event	Circuit	Winner	Nat.	Car	Time	Kph	Mph
1946									
1	01-Sep	Valentino GP	Valentino Park, Turin	Achille Varzi	ITA	Alfa Romeo 158	2h 35m 45.80s	103.996	64.620
2	23-Sep	Circuito di Milano	Sempione Park, Italy	Carlo Felice Trossi	ITA	Alfa Romeo 158	0h 56m 06.00s	89.463	55.590
3	03-Oct	GP du Salon, Paris	Bois de Boulogne, France	Raymond Sommer	FRA	Maserati 4CL	2h 12m 39.70s	115.342	71.670
1947									
4	09-Feb	Winter GP	Rommehed, Sweden	Reg Parnell	GBR	ERA A-Type	0h 59m 02.20s	105.235	65.390
5	23-Feb	Stockholm GP	Vallentuna, Sweden	Reg Parnell	GBR	ERA A-Type	1h 08m 18.80s	109.806	68.230
6	07-Apr	Pau GP	Pau, France	Nello Pagani	ITA	Maserati 4CL	3h 38m 31.00s	83.589	51.940
7	27-Apr	Roussillon GP	Perpignan, France	Eugène Chaboud	FRA	Talbot-Lago '39 MC	1h 35m 06.30s	92.811	57.670
8	08-May	Jersey Road Race	St. Helier	Reg Parnell	GBR	Maserati 4CL	1h 53m 33.00s	136.022	84.520
9	18-May	Marseille GP	Prado	Eugène Chaboud	FRA	Talbot-Lago '39 MC	2h 50m 23.60s	106.893	66.420
10	01-Jun	Nîmes GP	Nîmes-Courbessac, France	Luigi Villoresi	ITA	Maserati 4CL	3h 39m 59.40s	99.940	62.100
11	**08-Jun**	**SWISS GP**	**BREMGARTEN**	**JEAN-PIERRE WIMILLE**	**FRA**	**ALFA ROMEO 158**	**1h 25m 09.10s**	**154.787**	**96.180**
12	**29-Jun**	**BELGIAN GP**	**SPA-FRANCORCHAMPS**	**JEAN-PIERRE WIMILLE**	**FRA**	**ALFA ROMEO 158**	**3h 18m 28.64s**	**153.338**	**95.280**
13	06-Jul	Marne GP	Reims-Gueux, France	Christian Kautz	SUI	Maserati 4CL	2h 34m 50.70s	154.175	95.800
14	13-Jul	Albi GP	des Planques, France	Louis Rosier	FRA	Talbot-Lago T150C Sp.	2h 29m 48.70s	142.282	88.410
15	13-Jul	Bari GP	Bari, Italy	Achille Varzi	ITA	Alfa Romeo 158	2h 32m 27.20s	105.235	65.390
16	20-Jul	Nice GP	Nice, France	Luigi Villoresi	ITA	Maserati 4CL	3h 07m 07.10s	102.869	63.920
17	03-Aug	Alsace GP	Strasbourg, France	Luigi Villoresi	ITA	Maserati 4CL	2h 45m 41.90s	111.640	69.370

Race	Date	Event	Circuit	Winner	Nat.	Car	Time	Kph	Mph
18	09-Aug	Ulster Trophy	Ballyclare, N. Ireland	Bob Gerard	GBR	ERA B-Type	2h 05m 10.00s	115.036	71.480
19	10-Aug	GP du Comminges	St. Gaudens, France	Louis Chiron	FRA	Talbot-Lago '39 MC	2h 35m 37.40s	126.720	78.740
20	21-Aug	British Empire Trophy	Douglas, IoM	Bob Gerard	GBR	ERA B-Type	2h 16m 52.00s	109.468	68.020
21	**07-Sep**	**ITALIAN GP**	**SEMPIONE PARK, MILAN**	**CARLO FELICE TROSSI**	**ITA**	**ALFA ROMEO 158**	**3h 02m 25.00s**	**113.121**	**70.290**
22	**21-Sep**	**FRENCH GP (de l'ACF)**	**LYON-PARILLY**	**LOUIS CHIRON**	**FRA**	**TALBOT-LAGO '39 MC**	**4h 03m 40.70s**	**125.674**	**78.090**
23	05-Oct	Lausanne GP	Lausanne, Switzerland	Luigi Villoresi	ITA	Maserati 4CL	2h 49m 30.40s	151.150	93.920
24	16-Nov	GP du Salon	Montlhéry, Paris	Yves Giraud-Cabantous	FRA	Talbot-Lago '39 MD	2h 06m 28.20s	143.055	88.750

BOLD = GRANDE ÉPREUVE

1948

Race	Date	Event	Circuit	Winner	Nat.	Car	Time	Kph	Mph
25	29-Mar	Pau GP	Pau, France	Nello Pagani	ITA	Maserati 4CL	3h 33m 30.00s	87.597	54.430
26	29-Apr	Jersey Road Race	St. Helier	Bob Gerard	GBR	ERA B-Type	2h 00m 55.20s	141.349	87.830
27	02-May	GP des Nations	Genèva, Switzerland	Nino Farina	ITA	Maserati 4CLT	2h 23m 58.20s	98.782	61.380
28	**16-May**	**MONACO GP**	**MONTE CARLO**	**NINO FARINA**	**ITA**	**MASERATI 4CLT**	**3h 18m 26.90s**	**96.142**	**59.740**
29	25-May	British Empire Trophy	Douglas, IoM	Geoffrey Ansell	GBR	ERA B-Type	2h 03m 45.00s	108.936	67.690
30	30-May	Paris GP	Montlhéry	Yves Giraud-Cabantous	FRA	Talbot-Lago '39 MD	2h 08m 52.20s	140.496	87.300
31	27-Jun	San Remo GP	Ospedaletti, Italy	Alberto Ascari	ITA	Maserati 4CLT/48	3h 03m 34.00s	94.871	58.950
32	**04-Jul**	**SWISS GP**	**BREMGARTEN**	**CARLO FELICE TROSSI**	**ITA**	**ALFA ROMEO 158**	**1h 59m 17.30s**	**146.145**	**90.810**
33	**18-Jul**	**FRENCH GP (de l'ACF)**	**REIMS-GUEUX**	**JEAN-PIERRE WIMILLE**	**FRA**	**ALFA ROMEO 158**	**3h 01m 07.50s**	**165.698**	**102.960**
34	01-Aug	GP du Comminges	St. Gaudens, France	Luigi Villoresi	ITA	Maserati 4CLT/48	2h 11m 45.50s	150.313	93.400
35	07-Aug	Zandvoort GP	Zandvoort, Holland	'B.Bira'	THI	Maserati 4CL	1h 25m 22.20s	117.868	73.240
36	08-Aug	Ostschweiz GP	Erlen, Switzerland	Toulo de Graffenried	SUI	Maserati 4CL	1h 22m 14.80s	102.129	63.460
37	29-Aug	Albi GP	des Planques, France	Luigi Villoresi	ITA	Maserati 4CLT/48	1h 52m 57.90s	160.629	99.810
38	**05-Sep**	**ITALIAN GP**	**VALENTINO PARK, TURIN**	**JEAN-PIERRE WIMILLE**	**FRA**	**ALFA ROMEO 158**	**3h 10m 42.40s**	**113.266**	**70.380**
39	18-Sep	Goodwood Trophy	Goodwood, Gt. Britain	Reg Parnell	GBR	Maserati 4CLT/48	0h 08m 56.20s	129.649	80.560
40	02-Oct	British GP (RAC)	Silverstone	Luigi Villoresi	ITA	Maserati 4CLT/48	3h 18m 03.00s	116.323	72.280
41	10-Oct	GP du Salon	Montlhéry, Paris	Louis Rosier	FRA	Talbot-Lago T26C	2h 03m 52.90s	145.742	90.560
42	17-Oct	Autodrome GP	Monza, Italy	Jean-Pierre Wimille	FRA	Alfa Romeo 158	2h 50m 44.40s	177.108	110.050
43	31-Oct	Penya Rhin GP	Montjuïc, Spain	Luigi Villoresi	ITA	Maserati 4CLT/48	2h 10m 12.00s	143.940	89.440

BOLD = GRANDE ÉPREUVE

1949

Race	Date	Event	Circuit	Winner	Nat.	Car	Time	Kph	Mph
44	03-Apr	San Remo GP	Ospedaletti, Italy	Juan Manuel Fangio	ARG	Maserati 4CLT/48	3h 01m 28.60s	99.264	61.680
45	18-Apr	Pau GP	Pau, France	Juan Manuel Fangio	ARG	Maserati 4CLT/48	3h 36m 11.90s	86.518	53.760
46	18-Apr	Richmond Trophy	Goodwood, Gt. Britain	Reg Parnell	GBR	Maserati 4CLT/48	0h 17m 22.40s	133.399	82.890
47	24-Apr	Paris GP	Montlhéry	Philippe Étancelin	FRA	Talbot-Lago T26C	2h 05m 31.80s	149.862	93.120
48	28-Apr	Jersey Road Race	St. Helier	Bob Gerard	GBR	ERA B-Type	2h 16m 58.60s	124.080	77.100
49	07-May	Roussillon GP	Perpignan, France	Juan Manuel Fangio	ARG	Maserati 4CLT/48	2h 33m 16.70s	99.361	61.740
50	**14-May**	**BRITISH GP**	**SILVERSTONE**	**TOULO DE GRAFFENRIED**	**SUI**	**MASERATI 4CLT/48**	**3h 52m 50.20s**	**124.418**	**77.310**

Race	Date	Event	Circuit	Winner	Nat.	Car	Time	Kph	Mph
51	22-May	Marseille GP	Parc Borely, France	Juan Manuel Fangio	ARG	Simca-Gordini T15	1h 18m 33.00s	100.825	62.650
52	22-May	Ostschweiz GP	Erlen, Switzerland	Toulo de Graffenried	SUI	Maserati 4CL	1h 19m 29.80s	105.670	65.660
53	26-May	British Empire Trophy	Douglas, IoM	Bob Gerard	GBR	ERA B-Type	1h 57m 56.00s	114.360	71.060
54	05-Jun	GP des Frontières	Chimay, Belgium	Guy Mairesse	FRA	Talbot-Lago T26C	1h 10m 10.00s	139.417	86.630
55	**19-Jun**	**BELGIAN GP**	**SPA-FRANCORCHAMPS**	**LOUIS ROSIER**	**FRA**	**TALBOT-LAGO T26C**	**3h 15m 17.70s**	**156.026**	**96.950**
56	**03-Jul**	**SWISS GP**	**BREMGARTEN**	**ALBERTO ASCARI**	**ITA**	**FERRARI 125**	**1h 59m 24.60s**	**146.064**	**90.760**
57	10-Jul	Albi GP	des Planques, France	Juan Manuel Fangio	ARG	Maserati 4CLT/48	1h 54m 38.60s	158.021	98.190
58	**17-Jul**	**FRENCH GP**	**REIMS-GUEUX**	**LOUIS CHIRON**	**FRA**	**TALBOT-LAGO T26C**	**3h 02m 33.70s**	**160.870**	**99.960**
59	31-Jul	Zandvoort GP	Zandvoort, Holland	Luigi Villoresi	ITA	Ferrari 125	1h 21m 06.90s	124.113	77.120
60	20-Aug	International Trophy	Silverstone, Gt. Britain	Alberto Ascari	ITA	Ferrari 125	0h 59m 42.60s	145.549	90.440
61	27-Aug	Lausanne GP	Lausanne, Switzerland	Nino Farina	ITA	Maserati 4CLT/48	2h 44m 27.30s	105.911	65.810
62	**11-Sep**	**ITALIAN GP**	**MONZA**	**ALBERTO ASCARI**	**ITA**	**FERRARI 125**	**2h 58m 53.60s**	**169.045**	**105.040**
63	17-Sep	Goodwood Trophy	Goodwood, Gt. Britain	Reg Parnell	GBR	Maserati 4CLT/48	0h 16m 39.60s	139.096	86.430
64	25-Sep	Czechavlovakian GP	Masarykring, Brno	Peter Whitehead	GBR	Ferrari 125	2h 48m 41.00s	126.688	78.720
65	09-Oct	GP du Salon	Montlhéry, Paris	Raymond Sommer	FRA	Talbot-Lago T26C	2h 42m 18.00s	148.671	92.380

BOLD = GRANDE ÉPREUVE

1950

Race	Date	Event	Circuit	Winner	Nat.	Car	Time	Kph	Mph
66	10-Apr	Pau GP	Pau, France	Juan Manuel Fangio	ARG	Maserati 4CLT/48	3h 14m 20.00s	93.439	58.060
67	10-Apr	Richmond Trophy	Goodwood, Gt. Britain	Reg Parnell	GBR	Maserati 4CLT/48	0h 20m 14.40s	125.947	78.260
68	16-Apr	San Remo GP	Ospedaletti, Italy	Juan Manuel Fangio	ARG	Alfa Romeo 158	3h 10m 08.40s	95.901	59.590
69	30-Apr	Paris GP	Montlhéry	Georges Grignard	FRA	Talbot-Lago T26C	2h 05m 38.80s	150.264	93.370
70	15-Jun	British Empire Trophy	Douglas, IoM	Bob Gerard	GBR	ERA B-Type	1h 59m 36.80s	112.767	70.070
71	09-Jul	Bari GP	Bari, Italy	Nino Farina	ITA	Alfa Romeo 158	2h 34m 29.60s	124.660	77.460
72	13-Jul	Jersey Road Race	St. Helier	Peter Whitehead	GBR	Ferrari 125	1h 56m 02.60s	146.354	90.940
73	16-Jul	Albi GP	des Planques, France	Louis Rosier	FRA	Talbot-Lago T26C	1h 53m 08.60s	160.403	99.670
74	23-Jul	Dutch GP	Zandvoort	Louis Rosier	FRA	Talbot-Lago T26C-DA	3h 03m 36.30s	123.308	76.620
75	30-Jul	GP des Nations	Genèva, Switzerland	Juan Manuel Fangio	ARG	Alfa Romeo 158	2h 07m 55.00s	127.589	79.280
76	07-Aug	Nottingham Trophy	Gamston	David Hampshire	GBR	Maserati 4CLT/48	0h 25m 21.40s	146.611	91.100
77	12-Aug	Ulster Trophy	Dunrod, N. Ireland	Peter Whitehead	GBR	Ferrari 125	1h 19m 09.00s	135.700	84.320
78	15-Aug	Pescara GP	Pescara, Italy	Juan Manuel Fangio	ARG	Alfa Romeo 158	3h 02m 51.40s	136.231	84.650
79	26-Aug	International Trophy	Silverstone, Gt. Britain	Nino Farina	ITA	Alfa Romeo 158	1h 07m 17.00s	145.098	90.160
80	30-Sep	Goodwood Trophy	Goodwood, Gt. Britain	Reg Parnell	GBR	BRM P15	0h 20m 58.40s	132.739	82.480
81	29-Oct	Penya Rhin GP	Pedralbes, Spain	Alberto Ascari	ITA	Ferrari 375	2h 05m 14.80s	149.701	93.020

1951

Race	Date	Event	Circuit	Winner	Nat.	Car	Time	Kph	Mph
82	11-Mar	Syracuse GP	Syracuse, Sicily	Luigi Villoresi	ITA	Ferrari 375	2h 57m 31.60s	146.000	90.720
83	26-Mar	Pau GP	Pau, France	Luigi Villoresi	ITA	Ferrari 375	3h 17m 39.90s	82.801	51.450
84	26-Mar	Richmond Trophy	Goodwood, Gt. Britain	'B.Bira'	THI	Maserati 4CLT/48	0h 19m 44.00s	140.930	87.570
85	22-Apr	San Remo GP	Ospedaletti, Italy	Alberto Ascari	ITA	Ferrari 375	2h 57m 08.20s	101.694	63.190
86	29-Apr	Bordeaux GP	Bordeaux, France	Louis Rosier	FRA	Talbot-Lago T26C-DA	3h 07m 11.30s	96.899	60.210
87	05-May	International Trophy	Silverstone, Gt. Britain	Reg Parnell	GBR	Ferrari 375 'Thin Wall Sp.'	0h 16m 48.00s	99.602	61.890

Race	Date	Event	Circuit	Winner	Nat.	Car	Time	Kph	Mph
88	20-May	Paris GP	Bois de Boulogne	Nino Farina	ITA	Maserati 4CLT/48	2h 53m 12.50s	108.357	67.330
89	02-Jun	Ulster Trophy	Dunrod, N. Ireland	Nino Farina	ITA	Alfa Romeo 159	2h 11m 21.80s	147.191	91.460
90	21-Jul	Scottish GP	Winfield	Philip Fotheringham-Parker	GBR	Maserati 4CLT/48	1h 19m 27.00s	121.538	75.520
91	22-Jul	Dutch GP	Zandvoort	Louis Rosier	FRA	Talbot-Lago T26C-DA	2h 59m 19.40s	126.253	78.450
92	05-Aug	Albi GP	des Planques, France	Maurice Trintignant	FRA	Simca-Gordini T15	1h 51m 23.10s	163.944	101.870
93	15-Aug	Pescara GP	Pescara, Italy	Froilan Gonzalez	ARG	Ferrari 375	2h 14m 59.80s	137.695	85.560
94	02-Sep	Bari GP	Bari, Italy	Juan Manuel Fangio	ARG	Alfa Romeo 159	2h 39m 58.30s	135.008	83.890
95	29-Sep	Goodwood Trophy	Goodwood, Gt. Britain	Nino Farina	ITA	Alfa Romeo 159	0h 22m 31.20s	153.065	95.110
1952									
96	06-Apr	Valentino GP	Valentino Park, Turin	Luigi Villoresi	ITA	Ferrari 375	2h 06m 25.30s	119.494	74.250
97	14-Apr	Richmond Trophy	Goodwood, Gt. Britain	Froilan Gonzalez	ARG	Ferrari 375 'Thin Wall Sp.'	0h 19m 35.00s	141.992	88.230
98	11-May	Eläintarha-ajot	Djurgården, Helsinki	Roger Laurent	BEL	Talbot-Lago T26C	0h 30m 19.50s	98.926	61.47
99	01-Jun	Albi GP	des Planques, France	Louis Rosier	FRA	Ferrari 375	1h 50m 39.00s	163.992	101.900
100	07-Jun	Ulster Trophy	Dunrod, N. Ireland	Piero Taruffi	ITA	Ferrari 375	3h 05m 47.00s	131.049	81.430
101	02-Aug	Daily Mail Trophy	Boreham, Gt. Britain	Luigi Villoresi	ITA	Ferrari 375	2h 25m 36.00s	133.302	82.830
102	14-Sep	Skarpnacksloppet	Skarpnack, Sweden	Gunnar Carlsson	SWE	Mercury Special-Ford	0h 26m 49.40s	95.064	59.070
1953									
103	10-May	Eläintarha-ajot	Djurgården, Helsinki	Rodney Nuckey	GBR	Cooper-Bristol T23	0h 28m 55.20s	103.706	64.440
104	31-May	Albi GP	des Planques, France	Louis Rosier	FRA	Ferrari 375	0h 56m 36.80s	169.705	105.450
105	28-Jun	Rouen GP	Rouen-les-Essarts, France	Nino Farina	ITA	Ferrari 625	2h 15m 05.80s	135.909	84.450
106	13-Sep	Skarpnacksloppet	Skarpnack, Sweden	Erik Lundgren	SWE	Ford Special	0h 15m 41.90s	97.430	60.540
1954									
107	11-Apr	Syracuse GP	Syracuse, Sicily	Nino Farina	ITA	Ferrari 625	2h 51m 57.20s	153.403	95.320
108	19-Apr	Pau GP	Pau, France	Jean Behra	FRA	Gordini T16	3h 00m 02.20s	100.777	62.620
109	19-Apr	Lavant Cup	Goodwood, Gt. Britain	Reg Parnell	GBR	Ferrari 625	0h 11m 21.40s	142.861	88.770
110	09-May	Bordeaux GP	Bordeaux, France	Froilan Gonzalez	ARG	Ferrari 625	3h 05m 55.10s	97.558	60.620
111	15-May	International Trophy	Silverstone, Gt. Britain	Froilan Gonzalez	ARG	Ferrari 625	1h 06m 15.00s	149.315	92.780
112	22-May	Bari GP	Bari, Italy	Froilan Gonzalez	ARG	Ferrari 625	2h 21m 08.40s	141.300	87.800
113	05-Jun	Curtis Trophy	Snetterton, Gt. Britain	Roy Salvadori	GBR	Maserati 250F	0h 18m 26.40s	141.381	87.850
114	06-Jun	Rome GP	Castelfusano, Italy	Onofre Marimon	ARG	Maserati 250F	2h 18m 48.60s	170.912	106.200
115	06-Jun	GP des Frontières	Chimay, Belgium	'B.Bira'	THI	Maserati A6GCM	1h 22m 15.00s	158.021	98.190
116	07-Jun	BARC Formula 1 Race	Goodwood, Gt. Britain	Reg Parnell	GBR	Ferrari 625	0h 08m 13.20s	140.979	87.600
117	07-Jun	Cornwall MRC F1 Race	Davidstow, Gt. Britain	John Riseley-Prichard	GBR	Connaught-Lea Francis A-type	0h 29m 54.90s	119.429	74.210
118	19-Jun	Crystal Palace Trophy	Crystal Palace, London	Reg Parnell	GBR	Ferrari 625	0h 11m 26.60s	117.386	72.940
119	11-Jul	Rouen GP	Rouen-les-Essarts, France	Maurice Trintignant	FRA	Ferrari 625	3h 40m 34.50s	132.562	82.370
120	25-Jul	Caen GP	Caen, France	Maurice Trintignant	FRA	Ferrari 625	1h 29m 01.10s	142.491	88.540
121	02-Aug	August Trophy	Crystal Palace, London	Reg Parnell	GBR	Ferrari 625	0h 11m 18.80s	118.786	73.810
122	02-Aug	Cornwall MRC F1 Race	Davidstow, Gt. Britain	John Coombs	GBR	Lotus-Lea Francis 8	0h 28m 57.80s	123.356	76.650
123	07-Aug	International Gold Cup	Oulton Park, Gt. Britain	Stirling Moss	GBR	Maserati 250F	1h 11m 27.20s	134.348	83.480
124	14-Aug	RedeX Trophy	Snetterton, Gt. Britain	Reg Parnell	GBR	Ferrari 625	1h 13m 16.80s	142.298	88.420
125	15-Aug	Pescara GP	Pescara, Italy	Luigi Musso	ITA	Maserati 250F	2h 55m 54.51s	139.578	86.730
126	28-Aug	Joe Fry Memorial Trophy	Castle Combe, Gt. Britain	Horace Gould	GBR	Cooper-Bristol T23	0h 19m 49.00s	134.477	83.560
127	12-Sep	Circuit de Cadours	Cadours, France	Jean Behra	FRA	Gordini T16	0h 58m 49.80s	122.825	76.320

Race	Date	Event	Circuit	Winner	Nat.	Car	Time	Kph	Mph
128	19-Sep	Berlin GP	AVUS, Germany	Karl Kling	GER	Mercedes-Benz W196 'Str'	2h 19m 59.80s	213.496	132.660
129	25-Sep	Goodwood Trophy	Goodwood, Gt. Britain	Stirling Moss	GBR	Maserati 250F	0h 33m 03.20s	147.223	91.480
130	02-Oct	Daily Telegraph Trophy	Aintree, Gt. Britain	Stirling Moss	GBR	Maserati 250F	0h 35m 49.00s	137.486	85.430

1955

Race	Date	Event	Circuit	Winner	Nat.	Car	Time	Kph	Mph
131	27-Mar	Valentino GP	Valentino Park, Turin	Alberto Ascari	ITA	Lancia D50	2h 40m 21.20s	141.397	87.860
132	11-Apr	Pau GP	Pau, France	Jean Behra	FRA	Maserati 250F	3h 02m 09.60s	100.327	62.340
133	11-Apr	Glover Trophy	Goodwood, Gt. Britain	Roy Salvadori	GBR	Maserati 250F	0h 33m 53.00s	143.650	89.260
134	24-Apr	Bordeaux GP	Bordeaux, France	Jean Behra	FRA	Maserati 250F	2h 54m 12.60s	104.720	65.070
135	07-May	International Trophy	Silverstone, Gt. Britain	Peter Collins	GBR	Maserati 250F	1h 49m 50.00s	154.400	95.940
136	08-May	Naples GP	Posillipo, Italy	Alberto Ascari	ITA	Lancia D50	2h 13m 03.60s	111.576	69.330
137	29-May	Albi GP	Circuit Raymond Sommer, France	Andre Simon	FRA	Maserati 250F	2h 23m 22.10s	131.419	81.660
138	29-May	Curtis Trophy	Snetterton, Gt. Britain	Roy Salvadori	GBR	Maserati 250F	0h 18m 11.80s	143.280	89.030
139	30-May	Cornwall MRC F1 Race	Davidstow, Gt. Britain	Leslie Marr	GBR	Connaught-Alta B-type	0h 25m 57.20s	137.663	85.540
140	30-Jul	London Trophy	Crystal Palace, Gt. Britain	Mike Hawthorn	GBR	Maserati 250F	0h 16m 10.00s	124.402	77.300
141	06-Aug	Daily Record Trophy	Charterhall, Gt. Britain	Bob Gerard	GBR	Maserati 250F	0h 28m 49.00s	134.042	83.290
142	13-Aug	RedeX Trophy	Snetterton, Gt. Britain	Harry Schell	USA	Vanwall VW2	0h 50m 07.40s	130.035	80.800
143	03-Sep	Daily Telegraph Trophy	Aintree, Gt. Britain	Roy Salvadori	GBR	Maserati 250F	0h 36m 33.00s	134.734	83.720
144	07-Aug	International Gold Cup	Oulton Park, Gt. Britain	Stirling Moss	GBR	Maserati 250F	1h 44m 05.40s	138.307	85.940
145	01-Oct	Avon Trophy	Castle Combe, Gt. Britain	Harry Schell	USA	Vanwall VW2	1h 10m 32.80s	138.516	86.070
146	23-Oct	Syracuse GP	Syracuse, Sicily	Tony Brooks	GBR	Connaught-Alta B-type	2h 24m 55.70s	159.406	99.050

1956

Race	Date	Event	Circuit	Winner	Nat.	Car	Time	Kph	Mph
147	5-Feb	Buenos Aires City GP	Mendoza, Argentina	Juan Manuel Fangio	ARG	Lancia-Ferrari D50	1h 52m 38.90s	133.736	83.100
148	2-Apr	Glover Trophy	Goodwood, Gt. Britain	Stirling Moss	GBR	Maserati 250F	0h 48m 50.40s	151.842	94.350
149	15-Apr	Syracuse GP	Syracuse, Sicily	Juan Manuel Fangio	ARG	Lancia-Ferrari D50	2h 48m 59.90s	156.219	97.070
150	21-Apr	Aintree 200	Liverpool, Gt. Britain	Stirling Moss	GBR	Maserati 250F	2h 23m 06.40s	132.352	82.240
151	5-May	International Trophy	Silverstone, Gt. Britain	Stirling Moss	GBR	Vanwall VW2	1h 44m 53.00s	161.691	100.470
152	6-May	Naples GP	Posillipo, Italy	Robert Manzon	FRA	Gordini T16	2h 20m 43.80s	104.817	65.130
153	24-Jun	Aintree 100	Liverpool, Gt. Britain	Horace Gould	GBR	Maserati 250F	1h 13m 39.80s	133.704	83.080
154	22-Jul	Vanwall Trophy	Snetterton, Gt. Britain	Roy Salvadori	GBR	Maserati 250F	0h 26m 24.80s	148.607	92.340
155	26-Aug	Caen GP	Caen, France	Harry Schell	USA	Maserati 250F	1h 54m 19.40s	128.925	80.110
156	14-Oct	BRSCC Formula 1 Race	Brands Hatch, Gt. Britain	Archie Scott-Brown	GBR	Connaught-Alta B-type	0h 15m 07.60s	118.737	73.780

1957

Race	Date	Event	Circuit	Winner	Nat.	Car	Time	Kph	Mph
157	27-Jan	Buenos Aires City GP	Buenos Aires Autodromo, Argentina	Juan Manuel Fangio	ARG	Maserati 250F	2h 22m 30.30s	119.172	74.050
158	07-Apr	Syracuse GP	Syracuse, Sicily	Peter Collins	GBR	Lancia-Ferrari D50	2h 40m 11.90s	164.797	102.400
159	22-Apr	Pau GP	Pau, France	Jean Behra	FRA	Maserati 250F	3h 00m 13.70s	101.067	62.800
160	22-Apr	Glover Trophy	Goodwood, Gt. Britain	Stuart Lewis-Evans	GBR	Connaught-Alta B-type	0h 50m 49.80s	145.903	90.660
161	28-Apr	Naples GP	Posillipo, Italy	Peter Collins	GBR	Lancia-Ferrari D50	2h 10m 31.20s	113.089	70.270
162	14-Jul	Reims GP	Reims-Gueux	Luigi Musso	ITA	Lancia-Ferrari D50	2h 33m 02.60s	198.593	123.400
163	28-Jul	Caen GP	Caen, France	Jean Behra	FRA	BRM P25	2h 01m 55.00s	149.379	92.820

Race	Date	Event	Circuit	Winner	Nat.	Car	Time	Kph	Mph
164	14-Sep	International Trophy	Silverstone, Gt. Britain	Jean Behra	FRA	BRM P25	1h 01m 30.00s	160.854	99.950
165	22-Sep	Modena GP	Modena, Italy	Jean Behra	FRA	Maserati 250F	1h 24m 27.90s	130.502	81.090
166	27-Oct	Moroccan GP	Ain Diab, Casablanca	Jean Behra	FRA	Maserati 250F	2h 18m 23.00s	181.293	112.650
1958									
167	07-Apr	Glover Trophy	Goodwood, Gt. Britain	Mike Hawthorn	GBR	Ferrari Dino 246	1h 03m 44.40s	152.823	94.960
168	13-Apr	Syracuse GP	Syracuse, Sicily	Luigi Musso	ITA	Ferrari Dino 246	2h 02m 44.50s	161.321	100.240
169	19-Apr	Aintree 200	Liverpool, Gt. Britain	Stirling Moss	GBR	Cooper-Climax T45	2h 20m 47.00s	137.856	85.660
170	03-May	International Trophy	Silverstone, Gt. Britain	Peter Collins	GBR	Ferrari Dino 246	1h 26m 14.60s	163.863	101.820
171	20-Jul	Caen GP	Caen, France	Stirling Moss	GBR	Cooper-Climax T45	2h 00m 09.70s	151.166	93.930
1959									
172	30-Mar	Glover Trophy	Goodwood, Gt. Britain	Stirling Moss	GBR	Cooper-Climax T51	1h 06m 58.00s	145.340	90.310
173	18-Apr	Aintree 200	Liverpool, Gt. Britain	Jean Behra	FRA	Ferrari Dino 246	2h 15m 52.00s	142.845	88.760
174	02-May	International Trophy	Silverstone, Gt. Britain	Jack Brabham	AUS	Cooper-Climax T51	1h 25m 28.60s	165.328	102.730
175	07-Aug	International Gold Cup	Oulton Park, Gt. Britain	Stirling Moss	GBR	Cooper-Climax T51	1h 34m 37.20s	154.964	96.290
176	10-Oct	Silver City Trophy	Snetterton, Gt. Britain	Ron Flockhart	GBR	BRM P25	0h 39m 58.00s	163.686	101.710
1960									
177	18-Apr	Glover Trophy	Goodwood, Gt. Britain	Innes Ireland	GBR	Lotus-Climax 18	1h 00m 14.80s	161.562	100.390
178	14-May	International Trophy	Silverstone, Gt. Britain	Innes Ireland	GBR	Lotus-Climax 18	1h 20m 41.10s	175.129	108.820
179	01-Aug	Silver City Trophy	Brands Hatch, Gt. Britain	Jack Brabham	AUS	Cooper-Climax T53	1h 25m 36.60s	149.444	92.860
180	17-Sep	Lombank Trophy	Snetterton, Gt. Britain	Innes Ireland	GBR	Lotus-Climax 18	0h 58m 33.80s	165.328	102.730
181	24-Sep	International Gold Cup	Oulton Park, Gt. Britain	Stirling Moss	GBR	Lotus-Climax 18	1h 45m 54.00s	151.037	93.850
1961									
182	26-Mar	Lombank Trophy	Snetterton, Gt. Britain	John Surtees	GBR	Cooper-Climax T53	1h 00m 35.20s	155.430	96.580
183	03-Apr	Glover Trophy	Goodwood, Gt. Britain	John Surtees	GBR	Cooper-Climax T53	1h 03m 10.00s	154.111	95.760
184	03-Apr	Pau GP	Pau, France	Jim Clark	GBR	Lotus-Climax 18	2h 42m 00.30s	102.161	63.480
185	09-Apr	Brussels GP	Heysel, Belgium	Jack Brabham	AUS	Cooper-Climax T53	2h 19m 21.80s	129.343	80.370
186	16-Apr	Vienna GP	Aspern, Austria	Stirling Moss	GBR	Lotus-Climax 18	1h 10m 01.60s	128.989	80.150
187	22-Apr	Aintree 200	Liverpool, Gt. Britain	Jack Brabham	AUS	Cooper-Climax T55	1h 55m 17.20s	125.625	78.060
188	25-Apr	Syracuse GP	Syracuse, Sicily	Giancarlo Baghetti	ITA	Ferrari 156	1h 50m 08.02s	167.983	104.380
189	14-May	Naples GP	Posillipo, Italy	Giancarlo Baghetti	ITA	Ferrari 156	1h 22m 46.50s	108.872	67.650
190	22-May	London Trophy	Crystal Palace, Gt. Britain	Roy Salvadori	GBR	Cooper-Climax T53	0h 37m 22.80s	132.851	82.550
191	03-Jun	Silver City Trophy	Brands Hatch, Gt. Britain	Stirling Moss	GBR	Lotus-Climax 18/21	2h 11m 40.60s	147.706	91.780
192	23-Jul	Solitude GP	Stuttgart, Germany	Innes Ireland	GBR	Lotus-Climax 21	1h 41m 04.60s	169.400	105.260
193	20-Aug	Kannonloppet	Karlskoga, Sweden	Stirling Moss	GBR	Lotus-Climax 18/21	0h 46m 16.80s	111.463	69.260
194	26-Aug	Danish GP	Roskildering, Copenhagen	Stirling Moss	GBR	Lotus-Climax 18/21	0h 59m 28.50s	96.850	60.180
195	03-Sep	Modena GP	Modena, Italy	Stirling Moss	GBR	Lotus-Climax 18/21	1h 40m 08.10s	141.783	88.100
196	17-Sep	Flugplatzrennen	Zeltweg, Austria	Innes Ireland	GBR	Lotus-Climax 21	1h 44m 22.20s	147.175	91.450
197	23-Sep	International Gold Cup	Oulton Park, Gt. Britain	Stirling Moss	GBR	Ferguson-Climax P99	1h 51m 53.80s	142.958	88.830
198	01-Oct	Lewis-Evans Trophy	Brands Hatch, Gt. Britain	Tony Marsh	GBR	BRM-Climax P48	0h 52m 19.80s	146.692	91.150
199	10-Oct	Coppa Italia	Vallelunga, Rome	Giancarlo Baghetti	ITA	Porsche 718	1h 00m 53.90s	106.394	66.110

Race	Date	Event	Circuit	Winner	Nat.	Car	Time	Kph	Mph
200	09-Dec	Rand GP	Kyalami, South Africa	Jim Clark	GBR	Lotus-Climax 21	2h 06m 26.07s	145.726	90.550
201	17-Dec	Natal GP	Westmead, South Africa	Jim Clark	GBR	Lotus-Climax 21	2h 13m 58.40s	144.181	89.590
202	26-Dec	South African GP	East London	Jim Clark	GBR	Lotus-Climax 21	2h 06m 49.20s	148.382	92.200
1962									
203	02-Jan	Cape GP	Killarney, South Africa	Trevor Taylor	GBR	Lotus-Climax 21	1h 30m 54.00s	131.162	81.500
204	01-Apr	Brussels GP	Heysel, Belgium	Willy Mairesse	BEL	Ferrari 156	2h 18m 37.10s	130.115	80.850
205	14-Apr	Lombank Trophy	Snetterton, Gt. Britain	Jim Clark	GBR	Lotus-Climax 24	1h 20m 25.60s	162.689	101.090
206	23-Apr	Lavant Cup	Goodwood, Gt. Britain	Bruce McLaren	NZL	Cooper-Climax T55	0h 30m 31.80s	159.406	99.050
207	23-Apr	Glover Trophy	Goodwood, Gt. Britain	Graham Hill	GBR	BRM P57	0h 58m 55.20s	165.199	102.650
208	23-Apr	Pau GP	Pau, France	Maurice Trintignant	FRA	Lotus-Climax 18/21	2h 39m 35.50s	103.771	64.480
209	28-Apr	Aintree 200	Liverpool, Gt. Britain	Jim Clark	GBR	Lotus-Climax 24	1h 37m 08.20s	149.106	92.650
210	12-May	International Trophy	Silverstone, Gt. Britain	Graham Hill	GBR	BRM P57	1h 31m 34.20s	160.500	99.730
211	20-May	Naples GP	Posillipo, Italy	Willy Mairesse	BEL	Ferrari 156	1h 19m 36.10s	113.153	70.310
212	11-Jun	International 2000 Guineas	Mallory Park, Gt. Britain	John Surtees	GBR	Lola-Climax Mk4	1h 05m 03.60s	150.281	93.380
213	11-Jun	Crystal Palace Trophy	London, Gt. Britain	Innes Ireland	GBR	Lotus-BRM 24	0h 34m 46.40s	138.951	86.340
214	01-Jul	Reims GP	Reims-Gueux	Bruce McLaren	NZL	Cooper-Climax T60	2h 02m 30.20s	203.292	126.320
215	15-Jul	Solitude GP	Stuttgart, Germany	Dan Gurney	USA	Porsche 804	1h 45m 37.20s	162.093	100.720
216	12-Aug	Kannonloppet	Karlskoga, Sweden	Masten Gregory	USA	Lotus-BRM 24	0h 42m 51.30s	125.963	78.270
217	19-Aug	Mediterranean GP	Enna, Sicily	Lorenzo Bandini	ITA	Ferrari 156	1h 09m 25.80s	207.573	128.980
218	25-Aug	Danish GP	Roskildering, Copenhagen	Jack Brabham	AUS	Lotus-Climax 24	0h 59m 14.10s	96.496	59.960
219	01-Sep	International Gold Cup	Oulton Park, Gt. Britain	Jim Clark	GBR	Lotus-Climax 25	2h 03m 46.60s	157.233	97.700
220	04-Nov	Mexican GP	Magdalena Mixhuca, Mexico City	Trevor Taylor/Jim Clark	GBR	Lotus-Climax 25	2h 03m 50.90s	145.340	90.310
221	15-Dec	Rand GP	Kyalami, South Africa	Jim Clark	GBR	Lotus-Climax 25	1h 20m 47.42s	152.035	94.470
222	22-Dec	Natal GP	Westmead, South Africa	Trevor Taylor	GBR	Lotus-Climax 25	0h 48m 08.67s	148.816	92.470
1963									
223	30-Mar	Lombank Trophy	Snetterton, Gt. Britain	Graham Hill	GBR	BRM P57	1h 25m 09.60s	153.644	95.470
224	15-Apr	Glover Trophy	Goodwood, Gt. Britain	Innes Ireland	GBR	Lotus-BRM 24	0h 59m 02.40s	164.861	102.440
225	15-Apr	Pau GP	Pau, France	Jim Clark	GBR	Lotus-Climax 25	2h 46m 59.70s	99.168	61.620
226	21-Apr	Imola GP	Imola, Italy	Jim Clark	GBR	Lotus-Climax 25	1h 34m 07.40s	159.904	99.360
227	25-Apr	Syracuse GP	Syracuse, Sicily	Jo Siffert	SUI	Lotus-BRM 24	2h 06m 25.54s	146.080	90.770
228	27-Apr	Aintree 200	Liverpool, Gt. Britain	Graham Hill	GBR	BRM P57	1h 35m 20.80s	151.906	94.390
229	11-May	International Trophy	Silverstone, Gt. Britain	Jim Clark	GBR	Lotus-Climax 25	1h 24m 27.60s	174.002	108.120
230	19-May	Rome GP	Vallelunga, Italy	Bob Anderson	GBR	Lola-Climax Mk4	2h 02m 32.20s	127.042	78.940
231	28-Jul	Solitude GP	Stuttgart, Germany	Jack Brabham	AUS	Brabham-Climax BT3	1h 40m 06.90s	171.073	106.300
232	11-Aug	Kannonloppet	Karlskoga, Sweden	Jim Clark	GBR	Lotus-Climax 25	1h 04m 26.70s	111.656	69.380
233	18-Aug	Mediterranean GP	Enna, Sicily	John Surtees	GBR	Ferrari 156/63	1h 18m 00.80s	221.832	137.840
234	17-Sep	Austrian GP	Zeltweg	Jack Brabham	AUS	Brabham-Climax BT3	1h 09m 06.30s	155.060	96.350
235	21-Sep	International Gold Cup	Oulton Park, Gt. Britain	Jim Clark	GBR	Lotus-Climax 25	2h 02m 58.60s	158.263	98.340
236	14-Dec	Rand GP	Kyalami, South Africa	John Surtees	GBR	Ferrari 156 Aero	1h 20m 11.00s	153.210	95.200
1964									
237	14-Mar	Daily Mirror Trophy	Snetterton, Gt. Britain	Innes Ireland	GBR	BRP-BRM 1	1h 12m 53.40s	125.658	78.080
238	30-Mar	News of the World Trophy	Goodwood, Gt. Britain	Jim Clark	GBR	Lotus-Climax 25	0h 57m 39.00s	168.836	104.910
239	12-Apr	Syracuse GP	Syracuse, Sicily	John Surtees	GBR	Ferrari 158	1h 19m 51.80s	165.167	102.630
240	18-Apr	Aintree 200	Liverpool, Gt. Britain	Jack Brabham	AUS	Brabham-Climax BT7	2h 09m 02.60s	150.409	93.460
241	02-May	International Trophy	Silverstone, Gt. Britain	Jack Brabham	AUS	Brabham-Climax BT7	1h 22m 45.20s	177.591	110.350
242	19-Jul	Solitude GP	Stuttgart, Germany	Jim Clark	GBR	Lotus-Climax 33	1h 33m 02.20s	147.255	91.500

Race	Date	Event	Circuit	Winner	Nat.	Car	Time	Kph	Mph
243	16-Aug	Mediterranean GP	Enna, Sicily	Jo Siffert	SUI	Brabham-BRM BT11	1h 17m 59.30s	221.896	137.880
244	12-Dec	Rand GP	Kyalami, South Africa	Graham Hill	GBR	Brabham-BRM BT11	1h 22m 48.70s	148.382	92.200
1965									
245	13-Mar	Race of Champions	Brands Hatch, Gt. Britain	Mike Spence	GBR	Lotus-Climax 33	2h 11m 42.00s	156.428	97.200
246	04-Apr	Syracuse GP	Syracuse, Sicily	Jim Clark	GBR	Lotus-Climax 33	1h 43m 47.00s	177.993	110.600
247	19-Apr	Sunday Mirror Trophy	Goodwood, Gt. Britain	Jim Clark	GBR	Lotus-Climax 25	0h 57m 33.80s	169.094	105.070
248	15-May	International Trophy	Silverstone, Gt. Britain	Jackie Stewart	GBR	BRM P261	1h 21m 47.00s	179.699	111.660
249	15-Aug	Mediterranean GP	Enna-Pergusal, Sicily	Jo Siffert	SUI	Brabham-BRM BT11	1h 17m 05.20s	224.053	139.220
250	04-Dec	Rand GP	Kyalami, South Africa	Jack Brabham	AUS	Brabham-Climax BT11	1h 18m 11.20s	157.217	97.690
1966									
251	01-Jan	South African GP	East London	Mike Spence	GBR	Lotus-Climax 33	1h 29m 39.40s	157.313	97.750
252	01-May	Syracuse GP	Syracuse, Sicily	John Surtees	GBR	Ferrari 312	1h 40m 08.30s	184.543	114.670
253	14-May	International Trophy	Silverstone, Gt. Britain	Jack Brabham	AUS	Brabham-Repco BT19	0h 52m 45.60s	186.780	116.060
254	17-Sep	International Gold Cup	Oulton Park, Gt. Britain	Jack Brabham	AUS	Brabham-Repco BT19	1h 06m 14.20s	160.999	100.040
1967									
255	13-Mar	Race of Champions	Brands Hatch, Gt. Britain	Dan Gurney	USA	Eagle-Weslake T1G	1h 04m 30.60s	158.778	98.660
256	15-Apr	Spring Trophy	Oulton Park, Gt. Britain	Jack Brabham	AUS	Brabham-Repco BT20	0h 47m 21.40s	168.885	104.940
257	29-May	International Trophy	Silverstone, Gt. Britain	Mike Parkes	GBR	Ferrari 312	1h 19m 39.20s	184.511	114.650
258	21-May	Syracuse GP	Syracuse, Sicily	Mike Parkes/ Ludovico Scarfiotti^	GBR/ ITA	Ferrari 312/ Ferrari 312	1h 40m 58.40s	183.031	113.730
259	16-Sep	International Gold Cup	Oulton Park, Gt. Britain	Jack Brabham	AUS	Brabham-Repco BT24	1h 10m 07.00s	171.186	106.370
260	12-Nov	Spanish GP	Jarama, Madrid	Jim Clark	GBR	Lotus-Ford 49	1h 31m 10.40s	134.541	83.600
^ Dead heat									
1968									
261	17-Mar	Race of Champions	Brands Hatch, Gt. Britain	Bruce McLaren	NZL	McLaren-Ford M7A	1h 18m 53.40s	162.174	100.770
262	25-Apr	International Trophy	Silverstone, Gt. Britain	Denny Hulme	NZL	McLaren-Ford M7A	1h 14m 44.80s	196.614	122.170
263	17-Aug	International Gold Cup	Oulton Park, Gt. Britain	Jackie Stewart	GBR	Matra-Ford MS10	1h 00m 39.00s	175.885	109.290
1969									
264	16-Mar	Race of Champions	Brands Hatch, Gt. Britain	Jackie Stewart	GBR	Matra-Ford MS80	1h 13m 10.40s	174.855	108.650
265	30-Mar	International Trophy	Silverstone, Gt. Britain	Jack Brabham	AUS	Brabham-Ford BT26A	1h 25m 20.80s	172.200	107.000
266	13-Apr	Madrid GP	Jarama, Spain	Keith Holland	GBR	Lola-Chevrolet T142*	1h 03m 29.80s	128.699	79.970
267	16-Aug	International Gold Cup	Oulton Park, Gt. Britain	Jacky Ickx	BEL	Brabham-Ford BT26A	1h 00m 28.60s	176.336	109.570
* F5000 Car									
1970									
268	22-Mar	Race of Champions	Brands Hatch, Gt. Britain	Jackie Stewart	GBR	March-Ford 701	1h 12m 51.80s	175.596	109.110
269	26-Apr	International Trophy	Silverstone, Gt. Britain	Chris Amon	NZL	March-Ford 701	1h 13m 32.20s	199.864	124.190
270	22-Aug	International Gold Cup	Oulton Park, Gt. Britain	John Surtees	GBR	Surtees-Ford TS7	0h 59m 48.20s	178.315	110.800
1971									
271	24-Jan	Argentinean GP	Buenos Aires	Chris Amon	NZL	Matra MS120	2h 08m 19.29s	159.442	99.060
272	21-Mar	Race of Champions	Brands Hatch, Gt. Britain	Clay Regazzoni	SUI	Ferrari 312B2	1h 13m 35.00s	173.874	108.040
273	28-Mar	Questor GP	Ontario Speedway, California	Mario Andretti	USA	Ferrari 312B	1h 51m 48.41s	176.545	109.700
274	15-Apr	Spring Trophy	Oulton Park, Gt. Britain	Pedro Rodriguez	MEX	BRM P160	0h 57m 33.40s	185.252	115.110
275	08-May	International Trophy	Silverstone, Gt. Britain	Graham Hill	GBR	Brabham-Ford BT34	1h 11m 03.20s	206.801	128.500

Race	Date	Event	Circuit	Winner	Nat.	Car	Time	Kph	Mph
276	13-Jun	Jochen Rindt Memorial Trophy	Hockenheim, Germany	Jacky Ickx	BEL	Ferrari 312B	1h 10m 11.70s	203.099	126.200
277	22-Aug	International Gold Cup	Oulton Park, Gt. Britain	John Surtees	GBR	Surtees-Ford TS9	0h 57m 38.60s	185.010	114.960
278	24-Oct	Championships Victory Race	Brands Hatch, Gt. Britain	Peter Gethin	GBR	BRM P160	0h 19m 54.40s	179.957	111.820
1972									
279	19-Mar	Race of Champions	Brands Hatch, Gt. Britain	Emerson Fittipaldi	BRA	Lotus-Ford 72D	0h 56m 40.60s	180.601	112.220
280	30-Mar	Brazilian GP	Interlagos, São Paulo	Carlos Reutemann	ARG	Brabham-Ford BT34	1h 37m 16.25s	181.711	112.910
281	23-Apr	International Trophy	Silverstone, Gt. Britain	Emerson Fittipaldi	BRA	Lotus-Ford 72D	0h 53m 17.80s	212.128	131.810
282	29-May	International Gold Cup	Oulton Park, Gt. Britain	Denny Hulme	NZL	McLaren-Ford M19A	0h 57m 15.60s	185.348	115.170
283	18-Jun	Republica Italia GP	Vallelunga, Rome	Emerson Fittipaldi	BRA	Lotus-Ford 72D	1h 37m 31.90s	157.474	97.850
284	22-Oct	John Player Challenge Trophy	Brands Hatch, Gt. Britain	Jean-Pierre Beltoise	FRA	BRM P180	0h 59m 47.80s	167.951	104.360
1973									
285	17-Mar	Race of Champions	Brands Hatch, Gt. Britain	Peter Gethin	GBR	Chevron-Chevrolet B24*	0h 57m 22.90s	177.575	110.340
286	08-Apr	International Trophy	Silverstone, Gt. Britain	Jackie Stewart	GBR	Tyrrell-Ford 006	0h 52m 53.20s	213.753	132.820
* F5000 Car									
1974									
287	03-Feb	Presidente Medici GP	Brasilia, Brazil	Emerson Fittipaldi	BRA	McLaren-Ford M23	1h 15m 22.75s	174.244	108.270
288	17-Mar	Race of Champions	Brands Hatch, Gt. Britain	Jacky Ickx	BEL	Lotus-Ford 72D	1h 03m 37.60s	160.870	99.960
289	07-Apr	International Trophy	Silverstone, Gt. Britain	James Hunt	GBR	Hesketh-Ford 308	0h 52m 35.40s	214.976	133.580
1975									
290	16-Mar	Race of Champions	Brands Hatch, Gt. Britain	Tom Pryce	GBR	Shadow-Ford DN5A	0h 55m 53.50s	183.127	113.790
291	13-Apr	International Trophy	Silverstone, Gt. Britain	Niki Lauda	AUT	Ferrari 312T	0h 52m 17.60s	216.183	134.330
292	24-Aug	Swiss GP	Dijon-Prenois, France	Clay Regazzoni	SUI	Ferrari 312T	1h 01m 25.34s	194.103	120.610
1976									
293	14-Mar	Race of Champions	Brands Hatch, Gt. Britain	James Hunt	GBR	McLaren-Ford M23	0h 58m 01.23s	173.745	107.960
294	11-Apr	International Trophy	Silverstone, Gt. Britain	James Hunt	GBR	McLaren-Ford M23	0h 53m 04.57s	213.367	132.580
1977									
295	20-Mar	Race of Champions	Brands Hatch, Gt. Britain	James Hunt	GBR	McLaren-Ford M23	0h 53m 54.35s	187.263	116.360
1978									
296	19-Mar	International Trophy	Silverstone, Gt. Britain	Keke Rosberg	FIN	Theodore-Ford TR1	1h 12m 49.02s	155.527	96.640
1979									
297	15-Apr	Race of Champions	Brands Hatch, Gt. Britain	Gilles Villeneuve	CAN	Ferrari 312T3	0h 53m 17.12s	189.452	117.720
298	16-Sep	Gran Premio di Dino Ferrari	Imola, Italy	Niki Lauda	AUT	Brabham-Alfa Romeo BT48	1h 03m 55.89s	188.792	117.310
1980									
299	01-Jun	Spanish GP	Jarama, Madrid	Alan Jones	AUS	Williams-Ford FW07B	1h 43m 14.076s	153.998	95.690
1981									
300	07-Feb	South African GP	Kyalami, Johannesburg	Carlos Reutemann	ARG	Williams-Ford FW07B	1h 44m 54.030s	180.745	112.310
1982									
No Non-championship Races									
1983									
301	10-Apr	Race of Champions	Brands Hatch, Gt. Britain	Keke Rosberg	FIN	Williams-Ford FW08C	0h 53m 15.253s	189.719	117.886

Formula 1: All the winners

DRIVERS

		All F1 victories 1946-2011	All champ F1 victories 1950-2011	All non-champ F1 victories 1946-1983	All F2 champ victories 1952-1953
1	Michael Schumacher	91	91		
2	Alain Prost	51	51		
3	Jim Clark*	44	25	19	
4	Ayrton Senna	41	41		
5	Juan Manuel Fangio**	36	23	13	1
6	Stirling Moss*	34	16	18	
7	Jackie Stewart	32	27	5	
8	Nigel Mansell	31	31		
9	Jack Brabham	29	14	15	
10=	Niki Lauda	27	25	2	
	Fernando Alonso	27	27		
12	Nelson Piquet	23	23		
13	Damon Hill	22	22		
14	Sebastian Vettel	21	21		
15=	Graham Hill	20	14	6	
	Mika Häkkinen	20	20		
17=	Emerson Fittipaldi	18	14	4	
	Kimi Räikkönen	18	18		
19	Lewis Hamilton	17	17		
20	John Surtees	15	6	9	
21=	Nino Farina	14	4	10	1
	Reg Parnell	14		14	
	Carlos Reutemann	14	12	2	
	James Hunt	14	10	4	
25=	Luigi Villoresi	13		13	
	Mario Andretti	13	12	1	
	Alan Jones	13	12	1	
	David Coulthard	13	13		
29	Jenson Button	12	12		
30=	Jacky Ickx	11	8	3	
	Jacques Villeneuve	11	11		
	Felipe Massa	11	11		
	Rubens Barrichello	11	11		
34=	Alberto Ascari	10	2	8	11
	Jean Behra	10		10	
	Denny Hulme	10	8	2	
	Ronnie Peterson	10	10		
	Jody Scheckter	10	10		
	Gerhard Berger	10	10		
40=	Louis Rosier	9		9	
	Innes Ireland	9	1	8	
42=	Bob Gerard	7		7	
	José Froilán González	7	2	5	
	Peter Collins	7	3	4	
	Tony Brooks*	7	6	1	

		All F1 victories 1946-2011	All champ F1 victories 1950-2011	All non-champ F1 victories 1946-1983	All F2 champ victories 1952-1953
	Bruce McLaren	7	4	3	
	Clay Regazzoni	7	5	2	
	Gilles Villeneuve	7	6	1	
	Keke Rosberg	7	5	2	
	René Arnoux	7	7		
	Juan Pablo Montoya	7	7		
	Mark Webber	7	7		
53=	Roy Salvadori	6		6	
	Maurice Trintignant	6	2	4	
	Dan Gurney	6	4	2	
	Jochen Rindt	6	6		
	Jacques Laffite	6	6		
	Riccardo Patrese	6	6		
	Ralf Schumacher	6	6		
60=	Jean-Pierre Wimille	5		5	
	Jo Siffert	5	2	3	
	Michele Alboreto	5	5	0	
	John Watson	5	5	0	
64=	Luigi Musso*	4	1	3	
	Giancarlo Baghetti	4	1	3	
	Eddie Irvine	4	4	0	
67=	Carlo Felice Trossi	3		3	
	Louis Chiron	3		3	
	Toulo de Graffenried	3		3	
	'B.Bira'	3		3	
	Peter Whitehead	3		3	
	Harry Schell	3		3	
	Phil Hill	3	3	0	
	Pedro Rodriguez	3	2	1	
	Peter Gethin	3	1	2	
	Trevor Taylor*	3		3	
	Didier Pironi	3	3	0	
	Thierry Boutsen	3	3	0	
	Heinz-Harald Frentzen	3	3	0	
	Johnny Herbert	3	3	0	
	Giancarlo Fisichella	3	3	0	
82=	Achille Varzi	2		2	
	Raymond Sommer	2		2	
	Nello Pagani	2		2	
	Eugène Chaboud	2		2	
	Yves Giraud-Cabantous	2		2	
	Horace Gould	2		2	
	Mike Hawthorn	2	2	0	1
	Wolfgang von Trips	2	2	0	

DRIVERS (continued)

		All F1 victories 1946-2011	All champ F1 victories 1950-2011	All non-champ F1 victories 1946-1983	All F2 champ victories 1952-1953
	Willy Mairesse	2		2	
	Mike Spence	2		2	
	Mike Parkes^	2		2	
	Ludovico Scarfiotti^	2	1	1	
	Lorenzo Bandini	2	1	1	
	Chris Amon	2		2	
	Jean-Pierre Beltoise	2	1	1	
	Peter Revson	2	2	0	
	Patrick Depailler	2	2	0	
	Jean-Pierre Jabouille	2	2	0	
	Patrick Tambay	2	2	0	
	Elio de Angelis	2	2	0	
102=	Christian Kautz	1		1	
	Geoffrey Ansell	1		1	
	Philippe Étancelin	1		1	
	Guy Mairesse	1		1	
	Georges Grignard	1		1	
	David Hampshire	1		1	
	Philip Fotheringham-Parker	1		1	
	Roger Laurent	1		1	
	Gunnar Carlsson	1		1	
	Rodney Nuckey	1		1	
	Erik Lundgren	1		1	
	Onofre Marimon	1		1	
	Luigi Fagioli*	1	1		
	Piero Taruffi	1		1	1
	John Riseley-Pritchard	1		1	

		All F1 victories 1946-2011	All champ F1 victories 1950-2011	All non-champ F1 victories 1946-1983	All F2 champ victories 1952-19
	John Coombs	1		1	
	Karl Kling	1		1	
	Andre Simon	1		1	
	Leslie Marr	1		1	
	Robert Manzon	1		1	
	Archie Scott-Brown	1		1	
	Stuart Lewis-Evans	1		1	
	Ron Flockhart	1		1	
	Tony Marsh	1		1	
	Masten Gregory	1		1	
	Jo Bonnier	1	1		
	Richie Ginther	1	1		
	Bob Anderson	1		1	
	Keith Holland	1		1	
	Tom Pryce	1		1	
	François Cevert	1	1		
	Carlos Pace	1	1		
	Jochen Mass	1	1		
	Vittorio Brambilla	1	1		
	Gunnar Nilsson	1	1		
	Alessandro Nannini	1	1		
	Jean Alesi	1	1		
	Olivier Panis	1	1		
	Jarno Trulli	1	1		
	Robert Kubica	1	1		
	Heikki Kovalainen	1	1		

* One shared drive
** Two shared drives
^ One dead heat

CONSTRUCTORS

		All F1 victories 1946-2011	All champ F1 victories 1950-2011	All non-champ F1 victories 1946-1983	All F2 champ victories 1952-19
1	Ferrari^	260	202	58	14
2	McLaren	182	175	7	
3	Lotus	124	79	45	
4	Williams	116	113	3	
5	Maserati	68	8	60	1
6	Brabham	52	35	17	
7	Renault	35	35		
8	Cooper	31	16	15	
9	BRM	30	17	13	
10	Alfa Romeo	28	10	18	
11=	Benetton	27	27		
	Red Bull	27	27		
13	Tyrrell	24	23	1	
14	Talbot-Lago	19		19	
15=	Vanwall	12	9	3	
	Matra	12	9	3	
17	Mercedes-Benz	10	9	1	
18=	ERA	9		9	
	Ligier	9	9		
20	Brawn	8	8		
21=	Gordini	5		5	
	Connaught	5		5	
	March	5	3	2	
24	Jordan	4	4		
25=	Porsche	3	1	2	
	Lola	3		3	
	Wolf	3	3		
	Honda	3	3		
29=	Lancia	2		2	
	Eagle	2	1	1	
	Hesketh	2	1	1	
	Shadow	2	1	1	
	Surtees	2		2	
34=	Mercury Special	1		1	
	Ford Special	1		1	
	Ferguson	1		1	
	BRP	1		1	
	Chevron	1		1	
	Theodore	1		1	
	Penske	1	1		
	Stewart	1	1		
	BMW	1	1		
	Toro Rosso	1	1		

^ One dead heat

ENGINES

		All F1 victories 1946-2011	All champ F1 victories 1950-2011	All non-champ F1 victories 1946-1983	All F2 champ victories 1952-19
1	Ferrari^	261	203	58	14
2	Ford	207	176	31	
3	Renault	142	142		
4	Coventry-Climax	97	40	57	
5	Mercedes-Benz	89	88	1	
6	Honda	72	72		
7	Maserati	70	10	60	1
8	BRM	38	18	20	
9	Alfa Romeo	31	12	19	
10	TAG-Porsche	25	25		
11	BMW	20	20		
12	Talbot-Lago	19		19	
13=	Vanwall	12	9	3	
	Repco	12	8	4	
15	ERA	9		9	
16	Gordini	5		5	
17=	Alta	4		4	
	Matra	4	3	1	
	Mugen Honda	4	4		
20	Porsche	3	1	2	
21=	Bristol	2		2	
	Lea Francis	2		2	
	Lancia	2		2	
	Weslake	2	1	1	
	Chevrolet	2		2	

^ One dead heat

Formula 1: All the champions

Season	Champion driver	Nationality	Car(s) driven	Champion constructor	Nationality
1950	Nino Farina	ITA	Alfa Romeo		
1951	Juan Manuel Fangio	ARG	Alfa Romeo		
1952	Alberto Ascari	ITA	Ferrari		
1953	Alberto Ascari	ITA	Ferrari		
1954	Juan Manuel Fangio	ARG	Mercedes-Benz/Maserati		
1955	Juan Manuel Fangio	ARG	Mercedes-Benz		
1956	Juan Manuel Fangio	ARG	Ferrari		
1957	Juan Manuel Fangio	ARG	Maserati		
1958	Mike Hawthorn	GBR	Ferrari*	Vanwall	GBR
1959	Jack Brabham	AUS	Cooper-Climax	Cooper-Climax	GBR
1960	Jack Brabham	AUS	Cooper-Climax	Cooper-Climax	GBR
1961	Phil Hill	USA	Ferrari	Ferrari	ITA
1962	Graham Hill	GBR	BRM	BRM	GBR
1963	Jim Clark	GBR	Lotus-Climax	Lotus-Climax	GBR
1964	John Surtees	GBR	Ferrari	Ferrari	ITA
1965	Jim Clark	GBR	Lotus-Climax	Lotus-Climax	GBR
1966	Jack Brabham	AUS	Brabham-Repco	Brabham-Repco	AUS
1967	Denny Hulme	NZL	Brabham-Repco	Brabham-Repco	AUS
1968	Graham Hill	GBR	Lotus-Ford	Lotus-Ford	GBR
1969	Jackie Stewart	GBR	Matra-Ford	Matra-Ford	FRA
1970	Jochen Rindt	AUT	Lotus-Ford	Lotus-Ford	GBR
1971	Jackie Stewart	GBR	Tyrrell-Ford	Tyrrell-Ford	GBR
1972	Emerson Fittipaldi	BRA	Lotus-Ford	Lotus-Ford	GBR
1973	Jackie Stewart	GBR	Tyrrell-Ford*	Lotus-Ford	GBR
1974	Emerson Fittipaldi	BRA	McLaren-Ford	McLaren-Ford	NZL
1975	Niki Lauda	AUT	Ferrari	Ferrari	ITA
1976	James Hunt	GBR	McLaren-Ford*	Ferrari	ITA
1977	Niki Lauda	AUT	Ferrari	Ferrari	ITA
1978	Mario Andretti	USA	Lotus-Ford	Lotus-Ford	GBR
1979	Jody Scheckter	RSA	Ferrari	Ferrari	ITA
1980	Alan Jones	AUS	Williams-Ford	Williams-Ford	GBR
1981	Nelson Piquet	BRA	Brabham-Ford*	Williams-Ford	GBR
1982	Keke Rosberg	FIN	Williams-Ford*	Ferrari	ITA
1983	Nelson Piquet	BRA	Brabham-BMW*	Ferrari	ITA
1984	Niki Lauda	AUT	McLaren-TAG	McLaren-TAG	GBR
1985	Alain Prost	FRA	McLaren-TAG	McLaren-TAG	GBR
1986	Alain Prost	FRA	McLaren-TAG*	Williams-Honda	GBR
1987	Nelson Piquet	BRA	Williams-Honda	Williams-Honda	GBR
1988	Ayrton Senna	BRA	McLaren-Honda	McLaren-Honda	GBR
1989	Alain Prost	FRA	McLaren-Honda	McLaren-Honda	GBR
1990	Ayrton Senna	BRA	McLaren-Honda	McLaren-Honda	GBR
1991	Ayrton Senna	BRA	McLaren-Honda	McLaren-Honda	GBR
1992	Nigel Mansell	GBR	Williams-Renault	Williams-Renault	GBR
1993	Alain Prost	FRA	Williams-Renault	Williams-Renault	GBR
1994	Michael Schumacher	GER	Benetton-Ford*	Williams-Renault	GBR
1995	Michael Schumacher	GER	Benetton-Renault	Benetton-Renault	GBR
1996	Damon Hill	GBR	Williams-Renault	Williams-Renault	GBR
1997	Jacques Villeneuve	CAN	Williams-Renault	Williams-Renault	GBR
1998	Mika Hakkinen	FIN	McLaren-Mercedes	McLaren-Mercedes	GBR
1999	Mika Hakkinen	FIN	McLaren-Mercedes*	Ferrari	ITA
2000	Michael Schumacher	GER	Ferrari	Ferrari	ITA

Season	Champion driver	Nationality	Car(s) driven	Champion constructor	Nationality
2001	Michael Schumacher	GER	Ferrari	Ferrari	ITA
2002	Michael Schumacher	GER	Ferrari	Ferrari	ITA
2003	Michael Schumacher	GER	Ferrari	Ferrari	ITA
2004	Michael Schumacher	GER	Ferrari	Ferrari	ITA
2005	Fernando Alonso	ESP	Renault	Renault	FRA
2006	Fernando Alonso	ESP	Renault	Renault	FRA
2007	Kimi Raikkonen	FIN	Ferrari	Ferrari	ITA
2008	Lewis Hamilton	GBR	McLaren-Mercedes*	Ferrari	ITA
2009	Jenson Button	GBR	Brawn-Mercedes	Brawn-Mercedes	GBR
2010	Sebastian Vettel	GER	Red Bull-Renault	Red Bull-Renault	AUT
2011	Sebastian Vettel	GER	Red Bull-Renault	Red Bull-Renault	AUT

*Not Champion Constructor

CHAMPION CHAMPIONS (multiple title winners)

Drivers	Titles
Michael Schumacher*	7
Juan Manuel Fangio*	5
Alain Prost*	4
Jack Brabham*	3
Jackie Stewart	3
Niki Lauda	3
Nelson Piquet	3
Ayrton Senna*	3
Alberto Ascari*	2
Jim Clark	2
Graham Hill	2
Emerson Fittipaldi	2
Mika Häkkinen*	2
Fernando Alonso*	2
Sebastian Vettel*	2

* Back-to-back Champions

Constructors	Titles
Ferrari*	15
Williams*	9
McLaren*	8
Lotus*	7
Cooper*	2
Brabham*	2
Renault*	2
Red Bull*	2

* Back-to-back Champions

CHAMPIONS BY NATIONALITY

Country	Drivers' champions	Drivers' titles	Constructors' champions	Constructors' titles	Engine manufacturer 'titles'
Great Britain	10	14	9	30	16
Brazil	3	8	0	0	0
Finland	3	4	0	0	0
Germany	2	9	0	0	4
Australia	2	4	1	2	2
Austria	2	4	1	2	0
Italy	2	3	1	16	16
USA	2	2	0	0	0
Argentina	1	5	0	0	0
France	1	4	2	3	10
Spain	1	2	0	0	0
New Zealand	1	1	1	1	0
South Africa	1	1	0	0	0
Canada	1	1	0	0	0
Japan	0	0	0	0	6

BIBLIOGRAPHY

Magazines and annuals
Autocourse 1951–1960, 1969–2010
Autosport 1960–2011

Websites
forix on autosport.com
kolumbus.fi, Leif Snellman and Hans Etzrodt
silhouet.com, Darren Galpin

DVDs and videos
Official FIA season reviews
The History of Motor Racing 1950s, 1960s and 1970s (Duke Video)

Books
A Record of Grand Prix and Voiturette Racing, Paul Sheldon,
    St Leonard's Press: Vol 4, 1937–49 (1993); Vol 5, 1950–53
    (1989); Vol 6, 1954–59 (1987)
A-Z of Grand Prix Cars, David Hodges, Crowood Press Ltd, 2001
Alain Prost, Christopher Hilton, Corgi Books, 1993
Analysing Formula 1, Roger Smith, Haynes Publishing, 2008
Ayrton Senna – The hard edge of genius, Christopher Hilton,
    Corgi Books, 1995
Beyond the Limit, Professor Sid Watkins, Macmillan, 2001
British Grand Prix, Maurice Hamilton, PRC/Bookmart, 1992
BRM, Raymond Mays/Peter Roberts, Pan Books, 1964
Bruce McLaren – The man and his racing team, Eoin Young, Eyre
    & Spottiswoode, 1971
Damon Hill, David Tremayne, Parragon Book Service, 1996
DFV – The Inside Story of F1's Greatest Engine, Andrew Noakes,
    Haynes Publishing, 2007
Fangio – A Pirelli Album, Stirling Moss/Doug Nye, Pavilion
    Books, 1991
Ferrari – All the cars, Haynes Publishing, 2005
Ferrari – The Grand Prix Cars, Alan Henry, Hazleton
    Publishing, 1984
Formula 1 Paddock, Jean-François Galeron, Chronosports, 2003
Formula 1 The Autobiography, edited by Gerald Donaldson,
    Weidenfeld & Nicolson, 2002
From Brands Hatch to Indianapolis, Tommaso Tommasi, Hamlyn
    Publishing, 1974
Gilles Villeneuve – The life of the legendary racing driver, Gerald
    Donaldson, Virgin Books, 2003
Grand Prix Chronology, Stephen Hirst, Ian Allan Ltd, 1972
Grand Prix Data Book, David Hayhoe & David Holland, Haynes
    Publishing, 2006
Grand Prix Driver by Driver, Philip Raby, Green Umbrella
    Publishing, 2007
Grand Prix Who's Who, Steve Small, Travel Publishing Ltd, 2000
Grand Prix! – Volume 1 - 1950-1965, Mike Lang, Haynes
    Publishing, 1981
Grand Prix! – Volume 2 - 1966-1973, Mike Lang, Haynes
    Publishing, 1982
Grand Prix! – Volume 3 - 1974-1980, Mike Lang, Haynes
    Publishing, 1983
Grand Prix! – Volume 4 - 1981-1984, Mike Lang, Haynes
    Publishing, 1992
Hunt v Lauda, David Benson, Beaverbrook Newspapers, 1976
The International Motor Racing Guide, Peter Higham, David Bull
    Publishing, 2003
It was fun!, Tony Rudd, Patrick Stephens Ltd, 1993
James Hunt, Gerald Donaldson, Collins Willow, 1994
Jim Clark – Portrait of a great driver, Graham Gauld, Hamlyn
    Publishing, 1968
Jochen Rindt – The story of a World Champion, Heinz Prüller,
    William Kimber, 1973
Ken Tyrrell, Maurice Hamilton, Collins Willow, 2002
Kings of the Nürburgring, Chris Nixon, Transport Bookman
    Publications, 2005
Life at the Limit, Graham Hill, William Kimber, 1969
Mario Andretti, Gordon Kirby, David Bull Publishing, 2001
McLaren – The Grand Prix, Can-Am and Indy cars, Doug Nye,
    Hazleton Publishing, 1988
Michael Schumacher – The quest for redemption, James Allen,
    Transworld Publishers, 1999
Mon Ami Mate, Chris Nixon, Transport Bookman
    Publications, 1991
Nelson Piquet, Mike Doodson, Hazleton Publishing, 1991
Nigel Mansell – My Autobiography, Nigel Mansell/James Allen,
    Collins Willow, 1995
Niki Lauda Formula 1, Niki Lauda, William Kimber, 1979
Stirling Moss, Robert Edwards, Cassell & Co, 2001
Stirling Moss, Karl Ludvigsen, Patrick Stephens Ltd, 1997
The Autocourse History of the Grand Prix car – 1945–65, Doug
    Nye, Hazleton Publishing, 1993
The Autocourse History of the Grand Prix car – 1966–91, Doug
    Nye, Hazleton Publishing, 1992
The Book of Formula 1 Top Tens, Roger Smith, Haynes
    Publishing, 2008
The Complete Book of Formula One, Simon Arron and Mark
    Hughes, Motorbooks International, 2003
The Great Encyclopaedia of Formula 1, Pierre Ménard, Constable
    & Robinson Ltd, 2000
The Life of Senna, Tom Rubython, BusinessF1 Books, 2004
The Maserati 250F, Anthony Pritchard, Aston Publications, 1985
The Unofficial Formula One Encyclopaedia, Mark Hughes,
    Anness Publishing, 2004
Theme Lotus 1956–1986 – From Chapman to Ducarouge, Doug
    Nye, Motor Racing Publications, 1986
Vanwall, Ian Bamsey, Haynes Publishing, 1990
When the flag drops, Jack Brabham, William Kimber, 1971
Williams – Formula 1 racing team, Alan Henry, Haynes
    Publishing, 1998
Winning is not enough, Jackie Stewart, Headline Publishing
    Group, 2007